THE TEXAS CONSTITUTION IN STATE AND NATION

COMPARATIVE STATE CONSTITUTIONAL LAW IN THE FEDERAL SYSTEM

THE TEXAS CONSTITUTION IN STATE AND NATION

COMPARATIVE STATE CONSTITUTIONAL LAW IN THE FEDERAL SYSTEM

Charles W. "Rocky" Rhodes

Vinson & Elkins Research Professor & Professor of Law
South Texas College of Law, Houston, Texas

VANDEPLAS PUBLISHING, LLC

UNITED STATES OF AMERICA

The Texas constitution in state and nation
Comparative state constitutional law in the federal system

Rhodes, Charles W.

Published by:

Vandeplas Publishing, LLC – January 2014

801 International Parkway, 5th Floor
Lake Mary, FL. 32746
USA

www.vandeplaspublishing.com

ISBN 978-1-60042-215-7

TABLE OF CONTENTS

PREFACE AND ACKNOWLEDGMENTS

The most fun I've ever had teaching was my state constitutional law course in the spring semester of 2005. Since I've been blessed with many other outstanding groups of state constitutional law students, it wasn't just the students (although it was a stellar bunch). But what was so special about that course in that particular semester was the unique opportunity to teach with my mentor, colleague, and friend, Judge Tom Phillips.

Tom had just stepped down after more than sixteen years as the Chief Justice of the Supreme Court of Texas, and he spent a year at South Texas College of Law as the Spurgeon E. Bell Distinguished Visiting Professor of Law. I was able to finagle my way into co-teaching state constitutional law with him while he was here. I've had an interest in state constitutional law since law school, and that interest only intensified before I joined academia in my years as a briefing attorney and a staff attorney at the Supreme Court of Texas and as an appellate lawyer in private practice. I knew from these experiences that Tom's knowledge of state constitutional law, both in Texas and around the country, exceeds what could be contained in any book, so I relished the unique opportunity to engage with a true Texas legal legend.

Our collaboration that semester planted the seeds of this book. Unhappy with the lack of coverage of Texas state constitutional doctrine in any textbook, we compiled our own cases and other materials, which we provided to the students on a weekly basis throughout the semester. We were constantly consulting with each other on the materials and our approach to teaching the materials. Our classes were a give and take of lively banter between and among the students and ourselves. But whenever I had a chance, I was also fervently adding Tom's perspectives to my own class notes. The first draft of this book essentially contained those original materials we compiled and my notes from our classes.

I've continued to work on the book over the years, updating the materials, editing the cases, adding additional research, and revising sections based on class discussions. Although Tom's commitments as a partner at Baker & Botts prevented him from continuing our academic (but not our professional or personal) collaboration, his influence on all that is good in this book is immeasurable. Without him, this book would have never come to fruition. I can't thank him enough for his inspiration, guidance, and friendship.

I'm also indebted to the indefatigable research assistant I had during those early years of working on this book, Andy Torrant. His commitment was so great that he even offered to keep helping me after he graduated! But instead, he recruited the only person who could replace him as my research assistant on this book, Katie Chatterton, who later married Andy. This couple – who incidentally are expecting their first child shortly – were the best successive research assistants I could possibly imagine.

I've been further blessed with a dozen classes of state constitutional law students who have provided immense help with their feedback and comments. I particularly need to highlight Shane McDonald, who did the final cite checking of the book, and the fine proofreading skills of Leslie Hanna and Mike Kuykendall. Recognition is also due to all my students who have contributed to this book through their recitations, comments, and questions.

My focus on keeping this work accessible to students – while also providing a resource useful to practitioners and judges – has led me to employ some perhaps unusual conventions in this book, which mixes aspects of a textbook and a treatise. First, the book is heavily footnoted, allowing researchers to find the source materials for my assertions. The good news for students is that you only need to read the footnotes that are in the cases; you do not have to read the footnoted material in the introductory sections or in the notes that follow the cases. But you may want to hold on to this book, as that footnoted material will be helpful when you encounter these issues in the future.

In order to enhance the readability of the case and article excerpts, I have not indicated every omission from the source material. All additions to the cases or articles are noted by brackets, but I only used ellipses or asterisks for omissions when my edits interfered with the natural flow of the materials. In editing the cases, I sought to remove extraneous issues, repetitive authorities, and procedural discussions, while retaining the flavor of the court's analysis. Most footnotes have been removed from the cases and articles, but I kept a few consequential ones, which are numbered sequentially rather than retaining their original numbering.

I hope these efforts have aided my objective of providing a comprehensible text for students and a useful resource for practitioners and the judiciary in Texas. According to the Conference of Chief Justices, "being a competent and effective lawyer requires an understanding of both the federal Constitution and state constitutional law." My goal for this book is to provide a basis for that understanding.

It's been an extensive undertaking, and one that would not have been possible without the love and support of my family. As a result, this book is dedicated to my beautiful-in-every-way bride of twenty-plus years, Marcie, and our proudest accomplishment, our son Macen.

Charles W. "Rocky" Rhodes
South Texas College of Law
Houston, Texas

Chapter 1

DEVELOPMENT OF STATE CONSTITUTIONS

While most Americans are familiar with the United States Constitution, almost half are not aware that their state has its own constitution.[1] Even to lawyers, the mention of "constitutional law" rarely evokes thoughts of state constitutionalism. Yet state constitutions are the oldest surviving remnants of the political history of America, predating both the Articles of Confederation and the United States Constitution. They reflect the entirety of the American experience, from our early struggles to our modern challenges.

State constitutions remain vital today as they govern a realm outside the sphere of the United States Constitution. The United States Constitution creates a government of limited and enumerated powers, authorizing the federal government to act only within defined enclaves. For example, Congress is limited to those powers delegated to it by the constitutional text, which are primarily contained in Article I, Section 8, and the federal judiciary is limited to hearing the cases specified by Article III, Section 2. In contrast, the states retain an inherent "police power" to regulate personal and property rights for the public good, unless such regulation infringes on a constitutionally protected liberty. As James Madison remarked:

> The powers delegated by the proposed Constitution to the federal government are few and defined. Those which are to remain in the State government are numerous and indefinite. The former will be exercised principally on external objects, as war, peace, negotiation, and foreign commerce; with which last the power of taxation will, for the most part, be connected. The powers reserved to the several States will extend to all the objects which, in the ordinary course of affairs, concern the lives, liberties, and properties of the people, and the internal order, improvement, and prosperity of the State.[2]

The Tenth Amendment to the United States Constitution confirms that the states and the people retain the residual of sovereign authority, providing that "powers not delegated to the United States by the Constitution, nor prohibited by it to the States, are reserved to the States respectively, or to the people."[3] To define the function, structure, and the limitations of this sovereign authority, each state has adopted its own constitution.

Of course, these fifty different state constitutions, ratified at different times in our history, diverge in many respects. Even when a particular state constitutional provision is shared by more than one state, the judiciary in each state may interpret the provision differently. Nevertheless, many common currents run through the constitutions of the

---

[1] G. ALAN TARR, UNDERSTANDING STATE CONSTITUTIONS 1-2 & n.4 (1998).

[2] THE FEDERALIST NO. 45 (James Madison) (Clinton Rossiter ed., 1961).

[3] U.S. CONST. amend. X.

various states, allowing in many instances for a comparative analysis of these charters.

The first written state constitutions were adopted shortly before and after the Declaration of Independence. These new constitutions typically did not differ greatly from the colonial charters they replaced, except that executive power was weakened and sometimes declarations of rights announcing republican principles were incorporated due to concerns regarding potential tyranny from a powerful executive.[4] These concerns arose, of course, from the colonists' experiences under colonial governors chosen by or at least identified with the British Crown. As a result, these state constitutions concentrated almost all governing power to the branch deemed most responsive to the popular will–the legislature. Legislative elections were frequent, with short terms of office, that kept legislators accountable to the people. In every state except New York, the legislature selected the governor, who typically served for just a year, thereby subordinating the executive branch to the legislative branch.[5]

Over the next few years, states adopted their constitutions with more deliberation, sometimes revising constitutions adopted after Independence.[6] These "second-wave" constitutions typically provided at least some additional power to the executive and judicial branches as a potential check on legislative tyranny.[7] Legislatures under the revolutionary state constitutions had enacted laws for the confiscation of property and ex post facto debtor relief legislation that penalized commercial interests.[8] Such legislative excesses led the makers of these next state constitutions to secure some measure of gubernatorial independence from the legislature, frequently through direct popular election of the governor rather than legislative appointment. But these new state constitutions still did not meaningfully limit the boundaries of legislative authority, instead confining themselves to establishing the institutions, offices, mode of election, and foundational principles of the government.[9] James Madison and other supporters of the United States Constitution frequently bemoaned the resulting failure of the states to quell majoritarian impulses that they believed contravened the common good.[10]

Despite their defects, however, these early state constitutions contributed greatly to the establishment of our modern constitutional heritage. As historian Jack Rakove observed, these states and their early constitutions "had served, in effect, as the great political laboratory upon whose experiments the framers of 1787 drew to revise the theory of representative government."[11] In addition, two of these constitutions–at least in conjunction

---

[4]Robert F. Williams, *The State Constitutions of the Founding Decade: Pennsylvania's Radical 1776 Constitution and Its Influences on American Constitutionalism*, 62 TEMPLE L. REV. 541, 546-47 (1989).

[5]TARR, *supra* note 1, at 87.

[6]Williams, *supra* note 4, 62 TEMPLE L. REV. at 547.

[7]*Id.*

[8]GORDON WOOD, THE CREATION OF THE AMERICAN REPUBLIC, 1776-1787, 404-06 (1969).

[9]TARR, *supra* note 1, at 62.

[10]*See, e.g.*, James Madison, *Vices of the Political System of the United States*, *in* 9 THE PAPERS OF JAMES MADISON 345-58 (William T. Hutchinson et al. eds., 1962).

[11]JACK N. RAKOVE, ORIGINAL MEANINGS: POLITICS AND IDEAS IN THE MAKING OF THE CONSTITUTION 31 (1997).

with their subsequent amendments–have withstood the test of time: the Massachusetts Constitution of 1780 and the New Hampshire Constitution of 1784, the two oldest written republican constitutions still in effect in the world.

The ratification of the Federal Constitution did not halt the continuing development of a distinctive American state constitutional tradition. Existing states continued to modify their charters, sometimes wholly replacing them with new state constitutions. Additionally, as the boundaries of the new country expanded, the Union admitted new states, which then adopted new state constitutions. Sometimes these new states were formed out of federal territories that had been governed by Congress. For example, the states of Ohio, Indiana, Michigan, Illinois, and Wisconsin were formed from the Northwest Territory, which had been governed by the Northwest Ordinance of 1787. Perhaps not surprisingly, the constitutions of these states incorporated some provisions of the Ordinance.[12]

Territorial legislation, however, was not the only influence on the continued march of state constitutionalism. Newly admitted states and existing states revising their constitutions often borrowed from other state constitutions, or sometimes even from the United States Constitution. At the 1845 Texas Constitutional Convention, reliance on other constitutions became such a pervasive practice that the President of the Convention chided the delegates: "We can reflect for ourselves, and are capable of forming a Constitution for ourselves."[13] But in the delegates' defense, blazing a new constitutional trail without drawing from the experiences of other states and the federal government would have been shortsighted. A judicious consideration of pre-existing constitutions was not merely common–it was (and still is) appropriate.

The constitutions of both the newly admitted states and the existing states were also profoundly impacted by the social, economic, and political influences of the times. Jacksonian democracy, the Civil War, Reconstruction, the Grange movement, the Progressive movement, and post-World War II modernization, to name a few, influenced the state constitutions adopted or revised during each particular era. Constitutions ratified during the Jacksonian era, for example, often increased the number of elective governmental offices, including establishing a strong, elected judiciary accountable to the people.[14] And, of course, before the Civil War, state constitutional drafting was influenced by the issue of slavery, especially in those states in which the institution was controversial within the state's polity.[15] After the War, the states that had seceded were required to adopt new constitutions providing for voting rights for all men as a prerequisite for the restoration of self-governance. These postbellum constitutions, drafted predominantly by Republicans (as most southern Democrats had fought for the Confederacy and therefore were barred from participation), incorporated progressive ideas, such as free public education, civil and political rights for African Americans, and economic modernization.[16]

---

[12]Patrick Baude, *Interstate Dialogue in State Constitutional Law*, 28 RUTGERS L.J. 835, 843 (1997).

[13]WILLIAM F. WEEKS, DEBATES OF THE TEXAS CONVENTION 468 (1846) (remarks of Thomas J. Rusk).

[14]James A. Henretta, *Foreword: Rethinking the State Constitutional Tradition*, 22 RUTGERS L.J. 819, 833-35 (1991).

[15]TARR, *supra* note 1, at 129.

[16]ERIC FONER, RECONSTRUCTION: AMERICA'S UNFINISHED REVOLUTION 319-20, 325 (1988).

As Reconstruction ended, the majority of southern states replaced their Reconstruction constitutions with new charters that curtailed the scope of government.[17] But this anti-government movement was not merely confined to the south, as many northern states likewise were influenced by the agricultural Grange movement and the business Panic of 1873 to adopt new state constitutions limiting governmental power.[18] Decades later, many states revised their constitutions again during the Progressive movement, opening the franchise to women, providing mechanisms for citizens to participate in democratic governance through initiative and referendum, and authorizing the recall of elected officials. Paradoxically, however, state constitutions during this time too frequently incorporated changes designed to disenfranchise politically disfavored groups–such as African Americans in the south, Asian Americans in the west, and recent immigrants in the east–through a combination of literacy tests, poll taxes, educational requirements, and other similar devices that were finally abolished during the civil rights movement.

Since World War II, two more states have joined the Union, and at least eleven states have wholly revised their constitutions again, including Florida, which adopted a new constitution in 1968, Louisiana, which adopted its eleventh constitution in 1974, and Georgia, which adopted its tenth constitution in 1982.[19] These modern revisions typically incorporated reforms sought by political scientists and governmental administrators to adopt a more streamlined form of government in contrast to the sometimes unwieldy constitutions prevalent in the years between the Civil War and World War I.

Even when political, economic, and social movements at the national and local level did not result in the state's adoption of a new state constitution, the changing social order usually at least resulted in state constitutional amendments. The Texas experience provides a typical example. Texas has had a total of six constitutions since breaking away from Mexico: an 1836 Constitution establishing the Republic of Texas, an 1845 Constitution to join the Union, an 1861 Constitution to join the Confederacy, an 1866 Constitution to rejoin the Union, an 1869 Constitution in response to the demands of the Reconstruction Congress, and an 1876 Constitution after Democrats regained political control in the state. But the fact that Texas has now been operating under the same constitution for close to 140 years does not mean that no change has taken place–483 amendments to the Texas Constitution were ratified between 1876 and 2013, while only twelve amendments to the United States Constitution were ratified during that same period.[20] Many of these amendments stemmed from local, state, and national political and social movements, such as creating the Texas Railroad Commission in response to agrarian discontent, changing the funding and workings of the Texas public education system on numerous occasions, authorizing special

---

[17]*Id.* at 588.

[18]*Id.* at 518-19.

[19]*See* TARR, *supra* note 1, at137. Georgia has had three new state constitutions since World War II–in 1945, 1976, and 1982. The other states that adopted revised state constitutions since World War II are still operating under that constitution. Hawaii and Alaska also adopted their initial state constitutions after World War II, in 1950 and 1956, respectively. *Id.*

[20]The Texas experience is not unusual, as literally thousands of amendments were ratified by the states during the twentieth century. One study determined that the states ratified approximately 3,000 amendments during the years between 1970 and 1993 alone. *See* Janice C. May, *State Constitutions and Constitutional Revision, 1992-93, in* THE COUNCIL OF STATE GOVERNMENTS, THE BOOK OF THE STATES (1994).

conservation districts to conserve and develop water and other natural resources, and enacting the state equal rights amendment during the women's liberation movement.

State constitutional interpretation thus necessitates an understanding of the political, economic, and social forces of the times. The sections below describe some of the history behind the most important Texas constitutions for the study of state constitutional law: the 1836 Republic of Texas Constitution, the 1845 Statehood Constitution, and the present Texas Constitution ratified in 1876.[21]

A. THE 1836 REPUBLIC OF TEXAS CONSTITUTION

Early in the sixteenth century, Spain claimed the area that today is the State of Texas. The region was sparsely populated, with only around 5,000 people (including Native Americans) scattered over the area in 1800. Spain intermittently attempted to solicit settlers, but with little success.

In 1821, Mexico won its independence from Spain, and Texas was joined with Coahuila as a state in the new Mexican republic. At that time, a few Anglo-American immigrants were already in Texas, but American settlement began in earnest after Mexican independence. Drawn by the promise of cheap land and a new start from the Panic of 1819 in the United States, these Americans were hoping that the liberal Mexican Constitution of 1824, with an elected president and bicameral legislature, signaled a government much like their own.

But these American immigrants were disappointed. The Mexican judicial system lacked trial by jury, indictments, or bail, and the rights of assembly and to petition the government were curtailed under Mexican law. While these restrictions were often not enforced, a more objectionable requirement to the American settlers was that all Mexican residents were supposed to be Catholic. Mexican leaders were dismayed as well by the new immigrants, objecting to their practice of slavery, their failure to integrate into Mexican society by learning the language and adopting the religious and social traditions of the land, and their clinging to the American legal heritage. Although the Mexican government had originally encouraged at least some Anglo-American immigration, it came to fear the new settlers' intentions. So in 1830, Mexico began passing laws designed to limit the influx of settlers by forbidding future immigration, barring the introduction of slaves, and increasing taxation. The new Texans objected to these new measures, predominantly peaceably at first, with at least modest success.

But everything changed in 1835 when President Antonio López de Santa Anna voided the Mexican Constitution, placed all governmental power in his own hands, and repudiated the compromises that had been made. When Mexican military officials demanded the cannon the settlers at Gonzales kept for defense, Texans in that town responded to this demand with firepower. Additional battles followed, which provoked

[21]The provisions of the 1861 Confederate Constitution were almost identical to the 1845 Statehood Constitution, with the distinctions almost all traceable to Texas's membership in the Confederacy. The short-lived 1866 and 1869 Constitutions had no lasting impact.

Santa Anna to lead thousands of Mexican troops into Texas to quell the rebellion and remove the Americans from the state. While Santa Anna and his army were laying siege to the Alamo, a group of fifty-nine Texas delegates met at Washington-on-the-Brazos, beginning on March 1, 1836, to consider the appropriate political course of action.

David P. Currie, *The Constitution of the Republic of Texas Part 1*, 8 GREEN BAG 2D 145 (2005)*

Texas declared its independence from Mexico on March 2, 1836. "When a government has ceased to protect the lives, liberty and property of the people . . . [and] becomes an instrument in the hands of evil rulers for their oppression," the Declaration recites, "the first law of nature, the right of self-preservation[,]" enjoins the people "to abolish such government and create another, in its stead . . . ." There follows, as in the declaration adopted six decades earlier by the United States, a detailed list of specific grievances, ranging from the denial of trial by jury and freedom of conscience to military despotism and the failure to establish a system of public schools. The bottom line:

> We, therefore, the delegates . . . of the people of Texas, in solemn convention assembled, do hereby resolve and declare that our political connection with the Mexican nation has forever ended; and that the people of Texas do now constitute a free, sovereign and independent republic, and are fully invested with all the rights and attributes which properly belong to independent nations . . . .

Within a week a committee of the convention presented a draft constitution, which the convention itself approved with amendments on March 17. The constitution was ratified by the people in early September "by a practically unanimous vote."

The Text

"The constitution as adopted followed the general lines of that of the United States," except that "the federalistic features were eliminated because the new republic was a unit, and not divided into states." Beginning with a preamble that looks very much like our own, the constitution contains six Articles, a "Schedule," a set of "General Provisions," and a Declaration of Rights.

Article I begins with a separation-of-powers provision that is at best implicit in the U.S. Constitution:

> The powers of this government shall be divided into three departments, viz: legislative, executive and judicial, which shall remain forever separate and distinct.

Further sections of this article define the legislative branch, for the most part following the U.S. pattern. Legislative power was vested in a bicameral congress (§ 2). Members of the House of Representatives were to be elected annually (§ 3), Senators every three years–the

---

latter from "districts, as nearly equal in free population (free negroes and Indians excepted,) as practicable . . ." (§ 8). Most of the provisions in the first seven sections of the U.S. Article I were copied essentially verbatim; I note only departures from the U.S. model. The contempt power of Congress, implicit in the United States, was made express: "Each house may punish, by imprisonment, during the session, any person not a member, who shall be guilty of any disrespect to the house, by any disorderly conduct in their presence" (§ 16). The so-called Twenty-seventh Amendment, proposed in the United States in 1789 and allegedly ratified two centuries later, was incorporated with minor alterations into Article I, § 15. Except "in cases of emergency" certified by a two-thirds vote, bills were required to be "read on three several days in each house" (§ 20); if a bill was rejected, "no bill containing the same substance" could be adopted during the same session (§ 21); no holder or collector of public monies could be elected to Congress until he "acquitted himself of all responsibility" (§ 24); "[m]embers of either house m[ight] protest against any act or resolution, and . . . have such protest entered on the journals . . ." (id).

Article II embraces an enumeration of congressional powers remarkably reminiscent of the corresponding U.S. provisions. Nothing is said, however, of bankruptcy, naturalization, counterfeiting, piracy, offenses on the high seas or against the law of nations, or the seat of government. The commerce power was generalized, as befitted a unitary state: Congress was authorized simply "[t]o regulate commerce," with no limitation to that which was foreign, interstate, or Indian (§ 2). The clause respecting coinage was supplemented by the admonition that "nothing but gold and silver shall be made a lawful tender" (id), the clause dealing with patents and copyrights by express authority to grant "charters of incorporation" too (§ 3). The provision respecting organization of the militia, trimmed of its federalistic features, was transplanted to the Declaration of Rights (P Fifteenth).

It was only after I had carefully compared this enumeration with its U.S. counterpart that it occurred to me to wonder what it was doing there in the first place. In the United States, powers not enumerated are reserved to the individual states; in Texas there were no states to which they could be reserved. Could the Texan fathers have been such free spirits that they intended that unenumerated powers not be exercised at all?

The answer, if there is one, may lie in two provisions found in later articles of the constitution. The first, located in the final section of the judiciary article, enjoined it upon Congress, "as early as practicable," to

> introduce, by statute, the common law of England, with such modifications as our circumstances, in their judgment, may require; and in all criminal cases, the common law shall be the rule of decision (Art IV, § 13).

The second, tucked away among the "General Provisions" near the end of the document, required the adoption of a penal code as well as a general codification and revision of the laws. If "modifications" and "revisions" included statutes on topics previously unknown to the applicable law, then these provisions may have been the equivalent of the general grant of legislative authority one would expect to find in the constitution of a unitary state. Indeed it was not very long before the Texan Congress, possibly on the basis of these inauspicious clauses, enacted a bankruptcy code despite the absence of any reference to that subject in the enumeration of legislative powers. The mystery remains: If Congress was to have plenary powers, as the common-law and revision provisions arguably suggest, then what was the point of the enumeration?

Article III vested the executive authority in a popularly elected President serving for three years (two in the case of the first incumbent) and unable to succeed himself directly (§§ 1-2). Other provisions respecting the President, most of them quite familiar to the U.S. observer, are found in Article VI. Departures from the model include the following. If the Senate rejected a recess appointee, "the president shall not re-nominate the same individual to the same office" (§ 6). Heads of departments, appointed by the President with Senate approval, "shall remain in office during the term of service of the president, unless sooner removed by the president, with the advice and consent of the senate" (§ 10). The provision for presidential succession (§ 15) differs in several particulars from that of the United States. It applies not only in cases of removal, death, or resignation of the President, but also when he is impeached or absent from the country; it omits the U.S. reference to incapacity. It resolves an ambiguity in the U.S. version: in the cases specified the vice president "shall exercise the powers and discharge the duties of the president until a successor be duly qualified, or until the president, who may be absent or impeached, shall return or be acquitted."

Article IV, familiarly enough, vested the judicial power "in one supreme court, and such inferior courts as the congress may, from time to time, ordain and establish" (§ 1). There, however, the resemblance ends. The Texan Congress was required to divide the Republic into districts and to establish a court in each of them (§ 2). The Supreme Court was to consist of a chief justice and associate judges, but "the district judges shall compose the associate judges" (§ 7). Judges of both the supreme and district courts were to be elected "by joint ballot of both houses of congress," to serve four-year terms, and to be eligible for re-election (§§ 9, 1). Their compensation was "not to be increased or diminished" during their term (§ 1). There was also to be a set of county courts, together with "such justices' courts as the congress may, from time to time, establish" (§ 10).

The district courts were to have exclusive original jurisdiction "[i]n all admiralty and maritime cases, in all cases affecting ambassadors, public ministers or consuls, and in all capital cases," as well as original jurisdiction "in all civil cases when the matter in controversy amounts to one hundred dollars" (§ 3). Presumably this meant that cases within the "original" jurisdiction could be brought in county courts or before justices of the peace as well, along with those civil and criminal proceedings excluded from the district courts entirely. The supreme court was to have "appellate jurisdiction only," with the proviso (necessitated by the presence of district judges on the supreme bench) that "no judge shall sit in a case in the supreme court tried by him in the court below" (§ 8).

The "Schedule" consists of provisions respecting the transition from the old regime to the new constitution. The only ones of interest made provisional apportionments of House and Senate seats "until the first enumeration shall be made, as directed [or described] by this constitution" (§§ 6-7). Unfortunately, in their haste the framers managed to omit the original provision for a census; no enumeration was either "directed" or "described."

The "General Provisions" are a grab bag of clauses that, among other things, made it the duty of Congress to disqualify persons convicted of "bribery, perjury, or other high crimes and misdemeanors" from public office, from voting, and from sitting on juries (§ 1); required the legislature, "as soon as circumstances will permit, to provide by law, a general system of education" (§ 5); offered citizenship to white immigrants after six months' residence upon swearing allegiance to Texas (§ 6); protected existing slavery and the right to import additional slaves from the United States while forbidding free blacks to reside in Texas without the consent of Congress (§ 9); made detailed provision for the distribution of land (§ 10); and provided that the constitution itself might be amended by passage of a proposal by two successive legislatures (the second by a two-thirds vote in each house), followed by ratification by a simple "majority of the electors qualified to vote for members of congress voting thereon" (§ 11).

The Declaration of Rights combines elements of Article I, § 9 and Article III, § 3 of the U.S. Constitution with those of its Bill of Rights, with some significant variations. The first paragraph, which speaks of the "equal rights" of those who form a social compact, adds in cryptic terms that "no men or set of men are entitled to exclusive public privileges or emoluments from the community"; the second proclaims the "inalienable right" of the people "to alter their government." The third is either a paraphrase or a revision of our religion clauses:

> No preference shall be given by law to any religious denomination or mode of worship over another, but every person shall be permitted to worship God according to the dictates of his own conscience.

The fourth expands upon the freedom of expression:

> Every citizen shall be at liberty to speak, write, or publish his opinions on any subject, being responsible for the abuse of that privilege. No law shall ever be passed to curtail the liberty of speech or of the press; and in all prosecutions for libels, the truth may be given in evidence, and the jury shall have the right to determine the law and fact, under the directions of the court.

Amendments IV through VIII to the U.S. Constitution were reproduced almost word for word, except that the takings clause applied to the appropriation of services as well as property (P Thirteenth). The Second Amendment was modified in a way that seemed to resolve the controversial ambiguity of the original: "Every citizen shall have the right to bear arms in defence of himself and the republic" (P Fourteenth). The Third, which deals with the quartering of troops, was dropped entirely–as was the Ninth [and] Tenth. The guarantee of habeas corpus was preserved intact (P Tenth), but there is no reference to bills of attainder; the relevant clause provides that "[n]o retrospective or ex-post facto law, or laws impairing the obligation of contracts, shall be made" (P Sixteenth).

In addition to the first two paragraphs, the Declaration contains several other clauses unknown to the U.S. model. Imprisonment for debt was abolished (P Twelfth). The Declaration attempted to make a reality of Chief Justice Marshall's famous dictum that for every wrong there is a remedy: "All courts shall be open, and every man for any injury done him in his lands, goods, person, or reputation, shall have remedy by due course of law" (P Eleventh). Perpetuities, monopolies, entailments, and the law of primogeniture were forbidden (P Seventeenth); the military was expressly subordinated to "the civil power" (P Fourteenth). Article V, § 1 embodies a disqualification equally foreign to the U.S. Constitution:

> Ministers of the gospel being, by their profession, dedicated to God and the care of souls, ought not to be diverted from the great duties of their functions; therefore, no minister of the gospel, or priest of any denomination whatever, shall be eligible to the office of the executive of the republic, nor to a seat in either branch of the congress of the same.

These last two provisions, like numerous other novelties in the Texas constitution, were direct responses to grievances asserted in the Declaration of Independence.

Notes on the Republic of Texas Constitution

Influences of Spanish, Mexican, and American Constitutional and Legal Traditions: Almost all the framers of the 1836 Republic of Texas Constitution were steeped in the American constitutional legal tradition. Is it therefore surprising that the Texas national constitution, drafted in two weeks in the midst of a war, differed in as many respects as it did from the United States Constitution?

Some of these differences can be traced to the motivations that brought many founders to Texas. Debtors were frequently attracted to Texas, which promised a fresh start from creditors and land prices one-tenth or less of American prices. These motivations explain, for instance, the Texas constitutional bars against imprisonment for debt and against perpetuities, monopolies, entailments, and the law of primogeniture.

Other differences can be traced to the experiences of Texans under Mexican rule. In addition to the military subordination to the civil power and the ministry disqualification identified by Professor Curie, which other provisions of the 1836 Republic of Texas Constitution appear to have been enacted in response to the Texans' grievances against Mexican rule? On the other hand, are there other provisions of this constitution that followed Spanish and Mexican legal traditions?

The Enumeration of Legislative Power Enigma: Why did the Republic of Texas Constitution explicitly enumerate congressional powers? Was the hastiness of the deliberations a possible reason that the delegates included what could be viewed as an unnecessary enumeration of legislative power? Or was this enumeration desired by the delegates as a limitation on governmental power? If so, who received the reserved powers and how could they be exercised?

Texas's subsequent adoption of a bankruptcy code in the absence of a specific enumeration of power indicates, as Professor Currie notes, that the Texas Congress had plenary legislative authority, thereby rendering the enumeration surplusage. On the other hand, a constitutional amendment proposed during the 1840's, which would have explicitly authorized the Texas Congress "to pass naturalization laws," supports the proposition that the enumeration was intended to limit congressional power. This constitutional amendment would not have been necessary if the Texas Congress already had the power to enact any law under the common law and codification provisions of the constitution. Are there any explanations for Texas's apparent disparate treatment between bankruptcy laws and naturalization laws? Does the fact that the Republic of Texas Constitution specifically defined citizenship requirements suggest a potential answer?

Ratification of the Republic of Texas Constitution: The Texas Revolution ended with the Treaty of Velasco signed by President Santa Anna after his capture by Sam Houston's Texan army at the Battle of San Jacinto. The new nation then held an election a few months later in September 1836 to ratify the Republic of Texas Constitution and to select the officers of the government. The voters ratified the constitution nearly unanimously and elected Sam Houston in a landslide to serve as the first President of the Republic of Texas.

B. THE STATEHOOD CONSTITUTION OF 1845

In the inaugural September 1836 election for the Republic of Texas, the voters were also given the opportunity to express their views on whether Texas should seek admission to the United States. The voters overwhelmingly indicated their desire to be annexed. But while Texans were eager to join the United States, the United States was not ready.

United States Presidents Andrew Jackson and Martin Van Buren resisted Sam Houston's annexation requests primarily because of concerns regarding the United States's diplomatic relations with Mexico and the balance of power between slave states and free states. But a few years later, the political climate in Washington began to change as President John Tyler sought an issue that would support his election bid and James Knox Polk actively campaigned for the presidency on a platform to annex Texas. After Polk's election, but before he took office, Congress passed a joint resolution offering statehood for Texas over strident political opposition.[22] All that was left was for Texas to agree to the deal and establish an acceptable republican constitution for a state in a federal union.

John Cornyn, *The Roots of the Texas Constitution: Settlement to Statehood*, 26 Tex. Tech L. Rev. 1089 (1995)[*]

Daniel Webster characterized the new Texas charter [of 1845] as the "best of all American state constitutions." The New York Evening Post likewise rhapsodized that the new constitution "proved how much the spirit of legislation is advanced in the west, and the beneficial effects produced upon the young and growing minds of that region, by the controversies, struggles and experiences of the older portions of the United States."

---

[22]The joint resolution barely passed in the Senate, twenty-seven to twenty-five. *See* Earl M. Maltz, *The Constitution and the Annexation of Texas*, 23 Const. Comment. 381, 399 (2006). In addition to the political complaints that Texas statehood would lead to war with Mexico and additional sectional strife between slave and free states, opponents claimed that the very method of proceeding through a joint resolution violated the United States Constitution. Under their view, a treaty ratified by two-thirds of the Senate was a necessary prerequisite to Texas statehood. *See id.* at 386-90.

Still, self-interest, ideology, and culture were at least as influential on the Texas framers as were earlier constitutions. For all their diversity, the delegates who assembled in the frontier town of Austin beginning on July 4, 1845, had at least three things in common. The delegates were all: (1) recent immigrants seeking their fortune in the cheap and abundant lands of the Republic; (2) fleeing personal or financial misfortune; and (3) experienced fighters, having defended themselves, their families, and their possessions from both Indian depredations and an oppressive Mexican government.

As the delegates met, they had before them the constitutions of most other states, of the United States, and of the Republic of Texas. During the Convention, examples from other constitutions were addressed as either worthy of emulation or as examples of what should be avoided. The recently completed but unratified Constitution of Louisiana was held up as a model so often that the President of the Convention, forty-one year old Thomas Jefferson Rusk of Nacogdoches, exclaimed:

> I sincerely wish that the future Constitution of Louisiana had remained locked up until our labors were over. We have received no benefits from it, and have come very near to incorporating some articles which would have been ruinous to Texas. We can reflect for ourselves, and are capable of forming a Constitution for ourselves.

Another disapproving delegate similarly claimed that he "discovered a disposition to make everything conformable as far as possible to the system of the Federal government." Nevertheless, the delegates would refer by name to the constitutions of twenty states, as well as that of the United States, during their debates. Although state constitutions in the South were mentioned with relatively greater frequency–which is not surprising in light of where the delegates themselves hailed from and their common economic interest in the preservation of slavery–there was remarkable openness to examples set by states from all parts of the nation. Indeed, the constitutions of Pennsylvania and Mississippi were cited by the delegates with identical frequency, as were the constitutions of Arkansas, Illinois, Indiana, and Ohio. No single constitution, however, proved to be a template for the Texas document.

In the hierarchy of interests at stake in the Convention of 1845, one interest was clearly paramount: annexation. The concern for annexation counseled conservatism. As Rusk said in his opening remarks after he was selected President of the Convention: "We have one grand object in view; and that is to enter the great American confederacy with becoming dignity and self respect." To this end, he cautioned:

> The formation of a State Constitution upon Republican principles is the only act to be performed to incorporate us into the American Union. While we insert those great principles which have been sanctioned by time and experience, we should be careful to avoid the introduction of new and untried theories. We should leave those who are to follow us free to adopt such amendments to the system as their experience and intelligence shall suggest, and their circumstances render necessary.

The delegates were quite aware that their actions were being scrutinized by the outside world, including opponents of annexation. Above all else, the Texans wanted annexation. This proved an irresistible force in shaping the new constitution. * * * *

The Bill of Rights

The bill of rights, adopted [for the Republic of Texas] in 1836, was composed of seventeen sections. Its significance to Texas constitutionalism is evidenced by the fact that these sections formed the core of the twenty-one sections of the statehood bill of rights. With some exceptions, they were reproduced in Article I of the Constitution of 1876, still in effect today.

Such declarations were familiar to the delegates who gathered at Washington-on-the-Brazos in 1836. During the preceding six decades in America, bills of rights had become the customary means by which individual rights were proclaimed. American colonists had taken as their model similar declarations by their English forbears, such as the Magna Carta (1215), the Petition of Right (1628), and the English Bill of Rights (1689). Earlier colonial examples included Maryland's Toleration Act of 1649 and the Charter of Rhode Island, which guaranteed religious liberty. Massachusetts, even though it sponsored a state-supported religion, was in 1641 the first state to comprehensively guarantee, in its Body of Liberties, many other rights which we now consider fundamental: freedom of assembly and speech, equal protection of the laws, just compensation for public use of private property, freedom to emigrate, the right to bail, the right to employ counsel, the right to trial by jury in civil cases, the right to challenge jurors, limitations on imprisonment for debt, a guarantee of a speedy trial, and a prohibition on double jeopardy and cruel or excessive punishment.

The 1836 Texas Declaration of Rights was substantially identical to many state constitutions of the day and to the federal Bill of Rights. One historian bluntly stated: "The Declaration of Rights contains nothing new and consists substantially of what one can find attached to the constitution of almost any state."[23] The Virginia Bill of Rights, adopted in 1776, proved to be the model for all state constitutions that followed, including the Pennsylvania, New Hampshire, and South Carolina constitutions adopted in 1776, the New York Constitution adopted in 1777, and the Massachusetts Constitution adopted in 1780. Characteristic of all such declarations during this period was the invocation of natural law doctrine and the expressed conviction that governments were compacts between the government and the governed, founded upon the governed's consent.

The Declaration of Rights of the Republic provided for separation of church and state, freedom of speech and of the press, protection against unreasonable searches and seizures, and search warrants before search or seizure. In criminal cases, the accused was guaranteed the right to counsel, confrontation of witnesses, compulsory process, speedy and public jury trial, the right against self-incrimination, and presentment or indictment by grand jury. Denial of privileges of citizenship was prohibited except by due course of law. The Declaration of Rights also prohibited double jeopardy, the denial of bail except for capital

---

[23]Rupert N. Richardson, *Framing the Constitution of the Republic of Texas*, Vol. XXXI, No. 3, SW. HIST. Q. 191, 213 (1928).

crimes, and the conferral of any benefits from foreign states on persons in a position of public trust. The Declaration guaranteed the right to habeas corpus, prohibited excessive bail, fines, or cruel and unusual punishment, guaranteed that "all courts shall be open" and that a remedy would be provided by due course of law, forbade imprisonment for debt in consequence of inability to pay, required just compensation for the public taking of private property or services, guaranteed the right to bear arms, and subordinated the military to civil authority. In addition, the Declaration provided for a well-regulated militia, defined treason, and prohibited laws that were retroactive, ex post facto, or which impaired obligations of contract. The Declaration further outlawed perpetuities, monopolies, and the law of primogeniture or entailments. These now familiar guarantees were so similar to existing provisions of the federal and other state constitutions that one historian remarked:

> It appears that the framers of [the Declaration of Rights] had before them a copy of the Constitution of the United States and that of several of the southern and western states, and that they gathered from each whatever gems of political philosophy struck their fancy. But they rarely ever quote[d] verbatim; at least a word or two [was always] changed.[24]

At the [Statehood] Convention, on July 11, 1845, Issac Van Zandt, Chairman of the Committee on General Provisions and the Bill of Rights, reported the Committee's proposed bill of rights. Few new provisions were included. The Committee did add prohibitions against religious tests for officeholders (section 3) and bills of attainder. It also added a separate guarantee of "due course of law" (section 16), a limitation on the power to suspend laws (section 20), and a limitation on the power of eminent domain. The Due Course of Law provision was adopted without debate, as was the prohibition on perpetuities and monopolies, the latter being essentially a copy of a like provision in the Constitution of the Republic.

The final addition, section 21, provided that "everything in this 'Bill of Rights' is excepted out of the general powers of government, and shall forever remain inviolate, and all laws contrary thereto, or to the following provisions, shall be void." This proclamation originated in the Pennsylvania Constitution of 1790, Article IX, § 26, and when adopted by the Convention, nearly identical statements also existed in the constitutions of Pennsylvania, Kentucky, Mississippi, Alabama, and Florida. * * * *

C. THE TEXAS CONSTITUTION OF 1876

Texas became a part of the United States in 1845, as the tensions between the north and south regarding slavery and state's rights continued to escalate. Sixteen years later, these tensions erupted into the Civil War. Upon joining the Confederacy, Texas had to disavow its relationship with the United States and adopt a new state constitution. After the Civil War ended, yet another state constitution was then needed to rejoin the United States. The Texas Constitution of 1866 satisfied all the preconditions for statehood imposed by the reconciliatory policies of President Andrew Johnson. However, this constitution, as well as the other southern constitutions enacted immediately after the Civil War, did not meet the

[24] *Id.*

demands of the Radical Republicans in Congress, who wanted to safeguard voting and political rights of the former slaves and to limit such rights to those who had supported the Confederacy. Texas therefore had to adopt the Constitution of 1869 to appease the Radical Republicans in Congress. As Reconstruction ended, Texas had the opportunity to establish a new state charter.

John Walker Mauer, *State Constitutions in a Time of Crisis: The Case of the Texas Constitution of 1876*, 68 Tex. L. Rev. 1615 (1990)*

Before 1876, Texas had an unbroken tradition of liberal constitutionalism. All constitutions prior to 1876 imposed only limited controls on the financial authority of state and local governments. Those liberal constitutions include: the constitutions of 1845 and 1866, written by Democrats during constitutional conventions; the 1869 Constitution, drafted by Republicans during a constitutional convention; and the [never ratified] 1874 Constitution, fashioned by a Democrat-controlled legislature. While all these constitutions were liberal, the provisions dealing with government power varied from document to document. The liberal postwar Texas constitutions of 1866, 1869, and 1874 each contained measures that strengthened government. Those three documents established annual sessions of the legislature, higher salaries for state officials, longer terms of office for the judiciary, a government position for a state superintendent of education, and support to the banks, railroads or both.

In the sense that the Constitution of 1876 ended the postbellum flirtation with active government, this document was a return to an older style of constitutionalism, but it was also much more. The 1876 document broke with the liberal tradition that had dominated all earlier constitutions. As was common with other evolving restrictive organic laws, any deviation from tradition was dramatic. The restrictive Texas Constitution placed controls on state government in all four key areas of financial functioning[25] and also on local government in two of these areas. In addition, the 1876 document set maximum salaries for state officials and prohibited the legislature from passing many categories of legislation as special or local laws.

The Grangers were the most numerous and vocal advocates of a restrictive constitution, and their protests put them squarely in the mainstream of the emerging national trend towards restrictive constitutionalism. This new trend in constitutional creation was the result of popular dissatisfaction with the high cost of government, as well as the general belief that political leaders were unwilling to respond to the popular will. The Texas Grangers' executive committee criticized the state's Democratic leadership in an April 1875 document, in which it urged its membership to become involved in the selection of delegates. At the same time it condemned the earlier Republican officeholders, the executive committee made it clear that its primary complaint was against the current Democratic administration. The Grangers' dissatisfaction had a strong basis in fact.

---

[25]Dr. Mauer identified these four key controls as strict ceilings on taxes (expressed as maximum rates), explicit limits on public debt, the prohibition of governmental aid to private enterprise, and controls on the use of tax revenue (footnote added).

Democrats under Governor Coke had kept taxes at the historically high rates originally established by the Republicans. Furthermore, they mimicked their Republican predecessors by relying on deficit spending to fund the fiscal largess. Democrats, like Republicans before them, found the record-high taxation insufficient to pay for all the state's expenditures.

Yet, the focus of the Grangers' ire had an ironic twist. Because Texas had avoided debt before the Civil War through the windfall gained in the Compromise of 1850,[26] the debt of the mid-1870s seemed intolerable to many in the state. However, in comparison to some of the other southern states, Texas was carrying a light debt load. For example, in Alabama and Louisiana the Democratic leadership called constitutional conventions only because servicing the debt had become such a problem that it made reform by means of a new constitution unavoidable. The Texas Democratic hierarchy was able to stall holding a constitutional convention and have the legislature write the 1874 Constitution in part because it had a manageable debt.

When the Constitutional Convention of 1875 convened in Austin on September 6, it met in a decidedly different atmosphere from the one in which the legislative committee had written the abortive Constitution of 1874. Unlike the legislature, the Convention's only duty was to draft a new organic law. And unlike the legislature, the delegates came to the Convention after an extensive public airing of the constitutional revision issues. Moreover, because the Convention was a one-shot affair and a large number of delegates were not professional politicians, the success of the Constitutional Convention did not depend on the usual system of political rewards and punishments that dominate the traditional legislative process. Furthermore, the dominant players in the Convention were not the same players who had controlled the revision process in the legislature. Governor Coke and his allies in the Fourteenth Legislature had drafted a liberal, progovernment constitution [in 1874]. Grangers and the other rank-and-file Democrats dissatisfied with the Coke Administration dominated the Convention and wrote a restrictive organic law.

Ninety members–three elected from each of the thirty state senatorial districts–were present when the 1875 Convention began. Information relating to the Convention's membership is sketchy, but is sufficient to provide a rough idea of their backgrounds: twenty-eight were farmers, thirty-three were lawyers, and twenty-nine practiced other occupations. Thirty-seven identified themselves as Grangers, and of these, thirty claimed a farm-related occupation. The Grangers represented the largest single block in the Convention; therefore, they set the tone of the Convention. They provided leadership to the non-Granger delegates who favored a restrictive constitution. Lawyers were the second largest contingent, and at least one contemporary observer argued that a Granger-lawyer split existed in the Convention.[27] Analysis of the voting does not reveal a unified lawyer voting block within the Convention, but this occupation group generally comprised the largest minority element that was fighting to retain a liberal constitution.

---

[26]Under this Compromise, Texas surrendered its claim to all lands to the source of the Rio Grande (in what is now southern Wyoming) in exchange for $10 million in cash (footnote added).

[27]M. Perman, The Road to Redemption: Southern Politics 1869-1879, at 204 (1984).

The same fiscal concerns that prompted the delegates to draft a restrictive constitution motivated them to exercise fiscal responsibility in conducting the Convention. The Convention vigorously debated whether to hire a stenographer and whether to publish its debates. Further debate surrounded whether it should pay its delegates four dollars a day rather than the committee-recommended five dollars a day, which was still considerably below the eight dollars a day the legislators received. The Convention voted against hiring a stenographer and publishing the debates. However, the Grangers as well as the advocates of a liberal constitution supported the five dollars a day salary. The Convention's salary decision illustrated the limits to the majority's pursuit of retrenchment.

The Convention's actions on these early procedural matters prompted the first negative responses from the state's press. Most dailies became fervent critics of the Convention. The Shreveport Times published an especially perceptive critique of the Convention early in the process; the Dallas Herald republished the Times editorial, with a strong statement of approval. According to the Times editor, the Convention was split between "'the best men' and the 'retrenchers,'" and he described the latter as "men of good intentions, but who have absolutely no comprehension of the work entrusted to their wisdom."

The first article to emerge from committee was on the "Legislative Department," and it was strongly restrictive in character. Mandated to limit government's spendthrift ways, the Convention passed the provision with only minor changes. Abandoning the traditional liberal approach to fiscal responsibility, the Texas legislative article closely resembled the same articles contained in the new restrictive constitutions of other states. The Missouri Constitution of 1875 was a favorite model–most of the Texas's legislative article's restrictive provisions were taken, often verbatim, from that document. These new restrictive provisions limited the legislature's power to raise taxes, prohibited aid from state and local government to either private enterprise or cities, and denied the legislature the power to "release or extinguish" any financial obligation owed to state and local governments. Another section of the legislative article that was commonly associated with restrictive constitutions prohibited the legislature from passing twenty-five different categories of special and local laws. The Convention largely copied this article from the Missouri Constitution, which in turn had copied it from the Pennsylvania Constitution of 1874. Finally, another provision of the legislative article that had a restrictive effect was that providing for legislative pay. Not only were such salaries five dollars per day for the initial sixty days and two dollars per day thereafter, far below the eight dollars per day provided in the 1866, 1869, and 1874 constitutions, but they were also stated as constitutional maximums for the first time in history.

The taxation and revenue article provoked slightly more controversy than the legislative article, but that dissension did not involve constitutional issues. Delegates accepted the article's major restrictive constitutional provisions without much recorded dissent or even comment. The committee passed a version of the taxation and revenue article that was less restrictive than the one ultimately approved by the Convention. However, the details are scarce because the Convention did not record voting on the major amendments to the article. The committee version of the article included the traditional provisions that the legislature could select tax-exempt property by a two-thirds majority vote. Delegates eliminated this provision on the convention floor, while they added to the article a household property exemption of 250 dollars. A further change made on the convention floor was to include a provision that set a maximum on state property tax–the delegates extended this measure to also cover counties and towns. The Convention set the local government property tax rate at one-half of the state maximum of fifty cents per one hundred dollars of assessed value. In addition to these major restrictive features, the taxation and revenue article contained a variety of novel restrictive provisions that were narrower in scope. For example, the Convention modeled two sections after provisions contained in the Missouri Constitution. The first required that taxes be levied only by general laws "for public purposes only," and the second prohibited the legislature from passing a law that "surrendered or suspended" the authority to tax corporations.

In contrast to the relative ease with which the 1875 Convention passed the most important restrictive constitutional issues, other areas of its deliberations were extremely controversial. For the most part, these other issues were unrelated to the restrictive constitutional movement; however, one exception was the subject of salaries. The salary controversy differed depending upon the office. Furthermore, each of the Convention's committees approached its issues in different ways. As with the legislative article, the executive article emerged from committee with pay figures stated as constitutional maximums, but once on the convention floor, the latter article received a somewhat different reception because some delegates challenged the amount of pay provided. For example, the Convention lowered the governor's remuneration from 5,000 to 4,000 dollars. In comparison to other articles, salaries in the judicial article received quite different treatment. A majority in the judiciary committee were lawyers, and as reported from committee, the judicial article set no maximum on the salaries mentioned in it. For example, the committee provided a salary of 4,000 dollars for supreme court justices. On the convention floor, delegates added language making the salary figures the maximum allowed, but they resisted efforts to lower, by 500 dollars, the amount provided.

As the Convention wore on, the controversy over salaries and political rights turned many major newspapers into opponents, or at least into vocal critics, of the Convention. Early in the Convention the Galveston Daily News attacked that body's penny-pinching tendencies by observing:

> Government without expense is the ideal economy to which the heroic retrenchers aspire. Their faith in it is really touching. We know nothing comparable to it in simplicity and pathos. . . . Such retrenchment is not economy. It is essentially the worst kind of wastefulness.

The controversy surrounding financial matters, such as salaries for state officials, prompted opponents to refer to the delegates as "retrenchers," but as the anger grew, opponents began to openly attack the Grangers. [But] some small weekly newspapers continued to support the convention–openly cheering the Grangers in their parsimony.

The Convention's refusal to limit suffrage rights or intervene in the political process generated the most complaints. The goal sought by those that wanted some curtailment of political rights was "relief" to the black belt, as Speaker of the House Bryan put it in a letter to John Reagan (a leading Democrat who was one of the chief advocates of liberal constitutionalism in the convention). The most bitterly contested issue was whether to make the poll tax a suffrage requirement. Led by Grangers, delegates rejected proposals to transform the otherwise innocuous poll tax into a measure to restrict suffrage. Plans for a large house of representatives and territorial districts for the district courts also failed. Grangers and other white agrarian opponents of political discrimination did not oppose racial discrimination per se; rather, they believed that the poll tax proposals represented class legislation that threatened the political rights of poor whites. Thus, while accepting discrimination against blacks, those opposed to political discrimination believed it was more important to preserve the political rights of poor whites than to exclude the blacks from the political process.

After the Constitutional Convention of 1875 completed its work, the Democratic party's leadership found itself in a quandary. Most of the leaders advocated a new organic law, but the Convention-written document was far different from the one sought. Therefore, most leading Democrats, including Governor Coke, supported ratification of the 1876 Constitution because it was a Democratic party-sponsored replacement of the Reconstruction Constitution of 1869. Whether a determined opposition to the constitution by top Democrats would have prevented its ratification cannot be answered; because no internal resistance within the dominant party existed, the people overwhelmingly approved the 1876 Constitution in the ratification election. For many years to come the resulting document was caustically labeled "The Granger Constitution."

Notes on the Statehood Constitutions

The Granger Constitution? Grangers, who possessed what could be described as an "antigovernment" perspective, comprised the largest faction at the Constitutional Convention of 1875, as more than forty percent of the delegates were members of the Grange. Nevertheless, the caustic "Granger Constitution" label arguably overstates their influence, as the Grangers seldom voted as a bloc, and, even when they did, their votes alone were insufficient to pass their proposals.[28] As a reminder, the Grange movement in the United States was essentially a rural movement during the 1870's to obtain better business conditions for farmers. In Texas, the Grangers were particularly concerned with perceived governmental excesses during the postbellum period, especially with regards to taxation and spending. The Grangers, in general, desired a constitution that would limit both the power of state government and large business interests such as railroads. How well did the 1876 Texas Constitution serve these desires? Does the answer to this question explain in part the continued need for state constitutional amendments as the interests of Texas have changed over the approximately 140 intervening years?

The Judiciary as an Exception to Retrenchment? One commentator has urged that one section of the 1876 Constitution stood in marked contrast to the restrictive approach:

> The one section of the constitution that departed from the new organic charter's "systematically restrictive approach" was the hotly debated judiciary article, in which the delegates ultimately created courts with

---

[28]Patrick G. Williams, *Of Rutabagas and Redeemers: Rethinking the Texas Constitution of 1876*, 106 SW. HIST. Q. 231, 233-34, 244 (Oct. 2002).

> comprehensive powers, "charged with high and holy duties." The delegates had faith that the courts, more than any other state authority, would protect their individual liberties. At the same time, the delegates sought to ensure judicial accountability and check any promiscuous misuse of power through direct election of judges.[29]

Is this assessment correct? There are some unusual features to the Texas state government when it is compared to the federal government, such as the state legislature only meets once every two years in regular session, legislators are paid a nominal salary (currently set at $600 per month by article III, section 24) that requires them to have other occupations, and the powers of the governor are sometimes referred to as weak. But this commentary offered no evidentiary support for the proposition that the delegates to the Constitutional Convention of 1875 believed the courts would protect their individual liberties. Indeed, such a faith would have been somewhat remarkable as state constitutional litigation at that time "was rare and seldom involved civil-liberties issues."[30] Additionally, the decision by the Republican-dominated Texas Supreme Court just two years earlier in *Ex parte Rodriguez* that the gubernatorial election of Democrat Richard Coke violated the state constitution presumably created some distrust of the courts.[31] The state constitution in fact subordinates the court system to the legislature in some respects, granting the legislature the power to fund the court system, define its jurisdiction, and prescribe rules of practice and procedure.

Prolixity in State Constitutions: During the nineteenth century and early twentieth century, a perhaps unfortunate nationwide trend in state constitutions was their expanding length. Rather than staying within the confines of Chief Justice Marshall's famous statement that the nature of a constitution "requires that only its great outlines should be marked,"[32] state constitutions began to incorporate increasingly more specific and detailed provisions that appeared to be legislative in nature. These specific provisions concerned subjects that the predominant political forces wanted permanently ensconced in the fundamental charter of the state. Of great importance in this respect were provisions dealing with economic regulation of railroads, banks, and other corporations, limitations on the amount and types of governmental borrowing of money, and suffrage and apportionment. How many of these types of provisions are evident in Dr. Mauer's insightful discussion of the Texas Constitution of 1876? Does this help explain why the Texas Constitution is one of the longest in the nation, containing more than 85,000 words, or well over 170 pages of single-spaced text?

---

[29] James C. Harrington, *Free Speech, Press, and Assembly Liberties under the Texas Bill of Rights*, 68 TEX. L. REV. 1435, 1440 (1990).

[30] TARR, *supra* note 1, at 163.

[31] 39 Tex. 705 (1873). Article III, section 6 of the 1869 Texas Constitution contained two clauses, one mandating that the polls had to be open for four days and one granting the legislature the power to change the locale of elections, separated by a semi-colon. The court reasoned that, because of the semi-colon, the legislature could not limit an election to a single day as it had done for the 1873 gubernatorial election, earning the court the name "the semi-colon court."

[32] McCulloch v. Maryland, 17 U.S. (4 Wheat) 316, 407 (1819).

Failed Texas State Constitutions: Dr. Mauer's article highlights some of the contrasts between the failed proposed constitution of 1874 and the 1876 Constitution. In addition to the failed 1874 effort, several other state constitutions have been proposed for Texas yet never adopted. In 1833, Sam Houston chaired a committee that proposed a constitution for Texas as a separate state from Coahuila in the Republic of Mexico, but the Mexican government rejected the request. In the years since the 1876 Constitution, there have been a few abortive attempts to adopt a new state constitution. In 1919, Texas voters rejected the legislature's proposal to call a new constitutional convention. Between 1949 and 1961, some politicians and citizen groups sought and the legislature finally authorized a study of the state constitution, but the legislature did not take any action on the proposed recommendations. Further efforts from 1969 to 1975 culminated in a 1974 Texas Constitutional Convention and a proposed constitution that was approved by the legislature but defeated by the voters in a November 1975 election.

State Constitutional Interpretive Difficulties: How did the various political, social, and economic influences of the times influence the drafters of the 1836 Republic of Texas Constitution, the 1845 Statehood Constitution, and the 1876 Constitution? Should these influences still matter today when interpreting the Texas Constitution? Then-Supreme Court of Texas Justice John Cornyn points out in his article excerpted earlier in this chapter that the provisions of article I of the 1876 Constitution, which contains the existing "bill of rights" of the Texas Constitution, were derived in large part from the guarantees contained in the 1836 Republic of Texas Constitution and the 1845 Statehood Constitution. To the extent that it is possible to derive the "original intent" or "original meaning" of a constitutional provision, which intent or meaning should then control? The intent or meaning in 1836? 1845? 1876? Or some combination?

The particular challenges in interpreting state constitutions are highlighted throughout this book. While some interpretation problems are shared with the United States Constitution, state constitutions often have unique interpretation problems, such as frequently sketchy convention debates, multiple amendments and revisions to their constitutions over a long period of time, the prevalent borrowing of provisions from other sources (such as the Federal Constitution and other state constitutions), and the relative value of precedent from these disparate sources. In addition, state constitutions cannot be viewed in isolation, but must be integrated into the larger context of the federal system, as detailed in the next chapter.

Chapter 2

STATE CONSTITUTIONS AND THE FEDERAL SYSTEM

At our nation's founding, the states were truly sovereigns. The Declaration of Independence provided that, because of the enumerated abuses suffered under King George, the thirteen colonies had become "Free and Independent States . . . ; and that as Free and Independent States, they have full Power to levy War, conclude Peace, contract Alliances, establish Commerce, and to do all other Acts and Things which Independent States may of right do." The first charter governing the relations of these new states, the Articles of Confederation, specifically acknowledged that "each state retains its sovereignty, freedom, and independence, and every Power, Jurisdiction, and right, which is not by this confederation expressly delegated to the United States, in Congress assembled."[1]

Yet a nation so comprised was bound to have disagreements, which soon were evident among the states in the Union, particularly with respect to their interstate trade policies that were frequently motivated by economic self-interest. The Confederation Congress accordingly authorized a convention to be held in Philadelphia to propose changes to the Articles of Confederation. But instead of accomplishing its mandate, the Constitutional Convention, as it is now known, proposed abandoning the Articles of Confederation and adopting an entirely new Federal Constitution.[2]

The subsequent ratification of this Constitution changed the relationship between the state and federal governments. No longer did the states retain all aspects of their "sovereignty, freedom, and independence"–rather, the Federal Constitution and the laws and treaties made under it are declared "the supreme law of the land."[3] Thus, although the United States Constitution creates a federal government with only limited and enumerated powers, thereby providing the states a residuary sovereignty, the federal government is supreme within its sphere.

As a result of this preeminence, state constitutions cannot be studied in isolation. Instead, state constitutional law is influenced in many respects by the United States Constitution, federal laws and treaties, and the federal judicial system.

---

[1]ARTS. OF CONFED. art. II (1781).

[2]There is a rich literature on the motivations behind and the proceedings at the Constitutional Convention. *See, e.g.*, RICHARD BEEMAN, PLAIN, HONEST MEN: THE MAKING OF THE AMERICAN CONSTITUTION (2009); CATHERINE DRINKER BOWEN, MIRACLE AT PHILADELPHIA (1966); MAX FARRAND, THE FRAMING OF THE CONSTITUTION OF THE UNITED STATES (1913); JACK N. RAKOVE, ORIGINAL MEANINGS: POLITICS AND IDEAS IN THE MAKING OF THE CONSTITUTION (1996); GORDON S. WOOD, THE CREATION OF THE AMERICAN REPUBLIC, 1776-1787 (1972).

[3]U.S. CONST. art. VI.

A. THE GUARANTY CLAUSE AND FEDERAL POLITICAL INFLUENCES ON STATE CONSTITUTIONS

In less than two centuries, the United States grew from thirteen states to fifty states. The Constitution contains the authority for new states to be admitted in Article IV, Section 3, which provides that "New States may be admitted by Congress into this Union; but no new States shall be formed or erected within the Jurisdiction of any other States; nor any State be formed by the Junction of two or more States, or Parts of States, without the Consent of the Legislatures of the States concerned as well as of the Congress." Under this provision, Congress has the sole power to withhold or grant statehood, as long as it does not interfere with the boundaries of the existing states without their consent.

The Constitution is silent regarding the criteria Congress should employ in admitting new states into the Union. The only constitutional provision that arguably provides any potential limitation is the Guaranty Clause, Article IV, Section 4: "The United States shall guarantee to every State in this Union a Republican Form of Government, and shall protect each of them against Invasion; and on Application of the Legislature, or of the Executive (when the Legislature cannot be convened) against domestic violence." It would therefore appear that Congress should deny statehood if the proposed state does not possess a "Republican Form of Government."

But what are the characteristics of a "Republican Form of Government"? At the time the Constitution was being ratified, no other nation employed a similar "republican" governmental model that the United States could borrow. So did the framers merely intend to distinguish themselves from the existing aristocracies and monarchies prevalent in other nations? Or were the framers being more specific, envisioning a system of separation of powers to protect against the potential tyranny of factions? And who should decide whether a state's government is republican? Is this an issue that the federal courts should resolve, or is it a nonjusticiable political question that should be left to Congress?

***Largess v. Supreme Judicial Court of Massachusetts*, 373 F.3d 219 (1st Cir. 2004) (per curiam)**

Plaintiffs brought suit in United States District Court against the Supreme Judicial Court of Massachusetts (the "SJC") and others, alleging that the remedy adopted in the same-sex marriage decision, *Goodridge v. Department of Public Health,* 798 N.E.2d 941 (Mass. 2003), violated their rights under the Guarantee Clause of the federal Constitution. The SJC, in a divided opinion, held in *Goodridge* that "barring an individual from the protection, benefits, and obligations of civil marriage solely because that person would marry a person of the same sex violates the Massachusetts Constitution." As a remedy, the court ordered that the state of Massachusetts recognize the marriage of same-sex couples within six months of the opinion's issuance. The SJC later held that it was an insufficient remedy under the Massachusetts Constitution merely to afford same-sex partners the same benefits as married couples without also recognizing their marriage. *See Opinions of the Justices to the Senate,* 802 N.E.2d 565, 569-72 (Mass. 2004).

The plaintiffs, a Massachusetts citizen named Robert Largess and eleven members of the Massachusetts legislature acting as individuals, sought to enjoin the May 17, 2004 implementation of *Goodridge* and the issuance or recording of marriage licenses to same-sex couples. Julie Goodridge and her new spouse Hillary Goodridge, the named plaintiffs in the *Goodridge* case, along with several others, intervened in the federal action on the side of the defendants.

The plaintiffs' federal suit asserted that the remedy that the SJC adopted in *Goodridge* redefined marriage in violation of separation-of-powers principles in the Massachusetts Constitution. Under the state constitution, according to the plaintiffs, it is the prerogative of the state legislature, not the courts, to define the term "marriage." The plaintiffs also asserted that the Massachusetts Constitution itself defines the term "marriage" according to its historical meaning as a union between a man and a woman, and thus that *Goodridge* effected an impermissible amendment of the state constitution that further violated separation-of-powers principles. From the initial premise that the *state* constitution was violated, the plaintiffs next asserted that the remedy in *Goodridge* violated their rights under the *federal* Guarantee Clause of the U.S. Constitution by depriving them of a republican form of government.

A preliminary objection made by the defendants is that Guarantee Clause claims are *always* non-justiciable under the political question doctrine and related caselaw. *See Luther v. Borden,* 48 U.S. (7 How.) 1, 42 (1849) (finding non-justiciable a Guarantee Clause argument by an individual claiming to act under the authority of a state charter government because Congress, not the federal courts, should decide which of two competing Rhode Island governments should be recognized). At oral argument, the state defendants retreated from this absolutist position and acknowledged that there may be extreme cases in which a Guarantee Clause claim would be justiciable, such as those involving "permanent martial law, [the] declaration of a monarchy, [or] perhaps a hostile takeover of one branch by another." Another potential example, defendants acknowledged, might be a case presenting the same facts as this case but in which the state constitution had no mechanism for amendment, so that it was simply beyond the power of the people to alter the SJC's holding. These concessions by the state defendants demonstrate that resolving the issue of justiciability in the Guarantee Clause context may also turn on the resolution of the merits of the underlying claim.

Another preliminary objection advanced by the defendants is that this court should defer to the SJC's resolution of the Massachusetts constitutional law questions raised by the plaintiffs. Because the claimed federal Guarantee Clause violation here depends on supposed *state* constitutional violations that the SJC has specifically rejected, the defendants argue that the plaintiffs cannot establish a necessary premise to their federal case. The defendants are correct that federal courts should generally defer to a state's highest court on issues of state law. But it is at least arguable that the Guarantee Clause might provide an exception to that rule of deference in extreme cases, such as where the members of a state's highest court declared the state to be a monarchy and themselves its regents. This issue ultimately need not be resolved here, because, as we explain below, the plaintiffs have not established a *federal* Guarantee Clause violation on the facts here, regardless of whether the remedy in *Goodridge* offends the Massachusetts Constitution.

The crucial question raised by plaintiffs' case is why the state constitutional violations they allege, assuming they exist, amount to a violation of the federal Constitution's Guarantee Clause. Plaintiffs' argument is that the alleged transgressions of the Massachusetts Constitution have deprived them of a republican form of government by intruding on the people's rights to elect representatives and structure the government. According to the plaintiffs, not every separation-of-powers violation under a state constitution leads to this result, but this one does. Plaintiffs argue that this is because here three conditions have been met: (1) the delegation or limitation of power to one branch in the state constitution is express, (2) there is a "clear departure" from the historic status quo, and (3) this "clear departure" seriously impairs a representative form of government.

Whether or not the plaintiffs can satisfy their self-tailored test, they simply have no viable Guarantee Clause claim on these facts. First, the text of the Guarantee Clause does not support such a claim. Second, the Supreme Court's caselaw interpreting the Guarantee Clause rejects the plaintiffs' expansive reading of the provision. Third, recognizing the plaintiffs' claim would ultimately undermine the very purposes of the Guarantee Clause, as the Supreme Court has noted.

We begin with the text of the Guarantee Clause. It provides that:

> The United States shall guarantee to every State in this Union a Republican Form of Government, and shall protect each of them against Invasion; and on Application of the Legislature, or of the Executive (when the Legislature cannot be convened) against domestic Violence.

U.S. Const. art. IV, § 4. We do not purport to spell out the entire scope or meaning of the Clause's guarantee of a republican form of government. In fact, scholars have interpreted this portion of the Guarantee Clause in numerous, often conflicting, ways. *See* William M. Wiecek, *The Guarantee Clause of the U.S. Constitution* 293-303 (1972) (outlining different interpretations of the Guarantee Clause); *see also* Akhil Reed Amar, *The Central Meaning of Republican Government: Popular Sovereignty, Majority Rule, and the Denominator Problem,* 65 U. Colo. L. Rev. 749, 749 (1994); Erwin Chemerinsky, *Cases Under the Guarantee Clause Should be Justiciable,* 65 U. Colo. L. Rev. 849, 864-69 (1994); Henry Paul Monaghan, *We the Peoples, Original Understanding, and the Constitutional Amendment,* 96 Colum. L. Rev. 121, 164-65 (1996); G. Edward White, *Guaranteeing a Republican Form of Government: Reading the Guarantee Clause,* 65 U. Colo. L. Rev. 787, 803 (1994). And John Adams himself, twenty years after ratification of the Constitution, confessed that he "never understood" what the Guarantee Clause meant and that he "believ[ed] no man ever did or ever will." Letter from John Adams to Mercy Warren (July 20, 1807), *quoted in* Wiecek, *supra,* at 13.

Despite the conflicting views on the precise meaning of the Guarantee Clause, the text itself provides guidance. The first portion of the Clause is only implicated when there is a threat to a "Republican Form of Government." "Republican" is commonly defined as "of, relating to, or having the characteristics of a republic: having the form or based on the principles of a republic." *Webster's Third New International Dictionary* 1928 (1993). "Republic," in turn, is defined as "a government in which supreme power resides in a body of citizens entitled to vote and is exercised by elected officers and representatives responsible to them and governing according to law." *Id.; see also Oxford English Dictionary* (2d ed.1989) (defining "republic" as "[a] state in which the supreme power rests in the people and their elected representatives or officers, as opposed to one governed by a king or similar ruler"). The Guarantee Clause does not require a *particular* allocation of power within each state so long as a republican form of government is preserved. Indeed, the forms of each state government at the time of the adoption of the Constitution varied in terms of separations of powers, *see* Robert J. Pushaw, Jr., *Justiciability and Separation of Powers: A Neo-Federalist Approach,* 81 Cornell L. Rev. 393, 408-11 (1996), and are each presumed to have been "Republican" within the meaning of the Guarantee Clause, *see Minor v. Happersett,* 88 U.S. (21 Wall.) 162, 175-76 (1874). If there is any role for federal courts under the Clause, it is restricted to real threats to a republican form of government. The allocation of powers, including the amendment powers, set forth in the Massachusetts Constitution, at the time of adoption and now, self-evidently do not violate the Clause.

The Supreme Court cases addressing the Guarantee Clause confirm what the plain text of the Clause suggests: most disputes concerning the relationship among a state government's constituent branches do not offend the Constitution's guarantee of a republican form of government. The Supreme Court first said as much in *Forsyth v. City of Hammond,* 166 U.S. 506 (1897). Responding to a claim that powers belonging to a state legislature were given to the state courts in violation of the Guarantee Clause, the Supreme Court noted that "[t]he preservation of legislative control in such matters is not one of the essential elements of a republican form of government" that is guaranteed to the states. The Court later generalized this point, observing in response to a Guarantee Clause claim that "[h]ow power shall be distributed by a state among its governmental organs is commonly, if not always, a question for the state itself." *Highland Farms Dairy, Inc. v. Agnew,* 300 U.S. 608, 612 (1937); *see also Pac. States Tel. & Tel. Co. v. Oregon,* 223 U.S. 118, 150-57 (1912) (Guarantee Clause defense asserted by corporation against state's action to enforce payment of taxes is non-justiciable).

Plaintiffs argue that the Supreme Court has not closed the door to Guarantee Clause claims. They point out that the Court assumed arguendo that the Clause was applicable in *New York v. United States,* 505 U.S. 144, 185 (1992), and that it used some expansive language to describe the Clause in *Printz v. United States,* 521 U.S. 898, 919 (1997).[4] But as the plaintiffs acknowledge, neither *New York* nor *Printz* affirmatively held that the Guarantee Clause could appropriately be invoked on the facts in those cases. Both cases, moreover, are easily distinguishable from the present case because they involved claims by a state that the executive and legislative branches of the federal government were interfering with state matters. In this suit, by contrast, individuals are attempting to invoke the Guarantee Clause against state officials, and federalism concerns about the scope of congressional authority are simply absent.

Most importantly, though, *New York* and *Printz* do not establish that separation-of-powers violations within a state, such as those alleged by the plaintiffs,

---

[4]In *Printz,* the Court noted that the Guarantee Clause "presupposes the continued existence of the states and . . . those means and instrumentalities which are the creation of their sovereign and reserved rights." 521 U.S. at 919 (internal quotations omitted).

constitute Guarantee Clause violations. Much to the contrary, the Court in *New York* affirmed that the Guarantee Clause (if claims under it are justiciable at all) is only offended in highly limited circumstances. It held that there was no possible violation of the Clause in that case because the states retained "the ability to set their legislative agendas" and "state government officials remain[ed] accountable to the local electorate." The same is true here.

The obvious question here is why the possibility of amending the Massachusetts Constitution, *see* Mass. Const. amend. art. XLVIII, against the background of normal election of the legislature and governor by voters, is not sufficient to eliminate any plausible claim of a deprivation of a republican form of government under the Guarantee Clause. Although the possibility of amending the constitution is not the only safeguard, it is certainly the most direct.

Plaintiffs respond that the change in the definition of marriage is so momentous that it overshadows either of these checks available to the citizens of Massachusetts for two reasons. First, any amendment to the Massachusetts Constitution will take roughly two years to come into effect. Second, relying on the SJC's language in *Albano v. Attorney General*, 769 N.E.2d 1242, 1246 (Mass. 2002), the plaintiffs contend that the SJC would not permit a constitutional amendment to render ineffective actions taken *before* the date of the amendment. Thus, conclude the plaintiffs, even an amendment would not void *Goodridge*, so there is no way to undo the effect of *Goodridge* between its implementation and the passage of a subsequent initiative amendment. As a result, plaintiffs argue that "in the interim, [they] suffer loss of their representative form of government in the same way they would suffer loss if the SJC had abolished the legislature."

This argument goes too far. The SJC has not abolished the legislature. The amendment process enshrined in the Massachusetts Constitution is purposely designed to be slow; that choice is itself a result of the state's republican form of government. Moreover, even were the plaintiffs' reading of *Albano* correct, an issue we do not decide, then the inability of a constitutional amendment to void *Goodridge* retroactively is also the result of a republican form of government in action. It was the Massachusetts people who amended the state constitution in 1918 to provide for certain limitations in the process of constitutional amendment. *See* Mass. Const. amend. art. XLVIII, pt. II, § 2.

The resolution of the same-sex marriage issue by the judicial branch of the Massachusetts government, subject to override by the voters through the state constitutional amendment process, does not plausibly constitute a threat to a republican form of government. Absent such a threat, our federal constitutional system simply does not permit a federal court to intervene in the arrangement of state government under the guise of a federal Guarantee Clause question. Such an intervention would itself threaten federal court interference with the very form of government that the people of Massachusetts have chosen for themselves. Perhaps, in unusual and extreme cases, such as the establishment of a monarchy by a state in place of a republican form of government, individuals could utilize the federal courts to enforce the Guarantee Clause. *See The Federalist No. 43,* at 311 (J. Madison) (B. Wright ed., 1961) (the Guarantee Clause gives "the superintending government . . . authority to defend the system against aristocratic or monarchical innovations"). That is not this case.

Pacific States Telephone & Telegraph Co. v. Oregon, 223 U.S. 118 (1912)

MR. CHIEF JUSTICE WHITE delivered the opinion of the Court.

We premise by saying that while the controversy which this record presents is of much importance, it is not novel. It is important, since it calls upon us to decide whether it is the duty of the courts or the province of Congress to determine when a State has ceased to be republican in form and to enforce the guarantee of the Constitution on that subject. It is not novel, as that question has long since been determined by this court conformable to the practice of the Government from the beginning to be political in character, and therefore not cognizable by the judicial power, but solely committed by the Constitution to the judgment of Congress.

In 1902 Oregon amended its constitution (Art. IV, § 1). This amendment while retaining an existing clause vesting the exclusive legislative power in a General Assembly consisting of a senate and house of representatives added to that provision the following: "But the people reserve to themselves the power to propose laws and amendments to the constitution and to enact or reject the same at the polls, independent of the legislative assembly, and also reserve power at their own option to approve or reject at the polls any act of the legislative assembly." Specific means for the exercise of the power thus reserved was contained in further clauses authorizing both the amendment of the constitution and the enactment of laws to be accomplished by the method known as the initiative and that commonly referred to as the referendum. As to the first, the initiative, it suffices to say that a stated number of voters were given the right at any time to secure a submission to popular vote for approval of any matter which it was desired to have enacted into law, and providing that the proposition thus submitted when approved by popular vote should become the law of the State. The second, the referendum, provided for a reference to a popular vote, for approval or disapproval, of any law passed by the legislature, such reference to take place either as the result of the action of the legislature itself or of a petition filed for that purpose by a specified number of voters.

By resort to the initiative in 1906 a law taxing certain classes of corporations was submitted, voted on and promulgated by the Governor as having been duly adopted. By this law telephone and telegraph companies were taxed, by what was qualified as an annual license, two per centum upon their gross revenue derived from business done within the State. Penalties were provided for non-payment, and methods were created for enforcing payment in case of delinquency.

The Pacific States Telephone and Telegraph Company, an Oregon corporation engaged in business in that State, made a return of its gross receipts as required by the statute and was accordingly assessed two per centum upon the amount of such return. The suit which is now before us was commenced by the State to enforce payment of this assessment and the statutory penalties for delinquency.

The assignments of error filed are all based upon the single contention that the creation by a State of the power to legislate by the initiative and referendum causes the prior lawful state government to be bereft of its lawful character as the result of the provisions of § 4 of Art. IV of the Constitution, that "The United States shall guarantee to every State in this Union a Republican Form of Government . . . ." This being the basis of all the contentions, the case comes to the single issue whether the enforcement of that provision, because of its political character, is exclusively committed to Congress or is judicial in its character.

We shall not stop to consider the text to point out how absolutely barren it is of support for the contentions sought to be based upon it, since the repugnancy of those contentions to the letter and spirit of the text is so conclusively established by prior decisions of this court as to the cause the matter to be absolutely foreclosed. We do not content ourselves with a mere citation of the cases, but state more at length than we otherwise would the issues and the doctrine expounded in the leading and absolutely controlling case, *Luther v. Borden*, 7 How. 1 [(1849)].

The case came from a circuit court of the United States. It was an action of damages for trespass. The case grew out of what is commonly known as the Dorr Rebellion in Rhode Island, and the conflict which was brought about by the effort of the adherents of that alleged government, sometimes described as "the government established by a voluntary convention," to overthrow the established charter government. The defendants justified on the ground that the acts done by them, charged as a trespass, were done under the authority of the charter government during the prevalence of martial law, and for the purpose of aiding in the suppression of an armed revolt by the supporters of the insurrectionary government. The plaintiffs, on the contrary, asserted the validity of the voluntary government, and denied the legality of the charter government. In the course of the trial the plaintiffs, to support the contention of the illegality of the charter government and the legality of the voluntary government, "although that government never was able to exercise any authority in the state, nor to command obedience to its laws or to its officers," offered certain evidence tending to show that nevertheless it was "the lawful and established government," upon the ground that its powers to govern have been ratified by a large majority of the male people of the state of the age of twenty-one years and upwards, and also by a large majority of those who were entitled to vote for general officers cast in favor of a Constitution which was submitted as the result of a voluntarily assembled convention of what was alleged to be the people of the state of Rhode Island. The circuit court rejected this evidence and instructed the jury that, as the charter government was the established state government at the time the trespass occurred, the defendants were justified in acting under the authority of that government. This court, coming to review this ruling, at the outset pointed out "the novelty and serious nature" of the question which it was called upon to decide. Attention also was at the inception directed to the far-reaching effect and gravity of the consequences which would be produced by sustaining the right of the plaintiff to assail and set aside the established government by recovering damages from the defendants for acts done by them under the authority of, and for the purpose of sustaining, such established government. On this subject it was said (p. 38):

> For, if this court is authorized to enter upon this inquiry, as proposed by the plaintiff, and it should be decided that the charter government had no legal existence during the period of time above mentioned,–if it had been annulled by the adoption of the opposing government,–then the laws passed by its legislature during that time were nullities; its taxes wrongfully collected; its salaries and compensation to its officers illegally paid; its

> public accounts improperly settled; and the judgments and sentences of its courts in civil and criminal cases null and void, and the officers who carried their decisions into operation answerable as trespassers, if not in some cases as criminals.

Coming to review the question, attention was directed to the fact that the courts of Rhode Island had recognized the complete dominancy in fact of the charter government, and had refused to investigate the legality of the voluntary government for the purpose of decreeing the established government to be illegal, on the ground (p. 39) "that the inquiry proposed to be made belonged to the political power, and not to the judicial; that it rested with the political power to decide whether the charter government had been displaced or not; and when that decision was made, the judicial department would be bound to take notice of it as the paramount law of the state, without the aid of oral evidence or the examination of witnesses, etc."

Reviewing the grounds upon which these doctrines proceeded, their cogency was pointed out and the disastrous effect of any other view was emphasized, and from a point of view of the state law the conclusive effect of the judgments of the courts of Rhode Island was referred to. The court then came to consider the correctness of the principle applies by the Rhode Island court, in light of § 4 of article IV of the Constitution of the United States. In doing so it pointed out that owing to the inherent political character of such a question its decision was not by the Constitution vested in the judicial department of the Government, but was on the contrary exclusively committed to the legislative department by whose action on such subject the judiciary were absolutely controlled. The court said (p. 42):

> [It] rests with Congress to decide what government is the established one in a state. For, as the United States guarantee to each state a republican government, Congress must necessarily decide what government is established in the state before it can determine whether it is republican or not. And when the senators and representatives of a state are admitted into the councils of the Union, the authority of the government under which they are appointed, as well as its republican character, is recognized by the proper constitutional authority. And its decision is binding on every other department of the government, and could not be questioned in a judicial tribunal. It is true that the contest in this case did not last long enough to bring the matter to this issue; and as no senators or representatives were elected under the authority of the government of which Mr. Dorr was the head, Congress was not called upon to decide the controversy. Yet the right to decide is placed there, and not in the courts.

The fundamental doctrines thus so lucidly and cogently announced by the court, speaking through Mr. Chief Justice Taney in the case which we have thus reviewed, have never been doubted or questioned since, and have afforded the light guiding the orderly development of our constitutional system from the day of the deliverance of that decision up to the present time.

The defendant company does not contend here that it could not have been required to pay a license tax. It does not assert that it was denied an opportunity to be heard as to the amount for which it was taxed, or that there was anything inhering in the tax or involved intrinsically in the law which violated any of its constitutional rights. If such questions had been raised, they would have been justiciable, and therefore would have required the calling into operation of judicial power. Instead, however, of doing any of these things, the attack on the statute here made is of a wholly different character. Its essentially political nature is at once made manifest by understanding that the assault which the contention here advanced makes is not on the tax as a tax, but on the state as a state. It is addressed to the framework and political character of the government by which the statute levying the tax was passed. It is the government, the political entity, which (reducing the case to its essence) is called to the bar of this court, not for the purpose of testing judicially some exercise of power, assailed on the ground that its exertion has injuriously affected the rights of an individual because of repugnancy to some constitutional limitation, but to demand of the state that it establish its right to exist as a state, republican in form.

As the issues presented, in their very essence, are, and have long since by this court been, definitely determined to be political and governmental, and embraced within the scope of the powers conferred upon Congress, and not, therefore, within the reach of judicial power, it follows that the case presented is not within our jurisdiction.

Notes on the Guaranty Clause and the Admission of New States

Federal Judicial Enforcement of the Guaranty Clause: What is the difference in the approaches between the *Pacific States* Court and the *Largess* court? *Largess* opined that, in extreme cases, such as the establishment of a monarchy by a state, individuals might be able to use the federal courts to enforce the Guaranty Clause. But wouldn't such an extreme case provide exactly the type of crisis situation the Supreme Court in *Luther v. Borden* held should be resolved by Congress rather than the federal judiciary?

The underlying normative question is whether Guaranty Clause cases should be justiciable. As *Largess* points out, a number of scholars have urged (contrary to the seeming import of *Pacific States* and *Luther v. Borden*) that they should be resolved by the federal courts. The Supreme Court's 1992 decision in *New York v. United States*, which held that the Tenth Amendment barred the federal government from commandeering New York's legislative branch to enact and enforce a federal regulatory program, "indulg[ed] the assumption"–without deciding–that under some instances a claim under the Guaranty Clause might be justiciable. Nevertheless, the Court concluded that there was no possibility of a Guaranty Clause violation in that case as the federal law at issue did "not pose any realistic risk of altering the form or the method of functioning of New York's government."[5]

The Guaranty Clause claim asserted in *New York v. United States* envisioned a different role for the clause than contemplated in either *Pacific States* or *Largess*. *New York* considered a claim by a *state* that a *federal law* deprived it of a republican form of government, while the prior cases addressed whether an *individual* could assert that a *state's* actions violated the clause. Thus, the contention in *New York* was that the Guarantee Clause

---

[5]New York v. United States, 505 U.S. 144, 185 (1992).

protects the rights of states (as opposed to the rights of individuals).[6] Should the justiciability of Guaranty Clause claims depend on whether the clause is viewed as protecting a state right or individual right?

The Guaranty Clause in State Courts: Would the nonjusticiability of the Guaranty Clause in the federal courts preclude a state court from holding that its own constitution was in violation of the Guaranty Clause? As will be discussed in more detail in Chapter 3, state courts are not bound by the justiciability doctrines pronounced by the United States Supreme Court. The Kansas Supreme Court in *Van Sickle v. Shanahan* held that a Guarantee Clause claim in state court was justiciable, but determined (similar to the *Largess* court) that the purpose of the Guaranty Clause "is to protect the people of the several states against aristocratic and monarchial innovations, and against insurrections and domestic violence, and to prevent them from abolishing a republican form of government."[7] As a result, the court held that a state constitutional amendment authorizing the governor to issue reorganization orders of the executive department did not violate the Guaranty Clause even though it vested legislative power in the governor. Some other state courts have likewise rejected Guaranty Clause claims on the merits rather than dismissing the claims for lack of justiciability.[8]

Potential Meanings of the Guarantee Clause: Assuming Guaranty Clause cases are at least sometimes justiciable, is the "republican form of government" standard meaningful if all it prohibits are monarchies or aristocracies? Or is this exactly what the framers intended? As *Largess* notes, the state governments at the time of the ratification of the Constitution varied in many fundamental respects, yet James Madison wrote in *The Federalist* that all of them had "existing republican forms" that ought to be defended "against aristocratic or monarchial innovations."[9] Madison had earlier defined "a republic" as "a government which derives all of its powers directly or indirectly from the great body of the people, and is administered by persons holding their offices during pleasure for a limited period, or during good behavior."[10] He clarified that indirect appointments by officials elected by the people were authorized in a republic because otherwise no government in the United States would be republican–every state at that time "appointed indirectly only by the people" some officers of government.[11]

Some commentators have urged that the Guarantee Clause should prevent any undemocratic or procedurally invalid alterations of a state's constitution or laws, similar to

---

[6]This view of the Guaranty Clause is developed in Deborah Merritt, *The Guaranty Clause and State Autonomy: Federalism for a Third Century*, 88 COLUM. L. REV. 1 (1988).

[7]511 P.2d 223, 242-43 (Kan. 1973).

[8]*See, e.g., In re* Initiative Petition No. 348, 820 P.2d 772, 780-81 (Okla. 1991); Kadderly v. City of Portland, 74 P. 710, 719-20 (Or. 1903).

[9]THE FEDERALIST NO. 43 (James Madison) (Clinton Rossiter ed., 1961).

[10]THE FEDERALIST NO. 39 (James Madison) (Clinton Rossiter ed., 1961).

[11]*Id.*

the claim made in *Largess*.[12] But would federal court intervention to determine whether the state violated its own state constitution or laws be appropriate? Alexander Hamilton opined in *The Federalist* that the Guaranty Clause did not interfere with "reforms of the State constitutions by a majority of the people in a legal and peacable mode," but instead "only operate[d] against changes to be effected by violence."[13]

Another contention is that the Guaranty Clause may be violated by initiatives that are *too democratic* to be republican, which was the claim made in *Pacific States*. During the Progressive era, approximately twenty states, especially in the west, adopted some form of initiative process, which allow a specified number of citizens to submit proposed legislation to a popular vote and bypass the legislature. Opponents claimed that such direct democracy violated the republican principles of the Guaranty Clause and the federal constitutional commitment to controlling "the violence of faction."[14] However, those courts that have addressed this issue under the federal Guaranty Clause have concluded either that the claim was not justiciable or that the initiative process was not inconsistent with republican government.[15]

Yet a somewhat analogous claim obtained at least some success under the Texas state constitutional commitment in article I, section 2 "to the preservation of a republican form of government."[16] Although Texas has never had a statewide initiative,[17] some Texas cities have adopted city charters containing direct democracy devices such as the initiative, the referendum, and the recall. In *Ex parte Farnsworth*, the Texas Court of Criminal Appeals voided a Dallas city regulation of telephone service rates enacted directly by Dallas citizens that could not be repealed or amended without another city-wide vote.[18] The court reasoned that the ordinance contravened, among other constitutional provisions, article I, section 2 because it was "directly subversive of our constitutional form of government," which is one exclusively "by the people through their selected representatives," rather than through a grant of power by the legislature to the people.[19] But the state's other highest court, the Supreme Court of Texas, adopted a different view in holding that a direct

---

[12]*See* Timothy Sandefur, *A Private Little* Bush v. Gore*, or, How Nevada Violated the Republican Guarantee and Got Away With It*, 9 TEX. L. & POL. 105, 125 (2004); Thomas A. Smith, *The Rule of Law and the States: A New Interpretation of the Guarantee Clause*, 93 YALE L.J. 561, 561 (1984) (urging that the Guaranty Clause should require the states to "either observe their own constitutions and laws or change them by legally valid procedures").

[13]THE FEDERALIST NO. 21 (Alexander Hamilton) (Clinton Rossiter ed., 1961).

[14]THE FEDERALIST NO. 10 (James Madison) (Clinton Rossiter ed., 1961).

[15]*See, e.g.*, Pac. States Tel. & Tel. Co. v. Oregon, 223 U.S. 118, 143 (1912); *In re* Initiative Petition No. 348, 820 P.2d 772, 780-81 (Okla. 1991); Kadderly v. City of Portland, 74 P. 710, 719-20 (Or. 1903).

[16]TEX. CONST. art. I, § 2 ("All political power is inherent in the people, and all free governments are founded on their authority, and instituted for their benefit. The faith of the people of Texas stands pledged to the preservation of a republican form of government, and, subject to this limitation only, they have at all times the inalienable right to alter, reform or abolish their government in such manner as they may think expedient.").

[17]Texas voters rejected a proposed initiative and referendum amendment to the state constitution in November 1914. *See* 1 GEORGE D. BRADEN ET AL., THE CONSTITUTION OF THE STATE OF TEXAS: AN ANNOTATED AND COMPARATIVE ANALYSIS 13 (1977).

[18]135 S.W. 535 (Tex. Crim. App. 1911).

[19]*Id.* at 537.

democracy recall provision in the Dallas city charter did not violate the federal Guaranty Clause.[20] Quoting Thomas Jefferson, the court defined the republican form as "'a government by its citizens in mass, acting directly and not personally, according to the rules established by the majority; and that every other government is more or less republican in proportion as it has in its composition more or less of this ingredient of the direct action of its citizens.'"[21] Although the tension between these two decisions was never explicitly resolved, the "home rule" state constitutional amendment the next year granted cities with more than 5,000 citizens a constitutional right of self-governance through their city charters,[22] which apparently mollified the *Farnsworth* court's underlying concern that the state legislature, rather than the state constitution, had delegated lawmaking power to the people.

Some commentators have urged that only specified types of initiatives are incompatible with the principles of republican government. As one example, former Oregon Supreme Court Justice Hans Linde contended that majoritarian initiatives repealing or limiting aspects of the state's bill of rights may violate the Guaranty Clause. In 1984, through the initiative process, the citizens of Oregon added article I, section 40 to the Oregon Constitution, providing that the penalty for aggravated murder shall be death, notwithstanding the provisions of article I, sections 15 and 16, which respectively bar "vindictive justice" as the basis for the imposition of criminal penalties and "cruel and unusual punishments." The purpose underlying section 40 was to prevent the Oregon judiciary from holding that a death penalty imposed in an aggravated murder case violated the state constitutional guarantees against vindictive justice and cruel and unusual punishments. In a case challenging the imposition of a death penalty under section 40, Justice Linde, even while recognizing that the issue had not been raised by the defendant, was concerned "whether a plebiscite that bypasses the legislature and the governor in order to repeal parts of the Bill of Rights and to impose a penal regime which is morally repugnant to a substantial minority of citizens remains compatible with the state's obligation to maintain a republican form of government. An initiative measure not only short-circuits the hearings, study, debate and adjustments made in the normal legislative process, it replaces a representative body's resistance to overriding intensely felt minority concerns with a purely majoritarian plebiscite."[23]

If the proponents of these alternative views of the Guaranty Clause are right, what else might violate the Guaranty Clause? Is a constitutional provision requiring a super-majority of the state's highest court to declare a statute unconstitutional consistent with a republican form of government?[24] Article VI, section 4 of the North Dakota Constitution provides: "A majority of the supreme court shall be necessary to constitute a quorum or pronounce a decision, provided that the supreme court shall not declare a legislative enactment unconstitutional unless at least four of the members of the court so decide."

---

[20]Bonner v. Belsterling, 138 S.W. 571, 575 (1911).

[21]*Id.* at 574.

[22]TEX. CONST. art. XI, § 5.

[23]State v. Wagner, 752 P.2d 1136, 1197 n.8 (Or. 1988) (Linde, J., dissenting), *vacated on other grounds*, 492 U.S. 914 (1989).

[24]*See, e.g.*, NEB. CONST. art. V, § 2; N.D. CONST. art. VI, § 4.

Because the North Dakota Supreme Court consists of five members, legislation has been upheld against constitutional challenges even when a majority of the court concludes that it is unconstitutional. As an illustration, in *Bismarck Public School District No. 1 v. State*, three members of the court opined that the state system of providing funds for primary and secondary education was unconstitutional, while only two justices declared that the system was constitutional. Nevertheless, the final result was that the system was "not declared unconstitutional by a sufficient majority."[25] Should this be a Guaranty Clause violation?

Are there also potential challenges to state judicial election systems that could be asserted employing these alternative views of the Guaranty Clause? In the Eighth Circuit's en banc decision after remand from the Supreme Court in *Republican Party of Minnesota v. White*, the court suggested that the Minnesota Supreme Court's adoption of a judicial canon precluding certain political activities by candidates for judicial office "compromised any separation of powers framework established by Minnesota's constitution" by thrusting the state court, without apparent constitutional or statutory authority, "into the legislative arena in an attempt to regulate the political climate of statewide elections, an authority seemingly granted only to the Minnesota legislature under its plenary powers."[26] Could the promulgation of judicial codes of conduct by state supreme courts therefore, at least in some instances, violate the federal Guaranty Clause? On the other hand, could it be argued that a republican form of government requires the appearance of an impartial judiciary, which would support regulation of a judge's political activities, such as limiting campaign contributions by litigants and attorneys with cases before the court?[27]

Congressional Controls under the Guaranty Clause and Enabling Acts: Even though the judiciary has yet to articulate meaningful constraints under the Guaranty Clause, Congress often imposes its own requirements and limitations regarding the state constitutions of newly admitted states. For instance, in its enabling act authorizing the admission of North Dakota, South Dakota, Montana, and Washington into the United States, Congress mandated the number of delegates to each state constitution, the qualifications of the delegates, the method to select the delegates, and the place and date of the constitutional convention. Congress also required that their "constitutions shall be republican in form, and make no distinction in civil or political rights on account of race or color, except as to Indians not taxed, and not be repugnant to the Constitution of the United States and the principles of the Declaration of Independence."[28] Congress also specified that the "conventions shall provide, by ordinances irrevocable without the consent of the United States and the people of said States," that certain freedoms and rights be guaranteed, such as the "perfect toleration of religious sentiment" and "the establishment and maintenance of systems of public schools, which shall be open to all the children of said States, and free from sectarian control."[29]

---

[25]Bismarck Pub. Sch. Dist. No. 1 v. State, 511 N.W.2d 247 (N.D. 1994).

[26]416 F.3d 738, 752 n.7 (8th Cir. 2005) (en banc).

[27]*Cf.* Pub. Citizen, Inc. v. Bomer, 274 F.3d 212 (5th Cir. 2001) (dismissing on standing grounds a due process challenge to Texas's system for electing state court judges predicated on the appearance of impropriety through judicial solicitation and acceptance of large campaign contributions).

[28]Enabling Act of Feb. 22, 1889, Pub. L. No. 50-180, § 4, 25 Stat. 677 (1889).

[29]*Id.*

The Arizona Enabling Act of 1910 also contained a number of restrictions, including a provision outlawing polygamous marriages or cohabitation in the state, which apparently was directed against the Mormon population in the state.[30] If Congress could outlaw polygamous marriages in an enabling act, could Congress have enacted legislation under the Guaranty Clause declaring that the decision of the Massachusetts Supreme Judicial Court in *Goodridge* recognizing same-sex marriage was invalid? Would such congressional legislation be subject to federal judicial review, or would it be nonjusticiable?

The President's Role: The President also has a role in the admission of new states. In one well-known example, President William Howard Taft vetoed a joint resolution admitting the territories of New Mexico and Arizona as states into the Union on the ground that the Arizona Constitution authorized the recall of state and county judges six months after their election. President Taft explained:

> The provision of the Arizona constitution [authorizing recall of elective officers], in its application to county and State judges, seems to me so pernicious in its effect, so destructive of independence in the judiciary, so likely to subject the rights of the individual to the possible tyranny of a popular majority, and, therefore, to be so injurious to the cause of free government, that I must disapprove a constitution containing it. [In doing so,] I am discharging my constitutional function in respect to the enactment of laws, and my discretion is equal to that of the Houses of Congress. I must therefore withhold my approval from this resolution if in fact I do not approve it as a matter of governmental policy. Of course, a mere difference of opinion as to the wisdom of details in a State constitution ought not to lead me to set up my opinion against that of the people of the Territory. It is to be their government, and while the power of Congress to withhold or grant statehood is absolute, the people about to constitute a State should generally know better the kind of government and constitution suited to their needs than Congress or the Executive. But when such a constitution contains something so destructive of free government as the judicial recall, it should be disapproved.[31]

Should it be sufficient that the state constitution complies with the principles of the United States Constitution and the Declaration of Independence? Or does President Taft state the more persuasive position in his veto message?

The Limits of Enabling Acts: How long can the provisions of an enabling act bind the states in matters of their internal governance? In response to President Taft's veto, Congress sent another statehood resolution to President Taft, which he signed, that conditioned statehood for Arizona on deleting the judicial recall provision in a subsequent election.[32] Arizona complied with this requirement in December 1911, and was admitted

---

[30]Arizona and New Mexico Enabling Act of June 20, 1910, Pub. L. No. 61-219, § 20, 36 Stat. 557 (1910).

[31]Veto Message of August 11, 1911, 47 CONG. REC. 3964 (1911).

[32]S.J. Res. 47, 62nd Cong., 47 CONG. REC. 4127, 4242, 4381 (1911).

as a state early the next year. But less than a year later, in November 1912, Arizona voters ratified an amendment to their state constitution reincorporating the judicial recall that President Taft had vetoed.[33] Can a state always incorporate the required provisions into its constitution to placate Congress and the President, and then immediately amend its constitution? Or does the answer to the question depend on the type of provision at issue?

Coyle v. Smith, 221 U.S. 559 (1911)

MR. JUSTICE LURTON delivered the opinion of the Court.

[Petitioner claims] that the Oklahoma act of December 29, 1910, providing for the immediate location of the capital of the state at Oklahoma City, was void as repugnant to the enabling act of Congress of June 16, 1906, under which the state was admitted to the Union. The act referred to is entitled, "An Act to Enable the People of Oklahoma and of the Indian Territory to Form a Constitution and State Government and Be Admitted into the Union on an Equal Footing with the Original States." The same act provides for the admission of Arizona and New Mexico. The first twenty-two sections relate only to Oklahoma. The 2d section is lengthy and deals with the organization of a constitutional convention, and concludes in these words: "The capital of said state shall temporarily be at the city of Guthrie . . . . and shall not be changed therefrom previous to Anno Domini nineteen hundred and thirteen; but said capital shall, after said year, be located by the electors of said state at an election to be provided for by the legislature; provided, however, that the legislature of said state, except as shall be necessary for the convenient transaction of the public business of said state at said capital, shall not appropriate any public moneys of the state for the erection of buildings for capital purposes during said period."

The only question for review by us is whether the provision of the enabling act was a valid limitation upon the power of the state after its admission, which overrides any subsequent state legislation repugnant thereto.

The power to locate its own seat of government, and to determine when and how it shall be changed from one place to another, and to appropriate its own public funds for that purpose, are essentially and peculiarly state powers. That one of the original thirteen states could now be shorn of such powers by an act of Congress would not be for a moment entertained. The question, then, comes to this: Can a state be placed upon a plane of inequality with its sister states in the Union if the Congress chooses to impose conditions which so operate, at the time of its admission? The argument is, that while Congress may not deprive a state of any power which it *possesses*, it may, as a condition to the admission of a new state, constitutionally restrict its authority, to the extent, at least, of suspending its powers for a definite time in respect to the location of its seat of government. This contention is predicated upon the constitutional power of admitting new states to this Union, and the constitutional duty of guaranteeing to "every state in this Union a republican form of government."

The power of Congress in respect to the admission of new states is found in the 3d section of the 4th article of the Constitution. That provision is that, "new states may be

---

[33] *See* John D. Leshy, *The Making of the Arizona Constitution*, 20 ARIZ. ST. L.J. 1, 58 & n. 320 (1988).

admitted by the Congress into this Union." The only expressed restriction upon this power is that no new state shall be formed within the jurisdiction of any other state, nor by the junction of two or more states, or parts of states, without the consent of such states, as well as of the Congress.

But what is this power? It is not to admit political organizations which are less or greater, or different in dignity or power, from those political entities which constitute the Union. It is, as strongly put by counsel, a "power to admit states."

The definition of "a state" is found in the powers possessed by the original states which adopted the Constitution–a definition emphasized by the terms employed in all subsequent acts of Congress admitting new states into the Union. The first two states admitted into the Union were the states of Vermont and Kentucky, one as of March 4, 1791, and the other as of June 1, 1792. No terms or conditions were exacted from either. Each act declares that the state is admitted "as a new and *entire member* of the United States of America." Emphatic and significant as is the phrase admitted as "an entire member," even stronger was the declaration upon the admission in 1796 of Tennessee as the third new state, it being declared to be "one of the United States of America," "on an equal footing with the original states in all respects whatsoever,"– phraseology which has ever since been substantially followed in admission acts, concluding with the Oklahoma act, which declares that Oklahoma shall be admitted "on an equal footing with the original states."

The power is to admit "new states into *this* Union." "This Union" was and is a union of states, equal in power, dignity, and authority, each competent to exert that residuum of sovereignty not delegated to the United States by the Constitution itself. To maintain otherwise would be to say that the Union, through the power of Congress to admit new states, might come to be a union of states unequal in power, as including states whose powers were restricted only by the Constitution, with others whose powers had been further restricted by an act of Congress accepted as a condition of admission. Thus it would result, first, that the powers of Congress would not be defined by the Constitution alone, but in respect to new states, enlarged or restricted by the conditions imposed upon new states by its own legislation admitting them into the Union; and, second, that such new states might not exercise all of the powers which had not been delegated by the Constitution, but only such as had not been further bargained away as conditions of admission.

The argument that Congress derives from the duty of "guaranteeing to each state in this Union a republican form of government," power to impose restrictions upon a new state which deprive it of equality with other members of the Union, has no merit. It may imply the duty of such new state to provide itself with such state government, and impose upon Congress the duty of seeing that such form is not changed to one anti-republican, but it obviously does not confer power to admit a new state which shall be any less a state than those which compose the Union.

We come now to the question as to whether there is anything in the decisions of this court which sanctions the claim that Congress may, by the imposition of conditions in an enabling act, deprive a new state of any of those attributes essential to its equality in dignity and power with other states. In considering the decisions of this court bearing upon the question, we must distinguish, first, between provisions which are fulfilled by the admission of the state; second, between compacts or affirmative legislation intended to operate *in futuro*, which are within the scope of the conceded powers of Congress over the subject; and third, compacts or affirmative legislation which operates to restrict the powers of such new state in respect of matters which would otherwise be exclusively within the sphere of state power.

As to requirements in such enabling acts as relate only to the contents of the Constitution for the proposed new state, little need to be said. The constitutional provision concerning the admission of new states is not a mandate, but a power to be exercised with discretion. From this alone it would follow that Congress may require, under penalty of denying admission, that the organic law of a new state at the time of admission shall be such as to meet its approval. A Constitution thus supervised by Congress would, after all, be a Constitution of a state, and as such subject to alteration and amendment by the state after admission. Its force would be that of a state Constitution, and not that of an act of Congress.

It may well happen that Congress should embrace in an enactment introducing a new state into the Union legislation intended as a regulation of commerce among the states, or with Indian tribes situated within the limits of such new state, or regulations touching the sole care and disposition of the public lands or reservations therein, which might be upheld as legislation within the sphere of the plain power of Congress. But in every such case such legislation would derive its force not from any agreement or compact with the proposed new state, nor by reason of its acceptance of such enactment as a term of admission, but solely because the power of Congress extended to the subject, and therefore would not operate to restrict the state's legislative power in respect of any matter which was not plainly within the regulating power of Congress. *Willamette Iron Bridge Co. v. Hatch*, 125 U.S. 1, 9 [(1888)].

No such question is presented here. The legislation in the Oklahoma enabling act relating to the location of the capital of the state, if construed as forbidding a removal by the state after its admission as a state, is referable to no power granted to Congress over the subject, and if it is to be upheld at all, it must be implied from the power to admit new states. If power to impose such a restriction upon the general and undelegated power of a state be conceded as implied from the power to admit a new state, where is the line to be drawn against restrictions imposed upon new states?

We are unable to find in any of the decisions of this court cited by counsel for the plaintiff in error anything which contravenes the view we have expressed. *Green v. Biddle*, 8 Wheat. 1 [(1823)], involved the question as to whether a compact between two states, assented to by Congress, by which private land titles in Kentucky, derived from Virginia before the separation of Kentucky from Virginia, "should remain valid and secure under the laws of the proposed state of Kentucky, and should be determined by the laws now existing in this (Virginia) state." By subsequent legislation of the state of Kentucky these titles were adversely affected. This court held that this legislation impaired the obligation of a valid contract within that clause of the Constitution forbidding such impairment. Neither does *Virginia v. West Virginia*, 11 Wall. 39 [(1870)], have any bearing here. The question there was one of a compact between the two states, assented to by Congress, concerning the boundary between them. Both the cases last referred to concerned compacts between states, authorized by the Constitution when assented to by Congress. They were therefore compacts and agreements sanctioned by the Constitution, while the one here sought to be enforced is one having no sanction in that instrument.

Beecher v. Wetherby, 95 U. S. 517 [(1877)], involved the validity of the grant of every sixteenth section in each township for school purposes. The grant was made by the act providing for the organization of a state government for the territory of Wisconsin, and purported to be upon condition that the proposed state should never interfere with the primary disposal of the public lands of the United States, nor subject them to taxation. The grant was held to operate as a grant taking effect so soon as the necessary surveys were made. The conditions assented to by the state were obviously such as obtained no force from the assent of the state, since they might have been exacted as an exertion of the proper power of Congress to make rules and regulations as to the disposition of the public lands. *Minnesota v. Batchelder*, 1 Wall. 109 [(1863)], is another case which involved nothing more than an exertion by Congress of its power to regulate the disposition of the public lands.

Has Oklahoma been admitted upon an equal footing with the original states? If she has, she, by virtue of her jurisdictional sovereignty as such a state, may determine for her own people the proper location of the local seat of government. She is not equal in power to them if she cannot.

In *Texas v. White*, 7 Wall. 700, 725 [(1868)], Chief Justice Chase said in strong and memorable language that "the Constitution, in all of its provisions, looks to an indestructible Union, composed of indestructible states."

In *Lane County v. Oregon*, 7 Wall. 76 [(1868)], he said:

> The people of the United States constitute one nation, under one government; and this government, within the scope of the powers with which it is invested, is supreme. On the other hand, the people of each state compose state, having its own government, and endowed with all the functions essential to separate and independent existence. The states disunited might continue to exist. Without the states in union there could be no such political body as the United States.

To this we may add that the constitutional equality of the states is essential to the harmonious operation of the scheme upon which the Republic was organized. When that equality disappears we may remain a free people, but the Union will not be the Union of the Constitution.

Notes on State Sovereignty and Federal Restrictions on State Charters

The Bases for Federal Regulation: Carefully analyze the holding in *Coyle,* as well as the Court's discussion of the precedents relied upon by the parties, to determine the circumstances in which Congress may regulate the provisions of state constitutions and state laws. While Congress may be able to impose conditions on the substance of a state constitution as a prerequisite to obtaining admission to the United States, *Coyle* indicates such conditions may be subsequently repudiated by the state unless the restriction is buttressed by another independent congressional power, such as regulating interstate commerce, disposing of federal property, or approving compacts between the states. Is such a holding necessary to ensure that the states in the Union remain on "equal footing"?

Congressional powers to regulate interstate commerce and dispose of federal property are familiar topics from federal constitutional law. The other power *Coyle* discusses, compacts between the states, may not be so familiar. Article I, Section 10 of the United States Constitution provides: "No state shall, without the consent of Congress . . . enter into any Agreement or compact with another State." The rationale behind requiring the approval of Congress is to "check any infringement on the rights of the national government."[34] As a result, the Supreme Court has held that only those agreements that enhance the political power or influence of the compacting states or encroach upon or interfere with the authority of the federal government must be approved by Congress. Thus, in *United States Steel Corp. v. Multistate Tax Commission*, the Court held that an agreement of twenty-one states to establish a commission to study state tax systems and develop advisory regulations and proposals did not require the approval of Congress.[35] If Congress does approve the compact, however, it operates as federal law, such that its interpretation is a federal question that may override a state supreme court's interpretation of its own constitution.[36]

The Impact of Increasing Federal Power: Since *Coyle* was decided in 1911, the scope of congressional power has increased dramatically, even despite the Supreme Court's selective revival of some aspects of federalism. At the time of *Coyle*, the Court employed a very narrow interpretation of the scope of the Commerce Clause. *United States v. E.C. Knight* held that the Sherman Antitrust Act could not be used to prevent a sugar refining monopoly because the production and manufacture of sugar was not commerce.[37] *Carter v. Carter Coal Co.* similarly held that "the incidents leading up to and culminating in the mining of coal do not constitute [commerce]."[38] These narrow visions of the meaning of commerce were later repudiated by the New Deal Court in cases such as *NLRB v. Jones & Laughlin Steel Corp.*[39] and *Wickard v. Filburn.*[40] As the power of Congress has increased, does *Coyle v. Smith* have less reach today? For instance, could Congress rely on its Commerce Clause power to require that a state locate its capital in the locale most favorable to interstate travelers?

Recent Supreme Court cases interpret *Coyle* as imposing a limit on the federal government's power to affect the internal operations of a state,[41] similar to the federal

---

[34]J. Story, Commentaries on the Constitution § 1403 (1833).

[35]434 U.S. 454 (1978).

[36]West Virginia *ex. rel.* Dyer v. Sims, 341 U.S. 22 (1951).

[37]156 U.S. 1, 12-13 (1895).

[38]298 U.S. 238, 303 (1936).

[39]301 U.S. 1 (1937).

[40]317 U.S. 111 (1942). The continued vitality of *Wickard* was recently reaffirmed in *Gonzales v. Raich*, 545 U.S. 1, 17-22 (2005) (upholding congressional power under the Commerce Clause to criminalize the possession, for medical purposes, of home-grown marijuana).

[41]*See, e.g.*, Va. Office for Protection & Advocacy v. Stewart, 131 S. Ct. 1632, 1641 (2011).

government's inability to commandeer state legislative and executive officials.[42] *New York v. United States*, for example, in holding that Congress could not commandeer a state to adopt a federal regulatory program, relied on *Coyle* for the proposition that "the Constitution has never been understood to confer upon Congress the ability to require the state to govern according to Congress' instructions."[43] *Coyle* should thus invalidate, under principles of state autonomy, any congressional attempt to direct the location of a state's capital.

B. THE SUPREMACY CLAUSE AND CONFLICTS BETWEEN STATE CONSTITUTIONS AND FEDERAL LAW

The Supremacy Clause of the United States Constitution provides:

> The Constitution, and the Laws of the United States which shall be made in Pursuance thereof, and all Treaties made, or which shall be made, under the Authority of the United States, shall be the supreme law of the land; and the Judges in every State shall be bound thereby, any Thing in the Constitution or laws of any State to the Contrary notwithstanding.[44]

This Clause makes the United States Constitution and federal laws the supreme law of the land, notwithstanding "any Thing in the Constitution . . . of any State." The provisions of state constitutions are hence subject to federal constitutional judicial review. The Supreme Court first declared that a state constitutional enactment violated the United States Constitution in 1856 in *Dodge v. Woolsey*,[45] and has since held numerous state constitutional provisions unconstitutional under the federal charter.[46]

While perhaps the structure of our federalism might warrant that the federal courts should afford more deference to the federal constitutional validity of state constitutions in

---

[42]*See* Printz v. United States, 521 U.S. 898 (1997); New York v. United States, 505 U.S. 144 (1992).

[43]505 U.S. at 162 (citing *Coyle*).

[44]U.S. CONST. art. VI, cl. 2.

[45]59 U.S. 331, 360-61 (1856) (holding Ohio state constitutional provision providing for legislative establishment of new taxation scheme impaired the obligation of contracts).

[46]*See, e.g.,* Romer v. Evans, 517 U.S. 620 (1996) (holding initiative amendment to Colorado Constitution barring state or local legislation protecting gays and lesbians from discrimination violated Fourteenth Amendment); Hunter v. Underwood, 471 U.S. 222 (1985) (holding article VIII, section 182 of the Alabama Constitution, which disenfranchised persons convicted of a crime of moral turpitude, violated the Equal Protection Clause when it was motivated by a desire to discriminate and it had a disproportionate impact on African Americans); Reynolds v. Sims, 377 U.S. 533 (1964) (holding state legislative apportionment scheme partially contained in Alabama Constitution violated Equal Protection); Torcaso v. Watkins, 367 U.S. 488 (1961) (concluding Maryland Constitution requirement that public officers declare belief in God violated the First Amendment as incorporated against the states through the Fourteenth Amendment); Hawke v. Smith, 253 U.S. 221 (1920) (holding provision of Ohio Constitution providing for a referendum on any action of the legislature ratifying a proposed amendment to the Federal Constitution violated the amendment process of Article V); Cummings v. Missouri, 71 U.S. (4 Wall.) 277 (1867) (invalidating, under the Federal Constitution's prohibitions against ex post facto laws and bills of attainder, the Missouri Constitution's oath requirement of absolute prior loyalty in words and deeds to the Union).

comparison to mere state laws, the Supreme Court has never adopted this position. On the contrary, *Reynolds v. Sims* opined: "With respect to the operation of the Equal Protection Clause, it makes no difference whether a State's apportionment scheme is embodied in its constitution or in statutory provisions."[47] Indeed, in some instances, the Court appears to have adopted a more searching inquiry because the matter was contained in a state constitution. *Reitman v. Mulkey* invalidated, under the Federal Equal Protection Clause, a citizen initiative amendment to the California Constitution designed to overturn state laws barring discrimination by private sellers and lessors.[48] While recognizing that the state was not required to prevent private discrimination, the Court held that embodying the right to discriminate on racial grounds in the state constitution impermissibly involved "the State in private racial discrimination contrary to the Fourteenth Amendment."[49] While the state could have repealed all its state laws regarding private discrimination without violating the Federal Constitution, overturning such laws by incorporating a private right to discriminate into the state constitution violated the supreme federal charter.

The supreme federal law of the land is not limited to the provisions of the United States Constitution under the text of the Supremacy Clause, but also encompasses "the Laws of the United States" and "Treaties."[50] This additional text provides the basis for the Supreme Court's preemption doctrine, under which any state constitutional provision or state law that interferes with, or is contrary to, federal law is invalidated. While the federal law in a preemption analysis often is a statute enacted by Congress, an executive order or judicially-created federal common law can also override a state constitutional provision.[51] Even a federal regulation promulgated by an agency can preempt a state constitution, as the Supreme Court explained:

> Federal regulations have no less preemptive effect than federal statutes. Where Congress has directed an administrator to exercise his discretion, his judgments are subject to judicial review only to determine whether he has exceeded his statutory authority or acted arbitrarily. When the administrator promulgates regulations intended to pre-empt state law, the court's inquiry is similarly limited.[52]

---

[47]377 U.S. 533, 584 (1964). Although the Court continued that state constitutional provisions should only be invalidated if federal constitutional rights "could not otherwise be protected and effectuated," it then concluded that Alabama's legislative apportionment scheme was no less invalid merely because it was a part of the state constitution. *Id.*

[48]387 U.S. 369 (1967).

[49]*Id.* at 376-77.

[50]U.S. CONST. art. VI, cl. 2.

[51]*Cf.* Am. Ins. Ass'n v. Garamendi, 539 U.S. 396, 416-17 (2003) (recognizing preemptive effect of executive agreements); Hinderlider v. La Plata River & Cherry Creek Ditch Co., 304 U.S. 92 (1938) (holding state constitutional provisions on water rights were subordinate to federal common law); United States v. Belmont, 301 U.S. 324, 327 (1937) (holding that "no state policy can prevail against the international compact here involved").

[52]Fidelity Fed. Sav. & Loan Ass'n v. de la Cuesta, 458 U.S. 141, 153-54 (1982); *accord* Hillsborough Cnty., Fla. v. Automated Med. Labs., Inc., 471 U.S. 707, 713 (1985) ("We have repeatedly held that state laws can be pre-empted by federal regulations as well as by federal statutes.").

As long as Congress, the Executive, or an administrative agency acts within the proper scope of its authority, then, state constitutional provisions are ineffectual if they conflict with any type of federal law.[53] Several Texas constitutional provisions conflicting with federal law have been invalidated under such a preemption analysis.[54]

The Supreme Court recognizes two types of preemption. Express preemption requires explicit preemptive language, whereas implied preemption occurs if Congress has wholly occupied the field, compliance with both the federal and state regulations is impossible, or the state law impedes the accomplishment of Congress' objectives.[55] While these preemption tests are easy to state, the difficulty in practice is deciding whether a particular state constitutional provision or law is preempted. The Supreme Court has frequently stated that congressional intent is the dispositive issue in this analysis.[56] Yet Congress seldom makes its intent explicit, so the courts must make their best guess regarding the congressional purpose through a reading of the statutory text and legislative history. And this "guess" frequently will be colored by the court's view of the appropriate interrelationship of the federal and state governments.

The following case considers whether a provision of the Bankruptcy Code preempts the homestead protection contained in the Texas Constitution. While the majority and dissenting opinions clearly proffer differing interpretations of the federal statute at issue, a more fundamental disagreement between them is the deference to be afforded to Texas constitutional provisions.

Davis v. Davis (In re Davis), 170 F.3d 475 (5th Cir. 1999) (en banc)

EDITH H. JONES, Circuit Judge:

In 1987, Cullen and Karen Davis filed for bankruptcy relief and claimed as their exempt Texas homestead a residence valued at $500,000 which they owned free and clear. Cullen's former wife Sandra obtained a judgment from the bankruptcy court declaring that her $250,000-plus claim for alimony, child support, and maintenance was nondischargeable under 11 U.S.C. § 523(a)(5). To enforce the nondischargeability judgment, Sandra sought turnover relief in the form of an order permitting her to foreclose on Cullen's and Karen's homestead. The bankruptcy court and the district court held that she could not levy on the debtors' homestead because it is protected from execution under Texas law, and 11 U.S.C. § 522(c)(1), a provision of the Bankruptcy Code, did not preempt the debtors' state-law rights. A split panel of this court reversed the lower courts. This case was selected for en

[53]*Cf.* Texas v. Am. Blastfax, Inc., 121 F. Supp. 2d 1085, 1091 n.9 (W.D. Tex. 2000) (holding congressional act could not be invalidated by provision of Texas Constitution because of "basic Supremacy Clause law. It is axiomatic to our federal system of government that a federal law is not invalid solely because it violates one or more state constitutions.").

[54]*See, e.g.*, Hill v. Stone, 421 U.S. 289 (1975) (holding the property qualification for a municipal general obligation bond in Texas Constitution article VI, § 3a violated the Federal Equal Protection Clause); Texas *ex. rel.* Falkner v. Nat'l Bank of Commerce of San Antonio, Tex., 290 F.2d 229 (5th Cir. 1961) (holding former provisions of Texas Constitution article XVI, § 16 prohibiting branch banking were partially preempted by orders of the Secretary of Treasury regarding national banks).

[55]Gade v. Nat'l Solid Waste Mgmt. Ass'n, 505 U.S. 88, 98 (1992).

[56]*See, e.g.*, Medtronic Inc. v. Lohr, 518 U.S. 470, 485 (1996); *Gade*, 505 U.S. at 96.

banc rehearing because of its importance to federal bankruptcy law and to state exemption rules. We conclude that the lower courts were essentially correct.

FACTUAL AND PROCEDURAL HISTORY

When Sandra and Cullen divorced in 1968, they executed a property settlement, support and child custody agreement, and divorce judgment (collectively "divorce judgment"), and Cullen agreed to make monthly payments to Sandra through January 1, 1991, with certain contingent payments thereafter. In 1979, Cullen married Karen Davis. In 1984, Cullen and Karen purchased a house and lot for $750,000.

In 1987, Cullen and Karen stopped making payments to Sandra as required by the divorce judgment and filed for Chapter 7 bankruptcy relief, followed later by conversion to Chapter 11. As has been noted, Cullen's and Karen's costly, lien-free home was claimed as exempt property pursuant to § 522(b)(2)(A) and valued at $500,000 on their schedules.

Armed with the bankruptcy court's judgment that Cullen owed her $300,000 in nondischargeable alimony, maintenance and child support obligations and associated attorneys' fees, Sandra requested that the bankruptcy court seize and sell the debtors' homestead. Because a debtor's homestead is exempt from attachment, execution, or seizure under Tex. Const. art. XVI § 50 and Texas Property Code § 41.002(a), the bankruptcy court determined that the debtors' homestead was not subject to the Texas turnover statute. In so doing, the court rejected Sandra's argument that § 522(c)(1) of the Bankruptcy Code preempted the Texas homestead exemption for nondischargeable debts related to family support as defined in § 523(a)(5). Sandra appealed this ruling to the district court, which affirmed for substantially the same reasons. Sandra timely appealed to this court.

THE BANKRUPTCY EXEMPTION STATUTE

At issue in this case are the meaning and preemptive force, if any, of 11 U.S.C. § 522(c), a provision that is part of the Bankruptcy Code's framework for the treatment of exempt property. Federal bankruptcy law affords debtors a fresh start by enjoining collection of discharged debts, § 524, and by permitting the debtors to retain certain limited amounts and types of exempt property, § 522. Exemptions have been perennially controversial, because they reduce assets potentially available to pay creditors and arouse charges of abuse of bankruptcy. Exemptions are also fought over by states'-rights advocates, who value the traditional state legislative prerogative to adjust exemptions to local economic conditions, and by advocates of federal uniformity, who want to raise–or lower–exemptions based on conceptions of national equity. Congress allayed the controversy between state and federal advocates by providing in the 1978 Bankruptcy Code that states could opt out of prescribed federal exemptions altogether or could allow their citizens to select either schedule. *See* 11 U.S.C. § 522(b).

Exemptions are easy to claim. The debtor files a list of exempt property protected by applicable federal or state law with the court. *See* 11 U.S.C. § 522(*l*). If the exemptions are not objected to, the property becomes exempt and unavailable to be levied on by pre-petition creditors or managed by the trustee.

Moving from the general discussion of exemptions to the case before this court, the narrow terms of exception from the protected status of exempt property are described by the statute as follows:

> (c) Unless the case is dismissed, property exempted under this section is not liable during or after the case for any debt of the debtor that arose, or that is determined under section 502 of this title as if such debt had arisen, before the commencement of the case, except–
> (1) a debt of a kind specified in section 523(a)(1) or 523(a)(5) of this title [addressing nondischargeable divorce judgments] . . .

11 U.S.C. § 522(c). In order to prevail in this case, Sandra must demonstrate that § 522(c) creates a basis for execution on Cullen's homestead to enforce her nondischargeable divorce judgment and that, in enacting this provision, Congress expressly or impliedly preempted the Texas homestead law.

Sandra's argument as to § 522(c) is simple. She reads the section to say that property exempt from payment of discharged debts is "liable" for the types of debts listed as exceptions. But the statute does not say this. Rather, it states that exempt property "is not liable . . . for any debt . . . except . . . [a nondischargeable divorce judgment]." In other words, § 522(c) sought to leave exempt property exposed to postbankruptcy liability only to the extent it would have been exposed if the bankruptcy had not occurred.

We conclude that § 522(c)(1) does not "create" "liability" of exempt property for specified debts following bankruptcy. Instead, the section permits creditors holding such claims to proceed against the property after bankruptcy based on the rights and remedies they would have had under state law if bankruptcy had not been filed.

PREEMPTION

To prevail in her approach to § 522(c), Sandra must show that it preempts Texas law, thus subjecting Cullen's homestead to seizure and sale to satisfy her nondischargeable divorce judgment, despite the express prohibition on such foreclosure contained in the Texas constitution and statutes. *See Eggemeyer v. Eggemeyer,* 623 S.W.2d 462, 466 (Tex. App.-Waco 1981, writ dism'd) (homestead not subject to foreclosure to secure payment of accrued child support).

The Supremacy Clause enables Congress to override state laws if it so intends. Deference to our federalism counsels a presumption that areas of law traditionally reserved to the states, like police powers or property law, are not to be disturbed absent the "clear and manifest purpose of Congress." But preemption may be implied if state and federal laws conflict or a state law thwarts the "accomplishment and execution" of congressional intent. *See Pacific Gas & Elec. Co. v. State Energy Resources Conservation & Dev. Comm'n,* 461 U.S. 190, 204 (1983). Moreover, if Congress has passed a pervasive federal legislative scheme leaving states no room to supplement, then state law will also be preempted. Sandra has attempted to demonstrate (1) express preemption; (2) that §§ 523(a)(5) and 522(c) of the Bankruptcy Code create so pervasive a set of regulations as to impliedly preempt state laws regarding exempt property, and (3) that § 522(c) conflicts irreconcilably with the Texas homestead exemption. Express preemption is precluded by our rejection of Sandra's proffered interpretation of § 522(c).

The Bankruptcy Code's "policy" of strengthening enforcement of family support obligations is a weak reed on which to support implied preemption. Although § 522(c) entitles these obligations to special status against property otherwise exempt in bankruptcy, neither that provision nor § 523(a)(5), the provision for nondischargeability of family support obligations, which § 522(c) incorporates, expresses the full intent of the Code. A debtor who owes family support obligations is afforded a great deal of latitude and protection. First, the filing of the bankruptcy case automatically stays payments of support obligations, as it does all other payments to pre-petition creditors. *See* 11 U.S.C. § 362(a). An ex-spouse deprived of certain family support payments must file an adversary proceeding in bankruptcy court to enforce nondischargeability, and even then, the court may order reduction of certain payments if it finds that the defaulting spouse would suffer "hardship." *See* 11 U.S.C. §§ 523(c), 523(a)(15). A debtor may obtain a Chapter 7 discharge or confirm a Chapter 13 plan without being current in family support obligations. Bankruptcy law presently contains neither a pervasive or consistent approach toward family support obligations.

Reliance on the exemption provision of the Code as a source of implied preemption is also misplaced. Congress specifically preserved state exemptions under § 522(b), rejecting a proposal for uniform federal exemptions. Congress allowed states to define the existence and limits of exemptions. By expressly preserving a role for the state law in the Bankruptcy Code, it is clear that Congress has not devised a policy on federal exemptions so pervasive as to leave no room for a state to supplement bankruptcy law with respect to exemptions.

Even more important, there is no direct conflict between compliance with the Bankruptcy Code and the Texas homestead law. We concluded earlier that in specifying certain debts for which the exempt property is still liable, § 522(c) leaves the parties to their state law collection rights. To execute a judgment against Texas property, a judgment creditor must rely on the state mechanism for enforcement. Although Texas law does not permit the seizure of a homestead for a family support obligation, Sandra can still perfect a judgment lien against the property in question, even if it is a homestead. The property is thus liable, although it is immune from seizure while it is a homestead. This is all § 522(c)(1) requires. Section 522(c)(1) assures that the debtor remains ultimately liable, and the property or proceeds from the sale of property may be subject to seizure if the property ever ceases to be the debtor's homestead. Because the Texas homestead law does not bar the attachment of a perfected lien to homestead property, it does not conflict with § 522(c)(1).

CONCLUSION

Cullen and Karen Davis were entitled to exempt their homestead from claims of creditors under Texas and federal bankruptcy law, and they did so. Sandra is entitled, under § 522(c)(1), to enforce her nondischargeable judgment for family support obligations notwithstanding the exemption claim, but her remedy must be in accord with Texas law, since § 522(c) is not an execution statute and does not preempt relevant Texas law. Either Texas or, perhaps, the U.S. Congress could alter this situation, but it is our duty to enforce the present statute.

DENNIS, Circuit Judge, with whom POLITZ and ROBERT M. PARKER, Circuit Judges, join, dissenting:

To decide whether the Bankruptcy Code preempts the Texas homestead exemption laws, a court must begin by comparing § 522(c) with the state homestead constitutional and statutory provisions to determine if there is a conflict. Section 522(c) provides that during or after bankruptcy, exempt property is not liable for any debt that arose prepetition, or is deemed to have so arisen under § 502, except those debts specified in subparagraphs (1) through (3). This list includes: (1) debts for certain taxes and customs duties; (2) debts for alimony, maintenance, or support; (3) liens that cannot be avoided; (4) liens that are not void; (5) tax liens; and (6) certain nondischargeable debts owed to federal depository institutions.

Congress has plenary power to enact uniform federal bankruptcy laws. *See* U.S. CONST. art. 1, § 8, cl. 4. I recognize that Congress afforded significant deference to state law by allowing bankruptcy debtors to choose state exemptions and by further allowing states to opt out of the federal exemption scheme entirely. Yet, such deference does not warrant the conclusion that the detailed exceptions in § 522(c) to the general immunity from liability of the "property exempted" provided for by the same section must yield to or be controlled by the state exemption laws.

Only by adding a heavy Texas spin to gloss over the plain words and meaning of § 522(c) is the majority able to close its eyes to the obvious conflict between the state laws that exempt homestead property from liability to seizure and sale for alimony and child support debts and § 522(c)(1), which excepts nondischargeable alimony and child support debts from the effects of that exemption. The majority struggles to avoid acknowledging the conflict by theorizing that § 522(c)(1) does not mean what it says but strangely enough has a meaning that produces substantially the same result Texas courts have reached when a Texas court judgment creditor seeks to enforce her alimony and child support decree based solely on state law against the judgment debtor's homestead: The former spouse may have her lien attached to the property but she cannot enforce it until the debtor dies or abandons his homestead. In fact, as we have learned during the course of this case, under Texas law, she cannot enforce it against the proceeds of his sale of the homestead if he invests them in another Texas homestead within six months of the sale.

The conflict between the Bankruptcy Code and the Texas homestead exemption laws, however, is too sharp and too real to be covered up by any amount of ingenious judicial gloss. The state laws provide for an exemption of property from liability to seizure and sale for the owner's alimony and child support debts. The federal bankruptcy law in § 522(c)(1) provides for an exception to that exemption of the same property from liability to seizure and sale for the debtor-owner's alimony and child support debts. Consequently, there is a conflict between the state and federal laws. Therefore, it must be concluded that the state homestead laws are preempted by the federal Bankruptcy Code.

Notes on Federal Preemption Doctrine

Preemption and State Constitutions: Should the Texas homestead exemption receive more deference than other state laws in a preemption analysis because it is a part of the state constitution, justifying a state "spin" in evaluating the preemptive scope of an ambiguous federal statute? Or, conversely, is no additional deference warranted because debtor exemptions are a legislative matter in most states rather than a constitutional issue? Or is it irrelevant where or how Texas addresses the issue because preemption depends entirely on the federal government's actions?

As *Davis* acknowledges, the United States Congress could, by statutory amendment, alter the situation that precluded Sandra Davis from executing on her ex-husband's homestead to satisfy his nondischargeable family support obligations. Instead, though, Congress has given the states wide latitude with respect to federal bankruptcy exemptions. The Bankruptcy Code authorizes debtors to use state law property exemptions, which are quite generous in several states (including Texas, Florida, and California) that allow unlimited amounts of home equity to be shielded from creditors. While Congress has considered creating uniform national home equity limitations, it has not yet done so, primarily due to strong opposition from the debtor-friendly states' congressional contingents.

The Political Safeguards of Federalism: Many other examples exist where Congress *could* preempt a state constitutional provision but *chooses* not to do so. Some have accordingly argued that the political process in Congress provides the necessary protections for state sovereignty. Most famously, Professor Herbert Weschler urged that the election of senators from the state, the election of representatives from districts within the state, and the election of the president based on the votes of state electors would ensure that the states are adequately protected in the political process.[57] Does the political process provide adequate safeguards to ensure the state retains its residuary sovereign dignity and authority? Or is it necessary for the judiciary to carve out spheres of autonomy for the states? The Supreme Court has vacillated on this issue over the last century, acting to protect state autonomy before 1937,[58] then predominantly leaving the states to the mercy of the political process from 1937 until 1990.[59] Since 1990, the Supreme Court, under Chief Justices Rehnquist and Roberts, has reinvigorated judicial enforcement of state sovereignty

---

[57]Herbert Weschler, *The Political Safeguard of Federalism: The Role of the States in the Composition and Selection of the National Government*, 54 COLUM. L. REV. 543 (1954); *accord* JESSE CHOPER, JUDICIAL REVIEW AND THE NATIONAL POLITICAL PROCESS (1980).

[58]*See, e.g.,* Ashton v. Cameron Cnty. Water Improv. Dist., 298 U.S. 513, 527-31 (1936) (invalidating federal statute creating procedures for political subdivisions of a state to petition for bankruptcy as invading the states' freedom "to manage their own affairs"); Hammer v. Dagenhart, 247 U.S. 251, 273-76 (1918) (holding federal law barring the interstate transport of products made with child labor exceeded congressional power by intruding into the state's authority over "local trade and manufacture").

[59]*See, e.g.,* Garcia v. San Antonio Metro. Transit Auth., 469 U.S. 528, 551 (1985) (opining the states are protected by "the built-in restraints that our system provides through state participation in federal governmental action. The political process ensures that the laws that unduly burden the States will not be promulgated.").

to some extent by invalidating those laws that invade defined spheres of state autonomy.[60]

Federal Spending Conditions as a Preemption Alternative: Congress sometimes conditions the receipt of federal funds on the state's compliance with some mandate rather than actually preempting contrary state laws. For example, Congress has conditioned the receipt of a percentage of a state's federal highway funds on the state establishing a drinking age of twenty-one and prohibiting open containers of alcohol while in the car. A state does not have to comply with such conditions, but it will suffer a financial detriment if it refuses to do so. As long as the conditions are unambiguous and not unduly coercive, they fall within congressional power under the United States Constitution.[61]

But what if the state constitution precluded the state legislature from complying with the federal condition? Is the state constitution preempted in that situation, or does the state constitution have to be amended to obtain the federal benefit? *North Carolina ex rel. Morrow v. Califano* provides an example.[62] A state's qualification for financial grants under certain federal health plans required the establishment of a certificate of need program. But the North Carolina Supreme Court had previously held that such a program provided existing hospitals exclusive privileges and monopolizing powers that were prohibited by the state constitution.[63] A three-judge federal district court, in an opinion later affirmed by the Supreme Court, held that the only way to avoid the loss was by a state constitutional amendment–the federal legislation was not invalid merely because the state would have to change its constitution to obtain the benefit:

> Simply because one State, by some oddity of its Constitution may be prohibited from compliance is not sufficient ground, though, to invalidate a condition which is legitimately related to a national interest sought to be achieved by a federal appropriation and which does not operate adversely to the rights of other States to comply. Were this not so, any State, dissatisfied by some valid federal condition on a federal grant could thwart the congressional purpose by the expedient of amending its Constitution or by securing a decision of its own Supreme Court. The validity of the power of the federal government under the Constitution to impose a condition of

---

[60]*See, e.g.,* Shelby Cnty. v. Holder, 133 S. Ct. 2612, 2624-31 (2013) (invalidating coverage formula for preclearance under the Voting Rights Act as invading the equal sovereignty of the states without sufficient justification); Alden v. Maine, 527 U.S. 706, 751 (1999) (invalidating federal statute authorizing private suits for money damages against the states in their own courts that invaded the "State's most fundamental political processes" and struck "at the heart of the political accountability so essential to our liberty and republican form of government"); United States v. Lopez, 514 U.S. 549, 570-84 (1995) (Kennedy, J., concurring) (defending the Court's holding striking down the Gun-Free School Zones Act on the basis that judicial enforcement of federalism is necessary as "the federal balance is too essential a part of our constitutional structure and plays too vital a role in securing freedom for us to admit inability to intervene when one or the other level of Government has tipped the scales too far"); New York v. United States, 505 U.S. 144, 188 (1992) (holding that "[t]he Federal Government may not compel the States to enact or administer a federal regulatory program").

[61]*See* Nat'l Fed'n of Indep. Bus. v. Sebelius, 132 S. Ct. 2566, 2601-06 (2012) (holding that conditioning all state Medicaid funds on agreeing to the Medicaid expansion in the Patient Protection and Affordable Care Act was unduly coercive).

[62]445 F. Supp. 532 (E.D.N.C. 1977), *aff'd mem.*, 435 U.S. 962 (1978).

[63]*In re* Certificate of Need for Aston Park Hosp., Inc., 193 S.E.2d 729, 733-36 (N.C. 1973).

federal grants made under a proper Constitutional power does not exist at the mercy of the State Constitutions or decisions of State Courts.[64]

Preemption and Traditional State Powers: Should preemption also depend on whether the state constitutional provision or statute regulates an area traditionally considered a matter of state concern, such as criminal law, family law, or education? The Supreme Court has opined that the Supremacy Clause mandates "that if there is any conflict between federal and state law, federal law shall prevail," even when the state is providing necessities for its citizens' welfare in areas of traditional state concern.[65] Nevertheless, the following case reveals that judges may be less likely to find implied preemption if the state law is within the realm of the state's traditional police powers, although the appropriate characterization of the challenged law may not always be self-evident.

American Insurance Ass'n v. Garamendi, 539 U.S. 396 (2003)

Justice SOUTER delivered the opinion of the Court.

California's Holocaust Victim Insurance Relief Act of 1999 (HVIRA or Act), requires any insurer doing business in that State to disclose information about all policies sold in Europe between 1920 and 1945 by the company itself or any one "related" to it. The issue here is whether HVIRA interferes with the National Government's conduct of foreign relations. We hold that it does, with the consequence that the state statute is preempted.

I

A

The Nazi Government of Germany engaged not only in genocide and enslavement but theft of Jewish assets, including the value of insurance policies, and in particular policies of life insurance, a form of savings held by many Jews in Europe before the Second World War. Early on in the Nazi era, loss of livelihood forced Jews to cash in life insurance policies prematurely, only to have the government seize the proceeds of the repurchase, and many who tried to emigrate from Germany were forced to liquidate insurance policies to pay the steep "flight taxes" and other levies imposed by the Third Reich to keep Jewish assets from leaving the country. Before long, the Reich began simply seizing the remaining policies outright. After the war, even a policy that had escaped confiscation was likely to be dishonored, whether because insurers denied its existence or claimed it had lapsed from unpaid premiums during the persecution, or because the government would not provide heirs with documentation of the policyholder's death. Responsibility as between the government and insurance companies is disputed, but at the end of the day, the fact is that the value or proceeds of many insurance policies issued to Jews before and during the war were paid to the Reich or never paid at all.

West Germany enacted restitution laws in 1953 and 1956, and signed agreements with 16 countries for the compensation of their nationals, including the Luxembourg Agreement with Israel. Despite a payout of more than 100 billion deutsch marks as of 2000, these measures left out many claimants and certain types of claims, and when the agreement

---

[64]*Califano*, 445 F. Supp. at 535.

[65]Gonzales v. Raich, 545 U.S. 1, 29 & n.38 (2005).

reunifying East and West Germany was read by the German courts as lifting the London Debt Agreement's moratorium on Holocaust claims by foreign nationals, class-action lawsuits for restitution poured into United States courts against companies doing business in Germany during the Nazi era.

These suits generated much protest by the defendant companies and their governments, to the point that the Government of the United States took action. From the beginning, the Government's position, represented principally by Under Secretary of State (later Deputy Treasury Secretary) Stuart Eizenstat, stressed mediated settlement "as an alternative to endless litigation" promising little relief to aging Holocaust survivors. Ensuing negotiations at the national level produced the German Foundation Agreement, signed by President Clinton and German Chancellor Schröder in July 2000, in which Germany agreed to enact legislation establishing a foundation funded with 10 billion deutsch marks contributed equally by the German Government and German companies, to be used to compensate all those "who suffered at the hands of German companies during the National Socialist era."

The willingness of the Germans to create a voluntary compensation fund was conditioned on some expectation of security from lawsuits in United States courts, and after extended dickering President Clinton put his weight behind two specific measures toward that end. First, the Government agreed that whenever a German company was sued on a Holocaust-era claim in an American court, the Government of the United States would submit a statement that "it would be in the foreign policy interests of the United States for the Foundation to be the exclusive forum and remedy for the resolution of all asserted claims against German companies arising from their involvement in the National Socialist era and World War II." Though unwilling to guarantee that its foreign policy interests would "in themselves provide an independent legal basis for dismissal," that being an issue for the courts, the Government agreed to tell courts "that U.S. policy interests favor dismissal on any valid legal ground." On top of that undertaking, the Government promised to use its "best efforts, in a manner it considers appropriate," to get state and local governments to respect the foundation as the exclusive mechanism.

As for insurance claims specifically, both countries agreed that the German Foundation would work with the International Commission on Holocaust Era Insurance Claims (ICHEIC), a voluntary organization formed in 1998 by several European insurance companies, the State of Israel, Jewish and Holocaust survivor associations, and the National Association of Insurance Commissioners, the organization of American state insurance commissioners. The job of the ICHEIC, chaired by former Secretary of State Eagleburger, includes negotiation with European insurers to provide information about unpaid insurance policies issued to Holocaust victims and settlement of claims brought under them. It has thus set up procedures for handling demands against participating insurers.

The German Foundation pact has served as a model for similar agreements with Austria and France, and the United States Government continues to pursue comparable agreements with other countries.

B

While these international efforts were underway, California's Department of Insurance began its own enquiry into the issue of unpaid claims under Nazi-era insurance policies, prompting state legislation designed to force payment by defaulting insurers. The section of the bill codified as HVIRA, at issue here, requires "[a]ny insurer currently doing business in the state" to disclose the details of "life, property, liability, health, annuities, dowry, educational, or casualty insurance policies" issued "to persons in Europe, which were in effect between 1920 and 1945." The duty is to make disclosure not only about policies the particular insurer sold, but also about those sold by any "related company," including "any parent, subsidiary, reinsurer, successor in interest, managing general agent, or affiliate company of the insurer," whether or not the companies were related during the time when the policies subject to disclosure were sold. Nor is the obligation restricted to policies sold to "Holocaust victims" as defined in the Act; it covers policies sold to anyone during that time. The insurer must report the current status of each policy, the city of origin, domicile, or address of each policyholder, and the names of the beneficiaries, all of which is to be put in a central registry open to the public. The mandatory penalty for default is suspension of the company's license to do business in the State, and there are misdemeanor criminal sanctions for falsehood in certain required representations about whether and to whom the proceeds of each policy have been distributed.

After HVIRA was enacted, administrative subpoenas were issued against several subsidiaries of European insurance companies participating in the ICHEIC. Immediately, in November 1999, Deputy Secretary Eizenstat wrote to the insurance commissioner of California that although HVIRA "reflects a genuine commitment to justice for Holocaust victims and their families, it has the unfortunate effect of damaging the one effective means now at hand to process quickly and completely unpaid insurance claims from the Holocaust period, the [ICHEIC]." The Deputy Secretary said that "actions by California, pursuant to this law, have already threatened to damage the cooperative spirit which the [ICHEIC] requires to resolve the important issue for Holocaust survivors," and he also noted that ICHEIC Chairman Eagleburger had expressed his opposition to "sanctions and other pressures brought by California on companies with whom he is obtaining real cooperation." The same day, Deputy Secretary Eizenstat also wrote to California's Governor making the same points, and stressing that HVIRA would possibly derail the German Foundation Agreement. These expressions of the National Government's concern proved to be of no consequence, for the state commissioner announced at an investigatory hearing in December 1999 that he would enforce HVIRA to its fullest, requiring the affected insurers to make the disclosures, leave the State voluntarily, or lose their licenses.

II

After this ultimatum, the petitioners here, several American and European insurance companies and the American Insurance Association (a national trade association), filed suit for injunctive relief against respondent insurance commissioner of California, challenging the constitutionality of HVIRA. The District Court issued a preliminary injunction against enforcing the Act, reflecting its probability judgment that "HVIRA is unconstitutional based on a violation of the federal foreign affairs power and a violation of the Commerce Clause." On appeal, the Ninth Circuit rejected these grounds for questioning the Act.

Given the importance of the issue,[66] we granted certiorari, and now reverse.

III

The principal argument for preemption made by petitioners and the United States as *amicus curiae* is that HVIRA interferes with foreign policy of the Executive Branch, as expressed principally in the executive agreements with Germany, Austria, and France. The major premises of the argument, at least, are beyond dispute. There is, of course, no question that at some point an exercise of state power that touches on foreign relations must yield to the National Government's policy, given the "concern for uniformity in this country's dealings with foreign nations" that animated the Constitution's allocation of the foreign relations power to the National Government in the first place. *Banco Nacional de Cuba v. Sabbatino,* 376 U.S. 398, 427, n. 25 (1964); see The Federalist No. 44, p. 299 (J. Madison) (emphasizing "the advantage of uniformity in all points which relate to foreign powers"); The Federalist No. 42, p. 279 (J. Madison) ("If we are to be one nation in any respect, it clearly ought to be in respect to other nations").

Nor is there any question generally that there is executive authority to decide what that policy should be. Although the source of the President's power to act in foreign affairs does not enjoy any textual detail, the historical gloss on the "executive Power" vested in Article II of the Constitution has recognized the President's "vast share of responsibility for the conduct of our foreign relations." While Congress holds express authority to regulate public and private dealings with other nations in its war and foreign commerce powers, in foreign affairs the President has a degree of independent authority to act.

At a more specific level, our cases have recognized that the President has authority to make "executive agreements" with other countries, requiring no ratification by the Senate or approval by Congress, this power having been exercised since the early years of the Republic. [Valid] executive agreements are fit to preempt state law, just as treaties are, and if the agreements here had expressly preempted laws like HVIRA, the issue would be straightforward. But petitioners and the United States as *amicus curiae* both have to acknowledge that the agreements include no preemption clause, and so leave their claim of preemption to rest on asserted interference with the foreign policy those agreements embody. Reliance is placed on our decision in *Zschernig v. Miller,* 389 U.S. 429 (1968).

Zschernig dealt with an Oregon probate statute prohibiting inheritance by a nonresident alien, absent showings that the foreign heir would take the property "without confiscation" by his home country and that American citizens would enjoy reciprocal rights of inheritance there. By the time Zschernig (an East German resident) brought his challenge, it was clear that the Oregon law in practice had invited "minute inquiries concerning the actual administration of foreign law," and so was providing occasions for

[66]Several other States have passed laws similar to HVIRA. See Holocaust Victims Insurance Act, Fla. Stat. § 626.9543 (Cum.Supp.2003); Holocaust Victims Insurance Act, Md. Ins.Code Ann. §§ 28-101 to 28- 110 (2002); Holocaust Victims Insurance Relief Act of 2000, Minn.Stat. § 60A.053 (Cum.Supp.2003); Holocaust Victims Insurance Act of 1998, N.Y. Ins. Law §§ 2701-2711 (Consol.2000); Holocaust Victims Insurance Relief Act of 1999, Wash. Rev.Code §§ 48.104.010-48.104.903 (2003); see also Ariz.Rev.Stat. Ann. § 20-490 (West Cum.Supp.2003); Tex. Ins.Code Ann., Art. 21.74 (Vernon 2003). And similar bills have been proposed in other States. See, *e.g.,* Mass. Senate Bill No. 843 (Jan. 1, 2003).

state judges to disparage certain foreign regimes, employing the language of the anti-Communism prevalent here at the height of the Cold War. Although the Solicitor General, speaking for the State Department, denied that the state statute "unduly interfere[d] with the United States' conduct of foreign relations," the Court was not deterred from exercising its own judgment to invalidate the law as an "intrusion by the State into the field of foreign affairs which the Constitution entrusts to the President and the Congress."

The *Zschernig* majority relied on statements in a number of previous cases open to the reading that state action with more than incidental effect on foreign affairs is preempted, even absent any affirmative federal activity in the subject area of the state law, and hence without any showing of conflict. Justice Harlan, joined substantially by Justice White, disagreed with the *Zschernig* majority on this point, arguing that its implication of preemption of the entire field of foreign affairs was at odds with some other cases suggesting that in the absence of positive federal action "the States may legislate in areas of their traditional competence even though their statutes may have an incidental effect on foreign relations."

It is a fair question whether respect for the executive foreign relations power requires a categorical choice between the contrasting theories of field and conflict preemption evident in the *Zschernig* opinions,[67] but the question requires no answer here. For even on Justice Harlan's view, the likelihood that state legislation will produce something more than incidental effect in conflict with express foreign policy of the National Government would require preemption of the state law. And since on his view it is legislation within "areas of . . . traditional competence" that gives a State any claim to prevail, it would be reasonable to consider the strength of the state interest, judged by standards of traditional practice, when deciding how serious a conflict must be shown before declaring the state law preempted. Judged by these standards, we think petitioners and the Government have demonstrated a sufficiently clear conflict to require finding preemption here.

IV

A

To begin with, resolving Holocaust-era insurance claims that may be held by residents of this country is a matter well within the Executive's responsibility for foreign affairs. Since claims remaining in the aftermath of hostilities may be "sources of friction" acting as an "impediment to resumption of friendly relations" between the countries involved, there is a "longstanding practice" of the national Executive to settle them in discharging its responsibility to maintain the Nation's relationships with other countries. Vindicating victims injured by acts and omissions of enemy corporations in wartime is thus

---

[67]The two positions can be seen as complementary. If a State were simply to take a position on a matter of foreign policy with no serious claim to be addressing a traditional state responsibility, field preemption might be the appropriate doctrine, whether the National Government had acted and, if it had, without reference to the degree of any conflict, the principle having been established that the Constitution entrusts foreign policy exclusively to the National Government. Where, however, a State has acted within what Justice Harlan called its "traditional competence," but in a way that affects foreign relations, it might make good sense to require a conflict, of a clarity or substantiality that would vary with the strength or the traditional importance of the state concern asserted.

within the traditional subject matter of foreign policy in which national, not state, interests are overriding, and which the National Government has addressed.

The exercise of the federal executive authority means that state law must give way where, as here, there is evidence of clear conflict between the policies adopted by the two. The foregoing account of negotiations toward the three settlement agreements is enough to illustrate that the consistent Presidential foreign policy has been to encourage European governments and companies to volunteer settlement funds in preference to litigation or coercive sanctions. As for insurance claims in particular, the national position, expressed unmistakably in the executive agreements signed by the President with Germany and Austria, has been to encourage European insurers to work with the ICHEIC to develop acceptable claim procedures, including procedures governing disclosure of policy information.

California has taken a different tack of providing regulatory sanctions to compel disclosure and payment, supplemented by a new cause of action for Holocaust survivors if the other sanctions should fail. HVIRA's economic compulsion to make public disclosure, of far more information about far more policies than ICHEIC rules require, employs "a different, state system of economic pressure," and in doing so undercuts the President's diplomatic discretion and the choice he has made exercising it. Whereas the President's authority to provide for settling claims in winding up international hostilities requires flexibility in wielding "the coercive power of the national economy" as a tool of diplomacy, HVIRA denies this, by making exclusion from a large sector of the American insurance market the automatic sanction for noncompliance with the State's own policies on disclosure.

B

The express federal policy and the clear conflict raised by the state statute are alone enough to require state law to yield. If any doubt about the clarity of the conflict remained, however, it would have to be resolved in the National Government's favor, given the weakness of the State's interest, against the backdrop of traditional state legislative subject matter, in regulating disclosure of European Holocaust-era insurance policies in the manner of HVIRA.

The commissioner would justify HVIRA's ambitious disclosure requirement as protecting "legitimate consumer protection interests" in knowing which insurers have failed to pay insurance claims. But, quite unlike a generally applicable "blue sky" law, HVIRA effectively singles out only policies issued by European companies, in Europe, to European residents, at least 55 years ago. Limiting the public disclosure requirement to these policies raises great doubt that the purpose of the California law is an evaluation of corporate reliability in contemporary insuring in the State.

Indeed, there is no serious doubt that the state interest actually underlying HVIRA is concern for the several thousand Holocaust survivors said to be living in the State. But this fact does not displace general standards for evaluating a State's claim to apply its forum law to a particular controversy or transaction, under which the State's claim is not a strong one. "Even if a plaintiff evidences his desire for forum law by moving to the forum, we have generally accorded such a move little or no significance."

But should the general standard not be displaced, and the State's interest recognized as a powerful one, by virtue of the fact that California seeks to vindicate the claims of Holocaust survivors? The answer lies in recalling that the very same objective dignifies the interest of the National Government in devising its chosen mechanism for voluntary settlements, there being about 100,000 survivors in the country, only a small fraction of them in California. As against the responsibility of the United States of America, the humanity underlying the state statute could not give the State the benefit of any doubt in resolving the conflict with national policy.

C

The basic fact is that California seeks to use an iron fist where the President has consistently chosen kid gloves. We have heard powerful arguments that the iron fist would work better, and it may be that if the matter of compensation were considered in isolation from all other issues involving the European Allies, the iron fist would be the preferable policy. But our thoughts on the efficacy of the one approach versus the other are beside the point, since our business is not to judge the wisdom of the National Government's policy; dissatisfaction should be addressed to the President or, perhaps, Congress. The question relevant to preemption in this case is conflict, and the evidence here is "more than sufficient to demonstrate that the state Act stands in the way of [the President's] diplomatic objectives."

Justice GINSBURG, with whom Justice STEVENS, Justice SCALIA, and Justice THOMAS join, dissenting.

Although the federal approach [here] differs from California's, no executive agreement or other formal expression of foreign policy disapproves state disclosure laws like the HVIRA. Absent a clear statement aimed at disclosure requirements by the "one voice" to which courts properly defer in matters of foreign affairs, I would leave intact California's enactment.

Together, [our prior cases] confirm that executive agreements directed at claims settlement may sometimes preempt state law. The Court states that if the executive "agreements here had expressly preempted laws like HVIRA, the issue would be straightforward." One can safely demur to that statement, for, as the Court acknowledges, no executive agreement before us expressly preempts the HVIRA. Indeed, no agreement so much as mentions the HVIRA's sole concern: public disclosure.

Despite the absence of express preemption, the Court holds that the HVIRA interferes with foreign policy objectives implicit in the executive agreements. I would not venture down that path.

The Court's analysis draws substantially on *Zschernig v. Miller,* 389 U.S. 429 (1968). We have not relied on *Zschernig* since it was decided, and I would not resurrect that decision here. The notion of "dormant foreign affairs preemption" with which *Zschernig* is associated resonates most audibly when a state action "reflect[s] a state policy critical of foreign governments and involve[s] 'sitting in judgment' on them." L. Henkin, Foreign Affairs and the United States Constitution 164 (2d ed.1996). The HVIRA entails no such state action or policy. It takes no position on any contemporary foreign government and requires no assessment of any existing foreign regime. It is directed solely at private insurers doing business in California, and it requires them solely to disclose information in their or their affiliates' possession or control. I would not extend *Zschernig* into this dissimilar domain.

Neither would I stretch [our prior decisions] to support implied preemption by executive agreement. In each of those cases, the Court gave effect to the express terms of an executive agreement. Here, however, none of the executive agreements extinguish any underlying claim for relief. The United States has agreed to file precatory statements advising courts that dismissing Holocaust-era claims accords with American foreign policy, but the German Foundation Agreement confirms that such statements have no legally binding effect. It remains uncertain, therefore, whether even *litigation* on Holocaust-era insurance claims must be abated in deference to the German Foundation Agreement or the parallel agreements with Austria and France. Indeed, ambiguity on this point appears to have been the studied aim of the American negotiating team. See Eizenstat, Imperfect Justice, at 272-273 (describing the "double negative" that satisfied German negotiators and preserved the flexibility sought by Justice Department litigators).

If it is uncertain whether insurance *litigation* may continue given the executive agreements on which the Court relies, it should be abundantly clear that those agreements leave *disclosure* laws like the HVIRA untouched. Here, the Court invalidates a state disclosure law on grounds of conflict with foreign policy "embod[ied]" in certain executive agreements, although those agreements do not refer to state disclosure laws specifically, or even to information disclosure generally. It therefore is surely an exaggeration to assert that the "HVIRA threatens to frustrate the operation of the particular mechanism the President has chosen" to resolve Holocaust-era claims. If that were so, one might expect to find some reference to laws like the HVIRA in the later-in-time executive agreements. There is none.

Sustaining the HVIRA would not compromise the President's ability to speak with one voice for the Nation. To the contrary, by declining to invalidate the HVIRA in this case, we would reserve foreign affairs preemption for circumstances where the President, acting under statutory or constitutional authority, has spoken clearly to the issue at hand. "[T]he Framers did not make the judiciary the overseer of our government." And judges should not be the expositors of the Nation's foreign policy, which is the role they play by acting when the President himself has not taken a clear stand. As I see it, courts step out of their proper role when they rely on no legislative or even executive text, but only on inference and implication, to preempt state laws on foreign affairs grounds.

In sum, assuming, *arguendo,* that an executive agreement or similarly formal foreign policy statement targeting disclosure could override the HVIRA, there is no such declaration here. Accordingly, I would leave California's enactment in place.

Notes on Preemption of State Conduct Impacting International Affairs

Dormant Foreign Affairs Preemption: The Court acknowledges that the executive agreement could have explicitly preempted contrary state laws, but it did not. Why didn't the President include a preemption provision in the agreement? Shouldn't that count strongly against a finding of preemption? Because the executive did not demonstrate any intent to preempt state law in the agreement, *Garamendi* has been called a case of "dormant foreign affairs preemption." Is the basis of this type of preemption the view that states have little interest in regulating matters of foreign affairs?

Is *Garamendi*'s application of dormant foreign affairs preemption supported by *Zschernig*? The Oregon state judiciary in *Zschernig* was disparaging foreign regimes, while the HVIRA was a legislative enactment applying to private entities and their related companies wishing to do business in California. Do the same policies underlie the use of preemption in both situations?

State Courts and Transnational Law: What impact does the federal preeminence in foreign affairs have on state courts handling international law matters? The jurisdiction of the federal courts and state courts is typically coextensive regarding international or transnational law matters, although there are situations in which such cases may be removed to federal court.[68] Nevertheless, state courts in modern times probably handle more international law cases than do the federal courts.[69] Is there any tension between state judicial authority to resolve international law cases and the scope of the federal preemption doctrine applied to state laws impacting foreign affairs?

State Laws and Foreign Affairs: In spite of the potential for foreign affairs preemption, the states often do attempt to have a voice in matters of foreign affairs, illustrated by the number of states listed in *Garamendi*, including Texas, that promulgated laws similar to the HVIRA.

The statutes and constitutional provisions enacted by many states requiring divestment in South Africa as a result of the former system of apartheid provide another example. The Texas Constitution in article 16, section 70(r) contained a provision requiring businesses to disclose whether they did business in South Africa or Namibia before the state's Growth Fund could make an investment in the company. After apartheid was dismantled, this provision was finally repealed by Texas voters in 1999, following an unsuccessful attempt to repeal it in 1997. Before it was repealed, was this provision inoperable as a result of "dormant foreign affairs preemption"? The Office of Legal Counsel for President Reagan opined that such state divestment provisions were constitutional, concluding *Zschernig* merely "represents the Court's reaction to a particular regulatory statute, the operation of which intruded extraordinarily deeply into foreign

---

[68] *See, e.g.*, 28 U.S.C. § 1441(d) (authorizing foreign states to remove state court actions to federal court).

[69] Thomas R. Phillips, *State Supreme Courts: Local Courts in a Global World*, 38 TEX. INT'L L.J. 557, 564 (2003).

affairs."[70] Why did the Reagan administration conclude that these divestment provisions were constitutional, while the Clinton and Bush administrations challenged the HVIRA? If California's HVIRA had been supported by the President, would the Supreme Court have reached the same holding in *Garamendi*? If not, is dormant foreign affairs preemption merely a matter of the executive expressing after the fact disagreement with foreign affairs policy determinations made by the states?[71] Does this possibility have the effect of encouraging the states to express their views on foreign affairs in an attempt to influence the conduct of the federal government?

State laws impacting foreign affairs are typically justified under the rationale that states possess an inherent authority to govern that is derived, not from the United States Constitution, but from the people of the state. Absent a constitutional prohibition in either the United States or the state constitution, states may typically legislate on any matter, as discussed in greater detail in later chapters. Thus, the states are generally competent to enact legislation that touches on foreign affairs unless preempted by federal law. But are there other times when a state does not have any inherent authority and must be delegated that authority by the United States Constitution? If a state has no authority to regulate, is preemption analysis even necessary?

Cook v. Gralike, 531 U.S. 510 (2001)

JUSTICE STEVENS delivered the opinion of the Court.

In *U.S. Term Limits, Inc. v. Thornton,* 514 U.S. 779 (1995), we reviewed a challenge to an Arkansas law that prohibited the name of an otherwise eligible candidate for the United States Congress from appearing on the general election ballot if he or she had already served three terms in the House of Representatives or two terms in the Senate. We held that the ballot restriction was an indirect attempt to impose term limits on congressional incumbents that violated the Qualifications Clauses in Article I of the Constitution rather than a permissible exercise of the State's power to regulate the "Times, Places and Manner of holding Elections for Senators and Representatives."

In response to that decision, the voters of Missouri adopted in 1996 an amendment to Article VIII of their State Constitution designed to lead to the adoption of a specified "Congressional Term Limits Amendment" to the Federal Constitution. At issue in this case is the constitutionality of Article VIII.

I.

Article VIII "instruct[s]" each Member of Missouri's congressional delegation "to use all of his or her delegated powers to pass the Congressional Term Limits Amendment" set forth in § 16 of the Article. Mo. Const., Art. VIII, § 17(1). That proposed amendment would limit service in the United States Congress to three terms in the House of Representatives and two terms in the Senate.

---

[70] *See* Constitutionality of South African Divestment Statutes Enacted by State and Local Governments, 10 Op. Off. Legal Counsel 49, 50 (1986).

[71] *Cf.* Brandon P. Denning & Michael D. Ramsay, American Ins. Ass'n v. Garamendi *and Executive Preemption in Foreign Affairs*, 46 WM. & MARY L. REV. 825, 829-30 (2004).

Three provisions in Article VIII combine to advance its purpose. Section 17 prescribes that the statement "DISREGARDED VOTERS' INSTRUCTION ON TERM LIMITS" be printed on all primary and general ballots adjacent to the name of a Senator or Representative who fails to take any one of eight legislative acts in support of the proposed amendment. Section 18 provides that the statement "DECLINED TO PLEDGE TO SUPPORT TERM LIMITS" be printed on all primary and general election ballots next to the name of every nonincumbent congressional candidate who refuses to take a "Term Limit" pledge that commits the candidate, if elected, to performing the legislative acts enumerated in § 17. And § 19 directs the Missouri Secretary of State to determine and declare, pursuant to §§ 17 and 18, whether either statement should be printed alongside the name of each candidate for Congress.

Respondent Don Gralike was a nonincumbent candidate for election in 1998 to the United States House of Representatives from Missouri's Third Congressional District. A month after Article VIII was amended, Gralike brought [this] suit. The District Court decided the case on the pleadings, granting Gralike's motion for summary judgment. The United States Court of Appeals for the Eighth Circuit affirmed. Although the Court of Appeals' decision is consistent with the views of other courts that have passed on similar voter initiatives, the importance of the case prompted our grant of certiorari.

II.

Article VIII furthers the State's interest in adding a term limits amendment to the Federal Constitution in two ways. It encourages Missouri's congressional delegation to support such an amendment in order to avoid an unfavorable ballot designation when running for reelection. And it encourages the election of representatives who favor such an amendment. Petitioner argues that Article VIII is an exercise of the "right of the people to instruct" their representatives reserved by the Tenth Amendment, and that it is a permissible regulation of the "manner" of electing federal legislators within the authority delegated to the States by the Elections Clause. Because these two arguments rely on different sources of state power, it is appropriate at the outset to review the distinction in kind between powers reserved to the States and those delegated to the States by the Constitution.

As we discussed at length in *U.S. Term Limits,* the Constitution "draws a basic distinction between the powers of the newly created Federal Government and the powers retained by the pre-existing sovereign States." 514 U.S. at 801. On the one hand, in the words of Chief Justice Marshall, "it was neither necessary nor proper to define the powers retained by the States. These powers proceed, not from the people of America, but from the people of the several States; and remain, after the adoption of the constitution, what they were before, except so far as they may be abridged by that instrument." *Sturges v. Crowninshield,* 4 Wheat. 122, 193 (1819). The text of the Tenth Amendment delineates this principle:

> The powers not delegated to the United States by the Constitution, nor prohibited by it to the States, are reserved to the States respectively, or to the people.

On the other hand, as Justice Story observed, "the states can exercise no powers whatsoever, which exclusively spring out of the existence of the national government, which the constitution did not delegate to them." 1 Commentaries on the Constitution of the United States § 627 (3d ed. 1858) (hereinafter Story). Simply put, "[n]o state can say, that it has reserved, what it never possessed." *Ibid.*

III.

Petitioner relies heavily on the part instructions played in the Second Continental Congress, the Constitutional Convention, the early Congress, the selection of United States Senators before the passage of the Seventeenth Amendment, and the ratification of certain federal constitutional amendments. However, unlike Article VIII, none of petitioner's examples was coupled with an express legal sanction for disobedience. At best, as an *amicus curiae* for petitioner points out, and as petitioner herself acknowledges, such historical instructions at one point in the early Republic may have had "de facto binding force" because it might have been "political suicide" not to follow them.[72] This evidence falls short of demonstrating that either the people or the States had a right to give legally binding, *i.e.*, nonadvisory, instructions to their representatives that the Tenth Amendment reserved, much less that such a right would apply to federal representatives. See *U.S. Term Limits, Inc. v. Thornton,* 514 U.S. at 802 (Tenth Amendment "could only 'reserve' that which existed before"); cf. *McCulloch v. Maryland,* 4 Wheat. 316, 430 (1819) (rejecting argument that States had reserved power to tax corporations chartered by Congress because an "original right to tax" such federal entities "never existed").

Indeed, contrary evidence is provided by the fact that the First Congress rejected a proposal to insert a right of the people "to instruct their representatives" into what would become the First Amendment. 1 Annals of Cong. 732 (1789). The fact that the proposal was made suggests that its proponents thought it necessary, and the fact that it was rejected by a vote of 41 to 10, suggests that we should give weight to the views of those who opposed the proposal. It was their view that binding instructions would undermine an essential attribute of Congress by eviscerating the deliberative nature of that National Assembly. See, *e.g., id.,* at 735 (remarks of Rep. Sherman) ("[W]hen the people have chosen a representative, it is his duty to meet others from the different parts of the Union, and consult, and agree with them to such acts as are for the general benefit of the whole community. If they were to be guided by instructions, there would be no use in deliberation; all that a man would have to do, would be to produce his instructions, and lay them on the table, and let them speak for him"). As a result, James Madison, then a Representative from Virginia, concluded that a right to issue binding instructions would "run the risk of losing the whole system." *Id.,* at 739; see also *id.,* at 735 (remarks of Rep. Clymer) (proposed right to give binding instructions was "a most dangerous principle, utterly destructive of all ideas of an independent and deliberative body.").

In any event, even assuming the existence of the reserved right that petitioner asserts (and that Article VIII falls within its ambit), the question remains whether the State may use ballots for congressional elections as a means of giving its instructions binding force.

---

[72]But see 1 Annals of Cong. 744 (1789) (remarks of Rep. Wadsworth) ("I have known, myself, that [instructions] have been disobeyed, and yet the representative was not brought to account for it; on the contrary, he was caressed and re-elected, while those who have obeyed them, contrary to their private sentiments, have ever after been despised for it").

IV.

The federal offices at stake "aris[e] from the Constitution itself." *U.S. Term Limits, Inc. v. Thornton,* 514 U.S., at 805. Because any state authority to regulate election to those offices could not precede their very creation by the Constitution, such power "had to be delegated to, rather than reserved by, the States." *Id.,* at 804. Cf. 1 Story § 627 ("It is no original prerogative of state power to appoint a representative, a senator, or president for the union"). Through the Elections Clause, the Constitution delegated to the States the power to regulate the "Times, Places and Manner of holding Elections for Senators and Representatives," subject to a grant of authority to Congress to "make or alter such Regulations." Art. I, § 4, cl. 1. No other constitutional provision gives the States authority over congressional elections, and no such authority could be reserved under the Tenth Amendment. By process of elimination, the States may regulate the incidents of such elections, including balloting, only within the exclusive delegation of power under the Elections Clause.

With respect to the Elections Clause, petitioner argues that Article VIII "merely regulates the manner in which elections are held by disclosing information about congressional candidates." As such, petitioner concludes, Article VIII is a valid exercise of Missouri's delegated power.

We disagree. To be sure, the Elections Clause grants to the States "broad power" to prescribe the procedural mechanisms for holding congressional elections. Nevertheless, Article VIII falls outside of that grant of authority. As we made clear in *U.S. Term Limits,* "the Framers understood the Elections Clause as a grant of authority to issue procedural regulations, and not as a source of power to dictate electoral outcomes, to favor or disfavor a class of candidates, or to evade important constitutional restraints." 514 U.S., at 833-834. Article VIII is not a procedural regulation. It does not regulate the time of elections; it does not regulate the place of elections; nor, we believe, does it regulate the manner of elections. As to the last point, Article VIII bears no relation to the "manner" of elections as we understand it, for in our commonsense view that term encompasses matters like "notices, registration, supervision of voting, protection of voters, prevention of fraud and corrupt practices, counting of votes, duties of inspectors and canvassers, and making and publication of election returns." In short, Article VIII is not among "the numerous requirements as to procedure and safeguards which experience shows are necessary in order to enforce the fundamental right involved," ensuring that elections are "fair and honest," and that "some sort of order, rather than chaos, is to accompany the democratic process."

Rather, Article VIII is plainly designed to favor candidates who are willing to support the particular form of a term limits amendment set forth in its text and to disfavor those who either oppose term limits entirely or would prefer a different proposal. As noted, the state provision does not just "instruct" each member of Missouri's congressional delegation to promote in certain ways the passage of the specified term limits amendment. It also attaches a concrete consequence to noncompliance–the printing of the statement "DISREGARDED VOTERS' INSTRUCTIONS ON TERM LIMITS" by the candidate's name on all primary and general election ballots. Likewise, a nonincumbent candidate who does not pledge to follow the instruction receives the ballot designation "DECLINED TO PLEDGE TO SUPPORT TERM LIMITS."

In describing the two labels, the courts below have employed terms such as "pejorative," "negative," "derogatory," "intentionally intimidating," "particularly harmful," "politically damaging," "a serious sanction," "a penalty," and "official denunciation." The general counsel to petitioner's office, no less, has denominated the labels as "the Scarlet Letter." We agree with the sense of these descriptions. They convey the substantial political risk the ballot labels impose on current and prospective congressional members who, for one reason or another, fail to comply with the conditions set forth in Article VIII for passing its term limits amendment.

Indeed, it seems clear that the adverse labels handicap candidates "at the most crucial stage in the election process–the instant before the vote is cast." At the same time, "by directing the citizen's attention to the single consideration" of the candidates' fidelity to term limits, the labels imply that the issue "is an important–perhaps paramount–consideration in the citizen's choice, which may decisively influence the citizen to cast his ballot" against candidates branded as unfaithful. While the precise damage the labels may exact on candidates is disputed between the parties, the labels surely place their targets at a political disadvantage to unmarked candidates for congressional office. Thus, far from regulating the procedural mechanisms of elections, Article VIII attempts to "dictate electoral outcomes." *U.S. Term Limits, Inc. v. Thornton,* 514 U.S., at 833-834. Such "regulation" of congressional elections simply is not authorized by the Elections Clause.

Justice KENNEDY, concurring.

I join the opinion of the Court, holding Article VIII of the Missouri Constitution violative of the Constitution of the United States. It seems appropriate, however, to add these brief observations with respect to Part III of the opinion. The Court does not say the States are disabled from requesting specific action from Congress or from expressing their concerns to it. As the Court holds, however, the mechanism the State seeks to employ here goes well beyond this prerogative.

A State is not permitted to interpose itself between the people and their National Government as it seeks to do here. Whether a State's concern is with the proposed enactment of a constitutional amendment or an ordinary federal statute it simply lacks the power to impose any conditions on the election of Senators and Representatives, save neutral provisions as to the time, place, and manner of elections pursuant to Article I, § 4.

The dispositive principle in this case is fundamental to the Constitution, to the idea of federalism, and to the theory of representative government. The principle is that Senators and Representatives in the National Government are responsible to the people who elect them, not to the States in which they reside. The idea of federalism is that a National Legislature enacts laws which bind the people as individuals, not as citizens of a State; and, it follows, freedom is most secure if the people themselves, not the States as intermediaries, hold their federal legislators to account for the conduct of their office. If state enactments were allowed to condition or control certain actions of federal legislators, accountability would be blurred, with the legislators having the excuse of saying that they did not act in the exercise of their best judgment but simply in conformance with a state mandate. As noted in the concurring opinion in *Thornton,* "[n]othing in the Constitution or The Federalist Papers . . . supports the idea of state interference with the most basic relation between the

National Government and its citizens, the selection of legislative representatives." Yet that is just what Missouri seeks to do through its law–to wield the power granted to it by the Elections Clause to handicap those who seek federal office by affixing pejorative labels next to their names on the ballot if they do not pledge to support the State's preferred position on a certain issue. Neither the design of the Constitution nor sound principles of representative government are consistent with the right or power of a State to interfere with the direct line of accountability between the National Legislature and the people who elect it. For these reasons Article VIII is void.

This said, it must be noted that when the Constitution was enacted, respectful petitions to legislators were an accepted mode of urging legislative action. See W. Miller, Arguing About Slavery 105-107 (1995). This right is preserved to individuals (the people) in the First Amendment. Even if a State, as an entity, is not itself protected by the Petition Clause, there is no principle prohibiting a state legislature from following a parallel course and by a memorial resolution requesting the Congress of the United States to pay heed to certain state concerns. From the earliest days of our Republic to the present time, States have done so in the context of federal legislation. The fact that the Members of the First Congress decided not to codify a right to instruct legislative representatives does not, in my view, prove that they intended to prohibit nonbinding petitions or memorials by the State as an entity.

If there are to be cases in which a close question exists regarding whether the State has exceeded its constitutional authority in attempting to influence congressional action, this case is not one of them. In today's case the question is not close. Here the State attempts to intrude upon the relationship between the people and their congressional delegates by seeking to control or confine the discretion of those delegates, and the interference is not permissible.

[The concurring opinions of Justice Thomas and Chief Justice Rehnquist have been omitted.]

Notes on the Scope of State Powers

Delegated v. Reserved State Powers: States hold a plenary police power which was reserved by the Tenth Amendment, but this reserved power does not extend to encompass objects that would not exist in the absence of the federal government. As the Supreme Court reasoned early in our nation's history in *McCulloch v. Maryland*, the states cannot claim a reserved power to tax corporations chartered by Congress, such as the Bank of the United States, because an "original right to tax" such federal entities "never existed."[73] Without a federal government, there would be no Bank of the United States to tax, belying the claim that taxing the bank was an inherent state power protected by the Tenth Amendment.

This rationale is also evident in *Cook* and its predecessor case, *U.S. Term Limits v. Thornton*. Both of these cases determined that the states had no reserved powers to regulate elections for federal offices. Because these federal offices were created by the United States

[73] 17 U.S. (4 Wheat.) 316, 430 (1819).

Constitution, only the Federal Constitution could delegate the states regulatory authority over such elections. But *Cook* and *Thornton* differ from *McCulloch* in that the Constitution did delegate some electoral authority to the states, while it did not delegate any authority to tax federal entities. Thus, *Cook* was an extremely rare species of case in which the state depends on the powers *granted* to it by the *Federal* Constitution to support legislation, specifically the powers granted by the Elections Clause.

The Elections Clause: The Elections Clause of the United States Constitution provides: "The Times, Places, and Manner of holding Elections for Senators and Representative, shall be prescribed in each State by the Legislature thereof, but the Congress may at any time by law make or alter such Regulations."[74] The Court has long held that this clause only authorizes procedural regulations by the states, such as election dates, voter registration, voter qualifications, and vote tabulation, which explains its conclusions in *Thornton* and *Cook* that the clause did not allow the states to impose term limits on its federal representatives or dictate the outcomes of federal elections.

For a large part of this nation's history, the states had substantial discretion regarding many of the procedural aspects of elections, including the actual date to hold an election for Congress, the qualifications to vote in that election, and the mechanisms for recording and tabulating votes. But over the last 150 years, amendments to the Constitution and congressional statutes have constrained that discretion considerably, providing for uniform election dates and requiring that the right to vote cannot be denied to any citizen, who is at least eighteen years of age, based on gender, race, ethnicity, disability, or failure to pay a poll tax. Nevertheless, states still retain some discretion in the mechanisms for recording and tabulating votes, although the problems with the counting of the punch card ballots in Florida for the 2000 Presidential election has prompted recent federal action on this front. A commission on election reform co-chaired by former Presidents Jimmy Carter and Gerald Ford was instrumental in shaping a federal law known as the Help America Vote Act of 2002 ("HAVA"), which provides grants for states to replace punch card and lever voting machines and imposes certain voting system requirements on the states. As a result, the state's delegated power under the Elections Clause has been increasingly diminishing in importance.

Presidential Electors: A delegated state power over federal elections that has not diminished in importance is selecting the method of appointing electors to the Electoral College. The Constitution provides that each "State shall appoint, in such Manner as the Legislature thereof may direct, a Number of Electors, equal to the whole Number of Senators and Representatives to which the State may be entitled in Congress."[75] These electors then vote for the President.

While many states in the 1800's relied on their state legislature to appoint electors, all states now determine their slate of electors through popular elections. The electoral elections in each state use a "short ballot" that merely lists the names of the presidential candidates (rather than the common earlier practice of listing the names of the slate of

---

[74]U.S. CONST. art. I, § 4.

[75]U.S. CONST. art. II, § 2.

electors pledged to support that candidate), with the candidate receiving the most votes statewide obtaining his or her entire slate of pledged electors. But two states, Maine and Nebraska, currently deviate from this "winner takes all" formula, employing the "congressional district method" that awards two electors to the statewide winner and one elector to the winner in each congressional district. This resulted in a split electoral vote in Nebraska in 2008, with Barack Obama obtaining one electoral vote to John McCain's four electoral votes from the Cornhusker State. Some have advocated an alternative methodology that would select the electors for each candidate in proportion to the percentage of the vote the candidate received statewide, but none of the states have currently adopted such a system.

Some states have, however, enacted legislation pledging to select their electors according to the so-called National Popular Vote Plan upon passage of the act by enough states to control the outcome of the presidential election. Under this plan, the state's electors would be pledged to the winner of the *national* popular vote rather than to the winner of the statewide vote. However, by its terms, this plan will not take effect until states with a combined total of 270 electoral votes (the minimum number necessary for a candidate to win) have pledged their support.

Is the National Popular Vote Plan constitutional? Are there legally significant distinctions between it and the legislative appointment of electors existing in the nineteenth century? Would the National Popular Vote Plan violate *Cook*? Could it be a violation of the Guaranty Clause? Is the National Popular Vote Plan a compact between the states that will require congressional approval under the Compact Clause?

State Instructions to its Congressional Delegation: Justice Kennedy provided the crucial fifth vote for Part III of the Court's opinion, so his concurrence qualifies in some respects the Court's discussion regarding the state's power to instruct its representatives. Keeping in mind Kennedy's concurrence, what is the Court's holding regarding the extent to which a state can request specific actions from Congress or express its concerns to Congress? Can a state ever make such requests binding on its own representatives?

C. STATE COURTS IN THE FEDERAL SYSTEM AND THE DOCTRINE OF ADEQUATE AND INDEPENDENT STATE GROUNDS

The United States Constitution only creates the Supreme Court, leaving the establishment of lower federal courts to Congress. Article III, Section 1 provides: "The judicial power of the United States shall be vested in one Supreme Court, and in such inferior courts as the Congress shall from time to time ordain and establish." This provision originated from a compromise at the Constitutional Convention. While the delegates unanimously agreed on the necessity of one final arbiter of federal law, some urged there was no need to create lower federal courts as the state courts could serve as the inferior tribunals, with an appeal available to the Supreme Court. Others contended that lower federal courts were still needed to prevent the Supreme Court from being inundated with appeals and to provide a neutral forum free from bias against state nonresidents. In an attempt to placate both sides, James Wilson and James Madison formulated a proposal that was approved by the Convention granting Congress a discretionary power to establish lower federal courts with such jurisdiction as Congress thought appropriate.[76]

Although lower federal courts have been part of the national landscape since the first Congress enacted the Judiciary Act of 1789, the United States Constitution thus does not expressly require their existence, meaning Congress could arguably abolish all federal courts except the Supreme Court.[77] Even under such circumstances, though, Article III, Section 2 of the Constitution grants the Supreme Court "appellate Jurisdiction" over certain cases and controversies. This constitutional grant of appellate jurisdiction, even in the potential absence of lower federal courts, logically dictates that the Court may review state court decisions that fall within the limits of the federal judicial power as defined in Article III.[78]

The Constitution hence envisions state courts as a part of the federal system. Alexander Hamilton elaborated on this point, writing that "the national and State systems are to be regarded as ONE WHOLE. The courts of the latter will of course be natural auxiliaries to the execution of the laws of the Union, and an appeal from them will as naturally lie to that tribunal [the Supreme Court] which is destined to unite and assimilate the principles of national justice and the rules of national decisions."[79]

Hamilton also opined that, as a result of the "kindred" federal and state judicial systems that were part of "one whole," "the State courts would have a concurrent jurisdiction in all cases arising under the laws of the Union where it was not expressly prohibited."[80] In actuality, though, for almost the first century of the new nation, the state courts were the *only* available tribunal for the original adjudication of many federal claims, as the lower federal courts did not have general original jurisdiction over federal question cases.[81] Once Congress granted the lower federal courts federal question jurisdiction in 1875, the states still possessed concurrent jurisdiction to adjudicate federal claims.[82] State

---

[76] 1 THE RECORDS OF THE FEDERAL CONVENTION OF 1787, at 124-25 (Max Farrand ed., rev. ed. 1937).

[77] *See, e.g.*, Lockerty v. Phillips, 319 U.S. 182, 187 (1943) (Congress could have declined to create inferior federal courts); *but see* Martin v. Hunter's Lessee, 14 U.S. (1 Wheat) 304, 328-30 (1816) (arguing that all aspects of the federal judicial power described in Article III must be vested somewhere in the federal judicial system). Congressional abolition of the lower federal courts would also implicate Article III, Section 1, which provides that the "Judges, both of the supreme and inferior Courts, shall hold their Offices during good Behaviour, and shall, at stated Times, receive for their Services, a Compensation, which shall not be diminished during their Continuance in Office."

[78] *Cf. Martin*, 14 U.S. (1 Wheat.) at 340-42. The first Congress also shared this view, as the Judiciary Act of September 24, 1789, ch. 20, 1 Stat. 73, § 25 conferred appellate jurisdiction on the Supreme Court to review final judgments from the state courts that involved certain types of federal claims.

[79] THE FEDERALIST NO. 82 (Alexander Hamilton) (Clinton Rossiter ed., 1961).

[80] *Id.*

[81] The Judiciary Act of September 24, 1789, ch. 20, 1 Stat. 73, did not vest either the district courts or the circuit courts with jurisdiction of cases or controversies arising under the Constitution, laws, or treaties of the United States. For a short while, the "Midnight Judges" Act of February 13, 1801, 2 Stat. 89, did grant the district and circuit courts such jurisdiction, although this Act was repealed the following year. General federal question jurisdiction was not granted to the lower federal courts until the Act of March 3, 1875, 18 Stat. 470, which today is codified at 28 U.S.C. §1331.

[82] *See* Claflin v. Houseman, 93 U.S. 130, 136 (1876).

courts accordingly have a duty to entertain federal causes of action, absent rare circumstances.[83]

This obligation to adjudicate federal claims has occasionally led state courts to invalidate federal statutes on federal constitutional grounds. For instance, the South Carolina Supreme Court held that 28 U.S.C. § 1367(d), the tolling provision of the federal supplemental jurisdiction statute, was unconstitutional under the Tenth Amendment when applied to toll the statute of limitations against a political subdivision of the state,[84] and the Minnesota Supreme Court held the same provision violated the Eleventh Amendment when applied against an arm of the state.[85] In another example, the Washington Supreme Court concluded that a congressional statute shielding certain highway accident information collected by the states from discovery was unconstitutional as outside Congress's power under the Commerce Clause.[86] These state court determinations on federal issues were then subject to review by the Supreme Court, the final arbiter of the meaning of federal law, and in each of these examples the high Court granted certiorari to resolve the constitutional issues.[87]

Such federal law interpretations by the Supreme Court are, of course, binding on both lower federal courts and the state courts. But do federal circuit court interpretations of federal law similarly bind the state courts within that circuit? The answer, according to most courts, is no,[88] although state courts typically, as a matter of judicial policy, defer to the decisions of the federal circuits (but sometimes the state courts adopt the position of another circuit rather than the circuit that encompasses their state). As Supreme Court Justice Clarence Thomas summarized in a concurring opinion: "An Arkansas trial court is bound by this Court's (and by the Arkansas Supreme Court's and Arkansas Court of Appeals') interpretation of federal law, but if it follows the Eighth Circuit's interpretation of federal law, it does so only because it chooses to and not because it must."[89]

---

[83]*See, e.g.*, Mondou v. N.Y., New Haven & Hartford R.R. Co., 223 U.S. 1, 58 (1912) ("The existence of concurrent jurisdiction implies a duty to exercise it."). A state court can refuse to adjudicate a federal claim that has not been vested exclusively in the federal courts only pursuant to "neutral state rules regarding the administration of the courts," such as forum non conveniens. CHARLES ALAN WRIGHT & MARY KAY KANE, FEDERAL PRACTICE AND PROCEDURE: FEDERAL PRACTICE DESKBOOK § 47, at 391 (2002).

[84]Jinks v. Richland Cnty., 563 S.E.2d 104, 105-06 (S.C. 2002), *rev'd*, 538 U.S. 456 (2003).

[85]Regents of Univ. of Minn. v. Raygor, 620 N.W.2d 680, 681 (Minn. 2001), *aff'd on other grounds*, 534 U.S. 533 (2002).

[86]Guillen v. Pierce Cnty., 31 P.3d 628, 632-33 (Wash. 2001), *rev'd*, 537 U.S. 129 (2003).

[87]The Supreme Court did not agree with the state courts that the statutes at issue were unconstitutional. *See Jinks*, 538 U.S. at 461-65; *Guillen*, 537 U.S. at 147-48; *Raygor*, 534 U.S. at 546-47. Nevertheless, *Raygor* affirmed the state court's judgment as the Court held that section 1367(d) did not demonstrate the clear intent necessary to abrogate the state's sovereign immunity. *Raygor*, 534 U.S. at 546-47.

[88]*See, e.g.*, Freeman v. Lane, 962 F.2d 1252, 1257 (7th Cir. 1992); U.S. *ex rel.* Lawrence v. Woods, 432 F.2d 1072 (7th Cir. 1970); Owssley v. Peyton, 352 F.2d 804, 805 (4th Cir. 1965). *But see* Yniguez v. Arizona, 939 F.2d 727, 736 (9th Cir. 1991) (expressing "serious doubts" about the wisdom of allowing state courts to ignore decisions of the federal circuit courts regarding federal law).

[89]Lockhart v. Fretwell, 506 U.S. 364, 376 (1993) (Thomas, J., concurring).

A more vexing issue is the legal basis for this principle that state courts are not bound by circuit court decisions on federal law. Is this a constitutional structural prohibition, flowing from federalism principles and the separation of powers, or is it merely a default policy formulated in the absence of positive law? The answer is critical to determining whether the principle may be altered by Congress, which the Senate attempted to do in 1995 when it voted in favor of the "Product Liability Fairness Act." This legislative proposal would have mandated that a decision of a federal circuit court of appeals would be "considered a controlling precedent with respect to any subsequent decision made concerning the interpretation of any such provision [of this Act] by any Federal or State court within the geographical boundaries of the area under the jurisdiction of the circuit court of appeals."[90] The Conference of Chief Justices adopted a resolution opposing this provision, urging that the subsection "would, for the first time in our nation's history, make decisions of a United States Court of Appeals, or panels thereof, binding precedent for decision making by State Supreme courts located in that federal circuit."[91] Several potential constitutional infirmities of the Act were identified, including a potential violation of separation of powers principles and the Supremacy Clause. The separation of powers arguments were that, in the absence of direct judicial appellate review by the circuit courts of appeals over state court decisions, vesting the appellate courts with binding precedential powers might constitute a legislative rather than judicial function and that the Act may have intruded on the judiciary's core power to articulate the binding effect of its cases. The other argument was that the intersection of the Supremacy Clause and the provisions of Article III established that only the decisions of the Supreme Court could be binding on the states. Nevertheless, because the Act never became law, these questions were not addressed by the judiciary. The foundation for the principle is thus still uncertain, even though it is commonly accepted that, at least in the absence of contrary legislation within congressional power, states are bound only by the Supreme Court's interpretation of federal law, not the interpretation of any lower federal court.

While state court determinations on federal law issues may be reviewed by the Supreme Court, the state courts are supreme in the interpretation of their own law. *Erie Railroad Co. v. Tompkins* mandates that the federal courts are bound, except when construing federal law, by state substantive law as interpreted by that state's highest court.[92] Indeed, the preeminence of state courts on state constitutional, statutory, and common law matters is aptly illustrated by the fact that the Supreme Court's jurisdiction does not extend to state law issues resolved by state courts.[93]

---

[90]H.R. 956, 104th Cong. § 102(e) (as amended, May 10, 1995).

[91]Conference of Chief Justices, Resolution XVIII, In Opposition to Section 102(e) of H.R. 956, The Product Liability Fairness Act of 1995, as amended and passed by the U.S. Senate on May 10, 1995, adopted August 3, 1995.

[92]304 U.S. 64 (1938).

[93]*See* 28 U.S.C. § 1257(a). The Supreme Court has repeatedly recognized that it is bound by state court interpretations of state law. *See, e.g.*, City of Chicago v. Morales, 527 U.S. 41, 41 (1999) ("This Court has no authority to construe the language of a state statute more narrowly than the State's highest court."); Johnson v. Fankell, 520 U.S. 911, 916 (1997) ("Neither this Court nor any other federal tribunal has any authority to place a construction on a state statute different from the one rendered by the highest court of the State. This proposition, fundamental to our system of federalism, is applicable to procedural as well as substantive rules.") (citations omitted).

Thus, while state courts are a piece of the federal court system when deciding federal issues, being bound by, and their decisions reviewable by, the Supreme Court, their decisions on state law issues are binding on the federal courts and not subject to federal appellate review. Of course, in many cases, the state court resolves *both* federal and state issues. Are such cases involving both federal and state issues subject to review by the Supreme Court? Under what circumstances? The following cases consider these questions.

Eustis v. Bolles, 150 U.S. 361 (1893)

Mr. Justice SHIRAS

On February 14, 1887, Charles H. Bolles and George F. Wilde, as surviving members of the firm of B. Collender & Co., filed a petition in insolvency in the insolvency court within and for the county of Suffolk, state of Massachusetts. On February 16, 1887, they filed in the same insolvency court a written proposal for composition with their copartnership creditors, under the so-called "composition acts" of 1884 and 1885, and they therein proposed to pay 50 cents on the dollar of their debts in money.

In July, 1887, Eustis brought an action in the supreme judicial court against Bolles and Wilde, wherein he sought to recover the balance of his note remaining unpaid after the receipt of the one-half received under the insolvency proceedings. The supreme judicial court was of opinion that Eustis, by accepting the benefit of the composition, had waived any right that he might otherwise have had to object to the validity of the composition statutes as impairing the obligation of contracts.

It is settled law that, to give this court jurisdiction of a writ of error to a state court, it must appear, affirmatively, not only that a federal question was presented for decision by the state court, but that its decision was necessary to the determination of the cause, and that it was actually decided adversely to the party claiming a right under the federal laws or constitution, or that the judgment, as rendered, could not have been given without deciding it. *Murdock v. Memphis*, 20 Wall. 590 [(1874)].

It is likewise settled law that, where the record discloses that if a question has been raised and decided adversely to a party claiming the benefit of a provision of the constitution or laws of the United States, another question, not federal, has been also raised and decided against such party, and the decision of the latter question is sufficient, notwithstanding the federal question, to sustain the judgment, this court will not review the judgment.

In this state of the law, we are met at the threshold, in the present case, with the question whether the record discloses that the supreme judicial court of Massachusetts decided adversely to the plaintiffs in error any claim arising under the constitution or laws of the United States, or whether the judgment of that court was placed on another ground, not involving federal law, and sufficient of itself to sustain the judgment.

The defendants in the trial court depended on a discharge obtained by them under regular proceedings under the insolvency statutes of Massachusetts. This defense the plaintiffs met by alleging that the statutes under which the defendants had procured their discharge had been enacted after the promissory note sued on had been executed and delivered, and that to give effect to a discharge obtained under such subsequent laws would impair the obligation of a contract, within the meaning of the constitution of the United States. Upon such a state of facts, it is plain that a federal question, decisive of the case, was presented, and that if the judgment of the supreme judicial court of Massachusetts adjudged that question adversely to the plaintiffs, it would be the duty of this court to consider the soundness of such a judgment.

The record, however, further discloses that William T. Eustis represented in this court by his executors, had accepted and receipted for the money which had been awarded him as his portion under the insolvency proceedings, and that the court below, conceding that his cause of action could not be taken away from him, without his consent, by proceedings under statutes of insolvency passed subsequently to the vesting of his rights, held that the action of Eustis, in so accepting and receipting for his dividend in the insolvency proceedings, was a waiver of his right to object to the validity of the insolvency statutes, and that, accordingly, the defendants were entitled to the judgment.

The view of the court was that, when the composition was confirmed, Eustis was put to his election whether he would avail himself of the composition offer, or would reject it, and rely upon his right to enforce his debt against his debtors, notwithstanding their discharge.

In its discussion of this question the court below cited, and claimed to follow, the decision of this court in the case of *Clay v. Smith*, 3 Pet. 411 [(1830)], where it was held that the plaintiff, by proving his debt and taking a dividend under the bankrupt laws of Louisiana, waived his right to object that the law did not constitutionally apply to his debt, he being a creditor residing in another state. But in deciding that it was competent for Eustis to waive his legal rights, and that accepting his dividend under the insolvency proceedings was such a waiver, the court below did not decide a federal question. Whether that view of the case sound or not, it is not for us to inquire. It was broad enough, in itself, to support the final judgment, without reference to the federal question.

Having reached the conclusion that we are not called upon to determine any federal question, nor to consider whether the state court was right or wrong in its decision of the other question in the case, it only remains to inquire whether that conclusion requires us to affirm the judgment of the court below, or to dismiss the writ of error. An examination of our records will show that in similar cases this court has sometimes affirmed the judgment of the court below, and sometimes has dismissed the writ or error. This discrepancy may have originated in a difference of views as to the precise scope of the questions presented. However that may be, we think that when we find it unnecessary to decide any federal question, and when the state court had based its decision on a local or state question, our logical course is to dismiss the writ of error.

Notes on the Adequate and Independent State Grounds Doctrine

The Doctrine and its Policies: The rule enunciated in *Eustis* is known as the adequate and independent state grounds doctrine. The basic concept is that, if the state court would come to the same judgment irrespective of the resolution of the federal issues in the case, the Supreme Court will not review the judgment. Thus, while *Eustis* presented a federal constitutional issue as to whether the Massachusetts insolvency statutes violated the Contract Clause, the resolution of that issue was immaterial to the judgment because the defendant was nevertheless entitled to prevail on the state law ground that the plaintiff had waived his right to challenge the statutes by accepting payments made under them.

Justice Jackson, writing for the Court in *Herb v. Pitcairn*, proffered the following supporting rationale for the doctrine:

> This court from the time of its foundation has adhered to the principle that it will not review judgments of state courts that rest on adequate and independent state grounds. The reason is so obvious that it has rarely been thought to warrant statement. It is found in the partitioning of power between the state and federal judicial systems and in the limitations of our own jurisdiction. Our only power over state judgments is to correct them to the extent that they incorrectly adjudge federal rights. And our power is to correct wrong judgments not revise opinions. We are not permitted to render an advisory opinion, and if the same judgment would be rendered by the state court after we corrected its view of federal law, our review could amount to nothing more than an advisory opinion.[94]

Should this doctrine exist for the reasons expressed by Justice Jackson? Are there any disadvantages resulting from the adequate and independent state grounds rule? What impact does it have on the uniformity of federal law?

The Dilemma in Evaluating Adequate and Independent State Grounds: While the adequate and independent state grounds doctrine appears relatively simple at first glance, a "vexing" problem is determining when a state ground is adequate and independent under an ambiguous record. State courts often adjudicate both federal and state claims, "and because it is not necessary to make a sharp separation of the two their discussion is often interlaced."[95] In other words, state courts often do not make explicit whether they would have reached the same result in the absence of the federal issue. As an example, in *Eustis*, the state court had cited at least one United States Supreme Court decision in support of its waiver holding. Was the state court's waiver holding really independent of federal law, then? In such situations, as *Herb v. Pitcairn* noted, the Supreme Court had yet to adopt a consistent approach:

> In many cases the answer has been a strict adherence to the rule that it must affirmatively appear that the federal question was decided and that its decision was essential to disposition of the case; and that where it is not clear whether the judgment rests on a federal ground or an adequate state one, this Court will not review.

[94] 324 U.S. 117, 125-26 (1945).

[95] *Id.* at 127.

> In other cases where justice seemed to require it, for example because of supervening events, the Court has said that to set aside the judgment and remand the case to the state court for further consideration is not to review, in any proper sense of the term, the decision of the state court. And in *State of Minnesota v. National Tea Co.*, 309 U.S. 551, uncertainty as to the grounds of the decision below led the Court to vacate and remand for further consideration.
>
> It is no criticism of a state court that we are unable to say in a case where both state and federal questions are presented, discussed, and perhaps decided, that the judgment would have been the same had only one of the grounds been present. But we cannot perform our duty to refrain from interfering in state law questions and also to review federal ones without making a determination whether the one or the other controls the judgment. And in cases where the answer is not clear to us, it seems consistent with the respect due the highest courts of states of the Union that they be asked rather than told what they have intended. If this imposes an unwelcome burden it should be mitigated by the knowledge that it is to protect their jurisdiction from unwitting interference as well as to protect our own from unwitting renunciation.[96]

But despite the apparent finality in the preceding passage, *Herb* was not the final word on this problem. After continuing to struggle to find the appropriate approach for several decades, the Supreme Court adopted its current approach in *Michigan v. Long.*

Michigan v. Long, 463 U.S. 1032 (1983)

Justice O'CONNOR delivered the opinion of the Court.

In *Terry v. Ohio,* we upheld the validity of a protective search for weapons in the absence of probable cause to arrest because it is unreasonable to deny a police officer the right "to neutralize the threat of physical harm," when he possesses an articulable suspicion that an individual is armed and dangerous. We did not, however, expressly address whether such a protective search for weapons could extend to an area beyond the person in the absence of probable cause to arrest. In the present case, respondent David Long was convicted for possession of marijuana found by police in the passenger compartment and trunk of the automobile that he was driving. The police searched the passenger compartment because they had reason to believe that the vehicle contained weapons potentially dangerous to the officers. We hold that the protective search of the passenger compartment was reasonable under the principles articulated in *Terry* and other decisions of this Court. We also examine Long's argument that the decision below rests upon an adequate and independent state ground, and we decide in favor of our jurisdiction.

[Two Michigan police officers observed a car traveling erratically and at excessive speed before swerving into a ditch. When they went to investigate, they were met by Long, the only occupant of the vehicle, standing at the rear of his vehicle, with the driver's door

---

[96] *Id.* at 126-28.

still ajar. After the officers asked him a couple of questions, he started walking back toward his open car door and the officers both then observed a large hunting knife on the floorboard of his car. After stopping him, they conducted a pat-down frisk and shined their flashlights into the interior of his vehicle to search for other weapons. While no other weapons were found, they discovered a pouch with marijuana in the interior of the vehicle. After deciding to impound Long's car, the officers discovered another 75 pounds of marijuana in the trunk.]

The Barry County Circuit Court denied Long's motion to suppress the marijuana taken from both the interior of the car and its trunk. He was subsequently convicted of possession of marijuana. The Michigan Court of Appeals affirmed Long's conviction, holding that the search of the passenger compartment was valid as a protective search under *Terry*, and that the search of the trunk was valid as an inventory search. The Michigan Supreme Court reversed. The court held that "the sole justification of the *Terry* search, protection of the police officers and others nearby, cannot justify the search in this case."

Before reaching the merits, we must consider Long's argument that we are without jurisdiction to decide this case because the decision below rests on an adequate and independent state ground. The court below referred twice to the state constitution in its opinion, but otherwise relied exclusively on federal law.[97] Long argues that the Michigan courts have provided greater protection from searches and seizures under the state constitution than is afforded under the Fourth Amendment, and the references to the state constitution therefore establish an adequate and independent ground for the decision below.

Although we have announced a number of principles in order to help us determine whether various forms of references to state law constitute adequate and independent state grounds, we openly admit that we have thus far not developed a satisfying and consistent approach for resolving this vexing issue. In some instances, we have taken the strict view that if the ground of decision was at all unclear, we would dismiss the case. See, *e.g., Lynch v. New York,* 293 U.S. 52 (1934). In other instances, we have vacated, see, *e.g., Minnesota v. National Tea Co.,* 309 U.S. 551 (1940), or continued a case, see *e.g., Herb v. Pitcairn,* 324 U.S. 117 (1945), in order to obtain clarification about the nature of a state court decision. In more recent cases, we have ourselves examined state law to determine whether state courts have used federal law to guide their application of state law or to provide the actual basis for the decision that was reached. In *Oregon v. Kennedy,* 456 U.S. 667, 670-671 (1982), we rejected an invitation to remand to the state court for clarification even when the decision rested in part on a case from the state court, because we determined that the state case itself rested upon federal grounds. We added that "[e]ven if the case admitted of more doubt as to whether federal and state grounds for decision were intermixed, the fact that the state court relied to the extent it did on federal grounds requires us to reach the merits."

This *ad hoc* method of dealing with cases that involve possible adequate and independent state grounds is antithetical to the doctrinal consistency that is required when

---

[97]On the first occasion, the court merely cited in a footnote both the state and federal constitutions. See 320 N.W.2d, at 869, n. 4. On the second occasion, at the conclusion of the opinion, the court stated: "We hold, therefore, that the deputies' search of the vehicle was proscribed by the Fourth Amendment to the United States Constitution and art. 1, § 11 of the Michigan Constitution."

sensitive issues of federal-state relations are involved. Moreover, none of the various methods of disposition that we have employed thus far recommends itself as the preferred method that we should apply to the exclusion of others, and we therefore determine that it is appropriate to reexamine our treatment of this jurisdictional issue in order to achieve the consistency that is necessary.

The process of examining state law is unsatisfactory because it requires us to interpret state laws with which we are generally unfamiliar, and which often, as in this case, have not been discussed at length by the parties. Vacation and continuance for clarification have also been unsatisfactory both because of the delay and decrease in efficiency of judicial administration, see *Dixon v. Duffy,* 344 U.S. 143 (1952),[98] and, more important, because these methods of disposition place significant burdens on state courts to demonstrate the presence or absence of our jurisdiction. Finally, outright dismissal of cases is clearly not a panacea because it cannot be doubted that there is an important need for uniformity in federal law, and that this need goes unsatisfied when we fail to review an opinion that rests primarily upon federal grounds and where the *independence* of an alleged state ground is not apparent from the four corners of the opinion. We have long recognized that dismissal is inappropriate "where there is strong indication . . . that the federal constitution as judicially construed controlled the decision below." *National Tea Co., supra,* 309 U.S., at 556.

Respect for the independence of state courts, as well as avoidance of rendering advisory opinions, have been the cornerstones of this Court's refusal to decide cases where there is an adequate and independent state ground. It is precisely because of this respect for state courts, and this desire to avoid advisory opinions, that we do not wish to continue to decide issues of state law that go beyond the opinion that we review, or to require state courts to reconsider cases to clarify the grounds of their decisions. Accordingly, when, as in this case, a state court decision fairly appears to rest primarily on federal law, or to be interwoven with the federal law, and when the adequacy and independence of any possible state law ground is not clear from the face of the opinion, we will accept as the most reasonable explanation that the state court decided the case the way it did because it believed that federal law required it to do so. If a state court chooses merely to rely on federal precedents as it would on the precedents of all other jurisdictions, then it need only make clear by a plain statement in its judgment or opinion that the federal cases are being used only for the purpose of guidance, and do not themselves compel the result that the court has reached. In this way, both justice and judicial administration will be greatly improved. If the state court decision indicates clearly and expressly that it is alternatively based on bona fide separate, adequate, and independent grounds, we, of course, will not undertake to review the decision.

This approach obviates in most instances the need to examine state law in order to decide the nature of the state court decision, and will at the same time avoid the danger of

---

[98]Indeed, *Dixon v. Duffy* is also illustrative of another difficulty involved in our requiring state courts to reconsider their decisions for purposes of clarification. In *Dixon,* we continued the case on two occasions in order to obtain clarification, but none was forthcoming: "[T]he California court advised petitioner's counsel informally that it doubted its jurisdiction to render such a determination." 344 U.S., at 145. We then vacated the judgment of the state court, and remanded.

our rendering advisory opinions. It also avoids the unsatisfactory and intrusive practice of requiring state courts to clarify their decisions to the satisfaction of this Court. We believe that such an approach will provide state judges with a clearer opportunity to develop state jurisprudence unimpeded by federal interference, and yet will preserve the integrity of federal law. "It is fundamental that state courts be left free and unfettered by us in interpreting their state constitutions. But it is equally important that ambiguous or obscure adjudications by state courts do not stand as barriers to a determination by this Court of the validity under the federal constitution of state action." *National Tea Co., supra,* 309 U.S., at 557.

The principle that we will not review judgments of state courts that rest on adequate and independent state grounds is based, in part, on "the limitations of our own jurisdiction." *Herb v. Pitcairn,* 324 U.S. 117, 125 (1945). The jurisdictional concern is that we not "render an advisory opinion, and if the same judgment would be rendered by the state court after we corrected its views of federal laws, our review could amount to nothing more than an advisory opinion." *Id.,* at 126. Our requirement of a "plain statement" that a decision rests upon adequate and independent state grounds does not in any way authorize the rendering of advisory opinions. Rather, in determining, as we must, whether we have jurisdiction to review a case that is alleged to rest on adequate and independent state grounds, we merely assume that there are no such grounds when it is not clear from the opinion itself that the state court relied upon an adequate and independent state ground and when it fairly appears that the state court rested its decision primarily on federal law.[99]

Our review of the decision below under this framework leaves us unconvinced that it rests upon an independent state ground. Apart from its two citations to the state constitution, the court below relied *exclusively* on its understanding of *Terry* and other federal cases. Not a single state case was cited to support the state court's holding that the search of the passenger compartment was unconstitutional. Indeed, the court declared that the search in this case was unconstitutional because "[t]he Court of Appeals erroneously applied the principles of *Terry v. Ohio* . . . to the search of the interior of the vehicle in this case." 320 N.W.2d, at 869. The references to the state constitution in no way indicate that the decision below rested on grounds in any way *independent* from the state court's interpretation of federal law. Even if we accept that the Michigan constitution has been

[99]In dissent, Justice STEVENS proposes the novel view that this Court should never review a state court decision unless the Court wishes to vindicate a federal right that has been endangered. The rationale of the dissent is not restricted to cases where the decision is arguably supported by adequate and independent state grounds. Rather, Justice STEVENS appears to believe that even if the decision below rests exclusively on federal grounds, this Court should not review the decision as long as there is no federal right that is endangered.

The state courts handle the vast bulk of all criminal litigation in this country. In 1982, more than twelve million criminal actions (excluding juvenile and traffic charges) were filed in the 50 state court systems and the District of Columbia. See 7 State Court Journal 18 (1983). By comparison, approximately 32,700 criminal suits were filed in federal courts during that same year. See Annual Report of the Director of the Administrative Office of the United States Courts 6 (1982). The state courts are required to apply federal constitutional standards, and they necessarily create a considerable body of "federal law" in the process. It is not surprising that this Court has become more interested in the application and development of federal law by state courts in the light of the recent significant expansion of federally created standards that we have imposed on the States.

interpreted to provide independent protection for certain rights also secured under the Fourth Amendment, it fairly appears in this case that the Michigan Supreme Court rested its decision primarily on federal law.

[The Court then held that the search did not violate the Fourth Amendment.]

Justice STEVENS, dissenting.

The jurisprudential questions presented in this case are far more important than the question whether the Michigan police officer's search of respondent's car violated the Fourth Amendment. The case raises profoundly significant questions concerning the relationship between two sovereigns–the State of Michigan and the United States of America.

The Supreme Court of the State of Michigan expressly held "that the deputies' search of the vehicle was proscribed by the Fourth Amendment of the United States Constitution and art. 1, § 11 of the Michigan Constitution." The state law ground is clearly adequate to support the judgment, but the question whether it is independent of the Michigan Supreme Court's understanding of federal law is more difficult. Four possible ways of resolving that question present themselves: (1) asking the Michigan Supreme Court directly, (2) attempting to infer from all possible sources of state law what the Michigan Supreme Court meant, (3) presuming that adequate state grounds are independent unless it clearly appears otherwise, or (4) presuming that adequate state grounds are *not* independent unless it clearly appears otherwise. This Court has, on different occasions, employed each of the first three approaches; never until today has it even hinted at the fourth. In order to "achieve the consistency that is necessary," the Court today undertakes a reexamination of all the possibilities. It rejects the first approach as inefficient and unduly burdensome for state courts, and rejects the second approach as an inappropriate expenditure of our resources. Although I find both of those decisions defensible in themselves, I cannot accept the Court's decision to choose the fourth approach over the third–to presume that adequate state grounds are intended to be dependent on federal law unless the record plainly shows otherwise. I must therefore dissent.

If we reject the intermediate approaches, we are left with a choice between two presumptions: one in favor of our taking jurisdiction, and one against it. Historically, the latter presumption has always prevailed. The Court today points out that in several cases we have weakened the traditional presumption by using the other two intermediate approaches identified above. Since those two approaches are now to be rejected, however, I would think that *stare decisis* would call for a return to historical principle.

Even if I agreed with the Court that we are free to consider as a fresh proposition whether we may take presumptive jurisdiction over the decisions of sovereign states, I could not agree that an expansive attitude makes good sense. It appears to be common ground that any rule we adopt should show "respect for state courts, and [a] desire to avoid advisory opinions." And I am confident that all members of this Court agree that there is a vital interest in the sound management of scarce federal judicial resources. All of those policies counsel against the exercise of federal jurisdiction. They are fortified by my belief that a policy of judicial restraint–one that allows other decisional bodies to have the last word in legal interpretation until it is truly necessary for this Court to intervene–enables this Court to make its most effective contribution to our federal system of government.

The nature of the case before us hardly compels a departure from tradition. These are not cases in which an American citizen has been deprived of a right secured by the United States Constitution or a federal statute. Rather, they are cases in which a state court has upheld a citizen's assertion of a right, finding the citizen to be protected under both federal and state law. The complaining party is an officer of the state itself, who asks us to rule that the state court interpreted federal rights too broadly and "overprotected" the citizen.

Such cases should not be of inherent concern to this Court. The reason may be illuminated by assuming that the events underlying this case had arisen in another country, perhaps the Republic of Finland. If the Finnish police had arrested a Finnish citizen for possession of marijuana, and the Finnish courts had turned him loose, no American would have standing to object. If instead they had arrested an American citizen and acquitted him, we might have been concerned about the arrest but we surely could not have complained about the acquittal, even if the Finnish Court had based its decision on its understanding of the United States Constitution. That would be true even if we had a treaty with Finland requiring it to respect the rights of American citizens under the United States Constitution. We would only be motivated to intervene if an American citizen were unfairly arrested, tried, and convicted by the foreign tribunal.

In this case the State of Michigan has arrested one of its citizens and the Michigan Supreme Court has decided to turn him loose. The respondent is a United States citizen as well as a Michigan citizen, but since there is no claim that he has been mistreated by the State of Michigan, the final outcome of the state processes offended no federal interest whatever. Michigan simply provided greater protection to one of its citizens than some other State might provide or, indeed, than this Court might require throughout the country.

I believe that in reviewing the decisions of state courts, the primary role of this Court is to make sure that persons who seek to *vindicate* federal rights have been fairly heard. That belief resonates with statements in many of our prior cases.

Until recently we had virtually no interest in cases of this type. Thirty years ago, this Court reviewed only one. Indeed, that appears to have been the only case during the entire 1952 Term in which a state even sought review of a decision by its own judiciary. Fifteen years ago, we did not review any such cases, although the total number of requests had mounted to three. Some time during the past decade, our priorities shifted. The result is a docket swollen with requests by states to reverse judgments that their courts have rendered in favor of their citizens. I am confident that a future Court will recognize the error of this allocation of resources. When that day comes, I think it likely that the Court will also reconsider the propriety of today's expansion of our jurisdiction.

The Court offers only one reason for asserting authority over cases such as the one presented today: "an important need for uniformity in federal law [that] goes unsatisfied when we fail to review an opinion that rests primarily upon federal grounds and where the independence of an alleged state ground is not apparent from the four corners of the opinion." Of course, the supposed need to "review an opinion" clashes directly with our oft-repeated reminder that "our power is to correct wrong judgments, not to revise opinions." *Herb v. Pitcairn,* 324 U.S. 117, 126 (1945). The clash is not merely one of form: the "need for uniformity in federal law" is truly an ungovernable engine. That same need is no less present when it is perfectly clear that a state ground is both independent and adequate. In fact, it is equally present if a state prosecutor announces that he believes a certain policy of nonenforcement is commanded by federal law. Yet we have never claimed jurisdiction to correct such errors, no matter how egregious they may be, and no matter how much they may thwart the desires of the state electorate. We do not sit to expound our understanding of the Constitution to interested listeners in the legal community; we sit to resolve disputes. If it is not apparent that our views would affect the outcome of a particular case, we cannot presume to interfere.

Notes on the Plain Statement Rule

Applying the Plain Statement Rule: Does the plain statement rule apply in all cases in state court? *Long* noted that its presumption applies when the state court's decision "fairly appears to rest primarily on federal law, or to be interwoven with the federal law."[100] In the absence of these conditions, the presumption is not triggered. As a result, in cases in which the decision "fairly appears" to rest primarily on state rather than federal law, the Court will not review the case, despite the state court's failure to include a recitation that adequate and independent state law grounds supported the holding.[101]

In cases in which the presumption does apply, how can the state court rebut it? *Long* explained that the state court could rebut the presumption through "a plain statement in its judgment or opinion that the federal cases are being used only for the purpose of guidance, and do not themselves compel the result that the court has reached," such that the decision "clearly and expressly" indicates that it is "based on bona fide separate, adequate, and independent grounds."[102] Most state courts concerned about the presumption have employed language closely tracking this articulation from *Long*.[103]

Could a state supreme court make this necessary plain statement in advance, by indicating that "in all future situations in which this court cites federal opinions in interpreting our state constitution, we rely on those precedents merely for guidance and do

---

[100]Michigan v. Long, 463 U.S. 1032, 1040-41 (1983).

[101]*See, e.g.*, Coleman v. Thompson, 501 U.S. 722, 740 (1991) (holding that state court dismissal fairly appeared to rest on state law and was thus not subject to the *Long* presumption).

[102]*Long*, 463 U.S. at 1041.

[103]*See, e.g.*, Perry v. State, 741 A.2d 1162, 1188 n.11 (Md. 1999) (articulating "the 'plain statement' that, for purposes of interpreting Article 21 [of the Maryland Constitution], the holdings of the [federal courts] are being used for guidance only and do not themselves compel the result we reach here. The conclusions announced in this Opinion on this issue constitute our construction of the independent Maryland Constitutional provision."); Davenport v. Garcia, 834 S.W.2d 4, 10 n.17 (Tex. 1992) (addressing only state constitutional claims and noting that "to the extent this opinion cites any federal law, such precedent is used only for guidance, and in no way necessitates the result reached by this court today"); Am. Nat'l Can Corp. v. State Dep't of Rev., 787 P.2d 545, 552-53 (Wash. 1990) ("[O]ur discussion rests entirely upon our independent opinion of the requirements of the Washington State Constitution .... We have cited federal law in other separation of powers cases, but only for purposes of guidance. Federal law does not compel the results reached in this case.").

not consider ourselves bound by those decisions"?[104] Would such a generic statement satisfy the concerns the Supreme Court articulated in *Long*, especially regarding the interpretation and investigation of unfamiliar state laws?

The Competing Policies at Stake: What rationales support the *Long* presumption? Does it embody respect for the states? Does it encourage the states to develop their own independent state constitutional law doctrine? Is it efficient? Does it ensure uniformity in federal law interpretation?

In subsequent decisions, the Court has expanded on the policies underlying *Long*. The presumption works, according to the Court, "because in the majority of cases in which a state court decision fairly appears to rest primarily on federal law or to be interwoven with such law, and the state court does not plainly state that it is relying on an independent and adequate state ground, the state court decision did not in fact rest on an independent and adequate state ground."[105] The Court has also maintained that the presumption provides the states additional room for state constitutional experimentation by freeing them from misguided interpretations of supreme federal law.[106]

Justice Ginsburg, in a dissent joined by Justice Stevens, disagreed with these contentions, maintaining that *Long* "impedes the States' ability to serve as laboratories for testing solutions to novel legal problems" by improperly presuming that the state court intended to rely on federal law.[107] She also offered the following argument as to the presumption's practical defects:

> Application of the *Long* presumption has increased the incidence of non-dispositive U.S. Supreme Court determinations – instances in which state courts, on remand, have reinstated their prior judgment after clarifying their reliance on state grounds. Westling, *Advisory Opinions and the "Constitutionally Required" Adequate and Independent State Grounds Doctrine*, 63 TUL. L. REV. 379, 389 & n.47 (1988) (pre-*Long*, i.e., between January 1, 1978, and June 30, 1983, 14.3% of decisions (2 of 14) involving potentially adequate and independent state grounds were reinstated on state grounds upon remand; post-*Long*, i.e., between July 1, 1983 and January 1, 1988, 26.7% of such decisions (4 of 15) were reinstated on remand). Even if these reinstatements do not render the Supreme Court's opinion technically "advisory," they do suggest that the Court unnecessarily spent

[104]*Cf.* State v. Ball, 471 A.2d 347, 352 (N.H. 1983) ("We hereby make clear that when this court cites federal or other State court opinions in construing provisions of the New Hampshire Constitution or statutes, we rely on those precedents merely for guidance and do not consider our results bound by those decisions"); State v. Kennedy, 666 P.2d 1316, 1321 (Or. 1983) ("[W]hen this court cites federal opinions in interpreting a provision of Oregon law, it does so because it finds the views there expressed persuasive, not because it considers itself bound to do so by its understanding of federal doctrines"). Both the New Hampshire and Oregon Supreme Courts, though, have continued to reiterate versions of this plain statement in subsequent cases relying on their state constitutions.

[105]Coleman v. Thompson, 501 U.S. 722, 737 (1991).

[106]Arizona v. Evans, 514 U.S. 1, 8 (1995).

[107]*Id.* at 25 (Ginsburg, J., dissenting).

> its resources on cases better left, at the time in question, to state-court solution.[108]

Are Justice Ginsburg's two criticisms of *Long* contradictory? Does the *Long* presumption impede the states' ability to experiment if a state court on remand can clarify its reliance on state grounds and reinstate its prior judgment? On the other hand, does the fact that so few decisions actually do so indicate that the presumption generally works?

Another potential criticism of *Long* might have been its application to the case in which it was announced. While announcing such a rule prospectively would allow the states an opportunity to comply in future cases, applying the standard to a pending case when the state court had no notice of the necessity of such a plain statement has an element of unfairness. The Supreme Court did explain, however, in a footnote in *Long* that, even under pre-*Long* standards, it would have reached the same result:

> Even if we were to rest our decision on an evaluation of the state law relevant to Long's claim, as we have sometimes done in the past, our understanding of Michigan law would also result in our finding that we have jurisdiction to decide this case. Under state search and seizure law, a "higher standard" is imposed under art. 1, § 11 of the 1963 Michigan Constitution. If, however, the item seized is, *inter alia,* a "narcotic drug . . . seized by a peace officer outside the curtilage of any dwelling house in this state," art. 1, § 11 of the 1963 Michigan Constitution, then the seizure is governed by a standard identical to that imposed by the Fourth Amendment. In the light of our holding . . . that an interpretation of state law in our view compelled by federal constitutional considerations is not an independent state ground, we would have jurisdiction to decide the case.[109]

Justice Powell concurred, agreeing that jurisdiction existed, although he disagreed with both the efficiency and wisdom of the plain statement rule.[110] Justices Brennan and Marshall, while dissenting on the issue of the reasonableness of the search, agreed that jurisdiction was appropriate for the reasons expressed by the majority in the above quote.[111]

The Continued Need for Clarification: Is the plain statement presumption always dispositive? In another footnote, the Court in *Long* recognized that there "may be certain circumstances in which clarification is necessary or desirable, and we will not be foreclosed from taking the appropriate action."[112] For a high profile example of when such clarification was deemed to be necessary, *see Bush v. Palm Beach County Canvassing Board*, where the Supreme Court vacated and remanded the Florida Supreme Court's holding ordering manual

---

[108] *Id.* at 32.

[109] 463 U.S. 1032, 1044 n.10 (1983).

[110] *Id.* at 1054 (Powell, J., concurring).

[111] *Id.* at 1054 n.1 (Brennan, J., dissenting).

[112] *Id.* at 1041 n.6.

ballot recounts in the 2000 presidential election because of "'considerable uncertainty as to the precise grounds for the decision.'"[113] Further proceedings in the Florida courts eventually culminated with the Supreme Court's decision in *Bush v. Gore* stopping all recounts, thereby ensuring that Florida's electoral votes would be cast for George Bush.[114]

The Supreme Court and Expansive State Interpretations of Federal Rights: Is Justice Stevens' *Long* dissent more concerned with protecting state courts or with the appropriate role of the Court in vindicating individual rights? As a normative matter, should the Supreme Court review cases in which the state courts were more protective of the individual rights of their citizens? Before 1914, the Supreme Court did not even have appellate jurisdiction over a case from a state court in which the state sustained the federal claim (as in *Michigan v. Long*).[115] Is it a matter of federal concern if the states provide more rights to their citizens? Or is the problem that the fundamental rights protected by the Constitution should not vary from state to state?

Justice Stevens continued to urge during his tenure that an appropriate policy of judicial restraint would allow the state's highest court to be the final arbiter in cases in which the state court provided a litigant more protection from government action than required under the Federal Constitution.[116] Justice Scalia responded to Justice Stevens in *Kansas v. Marsh*, arguing that there were several reasons such cases merited the Court's attention, including ensuring the integrity and uniformity of federal law and correcting a state court's federal law errors, thereby allowing power to be returned to the states for decision making in accordance with their own principles of state governance.[117] Such state governance principles regarding the judicial power will be addressed in the next chapter.

CHAPTER 2 EXERCISES AND PROBLEMS

1. Bart is convicted in Texas state court of possession of marijuana. His appeal of his conviction is being heard by the Texas Court of Criminal Appeals. Bart asserts that his conviction was invalid because the marijuana was discovered during a search that violated (1) the Texas Code of Criminal Procedure, (2) article I, section 9 of the Texas Constitution, and (3) the Fourth Amendment of the United States Constitution. Evaluate each of the following circumstances to determine whether the United States Supreme Court could review the judgment of the Texas Court of Criminal Appeals:

(a) The court of criminal appeals upholds his conviction.

(b) The court of criminal appeals reverses his conviction solely on the basis that the search violated the statutory provision in the Texas Code of Criminal Procedure.

---

[113] 531 U.S. 70, 78 (2000) (quoting Minnesota v. Nat'l Tea Co, 309 U.S. 551, 555 (1940)).

[114] 531 U.S. 98, 110-11 (2000).

[115] *See* 20 CHARLES ALAN WRIGHT & MARY KAY KANE, FEDERAL PRACTICE & PROCEDURE § 114 (2000).

[116] *See, e.g.*, Kansas v. Marsh, 548 U.S. 163, 200-03 (2006) (Stevens, J., dissenting); Brigham City v. Stuart, 547 U.S. 398, 407-09 (2006) (Stevens, J., concurring).

[117] *Marsh*, 548 U.S. at 182-85 (Scalia, J., concurring).

(c) The court of criminal appeals reverses his conviction solely on the basis that the search violated article I, section 9 of the Texas Constitution.

(d) The court of criminal appeals reverses his conviction solely on the basis that the search violated the Fourth Amendment of the United States Constitution.

(e) The court of criminal appeals reverses his conviction, concluding that each of Bart's arguments are adequate and independent reasons for reversal.

2. The Texas Supreme Court holds that reporter Scoop Jones is protected in a civil lawsuit by both the First Amendment and article I, section 8 of the Texas Constitution from having to reveal his sources for an article he wrote. Evaluate each of the following circumstances to determine whether the United States Supreme Court could review the state court's First Amendment holding:

(a) The state court opinion has a unitary discussion of the state and federal arguments.

(b) The state court opinion makes a plain statement that article I, section 8 is an adequate and independent ground for its holding.

(c) The state court opinion clearly separates its discussion of article I, section 8 from its discussion of the First Amendment.

3. The New York Court of Appeals held that a police officer's entry into an automobile to determine its vehicle identification number violated the New York state constitution and the Fourth Amendment to the United States Constitution. The U.S. Supreme Court reversed, holding that the Fourth Amendment was not violated, and that the state constitutional holding was not supported by the requisite plain statement to constitute adequate and independent state grounds. On remand back to the New York Court of Appeals to reconsider the state constitutional holding, should the court's earlier holding impact its analysis? Since it already held that the state constitution had been violated, should the state court adhere to its earlier holding in the absence of some extraordinary or exceptional circumstances? Or should the state court instead reconsider the issue anew without being influenced by either its prior decision or the U.S. Supreme Court's holding? Or should the state court presume that its state constitutional holding, being informed by its erroneous view of the Fourth Amendment, is likewise suspect? When confronted with this situation, the New York Court of Appeals held that it would follow its earlier holding in the absence of extraordinary or compelling circumstances, *see People v. Class*, 494 N.E.2d 444, 445 (N.Y. 1986), but is this the best approach?

Chapter 3

STATE JUDICIAL POWER

The state judicial power is different in many respects from the "judicial power" vested by Article III of the Constitution in the federal courts. Article III, section 2 limits the subject matter jurisdiction of the federal judiciary to resolving certain categories of cases or controversies, such as admiralty cases, cases arising under federal law, controversies in which the United States is a party, or suits between citizens of different states. In contrast, state courts typically have general subject matter jurisdiction, authorizing some court in that state to adjudicate any type of controversy, except for those rare cases in which exclusive jurisdiction has been vested in the federal courts by Congress.

The Texas Constitution, for instance, vests the judicial power of the state in a system of trial and appellate courts without limiting the types of cases the system as a whole may adjudicate.[1] Texas district courts exercise "exclusive, appellate, and original jurisdiction of *all actions, proceedings, and remedies*, except in cases where exclusive, appellate, or original jurisdiction may be conferred by this Constitution or other law on some other court, tribunal, or administrative body."[2] Thus, the Texas Constitution explicitly grants the district courts a comprehensive default subject matter jurisdiction, authorizing these courts to adjudicate all actions that are not covered by another constitutional provision or state law. Other states, while employing a different allocation of judicial power within their state court system,[3] nevertheless likewise vest some trial court with general subject

---

[1]TEX. CONST. art. V, § 1.

[2]TEX. CONST. art. V, § 8 (emphasis added).

[3]A typical state judicial system has some type of trial court with general original jurisdiction and courts of appellate review, often divided into an intermediate appellate court and a state high court. *See* THE COUNCIL OF STATE GOVERNMENTS, THE BOOK OF THE STATES 304-07 (2012). In addition to the general jurisdiction trial courts, state court systems frequently have trial courts of limited original jurisdiction and specialized courts, like municipal courts, juvenile courts, and probate courts. The types and jurisdictional grants of these specialized courts vary from state to state. And not all the states even have a three-tier judicial system. Approximately ten states only have one appellate court, including Delaware, New Hampshire, and Nevada. *Id.* at 306-07. New Jersey has "superior courts" that are courts of general jurisdiction, but the superior courts are divided into an appellate division, a law division, and a chancery division, with a further appeal then possible to the New Jersey Supreme Court. N.J. CONST. art. VI, §§ 3-5. And there are remarkable variations even among the three-tiered systems. While Texas has a three-tier system, the state "high court" is actually two courts, a Court of Criminal Appeals for criminal matters and a Supreme Court of Texas for civil matters. *See* TEX. CONST. art. V, §§ 3, 5. Oklahoma also has divided its court structure to include both a Supreme Court and a Court of Criminal Appeals. OKLA. CONST. art. VII. All the other states have only one high court.

In addition to creating the Supreme Court of Texas and the Court of Criminal Appeals, the Texas Constitution establishes the courts of appeals, district courts , county courts, and justices of the peace courts. TEX. CONST. art. V, § 1. The constitution then grants the legislature the power to "establish such other courts as it may deem necessary and prescribe the jurisdiction and organization thereof, and may conform the jurisdiction of the district and other inferior courts thereto." *Id.* This grant of legislative authority has led to the current Byzantine nature of the Texas state judicial system–with at least nine different types of trial courts with varying jurisdictional limitations–as the legislature has created additional trial courts on an ad hoc basis. *See In re* United Servs. Auto Ass'n, 307 S.W.3d 299, 302-04 (Tex. 2010). The Texas Legislature attempted a partial

matter jurisdiction, establishing a presumption that the court has jurisdiction over a particular case unless a showing is made to the contrary. This general subject matter jurisdiction includes interpreting the state's constitution and laws, developing the common law of contracts, torts, property, and family relationships, and exercising concurrent power with the federal courts on most federal statutory and constitutional matters.

A state court's concurrent power on constitutional matters includes the power of judicial review, which was first exercised by the United States Supreme Court to invalidate federal legislation in the landmark case of *Marbury v. Madison*.[4] In that case, the Court, in an opinion by Chief Justice Marshall, held that Congress could not extend the original jurisdiction of the Supreme Court outside the bounds of Article III of the Constitution. Chief Justice Marshall reasoned that a legislative act repugnant to the Constitution is void, and, as it was "emphatically the province and the duty of the judicial department to say what the law is," the judiciary could make the determination.[5]

A long-standing criticism of *Marbury*, however, is that it arguably never adequately articulated *why* the Supreme Court, rather than the Congress, the President, or perhaps "the People" themselves, should be given the final word as to the constitutionality of a legislative or an executive act. The text of the Constitution does not explicitly grant the federal judiciary such a power. And the grant of such power has been frequently argued to be "a counter-majoritarian force in our system" and "a deviant institution in the American democracy."[6] Five (of nine) unelected Justices appointed for life by the President, with the Advice and Consent of the Senate, may negate the determination of the politically accountable branches regarding the constitutionality of either a legislative or executive act. This countermajoritarian difficulty has generated much debate regarding the legitimacy of judicial review under the Federal Constitution.[7]

But judicial review in the state courts, at least with respect to the coordinate branches of state government, is typically far less controversial. First, it has a longer pedigree, as scholars have traced the first appearance of judicial review in America to 1780, in the New Jersey case of *Holmes v. Walton*.[8] During the next few years before the Constitutional Convention, additional decisions recognized the state judiciary's power to

---

restructuring of the Texas judicial system in House Bill 79 enacted in 2011, *see* Act of June 29, 2011, 82d Leg., 1st. C.S., ch. 3, but a complete overhaul may be needed. *See In re* Reece, 341 S.W.3d 360, 378-85 (Tex. 2011) (Willet, J., dissenting) (highlighting the need for legislative structural reform of the Texas judiciary due to its complexities).

[4] 5 U.S. (1 Cranch) 137 (1803).

[5] *Id.* at 176-77.

[6] *See, e.g.*, ALEXANDER M. BICKEL, THE LEAST DANGEROUS BRANCH 16, 18 (2d ed. 1986).

[7] *See, e.g.*, Barry Friedman, *The Birth of an Academic Obsession: The History of the Countermajoritarian Difficulty Part V*, 112 YALE L.J. 153 (2002).

[8] Edward S. Corwin, *The Progress of Constitutional Theory Between the Declaration of Independence and the Meeting of the Philadelphia Convention*, 30 AM. HIST. REV. 511, 521-23 (1925); Albert L. Sturm, *The Development of American State Constitutions*, 12 PUBLIUS: THE JOURNAL OF FEDERALISM 57, 62 (1982).

void legislative acts contravening the state constitution.[9] Thus, the state courts experimented with the principle of judicial review well before *Marbury*.

In addition to its longer history, state court judicial review also has a stronger claim to legitimacy in many states. Since the majority of states have adopted more than one state constitution, the fact that judicial review has not been precluded in subsequent state constitutions arguably indicates a constitutional acquiescence to the practice. For instance, under the 1836 Republic of Texas Constitution, the Supreme Court of the Republic of Texas struck down several legislative acts as unconstitutional,[10] and in one of these cases, *Stockton v. Montgomery*, the court proffered the following ringing endorsement of judicial review in a system of separation of powers:

> the judiciary is not only a co-ordinate branch of the government, but a check interposed to keep the other branches . . . within the letter and spirit, the requisitions, the limitations and landmarks of the immutable constitutive law; that the exertion of this great and paramount duty is essential to the existence and transmission of freedom; and that this court is the last resort in which the people are protected, the constitution vindicated and the government preserved.[11]

If the citizens of Texas disagreed with this assessment, they would presumably have prohibited or limited the power of judicial review in one of the five statehood constitutions ratified after this decision.

This presumption is buttressed by constitutional provisions in some states that actually do preclude judicial review of certain questions,[12] or provide definitive structural limitations on its use.[13] The citizens of the states therefore know how to place limitations on judicial review, and have even done so on occasion. But no state today absolutely bars the judiciary from having the final word on the constitutionality of a statute, despite Theodore Roosevelt's proposal in 1912 that voters should be able to recall judicial decisions holding a law unconstitutional and reinstate the effectiveness of the statute. Indeed, a few state constitutions even have explicit provisions for judicial review. The Georgia Constitution of 1861 expressed: "Legislative Acts in violation of the fundamental law are

---

[9]BERNARD SCHWARTZ, A HISTORY OF THE SUPREME COURT 7-10 (1993); William Michael Traynor, *Judicial Review Before* Marbury, 58 STAN. L. REV. 455 (2005) (identifying more than thirty decisions engaging in judicial review before *Marbury*); Robert F. Utter, *Swimming in the Jaws of the Crocodile: State Court Comment on Federal Constitutional Issues When Disposing of Cases on State Constitutional Grounds*, 63 TEX. L. REV. 1025, 1031 (1985) (asserting at least ten of the existing seventeen states had asserted or exercised judicial review before *Marbury*).

[10]*See, e.g.*, David P. Currie, *The Constitution of the Republic of Texas Part 2: The Decisions*, 8 GREEN BAG 2D 239, 239-40 & nn.1-8 (2005) (citing cases).

[11]Dallam 473, 480-81 (Tex. 1842).

[12]*See, e.g.*, MICH. CONST. art. II, § 8 (recall of public officials "shall be a political rather than a judicial question.").

[13]*See* NEB. CONST. art. V, § 2 (mandating that legislation shall not "be declared unconstitutional except by the concurrence of five [of seven] judges"); N.D. CONST. art. VI, § 4 (precluding the supreme court from declaring "a legislative enactment unconstitutional unless at four of the [five] members of the court so decide.").

void; and the judiciary shall so declare them," a provision that still exists (with minor changes) in Georgia's Constitution today.[14]

Thus, although state courts are part of the federal judicial system, the state judiciaries do not operate under all the same constraints as the federal judiciary. Because a state's constitution, instead of the Federal Constitution, details the subject matter jurisdictional reach of its courts, the state courts do not have to follow the justiciability doctrines stemming from the "case" or "controversy" requirement of Article III, even when interpreting federal claims. Many states accordingly have developed their own independent justiciability doctrines. Moreover, the manner of selecting judges in most states varies markedly from the federal model. As a result of these and other differences, state judiciaries face their own unique problems in exercising the judicial power.

A. STATE JUSTICIABILITY DOCTRINES

The limitation on the federal judicial power in Article III of the United States Constitution to certain categories of "cases" and "controversies" has given rise to judicially-created doctrines of restraint known as the justiciability doctrines. These doctrines have several purposes, including ensuring that the federal courts will not intrude on the spheres of authority entrusted to the other branches of the federal government, and limiting the federal courts to issues presented in an adversary context, the context historically viewed as appropriate for judicial resolution.[15]

The federal justiciability doctrines include standing, ripeness, mootness, and the political question doctrine. The essence of standing is whether the plaintiff has the appropriate personal stake in the litigation as a result of suffering an injury that is fairly traceable to the defendant's conduct and is likely to be redressed by a favorable judicial decree.[16] Ripeness and mootness address the timing of the lawsuit; ripeness ensures that the suit is not filed too prematurely before a concrete adversary context exists,[17] and mootness prevents the continuation of the lawsuit after the injury has ceased.[18] Finally, the political question doctrine carves out certain subjects that the federal courts believe are inappropriate for judicial resolution because the decisions should be made by the politically accountable branches of government.[19] Although these doctrines emanating from the "case" or "controversy" requirement are easy enough to state, they "have an iceberg quality,

---

[14]GA. CONST. art. I, § 2, par. 5 ("Legislative acts in violation of this Constitution or the Constitution of the United States are void, and the judiciary shall so declare them."); *accord* LA. CONST. art. V, § 5 (granting Louisiana Supreme Court jurisdiction over cases in which a law or ordinance has been declared unconstitutional).

[15]Flast v. Cohen, 392 U.S. 83, 94-95 (1968).

[16]*See, e.g.*, Lujan v. Defenders of Wildlife, 504 U.S. 555, 560-61 (1992). There are other "prudential" limitations on standing as well, including that the plaintiff's interest falls within the "zone of interests" protected by the law, that the plaintiff not assert a *de minimis* "generalized grievance" shared by all or a large class of citizens, and that the plaintiff not assert the rights of third parties. *See* CHARLES ALAN WRIGHT & MARY KAY KANE, FEDERAL PRACTICE AND PROCEDURE: FEDERAL PRACTICE DESKBOOK § 14, at 107-08 (2002).

[17]*See, e.g.*, Abbott Labs. v. Gardner, 387 U.S. 136, 148-49 (1967).

[18]*See, e.g.*, U.S. Parole Comm'n v. Geraghty, 445 U.S. 388, 397 (1980).

[19]*See, e.g.*, Baker v. Carr, 369 U.S. 186, 210-26 (1962).

containing beneath their surface simplicity submerged complexities which go to the very heart of our constitutional form of government."[20]

But because these complexities arise from the express limitations in Article III on the federal judicial power, state courts are not required to adopt the same justiciability doctrines as the Supreme Court, not even when adjudicating a federal claim. Yet this leads to its own set of difficulties in our system of federalism.

ASARCO Inc. v. Kadish, 490 U.S. 605 (1989)

Justice KENNEDY delivered the opinion of the Court, except as to Part II-B-1 [which Justices Brennan, White, Marshall, and Blackmun deemed unnecessary to the holding].

The ultimate question for our decision is whether Arizona's statute governing mineral leases on state lands is void because it does not conform with the federal laws that originally granted those lands from the United States to Arizona. First, however, there is a difficult question about our own jurisdiction, a matter which touches on essential aspects of the proper relation between state and federal courts.

I

Various individual taxpayers and the Arizona Education Association, which represents approximately 20,000 public schoolteachers throughout the State, brought suit in Arizona state court, seeking a declaration that the state statute governing mineral leases on state lands, Ariz.Rev.Stat.Ann. § 27- 234(B) (Supp.1988), is void, and also seeking appropriate injunctive relief. The state statute was challenged on the ground that it does not comply with the methods Congress required the State to follow before it could lease or sell the lands granted from the United States in the New Mexico-Arizona Enabling Act of 1910, 36 Stat. 557, and which are repeated in the Arizona Constitution. [The Arizona Supreme Court found the statute unconstitutional and invalid, and the defendant mineral lessees sought review from the Supreme Court.]

II

Before we may undertake to consider whether the state legislation authorizing the leases is valid under federal law, we must rule on whether we have jurisdiction in the case. The parties and *amici* raise [several] jurisdictional issues, each of substance. The issues here [include] whether there is standing and an actual case or controversy that permits of a decision in federal court [and] whether the decision below is unreviewable in this Court because it rests on an adequate and independent state ground. . . .

B

1

The United States contends that the case should be dismissed for lack of standing, since neither respondent taxpayers nor respondent teachers association, who were the original plaintiffs, would have satisfied the requirements for bringing suit in federal court

[20]*Flast*, 392 U.S. at 94.

at the outset. [S]tanding in its most basic aspect can be one of the controlling elements in the definition of a case or controversy under Article III. The standing of respondents if they had filed suit in federal court at the trial level may be resolved by applying well-settled principles of federal law.

The question whether taxpayers or citizens have a sufficient personal stake to challenge laws of general application where their own injury is not distinct from that suffered in general by other taxpayers or citizens covers old and familiar ground. As an ordinary matter, suits premised on federal taxpayer status are not cognizable in the federal courts because a taxpayer's "interest in the moneys of the Treasury . . . is shared with millions of others, is comparatively minute and indeterminable; and the effect upon future taxation, of any payments out of the funds, so remote, fluctuating and uncertain, that no basis is afforded for [judicial intervention]." *Frothingham v. Mellon,* 262 U.S. 447, 487 (1923).

We have indicated that the same conclusion may not hold for municipal taxpayers, if it has been shown that the "peculiar relation of the corporate taxpayer to the [municipal] corporation" makes the taxpayer's interest in the application of municipal revenues "direct and immediate." *Frothingham, supra,* at 486-487. Yet we have likened state taxpayers to federal taxpayers, and thus we have refused to confer standing upon a state taxpayer absent a showing of "direct injury," pecuniary or otherwise. *Doremus v. Board of Education of Hawthorne,* 342 U.S. 429, 434 (1952).

No such showing has been made in this case. It follows that the suit would have been dismissed at the outset were the federal rule to apply.

2

But the state judiciary here chose a different path, as was their right, and took no account of federal standing rules in letting the case go to final judgment in the Arizona courts. That result properly follows from the allocation of authority in the federal system. We have recognized often that the constraints of Article III do not apply to state courts, and accordingly the state courts are not bound by the limitations of a case or controversy or other federal rules of justiciability even when they address issues of federal law, as when they are called upon to interpret the Constitution or, in this case, a federal statute. See, *e.g., Pennell v. San Jose,* 485 U.S. 1, 8 (1988).

Although the state courts are not bound to adhere to federal standing requirements, they possess the authority, absent a provision for exclusive federal jurisdiction, to render binding judicial decisions that rest on their own interpretations of federal law. See 28 U.S.C. § 1738; *Grubb v. Public Utilities Comm'n of Ohio,* 281 U.S. 470 (1930). Indeed, inferior federal courts are not required to exist under Article III, and the Supremacy Clause explicitly states that "the Judges in every State shall be bound" by federal law. U.S. Const., Art. VI, cl. 2.

The question now arises whether a judgment rendered by the state courts in these circumstances can support jurisdiction in this Court to review the case. At this juncture, petitioners allege a specific injury stemming from the state-court decree, a decree which rests on principles of federal law. Petitioners insist that, as a result of the state-court judgment, the case has taken on such definite shape that they are under a defined and specific legal obligation, one which causes them direct injury.

We agree. Although respondents would not have had standing to commence suit in federal court based on the allegations in the complaint, they are not the party attempting to invoke the federal judicial power. Instead it is petitioners, the defendants in the case and the losing parties below, who bring the case here and thus seek entry to the federal courts for the first time in the lawsuit. We determine that petitioners have standing to invoke the authority of a federal court and that this dispute now presents a justiciable case or controversy for resolution here.

Petitioners hold mineral leases that were granted under the state law the Arizona Supreme Court invalidated. Although no accounting of sums due under these leases remains at issue in this particular case, it is undisputed that the decision to be reviewed poses a serious and immediate threat to the continuing validity of those leases by virtue of its holding that they were granted under improper procedures and an invalid law.

Petitioners contend before us that the Arizona Supreme Court's decision rests on an erroneous interpretation of federal statutes. They claim that the declaratory judgment sought and secured by respondents, along with the relief that may flow from that ruling, is invalid under federal law. If we were to agree with petitioners, our reversal of the decision below would remove its disabling effects upon them. In these circumstances, we conclude that petitioners meet each prong of the constitutional standing requirements.

Although petitioners satisfy the requirements of federal standing and present an actual case or controversy for decision here, the United States contends that this showing is insufficient to support our jurisdiction. The Government suggests that the appropriate order is dismissal, and that petitioners are then free "to bring a declaratory judgment action in federal court" raising these same claims. Petitioners counter that if the Court finds it cannot review the judgment on the merits, the proper course is to vacate the judgment below and remand for appropriate further proceedings, as we have done at least on some occasions when a case becomes moot while it is pending on review from a state court. Neither disposition is appropriate here.

If we were to vacate the judgment below on the ground that respondents lacked federal standing when they brought suit initially, that disposition would render nugatory the entire proceedings in the state courts. The clear effect would be to impose federal standing requirements on the state courts whenever they adjudicate issues of federal law, if those judgments are to be conclusive on the parties. That result, however, would be contrary to established traditions and to our prior decisions recognizing that the state courts are not bound by Article III and yet have it within both their power and their proper role to render binding judgments on issues of federal law, subject only to review by this Court.

If we were merely to dismiss this case and leave the judgment below undisturbed, a different set of problems would ensue. The United States urges that the proper course for petitioners is to sue in federal trial court in order to readjudicate the very same issues that were determined in the state-court proceedings below. That action, in essence, would be an attempt to obtain direct review of the Arizona Supreme Court's decision in the lower federal courts, and would represent a partial inroad on *Rooker-Feldman*'s construction of 28 U.S.C. § 1257.

For these reasons, we believe it would be inappropriate to dismiss the case at this stage. That disposition would come at the cost of much disrespect to state-court proceedings and judgments. It also would require petitioners to commence a new action in federal court to vindicate their rights under federal law, even though right now they present us with a case or controversy that is justiciable under federal standards. Instead, we adopt the following rationale for our decision on this jurisdictional point: When a state court has issued a judgment in a case where plaintiffs in the original action had no standing to sue under the principles governing the federal courts, we may exercise our jurisdiction on certiorari if the judgment of the state court causes direct, specific, and concrete injury to the parties who petition for our review, where the requisites of a case or controversy are also met.

C

The last threshold procedural issue concerns the possibility that the decision below rested on an adequate and independent state ground that would defeat review of the federal issues by this Court. Here the state court mentioned the State Constitution several times in its opinion but otherwise relied exclusively on federal law, including an extended discussion of the applicable federal statutes and their legislative histories. In its conclusion, however, the Arizona Supreme Court directed the trial court "to enter a judgment declaring A.R.S. § 27-234 unconstitutional and invalid as it pertains to nonhydrocarbon mineral leases."

We conclude that the opinion below is not based on an adequate and independent state ground. Its discussion focuses solely on the federal statutes, and the State Constitution is never mentioned on its own apart from the Enabling Act. The Arizona Supreme Court explicitly considered itself "bound to adopt the construction advanced by [plaintiffs]" based on the prior decisions of this Court, and described Article 10 of the Arizona Constitution as simply a "rescript" of § 28 of the Enabling Act. In light of this description, the references to the Arizona Constitution simply reflect a holding which rests on the state court's interpretation of federal law. Although the Arizona Supreme Court was free to rest its holding on the State Constitution as an independent ground, the decision below did not divorce the state constitutional issue from the questions of federal law.

III

The issue on the merits is whether Arizona may lease mineral lands granted from the United States without meeting the specific requirements imposed by federal statute. [The Court then proceeded to affirm the judgment of the Arizona Supreme Court on the merits.]

Chief Justice REHNQUIST, with whom Justice SCALIA joins, concurring in part and dissenting in part.

For me, absence of standing disposes of this case and requires dismissal of the appeal. *Doremus v. Board of Education of Hawthorne,* 342 U.S. 429 (1952).

In *Doremus,* we dismissed an appeal from state court by taxpayers because they lacked standing. The Court now says that although the *Doremus* case is good law for plaintiffs who lack standing but lost in the state court on the merits of their federal claim, it is not good law for such plaintiffs who prevailed on the merits of their federal question in the state courts.

The Court is concerned with the fact that if it applies *Doremus* as sauce for the goose as well as for the gander state courts will remain free to decide important questions of federal statutory and constitutional law without the possibility of review in this Court. This is true, but I think it a rather unremarkable proposition. Some state courts render advisory decisions on federal law of no binding force even within the State. See, *e.g.*, Mass. Const., Art. LXXXV (amending the Massachusetts Constitution to provide: "Each branch of the legislature, as well as the governor or the council, shall have authority to require the opinions of the justices of the supreme judicial court, upon important questions of law, and upon solemn occasions"); Mich. Const., Art. 3, § 8 ("Either house of the legislature or the governor may request the opinion of the supreme court on important questions of law upon solemn occasions as to the constitutionality of legislation after it has been enacted into law but before its effective date"). In each instance, the interpretation of federal law may affect the governance of the State and thereby make some people better off and some worse off. Yet none of these decisions of federal law are reviewable in this or any other federal court. I see no reason to fear that our dismissal of the present appeal would lead to a legal landscape in which we would no longer have the opportunity to review many important decisions on questions of federal law. Therefore I see no reason why this Court should bend its Article III jurisprudence out of shape to avoid a largely imaginary problem.

Notes on the Relationship Between State and Federal Justiciability Doctrines

***State and Federal Standing in* ASARCO**: *ASARCO* addressed standing issues arising at two different junctures during the lawsuit. First, the Supreme Court considered the standing of the plaintiff state taxpayers to file their lawsuit urging federal law invalidated a state statute governing mineral leases. The Court concluded that, while the plaintiffs would not have had taxpayer standing in federal court, the Arizona state courts were not bound to apply the same federal justiciability standards even for a case arising under federal law. Why does the Supreme Court authorize this practice? How does the acceptability of the state courts applying different justiciability doctrines than the federal courts on matters of federal law compare with the *Erie* doctrine,[21] which generally requires the federal courts to employ state outcome-determinative rules when deciding issues of state law?

The Supreme Court then separately considered the standing of the defendant mineral lessees to seek federal review of the state court's holding on federal law. Based on the Court's view that the defendants suffered a harm from the state court's invalidation of their leases under federal law, the defendants were allowed to seek federal judicial review. But note that, if the taxpayers had lost in the Arizona Supreme Court, they would not have had standing to proceed to the Supreme Court, even if the Arizona Supreme Court had been wrong in its interpretation of federal law. Is it odd that the Supreme Court under these circumstances may review a state court's holding that a federal claim is valid but not a

[21]Erie R.R. Co. v. Tompkins, 304 U.S. 64 (1938).

holding that the federal claim is invalid? Can the Supreme Court ensure uniformity of federal law interpretation when the state courts use different justiciability standards?

Do other policies besides uniformity justify *ASARCO*'s holding? How does the *ASARCO* rule compare to the concerns articulated in Justice Stevens's dissent in *Michigan v. Long* in Chapter 2? Justice Stevens contended the business of the Supreme Court should be to protect rights secured by federal law rather than to prevent states from over-enforcing federal norms. Does *ASARCO* support this position?

State Justiciability Doctrines: Although it is not required by Article III, state courts typically have their own justiciability doctrines for cases coming within the "judicial power" that in large part are either similar to or borrow from the doctrines enunciated by the Supreme Court.[22] But almost every state has deviated from at least one, or more, of the "case or controversy" requirements imposed on the federal judiciary. As examples, several state courts have established an exception to the mootness doctrine for cases "of great public importance."[23] Other states have rejected the political question doctrine,[24] and some do not follow the prudential zone of interests test for standing to challenge administrative regulations.[25] The most common example, though, is that presented in *ASARCO*. Most states are more lenient than the United States Supreme Court with respect to allowing taxpayer suits against the state.[26] What factors might explain why the states have almost uniformly rejected this aspect of federal standing doctrine?

As Chief Justice Rehnquist noted in his *ASARCO* dissent, another difference is that several states authorize advisory opinions by the judiciary. Advisory opinions are absolutely prohibited in the federal courts. The most famous example was the refusal of the Supreme Court of the United States to issue an opinion in response to the request for advice from Secretary of State Thomas Jefferson, at the behest of President George Washington, regarding American treaty obligations under its neutrality proclamation in the war between France and England.[27] The Court explained in a letter to the President that the three branches of the government, "being in certain respects checks upon each other, and our

---

[22]*See, e.g.*, Life of the Land v. Land Use Comm'n, 623 P.2d 431, 438 (Haw. 1981) (opining that, even in the absence of a "case or controversy" requirement in the state constitution, the "judicial power to resolve public disputes in a system of government where there is a separation of powers should be limited to those questions capable of judicial resolution and presented in an adversary context").

[23]*See, e.g.*, *In re* Geraghty, 343 A.2d 737, 738-39 (N.J. 1975) ("[W] e have often recognized that courts may hear and decide cases which are technically moot where issues of great public importance are involved.").

[24]*See, e.g.*, Backman v. Sec'y of the Commonwealth, 441 N.E.2d 523, 526-27 (Mass. 1982) (assessing the procedural validity of a state constitutional amendment despite objections of nonjusticiability on political question grounds because "we have never explicitly incorporated the Federal doctrine into our State jurisprudence. We decline to avoid deciding the issue before us based on the conclusory label that it is a political question.").

[25]*See, e.g.*, Greer v. Ill. Hous. Dev. Auth., 524 N.E.2d 561, 574-75 (Ill. 1988).

[26]*See* JAMES A. GARDNER, INTERPRETING STATE CONSTITUTIONS 159 (2005). Typically this more expansive grant of taxpayer standing has been a result of judicial interpretation, but in other instances a state constitutional provision addresses the issue. *See, e.g.*, MICH. CONST. art. IX, § 32 (granting state taxpayers standing to allege certain taxes and expenditures violate specified constitutional restrictions).

[27]Correspondence of the Justices, Letter from Chief Justice John Jay and the Associate Justices to President George Washington, August 8, 1793.

being judges of a court of last resort, are considerations which afford strong arguments against the propriety of our extra-judicially deciding the questions alluded to."[28] The majority of the states, including Texas, follow the same standard–but a few states do not.

1. Advisory Opinions in State Courts

At least ten states authorize the state supreme court to render advisory opinions to the legislative and executive branches on specified subjects, either by constitutional provisions[29] or by statute.[30] While the provisions vary, the courts typically are limited to providing a member or members of the legislative or executive branch advice on the constitutionality or legality of a contemplated action or piece of legislation. On the other hand, other states, such as Texas, are firmly entrenched against issuing any type of advisory opinion, even when authorized by statute to do so.

Opinion of the Justices to the Senate, 802 N.E.2d 565 (Mass. 2004)

To the Honorable the Senate of the Commonwealth of Massachusetts:

The order indicates that there is pending before the General Court a bill, Senate No. 2175, entitled "An Act relative to civil unions." The order indicates that grave doubt exists as to the constitutionality of the bill if enacted into law and requests the opinions of the Justices on the following "important question of law":

> Does Senate, No. 2175, which prohibits same-sex couples from entering into marriage but allows them to form civil unions with all "benefits, protections, rights and responsibilities" of marriage, comply with the equal protection and due process requirements of the Constitution of the Commonwealth and articles 1, 6, 7, 10, 12 and 16 of the Declaration of Rights?

Under Part II, c. 3, art. 2, of the Constitution of the Commonwealth, as amended by art. 85 of the Amendments, "[e]ach branch of the legislature, as well as the governor or the council, shall have authority to require the opinions of the justices of the supreme judicial court, upon important questions of law, and upon solemn occasions." "[A] solemn occasion exists 'when the Governor or either branch of the Legislature, having some action in view, has serious doubts as to their power and authority to take such action, under the Constitution, or under existing statutes.'" *Answer of the Justices,* 302 N.E.2d 565 (Mass. 1973). The pending bill involves an important question of law and the Senate has indicated "grave doubt" as to its constitutionality. We therefore address the question.

---

[28] *Id.*

[29] *See, e.g.*, COLO. CONST. art. VI, § 3; FLA. CONST. art. V, § 3(b)(10); ME. CONST. art. VI, § 3; MASS. CONST. pt. II, ch. III, art. II; MICH. CONST. art. III, § 8; N.H. CONST. pt. II, art. 74; R.I. CONST. art. X, § 3; S.D. CONST. art. V, § 5.

[30] *See, e.g.*, ALA. CODE § 12-2-10; DEL. CODE ANN. tit. 10, § 141. But some state courts have held that a statutory authorization to issue advisory opinions is inadequate. *See, e.g.*, *In re* Constitutionality of House Bill No. 222, 90 S.W.2d 692, 692-93 (Ky. 1936); *In re* Op. of the Justices, 64 A.2d 169, 171-72 (Vt. 1949).

1. *Background of the proposed legislation.* In *Goodridge v. Department of Pub. Health,* 798 N.E.2d 941 (Mass. 2003) (*Goodridge*), the court considered the constitutional question "[w]hether the Commonwealth may use its formidable regulatory authority to bar same-sex couples from civil marriage." The court concluded that it may not do so, determining that the Commonwealth had failed to articulate a rational basis for denying civil marriage to same-sex couples. The court stated that the Massachusetts Constitution "affirms the dignity and equality of all individuals" and "forbids the creation of second-class citizens." The court concluded that in "[l]imiting the protections, benefits, and obligations of civil marriage to opposite-sex couples," G.L. c. 207, the marriage licensing law, "violates the basic premises of individual liberty and equality under law protected by the Massachusetts Constitution."

In so concluding, the court enumerated some of the concrete tangible benefits that flow from civil marriage, including, but not limited to, rights in property, probate, tax, and evidence law that are conferred on married couples. The court also noted that "intangible benefits flow from marriage," intangibles that are important components of marriage as a "civil right."

After reviewing the marriage ban under the deferential rational basis standard, the court concluded that the Department of Public Health "failed to identify any relevant characteristic that would justify shutting the door to civil marriage to a person who wishes to marry someone of the same sex."

The *Goodridge* decision by the court made no reference to the concept of "civil unions," nor did the separate concurring opinion of Justice Greaney. Rather, it was the lawfulness under the Massachusetts Constitution of the bar to civil marriage itself, "a vital social institution," that the court was asked to decide. The court decided the question after extensively reviewing the government's justifications for the marriage ban.

In response to the plaintiffs' specific request for relief, the court preserved the marriage licensing statute, but refined the common-law definition of civil marriage to mean "the voluntary union of two persons as spouses, to the exclusion of all others." The entry of judgment was stayed "for 180 days to permit the Legislature to take such action as it may deem appropriate." The purpose of the stay was to afford the Legislature an opportunity to conform the existing statutes to the provisions of the *Goodridge* decision.

2. *Provisions of the bill.* The order of the Senate plainly reflects that Senate No. 2175 is proposed action in response to the *Goodridge* opinion. The bill states that the "purpose" of the act is to provide "eligible same-sex couples the opportunity to obtain the benefits, protections, rights and responsibilities afforded to opposite sex couples by the marriage laws of the commonwealth, without entering into a marriage," declares that it is the "public policy" of the Commonwealth that "spouses in a civil union" "shall have all the benefits, protections, rights and responsibilities afforded by the marriage laws," and recites "that the Commonwealth's laws should be revised to give same-sex couples the opportunity to obtain the legal protections, benefits, rights and responsibilities associated with civil marriage, while preserving the traditional, historic nature and meaning of the institution of civil marriage." To that end, the bill proposes [to establish] the institution of "civil union," eligibility for which is limited to "[t]wo persons . . . [who] are of the same sex. . . ."

The proposed law states that "spouses" in a civil union shall be "joined in it with a legal status equivalent to marriage." Senate No. 2175, § 5. The bill expressly maintains that "marriage" is reserved exclusively for opposite-sex couples by providing that "[p]ersons eligible to form a civil union with each other under this chapter shall not be eligible to enter into a marriage with each other under chapter 207." *Id.* Notwithstanding, the proposed law purports to make the institution of a "civil union" parallel to the institution of civil "marriage." For example, the bill provides that "spouses in a civil union shall have all the same benefits, protections, rights and responsibilities under law as are granted to spouses in a marriage." In addition, terms that denote spousal relationships, such as "husband," "wife," "family," and "next of kin," are to be interpreted to include spouses in a civil union "as those terms are used in any law." *Id.* The bill goes on to enumerate a nonexclusive list of the legal benefits that will adhere to spouses in a civil union, including property rights, joint State income tax filing, evidentiary rights, rights to veteran benefits and group insurance, and the right to the issuance of a "civil union" license, identical to a marriage license under G.L. c. 207, "as if a civil union was a marriage."

3. *Analysis.* We have now been asked to render an advisory opinion on Senate No. 2175, which creates a new legal status, "civil union," that is purportedly equal to "marriage," yet separate from it. The constitutional difficulty of the proposed civil union bill is evident in its stated purpose to "preserv[e] the traditional, historic nature and meaning of the institution of civil marriage." Senate No. 2175, § 1. Preserving the institution of civil marriage is of course a legislative priority of the highest order, and one to which the Justices accord the General Court the greatest deference. We recognize the efforts of the Senate to draft a bill in conformity with the *Goodridge* opinion. Yet the bill, as we read it, does nothing to "preserve" the civil marriage law, only its constitutional infirmity. This is not a matter of social policy but of constitutional interpretation. As the court concluded in *Goodridge,* the traditional, historic nature and meaning of civil marriage in Massachusetts is as a wholly secular and dynamic legal institution, the governmental aim of which is to encourage stable adult relationships for the good of the individual and of the community, especially its children. The very nature and purpose of civil marriage, the court concluded, renders unconstitutional any attempt to ban all same-sex couples, *as* same-sex couples, from entering into civil marriage.

4. *Conclusion.* We are of the opinion that Senate No. 2175 violates the equal protection and due process requirements of the Constitution of the Commonwealth and the Massachusetts Declaration of Rights. Further, the particular provisions that render the pending bill unconstitutional, §§ 2 and 3 of proposed G.L. c. 207A, are not severable from the remainder. The bill maintains an unconstitutional, inferior, and discriminatory status for same-sex couples, and the bill's remaining provisions are too entwined with this purpose to stand independently.

The answer to the question is "No."

Morrow v. Corbin, 62 S.W.2d 641 (Tex. 1933)

CURETON, Chief Justice.

[In November 1932, Morrow sued Corbin seeking the foreclosure of a vendor's lien. A few months later, in an attempt to alleviate some of the hardships of the Great Depression, the Texas Legislature passed a statute providing for the judicial stay of lien foreclosure suits. Corbin then relied on the new law to seek a stay of Morrow's foreclosure suit. Morrow responded that his suit should not be stayed because the new law violated the federal and state constitutions. The trial judge, using a new procedure authorized by Senate Bill No. 173, issued a "certificate" on the question of the constitutionality of the judicial stay law to the court of civil appeals. The court of civil appeals then certified the questions contained in the certificate to the Supreme Court of Texas. But the Supreme Court held that it had no jurisdiction over the certificate because it sought an advisory opinion.]

The certificate is presented under Senate Bill No. 173, [which reads] as follows:

> Sec. 1. In any case now or hereafter pending in any District or County Court in this State, wherein the constitutionality of any law or any order, rule or regulation of any officer, board, or other State Commission is attacked as being violative of either the State or Federal Constitution, and wherein a decision on the same is material to the deciding of said case finally on its merits, the Judge of said Court shall have the power and authority to certify any such question or questions of law involved in said case directly to the Court of Civil Appeals in said District before trial on the merits for its decision.
>
> Sec. 3. In order to expedite the final determination of such question with dispatch, the Court of Civil Appeals may forthwith certify said question or questions immediately to the Supreme Court, as provided by Article 1758 of the Revised Civil Statutes of 1925, and other Articles relating to certifying questions to the Supreme Court. * * *
>
> Sec. 4. The trial court may hold the trial of said case in abeyance until its questions have been certified and answered. * * *

It is obvious that the purpose of this act is to obtain before judgment in the trial court the advice of the Court of Civil Appeals and the Supreme Court as to "the constitutionality of any law or any order, rule or regulation of any officer, board, or other State Commission," which may be involved in any case pending but undetermined in a trial court. In other words, by the terms of this enactment in so far as involved in the case before us we are required to advise the district and county judges how to try their cases as to all constitutional questions, not to revise, reverse, affirm, or otherwise affect their decrees. Ordinarily, we believe the rendition of advisory opinions is to be regarded as the exercise of executive rather than judicial power. This seems to have been the conception of those who framed the Constitution, since by that instrument the Attorney General, a member of the Executive Department, is the only state officer expressly authorized to render such opinions. State Constitution, article 4, §§ 1, 22. At any rate, the rendition of advisory opinions has generally been held not to be the exercise of judicial power. 7 Harvard Law Review, p. 153; Matter of State Industrial Commission, 224 N. Y. 13, 119 N. E. 1027; Laughlin v. Portland, 111 Me. 486, 90 A. 318; Opinion of Justices, 126 Mass. 567; Anway v. Grand Rapids R. Co., 211 Mich. 592, 179 N. W. 350. We shall inquire, however, whether or not such power may be exercised by the appellate courts of this state, either as an express grant under the Constitution or as incidental to any granted power.

Section 1, article 5, of the Constitution states in what "magistracy" the judicial power shall be vested. It declares: "The judicial power of this State shall be vested in one Supreme Court, in Courts of Civil Appeals, in a Court of Criminal Appeals, in District Courts, in County Courts, in Commissioners Courts, in Courts of Justices of the Peace, and in such other courts as may be provided by law." The Constitution has thus erected a system of trial and appellate courts quite similar to that of the United States and those of the American states generally, all of which are an outgrowth of the judicial system of England, out of which the common law grew and attained its renown.

The Constitution is specific in confiding trial jurisdiction to the district and county courts, and other inferior courts. State Constitution, article 5, §§ 8, 16, 19. These provisions mean that those courts are to exercise that portion of the judicial power allocated to them unimpeded by the supervision of any other tribunal, except in so far as powers of revision may be confided to other tribunals. The jurisdiction of these trial or inferior courts, without any exception, embraces the "power to hear and determine the matter in controversy according to established rules of law, and to carry the sentence or judgment of the court into execution."

We pass to a discussion of the constitutional powers of the Courts of Civil Appeals and Supreme Court, which should be interpreted in a manner consistent with the jurisdictional powers and concomitant duties of our trial tribunals, as outlined above, if this can be done. Section 3, article 5, of the State Constitution fixes the boundaries of the judicial power of the Supreme Court. An analysis of the vital portions of this section shows that:

(a) The Supreme Court has "appellate jurisdiction only" (except where authorized to exercise original jurisdiction);
(b) This "appellate jurisdiction only" is limited in two particulars, viz.:
  (1) "To questions of law,"
  (2) "Arising in cases of which the Courts of Civil Appeals have appellate jurisdiction."

The jurisdictional provisions of the Constitution relating to Courts of Civil Appeals are found in section 6 of article 5 of the Constitution, and in so far as here involved read: "Sec. 6. * * * Said Courts of Civil Appeals shall have appellate jurisdiction co-extensive with the limits of their respective districts, which shall extend to all civil cases of which the District Courts or County Courts have original or appellate jurisdiction, under such restrictions and regulations as may be prescribed by law. Provided, that the decision of said courts shall be conclusive on all questions of fact brought before them on appeal or error. * * * Said courts shall have such other jurisdiction, original and appellate as may be prescribed by law. * * *"

These provisions leave no room for doubt as to the types of jurisdiction which may be conferred upon Courts of Civil Appeals. They are (1) "original" and (2) "appellate."

We think the plain reading of the Constitution concludes the question that the Supreme Court and the Courts of Civil Appeals may exercise only these two classes of jurisdiction. Neither is given any advisory power by the organic law and since not given, under the rule expressio unius est exclusio alterius it is denied and can not be conferred by the Legislature.

Since advisory jurisdiction generally is not given under the Constitution and cannot be conferred by the Legislature, and since that authorized by the act before us is not original jurisdiction, it is obvious that if the enactment under which the certificate is before us is to stand the jurisdiction provided for must be found to be within the appellate powers of the Supreme Court and the Courts of Civil Appeals, either as an express grant or incidental to the exercise of the authority granted. The power to determine the constitutionality of a statute or order, etc., is certainly within the appellate power of the revisory courts, but this power can only be invoked in a case within their appellate jurisdiction (or in a case within their original jurisdiction), and in the manner and under conditions contemplated by the Constitution. The question then is when may the appellate jurisdiction of the Supreme Court and of the Courts of Civil Appeals be invoked. The rule in Texas, with exceptions to be hereafter noted, has always been that appellate jurisdiction may be invoked only after trial.

Not only must there be a trial in the inferior court, but the trial must result in a final judgment disposing of all issues and parties before appellate jurisdiction may attach. These rules have been stated and adhered to by the courts without any special discussion of the Constitution, but from a consideration of the statutes then existing. However, a proper interpretation of the Constitution leads us to the same conclusion. The Constitution does not in so many words say that appeals lie only from final judgments, but it does erect a system of trial and appellate courts and gives the latter (aside from their original jurisdiction) only appellate power. The Constitution is to be interpreted in the light of the common law, which has been the rule of decision with us since 1840. The common law limits and determines the meaning of words and phrases used in the Constitution when the context or some other provision of the instrument or some previous enactment existing when the Organic Law was framed does not determine them.

When the Constitution declares that our appellate courts shall have and exercise original and appellate jurisdiction, it means those types of original and appellate jurisdiction which from time immemorial the common-law courts have exercised. Beyond the limits of original and appellate power as comprehended by the common law the Legislature is without constitutional authority to confer jurisdiction, except in so far as the common law has been abrogated or modified directly or by necessary implication by the Constitution itself.

Under the common law in the law courts of England appellate jurisdiction could only be invoked after final judgment in the trial court. True, appeals could be taken before the judgment had been signed in order that writ of error might have the effect of a supersedeas, but an appeal could not be taken until after trial and judgment. The common-law rule as to the necessity of final judgments before appeal has become generally the rule throughout the United States. Interpreting our Constitution in the light of the common law as just stated, it is obvious that the jurisdictional sections quoted above mean that the appellate jurisdiction of the Supreme Court and that of the Courts of Civil Appeals can only be invoked after trial and final judgment in the trial courts.

The exceptions as to the necessity for final judgments before appeal to which we have referred above are those where the statutes permit appeals from certain interlocutory orders of trial courts, namely, those granting or refusing temporary injunctions, appointing receivers, and determining pleas of privilege. Under these statutes appeals are predicated upon judgments, which though interlocutory in form as effectively deprive the litigant of his rights or his property for the time being as do final judgments or decrees.

The validity of these statutes is referable to the practice in common law chancery courts, to "stare decisis" and the amendment and consequent re-adoption of the jurisdictional section of the Constitution as to the Supreme Court as previously interpreted, and is not here involved. In the case before us neither an interlocutory nor final judgment has ever been rendered and the statute in so far as here involved does not require the entry of decrees before certification.

The inquiry naturally suggests itself that if the giving of advisory opinions to the district courts is not the exercise of judicial power and not within the appellate jurisdiction of the Courts of Civil Appeals and the Supreme Court, and that the appellate powers of these courts cannot be invoked except upon appeal after judgment in the trial court, how may we justify the existing statutes and the practice under them relative to certified questions from the Courts of Civil Appeals to the Supreme Court? In all cases heretofore cognizable by certified question there have been actual trials and final judgments which the appellate courts may set aside, reform, or affirm and enforce under their appellate powers. In the case before us under the statute we are discussing in so far as involved in this proceeding nothing of this sort is provided for nor has any such action taken place in the instant case. The differences in the statutes and the state of the records under them determine the question in favor of the power of the appellate courts to certify in the one case, and as here shown, against it in the other. Originally the statutes permitting certified questions from Courts of Civil Appeals to the Supreme Court were of very doubtful validity. If there exists any constitutional authority for the statutes and the practice under them this court has never pointed it out. The question was before the court in 1893, shortly after the enactment of the certified question statutes in the case of Darnell v. Lyon, 85 Tex, 455, 22 S. W. 304, 960, and the majority of the court, Associate Justices Gaines and Henry, answered the questions certified by the Court of Civil Appeals without adverting to the constitutionality of the act under which the proceeding was before them. Chief Justice Stayton dissented in perhaps the strongest opinion he ever wrote, in which he held the certification statutes void. However, notwithstanding the strong dissenting opinion of Chief Justice Stayton, the statutes have been followed by this court for forty years. The question being one of practice in which the power has been consistently exercised for a long period of time, with no substantive right of the citizen involved, we will presume that there existed then and that there exists now a constitutional basis for the law, although elusive to us, and sustain the statute. The principle of stare decisis is, we think, applicable. In addition to the rule of stare decisis as a reason for sustaining the certification statutes we direct attention to the fact that in 1930 section 3 of article 5 of the Constitution, in which the jurisdiction of the Supreme Court is defined, was amended in such manner as to change only the length of the term of the court. This we are constrained to regard as a re-adoption of this section of the Constitution, with the construction previously placed thereon by the Legislature in enacting the certification statutes, and of the courts in treating the law as valid by acting thereunder.

We know of no rule by which the constitutional basis for existing certification statutes may be extended to the act before us, which calls for advisory action only, and requires no judgment or decree upon which the appellate power of the revisory courts may act.

Notes on the Impact of Advisory Opinions

The Precedential Value of Advisory Opinions: If advisory opinions are not part of the judicial power, as *Morrow v. Corbin* held, what is their precedential effect? Most state courts have held that advisory opinions, even when authorized by the state constitution, have no precedential effect in subsequent litigation.[31] Was there any indication in *Opinion of the Justices to the Senate* that the Massachusetts Legislature was bound by the court's decision? If advisory opinions are not binding, what purpose do they serve?

Does the fact that advisory opinions have no precedential value impact the propriety of a state court proffering such advice on a question of federal law? Chief Justice Rehnquist in his *ASARCO* dissent appeared not to be troubled by the possibility of state courts issuing advisory opinions on federal legal questions. Nevertheless, while some state courts have issued advisory opinions on federal constitutional issues, other courts have declined to do so, instead reserving their use for issues of state law.[32] What practical and theoretical arguments support a state court's refusal to issue advisory opinions on matters of federal law? What are the arguments to the contrary?

The Source of Authority for Advisory Opinions: What type of authorization is required for a state court to issue an advisory opinion? Can a state court claim an inherent

---

[31] *See, e.g.*, Op. of the Justices, 396 A.2d 219, 223 (Me. 1979) ("Even when the Justices are constitutionally empowered to render an advisory opinion, that opinion has no precedential value and no conclusive effect as to a judgment upon any party, and is not binding upon even the individual Justices rendering it in any subsequent litigated matter before their Court."); Commonwealth v. Welasky, 177 N.E. 656, 658 (Mass. 1931) ("It has been uniformly and many times held that such opinions, although necessarily the result of judicial examination and deliberation, are advisory in nature, given by the justices as individuals in their capacity as constitutional advisory of the other departments of government and without the aid of arguments, are not adjudications by the court, and do not fall within the doctrine of stare decisis. When the same questions are raised in litigation, the justices then composing the court are bound sedulously to guard against any influence flowing from the previous consideration, to examine the subject anew in the light of arguments presented by the parties without reliance upon the views theretofore expressed, and to give the case the most painstaking and impartial study and determination that an adequate appreciation of judicial duty can impel."); *In re* Op. of the Justices, 138 A. 284, 291 (N.H 1927) (noting the "opinion given is not a judicial decision of the questions propounded"); Op. to the Governor, 149 A.2d 341, 343 (R.I. 1959) (noting an advisory opinion "would not constitute a decision of the court, would not finally determine the question, and would have no binding effect on any person whose legal rights might be involved").

[32] *See, e.g., In re* Advisory Op. to the Governor, 509 So. 2d 292, 302 (Fla. 1987).

judicial power to issue an advisory opinion? Is a legislative authorization sufficient? Or are advisory opinions only permissible when explicitly authorized by the state constitution?

Although no state courts presently rely on an inherent power to issue advisory opinions, at least two states, Alabama and Delaware, have concluded that statutory authorization is sufficient.[33] Other courts disagree.[34] For instance, didn't the Supreme Court of Texas have a statutory authorization to issue the certificate in *Morrow v. Corbin*? Why didn't *Morrow* conclude that such a statutory authorization was enough, especially read in conjunction with the constitutional provision authorizing the courts of civil appeals to "have such other jurisdiction, original and appellate as may be prescribed by law"?

Morrow relied principally on an understanding of the Texas Constitution in light of common law principles to conclude that the constitutional grant of appellate jurisdiction did not authorize the issuance of advisory opinions. But was *Morrow*'s reliance on the common law final judgment rule appropriate in light of other historical principles? Before the United States Constitution was ratified, the accepted British practice allowed the Crown and the House of Lords to consult with judges extrajudicially and obtain advisory opinions regarding legal issues. Early American state courts frequently followed the British example and provided advisory opinions.[35] As the United States Supreme Court acknowledged, the federal prohibition against advisory opinions is thus predicated on "the implicit policies embodied in Article III, and not history alone."[36] Should *Morrow* have attempted to base its holding on similar implicit policies in the Texas Constitution, or is the common law itself such an implicit policy?

How persuasive is *Morrow*'s conclusion that the certificate procedure is an impermissible advisory opinion? Is the distinction drawn between a certificate on the constitutionality of a statute from a trial court and a similar certification by an appellate court to the Texas Supreme Court convincing? Is the court's exception for interlocutory appeals persuasive? In addition to these potential inconsistencies, *Morrow* is also difficult to reconcile with an earlier opinion of the Texas Supreme Court in *In re House Bill No. 537 of the Thirty-Eighth Legislature*.[37] In that case, the legislature enacted a statute imposing certain administrative duties on the Texas Supreme Court with respect to designating district judges to hold special terms of court in other districts. The court issued an opinion holding that the duties imposed by the statute did not fall within its constitutional grants of original and appellate jurisdiction and violated principles of separation of powers. But how did the Texas Supreme Court have jurisdiction to issue its opinion? No lawsuit had been filed, nor had any request for an opinion even been made by a coordinate branch. Instead, the court merely issued the opinion on its own initiative. Why wasn't that an advisory opinion outside of the court's judicial power?

---

[33] ALA. CODE § 12-2-10; DEL. CODE ANN. tit. 10, § 141.

[34] *See, e.g.*, *In re* Constitutionality of House Bill No. 222, 90 S.W.2d 692, 692-93 (Ky. 1936); *In re* Op. of the Justices, 64 A.2d 169, 171-72 (Vt. 1949).

[35] CHARLES ALAN WRIGHT & MARY KAY KANE, FEDERAL PRACTICE AND PROCEDURE: FEDERAL PRACTICE DESKBOOK § 13, at 87 (2002).

[36] Flast v. Cohen, 392 U.S. 83, 95 (1968).

[37] 256 S.W. 573 (Tex. 1923).

Advisory Opinions and Certified Questions: The stringency of the *Morrow* standard restricted the ability of the federal courts to obtain definitive construction of state laws in *Erie* cases, and was therefore subsequently partially modified by a state constitutional amendment. In *United Services Life Insurance Co. v. Delaney*, the Texas Supreme Court dismissed a state declaratory judgment action that had been filed to ascertain the meaning of insurance policies that were in dispute in a federal case.[38] The United States Court of Appeals for the Fifth Circuit had stayed the proceedings in federal court so that the parties could obtain a definitive interpretation of the governing Texas law from the Texas courts. But because the Fifth Circuit retained jurisdiction to render judgment, the Texas Supreme Court held, applying *Morrow*, that the state declaratory judgment action sought a nonjusticiable advisory opinion. This prevented the federal courts from obtaining definitive state interpretations of state law.

The legislature later acted to alleviate the problem through a state constitutional amendment, ratified by the voters in 1985, to allow federal appellate courts to obtain interpretations of state law from Texas' highest courts. Article V, section 3-c of the Texas Constitution grants the supreme court and the court of criminal appeals "jurisdiction to answer questions of law certified from a federal appellate court." The Senate Judiciary Committee noted that the constitutional amendment was necessary because "[t]he Texas Supreme Court has determined that under the Texas Constitution judicial power does not embrace giving advisory opinions."[39] Since the constitutional amendment, the court has only declined to answer a few questions while answering dozens of certified questions from the Fifth, Second, and Fourth Circuits.[40] Although the United States Supreme Court has not yet certified a question to the Texas Supreme Court, such a certification is possible in the appropriate case in light of the Supreme Court's past practice of certifying questions to other state high courts.[41]

Almost every state, except for Missouri and North Carolina, has some type of certification procedure, although these procedures vary in their scope. In Texas, article V, section 3-c is limited to certifications from "federal appellate courts," which does not extend to questions certified by other states or federal district courts. Other states, especially those relatively small in population, allow certified questions from federal district courts or sister

---

[38]396 S.W.2d 855, 860-63 (Tex. 1965).

[39]Senate Judiciary Committee, Bill Analysis, S.J.R. 10, § 1 R.S. (1985).

[40]*See* Pamela Stanton Baron, *Certified Questions To and From the Texas Supreme Court*, The Appellate Advocate XVII, No. 3, at 6, 9-10 (Winter 2005) (listing certified cases accepted and declined as of January 2005).

[41]*See, e.g.*, United States v. Juvenile Male, 130 S. Ct. 2518, 2519-20 (2010) (certifying question to Montana Supreme Court on the collateral state consequences of a juvenile's registration as a sex offender); Stewart v. Smith, 534 U.S. 157, 159-60 (2001) (certifying questions under Arizona certification procedure applicable to "federal courts" regarding proper interpretation of state rule of criminal procedure); Fiore v. White, 528 U.S. 23, 29-30 (1999) (certifying question to Pennsylvania Supreme Court regarding whether prior state court decision was a change in the law); Virginia v. Am. Booksellers Ass'n, Inc., 484 U.S. 383, 393-98 (1988) (certifying questions to Virginia Supreme Court regarding the reach of a state statute that made it unlawful to display sexually explicit material to juveniles); Aldrich v. Aldrich, 375 U.S. 249, 249-51 (1963) (certifying questions to Florida Supreme Court regarding the propriety under Florida law of decree ordering estate to continue to pay alimony); Dresner v. City of Tallahassee, 375 U.S. 136, 138-39 (1963) (certifying questions to Florida Supreme Court regarding appellate review of a state circuit court holding).

state appellate courts. The Supreme Court of Texas once employed one of these more expansive certification grants in a pending case, requesting the guidance of the Minnesota Supreme Court regarding a dispositive, unsettled issue of Minnesota law in *Minnesota Mining & Manufacturing Co. v. Nishika Ltd.*[42]

Declaratory Judgments and Advisory Opinions: How can Texas courts issue declaratory judgments without violating *Morrow*'s strict prohibition on advisory opinions? An uneasy tension exists between the prohibition on advisory opinions and declaratory judgments, which authorize a court to make a judicial declaration of the rights of the parties, sometimes before a tangible loss has actually been sustained.[43] Nevertheless, the two principles can be reconciled by restricting the availability of declaratory judgments to situations involving the binding adjudication of contested rights rather than a mere hypothetical future controversy. The Texas Supreme Court has accordingly held many declaratory judgment actions justiciable on the basis that a real controversy existed between the parties that would be actually determined by the requested declaration.[44]

In those situations, though, in which the controversy will not be resolved through a declaratory judgment, the action violates the prohibition on advisory opinions. *California Products, Inc. v. Puretex Lemon Juice, Inc.* provides an illustration.[45] California Products sought a declaration regarding whether a bottle it proposed to use to sell lemon and lime juice violated a prior injunction precluding the use of bottles resembling Puretex's bottles. The Texas Supreme Court held that the suit sought an advisory opinion because a decree that the bottle did violate the injunction would not settle the controversy between the parties. If the bottle violated the injunction, the court reasoned, California Products "could continue indefinitely to propose bottles of different sizes, shapes and colors on which it could seek an equally indefinite number of advisory opinions as to whether such bottles violate the injunction."[46] Thus, California Products's remedy was to sell its lemon and lime juice in a bottle that it did not believe violated the injunction and then defend its decision, if necessary, in a contempt proceeding. But what if the court had determined that the bottle did not violate the injunction? Would that have resolved the controversy between the parties? Why wasn't that sufficient to circumvent the prohibition on advisory opinions?

2. Texas Constitutional Justiciability Doctrines

Texas courts have long recognized doctrines of self-restraint limiting the types of cases appropriate for judicial disposition to those resolving mature, presently existing claims

---

[42]955 S.W.2d 853 (Tex. 1996) (certifying question on its own motion under Minnesota statutory procedure authorizing certification from other state appellate courts).

[43]*See* TEX. CIV. PRAC. & REM. CODE § 37.003-.004.

[44]*See, e.g.*, Farmers Tex. Cnty. Mut. Ins. Co. v. Griffin, 955 S.W.2d 81, 83 (Tex. 1997); Bd. of Water Eng's v. City of San Antonio, 283 S.W.2d 722, 724-25 (Tex. 1955); Cobb v. Harrington, 190 S.W.2d 709, 714-15 (Tex. 1945).

[45]334 S.W.2d 780 (Tex. 1960).

[46]*Id.* at 783.

concerning a justiciable interest between two or more adverse parties.[47] The core concern of these doctrines is preventing the courts from issuing advisory opinions impermissibly expounding on abstract questions of law,[48] which might occur, for instance, if the plaintiff's claim had not sufficiently matured,[49] the plaintiff did not have a justiciable interest to pursue,[50] or if the controversy had ceased and become moot.[51] In order to satisfy these justiciability constraints, there must be a real controversy between the parties that would be resolved by the requested relief.[52] Yet Texas courts had not explicitly grounded these doctrines in the text of the state constitution before the following case.

Texas Ass'n of Business v. Texas Air Control Board, 852 S.W.2d 440 (Tex. 1993)

CORNYN, Justice.

The Texas Association of Business (TAB), on behalf of its members, brought this declaratory judgment action seeking a ruling that statutes empowering two state administrative agencies to levy civil penalties for violations of their regulations conflict with the open courts and jury trial provisions of the Texas Constitution. The administrative agencies denied TAB's claims, and along with two Intervenors, filed counterclaims seeking a declaration that the same statutes and regulations comport with those constitutional provisions.

Following a bench trial, the trial court denied the relief sought by TAB, and as requested by the State and Intervenors, declared that section 4.041 of the Texas Clean Air Act, sections 26.136 and 27.1015 of the Texas Water Code, and section 8b of the Texas Solid Waste Disposal Act, as well as the rules and regulations promulgated under those statutes, are constitutional with regard to the open courts and jury trial provisions. We affirm the trial court's judgment as it relates to TAB's jury trial challenge and reverse its judgment as to TAB's open courts challenge.

Before we reach the merits of this case, we first consider the matter of the trial court's jurisdiction, as well as our own; specifically we determine whether TAB has standing to challenge the statutes and regulations in question. Because TAB's standing to bring this action is not readily apparent, and because our jurisdiction as well as that of the trial court depends on this issue, we requested supplemental briefing on standing at the oral argument of this case. In response, the parties insist that any question of standing has been

---

[47]*See* 1 ELAINE A. GRAFTON CARLSON, MCDONALD & CARLSON TEXAS CIVIL PRACTICE § 4.2 (2d ed. 2007).

[48]*See, e.g.*, Alamo Express, Inc. v. Union City Transfer, 309 S.W.2d 815, 827-28 (Tex. 1958); Bd. of Water Eng'rs v. City of San Antonio, 283 S.W.2d 722, 724 (Tex. 1955); City of New Braunfels v. City of San Antonio, 212 S.W.2d 817, 824-25 (Tex. Civ. App.–Austin 1948, writ ref'd n.r.e.); Brown Cnty. Life Ins. Co. v. Hagins, 110 S.W.2d 1162, 1163 (Tex. Civ. App.–Amarillo 1937, no writ); Stinson v. Graham, 286 S.W. 264, 265-66 (Tex. Civ. App.–Eastland 1926, writ ref'd).

[49]*See, e.g.*, *City of New Braunfels*, 212 S.W.2d at 824-25.

[50]*See, e.g.*, Davis v. First Nat'l Bank of Waco, 161 S.W.2d 467, 472-73 (Tex. 1942); Yett v. Cook, 281 S.W. 837, 841 (Tex. 1926); Harding v. Comm'rs Court of McLennan Cnty., 66 S.W. 44, 45 (Tex. 1902).

[51]*See, e.g.*, *Hagins*, 110 S.W.2d at 1163-64.

[52]*See, e.g.*, *Bd. of Water Eng'rs*, 283 S.W2d at 724.

waived in the trial court and cannot be raised by the court for the first time on appeal. We disagree.

Subject matter jurisdiction is essential to the authority of a court to decide a case. Standing is implicit in the concept of subject matter jurisdiction. The standing requirement stems from two limitations on subject matter jurisdiction: the separation of powers doctrine and, in Texas, the open courts provision. Subject matter jurisdiction is never presumed and cannot be waived.

One limit on courts' jurisdiction under both the state and federal constitutions is the separation of powers doctrine. *See* Tex. Const. art. II, § 1; *Valley Forge Christian College v. Americans United for Separation of Church and State,* 454 U.S. 464, 471-74 (1982). Under this doctrine, governmental authority vested in one department of government cannot be exercised by another department unless expressly permitted by the constitution. Thus we have construed our separation of powers article to prohibit courts from issuing advisory opinions because such is the function of the executive rather than the judicial department. *Firemen's Ins. Co. v. Burch,* 442 S.W.2d 331, 333 (Tex.1969); *Morrow v. Corbin*, 62 S.W.2d 641, 644 (Tex.1933).

The distinctive feature of an advisory opinion is that it decides an abstract question of law without binding the parties. *Alabama State Fed'n of Labor v. McAdory,* 325 U.S. 450, 461 (1945); *Firemen's Ins. Co.,* 442 S.W.2d at 333. An opinion issued in a case brought by a party without standing is advisory because rather than remedying an actual or imminent harm, the judgment addresses only a hypothetical injury. *See Allen v. Wright,* 468 U.S. 737, 751 (1984). Texas courts, like federal courts, have no jurisdiction to render such opinions.

The separation of powers doctrine is not the only constitutional basis for standing. Under federal law, standing is also an aspect of the Article III limitation of the judicial power to "cases" and "controversies." To comport with Article III, a federal court may hear a case only when the litigant has been threatened with or has sustained an injury. *Valley Forge Christian College,* 454 U.S. at 471. Under the Texas Constitution, standing is implicit in the open courts provision, which contemplates access to the courts only for those litigants suffering an injury. Specifically, the open courts provision provides:

> All courts shall be open, and every person for an **injury** done him, in his lands, goods, person or reputation, shall have remedy by due course of law.

Tex. Const. art. I, § 13 (emphasis added). Because standing is a constitutional prerequisite to maintaining a suit under both federal and Texas law, we look to the more extensive jurisprudential experience of the federal courts on this subject for any guidance it may yield.

Under federal law, a lack of standing deprives a court of subject matter jurisdiction because standing is an element of such jurisdiction. Other states have followed this analysis in construing their own constitutions. *See e.g., Prudential-Bache Sec., Inc. v. Commissioner of Revenue*, 588 N.E.2d 639, 642 (Mass. 1992); *Bennett v. Board of Trustees for Univ. of N. Colorado,* 782 P.2d 1214, 1216 (Colo.App.1989), *cert. denied,* 797 P.2d 748

(Colo.1990); *Pace Constr. Co. v. Missouri Highway and Transp. Comm'n*, 759 S.W.2d 272, 274 (Mo.App.1988); *Terracor v. Utah Bd. of State Lands & Forestry,* 716 P.2d 796, 798-99 (Utah 1986); *State by McClure v. Sports and Health Club, Inc.,* 370 N.W.2d 844, 850 (Minn.1985), *appeal dism'd,* 478 U.S. 1015 (1986); *Smith v. Allstate Ins. Co.,* 483 A.2d 344, 346 (Me.1984); *Ardmare Constr. Co. v. Freedman,* 467 A.2d 674, 675 n.4, 676-77 (Conn. 1983); *Horn v. County of Ventura,* 596 P.2d 1134, 1142 (Cal. 1979); *Stewart v. Board of County Comm'rs of Big Horn County,* 573 P.2d 184, 186, 188 (Mont. 1977); *State ex rel. Albritton v. Moore,* 116 So.2d 502, 504 (La. 1959).

Subject matter jurisdiction is an issue that may be raised for the first time on appeal; it may not be waived by the parties. This court recently reiterated that axiom in *Gorman v. Life Insurance Co.,* 811 S.W.2d 542, 547 (Tex.), *cert. denied*, 502 U.S. 824 (1991). Because we conclude that standing is a component of subject matter jurisdiction, it cannot be waived and may be raised for the first time on appeal.[53]

If we were to conclude that standing is unreviewable on appeal at least three undesirable consequences could result. First and foremost, appellate courts would be impotent to prevent lower courts from exceeding their constitutional and statutory limits of authority. Second, appellate courts could not arrest collusive suits. Third, by operation of the doctrines of res judicata and collateral estoppel, judgments rendered in suits addressing only hypothetical injuries could bar relitigation of issues by a litigant who eventually suffers an actual injury. We therefore hold that standing, as a component of subject matter jurisdiction, cannot be waived in this or any other case and may be raised for the first time on appeal by the parties or by the court.

We are aware that this holding conflicts with *Texas Industrial Traffic League v. Railroad Commission,* 633 S.W.2d 821, 823 (Tex.1982) (per curiam). The analysis that leads us to the conclusion we reach here, however, compels us to overrule *Texas Industrial Traffic League* and disapprove of all cases relying on it to the extent that they conflict with this opinion. Although our concern for the rule of stare decisis makes us hesitant to overrule any case, when constitutional principles are at issue this court as a practical matter is the only government institution with the power and duty to correct such errors.

Consequently, we proceed to determine here, on our own motion, whether TAB has standing to bring this suit.

TAB asserts standing on behalf of its members. The general test for standing in Texas requires that there "(a) shall be a real controversy between the parties, which (b) will be actually determined by the judicial declaration sought." *Board of Water Engineers v. City of San Antonio,* 283 S.W.2d 722, 724 (Tex. 1955). Texas, however, has no particular test for determining the standing of an organization, such as TAB. While we agree with the statement of the general test for standing set out in *Board of Water Engineers,* we foresee

---

[53]Justice Doggett disagrees that standing is a component of subject matter jurisdiction, yet he declines to explain what role standing plays in our jurisprudence. From his harsh critique of the doctrine, it seems that he not only objects to the conclusion that standing cannot be waived but also to the conclusion that standing is a requirement to initiate a lawsuit.

difficulties in relying on it alone to determine the standing of an organization like TAB.

The United States Supreme Court has articulated a standard for associational standing that lends itself to our use. We adopt that test today. In *Hunt v. Washington State Apple Advertising Commission,* the Court held that an association has standing to sue on behalf of its members when "(a) its members would otherwise have standing to sue in their own right; (b) the interests it seeks to protect are germane to the organization's purpose; and (c) neither the claim asserted nor the relief requested requires the participation of individual members in the lawsuit." 432 U.S. 333, 343 (1977). This standard incorporates the standing analysis we adopted in *Board of Water Engineers,* yet addresses the additional concerns we have noted.

We now apply the *Hunt* standard to the case before us. Reviewing the record in its entirety for evidence supporting subject matter jurisdiction, and resolving any doubt in TAB's favor, we conclude that TAB has standing to pursue the relief it seeks in this case.
* * * *

[The majority's holdings on the right to jury trial and open courts challenge are discussed in Chapter 5.]

DOGGETT, Justice, concurring & dissenting.

The issue of standing is a stranger to this litigation. No party before this court has ever asserted that the Texas Association of Business lacked capacity to challenge the actions of state government. How rare the occasion when all litigants agree on the proper resolution of an issue, but how truly extraordinary is such unanimity when the parties are two state regulatory agencies, the Texas Association of Business, the Sierra Club and the League of Women Voters. This, nonetheless, is the exceptional circumstance in which we find ourselves today as all of these diverse parties have urged the court not to decide this matter in the manner adopted. Addressing the question of standing solely at the belated insistence of the majority, all parties asserted that this issue was not in dispute; that, under recent precedent, standing had been waived; and, alternatively, that the record adequately demonstrated the right of the Texas Association of Business under Texas law to initiate this litigation.

This court has repeatedly held that the issue of standing may not be raised for the first time on appeal, either by the parties or by the court. In *Texas Industrial Traffic League v. Railroad Comm'n of Texas,* 633 S.W.2d 821, 822-23 (Tex.1982), we concluded:

> A party's lack of justiciable interest must be pointed out to the trial court . . . in a written plea in abatement, and a ruling thereon must be obtained or the matter is waived. No plea challenging the standing of [the party] was filed in the district court. *The issue of standing was therefore waived, and the court of appeals erred in writing on the issue at all.*

(Emphasis supplied). The sole issue presented in *Coffee v. William Marsh Rice University,* 403 S.W.2d 340 (Tex.1966), was whether the court of appeals erred in dismissing a case, on its own motion, for want of standing. This court held that, because standing had not been challenged in the trial court, that issue could not deprive the court of appeals of subject matter jurisdiction.

Time and time again, the courts of appeals have also refused to consider challenges to standing not first raised in the trial court. Until today, the only criticism of our prior holdings to this effect has consisted primarily of writings authored by one appellate judge.

[T]he majority vaults standing to a new and remarkable prominence by suddenly discovering that it has not just *one* but *two* constitutional bases. And what unusual constitutional pillars each of these new finds represents. First, the proscription of the separation of powers doctrine against issuance of advisory judicial opinions allegedly requires rigorous enforcement of standing even when no party debates its existence.

The second newly-announced constitutional basis is our state's vital guarantee that "[a]ll courts shall be open," Tex. Const. art. I, § 13, in some inexplicable way, mandates that they be closed to some and requires continual judicial monitoring of all who attempt to enter. No authority of any type is cited for this proposition that "open" courts really means "closed" courts. Nothing in the history or text of the provision justifies this reading nor has any Texas court previously attempted such converse interpretation.

Then, with a final flourish, standing is conveniently classified as a nonwaivable component of subject matter jurisdiction. Until today, Texas followed the rule, adopted by many of our sister states considering the issue, that objections to a party's standing are waived if not first raised in the trial court. No Texas case is cited for the proposition that standing is part of nonwaivable subject matter jurisdiction because, until today, this court had repeatedly stated precisely the very opposite – that standing is *not* jurisdictional.

Three purported policy justifications for the majority's actions are offered, with not a single supporting authority. The first concern is that a strict standing rule is necessary to prevent collusive litigation. Under Texas law, the filing of a fictitious suit constitutes contempt by counsel, Tex.R.Civ.P. 13, and may serve as the basis for a host of sanctions, including dismissal with prejudice. Adhering to precedent today would in no way undermine the power to dismiss fraudulent suits.

The second virtue proclaimed for today's holding is the guarantee that the lower courts will be restrained from exceeding their jurisdictional powers. This concern is derived solely from the federal law mandate that a federal appellate court is duty-bound to verify not only its own jurisdiction but that of the lower courts as well. Federal courts, however, have limited jurisdiction; Texas courts do not. Our Texas Constitution creates courts of general jurisdiction, investing them with all of the "judicial power of this State." Tex. Const. art. V, § 1.

Lastly, the majority expresses concern as to the res judicata effect on other potential litigants of a judgment rendered in the absence of genuine standing. Aware of this concern, the very federal judiciary that this majority is so eager to emulate has failed to perceive it as a problem of significance. If representation is inadequate, or a conflict of interest between members exists, any judgment will have minimal preclusive effect.

In defining state requirements for standing, we are in no way bound by federal jurisprudence founded upon converse jurisdictional principles from our own. Texas courts can afford their citizens access to justice in circumstances where they would have been unable to establish standing in the federal courts. *See City of Los Angeles v. Lyons,* 461 U.S. 95, 113 (1983) ("state courts need not impose the same standing . . . requirements that govern federal-court proceedings"); *Doremus v. Board of Education,* 342 U.S. 429, 434 (1952) (state courts not restrained by "case or controversy" limitations of Federal Constitution); *Greer v. Illinois Housing Development Auth.,* 524 N.E.2d 561 (Ill. 1988) ("We are not, of course, required to follow the Federal law on issues of justiciability and standing.").

The differences between our Texas Constitution and the Federal Constitution not only justify, but also require, that citizen groups be accorded a broader right of access to our state courts. The Texas Constitution contains no express limitation of courts' jurisdiction to "cases" or "controversies," as provided by the federal charter. U.S. Const. art. III, § 2. Instead, it affirmatively protects the rights of litigants to gain access to our judicial system:

> All courts shall be open, and every person for an injury done him, in his lands, goods, person or reputation, shall have remedy by due course of law.

Tex. Const. art. 1, § 13. This constitutional mandate is reflected in decisions of this court adopting an "open courts" approach to standing in general and associational standing in particular. On several occasions, we have recognized the power of the Legislature to exempt litigants from proof of "special injury." *Scott v. Board of Adjustment,* 405 S.W.2d 55, 56 (Tex.1966) (standing may be shown even in the absence of particular damage); *Spence v. Fenchler,* 180 S.W. 597 (Tex. 1915) (under statute, "any citizen" able to seek injunction, without showing particular interest or personal damage).

The majority works a grave disservice to our Texas Constitution by equating our open courts provision, affirmatively guaranteeing all Texans access to our judicial system, with an express federal constitutional limitation on the right to seek redress in court. Despite the fact that the two provisions are vastly different in language, history and purpose, the majority nonetheless determines to "look to the more extensive jurisprudential experience of the federal courts" to determine standing.

Notes on Standing and Justiciability in Texas

The Source and Substance of Texas Standing Doctrine: Because the Texas judicial article does not have a "case or controversy" requirement, what are the textual state constitutional bases for the standing doctrine in Texas? The court mentions two: (1) the separation of powers provision and (2) the "injury" language in the open courts provision. The supreme court and the courts of appeals have repeatedly reaffirmed since *Texas Ass'n of Business* that Texas standing doctrine is premised on both these provisions.[54] Although

---

[54] *See, e.g.*, Tex. Dep't of Transp. v. City of Sunset Valley, 146 S.W.3d 637, 646 (Tex. 2004); Brown v. Todd, 53 S.W.3d 297, 302 (Tex. 2001); M.D. Anderson Cancer Ctr. v. Novak, 52 S.W.3d 704, 708 (Tex. 2001).

predicating standing on separation of powers principles is common in both state and federal courts,[55] Texas appears to be the only jurisdiction out of forty with similar clauses to use its open courts provision as a basis for its standing doctrine. The more typical employment of the open courts guarantee as an individual right is discussed in Chapter 5.

After determining the constitutional sources for the state standing doctrine, the court next concluded that standing is part of subject matter jurisdiction, which means that it cannot be waived. Justice Doggett disagreed, relying on several Texas precedents holding that standing was waivable if not timely asserted. But if standing is not part of subject matter jurisdiction, what is it? Does Justice Doggett's dissent ever provide a satisfactory answer to that question? Can the dissent and the case it predominantly relied upon, *Texas Industrial Traffic League*, be reconciled with *Morrow v. Corbin*, discussed earlier in this chapter? Doesn't a suit brought by a litigant without standing seek an advisory opinion by definition?

Is the dissent's real concern with the *substance* of federal standing doctrine that the majority appears willing to examine for guidance? Federal standing doctrine has been frequently criticized by commentators, especially to the extent that it limits the ability of Congress to grant citizens standing to pursue environmental and other public interest claims.[56] In *Lujan v. Defenders of the Wildlife*, the Supreme Court held that, because standing is constitutionally based, Congress could not legislatively authorize plaintiffs who had not suffered a constitutionally sufficient injury to maintain claims in federal court.[57] In Texas, in contrast, earlier supreme court decisions have held that the legislature could authorize standing to individuals without a particularized individual injury.[58] Does *Texas Ass'n of Business* impact these holdings? In other words, does concluding that standing is a constitutional requirement and part of subject matter jurisdiction hamper the legislature's statutory authority to provide greater access to the courts?

---

[55] *See, e.g.*, Allen v. Wright, 468 U.S. 737, 752 (1984) (expressing that standing is "built on a single basic idea–the idea of separation of powers"); Bd. of Dirs., Metro Wastewater Reclamation Dist. v. Nat'l Union Fire Ins. Co. of Pittsburgh, Pa., 105 P.3d 653, 656 (Colo. 2005) ("In the separation of powers design of Colorado government, courts limit their exercise of judicial power through jurisprudential doctrines that include standing, mootness, and ripeness, to establish parameters for the principled exercise of judicial authority."); Nat'l Wildlife Fed'n v. Cleveland Cliffs Iron Co., 684 N.W.2d 800, 810 (Mich. 2004) ("Thus, we continue to adhere to . . . [the] holding that questions of standing implicate the constitutional separation of powers, and that forsaking this proposition 'would imperil the constitutional architecture.'"); Hinesburg Sand & Gravel Co. v. State, 693 A.2d 1045, 1048 (Vt. 1997) ("Standing doctrine is fundamentally rooted in respect for the separation of powers of the independent branches of government.").

[56] *See, e.g.*, William V. Dorsaneo, III, *The Enigma of Standing Doctrine in Texas Courts*, 28 REV. LITIG. 35, 37-57 (2008); William A. Fletcher, *The Structure of Standing*, 98 YALE L.J. 221, 221-24 (1988); Cass R. Sunstein, *What's Standing After* Lujan*? Of Citizens Suits, "Injuries," and Article III*, 91 MICH. L. REV. 163, 166-67 (1992).

[57] 504 U.S. 555, 573-78 (1992).

[58] *See, e.g.*, Scott v. Bd. of Adjustment, 405 S.W.2d 55, 56-57 (Tex. 1966) (holding that taxpayers had standing under state statute to maintain suit for an injunction against the erection of a large sign without a showing of a particularized injury); Spence v. Fenchler, 180 S.W. 597, 603 (Tex. 1915) (holding that taxpayers had standing under state statute to maintain suit for an injunction against a bawdyhouse without alleging a particularized injury). This exception only applies, however, if the statute specifically allows any citizen or any taxpayer to bring suit, rather than merely providing a remedy for persons "harmed," "aggrieved," or "adversely affected." *See Scott*, 405 S.W.2d at 56; *cf.* Andrade v. NAACP of Austin, 345 S.W.3d 1, 17 (Tex. 2011).

While a theoretical evaluation might arguably support a different conclusion, so far state judicial doctrine answers the question "no." Although the state supreme court has only mentioned the issue in dicta,[59] Texas courts of appeals have continued to uphold legislatively conferred standing after *Texas Ass'n of Business*.[60] This apparent continued approval of legislatively conferred standing comports with the state judiciary's approach in other aspects of standing doctrine. While Texas courts have borrowed from the "more extensive jurisprudential experience of the federal courts" in resolving standing issues not specifically addressed in prior Texas decisions, such as the standing of organizations,[61] legislators,[62] voters,[63] and those asserting common law claims,[64] the courts have declined to examine or follow federal standing doctrine if Texas cases have previously resolved the issue.[65] Texas courts have thus primarily borrowed from federal precedents to fill in gaps in state standing doctrine in those situations in which the federal standards can be harmonized with existing state law, instead of entirely adopting federal standing jurisprudence.

Other Texas Constitutional Justiciability Doctrines: Texas decisions addressing other state justiciability doctrines follow a similar pattern. The courts predominantly rely on past Texas precedent, but frequently borrow from consistent federal applications of the justiciability doctrines.

Ripeness: The Texas and federal standards on ripeness appear largely harmonious. In *Perry v. Del Rio*, the Texas Supreme Court, after holding that state law governed the ripeness of federal law claims in state court, concluded that, because there was no difference between the federal and state ripeness doctrines under the circumstances presented, it could rely equally on principles from federal case law.[66] The ripeness doctrines in both state and federal courts are designed to avoid premature adjudication of contingent or hypothetical claims by employing a functional approach examining the importance of the interest

---

[59]*See, e.g.*, Williams v. Lara, 52 S.W.3d 171, 178 (Tex. 2001) ("As a general rule of Texas law, to have standing, *unless it is conferred by statute*, a plaintiff must demonstrate that he or she possesses an interest in a conflict distinct from that of the general public, such that the defendant's actions have caused the plaintiff some particular injury.") (emphasis added).

[60]*See, e.g.*, Labrado v. Cnty. of El Paso, 132 S.W.3d 581, 587-88 (Tex. App.–El Paso 2004, no pet.) (holding losing bidder had statutory standing under the County Purchasing Act to seek an injunction against a contract alleged to violate the Act); Save Our Springs Alliance, Inc. v. Lowry, 934 S.W.2d 161, 163 (Tex. App.–Austin 1996, orig. proceeding) (holding group interested in the environment had standing to assert that a community college violated the Open Meetings Act in reaching its decision to acquire additional real estate to construct a new campus).

[61]Tex. Ass'n of Business v. Tex. Air Control Bd., 852 S.W.2d 440, 447 (Tex. 1993).

[62]*Brown*, 53 S.W.3d at 305.

[63]*Andrade*, 345 S.W.3d at 8-16.

[64]*See, e.g.*, DaimlerChrysler Corp. v. Inman, 252 S.W.3d 299, 304-07 (Tex. 2008) (borrowing requirements from federal law that plaintiff's injury must be "concrete and particularized, actual or imminent, not hypothetical").

[65]*See, e.g.*, W. Orange-Cove Consol. Indep. Sch. Dist. v. Alanis, 107 S.W.3d 558, 583-84 (Tex. 2003) (concluding school districts had standing under recent state standing precedents irrespective of the result under federal standing doctrine); Williams v. Lara, 52 S.W.3d 171, 179-82 (Tex. 2001) (employing state taxpayer standing rules rather than federal taxpayer standing doctrine).

[66]66 S.W.3d 239, 249-50 (Tex. 2001).

advanced, the extent of the injury or risk, the need for additional factual information to decide the substantive issues presented, and the sensitivity of the presented issues in the context of the federal system.[67] The Texas courts have accordingly frequently relied on cases and commentary regarding federal ripeness doctrine in resolving state ripeness queries.[68]

Mootness: Texas courts also borrow from federal mootness principles, as only slight differences exist between the state and federal doctrines. Mootness examines whether a controversy continues to exist between the parties at all stages of the proceedings.[69] Thus, if the defendant voluntarily satisfies the requested judgment,[70] if the right to possession expires in a forcible detainer action,[71] or if the defendant ceases to perform the types of services for which a prospective employee sought a position,[72] the case is moot. In most instances, Texas and federal courts appear to follow similar reasoning in ascertaining whether a proceeding is moot, despite certain distinctions between the state and federal doctrines regarding the appropriate judgment to be rendered in moot causes.[73] As one example, *Miga v. Jensen* held that the same rule exists in Texas and federal courts regarding the circumstances in which the payment of a judgment moots an appeal.[74]

Several exceptions to the mootness doctrine are recognized in both state and federal courts. These include those situations that are capable of repetition, yet evading review because the challenged action may occur to the plaintiff again while the short duration of each injury prevents final judicial resolution,[75] or that involve collateral consequences that will adversely impact the party seeking to appeal the judgment even if the underlying

---

[67]*See id.* at 251-52; Waco Indep. Sch. Dist. v. Gibson, 22 S.W.3d 849, 851-52 (Tex. 2000); Patterson v. Planned Parenthood of Houston & Se. Tex., Inc., 971 S.W.2d 439, 442-43 (Tex. 1998).

[68]*See, e.g.*, *Perry*, 66 S.W.3d at 249-52; *Patterson*, 971 S.W.2d at 442-43; Mayhew v. Town of Sunnyvale, 964 S.W.2d 922, 928 (Tex. 1998); City of Anson v. Harper, 216 S.W.3d 384, 390 (Tex. App.–Eastland 2006, no pet.). *But see* Hallco Tex., Inc. v. McMullen Cnty., 221 S.W.3d 50, 59 (Tex. 2006) (recognizing that the ripeness of a state taking claim cannot be measured by the same standard as the ripeness of a federal takings claim because a federal claim does not ripen until state court proceedings have been concluded).

[69]Marshall v. Housing Auth. of San Antonio, 198 S.W.3d 782, 787 (Tex. 2006); *Williams*, 52 S.W.3d at 184.

[70]Employees Finance Co. v. Lathram, 369 S.W.2d 927, 930 (Tex. 1963).

[71]*Marshall*, 198 S.W.3d at 787.

[72]Speer v. Presbyterian Children's Home & Serv. Agency, 847 S.W.2d 227, 228 (Tex. 1993).

[73]*See, e.g.*, Panterra Corp. v. Am. Dairy Queen, 908 S.W.2d 300, 300-01 (Tex. App.–San Antonio 1995, no writ) (discussing long-established Texas rule that all previous orders and judgments are vacated and the cause is dismissed when a cause becomes moot on appeal in Texas state court, despite the fact that vacatur is not automatically required in federal court under similar circumstances).

[74]96 S.W.3d 207, 212 (Tex. 2002). The dissent, however, claimed that Texas had previously followed a different rule. *See id.* at 223-26 (Schneider, J., dissenting).

[75]Tex. A&M Univ.–Kingsville v. Yarbrough, 347 S.W.3d 289, 290-91 (Tex. 2011) (holding suit challenging associate professor's performance evaluation mooted after professor granted tenure as potential challenges to future evaluations were not of such short duration that review could not be obtained); *Williams*, 52 S.W.3d at 184-85 (holding that inmates' claims were moot because it was not likely they would be incarcerated again); Blum v. Lanier, 997 S.W.2d 259, 264 (Tex. 1999) (holding suit challenging allegedly misleading ballot language was capable of repetition, yet evading review).

judgment is vacated.[76] Texas and federal courts also both recognize that a class action lawsuit does not become moot merely because the individual claims of the named plaintiffs are mooted.[77]

Some Texas appellate courts have also recognized an additional exception to the mootness doctrine that is not recognized under federal justiciability standards, the "public interest" exception, which authorizes "appellate review of an issue of considerable importance if that issue is capable of repetition between either the same parties or other members of the public, but for some reason evades appellate review."[78] The Texas Supreme Court, however, has not determined whether to recognize the exception. The supreme court refused to consider the issue in *FDIC v. Nueces County* because its suggested requirements had not even been met,[79] and then has not mentioned the exception at all in subsequent opinions, including *Williams v. Lara*, excerpted in the next subsection of this book. Other Texas appellate courts have accordingly declined to recognize the public interest exception.[80]

The only apparent difference between the public interest exception and the capable of repetition, yet evading review exception is that the public interest exception dispenses with the requirement that the issue be capable of repetition to the same parties as long as it is capable of repetition with other members of the public and it is of sufficient public importance. The public interest exception would thus presumably apply to cases such as *DeFunis v. Odegaard*, where the Supreme Court held that a challenge to a law school's admissions program was moot once the challenging student graduated because that student would never be considered by the admissions program again.[81] Under the public interest exception, as long as the admissions program was still being employed against other members of the public, and the courts had not previously resolved the issue, the controversy would not be moot. But only relatively infrequently would the application of the public interest exception lead to a different result in a particular case.

---

[76] *Yarbrough*, 347 S.W.3d at 291 (holding possible taint of a negative performance summary after professor granted tenure was not a sufficient collateral consequence to support an exception to mootness doctrine); *Marshall*, 198 S.W.3d at 788 (holding that vacating underlying judgment would preclude any collateral consequences from forcible detainer action); State v. Lodge, 608 S.W.2d 910, 912 (Tex. 1980) (holding collateral consequences existed from involuntary commitment to mental hospital); Carillo v. State, 480 S.W.2d 612, 616-17 (Tex. 1972) (holding collateral consequences existed for minor's adjudication as juvenile delinquent).

[77] Heckman v. Williamson Cnty., 369 S.W.3d 137, 162-65 (Tex. 2012) (adopting federal exception to mootness for class actions involving "inherently transitory" claims that are so short-lived that the certification determination cannot be made before the named plaintiffs' claims become moot).

[78] *See, e.g.*, Ngo v. Ngo, 133 S.W.3d 688, 692 (Tex. App.–Corpus Christi 2003, no pet.); Securtec, Inc. v. Cnty. of Gregg, 106 S.W.3d 803, 810-11 (Tex. App.–Texarkana 2003, pet. denied); Univ. Interscholastic League v. Buchanan, 848 S.W.2d 298, 304 (Tex. App.–Austin 1993, no writ) (adopting public interest exception and noting that thirty-six other states apparently follow the doctrine).

[79] 886 S.W.2d 766, 767 (Tex. 1994). The Court reasoned that the issue did not evade review because other courts had previously addressed the same issue. *Id.* at 767.

[80] *See, e.g.*, Houston Chronicle Publ'g Co. v. Thomas, 196 S.W.3d 396, 399-400 (Tex. App.–Houston [1st Dist.] 2006, no pet.) (refusing to recognize public interest exception and citing prior unpublished opinions as support); Olson v. Comm'n for Lawyer Discipline, 901 S.W.2d 520, 523 n.2 (Tex. App.–El Paso 1995, no writ).

[81] 416 U.S. 312, 318-20 (1974).

The Political Question Doctrine: Texas courts have long recognized that the final resolution of certain controversies is committed to the other departments of Texas government. In *Ferguson v. Maddox*, for example, the state supreme court reasoned that the Texas Senate, as long as it was acting within its constitutional jurisdiction, possessed the sole and final power regarding trying an impeachment proceeding against a state official.[82]

A related doctrine limits judicial review in Texas to only self-executing constitutional provisions, which are those supplying "a sufficient rule by means of which the right given may be enjoyed or protected, or the duty imposed may be enforced."[83] The underlying rationale is that, when the constitutional provision at issue only concerns mere abstractions or generalities, the judiciary has no basis to ascertain a legally enforceable standard. In the only state supreme court decision employing this doctrine to bar a judicial proceeding, *City of Corpus Christi v. City of Pleasanton*, the court held that article XVI, section 59 of the Texas Constitution, which requires the legislature to pass all such laws as may be appropriate to the conservation and development of the state's natural resources, did not provide the courts an appropriate basis to review the legislature's conservation efforts in establishing conduits and reservoirs.[84] But in other cases, the court has recognized that, while a specified constitutional provision may not provide a basis for the judiciary to decree the sole method for compliance, the provision is specific enough for the judiciary to invalidate any legislative solution that fails to satisfy constitutionally imposed mandates.[85]

These longstanding state doctrines share similar goals as the political question doctrine in the federal courts, which is designed to prevent judicial decisions on questions when there is a textually demonstrable constitutional commitment to a coordinate political department, a lack of judicially discoverable and manageable standards for resolution, or the potential for inter-branch embarrassment or conflict from a judicial disposition.[86] While the Texas Supreme Court has recognized the possibility that certain cases may involve nonjusticiable political questions under state separation of powers principles, it has never dismissed an action on the grounds that review was barred by the political question doctrine.[87] Nor has the supreme court adopted the same federal factors for analyzing political questions, instead merely "[a]ssuming that the same tests would serve equally well in defining the separation of powers in the state government under the Texas Constitution."[88]

---

[82]263 S.W. 888, 893-94 (Tex. 1924).

[83]Mitchell Cnty. v. City Nat'l Bank, 43 S.W. 880, 883-84 (Tex. 1898).

[84]276 S.W.2d 798, 803 (Tex. 1955).

[85]*See, e.g.*, Neeley v. W. Orange-Cove Consol. Indep. Sch. Dist., 176 S.W.3d 746, 782-83 (Tex. 2005) (holding that article VII, section 1 of the Texas Constitution, requiring the legislature to establish an efficient system of public free schools, was "self-executing insofar as it prohibits any system that fails to meet [its] standards"); *Mitchell Cnty.*, 43 S.W. at 883-84 (holding constitutional provisions regarding the financing and constructing of jails, courthouses, and bridges were self-executing only to the extent that conflicting laws were prohibited).

[86]Baker v. Carr, 369 U.S. 186, 217 (1963).

[87]*Neeley*, 176 S.W.3d at 780; Edgewood Indep. Sch. Dist. v. Kirby, 777 S.W.2d 391, 394 (Tex. 1989).

[88]*Neeley*, 176 S.W.3d at 778-79.

The political question doctrine in Texas state court is thus somewhat of an enigma. The typical federal political question criteria have not been adopted, although there are similarities between the federal political question doctrine and earlier Texas decisions on self-executing constitutional provisions and constitutional commitments to coordinate branches. But even assuming Texas courts borrowed from the federal *articulation* of the political question doctrine, the *application* would not necessarily be the same. As the division of powers among the branches or departments of government is not coextensive in the state and federal constitutions, federal determinations on textual commitments and the appropriate role of the judiciary could not control similar questions under the Texas Constitution.

State Justiciability and Adequate and Independent State Grounds: Would the holdings in cases such as *Texas Ass'n of Business* satisfy the strictures of the adequate and independent state grounds doctrine as expressed in *Michigan v. Long*? Or should questions of justiciability in state court always be presumed to rest on adequate and independent state grounds because of the nature of the federal system? The answer is evident from a significant silence–the United States Supreme Court has never held that a state court's justiciability determination did not rest on adequate and independent state grounds. Because the constraints of Article III of the United States Constitution do not apply to state courts, the only possible source of a state court justiciability holding is state law, precluding the possibility of Supreme Court review.

3. Texas Taxpayer Standing

Another frequently encountered justiciability doctrine in state constitutional law concerns taxpayer standing. As discussed previously in this chapter, the vast majority of the states authorize taxpayer standing to a greater extent than allowed under federal standing doctrine. The following case addresses taxpayer standing in Texas.

Williams v. Lara, 52 S.W.3d 171 (Tex. 2001)

Justice HANKINSON delivered the opinion of the Court.

This case involves a dispute over a religious-education program in a Tarrant County jail facility. Our inquiry focuses on the Chaplain's Education Unit (CEU), a separate unit within the Tarrant County Corrections Center (TCCC), where inmates can volunteer for instruction in a curriculum approved by the sheriff and director of chaplaincy at the jail as consistent with the sheriff's and chaplain's views of Christianity. Ruth Maree Lara and Lee Huff, former inmates at the TCCC, and Dr. Ronald Flowers, a Tarrant County resident, sued Tarrant County and its sheriff, David Williams (collectively, "the County"), for operating the CEU in violation of the Establishment, Free Exercise, and Equal Protection Clauses of the United States and Texas Constitutions, and for violating their civil rights under 42 U.S.C. § 1983. The plaintiffs asserted claims for damages, injunctive and declaratory relief, and attorney's fees.

I. Background

The Tarrant County Corrections Center is a county jail facility that houses inmates who are serving sentences, awaiting trial, or awaiting transfer to the Texas Department of

Criminal Justice. The Chaplain's Education Unit is one of many jail pods, or cluster of jail cells within the TCCC, where inmates live. Tarrant County, at the behest of Warden James Skidmore and other county employees, created the original CEU in 1992. It was initially open only to male inmates, but a women's CEU was added the following year. Admission to the CEU is voluntary. To be admitted, an inmate must receive security clearance. He or she also must sign an "Application and Agreement," acknowledging that the CEU is "based on orthodox Christian biblical principles" and confirming a willingness to "cooperate fully with the program." Inmates are admitted into the CEU for 120 days and then released back into the jail's general population.

The CEU's purported goals are to promote rehabilitation and reduce violence, which, according to the Director of Chaplaincy, Hugh Atwell, are best accomplished through the teaching of what Williams and Atwell labeled "orthodox Christianity." Atwell explained their views as "generally believing in Jesus Christ as deity, with the Bible being the scripture that is utilized in that belief system . . . and that the scripture is holy and it is accepted as an infallible truth," and that a person must be "born again" to attain salvation. Sheriff Williams and Chaplain Atwell testified that they would not allow instructors to discuss any other religious viewpoint, and the sheriff acknowledged that he would limit what could be taught in the CEU to that which comported with his own personal religious views. As part of the CEU program, inmates are taught in accordance with those views at least four hours a day. They spend the rest of their day completing assignments, studying the Bible, and reviewing other religious books or videotapes. Volunteer chaplains teach the inmates using donated materials. To maintain their positions, the volunteer chaplains must remain members in good standing of a local church.

Sheriff Williams had ultimate authority over and responsibility for the county jail, see Tex. Loc. Gov't Code § 351.041, which in this case includes the CEU and its curriculum. Chaplain Atwell was second-in-command. Like the sheriff, he was a paid employee of Tarrant County. Chaplain Atwell interviewed and selected the CEU's volunteer instructors, who were subject to background checks, and met with them weekly. He also met weekly with Sheriff Williams to apprise him of the CEU's progress and to discuss periodically the CEU's curriculum. Directly under Chaplain Atwell was Volunteer Chaplain Don Anderson, the CEU Director. Anderson was responsible for the CEU's daily operation. He was not a county-paid employee but was required to work a minimum of thirty hours a week to retain his position.

Except for a Tuesday night service, which is open to the jail's general population but follows the same curriculum as does the CEU, living in the CEU is the only opportunity county jail inmates have for any type of group religious study. Plaintiffs Ruth Maree Lara and Lee Huff are former TCCC inmates who did not participate in the CEU program. They, along with Dr. Ronald Flowers, a Tarrant County resident and taxpayer, sued Tarrant County and Sheriff Williams.

II. Standing

Standing is a constitutional prerequisite to maintaining suit in either federal or state court. *See Texas Ass'n of Bus. v. Texas Air Control Bd.,* 852 S.W.2d 440, 444 (Tex.1993). The parties in this case assert standing on various grounds. Alleging taxpayer standing, Flowers relies on his status as a Tarrant County property taxpayer, and Lara relies on her payment of rent and sales tax. Alternatively, Lara and Huff claim that as former TCCC inmates, they have suffered injuries sufficiently particular to confer standing. Relying on state law to analyze the standing issues, we address each of the parties' arguments separately. *See Bateman v. Arizona,* 429 U.S. 1302, 1305 (1976) ("The courts of a State are free to follow their own jurisprudence as to who may raise a federal constitutional question....").

Taxpayer Standing

As a general rule of Texas law, to have standing, unless it is conferred by statute, a plaintiff must demonstrate that he or she possesses an interest in a conflict distinct from that of the general public, such that the defendant's actions have caused the plaintiff some particular injury. *See Hunt v. Bass,* 664 S.W.2d 323, 324 (Tex.1984). Taxpayers, however, fall under a limited exception to this general rule. *See Bland Indep. Sch. Dist. v. Blue,* 34 S.W.3d 547, 556 (Tex.2000). Taxpayers in Texas have standing to enjoin the illegal expenditure of public funds, and need not demonstrate a particularized injury. *See id.; Calvert v. Hull,* 475 S.W.2d 907, 908 (Tex.1972); *Osborne v. Keith*, 177 S.W.2d 198, 200 (Tex. 1944). Implicit in this rule are two requirements: (1) that the plaintiff is a taxpayer; and (2) that public funds are expended on the allegedly illegal activity. *See Bland,* 34 S.W.3d at 556; *Calvert,* 475 S.W.2d at 908; *Osborne,* 177 S.W.2d at 200.

Flowers asserts that his status as a Tarrant County resident and property taxpayer gives him taxpayer standing to pursue his claims. He argues that because taxpayers have standing to enjoin the illegal expenditure of public funds, and public funds are required to administer the CEU, he has standing as a taxpayer to enjoin its illegal operation. According to Flowers, the County spends tax dollars to feed, clothe, and house the prisoners who participate in the CEU program. And he emphasizes that Sheriff Williams and Chaplain Atwell were county-paid employees, and that their time was partially occupied with supervising and monitoring the CEU.

Applying the same reasoning, Lara maintains that she too has standing as a taxpayer. Unlike Flowers, however, Lara does not own property and thus does not pay property taxes. She alleges that her taxpayer standing arises from her payment of rent on her Tarrant County residence and her payment of sales tax on the goods she purchases. Lara urges that her interest as a taxpayer is not lessened simply because she pays taxes when she purchases products rather than in connection with the ownership of property.

Tarrant County responds that neither Flowers nor Lara has standing as a taxpayer. First, it asserts that no authority supports Lara's contention that paying rent and sales tax confers taxpayer status. Second, the County contends that even if Lara is a taxpayer, neither she nor Flowers can prove that public funds are expended in operating the CEU. While we agree with the County that Lara is not a taxpayer for purposes of standing, we disagree that public funds are not expended in administering the CEU.

Whether Lara has taxpayer standing depends upon the type of tax she claims to have paid. Lara alleges that both her payment of rent on her Tarrant County residence and her payment of sales tax on the goods she purchases bestow taxpayer standing on her. We are unable to find any authority to support her contention that paying rent secures her status as a taxpayer. Lara is not liable to Tarrant County for the tax on the property she rents, and even if she presented proof that her landlord uses her rent to pay the tax, the connection between paying rent and her status as a taxpayer is too attenuated to confer taxpayer standing on her. We therefore decline to hold that paying rent confers taxpayer status.

Turning to Lara's argument that her payment of sales tax confers taxpayer standing, we first note that no Texas court has answered that question. Other jurisdictions, however, have held that merely paying sales tax does not confer taxpayer standing. In reaching this conclusion, these courts have determined, under their applicable state statutes, that a sales tax is imposed on the seller of goods, not on the purchaser. Thus they reason that although a retailer may pass the sales-tax cost on to the purchaser, paying sales tax cannot make a purchaser a taxpayer for purposes of standing.

Texas law characterizes our state sales tax differently. Texas courts recognize that although sellers have the legal duty to collect sales tax from purchasers, *see* Tex. Tax Code § 151.052, because it is a transaction tax, *see* Tex. Tax Code § 151.051 (tax imposed on "each sale" of a taxable item), both sellers and purchasers are liable to the state for sales tax. Therefore, in Texas, unlike the other jurisdictions, both sellers and purchasers are considered taxpayers. Despite this distinction, we are not persuaded that paying sales tax should be grounds for conferring taxpayer standing.

Taxpayer standing is a judicially created exception to the general standing rule. We have already limited the applicability of this exception by narrowly defining the type of action a taxpayer can maintain. A taxpayer may maintain an action solely to challenge proposed illegal expenditures; a taxpayer may not sue to recover funds previously expended, *Hoffman v. Davis,* 100 S.W.2d 94, 96 (Tex. 1937), or challenge expenditures that are merely "unwise or indiscreet," *Osborne,* 177 S.W.2d at 200. Underpinning these limitations is the realization that "'[g]overnments cannot operate if every citizen who concludes that a public official has abused his discretion is granted the right to come into court and bring such official's public acts under judicial review.'" *Bland,* 34 S.W.3d at 555. Extending taxpayer standing to those who pay only sales tax would mean that even a person who makes incidental purchases while temporarily in the state could maintain an action. This would eviscerate any limitation on taxpayer suits. It would allow a person with virtually no personal stake in how public funds are expended to come into court and bring the government's actions under judicial review. This is not what this Court envisioned in crafting the taxpayer-standing exception. *See Osborne,* 177 S.W.2d at 200. Accordingly, we hold, for prudential reasons, that paying sales tax does not confer taxpayer standing upon a party. Lara therefore does not have standing as a taxpayer to assert her claims.

In determining whether Flowers has taxpayer standing, we need not question whether he satisfies the taxpayer requirement; the parties do not dispute that Flowers is a Tarrant County resident who pays taxes on the property he owns. The dispositive issue regarding Flowers' standing is whether Tarrant County is actually expending public funds in operating the CEU. Because this Court has yet to consider what constitutes expending public funds, we look for guidance to the more extensive jurisprudential experience of the federal courts.

Under federal law, taxpayer standing is divided into three categories–federal, state, and municipal–depending on which entity's expenditures are being challenged. To have standing to challenge a federal expenditure, taxpayers must establish a logical nexus between being a taxpayer and the type of action challenged, and demonstrate a link between their taxpayer status and the precise nature of the constitutional violation alleged. *See Valley Forge Christian Coll. v. Americans United for Separation of Church & State, Inc.,* 454 U.S. 464, 479-80 (1982); *Flast v. Cohen,* 392 U.S. 83, 102-03 (1968). State taxpayer standing involves a similar test derived for the most part from *Doremus v. Board of Education,* 342 U.S. 429 (1952). In that case, which involved allegations of both state and municipal taxpayer standing, the Court rejected the taxpayers' standing to challenge a state statute providing for the reading of Old Testament verses at the opening of each public-school day. The Court held that the plaintiffs had not shown "the requisite financial interest that [was], or [was] threatened to be, injured by the unconstitutional conduct." The test for municipal taxpayer standing, on the other hand, clearly involves less stringent requirements. *See ASARCO Inc. v. Kadish,* 490 U.S. 605, 612 (1989) (Kennedy, J.) (explaining that the relative closeness between municipalities and their taxpayers justifies a more lenient test for establishing municipal taxpayer standing than for establishing federal-taxpayer standing). Municipal taxpayers need only establish that they pay taxes to the relevant entity, and that public funds are expended on the allegedly unconstitutional activity. Because these requirements mirror what is necessary to establish taxpayer standing in Texas, we look to the jurisprudence of municipal taxpayer standing to guide us in determining whether Tarrant County expends public funds in operating the CEU.

To be entitled to municipal taxpayer standing, a litigant must prove that the government is actually expending money on the activity that the taxpayer challenges; merely demonstrating that tax dollars are spent on something related to the allegedly illegal conduct is not enough. The County alleges that the operation of the CEU does not satisfy this requirement because the money used to feed, clothe, and house the CEU inmates would be spent regardless of the CEU's existence. While we agree with the County's argument regarding these specific expenditures, we are convinced that other aspects of the CEU's operation involve the use of public funds.

Both Sheriff Williams and Chaplain Atwell managed a religious program that involves numerous volunteers and hundreds of inmates. As the record shows, they selected the CEU curriculum, supervised the weekday volunteers, selected the volunteer chaplains, monitored the chaplains' hours and directed their activities, determined the requirements for inmate participation, met weekly to discuss the unit's affairs, and reviewed all information pertaining to the CEU. Based on their own testimony, we conclude that Sheriff Williams and Chaplain Atwell spent a significant amount of the County's time operating the CEU, and therefore that county funds were expended in operating the CEU.

Standing as Inmates

Lara maintains that even if she does not have standing as a taxpayer, she has standing as a former TCCC inmate. Huff similarly alleges that as a former inmate, he has suffered an injury sufficiently particular to confer standing. They argue that they were emotionally harmed by the County's unwelcome unconstitutional establishment of religion.

Tarrant County disagrees. It emphasizes that because Lara and Huff are no longer TCCC inmates, they are not currently subject to the allegedly unconstitutional activity they seek to enjoin, and thus their claims for injunctive and declaratory relief are moot. The County contends that the court of appeals erred in concluding that because Lara and Huff may again find themselves incarcerated in the TCCC, they satisfy the "capable of repetition, yet evading review" exception to the mootness doctrine.

For a plaintiff to have standing, a controversy must exist between the parties at every stage of the legal proceedings, including the appeal. *See United States v. Munsingwear, Inc.,* 340 U.S. 36, 39 (1950). If a controversy ceases to exist–"the issues presented are no longer 'live' or the parties lack a legally cognizable interest in the outcome"–the case becomes moot. *Murphy v. Hunt,* 455 U.S. 478, 481 (1982). If a case becomes moot, the parties lose standing to maintain their claims. *See generally City of Los Angeles v. Lyons,* 461 U.S. 95, 105-06 (1983); *Murphy,* 455 U.S. at 481. Because Lara and Huff have been released from jail, they lack a legally cognizable interest in obtaining injunctive or declaratory relief. They no longer face the unconstitutional conduct about which they complain, and thus any prospective relief we might grant cannot help them. Lara's and Huff's claims for injunctive and declaratory relief are therefore moot.

Lara and Huff contend that even if their claims are moot, they fall under the "capable of repetition, yet evading review" exception to the mootness doctrine. We disagree. This exception applies only in rare circumstances. *See Lyons,* 461 U.S. at 109. To invoke the exception, a plaintiff must prove that: (1) the challenged action was too short in duration to be litigated fully before the action ceased or expired; and (2) a reasonable expectation exists that the same complaining party will be subjected to the same action again. *See Murphy,* 455 U.S. at 482; *Weinstein v. Bradford,* 423 U.S. 147, 149 (1975); *Blum v. Lanier,* 997 S.W.2d 259, 264 (Tex.1999); *General Land Office v. OXY U.S.A., Inc.,* 789 S.W.2d 569, 571 (Tex.1990).

The TCCC is a county jail facility where inmates serve sentences or await trial, transfer, or release. The duration of any inmate's stay, however, may be so short that it would be unlikely that any inmate would reside in the TCCC during the entirety of a legal proceeding challenging the existence of the CEU. Therefore, Lara's and Huff's claims meet the evading-review element of the mootness-exception test.

Lara and Huff cannot, however, meet the capable-of-repetition element. Whether and when Lara and Huff may be charged with a crime that would lead to their incarceration in the TCCC is speculative. To conclude that there is a reasonable expectation that they will again be subjected to the allegedly unconstitutional operation of the CEU requires us to assume that Lara and Huff will commit another crime. But Lara and Huff are required by law to prevent their own recidivism. Only by ignoring well-established precedent can we conclude that Lara and Huff satisfy the "capable of repetition, yet evading review" exception to the mootness doctrine. Because we are unwilling to do so, we conclude that Lara's and Huff's claims for prospective relief are moot. Thus neither this Court nor the trial court has jurisdiction to render the injunctive and declaratory relief they seek. Accordingly, the County is entitled to summary judgment on Lara's and Huff's claims for injunctive and declaratory relief because Lara and Huff do not have standing to assert those claims. But Lara's and Huff's release from the TCCC does not render moot their claims for damages. . . .

Conclusion

Tarrant County's operation of the Chaplain's Education Unit so as to endorse one religion over other religions or nonreligion conveyed the impermissible message that the County preferred the personal religious views of the sheriff and chaplain over other views. This official endorsement of religion is, as a matter of law, unconstitutional. The trial court should determine whether injunctive relief, as sought by Flowers, is appropriate, and whether Lara is entitled to damages under section 1983 because of this constitutional violation.

Notes on State and Federal Taxpayer Standing

The Scope of Taxpayer Standing in Texas State Court: Carefully analyze the elements of taxpayer standing under Texas law and federal law as outlined in *Lara*. What is the difference between the federal and Texas standards? As *Lara* highlights, state taxpayers in Texas essentially receive the same treatment as municipal taxpayers are afforded in federal court under existing federal precedent.[89] What policies support such a result?

Has the Texas Supreme Court adopted the appropriate balance between ensuring elected official accountability and precluding a multitude of suits in taxpayer cases? In *Bland Independent School District v. Blue,* the court emphasized the narrowness of the taxpayer standing exception, holding it only applied to bar *future* illegal expenditures rather than to recover past illegal expenditures.[90] *Andrade v. Venable* held that the taxpayer had the burden to show that the government was "actually spending money on the alleged illegal activity–not on a related legal activity," which required proof of a significant "measurable, added expenditure" to perform the alleged illegal activity, or a significant amount of time spent by government employees on the alleged illegal activity.[91] And of course *Lara* refused to extend taxpayer standing to those paying only sales tax on policy grounds, concluding that such an extension would eviscerate any limitation on taxpayer suits. Are there other adequate mechanisms to ensure governmental compliance with the state constitution when no taxpayer can meet the limited exception for taxpayer standing?

Potential Changes in Federal Taxpayer Standing: The United States Supreme Court decisions on taxpayer standing in federal court have distinguished between three

---

[89] *Compare* Doremus v. Bd. of Educ., 342 U.S. 429, 433-35 (1952) (discussing the standards applicable to municipal and state taxpayers in federal court) *with* El Paso Cmty. Partners v. B&G/Sunrise J.V., 24 S.W.3d 620, 624-25 (Tex. App.–Austin 2000, no pet.) (discussing state taxpayer standing to enjoin a void or illegal expenditure of state funds) *and* Tex. State Employees Union/C.W.A. Local 6184 v. Tex. Workforce Comm'n, 16 S.W.3d 61, 68 (Tex. App.–Austin 2000, no pet.) (same), *disapproved on other grounds by* Tex. Dep't of Parks & Wildlife v. Miranda, 133 S.W.3d 217 (Tex. 2004).

[90] 34 S.W.3d 547, 556 (Tex.2000); *accord* S. Tex. Water Auth. v. Lomas, 223 S.W.3d 304, 308 (Tex. 2007) (holding that taxpayer standing was not adequately alleged based on the plaintiff's claim that funds under the challenged contract had been "misapplied" rather than the challenged contract was "illegal").

[91] 372 S.W.3d 134, 138-39 (Tex. 2012). *Andrade* held that a taxpayer did not have standing to assert that the designation of a candidate's party affiliation on election ballots violated certain provisions of the Texas Constitution because the taxpayer did not establish either that a significant, measurable amount of public funds were expended or that governmental officials spent significant time on the party designations. *See id.*

situations: federal taxpayers, who never have standing unless bringing a challenge under the Establishment Clause to an exercise of the taxing and spending power by Congress;[92] state taxpayers, who likewise almost never have standing;[93] and municipal taxpayers, who have been granted taxpayer standing to proceed in federal court to enjoin the "illegal use of the moneys of a municipal corporation" based on their "direct and immediate" interest in municipal funds.[94] But the rationale of a Roberts Court decision is in some tension with this longstanding approach to municipal taxpayer standing in federal court. *DaimlerChrysler Corp. v. Cuno* held that state taxpayers did not have standing to challenge a state franchise credit, reasoning in part that the plaintiffs had not suffered an injury in fact as it was speculative whether any financial savings from abolishing the challenged tax credit program would benefit the taxpayers due to the numerous other governmental programs that would compete for state funds.[95] This same logic could be extended to municipal taxpayer cases challenging expenditures, although *Cuno* did not purport to disturb its earlier municipal taxpayer precedents.[96] If the Supreme Court further limits taxpayer standing in federal court, should that make any difference to the scope of taxpayer standing in Texas state courts?

Borrowing from Federal Justiciability Doctrines: How did *Lara* evaluate the other presented justiciability arguments concerning the plaintiffs' standing as inmates? Is such borrowing from federal authorities when interpreting state justiciability doctrines appropriate? Or should Texas courts always create their own independent justiciability doctrines? If so, how should such doctrines be interpreted?

B. STATE JUDICIAL SELECTION

Another major difference between the state and federal judiciaries is the manner by which judges are selected. Under the federal system, the President "shall nominate, and by and with the Advice and Consent of the Senate, shall appoint . . . Judges of the supreme Court, and all other Officers of the United States."[97] After appointment, federal judges "hold their Offices during good Behavior, and shall, at stated Times, receive for their Service, a Compensation, which shall not be diminished during their Continuance in Office."[98] All judges of Article III courts thus receive a lifetime appointment during good behavior after their nomination and confirmation.[99]

---

[92]Flast v. Cohen, 392 U.S. 83, 105-06 (1968); Frothingham v. Mellon, 262 U.S. 447, 486-88 (1923).

[93]*Doremus*, 342 U.S. at 433-34.

[94]*Frothingham*, 262 U.S. at 486-87 (citing cases concluding that the "interest of a taxpayer of a municipality in the application of its moneys is direct and immediate" such that standing is appropriate).

[95]547 U.S. 332, 344-46 (2006).

[96]*See id.* at 349-50 (explaining that *Frothingham* "noted with approval the standing of municipal residents to enjoin the 'illegal use of the moneys of a municipal corporation,' relying on 'the peculiar relation of the corporate taxpayer to the corporation' to distinguish such a case from the general bar on taxpayer suits.").

[97]U.S. CONST. art. II, § 2.

[98]U.S. CONST. art. III, § 1.

[99]For an overview of the past and current appointment process for Supreme Court Justices, see Charles W. "Rocky" Rhodes, *Navigating the Path of the Supreme Appointment*, 38 FLA. ST. U. L. REV. 537 (2011). A number of excellent books also exist on the subject. *See, e.g.*, HENRY J. ABRAHAM, JUSTICES, PRESIDENTS AND

The states, on the other hand, use a variety of methods for selecting judges, including different types of elective and appointive systems. These include partisan elections, nonpartisan elections, appointments for varying periods of time by the executive or legislative branches, and initial appointments followed by retention elections. In all, approximately forty of the states rely on some type of election to select some or all of their appellate and general-jurisdiction trial judges, even though popular elections for the judiciary are rare worldwide. The following article overviews the development of judicial elections in the states and the difficulties arising from popular elections.

Thomas R. Phillips, *Keynote Address: Electoral Accountability and Judicial Independence*, 64 OHIO ST. L. J. 137 (2003)*

In the early [American] Republic, no judges, or at least no judges with any substantial jurisdiction, were elected. The federal constitution provided for executive appointment with senatorial confirmation for a life term during good behavior, while most states opted for legislative elections or appointments for limited terms. But Georgia broke new ground in electing its trial judges in 1812, and Indiana followed suit in 1816. Mississippi's 1832 Constitution made all judges elected, as did New York's in 1846. After that, every new state until Alaska provided for elected judges, and more than two-thirds of the existing states moved to judicial elections in the fifteen years between the New York Convention and the outbreak of the Civil War. Among the states making this change were Texas in 1850 and Ohio in 1851.

Logically, one might suppose that the move to elections was purely an assertion of increased accountability–that constitutional framers and ratifiers finally tired of arrogant, activist judges. This is the traditional explanation, and no doubt it is at least in part true. Many framers shared the resentment of the Kentucky delegate to that state's 1849-1850 Convention who called appointed judges "the last dying kick of aristocracy."

But in recent years, other plausible explanations have been offered. Political scientist Kermit Hall has concluded that many reformers supported elections as a way to enhance judicial independence. Hall asserts that "[p]roponents of popular election insisted that the appellate judiciary had suffered because governors and legislators had distributed judgeships on the basis of 'service to the party' rather than on the 'legal skills or judicial temperament' of appointees."[100] Thus, "[t]he rise of popular, partisan election of appellate judges is best understood as an essentially thoughtful response by constitutionally moderate lawyers and judges . . . [who] wanted the appellate judiciary to command more, rather than less, power and prestige." One Ohio advocate of judicial elections inquired if it were not

---

SENATORS: A HISTORY OF U.S. SUPREME COURT APPOINTMENTS FROM WASHINGTON TO BUSH II (5th ed. 2008); MICHAEL J. GERHARDT, THE FEDERAL APPOINTMENTS PROCESS (rev. ed. 2003); JOHN ANTHONY MALTESE, THE SELLING OF SUPREME COURT NOMINEES (1995).

*Originally published in 64 Ohio St. L.J. 137 (2003).

[100] Kermit L. Hall, Progressive Reform and the Decline of Democratic Accountability: The Popular Election of State Supreme Court Justices, 1850-1920, 1984 AM. B. FOUND. RES. J. 345, 348 (quoting Samuel Medary, The New Constitution 171 (1849)).

true that "a blindfold[ed] man might . . . go into a crowd of fifty and select, at random, a man competent to fill the office of Governor of Ohio," while a Supreme Court judge must possess "learning, ability, experience, purity of character."

Yet another scholar, Caleb Nelson, has more recently asserted that the move to elections was intended neither to weaken nor to strengthen judicial power per se, but rather was part of a larger movement "[to] weaken [ ] officialdom as a whole" and "rein in the power of all officials to act independently of the people."[101] As one Kentucky delegate, quoted by Nelson, complained: "[W]e have provided for the popular election of every public officer save the dog catcher, and if the dogs could vote, we should have that as well."

Whatever the reason, elected judges met with initial satisfaction, but disillusion soon set in. Many eminent judges, including Chief Justices and law school namesakes Thomas Cooley in Michigan and William Mitchell in Minnesota, were tossed out in partisan sweeps. To some reformers' apparent surprise, political caucuses and conventions proved as adept as governors in rewarding faithful hacks with judicial sinecures. By the beginning of the twentieth century, many leaders of the bench and bar were calling for change.

Many states, particularly those most influenced by the Progressive movement, moved to non-partisan elections, sometimes held at different times than other elections. Ohio adopted this change in 1911. But nonpartisan elections had problems of their own, including low voter interest and the lack of a ready pool of campaign volunteers.

In 1940, Missouri became the first state to adopt the so-called merit selection system for some of its judges. Long advocated by the American Judicature Society, the plan called for initial appointment of judges by the Governor from a short list of nominees submitted by a panel of worthies, then periodic "yes/no" retention elections. Most new constitutions in the 1960s and 1970s adopted this system, and several states amended their constitutions to provide for it. But critics asserted that the scheme was in essence a lifetime appointment, and indeed in many states no judge ever failed to be retained. Many uninspiring or even corrupt judges stayed in office because the bar was unwilling to mount campaigns to beat somebody with nobody. In the 1980s and 1990s, three states adopted some form of merit selection, but the movement to any kind of merit system stalled with crushing defeats at the polls in Ohio in 1987 and Florida in 2000.

In many states, the judicial selection system still works to provide a stable, competent judiciary. But whether a judge faces a "good government" non-partisan election, as in Wisconsin or Idaho, a "phony" non-partisan election, as in Michigan or Ohio, a merit retention election, as in Florida or Tennessee, or a blatantly partisan election, as in Alabama or Texas, modern judicial elections have been manipulated and abused in ways that diminish respect for the rule of law. Each election cycle, additional states experience divisive, expensive, agenda-driven campaigns, increasingly accompanied by independent expenditures from national interest groups. The problem is now national in scope, and it demands national attention.

---

[101] Caleb Nelson, A Re-Evaluation of Scholarly Explanations for the Rise of the Elective Judiciary in Antebellum America, 37 AM. J. LEGAL HIST. 190, 224 (1993).

Why did a judicial election system that reportedly worked well in Millard Fillmore's day cause dissatisfaction by the end of the nineteenth century, and become almost totally broken now? There may be many reasons, but I believe that, more than anything else, fundamental changes in the electoral process have made the traditional judicial election methods untenable.

In the 1850s, elections still had the flavor of Athenian democracy, or at least a New England town meeting. There were no filing deadlines, no secret ballots, no billboards. Aside from a few handbills and some libations for thirsty voters at the polls, candidates incurred no expenses. Small populations and a restricted franchise resulted in a very small electorate, who knew most of the candidates personally or by reputation. The Ohio Constitution of 1851, for example, provided for five Supreme Court justices and twenty-seven common pleas judges elected from nine districts. Texas, being smaller, had even fewer judges.[102]

Today, urban voters face massive ballots. In 1994, for example, the general election ballot in Harris County, Texas featured fifty-five contested judicial races. Most voters probably did not know any of the candidates, and many may not have recognized a single candidate's name. Almost without exception, judicial campaigns generate few issues and no free media. Candidates must inform the voters through their own campaigns, and that isn't easy. If judicial candidates could get a few minutes on the public address systems during the Michigan-Ohio State halftime, maybe they could get their message out. But in a nation that increasingly is "bowling alone,"[103] the traditional venues of county fairs, Rotary meetings and political rallies are almost pathetically ineffective in reaching voters. As the Supreme Court observed in *Buckley v. Valeo*, "virtually every means of communicating ideas in today's mass society requires the expenditure of money."[104] You may call a candidate who thinks otherwise many things, but you probably will never call him or her "judge."

This state of affairs has diminished our judiciary in many ways, of which I will mention three. First, it discourages many of our best lawyers from becoming state judges. Whenever a federal bench opens in Texas, literally dozens of qualified lawyers make known their availability to serve. Justices on both the Ohio and Texas Supreme Court are currently awaiting Senate confirmation for a "promotion" to an intermediate federal bench. Open seats for state courts seldom draw a crowd. Two Texas Supreme Court justices are retiring at the end of their terms this year; a total of four Republicans and two Democrats filed to succeed them.

Second, increasingly competitive elections have destabilized the judiciary, at least in some states. [Nationwide,] about 20% of partisan judges are defeated if they are opposed for re-election. In Texas, it has been higher. Between 1980 and 2000, 208 state trial and

---

[102]See Tex. Const. of 1876, art. V, §§ 2, 7 (providing for only three Supreme Court justices and twenty-six district judges).

[103]See ROBERT D. PUTNAM, BOWLING ALONE: THE COLLAPSE AND REVIVAL OF AMERICAN COMMUNITY (2000).

[104]424 U.S. 1, 19 (1976) (per curiam).

appellate judges have been defeated at the polls. That amounts to a loss rate of 29% of our district judges and 41% of our appellate judges when opposed. Need I add that performance in office has seldom, if ever, been decisive to the outcome? When this electoral instability affects the state's supreme court, it is particularly likely to produce jurisprudential instability. Who can argue that more pronounced swings have not occurred in the judicial philosophy of elected high courts in Texas, Ohio, Michigan, Alabama, and Mississippi, for example, than in any five merit selection supreme courts that one cares to name?

Third, and most significantly, judicial elections are undermining public confidence in the fairness and impartiality of the courts. Long ago, Chief Justice John Jay said, "[n]ext to doing right, the great object in the administration of justice should be to give public satisfaction." That is because the authority of "the least dangerous branch" rests almost entirely on the voluntary compliance with its rulings by the other branches of government and by the public at large. How can judges convince the public that their only constituency is the law when their tenure in office depends on campaign contributions from lawyers and litigants?

There is widespread public skepticism that elected judges can be more than mere politicians in robes. While general public confidence in our courts remains high, polls commissioned for the National Center for State Court's initiative on Public Trust and Confidence in the Courts reveal that about three-fourths of Americans believe that judicial outcomes are affected by campaign contributions. A new nationwide poll, released just last month by Greenberg Quinlan Rosner Research for the Justice at Stake Campaign, confirms those findings. Moreover, the Greenberg poll showed additional, albeit inconclusive, evidence of further public cynicism about the courts in states with elected judiciaries.

Yet the Greenberg poll shows clearly that voters cherish their franchise and in elected states they generally prefer to retain it by a two to one margin. They support merit selection only when the question stresses the component that every judge gets to face every voter in the district at frequent intervals.

If merit selection is a good idea that cannot be compressed into a marketable "sound bite," what, then, is to be done? First, we can reduce the number of judicial elections by lengthening judicial terms. Second, where the Voting Rights Act permits, we can enhance qualifications for judicial office. Third, we can elevate the tenor of judicial campaigns by clarifying our codes of judicial conduct, improving our systems of judicial discipline, encouraging voluntary aspirational codes, and by following Ohio's lead in creating citizens' campaign monitoring groups. To the extent the Unites States Supreme Court will permit, we should require disclosure of all independent expenditures that pertain to judicial elections or elected judges. Fourth, and of paramount importance, we should educate voters about judicial candidates in ways that reduce the need for campaign contributions. Every state should prepare and distribute judicial voters' guides, at no cost to the candidates, in print and electronic form. Congress should provide a free frank for mailing these guides. The media and other groups should sponsor candidate forums and debates, which should be broadcast on television or radio and over the Internet. Finally, we should work toward full public funding of judicial elections, at least for the highest state courts.

The Greenberg poll shows widespread public support for public funding of judicial races: 80% are for it, and 77% would favor eliminating any private contributions in such a system. Interestingly, an accompanying Greenberg poll of over 2400 state judges revealed support for full public funding by 61% to 29%, while merit selection was opposed, 50% to 45%. The ninety-nine Ohio judges surveyed favored public financing, 57% to 39%, while they opposed merit selection, 30% to 66%. Even the 110 Texas judges favored public financing by a 10% margin but merit selection, long the first choice of our reform movement, by only a statistically insignificant 1%.

Just as partisan elections swept the country in the mid-1850s, and nonpartisan elections and merit selection later found favor, it may be time for a new paradigm in state judicial selection. At least at the supreme court level, it seems that the paradigm could be public financing. State high courts make enough public policy through their judicial opinions and their administrative responsibilities that popular choice can be intellectually defended, and the state could fund this limited number of contests at minimal expense.

Notes on Selecting State Judges

The Movement Towards Elections: Why did the states move to elected judiciaries? As former Texas Supreme Court Chief Justice Thomas Phillips discussed in the above article, various explanations have been offered, including that popular judicial elections limited legislative power, enhanced judicial independence, and ensured electoral accountability.[105] What then caused some states to employ alternative procedures, such as merit selection with retention elections and nonpartisan elections? From a policy perspective, what is the best method of selecting judges?

The states certainly cannot agree on the best method: "America has almost as many different ways of selecting state judges as it has states."[106] Only three states employ something akin to the federal idea of judges continuously serving during good behavior for life, but two of these states set a mandatory retirement age, and all three require the governor's appointment to be made in consultation with a judicial nominating council or elected executive council.[107] Of the remaining states, approximately twenty-two states initially elect their judges to full terms on their highest court either through partisan or nonpartisan elections, sixteen states adopt some type of system of executive branch appointments followed by retention elections, seven states provide for some manner of executive branch appointment for a specified term followed by potential reappointment by the governor, a commission, or the legislature, and two states have legislative appointment or election with legislative reappointments.[108] Although most states use some type of executive branch appointment process to fill the unexpired portion of a term when a judge resigns or is removed from office, a few states allow the court itself or the legislature to

---

[105] *Accord* G. ALAN TARR, UNDERSTANDING STATE CONSTITUTIONS 122 (1998).

[106] Thomas R. Phillips, *The Merits of Merit Selection*, 32 HARV. J.L. & PUB. POL'Y 67, 68 (2009).

[107] *See* THE COUNCIL OF STATE GOVERNMENTS, THE BOOK OF THE STATES 313-15 (2012). The three states are Massachusetts, New Hampshire, and Rhode Island, with only Rhode Island providing for life tenure. *See id.*

[108] *See id.*; *cf.* JAMES A. GARDNER, INTERPRETING STATE CONSTITUTIONS 213 (2005).

make the appointment.[109] Moreover, additional variations exist when considering state trial court judges, as several states employ distinct systems for selecting different types of judges.[110]

Merit Selection: The Best of Both Worlds? Merit selection is designed "to emphasize the best and minimize the worst of all existing judicial selection methods." Judge Phillips provided the following summary of both the process and its benefits in another article:

> When a vacancy arises, a select but diverse committee screens potential nominees and sends several names to the governor. In most states, the governor must choose a judge from this list, sometimes with an option to request alternative or additional names. In some states, the appointee takes office immediately; in others, confirmation by the governor's council or the legislature is required. At the end of each term, every judge runs against his own record in a "retention" election. A judge who receives more "yes" than "no" votes stays in office. If the judge dies, resigns, declines to stand again, or receives more "no" than "yes" votes, the process starts anew. . .
>
> In the face of all the[] problems [discussed previously regarding partisan and nonpartisan judicial elections, the] merit selection plan, for all its flaws, is the best option for maintaining dignity, stability, and accountability in the judiciary. In theory, merit selection should produce more judges who will respect their proper role in the governmental process. In practice, merit selection has worked well most of the time in most places. Taken together, these benefits should be sufficient to command support from the bench, the bar, and a concerned public in general . . . .[111]

Judge Phillips then continued to highlight the advantages of merit selection over elections with respect to minimizing both the turnover in the judiciary and the need for judges to raise campaign funds. Out of the more than 650 retention elections held nationwide before 2012 for state high courts, only eleven judges lost their seats.[112] Appellate judges and trial judges have an even better record of success, with less than one percent of lower court judges losing retention elections.[113] This means judges in merit selection states typically have very little need to campaign or solicit funds in order to retain their positions.

---

[109]BOOK OF THE STATES at 313-15.

[110]*See id.* at 313-20. For example, some states appoint appellate judges, but elect trial judges, probably on the theory that the electorate can be informed regarding the performance of such local officials. *See, e.g.*, KAN. CONST. art. III, § 6 (authorizing voters in each of the state's judicial districts to decide whether to employ elections or a nonpartisan selection method for trial judges).

[111]Phillips, *The Merits of Merit Selection*, 32 HARV. J.L. & PUB. POL'Y at 76-77.

[112]*See* Mark Curriden, *Judging the Judges*, 96 A.B.A. J. 56 (Jan. 2011).

[113]*See id.* (citing research of Albert Klumpp showing that only two of 1722 appellate judges and 70 out of 7535 trial judges lost their seats in retention elections).

The rare exceptions are illustrative of the general benefits of merit selection. The eleven state high court judges who lost retention elections over the years all sparked controversy with their holdings in high profile cases that led to a concerted effort to defeat them. The most recent example is the three Iowa Supreme Court justices who lost 2010 retention elections after ruling in 2009 that same-sex marriage was mandated by the Iowa Constitution. Soon after the 2009 decision, an anti-retention association was formed by conservative Iowans, who received hundreds of thousands of dollars in support from out-of-state interest groups fighting against same-sex marriage. Despite the concerted effort against them, the Iowa justices did not campaign or solicit contributions, and all were narrowly defeated. A similar dynamic occurred in California in 1986, where three California Supreme Court justices lost a retention election after being portrayed by opponents as soft on crime. Although these outcomes arguably contravene the ideal of judicial independence, they were less random than the frequent ousters in election states (such as Texas) based on nothing more than a partisan sweep or an unfortunate ballot name.

***Texas Judicial Elections and the Code of Judicial Conduct*:** Texas employs direct, partisan elections to fill both the full six-year terms of appellate judges (including the nine Justices of the Supreme Court of Texas, the nine Judges of the Court of Criminal Appeals, and the eighty Justices of the fourteen Texas courts of appeals) and the full four-year terms of trial judges. This means that judicial candidates must organize campaigns and run for office like other candidates for elective positions, although there are certain unique qualifications for candidates seeking to serve on most of the courts established by the Texas Constitution. Members of the Supreme Court of Texas, the Court of Criminal Appeals, and the various Texas courts of appeals must be thirty-five years old, licensed to practice law in Texas, and have previously practiced law at least ten years as of the date of the general election.[114] District judges must similarly be licensed to practice law in Texas and have practiced law for at least four years.[115] Judges of the constitutionally-created county courts must merely be "well informed in the law of the State," but do not have to be attorneys.[116] There are no constitutional or statutory qualifications other than age to serve as a justice of the peace, and the qualifications to serve as a judge of legislatively-created courts such as county courts at law and statutory probate courts depend on the specific statute creating the court.

Texas judicial elections are also governed by various statutes and rules. In addition to the generally applicable statutory regulations of elections contained in the Texas Election Code and other state laws, the Texas Judicial Campaign Fairness Act of 1995 establishes limits on contributions by individuals, law firms, and political action committees to

---

[114]TEX. CONST. art. V, §§ 2, 4 & 6; Sears v. Bayoud, 786 S.W.2d 248, 254-55 (Tex. 1990) (holding candidate for supreme court who was a few days short of being a licensed attorney for ten years as of the date of the general election was constitutionally ineligible to hold office).

[115]TEX. CONST. art. V, § 7.

[116]TEX. CONST. art. V, § 15; Little v. State, 12 S.W. 965, 967 (Tex. 1890) (holding that the "well informed in the law of the State requirement" is directed to the voters and does not require a county judge to either be an attorney or have studied law).

candidates for judicial office.[117] The Texas judiciary and judicial candidates are also subject to the Code of Judicial Conduct promulgated by the Texas Supreme Court.[118] The supreme court promulgated the state's first Code of Judicial Conduct in 1974 (which was modeled in large part on the American Bar Association's 1972 Model Code of Judicial Conduct), and then promulgated a completely updated Code, based on the 1990 Model Code from the ABA, in 1993. With respect to elections, the Code currently prohibits judges and judicial candidates from making public comments suggesting the judge's probable decision regarding matters pending or impending in the court in which the judge serves or the candidate would serve if elected.[119] Additionally, judges and judicial candidates may not make pledges or promises that would reasonably suggest a predisposition to decide specified cases in a certain manner, nor can they endorse another candidate for any public office other than indicating support for a political party.[120]

Yet there are some questions regarding the constitutionality of these restrictions on the political speech of judicial candidates under the First Amendment. One of the suggestions in the preceding article for judicial reform was to "elevate the tenor of judicial campaigns" through "clarifying our codes of judicial conduct" and requiring "disclosure of all independent expenditures that pertain to judicial elections or elected judges," limited by "the extent the United States Supreme Court will permit." The reason for this cautionary note is that the Supreme Court in 2002 held that one aspect of Minnesota's Code of Judicial Conduct regulating judicial elections violated the free speech rights of the candidates.

Republican Party of Minnesota v. White, 536 U.S. 765 (2002)

Justice SCALIA delivered the opinion of the Court.

The question presented in this case is whether the First Amendment permits the Minnesota Supreme Court to prohibit candidates for judicial election in that State from announcing their views on disputed legal and political issues.

I

Since Minnesota's admission to the Union in 1858, the State's Constitution has provided for the selection of all state judges by popular election. Minn. Const., Art. VI, § 7. Since 1912, those elections have been nonpartisan. Act of June 19, ch. 2, 1912 Minn. Laws Special Sess., pp. 4-6. Since 1974, they have been subject to a legal restriction which states that a "candidate for a judicial office, including an incumbent judge," shall not "announce his or her views on disputed legal or political issues." Minn.Code of Judicial Conduct, Canon 5(A)(3)(d)(i). This prohibition, promulgated by the Minnesota Supreme Court and based on Canon 7(B) of the 1972 American Bar Association (ABA) Model Code of Judicial Conduct, is known as the "announce clause." Incumbent judges who violate it

---

[117]The Judicial Campaign Fairness Act of 1995, 74 Leg. R.S., ch. 763, 1995 Tex. Gen. Laws 3956-68 (codified at TEX. ELEC. CODE § 253.151, *et seq.* & TEX. LOC. GOV'T CODE § 159.051-.056).

[118]TEX. CONST. art. V, § 1-a (authorizing the removal of any Texas Justice or Judge willfully violating the Code of Judicial Conduct); TEX. GOV'T CODE § 34.001 (subjecting judicial candidates to the requirements of the Code of Judicial Conduct).

[119]Tex. Code of Judicial Conduct Canon 3(B)(10).

[120]Tex. Code of Judicial Conduct Canon 5(1)-(2).

are subject to discipline, including removal, censure, civil penalties, and suspension without pay. Minn. Rules of Board on Judicial Standards 4(a)(6), 11(d). Lawyers who run for judicial office also must comply with the announce clause. Minn. Rule of Professional Conduct 8.2(b). Those who violate it are subject to, *inter alia,* disbarment, suspension, and probation. Rule 8.4(a); Minn. Rules on Lawyers Professional Responsibility 8-14, 15(a).

In 1996, one of the petitioners, Gregory Wersal, ran for associate justice of the Minnesota Supreme Court. In the course of the campaign, he distributed literature criticizing several Minnesota Supreme Court decisions on issues such as crime, welfare, and abortion. A complaint against Wersal challenging, among other things, the propriety of this literature was filed with the Office of Lawyers Professional Responsibility, the agency which, under the direction of the Minnesota Lawyers Professional Responsibility Board, investigates and prosecutes ethical violations of lawyer candidates for judicial office. The Lawyers Board dismissed the complaint; with regard to the charges that his campaign materials violated the announce clause, it expressed doubt whether the clause could constitutionally be enforced. Nonetheless, fearing that further ethical complaints would jeopardize his ability to practice law, Wersal withdrew from the election. In 1998, Wersal ran again for the same office. Early in that race, he sought an advisory opinion from the Lawyers Board with regard to whether it planned to enforce the announce clause. The Lawyers Board responded equivocally, stating that, although it had significant doubts about the constitutionality of the provision, it was unable to answer his question because he had not submitted a list of the announcements he wished to make.

Shortly thereafter, Wersal filed this lawsuit in Federal District Court against respondents, seeking, *inter alia,* a declaration that the announce clause violates the First Amendment and an injunction against its enforcement. Wersal alleged that he was forced to refrain from announcing his views on disputed issues during the 1998 campaign, to the point where he declined response to questions put to him by the press and public, out of concern that he might run afoul of the announce clause. Other plaintiffs in the suit, including the Minnesota Republican Party, alleged that, because the clause kept Wersal from announcing his views, they were unable to learn those views and support or oppose his candidacy accordingly. The parties filed cross-motions for summary judgment, and the District Court found in favor of respondents, holding that the announce clause did not violate the First Amendment. Over a dissent by Judge Beam, the United States Court of Appeals for the Eighth Circuit affirmed. We granted certiorari.

II

Before considering the constitutionality of the announce clause, we must be clear about its meaning. Its text says that a candidate for judicial office shall not "announce his or her views on disputed legal or political issues." Minn.Code of Judicial Conduct, Canon 5(A)(3)(d)(i).

We know that "announc[ing] . . . views" on an issue covers much more than *promising* to decide an issue a particular way. The prohibition extends to the candidate's mere statement of his current position, even if he does not bind himself to maintain that position after election. All the parties agree this is the case, because the Minnesota Code contains a so-called "pledges or promises" clause, which *separately* prohibits judicial candidates from making "pledges or promises of conduct in office other than the faithful and impartial performance of the duties of the office," *ibid.*–a prohibition that is not challenged here and on which we express no view.

In any event, it is clear that the announce clause prohibits a judicial candidate from stating his views on any specific nonfanciful legal question within the province of the court for which he is running, except in the context of discussing past decisions–and in the latter context as well, if he expresses the view that he is not bound by *stare decisis.*

Respondents contend that this still leaves plenty of topics for discussion on the campaign trail. These include a candidate's "character," "education," "work habits," and "how [he] would handle administrative duties if elected." Indeed, the Judicial Board has printed a list of preapproved questions which judicial candidates are allowed to answer. These include how the candidate feels about cameras in the courtroom, how he would go about reducing the caseload, how the costs of judicial administration can be reduced, and how he proposes to ensure that minorities and women are treated more fairly by the court system. Whether this list of preapproved subjects, and other topics not prohibited by the announce clause, adequately fulfill the First Amendment's guarantee of freedom of speech is the question to which we now turn.

III

As the Court of Appeals recognized, the announce clause both prohibits speech on the basis of its content and burdens a category of speech that is "at the core of our First Amendment freedoms"–speech about the qualifications of candidates for public office. The Court of Appeals concluded that the proper test to be applied to determine the constitutionality of such a restriction is what our cases have called strict scrutiny; the parties do not dispute that this is correct. Under the strict-scrutiny test, respondents have the burden to prove that the announce clause is (1) narrowly tailored, to serve (2) a compelling state interest.

The Court of Appeals concluded that respondents had established two interests as sufficiently compelling to justify the announce clause: preserving the impartiality of the state judiciary and preserving the appearance of the impartiality of the state judiciary. Respondents reassert these two interests before us, arguing that the first is compelling because it protects the due process rights of litigants, and that the second is compelling because it preserves public confidence in the judiciary. Respondents are rather vague, however, about what they mean by "impartiality."

A

One meaning of "impartiality" in the judicial context–and of course its root meaning–is the lack of bias for or against either *party* to the proceeding. Impartiality in this sense assures equal application of the law. That is, it guarantees a party that the judge who hears his case will apply the law to him in the same way he applies it to any other party. This is the traditional sense in which the term is used. See Webster's New International Dictionary 1247 (2d ed.1950). It is also the sense in which it is used in the cases cited by respondents and *amici* for the proposition that an impartial judge is essential to due process. *Tumey v. Ohio,* 273 U.S. 510, 523, 531-534 (1927) (judge violated due process by sitting in a case in which it would be in his financial interest to find against one of the parties); *Aetna Life Ins. Co. v. Lavoie,* 475 U.S. 813, 822-825 (1986) (same); *Johnson v. Mississippi,* 403

U.S. 212, 215-216 (1971) *(per curiam)* (judge violated due process by sitting in a case in which one of the parties was a previously successful litigant against him).

We think it plain that the announce clause is not narrowly tailored to serve impartiality (or the appearance of impartiality) in this sense. Indeed, the clause is barely tailored to serve that interest *at all,* inasmuch as it does not restrict speech for or against particular *parties,* but rather speech for or against particular *issues.* To be sure, when a case arises that turns on a legal issue on which the judge (as a candidate) had taken a particular stand, the party taking the opposite stand is likely to lose. But not because of any bias against that party, or favoritism toward the other party. *Any* party taking that position is just as likely to lose. The judge is applying the law (as he sees it) evenhandedly.

B

It is perhaps possible to use the term "impartiality" in the judicial context (though this is certainly not a common usage) to mean lack of preconception in favor of or against a particular *legal view.* This sort of impartiality would be concerned, not with guaranteeing litigants equal application of the law, but rather with guaranteeing them an equal chance to persuade the court on the legal points in their case. Impartiality in this sense may well be an interest served by the announce clause, but it is not a *compelling* state interest, as strict scrutiny requires. A judge's lack of predisposition regarding the relevant legal issues in a case has never been thought a necessary component of equal justice, and with good reason. For one thing, it is virtually impossible to find a judge who does not have preconceptions about the law. As then-Justice REHNQUIST observed of our own Court: "Since most Justices come to this bench no earlier than their middle years, it would be unusual if they had not by that time formulated at least some tentative notions that would influence them in their interpretation of the sweeping clauses of the Constitution and their interaction with one another." *Laird v. Tatum,* 409 U.S. 824, 835 (1972) (memorandum opinion). Indeed, even if it were possible to select judges who did not have preconceived views on legal issues, it would hardly be desirable to do so. "Proof that a Justice's mind at the time he joined the Court was a complete *tabula rasa* in the area of constitutional adjudication would be evidence of lack of qualification, not lack of bias." *Ibid.* The Minnesota Constitution positively forbids the selection to courts of general jurisdiction of judges who are impartial in the sense of having no views on the law. Minn. Const., Art. VI, § 5 ("Judges of the supreme court, the court of appeals and the district court shall be learned in the law"). And since avoiding judicial preconceptions on legal issues is neither possible nor desirable, pretending otherwise by attempting to preserve the "appearance" of that type of impartiality can hardly be a compelling state interest either.

C

A third possible meaning of "impartiality" (again not a common one) might be described as open-mindedness. This quality in a judge demands, not that he have no preconceptions on legal issues, but that he be willing to consider views that oppose his preconceptions, and remain open to persuasion, when the issues arise in a pending case. This sort of impartiality seeks to guarantee each litigant, not an *equal* chance to win the legal points in the case, but at least *some* chance of doing so. It may well be that impartiality in this sense, and the appearance of it, are desirable in the judiciary, but we need not pursue that inquiry, since we do not believe the Minnesota Supreme Court adopted the announce clause for that purpose.

The short of the matter is this: In Minnesota, a candidate for judicial office may not say "I think it is constitutional for the legislature to prohibit same-sex marriages." He may say the very same thing, however, up until the very day before he declares himself a candidate, and may say it repeatedly (until litigation is pending) after he is elected. As a means of pursuing the objective of open-mindedness that respondents now articulate, the announce clause is so woefully underinclusive as to render belief in that purpose a challenge to the credulous.

Justice STEVENS asserts that statements made in an election campaign pose a special threat to open-mindedness because the candidate, when elected judge, will have a *particular* reluctance to contradict them. That might be plausible, perhaps, with regard to campaign *promises*. A candidate who says "If elected, I will vote to uphold the legislature's power to prohibit same-sex marriages" will positively be breaking his word if he does not do so (although one would be naive not to recognize that campaign promises are–by long democratic tradition–the least binding form of human commitment). But, as noted earlier, the Minnesota Supreme Court has adopted a separate prohibition on campaign "pledges or promises," which is not challenged here. The proposition that judges feel significantly greater compulsion, or appear to feel significantly greater compulsion, to maintain consistency with *nonpromissory* statements made during a judicial campaign than with such statements made before or after the campaign is not self-evidently true. It seems to us quite likely, in fact, that in many cases the opposite is true. We doubt, for example, that a mere statement of position enunciated during the pendency of an election will be regarded by a judge as more binding–or as more likely to subject him to popular disfavor if reconsidered–than a carefully considered holding that the judge set forth in an earlier opinion denying some individual's claim to justice. In any event, it suffices to say that respondents have not carried the burden imposed by our strict-scrutiny test to establish this proposition (that campaign statements are uniquely destructive of open-mindedness) on which the validity of the announce clause rests.

Moreover, the notion that the special context of electioneering justifies an *abridgment* of the right to speak out on disputed issues sets our First Amendment jurisprudence on its head. "The role that elected officials play in our society makes it all the more imperative that they be allowed freely to express themselves on matters of current public importance." *Wood v. Georgia,* 370 U.S. 375, 395 (1962). We have never allowed the government to prohibit candidates from communicating relevant information to voters during an election.

Justice GINSBURG would do so–and much of her dissent confirms rather than refutes our conclusion that the purpose behind the announce clause is not openmindedness in the judiciary, but the undermining of judicial elections. She contends that the announce clause must be constitutional because due process would be denied if an elected judge sat in a case involving an issue on which he had previously announced his view. She reaches this conclusion because, she says, such a judge would have a "direct, personal, substantial, and pecuniary interest" in ruling consistently with his previously announced view, in order to reduce the risk that he will be "voted off the bench and thereby lose [his] salary and emoluments." But elected judges–regardless of whether they have announced any views beforehand–*always* face the pressure of an electorate who might disagree with their rulings and therefore vote them off the bench. Surely the judge who frees Timothy McVeigh places his job much more at risk than the judge who (horror of horrors!) reconsiders his previously announced view on a disputed legal issue. So if, as Justice GINSBURG claims, it violates due process for a judge to sit in a case in which ruling one way rather than another increases his prospects for reelection, then–quite simply–the practice of electing judges is itself a violation of due process. It is not difficult to understand how one with these views would approve the election-nullifying effect of the announce clause. They are not, however, the views reflected in the Due Process Clause of the Fourteenth Amendment, which has coexisted with the election of judges ever since it was adopted.

Justice GINSBURG greatly exaggerates the difference between judicial and legislative elections. She asserts that "the rationale underlying unconstrained speech in elections for political office–that representative government depends on the public's ability to choose agents who will act at its behest–does not carry over to campaigns for the bench." This complete separation of the judiciary from the enterprise of "representative government" might have some truth in those countries where judges neither make law themselves nor set aside the laws enacted by the legislature. It is not a true picture of the American system. Not only do state-court judges possess the power to "make" common law, but they have the immense power to shape the States' constitutions as well. See, *e.g., Baker v. State,* 744 A.2d 864 (Vt. 1999). Which is precisely why the election of state judges became popular.

IV

To sustain the announce clause, the Eighth Circuit relied heavily on the fact that a pervasive practice of prohibiting judicial candidates from discussing disputed legal and political issues developed during the last half of the 20th century. It is true that a "universal and long-established" tradition of prohibiting certain conduct creates "a strong presumption" that the prohibition is constitutional. *McIntyre v. Ohio Elections Comm'n,* 514 U.S. 334, 375-377 (1995) (SCALIA, J., dissenting). The practice of prohibiting speech by judicial candidates on disputed issues, however, is neither long nor universal.

At the time of the founding, only Vermont (before it became a State) selected any of its judges by election. Starting with Georgia in 1812, States began to provide for judicial election, a development rapidly accelerated by Jacksonian democracy. By the time of the Civil War, the great majority of States elected their judges. E. Haynes, Selection and Tenure of Judges 99-135 (1944); Berkson, Judicial Selection in the United States: A Special Report, 64 Judicature 176 (1980). We know of no restrictions upon statements that could be made by judicial candidates (including judges) throughout the 19th and the first quarter of the 20th century. Indeed, judicial elections were generally partisan during this period, the movement toward nonpartisan judicial elections not even beginning until the 1870's. Thus, not only were judicial candidates (including judges) discussing disputed legal and political issues on the campaign trail, but they were touting party affiliations and angling for party nominations all the while.

The first code regulating judicial conduct was adopted by the ABA in 1924. 48 ABA Reports 74 (1923) (report of Chief Justice Taft). It contained a provision akin to the announce clause: "A candidate for judicial position . . . should not announce in advance his conclusions of law on disputed issues to secure class support . . . ." ABA Canon of Judicial Ethics 30 (1924). The States were slow to adopt the canons, however. "By the end of World War II, the canons . . . were binding by the bar associations or supreme courts of only eleven states." J. MacKenzie, The Appearance of Justice 191 (1974). Even today, although a majority of States have adopted either the announce clause or its 1990 ABA successor, adoption is not unanimous. Of the 31 States that select some or all of their appellate and general-jurisdiction judges by election, 4 have adopted no candidate-speech restriction comparable to the announce clause, and 1 prohibits only the discussion of "pending litigation." This practice, relatively new to judicial elections and still not universally adopted, does not compare well with the traditions deemed worthy of our attention in prior cases.

* * *

There is an obvious tension between the article of Minnesota's popularly approved Constitution which provides that judges shall be elected, and the Minnesota Supreme Court's announce clause which places most subjects of interest to the voters off limits. (The candidate-speech restrictions of all the other States that have them are also the product of judicial fiat.) The disparity is perhaps unsurprising, since the ABA, which originated the announce clause, has long been an opponent of judicial elections. That opposition may be well taken (it certainly had the support of the Founders of the Federal Government), but the First Amendment does not permit it to achieve its goal by leaving the principle of elections in place while preventing candidates from discussing what the elections are about.

The Minnesota Supreme Court's canon of judicial conduct prohibiting candidates for judicial election from announcing their views on disputed legal and political issues violates the First Amendment. Accordingly, we reverse . . . .

Justice O'CONNOR, concurring.

I join the opinion of the Court but write separately to express my concerns about judicial elections generally.

We of course want judges to be impartial, in the sense of being free from any personal stake in the outcome of the cases to which they are assigned. But if judges are subject to regular elections they are likely to feel that they have at least some personal stake in the outcome of every publicized case. Elected judges cannot help being aware that if the public is not satisfied with the outcome of a particular case, it could hurt their reelection prospects. Even if judges were able to suppress their awareness of the potential electoral consequences of their decisions and refrain from acting on it, the public's confidence in the judiciary could be undermined simply by the possibility that judges would be unable to do so.

Moreover, contested elections generally entail campaigning. And campaigning for a judicial post today can require substantial funds. See Schotland, Financing Judicial Elections, 2000: Change and Challenge, 2001 L.Rev. Mich. State U. Detroit College of Law 849, 866 (reporting that in 2000, the 13 candidates in a partisan election for 5 seats on the Alabama Supreme Court spent an average of $1,092,076 on their campaigns). Unless the pool of judicial candidates is limited to those wealthy enough to independently fund their campaigns, a limitation unrelated to judicial skill, the cost of campaigning requires judicial candidates to engage in fundraising. Yet relying on campaign donations may leave judges feeling indebted to certain parties or interest groups. See Thomas, National L. J., Mar. 16,

1998, p. A8, col. 1 (reporting that a study by the public interest group Texans for Public Justice found that 40 percent of the $9,200,000 in contributions of $100 or more raised by seven of Texas' nine Supreme Court justices for their 1994 and 1996 elections "came from parties and lawyers with cases before the court or contributors closely linked to these parties"). Even if judges were able to refrain from favoring donors, the mere possibility that judges' decisions may be motivated by the desire to repay campaign contributors is likely to undermine the public's confidence in the judiciary.

Despite these significant problems, 39 States currently employ some form of judicial elections for their appellate courts, general jurisdiction trial courts, or both. Judicial elections were not always so prevalent. The first 29 States of the Union adopted methods for selecting judges that did not involve popular elections. [But] beginning with Georgia in 1812, States began adopting systems for judicial elections. From the 1830's until the 1850's, as part of the Jacksonian movement toward greater popular control of public office, this trend accelerated, and by the Civil War, 22 of the 34 States elected their judges. By the beginning of the 20th century, however, elected judiciaries increasingly came to be viewed as incompetent and corrupt, and criticism of partisan judicial elections mounted. In 1906, Roscoe Pound gave a speech to the American Bar Association in which he claimed that "compelling judges to become politicians, in many jurisdictions has almost destroyed the traditional respect for the bench." The Causes of Popular Dissatisfaction with the Administration of Justice, 8 Baylor L.Rev. 1, 23 (1956) (reprinting Pound's speech).

In response to such concerns, some States adopted a modified system of judicial selection that became known as the Missouri Plan. Under the Missouri Plan, judges are appointed by a high elected official, generally from a list of nominees put together by a nonpartisan nominating commission, and then subsequently stand for unopposed retention elections in which voters are asked whether the judges should be recalled. If a judge is recalled, the vacancy is filled through a new nomination and appointment. This system obviously reduces threats to judicial impartiality, even if it does not eliminate all popular pressure on judges. The Missouri Plan is currently used to fill at least some judicial offices in 15 States.

Thirty-one States, however, still use popular elections to select some or all of their appellate and/or general jurisdiction trial court judges, who thereafter run for reelection periodically. Of these, slightly more than half use nonpartisan elections, and the rest use partisan elections. Most of the States that do not have any form of judicial elections choose judges through executive nomination and legislative confirmation.

Minnesota has chosen to select its judges through contested popular elections instead of through an appointment system or a combined appointment and retention election system along the lines of the Missouri Plan. In doing so the State has voluntarily taken on the risks to judicial bias described above. As a result, the State's claim that it needs to significantly restrict judges' speech in order to protect judicial impartiality is particularly troubling. If the State has a problem with judicial impartiality, it is largely one the State brought upon itself by continuing the practice of popularly electing judges.

Justice STEVENS, with whom Justice SOUTER, Justice GINSBURG, and Justice BREYER join, dissenting.

The Court's disposition rests on two seriously flawed premises–an inaccurate appraisal of the importance of judicial independence and impartiality, and an assumption that judicial candidates should have the same freedom "'to express themselves on matters of current public importance'" as do all other elected officials. Elected judges, no less than appointed judges, occupy an office of trust that is fundamentally different from that occupied by policymaking officials. Although the fact that they must stand for election makes their job more difficult than that of the tenured judge, that fact does not lessen their duty to respect essential attributes of the judicial office that have been embedded in Anglo-American law for centuries.

There is a critical difference between the work of the judge and the work of other public officials. In a democracy, issues of policy are properly decided by majority vote; it is the business of legislators and executives to be popular. But in litigation, issues of law or fact should not be determined by popular vote; it is the business of judges to be indifferent to unpopularity.

Consistent with that fundamental attribute of the office, countless judges in countless cases routinely make rulings that are unpopular and surely disliked by at least 50 percent of the litigants who appear before them. It is equally common for them to enforce rules that they think unwise, or that are contrary to their personal predilections. For this reason, opinions that a lawyer may have expressed before becoming a judge, or a judicial candidate, do not disqualify anyone for judicial service because every good judge is fully aware of the distinction between the law and a personal point of view.

[W]e do not have to put States to an all or nothing choice of abandoning judicial elections or having elections in which anything goes. As a practical matter, we cannot know for sure whether an elected judge's decisions are based on his interpretation of the law or political expediency. In the absence of reliable evidence one way or the other, a State may reasonably presume that elected judges are motivated by the highest aspirations of their office. But we do know that a judicial candidate, who announces his views in the context of a campaign, is effectively telling the electorate: "Vote for me because I believe X, and I will judge cases accordingly." Once elected, he may feel free to disregard his campaign statements, but that does not change the fact that the judge announced his position on an issue likely to come before him *as a reason to vote for him*. Minnesota has a compelling interest in sanctioning such statements.

Justice GINSBURG, with whom Justice STEVENS, Justice SOUTER, and Justice BREYER join, dissenting.

[Judges] perform a function fundamentally different from that of the people's elected representatives. Legislative and executive officials act on behalf of the voters who placed them in office; "judge[s] represen[t] the Law." *Chisom v. Roemer,* 501 U.S. 380, 411 (1991) (SCALIA, J., dissenting). Unlike their counterparts in the political branches, judges are expected to refrain from catering to particular constituencies or committing themselves on controversial issues in advance of adversarial presentation.

Thus, the rationale underlying unconstrained speech in elections for political office–that representative government depends on the public's ability to choose agents who will act at its behest–does not carry over to campaigns for the bench. As to persons aiming to occupy the seat of judgment, the Court's unrelenting reliance on decisions involving contests for legislative and executive posts is manifestly out of place. In view of the magisterial role judges must fill in a system of justice, a role that removes them from the partisan fray, States may limit judicial campaign speech by measures impermissible in elections for political office.

The Court sees in this conclusion, and in the Announce Clause that embraces it, "an obvious tension": The Minnesota electorate is permitted to select its judges by popular vote, but is not provided information on "subjects of interest to the voters"–in particular, the voters are not told how the candidate would decide controversial cases or issues if elected. This supposed tension, however, rests on the false premise that by departing from the federal model with respect to who *chooses* judges, Minnesota necessarily departed from the federal position on the *criteria* relevant to the exercise of that choice.

Minnesota did not choose a judicial selection system with all the trappings of legislative and executive races. While providing for public participation, it tailored judicial selection to fit the character of third branch office holding. The balance the State sought to achieve–allowing the people to elect judges, but safeguarding the process so that the integrity of the judiciary would not be compromised–should encounter no First Amendment shoal.

Notes on State Judicial Elections and their Regulation

***The First Amendment Constraints on Judicial Codes of Conduct*:** What impact does *Republican Party of Minnesota v. White* have on the judicial selection process in other states? Within two months of *White*, the Texas Supreme Court amended the Texas Code of Judicial Conduct, deleting the Texas version of the "announce" clause and modifying the "public comment" and the "pledges or promises" clauses. The Texas provisions now prevent a judge from making public comments suggesting the judge's probable decision regarding matters pending or impending in the court in which the judge serves or the candidate would serve if elected, making specific pledges or promises that would reasonably suggest a predisposition to a probable decision in covered cases, or endorsing another candidate for any public office other than indicating support for a political party.[121] Do these provisions as amended satisfy the First Amendment concerns raised by the Supreme Court in *White*?

White expressed no view on Minnesota's "pledges or promises" clause, which as written barred candidates from making any pledges or promises other than the faithful and impartial performance of judicial duties. Some federal district courts have nevertheless

[121]Tex. Code of Judicial Conduct Canons 3(B)(10), 5(1)-(2).

invalidated similar clauses.[122] However, the amended Texas clause is narrower, only prohibiting pledges or promises "regarding pending or impending cases, specific classes of cases, specific classes of litigants, or specific propositions of law that would suggest to a reasonable person that the judge is predisposed to a probable decision in cases within the scope of the pledge."[123] Is prohibiting such pledges or promises by candidates for judicial office narrowly tailored to serve a compelling interest? At least one court concluded that such a narrower pledge or promise clause, which was construed only to apply to post-election commitments to decide an issue or a case in a particular way, was narrowly tailored to serve compelling interests in preserving an open-minded judiciary and protecting the due process rights of future litigants.[124]

What about the provisions of the Texas Code of Judicial Conduct precluding a judge or candidate for judicial office from commenting on pending or impending matters or endorsing another candidate for office? Are these restrictions constitutional? The State Commission on Judicial Conduct in 2006 admonished state supreme court Justice Nathan Hecht for statements he made to the media in support of the nomination of Harriet Miers to the United States Supreme Court. Justice Hecht challenged the admonition before a special court of review, which concluded that he had not violated any of the applicable canons.[125] A concurring opinion reached Justice Hecht's constitutional challenge under *White*, concluding that the endorsement canon was unconstitutional due to the severe underinclusiveness evidenced in its ban of verbal endorsements while allowing political campaign contributions.[126] However, the Seventh and Eighth Circuits have upheld analogous endorsement canons from Wisconsin and Minnesota, respectively.[127]

Are there other provisions of state judicial codes of conduct that might be unconstitutional under *White*?[128] The Eighth Circuit considered some of the other provisions of the Minnesota Code of Judicial Conduct in an en banc decision after remand from the Supreme Court in *Republican Party of Minnesota v. White*.[129] The Eighth Circuit invalidated Minnesota's ban on judicial candidates personally soliciting campaign contributions even from large groups or through signed letters,[130] and also invalidated

---

[122]*See, e.g.*, N.D. Family Alliance, Inc. v. Bader, 361 F. Supp. 2d 1021, 1038-39 (D.N.D. 2005); Family Trust Found. of Ky., Inc. v. Wolnitzek, 345 F. Supp. 2d 672, 704 (E.D. Ky. 2004). *But see In re* Kinsey, 842 So. 2d 77, 87 (Fla. 2003) (upholding Florida pledge or promise clause against First Amendment challenge); *In re* Watson, 794 N.E.2d 1, 6-8 (N.Y. 2003) (upholding similar New York pledge or promise clause).

[123]Tex. Code of Judicial Conduct Canon 5(1).

[124]*See, e.g.*, Pa. Family Inst., Inc. v. Celluci, 521 F. Supp. 2d 351, 383-84 (E.D. Pa. 2007).

[125]*In re* Hecht, 213 S.W.3d 547, 580 (Tex. Spec. Ct. Rev. 2006).

[126]*See id.* at 595 (McClure, J., concurring).

[127]Wersal v. Sexton, 674 F.3d 1010, 1025-28 (8th Cir. 2012) (Bye, J., plurality op.) (en banc); Siefert v. Alexander, 608 F.3d 974, 983-88 (7th Cir. 2010).

[128]*Compare* Carey v. Wolnitzek, 614 F.3d 189, 211-18 (6th Cir. 2010) (appendices listing state judicial code provisions).

[129]416 F.3d 738 (8th Cir. 2005) (en banc).

[130]*Id.* at 763-66. The Sixth and Eleventh Circuits have also invalidated solicitation clauses. *See Carey*, 614 F.3d at 204-06; Weaver v. Bonner, 309 F.3d 1312, 1322-23 (11th Cir. 2002). However, the Eighth Circuit subsequently upheld a narrower solicitation ban in Minnesota that only applied to personal solicitations of groups of less than twenty people. *Wersal*, 674 F.3d at 1029-31. And the Seventh Circuit upheld Wisconsin's

Minnesota's "partisan-activities clause," which precluded judges and candidates in Minnesota's non-partisan elections for judicial offices from identifying with or seeking an endorsement from a political party.[131] The Sixth and Seventh Circuits have also invalidated similar party affiliation clauses that generally prohibited judges in non-partisan elections from disclosing their party affiliation,[132] and the Ninth Circuit invalidated a bar on political party endorsements of judicial candidates in Montana's non-partisan elections.[133]

If candidates for judicial office cannot be prohibited from associating with political parties or disclosing their party affiliation, and political parties cannot be prohibited from endorsing judicial candidates, are non-partisan elections meaningful? What impact might these holdings have on other suggested judicial reforms, such as public financing schemes?

The Remedy for the Appearance of Impartiality: What happens if the speech or campaign conduct of the judge or judicial candidate raises doubts about his or her ability to be impartial in a particular lawsuit? Judicial canons typically require the recusal of a judge when his or her actions create the perception that the judge has been impaired in his or her ability to perform adjudicative duties with integrity, impartiality, and competence.[134] In addition, the Due Process Clause requires that, at least in some situations, a judge must recuse to ensure a litigant's right to a fair trial.

Caperton v. A.T. Massey Coal Co., for instance, held that excessive campaign expenditures in a state court judicial election could raise a constitutionally intolerable probability of bias.[135] After a West Virginia state court jury returned a $50 million verdict against A.T. Massey Coal Co., the company's chairman, CEO, and president, Don Blakenship, spent $3 million to unseat an incumbent judge on the West Virginia Supreme Court and elect attorney Brent Benjamin in his place. Blakenship's expenditures provided sixty percent of the funds supporting Benjamin's candidacy in a race Benjamin won by less than 50,000 votes. When the appeal of the $50 million judgment against Massey Coal was heard by the West Virginia Supreme Court, Justice Benjamin refused to recuse, casting the deciding vote in favor of Massey Coal. But the United States Supreme Court held that Justice Benjamin's failure to recuse violated due process in light of the exceptional nature of the expenditures, which led to the conclusion that "a person with a personal stake in a particular case had a significant and disproportionate influence in placing the judge on the case by raising funds or directing the judge's election campaign when the case was pending or imminent."[136] Examining the relative size of the expenditures, their timing, and their apparent impact, the Court opined that serious fears of bias arose when a litigant, without the consent of the other parties, chooses the judge in its own cause.

---

solicitation ban, employing reasoning borrowed from the Supreme Court's campaign finance regulation cases. *Siefert*, 608 F.3d at 988-90.

[131] 416 F.3d at 754-63.

[132] *Carey*, 614 F.3d at 201-04; *Siefert*, 608 F.3d at 981-83.

[133] Sanders Cnty. Republican Cent. Comm. v. Bullock, 698 F.3d 741, 745-49 (9th Cir. 2012).

[134] *See* ABA Annotated Model Code of Judicial Conduct.

[135] 556 U.S. 868 (2009).

[136] *Id.* at 884.

But how far does *Caperton* extend? While the majority repeatedly emphasized the "exceptional" and "extraordinary" nature of the campaign contributions in the case, the dissent listed forty questions left unanswered by the majority's holding, which will have to be resolved in future cases.[137] Some of these questions may impact the Texas judiciary, as raising funds for political campaigns often entails accepting contributions from litigants and attorneys appearing in the judge's courtroom.

Federal Judicial Criticisms of Elected State Judiciaries: Is it possible that *White*'s holding was influenced by the promulgation of the announce clause by the judiciary rather than the clause being a part of the state constitution or enacted into law by the legislature? The Supreme Court did highlight that this limitation and all other existing judicial-candidate speech limitations were imposed "by judicial fiat." The Eighth Circuit, perhaps perceiving a hint here, suggested in a footnote on remand that the regulations of election activities in Minnesota's Judicial Code of Conduct "compromised any separation of powers framework established by Minnesota's constitution" by infringing on "an authority seemingly granted only to the Minnesota legislature under its plenary powers."[138]

Why did Justice O'Connor write her concurrence criticizing state judicial elections? Was this an appropriate opinion from a Supreme Court Justice in our federal system, especially one who frequently espoused a commitment to the rights of states? Justice Kennedy offered the following responsive comments in his own concurrence:

> There is general consensus that the design of the Federal Constitution, including lifetime tenure and appointment by nomination and confirmation, has preserved the independence of the Federal Judiciary. In resolving this case, however, we should refrain from criticism of the State's choice to use open elections to select those persons most likely to achieve judicial excellence. States are free to choose this mechanism rather than, say, appointment and confirmation. By condemning judicial elections across the board, we implicitly condemn countless elected state judges and without warrant. Many of them, despite the difficulties imposed by the election system, have discovered in the law the enlightenment, instruction, and inspiration that make them independent-minded and faithful jurists of real integrity. We should not, even by inadvertence, "impute to judges a lack of firmness, wisdom, or honor." *Bridges v. California,* 314 U.S. 252, 273 (1941).[139]

The Role of Elected State Judges: Do state judges have a different role than federal judges? The Supreme Court opined in *White*: "Not only do state-court judges possess the power to 'make' common law, but they have the immense power to shape the States' constitutions as well. See, *e.g., Baker v. State,* 744 A.2d 864 (Vt. 1999). Which is precisely why the election of state judges became popular."[140] Is Justice Scalia's majority opinion

---

[137] *Id.* at 893-98 (Roberts, C.J., dissenting).

[138] 416 F.3d 738, 752 n.7 (8th Cir. 2005).

[139] *White,* 536 U.S. at 795-96 (Kennedy, J., concurring).

[140] *Id.* at 784.

implying that there is more of a need for electoral oversight of state judiciaries because of their common law power (a power which is extremely limited in the federal courts) and a fear of state constitutionalism run amuck? The *Baker v. State* reference is to a Vermont Supreme Court decision holding that the Vermont Constitution required the state to offer legal benefits to same-sex couples identical to the benefits afforded to married couples, which caused the Vermont legislature to adopt civil unions for same-sex couples (as will be discussed in Chapter 4).

Should elected judges be more attuned to the popular will and less concerned with precedent than appointed judges? Some have made variations of this argument. In his concurrence in *Melody Homes Manufacturing Co. v. Barnes*, Texas Supreme Court Justice Oscar Mauzy offered the following reply to the charge that the majority opinion overruled a two-year old precedent: "The answer to that question is that the makeup of this court has changed. . . . The people, speaking through the elective process, have constituted a new majority of this court which has not only the power but the duty to correct the incorrect conclusion arrived at by the then-majority in 1985 on this question."[141] Justice Hans Linde of Oregon argued that, when judges are "elected representatives, like legislators," they "feel less hesitant to offer their policy views than do appointed judges."[142] Moreover, some studies have revealed that electoral accountability does–at least to the extent that the public is informed of judicial performance–tend to keep judicial decisions consistent with popular sentiment.[143] Should elected judges thus be more active in interpreting their state charters than appointed justices? Does a state's method of selecting judges impact the correct understanding of the judicial role in the scheme of separation of powers?

C. THE INTERPRETATION OF STATE CONSTITUTIONS

Judicial review is properly a power to interpret an existing constitution; it should not be a guise for the judiciary to impose its own personal values by invalidating legislation it does not like. As Alexander Hamilton remarked in defending the entrustment of this power to a life-tenured federal judiciary, "they should be bound down by strict rules and precedents which serve to define and point out their duty in every particular case that comes before them."[144] Judges, he continued, have no ultimate "influence over either the sword or the purse;" the judiciary possesses "neither FORCE nor WILL but merely judgment."[145] Because the judiciary depends on the other branches to enforce its decrees, judges must stay within the confines of governing interpretive rules and precedents such that their judgments will be respected by the other governmental departments and the People themselves.

Yet a difficulty is that the interpretation of a particular constitutional provision cannot always be determined by resort to "strict rules and precedents." Numerous problems

---

[141]741 S.W.2d 349, 362 (Tex. 1987) (Mauzy, J., concurring).

[142]Hans A. Linde, *Observations of a State Judge*, *in* JUDGES AND LEGISLATORS: TOWARD INSTITUTIONAL COMITY 117 (Robert A Katzmann ed., 1988).

[143]*See* JAMES A. GARDNER, INTERPRETING STATE CONSTITUTIONS 212-13 (2005) (discussing studies).

[144]THE FEDERALIST NO. 78, at 471 (Alexander Hamilton) (Clinton Rossiter ed., 1961).

[145]*Id.* at 465.

arise that are not addressed either by prior decisions or the constitutional text. And even if there is relevant text or precedent, it may not resolve the controversy. The constitutional text is frequently too open-textured to establish a definitive outcome, and prior decisions may not be exactly on point or they may have been rendered obsolete by subsequent legal or societal changes. As a result, a constant theme throughout the study of both federal and state constitutional law is the proper methodology for interpreting a given constitutional provision.

The interpretation of state constitutions poses many of the same issues as construing the United States Constitution. The interpreter must determine how much weight to afford each of the accepted modes of constitutional argument, such as the text of the constitutional provision, the structure of the document, the original meaning of the provision, the intent of the framers and ratifiers, historical evidence regarding the times, past judicial precedent, fundamental values of the people manifest in its provisions, and the prudential function of the judiciary in our scheme of separation of powers.[146] A variety of theories have been proposed on the appropriate hierarchy of these modes of constitutional analysis. These theories are frequently characterized as either "originalist" or "nonoriginalist." Briefly stated, originalism is the view that constitutions should be interpreted in accord with the express text of the constitutional provision and the original meaning, understanding, or intent of the framers and ratifiers.[147] In contrast, nonoriginalism, which has also been called living constitutionalism, espouses that the courts may adopt interpretations that diverge from the intent of the framers.[148] But in many respects, this categorization is misleading because numerous alternative visions exist within these two schools of thought. Within "originalism," for instance, there are textualists, strict originalists, moderate originalists, original meaning originalists, and original intent originalists, to name a few. Nonoriginalists are perhaps even less uniform in their views, as they have offered theories based on everything from natural law and fundamental moral values to democratic process to pragmatism. State court judges, whether or not subscribing to one of these overarching constitutional theories, must contemplate the appropriate hierarchy of constitutional arguments when interpreting the provisions of their state constitution.

In addition, state constitutions typically pose some unique interpretive challenges. One set of these challenges stems from the length of state constitutions in comparison to the Federal Constitution. Rather than abiding by Chief Justice Marshall's admonition that the nature of a constitution "requires that only its great outlines should be marked,"[149] many state constitutional provisions are extremely detailed, closely resembling statutes. In at least one instance in Texas, this has led to directly conflicting constitutional text. The Supreme Court of Texas in *Stringer v. Cendant Mortgage Co.*, in answering a certified question from the Fifth Circuit, confronted the dilemma of conflicting constitutional provisions proposed

---

[146]*See, e.g.*, PHILLIP BOBBITT, CONSTITUTIONAL INTERPRETATION 12-13 (1991); 1 LAURENCE H. TRIBE, AMERICAN CONSTITUTIONAL LAW § 1-11, at 31 (3d ed. 2000).

[147]*See, e.g.*, JOHN HART ELY, DEMOCRACY AND DISTRUST 1 (1980). Professor Ely's seminal work, however, employed alternative nomenclature, calling originalism "interpretivism" and nonoriginalism "noninterpretivism." *Id.*

[148]*Id.*

[149]McCulloch v. Maryland, 17 U.S. (4 Wheat) 316, 407 (1819).

and ratified simultaneously in 1997 to allow home equity loans in Texas. The court explained the problem as follows:

> Section 50(a)(6) [of the Texas Constitution] allows a home-equity lender to require the borrower to use loan proceeds to pay: (1) debts secured by the homestead; and (2) non-homestead debts to third-party creditors. *See* TEX. CONST. art. XVI, § 50(a)(6)(Q)(i). On the other hand, section 50(g) provides that a home-equity lender cannot require a borrower to apply loan proceeds to another debt that is not secured by the home or to another debt to the same lender.
>
> We agree with the Fifth Circuit that the plain language of section 50(a)(6)(Q)(i) and section 50 (g)(Q)(1) conflict. And, there is nothing in the amendment, its legislative history, or the parties' arguments that hints at a legislative reason for the conflict other than speculation that the difference in language results from an oversight.[150]

The court, after analyzing the structure of the constitutional amendment, reasoned that the provision authorizing a lender to pay non-homestead debts to third parties was the substantive provision establishing the lender's rights while the other provision merely provided the terms to be included in a constitutionally required notice to borrowers.[151] This led to the interesting conclusion that the Texas Constitution allowed a lender to require the payment of third-party non-homestead debts while at the same time requiring the lender to provide a notice to the borrower stating that it could not do so. To alleviate the potential confusion, the court then drafted its own additional notice that lenders should provide to borrowers explaining the contradiction.[152] This type of explicit contradiction simply does not exist in the United States Constitution.[153]

The length of many state constitutions causes difficulties with structural arguments as well. The interrelationship of the various textual provisions is more evident in the United States Constitution, which is relatively short, than in longer state constitutions, like the Texas Constitution, that may span hundreds of pages. The Texas Constitution, according to Professor Janice May, contains more than 80,000 words (which is more than eight times longer than the United States Constitution) and "is one of the longest in the nation (possibly second only to the Alabama charter)."[154] The prolixity of the Texas Constitution is also

---

[150]23 S.W.3d 353, 356 (Tex. 2000).

[151]*Id.* at 357.

[152]*Id.* at 357-58.

[153]Of course, even under the United States Constitution, implicit contradictions frequently arise between constitutional provisions, especially those adopted in different eras. For instance, the Court in *Granholm v. Heald*, 544 U.S. 460, 466 (2005), had to determine whether the Twenty-first Amendment, which repealed prohibition and also barred the transportation of intoxicating liquors into a state in violation of state law, prevented dormant Commerce Clause scrutiny of state laws prohibiting out-of-state wineries from shipping wine directly to in-state consumers.

[154]JANICE C. MAY, THE TEXAS STATE CONSTITUTION, A REFERENCE GUIDE xxxv (1995). Statistics compiled by the Council of State Governments also indicate that the Texas Constitution, at slightly under 87,000 words, is the second longest in the nation, behind only Alabama. THE COUNCIL OF STATE GOVERNMENTS, THE

indicated by its several hundred sections in sixteen separate articles, in contrast to the twenty-one sections in seven articles in the United States Constitution.

Contributing to this complexity is the fact that the Texas Constitution has been amended almost 500 times since it was adopted in 1876 (in comparison, only twenty-seven amendments have been made to the United States Constitution since 1788, with ten of those amendments being passed within a couple of years of the ratification of the Constitution). Texas, along with most other states today operating under constitutions ratified since the Civil War, has a relatively easy state constitutional amendment process. The resulting almost continual constitutional change has decreased the likelihood that the words used in the various parts of a lengthy constitution may be linked in a coherent pattern.

The length, detail, and breadth of provisions contained in state constitutions have contributed to the contention that state constitutions (or at least their "lesser" provisions that do not announce fundamental principles of government) should be interpreted in accordance with principles of statutory construction rather than employing the accepted modes of federal constitutional interpretation.[155] Arguably, however, this prolixity in state constitutions is partially necessary due to the somewhat different functions state charters serve. In theory at least, the United States Constitution primarily *grants* power to the federal government, whereas the state constitutions serve to *limit* the plenary power the states would otherwise enjoy. Establishing limitations on all potential plenary powers would logically appear to require more detail than merely granting certain defined limited powers to the government, although all the verbosity in the Texas Constitution and many other charters can hardly be attributed to this distinction.

Another unique aspect to interpreting state constitutions is the continuing interrelationship of the constitution and the development of the common law. As seen in *Morrow v. Corbin* earlier in this chapter, state constitutional provisions are sometimes interpreted in light of the common law. This is not surprising, and takes place at the federal level as well, because many constitutional rights had common law antecedents in both English decisions and American decisions in the colonial and early republic periods.[156] But state courts, unlike federal courts, are charged with the continued responsibility to develop the common law. This can lead to interpretive difficulties, as when the Supreme Court of Texas in *Sipriano v. Great Spring Waters of America, Inc.*[157] considered whether it should

BOOK OF THE STATES 11-12 (2012).

[155] *See, e.g.*, Vreeland v. Byrne, 370 A.2d 825, 832 (N.J. 1977) (opining that the "a literal adherence to the words of the clause" is required for those provisions that are not among the "great ordinances" of the constitution and instead merely set forth the details of governmental administration); Kiser v. Kiser, 385 S.E.2d 487, 491 (N.C. 1989) (explaining that the constitutional "'great ordinances' are interpreted as evolving responsively to the felt needs of the times, whereas lesser provisions are not broadly or expansively applied"); State *ex rel.* Sanstead v. Freed, 251 N.W.2d 898, 908 (N.D. 1977) ("Generally, principles of construction applicable to statutes are also applicable to constitutional provisions"), *superseded by state constitutional amendment*, N.D. CONST. art. V, § 7.

[156] *See, e.g.*, Judith S. Kaye, *Foreword: The Common Law and State Constitutional Law as Full Partners in the Protection of Individual Rights*, 23 RUTGERS L.J. 727 (1992); Ellen A. Peters, *Common Law Antecedents of Constitutional Law in Connecticut*, 53 ALB. L. REV. 259, 261 (1989).

[157] 1 S.W.3d 75 (Tex. 1999).

adhere to the common law rule of capture for groundwater that had been recognized before a Texas constitutional amendment authorizing the state legislature to regulate the state's natural resources.[158] The court concluded any modification of this common law rule would have "to be guided and constrained by constitutional and statutory considerations."[159] Accordingly, the court declined to modify the common law rule even though every other jurisdiction in the United States, and England itself, had ceased to follow it. But the court did indicate that it might be inclined to revisit the issue if the legislature did not satisfactorily undertake its constitutional obligation. Such a juxtaposition of common law and constitutional interpretation occurs less frequently at the federal level, as the federal courts may recognize federal common law only in a "few and restricted" instances.[160]

In addition to the preceding difficulties, the various types of historical arguments, especially original intent and original meaning, typically require more effort to unearth under the state constitutions. A relative wealth of such information exists at the federal level, as James Madison took copious notes at the Constitutional Convention and *The Federalist* and numerous other writings were published thereafter.[161] The Constitution was then ratified by the states sitting in conventions, and many of the debates in these state conventions were even published.[162] But such materials do not usually exist to the same extent for state constitutions. As an example, the delegates to the Texas Constitutional Convention of 1875 decided not to pay a stenographer to record their arguments, so the existing accounts primarily must be taken from newspaper reports, which are incomplete and perhaps somewhat slanted by the newspaper's political ideology.[163] Moreover, the Texas framers did not engage in systematic written debates as to the merits of our existing state constitution like the Federalists and Anti-Federalists did. Finally, there are almost no written records of the thoughts of the ratifiers in Texas, who, after all, were the individual voters of the state.

A further complexity arises because most states have had more than one constitution. Texas, for example, has had six constitutions, and, in some instances, a provision from an earlier constitution was adopted in a later constitution without change, or perhaps with only minor changes. This compounds the problem of determining original intent or meaning when the same provision may have been considered and debated over the course of several different constitutional conventions.

---

[158]*See* TEX. CONST. art. XVI, § 59.

[159]*Sipriano*, 1 S.W.3d at 80.

[160]City of Milwaukee v. Illinois, 451 U.S. 304, 313 (1981).

[161]*See* THE RECORDS OF THE FEDERAL CONVENTION OF 1787 (Max Farrand ed., rev. ed. 1937); THE FEDERALIST PAPERS (Clinton Rossiter ed., 1961).

[162]JONATHAN ELLIOT, THE DEBATES IN THE SEVERAL STATE CONVENTIONS, ON THE ADOPTION OF THE FEDERAL CONSTITUTION, AS RECOMMENDED BY THE GENERAL CONVENTION AT PHILADELPHIA, IN 1787 (2d ed. 1854). In addition, the Wisconsin Historical Society is in the midst of a multi-volume compilation project collecting and publishing the entire documentary record of the debate over ratification.

[163]*See* SETH SHEPARD MCKAY, DEBATES IN THE TEXAS CONSTITUTIONAL CONVENTION OF 1875 (1930). Indeed, of all the Texas Constitutions, only the convention debates of the 1845 Statehood Constitution were recorded. WILLIAM F. WEEKS, DEBATES OF THE TEXAS CONVENTION (1846).

A final difficulty that has troubled commentators and courts is the appropriate interpretation of "borrowed" provisions. As discussed in Chapter 1, state constitutions often borrow from language contained in the United States Constitution and the constitutions of other states. When a state has constitutional text similar to the United States Constitution, should the United States Supreme Court's interpretation of the federal provision be binding, highly persuasive, or merely another precedent to be considered in construing the state constitution? And which Supreme Court interpretation? The one at the time the language was first adopted in the state constitution, the one at the time of the most recent constitution with the same language, or the current Supreme Court interpretation? Does the fact that state constitutions are easier to amend justify a more activist approach than that adopted by the Supreme Court because state citizens may resort to the amendment process to override judicial interpretations, or does it support a less activist position under the theory that state constitutions should evolve by amendment rather than interpretation? In addition, how much deference should be given to decisions of other jurisdictions with a similar provision? Should more deference be paid to judicial interpretations in other states predating a constitution's adoption, or to more recent doctrine? Finally, returning to the issues raised in the last section, does a state's method of selecting its judiciary have an impact on the deference it affords to decisions from other jurisdictions? The next two chapters examine these and other interpretive questions in the context of state constitutional rights guarantees.

CHAPTER 3 EXERCISES AND PROBLEMS

1. The Texas Supreme Court held in *Lara v. Williams* that payment of sales tax was insufficient to confer taxpayer standing for prudential reasons. Should the same rule apply to governmental entities, like some public transportation agencies, that only receive revenues from sales tax? Which prudential policy should be followed: the concern regarding a multitude of suits or the policy favoring governmental accountability?

2. The Texas Code of Judicial Conduct prohibits judges and judicial candidates from making pledges or promises that would suggest to a reasonable person that the judge is predisposed to a probable decision within the scope of the pledge. Evaluate whether a judicial candidate could respond to each of the following inquiries in a judicial questionnaire without violating the Code. If responding to an inquiry would violate the Code, evaluate whether the First Amendment would allow the judge to respond:

> (a) Would you promise to apply only the text and original meaning of the Texas Constitution in interpreting its provisions?
>
> (b) Would you promise to uphold all abortion laws enacted by the Texas Legislature unless binding U.S. Supreme Court precedent requires the law's invalidation?

Chapter 4

DUALLY PROTECTED INDIVIDUAL RIGHTS UNDER STATE CONSTITUTIONS

As the former colonies revolted from Great Britain, they were faced with the prospect of establishing their own forms of government. To accomplish this task, ten of the states adopted new state constitutions within a year of the Declaration of Independence.[1] Beginning with Virginia and its Declaration of Rights in 1776, most of these states adopted or incorporated formal declarations or bills of rights as part of their fundamental law.[2]

Virginia adopted its Declaration of Rights *before* its constitution (and before the nation even declared independence).[3] Other revolutionary state declarations of rights, while incorporated within state charters, preceded the constitutional provisions that created the departments of government and distributed powers among them.[4] A compilation of these early rights provisions would encompass almost all the individual rights familiar to Americans today: freedom of the press, free exercise of religion, trial by jury, due process, protection against unreasonable searches and seizures, freedom of speech, double jeopardy, and the protection against establishment of religion.[5] By the time the Revolutionary War ended, the principle that one function of constitutions was to outline the republican rights of the people had become entrenched in the American experience.

Nevertheless, the Federal Constitutional Convention rejected a proposal made in its waning days by George Mason, the author of the Virginia Declaration of Rights, to include a "bill of rights" in the proposed Constitution.[6] During the ratification debates, this omission of a rights enumeration was the most resonating criticism of the new proposed charter. The Federalist supporters of the Constitution replied that a bill of rights, while perhaps necessary to announce the rights of citizens in light of the plenary power of the states, was unnecessary in the Federal Constitution (due to the limited nature of the federal government) and perhaps dangerous (as a potential pretext to assert governmental power

---

[1]G. ALAN TARR, UNDERSTANDING STATE CONSTITUTIONS 60 (1998). Four states–New Hampshire, South Carolina, Virginia, and New Jersey–drafted their state constitutions before the Declaration of Independence. Six other states–Delaware, Georgia, Maryland, New York, North Carolina, and Pennsylvania–did so in the first year after the Declaration of Independence. *Id.* Massachusetts waited until 1780, and Connecticut and Rhode Island retained their colonial charters with minor modifications as their fundamental law. *Id.*

[2]*Id.* at 62-63, 75.

[3]JACK RAKOVE, REVOLUTIONARIES: A NEW HISTORY OF THE INVENTION OF AMERICA 172-78 (2010). The Virginia fifth provincial convention approved the Virginia Declaration of Rights on June 12, 1776, and then approved the new state constitution on June 29, 1776. *See id.*

[4]TARR, *supra* note 1, at 78.

[5]BERNARD SCHWARTZ, THE GREAT RIGHTS OF MANKIND: A HISTORY OF THE AMERICAN BILL OF RIGHTS 90-91 (1977). However, some of these rights, like freedom of speech, the prohibition on establishment of religion, and the protection against double jeopardy, were only protected by one or two state constitutions. *Id.*

[6]2 THE RECORDS OF THE FEDERAL CONVENTION OF 1787, at 587-88 (Max Farrand ed., rev. ed. 1937); 1 BERNARD SCHWARTZ, THE BILL OF RIGHTS: A DOCUMENTARY HISTORY 438 (1971).

over non-enumerated rights that were properly outside the federal government's constitutional powers).[7] Yet as the majority of the ratifying states requested the inclusion of a bill of rights, and the New York and Virginia state legislatures applied to Congress under the Article V amendment process to call another constitutional convention for proposing amendments, Federalists capitulated.[8]

James Madison, then a member of the House of Representatives, borrowed pervasively from the existing state bills and declarations of rights to recommend seventeen amendments to the United States Constitution, twelve of which were passed by both Houses of Congress and ten of which were soon thereafter ratified by the states.[9] State constitutions were thus the original wellspring of the American conception of civil liberties. Indeed, all the rights in the Bill of Rights except those that flow from the federal structure (such as the states-rights reservation of the Tenth Amendment) were contained in at least one state's declaration of rights. This is not to say that the early state declarations comported with contemporary understandings of civil liberties, as only a handful guaranteed such important rights as freedom of speech, establishment, and double jeopardy.[10] These state bills of rights also typically employed hortatory language rather than mandatory phrasing–using "ought" instead of "shall"–and articulated principles of good republican government rather than judicially enforceable individual rights.[11] James Madison complained that "some states have no bills of rights, there are others provided with very defective ones, and there are others whose bills of rights are not only defective, but absolutely improper."[12] Yet in the absence of the prior American familiarity with state declarations of rights, the impetus for a Federal Bill of Rights shortly after the Constitution's ratification might not have come to fruition.

Most states later amended or adopted new bills and declarations of rights, employing mandatory language and safeguarding more of the rights protected at the federal level. But important differences still exist between the federal and state declarations. One of these differences is structural: the bills of rights of most states are still located at the beginning of the constitution. For example, the Texas Bill of Rights is contained in article I of the Texas Constitution.[13] This state constitutional structure suggests that the study of judicial review under state constitutions might begin with an analysis of individual rights.

---

[7]THE FEDERALIST NO. 84 (Alexander Hamilton) (Clinton Rossiter ed., 1961).

[8]*See, e.g.*, 3 JONATHAN ELLIOT, THE DEBATES IN THE SEVERAL STATE CONVENTIONS ON THE ADOPTION OF THE FEDERAL CONSTITUTION AS RECOMMENDED BY THE GENERAL CONVENTION IN PHILADELPHIA IN 1787, at 657-661 (2d ed. 1854).

[9]5 BERNARD SCHWARTZ, ROOTS OF THE BILL OF RIGHTS 1145-47, 1171 (1980).

[10]SCHWARTZ, THE GREAT RIGHTS OF MANKIND, *supra* note 4, at 90-91.

[11]TARR, *supra* note 1, at 76-78.

[12]1 ANNALS OF CONGRESS 439 (J. Gales ed., 1789). South Carolina illustrates Madison's complaints. The South Carolina Constitution of 1776 did not guarantee any individual rights, and the South Carolina Constitution of 1778 only guaranteed three: the right of Christian Protestants to worship freely, the right of due process under the law of the land, and the liberty of the press. S.C. CONST. of 1778, arts. XXXVIII, XLI, & XLIII.

[13]TEX. CONST. art. I.

But another structural distinction renders this study somewhat more complicated under state constitutions. The individual rights contained in state constitutions only protect against state intrusions; they cannot protect against any interference from the federal government operating within the scope of its enumerated powers as a result of the Supremacy Clause considered in Chapter 2. In the antebellum period, this corresponded nicely with the original understanding that the Federal Bill of Rights only protected citizens against the actions of the federal government.[14] A symmetry existed: state constitutions protected individuals against state usurpations, and the Federal Constitution protected individuals against the federal government. The two separate systems did borrow from each other in defining the appropriate relationship between the government and the individual in accord with the common antebellum natural law judicial philosophy that constitutions evinced universal principles of self-governance.[15] Yet even though state courts voluntarily employed principles drawn from the Federal Constitution or its interpretation when considering state constitutional claims before the Civil War, the individual rights in the Federal Constitution were not binding protections a state had to afford its own citizens.

Later, however, the adoption of the Fourteenth Amendment radically changed the federal government's role in the protection of liberty against state interference. It prevented the *states* from depriving any person "of life, liberty, or property, without due process of law" or from depriving persons within their jurisdiction "the equal protection of the laws."[16] As the nineteenth century faded into the twentieth, the Supreme Court began using the Fourteenth Amendment as a vehicle to apply provisions of the Federal Bill of Rights against the states.[17] Through this process, almost all the provisions of the Bill of Rights have been incorporated through the Due Process Clause to guarantee against state intrusions.[18]

Because these incorporated liberties contained in the Federal Bill of Rights are also almost always protected by state charters as well, these rights can be said to be "dually protected" from interference by state and local governments. The citizens of a state can assert their *federal* constitutional rights to protect against actions taken by state and local governments because of the incorporation doctrine. Additionally, state citizens may assert their *state* constitutional rights to protect themselves from unconstitutional actions of state and local governments (but remember that only federal constitutional rights safeguard against the federal government's actions).

---

[14]Barron v. City of Baltimore, 32 U.S. (7 Pet.) 243 (1833).

[15]JAMES A. GARDNER, INTERPRETING STATE CONSTITUTIONS 30-32 (2005).

[16]U.S. CONST. amend. XIV.

[17]*See, e.g.*, JOHN E. NOWAK & RONALD D. ROTUNDA, CONSTITUTIONAL LAW § 11.6, at 462-64 (7th ed. 2004).

[18]*See, e.g.*, *id.* § 10.2, at 397-99; *id.* § 11.6, at 465-66. The Court has rejected the incorporation of the Fifth Amendment's requirement of a grand jury indictment and the Seventh Amendment's right to a jury trial in civil cases. The Court has not specifically held that the Third Amendment's ban against quartering soldiers or the Eighth Amendment's prohibitions against excessive bail and excessive fines are incorporated against the states, although it has assumed the excessive bail proscription applies to the states. All the other guarantees contained in the first eight amendments of the Bill of Rights have been incorporated. *See id.*; *accord* Duncan v. Louisiana, 391 U.S. 145, 148-49 (1968) (listing the provisions of the Bill of Rights that have been incorporated to apply against the states); McDonald v. City of Chicago, 131 S. Ct. 3020 (2010) (incorporating Second Amendment).

The appropriate interpretation of these dually protected state and federal rights has been a source of ongoing debate in state constitutional law. From the turn of the twentieth century to the late 1960's, while the Supreme Court federalized individual rights through the incorporation doctrine, state courts seldom turned to their own constitutions to protect individual liberties, although some notable exceptions did exist. The Supreme Court's holding in *Mapp v. Ohio* that the exclusionary rule suppressing unconstitutionally seized evidence applied to the states under the Fourteenth Amendment, for example, was heavily influenced by the number of states that had already adopted an exclusionary rule under their own state constitutions and laws.[19] But for the most part during this time period, state courts followed the federal court lead in defining the scope of dually protected rights.

As the Burger Court replaced the Warren Court, though, and incorporation reached its culmination, a new debate emerged as to the proper methodology to interpret such dually protected rights. This debate was fueled by the rise of the "new judicial federalism," which urged that the Supreme Court's interpretation of the Federal Constitution should not be considered dispositive of civil liberties guaranteed by textually similar state constitutional counterparts. Although neither the first nor the most sophisticated, the best-known article supporting this position is former Supreme Court Justice William J. Brennan's article *State Constitutions and the Protections of Individual Rights.*[20] Justice Brennan maintained that state courts vindicate state autonomy in the federal structure by conducting a searching independent analysis of their own constitutions without parroting the determinations of the Supreme Court on counterpart federal constitutional provisions.[21] Many commentators have echoed Justice Brennan's conclusions, sometimes presenting additional arguments in favor of the new judicial federalism, such as the state courts' freedom from the judicial constraints on the Supreme Court in the American federal system.[22] Yet others offered contrary views regarding the desirability of independent state court constitutional adjudication,[23] leading to an ongoing controversy. Should the state right be interpreted as merely offering the same protection as the corresponding federal right? Should the state right offer broader protection? Should the answer instead depend on a clause-by-clause analysis of the text, structure, history, and precedent regarding the state provision in comparison to the federally protected right, which might mean in some instances greater state protection, in other instances the same, and other times less protection? Or, alternatively, is the federal interpretation mostly or even wholly irrelevant to the interpretation of the state charter?

Another aspect of this continuing debate concerns the appropriate order for resolving corresponding rights asserted under both the federal and state constitutions.

---

[19] 367 U.S. 643, 651 (1961). Texas first adopted the exclusionary rule in 1925 by a statute that is currently codified at Texas Code of Criminal Procedure article 38.23.

[20] William J. Brennan, Jr., *State Constitutions and the Protections of Individual Rights*, 90 HARV. L. REV. 489 (1977).

[21] *Id.* at 502-04.

[22] *See, e.g.*, Robert F. Williams, *In the Supreme Court's Shadow: Legitimacy of State Rejection of Supreme Court Reasoning and Result*, 35 S.C. L. REV. 353 (1984).

[23] *See, e.g.*, James A. Gardner, *The Failed Discourse of State Constitutionalism*, 90 MICH. L. REV. 761 (1992); Earl M. Malz, *False Prophet–Justice Brennan and the Theory of State Constitutional Law*, 15 HASTINGS CONST. L.Q. 429 (1988).

Several approaches have been proposed. One view is the primacy approach, under which the state court should decide the state constitutional issue first and only resolve the federal issue if the court concludes that the right is not protected under the state constitution.[24] The opposing view is the interstitial method, under which the state court should decide the federal issue first and then examine the state constitution only if the Federal Constitution does not protect the right at issue.[25] An alternative approach is the dual reliance method, under which the state court always considers both the federal and state issues independently.[26] Yet others have argued that all of these approaches are artificial constructs that unnecessarily constrain judicial resolution of constitutional claims.[27]

Such concerns underlie the state constitutional law decisions of Texas, as well as most other states. This chapter considers these issues by examining various dually protected guarantees under the Texas Constitution and then comparing the results with judicial decisions from other states. In analyzing these opinions, the normative questions should be kept in mind. Why did the court embrace the methodology that it followed? How did the court view the interrelationship of the rights protected by the federal and state constitutions?

A. SEARCHES AND SEIZURES AND RIGHTS OF THE ACCUSED

The Fourth Amendment to the United States Constitution prohibits unreasonable searches and seizures in the following language:

> The right of the people to be secure in their persons, houses, papers, and effects, against unreasonable searches and seizures, shall not be violated, and no Warrants shall issue, but upon probable cause, supported by Oath or affirmation, and particularly describing the place to be searched, and the person or things to be seized.

Every state constitution contains an analogous prohibition, typically with similar wording. Article I, section 9 of the Texas Constitution is illustrative, encompassing all the same concepts with only minor differences in word choice and ordering:

> The people shall be secure in their persons, houses, papers and possessions, from all unreasonable seizures or searches, and no warrant to search any place, or to seize any person or thing, shall issue without describing them as near as may be, nor without probable cause, supported by oath or affirmation.

---

[24]*See, e.g.*, Hans A. Linde, *First Things First: Rediscovering the States' Bills of Rights*, 9 U. BAL. L. REV. 379 (1980).

[25]*See, e.g.*, Stewart G. Pollock, *Adequate and Independent Grounds as a Means of Balancing the Relationship Between State and Federal Courts*, 63 TEX. L. REV. 977 (1985).

[26]*See, e.g.*, Robert F. Utter, *"Swimming in the Jaws of the Crocodile:" State Court Comment on Federal Constitutional Issues When Disposing of Cases on State Constitutional Grounds*, 63 TEX. L. REV. 1025 (1985).

[27]*See, e.g.*, *Ex parte* Tucci, 859 S.W.2d 1, 33 (Phillips, C.J., concurring).

The Texas Court of Criminal Appeals recognized in the 1940's that the language of article I, section 9 and the Fourth Amendment were, "in all material aspects, the same."[28] Moreover, in a number of cases, the court had treated the two provisions as providing the same protections.[29] Nevertheless, some decisions during the late 1980's had hinted that the court might be ready to embrace the new judicial federalism movement and construct an independent state civil rights jurisprudence even with respect to textually similar dually protected rights.[30] The Court of Criminal Appeals squarely addressed the issue in the following case.

Heitman v. State, 815 S.W.2d 681 (Tex. Crim. App. 1991)

MILLER, JUDGE.

The trial court convicted appellant on his plea of nolo contendere to the offense of possession of methamphetamine with intent to deliver, and he appealed to contest the court's adverse ruling on his motion to suppress the methamphetamine which was discovered during an inventory search of his car. Art. 44.02 V.A.C.C.P. The Court of Appeals affirmed. 776 S.W.2d 324. A detailed rendition of the pertinent facts is set out in the Court of Appeals opinion. Briefly, police discovered the appellant slumped forward in his car outside a store at about 5:30 a.m. Officers found a loaded 9mm pistol on appellant and arrested him for UCW. As appellant was transported to jail, the officers inventoried his car and found a locked briefcase in the passenger compartment. The officers "jimmied" open the briefcase and found the methamphetamine. Appellant claims the inventory search violated both the Fourth Amendment and Art. I, § 9. We granted appellant's petition for discretionary review to determine whether either claim has merit.

Without commenting on the correctness of the result reached in the Court of Appeals disposition of the Fourth Amendment claim, we note that cursory treatment was given to the Art. I, § 9 claim. Guided by language in some caselaw and distinguishing language in other caselaw, all from this Court, the Court of Appeals disposed of the Art. I § 9 claim solely by construing it in harmony with the Fourth Amendment. Today we reserve for ourselves the power to interpret our own constitution. We will reverse the decision of the Court of Appeals and remand the case to them for an independent analysis of the state constitutional claim.

We herein confront the question of whether this Court will automatically adopt and apply to Art. I, § 9, of the Texas Constitution the Supreme Court's interpretations of the Fourth Amendment. This Court has repeatedly recognized that Art. I, § 9 of the Texas Constitution and the Fourth Amendment to the United States Constitution are the same in

---

[28]Crowell v. State, 180 S.W.2d 343, 346 (Tex. Crim. App. 1944).

[29]*See, e.g.*, Johnson v. State, 803 S.W.2d 272, 288 (Tex. Crim. App. 1990), *overruled to the extent in conflict with* Heitman v. State, 815 S.W.2d 681, 690 (Tex. Crim. App. 1991); Osban v. State, 726 S.W.2d 107, 111 (Tex. Crim. App. 1986), *overruled to the extent in conflict with Heitman*, 815 S.W.2d at 690; Brown v. State, 657 S.W.2d 797, 798 (Tex. Crim. App. 1983) (plurality op.), *overruled to the extent in conflict with Heitman*, 815 S.W.2d at 690; *Crowell*, 180 S.W.2d at 346.

[30]*See, e.g.*, *Ex parte* Patterson, 740 S.W.2d 766, 770-75 (Tex. Crim. App. 1987) (holding convicted felon had protected liberty interest in parole under the Texas Constitution despite contrary United States Supreme Court precedent), *overruled on other grounds*, *Ex parte* Beck, 769 S.W.2d 525, 528 (Tex. Crim. App. 1989).

all material aspects. The two provisions serve to safeguard individuals' privacy and security against arbitrary invasion by governmental officials. *Evers v. State,* 576 S.W.2d 46 (Tex.Cr.App.1979), and *Kolb v. State,* 532 S.W.2d 87 (Tex.Cr.App.1976).

Under our system of federalism, however, the states are free to reject federal holdings as long as state action does not fall below the minimum standards provided by federal constitutional protections. See *Cooper v. California,* 386 U.S. 58 (1967). Likewise, a state is free as a matter of its own law to impose greater restrictions on police activity than those the Supreme Court holds to be necessary upon federal constitutional standards. *Oregon v. Hass,* 420 U.S. 714 (1975). Although recognizing these precepts of federalism, this Court has not chosen to interpret Art. I, § 9 in a manner that accords the citizens of this State greater protections than those accorded by the Fourth Amendment.[31] We write today to finally resolve this question of interpretation of our state constitution. We find that there are several reasons and situations other than similarity of wording or absence of statutory or constitutional mandates which justify, if not compel, a state court to independently judicially interpret its own state constitutional provisions.

Initially, using similarity of wording as the foundation for the theory of harmonious interpretation assumes that state constitutional framers desired that this be done. We believe this assumption to be erroneous. There is no historical factual basis for such an assumption. A recent law review article points out that as early as 1855, several state appellate courts had already looked to their own state constitutional conventions in interpreting the provisions of their constitutions. Although some states used the federal constitution as a guideline for their own, arguably the framers of the states' constitutions were unaware of the original intent of the framers of the federal constitution when it was drafted. Thus, even under an original intent theory, looking to federal constitutional jurisprudence in interpreting state constitutional provisions was not necessarily prudent.

Historically, criminal procedure was primarily governed by state constitutions and by each state's judicial interpretation of its own statutory and constitutional provisions. Abrahamson, *Criminal Law and State Constitutions: The Emergence of State Constitutional Law,* 63 Tex. L. Rev. 1141, 1144 (1985). Until the passage of the Fourteenth Amendment and its selective incorporation, only state judiciaries relying on state constitutions protected individual rights from state governments. Thus, state courts and state constitutions originally were the primary guarantors of individual rights and of liberty in criminal cases. State courts have thus been considered "laboratories" of constitutional law. State courts have the opportunity to experiment with constitutional rights and lay potential guidelines for future constitutional decisions of not only state courts but the Supreme Court as well. The United States Supreme Court has in fact looked to state constitutional jurisprudence and experience in determining to apply the federal Bill of Rights to the states. For example, in

---

[31]The Texas legislature and the voters have exercised this freedom to afford the state's citizens greater protections than the minimum requirements of the federal constitution. See e.g. Art. I, § 10, Tex. Const., (requiring indictment by grand jury in felonies although states are not subject to the indictment requirement of the Fifth Amendment); *Whisenant v. State,* 557 S.W.2d 102 (Tex.Cr.App.1977) (Texas procedure for revoking probations affords greater protection than that required by Fourteenth Amendment); and *Butler v. State,* 493 S.W.2d 190 (Tex.Cr.App. 1973) (Art. 38.22, V.A.C.C.P., more strict than Fifth Amendment regarding oral confessions).

Mapp v. Ohio, 367 U.S. 643, 650 (1961), in discussing the exclusionary rule from *Weeks v. United States,* 232 U.S. 383 (1914), the Supreme Court noted that although it had not imposed the rule upon the states as an essential ingredient of the Fourth Amendment, numerous states had. In reaching its decision that the exclusionary rule applied to the states via the Fourteenth Amendment, the Supreme Court discussed the experience the states had had with alternative means of protecting the Fourth Amendment right to privacy.

Furthermore, the state courts are better able to approach state constitutional interpretation with a more innovative and responsive approach to local interests than the Supreme Court whose decisions bear the onus of nationwide applicability. The state court is best able to address the interests of the citizens of its state and balance those against the interests of that state as it does not have to operate from a national vision, seeking the lowest common denominator and considering all the variations from state to state.

Riding in tandem with this idea that state courts can better respond to local interests is the concept of diversity. Our society is at once homogeneous and heterogenous, and our legal culture should correspondingly be homogenous (national) and heterogenous (state). Moreover, the very concept of federalism embraces such an approach. State courts may review and "rethink" federal constitutional decisions and thereby ensure that, when interpreting state constitutions, their citizens will have the "double security" the federal constitution was intended to provide. Finally, failure to independently interpret the state constitution effectively repeals or renders moot the state constitutional provisions, and allows the Supreme Court, nine appointed justices who are not responsible to this state's electorate, to have the final say on our state constitutional rights.

Merely following Supreme Court decisions ignores state precedent that existed before the comparable federal right was applied to the states. Moreover, our state constitution is a doctrine independent of the federal constitution and its guarantees are not dependent upon those in the federal constitution.[32] The wording of our constitution is not identical to that of the federal constitution, although the rights and provisions are similar, and to interpret our state constitutional provisions in accordance with federal court interpretations of comparable rights ignores our own constitutional history. When the country known as the Republic of Texas became a state in 1846, it came into the Union with its own constitution. The statehood constitution of 1845, which had 21 rights guarantees under its Bill of Rights, "drew heavily on the newly-adopted constitution of Louisiana, and on the proposed constitution for the State of Texas drawn up in 1833, but, apparently, used the Constitution of 1836 as a working model as far as the general plan of government and the bill of rights were concerned." Vernon's Ann.Tex. Const., Preamble (Interpretive Commentary). The 1876 Constitution, under which Texas operates today, had 29 Bill of Rights sections, and, in drafting this constitution, the authors relied on the wisdom of other states' constitutions.

---

[32]Article I, section 1, of the Texas Constitution provides: "Texas is a free and independent State, subject only to the Constitution of the United States, and the maintenance of our free institutions and the perpetuity of the Union depend upon the preservation of the right of local self-government, unimpaired to all the States."

[I]t is, we believe, significant that our Bill of Rights is the first article in our state constitution and that it held this position in each of Texas's five state constitutions. Such placement indicates the degree of importance of these provisions to the drafters of the constitution and the citizens of this state, as opposed to the federal Bill of Rights which was *amended to* the end of the federal counterpart.

Further, there is *direct* evidence which indicates the framers of the 1845 constitution did not intend for our state constitution to be interpreted in lock-step with the federal constitution. A Washington County constitutional delegate proposed that the 1845 document be construed *in pari materia* with the Bill of Rights to the United States Constitution. This proposal was not adopted, thus indicating the framers did not intend to limit the rights of citizens of this State to that which protects them under the federal constitution. Ponton, Arvel (Rod), III, *Sources of Liberty in the Texas Bill of Rights,* 20 St. Mary's L.J. 93, 109 (1988). Clearly our own state constitution was not intended by our own founding fathers to mirror that of the federal government.

Therefore, given the foregoing reasons and the numerous decisions tacitly addressing the "interpretation issue", we now expressly conclude that this Court, when analyzing and interpreting Art. I, § 9, Tex. Const., will not be bound by Supreme Court decisions addressing the comparable Fourth Amendment issue.[33] In reaching this conclusion, we recognize that state constitutions cannot subtract from the rights guaranteed by the United States Constitution, but they can provide additional rights to their citizens. The decisions of the Supreme Court represent the *minimum* protections which a state must afford its citizens.

As to the issue presented in the case *sub judice,* the legality of an inventory search, we decline to blindly follow the Supreme Court's decisions interpreting the Fourth Amendment in addressing the issue under Art. I, § 9. Cases, including those cited herein, in conflict are overruled to the extent of that conflict. [T]his cause is remanded to the court of appeals for consideration of appellant's state constitutional claim in light of this decision.

[The dissenting opinion of Presiding Judge McCormack has been omitted. Judge White also noted his dissent].

Notes on Interpreting Textually Similar Constitutional Provisions

Independent and Lockstep Interpretations: Under what circumstances should provisions in the federal and state constitutions with similar wording that do not differ in any "material aspect" be interpreted differently? If the words are the same or close to the same, and there is no relevant historical evidence or precedent suggesting a different intended meaning, is it legitimate for a state court to adopt an independent meaning for the state provision? On the other hand, is the contrary methodology, which adopts the same meaning for the federal and state guarantees, legitimate when it renders state constitutional rights largely superfluous?

---

[33]This is not to say that United States Supreme Court cases will not be permissive authority, just as court decisions from other states may be.

A state court confronted with interpreting a state constitutional individual right with analogous text, purposes, history, and prior precedent as a federal guarantee has two basic interpretational choices: (1) an independent analysis of the state constitutional provision or (2) the so-called lockstep approach that continues to interpret the state right identically to the federal right. In *Heitman*, the Texas Court of Criminal Appeals chose an independent analysis for the Texas search and seizure provision. It first reasoned that there was no "historical factual basis" for the assumption that the state constitutional framers intended that the state constitution be interpreted in harmony with the Federal Constitution, later mentioning that a proposal to interpret all of the Texas rights guarantees *in pari materia* with the Federal Bill of Rights was not adopted. But why isn't the fact that some of the provisions of the Texas Bill of Rights are drafted in almost identical language to the Federal Bill of Rights, while others are not, a "factual basis" for an analogous interpretation of similar clauses? Many state courts have reasoned that the presence of identical language in the federal and state provisions supports a uniform interpretation of the clauses.[34] The Texas Court of Criminal Appeals appeared to respond that, because the states were unaware of the original "secret" intent of the federal framers contained in their journals, diaries, and correspondence that were published posthumously, the states should not be bound by that intent. But is a textually-based theory that like-worded phrases should be interpreted similarly the same as original intent? Could a state court adopt the lockstep approach without subscribing to a theory of original intent?

Heitman next highlighted that state courts and state constitutions originally were the primary guarantors of rights against the actions of state governments. While this is undoubtedly true, the failure of many states to adequately fulfill this role motivated the United States Supreme Court to incorporate most of the provisions of the Federal Bill of Rights through the Due Process Clause to ensure citizens would be safeguarded from the actions of state governments. Does the original position of the state constitutions justify an independent approach today if the courts of a particular state had never adopted a robust and independent protection for individual rights before the incorporation of provisions of the Federal Bill of Rights?

Heitman finally contended that the nature of our federal system supported independent state constitutional interpretation. The states exist in part to secure a dual security for the people, responding to local needs and serving as laboratories to engage in constitutional experimentation. But do these arguments, as strong as they are, provide a basis for the state's *judiciary* to independently interpret textually similar, dually protected rights at the expense of the other branches of state government?

In the first footnote in *Heitman*, the court recognized that the Texas Legislature has enacted statutes and, with the aid of Texas voters, adopted constitutional amendments authorizing certain additional state protections for criminal defendants over those required

---

[34]*See, e.g.*, People v. Harris, 570 N.E.2d 1051, 1053 (N.Y. 1991) ("Because the language of the Fourth Amendment . . . and section 12 of article I of the New York State Constitution prohibiting unreasonable searches and seizures is identical, it may be assumed, as a general proposition, that the two provisions confer similar rights."); People v. Reynolds, 523 N.E.2d 291, 293 (N.Y. 1988) (noting "the identity of language in the two clauses supports a policy of uniformity" in interpretation). *But see* People v. Scott, 593 N.E.2d 1328 (N.Y. 1992) (rejecting federal open fields exception to searches for posted land).

by the Federal Constitution, such as requiring grand jury indictments for felonies even though the Fifth Amendment's grand jury requirement does not apply against the states. The Texas Constitution also absolutely prohibits the writ of habeas corpus from being suspended, unlike the United States Constitution and the constitutions of most states that authorize the suspension of the great writ in cases of rebellion or invasion.[35] Further, Texas adopted the exclusionary rule by statute decades before the Supreme Court in *Mapp v. Ohio* required the states to do so, and in some respects this statutory exclusionary rule offers more protection than required by the Fourth Amendment.[36] Similarly, the Texas Code of Criminal Procedure defines the situations in which a police officer may make a warrantless arrest, which are also more strict in some circumstances than the Fourth Amendment.[37] Are such uses of the political process a better method for a state to expand its citizens' rights? Or is it preferable for state courts to create additional protections via constitutional interpretation of rights textually similar to those protected by the Federal Constitution?

Professor Earl Maltz noted that, in the absence of binding constitutional limitations, the legislature may create rights by statute and courts may determine rights by common law such that "*some* governmental process will determine the distribution of legal rights in society–with or without the innovation of constitutional analysis." He continued:

> The key question in state constitutional analysis is how the authority to make this determination will be distributed within state governments. A general rule that limits the activism of state courts in individual rights cases allocates maximum authority to state legislatures. More activist theories, by contrast, increase the power of the courts to make decisions and place them beyond the control of the normal legislative process.[38]

Is Professor Maltz's assessment correct? Are there potential problems in allocating "maximum authority to state legislatures"?

---

[35]*Compare* TEX. CONST. art. I, § 12 ("The writ of habeas corpus is a writ of right, and shall never be suspended.") *with* U.S. CONST. art. I, § 9 ("The Privilege of the Writ of Habeas Corpus shall not be suspended, unless when in Cases of Rebellion or Invasion the public Safety may require it."). Texas constitutions before 1876 allowed the suspension of the privilege of the writ in cases of rebellion and invasion, but perceived abuses of this suspension power during Reconstruction led to the current state constitutional prohibition against the suspension of the writ. *See* 1 GEORGE D. BRADEN ET AL., THE CONSTITUTION OF THE STATE OF TEXAS: AN ANNOTATED AND COMPARATIVE ANALYSIS 46 (1977). Approximately nine other state constitutions contain a similar absolute bar. *Id.* at 47.

[36]TEX. CODE CRIM. PROC. art. 38.23. This statutory exclusionary rule is broader in at least two respects than the Fourth Amendment: first, it applies to violations of the law by private citizens and government agents, unlike the Fourth Amendment that just applies to government agents, *see* Miles v. State, 241 S.W.3d 28, 32-36 (Tex. Crim. App. 2007); and second, the good faith exception to the exclusionary rule under the statute requires a finding of probable cause whereas the Fourth Amendment employs a more flexible standard. *See* Gordon v. State, 801 S.W.2d 899, 912-13 (Tex. Crim. App. 1990). In *Garcia v. State*, 829 S.W.2d 796, 797-800 (Tex. Crim. App. 1992) (Benavides, J., plurality op.), a plurality of the court concluded that the statutory standard was also more protective in that it did not incorporate an inevitable discovery exception as under the Fourth Amendment.

[37]*See* TEX. CODE CRIM. PROC. arts. 14.01-.06.

[38]Earl M. Maltz, *The Political Dynamic of the "New Judicial Federalism"*, 2 EMERGING ISSUES IN STATE CONST. L. 233, 233-34 (1989).

Policy Implications of Independent Search and Seizure Doctrine: The states may afford their citizens greater protection against state governmental action than the Federal Constitution would provide, assuming in the process no federal law is violated. Nevertheless, merely because a state *can* do something does not mean that it *should.* What are the policy arguments in favor of providing additional protections to citizens against governmental searches and seizures? What are the policy arguments against such additional protections? Or should such policy concerns not be a consideration in constitutional interpretation?

Some courts and commentators have urged that employing different standards under the federal and state constitutions creates unnecessary confusion, especially as state and federal law enforcement officers working together on the same investigation would have disparate obligations to the citizens under investigation.[39] But wouldn't this problem exist anyway as a result of deviations between federal and state criminal procedure statutes and rules? Or is this not as severe a problem because statutes and rules are easier to follow than constitutional standards?

What if a federal law enforcement officer, performing a valid search under the Fourth Amendment, shared evidence that would be inadmissible under a state's constitution with a state law enforcement officer or prosecutor? Could the evidence be used in state court even though it was gathered in violation of the state constitution? Although Texas cases have not definitively resolved this issue,[40] most other jurisdictions allow the evidence to be used under the reverse "silver platter" doctrine, as long as the federal officer was not acting as an agent of state officials.[41]

Heitman*'s Holding and Impact*: *Heitman* did not hold that the search at issue violated article I, section 9, instead merely remanding the case to the court of appeals for an independent state constitutional analysis. On remand, the court of appeals, sitting en banc, reasoned that the search of Heitman's briefcase was a reasonable inventory search under prior Texas and federal case law rather than an unreasonable search precluded by article I, section 9.[42] Was the court of appeals' holding on remand consistent with the spirit of the

---

[39]*See, e.g.*, McCrory v. State, 342 So. 2d 897, 900 (Miss. 1977); State v. Seibel, 471 N.W.2d 226, 235 n.15 (Wis. 1991); Cathleen C. Herasimchuk, *The New Federalism: Judicial Legislation by the Texas Court of Criminal Appeals?*, 68 TEX. L. REV. 1481, 1510-11 (1990). *Compare* State v. Florance, 527 P.2d 1202, 1209 (Or. 1974) (reasoning that uniformity between federal and state search and seizure standards would be simpler for law enforcement personnel) *with* State v. Caraher, 653 P.2d 942, 946-47 (Or. 1982) (concluding, contrary to *Florance*, that simplicity would be better served by relying on an independent analysis of the state constitution rather than guessing at the appropriate Fourth Amendment standard to apply).

[40]*See* State v. Toone, 823 S.W.2d 744, 747-48 (Tex. App.–Dallas 1992) (employing reverse silver platter doctrine), *aff'd on other grounds*, 872 S.W.2d 750, 752 & n.7 (Tex. Crim. App. 1994) (determining it was unnecessary to reach the silver platter issue).

[41]*See, e.g.*, Pooley v. State, 705 P.2d 1293, 1301-03 (Alaska App. 1985); State v. Bridges, 925 P.2d 357, 364-72 (Haw. 1996); State v. Mollica, 554 A.2d 1315, 1324-30 (N.J. 1989); State v. Dreibelbis, 511 A.2d 307, 308 (Vt. 1986). *But see* State v. Cardenas-Alvarez, 25 P.3d 225, 232 (N.M. 2001); State v. Davis, 834 P.2d 1008, 1012-13 (Or. 1992). The original formulation of the silver platter doctrine, allowing federal officials to use evidence obtained by state officials before the Fourth Amendment was wholly incorporated against the states, was rejected by the Supreme Court in *Elkins v. United States*, 364 U.S. 206, 223 (1960).

[42]836 S.W.2d 840, 842-43 (Tex. App.–Fort Worth 1992, no pet.) (en banc).

opinion of the Court of Criminal Appeals? The dissent in the court of appeals complained that the majority had limited "the privacy protections afforded all Texans under our State Constitution by interpreting article I, section 9 with the same interpretive constriction as the United States Supreme Court has used in delineating the privacy provision of the Fourth Amendment to the United States Constitution."[43] While a few state court decisions from other jurisdictions have restricted inventory searches under their state constitutions as urged by the dissent in the court of appeals, most state courts have not done so.[44]

Heitman's impact was limited in part because, despite its ringing endorsement of independent state constitutional interpretation of textually similar clauses, the court did not actually indicate *how* such an independent interpretation should be conducted. The court's opinion might be compared to a recipe book extolling the delicacy of a dish without providing either the ingredients or the directions for making it. Chief Justice Walker of the Beaumont Court of Appeals employed his own colorful metaphor, complaining that the Court of Criminal Appeals, by requiring independent analysis without any guidance, had parachuted the fourteen Texas courts of appeals "into the Okefenokee Swamp, without a compass, at night."[45]

Texas appellate decisions for the next few years after *Heitman*, although recognizing that a claim under article I, section 9 had to be analyzed separately from the Fourth Amendment, typically adopted a coextensive interpretation of the state and federal prohibitions on searches and seizures in the particular context under consideration.[46] There were, however, some exceptions. Most notably, in *Richardson v. State*, the Court of Criminal Appeals held that the use of a pen register by law enforcement personnel to record outgoing numbers dialed from a telephone line was a search under article I, section 9,[47] despite the United States Supreme Court's holding in *Smith v. Maryland* that an individual has no expectation of privacy implicating the Fourth Amendment with respect to dialed phone numbers.[48] The Court of Criminal Appeals primarily relied on commentators that had criticized *Smith* and the state courts that had rejected *Smith*'s reasoning under their own constitutions.[49] These other states had concluded, and the Texas Court of Criminal Appeals

---

[43] *Id.* at 843-44 (Lattimore, J., dissenting).

[44] *See* 2 JENNIFER FRIESEN, STATE CONSTITUTIONAL LAW: LITIGATING INDIVIDUAL RIGHTS, CLAIMS AND DEFENSES § 11.07[2] (4th ed. 2006).

[45] Autran v. State, 830 S.W.2d 807, 817 (Tex. App.–Beaumont 1992) (Walker, C.J., concurring), *rev'd*, 887 S.W.2d 31 (Tex. Crim. App. 1994). *See generally* Catherine Greene Burnett & Neil Colman McCabe, *A Compass in the Swamp: A Guide to Tactics in State Constitutional Law Challenges*, 25 TEX. TECH L. REV. 75 (1993) (providing an overview of the problem and a suggested interpretive analysis).

[46] *See, e.g.*, Johnson v. State, 912 S.W.2d 227, 232-34 (Tex. Crim. App. 1995) (plurality op.) (employing same definition of seizure under article I, section 9 as United States Supreme Court articulated for the Fourth Amendment); Aitch v. State, 879 S.W.2d 167, 171-74 (Tex. App.–Houston [14th Dist.] 1994, pet. ref'd) (employing federal standards to adjudge constitutionality under Texas Constitution of search of automobile); Hernandez v. State, 867 S.W.2d 900, 908 (Tex. App.–Texarkana 1993, no pet.) (holding neither precedent nor legislation supported a distinction between Texas and United States Constitutions regarding constitutionality of stop of motorist and subsequent search of vehicle).

[47] 865 S.W.2d 944, 953 (Tex. Crim. App. 1993).

[48] 442 U.S. 735, 743 (1979).

[49] *Richardson*, 865 S.W.2d at 950-51 (citing cases).

agreed, that the mere fact that the telephone company collected the numbers dialed from the line did not diminish the individual's expectation that the government would not intrude into his or her affairs.[50] Yet the Court of Criminal Appeals did not determine whether such a search would be unreasonable in the absence of probable cause, instead remanding that determination and the other remaining issues in the case back to the court of appeals. The court of appeals then disposed of the case on the grounds that the defendant did not have standing to complain about the pen register because it was not placed on his phone and that, in any event, the pen register was immaterial because it was not used as a basis to establish probable cause for the subsequent wiretap that recorded the defendant's incriminating statements.[51]

The Lockstep Conundrum: A state court's determination to interpret a state constitutional right coextensively with a federal guarantee creates its own set of conceptual difficulties. Should the scope of the federal guarantee at the time of the state's adoption of its constitution control, or should the state adopt a lockstep interpretation that continuously maintains equivalent treatment? What happens when the United States Supreme Court later alters or diminishes the scope of the federal right?

The Texas Court of Criminal Appeals' decision in *Johnson v. State* provides an illustration of these problems in the context of determining when a seizure occurs under article I, section 9.[52] Before 1991, the primary consideration in the Supreme Court's Fourth Amendment seizure cases was whether a reasonable person would feel free to leave, which the Texas Court of Criminal Appeals had likewise adopted under article I, section 9.[53] Subsequently, in its 1991 decision in *California v. Hodari D.*, the Supreme Court added to the analysis whether there was physical force by the law enforcement officer or an actual submission to the assertion of authority.[54] The Court of Criminal Appeals in *Johnson* then had to consider whether to adopt the new *Hodari D.* analysis for Fourth Amendment seizures under article I, section 9.[55] Although there was no majority opinion, *Johnson*'s holding comported with the limitations imposed by *Hodari D.* In other words, the court kept article I, section 9 and the Fourth Amendment protections against seizures in "lockstep" as the Supreme Court restricted federal rights.

Other states have also employed a "lockstep" analysis when interpreting their state constitutional search and seizure provisions,[56] including adopting the *Hodari D.* analysis for

---

[50]*Id.*

[51]Richardson v. State, 902 S.W.2d 689, 691-92 (Tex. App.–Amarillo 1995, no pet.).

[52]912 S.W.2d 227 (Tex. Crim. App. 1995).

[53]*Id.* at 232.

[54]499 U.S. 621, 626 (1991).

[55]912 S.W.2d at 232.

[56]*See, e.g.*, People v. Lampitok, 798 N.E.2d 91, 99 (Ill. 2003) (noting Illinois follows the lockstep doctrine providing the same protection against searches and seizures under the state constitution as provided by the Fourth Amendment with one narrow exception); State v. Malone, 683 N.W.2d 1, 6 (Wis. 2004) ("The interpretation of our state constitution's analogous provision has evolved in virtual lockstep with the United States Supreme Court's jurisprudence construing the Fourth Amendment.").

seizures under their state constitutions.[57] In one of these states, Florida, such a result is mandated by a 1982 amendment to its constitution that requires Florida courts to construe the state constitutional protection against searches and seizures "in conformity with the 4th amendment to the United States Constitution, as interpreted by the United States Supreme Court."[58]

Yet other states disagree that a state should change its state constitutional protections as federal standards fluctuate. Some state courts that previously interpreted their state constitutions in accordance with federal constitutional standards have declined to keep their state constitutions in step as Supreme Court interpretations change.[59] As a result, a number of states have refused to use *Hodari D.* as a model for defining when a seizure occurs under their state constitutions, instead preferring to adhere solely to the test examining whether a reasonable person would feel free to leave.[60]

Is it preferable to keep the federal and state constitutions in "lockstep," or to abide by prior interpretations of the state constitution that relied on federal law? Or does the answer depend on the particular circumstances and whether the Supreme Court's reasons for altering the federal right also apply to the state constitution? Of course, one way to avoid this dilemma is to interpret the state constitution entirely independently from the Federal Constitution, a method that the Court of Criminal Appeals employed again in the following case, albeit with an interesting twist.

---

[57] *See, e.g.*, State v. Bartee, 623 So. 2d 458, 459 (Fla. 1993); Harper v. State, 635 So. 2d 864, 867 (Miss. 1994); State v. Cronin, 509 N.W.2d 673, 676 (Neb. Ct. App. 1993).

[58] FLA. CONST. art. I, § 12. This amendment requires Florida courts to follow decisions of the Supreme Court under the Fourth Amendment when interpreting their own search and seizure state constitutional provision. *See, e.g.*, Bernie v. State, 524 So. 2d 988, 990-91 (Fla. 1988). However, the Florida Supreme Court has held that it does not require adherence to plurality opinions, *see* State v. Welker, 536 So. 2d 1017, 1019 (Fla. 1988), nor to issues that have been decided by federal appellate courts rather than the Supreme Court. State v. Cross, 487 So. 2d 1056, 1057-58 (Fla. 1986). The Florida courts must likewise construe the state constitutional prohibition on cruel or unusual punishments "in conformity with decisions of the United States Supreme Court which interpret the prohibition against cruel and unusual punishment provided in the Eighth Amendment to the United States Constitution." FLA. CONST. art. I, § 17. California has since adopted a similar constitutional provision that bars the state courts from affording greater rights to criminal defendants than those afforded by the United States Constitution. CAL. CONST. art. I, § 24.

[59] *See, e.g.*, Robins v. Pruneyard Shopping Ctr., 592 P.2d 341, 346 (Cal. 1979) (noting prior state decisions interpreting state constitution were still useful precedents supporting free speech rights at a privately owned shopping center even though the prior decisions relied on and cited "federal law that took a divergent course"); State v. Novembrino, 519 A.2d 820, 856-57 (N.J. 1987) (refusing to adopt good faith exception to exclusionary rule under state constitution as court would adhere to its prior interpretations of the rule over the last twenty-five years); BARRY LATZER, STATE CONSTITUTIONS AND CRIMINAL JUSTICE 73-74 (1991) (discussing cases in which a state court rejected current Supreme Court doctrine to preserve a previous interpretation of its state constitution that had relied on then-existing federal precedent).

[60] *See, e.g.*, State v. Oquendo, 613 A.2d 1300, 1307-10 (Conn. 1993) (declining to adopt *Hodari D.* definition of seizure and instead adhering to prior state precedents that relied on earlier federal seizure definition); State v. Quino, 840 P.2d 358, 362 (Haw. 1992) (same); *In re* E.D.J., 502 N.W.2d 779, 780-83 (Minn. 1993) (same); State v. Clayton, 45 P.3d 30, 34 (Mont. 2002) (same); State v. Tucker, 642 A.2d 401, 404-05 (N.J. 1994) (same); Commonwealth v. Matos, 672 A.2d 769, 776 (Pa. 1996) (same); State v. Randolph, 74 S.W.2d 330, 337 (Tenn. 2002) (same); State v. Young, 957 P.2d 681, 687 (Wash. 1998) (same).

Hulit v. State, 982 S.W.2d 431 (Tex. Crim. App. 1998)

WOMACK, J., delivered the opinion of the Court, in which McCORMICK, P.J., and MANSFIELD, KELLER, and HOLLAND, JJ., joined.

This case calls on us to decide whether the search and seizure provision of the Texas Constitution was violated when a peace officer went to the aid of a motorist who was unconscious in his vehicle on a public highway.

I.

About 2:00 a.m. on April 29, 1995, Officer T.A. Page of the Benbrook Police Department was dispatched to the intersection of the westbound service road of Southwest Loop 820 and Winscott "to assist another officer on an ambulance call. A woman–it was reported that there was a woman possibly having a heart attack in a vehicle at that address." Page was the first officer to arrive. He found a pickup truck "sitting in the inside lane" of the service road, which is marked for a turn lane, about 50 feet back from the intersection. An individual with "long hair in a ponytail" was "slumped over the steering wheel. Just like he was asleep or passed out or possibly had a heart attack." The truck's engine was running; all the windows were rolled up. There was no other traffic on the road.

Page got out of his vehicle, walked up to the truck, and started rapping on the window to try to awaken the driver, who he could now see was a man. At first the driver did not respond at all. Another officer, Doug Bird, arrived, and both officers kept rapping at the window and yelling at the driver to wake up. "He eventually woke up and pulled the handle on the door and opened the door." The driver seemed to be disoriented, and Page smelled an odor of alcohol about him.

The officers began an investigation for DWI. The parties stipulated that the driver was the appellant, and that at a trial the State would offer additional testimony about the investigation that the State "would not be able to elicit in fact but for the initial detention."

The appellant was indicted for the offense of driving while intoxicated which was enhanced by two previous DWI convictions. He filed a written motion to suppress evidence "because of the violation of the Defendant's rights against unreasonable search and seizure solely under Tex. Const. Art. I, Sec. 9, 10 and 19; and Tex.Code Crim. Proc. Ann. Arts. 1.04, 1.05, 1.06, 38.21, 38.22 and 38.23." The appellant withdrew an earlier motion which had invoked both state and federal constitutions. He told the trial court that "the Texas Constitution and law . . . are the only issues that are before the Court in this motion."

The trial court denied the motion to suppress evidence after hearing the testimony and stipulations which we have summarized. The appellant waived trial by jury and pleaded guilty. This appeal is based on the trial court's denial of the appellant's motion to suppress evidence. . . .

III.

Article I, Section 9 of the Texas Constitution recognizes the right of the people to be secure from all unreasonable seizures or searches. [W]e have "expressly conclude[d] that this Court, when analyzing and interpreting Art. I, § 9, Tex. Const., will not be bound by Supreme Court decisions addressing the comparable Fourth Amendment issue." *Heitman v. State,* 815 S.W.2d 681, 690 (Tex.Cr.App.1991).

The appellant argues that the warrant requirement of the Texas Constitution was violated when he was seized without a warrant under circumstances that did not fall within an established exception. By "the warrant requirement," he means a requirement that a seizure be authorized by a warrant, in the absence of which the seizure would be unlawful even if it were otherwise reasonable. Is there such a requirement in Article I, Section 9 of the Texas Constitution? We shall examine the text of the Constitution, refer to our prior decisions, consider the history of the common law, and consider Fourth Amendment jurisprudence.

Article I, Section 9 reads:

> The people shall be secure in their persons, houses, papers and possessions, from all unreasonable seizures or searches, and no warrant to search any place, or to seize any person or thing, shall issue without describing them as near as may be, nor without probable cause, supported by oath or affirmation.

Section 9, like the Fourth Amendment, comprises two, independent clauses. The first recognizes the right to be free from unreasonable seizures or searches. The second imposes limits on warrants. Neither clause requires a warrant or even authorizes a warrant. The warrant clause does not say when a warrant must issue, or when it may issue; it says only when warrants may not issue. It is cast in the negative ("*no* warrant . . . shall issue"). And even if a warrant met the minimum requirements of the warrant clause (description, probable cause, and affidavit), the warrant still would be unlawful if the seizure or search that it authorized were unreasonable. The natural reading of Section 9 does not support the appellant's assertion that it requires a warrant for a reasonable seizure.

In our prior decisions, we have not found a warrant requirement in Article I, Section 9. In finding constitutional a statute which required common carriers to allow peace officers to inspect their records of shipments of intoxicating liquors, this Court pointed out, "It is not every search that our Constitution inhibits. It is only *unreasonable* searches. In our opinion that provision of our Bill of Rights prohibiting unreasonable seizures and searches, if it has any application whatever to the statute in question in this case, has in no way been violated, and said act of the Legislature is, in our opinion, in every way valid and constitutional." *Hughes v. State,* 149 S.W. 173, 184 (Tex. Crim. App. 1912). Therefore the warrant clause in Section 9 does not mean that a warrant is indispensable to a valid search and seizure.

Historical considerations give no support to the contention that the Texas Constitution imposes a general requirement of a warrant to seize a person. At common law, seizure of a person (that is, arrest) was permitted when an officer had probable cause to believe that the person was committing, or had committed, a felony, or that the person was committing a misdemeanor involving a breach of the peace in the officer's presence. *See Carroll v. United States,* 267 U.S. 132, 156-57 (1925). The arrest statutes of Texas follow the common law pattern, except that they expand the officer's authority by permitting warrantless arrest for any misdemeanor committed in the officer's presence regardless of whether it involves a breach of the peace, and for certain misdemeanors that are not committed in the officer's presence.

We have recognized that, because of the similarities of the search and seizure provisions in the state and federal constitutions, United States Supreme Court cases may be permissive authority in interpreting the Texas Constitution. *See Heitman v. State,* 815 S.W.2d at 690 n.22. But we do not find persuasive the appellant's citation of Fourth Amendment law from the Supreme Court on this subject. First, the holding that the Fourth Amendment requires a warrant is, as the appellant's brief says, a requirement for searches. The Fourth Amendment does not require a warrant for a seizure of a person that does not involve an intrusion into a home. *United States v. Watson,* 423 U.S. 411 (1976).

Second, although the Supreme Court has frequently said that the Fourth Amendment imposes a general warrant requirement for searches, these statements have often been followed by the Court's statements that the central inquiry under the Fourth Amendment is the reasonableness of the search or seizure under the totality of the circumstances.[61] It is the latter approach which we find consistent with the language of Article I, Section 9 of the Texas Constitution.

Third, historical research indicates that the Framers' primary, if not sole, concern in drafting the Fourth Amendment was avoiding a repetition of the British colonial practice of issuing general warrants or warrants based on bare suspicion.[62] Such warrants were doubly pernicious because they not only authorized intrusions on the privacy of the colonists, they prevented civil redress by shielding the executing officers from civil liability. Supreme Court cases which have held that the Fourth Amendment was intended to impose a warrant requirement are not well founded in historical fact. Insofar as Article I, Section 9 of the Texas Constitution was directed at preventing the same evil that the Fourth Amendment was intended to prevent, the history of the Fourth Amendment informs our interpretation of its meaning.

Fourth, by finding a general requirement of a warrant to which there are exceptions, the Supreme Court has created a jurisprudential mare's nest. There are so many exceptions to the warrant requirement that most searches and seizures are conducted without warrants and justified under one of the exceptions. Such a model of the Fourth Amendment not only makes a mockery of the supposed requirement, it interferes with a more fine-tuned assessment of the competing interests at stake. For these reasons we find the Supreme Court's statements about a warrant requirement unpersuasive.

It is our holding that Article I, Section 9 of the Texas Constitution contains no requirement that a seizure or search be authorized by a warrant, and that a seizure or search

---

[61] *E.g., Terry v. Ohio,* 392 U.S. 1 (1968). *See United States v. Rabinowitz,* 339 U.S. 56 (1950).

[62] Charles H. Whitebread & Christopher Slobogin, CRIMINAL PROCEDURE 130 (3d. ed 1993) ("There is considerable historical support . . . "); Akhil Reed Amar, THE CONSTITUTION AND CRIMINAL PROCEDURE 10-13 (1997); Telford Taylor, TWO STUDIES IN CONSTITUTIONAL INTERPRETATION 41 (1969) ("[O]ur constitutional fathers were not concerned about warrantless searches, but about overreaching warrants").

that is otherwise reasonable will not be found to be in violation of that section because it was not authorized by a warrant.

This is not to say that statutes which require warrants for seizure or search may be ignored. Nor do we say that the issuance of a warrant by a neutral magistrate may not be a factor in the totality of circumstances by which we judge whether a seizure or search was reasonable.

We understand that our holding means that Section 9 of our Bill of Rights does not offer greater protection to the individual than the Fourth Amendment to the United States Constitution, and it may offer less protection. But our holding is the construction that is faithful to the Constitution which our people have adopted, and it is our duty to interpret that Constitution independent of the interpretations of federal courts. *Heitman v. State, supra.*

Heitman does not mean that the Texas Constitution cannot be interpreted to give less protection than the federal constitution. It only means that the Texas Constitution will be interpreted independently. *See Hulit v. State,* 947 S.W.2d at 709. Its protections may be lesser, greater, or the same as those of the federal constitution.[63]

In *Heitman,* we repeated the dictum of our sister court: "The federal constitution sets the floor for individual rights; state constitutions establish the ceiling." *LeCroy v. Hanlon,* 713 S.W.2d 335, 338 (Tex.Sup.1986). With all respect to our Sister Court, we think its metaphor is wrong. The state constitution and the federal constitution are not parts of one legal building; each is its own structure. Their shapes may be different, as may their parts. Each may shield rights that the other does not. The ceiling of one may be lower than the floor of the other. Because of the Supremacy Clause of the United States Constitution, a defendant who is entitled to claim the protection of a federal provision may receive a greater protection from that floor than the greatest protection that the ceiling of the Texas Constitution would give him. But that does not mean that the Texas Constitution has no ceilings that are lower than those of the federal constitution. *See Welchek v. State,* 247 S.W. 524 (Tex. Crim. App. 1922) (Article I, Section 9 creates no exclusionary rule similar to that found in Fourth Amendment for federal prosecutions).

In our holding there is no violation of the Supremacy Clause of Article VI of the United States Constitution.

> State courts are the final interpreters of state law even though their actions are reviewable under the federal constitution, treaties, or laws. The supreme court of a state is truly the highest court in terms of this body of

---

[63]The dissent is mistaken in saying that this court cannot interpret our state constitution as affording less protection than the federal constitution. As a distinguished state jurist and leader of the new federalism said, "The right question is not whether a state's guarantee is the same as or broader than its federal counterpart as interpreted by the Supreme Court. The right question is what the state's guarantee means and how it applies to the case at hand. The answer may turn out the same as it would under federal law. The state's law may prove to be more protective than federal law. The state law also may be less protective. In that case the court must go on to decide the claim under federal law, assuming it has been raised." Hans A. Linde, *E Pluribus–Constitutional Theory and State Courts,* 18 GA. L. REV. 165, 179 (1984).

> law and it is not a "lower court" even in relation to the Supreme Court of the United States. It must follow the Supreme Court's rulings on the meaning of the Constitution of the United States or federal law, but it is free to interpret state laws or the state constitution in any way that does not violate principles of federal law.

John E. Nowak, Ronald D. Rotunda, J. Nelson Young, 1 Treatise on Constitutional Law 31 (1986). We do not make any holding about the appellant's rights under federal law. In this case, the appellant has chosen not to seek any shelter in the federal constitution. (In our architectural metaphor, he may not be able to fit his facts under the federal ceiling.) This case has called on us to decide whether our constitution will give him the shelter he wants. It does not.

The Supremacy Clause means that, in practical terms, persons will always be able to avail themselves of the greater right. This is very important to litigants and their counsel, who are naturally and properly result-oriented. But it does not mean that a court, faithfully interpreting state laws, can only find in them protections that equal or exceed federal laws.

We find that the police officers acted reasonably when they approached the vehicle in which the appellant was slumped unconscious on a public highway, awakened the appellant, and asked him to step out so they could see if he was in need of assistance. We hold that Article I, Section 9 of the Texas Constitution was not violated by their actions. We do this, not by finding that there is a community care-taking exception to a warrant requirement, but by asking whether, from the totality of the circumstances, after considering the public and private interests that are at stake, their action was an unreasonable seizure. It was not.

BAIRD, J., delivered a dissenting opinion, joined by OVERSTREET, J.

The majority disregards the Supremacy Clause, the Fourth Amendment of the United States Constitution, and Supreme Court precedent to hold there is no actual warrant requirement under the Texas Constitution, only an ethereal requirement a search or seizure be "reasonable." This is incorrect. The United States Supreme Court has interpreted the Fourth Amendment as requiring that searches and seizures be pursuant to a warrant, or a legal exception to the warrant requirement. Because art. I, § 9 of the Texas Constitution must provide at least the same protection as the Fourth Amendment to the United States Constitution, including warrants or valid legal exceptions to the warrant requirement, I dissent.

I.

The Supremacy Clause

The Supremacy Clause is a clear directive to this Court that we are bound by the United States Constitution and its interpretation by the United States Supreme Court. Art. VI, cl. 2. There are two major Supremacy Clause problems with the majority opinion.

First, it is of no legal consequence whether the Judges on this Court " . . . find the Supreme Court's statements about a warrant requirement unpersuasive", because we are bound by Supreme Court precedent interpreting the United States Constitution.

The second major Supremacy Clause problem presented by the majority opinion is that because the Fourth Amendment and United States Supreme Court are clear there is a warrant requirement, the Texas Constitution must *at least* require the same protection. Pursuant to *Heitman v. State,* 815 S.W.2d 681 (Tex.Cr.App.1991), we are free to interpret the Texas Constitution as bestowing *greater protection* than its federal counterpart, but we cannot interpret it as affording less protection.

II.
Warrant Requirement

Appellant makes no argument under the United States Constitution. Instead, he relies exclusively on the protection of the Texas Constitution and argues art. I, § 9 provides greater protection than the Fourth Amendment. The majority disagrees with this contention but does not stop there. The majority oversteps its bounds by interpreting art. I, § 9 of the Texas Constitution as affording *less* protection than its Federal counterpart.

III.
Heitman v. State–New Federalism

In *Heitman v. State,* we were presented with the question of whether art. I, § 9 provided greater protection than the Fourth Amendment. We explained that traditionally this Court had treated art. I, § 9 the same as the Fourth Amendment. *Heitman,* 815 S.W.2d at 682-83. The *Heitman* Court announced that under our system of federalism we "are free to reject federal holdings *as long as state action does not fall below the minimum standards provided by federal constitutional protections.*" *Id.,* 815 S.W.2d at 682 *citing Cooper v. California,* 386 U.S. 58 (1967). *See also, Oregon v. Kennedy,* 456 U.S. 667, 681 (1982) (state constitutions can provide additional rights for their citizens); *PruneYard Shopping Center v. Robins,* 447 U.S. 74, 81 (1980) (state has sovereign right to adopt in its own Constitution individual liberties more expansive than those conferred by the Federal Constitution); *and, LeCroy v. Hanlon,* 713 S.W.2d 335, 338 (Tex.1986) (the federal constitution sets the floor for individual rights; state constitutions establish the ceiling).

The majority completely misstates *Heitman* as standing for the proposition that this Court can interpret art. I, § 9 as providing *less* protection than the Fourth Amendment. But neither *Heitman* nor its underpinnings suggest this Court is free to interpret the Texas Constitution as providing less protection or fewer rights than its Federal counterpart. To the contrary, in *Heitman,* we *clearly* explained:

> . . . we recognize that *state constitutions cannot subtract from the rights guaranteed by the United States Constitution,* but they can provide additional rights to their citizens. The decisions of the Supreme Court represent the minimum protections which a state must afford its citizens. "The federal constitution sets the floor for individual rights; state constitutions establish the ceiling."

Heitman, 815 S.W.2d at 690 (internal citation omitted). In fact, my research does not reveal a single case where this Court has construed our Constitution as providing less protection or fewer rights than the United States Constitution. The majority fails to cite such a case. What was clear to a majority of this Court in *Heitman* is lost on today's majority.

IV.
The "new" New Federalism

"The term 'federalism' in American history and law traditionally referred to the coordinate relationship and distribution of power between the individual states and the national government." Cathleen Herasimchuk, *The New Federalism: Judicial Legislation by the Texas Court of Criminal Appeals,* 68 Tex. L. Rev. 1481, 1485 (1990). When this Court issued *Heitman,* cries of "New Federalism" were heard, as were accusations that *Heitman* was the work of activist judges using the state constitution to expand state constitutional protections. *See, e.g.* Herasimchuk, *supra; and,* Matthew W. Paul & Jeffrey Van Horn, *Heitman v. State: The Question Left Unanswered,* 23 St. Mary's L.J. 929 (1992). In explaining the New Federalism, opponents opined that state court judges, unhappy with the Supreme Court's decisions limiting the rights of defendants, would invoke state constitutional protections in order to reach alternate results in conflict with the Supreme Court's decisions.

Today, by holding "that Section 9 of our Bill of Rights does not offer greater protection to the individual than the Fourth Amendment to the United States Constitution, and it may offer less protection," the majority is engaging in a "new" New Federalism by diminishing our state constitutional guarantees. The same critics of *Heitman* should be equally outraged with the majority's attempt to interpret state constitutional protections as affording less protection than its federal counterpart, in order to avoid Supreme Court precedent. If providing more rights under our state constitution is judicial activism, surely providing less rights is within that same realm.

V.
Conclusion

First year law students learn that the federal constitution sets the floor for individual rights and state constitutions establish the ceiling. *See,* U.S. Const. art. VI, cl. 2; *Heitman,* 815 S.W.2d at 690; *and, LeCroy v. Hanlon,* 713 S.W.2d at 338. By holding art. I, § 9 does not require that a search or seizure be authorized by a warrant, a majority of this Court no longer reaches for the constitutional ceiling but instead stoops to dig a constitutional basement wherein the Texas Constitution is housed below the floor of the Fourth Amendment. Texans should not have less protections than those enjoyed by the people of the other 49 states.

[The concurring opinions have been omitted.]

Notes on Independent Interpretations and the Floor-Ceiling Metaphor

Diminished Rights under Independent State Constitutional Analysis: Can a state constitutional provision properly be interpreted as providing less rights than guaranteed by an analogous federal provision? *Hulit* is not the only state court decision that has interpreted its state charter as providing less protection in certain contexts.[64] Another good example is

---

[64] *See, e.g.*, State v. Bleyl, 435 A.2d 1349, 1357-58 (Me. 1981) (noting that it had never been decided whether the Maine Constitution required *Miranda* warnings under penalty of exclusion of the evidence); State v. Hopper, 822 P.2d 775, 778 (Wash. 1992) (reasoning Federal Constitution required "a more stringently drafted

State v. Smith, where a plurality of the Oregon Supreme Court explained its conclusion that *Miranda*-type warnings should not be required under the state constitution as follows:

> We do not understand how an Oregon rule identical to the federal [*Miranda*] rule would [be beneficial.] If we adopted a different Oregon *Miranda* rule or placed a different interpretation upon the present federal rule, then we have created confusion. . . . We have the federal *Miranda* warnings. By virtue of the Fifth Amendment and the Fourteenth Amendment we have no choice. We are not arguing about that. *Miranda v. Arizona* is now 20 years old. A whole generation of police, lawyers, and judges has grown up with the federal *Miranda* warnings. We will not speculate what Oregon would be like without them. We also have a body of law on confessions. The bottom line in Oregon for over 100 years has been that before a confession or admission can be received in evidence, the state must prove that it was free and voluntary. For the most part during the last 20 years our law on confessions has been in a standby position gathering rust. Most of the questionable confessions and admissions have been eliminated by the federal *Miranda* rule. However, it is possible to have an involuntary confession or admission even though the *Miranda* warnings have been properly given. We think that it is important to keep the Oregon law on confessions and admissions intact.
>
> To adopt an Oregon *Miranda* rule identical to the federal rule without any commitment to future interpretation would be unwise. We would be in the same position as we are today, except that the ranch would have been sold with no down payment. To adopt an Oregon *Miranda* rule identical to the federal rule and tie it to future interpretation by the federal caselaw would be foolish. We do not know what may be waiting in the alley. To adopt an Oregon *Miranda* rule identical to the federal rule and place our own future interpretation on it would only further confuse an already confused area of the law. To adopt an Oregon *Miranda* rule different from the federal rule is not warranted.
>
> Article I, section 12, of the Oregon Constitution prohibits compulsion, which we interpret to require voluntariness. . . . In a case where the state has given *Miranda*-type warnings and avoided any form of compulsion, the state has met its burden. Where the *Miranda*-type warnings were not given, the burden fully remains on the state to establish that the confession was voluntary. We know of no strong and compelling reason to overturn a long-standing precedent of this court in order to adopt a rule which we consider to be unnecessary and confusing under the present circumstances.[65]

---

charging instrument" than required by the state constitution).

[65]725 P.2d 894, 901-02 (Or. 1986) (Campbell, J., plurality op.). In subsequent decisions, the Oregon Supreme Court, while not adopting the full panoply of *Miranda* warnings under the state constitution, has recognized that the state constitution prohibits the police from continuing to interrogate a suspect after an

The Texas Supreme Court has also recognized that a state constitutional provision can be interpreted as providing less rights than the Federal Constitution,[66] and the plain text of several state constitutional provisions explicitly provides for less protection than under the federal charter.[67] For instance, California Constitution article I, section 28(f)(2) precludes the California state courts from excluding any relevant evidence from a criminal proceeding except as authorized by a two-thirds vote of the state legislature.[68]

Nevertheless, as a practical matter, when state constitutional protections dip below the United States Constitution, the Supremacy Clause requires the application of the federal standard, *assuming* the federal issue has been properly preserved and asserted. Thus, the bar in the California state constitution against the exclusionary rule must yield if a defendant in California state court asserts his *federal* constitutional right to have illegally seized evidence excluded from his criminal trial.[69] Likewise, as *Hulit* recognized, the fact that the court declined to impose a warrant requirement under the Texas Constitution does not preclude a defendant from relying on the warrant requirement of the Fourth Amendment. As *Hulit* noted: "The Supremacy Clause means that, in practical terms, persons will always be able to avail themselves of the greater right." In this respect, the concept of federal supremacy mandates that incorporated federal rights provide a minimum level of protection against the state, or floor, that the state can only alter in practice by providing additional rights. But if this is the case, why did Hulit only receive the benefit of the lesser constitutional protection provided by the state constitution?

Hulit was unusual because the defendant explicitly waived his federal constitutional rights, instead asserting rights solely under the state constitution. Federal constitutional rights, like other arguments in litigation, may be waived either explicitly or implicitly by failure to properly assert them. What might explain Hulit's failure to assert that his seizure violated the Fourth Amendment to the United States Constitution?

The Independent Interpretation of the Texas Search and Seizure Provision: Did *Hulit* answer the question left open in *Heitman* regarding the appropriate method to conduct an independent interpretation of the Texas search and seizure provision? *Hulit* examined the constitutional text, prior state precedent, the history of the common law, and comparative federal jurisprudence in adjudging whether a warrant requirement existed for seizures under the Texas Constitution. Are there other appropriate considerations in interpreting a state constitutional clause with the same language as a federal provision?

---

unequivocal request for an attorney, State v. Isom, 761 P.2d 524, 527-29 (Or. 1988), or from interrogating a suspect in custody at the police station without adequate warnings. State v. Magee, 744 P.2d 250, 252-53 (Or. 1987).

[66] *Ex parte* Tucci, 859 S.W.2d 1, 13 (Tex. 1993) (Doggett, J., plurality op.); *id.* at 32 & n.34 (Phillips, C.J., concurring) (presented *infra* section B).

[67] *See, e.g.*, Sitz v. Dep't of State Police, 506 N.W.2d 209, 216-17 (Mich. 1993) (acknowledging that anti-exclusionary rule provision of Michigan Constitution provided lesser protection than the Fourth Amendment).

[68] CAL. CONST. art. I, § 28(f)(2) (providing, in pertinent part, that "relevant evident shall not be excluded in any criminal proceedings" unless provided by state statute "enacted by two-thirds vote").

[69] *See, e.g.*, People v. Hines, 938 P.2d 388 (Cal. 1997) ("In general, relevant evidence that is illegally obtained under California law is nonetheless admissible, so long as federal law does not bar its admission.").

Do *Hulit* and *Heitman* mean that the state courts in Texas must make an independent reasonableness evaluation under the totality of the circumstances in every case in which a search or seizure is challenged under article I, section 9? If so, what guidance do these cases provide for subsequent Texas cases considering the same problem? How should a court determine when a particular search or seizure is reasonable? Could it ever be possible that the Texas approach would offer greater protections in some instances than the federal approach, perhaps by concluding that a permissible stacking of the approximately two dozen federal warrant exceptions in a particular case was not reasonable?

Texas cases after *Hulit* have not to date provided this type of broader protection against searches and seizures under the reasonableness standard. Yet there are still rare circumstances in which article I, section 9 has been held to provide slightly more protection than the Fourth Amendment. For instance, under the Federal Constitution, voluntary consent to a search must be established by a preponderance of the evidence, while article I, section 9 has been repeatedly interpreted to require clear and convincing evidence of the voluntariness of the consent to the search.[70] But for the most part, the dually protected Texas constitutional guarantees in the criminal context, including the search and seizure protection, have been interpreted to provide no greater rights than afforded under the incorporated protections of the Federal Constitution,[71] although some Texas statutes afford greater protections to the accused.[72]

Search and Seizure Protections and the Rights of the Accused in Other States: While Texas has generally relied on statutes rather than constitutional interpretation to expand protections against governmental searches and seizures, one study concluded that a little over half of search and seizure cases decided by a random sample of twenty-five state supreme courts over a twenty-five year period had provided broader rights under their state constitutions.[73] Professor Jennifer Friesen's treatise on litigating state constitutional claims

---

[70]*See, e.g.*, Montanez v. State, 195 S.W.3d 101, 105 (Tex. Crim. App. 2006); State v. Ibarra, 953 S.W.2d 242, 243-45 (Tex. Crim. App. 1997) (citing prior cases).

[71]*See, e.g.*, Michael E. Keasler, *The Texas Experience: A Case for the Lockstep Approach*, 77 MISS. L.J. 345, 366 (2007). From 1996 until 2007, the Texas Court of Criminal Appeals interpreted article I, section 14, the Texas Double Jeopardy Clause, to bar retrial based on prosecutorial misconduct "under slightly more expansive conditions than those allowed by the United States Supreme Court." Bauder v. State, 921 S.W.2d 696, 698-700 (Tex. Crim. App. 1996), *overruled in Ex parte* Lewis, 219 S.W.3d 335, 337 (Tex. Crim. App. 2007). Under federal law, a retrial is barred only for intentional or deliberate prosecutorial misconduct, while the *Bauder* standard also barred retrials if the prosecutor "was aware but consciously disregarded the risk that an objectionable event for which he was responsible would cause a mistrial at the defendant's request." *Id.* at 699. Several other states had similarly rejected the federal standard. *See, e.g.*, Pool v. Superior Court, 677 P.2d 261 (Ariz. 1984); People v. Batts, 68 P.3d 357 (Cal. 2003); State v. Rogan, 984 P.2d 1231 (Haw. 1999); State v. Breit, 930 P.2d 792 (N.M. 1996); State v. Kennedy, 666 P.2d 1316 (Or. 1983); Commonwealth v. Smith, 615 A.2d 321 (Pa. 1992). But just as many states have accepted it. *See, e.g.*, Harris v. People, 888 P.2d 259 (Colo. 1995); State v. Bell, 322 N.W.2d 93 (Iowa 1982); State v. Williams, 988 P.2d 722 (Kan. 1999); State v. Chapman, 496 A.2d 297 (Me. 1985); State v. Dawson, 427 N.W.2d 886 (Mich. 1988); State v. White, 369 S.E.2d 813 (N.C. 1988); State v. Diaz, 521 A.2d 129 (R.I. 1987). In *Ex parte Lewis*, the Texas Court of Criminal Appeals overruled *Bauder* and adopted the rule followed by the United States Supreme Court. 219 S.W.3d at 337.

[72]*See, e.g.*, TEX. CODE CRIM. PROC. arts. 14.01-.06, 38.22-.23.

[73]James N.G. Cauthen, *Expanding Rights under State Constitutions: A Quantitative Analysis*, 63 ALB. L. REV. 1183, 1195-96 (2000).

likewise notes that "no other area of constitutional rights has seen a wider and more frequent divergence between state and federal supreme courts" than search and seizure.[74] Professor Friesen then discusses numerous–and cites to hundreds of–state court decisions expanding constitutional protections in the search and seizure context.[75] She concludes that some of the federal rules that are most frequently rejected by state supreme courts include the good faith exception to the exclusionary rule, the absence of any protection for searches of open fields and curbside garbage, the approach for measuring probable cause for a search warrant when the information is supplied by an informant, the allowance of broad searches incident to an arrest, and the lessened protection for sobriety roadblocks.[76]

Yet outside the search and seizure context, state courts appear to be more likely to follow the federal lead on constitutional criminal procedure issues. A 1991 study of criminal procedure decisions found that state courts construe state constitutions in conformity with the Federal Constitution nearly seventy percent of the time.[77] These results were essentially duplicated in a 2000 study covering a twenty-five year period.[78] What might account for the willingness of state courts to depart from federal search and seizure doctrine while typically following other aspects of federal criminal procedure under their state constitutions?

The Impact of Textual Distinctions in Dually Protected Rights: Although many states are similar to Texas in that their state constitutional prohibitions on unreasonable searches and seizures are nearly identical to the Fourth Amendment, some of the states that have expanded protection under their state constitutions have significant textual differences in their search and seizure provision. As one example, Washington Constitution article I, section 7 provides "[n]o person shall be disturbed in his private affairs, or his home invaded, without authority of law." Relying on this provision, the Washington Supreme Court has rejected the Fourth Amendment's polestar of a "reasonable expectation of privacy," instead analyzing whether the state unreasonably intruded into a defendant's private affairs.[79] Under this rationale, the Washington Supreme Court has frequently deviated from federal standards.[80] Hawaii, Illinois, Louisiana, and South Carolina also have search and seizure

---

[74]2 JENNIFER FRIESEN, STATE CONSTITUTIONAL LAW: LITIGATING INDIVIDUAL RIGHTS, CLAIMS AND DEFENSES § 11.02[1] (4th ed. 2006).

[75]*Id.* §§ 11.01-.017, at pp. 11-3 to 11-173.

[76]*Id. See also* Michael J. Gorman, *Survey: State Search and Seizure Analogs*, 77 MISS. L.J. 417 (2007).

[77]Barry Latzer, *The Hidden Conservatism of the State Court "Revolution"*, 74 JUDICATURE 190, 193 (1991).

[78]This study found that state courts followed federal doctrine approximately 70% of the time in interpreting their own state constitutional protections for civil liberties, but the states were much more likely to find expansive rights under their state constitutions in the areas of search and seizure, jury trial, and free exercise of religion. Cauthen, *supra* note 73, 63 ALB. L. REV. at 1195-96. Professor Cauthen concluded that, in most of these areas in which the state courts were likely to provide more expansive rights, the United States Supreme Court "has become more conservative in its decision-making." *Id.* at 1201.

[79]*See, e.g.*, State v. Myrick, 688 P.2d 151, 154 (Wash. 1984) .

[80]*See, e.g.*, York v. Wahkiakum Sch. Dist. No. 200, 178 P.3d 995, 1001-06 (Wash. 2008) (holding random and suspicionless drug testing of student athletes violated state constitution despite contrary Fourth Amendment precedent); State v. Young, 957 P.2d 681, 687-89 (Wash. 1998) (rejecting *Hodari D.* standard for seizures and instead employing analysis of whether police disturbed citizens' private affairs); State v. Boland,

clauses explicitly protecting an individual's privacy, a distinction which their courts have relied upon to provide more expansive rights in some cases than granted by the Fourth Amendment.[81] How important should such textual differences be to a state court interpreting a dually protected right?

One well-known early decision interpreting a dually protected right more broadly under the state constitution involved such a textual distinction. In *People v. Anderson*, the California Supreme Court invalidated the death penalty under the state constitutional prohibition on "cruel or unusual punishment."[82] The court seized on the disjunctive use of the word "or" between "cruel" and "unusual" in the state constitution, in contrast to the conjunctive form "cruel and unusual punishment" contained in the Eighth Amendment.[83] As a result of this difference, the court reasoned that the California Constitution prohibited punishments that were *either* cruel or unusual, while the Federal Constitution only barred punishments that were *both* cruel and unusual.[84] While the decision in *Anderson* was later overturned by a state constitutional amendment reinstating the death penalty,[85] other courts have also relied on such textual variations to justify an independent state constitutional result.[86] Does this mean the Texas Constitution, and approximately twenty other state constitutions, provide greater protection than the Eighth Amendment, as they likewise preclude the infliction of "cruel or unusual punishment"?[87] Are textual variations between constitutions always indicative of different meanings?

---

800 P.2d 1112, 1116 (Wash. 1990) (holding law enforcement officers searching defendant's trash placed at his curb intruded upon his private affairs despite contrary holding of United States Supreme Court); State v. Gunwall, 720 P.2d 808, 816 (Wash. 1986) (holding use of pen register intruded upon defendant's private affairs and implicated state constitutional prohibition although Supreme Court had held that the use of such a device was not a search under Fourth Amendment); State v. Chrisman, 676 P.2d 419, 423 (Wash. 1984) (holding on remand from Supreme Court that search of student's dormitory violated state constitution even though Supreme Court had held that same search did not violate the Fourth Amendment).

[81]HAW. CONST. art. I, § 7; ILL. CONST. art. I, § 6; LA. CONST. art. I, § 5; S.C. CONST. art. I, § 10. *See* Charles W. "Rocky" Rhodes, *State Constitution, Privacy Provisions, in* 3 ENCYCLOPEDIA OF AMERICAN CIVIL LIBERTIES 1532 (Paul Finkelman ed., 2006).

[82]493 P.2d 880 (Cal. 1972).

[83]*Id.* at 883-84.

[84]*Id.*

[85]CAL. CONST. art. I, § 27.

[86]*See, e.g.*, People v. Fitzpatrick, 633 N.E.2d 685, 687-88 (Ill. 1994) (invalidating state law allowing child abuse victims to testify by closed-circuit television outside the presence of the defendant because it violated the defendant's state constitutional right for the accused "to meet witnesses face to face," a phrase that does not appear in the United States Constitution); People v. Bullock, 485 N.W.2d 866, 872-73 (Mich. 1992) (rejecting federal standard under state constitution in part because of textual differences between the Eighth Amendment and state constitutional prohibition against "cruel or unusual" punishment); Commonwealth v. Ludwig, 594 A.2d 281, 282-84 (Pa. 1991) (same holding as *Fitzpatrick*).

[87]TEX. CONST. art. I, § 13 ("Excessive bail shall not be required, nor excessive fines imposed, nor cruel or unusual punishment inflicted."). The Texas Court of Criminal Appeals has not determined whether this means the state constitutional provision is broader than the Eighth Amendment. While this issue arose in one death penalty case, the court sidestepped it: "Assuming that the word 'or' requires a disjunctive reading of the words 'cruel' and 'unusual,' we find that the death penalty is neither." Anderson v. State, 932 S.W.2d 502, 509 (Tex. Crim. App. 1996).

The Utah Supreme Court debated this question in two separate decisions regarding its privilege against self-incrimination. The Fifth Amendment to the United States Constitution provides that no person can be compelled "to *be a witness* against himself."[88] In contrast, the Utah Constitution states that an "accused shall not be compelled to *give evidence* against himself."[89] In *Hansen v. Owens*, the Utah Supreme Court reasoned that, since the Utah Constitution used different words to express the privilege, the provision must "mean something different and broader than" the federal guarantee.[90] Specifically, the court held that its privilege, unlike the federal standard, prevented the state from requiring an accused to furnish a handwriting sample because that would constitute an affirmative act of giving "evidence" against himself.[91] But five years later, the court overruled *Hansen* in *American Fork City v. Crosgove.*[92] *Crosgove* concluded that *Hansen*'s reasoning had "little support in history" as the accepted view at the time of the adoption of the Utah Constitution was that this differentiation between giving "evidence" and being a "witness" was "insignificant" with no distinction "'in spirit and principle.'"[93] While recognizing that constitutional guarantees are not necessarily limited in scope to their historical roots, the court determined that, as history undercut *Hansen*'s textual foundation and modern policy considerations did not support its holding, it would henceforth limit its self-incrimination privilege to "evidence of a testimonial or communicative nature."[94] Which should be more important to a state court interpreting its constitution: textual differences between the federal and state constitutions or the rationale behind such distinctions?

B. FREE EXPRESSION

Unlike the typical search and seizure provision, the text of the free expression guarantees in most states differs from the language of the First Amendment. The familiar language of the First Amendment provides that "Congress shall make no law . . . abridging the freedom of speech, or of the press."[95] In contrast, most state constitutions, including the Texas Constitution, employ language traceable to William Blackstone's description of English common law, which provided a right to publish without prior restraints but not freedom from after-the-fact punishment for the content of the publication.[96] Article I, section 8 of the Texas Constitution provides:

> Every person shall be at liberty to speak, write or publish his opinions on any subject, being responsible for the abuse of that privilege; and no law shall ever be passed curtailing the liberty of speech or of the press. In

---

[88]U.S. CONST. amend. V (emphasis added).

[89]UTAH CONST. art. I, § 12 (emphasis added).

[90]619 P.2d 315, 317 (Utah 1980), *overruled by* Am. Fork City v. Crosgove, 701 P.2d 1069 (Utah 1985).

[91]*Id.* at 316-17.

[92]701 P.2d 1069 (1985).

[93]*Id.* at 1072 (quoting Counselman v. Hitchcock, 142 U.S. 547, 584-86 (1892)).

[94]*Id.* at 1073-75.

[95]U.S. CONST. amend. I.

[96]4 WILLIAM BLACKSTONE, COMMENTARIES 151-52.

> prosecutions for the publication of papers, investigating the conduct of officers, or men in public capacity, or when the matter published is proper for public information, the truth thereof may be given in evidence. And in all indictments for libels, the jury shall have the right to determine the law and the facts, under the direction of the court, as in other cases.[97]

Although the textual differences between the provisions are obvious, the more important question is the significance of such distinctions. Do these distinctions mean that the Texas guarantee must be interpreted differently? If so, how? Is the interpretation of similarly worded free expression provisions in other states a relevant consideration? The following materials consider these and other questions, first by examining the contours of the Texas free expression right and then by considering an issue frequently addressed by state courts nationwide, free speech rights on private property.

1. Texas Free Expression Doctrine

Davenport v. Garcia, 834 S.W.2d 4 (Tex. 1992)

DOGGETT, Justice.

In this mandamus proceeding, we address three issues: (1) the ability of a judge to suppress speech with a "gag order;" (2) whether Relator was impermissibly denied access to court records; and (3) the appropriate standard for removal of a guardian ad litem. Applying our state constitutional guarantee of free expression to invalidate the trial court's unconstitutional prior restraint on speech, we grant this part of the petition for writ of mandamus. Because the trial court did not otherwise abuse its discretion, the remainder of the petition is denied.

A guardian ad litem was appointed to represent two hundred and thirteen children among numerous persons who brought suit concerning toxic chemical exposure at the Brio Dump site in Harris County. In a 1987 settlement the adults released all claims to future medical benefits for their children, and in 1989 the ad litem withdrew. In February 1990 Judge Alice Trevathan, then the presiding judge, appointed Valorie Davenport, Relator herein, as guardian ad litem.

After eighteen months of work, Davenport submitted a bill for her services on August 21, 1991. At a hearing two days later, Judge Carolyn Garcia, who had become the presiding trial judge, on her own motion, questioned the continued need for a guardian ad litem. Additionally, the court entered an oral injunction, described as a "gag order," instructing the ad litem, parties and counsel to "cease and desist any discussion of this case outside the court hearing" and prohibiting any "communications with any other lawyer or discussion at all about the matters that have transpired in this case."

On September 10 the trial court dismissed Davenport, concluding that because the parents were no longer seeking either individual recovery or expense reimbursement, no

[97] TEX. CONST. art. I, § 8.

conflict of interest existed to justify continuation of the ad litem. The court also found unnecessary ad litem oversight of a medical monitoring program proposed by defendants as part of a settlement.

I. The Gag Order

The trial court correctly characterized as a "gag order" its oral injunction of August 23, which prohibited all discussion of the Brio case outside the courtroom. Relator risked contempt should she speak either in public or even in private to any of the children whose interests she had represented. Nor did the order permit any party to discuss the case or the pending settlement with a family physician, medical expert, or another attorney.

These limitations were reiterated in the written protective order of September 12, which prohibited *any* public comment or discussion of the litigation with anyone not involved in the "necessary course of business of this case." Counsel were also directed to inform their clients of the order's applicability to each of them. The sole reason given for this sweeping injunction was the finding that "conflicts between counsel and the parents of the minor children were resulting in miscommunications with the parents of the children and with the media and general public."

We consider whether the court's gag orders violate the guarantee of free expression contained in article I, section 8 of the Texas Constitution, which provides in pertinent part:

> Every person shall be at liberty to speak, write or publish his opinions on any subject, being responsible for the abuse of that privilege . . . .

The history of this provision is a rich one, and its language demonstrates Texas' strong and longstanding commitment to free speech. By the plain language of our constitution, this fundamental liberty "shall forever remain inviolate." Tex. Const. art. I, § 29.

From the outset of this state's history, freedom of expression was a priority. As rural communities developed from the wilderness in the young region, Mexico passed the Constitutive Act of 1824, uniting Coahuila and Texas into one Mexican state. Already integrated into the government and with nine times the population of Texas, Coahuila predominated. After unsuccessful efforts to have the new state government forward their written complaints or remonstrances to the central government, dissatisfied Texans sought in 1833 a Mexican state constitution separate from Coahuila. This first proposed constitution incorporated the strong desire of Texans to speak without fear of governmental repression:

> The free communication of thoughts and opinions, is one of the inviolable rights of man; and every person may freely speak, write, print, and publish, on any subject, being responsible for the abuse of that liberty.

Proposed Constitution for the State of Texas (1833) art. 16. As an early advocate of a strong state constitution, Stephen F. Austin was jailed for his outspokenness in personally carrying this proposed charter and other remonstrances to Mexico City. The authoritarianism and unresponsiveness of Mexico to these attempts to exercise and establish protection of free speech were a contributing factor to Texas' revolution and independence.

Although the 1836 Texas Independence Constitution in general closely tracked the wording of the United States Constitution, different language was chosen to protect speech:

> Every citizen shall be at liberty to speak, write, or publish his opinions on any subject, being responsible for the abuse of that privilege. No law shall ever be passed to curtail the liberty of speech or of the press; and in all prosecutions for libels, the truth may be given in evidence, and the jury shall have the right to determine the law and fact, under the direction of the court.

Constitution of the Republic of Texas, Declaration of Rights § 4 (1836). Rather than a restriction on governmental interference with speech such as that provided by the First Amendment of the United State Constitution, Texans chose from the beginning to assure the liberties for which they were struggling with a specific guarantee of an affirmative right to speak. This language of the Texas Independence Constitution became the model for all of our subsequent state constitutions.

The drafters of the 1876 Constitution began their convention with a heightened sensitivity of the need for a strong state constitution. While major changes in the Bill of Rights were not initially anticipated, vigorous debate ensued. Delegate McLean's efforts to tie freedom of speech to "good motives" in the libel section was disapproved. Additionally, a proposal to replace the existing free expression provision with alternative language more similar to that of the First Amendment of the United States Constitution was explicitly rejected. By substituting the word "person" for the prior "citizen" in the current language of article one, section eight, "[e]very person shall be at liberty to speak, write, or publish his opinions on any subject," the delegates removed any citizenship requirement. *Compare* Tex. Const. of 1845, art. I, §§ 5-6. In their careful attention to its language, Texans once again chose protection in article one, section eight that is highly distinct from the First Amendment.

Consistent with this history, we have recognized that in some aspects our free speech provision is broader than the First Amendment. *O'Quinn v. State Bar of Texas,* 763 S.W.2d 397, 402 (Tex.1988) (noting that "Texas' free speech right [has been characterized] as being broader than its federal equivalent," the court concluded that "it is quite obvious that the Texas Constitution's affirmative grant of free speech is more broadly worded than the first amendment").

Under our broader guarantee, it has been and remains the preference of this court to sanction a speaker after, rather than before, the speech occurs. This comports with article one, section eight of the Texas Constitution, which both grants an affirmative right to "speak . . . on any subject," but also holds the speaker "responsible for the abuse of that privilege." The presumption in all cases under section eight is that pre-speech sanctions or "prior restraints" are unconstitutional.

In *Ex Parte Tucker,* 110 Tex. 335, 220 S.W. 75 (1920), this court applied section eight to safeguard speech which may not otherwise have been guaranteed under the First Amendment as interpreted in that era. That case involved an injunction prohibiting union members from "vilifying, abusing, or using . . . epithets" against the employees of a particular company. While such "fighting words" may not have been federally protected, the court relied upon our own constitution:

> The purpose of [article one, section eight] is to preserve what we call "liberty of speech" and "the freedom of the press," and at the same time hold all persons accountable to the law for the misuse of that liberty or freedom. Responsibility for the abuse of the privilege is as fully emphasized by its language as that the privilege itself shall be free from all species of restraint. But the abuse of the privilege . . . shall be dealt with in no other way. It is not to be remedied by denial of the right to speak, but only by appropriate penalties for what is wrongfully spoken. Punishment for the abuse of the right, not prevention of its exercise, is what the provision contemplates.

220 S.W. at 76.

This court previously indicated that a prior restraint would be permissible only when essential to the avoidance of an impending danger. *Hajek v. Bill Mowbray Motors, Inc.,* 647 S.W.2d 253, 255 (Tex.1983) (striking down an injunction because the language at issue "evoked no threat of danger to anyone and, therefore, may not be subject to the prior restraint of a temporary injunction."). *See also Ex Parte Tucker,* 220 S.W. at 76 (speech is properly restrained only when involving an actionable and immediate threat).

Since the dimensions of our constitutionally guaranteed liberties are continually evolving, today we build on our prior decisions by affirming that a prior restraint on expression is presumptively unconstitutional. With this concept in mind, we adopt the following test: a gag order in civil judicial proceedings will withstand constitutional scrutiny only where there are specific findings supported by evidence that (1) an imminent and irreparable harm to the judicial process will deprive litigants of a just resolution of their dispute, and (2) the judicial action represents the least restrictive means to prevent that harm. Assisting our analysis are federal cases that have addressed prior restraints. The standard enunciated in *Nebraska Press Ass'n v. Stuart,* 427 U.S. 539, 563-64 (1976), does not, however, sufficiently protect the rights of free expression that we believe that the fundamental law of our state secures. Today we adopt a test recognizing that article one, section eight of the Texas Constitution provides greater rights of free expression than its federal equivalent.

We are fully aware that a prior restraint will withstand scrutiny under this test only under the most extraordinary circumstances. That result is consistent with the mandate of our constitution recognizing our broad right to freedom of expression in Texas.

The first requirement of our standard advances from the prior holdings of Texas courts that only an imminent, severe harm can justify prior restraint, and in the context of gag orders, that harm must be to the judicial process. The mandate that findings of irreparable harm be made is based on our state constitutional preference for post-speech remedies. Only when no such meaningful remedies exist will prior restraints be tolerated in this context.

The second part of the test is intended to ensure that no alternative exists to treat the specific threat to the judicial process which would be less restrictive of state speech rights. While this element is shared in common with the ruling in *Nebraska Press,* 427 U.S. at 563-64, we view the federal test announced therein as too permissive toward prior restraints and decline to adopt it. The federal approach offers only limited guidance concerning gag orders such as that involved here, which restrict access to information by prohibiting individuals from discussing a case. Such orders should be treated like any other prior restraint.

Applying this test to the facts of this case, there can be no doubt but that the gag orders violated article one, section eight of the Texas Constitution. The orders fail to identify any miscommunication that the trial court may have perceived, does not indicate any specific, imminent harm to the litigation, and offers no explanation of why such harm could not be sufficiently cured by remedial action. For instance, had any miscommunication stemmed from improper statements by Relator, as implied by the court, the proper response may have been to sanction her conduct. By stopping not only the purported miscommunications but *any* communications, the broadly worded injunction certainly fails the second part of our test.

II. The Role of the State Constitution

Having found that the trial court's gag orders violate article I, section 8 of the Texas Constitution, this court need not consider whether the United States Constitution has also been violated. Today we reaffirm our prior pronouncement that "[o]ur constitution has independent vitality, and this court has the power and duty to protect the additional state guaranteed rights of all Texans." *LeCroy v. Hanlon,* 713 S.W.2d 335, 339 (Tex.1986). We decline to limit the liberties of Texans to those found in the Federal Constitution when this court is responsible for the preservation of Texas' own fundamental charter. When a state court interprets the constitution of its state merely as a restatement of the Federal Constitution, it both insults the dignity of the state charter and denies citizens the fullest protection of their rights.

A.

Over the past twenty years, state courts have increasingly looked to their own constitutions, rather than the Federal Constitution, in examining the extent of their citizens' liberties.[98] This trend toward what has variously been called "state constitutionalism" and "new federalism" has met with broad approval. Numerous commentators and courts, both state and federal, have advocated and applied a method of constitutional analysis wherein the state court may examine its own constitution first to determine whether the right in question is protected. Within the context of such an analysis, a state court can benefit from the insights of well-reasoned and developed federal jurisprudence, but is not compelled to reach identical results.

---

[98]From 1970 to 1989, approximately six hundred published opinions relied on state constitutional grounds to provide protections broader than federally interpreted guarantees under the United States Constitution. Linda B. Matarese, *Other Voices: The Role of Justices Durham, Kaye and Abrahamson in Shaping the "New Judicial Federalism",* 2 Emerging Issues in St. Const.L. 239, 246 (1989).

Our courts recognized the importance of our state constitution long before "new federalism" even had a name. A century-long line of Texas cases support applying our state's constitution, particularly in the area of free speech. Our decision in 1920 to rely on the plain language of article I, section 8 in striking down a prior restraint in *Ex Parte Tucker,* 220 S.W. at 76, predated the application of the First Amendment to the states.

In *Sax v. Votteler,* 648 S.W.2d 661 (Tex.1983), we invalidated a statute of limitations under the Texas Constitution's open courts provision. While expressly recognizing that the appeal was brought under both federal and state law, *id.* at 663, the court concluded that because article I, section 13 "does accord Texas citizens additional rights, we choose not to decide this case on the basis of the United States Constitution." *Id.* at 664. Holding legislation increasing a filing fee unconstitutional under the state open courts provision, we noted in *LeCroy,* 713 S.W.2d at 338, that "state constitutions can and often do provide additional rights for their citizens." We relied on the Texas Constitution because "[b]y enforcing *our* constitution, we provide Texans with their full individual rights and strengthen federalism." *Id.* at 339 (emphasis added). In doing so we observed that Texas is "in the mainstream of this [state constitutionalism] movement." *Id.* at 338. The next year, the court voided a gender-based distinction in the Family Code based solely on the Texas Constitution. *In re Baby McLean,* 725 S.W.2d 696, 698 (Tex.1987) ("[b]ecause we hold that [a provision] of the Texas Family Code violates the Texas Constitution, we need not reach the federal law issues"). Hence, in the past decade this court has strongly reaffirmed its continued commitment to our state constitution.

This commitment of Texas to its own constitution is consistent with the principle of federalism embodied in the United States Constitution. Its authors intended that "[i]n the compound republic of America, the power surrendered by the people is divided between two distinct governments . . . . *Hence a double security arises to the rights of the people.*" *The Federalist* No. 51, at 323 (James Madison) (Clinton Rossiter ed., 1961) (emphasis added).

The only limit on the states is that, in relying on their constitutions, they may not deny individuals the minimum level of protection mandated by the Federal Constitution. *See Sax,* 648 S.W.2d at 664; *LeCroy v. Hanlon,* 713 S.W.2d at 338. This approach has been referred to as a "federal safety net," ensuring that individuals receive all available guarantees of their rights.

The involvement of state courts is particularly appropriate in the protection of free speech rights. Particularly in the context of judicial proceedings, state courts have long been involved with the protection of speech rights. In the current case, the state interest is all the greater since at issue is the order of a Texas judge instructing members of the Texas bar and their Texan clients not to discuss a case ongoing in a Texas court with anyone.

B.

Our Texas charter bears the distinction of being one of the few state constitutions that were derived from its own independent, national constitution. As we emphasized in *LeCroy,* "[t]he powers restricted and the individual rights guaranteed in the present constitution reflect Texas' values, customs, and traditions." 713 S.W.2d at 339. The diverse drafters of our Constitution represented a "heterogenous miscellany of opinions." The experiences and philosophies of this group were far different than those who sat in a

Philadelphia meeting hall a century earlier. As expressed by one commentator, "[o]ur Texas Forbears surely never contemplated that the fundamental state charter, crafted after years of rugged experience on the frontier and molded after reflection on the constitutions of other states, would itself veer in meaning each time the United States Supreme Court issued a new decision." James C. Harrington, *The Texas Bill of Rights* 41 (1987).

Basing decisions on the state constitution whenever possible avoids unnecessary federal review. This not only lessens federal interference into state issues, but also results in "efficient judicial management." This approach relieves the overburdened docket of the United States Supreme Court, and spares state courts from having to deal anew with cases on remand.

As a state court, sitting in Texas, our expertise is in Texas law, our judges are Texas citizens and members of the Texas Bar, and our concerns are Texas concerns. If we simply apply federal law in all cases, why have a Texas Constitution, and why have a Texas Supreme Court?

C.

Having concluded that there are numerous reasons *why* the state constitution should be applied, we are left to consider *how* to apply it. Today's opinion has centered on a historical review to understand the origins of our liberties as Texans and the intentions of our forebears. This focus should not, however, be misconstrued to suggest any deviation from our traditional method of constitutional interpretation. In *Edgewood Indep. Sch. Dist. v. Kirby,* 777 S.W.2d 391 (Tex.1989), we outlined an appropriate approach:

> In construing [a provision of the Texas Constitution], we consider "the intent of the people who adopted it." In determining that intent, "the history of the times out of which it grew and to which it may be rationally supposed to have direct relationship, the evils intended to be remedied and the good to be accomplished, are proper subjects of the inquiry." However, because of the difficulties inherent in determining the intent of voters over a century ago, we rely heavily on the literal text. We seek its meaning with the understanding that the Constitution was ratified to function as an organic document to govern society and institutions as they evolve through time.

Our rich history demonstrates a longstanding commitment in Texas to freedom of expression as well as a determination that state constitutional guarantees be given full meaning to protect our citizens. But historical analysis is only a starting point. The constitution of our state is an organic document. *Edgewood,* 777 S.W.2d at 394. In no way must our understanding of its guarantees be frozen in the past; rather, our concept of freedom of expression continues to evolve over time. *See id.* Forms of expression not widely approved in 1875 may well demand state constitutional protection today, just as new methods of infringing on speech may require new methods of protection tomorrow.

In interpreting our constitution, this state's courts should be neither unduly active nor deferential; rather, they should be independent and thoughtful in considering the unique values, customs, and traditions of our citizens. With a strongly independent state judiciary,

Texas should borrow from well-reasoned and persuasive federal procedural and substantive precedent when this is deemed helpful, but should never feel compelled to parrot the federal judiciary. With the approach we adopt, the appropriate role of relevant federal case law should be clearly noted, in accord with *Michigan v. Long,* 463 U.S. 1032, 1040-41 (1983) (presuming that a state court opinion not explicitly announcing reliance on state law is assumed to rest on reviewable federal law). A state court must definitely provide a "plain statement" that it is relying on independent and adequate state law, and that federal cases are cited only for guidance and do not compel the result reached. *Id.* at 1040-41. *Long* offers further reason for developing state constitutional law, since now courts, rather than merely adjudicating state constitutional claims, must be prepared to defend their integrity by both quantitatively and qualitatively supporting their opinion with state authority. Consistent with this method, we may also look to helpful precedent from sister states in what New Jersey Justice Stewart Pollock has described as "horizontal federalism." Stewart G. Pollock, *Adequate and Independent State Grounds as a Means of Balancing the Relationship Between State and Federal Courts,* 63 Tex.L.Rev. 977, 992 (1985).

Our consideration of state constitutional issues is encumbered when they are not fully developed by counsel. Many of our sister states, when confronted with similar difficulties, have nevertheless decided cases solely on state grounds or ordered additional briefing of the state issue. We will follow this procedure as necessary and appropriate, when asserted state grounds have not been adequately briefed.

D.

Rejecting our careful and detailed analysis of the development and interpretation of article one, section eight, the concurrence advances an alternative–Texas judges should follow, but never lead, federal jurisprudence. Whenever both federal and state constitutional provisions "overlap or correspond," the Texas judge should never diverge from the path taken by the federal judiciary. No aspect of Texas history, no series of Texas decisions such as that present here should obscure the obligation of adherence to federal authority.

We prefer self-reliance. What we accept today is the responsibility to conduct a thoughtful, complete, and independent search for a sound understanding of our most fundamental law. . . .

HECHT, Justice, joined by COOK and CORNYN, Justices, concurring in the judgment.

I join in the Court's judgment, but not in its opinion. I agree that mandamus should issue directing the respondent district court to vacate the gag orders of which relator complains, but not to reinstate relator as guardian ad litem. I also agree that we should not direct the district court to allow relator access to court records when relator has failed to establish that her access to those records has been restricted. I differ with the Court's reasons for these decisions, however, and write to explain why.

I

Deciding whether the two gag orders which the district court issued in the pending litigation are invalid is not the principal occupation of the Court's opinion. Those orders have already been ordered vacated in response to relator's request for emergency relief. 837 S.W.2d 73. Our reasons for granting this relief do not require elaborate explanation. The Court is unanimous in the view that the gag orders are invalid because they are too broad, they are not necessary to protect against an imminent threat to the administration of justice, and they were issued without following procedures to safeguard against suppression of relator's constitutionally protected speech. Issuance of the orders was a clear abuse of discretion from which relator has no adequate remedy by appeal. Thus, relator is entitled to mandamus relief to have the orders set aside.

Relator complains that the gag orders infringe unlawfully upon her right to freedom of speech under the First Amendment to the United States Constitution. The United States Supreme Court has had several occasions to consider the validity of gag orders in criminal cases. *Gentile v. State Bar of Nevada,* 501 U.S. 1030 (1991); *Nebraska Press Ass'n v. Stuart,* 427 U.S. 539 (1976). The principal authority applying the First Amendment to gag orders on the participants in a civil case, however, is *Bernard v. Gulf Oil Co.,* 619 F.2d 459, 467 (5th Cir.1980) (en banc), *aff'd on other grounds,* 452 U.S. 89 (1981), in which the court held that an order restricting the named plaintiffs in a class action and their attorneys from communicating freely with prospective class members violated the First Amendment. The court determined that such gag orders are prior restraints upon free speech. *Id.* at 467.

According to *Bernard,* a gag order is permitted by the First Amendment only if it meets three conditions. First, "'before a prior restraint may be imposed by a judge, even in the interest of assuring a fair trial, there must be "an imminent, not merely a likely, threat to the administration of justice. The danger must not be remote or even probable; it must immediately imperil."''" *Bernard,* 619 F.2d at 474 (quoting *United States v. Columbia Broadcasting System, Inc.,* 497 F.2d 102, 104 (5th Cir.1974) (quoting *Craig v. Harney,* 331 U.S. 367, 376 (1947))). "In general, a prior restraint may be justified only if the expression sought to be restrained 'surely [will] result in direct, immediate, and irreparable damage.'" *Bernard,* 619 F.2d at 473 (quoting *International Soc'y for Krishna Consciousness v. Eaves,* 601 F.2d 809, 833 (5th Cir.1979)). Second, a valid prior restraint "must not sweep too broadly. Rather it 'must be narrowly drawn and cannot be upheld if reasonable alternatives are available having a lesser impact on First Amendment freedoms.'" *Bernard,* 619 F.2d at 476 (quoting *CBS, Inc. v. Young,* 522 F.2d 234, 238 (6th Cir.1975)). Third, "the restraint 'must have been accomplished with procedural safeguards that reduce the danger of suppressing constitutionally protected speech.'" *Bernard,* 619 F.2d at 477 (quoting *Southeastern Promotions [v. Conrad],* 420 U.S. [546,] 559 [(1975)]). These safeguards include evidence and findings.

The district court's gag orders do not meet First Amendment standards. The orders were not necessitated by any imminent threat imperiling the administration of justice. Moreover, the orders were overly broad and were not the only reasonable alternative for addressing the problems the district court confronted. The district court prohibited relator from talking with anyone about the case under any circumstances except in the course of proceedings. Finally, the district court did not follow procedures that would safeguard against an unwarranted infringement of relator's First Amendment rights. . . .

B

The Court reaches this result but not by the well-traveled road of First Amendment jurisprudence. It insists instead on traversing the largely uncharted terrain of article I, section 8 of the Texas Constitution.

1

I say "insists" because the idea that this case should be decided on state constitutional grounds alone did not originate with the parties but with one Member of this Court. Article I, section 8 was not even mentioned in this case until relator's counsel alluded to it in passing in oral argument, after which the following colloquy occurred:

> JUSTICE DOGGETT: Are you asserting–you made reference to the Texas Constitution earlier–are you asserting free speech rights under the Texas Constitution as well as the U.S. Constitution?
> RELATOR'S COUNSEL: That is correct, Your Honor. I read article I, section 8 of the Texas Constitution as going beyond the First Amendment.
> JUSTICE DOGGETT: Have you briefed that and cited us any authority on the broader protections afforded by the Texas Constitution?
> RELATOR'S COUNSEL: No, we haven't, Your Honor. I entered this case after the briefing was terminated.
> JUSTICE DOGGETT: Are you interested in filing any supplemental briefing on that issue?
> RELATOR'S COUNSEL: We would welcome the opportunity to file supplemental briefing with this Court on the First Amendment issues.

There was no further discussion of article I, section 8 during oral argument. Relator subsequently filed a supplemental brief arguing that the gag orders were not permitted by the First Amendment, and secondarily, that article I, section 8 provides an independent basis for overturning them. Respondent never replied to this brief.

Thus, in considering the applicability of article I, section 8 to this case, the Court has the benefit of no argument and approximately four pages of briefing which relator filed at the invitation of one Justice. The Court may choose to rest a significant decision on grounds which the parties have not fully presented, but there are always risks in doing so, and the more important the issue, the greater the risks. . . .

4

The Court also examines the text of article I, section 8, pointing out the inescapable facts that the language is not identical to that of the First Amendment, that it is stated partly in the affirmative ("Every person shall be at liberty to speak") rather than entirely in the negative ("Congress shall make no law"), and that it appears toward the front of the constitution rather than at the end. These facts prove conclusively that the language of article I, section 8 is different from the First Amendment, something that is plain as day. The issue, however, is not whether there are differences, but what, if anything, those differences mean, and the Court's observations shed no light on this issue.

The Court's contention that the language of article I, section 8 is "different" and "highly distinct" is misleading. Texas, like most states, appears to have derived its constitutional provision protecting the right to free speech from Blackstone, who articulated that right as follows: "Every freeman has an undoubted right to lay what sentiments he pleases before the public; to forbid this, is to destroy the freedom of the press: but if he publishes what is improper, mischievous, or illegal, he must take the consequences of his own temerity." 4 WILLIAM BLACKSTONE, COMMENTARIES 152. By 1833, when a constitution was first proposed for Texas, 15 of the 24 states then in the United States had constitutional provisions protecting free speech in words similar to Blackstone's. The language proposed for Texas' constitution in 1833, and the language incorporated in the 1876 constitution, are obviously related to Blackstone's formulation of the common law, and are strikingly similar to the provisions of what were then almost two-thirds of the state constitutions except in one respect: the language of our 1876 constitution, unlike the language proposed in 1833, extended freedom of speech to persons instead of citizens. Even in this respect, however, Texas was neither unique nor first: Missouri had already adopted such a provision.

The close relationship between the free speech guarantees in the constitutions of Texas and many other states should not be surprising. The idea that freedom of speech is a fundamental right is not unique to Texas or any other state, but one inherent in our political structure and shared generally by the people of this nation. While the right has been described in somewhat different words at different times and places, the basic ideas certainly transcend state lines. Free speech is a national idea, not only a Texas idea. The Court's attempt to distinguish Texas free speech as significantly different from First Amendment free speech–and presumably also from New York free speech or California free speech–is not supported by the texts of the various guarantees.

5

The only serious effort the Court makes to determine how article I, section 8 should apply to gag orders is by examining our own precedents, and this effort, though flawed, is exhaustive. For it should be noted that in more than 150 years article I, section 8 has been *mentioned* in this Court's opinions in only 19 cases, and twice the reference was in a separate opinion. In only five of these 19 cases has this Court written more than a few words about article I, section 8, and only three of those five involved prior restraints. Two of the three prior restraint cases relied entirely on the third, *Ex parte Tucker,* 110 Tex. 335, 220 S.W. 75 (1920). This is the totality of our prior restraint jurisprudence under the Texas Constitution.

Tucker, decided before the First Amendment was applied to the states through the Fourteenth Amendment in *Gitlow v. New York,* 268 U.S. 652 (1925), held that an injunction prohibiting union employees from "'vilifying, abusing, or using opprobrious epithets to'" other employees violated article I, section 8. The Court cites *Tucker* and quotes from it extensively as an example of the independence of article I, section 8 from the First Amendment. But the Court does not quote the following:

> The experience of the English nation and some of the American colonies under the tyranny of such systems is the reason this provision in the Bill of Rights [article I, section 8] is one common to the Constitutions of the American States, and for its incorporation, *in like words,* in the First Amendment to the Federal Constitution.

Id. at 76 (emphasis added). *Tucker* did not ignore the First Amendment in its analysis of article I, section 8, as the Court has, nor did it differentiate the two provisions, as the Court attempts to do today. Rather, it linked them in two respects: they were founded on common experience, that of the English nation and the American colonies, and they were framed in "like words".

The other two cases which utilize article I, section 8 to invalidate prior restraints rely entirely upon *Tucker.* In *Dallas General Drivers v. Wamix, Inc.,* 156 Tex. 408, 295 S.W.2d 873, 879 (Tex.1956), the Court dissolved an injunction prohibiting striking employees from "us[ing] . . . insulting, threatening and indecent language" toward non-striking employees "without prejudice to the right of the trial court to reinstate it if future conduct of the [striking employees] should authorize it." Thus, the Court invalidated an injunction as a prior restraint but did not preclude the trial court from reissuing it if the circumstances warranted. This is certainly not a very broad reading of article I, section 8, and may well be narrower than the First Amendment. In *Hajek v. Bill Mowbray Motors, Inc.,* 647 S.W.2d 253, 255 (Tex.1983) (per curiam), the Court dissolved an injunction prohibiting an owner from driving his car on which he had prominently labeled as a "lemon". Although the Court did not refer to the First Amendment, it also did not state that article I, section 8 afforded broader protection of speech.

The truth of the matter is that all our prior caselaw either assumes a close identity between the First Amendment and article I, section 8, or is silent on the subject. Not before today has this Court insisted that the two provisions are different in substance, and so much so that we should not even consider the former in construing the latter.

6

As flawed as the Court considers *Nebraska Press* and *Bernard* to be, it is difficult to conceive how the Court can state a test for gag orders under article I, section 8 that is identical to *Bernard*'s First Amendment standards. The presumption against the constitutionality of gag orders is the same. The first element of the Court's test–"an imminent and irreparable harm to the judicial process [that] will deprive litigants of a just resolution of their dispute"–is the same as *Bernard*'s–"an imminent, not merely a likely, threat to the administration of justice", 619 F.2d at 474, that "surely [will] result in direct, immediate, and irreparable damage", 619 F.2d at 473. The second element of the Court's test–"the judicial action represents the least restrictive means to prevent that harm"– is also the same as *Bernard*'s–the gag order "'must be narrowly drawn and cannot be upheld if reasonable alternatives are available having a lesser impact on First Amendment freedoms'", 619 F.2d at 476. The Court's requirement that there be specific findings supported by evidence is the same as *Bernard*'s third condition that there be "procedural safeguards" including evidence and findings, 619 F.2d at 477.

If the two constitutional provisions are really as different as the Court insists they are, it is a remarkable coincidence that the standards for applying them to gag orders happen to be identical. But if the standards really are the same, then there is no practical difference in the two provisions, contrary to the Court's insistence. Thus, the Court's analysis strains credulity and finally disproves its own thesis.

7

Without reference to the First Amendment, or to the hundreds of cases construing it, this Court attempts to formulate independent standards for applying the guarantee of free speech in article I, section 8 of the Texas Constitution to one form of prior restraints, gag orders like the ones in this case. The task is daunting, even though the law the Court attempts to create on its own is but a small part of what Americans have come to understand as freedom of speech. And in the end the Court fails in its efforts. Barely managing to cobble together a few fragments of history, obvious truisms about the constitutional language, exaggerated claims about its distinctiveness, and phrases taken out of context from a few of our cases, the Court produces a test that is identical to more fully developed First Amendment standards. The Court achieves the very end it sought to avoid–adoption of First Amendment standards–without admitting it.

C.

As the Court notes, many of the authorities I have cited support judicial reliance upon state constitutions. So do I. Contrary to the Court's assertions, I do not argue that state constitutions should be ignored, or that federal law always controls their construction. I contend only that federal constitutional law should be considered when a state constitutional provision is applied. The Court's new analytical method treats the resource of federal law with marked ambivalence. On the one hand, the Court includes federal law among the considerations its new method is to use: "Within the context of such an analysis, a state court can benefit from the insights of well-reasoned and developed federal jurisprudence, but is not compelled to reach identical results." On the other hand, the Court avoids any useful reference to federal law in this case. The Court *claims* that it "quite obviously" does not disregard federal law, yet it ignores *Bernard* and the United States Supreme Court decisions on which it relies. The Court *says* First Amendment jurisprudence is "not irrelevant", but it also says that it "need not consider whether the United States Constitution has also been violated." In sum, the Court *says* federal law can be useful in applying the state constitution, but the Court does not use it in this case.

It cannot be denied that there are rights protected by state constitutions that extend beyond those guaranteed by the United States Constitution. Many state constitutional provisions simply have no federal analogue. Three of the most important decisions this Court has ever issued were based upon such provisions. *Carrollton-Farmers Branch Indep. Sch. Dist. v. Edgewood Indep. Sch. Dist.,* 826 S.W.2d 489 (Tex.1992); *Edgewood Indep. Sch. Dist. v. Kirby,* 804 S.W.2d 491 (Tex.1991); *Edgewood Indep. Sch. Dist. v. Kirby,* 777 S.W.2d 391 (Tex.1989). In construing state constitutional provisions which have no federal counterpart, reference to federal law is usually of little utility.

When state and federal provisions overlap or correspond, state law, as well as federal law and the law of other states, may be helpful in analyzing their proper application. To ignore all federal constitutional law in construing state constitutional provisions guaranteeing rights common to both is as wrong as ignoring state constitutional provisions altogether. If nothing else, it is inefficient to blaze a trail through the wilderness when there is a perfectly good highway there already, built at considerable expense, and well traveled. But the problems of the Court's method run even deeper. The Court does not merely ignore federal law; it rejects it. And the rejection has a disturbing tone to it. "[O]ur concerns are Texas concerns," the Court asserts, a viewpoint that cannot be very comforting to out-of-state parties litigating in Texas courts. . . .

2

The Court's claim that Texas courts have "recognized the importance of our state constitution" for more than a century cannot be disputed. Certainly, if state courts have not recognized the importance of our state constitution, they should have. This does not mean, of course, that any Texas court has ever employed the constitutional analysis used by the Court today. If the Court's new analytical method had really been followed in Texas for 100 years, as the Court means to suggest, it would hardly need the major defense the Court attempts to provide in this case. Today's opinion is significant only because the Court's methodology has not previously been the accepted model in Texas. In five of the cases the Court cites, we applied provisions of our constitution which have no federal counterpart: *In re Baby McLean,* 725 S.W.2d 696, 698 (Tex.1987) (equal rights amendment); *LeCroy v. Hanlon,* 713 S.W.2d 335, 341-42 (Tex.1986) (open courts); *Nelson v. Krusen,* 678 S.W.2d 918, 922 (Tex.1984) (open courts); *Sax v. Votteler,* 648 S.W.2d 661, 664 (Tex.1983) (open courts); *Bell v. Indian Live-Stock Co.,* 11 S.W. 344, 345 (Tex.1889) (protecting current wages for personal service from garnishment). In *Tucker,* as we have noted, the Court referred to article I, section 8 and the First Amendment as "like" provisions, and *Hajek* relies entirely on *Tucker.* None of the Texas cases the Court cites uses the method it endorses.

3

One argument the Court makes for its new method–avoidance of "unnecessary" federal review–is more subtle and requires more attention. The Court contends that its approach is more efficient because if a case is decided on state constitutional grounds, the United States Supreme Court cannot review it, and thus that Court's workload is reduced and the parties' dispute more quickly resolved. As evidence of the savings to be achieved using its approach, the Court cites a total of four decisions by state courts in the past seventeen years in which review by the United States Supreme Court could have been avoided. Even if it is assumed that all four cases could have been decided on state constitutional grounds unreviewable by the Supreme Court, reducing that Court's workload by four cases in 17 years would not measurably improve its efficiency. Nor do delays in so few cases over so long a period indicate a problem of any magnitude. Efficiency is not a very compelling basis for the Court's argument.

But the Court has more serious reasons for wanting to avoid "unnecessary" federal review. The goal of the Court's methodology is not merely to augment a state's voice in national affairs, but to still the national voice in state affairs. The approach adopted by the Court is not limited to producing state participation in the national debate over fundamental issues; it seeks state autonomy.

That autonomy, the Court recognizes, is accomplished not by the state constitution itself, but by the *interpretation* of the constitution by the state's highest court. And this brings us to what lies at the very heart of the Court's position: the Justices of this Court, and not the United States Supreme Court, should determine the people's fundamental rights, and if our determinations are unsatisfactory, we can be replaced.

There are several difficulties with the Court's position. First, it weakens the validity of constitutionalism and the rule of law. The essence of constitutionalism is that certain principles, endorsed by the people, become fundamental rules of law. How these rules apply in changing circumstances is often disputed, and the judiciary in this country has taken upon itself the ultimate responsibility of resolving those disputes, beginning with *Marbury v. Madison,* 5 U.S. (1 Cranch) 137 (1803). The people and the other branches of government have acquiesced in this delegation of responsibility in part, I think, because of their perception that the judiciary is bound in its construction and application of constitutional provisions by definite rules of law which preclude judges from substituting their personal policies for constitutional principles in the guise of construing those principles. Adherence to these rules is essential to the validity and the credibility of constitutionalism. For this reason, constitutional construction must be founded upon a careful construction of each provision's language, purpose, history and intent, as well as upon precedent, theory and fundamental values. If the analytical process is inadequate or flawed, the result may appear to be based primarily on the judge's policy preferences and not the constitutional principle itself.

It is no answer to say that "unsatisfactory" constructions of the constitution can be corrected simply by removing the judges. This is not the way to amend the constitution. And while it might correct the result in particular cases for a time, it leaves the process of constitutionalism itself fatally flawed. Substituting one judge for another in order to change the meaning of the constitution concedes that the constitution has no meaning apart from judges' views. The importance of individual judicial views cannot be denied, but they do not substitute for rules of law. Thus, constitutional construction must not be reduced to the issue of who is doing the construction, "we" or "they". Yet this is the result of the Court's approach, carried to its logical extreme.

The second difficulty with the Court's view that we should define fundamental constitutional rights without interference from outside the state is that it is premised on a one-dimensional view of those rights which is rarely accurate. If relator were constitutionally entitled to say whatever she pleased, this would be an easy case. But her right to speak freely is not absolute, under either the First Amendment or article I, section 8. In this case, relator's right conflicts with the district court's interest in protecting minor litigants, and the issue is whether the district court's interest warrants the restriction imposed on relator's right. This tension among competing rights and interests gives constitutional construction a multi-dimensional aspect. Thus, the Court's view that federal constitutional rights, which states cannot diminish, are a "federal safety net" is overly simplistic. Federal constitutional construction does not merely set minimum standards for protected rights which the states are free to increase; it strikes a balance among competing rights and interests that is itself of constitutional significance. While states may have more latitude in adjusting this balance than they do in reducing guaranteed protections, that latitude is not unlimited. State courts are not free from federal constitutional considerations in determining fundamental rights. The delicate balance among those rights and other interests must also be maintained.

Finally, the we-better-than-they argument evinces an inappropriate chauvinism toward the federal courts and other state courts. The concept of freedom of speech in this country did not originate in any one state, nor does any one court have a monopoly on its application. As it happens, the federal courts have been at construing the First Amendment much longer and far more often than Texas courts have had occasion to consider article I, section 8. The federal courts' experience in defining the contours of freedom of speech ought to be invaluable. To ignore it simply because we can is both imprudent and arrogant.

PHILLIPS, C.J., did not participate.

Notes on *Davenport* and the Methods for Resolving Dually Protected Rights

***The Issues in* Davenport**: *Davenport* addressed two conceptually distinct but related issues. The first issue the court considered was whether, based on the text, history, and precedent of the Texas free speech provision, the gag order violated article I, section 8. The court then explained in the second part of its opinion its rationale for commencing (and ending) its analysis with the Texas free expression provision rather than evaluating the First Amendment. Although logically these issues might have been decided in the reverse order, the court presumably believed that its opinion would be more persuasive if the defense of state constitutionalism appeared as a foregone conclusion.

The Primacy Approach to Dually Protected Rights: What reasons did the *Davenport* majority provide for examining the state constitution first? How did the concurrence respond to each of these rationales? The issue of whether state constitutional rights or federal constitutional rights should be addressed first by a state court has been debated by numerous judges and scholars. The *Davenport* majority followed the primacy approach, which advocates that state constitutional issues should be decided first, and only if the state constitutional right is not protected should the court consider the federal issue.

The advocates of the primacy approach rely on many of the arguments expressed in *Davenport*: primacy comports with principles of federalism, it aids in the development of an independent state constitutional jurisprudence, and it promotes judicial economy. Consider this articulation of primacy's benefits from the Florida Supreme Court in *State v. Traylor*:

> The federal Constitution secures a common degree of protection for the citizens of all fifty states, but the federal Court has wisely exercised restraint in construing the extent of this protection for several reasons. First, under our federalist system, many important decisions concerning basic freedoms have traditionally inhered in the states. Second, the federal Court's precedent is binding on all jurisdictions within the union; once it settles a matter, further experimentation with potentially rewarding alternative approaches in other jurisdictions is foreclosed. Third, federal precedent applies equally throughout fifty diverse and independent states; a ruling that may be suitable in one may be inappropriate in others. And fourth, the federal union embraces a multitude of localities; the Court oftentimes is simply unfamiliar with local problems, conditions and traditions. *See generally San Antonio Indep. Sch. Dist. v. Rodriguez,* 411 U.S. 1 (1973).
>
> State courts do not suffer these prudential concerns to the same degree as the federal Court. First, unlike their federal counterparts, state

> courts and constitutions have traditionally served as the prime protectors of their citizens' basic freedoms. State constitutions were the initial and prime charters of individual rights throughout most of our nation's existence . . . . State courts function daily as the prime arbiters of personal rights. An assertive state court thus impinges on no traditional federal prerogative where basic rights are concerned.
>
> Second, unlike the federal Court, a state court's decision construing its own constitution is controlling only as to courts within that state; the ruling will not stifle the development of alternative methods of constitutional analysis in other jurisdictions. . . . And finally, no court is more sensitive or responsive to the needs of the diverse localities within a state, or the state as a whole, than that state's own high court.[99]

Justice Kogan, who concurred in part and dissented in part in *Traylor*, added:

> I fully concur in [the majority's] statement regarding the primacy of the Florida Constitution in state courts. Clearly, state constitutional issues must be considered first whenever fundamental rights are at stake. Far too often, both bench and bar fail even to consider the possibility that some principle of the Florida Constitution may be dispositive of the issue. This practice clearly is contrary to the two central policies upon which the doctrine of primacy rests.
>
> First, primacy promotes judicial economy. If the state constitution provides greater rights than the federal, then there is no need for litigants to waste further time and resources in appeals or other challenges mounted in the federal courts. Second and most importantly, primacy gives the state Constitution the respect and effect its framers manifestly intended it to have. The Florida Constitution is not a nullity to be ignored. Its words are not meaningless. When the state Constitution creates a fundamental right, that right must be respected, even if no similar right is recognized by the federal courts.
>
> To this end, the doctrine of primacy promotes the long-standing tradition of American states interpreting their own constitutions independently. Only starting in the middle part of this century did the federal courts gradually expand the scope of the Fourteenth Amendment to "incorporate" virtually the entire range of rights contained in the first eight amendments to the federal Constitution.

---

[99] 596 So. 2d 957, 961-62 (Fla. 1992). *State v. Traylor* addressed whether the defendant's confessions were obtained in violation of the right to counsel and the privilege against self-incrimination protected by both the federal and state constitutions. While adopting the primacy approach, the court's interpretation of these state constitutional guarantees did not depart materially from federal standards. After concluding the admission of one of the confessions violated the state constitutional right to counsel, the court proceeded to hold that the error was harmless. *Id.* at 970-73.

> Prior to this time, the *only* guardians protecting individual liberty were the state constitutions and the courts that interpreted them. Without these independent efforts, nothing would have prevented an American state from establishing an official religion, prohibiting free speech, forbidding public assemblies, or authorizing medieval methods of extracting confessions from defendants. All of these evils were avoided when the people of the states, including Florida, adopted freestanding constitutional guarantees expressly forbidding such practices. Thus, the doctrine of primacy recognized by the majority is a vital and living concept whose antecedents extend back to the earliest days of Florida history.[100]

Other states have similarly extolled the virtues of the primacy approach when confronted with dually protected rights, including New Hampshire, Maine, Oregon, Utah, Vermont, Washington, and Wyoming.[101] These state courts have urged that the primacy approach is desirable as it encourages an independent analysis of state constitutional rights outside the shadow of federal reasoning.

Professor (later Oregon Supreme Court Justice) Hans Linde contended that the primacy approach is not only preferable, but essentially required because the state cannot violate the Fourteenth Amendment through a law that is invalid under its state constitution:

> The federal source of all "due process" and "equal protection" attacks on state regulation is the fourteenth's amendment command that "No state shall . . . deprive any person of life, liberty, or property, without due process of law; nor deny to any person within its jurisdiction the equal protection of the laws." Whether this command has been violated depends on what the state has finally done. Many low-level errors that potentially deny due process or equal protection are corrected within the state court system; that is what it is for. The state constitution is part of the state law, and decisions applying it are part of the total state action in a case. When the state court holds that a given state law, regulation, ordinance, or official action is invalid and must be set aside under the state constitution, then the state is not violating the fourteenth amendment.[102]

Does Professor Linde's argument prove too much? If he is correct, would that require federal courts to investigate state constitutional law before reaching federal constitutional issues?

---

[100] *Id.* at 982-83 (Kogan, J., concurring & dissenting).

[101] *See, e.g.*, State v. Ball, 471 A.2d 347, 350-51 (N.H. 1983); State v. Cadman, 476 A.2d 1148, 1150 (Me. 1984); Sterling v. Cupp, 625 P.2d 123, 126 (Or. 1981); West v. Thomson Newspapers, 872 P.2d 999, 1005-07 (Utah 1994); State v. Badger, 450 A.2d 336, 346-47 (Vt. 1982); State v. Coe, 679 P.2d 353, 359 (Wash. 1984); Vasquez v. State, 990 P.2d 476, 485-86 & n.4 (Wyo. 1999).

[102] Hans A. Linde, *Without "Due Process": Unconstitutional Law in Oregon*, 49 OR. L. REV. 125, 133-34 (1970).

Criticisms of the Primacy Approach: What are some of the arguments against the primacy approach? Justice Hecht's *Davenport* concurrence notes that "it is inefficient to blaze a trail through the wilderness when there is a perfectly good highway there already, built at considerable expense, and well traveled." In other words, creating a state constitutional jurisprudence from scratch is a time-consuming and difficult process, especially as a result of the difficulties inherent in state constitutional interpretation discussed in Chapter 2. As elaborated in an article by this text's author:

> It is indisputable that the framers originally envisioned the states as the principal guardians of individual rights. But, it is equally true that, throughout [the last] century, the United States Supreme Court and the federal courts assumed the dominant role in the protection of these sacred rights. In Texas, state guarantees with corresponding federal guarantees received scant attention until the emergence of the new federalism movement, as aptly illustrated by the paucity of cases mustered by the *Davenport* court as support for its primacy methodology .... On the other hand, the United States Supreme Court has engendered an intricate framework, developed by some of the most respected jurists in our nation's history, for resolving free expression cases. It would be pure folly to wholly reject this learned body of law and start anew.[103]

However, would the primacy approach be more efficient in the long run if a state consistently adhered to its principles? While indeed a possibility, the answer is uncertain as no state has demonstrated an unflappable devotion to primacy precepts.[104] Florida, despite its ringing endorsement and apparent adoption of primacy in *State v. Traylor*, has been inconsistent in adhering to the model in subsequent cases.[105] Even the very use of primacy in *Traylor* itself is somewhat suspect as the court created a state constitutional right that was merely coextensive with the federal right.[106] Some states candidly admit that their commitment to primacy has been uneven, although this is partly because of the shortcomings of litigants in presenting state constitutional issues.[107] This has led one critique to conclude:

> The failing of the primacy model is that [its] assumption no longer resembles reality. Nor does it reflect the fact that litigants typically present

---

[103]Charles W. "Rocky" Rhodes, *A Proposal for Interpreting Corresponding United States and Texas Constitutional Guarantees in the New Millenium*, 51 BAYLOR L. REV. 269, 316 (1999).

[104]*See* JAMES A. GARDNER, INTERPRETING STATE CONSTITUTIONS 47 (2005). New Hampshire probably has been the most consistent primacy adherent, *see* State v. Beauchesne, 868 A.2d 972, 975 (N.H. 2005) (maintaining state supreme court had consistently followed the primacy approach since 1983), although its experience may be unique due to its relatively small populace and a state constitution that predated the Federal Constitution.

[105]*Compare* N. Fla. Women's Health & Counseling Servs., Inc. v. State, 866 So. 2d 612 (Fla. 2003) (deciding parental notification law for abortions unconstitutional under Florida's explicit right to privacy) *with* State v. Owen, 696 So. 2d 715 (Fla. 1997) (resolving federal constitutional issue regarding *Miranda* warning before determining that the state constitution provided a similar protection).

[106]*See, e.g.*, *Owen*, 696 So. 2d at 719-20 (interpreting *Traylor* to have required warnings to the accused under the state constitution that were coextensive with the *Miranda* warnings).

[107]*See, e.g.*, State v. Tiedemann, 162 P.3d 1106, 1113 (Utah 2007).

> state constitutional issues only when they expect an unfavorable federal constitutional result. Federal assumption of the dominant role in the federal system–and particularly in the protection of individual rights–has rendered the primacy model obsolete. When federal protections are extensive and well articulated, state court decisionmaking that eschews consideration of, or reliance on, federal doctrine not only will often be an inefficient route to an inevitable result, but also will lack the cogency that a reasoned reaction to the federal view could provide, particularly when parallel federal issues have been exhaustively discussed by the Supreme Court and commentators. In a community that perceives the Supreme Court to be the primary interpreter of constitutional rights, reliance on Supreme Court reasoning can help to legitimate state constitutional decisions that build on the federal base. When a state court diverges from the federal view, a reasoned explanation of the divergence may be necessary if the decision is to command respect.[108]

Are any of the other claimed advantages of primacy likewise contrary to reality? Proponents of primacy frequently assert that the approach promotes judicial economy by limiting United States Supreme Court review and the necessity of remands to address state constitutional issues not resolved on adequate and independent state grounds. But this result, as Justice Hecht's *Davenport* concurrence noted, occurs very rarely–only once every few years. At the same time, the primacy approach has led to its own meaningless judicial holdings, as several states have ratified state constitutional amendments to overturn judicial decisions adopting an independent state constitutional doctrine for a dually protected right.[109]

A final concern is whether the primacy approach is as practical in a state like Texas with two coequal high courts. What if the Court of Criminal Appeals preferred to mirror federal First Amendment doctrine rather than employing the primacy method to establish an independent meaning for article I, section 8? Is this simply an inherent risk of the unique high court division in Texas? Even before federal incorporation, the Texas high courts sometimes reached conflicting holdings regarding the appropriate interpretation of the state constitution.[110] Yet does employing a primacy methodology enhance the risk of such conflicts?

---

[108]Note, *Developments in the Law–The Interpretation of State Constitutional Rights,* 95 HARV. L. REV. 1324, 1357 (1982) (footnotes omitted).

[109]California provides a good illustration, as several constitutional amendments have been adopted in response to independent judicial interpretations of the state constitution. *See, e.g.*, CAL. CONST. art. I, §7 (barring judicially mandated student busing except as required by the Federal Constitution); *id.* § 24 (requiring the rights of criminal defendants be interpreted consistently with the United States Constitution); *id.* § 27 (reinstating the death penalty); *id.* § 28(f)(2) (overruling judicially created exclusionary rule under state law).

[110]*Compare* Brown v. City of Galveston, 75 S.W. 488, 495-96 (Tex. 1903) (upholding taxation ordinances adopted by the Galveston government, which had been appointed by the governor pursuant to legislative authorization after the Galveston hurricane) *with Ex parte* Lewis, 73 S.W. 811, 818-19 (Tex. Crim. App. 1903) (invalidating criminal ordinances passed by the Galveston government appointed by the governor).

The Interstitial and Dual Reliance Methods: The opposing view to the primacy model is known as the interstitial or supplemental approach. Under this approach, the federal component of a dually protected right should be addressed first, meaning that the state constitutional issue will only be addressed if the right is not protected under the United States Constitution. Proponents of this methodology maintain that it better matches the reality of contemporary constitutional practice–namely, that federal constitutional law dominates the field, with the states only having a gap-filling role. Under this view, the state court's role is not to "construct a complete system of fundamental rights from the ground up," but rather to criticize or supplement federal constitutional doctrine.[111] This is said to fulfill one of the state's primary functions in safeguarding the liberty of its citizens from governmental tyranny at both the federal and state levels.

Although very few states have officially adopted this approach as the preferred methodology,[112] in practice it is frequently encountered, especially in those states that only occasionally diverge from federal doctrine in interpreting dually protected rights.[113] Despite its frequent use, it has been heavily criticized by commentators. Because the state constitutional issue is only addressed in the absence of a federally protected right, the interstitial approach will not lead to the development of a robust and independent state constitutional doctrine. Moreover, the approach appears to diminish the legitimacy of state constitutions by relegating them to second-tier status.

A third approach has also been advocated, the dual reliance method, under which both the federal and state constitutional rights are always separately analyzed in each case.[114] However, as a practical matter, it has not been frequently employed by the courts, which is not that surprising in view of its inherent inefficiencies in conducting a full and separate analysis under both the federal and state constitution in every case.

The Texas and Federal Approaches to Gag Orders: With respect to *Davenport*'s holding that the gag order violated article I, section 8, what differences are there, if any, between its test to evaluate gag orders and the federal standard? In *Nebraska Press Ass'n v. Stuart*, the Supreme Court considered a First Amendment challenge to a state district judge's pretrial speech restraint of the news media before jury selection in a highly publicized mass murder case. The Court reasoned that such a case required the balancing of the criminal defendant's Sixth Amendment right to a fair jury trial, which is "fundamental to the American scheme of justice," against the First Amendment's disdain for prior restraints, "the most serious and least tolerable infringement" on free expression.[115] Because the Court believed it could not establish which amendment possessed priority under all circumstances, it designed a very fact-specific test applying only to pre-trial gag orders on

---

[111]*Developments in the Law*, *supra* note 108, 95 HARV. L. REV. at 1357-58.

[112]*See, e.g.*, State v. Gomez, 932 P.2d 1, 7-8 (N.M. 1997).

[113]*See, e.g.*, People v. Caballes, 851 N.E.2d 26, 42-43 (Ill. 2006) (noting court had typically employed interstitial approach without adopting it to govern all cases).

[114]*See, e.g.*, Robert F. Utter, *"Swimming in the Jaws of the Crocodile:" State Court Comment on Federal Constitutional Issues When Disposing of Cases on State Constitutional Grounds*, 63 TEX. L. REV. 1025, 1029 (1985).

[115]427 U.S. 539, 551, 559 (1976).

the media in criminal trials. But five Justices, in concurring opinions, questioned whether such a gag order on pretrial publicity could ever be justified.[116]

Because the Supreme Court did not specify a standard to govern all gag orders, the United States Court of Appeals for the Fifth Circuit in *Bernard v. Gulf Oil Co.* pronounced its own standard for gag orders on litigants and attorneys in civil proceedings, a standard that it pieced together from various Supreme Court precedents.[117] Justice Hecht discusses the *Bernard* standard at length in his *Davenport* concurrence. Are there meaningful differences between the tests enunciated in *Bernard* and *Davenport*? If not, does that undercut *Davenport*'s position that the Texas free speech provision is broader than the First Amendment? Consider this view:

> At most, therefore, the [existing] federal law was coextensive with the standard promulgated in *Davenport* for reviewing a gag order under the Texas Constitution. If the Texas Supreme Court desired to create a broader standard, it should have utilized the reasoning from Justice Brennan's concurrence in *Nebraska Press* to hold that the speculative nature of any alleged injury to the judicial process could never justify a gag order infringing upon the sacred right of free expression . . . .
>
> The court could have commenced its opinion by delineating the standards articulated in the various *Nebraska Press* opinions. It then could have focused on the text of the Texas Constitution in article I, section 8, which, in its first clause, provides every person the liberty to speak. While recognizing that the Texas free speech provision could not always be broader because of the language in the subsequent clauses, the court could have constructed an argument that the affirmative grant of speech in the first clause, the Texas judicial disdain for prior restraints evinced in its earlier opinions, and well-reasoned judicial theory, as articulated by Justice Brennan's concurring opinion in *Nebraska Press*, mandated, in all instances, that a gag order in a judicial proceeding violates article I, section 8. Such an approach would have had more secure moorings in constitutional jurisprudence and in the text, history, and purpose of article I, section 8.[118]

Do you agree or disagree? What practical problems may have been caused by employing such an absolutist approach to prior restraints?

---

[116] *Id.* at 604 (Brennan, J., concurring, joined by Stewart & Marshall, JJ.) (concluding resort to gag orders restraining freedom of press was under all circumstances constitutionally impermissible); *id.* at 617 (Stevens, J., concurring) (agreeing "to most of what Mr. Justice Brennan says and, if ever required to face the issue squarely, may well accept his ultimate conclusion."); *id.* at 570-71 (White, J., concurring) (stating he doubted "whether orders with respect to the press such as were entered in this case would ever be justifiable").

[117] 619 F.2d 459, 473-77 (5th Cir. 1980), *aff'd on other grounds*, 452 U.S. 89 (1981).

[118] Charles W. "Rocky" Rhodes, *A Proposal for Interpreting Corresponding United States and Texas Constitutional Guarantees in the New Millennium*, 51 BAYLOR L. REV. 269, 297-98, 318 (1999).

The *Davenport* test remains the standard for determining the validity of judicial gag orders under the Texas Constitution. In *Star-Telegram, Inc. v. Walker*, the majority held that a gag order imposed on a media defendant must comply with the two-part test developed in *Davenport*, with Justice Hecht concurring on First Amendment grounds.[119] Later, the supreme court held in a short per curiam opinion, *Grigsby v. Coker*, that a gag order on the litigants in a child custody modification proceeding was unconstitutional when the trial court did not make the findings required by *Davenport*.[120] But the *Davenport* test has not been extended to other situations, as illustrated by the following cases.

Ex Parte Tucci, 859 S.W.2d 1 (Tex. 1993)

DOGGETT, Justice (plurality opinion).

We consider the scope of our state constitutional guarantee of freedom of expression. Keith Tucci [and six others] were convicted of civil contempt for public protests in which each of them disregarded a provision of a temporary restraining order. As relators, they bring this original habeas corpus proceeding asserting that they have been confined for expression which is protected under article I, section 8 of the Texas Constitution.

I.

The importance attached to freedom of expression in our state's jurisprudence is reflected in the longstanding rule that one imprisoned for disregarding a court order restraining speech may challenge the underlying restraint as void through a habeas proceeding such as this. Texas courts have repeatedly granted habeas relief to release those confined for disregarding an unconstitutional restriction on varying types of expression. *See Ex parte Henry,* 215 S.W.2d 588 (Tex. 1948) (peaceful picketing); *Ex parte Tucker,* 220 S.W. 75 (Tex. 1920) ("vilifying, abusing or using opprobrious epithets"); *Ex parte McCormick,* 88 S.W.2d 104 (Tex. Crim. App. 1935) (gag order).

Underlying our state law is the principle that speech delayed often translates into speech denied. The Texas approach represents the converse of the federal collateral bar rule, which was relied upon in *Walker v. City of Birmingham,* 388 U.S. 307 (1967), to bar the release of Dr. Martin Luther King, Jr. and others from the Birmingham jail for disregarding unconstitutional restrictions upon their civil rights marches. Nor is Texas alone in recognizing the unduly restrictive nature of a collateral bar rule. *See, e.g., In re Berry,* 436 P.2d 273, 280 (Cal. 1968) (en banc); *Wood v. Goodson*, 485 S.W.2d 213, 217 (Ark. 1972); *State ex. rel. Superior Court v. Sperry,* 483 P.2d 608, 611 (Wash. 1971); *Phoenix Newspapers, Inc. v. Superior Court,* 418 P.2d 594, 596 (Ariz. 1966).

II.

Fearful that former President George Bush would weaken the Republican Party's opposition to a woman's constitutional right to choose whether to have an abortion, Relators initiated "Operation G.O.P." to express vehemently their anti-choice views during the 1992 Republican National Convention in Houston. To attract maximum attention, Relators

---

[119]834 S.W.2d 54, 56-58 (Tex. 1992).

[120]904 S.W.2d 619, 620-21 (Tex. 1995).

scheduled their protests at local family planning clinics. Concerned that they and their clients would be caught up in the intra-Republican crossfire, these clinics, joined by others, obtained temporary restraining orders to protect clinic access. Nevertheless, Relators gave various speeches–one imploring President Bush to appoint additional anti-choice judges and others condemning abortions–within a judicially prohibited area of "one-hundred (100) feet" from "either side of or in front of any doorway entrance or exit, parking lot, parking lot entrance or exit, driveway, or driveway entrance or exit" of a clinic.

Each Relator was fined $500 and committed to the Harris County jail for six months or for a lesser time if purged of contempt by paying the fine and announcing in open court a willingness to abide by the restraining orders. All seven sought habeas relief, asserting that the contempt judgment by which they were incarcerated was based upon a void, unconstitutional temporary restraining order. After the court of appeals denied relief, this court ordered Relators released upon bond.

III.

In support of the temporary restraining orders, it was asserted that clinic demonstrations posed an immediate and irreparable threat to the ability of women to seek counseling at the clinics and, if desired, to obtain abortion-related services without intimidation, threats of violence, harassment or physical obstruction. A woman's right to terminate a pregnancy is constitutionally protected. *Roe v. Wade,* 410 U.S. 113 (1973). We have found merit in the reasoning of this decision in recognizing our own independent right of privacy under the Texas Constitution in *Texas State Employees Union v. Texas Dep't of Mental Health and Mental Retardation,* 746 S.W.2d 203, 205 (Tex.1987) (citing *Roe*). Without unimpaired access to appropriate counseling and medical facilities, a woman's constitutional guarantee of choice would be no choice at all.

Additionally, the clinics and intervenor businesses claimed injury would result from trespasses, blocked access and the intimidation of patients, staff and customers. This court has recognized that "[c]onstitutional protection of the rights of free speech and assembly does not license . . . obstruction of public ways or of entrances to and exits from places of business." *Ex parte Pierce,* 342 S.W.2d [424,] 427 (Tex. 1961). Uncontroverted evidence offered in support of the temporary restraining orders established that the threat of injury posed by Operation G.O.P. to the women plaintiffs' right of access to the clinics and to the ability of clinics and businesses to operate was both imminent and irreparable.

IV.

The trial court issued two temporary restraining orders containing a number of provisions clearly directed to protecting against the specific injuries alleged by the women, clinics and businesses. [C]onfinement of relators was premised solely on their having disregarded portions of the temporary restraining orders that barred:

> Demonstrating within one-hundred (100) feet from either side of or in front of any doorway entrance or exit, parking lot, parking lot entrance or exit, driveway, or driveway entrance or exit at [any of the] clinics[s] or parking lots.

Relators thus do not attack any of the other provisions of the restraining orders but challenge only the one-hundred foot limitation as unconstitutional.

V.

In reviewing the validity of the particular one-hundred foot limitation in these orders, we must look first to our Texas Constitution. *See Davenport v. Garcia,* 834 S.W.2d 4, 12 (Tex.1992). With its broad command that "'[e]very person shall be at liberty to speak . . . opinions on any subject,' article one, section eight . . . provides greater rights of free expression than its federal equivalent." *Id.* at 10. "[I]ts language demonstrates Texas' strong and longstanding commitment to free speech." *Id.* at 7.

Relying upon this fundamental state guarantee, our courts have repeatedly rejected both legislative and judicial attempts to restrict expression. . . . Consistent with [our prior] jurisprudence and the history of our state constitution, this court announced in *Davenport* that restrictions must be targeted at the effect of expression rather than at the expression itself. There, "an imminent and irreparable harm to the judicial process [that] deprive[s] litigants of a just resolution of their dispute" was determined to be the effect of expression to which a judicial order could be directed. 834 S.W.2d at 10. Second, we emphasized the need to ensure that any limitation "represents the least restrictive means to prevent that harm[ful effect.]" *Id.*

That same standard controls here. Freedom of expression may not be restricted solely on grounds that its exercise will have the effect of producing imminent and irreparable harm. Restraints may be imposed only if the injunctive relief granted encompasses the least restrictive means of protecting against the alleged harmful effect. In resolving both whether the alleged effect was imminent and irreparable and whether the temporary injunctive relief granted here was the least restrictive means to prevent that harm, we look to the injury asserted, the relief requested, and the underlying evidence.

VI.

Encompassed within this large "speech-free" zone around each of the clinics was not just clinic property and the area immediately in front of entrances and exits of the clinics and their parking lots, but public streets and sidewalks as well. This restriction had the effect of closing to protestors during the Republican Convention the entire city block on which the Planned Parenthood clinic was located, and displacing them across several of Houston's busiest streets. While the one-hundred foot limitation here, simply by the mere fact of distance, might have had the general effect of preserving clinic access and protecting patients, staff and customers against intimidation and harassment, it was not proved at the trial court hearing that this large zone was the least restrictive means for guarding against these injuries. Without specific findings supported by evidence that the 100-foot speech-free zone was the least restrictive means to ensure unimpeded access to clinics and guard against intimidation and harassment, we hold that this limitation in the restraining orders violates article I, section 8 of the Texas Constitution.

APPENDIX I
Response to Concurrence of Chief Justice Phillips

Today at least five members of this Court continue to subscribe to the broad conception of individual liberty guaranteed under our state constitution and embodied in *Davenport v. Garcia,* 834 S.W.2d 4 (Tex.1992, orig. proceeding). While requiring a mere nine paragraphs to explain his own rationale for agreeing with the judgment entered today, Chief Justice Phillips writes at length about a guarantee of the Texas Constitution that he then chooses to ignore completely, since he is personally unable "to articulate its meaning with confidence." Instead, he prefers to resolve this case solely on federal constitutional grounds which are "more familiar" to him.

[Chief Justice Phillips] denigrate[s] the work of the Texas drafters of [the revolutionary] era on the unusual grounds that they must have considered the constitutional experience of others and because the strong language they chose in 1836 did not attract the enthusiasm of one historian a century later. Certainly Texans did not live wholly isolated from the rest of the world and human experience in 1836, 1845, or 1876, nor do they now. Of course, there are others here and abroad who have made enormous contributions to freedom. The question resolved by the court in *Davenport* and addressed once again today is whether the Texas judiciary will contribute to that effort with independent decisionmaking or serve only to parrot the thinking of an omniscient federal judiciary on every civil liberties question.

We are told that our Texas guarantee of freedom of expression is but a poor copy of an earlier Pennsylvania Constitution. Even were it true that our forbears simply copied identical language from the federal constitution or that of another state, that does not mean that they accepted the identical meaning attached by that other forum, either then or now. But in this particular instance, what we are not told is that the Pennsylvania courts have regularly interpreted this language as "independently protect[ing]" expression, *William Goldman Theaters, Inc. v. Dana,* 173 A.2d 59 (Pa. 1961), and as "even more protective of speech than the federal Constitution." *Franklin Chalfont Assoc. v. Kalikow,* 573 A.2d 550, 556 (Pa. Super. Ct. 1990); *see also Commonwealth v. Tate,* 432 A.2d 1382 (Pa. 1981). Nor are they alone. Almost a century ago wording similar to that contained in article I, section 8 was described as "terse and vigorous" and "broader" than the comparable federal provision with which it "varies" and as "giv[ing] [citizens] greater liberty in the exercise of the right granted." *Dailey v. Superior Court,* 44 P. 458, 459 (Cal. 1896).

Both this court and our sister court, the Court of Criminal Appeals have recognized the independent vitality of our Texas Constitution rather than relying exclusively on the federal judiciary. *See, e.g., LeCroy v. Hanlon,* 713 S.W.2d 335, 338-39 (Tex.1986); *In re Baby McLean,* 725 S.W.2d 696, 698 (Tex.1987); *Sax v. Votteler,* 648 S.W.2d 661, 664 (Tex.1983); *Heitman v. State,* 815 S.W.2d 681, 690 (Tex.Crim.App.1991). Chief Justice Phillips declares these rulings of our highest Texas courts "simply wrong" in describing a federal constitutional floor for individual liberties, which the states may equal or exceed with a ceiling–a greater level of protection. When both federal and state constitutional claims are raised, a state court may not, under the supremacy clause, U.S. Const. art. VI, cl. 2, afford less protection to individual rights than that guaranteed by our national Bill of Rights. In that sense, the prior writings of this court are fully accurate regarding a "federal safety net"–a floor for our liberties and a potentially higher state ceiling. It is also true that an independent state judiciary may interpret its fundamental law as affording less protection than our federal charter. Chief Justice Phillips prefers the latter. In his view not only does our state charter fail to offer a more expansive ceiling for broader freedoms but it fails even to offer a floor.

Chief Justice Phillips insists that the poor wording selected by the Texas frontiersmen provides even less protection than those guarantees found elsewhere; apparently our State Constitution offers only superfluous subflooring for individual rights. In essence his position is that anything not already written about the scope of freedom of expression can best be obtained from Washington. The possibility that state jurists have the capacity for thoughtful, independent consideration of even identical constitutional language is not even a conceivable possibility.

Our Texas Constitution is not a collection of meaningless paper promises, mere surplusage to the federal guarantees. Rather we as jurists are summoned to give effect to its terms whenever liberty is threatened.

PHILLIPS, Chief Justice, concurring, joined by Justice Cornyn.

The decisions of five justices in two opinions are based on the fundamentally flawed premise that the Free Expression Clause of the Texas Constitution, Tex. Const. art. I, § 8, is in some relevant way "broader" or more protective of free expression than the First Amendment to the United States Constitution. Because of this alleged greater breadth, a majority of the Court strikes down the trial court's order.

I disagree that our clause is "broader" than its federal counterpart in any sense that affects this case. In fact, I am not certain that the order of the trial court below violates the Texas Constitution in any respect. Only because I conclude that the order violates the guarantees of the First Amendment do I join in the Court's judgment discharging the Relators. Accordingly, I write separately.

I.

A.

The comparative breadth construct to which the Court adheres can mean very different things to different beholders. Here, it does not dissuade Justice Gonzalez from recognizing the fundamental dichotomy between direct and indirect governmental regulation, long a starting point in most state and federal analyses of free speech. It does lead him, however, to require a higher countervailing interest to justify in restricting speech than do the federal courts or most state courts. In contrast, the doctrine leads the plurality to erect a test that, as Justice Gonzalez explains, virtually eviscerates the notion of protecting any competing interests or rights that are harmed by speech. Both writings, however, purport to rely on *Davenport v. Garcia,* 834 S.W.2d 4 (1992), in which this Court first adopted the comparative breadth construct.

One obvious reason for such divergent results is that comparative breadth is not a one-dimensional concept. In the free expression context, for example, a constitutional provision may be "broad" or "narrow" on at least six axes, including: 1) the types of expression deemed protected, 2) the range of potential infringers against which the provision is operable, 3) the range of potential persons and entities who may invoke the protection, 4) the type of permissible restrictions and sanctions on free expression, 5) the degree of importance necessary for a competing interest or right to restrict free expression, and 6) how narrowly the infringement on free expression must be tailored to accommodate that competing interest or right. Thus, to pronounce one free expression clause as broader than another is, standing alone, of little help.

As to any axes along which breadth may appropriately be measured in this case, I maintain that the Texas Free Expression Clause is not "broader" than the corresponding guarantee of the First Amendment. A closer examination of our provision demonstrates why I reject the Court's conclusion, and why I find it necessary only to reach Relators' First Amendment claims.

B.

It seems obvious that no provision which expressly recognizes criminal libel prosecutions can be read as approaching Justice Black's absolutist vision of free expression. The unadorned text, however, does not reveal whether this guarantee should properly be read as any "broader" in protecting Relators' free expression rights than the prevailing understanding of the First Amendment. To make such a determination, we must search for the import of terms like "liberty," "speak, write or publish," "subject," "responsible," "abuse," "law," and "curtailing," as they relate to the provision as a whole. Only after we make an independent determination of our guarantee's meaning should we attempt to compare its reach with another guarantee.

To interpret any provision of the Texas Constitution, we start with our recent pronouncement in *Edgewood Indep. Sch. Dist. v. Kirby,* 777 S.W.2d 391, 394 (Tex.1989):

> In construing [a section of the Texas Constitution], we consider "the intent of the people who adopted it." [citations omitted] In determining that intent, "the history of the times out of which it grew and to which it may be rationally supposed to have direct relationship, the evils intended to be remedied and the good to be accomplished, are proper subjects of the inquiry." [citation omitted] However, because of the difficulties inherent in determining the intent of voters over a century ago, we rely heavily on the literal text. We seek its meaning with the understanding that the Constitution was ratified to function as an organic document to govern society and institutions as they evolve through time. [citation omitted][121]

---

[121] A somewhat different articulation, set forth in the concurring opinion in *Davenport* and slightly modified by me, suggests that we "ordinarily look to such things as the language of the constitutional provision itself, its purpose, the historical context in which it was written, the intentions of the framers [and ratifiers], the application in prior judicial decisions, the relation of the provision to [other parts of the constitution and] the law as a whole, the understanding of other branches of government, the law in other jurisdictions, state and federal, constitutional and legal theory, and fundamental values including justice and social policy." *Davenport,* 834 S.W.2d at 30 (Hecht, J., concurring, with my additions noted). Both this and the *Edgewood* formulation, which it "closely parallels," *Davenport,* 834 S.W.2d at 22, are useful constructs for constitutional analysis.

In applying this standard to Article I, Section 8, I thus look to the literal text, to the general historical context from which it arose, to the sources from which our framers derived it, to their deliberations in choosing it, to the understanding of the voters in adopting it, to its development in the judicial opinions of this and other states, and to its need to serve an evolving and expanding society. I also look to the entire provision and the relationship between its component parts, not, as do the plurality and concurrence, merely to the first clause of the first half of the first sentence. After all, the whole guarantee, although separated into two adjoining sections in prior Texas Constitutions, was combined by the framers of the current Constitution into a single section, presumably for a reason.

Finally, I consider also the experience of other jurisdictions, many of whom share similar free expression guarantees. Closely corresponding provisions existed in thirteen of the 25 American states at the time of our 1836 Independence Convention, including every state which had joined the Union after 1791. By our 1875 Convention, 26 of the 36 other states had such a clause, as do 36 of the 49 other states today. I am convinced that our language reflects not an attempt to glorify "all that is unique to Texas," *Davenport,* 834 S.W.2d at 22, but a conscious desire to examine "the action of the other States" and "profit by their example and experience." DEBATES OF THE TEXAS CONVENTION OF 1845 at 89 (William F. Weeks, reporter) (1846) (remarks of Delegate Isaac Van Zandt of Harrison County).[122]

With these general principles in mind, I turn to the words of our guarantee to determine "the evils intended to be remedied and the good to be accomplished."

II.

A.

Article I, Section 8, begins as follows:

> *Every person shall be at liberty to speak, write, and publish his opinions on any subject, being responsible for the abuse of that privilege....*

By its plain terms, this portion of the guarantee both grants and limits the freedom of expression, for one may later be called to account for exercising the "privilege" of the "liberty" of expression. The language derives from the eighteenth century right at English common law to publish books and pamphlets without prior government approval. *See generally* Philip Hamburger, *The Development of the Law of Seditious Libel and the Control of the Press,* 37 STAN. L. REV. 661 (1985). This English "liberty of the press," while no doubt advanced in its time, was a far cry from modern notions of free expression. *See*

---

[122]Although *Davenport* acknowledges that "we may also look to helpful precedent from sister states" as "we build from experience in Texas and elsewhere to enhance individual liberty," 834 S.W.2d at 20, 22, in fact its interpretative analysis wholly ignores the rest of the Anglo-American experience. The opinion never acknowledges that our Texas free expression provision resembles *any* other jurisdiction, much less nearly three-quarters of the American states. It cites no other state constitution, convention journal, convention debate, legislative provision or judicial decision in analyzing the Texas Constitution. While the Court expressly invited "other states [to] rely on unique Texas law developed independently by the legislature and judiciary of this state," *id.* at 18, it returned the favor only to this extent: "We do not say that the Texas guarantee of free expression inevitably varies in all particulars from the federal, or that of New York or California." *Id.* at 22.

JONATHAN EMORD, FREEDOM, TECHNOLOGY, AND THE FIRST AMENDMENT (1991). It was truly a situation of "let the publisher beware," for the mere absence of censors afforded no protection against a myriad of common law and statutory mechanisms by which an expression could be sanctioned *after* publication. As Blackstone explained:

> The liberty of the press is indeed essential to the nature of a free state; but this consists in laying no previous restraints upon publications, and not in freedom from censure for criminal matters when published. Every freeman has an undoubted right to lay what sentiments he pleases before the public: to forbid this, is to destroy the freedom of the press: but if he publishes what is improper, mischievous, or illegal, he must take the consequences of his own temerity.

4 WILLIAM BLACKSTONE, COMMENTARIES 151-52. Some of these very words were enshrined in the speech and press guarantees of the Pennsylvania Constitution of 1790. What "Blackstone thus recognized as the law of England came to be . . . an established constitutional right in Pennsylvania as to both speech and press." *William Goldman Theatres, Inc. v. Dana,* 173 A.2d 59, 62 (Pa. 1961). This language eventually spread to most other American states, and has been included in all the constitutions of Texas.

Texas courts have traditionally adhered to this limited view of the state's free expression guarantee. As was explained in *Ex parte Tucker,* 220 S.W. 75 (Tex. 1920):

> The purpose of this provision is to preserve what we call "liberty of speech" and the "freedom of the press," and at the same time hold all persons accountable to the law for the misuse of that liberty or freedom. Responsibility for the abuse of that privilege is as fully emphasized by its language as that the privilege itself shall be free from all species of restraint . . . Punishment for the abuse of the right, not prevention of its exercise, is what the provision contemplates.

220 S.W. at 76. Thus, prior restraint is always prohibited, assuming the expression does not rise to the level of "conduct," but the government can require accountability for expressions, once made, that constitute "abuse" of the privilege of free expression.

B.

The Texas Free Expression Clause provides an additional guarantee in the second clause of the first sentence:

> *[A]nd no law shall ever be passed curtailing the liberty of speech, or of the press.*

This provision, which has also been included in every adopted Texas Constitution, enjoys far less general acceptance in other American jurisdictions. Only four states had similar language in 1836, and only 16 other states had it when the Constitution of 1876 was framed. Even today, fewer than half the states afford such protection in their constitutions.

As with the first clause, the delegates to the various Texas constitutional conventions expended little effort in framing this language. In all probability, the text was borrowed, directly or indirectly, from the First Amendment to the United States Constitution. What the framers and ratifiers originally intended to protect by these words is less certain.

[I]t must be remembered that, whatever its original purpose, during the time our constitutions were framed the free expression guarantees of the First Amendment were generally applied only to forbid prior restraints. *See, e.g., Patterson v. Colorado,* 205 U.S. 454, 462 (1907). For all practical purposes, therefore, the state and federal guarantees were regarded as the same. *See Ex parte Tucker,* 220 S.W. at 76 ("The experience of the English nation and some of the American colonies under the tyranny of [licensing] systems is the reason [the ban on prior restraints] is one common to the Constitutions of the American States, and for its incorporation, in like words, in the First Amendment to the Federal Constitution"). While the federal experience demonstrates the elasticity of these elegant words, no Texas case has yet suggested that the second clause imparts protection greater than either the "liberty and responsibility" clause or the First Amendment, or that it modifies the state's ability to impose punishment for expressions deemed an "abuse."

C.

The next clause of Article I, Section 8 provides as follows:

In prosecutions for the publications of papers, investigating the conduct of officers, or men in public capacity, or when the matter published is proper for public information, the truth thereof may be given in evidence.

Ironically, because the United States Supreme Court now apparently interprets the First Amendment to prohibit criminal sanctions for any true statement, *see Garrison v. Louisiana,* 379 U.S. 64 (1964), the provisions of the third clause fail to resonate with modern concepts of free expression.

[B]y 1876, the Texas Constitution was hardly on the cutting edge of free expression; it was not even in the mainstream. Only six other state constitutions still provided for such a circumscribed truth defense, while nineteen used [broader] models. Even Pennsylvania, which originated the Texas approach, had abandoned it for a more liberal standard, as had Great Britain, where Lord Campbell's Act of 1843 had made truth with good motives a defense in a prosecution for criminal libel.

D.

The final clause of Article I, Section 8 provides:

And in all indictments for libels, the jury shall have the right to determine the law and the facts, under the direction of the court, as in other cases.

This clause expands the common law role of fact finders in criminal libel prosecutions, ensuring them the right to render a general verdict in the same manner as they do in other criminal cases. That is to say, the clause permits a jury to decide guilt or innocence by applying the relevant legal standards to its view of the evidence, resolving each of the subsidiary issues legally necessary to reach its verdict: whether the material is libelous, whether the defendant published it, and the sense in which the material should be read. Some states trace similar constitutional provisions directly to the Fox Libel Act, while others have suggested that the provision was inspired by the Peter Zenger trial of 1735. Today, nineteen other states incorporate a parallel guarantee in their free expression clause.

III.

A.

What is one to make of all this? Many of the framers' deliberations now seem obscure, and, as we have seen, the provisions most important to them have been effectively superseded by the evolving guarantees of the First Amendment. Yet in applying these antique words to contemporary situations, we must remain faithful to the essential purposes of the framers and ratifiers. Several conclusions stand out.

First, the broad, majestic guarantees of the first two clauses were combined with the precise, technical provisions of the last two. Any fair reading of our free expression guarantee must consider the provision as a whole, not merely the first portion thereof. In addition to the truth defense clause, our Constitution characterizes expression as a "privilege" in the first clause, and qualifies the jury's role as "under the direction of the court, as in other cases" in the fourth clause. Third, there was little desire to sanction the actions of those who would "discuss and scan every private act of our lives." While speech could not be censored in advance, protection would not be afforded for those who invaded the "private relations of private citizens."

B.

To apply what we have learned to the facts at hand, we must first determine whether the trial court's orders constitute prior restraints on speech. If they do, they are unconstitutional, as there is no assertion that the expression here constituted "conduct" or "threatened conduct." *Ex parte Tucker,* 220 S.W. at 76. In the present order, however, the trial court was not acting as a censor either as to the content of Relators' expression or as to the identity of persons allowed to speak. Instead, the challenged portions of the injunctive relief regulated only where Relators might stand while demonstrating. While some restriction of time, place and manner may be so spatially extensive as to constitute a prohibition against a speaker or his or her message, not every limitation rises to this level. Hence, a citywide ban on the sale of a newspaper would be barred by Article I, Section 8, but a restriction of a few feet on abusive or damaging speech surely would not. Such a limited restriction would enable the speakers to deliver their message to whom they want, but in a manner that accords some weight to the rights of others.

For precisely the reasons articulated by Justice Gonzalez, I conclude that 100-foot bans on demonstrators who seek to confront women and call public attention to their choice decision to seek abortion services are not prior restraints. They instead merely regulate the location of expression, and their validity must be tested under our Constitution by whether the expression constitutes an "abuse" for which the speakers have been held "responsible."

* * * *

D.

I conclude that nothing in the language or purpose of the Texas Free Expression Clause authorizes us to abandon the notion of accommodating competing interests, as the plurality has done, or even to afford greater weight in the balancing of interests to free expression than we would under the First Amendment, as Justice Gonzalez proposes. Under the first clause, with its explicit reference to abuse, I would be inclined to give even less weight to expression interests than the expansive wording of the First Amendment provides. One could argue that the second clause, which so closely parallels the First Amendment, *cf. Ex parte Tucker,* 220 S.W. at 76, mandates a similar balance. We are not required, however, to use past or present First Amendment doctrine as a minimum "floor" which our independent guarantee must be interpreted to meet or exceed. Previous intimations to the contrary in some of our opinions are, in my view, simply wrong. *See LeCroy v. Hanlon,* 713 S.W.2d 335, 338 (Tex.1986); *Sax v. Votteler,* 648 S.W.2d 661 (Tex.1983); *see also Heitman v. State,* 815 S.W.2d 681 (Tex.Crim.App.1991).[123]

Given the many difficulties with our guarantee, it would be difficult to articulate its precise meaning with confidence. I decline to make the attempt for a simple, but to me compelling reason: the trial court's orders fail to meet constitutional muster under the more familiar contours of the First Amendment.

IV.

In turning to the First Amendment to resolve this case, I am by no means avoiding the issue before us. In fact, while Relators request relief under both the federal and state constitutions, they devote barely 15 percent of their briefs before this Court to the latter claims; the rest pertains solely to their First Amendment arguments. Respondents undertake no independent discussion of Article I, Section 8 jurisprudence at all, simply distinguishing such cases as *Davenport* and *Tucker,* along with First Amendment prior restraint cases, from the place and manner regulations at issue here. Only because of the false construct of considering state constitutional issues first, pronounced by this Court in *Davenport,* has it been necessary for seven justices who join in the judgment to write three separate,

---

[123]This position was again apparently asserted by the Court in *Davenport,* which suggested that, in interpreting their own constitutions, state courts "may not deny individuals the minimum level of protection mandated by the Federal Constitution." *Id.* at 15. Literally read, this position makes no logical sense. If our text was written at a different time by different people with different concerns, then the protection it affords may be greater, lesser, or the same as that provided by a different provision in the United States Constitution.

The suggestion that state bills of rights cannot afford less liberty protection than their federal counterparts confuses independent state constitutionalism with the mandate of the Supremacy Clause, U.S. Const. art. VI, cl. 2, that federal rights, if asserted, not be ignored. Thus, in this case, our Court could not deny relief to the relators on state constitutional grounds without also considering all properly pled federal constitutional claims. But the "federal safety net" is a false construct, now rejected by an increasing number of courts and scholars. *See, e.g., State v. Smith,* 725 P.2d 894 (Ore. 1986) (Oregon Constitution does not require Miranda warnings); *Serna v. Superior Court,* 707 P.2d 793 (Cal. 1985) (California Constitution requires less stringent speedy trial standards than federal counterpart).

Fortunately, today's plurality opinion recognizes that "an independent state judiciary may interpret its fundamental law as affording less protection than our federal charter." 859 S.W.2d at 13. Regardless of what conclusions we reach in this or other cases, this recognition will enhance the possibility of principled state constitutional development.

time-consuming opinions.[124]

It is clear under federal law that the restrictions imposed in this case were an attempt at a "time, place, and manner" restriction rather than an "absolute prohibition on a particular type of expression" or prior restraint. Under the first "prong" of the "time, place, and manner" analysis, courts have consistently held restrictions similar to the ones challenged here to be "content-neutral." Under the remaining elements of the time, place, and manner test, we are required to balance carefully the interests the orders are intended to vindicate with the need to protect and preserve the "uninhibited, robust, and wide-open" debate that the First Amendment envisions. I would agree with Justice Gonzalez that the interests advanced in support of the challenged orders, the patients' right to an abortion and the clinic owners' right to engage in lawful activities, are at least "significant" for purposes of the time, place, and manner analysis.

There are, however, two related difficulties in the challenged orders. First, there is nothing in the record concerning the physical layouts of the numerous clinics in relation to public sidewalks and roads, or the features of the areas in which the clinics were located. [B]y failing to provide any information concerning the surroundings and location of individual clinics, we have no way of judging the propriety of the 100-foot restriction in each location and whether such provisions ensure adequate alternative channels of communication. Second, there are a number of other provisions in the orders, not challenged by Relators, designed to effectuate the interests that Plaintiffs assert. I would accordingly hold that Plaintiffs have failed to demonstrate that the challenged 100-foot restrictions are sufficiently narrowly tailored and leave open adequate alternative channels of communication to pass muster under the First Amendment. . . .

VI.

The revitalized commitment to state constitutions has been one of the most important jurisprudential developments of our generation. Contrary to the repeated insinuations of the plurality, I question neither the power nor the obligation of our Court to apply state, as well as national, constitutional guarantees to the claims before us. Moreover, our application of the state constitution need not be controlled, or even informed, by how past or current federal courts have read corresponding guarantees of the United States Constitution.

Unfortunately, however, the manner in which some state courts have exercised this authority has led some commentators to view state constitutional guarantees as merely a convenient vehicle for result-oriented pronouncements. *See* authorities cited at *Davenport,* 834 S.W.2d at 38 n.10 (Hecht, J., concurring). Our recent writings in the free expression area have also done little to dispel this notion. From the unseemly chauvinism of *Davenport* to the blatantly partisan factual recitation of today's plurality opinion, it would appear that some see our Texas Constitution as little more than "a handy grab bag filled with a bevy of

[124] In insisting that courts and litigants "rely on the state constitution in the first instance," *id.* at 18, the Court builds unnecessary rigidity into our decision-making process. Just as we do not insist that all contract claims be considered before accompanying tort claims, I see no need for the artificial construct in constitutional litigation.

clauses that may be exploited" to achieve "some particular social goal." Ronald R.K. Collins, *Reliance on State Constitutions–Away From a Reactionary Approach,* 9 HASTINGS CONST. L.Q. 1, 2 (1981). If I have authored an "expansive writing . . . to dissent from each and every underpinning of" *Davenport,* it is only because that opinion is so perforated with error, constructs so flawed a foundation for a methodological framework for future decisions. I do, indeed, "fret" over such a writing by this Court, and I fervently hope that our subsequent efforts in this area will prove more substantial. For this case, as the guarantees of the First Amendment to the United States Constitution provide all the relief sought by Relators, I rely solely on that authority to concur in the judgment that Relators remain discharged.

GONZALEZ, Justice, concurring.

In *Davenport v. Garcia,* 834 S.W.2d 4, 12-13 (Tex.1992), this Court stated that "we can benefit from the insights of well-reasoned and developed federal jurisprudence" in analyzing our state constitution. However, in today's opinion, the plurality ignores years of federal and state jurisprudence without offering any reasoning for its departure from the well-known "time, place, and manner" standard and adopts an overly restrictive test for analyzing restrictions on speech. I would instead utilize a modified version of the time, place, and manner test to hold that the creation of the one-hundred (100) foot free speech zone around the entrances, exits, and parking lots of various Houston abortion clinics during the Republican National Convention was unconstitutional. Therefore, although I concur in the judgment of the Court, I do not join the plurality opinion.

I.

I commence my analysis by examining the traditional and fundamental dichotomy between direct and indirect speech regulation that has been utilized by the courts of this state and the courts of this nation for generations. I believe that such an analysis is necessary to remain faithful to *Davenport* and its directive that this Court should "borrow from well-reasoned and persuasive federal procedural and substantive precedent when this is deemed helpful . . . ." *Davenport,* 834 S.W.2d at 20. In order to determine whether the course of our sister states and the federal judiciary is helpful, we must at some point examine the rationale developed by these other courts. This Court should not develop constitutional law in a complete vacuum, but instead we should examine the development of the law in the other states and the federal system and benefit from their experiences. The federal courts, and especially the United States Supreme Court, have developed a two-track model for examining speech regulations that has been followed to some extent by the vast majority of other jurisdictions in this nation. Before we reject such a well-accepted model, we should at least examine it.

Although this dichotomy between direct speech regulation and indirect speech regulation is not without its critics, the United States Supreme Court and the lower federal courts have utilized this dichotomy for over fifty years. *See Hague v. C.I.O.,* 307 U.S. at 515-16 (1939); *Cox v. New Hampshire,* 312 U.S. at 574 (1941). Moreover, the courts of every other state likewise utilize this same distinction. *See, e.g., Planned Parenthood v. Operation Rescue,* 550 N.E.2d 1361, 1370 (Mass. 1990); *Bering v. SHARE,* 721 P.2d 918 (Wash. 1986). Even this state has recognized this dichotomy in previous decisions. *Iranian Muslim Organization v. City of San Antonio,* 615 S.W.2d 202, 205-06 (Tex.1981); *Olvera v. State,* 806 S.W.2d 546, 548-50 (Tex.Crim.App.1991). Furthermore, not only do most jurisdictions in the nation recognize the dichotomy between direct and indirect speech regulations, such a distinction just makes sense. Why should indirect restrictions attempting to balance competing rights be subject to the same high degree of scrutiny as direct restrictions that completely ban a type of expression? However, in today's opinion, without analysis or discussion, the plurality fails to recognize this dichotomy under the Texas Constitution. I instead would utilize the experiences of this state and other jurisdictions and recognize the traditional distinction between indirect speech regulation and direct speech regulation; therefore, I would subject indirect speech regulations to a less onerous test than direct speech regulations.

II.

However, I am a vigorous proponent of the right of free expression, and I have on many occasions expressed my belief that the free speech guarantees of the Texas Constitution are greater than the guarantees provided by the First Amendment. *See, e.g., Casso v. Brand,* 776 S.W.2d 551, 564 (Tex.1989) (Gonzalez, J., concurring and dissenting); *Channel 4, KGBT v. Briggs,* 759 S.W.2d 939, 944 (Tex.1988) (Gonzalez, J., concurring). This is now also the opinion of this Court. *Davenport,* 834 S.W.2d at 10. Consistent with "Texas' strong and longstanding commitment to free speech," *id.* at 7, I would modify the time, place, and manner test to reflect the greater free speech guarantee contained in article I, section 8. Rather than utilizing the normal standard requiring that the restriction be narrowly tailored to serve an significant government interest, I would require that the restriction be narrowly tailored to serve a compelling government interest.

III.

Although I differ from the plurality opinion in the method by which I analyze the constitutionality of these temporary restraining orders, I reach the same result.

I commence this analysis by determining whether the temporary restraining orders in this case are content neutral. I believe that the orders are indeed content neutral. The restraining orders apply equally to all protests; no differentiation is made based upon the particular message conveyed by the relators. It is true that the restraining orders only applied to the relators, but that is because they are the only defendants the clinics have established create the requisite threat of harm to support injunctive relief.

The second prong of this modified time, place, and manner test is whether the restraining order is narrowly tailored to serve a compelling government interest. [T]here is no compelling interest in keeping the relators one-hundred feet from all clinic entrances, exits, and parking lots when access to the clinic has been guaranteed by the other, more narrowly drawn prohibitions of the temporary restraining orders. In other words, the one-hundred foot free speech zones in this case are not narrowly tailored to serve any compelling interest not already served by the other restrictions in the temporary restraining orders.

Therefore, under the modified time, place, and manner test, the one-hundred foot distance limitation in the temporary restraining orders violates article I, section 8 of the Texas Constitution. I thus concur in the judgment of the Court that relators be discharged.

HECHT, Justice, dissenting, joined by Justice Enoch.

I agree that the district court's temporary restraining orders impermissibly infringed upon relators' First Amendment rights for the reasons explained by CHIEF JUSTICE PHILLIPS in his concurring opinion. I do not agree, however, that relators were entitled to violate those orders with impunity without first exhausting all available efforts to have them set aside. Relators chose a course of action which they expected would land them in jail. I would not disappoint them; I would remand them into the custody of the Sheriff of Harris County until they served their full punishment.

Notes on the Breadth of the *Davenport* Standard

A Broader Texas Expressive Right?: What is meant by the statement in Justice Doggett's plurality opinion and Justice Gonzalez's concurrence that the state constitutional guarantee is "broader" than the First Amendment? Why do the two Justices disagree on the appropriate test to apply to this temporary restraining order when both maintain that article I, section 8 offers greater protection than federal doctrine?

Does the determination that the Texas expressive right is broader indicate an appropriate methodology for analyzing the scope of the guarantee in a given case? Does this mean that the court should start with the protections of the First Amendment, and then provide additional protections thereafter? If so, how should the scope of such additional protections be determined in the first instance?

Instead of a generalized conclusion regarding breadth, is it better to analyze the text, purposes, history, and precedent supporting each particular application of a state constitutional provision? If so, how should this be done? In his concurrence, Chief Justice Phillips articulates two slightly different versions of the proper methodology to interpret a state constitution. Which one is preferable and why? How does the methodology articulated by Chief Justice Phillips compare to the methodology employed by the Texas Court of Criminal Appeals in *Heitman* and *Hulit* presented in the prior section? How does the plurality's rationale in *Ex parte Tucci* compare to *Heitman* and *Hulit*? Does the disagreement regarding the appropriate interpretive methodology assist in explaining the need for the seven justices that agreed the relators should be discharged to write three separate opinions, none of which commanded a majority?

First Amendment Standard for Time, Place, and Manner Injunctions: Five years after *Ex parte Tucci*, the Texas Supreme Court decided another case involving the same group of anti-abortion protestors, *Operation Rescue-National v. Planned Parenthood of Houston & Southeast Texas, Inc.*[125] After the supreme court ordered the protestors released in *Tucci* on the basis that the district court's temporary restraining order violated the state constitution, the district court proceeded to issue a temporary injunction and then a permanent injunction against the protestors, which was appealed to the supreme court.

---

[125] 975 S.W.2d 546 (Tex. 1998).

The first issue for the *Operation Rescue* court was determining the appropriate standard for reviewing the district court's injunction. At the time *Tucci* was decided, there was some debate regarding whether strict scrutiny or intermediate scrutiny was the appropriate standard under the First Amendment for an injunction regulating the time, place, and manner of expressive activity. In the intervening five years between *Tucci* and *Operation Rescue*, the United States Supreme Court resolved the First Amendment issue, concluding in *Madsen v. Women's Health Center, Inc.* that such injunctions must "burden no more speech than necessary to serve a significant government interest."[126] The *Madsen* test falls somewhere between federal intermediate and strict scrutiny, requiring a closer fit between the injunction and the government's interest as in strict scrutiny but employing a "significant governmental interest" standard as in intermediate scrutiny. After explaining the First Amendment standard under *Madsen*, Justice Hecht's opinion for the Texas Supreme Court in *Operation Rescue* then turned to the proper free speech analysis under the Texas Constitution:

Operation Rescue-National v. Planned Parenthood of Houston & Southeast Texas, Inc., 975 S.W.2d 546 (Tex. 1998)

We next consider the standard under Article I, Section 8 of the Texas Constitution. If it is the same as the First Amendment standard, or if it is less protective of speech, then we need only apply the federal standard. If the state constitutional standard is more protective of speech, then we must determine how to apply it in the context of this case, which involves a balancing of competing and conflicting rights and interests.

In two cases, *Davenport v. Garcia* and *Ex Parte Tucci,* this Court has said that Article I, Section 8 of the Texas Constitution is "broader" or affords "greater" protection of speech than the First Amendment. In neither case, however, did the Court actually apply a different standard under the state constitutional provision than required by the First Amendment.

Davenport involved a content-specific gag order that the trial court imposed on a guardian ad litem in pending civil litigation. This Court concluded that the First Amendment standard for reviewing such an order had not been clearly defined in federal case law and adopted its own test under Article I, Section 8. But even if federal law was unclear, the state standard enunciated by the Court did not conflict with federal law. The Court did not reject a federal standard as inadequate for the state constitutional protection. In any event, because *Davenport* dealt with a content-based restriction, it provides no guidance to us here.

Tucci, it so happens, arose out of the same litigation before us today. As already explained above, relators in that case, some of whom are petitioners here, were held in contempt for violating the district court's temporary restraining order. The Court unanimously agreed that the order violated relators' rights under Article I, Section 8 of the Texas Constitution. Five Justices expressed the view that this provision provides greater protection of speech than the First Amendment. But this majority could not agree on the

---

[126] 512 U.S. 753, 765 (1994).

applicable standard. At the time, *Madsen* had not been decided.

JUSTICE GONZALEZ's test requires that injunctive relief serve a higher interest than *Madsen*–compelling rather than significant–but allows a looser fit between the relief and the interest–narrowly tailored rather than no more burden than necessary. The requirement of a compelling government interest resembles the strict scrutiny reserved for content-based restrictions, but JUSTICE GONZALEZ did not argue for strict scrutiny. On the contrary, he viewed his standard as less demanding than JUSTICE DOGGETT's. Thus, both JUSTICE GONZALEZ's test and the *Madsen* test fall between the federal strict scrutiny and intermediate scrutiny standards. If they operate differently, it is not clear how.

The "least restrictive means" component of JUSTICE DOGGETT's test is indistinguishable from the "burden no more speech than necessary" element of the *Madsen* test. Under either formulation, the goal is to protect the interests at stake while minimizing the speech proscribed. An injunction that safeguards relevant interests by excessively proscribing speech would not only burden speech more than necessary, but would not be the least restrictive means available. But it is not clear how JUSTICE DOGGETT's requirement that restrictions be used only to protect against imminent and irreparable harm compares to *Madsen*'s requirement that restrictions must serve a significant government interest. The threat of irreparable harm is necessary for issuance of an injunction under federal law, and is therefore implicit in the *Madsen* test. No injunction can issue except to protect against imminent harm. It thus appears that the *Madsen* test contains both the elements in JUSTICE DOGGETT's test and adds a significant-government-interest limitation missing from JUSTICE DOGGETT's test.

But if the *Madsen* test is more protective of speech than JUSTICE DOGGETT's test in *Tucci,* then it is perforce more protective than JUSTICE GONZALEZ's test, belying both their assertions that Article I, Section 8 is more protective of speech than the First Amendment. On the other hand, if the *Madsen* test is less protective than both the others, even though it is more protective than federal intermediate scrutiny, then the differences are too minuscule to matter. The notion that not one, but three different tests can be formulated and applied in between traditional federal intermediate scrutiny and strict scrutiny presupposes a continuum more metaphysical than legal.

It is possible that Article I, Section 8 may be more protective of speech in some instances than the First Amendment, but if it is, it must be because of the text, history, and purpose of the provision, not just simply *because.* Starting from the premise that the state constitutional provision *must* be more protective than its federal counterpart illegitimizes any effort to determine state constitutional standards. To define the protections of Article I, Section 8 simply as one notch above First Amendment protections is to deny state constitutional guarantees any principled moorings whatever. We reject this approach.

The text, history, and purposes of Article I, Section 8 have been thoroughly examined by this Court.[127] We know of nothing to suggest that injunctions restricting

---

[127]*Davenport,* 834 S.W.2d at 30-35 (Hecht, J., concurring); *Tucci,* 859 S.W.2d at 16-32 (Phillips, C.J., concurring).

speech should be judged by a different standard under the state constitution than the First Amendment. We are concerned that the fact that an injunction suit necessarily focuses on particular speech in particular circumstances makes it difficult to consider relief without regard to the content of the speech involved. We are therefore persuaded, as the Supreme Court has been, that injunctive restrictions must be judged more strictly than legislative restrictions, but like the Supreme Court, we hesitate to apply the same strict scrutiny to content-neutral injunctions as is applied to content-based statutes.

The considerations relevant to determining the protection to be afforded speech in the present context are the same under both the federal and state constitutions. Accordingly, we conclude that an injunction in these circumstances must burden no more speech than necessary to serve a significant government interest. . . .

[The court then proceeded to apply the *Madsen* test to the challenged permanent injunction, upholding some provisions while modifying or deleting other provisions of the detailed injunction.]

Notes on the Current Texas Approach to Free Speech

The Factor Analysis: What factors, according to the *Operation Rescue* court, might justify interpreting the free speech provision of the Texas Constitution to afford greater protections than the First Amendment? Since *Operation Rescue*, subsequent supreme court decisions have confirmed that article I, section 8 will not be interpreted as more expansive than the First Amendment without some "textual or contextual reason."[128] How does this currently prevailing rationale compare with *Davenport*?

Are the factors that *Operation Rescue* mentions–the text, history, and purpose of the provision–encompassing enough? Several other states have adopted criteria for evaluating whether more protection should be afforded for dually protected guarantees under state constitutions. Justice Handler of the New Jersey Supreme Court apparently was the first judge to articulate such a set of standards. He formulated seven: (1) significantly different textual language, (2) legislative and ratification history of the provision indicating a broader meaning, (3) preexisting state law defining the scope of a right later established, (4) structural differences between the state and federal charters, (5) matters of particular state interest and local concern, (6) unique state history or traditions, and (7) distinctive attitudes

[128] Tex. Dep't of Transp. v. Barber, 111 S.W.3d 86, 106 (Tex. 2003) (holding litigant had not "articulated any reasons based on the text, history, and purpose of Article I, Section 8 to show that its protection of noncommercial speech is broader than that provided by the First Amendment under the circumstances presented."); Comm'n for Lawyer Discipline v. Benton, 980 S.W.2d 425, 434 (Tex. 1998) (rejecting claim that Texas Constitution provided heightened free speech protection because it was "aware of no textual or contextual reason to construe Article I, Section 8 as more protective than the First Amendment standard we apply today in the area of ethical restrictions on attorneys' professional speech"); *see also* New Times, Inc. v. Isaacks, 146 S.W.3d 144, 150 (Tex. 2004) (assuming that federal and state constitutional free speech guarantees had same scope when it was not neither apparent, nor had the parties argued, that the textual differences were material in the defamation context); Bentley v. Bunton, 94 S.W.3d 561, 579 (Tex. 2002) (same); Osterberg v. Peca, 12 S.W.3d 31, 40-41 (Tex. 2000) (considering arguments only under the First Amendment of the United States Constitution when the litigants had provided no rationale to support a holding under article I, section 8).

of the state's citizenry.[129] The New Jersey Supreme Court then explicitly adopted these seven criteria as controlling in *State v. Williams*.[130] Washington subsequently adopted its own list of similar factors for interpreting its constitution in *State v. Gunwall*,[131] and Connecticut, Michigan, Pennsylvania, and Wyoming have also employed analogous factors to assist in state constitutional interpretation.[132] How do these factors compare with those highlighted by the Texas Supreme Court?

Are any other factors important? Consider the following 1974 amendment to the California Constitution: "Rights guaranteed by this Constitution are not dependent on those guaranteed by the United States Constitution."[133] Rhode Island also ratified an almost identical amendment to its constitution in 1986.[134] How should these amendments impact the interpretation of dually protected constitutional guarantees under the state constitution? Do these amendments guarantee "broader" rights or are they merely reminders that the state constitution does not have to be interpreted in lockstep with the Federal Constitution?[135]

Under the factor analysis, who must raise the distinctions between the federal and state constitutions? In Texas, as well as in many other states, the parties typically have the responsibility to urge that differences between the state and federal constitutional guarantees are material to the case. If the parties do not make such an argument, both the Texas Supreme Court and the Court of Criminal Appeals usually assume without deciding that the guarantees are coextensive, even though *Davenport* articulated that the court would

---

[129]State v. Hunt, 450 A.2d 952, 965-67 (N.J. 1982) (Handler, J., concurring).

[130]459 A.2d 641, 650 (N.J. 1983).

[131]720 P.2d 808, 811-13 (Wash. 1986) (adopting six nonexclusive factors to determine whether Washington Constitution should be interpreted more broadly than the United States Constitution: (1) textual language, (2) differences in the text, (3) state constitutional and common law history, (4) preexisting state law, (5) structural differences, and (6) matters of particular state or local concern).

[132]*See, e.g.*, State v. Geisler, 610 A.2d 1225, 1232 (Conn. 1992) (explaining the court will examine state constitutional text, state and federal precedent, sister state decisions, the historical constitutional setting and constitutional debates, and economical and sociological considerations); People v. Catania, 398 N.W.2d 343, 351 n.12 (Mich. 1986) (noting factors similar to those adopted in *Gunwall* would aid the court in determining the proper independent scope of state constitution); Commonwealth v. Edmunds, 586 A.2d 887, 895 (Pa. 1991) (culling the following four factors from its prior decisions: "(1) text of the Pennsylvania constitutional provision; (2) history of the provision, including Pennsylvania case-law; (3) related case-law from other states; and (4) policy considerations, including unique issues of state and local concern, and applicability with modern Pennsylvania jurisprudence."); Saldana v. State, 846 P.2d 604, 622 (Wyo. 1993) (adopting *Gunwall* factors as non-exclusive criteria for interpreting state constitutional provisions); *accord* Commonwealth v. Wason, 842 S.W.2d 487, 492 (Ky. 1992) (examining textual, structural, and precedential distinctions between Kentucky and United States Constitution to protect deviate sexual intercourse in private by consenting adults despite then-existing contrary federal precedent).

[133]CAL. CONST. art. I, § 24.

[134]R.I. CONST. art. I, § 24 ("The rights guaranteed by this Constitution are not dependent on those guaranteed by the Constitution of the United States.").

[135]*Cf.* People v. Brisendine, 531 P.2d 1099, 1144 (Cal. 1975) (opining article I, section 24 "was a mere reaffirmation of existing law"); People v. Norman, 538 P.2d 237, 245 n.10 (Cal. 1975) (referring to article I, section 24 as a "declaration of constitutional independence").

undertake its own analysis without the benefit of briefing.[136] But despite the fact that the resolution of state constitutional claims in Texas and other states depends on the parties' briefing, the parties frequently do not adequately assert a state constitutional claim. This has led some state supreme courts to admonish counsel of the need to provide better briefing on state constitutional issues.[137]

Davenport*'s Legacy*: After *Operation Rescue*, what, if anything, is the lasting import of *Davenport*? One (perhaps overly) optimistic view is that "it will hopefully benefit the future of Texas jurisprudence by forcing litigants to focus on the guarantees contained in the state constitution. The text, history, and purpose of these provisions may indeed compel, under certain circumstances, a broader or more expansive right than provided by the United States Constitution. . . . If counsel will divine from *Davenport* an additional opportunity to protect the fundamental rights of the citizens of Texas, the case will be of lasting benefit even though its foundations were fundamentally flawed."[138]

Under what circumstances (if any) could the text, history, and purposes of article I, section 8 perhaps support greater free speech rights than the United States Constitution? The Texas Supreme Court in *Republican Party of Texas v. Dietz*, while refusing to resolve the issue as the parties had not briefed or argued it, noted that some state courts in other jurisdictions had determined that their free expression guarantees could be asserted against privately-owned shopping centers and universities.[139] Is there a textual or contextual basis for such an expansion of expressive rights in Texas?

2. Free Speech Rights on Private Property

The judiciary frequently has been required to resolve the conflict between the right of free expression and the private property rights of individuals and corporations. The United States Supreme Court initially sided with the First Amendment, holding in *Amalgamated Food Employees Union Local 590 v. Logan Valley Plaza, Inc.* that union members had a constitutionally protected right to picket a nonunion store on privately

---

[136] *See, e.g.*, *In re* B.G., 317 S.W.3d 250, 252 n.2 (Tex. 2010) (treating federal and state due process guarantees as the same when the parties did not identify any material differences); *In re* Fisher, 164 S.W.3d 637, 645 (Tex. 2005) (limiting analysis to federal constitutional issues when parties had not argued that differences between the federal and state guarantees were material to the case); Sheffield Dev. Co. v. City of Glenn Heights, 140 S.W.3d 660, 669 (Tex. 2004) (noting neither party had urged that the differences in wording between the federal and state taking clauses were significant such that the court could look to federal jurisprudence for guidance in interpreting the state constitution); *In re* Bay Area Citizens Against Lawsuit Abuse, 982 S.W.2d 371, 375 n.4 (Tex. 1998) (declining to consider right to associate under state constitution when litigant's briefing exclusively relied on federal authority); Tilton v. Marshall, 925 S.W.2d 672, 677 n.6 (Tex. 1996) (assuming federal and state constitutional protections for free exercise of religion were coextensive in absence of contrary argument); Arnold v. State, 873 S.W.2d 27, 33 (Tex. Crim. App. 1993) (appellant claiming relief under both the federal and state constitutions must "analyze, argue or provide authority to establish that his protection under the Texas Constitution exceeds or differs from that provided to him by the Federal Constitution.").

[137] *See, e.g.*, State v. Ball, 685 P.2d 1055, 1061 (Utah 1984) (noting state constitutional issues not briefed in the case deserved "thorough treatment by counsel").

[138] Charles W. "Rocky" Rhodes, *A Proposal for Interpreting Corresponding United States and Texas Constitutional Guarantees in the New Millenium*, 51 BAYLOR L. REV. 269, 316-17 (1999).

[139] 940 S.W.2d 86, 90 n.5 (Tex. 1997).

owned shopping center property.[140] The Court then limited *Logan Valley* in *Lloyd Corp. v. Tanner*, which held that the distribution of handbills in a shopping center protesting military operations in Vietnam was not constitutionally protected because *Logan Valley* only applied to picketing directed at a store on the premises with no other reasonable opportunity to reach the intended audience.[141] Finally, the Court retreated entirely from the proposition that the First Amendment protected free speech rights on private property, even in the context of labor picketing targeted at a store on the premises, in *Hudgens v. NLRB*.[142]

In the meantime, however, the issue was also percolating in the state courts under state constitutions. And while *Hudgens* was the last word on the reach of the First Amendment, it did not resolve the issue under the free speech provisions of the state constitutions. Some state supreme courts have concluded that their expression guarantees do protect free speech rights on private property, based in part on the affirmative grant in the text of the right of every person to speak, subject to the responsibility for abuse of the privilege. The first state high court to ground such a holding exclusively under the state constitution was the California Supreme Court, in a case that eventually went before the United States Supreme Court.

Robins v. Pruneyard Shopping Center, 592 P.2d 341 (Cal. 1979)

NEWMAN, Justice.

In this appeal from a judgment denying an injunction we hold that the soliciting at a shopping center of signatures for a petition to the government is an activity protected by the California Constitution.

Pruneyard Shopping Center is a privately owned center that consists of approximately 21 acres, 5 devoted to parking and 16 occupied by walkways, plazas, and buildings that contain 65 shops, 10 restaurants, and a cinema. The public is invited to visit for the purpose of patronizing the many businesses. Pruneyard's policy is not to permit any tenant or visitor to engage in publicly expressive activity, including the circulating of petitions, that is not directly related to the commercial purposes. The policy seems to have been strictly and disinterestedly enforced.

Appellants are high school students who attempted one Saturday afternoon to solicit support for their opposition to a United Nations resolution against "Zionism." They set up a cardtable in a corner of Pruneyard's central courtyard and sought to discuss their concerns with shoppers and to solicit signatures for a petition to be sent to the White House in Washington. Their activity was peaceful and apparently well-received by Pruneyard patrons.

Soon after they had begun their soliciting they were approached by a security guard who informed them that their conduct violated Pruneyard regulations. They spoke to the guard's superior, who informed them they would have to leave because they did not have

---

[140] 391 U.S. 308, 319-25 (1968), *overruled by Hudgens v. NLRB*, 424 U.S. 507 (1976).

[141] 407 U.S. 551, 561-67 (1972).

[142] 424 U.S. 507, 518-21 (1976).

permission to solicit. The officers suggested that appellants continue their activities on the public sidewalk at the center's perimeter.

Appellants immediately left the premises and later brought suit. The trial court rejected their request that Pruneyard be enjoined from denying them access.

Our main questions are: (1) Did Lloyd v. Tanner (1972) 407 U.S. 551 recognize federally protected property rights of such a nature that we now are barred from ruling that the California Constitution creates broader speech rights as to private property than does the federal Constitution? (2) If not, does the California Constitution protect speech and petitioning at shopping centers?

DOES LLOYD IDENTIFY SPECIAL PROPERTY RIGHTS PROTECTED BY THE FEDERAL CONSTITUTION?

Lloyd held that a shopping center owner could prohibit distribution of leaflets when they communicated no information relating to the center's business and when there was an adequate, alternate means of communication. The court stated, "We hold that there has been no such dedication of Lloyd's privately owned and operated shopping center to public use as to entitle respondents to exercise therein the asserted First Amendment rights." (407 U.S. at p. 570.)

Appellants correctly assert that Lloyd is primarily a First Amendment case. The references to Fifth and Fourteenth Amendment rights were made specifically in connection with the court's discussion of state action requirements. The court was focusing on Marsh v. Alabama (1946) 326 U.S. 501, which held that a property owner's actions in some circumstances are equivalent to state action because of public functions performed by the property. The court in Lloyd examined the functions performed by Lloyd's center but did not purport to define the nature or scope of Fifth and Fourteenth Amendment rights of shopping center owners generally.

Subsequent decisions support that reading of Lloyd. In Hudgens v. NLRB (1976) 424 U.S. 507, the court again considered First Amendment rights in relation to private property. Though it concluded that the First Amendment did not protect picketing in a shopping center, it acknowledged that "statutory or common law may in some situations extend protection or provide redress against a private corporation or person who seeks to abridge the free expression of others . . . ." (Id. p. 513.) The court's conclusion that the National Labor Relations Act controlled the issues there presented indicates that Lloyd by no means created any property right immune from regulation.

Lloyd when viewed in conjunction with Hudgens does not preclude law-making in California which requires that shopping center owners permit expressive activity on their property. To hold otherwise would flout the whole development of law regarding states' power to regulate uses of property and would place a state's interest in strengthening First Amendment rights in an inferior rather than a preferred position. "(A)ll private property is held subject to the power of the government to regulate its use for the public welfare." (Agricultural Labor Relations Bd. v. Superior Court (1976), 546 P.2d 687, 694; app. dism. for want of substantial federal question, 429 U.S. 802.)

[C]entral business districts apparently have continued to yield their functions more and more to suburban centers. Evidence submitted by appellants in this case helps dramatize the potential impact of the public forums sought here. [Retail sales in the central business district continue to decline, while outlying shopping centers are frequently visited as they provide the location, goods, and services to satisfy the needs and wants of suburban and rural communities.]

In assessing the significance of the growing importance of the shopping center we stress also that to prohibit expressive activity in the centers would impinge on constitutional rights beyond speech rights. Courts have long protected the right to petition as an essential attribute of governing. (United States v. Cruikshank (1875) 92 U.S. 542-52.) The California Constitution declares that "people have the right to . . . petition government for redress of grievances . . . ." (Art. I, s 3.) That right in California is, moreover, vital to a basic process in the state's constitutional scheme direct initiation of change by the citizenry through initiative, referendum, and recall.

To protect free speech and petitioning is a goal that surely matches the protecting of health and safety, the environment, aesthetics, property values and other societal goals that have been held to justify reasonable restrictions on private property rights.

DOES THE CALIFORNIA CONSTITUTION GUARANTEE THE RIGHT TO GATHER SIGNATURES AT SHOPPING CENTERS?

No California statute prescribes that shopping center owners provide public forums. But article I, section 2 of the state Constitution reads: "Every person may freely speak, write and publish his or her sentiments on all subjects, being responsible for the abuse of this right. A law may not restrain or abridge liberty of speech or press." Though the framers could have adopted the words of the federal Bill of Rights they chose not to do so. (See Note, Rediscovering the California Declaration of Rights (1974) 26 Hastings L.J. 481.) Special protections thus accorded speech are marked in this court's opinions. Wilson v. Superior Court (1975), 532 P.2d 116, 120, for instance, noted that "(a) protective provision more definitive and inclusive than the First Amendment is contained in our state constitutional guarantee of the right of free speech and press."

Past decisions on speech and private property testify to the strength of "liberty of speech" in this state. Diamond I held that distributing leaflets and soliciting initiative signatures at a shopping center are constitutionally protected. [477 P.2d 733 (Cal. 1970)]. Though the court relied partly on federal law, California precedents also were cited. (E.g., Schwartz-Torrance Investment Corp. v. Bakery & Confectionery Workers' Union (1964), 394 P.2d 921; In re Lane (1969), 457 P.2d 561; In re Hoffman (1967), 434 P.2d 353.) The fact that those opinions cited federal law that subsequently took a divergent course does not diminish their usefulness as precedent. The duty of this court is to help determine what "liberty of speech" means in California. Federal principles are relevant but not conclusive so long as federal rights are protected.

Schwartz-Torrance, supra, held that a labor union has the right to picket a bakery located in a shopping center. The opinion noted that the basic problem is one of "accommodating conflicting interests: plaintiff's assertion of its right to the exclusive use of the shopping center premises to which the public in general has been invited as against the union's right of communication of its position which, it asserts, rests upon public policy and constitutional protection." (394 P.2d at p. 922.)

The issue arose too in In re Hoffman (1967), 434 P.2d 353, where Vietnam War protesters had attempted to distribute leaflets in the Los Angeles Union Station, owned by three private companies. It housed a restaurant, snack bar, cocktail lounge, and magazine stand in addition to facilities directly related to transporting passengers. The public was free to use the whole station. Chief Justice Traynor's opinion made it clear that property owners as well as government may regulate speech as to time, place, and manner. (434 P.2d 353.) Nonetheless, "a railway station is like a public street or park." (Id. at p. 356.) Further, "the test is not whether petitioners' use of the station was a railway use but whether it interfered with that use." (Id.) The opinion thus affirms that the public interest in peaceful speech outweighs the desire of property owners for control over their property. (See too In re Cox (1970), 474 P.2d 992, 1000. "The shopping center may no more exclude individuals who wear long hair . . . who are black, who are members of the John Birch Society, or who belong to the American Civil Liberties Union, merely because of these characteristics or associations, than may the City of San Rafael.")

A closer look at Lloyd, supra, 407 U.S. 551, has revealed that it does not prevent California's providing greater protection than the First Amendment now seems to provide. We conclude that sections 2 and 3 of article I of the California Constitution protect speech and petitioning, reasonably exercised, in shopping centers even when the centers are privately owned.

The judgment rejecting appellants' request that Pruneyard be enjoined from denying access to circulate the petition is reversed.

BIRD, C. J., and TOBRINER and MOSK, JJ., concur.

RICHARDSON, Justice, dissenting.

I respectfully dissent. The majority relegates the private property rights of the shopping center owner to a secondary, disfavored, and subservient position vis-a-vis the "free speech" claims of the plaintiffs. Such a holding clearly violates Federal constitutional guarantees announced in Lloyd Corp. v. Tanner (1972) 407 U.S. 551.

However, the majority attempts to circumvent Lloyd by relying upon the "liberty of speech clauses" of the California Constitution. I believe that such an analysis is clearly incorrect, because the owners of defendant Pruneyard Shopping Center possess Federally protected property rights which do not depend upon the varying and shifting interpretations of state constitutional law for their safeguard and survival.

The lesson to be learned from Lloyd is unmistakable and irrefutable: A private shopping center owner is protected by the Federal Constitution from unauthorized invasions by persons who enter the premises to conduct general "free speech" activities unrelated to the shopping center's purposes and functions. Nor is the foregoing principle in any way diminished or affected by the fact that the claimed free speech rights are purportedly sanctioned by the California Constitution, given the overriding supremacy of the federal Constitution.

Because, as the trial court expressly found, plaintiffs had adequate public forums in which to conduct their activities, their unauthorized entries on Pruneyard property manifestly cannot be excused on the basis of any state policy or goal "to protect free speech and petitioning." The Lloyd rationale is applicable and unanswerable. The majority may not evade it by resort, in this instance, to the California Constitution, which must yield to a paramount federal constitutional imperative.

Notes on State Constitutional Expressive Rights

Free Speech v. Private Property: *Robins* had to resolve two primary questions: first, whether *Lloyd* had foreclosed the states from protecting free speech rights on private property, and second, whether the California Constitution provided such protection. Examining the second question first, what arguments did the California Supreme Court use to support its holding that article I, section 2 of its state constitution protected free speech rights on private property? Are these arguments persuasive?

The court heavily emphasized the constitutional text, noting that it was more inclusive than the First Amendment because it affirmatively granted the right of every person to freely speak, write, and publish. But was there any indication that this text was originally considered or intended to protect expressive rights on private property? Or was it merely intended to ensure protection from governmental licensing and censorship in the manner articulated by the original source for this phraseology, William Blackstone?

The court also emphasized the significance of the shopping center as a forum for speech, especially in the context of the right to petition under the initiative, referendum, and recall provisions of the California Constitution. Finally, the court cited to its prior precedents, even though some of these cases relied on "federal law that subsequently took a divergent course."

Despite such arguments, however, most states that have considered the issue have rejected the *Robins* approach and held that their state constitutions do not protect expressive activities on private property.[143] Only a couple of state courts have followed *Robins*.[144]

---

[143] *See, e.g.*, Cologne v. Westfarms Assocs., 469 A.2d 1201, 1207-10 (Conn. 1984); Citizens for Ethical Gov't, Inc. v. Gwinnet Place Assocs., L.P., 392 S.E.2d 8, 19 (Ga. 1990); Estes v. Kapiolani Women's & Children's Med. Ctr., 787 P.2d 216, 221 (Haw. 1990); State v. Lacey, 465 N.W.2d 537, 539-40 (Iowa 1991); Woodland v. Mich. Citizens Lobby, 378 N.W.2d 337, 344-48 (Mich. 1985); S.O.C., Inc. v. Mirage Casino-Hotel, 23 P.3d 243, 250-51 (Nev. 2001); SHAD Alliance v. Smith Haven Mall, 488 N.E.2d 1211, 1214-17 (N.Y. 1985); State v. Felmet, 273 S.E.2d 708, 712 (N.C. 1981); Eastwood Mall, Inc. v. Slanco, 626 N.E.2d 59, 61 (Ohio 1994); Charleston Joint Venture v. McPherson, 417 S.E.2d 544, 548-49 (S.C. 1992); Southcenter Joint Venture v. Nat'l Democratic Policy Comm., 780 P.2d 1282, 1285-92 (Wash. 1989); Jacobs v. Major, 407 N.W.2d 832, 839 (Wis. 1987).

[144] *See, e.g.*, Bock v. Westminster Mall Co., 819 P.2d 55, 60 (Colo. 1991) (holding state free speech guarantee protected leafleting opposing American foreign policy at privately owned mall); N.J. Coalition Against War in the Middle East v. J.M.B. Realty Corp., 650 A.2d 757, 758 (N.J. 1994) (protecting right to leaflet on societal issues at regional and community shopping centers); State v. Schmid, 423 A.2d 615, 626-30 (N.J. 1980)

The New Jersey courts have followed California's lead to safeguard fairly extensive state constitutional free speech rights on private property. In *State v. Schmid*, the New Jersey Supreme Court overturned the defendant's trespassing conviction for distributing political literature on Princeton University's campus. Reasoning that New Jersey's guarantee protecting the right to "freely speak, write, and publish his sentiments" was "more sweeping in scope than the language of the First Amendment," the court adopted a balancing test to govern expressive activities on private property, evaluating the property's normal use, the parameters of the invitation to the public, and the purpose of the expressive activity.[145] Subsequently, in *New Jersey Coalition Against War in the Middle East v. J.M.B. Realty Corp.*, the *Schmid* balancing test was employed to hold that a large, regional shopping center had to allow leafleting regarding issues of public import, although it could regulate the time, place, and manner of the exercise of the free speech rights.[146] The *Coalition* court also emphasized that its holding was limited and would not apply to a solitary business or even to a small-to-medium sized shopping center.[147] In accord with this limited understanding, the New Jersey Supreme Court most recently held that homeowners could not assert state constitutional free speech rights against their residential community association.[148] California has similarly recognized limits on the scope of expressive rights on private property, concluding in *Golden Gateway Center v. Golden Gateway Tenants Ass'n* that tenants did not have a state constitutional right to distribute a newsletter and leaflets in a privately owned residential apartment complex.[149]

Another potential restriction is that almost all the state cases protecting speech on private property have involved political speech at the core of expressive rights. Would these decisions also protect other forms of speech, such as commercial or indecent speech, on private property? As an example, could a rival shopping center advertise by leafleting in the Pruneyard Shopping Center? The California Supreme Court held in *Fashion Valley Mall, LLC v. NLRB* that a union had a right to distribute leaflets urging a boycott of a store in the mall in protest of the store's advertisements in a paper employing nonunion employees.[150] Yet this still arguably involved political speech related to labor relations, which the court's opinion emphasized by discussing the tradition of boycotts as a form of protected speech.[151] Do the difficulties in defining the appropriate scope and balancing of expressive rights on private property explain why so many courts have refused to recognize such a state constitutional right, allowing legislative bodies to accommodate the competing interests?

The Scope of Other States' Free Speech Guarantees: Are there other arguments in addition to textual distinctions that might justify a different scope of free speech rights

---

(holding state free speech guarantee protected political leafleting at private university).

[145]423 A.2d 615, 626-30 (N.J. 1980).

[146]650 A.2d 757, 775-79 (N.J. 1994).

[147]*Id.* at 781.

[148]Comm. for a Better Twin Rivers v. Twin Rivers Homeowners' Ass'n, 929 A.2d 1060, 1073-74 (N.J. 2007).

[149]29 P.3d 797, 803-10 (Cal. 2001) (Brown, J., plurality op.).

[150]172 P.3d 742 (Cal. 2007).

[151]*Id.* at 753-54.

under state constitutions? Some aspects of First Amendment law incorporate community standards, such as the test for obscenity, which examines the prurience and offensiveness of the displayed or depicted sexual conduct in light of contemporary community standards.[152] Does this mean that obscenity is a matter of local concern rather than national concern, diminishing any deference owed to United States Supreme Court decisions? New York has taken this position, extending its free speech protections for a sexually explicit bookstore beyond that required by the First Amendment, reasoning that New York often tolerates and supports "works which in other states would be found offensive to the community."[153] New York has also relied on its "hospitable climate for the free exchange of ideas" to restrict the right to recover in state tort law claims for defamation.[154]

Other states have likewise concluded that their history and traditions evince a unique commitment to free speech rights. Rhode Island has provided additional state constitutional protections against defamation actions because of the vitality of "opinion and debate" in the state's history, from its founding by dissenters to its pride "on its role in serving as the cradle of religious liberty in America."[155] Oregon has probably developed the most expansive free speech jurisprudence in the nation, concluding that its expressive guarantee encompasses all means of expressions on "any subject whatever" unless the expression falls within "an historically established exception" to the state constitutional guarantee.[156] These exceptions have been interpreted narrowly to apply only to matters such as libel, perjury, criminal solicitation, forgery, and fraud.[157] Thus, the Oregon Constitution protects obscenity, profanity, nude dancing, and even sexual conduct with an expressive component.[158] But the vast majority of states have not adopted an independent state constitutional free expression doctrine, instead employing traditional First Amendment precepts when interpreting the speech guarantees of their state constitutions.[159]

---

[152]Miller v. California, 413 U.S. 15, 24-33 (1973).

[153]People *ex rel.* Arcara v. Cloud Books, Inc., 503 N.E.2d 492, 494-95 (N.Y. 1986) (concluding, after remand from the Supreme Court's determination that the First Amendment was not implicated by a state court order closing an adult bookstore as a public nuisance for illegal on-premises sexual activities, that the state constitutional free speech guarantee invalidated the order).

[154]Immuno AG. v. Moor-Jankowski, 567 N.E.2d 1270, 1278-80 (N.Y. 1991).

[155]Beattie v. Fleet Nat'l Bank, 746 A.2d 717, 724-25 (R.I. 2000).

[156]State v. Henry, 732 P.2d 9, 11 (Or. 1987).

[157]*Id.*

[158]*See, e.g.*, City of Nyssa v. Dufloth, 121 P.3d 639, 642-44 (Or. 2005) (holding city ordinance requiring nude dancers to remain four feet away from audience infringed upon protected expressive activity that did not fall within any well-established historical exception to free speech protection); State v. Ciancanelli, 121 P.3d 613, 629-35 (Or. 2005) (holding statute prohibiting "live public show" in which participants engage in "sexual conduct" violated Oregon free speech provision); *Henry*, 732 P.2d at 11-16 (holding statute prohibiting the possession of obscene material violated state free expression guarantee). Although acknowledging that laws against obscenity have existed for a long time, Oregon has discounted the existence of such laws as being primarily directed at protecting youth from obscene materials and preventing sacrilegious expression, concerns it does not believe apply in modern times when adults possess such materials. *Henry*, 732 P.2d at 11-16.

[159]1 JENNIFER FRIESEN, STATE CONSTITUTIONAL LAW: LITIGATING INDIVIDUAL RIGHTS, CLAIMS AND DEFENSES § 5.01 (4th ed. 2006).

Countervailing Federally Protected Rights: What are the limits on the state's ability to expand protections of free speech rights beyond that established by the First Amendment? For instance, are there provisions of the United States Constitution that may be violated if the state court extends free speech rights to private property? The California Supreme Court in *Robins* concluded that *Lloyd* had not, as a matter of federal constitutional law, foreclosed the states from protecting free speech rights on private property. But the possibility that the Pruneyard Shopping Center's federal rights were violated through the California Supreme Court's interpretation of the state constitution in *Robins* provided the United States Supreme Court an opportunity to review the decision.

PruneYard Shopping Center v. Robins, 447 U.S. 74 (1980)

Mr. Justice REHNQUIST delivered the opinion of the Court.

We [consider] whether state constitutional provisions, which permit individuals to exercise free speech and petition rights on the property of a privately owned shopping center to which the public is invited, violate the shopping center owner's property rights under the Fifth and Fourteenth Amendments or his free speech rights under the First and Fourteenth Amendments. . . .

III

Appellants first contend that *Lloyd Corp. v. Tanner*, 407 U.S. 551 (1972), prevents the State from requiring a private shopping center owner to provide access to persons exercising their state constitutional rights of free speech and petition when adequate alternative avenues of communication are available. *Lloyd* dealt with the question whether under the Federal Constitution a privately owned shopping center may prohibit the distribution of handbills on its property when the handbilling is unrelated to the shopping center's operations. *Id.*, at 552. The shopping center had adopted a strict policy against the distribution of handbills within the building complex and its malls, and it made no exceptions to this rule. *Id.*, at 555. Respondents in *Lloyd* argued that because the shopping center was open to the public, the First Amendment prevents the private owner from enforcing the handbilling restriction on shopping center premises. *Id.*, at 564. In rejecting this claim we substantially repudiated the rationale of *Food Employees v. Logan Valley Plaza*, 391 U.S. 308 (1968), which was later overruled in *Hudgens v. NLRB*, 424 U.S. 507 (1976). We stated that property does not "lose its private character merely because the public is generally invited to use it for designated purposes," and that "[t]he essentially private character of a store and its privately owned abutting property does not change by virtue of being large or clustered with other stores in a modern shopping center."

Our reasoning in *Lloyd*, however, does not *ex proprio vigore* limit the authority of the State to exercise its police power or its sovereign right to adopt in its own Constitution individual liberties more expansive than those conferred by the Federal Constitution. *Cooper v. California*, 386 U.S. 58, 62 (1967). In *Lloyd, supra*, there was no state constitutional or statutory provision that had been construed to create rights to the use of private property by strangers, comparable to those found to exist by the California Supreme Court here. It is, of course, well established that a State in the exercise of its police power may adopt reasonable restrictions on private property so long as the restrictions do not amount to a taking without just compensation or contravene any other federal constitutional provision. See, *e.g., Euclid v. Ambler Realty Co.*, 272 U.S. 365 (1926); *Young v. American Mini Theatres, Inc.*, 427 U.S. 50 (1976). *Lloyd* held that when a shopping center owner opens his private property to the public for the purpose of shopping, the First Amendment to the United States Constitution does not thereby create individual rights in expression beyond those already existing under applicable law.

IV

Appellants next contend that a right to exclude others underlies the Fifth Amendment guarantee against the taking of property without just compensation and the Fourteenth Amendment guarantee against the deprivation of property without due process of law.

It is true that one of the essential sticks in the bundle of property rights is the right to exclude others. *Kaiser Aetna v. United States*, 444 U.S. 164, 179-180 (1979). And here there has literally been a "taking" of that right to the extent that the California Supreme Court has interpreted the State Constitution to entitle its citizens to exercise free expression and petition rights on shopping center property. But it is well established that "not every destruction or injury to property by governmental action has been held to be a 'taking' in the constitutional sense." *Armstrong v. United States*, 364 U.S. 40, 48 (1960). Rather, the determination whether a state law unlawfully infringes a landowner's property in violation of the Taking Clause requires an examination of whether the restriction on private property "forc[es] some people alone to bear public burdens which, in all fairness and justice, should be borne by the public as a whole." *Id.*, at 49. This examination entails inquiry into such factors as the character of the governmental action, its economic impact, and its interference with reasonable investment-backed expectations. *Kaiser Aetna v. United States, supra*, at 175. When "regulation goes too far it will be recognized as a taking." *Pennsylvania Coal Co. v. Mahon*, 260 U.S. 393, 415 (1922).

Here the requirement that appellants permit appellees to exercise state-protected rights of free expression and petition on shopping center property clearly does not amount to an unconstitutional infringement of appellants' property rights under the Taking Clause. There is nothing to suggest that preventing appellants from prohibiting this sort of activity will unreasonably impair the value or use of their property as a shopping center. The PruneYard is a large commercial complex that covers several city blocks, contains numerous separate business establishments, and is open to the public at large. The decision of the California Supreme Court makes it clear that the PruneYard may restrict expressive activity by adopting time, place, and manner regulations that will minimize any interference with its commercial functions. Appellees were orderly, and they limited their activity to the common areas of the shopping center. In these circumstances, the fact that they may have "physically invaded" appellants' property cannot be viewed as determinative.

There is also little merit to appellants' argument that they have been denied their property without due process of law. In *Nebbia v. New York*, 291 U.S. 502 (1934), this Court stated:

> [N]either property rights nor contract rights are absolute . . . Equally fundamental with the private right is that of the public to regulate it in the common interest. . . .

* * *

> . . . [T]he guaranty of due process, as has often been held, demands only that the law shall not be unreasonable, arbitrary or capricious, and that the means selected shall have a real and substantial relation to the objective sought to be attained.

Id., at 523,525. Appellants have failed to provide sufficient justification for concluding that this test is not satisfied by the State's asserted interest in promoting more expansive rights of free speech and petition than conferred by the Federal Constitution.

V

Appellants finally contend that a private property owner has a First Amendment right not to be forced by the State to use his property as a forum for the speech of others. They state that in *Wooley v. Maynard*, 430 U.S. 705 (1977), this Court concluded that a State may not constitutionally require an individual to participate in the dissemination of an ideological message by displaying it on his private property in a manner and for the express purpose that it be observed and read by the public. This rationale applies here, they argue, because the message of *Wooley* is that the State may not force an individual to display any message at all.

Wooley, however, was a case in which the government itself prescribed the message ["Live Free or Die"], required it to be displayed openly on appellee's personal property that was used "as part of his daily life," and refused to permit him to take any measures to cover up the motto [on his license plate] even though the Court found that the display of the motto served no important state interest. Here, by contrast, there are a number of distinguishing factors. Most important, the shopping center by choice of its owner is not limited to the personal use of appellants. It is instead a business establishment that is open to the public to come and go as they please. The views expressed by members of the public in passing out pamphlets or seeking signatures for a petition thus will not likely be identified with those of the owner. Second, no specific message is dictated by the State to be displayed on appellants' property. There consequently is no danger of governmental discrimination for or against a particular message. Finally, as far as appears here appellants can expressly disavow any connection with the message by simply posting signs in the area where the speakers or handbillers stand. Such signs, for example, could disclaim any sponsorship of the message and could explain that the persons are communicating their own messages by virtue of state law.

Appellants also argue that their First Amendment rights have been infringed in light of *West Virginia State Board of Education v. Barnette*, 319 U.S. 624 (1943), and *Miami Herald Publishing Co. v. Tornillo*, 418 U.S. 241 (1974). *Barnette* is inapposite because it involved the compelled recitation of [the Pledge of Allegiance,] a message containing an affirmation of belief. This Court held such compulsion unconstitutional because it "require[d] the individual to communicate by word and sign his acceptance" of government-dictated political ideas, whether or not he subscribed to them. 319 U.S., at 633. Appellants are not similarly being compelled to affirm their belief in any governmentally prescribed position or view, and they are free to publicly dissociate themselves from the views of the speakers or handbillers.

Tornillo struck down a Florida statute requiring a newspaper to publish a political candidate's reply to criticism previously published in that newspaper. It rests on the principle that the State cannot tell a newspaper what it must print. These concerns obviously are not present here.

We conclude that neither appellants' federally recognized property rights nor their First Amendment rights have been infringed by the California Supreme Court's decision.

C. STATE ACTION

With the exception of the Thirteenth Amendment preventing slavery or involuntary servitude, the individual rights guaranteed by the United States Constitution only protect against governmental infringement, not private infringement. This state action requirement originated in *The Civil Rights Cases*, where the Supreme Court explained that private action was generally governed by state law rather than the United States Constitution:

> The wrongful act of an individual, unsupported by any such [state] authority is simply a private wrong, or a crime of that individual; an invasion of the rights of the injured party, it is true, whether they affect his person, his property, or his reputation; but if not sanctioned in some way by the State, or done under State authority, his rights remain in full force, and may presumably be vindicated by resort to the laws of the State for redress.[160]

Thus, unless a private infringer's conduct can in some manner be fairly attributed to the state, the United States Constitution does not provide a means of redress. But the question of when a private infringer's conduct is attributable to the state is extremely fact-intensive and policy bound.[161] The Court has adopted various tests and categories to aid in the inquiry, such as the public function doctrine, joint state participation, the symbiotic relationship test, and governmental coercion, but these "criteria lack rigid simplicity" as "no one fact can function as a necessary condition across the board for finding state action; nor is any set of circumstances absolutely sufficient."[162]

Do the same state action constraints apply to the individual rights guaranteed by the state constitutions? What are the competing policies at stake? Should the answer depend on the nature of the particular right at issue? The following cases and materials consider these issues, beginning with the first Texas Supreme Court case to address state action under the state constitution.

---

[160] 109 U.S. 3, 17 (1883).

[161] *See, e.g.*, Brentwood Academy v. Tenn. Secondary Sch. Athletic Ass'n, 531 U.S. 288, 295-96 (2001).

[162] *Id.*

Republican Party of Texas v. Dietz, 940 S.W.2d 86 (Tex. 1997)

ABBOTT, Justice, delivered the opinion of the Court, in which PHILLIPS, Chief Justice, and HECHT, CORNYN, ENOCH, OWEN and BAKER, Justices, joined.

On June 14, 1996, a Travis County district court issued a temporary injunction that essentially required the Republican Party of Texas to provide a convention booth and program advertisement space to the Log Cabin Republicans at the 1996 Republican Party of Texas Convention. In a per curiam opinion issued on June 19, 1996, we stayed the district court's temporary injunction because we were "tentatively of the opinion that state action is required for there to have been a violation of the constitutional rights asserted by the Log Cabin Republicans and that such action was not present under the facts of this case; that the contract claims of the Log Cabin Republicans do not warrant the relief granted by the district court; and that mandamus relief may be appropriate under the unique and compelling circumstances of this case." 924 S.W.2d 932, 932-33. We retained jurisdiction to issue an opinion explaining in detail the rationale for the stay order.

I

The Log Cabin Republicans of Texas and the Texas Log Cabin Republicans, Inc. (collectively LCR) are Texas non-profit corporations of Republicans who support equal civil rights for gay and lesbian individuals. In April 1996, LCR applied for an exhibitor's booth at the 1996 Republican Party of Texas Convention which began on June 20. As part of the booth application, LCR agreed to abide by the rules and regulations issued by the Republican Party of Texas for the convention. One of these rules allowed the Republican Party "the right to restrict exhibits which, because of undue noise, method of operation, material, content, or any other reason, become objectionable."

The Exhibits Chairman for the convention orally informed LCR's President, Dale Carpenter, that the group's booth application was approved. The Republican Party also cashed the $400 check Carpenter submitted for the booth. On May 15, 1996, LCR submitted to the Republican Party an advertisement to be included in the convention program along with a $750 check for the cost of the advertisement. The advertisement asserted LCR's beliefs that equal rights should be provided for gay and lesbian individuals. On May 21, 1996, the Republican Party Executive Director sent a letter to LCR rejecting the advertisement and the booth request. The Party returned the $750 check and refunded the cost of the booth.

On May 30, 1996, LCR filed this lawsuit in Travis County seeking injunctive relief. LCR alleged that the Republican Party's actions unconstitutionally infringed upon LCR's rights to free speech, equal rights, and due course of law under the Texas Constitution. LCR also claimed a right to specific performance of its contract with the Republican Party of Texas for a booth and an advertisement. The district court held a hearing on Friday, June 14, 1996. At the conclusion of the hearing, the court issued a temporary injunction precluding the Republican Party from refusing to provide the booth and advertisement.

On Monday, June 17, 1996, the Republican Party filed with this Court a motion for leave to file a petition for writ of mandamus and an emergency motion to stay the district court's temporary injunction order. The next day, we requested an expedited response from LCR, and set oral argument for June 19, 1996–one day before the convention began. After hearing oral argument, we granted the emergency stay in a per curiam opinion. We now explain why we concluded that the Republican Party was entitled to extraordinary relief.

II

The district court's injunction was based on a finding that LCR would probably prevail on its breach of contract claims and its free speech, equal rights, and due course of law claims under the Texas Constitution.[163] The Republican Party urges that LCR's state constitutional claims cannot be maintained because the Party's conduct did not constitute "state action." The Party further argues that there is no basis for LCR's breach of contract claims.

STATE ACTION

Under the "state action" doctrine developed by the federal courts, the United States constitutional guarantees of free speech, equal protection, and due process impose restrictions or obligations only on "state actors." As such, United States constitutional civil rights protect only against governmental action, either actual or constructive, in the shape of laws, customs, or judicial or executive proceedings. The rights and liberties guaranteed by the United States Constitution therefore "erec[t] no shield against merely private conduct." *Shelley v. Kraemer,* 334 U.S. 1, 13 (1948).

However, LCR's claims do not arise under provisions in the United States Constitution; rather, LCR's causes of action are based on guarantees contained in article I of the Texas Constitution, which is known as the Texas Bill of Rights. Thus, we must decide whether the "state action" doctrine applied in federal courts is required for a party to maintain a claim for a violation of the Texas free speech, equal rights, and due course of law guarantees. Several Texas courts of appeals have concluded that some quantum of state action is required before a litigant can maintain a lawsuit for the deprivation of a Texas constitutional right, *see, e.g., Weaver v. AIDS Services of Austin, Inc.,* 835 S.W.2d 798, 802 (Tex.App.–Austin 1992, writ denied); *Jones v. Memorial Hosp. System,* 746 S.W.2d 891, 894-95 (Tex.App.–Houston [1st Dist.] 1988, no writ); but this Court has never squarely confronted the issue before today.

(a)

We first turn our attention to whether the constitutional claims advanced by LCR require state action. When interpreting our state Constitution, we rely heavily on its literal text, *Edgewood Indep. Sch. Dist. v. Kirby,* 777 S.W.2d 391, 394 (Tex.1989), and are to give effect to its plain language. *City of Beaumont v. Bouillion,* 896 S.W.2d 143, 148 (Tex.1995). We also may consider such things as the purpose of the constitutional provision, the historical context in which it was written, the collective intent, if it can be ascertained, of the framers and the people who adopted it, our prior judicial decisions, the interpretations of analogous constitutional provisions by other jurisdictions, and constitutional theory.

[163]LCR did not assert any cause of action arising under the United States Constitution.

The text of our state charter demonstrates that the guarantees of the Texas Bill of Rights generally apply only against the government. The Texas Constitution contains a specific provision, article I, section 29, that defines the scope and application of the Texas Bill of Rights. Section 29 is titled "Provisions of Bill of Rights excepted from powers of government; to forever remain inviolate" and provides as follows:

> To guard against transgressions of the high powers herein delegated, we declare that everything in this "Bill of Rights" is excepted out of the general powers of government, and shall forever remain inviolate, and all laws contrary thereto, or to the following provisions, shall be void.

TEX. CONST. art. I, § 29. The first clause of section 29 establishes that the purpose of the Texas Bill of Rights is to "guard against transgressions of the high powers" delegated to the state government by the Texas Constitution. Nowhere does the Texas Constitution contain similar language indicating an intent to have the Bill of Rights generally guard against transgressions by individuals. Further, the provisions in section 29 excepting everything in the Bill of Rights "out of the general powers of government" and providing that "all laws" contrary to the Bill of Rights shall be void demonstrates that the Bill of Rights serves as a shield against the powers and laws of government. Similar protections do not exist for actions by private individuals.

Our conclusion is buttressed by two prior decisions of this Court which recognized that the Texas Bill of Rights establishes limitations on the powers of government. In *Travelers' Ins. Co. v. Marshall,* 124 Tex. 45, 76 S.W.2d 1007 (Tex.1934), we stated that the Bill of Rights "consists of *express limitations of power*" on the legislature, executive officers, and the judiciary. *Id.* at 1009 (emphasis in original). More recently, we held in *City of Beaumont v. Bouillion* that a law conflicting with rights guaranteed by the Texas Bill of Rights is void "because the Bill of Rights is a *limit on State power.*" 896 S.W.2d at 149 (emphasis added).

Separate from the actual text, there is no indication that our Constitution's framers intended that the free speech, equal rights, and due course of law guarantees of the Texas Bill of Rights would apply to purely private conduct. Instead, the framers appear to have borrowed liberally from the federal Bill of Rights and the bills of rights in other state constitutions. *See generally* Ericson, *Origins of the Texas Bill of Rights,* Vol. LXII, No. 4, S.W. HIST. Q. 457, 457-58 (1959); *see also* Cornyn, *The Roots of the Texas Constitution: Settlement to Statehood,* 26 TEX. TECH L. REV. 1089, 1127 (1995). As noted previously, the federal courts have consistently applied the state action principle. Moreover, we are not aware of any sister state that has generally applied its constitutional guarantees to regulate private conduct.[164] Accordingly, the bills of rights from which the Texas framers borrowed

[164] There are, however, a handful of states that have determined that their free expression guarantees can be asserted against privately-owned shopping centers and universities. [Citations omitted.] These decisions have been based on two primary factors: (1) the unique character of such businesses in contemporary society as the functional equivalent of the traditional town square, where historically the public's free expression rights were exercised; and (2) the state constitution's free speech guarantee being phrased in affirmative language, i.e., "every person shall be at liberty to speak," rather than in the familiar negative language of the First Amendment to the United States Constitution that "Congress shall make no law . . . abridging the freedom of speech." [These]

have been construed to provide for state action, and there is no indication that our framers intended otherwise.

Our holding today is consistent with well-reasoned constitutional theory. A "constitution" has been defined as "a charter of government deriving its whole authority from the governed." BLACK'S LAW DICTIONARY 311 (6th ed. 1990). In essence, a constitution is a compact between the government and the people in which the people delegate powers to the government and in which the powers of the government are prescribed. *See* THE ORIGINS OF THE AMERICAN CONSTITUTION: A DOCUMENTARY HISTORY ix (Michael G. Kammen ed., 1986).[165] Bills of rights are often included as part of this compact between governments and citizens and are intended to protect citizens from governmental transgressions of certain fundamental rights. *See* COOLEY, A TREATISE ON THE CONSTITUTIONAL LIMITATIONS 176 (1868); *see also* BRADEN ET AL., THE CONSTITUTION OF THE STATE OF TEXAS: AN ANNOTATED AND COMPARATIVE ANALYSIS 2-3 (1977). They are not designed, however, to protect from the invasion of such rights by individuals. Indeed, as noted by one constitutional scholar, enforcing constitutional guarantees against private individuals would actually restrict liberty because it would deny individuals "the freedom to make certain choices, such as choices of the persons with whom they will associate." TRIBE, AMERICAN CONSTITUTIONAL LAW § 18-2, at 1691 (2d ed. 1988).

Accordingly, based on the text of the Texas Bill of Rights, its history and purpose, our prior judicial decisions, the law in other jurisdictions, constitutional theory, and the concern for the liberty of all Texas citizens, we conclude that state action is required before a litigant can maintain a claim for deprivation of a right secured by the free speech, equal rights, and due course of law guarantees of the Texas Bill of Rights.

(b)

Having concluded that "state action" is required, we must now consider how to apply the principle. Generally, state action is only present for otherwise private conduct

---

decisions have been limited to their facts and only applied to free speech claims made against large shopping centers and similar public enterprises.

Conversely, a greater number of state courts have determined that free speech rights can only be asserted against private property owners when the property has assumed all the characteristics of a municipality, in accord with the United States Supreme Court's decision in *Hudgens v. NLRB*, 424 U.S. 507, 516-21 (1976). [Citations omitted.]

In this case, LCR never alleged that it was entitled to a temporary injunction on the basis that the Texas Constitution's free speech guarantee applied on private property. Moreover, neither party has briefed nor argued this point to this Court. Accordingly, it would be inappropriate to resolve this complex issue under the facts before us.

[165] The framers of the Texas Constitution apparently shared the belief that a constitution was a compact between the government and its citizens. TEX. CONST. art I, § 2 ("All political power is inherent in the people, and all free governments are founded on their authority, and instituted for their benefit."); DEBATES OF THE TEXAS CONVENTION at 330 (William F. Weeks, reporter)(1846)("We are . . . about to form a new government. . . . Then, as I believe, we are just in the position of a people in a natural state of society, about to form a social compact; . . . ") (remarks of delegate Isaac Van Zandt).

when the conduct can be fairly attributed to the government. *See generally Blum v. Yaretsky,* 457 U.S. 991, 1004 (1982). Determining whether the government is sufficiently involved in the challenged conduct requires us to make a legal determination based upon the circumstances of each case.

Federal court decisions provide a wealth of guidance in our resolution of state action issues. *See generally Davenport v. Garcia,* 834 S.W.2d 4, 20 (Tex.1992)("Texas should borrow from well-reasoned and persuasive federal procedural and substantive precedent when this is deemed helpful . . . ."). Among the variety of circumstances under which the federal courts have analyzed state action, several decisions have considered the circumstances under which a political party (such as the Republican Party of Texas) is a state actor.

In the *White Primary Cases,* the Supreme Court considered whether the Texas Democratic Party could exclude African-Americans from voting in its primaries. In prohibiting such exclusions, the Court declared that political parties were state actors when they held primary elections. While state action may exist when political parties exercise the "traditional government function" of conducting elections, it is not true that every act of a political party is state action.

[Some] party activities are private. In *Seergy v. Kings County Republican County Comm.,* 459 F.2d 308, 314 (2d Cir.1972), the Second Circuit declined to extend "the Equal Protection requirement of the Fourteenth Amendment to . . . the county committee in the conduct of its internal party affairs which have no direct relation to the electoral process." Similarly, in *Lynch v. Torquato,* 343 F.2d 370, 372 (3d Cir.1965), the Third Circuit held that "the normal role of party leaders in conducting internal affairs of their party, other than primary or general elections, does not make their party offices governmental offices or the filling of these offices state action." In *Kay v. New Hampshire Democratic Party,* 821 F.2d 31, 33 (1st Cir.1987), the First Circuit held that the New Hampshire Democratic Party did not engage in state action in holding a presidential candidates' forum because the forum was not an integral part of the election process. Accordingly, the Democratic Party had the absolute right to exclude a Democratic presidential candidate from the forum, even though the candidate had originally been invited to participate. The Sixth Circuit concluded in *Banchy v. Republican Party of Hamilton County,* 898 F.2d 1192, 1196 (6th Cir.1990), that the election of party ward chairmen was not state action because there was no evidence that the chairmen played an "integral part" in the election process.

We agree that a political party is a state actor in some instances, such as when it is conducting elections, but a private organization in other instances, such as when it is conducting certain of its internal affairs. We must determine where, along this spectrum, the Republican Party's conduct falls. We hold that the actions of the Republican Party in denying LCR the booth and advertisement were mere internal party affairs. The stated purpose of LCR in attempting to obtain a booth and advertising space was to work toward changing the Party's internal platform. However, a Party's platform is not an element of the electoral process. Party candidates are free to accept in part and reject in part the platform, and there is no requirement that a party member adhere to all portions of the platform. While there are many provisions of the Texas Election Code regulating the conduct of political parties, these provisions do not regulate or even require that a political party have a platform. *See* TEX. ELEC.CODE §§ 161-192.

The fact that the Republican Party has adopted by reference the Texas Constitution "in so far as [it] may be applicable" does not affect our analysis. As we have held, the free speech, equal rights, and due course of law provisions of the Texas Bill of Rights are only applicable when state action is present; thus, the fact that the Party agreed to abide by the Constitution when "applicable" does not change the controlling issue. Because the Republican Party's conduct in denying LCR a booth and advertisement at the convention is an internal party affair rather than an integral part of the election process, the Republican Party is not a state actor under the undisputed facts of this case. Therefore, LCR cannot maintain its state constitutional claims against the Party . . . .

SPECTOR, Justice, concurring.

I first disagree with the majority's overbroad rationale for adopting a state action requirement for equal rights, due course of law, and free speech claims under the Texas Constitution. In the hundred and fourteen years since the United States Supreme Court first recognized a state action requirement under the federal Fourteenth Amendment, *see The Civil Rights Cases,* 109 U.S. 3, 23 (1883), this Court has never found a proper occasion to determine whether any provision of our state Bill of Rights contains a similar limitation.

The majority's heavy reliance on federal state action doctrine under the federal Fourteenth Amendment and the portions of the Bill of Rights incorporated through that amendment is misplaced. Both the Fourteenth Amendment and the First Amendment, by their plain language, pertain only to governmental actions. *See* U.S. Const. amends. I ("Congress shall pass no law . . ."), XIV ("[N]or shall any state . . ."). The Texas Bill of Rights contains nothing comparable to this strong language: to the extent that it is regarded as having any meaning at all, article I, section 29 has previously been read to strengthen–not to limit–the other provisions of the Bill of Rights. *See* 1 George D. Braden, The Constitution of the State of Texas: An Annotated and Comparative Analysis 85-86 (1977). Further, the federal state action requirement is a product of the twin concerns of federalism and separation of powers within the federal government. Laurence H. Tribe, American Constitutional Law § 18-2, at 1691 (2d ed. 1988). These concerns relate differently to our state constitution than to the federal constitution.

The majority disregards significant differences between the language of the Texas and federal constitutions. For example, the federal Due Process Clause has a limited reach because it "is phrased as a limitation on the State's power to act, not as a guarantee of certain minimal levels of safety and security." *DeShaney v. Winnebago County Dept. of Social Services,* 489 U.S. 189, 195 (1989). Like other state courts that have applied state free speech provisions to the acts of private parties, however, this Court has repeatedly drawn attention to the affirmative right conferred by article I, section 8:

> *Rather than a restriction on governmental interference* with speech such as that provided by the First Amendment of the United States Constitution, Texans chose from the beginning to assure the liberties for which they were struggling with a specific guarantee of an affirmative right to speak.

Davenport v. Garcia, 834 S.W.2d 4, 7-8 (1992) (emphasis added); *see also Ex parte Tucci,* 859 S.W.2d 1, 5 (Tex.1993) (plurality opinion); *O'Quinn v. State Bar of Texas*, 763 S.W.2d 397, 402 (Tex.1988). The majority discounts persuasive decisions by other state courts interpreting similar state constitutional provisions, merely because the Log Cabin Republicans "never alleged that [they were] entitled to a temporary injunction on the basis that the Texas Constitution's free speech guarantee applied on private property." Here, of course, such a claim would have been inappropriate because the Party's convention took place on public property at San Antonio's Alamodome.

Even assuming a state action requirement should apply to the Log Cabin Republicans' claims, the majority does not offer a satisfactory justification for finding an absence of state action here. In construing the federal state action requirement, the United States Supreme Court has recognized that even an entirely private person may be considered a state actor, when the person acts in conjunction with or obtains significant aid from the state. *See Lugar v. Edmondson Oil Co.,* 457 U.S. 922, 941 (1982).

Whether sufficient state action exists here must turn on the extent to which the Party's state convention implicates the state's authority and the electoral process. The majority recognizes that the behavior of political parties has risen to the level of state action in various circumstances. 940 S.W.2d at 92-93. Today's opinion, however, does not articulate any standard or principle that determines where the threshold for state action lies.

Notes on State Action under the Texas Constitution

The Justifications for the State Action Requirement: What are the court's justifications for imposing a state action requirement under the free speech, equal rights, and due course of law provisions of the Texas Constitution? Was it appropriate for the court to rely on structural implications from the Texas Bill of Rights, prior state and sister state precedent, and constitutional theory in reaching this holding? What contrary arguments did the concurring opinion raise concerning textual distinctions between the federal and state provisions at issue?

The court outlined in a footnote the debate discussed in the previous section regarding whether free speech rights under state constitutions could be asserted on private property.[166] But the court determined that resolution of this issue was inappropriate as it had not been briefed or argued.[167] How does this compare to the willingness of the court in

---

[166]940 S.W.2d 86, 90 n.5 (Tex. 1997).

[167]Although the Texas Supreme Court has not resolved this issue, it has been considered on a few occasions by Texas appellate courts. *See, e.g.*, Zarsky v. State, 827 S.W.2d 408, 411-13 (Tex. App.–Corpus Christi 1992, pet. ref'd) (holding state constitutional free speech rights did not extend to privately owned walkway outside abortion clinic in office complex); Right to Life Advocates, Inc. v. Aaron Women's Clinic, 737 S.W.2d 564, 567-69 (Tex. App.–Houston [14th Dist.] 1987, writ denied) (Sears, J., lead op.) (employing balancing test to conclude speech rights under the Texas Constitution did not extend to privately owned office building); Savoy v. Graham Mem'l Auditorium Ass'n, Inc., 329 S.W.2d 352, 354 (Tex. Civ. App.–Fort Worth 1959, no writ) (holding federal and state constitutional assembly, speech, and worship rights did not extend to using a private auditorium); Good v. Dow Chem. Co., 247 S.W.2d 608, 610-11 (Tex. Civ. App.–Galveston 1952, writ ref'd n.r.e.) (holding federal and state constitutional rights did not extend to use of privately owned park).

Davenport to decide state constitutional issues? Do the opinions in *Republican Party* and *Operation Rescue* provide any clues regarding the court's view of the free speech on private property issue?

Is it surprising that the Texas Supreme Court had never addressed the issue of state action under the Texas Constitution before it decided this case in 1997, even though this doctrine was established in the federal courts more than a century earlier? Is this just more proof that some aspects of state constitutional jurisprudence are underdeveloped in comparison to federal doctrine?

The Scope of the State Action Requirement: The court carefully limited its holding to requiring state action under the Texas free speech, equal rights, and due course of law guarantees. Are there other provisions of the Texas Bill of Rights that might not require state action? Are there circumstances in which it might it be appropriate to modify the state action requirement under the state constitution?

While the Texas Supreme Court has not addressed these issues, decisions from other jurisdictions have deviated from the federal state action requirement in two basic circumstances: (1) when the text, history, or purpose of a particular constitutional provision indicates that state action is not required, or (2) when the state court's own review of the interconnection between a private individual and the government weighs the factual circumstances in a different manner than the United States Supreme Court. The following cases illustrate these principles.

Hill v. National Collegiate Athletic Ass'n, 865 P.2d 633 (Cal. 1994)

LUCAS, Chief Justice.

The National Collegiate Athletic Association sponsors and regulates intercollegiate athletic competition throughout the United States. Under the NCAA's drug testing program, randomly selected college student athletes competing in postseason championships and football bowl games are required to provide samples of their urine under closely monitored conditions. Urine samples are chemically analyzed for proscribed substances. Athletes testing "positive" are subject to disqualification.

Plaintiffs, who were student athletes attending Stanford University at the time of trial, sued the NCAA, contending its drug testing program violated their right to privacy secured by article I, section 1 of the California Constitution. Stanford intervened in the suit and adopted plaintiffs' position. Finding the NCAA's program to be an invasion of plaintiffs' right to privacy, the superior court permanently enjoined its enforcement against plaintiffs and other Stanford athletes. The Court of Appeal upheld the injunction.

By its nature, sports competition demands highly disciplined physical activity conducted in accordance with a special set of social norms. Unlike the general population, student athletes undergo frequent physical examinations, reveal their bodily and medical conditions to coaches and trainers, and often dress and undress in same-sex locker rooms. In so doing, they normally and reasonably forgo a measure of their privacy in exchange for the personal and professional benefits of extracurricular athletics.

A student athlete's already diminished expectation of privacy is outweighed by the NCAA's legitimate regulatory objectives in conducting testing for proscribed drugs. As a sponsor and regulator of sporting events, the NCAA has self-evident interests in ensuring fair and vigorous competition, as well as protecting the health and safety of student athletes. These interests justify a set of drug testing rules reasonably calculated to achieve drug-free athletic competition.

Discussion

Article I, section 1 of the California Constitution provides: "All people are by nature free and independent and have inalienable rights. Among these are enjoying and defending life and liberty, acquiring, possessing, and protecting property, and pursuing and obtaining safety, happiness, *and privacy*." (Italics added.) The phrase "and privacy" was added by an initiative adopted by the voters on November 7, 1972 (the Privacy Initiative or Amendment).

To resolve the dispute between the parties, we address three questions of first impression in this court: (1) Does the Privacy Initiative govern the conduct of private, nongovernmental entities such as the NCAA; and (2) if it does, what legal standard is to be applied in assessing alleged invasions of privacy; and (3) under that standard, is the NCAA's drug testing program a violation of the state constitutional privacy right?

1. Application of the California Constitutional Right to Privacy to Nongovernmental Entities

Neither plaintiffs nor Stanford assert that the NCAA is an agency or instrumentality of government or a vehicle for state action. Case law generally confirms the status of the NCAA as a private organization, comprised of American colleges and universities, and democratically governed by its own membership. (*National Collegiate Athletic Assn. v. Tarkanian* (1988) 488 U.S. 179, 197 [NCAA is private actor that "enjoy[s] no governmental powers"].)

In its opening attack on the judgment, the NCAA asserts that its private status is dispositive of this action because the Privacy Initiative does not embody a right of action against nongovernmental entities. We disagree.

Article I, section 1 of the California Constitution is an enumeration of the "inalienable rights" of all Californians. "Privacy" is declared to be among those rights. Typical of broad constitutional declarations of rights, the section does not define "privacy" or explain its relationship to other rights or interests. Nor does it specify how or against whom the right of privacy is to be safeguarded. Mere use of the word "privacy" is not definitive in this regard–at the time of the Privacy Initiative there were two distinct and well established legal sources of privacy rights–the federal Constitution (applicable only to government action) and common law and statutory provisions (applicable as well against nongovernmental entities).

The Privacy Initiative is to be interpreted and applied in a manner consistent with the probable intent of the body enacting it: the voters of the State of California. The official ballot pamphlet section dealing with Proposition 11, the Privacy Initiative, contains arguments for and against the measure as well as rebuttals. The argument in favor of

Proposition 11 is replete with references to information-amassing practices of both "government" and "business." The authors of the argument, then-Assemblyman Kenneth Cory and then-Senator George Moscone, emphasized the capacity of both governmental and nongovernmental agencies to gather, keep, and disseminate sensitive personal information without checking its accuracy or restricting its use to mutually agreed or otherwise legitimate purposes.

The rebuttal to the argument in favor of Proposition 11 and the argument against Proposition 11, both of which were written by then-Senator James Whetmore, do not contest the privacy measure's potential impact on "business" as well as "government." Rather, they challenge only the need for additional privacy safeguards, observing: "To say there are at present no effective restraints on the information activities of government *and business* is simply untrue." Opponents further argued that the receipt of personal information is essential to effectuate the *private* party relationships and transactions referred to by proponents of the measure, e.g., credit cards, life insurance policies, and employment interviews.

In its day-to-day operations, the NCAA is in a position to generate, retain, and use personal information about student athletes and others. In this respect, it is no different from a credit card purveyor, an insurance company, or a private employer (the private entity examples used in the ballot arguments) in its capacity to affect the privacy interests of those with whom it deals.

The NCAA nonetheless urges us to impose a state action prerequisite to suits under the Privacy Initiative because it adds "privacy" to the declaration of rights portion of our state Constitution. The NCAA correctly observes that our decisions construing *other* provisions in the declaration of rights impose a state action requirement (e.g., *People v. Zelinski* (1979) 594 P.2d 1000 [search and seizure]; *Garfinkle v. Superior Court* (1978) 578 P.2d 925, app. dism. (1978) 439 U.S. 949 [due process]). But those decisions were not premised on the *mere location* of the respective provisions in the constitutional text, but on their distinct language and histories. [W]hat the voters intended in enacting the Privacy Initiative must determine the propriety of any state action requirement in this case. As we have seen, the ballot arguments contain persuasive evidence of drafter and voter intent to recognize a right of action for invasion of privacy against private as well as government entities.

[A] reasonable voter would most likely have concluded he or she was casting a ballot to safeguard his or her personal privacy against private as well as government entities. After the case was so presented, the voters were persuaded. To remove by judicial construction a significant part of what the voters desired would amount to an electoral "bait and switch."

In summary, the Privacy Initiative in article I, section 1 of the California Constitution creates a right of action against private as well as government entities. The legal concept of "privacy" as embodied in the initiative is susceptible of such an interpretation; the ballot arguments strongly support it. Our holding in this regard is necessarily confined to the Privacy Initiative. We intimate nothing about the existence of rights of action or permissible defendants in legal proceedings that may be brought either under other clauses in article I, section 1 or other parts of our state Constitution.

2. Standards for Determining Invasion of Privacy Under Article I, Section 1

In evaluating the NCAA's drug testing program, the trial court and the Court of Appeal assumed that private entities were subject to the same legal standards as government agencies with respect to claims of invasion of privacy. Borrowing from a few of our cases involving the conduct of government in its dealings with individual citizens, the lower courts imposed on the NCAA the burden of proving both: (1) a "compelling state interest" in support of drug testing; and (2) the absence of any alternative means of accomplishing that interest. Because the NCAA failed to shoulder the purported burden, it was enjoined from carrying out its drug testing program.

The principal focus of the Privacy Initiative is readily discernible. The Ballot Argument warns of unnecessary information gathering, use, and dissemination by public and private entities–images of "government snooping," computer stored and generated "dossiers" and "'cradle-to-grave' profiles on every American" dominate the framers' appeal to the voters. The evil addressed is government and business conduct in "collecting and stockpiling unnecessary information . . . and misusing information gathered for one purpose in order to serve other purposes or to embarrass."

Although the argument in favor does contain a cryptic reference to a "compelling public need" for abridgement of privacy, the reference occurs in the context of informational privacy rights against government. The argument states in part: "The right of privacy is an important American heritage and essential to the fundamental rights guaranteed by the First, Third, Fourth, Fifth, and Ninth Amendments to the U.S. Constitution. This right should be abridged only when there is compelling *public* need. Some *information* may remain as designated *public* records but only when the availability of such *information* is clearly in the *public* interest." Nothing in this passage compels the conclusion that the phrase "compelling public need" was intended to supply a single, all-encompassing legal test for privacy rights.

Even within the context of government information-gathering, the limited references in the ballot arguments to "compelling" necessity in the ballot arguments are not consistent. When pressed by the opponents of the Privacy Initiative, who maintained that the new right to privacy would place unwieldy burdens on government efforts to obtain information needed to police the welfare system, the framers equivocated, narrowing their description of the initiative's effect. In a rebuttal to the argument against the Privacy Initiative, Assemblyman Cory stated in part: "The right to privacy will not destroy welfare nor undermine any important government program. It is limited by 'compelling public necessity' *and the public's need to know. [The Privacy Initiative] will not prevent the government from collecting any information it legitimately needs. It will only prevent misuse of this information for unauthorized purposes and preclude the collection of extraneous or frivolous information.*"

As applied to private entities, a "compelling public interest" standard poses additional difficulties. Private entities pursue private ends and interests, not those of government. If every private organization had to establish a "compelling *public* interest" or "compelling *state* interest" to justify any activity that had an impact on individual privacy, it would fail to do so in most, if not all, conceivable cases. To use an example referred to in the ballot arguments, a private business extending credit or selling insurance may have a legitimate commercial need for obtaining personal information, but such a need is not thereby legally transformed into a "state interest," let alone a "compelling" one.

The Ballot Argument on the Privacy Initiative is useful in identifying the general evils that concerned its authors, but it does not provide clear or unequivocal support for a universal "compelling public interest" standard for privacy rights, regardless of context or circumstances. At the time the Privacy Initiative was considered and adopted by the voters, a right to privacy had been recognized and defined in several distinct branches of the law. Therefore, in order to discern the meaning of "privacy" as used in the Privacy Initiative, we must examine the various legal roots of the privacy concept.

a. Sources of the Right to Privacy

The pre-initiative judicial construction of the right to privacy developed along two distinct lines: (1) a common law right, supplemented in some instances by statutes, protecting a diverse set of individual interests from interference by nongovernmental entities; and (2) a federal constitutional right, derived from various provisions of the Bill of Rights, that took distinct shape in United States Supreme Court decisions in the 1960's safeguarding the rights of individuals and private entities from government invasion.

[T]he common law right of privacy is neither absolute nor globally vague, but is carefully confined to specific sets of interests that must inevitably be weighed in the balance against competing interests before the right is judicially recognized. A plaintiff's expectation of privacy in a specific context must be objectively reasonable under the circumstances, especially in light of the competing social interests involved.

[T]he federal constitutional right to privacy as recognized in decisions of the United States Supreme Court "have in fact involved at least two different kinds of interests. One is the individual interest in avoiding disclosure of personal matters, and another is the interest in independence in making certain kinds of important decisions." (*Whalen v. Roe* (1977) 429 U.S. 589, 598-600.) The former interest is informational or data-based; the latter involves issues of personal freedom of action and autonomy in individual encounters with government. The distinction between the two interests is not sharply drawn–disclosure of information, e.g., information about one's financial affairs, may have an impact on personal decisions and relationships between individuals and government.

b. Elements of a Cause of Action for Invasion of the State Constitutional Right of Privacy

[W]e decline to hold that every assertion of a privacy interest under article I, section 1 must be overcome by a "compelling interest." Neither the language nor history of the Privacy Initiative unambiguously supports such a standard. In view of the far-reaching and multifaceted character of the right to privacy, such a standard imports an impermissible inflexibility into the process of constitutional adjudication.

There remains, however, the question of the correct legal standard to be applied in assessing plaintiffs' claims for invasion of privacy. Based on our review of the history of the Privacy Initiative, we will describe in the remainder of this part the elements of the cause of action for violation of the state constitutional right to privacy and the defenses that might be asserted against such a cause of action.

(1) A legally protected privacy interest

The first essential element of a state constitutional cause of action for invasion of privacy is the identification of a specific, legally protected privacy interest. Whatever their common denominator, privacy interests are best assessed separately and in context. Just as the right to privacy is not absolute, privacy interests do not encompass all conceivable assertions of individual rights. Legally recognized privacy interests are generally of two classes: (1) interests in precluding the dissemination or misuse of sensitive and confidential information ("informational privacy"); and (2) interests in making intimate personal decisions or conducting personal activities without observation, intrusion, or interference ("autonomy privacy").

(2) Reasonable Expectation of Privacy

The second essential element of a state constitutional cause of action for invasion of privacy is a reasonable expectation of privacy on plaintiff's part. A "reasonable" expectation of privacy is an objective entitlement founded on broadly based and widely accepted community norms.

(3) Serious invasion of privacy interest

No community could function if every intrusion into the realm of private action, no matter how slight or trivial, gave rise to a cause of action for invasion of privacy. Actionable invasions of privacy must be sufficiently serious in their nature, scope, and actual or potential impact to constitute an egregious breach of the social norms underlying the privacy right. Thus, the extent and gravity of the invasion is an indispensable consideration in assessing an alleged invasion of privacy.

c. Defenses to a State Constitutional Privacy Cause of Action

Invasion of a privacy interest is not a violation of the state constitutional right to privacy if the invasion is justified by a competing interest. Legitimate interests derive from the legally authorized and socially beneficial activities of government and private entities. Their relative importance is determined by their proximity to the central functions of a particular public or private enterprise. Conduct alleged to be an invasion of privacy is to be evaluated based on the extent to which it furthers legitimate and important competing interests.

The NCAA is a private organization, not a government agency. Judicial assessment of the relative strength and importance of privacy norms and countervailing interests may differ in cases of private, as opposed to government, action.

First, the pervasive presence of coercive government power in basic areas of human life typically poses greater dangers to the freedoms of the citizenry than actions by private persons. "The government not only has the ability to affect more than a limited sector of the populace through its actions, it has both economic power, in the form of taxes, grants, and control over social welfare programs, and physical power, through law enforcement agencies, which are capable of coercion far beyond that of the most powerful private actors." (Sundby, *Is Abandoning State Action Asking Too Much of the Constitution?* (1989) 17 Hastings Const. L.Q. 139, 142-143 [hereafter Sundby].)

Second, "an individual generally has greater choice and alternatives in dealing with private actors than when dealing with the government." (Sundby, *supra*.) Initially, individuals usually have a range of choice among landlords, employers, vendors and others with whom they deal. To be sure, varying degrees of competition in the marketplace may broaden or narrow the range. But even in cases of limited or no competition, individuals and groups may turn to the Legislature to seek a statutory remedy against a specific business practice regarded as undesirable. State and federal governments routinely engage in extensive regulation of all aspects of business. Neither our Legislature nor Congress has been unresponsive to concerns based on activities of nongovernment entities that are perceived to affect the right of privacy.

Third, private conduct, particularly the activities of voluntary associations of persons, carries its own mantle of constitutional protection in the form of freedom of association. Private citizens have a right, not secured to government, to communicate and associate with one another on mutually negotiated terms and conditions. The ballot argument recognizes that state constitutional privacy protects in part "our freedom of communion and our freedom to associate with the people we choose." Freedom of association is also protected by the First Amendment and extends to all legitimate organizations, whether popular or unpopular.

These generalized differences between public and private action may affect privacy rights differently in different contexts. If, for example, a plaintiff claiming a violation of the state constitutional right to privacy was able to choose freely among competing public or private entities in obtaining access to some opportunity, commodity, or service, his or her privacy interest may weigh less in the balance. In contrast, if a public or private entity controls access to a vitally necessary item, it may have a correspondingly greater impact on the privacy rights of those with whom it deals.

3. Application of the Elements of Invasion of Privacy to This Case

The NCAA challenges the decision of the Court of Appeal upholding a permanent injunction against its drug testing program as a violation of the state constitutional right to privacy. We will therefore review the record, including the findings made by the trial court, in light of the elements of a cause of action for invasion of privacy as we have just discussed them. . . .

Disposition

The NCAA's drug testing program does not violate the state constitutional right to privacy. Therefore, the NCAA is entitled to judgment in its favor. As a result of our disposition, we do not decide whether the recognition of a state constitutional right to privacy in these circumstances would violate the [federal] commerce clause.

Notes on State Constitutional Provisions Applying to Private Conduct

Hill ***and the California Privacy Initiative***: Even when the state constitution generally requires state action, the text, history, or purpose of a particular state constitutional provision may evidence an intent that it be applied to private actors, just like the Thirteenth Amendment to the United States Constitution applies to private and state actors while the rest of the Federal Constitution only applies to government actors. What considerations influenced *Hill*'s holding that state action was not required under the Privacy Initiative? Did the framers and ratifiers of the Initiative adequately display a purpose to dispense with the state action requirement even though other provisions of the California Bill of Rights require state action? While other states with express constitutional privacy provisions have not applied them to private actors, the same unique persuasive evidence of drafter and voter intent to recognize a constitutional privacy claim against private actors did not exist in these other states.[168]

Yet after concluding that the Privacy Initiative applied to private actors, *Hill* declined to review the NCAA's drug testing program under strict scrutiny, instead adopting a balancing approach weighing the seriousness of the privacy invasion against the legitimate countervailing interests in the program. By creating such a less stringent standard for purely private actors, did the court entirely dispense with the state action requirement? Or was the court's holding more in line with pre-existing common law causes of action that do not depend upon state action? Under the common law, a cause of action for invasion of privacy by public disclosure of private facts requires that the actionable disclosure be widely published and not confined to a few persons or limited circumstances.[169] In contrast, *Hill* noted that the Privacy Initiative did not require broad dissemination because private information could be misused even if its disclosure was limited.[170] Should the students in *Hill* also have sought a modification of the common law rather than merely relying on the Privacy Initiative? What would have been the potential advantages and disadvantages of such a strategy?

If the court had held that the drug testing program violated the state constitution, what practical and conceptual legal difficulties might have arisen? The NCAA argued that recognizing a state constitutional right to privacy in these circumstances would violate the Commerce Clause of the United States Constitution by placing an undue burden on its ability to regulate prohibited substances and to ensure the integrity of interstate athletic contests. If Stanford students obtained a state constitutional right to forego drug testing, would that be fair to conference opponents such as Oregon, Washington, and Washington State? Do such difficulties suggest state courts should employ a cautious approach in cases

---

[168] *See, e.g.*, Miller v. Safeway, Inc., 102 P.3d 282, 288-90 (Alaska 2004); Resha v. Tucker, 670 So. 2d 56, 58 (Fla. 1996); City of N. Miami v. Kurtz, 653 So. 2d 1025, 1027-28 (Fla. 1995); City of Pasco v. Shaw, 166 P.3d 1157, 1162 (Wash. 2006). Two Louisiana Supreme Court decisions have indicated that the Louisiana privacy clause "goes beyond limiting state action," but the court has not explored the extent to which it applies to private actors. *See, e.g.*, Moresi v. State, 567 So. 2d 1081, 1092 (La. 1990); Jaubert v. Crowley Post-Signal, Inc., 375 So. 2d 1386, 1387-88 n.2 (La. 1979).

[169] RESTATEMENT (SECOND) OF TORTS, § 652D, cmt. a.

[170] 865 P.2d 633, 649 (Cal. 1994).

with a nationwide impact that request a broader interpretation of state constitutional guarantees?

Other Provisions Potentially Dispensing with State Action: Are there other state constitutional provisions whose text, history, or purpose indicates that state action is not required? Article I, paragraph 19 of the New Jersey Constitution provides: "Persons in private employment shall have the right to organize and bargain collectively." Does the text of this provision explicitly dispense with state action?

How about article I, section 26 of the Texas Constitution, which provides in part: "Perpetuities and monopolies are contrary to the genius of a free government, and shall never be allowed"? Is this provision merely a non-enforceable directive to the legislature? If it is enforceable, does it only apply to perpetuities or monopolies created by the government, or does it actually authorize constitutional claims for injunctive relief any time a perpetuity or monopoly is allowed through legislative inaction? Although there is some dictum implying that even privately created monopolies may violate this provision,[171] most of the cases involving section 26 have addressed monopolies granted by the government rather than those established purely by the actions of private persons or corporations.[172]

In addition to the claim that a particular state constitutional provision does not require state action, sometimes state courts have weighed the facts and sifted the circumstances regarding whether a private actor's conduct can be fairly attributed to the government in a different manner than the United States Supreme Court. Is this appropriate? The following case addresses whether the requisite state action existed under New York's due process clause, even though the United States Supreme Court had held that a similar self-help regulatory scheme was not state action under the Federal Constitution.

Sharrock v. Dell Buick-Cadillac, Inc., 379 N.E.2d 1169 (N.Y. 1978)

COOKE, Judge.

Challenged here as violative of the due process clauses of the State Constitution (N.Y.Const. art. I, s 6) and the Fourteenth Amendment of the Federal Constitution is the statutory authorization afforded a garageman to foreclose his possessory statutory lien for repair and storage charges (Lien Law, s 184), by means of a public sale of the vehicle in his possession. We hold that sections 200, 201, 202 and 204 of the Lien Law, insofar as they empower a garageman to conduct an ex parte sale of a bailed automobile, fail to comport with traditional notions of procedural due process embodied in the State Constitution, as they deprive the owner of the vehicle of a significant property interest without providing any opportunity to be heard.

On October 12, 1975, plaintiff's husband took her 1970 Cadillac to Dell Buick-Cadillac, Inc. (Dell), for installation of a replacement engine he had purchased

---

[171] *See* After Hours, Inc. v. Sherrard, 456 S.W.2d 227, 228 & n.1 (Tex. Civ. App.–Austin 1970), *rev'd on other grounds*, 464 S.W.2d 87 (Tex. 1971).

[172] *See, e.g.*, City of Mason v. W. Tex. Util. Co., 237 S.W.2d 273, 279 (Tex. 1951); City of Brenham v. Brenham Water Co., 4 S.W. 143, 153-56 (Tex. 1887).

elsewhere. The husband signed a work authorization wherein it was agreed that Dell was to remove the defective engine and install its replacement for the sum of $225. The affidavits of plaintiff and her husband recite that the work authorization form contained no provisions with respect to storage charges which were subsequently unilaterally imposed by Dell. Approximately one week later, plaintiff's husband offered to pay the $225 to Dell, but was advised by its service manager to withhold payment until the engine was installed.

Unfortunately, the replacement engine proved to be defective and had to be removed. Delivery of a replacement engine was then arranged. When the new replacement engine arrived, Dell informed plaintiff's husband that it would not be installed until Dell was paid the $225 due for the installation of the original defective engine. Although he agreed to pay this sum, plaintiff's husband did not have that amount of money with him at the time and soon thereafter was hospitalized, rendering him incapable of continuing his business dealings with Dell.

On January 14, 1976 plaintiff received a "Notice of Lien and Sale" by certified mail, informing her that pursuant to section 184 of the Lien Law Dell had imposed a possessory lien against the Cadillac in the amount of $304.95. That notice further advised that if plaintiff did not tender this sum within 30 days, the automobile would be sold at public auction on March 15, 1976 (see Lien Law, s 200). Plaintiff was subsequently informed by one of the auctioneers listed on the notice of sale that, her belief to the contrary notwithstanding, included in the lien was the sum of $79.95, representing storage charges. However, the auctioneer did agree to contact Dell in order to ascertain whether they would "take off" the storage charge from the amount due.

Several days later, the auctioneer informed plaintiff that Dell refused to waive its storage charge and that the amount now due had been increased to $545. He also advised her that since the book value of the car was appreciably greater than $545, it would be to plaintiff's advantage to pay the charges since Dell "had her over a barrel" because her husband had taken the car there for repair. On the day of the auction, March 15, 1976, Dell again modified its claim and informed plaintiff that the amount due had been reduced to $502. Later that day, plaintiff's 1970 Cadillac, having an established resale value of between $1,200 and $1,400, was sold to Dell for the sum of $502.

Plaintiff then commenced the instant action for declaratory and injunctive relief, as well as damages, claiming that the sale provisions of the Lien Law are violative of her due process rights as they authorize public sale of her automobile without affording the opportunity for a hearing.

The threshold question in any judicial inquiry into conduct claimed to be violative of the due process clause of the Fourteenth Amendment is whether the State has in some fashion involved itself in what, in another setting, would otherwise be deemed private activity (see U.S.Code, tit. 42, s 1983; Jones v. Mayer Co., 392 U.S. 409, 422-424). That much is made plain by the express terms of the amendment which specifies that "nor shall Any State deprive any person of life, liberty, or property without due process of law." Purely private conduct, however egregious or unreasonable, does not rise to the level of constitutional significance absent a significant nexus between the State and the actors or the conduct (see Civil Rights Cases, 109 U.S. 3, 11). This nexus has been denominated "State action" and is an essential requisite to any action grounded on violation of equal protection of the laws or a deprivation of due process of law.

Despite its outward simplicity as a concept, State action is in fact an elusive principle, one which cannot be easily discerned by resort to ritualistic incantations or precise formalisms (see Burton v. Wilmington Parking Auth., 365 U.S. 715, 722). Instead, a number of factors must be considered in determining whether a State is significantly involved in statutorily authorized private conduct. These factors include: the source of authority for the private action; whether the State is so entwined with the regulation of the private conduct as to constitute State activity; whether there is meaningful State participation in the activity; and whether there has been a delegation of what has traditionally been a State function to a private person (Melara v. Kennedy, 9 Cir., 541 F.2d 802, 805). As the test is not simply State involvement, but rather significant State involvement, satisfaction of one of these criteria may not necessarily be determinative to a finding of State action.

We need not address plaintiff's contention that the actions taken by Dell are attributable to the State of New York for purposes of the due process clause of the Fourteenth Amendment. Recently, in Flagg Bros. v. Brooks (436 U.S. 149), the Supreme Court rejected the argument that a private sale of property subject to a warehouseman's possessory lien pursuant to section 7-210 of the Uniform Commercial Code constitutes State action. The similarities between section 7-210 and the statutes at issue here might preclude any contrary finding by this court.[173]

But the mere fact that an activity might not constitute State action for purposes of the Federal Constitution does not perforce necessitate that the same conclusion be reached when that conduct is claimed to be violative of the State Constitution (see Ives v. South Buffalo Ry. Co., 94 N.E. 431, 449; Oregon v. Hass, 420 U.S. 714, 719). Indeed, on innumerable occasions this court has given our State Constitution an independent construction, affording the rights and liberties of the citizens of this State even more protection than may be secured under the United States Constitution. This independent construction finds its genesis specifically in the unique language of the due process clause of the New York Constitution as well as the long history of due process protections afforded

---

[173]There are, of course, substantial differences between the private sale of goods authorized by the warehouseman's lien law and the private sale authorized by sections 200, 201, 202 and 204 of the Lien Law. Critical to the determination in Flagg Bros. that the private sale did not constitute State action was the "total absence of overt official involvement." Here, that overt governmental involvement absent in Flagg Bros. is present to some degree. In this State, title to an automobile cannot be transferred, and thus a sale cannot be accomplished under the Lien Law, without registration of the vehicle by the Department of Motor Vehicles and its issuance of a certificate of title (Vehicle and Traffic Law, ss 401, 420, 2104, 2107, 2113-2115, 2117). Thus, the fact that initiation of the sale stems from a private source does not detract from the necessity that the garageman invoke both the power of the sovereign and the participation of public officials to bring about the involuntary transfer of title. The power of the State utilized to implement the involuntary transfer of title pursuant to the Lien Law may be sufficiently analogous to the issuance of a writ by a court clerk in Sniadach v. Family Fin. Corp. (395 U.S. 337), Fuentes v. Shevin (407 U.S. 67) and North Ga. Finishing v. Di-Chem (419 U.S. 601) to support a finding of overt State involvement in the garagemen's sale. However, in view of our determination that the challenged provisions of the Lien Law are violative of the due process clause of the State Constitution, it is unnecessary for us to decide that question.

the citizens of this State and, more generally, in fundamental principles of federalism.

In contrast to the due process clause of the Fourteenth Amendment, which is phrased in terms of State deprivation of life, liberty or property, section 6 of article I of the New York Constitution guarantees that "(n)o person shall be deprived of life, liberty or property without due process of law." Conspicuously absent from the State Constitution is any language requiring State action before an individual may find refuge in its protections. That is not to say, of course, that the due process clause of the State Constitution eliminates the necessity of any State involvement in the objected to activity (see Stuart v. Palmer, 74 N.Y. 183, 188). Rather, the absence of any express State action language simply provides a basis to apply a more flexible State involvement requirement than is currently being imposed by the Supreme Court with respect to the Federal provision.

The historical differences between the Federal and State due process clauses make clear that they were adopted to combat entirely different evils (see Schwartz, The Bill of Rights: A Documentary History, pp. 161, 165, 387, 855- 856). Prior to the Civil War, the Federal Constitution had as its major concern governmental structures and relationships. Indeed, prior to the enactment of the Fourteenth Amendment, the Bill of Rights delimited only the power of the National Government, imposing few restrictions on State authority and offering virtually no protections of individual liberties (see Barron v. Mayor & City Council of Baltimore, 7 Pet. (32 U.S.) 243). The Fourteenth Amendment was a watershed–an attempt to extend and catalogue a series of national privileges and immunities, thereby furnishing minimum standards designed to guarantee the individual protection against the potential abuses of a monolithic government, whether that government be national, State or local (see Brennan, State Constitutions and the Protection of Individual Rights, 90 Harv. L. Rev. 489, 501). In contrast, State Constitutions in general, and the New York Constitution in particular, have long safeguarded any threat to individual liberties, irrespective of from what quarter that peril arose. Thus, as early as 1843, Justice Bronson, in speaking of the due process clause of our State Constitution, noted: "The meaning of the section then seems to be, that no member of the state shall be disfranchised, or deprived of any of his rights and privileges, unless the matter be adjudged against him upon trial and according to the course of the common law. It must be ascertained judicially that he has forfeited his privileges, or that some one else has a superior title to the property he possesses, before either of them can be taken from him" (Taylor v. Porter, 4 Hill 140, 146; see, also, Wynehamer v. People, 13 N.Y. 378, 394 (1856)).

Examination of the indices of State participation in nonjudicial foreclosure pursuant to the provisions of the Lien Law at issue here compels the conclusion that New York has so entwined itself into the debtor-creditor relationship as to constitute sufficient and meaningful State participation which triggers the protections afforded by our Constitution.

[C]ommon law afforded the garageman only the right to possession; it was the State which authorized enforcement of the lien by means of ex parte sale of the vehicle without first affording its owner an opportunity to be heard (see L.1909, ch. 38, as amd.). Thus, New York has done more than simply furnish its statutory imprimatur to purely private action. Rather, it has entwined itself into the debtor-creditor relationship arising out of otherwise regular consumer transactions. The enactment of substantive provisions of law which authorize the creditor to bypass the courts to carry out the foreclosure sale encourages him to adopt this procedure rather than to rely on more cumbersome methods which might comport with constitutional due process guarantees. Indeed, not only does the State encourage adoption of this patently unfair procedure, it insulates the garageman from civil or criminal liability arising out of the sale and requires one of its agencies, the Department of Motor Vehicles, to recognize and record the transfer of title (see Vehicle and Traffic Law, s 401), thus enabling the garageman to transfer title to a vehicle he would not otherwise be deemed to own.

Even more fundamentally, the underlying purpose of the sale provisions of the Lien Law–that of conflict resolution–has always been deemed one of the essential attributes of sovereignty. Absent consent of the debtor, the power to fashion the means to order legally binding surrenders of property has always been exclusively vested in the State. However strong the interest of the garageman in the vehicle may be, his power of foreclosure has no vitality until it is sanctioned by the State. It follows, then, that such a person vested by the State with the power to resolve unilaterally an otherwise judicially cognizable controversy, is nothing more than a delegate of an exclusively governmental function (cf. North Ga. Finishing v. Di-Chem, 419 U.S. 601, Supra; Fuentes v. Shevin, 407 U.S. 67, 93, Supra). For this reason, the debtor must be provided with that measure of due process as would be afforded in a court of law.

Having determined that enforcement of the garageman's lien constitutes meaningful State participation inasmuch as New York has delegated to private parties functions traditionally associated with sovereignty, we therefore reach the substantive constitutional question. Fundamental notions of procedural due process require that before the State may deprive a person of a significant property interest in aid of a creditor, that person be given notice and an opportunity to be heard prior to deprivation of that interest. Tested by this requirement, the statutes do not pass muster in light of the due process standards articulated in analogous circumstances by the Supreme Court. Sniadach v. Family Fin. Corp. (395 U.S. 337, Supra) and Fuentes v. Shevin (407 U.S. 67, Supra) teach that even a temporary deprivation of property is entitled to due process protection.

While the owner of a vehicle ordinarily understands that a garageman expects payment upon completion of the work, the contested provisions of the Lien Law afford him little redress to the garageman's retention and ex parte sale if the charges demanded exceed the previous estimate or there is a dispute as to the quality of workmanship. Instead, pursuant to his statutory grant of authority, a garageman may sell any vehicle, no matter how valuable, to satisfy any lien, no matter how small (Parks v. "Mr. Ford", 3 Cir., 556 F.2d 132, 143, Supra). To be sure, it is a reasonable exercise of the State's police power to give the garageman a security interest in vehicles which he has enhanced in value. However, it is unreasonable and constitutionally impermissible to provide absolutely no safeguards against unauthorized or unnecessary repairs or storage charges which may underlie the whole transaction, especially where an ownership interest hangs in the balance. Where by permitting a creditor to hold and sell a debtor's property unless his demands are met, the State empowers the garageman to engage in conduct which is tantamount to blackmail. In these circumstances, it is essential that the debtor be provided a forum to air his defenses.

It must be concluded, therefore, that the sale provisions of sections 200, 201, 202 and 204 of the Lien Law violate the due process clause of the New York Constitution inasmuch as they fail to provide the owner of a vehicle an opportunity to be heard prior to permanent deprivation of a significant property interest. The garageman's right to retain his possessory lien is unaffected by this decision, but he may not sell the vehicle to satisfy his claim unless and until a method is devised, consistent with due process, of affording the owner some opportunity to be heard.[174]

JASEN, Judge (dissenting).

Confronted by a controlling decision of the United States Supreme Court, the majority declines, as indeed it must, to hold these statutes violative of the due process clause of the Federal Constitution. In Flagg Bros. v. Brooks, the argument was rejected that a private sale of goods subject to a warehouseman's lien as authorized by section 7-210 of the Uniform Commercial Code, a statute strikingly similar to those challenged in this case, constitutes State action.

I believe the analysis in Flagg applies with equal force to the statutes challenged today. Not only is a private commercial transaction involved here, but the interest of the garageman in a chattel, having stored it and having enhanced its value, is more substantial than the interest of a warehouseman, who merely stores a chattel.

The majority, however, asserts that "the mere fact that an activity might not constitute State action for purposes of the Federal Constitution does not perforce necessitate that the same conclusion be reached when that conduct is claimed to be violative of the State Constitution." Particularly in a case such as this involving commercial transactions, I would be reluctant to hold, as the majority does, that State and Federal due process protections are not coextensive. "The clauses", we said in Central Sav. Bank v. City of New York (19 N.E.2d 659, 659), "are formulated in the same words and are intended for the protection of the same fundamental rights of the individual and there is, logically, no room for distinction in definition of the scope of the two clauses." There is little difference of constitutional dimension for State action purposes between the two clauses. Both clauses are aimed directly at limiting the ability of State government to deal unfairly with its citizens. Clearly, then, the due process clauses are limited in their operation to situations where there is State involvement. This emphasis on State action ensures that citizens are protected from arbitrary and capricious action by the State.

While the challenged statutory scheme authorizes more than a mere possessory lien, permitting the lienor to conduct a foreclosure sale of the chattel (Lien Law, s 200) subject to strict notice requirements (Lien Law, ss 201, 202), such an expansion of rights is merely an exercise of the State's regulatory powers to provide guidelines for the resolution of legitimate divergent interests. The garageman, having enhanced the value of the chattel, has obtained a significant property interest in it. This interest served as the springboard for the

[174]There are a number of statements in the dissenting opinion which merit comment. Most importantly, we do not hold or even intimate that the statutes at issue here are not violative of the due process clause of the Federal Constitution. Rather, when tested by the dictates of the State due process clause, the statutes fail to pass constitutional muster thus rendering any inquiry of State action for purposes of the Fourteenth Amendment wholly academic. Noticeably, the dissenters do not address the issue of whether the deprivation of a motor vehicle under the questioned statutes accords with fundamental concepts of justice and fairness.

creation of the common-law artisan's lien, and it similarly supports statutory authorization for the lienor to foreclose the lien. Indeed, a mere possessory lien without the right to sell would offer little benefit to the garageman who might ultimately bear the expense and inconvenience of storage of the vehicle indefinitely. Such a burden could defeat the very purpose sought to be achieved by the lien. The right to foreclose, upon proper prior notice to the owner, is therefore both a reasonable and necessary means of insuring that the lien will serve its intended purpose. By contrast, the rights of the owner of the chattel are affected only minimally by the sale, since the lienor's right to possession continues indefinitely until satisfied. The substantial interests of the garageman in the chattel, and the lesser impact that these statutes have on the interests of the owner, compel the conclusion that these statutes have not worked a significant reordering of the interests involved. The challenged private conduct should therefore not be attributed to the State.

Moreover, the other indices of State action are not present to any significant degree. No benefit inures to the State by operation of these statutes, nor is the State encouraging the lienor to take any action whatever; the initiative rests with the lienor. As to governmental participation, it cannot be argued persuasively that the purely incidental involvement of a licensed auctioneer, who conducted the sale, or of the Department of Motor Vehicles, which transfers title of vehicles, rises to the level of State action, any more than that the use of the post office to mail the notice of sale constitutes Federal action.

Due process of law is a Constitutional mandate, not an excuse for the imposition of one's predilections. Rejecting sound analysis, the majority insists on voiding a reasonable statutory framework in the name of due process, when this decision will deal another blow to the economic welfare of the State. I cannot concur in such a result.

Notes on State Resistance to Federal State Action Doctrine

Comparing* Sharrock*'s Holding to Federal Law: Was state action present under the Federal Constitution in *Sharrock*? The majority opinion vacillated somewhat on this issue, stating that distinctions between the New York lien laws and the statutory scheme examined by the Supreme Court in *Flagg Bros.* might support a different result under the Fourteenth Amendment, but the dissent discounted this possibility. Subsequently, the New York high court in a short memorandum opinion relied on *Sharrock* to invalidate under its state constitution a provision identical to the one that was upheld in *Flagg Bros.*[175] The New York legislature subsequently adopted notice procedures to cure the state constitutional infirmities in both statutory schemes.

Sharrock refused to follow *Flagg Bros.* due to differences in text between the federal and state due process clauses, differences in constitutional history, and the importance of conflict resolution as a matter of state sovereignty. How did the dissent respond to these arguments? Whose arguments were more convincing? Were there other factors that might have influenced the *Sharrock* court? Could the sympathetic plight of the plaintiff have been a factor? Could the belief that federal state action doctrine has become too complicated, confusing, and elusive have influenced the court? Or did the court's

---

[175] Svendsen v. Smith's Moving & Trucking Co., 429 N.E.2d 411, 411 (N.Y. 1981).

holding stem from a fundamental disagreement with the Supreme Court's reasoning in *Flagg Bros.*?

The New York high court has not otherwise developed an independent state action jurisprudence outside the foreclosure and lien context,[176] indicating that the court disagreed with the particular application of the state action requirement in *Flagg Bros.* to the case before it without necessarily desiring a wholesale departure from Supreme Court standards. Some commentators have charged that such a methodology improperly views state constitutions as "a handy grab bag filled with a bevy of clauses that may be exploited" to achieve "some particular social goal."[177] Yet others view such disagreements as appropriate because of the difficulty of interpreting constitutional language and applying it to a given factual scenario, which necessarily would lead to differences of opinion.[178]

Independence in State Action Doctrine: Would it have been better for the New York Court of Appeals to create its own independent test for state action? State court decisions typically have not done so outside the handful of cases protecting the exercise of free speech rights on private property, instead intermixing federal and state authorities when evaluating state action issues under state charters.[179] But there are rare cases that have tried to create an independent state action doctrine, including perhaps one Texas appellate court decision.

In *Jones v. Memorial Hospital System*, the First Court of Appeals in Texas adopted, for purposes of deciding a summary judgment motion, a state action test analyzing whether the defendant "was so substantially involved with state and federal activity, that its actions should be treated as those of a public entity for the purposes of constitutional adjudication."[180] While the court hinted that this test required a lower quantum of state involvement to satisfy the state action requirement, it is not clear that it actually did so. As another appellate court stated, "Although the *Jones* court implies that its test requires a lower threshold of public activities, it does not distinguish its test from federal precedent. We are not persuaded that the *Jones* court articulated a test that differs substantially from federal precedent."[181] No other Texas court has attempted to employ *Jones* to adopt an independent state action standard, and the Texas Supreme Court in *Republican Party*

---

[176]*See, e.g.*, SHAD Alliance v. Smith Haven Mall, 488 N.E.2d 1211, 1215 (N.Y. 1985) (refusing to extend free speech rights to private property as the state action doctrine "is not only deeply rooted in constitutional tradition, it is at the foundation of the very nature of a constitutional democracy").

[177]Ronald R.K. Collins, *Reliance on State Constitutions–Away From a Reactionary Approach*, 9 HASTINGS CONST. L.Q. 1, 2 (1981).

[178]*See, e.g.*, Shirley S. Abrahamson, *Divided We Stand: State Constitutions in a More Perfect Union*, 18 HASTINGS CONST. L.Q. 723, 731 (1991).

[179]*See, e.g.*, Ala. Power Co. v. Smith, 575 So. 2d 1084, 1086 (Ala. 1991); Savage v. Aronson, 571 A.2d 696, 711 (Conn. 1990); Barr v. Kelso-Burnett Co., 478 N.E.2d 1354, 1356-57 (Ill. 1985); Green v. Racing Ass'n of Cent. Iowa, 713 N.W.2d 234, 238-43 (Iowa 2006); Onat v. Penobscot Bay Med. Ctr., 574 A.2d 872, 875-76 (Me. 1990); Campbell v. St. Mary's Hosp., 252 N.W.2d 581, 585-86 (Minn. 1977); Pete Lien & Sons, Inc. v. Ellsworth Peck Constr. Co., 896 P.2d 761, 764 (Wyo. 1995).

[180]746 S.W.2d 891, 895 (Tex. App.–Houston [1st Dist.] 1988, no writ).

[181]Weaver v. AIDS Servs. of Austin, Inc., 835 S.W.2d 798, 802 n.5 (Tex. App.–Austin 1992, writ denied).

pointed to *Jones* as a case requiring at least some quantum of state action under the state constitution.

Would it have been preferable for the Texas courts to create a state action doctrine that was less fact-intensive than the federal standards? Or have the Texas courts appropriately followed federal doctrine in the few instances in which they have addressed state action under the Texas Constitution?

D. FUNDAMENTAL PERSONAL AUTONOMY RIGHTS

Under the Fifth and Fourteenth Amendments to the United States Constitution, certain liberties, even though not explicitly mentioned the text of the Constitution, are considered to be "fundamental," requiring the government to have a compelling justification before infringing upon them. These include the personal autonomy rights, sometimes imprecisely referred to as "privacy" rights, such as marriage, procreation, child rearing, medical treatment determinations, contraception, and abortion.

State courts have likewise protected such personal autonomy rights under their state constitutions. In some instances, the state courts have formulated these rights from state constitutional due process or equal protection provisions that are very similar to the guarantees contained in the United States Constitution. As an example, *Texas State Employees Union v. Texas Department of Mental Health & Mental Retardation* held that "the Texas Constitution protects personal privacy from unreasonable intrusion" because "it contains several provisions similar to those in the United States Constitution that have been recognized as implicitly creating protected 'zones of privacy.'"[182] Yet in other states, the existence of privacy rights does not have to be inferred because textual privacy guarantees in their constitutions explicitly protect their citizens' right to privacy or right to be let alone.[183]

How willing should state courts be to protect non-enumerated rights under their state constitutions? Should the relative ease of the state amendment process in comparison to the federal process influence the court's willingness to do so? If the state constitution has an explicit privacy guarantee, how should this be interpreted?

---

[182]746 S.W.2d 203, 205 (Tex. 1987). The court relied on various provisions of the Texas Bill of Rights to support its holding, including the due course of law guarantee in section 19, the free expression guarantee of section 8, the rights of the accused protected by section 10, the prohibitions against unreasonable searches and seizures in section 9 and against quartering soldiers in section 25, and the protection of religious conscience in section 6. *Id.*

[183]*See, e.g.*, ALASKA CONST. art. I, § 22; CAL. CONST. art. I, § 1; FLA. CONST. art. I, § 23; HAW. CONST. art. I, § 6; MONT. CONST. art. II, § 10.

City of Sherman v. Henry, 928 S.W.2d 464 (Tex. 1996)

ABBOTT, Justice, delivered the opinion of the Court, in which PHILLIPS, Chief Justice, and GONZALEZ, HECHT, CORNYN, ENOCH and BAKER, Justices, join.

The City of Sherman Police Chief denied Patrolman Otis Henry a promotion to the rank of sergeant because Henry was having a sexual affair with the wife of a fellow police officer. The Firemen's and Police Officers' Civil Service Commission of the City of Sherman, Texas (the Commission) upheld that decision by finding that the Police Chief had a valid reason for not promoting Henry. Henry appealed to district court which held that the basis of the Police Chief's decision violated Henry's right to privacy under the United States and Texas Constitutions and was not a valid reason for denying the promotion. Accordingly, the district court ordered the promotion of Henry. That decision was affirmed by the court of appeals. 910 S.W.2d 542. We reverse the judgment of the court of appeals and hold that Henry's constitutional rights were not violated when he was denied a promotion for having a sexual affair with another officer's wife.

I

Sergeant Tom Pollard and Dispatcher Kelly Olson worked for the Sherman Police Department. Pollard and Olson were married in September 1989, but kept their marriage secret for nearly two years because they believed the police department had a nepotism policy prohibiting marriage between employees.

Henry and Olson developed a relationship in April 1991 that progressed into a sexual affair. When the relationship began, Henry knew that Olson and Pollard lived together and were dating, but he did not know they were married. In June 1991, Olson admitted to Henry that she was married to Pollard. A month later, Olson and Pollard informed the department they were married. Olson and Pollard separated in December 1991 and Pollard filed for divorce. Meanwhile, the sexual affair between Henry and Olson continued.

Police Chief Stephen Pilant first heard allegations of the affair in the late summer or early fall of 1991. After that, Chief Pilant noticed that Pollard seemed distraught on occasion and missed work due to illness. Rumor and innuendo about the affair increased in December 1991, about the same time it became known in the department that a sergeant's position would become available in January 1992. Absent a valid reason to the contrary, Henry was entitled to the promotion to sergeant.

In mid-January, and before making the promotion decision, Chief Pilant asked Lieutenant Mayo to investigate the validity of the rumors regarding Henry's relationship with Olson. The investigation consisted of Lieutenant Mayo getting from Pollard a memorandum detailing facts about the affair and a love letter from Henry to Olson. Pollard's memorandum simply described how he had already verified the existence of the affair. The record reveals that several months *before* Chief Pilant requested an informal investigation, Pollard had already confirmed the affair between Olson and Henry. Moreover, Pollard did not engage in clandestine conduct to "investigate" the affair; instead, he discovered Olson and Henry together while he was driving on the public streets. He also found in his own home love letters from Henry to Olson. Mayo did not pursue further investigation after receiving Pollard's memorandum, and he did not interrogate Henry or anyone else about the matter.

On January 17, 1992, a sign appeared on a department bulletin board and in the departmental mailboxes of most police officers that stated in its entirety: "If you can't trust another officer with your wife, how can you trust him with your life?" Henry assumed the author directed the jab at him and complained about the sign to Lieutenant Mayo and another Lieutenant. Henry also requested an investigation by the Internal Affairs Division.

One month later, Chief Pilant announced that Henry would be passed over for the promotion. In a written memorandum, Chief Pilant stated the reason for denying the promotion was his belief that Henry would not command respect and trust from rank-and-file officers and that promoting Henry would adversely affect the efficiency and morale of the department. Chief Pilant orally expressed to Henry that the sole basis of these conclusions was the affair Henry had with Olson.

Henry appealed Chief Pilant's decision to the Commission. At the hearing, Chief Pilant admitted that Henry was very qualified for the sergeant's position. Nevertheless, Pilant testified that he did not promote Henry because of the impact the relationship between Henry and Olson would have both on Henry's ability to perform his work and on the morale of the department. As evidence that the affair was disruptive, the Chief pointed to the rumors and innuendo among officers, the sign posted on the bulletin board, and the emotional distress suffered by Pollard.

Several more witnesses testified at the Commission hearing that the affair adversely affected the department and that Henry's promotion would have a detrimental impact on morale and on Henry's ability to perform his job. That evidence was contested by testimony from Henry and Olson.

After hearing all of the evidence presented by the City and by Henry, the Civil Service Commission voted unanimously that Chief Pilant had a valid reason for not promoting Henry. Henry appealed the Commission's decision to state district court where both Henry and the City of Sherman moved for summary judgment. Significantly, neither party challenged the Commission's fact findings or claimed the Commission's decision was not based on substantial evidence. Indeed, both parties submitted their summary judgment motions to the district court upon stipulated facts.

During the oral argument of this case, the parties represented that, after the trial court's judgment, Henry was promoted to sergeant and the Pollards subsequently remarried. Thus, the issue for us to decide is whether Henry is entitled to the back pay and the attorney's fees awarded to him by the trial court. To make that determination, we must decide whether the Police Chief's reason for denying Henry the promotion infringed upon Henry's constitutional rights.

* * * *

III

Henry maintains his conduct is protected by the right to privacy under both the United States and Texas Constitutions. Neither Constitution expressly provides a right of privacy. Indeed, neither Constitution even contains the word "privacy." However, the United States Supreme Court has recognized that at least two different kinds of privacy interests are protected by the United States Constitution.

The first type of privacy protects an individual's interest in avoiding the disclosure of personal information. *Whalen v. Roe,* 429 U.S. 589, 599 (1977). This interest is the "right to be let alone," which has been characterized as "the right most valued by civilized men." *Id.* at 599 & n. 25 (quoting *Olmstead v. United States,* 277 U.S. 438, 478 (1928)(Brandeis, J., dissenting)). The second constitutionally protected privacy interest is the right to make certain kinds of important decisions and to engage in certain kinds of conduct. *Whalen,* 429 U.S. at 600. This interest protects individual autonomy in making decisions and conduct relating to marriage, procreation, contraception, family relationships, child rearing, and education. The first privacy interest focuses on government action that is intrusive or invasive; the second concerns decisions or conduct by individuals. The United States Supreme Court and lower federal courts have consistently recognized the dichotomy between these two distinct aspects of the privacy right.

In *Texas State Employees Union v. Texas Department of Mental Health & Mental Retardation,* 746 S.W.2d 203 (Tex.1987)(hereinafter *TSEU*), this Court noted that the Texas Constitution contains "several provisions similar to those in the United States Constitution that have been recognized as implicitly creating protected 'zones of privacy.'" *Id.* at 205. We also noted that "a right of individual privacy is implicit among those 'general, great, and essential principles of liberty and free government' established by the Texas Bill of Rights." *Id.* (quoting TEX. CONST. art. I, Introduction to the Bill of Rights).

In *TSEU,* the Texas Department of Mental Health and Mental Retardation had instituted a mandatory polygraph policy requiring employees to submit to a polygraph during the course of an investigation of suspected patient abuse, theft, or other criminal behavior. *Id.* at 204. The case did not concern the constitutionality of individual conduct; instead it focused on the constitutionality of the governmental intrusion. Obviously, patient abuse or criminal behavior is not constitutionally protected by the autonomy aspect of privacy. The government could typically regulate such conduct or make an employment decision based on such conduct. But the government nevertheless does not have license to intrusively pry into the affairs of its employees. Thus, we held in *TSEU* that the Texas Constitution protected the personal privacy of the employees from the unreasonable intrusion of the mandatory polygraph policy. The meaning of *TSEU* was not that the employees' conduct was constitutionally protected; but rather that the government impermissibly intruded on the employees' "right to be let alone."

Henry's claim presents the opposite scenario. Henry does not claim that Chief Pilant or the City of Sherman invaded his right to be let alone. Similarly, he does not complain that the government's method of obtaining information regarding his affair with Olson constituted any type of intrusion into his personal life. Instead, Henry urges that the *basis* of Chief Pilant's decision (Henry's adulterous affair with another officer's wife) was invalid because it violated his constitutionally protected privacy rights. This is a claim only under the autonomy aspect of the right to privacy–the right to make certain fundamental decisions and engage in certain conduct without state interference. Thus, the sole issue for our review is whether conduct involving an affair by one police officer with the wife of another officer is a fundamental, constitutionally protected right.

A

The United States Supreme Court has construed the United States Constitution to confer a limited right of privacy for individuals to make certain fundamental decisions or engage in certain conduct. *Whalen,* 429 U.S. at 600. In *Bowers v. Hardwick,* 478 U.S. 186, 190 (1986), the Supreme Court thoroughly analyzed this right to privacy and concluded that its scope has been limited to child rearing and education, *see Pierce v. Society of Sisters,* 268 U.S. 510, 534-35 (1925) and *Meyer v. Nebraska,* 262 U.S. 390 (1923); family relationships, *see Prince v. Massachusetts,* 321 U.S. 158 (1944); procreation, *see Skinner v. Oklahoma,* 316 U.S. 535 (1942); marriage, *see Loving v. Virginia,* 388 U.S. 1 (1967); contraception, *see Eisenstadt v. Baird,* 405 U.S. 438 (1972) and *Griswold v. Connecticut,* 381 U.S. 479 (1965); and abortion, *see Roe v. Wade,* 410 U.S. 113 (1973).

Bowers concerned a challenge to Georgia's sodomy statute brought by a homosexual adult male who had been charged with (but not indicted for) violating the sodomy law. The Court ruled there was no fundamental right to engage in homosexual sodomy. 478 U.S. at 191. In so doing, it emphasized that its prior decisions do not "stand for the proposition that any kind of private sexual conduct between consenting adults is constitutionally insulated." *Id.* The Court reasoned that there was no resemblance or connection between the claimed constitutional right to engage in homosexual sodomy and the recognized privacy rights concerning marriage, procreation, and family.

The *Bowers* Court also analyzed whether it should recognize a substantive due process right for homosexual activity under the Fourteenth Amendment. It held that only those rights which are "implicit in the concept of ordered liberty" such that "neither liberty nor justice would exist" if they were sacrificed, or those liberties which are "deeply rooted in this Nation's history and tradition" receive constitutional protection under the substantive component of the due process clause. *Id.* at 191-92. The Court held that neither of these formulations applied to create a fundamental right for homosexuals to engage in acts of consensual sodomy. *Id.* at 192.

In reviewing the history of sodomy, the Court noted it was a criminal offense at common law, forbidden by all the original thirteen states when they ratified the Bill of Rights, and the vast majority of the states when the Fourteenth Amendment became the law of the land. The Court concluded that, based on this history, the claim that the right to engage in homosexual sodomy was "implicit in the concept of ordered liberty" or "deeply rooted in this Nation's history and tradition" was, at best, facetious.

Using the Supreme Court's framework, we conclude that Henry's affair with Pollard's wife is unlike the recognized privacy rights concerning child rearing, family relationships, procreation, marriage, contraception, and abortion. Indeed, Henry's adulterous conduct is the very antithesis of marriage and family. Adultery, by its very nature, undermines the marital relationship and often rips apart families. Rather than suffering an invasion of privacy, Henry invaded the "privacy surrounding the marriage relationship" so revered by Justice Douglas in *Griswold.* 381 U.S. at 486.

Moreover, sexual relations with the spouse of another is not a right that is "implicit in the concept of ordered liberty" or "deeply rooted in this Nation's history and tradition." Prohibitions against adultery have ancient roots. In the latter half of the 17th century in England, adultery was a capital offense. 4 WILLIAM BLACKSTONE, COMMENTARIES *64. The common law brought to this country by the American colonists included the crime of adultery as previously defined by the canon law of England. *United States v. Clapox,* 35 F. 575, 578 (D.Or.1888); FRANCIS WHARTON, A TREATISE ON CRIMINAL LAW vol. 11, §§ 1719-20, p. 524 (9th ed. 1885). Adultery was still considered a crime by courts and commentators in the latter half of the 19th century when the Fourteenth Amendment was ratified. *See Clapox,* 35 F. at 578; WHARTON, *supra.* In fact, adultery is a crime today in half of the states and the District of Columbia.

While other states, including Texas, have recently repealed laws criminalizing adultery, the mere fact that such conduct is no longer illegal in some states does not cloak it with constitutional protection. Even in most states where adultery is not criminal behavior, civil laws still burden those engaging in adulterous activity. *See* Note, *Constitutional Barriers to Civil and Criminal Restrictions on Pre- and Extramarital Sex,* 104 HARV. L. REV. 1660, 1672-74 (1991). A right to engage in adultery simply cannot be said to be either "implicit in the concept of ordered liberty" or "deeply rooted in this Nation's history and tradition."

Our conclusion that adultery is not a fundamental right protected under the United States Constitution is buttressed by dicta contained in several Supreme Court opinions. Justice Goldberg's concurrence in *Griswold,* which was joined by Chief Justice Warren and Justice Brennan, stated that the constitutionality of statutes prohibiting adultery and fornication was "beyond doubt." 381 U.S. at 498 (Goldberg, J., concurring). Similarly, the Court in *Bowers* expressed concern that, if it granted a right of privacy to homosexual conduct, "adultery, incest, and other sexual crimes" would also be protected. 478 U.S. at 195-96. The Court opined that it was "unwilling to start down that road." *Id.* at 196. Even the dissenting justices in *Bowers* (Justices Blackmun, Brennan, Marshall, and Stevens) claimed that a court "could find simple, analytically sound distinctions between certain private, consensual sexual conduct, on the one hand, and adultery . . . on the other." *Id.* at 209 n. 4 (Blackmun, J., dissenting). One major distinction noted by the dissent was that adultery often injures third persons, such as spouses and children.

We conclude that the right to privacy under the United States Constitution does not include the right to maintain a sexual relationship with the spouse of someone else. We turn now to Henry's claim to a privacy right under the Texas Constitution.

B

Although the Texas Constitution does not expressly provide a right of privacy, our opinion in *TSEU* recognized constitutionally protected zones of privacy emanating from several sections of article I of the Texas Constitution: section 6, concerning freedom of worship; section 8, concerning freedom of speech and press; section 9, concerning searches and seizures; section 10, concerning the rights of an accused in criminal prosecutions; section 19, concerning deprivation of life, liberty and property, and due course of law; and section 25, concerning quartering soldiers in houses. *TSEU,* 746 S.W.2d at 205. No court has recognized any other provision of the Texas Constitution as establishing a right to privacy. Other than section 19, none of these provisions even remotely addresses the situation of an individual who is denied a promotion because he is having an affair with the wife of someone else. We are thus faced with the task of determining whether Henry's conduct is protected by article I, section 19 of the Texas Constitution.

[T]here is no reason to believe that article I, section 19 of the Texas Constitution provides a right of privacy for Henry's conduct. That constitutional provision states:

> No citizen of this State shall be deprived of life, liberty, property, privileges or immunities, or in any manner disfranchised, except by the due course of the law of the land.

This language is remarkably similar to the Fourteenth Amendment to the United States Constitution[184] upon which the United States Supreme Court has relied when defining right to privacy parameters. While the Texas Constitution has been recognized to possess independent vitality, separate and apart from the guarantees provided by the United States Constitution, *see In the Interest of J.W.T.,* 872 S.W.2d 189, 197 (Tex.1994) and *LeCroy v. Hanlon,* 713 S.W.2d 335, 339 (Tex.1986), there is no reason to expand Texas constitutional protections to protect Henry's conduct.

Neither Henry nor Justice Spector's concurring opinion provides any support for the proposition that the framers or ratifiers of the Texas Constitution would have considered the right to have a sexual affair with the wife of another an essential component of life, liberty, or property. Nor has there been any showing that Henry's conduct is among those "general, great, and essential principles" of our government. In fact, when our state charter was ratified in 1876, article 392 of the Texas Penal Code of 1857 provided that adultery was a crime punishable by fine. A mere three years after the passage of the 1876 Texas Constitution, the Texas Legislature revised the Penal Code, but retained the provision criminalizing adultery. *See* Tex. Penal Code art. 336 (1879). The prohibition against adultery continued for almost a century until it was finally repealed in 1973. *See* Act of June 14, 1973, 63d Leg., R.S., ch. 399, § 3, 1973 Tex. Gen. Laws 883, 992, *repealing* Tex. Penal Code art. 499 (1925). While the constitution's framers may have been willing to die for the right of free expression, *see Davenport,* 834 S.W.2d at 7, there is no indication they were willing to make any sacrifice for the right to commit adultery.

Implicitly conceding that the original intent of the Texas Constitution did not encompass a right to commit adultery, Henry contends his conduct is constitutionally protected because it is no longer illegal. However, there are two major fallacies with this argument. First, the mere fact that conduct is no longer illegal does not make it constitutionally protected. Adultery is no longer a statutory violation in Texas, but it is still

---

[184]The Fourteenth Amendment provides: "No State shall make or enforce any law which shall abridge the privileges or immunities of citizens of the United States; nor shall any State deprive any person of life, liberty, or property without due process of law . . . ." We have previously recognized the textual similarity between article I, section 19 and the Fourteenth Amendment. *See, e.g., University of Tex. Med. Sch. v. Than,* 901 S.W.2d 926, 929 (Tex.1995); *Mellinger v. City of Houston,* 68 Tex. 37, 3 S.W. 249, 252-53 (1887).

not favored by the law. In fact, Texas specifically allows courts to consider adultery in granting a divorce or in dividing community assets. *See* Tex. Fam. Code §§ 3.03, 3.63; *Young v. Young,* 609 S.W.2d 758, 761 (Tex.1980). Second, the fact that constitutional guarantees continue to evolve over time does not mean that we are allowed to create new guarantees that are not present in either the text or the intent of the constitution. Moreover, Henry's argument is illogical. To follow Henry's argument to its logical end would require us to rule that legislative action concerning any type of conduct would establish its constitutionality. Such an untenable position would place the Constitution at the mercy of the Legislature.

Accordingly, we find no basis for the argument that adultery is protected as a fundamental right under the Texas Constitution. Borrowing from the *Bowers* analysis, Henry's conduct is not a right implicit in the concept of liberty in Texas or deeply rooted in this state's history and tradition.

Considering the Texas Constitution as a whole and article I, section 19 in particular, the historical context in which the Texas Constitution was conceived and has lived, actions by the Texas Legislature, and judicial decisions, we conclude that the Texas Constitution does not provide a right of privacy for a police officer who was denied a promotion because he had a sexual affair with the wife of another police officer. This conclusion does not mean, however, that the government is free to engage in intrusive investigation methods to determine the sexual practices of individuals.

SPECTOR, Justice, concurring.

Nine years ago, the right of privacy under the Texas Constitution prevented the state from asking employees whether they had ever stolen or whether they had beaten their children. Today, the majority announces that the Texas constitutional right of privacy has somehow shriveled to the point that the most personal aspects of our lives are the government's business.

The only issue here concerns the individual's right to enter into intimate personal relationships, secure in the knowledge that our Constitution protects the relationship from intrusion by the government in the absence of a compelling state interest. *See TSEU,* 746 S.W.2d at 206; *see also Stanley v. Georgia,* 394 U.S. 557, 564 (1969). I strongly disagree that Henry's claim does not implicate a privacy interest protected by the Texas Constitution. If the right Henry asserts is not "implicit in the concept of liberty," then the right we recognized in *TSEU* is no more than a hollow shell.

I believe that the City infringed Henry's privacy rights at two points: First, when the police chief ordered his internal affairs division to investigate rumors of Henry's liaison, and later, when it denied Henry the promotion to which he would clearly have been entitled. *See Thorne v. City of Segundo,* 726 F.2d 459, 468 (9th Cir.1983) (stating that the plaintiff's constitutional privacy interests were implicated both when the defendants "forc[ed] her to disclose information regarding personal sexual matters" in a polygraph test and when the defendants "refused to hire her as a police officer based in part on her prior sexual activities").

Even if there had been no investigation and Henry had voluntarily disclosed the affair, however, Henry's privacy rights were implicated when the police chief denied the promotion based solely upon his affair with Olson. *See Thorne v. City of Segundo,* 726 F.2d at 468, 471. The majority's conclusion that Henry does not assert a constitutionally-protected right rests almost entirely on the fact that "adultery was a crime" at the time our Constitution was ratified. 928 S.W.2d at 473. The majority's constitutional analysis thus implies that the scope of individual rights under the Texas Constitution is frozen in time, limited to conduct or actions that were legal and accepted more than one hundred years ago. This analysis is inconsistent with this Court's opinion in *Davenport v. Garcia,* 834 S.W.2d 4, 10, 19 (Tex.1992). If it is true that Henry asserts no constitutionally-protected right because adultery was illegal in 1876, then the privacy right we recognized in *TSEU* also does not protect a woman's right to choose to terminate a pregnancy, *see* Tex. Penal Code art. 536 (1879), or the right of an interracial couple to marry, *see* Tex. Penal Code art. 326 (1879).

The fact that Henry asserts a constitutionally-protected right to privacy is not dispositive, however. In *TSEU,* we recognized that the right to privacy is not unlimited, but should "yield . . . when the government can demonstrate that the intrusion is reasonably warranted for the achievement of a compelling governmental objective . . . ." *TSEU,* 746 S.W.2d at 205. The trial court in this case concluded that the police chief erred in denying Henry's promotion. I differ from the trial court because I believe the record shows that the department had a compelling interest justifying its action.

We acknowledged in *TSEU* that police departments, unlike most public agencies, are quasi-military organizations that may require "unquestioning obedience." *Id.* at 206. Here, the record contains substantial evidence that Henry's conduct had, at some point, intruded into the workplace and cast doubt upon his ability to command the trust and obedience necessary in a paramilitary organization. It was not unreasonable for the chief to conclude that Henry's betrayal of his fellow officer's trust had undermined his ability to assume a leadership position. Under these circumstances, the police chief's decision to pass Henry over until this volatile situation was resolved was justified.

Because I believe that the record contains substantial evidence that the City had a compelling interest in denying Henry's promotion, I join in the Court's judgment. I cannot, however, join in the majority's unnecessary and unjustified constriction of the fundamental constitutional right to privacy.

OWEN, Justice, concurring.

I join only in the judgment of the Court. The opinion of the Court is broader than necessary to decide the very narrow issue in this case, which is: *assuming* Officer Henry had a cognizable constitutional right, could the City of Sherman deny him a promotion when his adulterous affair with the wife of a fellow police officer led to disruption in the department. The answer obviously is yes. The Court need not engage in an extended discussion of a host of constitutional issues and principles of constitutional law to resolve this case.

Notes on the Texas Constitutional Right to Privacy

The Development of Texas Constitutional Privacy Rights: The Texas Supreme Court first recognized a right to privacy under the state constitution in *Texas State Employees Union v. Texas Department of Mental Health & Mental Retardation*.[185] In that case, the Department of Mental Health and Mental Retardation had established a mandatory polygraph policy for its employees during investigations for suspected patient abuse, criminal activity, or health or safety threats. The supreme court, however, invalidated the policy under the state constitution. The court reasoned that a number of provisions in the Texas Bill of Rights implicitly established a right of individual privacy that should "yield only when the government can demonstrate that an intrusion is reasonably warranted for the achievement of a compelling governmental objective that can be achieved by no less intrusive, more reasonable means."[186] Based on the trial court's findings that polygraph testing was unreliable and the testing protocol included highly intrusive personal questions, the court held that the Department had not selected a reasonable means to accomplish its objectives.

The Texas Supreme Court in *TSEU*, and again in *Henry*, discussed several sources for the implicit right of privacy under the Texas Constitution. How does this enumeration compare to the federal right of privacy and federal substantive due process analysis in general? While the federal right to zones of privacy was initially derived from "penumbras, formed by emanations from [the specific] guarantees [in the Bill of Rights] that help give them life and substance,"[187] more recent federal decisions have minimized the reliance on "privacy," instead examining the strength of the asserted liberty interest under the Due Process Clause.[188] Did the *Henry* court acknowledge this shift by using the state due course of law clause in article I, section 19 as the sole supporting textual basis for analyzing Henry's claims?

When is the right of privacy under the Texas Constitution implicated? *Henry* discusses two interests protected by the state right of privacy: first, the interest in avoiding intrusive or invasive governmental actions regarding personal matters; and second, the right to individual autonomy in making decisions and engaging in conduct related to marriage, procreation, contraception, family relationships, and child rearing. Which of these interests were at stake in *TSEU*? Which of these interests were at stake in *Henry*? Does the majority or Justice Spector's concurrence have the better of the argument regarding the implicated interests in *Henry*?

Could a privacy right be protected under the state constitution but not be protected by the federal charter? If so, under what circumstances? While essentially following federal standards, the *Henry* court did employ a subtle shift, analyzing whether Henry's conduct was a "right implicit in the concept of liberty *in Texas* or deeply rooted in *this*

---

[185] 746 S.W.2d 203 (Tex. 1987).

[186] *Id.* at 205.

[187] Griswold v. Connecticut, 381 U.S. 479, 484 (1965).

[188] *See, e.g.*, Lawrence v. Texas, 539 U.S. 558, 562-79 (2003); Casey v. Planned Parenthood of Se. Pa., 505 U.S. 833, 851 (1992) (joint plurality op.).

state's history and tradition."[189] In other words, rather than examining the nation's history and traditions, *Henry* relied on the state's history and traditions to evaluate whether Henry's actions were protected. Other states have likewise focused on their own state's history, traditions, and conceptions of liberty in evaluating the scope of protected privacy interests under their state constitutions, which has led in some cases to protected state constitutional rights that are not recognized under the Federal Constitution.[190]

Expanding Federal Autonomy Rights: Why didn't the City's conduct violate Officer Henry's federal constitutional rights? In analyzing the federal constitutional issue, the Texas Supreme Court followed *Bowers v. Hardwick*, which at that time was binding precedent although it was later overruled by the United States Supreme Court in *Lawrence v. Texas*.[191] In *Lawrence*, the Court held that Texas Penal Code § 21.06, which precluded certain sexual acts between members of the same sex, infringed upon a protected liberty interest without any legitimate state justification, even though the Court did not hold that a fundamental right was at issue. Justice Scalia's dissent in *Lawrence* noted that the Texas Supreme Court's holding in *City of Sherman v. Henry* followed *Bowers*, leading to the possibility that laws against adultery were "called into question" by *Lawrence*.[192] Would adultery now be constitutionally protected conduct under the United States Constitution, or is there a valid distinction between adultery and the statute at issue in *Lawrence*? What effect does *Lawrence* have on the Texas Supreme Court's interpretation of its own constitution in *City of Sherman v. Henry*? Would the persuasiveness of *Lawrence* in this regard be impacted if the text of the Texas Constitution could more readily be distinguished from the Fourteenth Amendment?

1. State Constitutional Privacy Provisions

As illustrated by *City of Sherman v. Henry*, the methodology for protecting autonomy rights under state constitutions without an explicit privacy guarantee is similar to that employed by the United States Supreme Court in its substantive due process cases. This is not to say that the state courts always reach the same results as the United States Supreme Court, as several states have interpreted their implicit autonomy rights to afford greater protection than the federal right under a variety of rationales.[193] Nevertheless, in all

---

[189] 928 S.W.2d 464, 473 (Tex. 1996) (emphasis added).

[190] *See, e.g.*, Jegley v. Picado, 80 S.W.3d 332, 346-50 (Ark. 2002) (relying in part on state's "rich and compelling tradition of protecting individual privacy" in invalidating state sodomy statute despite contrary then-existing federal law); Powell v. State, 510 S.E.2d 18, 21-26 (Ga. 1998) (similar holding); Commonwealth v. Wasson, 842 S.W.2d 487, 492-99 (Ky. 1992) (similar holding). Subsequently, the United States Supreme Court relied on these and other state court decisions in overruling *Bowers* and holding that the Federal Constitution was violated by prohibitions against private, consensual sexual acts between adults of the same sex. *Lawrence*, 539 U.S. at 576.

[191] 539 U.S. 558 (2003).

[192] *Id.* at 590 (Scalia, J., dissenting).

[193] *See, e.g.,* Planned Parenthood League of Mass., Inc. v. Attorney General, 677 N.E.2d 101, 108 (Mass. 1997) (holding state statute requiring pregnant unmarried minor to either obtain consent of both her parents or a judicial bypass before obtaining an abortion violated state constitutional right to abortion); Women of Minn. v. Gomez, 542 N.W.2d 17, 30-31 (Minn. 1995) (interpreting Minnesota Constitution to provide more protection for abortion funding than that afforded under the Federal Constitution); Planned Parenthood of Middle

the states without privacy provisions, the courts must define the contours of any protected autonomy rights from structural implications rather than constitutional text.

Ten states, however, have adopted state constitutional provisions explicitly guaranteeing an individual's "privacy," "private life," or "private affairs." The guarantees in five of these states at least textually appear to relate primarily to the prohibition on unreasonable governmental searches and seizures,[194] although occasionally they are interpreted to encompass other privacy interests as well.[195] The other five states–Alaska, California, Florida, Hawaii, and Montana–have separated their guarantees from constitutional clauses regarding searches and seizures, thereby enumerating an explicit individual autonomy and informational privacy right. None of these provisions are identical: Alaska recognizes a "right of the people to privacy" that "shall not be infringed," California simply includes "privacy" as one of the "inalienable rights" protected by the state constitution, Florida guarantees a "right to be let alone and free from governmental intrusion into the person's private life," Hawaii protects a "right of the people to privacy" that cannot "be infringed without the showing of a compelling state interest," and Montana protects a "right of individual privacy" that also cannot be infringed without a compelling interest.[196] But in each of these states, explicit state privacy rights have been granted a textual status divorced from the search and seizure context.[197]

Do such state constitutional provisions support a more expansive state autonomy guarantee? In what ways might the protected privacy rights be broader? In *Hill v. NCAA*, discussed in the previous section, the California Constitution's right to privacy was held to dispense with the state action requirement in a drug testing case. Additionally, in California and other states with explicit privacy guarantees, the courts have found autonomy protections not available under the United States Constitution.

Tenn. v. Sundquist, 38 S.W.3d 1, 15-17 (Tenn. 2000) (adopting more stringent standard under Tennessee Constitution for reviewing regulations of abortion).

[194]ARIZ. CONST. art. II, § 8 ("No person shall be disturbed in his private affairs, or his home invaded, without authority of law."); ILL. CONST. art. I, § 6 ("The people shall have the right to be secure in their persons, houses, papers, and other possessions against unreasonable searches, seizures, invasions of privacy or interceptions of communications . . . ."); LA. CONST. art. I, § 5 ("Every person shall be secure in his person, property, communications, houses, papers, and effects against unreasonable searches, seizures, or invasions of privacy."); S.C. CONST. art. I, § 10 ("The right of the people to be secure in their persons, houses, papers, and effects against unreasonable searches and seizures and unreasonable invasions of privacy shall not be violated . . . ."); WASH. CONST. art. I, § 7 ("No person shall be disturbed in his private affairs, or his home invaded, without authority of law."). Hawaii also has a similar provision, as well as another freestanding privacy provision. *See* HAW. CONST. art I, §§ 6-7.

[195]*See, e.g.*, Rasmussen v. Fleming, 741 P.2d 674, 682 (Ariz. 1987) (extending Arizona's freedom from disturbance in private affairs to an individual's right to refuse medical treatment); Singleton v. State, 437 S.E.2d 53, 61 (S.C. 1993) (holding state constitutional right of privacy protected against unwarranted medical intrusions).

[196]ALASKA CONST. art. I, § 22; CAL. CONST. art. I, § 1; FLA. CONST. art. I, § 23; HAW. CONST. art. I, § 6; MONT. CONST. art. II, § 10.

[197]Charles W. "Rocky" Rhodes, *State Constitution, Privacy Provisions*, *in* 3 ENCYCLOPEDIA OF AMERICAN CIVIL LIBERTIES 1532 (Paul Finkelman ed., 2006).

In re T.W., 551 So. 2d 1186 (Fla. 1989)

SHAW, Justice.

We have on appeal *In re T.W.*, 543 So.2d 837 (Fla. 5th DCA 1989), which declared unconstitutional section 390.001(4)(a), Florida Statutes (Supp.1988), the parental consent statute.

I.

The procedure that a minor must follow to obtain an abortion in Florida is set out in the parental consent statute and related rules. Prior to undergoing an abortion, a minor must obtain parental consent or, alternatively, must convince a court that she is sufficiently mature to make the decision herself or that, if she is immature, the abortion nevertheless is in her best interests. Pursuant to this procedure, T.W., a pregnant, unmarried, fifteen-year-old, petitioned for a waiver of parental consent under the judicial bypass provision on the alternative grounds that (1) she was sufficiently mature to give an informed consent to the abortion, (2) she had a justified fear of physical or emotional abuse if her parents were requested to consent, and (3) her mother was seriously ill and informing her of the pregnancy would be an added burden.

The relevant portions of the hearing consisted of T.W.'s uncontroverted testimony that she was a high-school student, participated in band and flag corps, worked twenty hours a week, baby-sat for her mother and neighbors, planned on finishing high school and attending vocational school or community college, had observed an instructional film on abortion, had taken a sex education course at school, would not put her child up for adoption, and had discussed her plans with the child's father and obtained his approval. She informed the court that due to her mother's illness, she had assumed extra duties at home caring for her sibling and that if she told her mother about the abortion, "it would kill her." Evidence was introduced showing that the pregnancy was in the first trimester.

The seminal case in United States abortion law is *Roe v. Wade,* 410 U.S. 113 (1973). There, the Court ruled that a right to privacy implicit in the fourteenth amendment embraces a woman's decision concerning abortion. Autonomy to make this decision constitutes a fundamental right and states may impose restrictions only when narrowly drawn to serve a compelling state interest. The Court recognized two important state interests, protecting the health of the mother and the potentiality of life in the fetus, and ruled that these interests become compelling at the completion of the first trimester of pregnancy and upon viability of the fetus (approximately at the end of the second trimester), respectively. Thus, during the first trimester, states must leave the abortion decision to the woman and her doctor; during the second trimester, states may impose measures to protect the mother's health; and during the period following viability, states may possibly forbid abortions altogether. Although the workability of the trimester system and the soundness of *Roe* itself have been seriously questioned in *Webster v. Reproductive Health Services,* 492 U.S. 490 (1989), the decision for now remains the federal law. Subsequent to *Roe,* the Court issued several decisions dealing directly with the matter of parental consent for minors seeking abortions. *See Planned Parenthood Ass'n v. Ashcroft,* 462 U.S. 476 (1983); *City of Akron v. Akron Center for Reproductive Health Inc.,* 462 U.S. 416 (1983); *Bellotti v. Baird,* 443 U.S. 622 (1979) (plurality opinion); *Planned Parenthood v. Danforth,* 428 U.S. 52 (1976).

To be held constitutional, the instant statute must pass muster under both the federal and state constitutions. Were we to examine it solely under the federal Constitution, our analysis necessarily would track the decisions noted above. However, Florida is unusual in that it is one of at least four states having its own express constitutional provision guaranteeing an independent right to privacy, and we opt to examine the statute first under the Florida Constitution. If it fails here, then no further analysis under federal law is required.

As we noted in *Winfield v. Division of Pari-Mutuel Wagering,* 477 So.2d 544 (Fla.1985), the essential concept of privacy is deeply rooted in our nation's political and philosophical heritage. Justice Brandeis in *Olmstead v. United States,* 277 U.S. 438, 478 (1928) (Brandeis, J., dissenting), eloquently expressed the fundamental and wide-ranging "right to be let alone":

> The makers of our Constitution undertook to secure conditions favorable to the pursuit of happiness. They recognized the significance of man's spiritual nature, of his feelings and of his intellect. . . . They sought to protect Americans in their beliefs, their thoughts, their emotions and their sensations. They conferred, as against the government, the right to be let alone–the most comprehensive of rights and the right most valued by civilized men.

Pursuant to this principle, the United States Supreme Court has recognized a privacy right that shields an individual's autonomy in deciding matters concerning marriage, procreation, contraception, family relationships, and child rearing and education. *Roe,* 410 U.S. at 152-53. It is this general right to privacy that protects against the public disclosure of private matters. *Nixon v. Administrator of General Servs.,* 433 U.S. 425 (1977); *Whalen v. Roe,* 429 U.S. 589 (1977). The Court, however, has made it clear that the states, not the federal government, are the final guarantors of personal privacy: "But the protection of a person's *general* right to privacy–his right to be let alone by other people–is, like the protection of his property and of his very life, left largely to the law of the individual States." *Katz v. United States,* 389 U.S. 347, 350-51 (1967) (footnotes omitted; emphasis in original). While the federal Constitution traditionally shields enumerated and implied individual liberties from encroachment by state or federal government, the federal Court has long held that state constitutions may provide even greater protection.

In 1980, Florida voters by general election amended our state constitution to provide:

> Section 23. Right of privacy.–Every natural person has the right to be let alone and free from governmental intrusion into his private life except as otherwise provided herein. This section shall not be construed to limit the public's right of access to public records and meetings as provided by law.

This Court in *Winfield* described the far-reaching impact of the Florida amendment:

> The citizens of Florida opted for more protection from governmental intrusion when they approved article I, section 23, of the Florida

> Constitution. This amendment is an independent, freestanding constitutional provision which declares the fundamental right to privacy. Article I, section 23, was intentionally phrased in strong terms. The drafters of the amendment rejected the use of the words "unreasonable" or "unwarranted" before the phrase "governmental intrusion" in order to make the privacy right as strong as possible. Since the people of this state exercised their prerogative and enacted an amendment to the Florida Constitution which expressly and succinctly provides for a strong right of privacy not found in the United States Constitution, it can only be concluded that the right is much broader in scope than that of the Federal Constitution.

Winfield, 477 So.2d at 548. In other words, the amendment embraces more privacy interests, and extends more protection to the individual in those interests, than does the federal Constitution.

Consistent with this analysis, we have said that the amendment provides "an explicit textual foundation for those privacy interests inherent in the concept of liberty which may not otherwise be protected by specific constitutional provisions." *Rasmussen v. South Fla. Blood Serv.,* 500 So.2d 533, 536 (Fla.1987). We have found the right implicated in a wide range of activities dealing with the public disclosure of personal matters. *See Barron v. Florida Freedom Newspapers,* 531 So.2d 113 (Fla.1988) (closure of court proceedings and records); *Rasmussen* (confidential donor information concerning AIDS-tainted blood supply); *Winfield* (banking records); *Florida Bd. of Bar Examiners re: Applicant,* 443 So.2d 71 (Fla.1983) (bar application questions concerning disclosure of psychiatric counseling). Florida courts have also found the right involved in a number of cases dealing with personal decisionmaking. *See Public Health Trust v. Wons,* 541 So.2d 96 (Fla.1989) (refusal of blood transfusion that is necessary to sustain life); *Corbett v. D'Alessandro,* 487 So.2d 368 (Fla. 2d DCA), *review denied,* 492 So.2d 1331 (Fla.1986) (removal of nasogastric feeding tube from adult in permanent vegetative state); *In re Guardianship of Barry,* 445 So.2d 365 (Fla. 2d DCA 1984) (removal of life support system from brain-dead infant).

The privacy section contains no express standard of review for evaluating the lawfulness of a government intrusion into one's private life, and this Court when called upon, adopted the following standard:

> Since the privacy section as adopted contains no textual standard of review, it is important for us to identify an explicit standard to be applied in order to give proper force and effect to the amendment. The right of privacy is a fundamental right which we believe demands the compelling state interest standard. This test shifts the burden of proof to the state to justify an intrusion on privacy. The burden can be met by demonstrating that the challenged regulation serves a compelling state interest and accomplishes its goal through the use of the least intrusive means.

Winfield, 477 So.2d at 547. When this standard was applied in disclosural cases, government intrusion generally was upheld as sufficiently compelling to overcome the individual's right to privacy. We reaffirm, however, that this is a highly stringent standard, emphasized by the fact that no government intrusion in the personal decisionmaking cases cited above has survived.

Florida's privacy provision is clearly implicated in a woman's decision of whether or not to continue her pregnancy. We can conceive of few more personal or private decisions concerning one's body that one can make in the course of a lifetime, except perhaps the decision of the terminally ill in their choice of whether to discontinue necessary medical treatment.

The next question to be addressed is whether this freedom of choice concerning abortion extends to minors. We conclude that it does, based on the unambiguous language of the amendment: The right of privacy extends to "[e]very natural person." Minors are natural persons in the eyes of the law and "[c]onstitutional rights do not mature and come into being magically only when one attains the state-defined age of majority. Minors, as well as adults, . . . possess constitutional rights." *Danforth,* 428 U.S. at 74.

II.

Common sense dictates that a minor's rights are not absolute; in order to overcome these constitutional rights, a statute must survive the stringent test announced in *Winfield*: The state must prove that the statute furthers a compelling state interest through the least intrusive means. The *Roe* Court recognized two state interests implicated in the abortion decision: the health of the mother and the potentiality of life in the fetus. Under *Roe,* the health of the mother does not become a compelling state interest until immediately following the end of the first trimester because until that time, "mortality in abortion may be less than mortality in normal childbirth." *Roe,* 410 U.S. at 163. Due to technological developments in second-trimester abortion procedures, the point at which abortions are safer than childbirth may have been extended into the second trimester. *See City of Akron,* 462 U.S. at 429 n. 11. We nevertheless adopt the end of the first trimester as the time at which the state's interest in maternal health becomes compelling under Florida law because it is clear that prior to this point no interest in maternal health could be served by significantly restricting the manner in which abortions are performed by qualified doctors, whereas after this point the matter becomes a genuine concern. Under Florida law, prior to the end of the first trimester, the abortion decision must be left to the woman and may not be significantly restricted by the state. Following this point, the state may impose significant restrictions only in the least intrusive manner designed to safeguard the health of the mother. Insignificant burdens during either period must substantially further important state interests.

Under *Roe,* the potentiality of life in the fetus becomes compelling at the point in time when the fetus becomes viable, which the Court defined as the time at which the fetus becomes capable of meaningful life outside the womb, albeit with artificial aid. *Roe,* 410 U.S. at 160, 163. Under our Florida Constitution, the state's interest becomes compelling upon viability, as defined below. Until this point, the fetus is a highly specialized set of cells that is entirely dependent upon the mother for sustenance. No other member of society can provide this nourishment. The mother and fetus are so inextricably intertwined that their interests can be said to coincide. Upon viability, however, society becomes capable of sustaining the fetus, and its interest in preserving its potential for life thus becomes compelling. Viability under Florida law occurs at that point in time when the fetus becomes capable of meaningful life outside the womb through standard medical measures. Under current standards, this point generally occurs upon completion of the second trimester.

III.

The challenged statute fails because it intrudes upon the privacy of the pregnant minor from conception to birth. Such a substantial invasion of a pregnant female's privacy by the state for the full term of the pregnancy is not necessary for the preservation of maternal health or the potentiality of life. However, where parental rights over a minor child are concerned, society has recognized additional state interests–protection of the immature minor and preservation of the family unit. For reasons set out below, we find that neither of these interests is sufficiently compelling under Florida law to override Florida's privacy amendment.

In evaluating the validity of parental consent and notice statutes, the federal Court has taken into consideration the state's interests in the well-being of the immature minor, *see Ashcroft; City of Akron; Matheson; Bellotti; Danforth,* and in the integrity of the family, *see Matheson; Bellotti.* In *Bellotti,* the Court set forth three reasons justifying the conclusion that states can impose more restrictions on the right of minors to obtain abortions than they can impose on the right of adults: "[T]he peculiar vulnerability of children; their inability to make critical decisions in an informed, mature manner; and the importance of the parental role in child rearing." *Bellotti,* 443 U.S. at 634. The Court pointed out that "during the formative years of childhood and adolescence, minors often lack the experience, perspective, and judgment to recognize and avoid choices that could be detrimental to them," *id.* at 635, and that the role of parents in "teaching, guiding, and inspiring by precept and example is essential to the growth of young people into mature, socially responsible citizens," *id.* at 638. In assessing the validity of parental consent statutes, the federal Court applied a relaxed standard; the state interest need only be "significant," not "compelling," to support the intrusion.

We agree that the state's interests in protecting minors and in preserving family unity are worthy objectives. Unlike the federal Constitution, however, which allows intrusion based on a "significant" state interest, the Florida Constitution requires a "compelling" state interest in all cases where the right to privacy is implicated. *Winfield.* We note that Florida does not recognize these two interests as being sufficiently compelling to justify a parental consent requirement where procedures other than abortion are concerned. Section 743.065, Florida Statutes (1987), provides [that] a minor may consent, without parental approval, to any medical procedure involving her pregnancy or her existing child–no matter how dire the possible consequences–except abortion. Under *In re Guardianship of Barry,* 445 So.2d 365 (Fla. 2d DCA 1984) (parents permitted to authorize removal of life support system from infant in permanent coma), this could include authority in certain circumstances to order life support discontinued for a comatose child. In light of this wide authority that the state grants an unwed minor to make life-or-death decisions concerning herself or an existing child without parental consent, we are unable to discern a special compelling interest on the part of the state under Florida law in protecting the minor only where abortion is concerned. We fail to see the qualitative difference in terms of impact on the well-being of the minor between allowing the life of an existing child to come to an end and terminating a pregnancy, or between undergoing a highly dangerous medical procedure on oneself and undergoing a far less dangerous procedure to end one's pregnancy. If any qualitative difference exists, it certainly is insufficient in terms of state interest.

The parental consent statute also fails the second prong of the *Winfield* standard, i.e., it is not the least intrusive means of furthering the state interest. Any inquiry under this prong must consider procedural safeguards relative to the intrusion. As pointed out by the district court below, although the instant statute does provide for a judicial bypass procedure, it makes no provision for a lawyer for the minor or for a record hearing.

Based on the foregoing analysis of our state law, we hold that section 390.001(4)(a), Florida Statutes (Supp.1988), violates the Florida Constitution. Accordingly, no further analysis under federal law is required. We expressly decide this case on state law grounds and cite federal precedent only to the extent that it illuminates Florida law.

OVERTON, Justice, concurring in part, dissenting in part.

I concur in parts I and II; however, I must dissent from the majority's holding in part III. While I agree that section 390.001(4)(a), Florida Statutes (Supp.1988), is unconstitutional as it was interpreted and applied by the trial court, I would not declare the statute unconstitutional *vel non* but would interpret the statute so that it can be applied in accordance with the principles set forth by the United States Supreme Court in *Bellotti v. Baird,* 443 U.S. 622 (1979). In that decision, the United States Supreme Court approved this type of statute and stated: "[T]he [judicial alternative] procedure must ensure that the provision requiring parental consent does not in fact amount to the 'absolute, and possibly arbitrary, veto' that was found impermissible in *Danforth,*" *id.* at 644 (citation omitted), but must "provide an effective opportunity for an abortion to be obtained." *Id.*

As previously noted, the United States Supreme Court had clearly established the principles by which the constitutionality of this type of parental consent legislation must be judged before the legislature enacted section 390.001(4)(a). I believe that the legislature intended this statute to be constitutional within those principles. I find that the statute can be interpreted to ensure that parental consent does not amount to an absolute veto and this Court can adopt procedures to provide minors with effective opportunities to obtain abortions. Further, I conclude that the majority has abdicated its responsibility by not so construing the statute, thus leaving the legislature with the problem of redrafting a constitutional statute.

GRIMES, Justice, concurring in part, dissenting in part.

The United States Constitution does not explicitly refer to the right of privacy. However, in *Roe v. Wade,* 410 U.S. 113 (1973), the United States Supreme Court construed the due process clause of the fourteenth amendment to provide a right of privacy with respect to a woman's decision to have an abortion. In several subsequent decisions, the United States Supreme Court has delineated the extent to which the state may qualify or otherwise burden a woman's right to have an abortion.

In 1980, the Florida Constitution was amended to specifically guarantee persons the right to privacy. As a consequence, it was thereafter unnecessary to read a right of privacy into the due process provision of Florida's equivalent to the fourteenth amendment. However, this did not mean that Florida voters had elected to create more privacy rights concerning abortion than those already guaranteed by the United States Supreme Court. By 1980, abortion rights were well established under the federal Constitution, and I believe the privacy amendment had the practical effect of guaranteeing these same rights under the Florida Constitution. If the United States Supreme Court were to subsequently recede from *Roe v. Wade,* this would not diminish the abortion rights now provided by the privacy amendment of the Florida Constitution. Consequently, I agree with the analysis contained in parts I and II of the majority opinion, which I read as adopting, for purposes of the Florida Constitution, the qualified right to have an abortion established in *Roe v. Wade.*

In part III, however, the majority opinion interprets the Florida Constitution differently than the United States Supreme Court has interpreted the federal Constitution with respect to a minor's right to an abortion. [T]he United States Supreme Court has consistently recognized that a state statute requiring parental consent to a minor's abortion is constitutional if it provides a judicial alternative in which the consent is obviated if the court finds that the minor is mature enough to make the abortion decision or, in the absence of the requisite maturity, the abortion is in the minor's best interest. *Planned Parenthood Ass'n v. Ashcroft,* 462 U.S. 476 (1983); *Bellotti.*

While purporting to acknowledge the state's interest in protecting minors and in preserving family unity, the majority reaches the conclusion that these interests as reflected in the instant statute must fall in the face of its broad interpretation of the privacy amendment. In effect, the Court has said that the state's interest in regulating abortions is no different with respect to minors than it is with adults. Under this ruling, even immature minors may decide to have an abortion without parental consent. I do not agree with either the majority's broad interpretation of the privacy amendment or its limited view of the state's interest concerning the conduct of minors.

It is this Court's duty to uphold the constitutionality of statutes whenever this can be done consistent with sound legal principles. *Corn v. State,* 332 So.2d 4 (Fla.1976). Clearly, this statute is valid under our federal Constitution as interpreted by the United States Supreme Court. Admittedly, this Court has the authority to give the Florida Constitution a broader interpretation, but there should be a compelling reason for taking such a step.

Notes on Abortion Rights and Privacy Clauses

The Constitutional Struggle Over Minors' Abortion Rights in Florida: After *In re T.W.* invalidated the Florida Legislature's parental *consent* statute governing minors' abortions, the Florida Legislature enacted a parental *notification* statute that was likewise declared unconstitutional by the Florida Supreme Court. *North Florida Women's Health & Counseling Services, Inc. v. State* relied on *T.W.* to hold that the state's stated justifications for mandating parental notification were not sufficiently compelling to satisfy strict scrutiny.[198] In response, the Florida Legislature proposed a constitutional amendment, which was ratified by Florida voters in November 2004, authorizing the state legislature "to require by general law for notification to a parent or guardian of a minor before the termination of a minor's pregnancy," notwithstanding the minor's right of privacy protected by article I, section 23.[199] As a result of this constitutional amendment, *North Florida Women's Health* was effectively overruled and the state legislature was allowed to enact a parental notification statute.

What impact should the frequent resort to constitutional amendments in many states such as Florida have on state constitutional interpretation? In comparison to the United States Constitution, state constitutional amendments are a common occurrence–indeed, California and Arizona alone have combined to amend their state constitutions more than 1,000 times since 1879.[200] Moreover, state constitutional amendments are frequently designed to override a prior (or sometimes prevent a contrary) judicial interpretation, whereas this has happened only a few times at the federal level. The Florida Constitution, for example, has been amended several times since 1982 in response to state constitutional decisions. In addition to article X, section 22 being added to override *North Florida Women's Health*, article I, section 17 was amended in 2002 in several respects to ensure the continued viability of the death penalty in response to concerns that the Florida Supreme Court might invalidate it.[201] In 1982, article I, section 12 of the Florida Constitution was amended to require Florida courts to apply United States Supreme Court decisions to Florida search and seizure issues after the Florida Supreme Court indicated that the state constitution provided additional protections against governmental intrusions.[202] In contrast, the last amendment to the United States Constitution in response to a Supreme Court decision was the Twenty-Sixth Amendment ratified in 1971. Does the more ready availability of constitutional amendment to override state constitutional decisions justify an activist approach to state constitutional interpretation? Or does the relative ease of state constitutional amendment indicate that constitutional change should predominantly be accomplished by the political process rather than the judicial process?

---

[198]866 So. 2d 612, 631-34 (Fla. 2003), *abrogated by constitutional amendment*, FLA. CONST. art. X, § 22.

[199]FLA. CONST. art. X, § 22.

[200]G. ALAN TARR, UNDERSTANDING STATE CONSTITUTIONS 24 (1998).

[201]In *Jones v. State*, 701 So. 2d 76 (Fla. 1997), the Florida Supreme Court held that the state's use of the electric chair did not constitute cruel or unusual punishment under the state constitution, but three judges strongly dissented and even a concurring opinion cautioned that the legislature needed to take some action. Earlier opinions from the court had indicated that the disjunctive phrasing "cruel or unusual punishment" in the state constitution created "arguably a broader constitutional provision." Hale v. State, 630 So. 2d 521, 526 (Fla. 1993); *cf.* Allen v. State, 636 So. 2d 494, 497 n.5 (Fla. 1994). The 2002 constitutional amendments changed the prior constitutional prohibition against "cruel or unusual punishment" to a prohibition against "cruel and unusual punishment," and then an additional clause was inserted mandating that the section be "construed in conformity with decisions of the United States Supreme Court which interpret the prohibition against cruel and unusual punishment provided in the Eighth Amendment to the United States Constitution." FLA. CONST. art. I, § 17. The section was also amended to provide that the "death penalty is an authorized punishment for capital crimes designated by the legislature" and that "[a]ny method of execution shall be allowed, unless prohibited by the United States Constitution." *Id.*

[202]State v. Sarmiento, 397 So. 2d 643 (Fla. 1981) (indicating that undercover officers and informants could not record conversations in a suspect's home despite contrary federal precedent).

***The Continuing Impact of* T.W.**: What is the import of *In re T.W.* today after Florida's 2004 constitutional amendment adding article X, section 22? In other words, does the Florida Constitution provide broader abortion rights in contexts other than parental consent statutes? The answer might be "yes." Despite the United States Supreme Court's retreat from the *Roe v. Wade* trimester framework in *Planned Parenthood of Southeastern Pennsylvania v. Casey*,[203] a Florida appellate court employed strict scrutiny under the state constitution rather than the undue burden standard from *Casey* in reviewing a Florida statute requiring a woman's informed consent before obtaining an abortion.[204]

Even Justice Grimes, who dissented in part in *T.W.*, apparently would agree that strict scrutiny rather than the undue burden test should be applied to abortion regulations infringing on the state constitutional right to privacy. His dissent urged that article I, section 23 of the Florida Constitution "had the practical effect of guaranteeing these same [federal abortion] rights under the Florida Constitution. If the United States Supreme Court were to subsequently recede from *Roe v. Wade*, this would not diminish the abortion rights now provided by the privacy amendment of the Florida Constitution." Thus, although Justice Grimes did not think that the privacy amendment added to abortion rights, he apparently viewed the amendment as adopting prevailing federal autonomy rights at the time of its ratification. Is this an appropriate view? Or is the majority's argument stronger that state autonomy rights must be interpreted as broader in scope than under federal law because "'the people of this state exercised their prerogative and enacted an amendment to the Florida Constitution which expressly and succinctly provides for a strong right of privacy not found in the United States Constitution'"?[205] Or is there yet perhaps another argument that, because the text of the Florida privacy amendment appears predominantly concerned with informational privacy rather than autonomy rights, it should be limited to that specific context?

Abortion Rights in Texas and Other States: Several other states with privacy clauses have also extended additional protections to the right to an abortion under their state constitutions. The California Supreme Court, citing *In re T.W.* as support, held that the legislature's enactment of a parental consent statute violated the state's Privacy Initiative.[206] The Alaska Supreme Court similarly relied on its state privacy guarantee in holding that a parental consent statute was not the least restrictive means of advancing the compelling governmental interests in safeguarding minors and aiding parental responsibilities, as parental notification constituted a less restrictive alternative to accomplish the state's purposes.[207] The Alaska high court decided in another case that the privacy provision

---

[203]505 U.S. 833 (1992).

[204]State v. Presidential Women's Ctr., 707 So. 2d 1145, 1149-50 (Fla. App. 1998). In a subsequent appeal, the appellate court invalidated the statute, but the Florida Supreme Court determined that the statute did not implicate privacy rights any more than any other statute requiring a patient's informed consent before a medical procedure. State v. Presidential Women's Ctr., 884 So. 2d 526 (Fla. App. 2004), *rev'd*, 937 So. 2d 114 (Fla. 2006).

[205]*In re* T.W., 551 So. 2d 1186, 1191-92 (Fla. 1989) (quoting Winfield v. Div. of Pari-Mutual Wagering, 477 So. 2d 544, 548 (Fla. 1985)).

[206]Am. Academy of Pediatrics v. Lungren, 940 P.2d 797, 825-28 (Cal. 1997).

[207]State v. Planned Parenthood of Alaska, 171 P.3d 577, 581-85 (Alaska 2007).

created broader protections for reproductive autonomy, such that a "quasi-public institution" could not decline to perform abortions.[208] Montana's high court likewise determined that the state privacy clause necessitated a heightened strict scrutiny evaluation of legislation infringing on procreative autonomy rights, and that this heightened scrutiny invalidated a state statute requiring pre-viability abortions to be performed by physicians.[209]

But the existence of an explicit privacy clause does not appear to be a prerequisite to affording greater abortion rights. Several states without such clauses have granted broader protection to the right to choose an abortion under their state constitutions.[210] Yet the vast majority of states have avoided the issue and not addressed the scope of abortion rights under their state constitutions.[211]

Texas is among the states not addressing the issue. The Texas Supreme Court noted in *Bell v. Low Income Women of Texas* that it had "never decided whether the Texas Constitution creates privacy rights coextensive with those recognized under the United States Constitution" in the abortion context.[212] Although the court subsequently construed the Texas statutory requirements for a judicial bypass under a parental notification statute in a series of cases, none of these cases addressed any state or federal constitutional issues.[213]

Interpreting Privacy Clauses: If both states that have privacy clauses and states without such provisions have interpreted their state constitutions to provide broader autonomy rights, what is the practical effect of explicit privacy texts? Is it merely that states with privacy clauses are more likely to conclude that their citizens enjoy broader autonomy rights? Or do these privacy clauses predominantly concern only informational privacy? What should be the impact of privacy clauses, and what limitations should a court impose upon itself in interpreting its privacy guarantee?

Ravin v. State, 537 P.2d 494 (Alaska 1975)

RABINOWITZ, Chief Justice.

The constitutionality of Alaska's statute prohibiting possession of marijuana is put in issue in this case. Petitioner Ravin raises two basic claims: first, that there is no

---

[208]Valley Hosp. Ass'n v. Mat-Su Coalition for Choice, 948 P.2d 963, 968-72 (Alaska 1997).

[209]Armstrong v. State, 989 P.2d 364, 375-82 (Mont. 1999).

[210]*See, e.g.*, Planned Parenthood League of Mass., Inc. v. Attorney General, 677 N.E.2d 101, 108 (Mass. 1997) (holding state statute requiring pregnant unmarried minor to either obtain consent of both her parents or a judicial bypass before obtaining abortion violated state constitutional right to abortion); Women of Minn. v. Gomez, 542 N.W.2d 17, 30-31 (Minn. 1995) (interpreting Minnesota Constitution to provide more protection for abortion than that afforded under the Federal Constitution); Planned Parenthood of Middle Tenn. v. Sundquist, 38 S.W.3d 1, 15-17 (Tenn. 2000) (adopting more stringent standard under Tennessee Constitution for reviewing regulations of abortion).

[211]*See, e.g.*, 1 JENNIFER FRIESEN, STATE CONSTITUTIONAL LAW: LITIGATING INDIVIDUAL RIGHTS, CLAIMS AND DEFENSES § 2.05[2] (4th ed. 2006).

[212]95 S.W.3d 253, 265 (Tex. 2002).

[213]*See, e.g.*, *In re* Doe 11, 92 S.W.3d 511, 512 (Tex. 2002); *In re* Doe 2, 19 S.W.3d 278, 284 (Tex. 2000).

legitimate state interest in prohibiting possession of marijuana by adults for personal use, in view of the right to privacy; and secondly, that the statutory classification of marijuana as a dangerous drug, while use of alcohol and tobacco is not prohibited, denies him due process and equal protection of law.

We first address petitioner's contentions that his constitutionally protected right to privacy compels the conclusion that the State of Alaska is prohibited from penalizing the private possession and use of marijuana. Ravin's basic thesis is that there exists under the federal and Alaska constitutions a fundamental right to privacy, the scope of which is sufficiently broad to encompass and protect the possession of marijuana for personal use. Given this fundamental constitutional right, the State would then have the burden of demonstrating a compelling state interest in prohibiting possession of marijuana.

We have previously stated the tests to be applied when a claim is made that state action encroaches upon an individual's constitutional rights. In Breese v. Smith, 501 P.2d 159 (Alaska 1972), we had before us a school hairlength regulation which encroached on what we determined to be the individual's fundamental right to determine his own personal appearance. There we stated:

> Once a fundamental right under the constitution of Alaska has been shown to be involved and it has been further shown that this constitutionally protected right has been impaired by governmental action, then the government must come forward and meet its substantial burden of establishing that the abridgement in question was justified by a compelling governmental interest.

When, on the other hand, governmental action interferes with an individual's freedom in an area which is not characterized as fundamental, a less stringent test is ordinarily applied. In such cases our task is to determine whether the legislative enactment has a reasonable relationship to a legitimate governmental purpose. Under this latter test, which is sometimes referred to as the 'rational basis' test, the State need only demonstrate the existence of facts which can serve as a rational basis for belief that the measure would properly serve the public interest.

In our recent opinion in Lynden Transport, Inc. v. State, 532 P.2d 700 (Alaska 1975), we recognized the existence of considerable dissatisfaction with the fundamental right-compelling state interest test. There we said:

> It has been suggested that there is mounting discontent with the rigid two-tier formulation of the equal protection doctrine, and that the United States Supreme Court is prepared to use the clause more rigorously to invalidate legislation without expansion of 'fundamental rights' or 'suspect' categories and the concomitant resort to the 'strict scrutiny' tests. We are in agreement with the view that the Supreme Court's recent equal protection decisions have shown a tendency towards less speculative, less deferential, more intensified means-to-end inquiry when it is applying the traditional rational basis test and we approve of this development.

This court has previously applied a test different from the rigid two-tier formulation to state regulations. In State v. Wylie, [515 P.2d 142 (Alaska 1973)], we tested durational residency requirements for state employment by both the compelling state interest test and a test which examined whether the means chosen suitably furthered an appropriate governmental interest. It is appropriate in this case to resolve Ravin's privacy claims by determining whether there is a proper governmental interest in imposing restrictions on marijuana use and whether the means chosen bear a substantial relationship to the legislative purpose. If governmental restrictions interfere with the individual's right to privacy, we will require that the relationship between means and ends be not merely reasonable but close and substantial.

Thus, our undertaking is two-fold: we must first determine the nature of Ravin's rights, if any, abridged by AS 17.12.010, and, if any rights have been infringed upon, then resolve the further question as to whether the statutory impingement is justified.

In Alaska this court has dealt with the concept of privacy on only a few occasions. One of the most significant decisions in this area is Breese v. Smith, where we considered the applicability of the guarantee of 'life, liberty, the pursuit of happiness' found in the Alaska Constitution, to a school hairlength regulation. Noting that hairstyles are a highly personal matter in which the individual is traditionally autonomous, we concluded that governmental control of personal appearance would be antithetical to the concept of personal liberty under Alaska's constitution. Since the student would be forced to choose between controlling his own personal appearance and asserting his right to an education if the regulations were upheld, we concluded that the constitutional language quoted above embodied an affirmative grant of liberty to public school students to choose their own hairstyles, for "at the core of (the concept of liberty) is the notion of total personal immunity from government control: the right 'to be let alone.'" That right is not absolute, however; we also noted that this 'liberty' must yield where it 'intrude(s) upon the freedom of others.'

Subsequent to our decision in Breese, a right to privacy amendment was added to the Alaska Constitution. Article I, section 22 reads:

> The right of the people to privacy is recognized and shall not be infringed.
> The legislature shall implement this section.

The effect of this amendment is to place privacy among the specifically enumerated rights in Alaska's constitution. But this fact alone does not, in and of itself, yield answers concerning what scope should be accorded to this right of privacy. We have suggested that the right to privacy may afford less than absolute protection to 'the ingestion of food, beverages or other substances'. For any such protection must be limited by the legitimate needs of the State to protect the health and welfare of its citizens.

Assuming this court were to continue to utilize the fundamental right-compelling state interest test in resolving privacy issues under article I, section 22 of Alaska's constitution, we would conclude that there is not a fundamental constitutional right to possess or ingest marijuana in Alaska. For in our view, the right to privacy amendment to the Alaska Constitution cannot be read so as to make the possession or ingestion of marijuana itself a fundamental right. Nor can we conclude that such a fundamental right is shown by virtue of the analysis we employed in Breese. In that case, the student's traditional liberty pertaining to autonomy in personal appearance was threatened in such a way that his constitutionally guaranteed right to an education was jeopardized. Hairstyle, as emphasized in Breese, is a highly personal matter involving the individual and his body. In this sense this aspect of liberty-privacy is akin to the significantly personal areas at stake in Griswold and Eisenstadt v. Baird. Few would believe they have been deprived of something of critical importance if deprived of marijuana, though they would if stripped of control over their personal appearance. And, as mentioned previously, a discrete federal right of privacy separate from the penumbras of specifically enumerated constitutional rights has not as yet been articulated by the Supreme Court of the United States. Therefore, if we were employing our former test, we would hold that there is no fundamental right, either under the Alaska or federal constitutions, either to possess or ingest marijuana.

This leads us to a more detailed examination of the right to privacy and the relevancy of where the right is exercised. At one end of the scale of the scope of the right to privacy is possession or ingestion in the individual's home. If there is any area of human activity to which a right to privacy pertains more than any other, it is the home. The importance of the home has been amply demonstrated in constitutional law. Among the enumerated rights in the federal Bill of Rights are the guarantee against quartering of troops in a private house in peacetime (Third Amendment) and the right to be 'secure in their . . . houses . . . against unreasonable searches and seizures . . .' (Fourth Amendment). The First Amendment has been held to protect the right to 'privacy and freedom of association in the home.' The Fifth Amendment has been described as providing protection against all governmental invasions 'of the sanctity of a man's home and the privacies of life.' The protection of the right to receive birth control information in Griswold was predicated on the sanctity of the marriage relationship and the harm to this fundamental area of privacy if police were allowed to 'search the sacred precincts of marital bedrooms.' And in Stanley v. Georgia, the Court emphasized the home as the situs of protected 'private activities'. The right to receive information and ideas was found in Stanley to take on an added dimension precisely because it was a prosecution for possession in the home: 'For also fundamental is the right to be free, except in very limited circumstances, from unwanted governmental intrusions into one's privacy.' In a later case, the Supreme Court noted that Stanley was not based on the notion that the obscene matter was itself protected by a constitutional penumbra of privacy, but rather was a "reaffirmation that 'a man's home is his castle.'" At the same time the Court noted, 'the Constitution extends special safeguards to the privacy of the home, just as it protects other special privacy rights such as those of marriage, procreation, motherhood, child rearing, and education.' And as the Supreme Court pointed out, there exists a 'myriad' of activities which may be lawfully conducted within the privacy and confines of the home, but may be prohibited in public.

In Alaska we have also recognized the distinctive nature of the home as a place where the individual's privacy receives special protection. This court has consistently recognized that the home is constitutionally protected from unreasonable searches and seizures, reasoning that the home itself retains a protected status under the Fourth Amendment and Alaska's constitution distinct from that of the occupant's person. The privacy amendment to the Alaska Constitution was intended to give recognition and protection to the home. Such a reading is consonant with the character of life in Alaska. Our territory and now state has traditionally been the home of people who prize their individuality and who have chosen to settle or to continue living here in order to achieve a measure of control over their own lifestyles which is now virtually unattainable in many of our sister states.

The home, then, carries with it associations and meanings which make it particularly important as the situs of privacy. Privacy in the home is a fundamental right, under both the federal and Alaska constitutions. We do not mean by this that a person may do anything at anytime as long as the activity takes place within a person's home. There are two important limitations on this facet of the right to privacy. First, we agree with the Supreme Court of the United States, which has strictly limited the Stanley guarantee to possession for purely private, noncommercial use in the home. And secondly, we think this right must yield when it interferes in a serious manner with the health, safety, rights and privileges of others or with the public welfare. No one has an absolute right to do things in the privacy of his own home which will affect himself or others adversely. Indeed, one aspect of a private matter is that it is private, that is, that it does not adversely affect persons beyond the actor, and hence is none of their business. When a matter does affect the public, directly or indirectly, it loses its wholly private character, and can be made to yield when an appropriate public need is demonstrated.

Thus, we conclude that citizens of the State of Alaska have a basic right to privacy in their homes under Alaska's constitution. This right to privacy would encompass the possession and ingestion of substances such as marijuana in a purely personal, non-commercial context in the home unless the state can meet its substantial burden and show that proscription of possession of marijuana in the home is supportable by achievement of a legitimate state interest.

This leads us to the second facet of our inquiry, namely, whether the State has demonstrated sufficient justification for the prohibition of possession of marijuana in general in the interest of public welfare; and further, whether the State has met the greater burden of showing a close and substantial relationship between the public welfare and control of ingestion or possession of marijuana in the home for personal use.

The evidence which was presented at the hearing before the district court consisted primarily of several expert witnesses familiar with various medical and social aspects of marijuana use. Numerous written reports and books were also introduced into evidence. The State relies upon a number of medical researchers who have raised questions as to the substance's effect on the body's immune system, on chromosomal structure, and on the functioning of the brain. On the other hand, in almost every instance of reports of potential danger arising from marijuana use, reports can be found reaching contradictory results. It appears that there is no firm evidence that marijuana, as presently used in this country, is generally a danger to the user or to others. But neither is there conclusive evidence to the effect that it is harmless. The one significant risk in use of marijuana which we do find established to a reasonable degree of certainty is the effect of marijuana intoxication on driving.

Possibly implicit in the State's catalogue of possible dangers of marijuana use is the assumption that the State has the authority to protect the individual from his own folly, that is, that the State can control activities which present no harm to anyone except those enjoying them. Although some courts have found the 'public interest' to be broad enough to justify protecting the individual against himself, most have found inherent limitations on the police power of the state. The state cannot impose its own notions of morality, propriety, or fashion on individuals when the public has no legitimate interest in the affairs of those individuals. The right of the individual to do as he pleases is not absolute, of course: it can be made to yield when it begins to infringe on the rights and welfare of others.

Further, the authority of the state to control the activities of its citizens is not limited to activities which have a present and immediate impact on the public health or welfare. It is conceivable, for example, that a drug could so seriously develop in its user a withdrawal or a motivational syndrome, that widespread use of the drug could significantly debilitate the fabric of our society. Faced with a substantial possibility of such a result, the state could take measures to combat the possibility. The state is under no obligation to allow otherwise 'private' activity which will result in numbers of people becoming public charges or otherwise burdening the public welfare. But we do not find that such a situation exists today regarding marijuana. It appears that effects of marijuana on the individual are not serious enough to justify widespread concern, at least as compared with the far more dangerous effects of alcohol, barbiturates and amphetamines. Moreover, the current patterns of use in the United States are not such as would warrant concern that in the future consumption patterns are likely to change.

But one way in which use of marijuana most clearly does affect the general public is in regard to its effect on driving. All of which brings us to the opposite (from the home) end of the scale of the right to privacy in the context of ingestion or possession of marijuana, namely, when the individual is operating a motor vehicle. Recent research has produced increasing evidence of significant impairment of the driving ability of persons under the influence of cannabis.

In view of the foregoing, we believe that at present, the need for control of drivers under the influence of marijuana and the existing doubts as to the safety of marijuana, demonstrate a sufficient justification for the prohibition found in AS 17.12.010 as an exercise of the state's police power for the public welfare. Given the evidence of the effect of marijuana on driving an individual's right to possess or ingest marijuana while driving would be subject to the prohibition provided for in AS 17.12.010. However, given the relative insignificance of marijuana consumption as a health problem in our society at present, we do not believe that the potential harm generated by drivers under the influence of marijuana, standing alone, creates a close and substantial relationship between the public welfare and control of ingestion of marijuana or possession of it in the home for personal use. Thus we conclude that no adequate justification for the state's intrusion into the citizen's right to privacy by its prohibition of possession of marijuana by an adult for personal consumption in the home has been shown. The privacy of the individual's home cannot be breached absent a persuasive showing of a close and substantial relationship of the intrusion to a legitimate governmental interest. Here, mere scientific doubts will not suffice. The state must demonstrate a need based on proof that the public health or welfare will in fact suffer if the controls are not applied.

The state has a legitimate concern with avoiding the spread of marijuana use to adolescents who may not be equipped with the maturity to handle the experience prudently, as well as a legitimate concern with the problem of driving under the influence of marijuana. Yet these interests are insufficient to justify intrusions into the rights of adults in the privacy of their own homes. Further, neither the federal or Alaska constitution affords protection for the buying or selling of marijuana, nor absolute protection for its use or possession in public. Possession at home of amounts of marijuana indicative of intent to sell rather than possession for personal use is likewise unprotected.

The record does not disclose any facts as to the situs of Ravin's arrest and his alleged possession of marijuana. In view of these circumstances, we hold that the matter must be remanded to the district court for the purpose of developing the facts concerning Ravin's arrest and circumstances of his possession of marijuana. Once this is accomplished, the district court is to consider Ravin's motion to dismiss in conformity with this opinion.

Notes on Privacy and Unique State Values

Ravin*'s Scope and the Rest of the Story*: What right does the *Ravin* court protect? How far does this right extend? Does it offer any protection for an Alaskan citizen to purchase, grow, or otherwise obtain marijuana? Subsequent Alaskan decisions confirm that *Ravin* is confined to the possession of marijuana for personal use in the home or other private place; *Ravin* has not been extended to encompass other situations or other types of banned substances.[214]

In response to *Ravin*, the Alaska Legislature rewrote state law regarding possession of marijuana. The law as amended in 1982 precluded possession of more than four ounces of marijuana, even in a private place, on the basis that this quantity indicated an intent to sell rather than being merely for personal use.[215] Yet there was no punishment for the possession of four ounces or less of marijuana in private.

Subsequently, however, Alaskan voters passed an initiative to again criminalize all use and possession of marijuana, and the governing statute was therefore amended in 1990 in conformity with the initiative to prohibit all possession of marijuana.[216] The Alaska Supreme Court never addressed the conflict between *Ravin* and the 1990 amendments to the statute.[217] However, an Alaskan appellate court held that the new statute was unconstitutional under *Ravin* to the extent that it criminalized the possession of less than four ounces of marijuana in one's home.[218]

This did not defer the state's legislature from trying again in 2006 to re-criminalize possession of small amounts of marijuana by adults in the privacy of their homes in House Bill 149. The legislature included in the bill a set of findings intended to prove that

---

[214]*See, e.g.*, State v. Erickson, 574 P.2d 1 (Alaska 1978) (state constitutional right of privacy does not extend to possession of cocaine); Belgrade v. State, 543 P.2d 206 (Alaska 1975) (no privacy right for possession of marijuana in a public place).

[215]*See* Ch. 45, § 2, SLA 1982.

[216]A.S. 11.71.060.

[217]*See* Brown v. Ely, 14 P.3d 257, 260 (Alaska 2000).

[218]Noy v. State, 83 P.3d 538, 543, *reh'g denied*, 83 P.3d 545 (Alaska App. 2003).

marijuana has increased in potency since the decision in *Ravin* and has therefore become more dangerous. The ACLU immediately sued to invalidate the new law, but the Alaska Supreme Court dismissed the ACLU's pre-enforcement challenge on ripeness grounds, reasoning that the risk of enforcement of *federal* laws outlawing possession of marijuana curtailed any hardship from the presence of the *state* law.[219] As a result, the 2006 statute can only be challenged in court by an adult arrested by the state for possession of marijuana for personal use in the home or other similar private place.

Does this struggle between the Alaskan courts on one side and the legislature, governor, and the citizen initiative process on the other side indicate a disagreement regarding the balance struck in *Ravin*? Does this struggle undercut *Ravin*'s view of Alaska as the home of people who prize a libertarian view of individuality?

Why hasn't the legislature simply attempted to amend the Alaska Constitution to overturn the *Ravin* decision? The Alaska Constitution is not particularly hard to amend, requiring a two-thirds vote in each house of the legislature and a majority vote of the electorate.[220] Yet the failure to attempt to amend the constitution may reflect a concern regarding whether enough support exists for a constitutional amendment.

Contrary Federal Drug Laws: Isn't any constitutional right of privacy under the Alaska Constitution to possess and ingest marijuana for personal use not enforceable against federal drug laws under the Supremacy Clause? The Controlled Substances Act, 21 U.S.C. § 844, makes possession of marijuana a federal crime. In *Gonzales v. Raich*, the United States Supreme Court upheld the power of Congress to prohibit the local cultivation and use of marijuana under the Controlled Substances Act even when it is authorized by state law.[221] Do *Ravin* and its progeny have any practical import at all, then? Does it just mean that a state law enforcement officer cannot charge an Alaskan with a state crime for possessing a small amount of marijuana in the home? Or is there a larger significance in the Alaska judiciary's declaration of resistance to the wide scope of the national war on drugs?

Unique State Identity: The Alaska Supreme Court relied heavily in *Ravin* on the claimed unique attributes and characteristics of Alaskan citizens. However, Professor James Gardner, in a well-known critique of prevailing state constitutional jurisprudence, contended that "Americans are now a people who are so alike from state to state, and whose identity is so much associated with national values and institutions, that the notion of significant local variations in character and identity is just too implausible to take seriously as the basis for a distinct constitutional discourse."[222] Based on *Ravin*, would the Alaska Supreme Court agree with Professor Gardner? Does the fact that other state supreme courts, even those with privacy clauses, rejected any constitutional protection for marijuana possession in the

---

[219] State v. ACLU of Alaska, 204 P.3d 364, 369 (Alaska 2009).

[220] ALASKA CONST. art. XIII, § 1.

[221] 545 U.S. 1, 31-33 (2005).

[222] James A. Gardner, *The Failed Discourse of State Constitutionalism*, 90 MICH. L. REV. 761, 818 (1992).

privacy of the home lend some support to the individualistic nature of Alaska?[223] On the other hand, does the initiative later passed by Alaskan citizens offer support for Professor Gardner's views? In reality, how much difference is there between the citizens of different states? Do the same-sex marriage decisions offer further insight on this question?

2. Same-Sex Marriage

A highly publicized legal controversy arising under state constitutions is whether same-sex couples have or should have the right to marry on the same terms as opposite-sex couples. In 1993, the Hawaii Supreme Court became the first state high court to address this issue under its state charter. Although the court held that the Hawaii privacy clause did not provide a right for same-sex couples to marry, a plurality concluded that the statutory reservation of marriage to opposite-sex couples was a sex-based classification that could only be sustained if the statute was narrowly drawn to serve a compelling state interest.[224] The court then remanded the case for further proceedings, and, on remand, the trial court declared that the opposite-sex limitation on marriage did not satisfy the strict scrutiny standard for sex-based classifications. Before the case could be appealed again to the state supreme court, Hawaii citizens mooted the controversy through a constitutional amendment granting the state legislature "the power to reserve marriage to opposite-sex couples."[225] About the same time, Alaska also adopted a state constitutional amendment providing that "a marriage may exist only between one man and one woman," thereby similarly mooting a pending state constitutional challenge.[226]

In 1999, the Vermont Supreme Court held that the denial of the benefits incident to marriage to same-sex partners violated the "common benefits" provision of the Vermont Constitution (the state analogue to the Federal Equal Protection Clause), but that this violation could be cured by enacting a statute authorizing civil unions,[227] which the state legislature subsequently passed.[228] However, no other state constitutional challenge to the limitation of marriage to opposite-sex couples had been successful until the following decision in Massachusetts.[229]

---

[223] *See, e.g.*, Nat'l Org. for Reform of Marijuana Laws v. Gain, 161 Cal. Rptr. 181, 184 (Cal. App. 1979); Laird v. State, 342 So. 2d 962, 963-65 (Fla. 1977); State v. Mallan, 950 P.2d 178, 188 (Haw. 1998).

[224] Baehr v. Lewin, 852 P.2d 44, 56-66 (Levinson, J., plurality op.), *reconsideration & clarification granted in part*, 875 P.2d 74 (Haw. 1993).

[225] HAW. CONST. art. I, § 23.

[226] ALASKA CONST. art. I, § 25. An Alaskan superior court had held that choosing a marital partner is a fundamental right that cannot be denied without a compelling reason. Brause v. Bureau of Vital Statistics, No. 3AN-95-6562 CI, 1998 WL 88743, at *5-6 (Alaska Super. Ct. Feb. 27, 1998).

[227] Baker v. State, 744 A.2d 864, 886-87 (Vt. 1999).

[228] VT. STAT. tit. 15, §§ 1201-07.

[229] *See, e.g.*, Dean v. Dist. of Columbia, 653 A.2d 307 (D.C. 1995); Baker v. Nelson, 191 N.W.2d 185 (Minn. 1971), *appeal dism'd for want of a substantial federal question*, 409 U.S. 810 (1972).

Goodridge v. Department of Public Health, 798 N.E.2d 941 (Mass. 2003)

MARSHALL, C.J.

Marriage is a vital social institution. The exclusive commitment of two individuals to each other nurtures love and mutual support; it brings stability to our society. For those who choose to marry, and for their children, marriage provides an abundance of legal, financial, and social benefits. In return it imposes weighty legal, financial, and social obligations. The question before us is whether, consistent with the Massachusetts Constitution, the Commonwealth may deny the protections, benefits, and obligations conferred by civil marriage to two individuals of the same sex who wish to marry. We conclude that it may not. The Massachusetts Constitution affirms the dignity and equality of all individuals. It forbids the creation of second-class citizens.

We are mindful that our decision marks a change in the history of our marriage law. Many people hold deep-seated religious, moral, and ethical convictions that marriage should be limited to the union of one man and one woman, and that homosexual conduct is immoral. Many hold equally strong religious, moral, and ethical convictions that same-sex couples are entitled to be married, and that homosexual persons should be treated no differently than their heterosexual neighbors. Neither view answers the question before us. Our concern is with the Massachusetts Constitution as a charter of governance for every person properly within its reach. "Our obligation is to define the liberty of all, not to mandate our own moral code." *Lawrence v. Texas,* 539 U.S. 558 (2003).

Whether the Commonwealth may use its formidable regulatory authority to bar same-sex couples from civil marriage is a question not previously addressed by a Massachusetts appellate court. It is a question the United States Supreme Court left open as a matter of Federal law in *Lawrence,* where it was not an issue. The Massachusetts Constitution is, if anything, more protective of individual liberty and equality than the Federal Constitution; it may demand broader protection for fundamental rights; and it is less tolerant of government intrusion into the protected spheres of private life.

I

The plaintiffs are fourteen individuals from five Massachusetts counties. The plaintiffs include business executives, lawyers, an investment banker, educators, therapists, and a computer engineer. Many are active in church, community, and school groups. They have employed such legal means as are available to them–for example, joint adoption, powers of attorney, and joint ownership of real property–to secure aspects of their relationships. Each plaintiff attests a desire to marry his or her partner in order to affirm publicly their commitment to each other and to secure the legal protections and benefits afforded to married couples and their children.

On April 11, 2001, the plaintiffs filed suit in the Superior Court against the department and the commissioner seeking a judgment that "the exclusion of the [p]laintiff couples and other qualified same-sex couples from access to marriage licenses, and the legal and social status of civil marriage, as well as the protections, benefits and obligations of marriage, violates Massachusetts law." The department, represented by the Attorney General, admitted to a policy and practice of denying marriage licenses to same-sex couples.

It denied that its actions violated any law or that the plaintiffs were entitled to relief. The parties filed cross motions for summary judgment. A Superior Court judge ruled for the department. After the complaint was dismissed and summary judgment entered for the defendants, the plaintiffs appealed.

II

General Laws c. 207 is both a gatekeeping and a public records statute. It sets minimum qualifications for obtaining a marriage license and directs city and town clerks, the registrar, and the department to keep and maintain certain "vital records" of civil marriages. The gatekeeping provisions of G.L. c. 207 are minimal. They forbid marriage of individuals within certain degrees of consanguinity, §§ 1 and 2, and polygamous marriages. See G.L. c. 207, § 4. They prohibit marriage if one of the parties has communicable syphilis, see G.L. c. 207, § 28A, and restrict the circumstances in which a person under eighteen years of age may marry. See G.L. c. 207, §§ 7, 25, and 27. The statute requires that civil marriage be solemnized only by those so authorized.

The record-keeping provisions of G.L. c. 207 are more extensive. Marriage applicants file standard information forms and a medical certificate in any Massachusetts city or town clerk's office and tender a filing fee. G.L. c. 207, §§ 19-20, 28A. The clerk issues the marriage license, and when the marriage is solemnized, the individual authorized to solemnize the marriage adds additional information to the form and returns it (or a copy) to the clerk's office. G.L. c. 207, §§ 28, 30, 38-40 (this completed form is commonly known as the "marriage certificate"). The clerk sends a copy of the information to the registrar, and that information becomes a public record.

In short, for all the joy and solemnity that normally attend a marriage, G.L. c. 207, governing entrance to marriage, is a licensing law. The plaintiffs argue that because nothing in that licensing law specifically prohibits marriages between persons of the same sex, we may interpret the statute to permit "qualified same sex couples" to obtain marriage licenses, thereby avoiding the question whether the law is constitutional.

The everyday meaning of "marriage" is "[t]he legal union of a man and woman as husband and wife," Black's Law Dictionary 986 (7th ed.1999), and the plaintiffs do not argue that the term "marriage" has ever had a different meaning under Massachusetts law. This definition of marriage, as both the department and the Superior Court judge point out, derives from the common law. See *Commonwealth v. Knowlton,* 2 Mass. 530, 535 (1807)(Massachusetts common law derives from English common law except as otherwise altered by Massachusetts statutes and Constitution). Far from being ambiguous, the undefined word "marriage," as used in G.L. c. 207, confirms the General Court's intent to hew to the term's common-law and quotidian meaning concerning the genders of the marriage partners.

III

A

The plaintiffs' claim that the marriage restriction violates the Massachusetts Constitution can be analyzed in two ways. Does it offend the Constitution's guarantees of equality before the law? Or do the liberty and due process provisions of the Massachusetts Constitution secure the plaintiffs' right to marry their chosen partner? In matters implicating marriage, family life, and the upbringing of children, the two constitutional concepts frequently overlap, as they do here. See, e.g., *M.L.B. v. S.L.J.,* 519 U.S. 102 (1996) (noting convergence of due process and equal protection principles in cases concerning parent-child relationships). See also *Lawrence, supra* ("Equality of treatment and the due process right to demand respect for conduct protected by the substantive guarantee of liberty are linked in important respects, and a decision on the latter point advances both interests"). Much of what we say concerning one standard applies to the other.

We begin by considering the nature of civil marriage itself. Simply put, the government creates civil marriage. In Massachusetts, civil marriage is, and since pre-Colonial days has been, precisely what its name implies: a wholly secular institution. See *Commonwealth v. Munson,* 127 Mass. 459, 460-466 (1879). No religious ceremony has ever been required to validate a Massachusetts marriage. *Id.*

Civil marriage is created and regulated through exercise of the police power. See *Commonwealth v. Stowell,* 389 Mass. 171, 175, 449 N.E.2d 357 (1983) (regulation of marriage is properly within the scope of the police power). "Police power" (now more commonly termed the State's regulatory authority) is an old-fashioned term for the Commonwealth's lawmaking authority, as bounded by the liberty and equality guarantees of the Massachusetts Constitution and its express delegation of power from the people to their government. In broad terms, it is the Legislature's power to enact rules to regulate conduct, to the extent that such laws are "necessary to secure the health, safety, good order, comfort, or general welfare of the community" (citations omitted). *Opinion of the Justices,* 341 Mass. 760, 785, 168 N.E.2d 858 (1960).

Without question, civil marriage enhances the "welfare of the community." It is a "social institution of the highest importance." Civil marriage anchors an ordered society by encouraging stable relationships over transient ones. It is central to the way the Commonwealth identifies individuals, provides for the orderly distribution of property, ensures that children and adults are cared for and supported whenever possible from private rather than public funds, and tracks important epidemiological and demographic data.

The benefits accessible only by way of a marriage license are enormous, touching nearly every aspect of life and death. It is undoubtedly for these concrete reasons, as well as for its intimately personal significance, that civil marriage has long been termed a "civil right." See, e.g., *Loving v. Virginia,* 388 U.S. 1, 12 (1967) ("Marriage is one of the 'basic civil rights of man,' fundamental to our very existence and survival"); *Milford v. Worcester,* 7 Mass. 48, 56 (1810) (referring to "civil rights incident to marriages"). The United States Supreme Court has described the right to marry as "of fundamental importance for all individuals" and as "part of the fundamental 'right of privacy' implicit in the Fourteenth Amendment's Due Process Clause." *Zablocki v. Redhail,* 434 U.S. 374, 384 (1978).

Without the right to marry–or more properly, the right to choose to marry–one is excluded from the full range of human experience and denied full protection of the laws for one's "avowed commitment to an intimate and lasting human relationship." Because civil marriage is central to the lives of individuals and the welfare of the community, our laws assiduously protect the individual's right to marry against undue government incursion. Laws may not "interfere directly and substantially with the right to marry."

Unquestionably, the regulatory power of the Commonwealth over civil marriage is broad, as is the Commonwealth's discretion to award public benefits. See *Commonwealth v. Stowell,* 389 Mass. 171, 175, 449 N.E.2d 357 (1983) (marriage); *Moe v. Secretary of Admin. & Fin.,* 382 Mass. 629, 652, 417 N.E.2d 387 (1981) (Medicaid benefits). Individuals who have the choice to marry each other and nevertheless choose not to may properly be denied the legal benefits of marriage. But that same logic cannot hold for a qualified individual who would marry if she or he only could.

B

For decades, indeed centuries, in much of this country (including Massachusetts) no lawful marriage was possible between white and black Americans. That long history availed not when the Supreme Court of California held in 1948 that a legislative prohibition against interracial marriage violated the due process and equality guarantees of the Fourteenth Amendment, *Perez v. Sharp,* 32 Cal.2d 711, 728, 198 P.2d 17 (1948), or when, nineteen years later, the United States Supreme Court also held that a statutory bar to interracial marriage violated the Fourteenth Amendment, *Loving v. Virginia,* 388 U.S. 1 (1967). As both *Perez* and *Loving* make clear, the right to marry means little if it does not include the right to marry the person of one's choice, subject to appropriate government restrictions in the interests of public health, safety, and welfare. In this case, as in *Perez* and *Loving,* a statute deprives individuals of access to an institution of fundamental legal, personal, and social significance–the institution of marriage–because of a single trait: skin color in *Perez* and *Loving,* sexual orientation here. As it did in *Perez* and *Loving,* history must yield to a more fully developed understanding of the invidious quality of the discrimination.

The Massachusetts Constitution protects matters of personal liberty against government incursion as zealously, and often more so, than does the Federal Constitution, even where both Constitutions employ essentially the same language. See *Planned Parenthood League of Mass., Inc. v. Attorney Gen.,* 424 Mass. 586, 590, 677 N.E.2d 101 (1997); *Corning Glass Works v. Ann & Hope, Inc. of Danvers,* 363 Mass. 409, 416, 294 N.E.2d 354 (1973). That the Massachusetts Constitution is in some instances more protective of individual liberty interests than is the Federal Constitution is not surprising. Fundamental to the vigor of our Federal system of government is that "state courts are absolutely free to interpret state constitutional provisions to accord greater protection to individual rights than do similar provisions of the United States Constitution." *Arizona v. Evans,* 514 U.S. 1, 8 (1995).

The Massachusetts Constitution requires, at a minimum, that the exercise of the State's regulatory authority not be "arbitrary or capricious." *Commonwealth v. Henry's Drywall Co.,* 366 Mass. 539, 542, 320 N.E.2d 911 (1974).[230] Under both the equality and liberty guarantees, regulatory authority must, at very least, serve "a legitimate purpose in a rational way"; a statute must "bear a reasonable relation to a permissible legislative

[230]The Massachusetts Constitution empowers the General Court to enact only those orders, laws, statutes, and ordinances "wholesome and reasonable," that are not "repugnant or contrary" to the Constitution, and that, in the Legislature's judgment, advance the "good and welfare" of the Commonwealth, its government, and all of its subjects. Part II, c. 1, § 1, art. 4.

objective." *Rushworth v. Registrar of Motor Vehicles,* 413 Mass. 265, 270, 596 N.E.2d 340 (1992). Any law failing to satisfy the basic standards of rationality is void.

The department argues that no fundamental right or "suspect" class is at issue here, and rational basis is the appropriate standard of review. For the reasons we explain below, we conclude that the marriage ban does not meet the rational basis test for either due process or equal protection. Because the statute does not survive rational basis review, we do not consider the plaintiffs' arguments that this case merits strict judicial scrutiny.

The department posits three legislative rationales for prohibiting same-sex couples from marrying: (1) providing a "favorable setting for procreation"; (2) ensuring the optimal setting for child rearing, which the department defines as "a two-parent family with one parent of each sex"; and (3) preserving scarce State and private financial resources. We consider each in turn.

The judge in the Superior Court endorsed the first rationale, holding that "the state's interest in regulating marriage is based on the traditional concept that marriage's primary purpose is procreation." This is incorrect. Our laws of civil marriage do not privilege procreative heterosexual intercourse between married people above every other form of adult intimacy and every other means of creating a family. General Laws c. 207 contains no requirement that the applicants for a marriage license attest to their ability or intention to conceive children by coitus. Fertility is not a condition of marriage, nor is it grounds for divorce. People who have never consummated their marriage, and never plan to, may be and stay married. While it is certainly true that many, perhaps most, married couples have children together (assisted or unassisted), it is the exclusive and permanent commitment of the marriage partners to one another, not the begetting of children, that is the sine qua non of civil marriage.

Moreover, the Commonwealth affirmatively facilitates bringing children into a family regardless of whether the intended parent is married or unmarried, whether the child is adopted or born into a family, whether assistive technology was used to conceive the child, and whether the parent or her partner is heterosexual, homosexual, or bisexual. If procreation were a necessary component of civil marriage, our statutes would draw a tighter circle around the permissible bounds of nonmarital child bearing and the creation of families by noncoital means.

The "marriage is procreation" argument singles out the one unbridgeable difference between same-sex and opposite-sex couples, and transforms that difference into the essence of legal marriage. Like "Amendment 2" to the Constitution of Colorado, which effectively denied homosexual persons equality under the law and full access to the political process, the marriage restriction impermissibly "identifies persons by a single trait and then denies them protection across the board." *Romer v. Evans,* 517 U.S. 620, 633 (1996). In so doing, the State's action confers an official stamp of approval on the destructive stereotype that same-sex relationships are inherently unstable and inferior to opposite-sex relationships and are not worthy of respect.

The department's first stated rationale, equating marriage with unassisted heterosexual procreation, shades imperceptibly into its second: that confining marriage to opposite-sex couples ensures that children are raised in the "optimal" setting. Protecting the welfare of children is a paramount State policy. Restricting marriage to opposite-sex couples, however, cannot plausibly further this policy. The "best interests of the child" standard does not turn on a parent's sexual orientation or marital status. See e.g., *Doe v. Doe,* 16 Mass.App.Ct. 499, 503, 452 N.E.2d 293 (1983) (parent's sexual orientation insufficient ground to deny custody of child in divorce action).

The department has offered no evidence that forbidding marriage to people of the same sex will increase the number of couples choosing to enter into opposite-sex marriages in order to have and raise children. There is thus no rational relationship between the marriage statute and the Commonwealth's proffered goal of protecting the "optimal" child rearing unit. Moreover, the department readily concedes that people in same-sex couples may be "excellent" parents. These couples (including four of the plaintiff couples) have children for the reasons others do–to love them, to care for them, to nurture them. But the task of child rearing for same-sex couples is made infinitely harder by their status as outliers to the marriage laws. Excluding same-sex couples from civil marriage will not make children of opposite-sex marriages more secure, but it does prevent children of same-sex couples from enjoying the immeasurable advantages that flow from the assurance of "a stable family structure in which children will be reared, educated, and socialized."

The third rationale advanced by the department is that limiting marriage to opposite-sex couples furthers the Legislature's interest in conserving scarce State and private financial resources. The marriage restriction is rational, it argues, because the General Court logically could assume that same-sex couples are more financially independent than married couples and thus less needy of public marital benefits, such as tax advantages, or private marital benefits, such as employer-financed health plans that include spouses in their coverage.

An absolute statutory ban on same-sex marriage bears no rational relationship to the goal of economy. First, the department's conclusory generalization–that same-sex couples are less financially dependent on each other than opposite-sex couples–ignores that many same-sex couples, such as many of the plaintiffs in this case, have children and other dependents (here, aged parents) in their care. The department does not contend, nor could it, that these dependents are less needy or deserving than the dependents of married couples. Second, Massachusetts marriage laws do not condition receipt of public and private financial benefits to married individuals on a demonstration of financial dependence on each other; the benefits are available to married couples regardless of whether they mingle their finances or actually depend on each other for support.

It has been argued that, due to the State's strong interest in the institution of marriage as a stabilizing social structure, only the Legislature can control and define its boundaries. Accordingly, our elected representatives legitimately may choose to exclude same-sex couples from civil marriage in order to assure all citizens of the Commonwealth that (1) the benefits of our marriage laws are available explicitly to create and support a family setting that is, in the Legislature's view, optimal for child rearing, and (2) the State does not endorse gay and lesbian parenthood as the equivalent of being raised by one's married biological parents. These arguments miss the point. The Massachusetts Constitution requires that legislation meet certain criteria and not extend beyond certain limits. It is the function of courts to determine whether these criteria are met and whether these limits are exceeded. In most instances, these limits are defined by whether a rational basis exists to conclude that legislation will bring about a rational result. The Legislature in the first instance, and the courts in the last instance, must ascertain whether such a rational basis exists.

The history of constitutional law "is the story of the extension of constitutional rights and protections to people once ignored or excluded." *United States v. Virginia,* 518 U.S. 515, 557 (1996) (construing equal protection clause of Fourteenth Amendment to prohibit categorical exclusion of women from public military institute). This statement is as true in the area of civil marriage as in any other area of civil rights. As a public institution and a right of fundamental importance, civil marriage is an evolving paradigm. The common law was exceptionally harsh toward women who became wives: a woman's legal identity all but evaporated into that of her husband. But since at least the middle of the Nineteenth Century, both the courts and the Legislature have acted to ameliorate the harshness of the common-law regime. Alarms about the imminent erosion of the "natural" order of marriage were sounded over the demise of antimiscegenation laws, the expansion of the rights of married women, and the introduction of "no-fault" divorce. Marriage has survived all of these transformations, and we have no doubt that marriage will continue to be a vibrant and revered institution.

We also reject the argument suggested by the department, and elaborated by some amici, that expanding the institution of civil marriage in Massachusetts to include same-sex couples will lead to interstate conflict. We would not presume to dictate how another State should respond to today's decision. But neither should considerations of comity prevent us from according Massachusetts residents the full measure of protection available under the Massachusetts Constitution. The genius of our Federal system is that each State's Constitution has vitality specific to its own traditions, and that, subject to the minimum requirements of the Fourteenth Amendment, each State is free to address difficult issues of individual liberty in the manner its own Constitution demands.

Several amici suggest that prohibiting marriage by same-sex couples reflects community consensus that homosexual conduct is immoral. Yet Massachusetts has a strong affirmative policy of preventing discrimination on the basis of sexual orientation. See G.L. c. 151B (employment, housing, credit, services); G.L. c. 265, § 39 (hate crimes); G.L. c. 272, § 98 (public accommodation); G.L. c. 76, § 5 (public education). See also, e.g., *Commonwealth v. Balthazar,* 366 Mass. 298, 318 N.E.2d 478 (1974)(decriminalization of private consensual adult conduct); *Doe v. Doe,* 16 Mass.App.Ct. 499, 503, 452 N.E.2d 293 (1983)(custody to homosexual parent not per se prohibited).

IV

We construe civil marriage to mean the voluntary union of two persons as spouses, to the exclusion of all others. This reformulation redresses the plaintiffs' constitutional injury and furthers the aim of marriage to promote stable, exclusive relationships. It advances the two legitimate State interests the department has identified: providing a stable setting for child rearing and conserving State resources. It leaves intact the Legislature's broad discretion to regulate marriage.

We declare that barring an individual from the protections, benefits, and obligations of civil marriage solely because that person would marry a person of the same sex violates the Massachusetts Constitution. We vacate the summary judgment for the department. We remand this case to the Superior Court for entry of judgment consistent with this opinion. Entry of judgment shall be stayed for 180 days to permit the Legislature to take such action as it may deem appropriate in light of this opinion.

GREANEY, J. (concurring).

I agree with the result reached by the court, the remedy ordered, and much of the reasoning in the court's opinion. In my view, however, the case is more directly resolved using traditional equal protection analysis.

Article 1 of the Declaration of Rights, as amended by art. 106 of the Amendments to the Massachusetts Constitution, provides:

> All people are born free and equal and have certain natural, essential and unalienable rights; among which may be reckoned the right of enjoying and defending their lives and liberties; that of acquiring, possessing and protecting property; in fine, that of seeking and obtaining their safety and happiness. Equality under the law shall not be denied or abridged because of sex, race, color, creed or national origin.

This provision, even prior to its amendment, guaranteed to all people in the Commonwealth–equally–the enjoyment of rights that are deemed important or fundamental. The withholding of relief from the plaintiffs, who wish to marry, and are otherwise eligible to marry, on the ground that the couples are of the same gender, constitutes a categorical restriction of a fundamental right. The restriction creates a straightforward case of discrimination that disqualifies an entire group of our citizens and their families from participation in an institution of paramount legal and social importance. This is impermissible under art. 1.

Because our marriage statutes intend, and state, the ordinary understanding that marriage under our law consists only of a union between a man and a woman, they create a statutory classification based on the sex of the two people who wish to marry. See *Baehr v. Lewin,* 74 Haw. 530, 564, 852 P.2d 44 (1993) (plurality opinion) (Hawaii marriage statutes created sex-based classification). That the classification is sex based is self-evident. The marriage statutes prohibit some applicants, such as the plaintiffs, from obtaining a marriage license, and that prohibition is based solely on the applicants' gender. As a factual matter, an individual's choice of marital partner is constrained because of his or her own sex. Stated in particular terms, Hillary Goodridge cannot marry Julie Goodridge because she (Hillary) is a woman. Likewise, Gary Chalmers cannot marry Richard Linnell because he (Gary) is a man. Only their gender prevents Hillary and Gary from marrying their chosen partners under the present law.

The equal protection infirmity at work here is strikingly similar to (although, perhaps, more subtle than) the invidious discrimination perpetuated by Virginia's antimiscegenation laws and unveiled in the decision of *Loving v. Virginia, supra.* In its landmark decision striking down Virginia's ban on marriages between Caucasians and members of any other race on both equal protection and substantive due process grounds, the United States Supreme Court soundly rejected the proposition that the equal application of the ban (i.e., that it applied equally to whites and blacks) made unnecessary the strict scrutiny analysis traditionally required of statutes drawing classifications according to race, see *id.* at 8-9, and concluded that "restricting the freedom to marry solely because of racial classifications violates the central meaning of the Equal Protection Clause." *Id.* at 12. That our marriage laws, unlike antimiscegenation laws, were not enacted purposely to discriminate in no way neutralizes their present discriminatory character.

With these two propositions established (the infringement on a fundamental right and a sex-based classification), the enforcement of the marriage statutes as they are currently understood is forbidden by our Constitution unless the State can present a compelling purpose furthered by the statutes that can be accomplished in no other reasonable manner. This the State has not done. The justifications put forth by the State to sustain the statute's exclusion of the plaintiffs are insufficient for the reasons explained by the court.

SPINA, J. (dissenting, with whom Sosman and Cordy, JJ., join).

What is at stake in this case is not the unequal treatment of individuals or whether individual rights have been impermissibly burdened, but the power of the Legislature to effectuate social change without interference from the courts, pursuant to art. 30 of the Massachusetts Declaration of Rights. The power to regulate marriage lies with the Legislature, not with the judiciary. See *Commonwealth v. Stowell,* 389 Mass. 171, 175, 449 N.E.2d 357 (1983). Today, the court has transformed its role as protector of individual rights into the role of creator of rights, and I respectfully dissent.

1. *Equal protection.* Although the court did not address the plaintiffs' gender discrimination claim, G.L. c. 207 does not unconstitutionally discriminate on the basis of gender. A claim of gender discrimination will lie where it is shown that differential treatment disadvantages one sex over the other. See *Attorney Gen. v. Massachusetts Interscholastic Athletic Ass'n,* 378 Mass. 342, 349-352, 393 N.E.2d 284 (1979). General Laws c. 207 enumerates certain qualifications for obtaining a marriage license. It creates no distinction between the sexes, but applies to men and women in precisely the same way. It does not create any disadvantage identified with gender, as both men and women are similarly limited to marrying a person of the opposite sex. See *Commonwealth v. King,* 374 Mass. 5, 15-22, 372 N.E.2d 196 (1977)(law prohibiting prostitution not discriminatory based on gender because of equal application to men and women).

Similarly, the marriage statutes do not discriminate on the basis of sexual orientation. As the court correctly recognizes, constitutional protections are extended to individuals, not couples. The marriage statutes do not disqualify individuals on the basis of sexual orientation from entering into marriage. All individuals, with certain exceptions not relevant here, are free to marry. Whether an individual chooses not to marry because of sexual orientation or any other reason should be of no concern to the court.

The court concludes, however, that G.L. c. 207 unconstitutionally discriminates against the individual plaintiffs because it denies them the "right to marry the person of one's choice" where that person is of the same sex. To reach this result the court relies on *Loving v. Virginia,* 388 U.S. 1, 12 (1967), and transforms "choice" into the essential element of the institution of marriage. The *Loving* case did not use the word "choice" in this manner, and it did not point to the result that the court reaches today.

Unlike the *Loving* and *Sharp* cases, the Massachusetts Legislature has erected no barrier to marriage that intentionally discriminates against anyone. Within the institution of marriage, anyone is free to marry, with certain exceptions that are not challenged. In the absence of any discriminatory purpose, the State's marriage statutes do not violate principles of equal protection. See *Washington v. Davis,* 426 U.S. 229, 240 (1976) ("invidious quality of a law claimed to be . . . discriminatory must ultimately be traced to a . . . discriminatory purpose"); *Dickerson v. Attorney Gen.,* 396 Mass. 740, 743, 488 N.E.2d 757 (1986) (for purpose of equal protection analysis, standard of review under State and Federal Constitutions is identical). This court should not have invoked even the most deferential standard of review within equal protection analysis because no individual was denied access to the institution of marriage.

2. *Due process.* The marriage statutes do not impermissibly burden a right protected by our constitutional guarantee of due process implicit in art. 10 of our Declaration of Rights. There is no restriction on the right of any plaintiff to enter into marriage. Each is free to marry a willing person of the opposite sex. Cf. *Zablocki v. Redhail,* 434 U.S. 374 (1978) (fundamental right to marry impermissibly burdened by statute requiring court approval when subject to child support order).

Although this court did not state that same-sex marriage is a fundamental right worthy of strict scrutiny protection, it nonetheless deemed it a constitutionally protected right by applying rational basis review. Before applying any level of constitutional analysis there must be a recognized right at stake. Same-sex marriage, or the "right to marry the person of one's choice" as the court today defines that right, does not fall within the fundamental right to marry. Same-sex marriage is not "deeply rooted in this Nation's history," and the court does not suggest that it is. Except for the occasional isolated decision in recent years, see, e.g., *Baker v. State,* 170 Vt. 194, 744 A.2d 864 (1999), same-sex marriage is not a right, fundamental or otherwise, recognized in this country. Just one example of the Legislature's refusal to recognize same-sex marriage can be found in a section of the legislation amending G.L. c. 151B to prohibit discrimination in the workplace on the basis of sexual orientation, which states: "Nothing in this act shall be construed so as to legitimize or validate a 'homosexual marriage' . . . ." St.1989, c. 516, § 19. In this Commonwealth and in this country, the roots of the institution of marriage are deeply set in history as a civil union between a single man and a single woman. There is no basis for the court to recognize same-sex marriage as a constitutionally protected right.

3. *Remedy.* The remedy that the court has fashioned both in the name of equal protection and due process exceeds the bounds of judicial restraint mandated by art. 30. The remedy that construes gender-specific language as gender-neutral amounts to a statutory revision that replaces the intent of the Legislature with that of the court. Article 30 permits the court to apply principles of equal protection and to modify statutory language only if legislative intent is preserved. See, e.g., *Commonwealth v. Chou,* 433 Mass. 229, 238-239, 741 N.E.2d 17 (2001) (judicial rewriting of gender language permissible only when

Legislature intended to include both men and women). Here, the alteration of the gender-specific language alters precisely what the Legislature unambiguously intended to preserve, the marital rights of single men and women. Such a dramatic change in social institutions must remain at the behest of the people through the democratic process.

SOSMAN, J. (dissenting, with whom Spina and Cordy, JJ., join).

Although ostensibly applying the rational basis test to the civil marriage statutes, it is abundantly apparent that the court is in fact applying some undefined stricter standard to assess the constitutionality of the marriage statutes' exclusion of same-sex couples. While avoiding any express conclusion as to any of the proffered routes by which that exclusion would be subjected to a test of strict scrutiny–infringement of a fundamental right, discrimination based on gender, or discrimination against gays and lesbians as a suspect classification–the opinion repeatedly alludes to those concepts in a prolonged and eloquent prelude before articulating its view that the exclusion lacks even a rational basis. In short, while claiming to apply a mere rational basis test, the court's opinion works up an enormous head of steam by repeated invocations of avenues by which to subject the statute to strict scrutiny, apparently hoping that that head of steam will generate momentum sufficient to propel the opinion across the yawning chasm of the very deferential rational basis test.

Shorn of these emotion-laden invocations, the opinion ultimately opines that the Legislature is acting irrationally when it grants benefits to a proven successful family structure while denying the same benefits to a recent, perhaps promising, but essentially untested alternate family structure. Placed in a more neutral context, the court would never find any irrationality in such an approach. For example, if the issue were government subsidies and tax benefits promoting use of an established technology for energy efficient heating, the court would find no equal protection or due process violation in the Legislature's decision not to grant the same benefits to an inventor or manufacturer of some new, alternative technology who did not yet have sufficient data to prove that that new technology was just as good as the established technology.

Through the political process, the people may decide when the benefits of extending civil marriage to same-sex couples have been shown to outweigh whatever risks–be they palpable or ephemeral–are involved. However minimal the risks of that redefinition of marriage may seem to us from our vantage point, it is not up to us to decide what risks society must run, and it is inappropriate for us to arrogate that power to ourselves merely because we are confident that "it is the right thing to do."

CORDY, J. (dissenting, with whom Spina and Sosman, JJ., join).

The Massachusetts marriage statute does not impair the exercise of a recognized fundamental right, or discriminate on the basis of sex in violation of the equal rights amendment to the Massachusetts Constitution. Consequently, it is subject to review only to determine whether it satisfies the rational basis test. Because a conceivable rational basis exists upon which the Legislature could conclude that the marriage statute furthers the legitimate State purpose of ensuring, promoting, and supporting an optimal social structure for the bearing and raising of children, it is a valid exercise of the State's police power.

A. *Limiting marriage to the union of one man and one woman does not impair the exercise of a fundamental right.*

Supreme Court cases that have described marriage or the right to marry as "fundamental" have focused primarily on the underlying interest of every individual in procreation, which, historically, could only legally occur within the construct of marriage because sexual intercourse outside of marriage was a criminal act. In *Skinner v. Oklahoma, supra,* the first case to characterize marriage as a "fundamental" right, the Supreme Court stated, as its rationale for striking down a sterilization statute, that "[m]arriage and procreation are fundamental to the very existence of the race." *Id.* at 541. In concluding that a sterilized individual "is forever deprived of a basic liberty," *id.*, the Court was obviously referring to procreation rather than marriage. Similarly, in *Loving v. Virginia, supra,* in which the United States Supreme Court struck down Virginia's antimiscegenation statute, the Court implicitly linked marriage with procreation in describing marriage as "fundamental to our very existence." *Id.* at 12. In *Zablocki v. Redhail, supra,* the Court expressly linked the right to marry with the right to procreate, concluding that "if [the plaintiff's] right to procreate means anything at all, it must imply some right to enter the only relationship in which the State . . . allows sexual relations legally to take place." *Id.* at 386. Once again, in *Turner v. Safley, supra,* striking a State regulation that curtailed the right of an inmate to marry, the Court included among the important attributes of such marriages the "expectation that [the marriage] ultimately will be fully consummated." *Id.* at 96. See *Milford v. Worcester,* 7 Mass. 48, 52 (1810) (purpose of marriage is "to regulate, chasten, and refine, the intercourse between the sexes; and to multiply [and] preserve . . . the species"). Because same-sex couples are unable to procreate on their own, any right to marriage they may possess cannot be based on their interest in procreation, which has been essential to the Supreme Court's denomination of the right to marry as fundamental.

Finally, the constitutionally protected interest in child rearing, recognized in *Meyer v. Nebraska,* 262 U.S. 390, 399 (1923); *Pierce v. Society of Sisters,* 268 U.S. 510, 534-535 (1925); and *Care & Protection of Robert, supra* at 58, 60, 556 N.E.2d 993, is not implicated or infringed by the marriage statute here. The fact that the plaintiffs cannot marry has no bearing on their independently protected constitutional rights as parents which, as with opposite-sex parents, are limited only by their continued fitness and the best interests of their children. *Bezio v. Patenaude,* 381 Mass. 563, 579, 410 N.E.2d 1207 (1980) (courts may not use parent's sexual orientation as reason to deny child custody).

Because the rights and interests discussed above do not afford the plaintiffs any fundamental right that would be impaired by a statute limiting marriage to members of the opposite sex, they have no fundamental right to be declared "married" by the State.

B. *The marriage statute, in limiting marriage to heterosexual couples, does not constitute discrimination on the basis of sex in violation of the Equal Rights Amendment to the Massachusetts Constitution.*

The central purpose of the ERA was to eradicate discrimination against women and in favor of men or vice versa. See *Attorney Gen. v. Massachusetts Interscholastic Athletic Ass'n,* 378 Mass. 342, 357, 393 N.E.2d 284 (1979). Consistent with this purpose, we have construed the ERA to prohibit laws that advantage one sex at the expense of the other, but not laws that treat men and women equally. The Massachusetts marriage statute does not subject men to different treatment from women; each is equally prohibited from precisely the same conduct.

Of course, a statute that on its face treats protected groups equally may still harm, stigmatize, or advantage one over the other. Such was the circumstance in *Loving v. Virginia,* 388 U.S. 1 (1967), where the Supreme Court struck down a State statute that made interracial marriage a crime, as constituting invidious discrimination on the basis of race. While the statute purported to apply equally to whites and nonwhites, the Court found that it was intended and structured to favor one race (white) and disfavor all others (nonwhites). The statute's legislative history demonstrated that its purpose was not merely to punish interracial marriage, but to do so for the sole benefit of the white race.

By contrast, here there is no evidence that limiting marriage to opposite-sex couples was motivated by sexism in general or a desire to disadvantage men or women in particular. Moreover, no one has identified any harm, burden, disadvantage, or advantage accruing to either gender as a consequence of the Massachusetts marriage statute. In the absence of such effect, the statute limiting marriage to couples of the opposite sex does not violate the ERA's prohibition of sex discrimination.

In anticipation of [the ERA's] adoption, the Legislature enacted and, on June 21, 1975, the Governor approved a "Resolve providing for an investigation and study by a special commission relative to the effect of the ratification of the proposed amendments to the Constitution of the Commonwealth of Massachusetts and the Constitution of the United States prohibiting discrimination on account of sex upon the laws, business communities and public in the Commonwealth." Res.1975, c. 26. One of the principal tasks of the commission was to catalog the aspects of the General Laws that would have to be amended for the statutory code to comply with the mandate of the proposed amendment that equality not be abridged on the basis of sex.

On October 19, 1976, just before the general election at which the amendment was to be considered, the commission filed its Interim Report, which focused on the effect of the Massachusetts ERA on the laws of the Commonwealth. A section of the report, entitled "Areas Unaffected by the Equal Rights Amendment," addressed some of the legal regimes that would *not* be affected by the adoption of the ERA. One such area was "Homosexual Marriage," about which the commission stated:

> An equal rights amendment will have no effect upon the allowance or denial of homosexual marriages. The equal rights amendment is not concerned with the relationship of two persons of the same sex; it only addresses those laws or public-related actions which treat persons of opposite sexes differently.

The views of the commission were reflected in the public debate surrounding the passage of the ERA that focused on gender equality. Claims that the ERA might be the basis for validating marriages between same-sex couples were labeled as "exaggerated" and "unfounded."

C. *The marriage statute satisfies the rational basis standard.*

In analyzing whether a statute satisfies the rational basis standard, we look to the nature of the classification embodied in the enactment, then to whether the statute serves a legitimate State purpose, and finally to whether the classification is reasonably related to the furtherance of that purpose. With this framework, we turn to the challenged statute, G.L. c. 207, which authorizes local town officials to issue licenses to couples of the opposite sex authorizing them to enter the institution of civil marriage.

1. *Classification.* The nature of the classification at issue is readily apparent. Opposite-sex couples can obtain a license and same-sex couples cannot. The granting of this license, and the completion of the required solemnization of the marriage, opens the door to many statutory benefits and imposes numerous responsibilities. The fact that the statute does not permit such licenses to be issued to couples of the same sex thus bars them from civil marriage. The classification is not drawn between men and women or between heterosexuals and homosexuals, any of whom can obtain a license to marry a member of the opposite sex; rather, it is drawn between same-sex couples and opposite-sex couples.

2. *State purpose.* The court's opinion concedes that the civil marriage statute serves legitimate State purposes, but further investigation and elaboration of those purposes is both helpful and necessary.

Civil marriage is the institutional mechanism by which societies have sanctioned and recognized particular family structures, and the institution of marriage has existed as one of the fundamental organizing principles of human society. Marriage has not been merely a contractual arrangement for legally defining the private relationship between two individuals (although that is certainly part of any marriage). Rather, on an institutional level, marriage is the "very basis of the whole fabric of civilized society," J.P. Bishop, Commentaries on the Law of Marriage and Divorce, and Evidence in Matrimonial Suits § 32 (1852), and it serves many important political, economic, social, educational, procreational, and personal functions.

Paramount among its many important functions, the institution of marriage has systematically provided for the regulation of heterosexual behavior, brought order to the resulting procreation, and ensured a stable family structure in which children will be reared, educated, and socialized. See *Milford v. Worcester,* 7 Mass. 48, 52 (1810) (civil marriage "intended to regulate, chasten, and refine, the intercourse between the sexes; and to multiply, preserve, and improve the species"). Admittedly, heterosexual intercourse, procreation, and child care are not necessarily conjoined (particularly in the modern age of widespread effective contraception and supportive social welfare programs), but an orderly society requires some mechanism for coping with the fact that sexual intercourse commonly results in pregnancy and childbirth. The institution of marriage is that mechanism.

The institution of marriage provides the important legal and normative link between heterosexual intercourse and procreation on the one hand and family responsibilities on the other. The partners in a marriage are expected to engage in exclusive sexual relations, with children the probable result and paternity presumed. See G.L. c. 209C, § 6 ("a man is presumed to be the father of a child . . . if he is or has been married to the mother and the child was born during the marriage, or within three hundred days after the marriage was terminated by death, annulment or divorce").

The marital family is also the foremost setting for the education and socialization of children. Children learn about the world and their place in it primarily from those who raise them, and those children eventually grow up to exert some influence, great or small, positive or negative, on society. The institution of marriage encourages parents to remain committed to each other and to their children as they grow, thereby encouraging a stable venue for the education and socialization of children. More macroscopically, construction of a family through marriage also formalizes the bonds between people in an ordered and institutional manner, thereby facilitating a foundation of interconnectedness and interdependency on which more intricate stabilizing social structures might be built.

It is difficult to imagine a State purpose more important and legitimate than ensuring, promoting, and supporting an optimal social structure within which to bear and raise children. At the very least, the marriage statute continues to serve this important State purpose.

3. *Rational relationship.* The question we must turn to next is whether the statute, construed as limiting marriage to couples of the opposite sex, remains a rational way to further that purpose. We must assume that the Legislature (1) might conclude that the institution of civil marriage has successfully and continually provided this structure over several centuries; (2) might consider and credit studies that document negative consequences that too often follow children either born outside of marriage or raised in households lacking either a father or a mother figure, and scholarly commentary contending that children and families develop best when mothers and fathers are partners in their parenting; and (3) would be familiar with many recent studies that variously support the proposition that children raised in intact families headed by same-sex couples fare as well on many measures as children raised in similar families headed by opposite-sex couples; support the proposition that children of same-sex couples fare worse on some measures; or reveal notable differences between the two groups of children that warrant further study.

Taking all of this available information into account, the Legislature could rationally conclude that a family environment with married opposite-sex parents remains the optimal social structure in which to bear children, and that the raising of children by same-sex couples, who by definition cannot be the two sole biological parents of a child and cannot provide children with a parental authority figure of each gender, presents an alternative structure for child rearing that has not yet proved itself beyond reasonable scientific dispute to be as optimal as the biologically based marriage norm. Working from the assumption that a recognition of same-sex marriages will increase the number of children experiencing this alternative, the Legislature could conceivably conclude that declining to recognize same-sex marriages remains prudent until empirical questions about its impact on the upbringing of children are resolved.

The fact that the Commonwealth currently allows same-sex couples to adopt, does not affect the rationality of this conclusion. The eligibility of a child for adoption presupposes that at least one of the child's biological parents is unable or unwilling, for some reason, to participate in raising the child. In that sense, society has "lost" the optimal setting in which to raise that child–it is simply not available. In these circumstances, the principal and overriding consideration is the "best interests of the child," considering his or her unique circumstances and the options that are available for that child. The objective is an individualized determination of the best environment for a particular child, where the normative social structure–a home with both the child's biological father and mother–is not an option. That such a focused determination may lead to the approval of a same-sex couple's adoption of a child does not mean that it would be irrational for a legislator, in fashioning statutory laws that cannot make such individualized determinations, to conclude generally that being raised by a same-sex couple has not yet been shown to be the absolute equivalent of being raised by one's married biological parents.

There is no question that many same-sex couples are capable of being good parents, and should be (and are) permitted to be so. The policy question that a legislator must resolve is a different one, and turns on an assessment of whether the marriage structure proposed by the plaintiffs will, over time, if endorsed and supported by the State, prove to be as stable and successful a model as the one that has formed a cornerstone of our society since colonial times, or prove to be less than optimal, and result in consequences, perhaps now unforeseen, adverse to the State's legitimate interest in promoting and supporting the best possible social structure in which children should be born and raised. Given the critical importance of civil marriage as an organizing and stabilizing institution of society, it is eminently rational for the Legislature to postpone making fundamental changes to it until such time as there is unanimous scientific evidence, or popular consensus, or both, that such changes can safely be made.

Notes on Same-Sex Unions

Goodridge*'s Reasoning*: Could the Massachusetts Supreme Judicial Court have avoided the constitutional issue in *Goodridge*? Why didn't it do so? In answering this question, it may be helpful to review the plurality's reasoning. First the plurality determined that marriage under Massachusetts statutory law was between a man and a woman as a result of the "common law and quotidian meaning" of marriage. Then, despite a lengthy exposition of the constitutional implications of the marital relationship, the plurality did not address whether strict scrutiny should be applied. Instead, the plurality purported to invalidate the limitation to opposite-sex marriage on the basis that it was not rationally related to the state's claimed interests in procreation and child rearing. Why did the plurality proceed in this manner? Was this the plurality's attempt to initiate a dialogue on the rationales supporting and opposing same-sex marriage?

Should individuals have a fundamental right to marry a spouse of their choice, irrespective of gender? If so, how far should this right extend? So far, all the United States Supreme Court decisions that have recognized marriage as a fundamental right have been predicated at least in part on the procreative aspects of the marital relationship that are necessary for the survival of the human race.[231] Even *Lawrence v. Texas*, which invalidated statutes criminalizing private same-sex sexual conduct, cautioned that it was not requiring

[231] *See, e.g.*, Zablocki v. Redhail, 434 U.S. 374, 386 (1978); Skinner v. Oklahoma, 316 U.S. 535, 541 (1942).

states to affirmatively recognize or provide benefits to same-sex couples.[232] Of course, such federal constitutional law principles do not preclude a state court from establishing a more encompassing fundamental right under its state constitution. The California Supreme Court, for instance, held that its privacy and due process guarantees granted same-sex couples the same fundamental right enjoyed by opposite-sex couples "to choose one's life partner and enter with that person into a committed, officially recognized, and protected family relationship that enjoys all the constitutionally based incidents of marriage."[233] The court reasoned that the fundamental right to marry, while historically limited to opposite-sex couples, should be extended to all persons under the California Constitution, including same-sex couples.[234] Although opponents of same-sex marriage succeeded in amending the California Constitution through California's initiative process to effectively overrule the decision for a time,[235] this constitutional initiative amendment (known as Proposition 8) was later held invalid under the United States Constitution,[236] reinstating the fundamental right of same-sex couples to marry in California.

Is denying marriage to same-sex couples gender discrimination? Justice Greaney opined that it was in his *Goodridge* concurrence. In Texas, the Court of Appeals for the Fourteenth District of Texas, sitting en banc, rejected a similar argument (after it had been accepted by two out of the three justices in a panel decision) in *Lawrence v. State*.[237] In holding that the Texas Penal Code's prohibition against certain sexual acts between members of the same sex did not violate equal protection, the court determined that the statute did not discriminate on the basis of gender. The court reasoned that the statute applied equally to men and women and that the statute was not "intended to promote any hostility between the sexes, preserve any unequal treatment as between men and women, or perpetuate any societal or cultural bias with respect to gender." Most states considering the issue have agreed with this reasoning in holding that same-sex marriage prohibitions do not constitute gender discrimination,[238] although contrary authority exists.[239] Do same-sex marriage bans classify based on gender? Or is the classification based on sexual orientation or some other ground?

Should sexual orientation be considered a suspect or semi-suspect classification for equal protection purposes? The United States Supreme Court in *Lawrence* never articulated that a suspect or semi-suspect classification was at issue, and neither did the Massachusetts

---

[232]539 U.S. 558, 578-79 (2003).

[233]*In re* Marriage Cases, 183 P.3d 384, 433-34 (Cal. 2008).

[234]*Id.* at 429-31.

[235]CAL. CONST. art. I, § 7.5.

[236]*See* Perry v. Schwarzenegger, 704 F. Supp. 2d 921, 1004 (N.D. Cal. 2010), *aff'd sub nom.* Perry v. Brown, 671 F.3d 1052 (9th Cir. 2012), *appeal dism'd sub nom.* Hollingsworth v. Perry, 133 S. Ct. 2652 (2013).

[237]41 S.W.3d 349, 357-58 (Tex. App.–Houston [14th Dist.] 2001), *rev'd on other grounds*, 539 U.S. 558 (2003).

[238]*See, e.g.*, Conaway v. Deane, 932 A.2d 571, 585-99 (Md. 2007); Hernandez v. Robles, 855 N.E.2d 1, 6 (N.Y. 2006) (Smith, J., plurality op.); Baker v. State, 744 A.2d 864, 880-81 n.13 (Vt. 1999); Andersen v. King Cnty., 138 P.3d 963, 987-89 (Wash. 2006) (Madsen, J., plurality op.).

[239]*E.g.*, Baehr v. Lewin, 852 P.2d 44, 56-66 (Levinson, J., plurality op.), *reconsideration and clarification granted in part*, 875 P.2d 74 (Haw. 1993).

Supreme Judicial Court in *Goodridge* (although Justice Greaney's concurrence argued for strict scrutiny). Nevertheless, did the courts in either case apply traditional rational basis review, or did they engage in a more searching inquiry? If a more searching inquiry was applied, was it appropriate to do so?

State high courts in California, Connecticut, and Iowa have held that discrimination on the basis of sexual orientation in marriage violates state equal protection principles.[240] These state supreme courts have all relied on state precedent and state legislative enactments protecting gays and lesbians from specific types of discrimination to conclude that classifications based on sexual orientation are subject to heightened scrutiny under their respective state constitutions. Yet the California decision was later effectively overruled by California voters for a time through an initiative amendment, Proposition 8. Voters also expressed their displeasure in Iowa, where the three Iowa Supreme Court Justices facing a merit retention election shortly after the decision were defeated–the first time Iowa judges lost a retention election since the state moved to the merit selection process in 1962. Do the voters' reactions in California and Iowa indicate that this is an issue better reserved for the political process, especially as a number of states have now adopted same-sex marriage through ordinary political means? Or was judicial intervention a needed catalyst to begin the political process?

Subsequent Developments in Massachusetts: In response to *Goodridge*, the Massachusetts Senate proposed Senate No. 2175, which established a "civil union" procedure for same-sex partners that created "a legal status equivalent to marriage." The Senate requested the Massachusetts Supreme Judicial Court to provide an opinion on the constitutionality of the proposed bill. In *Opinion of the Justices to the Senate*, more fully excerpted in Chapter 3, the court concluded that the proposal for civil unions was likewise unconstitutional. The majority reasoned:

> Segregating same-sex unions from opposite-sex unions cannot possibly be held rationally to advance or "preserve" what we stated in *Goodridge* were the Commonwealth's legitimate interests in procreation, child rearing, and the conservation of resources. Because the proposed law by its express terms forbids same-sex couples entry into civil marriage, it continues to relegate same-sex couples to a different status. The holding in *Goodridge,* by which we are bound, is that group classifications based on unsupportable distinctions, such as that embodied in the proposed bill, are invalid under the Massachusetts Constitution.[241]

The court continued that the bill improperly relegated same-sex marriages to "second-class status" that could not be condoned under the Massachusetts Constitution, even though the

[240]*In re* Marriage Cases, 183 P.3d 384 (Cal. 2008) (applying strict scrutiny to distinctions in state marriage laws between opposite-sex and same-sex couples); Kerrigan v. Comm'r of Pub. Health, 957 A.2d 407 (Conn. 2008) (employing intermediate scrutiny to sexual orientation discrimination in state's ban on same-sex marriages); Varnum v. Brien, 763 N.W.2d 862 (Iowa 2009) (applying intermediate scrutiny to ban on same-sex marriages).

[241]802 N.E.2d 565, 569 (Mass. 2004).

court recognized that same-sex couples would not be entitled to federal marital benefits under the then-valid federal Defense of Marriage Act.[242] The three dissenters opined that it was indeed "rational" for the legislature to employ different terminology for same-sex unions as such unions would have a different status than opposite-sex unions with respect to the benefits afforded at the time by federal law and the laws of other states.[243]

Massachusetts started issuing marriage licenses to same-sex couples in May 2004. Immediately thereafter, opponents of same-sex marriage began attempts to amend the Massachusetts Constitution to halt the practice. The state legislature first considered a state constitutional amendment that would limit "marriage" to persons of the opposite sex while allowing civil unions for same-sex couples. To ratify an amendment to the Massachusetts Constitution initiated by the state legislature, the proposed amendment must be passed in two successive legislative sessions and then the amendment must receive a majority of the popular vote in a statewide election. While the proposed amendment passed in the first legislative session, it failed in the second. Various Massachusetts citizen groups then attempted an alternative amendment mechanism, the initiative process, to ban future single-sex marriages, although without invalidating existing same-sex marriages. The initiative procedure requires certified signatures from more than three percent of the number of voters in the immediately-preceding gubernatorial election, the backing of at least fifty members of the 200-member Legislature in two successive legislative sessions, and then a statewide popular election. The citizen groups successfully cleared the first hurdle, submitting approximately 150,000 certified signatures in support of their amendment. But while the proposed initiative cleared the necessary vote requirement in the first legislative session, it only received forty-five in the second legislative session in June 2007. This rejection killed the prospect of any constitutional amendment regarding same-sex marriage in Massachusetts from becoming effective for a number of years, and same-sex marriage opponents gave up the fight there.

State Constitutional Amendments Defining Marriage in Texas and Other States: Although Massachusetts never amended its constitution, *Goodridge* spurred state constitutional amendments across the nation defining marriage as between a man and a woman. Before *Goodridge*, only three states (Alaska, Nebraska, and Nevada) had amended their state constitutions to prohibit recognizing marriages other than those between one man and one woman.[244] But between the *Goodridge* decision in late 2003 and the end of 2008, twenty-six more states, including Texas, did so, with one more state adopting a similar state constitutional amendment in 2012.[245]

---

[242] *Id.* at 570-71.

[243] *Id.* at 574-75 (Sosman, J., dissenting).

[244] ALASKA CONST. art. I, § 25; NEB. CONST. art. I, § 29; NEV. CONST. art. I, § 21. Nebraska's state constitutional amendment is more expansive than the other two, preventing the validity or recognition of "a civil union, domestic partnership, or other similar same-sex relationship." Hawaii also adopted a state constitutional amendment regarding same-sex marriage before 2004, but its amendment is solely directed at barring judicial action by granting the legislature "the power to reserve marriage to opposite-sex couples." HAW. CONST. art. I, § 23.

[245] ALA. CONST. art. I, § 36.03; ARIZ. CONST. art. XXX, § 1; ARK. CONST. art. I, § 25; CAL. CONST. art. I, § 7.5; COLO. CONST. art. II, § 31; FLA. CONST. art. I, § 27; GA. CONST. art. I, § 4, par. 1; IDAHO CONST. art. III, § 28; KAN. CONST. art. XV, § 16; KY. CONST. § 233A; LA. CONST. art. XII, § 15; MICH. CONST. art. I, § 25;

All these amendments define marriage as between one man and one woman, and bar recognition of any marriage that is not between members of the opposite sex. Further, approximately twenty of the twenty-nine state defense of marriage constitutional amendments enforceable today also ban the recognition of civil unions or other legal states substantially similar to marriage. The 2005 Texas constitutional amendment adding article I, section 32 to the state constitution is illustrative of this latter category, providing:

> (a) Marriage in this state shall consist only of the union of one man and one woman.
> (b) This state or a political subdivision of this state may not create or recognize any legal status identical or similar to marriage.[246]

The joint resolution proposing the Texas amendment perhaps somewhat limited its scope, specifying that, "through the designation of guardians, the appointment of agents, and the use of private contracts," persons may arrange certain rights "without the existence of any legal status identical or similar to marriage."[247] But although this resolution may be indicative of the intent of the legislature in proposing article I, section 32, it is not part of the constitutional text ratified by Texas voters.

Assuming amendments such as article I, section 32 of the Texas Constitution are properly ratified in accordance with state constitutional procedures, they preclude any state authorization or recognition of the specified unions under state law. The only question that remains, then, is whether such state defense of marriage amendments violate the United States Constitution.

With one notable exception, so far these state marriage amendments have survived federal constitutional challenges,[248] although some thirty additional challenges are pending as this book is going to press. The Eighth Circuit's decision in *Citizens for Equal Protection v. Bruning* provides a good illustration of the rationale of the cases that have upheld state constitutional marriage provisions against federal constitutional claims.[249] After a federal district court invalidated Nebraska's state constitutional ban on recognizing same-sex marriage, civil unions, domestic partnerships, and other similar same-sex relationships on

---

MISS. CONST. art. XIV, § 263-A; MO. CONST. art. I, § 33; MONT. CONST. art. XIII, § 7; N.D. CONST. art. XI, § 28; OHIO CONST. art. XV, § 11; OKLA. CONST. art. II, § 35; OR. CONST. art. XV, § 5a; S.C. CONST. art. XVII, § 15; S.D. CONST. art. XXI, § 9; TENN. CONST. art. XI, § 18; TEX. CONST. art. I, § 32; UTAH CONST. art. I, § 29; VA. CONST. art. I, § 15-A; WIS. CONST. art. XIII, § 13. A federal district court subsequently enjoined officials from enforcing California's amendment. *See* supra note 237 and accompanying text. North Carolina adopted its defense of marriage amendment in 2012. N.C. CONST. art. XIV, § 6.

[246] TEX. CONST. art. I, § 32.

[247] TEX. H.J.R. No. 6, § 2 (2005).

[248] *See, e.g.*, Citizens for Equal Protection v. Bruning, 455 F.3d 859, 867-68 (8th Cir. 2006); *see also* Standhardt v. Superior Court, 77 P.3d 451 (Ariz. App. 2003) (upholding Arizona's statutory defense of marriage act against state and federal due process and equal protection challenges); Morrison v. Sadler, 821 N.E.2d 15 (Ind. App. 2005) (holding Indiana's statutory defense of marriage act did not violate either the federal or state constitutions).

[249] 455 F.3d 859 (8th Cir. 2006).

federal associational and equal protection grounds,[250] the Eighth Circuit reversed.[251] The Eighth Circuit held that the Nebraska amendment was rationally related to a valid purpose of "steering heterosexual procreation into marriage" under federal constitutional analysis. It further concluded that a more searching inquiry than the rational basis test was not required because the amendment was not so broad as to render its enactment inexplicable by anything but animus toward same-sex couples.[252] Finally, the court opined that canons of judicial restraint required caution before creating a new federal constitutional right that would interfere with traditional state prerogatives over marriage.[253]

The one state marriage amendment that did not survive a federal constitutional challenge was California's Proposition 8. The California same-sex couples challenging Proposition 8, the federal district court held, had a fundamental right under the federal Due Process Clause to marry someone of the same sex in light of the evolution of matrimony in America with respect to both gender roles and miscegenation.[254] The district court also concluded that Proposition 8 denied the federal equal protection rights of same-sex couples by preventing their marriage based on nothing more than a "private moral view that same-sex couples are inferior to opposite-sex couples."[255] The district court therefore enjoined California state officials from enforcing Proposition 8.[256] While the enjoined California officials did not appeal, the official citizen proponents of Proposition 8 did. On appeal, the Ninth Circuit affirmed the district court's judgment, but on narrower grounds. The appellate court reasoned that, because same-sex marriage had been granted in California before Proposition 8, the subsequent denial of that right violated equal protection when the denial was not rationally related to the government's asserted interests in child rearing, responsible procreation, incremental social change, religious liberty, or moral education in public schools.[257] The court emphasized as precedential support the United States Supreme Court's holding in *Romer v. Evans* that a state constitutional amendment in Colorado, which effectively repealed local laws banning sexual orientation discrimination and prohibited the enactment of such laws in the future, invidiously singled out gays and lesbians for disfavored legal status.[258] The Ninth Circuit viewed Proposition 8 as similarly motivated by an animus against gays and lesbians prohibited by the Equal Protection Clause. Proposition 8, the court explained, stripped same-sex couples of the ability to describe their relationship as "marriage" without any legitimate reason, as California law provided same-sex couples with the same state rights as opposite-sex married couples.[259] The Proposition

---

[250]Citizens for Equal Protection v. Bruning, 368 F. Supp. 2d 980, 985-1002 (D. Neb. 2005), *rev'd*, 455 F.3d 859 (8th Cir. 2006).

[251]*Bruning*, 455 F.3d at 867-68.

[252]*Id.*

[253]*Id.* at 870-71.

[254]Perry v. Schwarzenegger, 704 F. Supp. 2d 921, 992-95 (N.D. Cal. 2010), *aff'd sub nom.* Perry v. Brown, 671 F.3d 1052 (9th Cir. 2012), *appeal dism'd sub nom.* Hollingsworth v. Perry, 133 S. Ct. 2652 (2013).

[255]*Id.* at 1002-03.

[256]*Id.* at 1004.

[257]671 F.3d at 1063-64.

[258]517 U.S. 620, 633-35 (1996).

[259]671 F.3d at 1083-95.

8 proponents then sought review from the United States Supreme Court, but the Supreme Court held that the proponents had no standing to appeal the district court's judgment under federal justiciability doctrines.[260] The Supreme Court therefore vacated the Ninth Circuit's judgment, leaving the district court's judgment invalidating Proposition 8 intact.

While the Supreme Court thus avoided resolving the federal constitutional challenges to Proposition 8, dozens of other federal constitutional challenges to state constitutional marriage amendments barring same-sex marriage are percolating in lower federal and state courts. The United States Supreme Court at some point will have to settle whether the United States Constitution requires state creation and recognition of marriages between couples of the same sex.

Judicial Decisions and Legislative Actions in Other States: As of November 2013, sixteen states and the District of Columbia have granted same-sex couples the right to marry. Five of these states adopted same-sex marriage after judicial determinations under their state constitutions: Massachusetts, California, Connecticut, Iowa, and New Jersey.[261] Eleven other states–Vermont, New Hampshire, New York, Washington, Maine, Maryland, Delaware, Rhode Island, Minnesota, Hawaii, and Illinois–adopted same-sex marriage through legislation or a referendum, as did the District of Columbia.

A few other states currently allow same-sex couples to enter into civil unions or domestic partnerships that confer substantially all the benefits of marriage. The legislature in Vermont enacted the nation's first civil union law, which Vermont later amended to become the first state to legislatively adopt same-sex marriage.[262] Civil unions or domestic partnerships conferring substantially all the benefits of marriage to same-sex couples exist

---

[260]*Hollingsworth*, 133 S. Ct. at 2668.

[261]Goodridge v. Dep't of Pub. Health, 798 N.E.2d 941 (Mass. 2003); *In re* Marriage Cases, 183 P.3d 384 (Cal. 2008); Kerrigan v. Comm'r of Pub. Health, 957 A.2d 407 (Conn. 2008); Varnum v. Brien, 763 N.W.2d 862 (Iowa 2009); Garden State Equality v. Dow, __ A.3d __, 2013 WL 5687193 (N.J. Oct. 18, 2013). Same-sex marriage arrived in New Jersey after a prolonged struggle involving the New Jersey courts, the state's political branches, and the United States Supreme Court. In *Lewis v. Harris,* 908 A.2d 196, 220-24 (N.J. 2006), the New Jersey Supreme Court held that same-sex couples were guaranteed the same rights and benefits enjoyed by married opposite sex-couples under the state constitution's implicit protection against unequal treatment. In response to *Lewis*, New Jersey's legislature enacted a civil union statute providing same-sex partners all the rights and benefits of marriage. In 2011, the advocacy group Garden State Equality, joined by several same-sex couples, filed suit against various state officials, arguing that the state civil union statute did not truly provide equal treatment to same-sex couples as required by *Lewis.* Their lawsuit was bolstered when the United States Supreme Court invalidated the federal Defense of Marriage Act in *United States v. Windsor*, 133 S. Ct. 2675, 2695-96 (2013), effectively granting federal recognition to lawful state same-sex "marriages," but not to civil unions or other forms of partnerships. The *Garden State Equality* trial court ordered after *Windsor* that New Jersey officials had to begin allowing same-sex couples to marry within twenty-four days to ensure that same-sex couples would have the required equal "rights and benefits" available to opposite-sex couples. After unsuccessful attempts to stay this order in the lower courts, state officials sought a stay from the state's highest court. In a unanimous opinion, the New Jersey Supreme Court rejected the stay request, holding that the state did not show a reasonable probability of success on the merits when "same-sex couples who cannot marry are not treated equally under the law today. The harm to them is real, not abstract or speculative." *Garden State Equality* at *1. After the court's decision, Governor Chris Christie–who had vetoed a same-sex marriage bill passed by the New Jersey Legislature in 2012–directed state officials to drop the appeal and comply with the trial court's order.

[262]*See* VT. STAT. tit. 15, §8.

as of November 2013 in Colorado, Nevada, and Oregon, while a more limited form of domestic same-sex partnership exists in Wisconsin. Every other state except New Mexico (where the issue is currently pending before the state supreme court) has by constitutional amendment, statute, or judicial decision limited marriage or any similar status to opposite-sex couples.

Federal Recognition of Lawful Same-Sex State Marriages: Soon after same-sex marriage became a national political issue, Congress enacted, and President Bill Clinton signed into law, the Defense of Marriage Act of 1996 ("DOMA"),[263] which in section 3 defined the term "marriage" for all federal statutes and regulations as including opposite-sex couples only: "In determining the meaning of any Act of Congress, or of any ruling, regulation, or interpretation of the various administrative bureaus and agencies of the United States, the word 'marriage' means only a legal union between one man and one woman as husband and wife, and the word 'spouse' refers only to a person of the opposite sex who is a husband or a wife."[264] Under DOMA § 3, then, same-sex couples lawfully married under state law were not treated as married for federal law purposes, including income and estate taxation, social security and veterans' benefits, Medicaid and Medicare, and more than 1,000 other federal laws and programs where marital status was a factor in defining benefits, rights, and privileges.[265]

But the Supreme Court in *United States v. Windsor* invalidated DOMA § 3 under the Fifth Amendment's Due Process Clause.[266] Edith Windsor had attempted to claim the estate tax exemption for surviving spouses after the death of her same-sex spouse, Thea Spyer, but could not because of DOMA § 3, which she then challenged in federal court. In addressing her challenge, the Supreme Court first recognized that the definition and regulation of marriage had traditionally been viewed as a virtually exclusive state prerogative, whereby each state established its own scheme governing all marriages within the state.[267] Section 3 intruded on state-sanctioned marriages in an unusual and discriminatory fashion, the Court reasoned, as Congress had no sufficient justification for disparaging and imposing disabilities upon lawful same-sex marriages recognized and protected by state law.[268] Section 3 therefore was unconstitutional to the extent it barred federal recognition of lawful same-sex state marriages.

Yet the Supreme Court's holding in *Windsor* was limited to federal recognition of valid same-sex marriages. *Windsor* did not compel states to allow same-sex couples to marry. Nor did it invalidate section 2 of DOMA, which authorizes a state to refuse to recognize same-sex marriages performed under the laws of a sister state.

---

[263] Pub. L. No. 104-100, 110 Stat. 2419 (1996).

[264] 1 U.S.C. § 7.

[265] *See* GENERAL ACCOUNTING OFFICE, GAO-04-353R DEFENSE OF MARRIAGE ACT (Jan. 23, 2004) (identifying 1,138 federal statutory provisions based on marital status as of Dec. 31, 2003).

[266] 133 S. Ct. 2675, 2695-96 (2013).

[267] *Id.* at 2689-92.

[268] *Id.* at 2693-95.

Interstate Recognition and Full Faith and Credit Issues with Same-Sex Marriages and Civil Unions: The Full Faith and Credit Clause to the United States Constitution provides:

> Full Faith and Credit shall be given in each State to the public Acts, Records, and judicial Proceedings of every other State; and the Congress may by general Laws prescribe the Manner in which such Acts, Records and Proceedings shall be proved, and the Effect thereof.[269]

Yet the Full Faith and Credit Clause has little application to state recognition of marriages from other states. States apply the doctrine of comity to out-of-state marriages, recognizing such marriages out of mutual respect for sister states unless recognition is either specifically prohibited by state law or repugnant to the state's public policy. Full faith and credit principles have never been held to require "states to recognize marriages that violate their own public policies concerning who may marry" because the "states have always had the power to decline to recognize marriages from other states."[270]

This means each state can decide, without violating the Full Faith and Credit Clause, whether to recognize same-sex marriages from sister states for state law purposes (such as extending state marital benefits to same-sex couples or granting same-sex divorces). In conjunction with divorce residency requirements in many states, this often creates a dilemma for same-sex couples attempting to dissolve their relationship after moving to another state that does not recognize same-sex marriage.[271] While some courts in states disallowing the creation of same-sex marriages have held that recognizing same-sex marriages for purposes of divorce does not violate either state law or the state's public policy,[272] other state courts have not permitted same-sex married couples from sister states to divorce.[273]

The propriety of same-sex divorce in Texas is currently before the state supreme court in two cases consolidated for oral argument, *In re Marriage of J.B. & H.B* and *State*

---

[269]U.S. CONST. art. IV, § 1.

[270]ANDREW KOPPELMAN, SAME SEX, DIFFERENT STATES: WHEN SAME SEX MARRIAGES CROSS STATE LINES 117-18 (2006).

[271]Some same-sex marriage jurisdictions statutorily exempt same-sex marriages from the typical residency requirement for divorces if the couple's home state refuses to dissolve the marriage. *See, e.g.*, CAL. FAM CODE § 2320; 13 DEL. CODE § 129(f); D.C. CODE § 16-902(b)(1); MINN. STATE. § 518.07; 15 VT. STAT. § 592.

[272]*See, e.g.*, Christiansen v. Christiansen, 253 P.3d 153, 157 (Wyo. 2011) (holding recognition of valid Canadian same-sex marriage for purposes of a domestic divorce proceeding did not violate state public policy or statutory prohibition on creation of same-sex marriage). Before Maryland and New York adopted same-sex marriage, judicial decisions in those states similarly allowed same-sex couples from other states to divorce. *See, e.g.*, Port v. Cowan, 44 A.3d 970, 977-82 (Md. 2012); Dickerson v. Thompson, 897 N.Y.S.2d 298, 299-301 (N.Y. App. Div. 2010) (divorce from civil union).

[273]See, e.g., Kern v. Taney, 11 Pa. D. & C. 5th 558, 562-63 (Ct. Com. Pl. 2010) (holding that Pennsylvania statute voiding same-sex marriages from sister states prevented the granting of a divorce to same-sex couple married in Massachusetts); Chambers v. Ormiston, 935 A.2d 956, 967 (R.I. 2007) (holding that limited statutory jurisdiction of state family court to hear divorces from a "marriage" did not extend to entertaining a same-sex divorce petition).

v. Naylor. In both cases, same-sex couples were married in Massachusetts, later moved to Texas, and then filed for divorce. After J.B. filed for divorce in a Dallas trial court, the State (through the Texas Attorney General) intervened, arguing that Texas courts had no subject matter jurisdiction to adjudicate a same-sex divorce under the Texas Constitution and the Family Code. The Dallas Court of Appeals agreed with the State, holding that the proper procedure is a suit to declare the marriage void.[274] The appellate court further held that the state's denial of a same-sex divorce did not violate equal protection as it was rationally related to the state's overall family law scheme to promote procreation and the optimal setting for child rearing.[275] In the other case, Naylor filed for divorce in an Austin trial court, with the State attempting to intervene after the court rendered judgment granting the divorce. The State appealed, but the Austin Court of Appeals dismissed the appeal because the State was not a party to the suit and had not timely intervened in the action.[276] The Texas Supreme Court's review of these cases likely will address whether Texas law authorizes same-sex divorce and, if not, whether the alternative procedure of voiding same-sex marriages comports with equal protection.

The Full Faith and Credit Clause becomes a key concern in those cases involving a *judgment* from a sister state court, which might occur, for instance, in a Texas lawsuit seeking to enforce a sister state's same-sex divorce judgment transferring property in Texas. There is "no roving 'public policy exception' to the full faith and credit due *judgments*."[277] State courts thus must recognize and give effect to all valid sister court judgments–even those against the state's public policy. Yet Congress attempted to limit the full faith and credit due to judgments related to same-sex marriages in DOMA § 2, which authorizes states to refuse to give effect to or recognize any right from "any public act, record, or judicial proceeding" from another state respecting "a relationship between persons of the same sex that is treated as a marriage under the laws of [another] State."[278] In enacting this section, Congress relied on the Full Faith and Credit Clause's grant of legislative authority to prescribe, by general laws, the manner and effect of records and judgments. But congressional power to establish a blanket recognition exemption for all state court judgments respecting same-sex marriage is anything but clear and has yet to be addressed by the courts.[279] This is another of the many constitutional and public policy issues courts in future cases will likely have to resolve touching upon same-sex marital relations.

---

[274]*In re* Marriage of J.B. & H.B., 326 S.W.3d 654, 665-67 (Tex. App.–Dallas 2010, pet. granted).

[275]*Id.* at 676-79.

[276]State v. Naylor, 330 S.W.3d 434, 436 (Tex. App.–Austin 2011, pet. granted).

[277]Baker *ex rel.* Thomas v. Gen. Motors Corp., 522 U.S. 222, 233 (1998).

[278]28 U.S.C. § 1738C.

[279]*Compare* Wilson v. Ake, 345 F. Supp. 2d 1298 (M.D. Fla. 2005) (upholding DOMA § 2 against challenge by same-sex couple married in Massachusetts seeking to have their marriage recognized in Florida, although no sister court judgment was at issue). Two cases from federal circuit courts have addressed issues related to the full faith and credit owed to state court adoption decrees in favor of same-sex couples, although neither case considered the constitutionality of DOMA § 2. See, e.g., Adar v. Smith, 639 F.3d 146 (5th Cir. 2011); Finstuen v. Crutcher, 496 F.3d 1139 (10th Cir. 2007).

E. DUE PROCESS AND DUE COURSE OF LAW

Almost every state has a constitutional provision either similar to or that can be read to provide equivalent protection as the Federal Due Process Clauses, which bar the government from depriving any person "of life, liberty, or property without due process of law."[280] Historically, such clauses have been linked to the Magna Carta, which can be translated as follows: "No freeman shall be taken or imprisoned, or disseized or outlawed, or exiled, or anyways destroyed; nor will we go upon him, unless by the lawful judgment of his peers, or by the law of the land."[281] Under the Magna Carta, though, an Act of Parliament was by definition "the law of the land," such that governmental action in accordance with legislative acts was always valid. In contrast, in the United States, the courts held early in our Nation's history that due process concepts could be employed to invalidate legislative actions that were procedurally unfair or arbitrary and capricious.

The state courts led the way in employing their due process or "law of the land" provisions against legislative actions.[282] An 1805 North Carolina decision invalidated a statutory repeal of a property grant to the University of North Carolina that had the effect of divesting the trustees of property because the legislature could not deprive individuals "of their liberties or property, unless by a trial by Jury in a court of Justice, according to the known and established rules of decision, derived from the common law, and such acts of the Legislature as are consistent with the constitution."[283] Another formative decision from Tennessee invalidated a state law creating a special equity court with special powers for adjudicating claims by the state bank against certain debtors because the "law of the land" was violated when procedural rights, including the right to trial by jury and to appeal, were "taken away in these special cases, while every other member of the community, having incurred similar liabilities, enjoys them."[284] Other state antebellum decisions likewise invalidated legislation creating special methods for resolving certain claims.[285] The United States Supreme Court adopted a similar understanding before the Civil War, holding that the Due Process Clause barred legislative actions that violated "settled usages and modes of proceeding,"[286] which subsequently became well-accepted doctrine throughout the United States, including Texas.[287]

---

[280]U.S. CONST. amends. V & XIV.

[281]MAGNA CARTA § 39 (1225).

[282]*See* Edwin S. Corwin, *The Doctrine of Due Process of Law Before the Civil War*, 24 HARV. L. REV. 366, 380-85 (1911).

[283]Trustees of Univ. of N.C. v. Foy, 5 N.C. (1 Mur.) 58, 87-89 (1805).

[284]Bank of the State v. Cooper, 10 Tenn. (2 Yer.) 599, 607-08 (1831) (Green, J., seriatim op.); *accord id.* at 613-15 (Peck, J., seriatim op.); *id.* at 618-23 (Kennedy, J., seriatim op.).

[285]*See, e.g.*, Reid v. Wright, 2 Greene 15, 25-30 (Iowa 1849) (invalidating special procedures for settlement titles for certain lands under the Northwest Ordinance as not comporting with "course of the common law" or the "law of the land").

[286]Murray's Lessee v. Hoboken Land & Improv. Co., 59 U.S. (18 How.) 272, 276-77 (1856).

[287]*See, e.g.*, Union Cent. Life Ins. Co. v. Chowning, 26 S.W. 982, 984 (Tex. 1894) (noting due course of law required a general law authorizing a judicial hearing, proper procedures, and a judgment only after trial).

But even though the federal and state clauses share a common developmental tradition, textual differences between the provisions are frequently encountered. As an example, article I, section 19 of the Texas Constitution provides: "No citizen of this State shall be deprived of life, liberty, property, privileges or immunities, or in any manner disfranchised, except by the due course of the law of the land." The Texas clause thus extends due course protections to "privileges or immunities" and "disfranchisement." Additionally, the Texas guarantee is "due course of the law of the land" rather than "due process of law." Do such textual differences support differing interpretations? Could the Texas Due Course of Law Clause, and similar clauses from other states, avoid the recognized difficulty of creating a substantive component to "due process"?

In re J.W.T., 872 S.W.2d 189 (Tex. 1994)

> DOGGETT, Justice, delivered the opinion of the Court, in which PHILLIPS, Chief Justice, and GONZALEZ, HIGHTOWER, GAMMAGE, and SPECTOR, Justices, join.

In this case we consider whether, under the Texas due course of law guarantee, a biological father may be denied an opportunity to establish his paternity and claim parental rights. While living together in 1988, Larry G. and Judy T. conceived a child later named J.W.T. Though still married to Randy T., Judy had planned to marry Larry after resolution of her pending divorce. Judy and Larry together arranged for prenatal care with a local clinic in a contract acknowledging Larry's paternity. Pursuant to that agreement Larry made several payments for obstetric treatment.

Judy and Randy later reconciled and dismissed their divorce action. Before the child's birth, Larry brought an action under the Texas Family Code alleging that he was the father of J.W.T., acknowledging responsibility for child support payments, and requesting a judicial declaration of paternity and recognition of his visitation rights. After the birth, Larry unsuccessfully attempted to maintain contact with J.W.T. Under court order, the parties submitted to scientific paternity testing, which showed a 99.41% probability that Larry was J.W.T.'s biological father.

Accepting the contention of Randy and Judy that Larry lacked standing under the Texas Family Code to bring any action relating to J.W.T., the trial court rejected Larry's assertion of constitutional rights and dismissed his claim. The court of appeals reversed, determining that Section 11.03(a)(7) of the Texas Family Code, under which Larry was denied standing to sue, violated the due course of law guarantee contained in article I, section 19 of the Texas Constitution. We affirm the judgment of the court of appeals.

I.

Critical to this appeal is an understanding of the various provisions of the Texas Family Code that affect a putative father's ability to establish parental rights. If, when a child is born, the mother is married to someone other than the biological father, her husband is "presumed" to be the child's actual father, and this "marital presumption" may not be attacked by any party outside the marriage except a government entity. *See* Tex.Fam.Code §§ 12.02(a), 12.06(a)(Vernon Supp.1994).

Several provisions of the Code operate in tandem to prevent a man claiming to be a child's biological father from suing either to rebut the marital presumption or to claim parental rights by establishing his paternity. A biological father has standing to sue under the Family Code only if the child he claims has no presumed father, Tex.Fam.Code § 11.03(a)(7); and the only type of action he may bring is a paternity suit under Chapter 13, which is limited to children who have no presumed father. Id.; Tex.Fam.Code § 13.21(a). The marital presumption is irrebuttable in a Chapter 13 suit and, even under Chapter 12, only the husband or wife may deny the husband's paternity of a child born during their marriage. Tex.Fam.Code § 12.06(a).

Thus, a biological father of a child with a presumed father is given the opportunity for a hearing before a court to establish parental rights only at the request of another party; he may not himself initiate such proceedings. With Randy's paternity of J.W.T. denied by neither Judy nor himself, Randy remains the legally recognized, "presumed" biological father. Under the provisions of the Family Code, Larry is completely barred from asserting his paternity and claiming any relationship with his apparent natural son, J.W.T.

II.

Relying on both his biological connection with and actions to accept responsibility for J.W.T., Larry contends that the Family Code's denial of his parental rights violates the command of Article I, section 19 of the Texas Constitution that:

> No citizen of this State shall be deprived of life, liberty, property, privileges or immunities, or in any manner disfranchised, except by the due course of the law of the land.

Under this provision, Larry seeks an opportunity to prove paternity[288] and to obtain a judicial declaration entitling him to both the rights and the obligations of a "parent." As a "parent," Larry could be appointed a managing or possessory conservator of J.W.T., unless shown not to be in J.W.T.'s best interest. If appointed, Larry would be invested with all of the parental rights recognized by the Family Code, except those that the trial court orders are to be exercised exclusively by Judy, including direction of the child's moral and religious training, management of his estate, access to his services and earnings, right to consent to his marriage or participation in the military, and representation of the child in any legal action.

A declaration of paternity would also impose parental duties, including that of financial support and provision for the child of clothing, food, shelter, medical care, and education, as well as contribution to the mother's pre- and post-natal health care expenses. These duties may be forced upon Larry regardless of whether he attempts to exercise any concurrent rights of parenthood–a paternity suit may be brought at any time by a number of other interested parties whose standing to sue does not depend on the absence of a presumed

[288]Procedurally, this case is unusual in that the factual foundation for establishing paternity was confirmed by court ordered blood tests before the trial court determined that the biological father lacked standing. In contrast, we contemplate a blood test only after a showing at an initial hearing by the putative father that he has met the standard announced in this writing.

father. *See, e.g., In re S.C.V.,* 750 S.W.2d 762 (Tex.1988) (mother's suit to enforce child support against biological father of child born during her marriage to another man).

III.

Acceptance of Larry's argument that the due course of law provision guarantees him an opportunity to prove paternity would have been highly improbable at the time of the ratification of our Texas Constitution in 1876. A paternity suit was not permitted in Texas at common law. Under English common law, an onerous burden of overcoming the marital presumption was designed to protect a child from the harsh consequences of a finding of illegitimacy, which included an inability to obtain support from the father or to inherit from either parent. A child could not be delegitimized by proof of the spouses' lack of access to one another if the husband was present "within the four seas" surrounding England at the time of conception, unless his impotence or sterility was proven. An evidentiary rule known as Lord Mansfield's Rule, first articulated in 1777, further prohibited either the husband or the wife from testifying about lack of access, thus requiring evidence or testimony from sources outside the marriage, which were more difficult to secure. Although widely criticized by legal scholars, this rule was generally embraced by the courts, and then gradually rejected in the twentieth century as the legal disabilities associated with illegitimacy diminished.

IV.

Significant twentieth century changes in the resolution of issues affecting the family are reflected in statutes, demographics, alteration of social attitudes toward illegitimate children, and decisions of the Texas courts. With the enactment of the Texas Family Code in 1973, a method was statutorily afforded a putative father to establish his paternity voluntarily. Adoption in 1975 of an involuntary paternity action, by which others could enforce parental duties upon biological fathers, finally secured the right of illegitimate children to obtain paternal support, as mandated in *Gomez v. Perez,* 409 U.S. 535 (1973). The new statutory paternity action applied, however, only with regard to those children born to an unwed mother, and the marital presumption was codified without any mechanism for its rebuttal.

After paternity suits became statutorily available, this court overruled its prior recognition of Lord Mansfield's Rule. *Davis v. Davis,* 521 S.W.2d 603 (Tex.1975). Because an illegitimate child had rights vis-a-vis the true biological father, attempts to preserve the fiction that the mother's husband was the father no longer necessarily protected the child's best interest.

Under *Davis,* however, the marital presumption continued to bar delegitimization absent testimony regarding non-access or sterility. If married and living together as husband and wife, neither spouse could rebut the marital presumption, not even with scientific evidence of another's paternity. Not until 1983 was the husband/presumed father statutorily permitted, under Section 12.06 of the Family Code, to deny paternity of a child born to his wife during their marriage, and to seek court-ordered blood testing to disprove paternity. In 1987, the same right was accorded the wife.

Human physiology has not changed, but our understanding of it has. Current methods of scientific testing provide more reliable and less intrusive means of determining paternity. Under the current Family Code, the court is required to order the mother, alleged father, and child to submit to scientifically accepted paternity testing that excludes at least 99% of the male population from the possibility of parentage. Tex.Fam.Code § 13.02. And advances in genetic testing techniques can accommodate this requirement.

V.

We have recognized the adaptability to such changes of our state's fundamental governing law and found considerable strength in the organic nature of its command. *Davenport v. Garcia,* 834 S.W.2d 4, 19 (Tex.1992, orig. proceeding).

In asserting a due course of law claim, Larry must establish that his interest is constitutionally protected. *See Tarrant County v. Ashmore,* 635 S.W.2d 417, 422 (Tex.1982) (extending due course protection to interest of official in elected position). In previous decisions, we have accorded great respect for the biological bond between parent and child. In *Wiley v. Spratlan,* 543 S.W.2d 349, 352 (Tex.1976), we recognized that "[t]he natural right which exists between parents and their children is one of constitutional dimensions." Similarly, in *Gunn v. Cavanaugh,* 391 S.W.2d 723 (Tex.1965), we declared that

> the rights of the natural parent are of high importance and due process properly requires that the burden of proof to show forfeiture of parental rights rests upon [whomever challenges those rights].

We have nonetheless tempered these decisions by recognizing that the rights of natural parents are not absolute; protection of the child is paramount. *See id.* The rights of parenthood are accorded only to those fit to accept the accompanying responsibilities.

To determine the extent of procedural rights to which a biological father is entitled, we must consider the public interest in protecting the child along with the father's constitutional interest in establishing a relationship with his child. In a situation such as that presented here where the biological father does assert his interest near the time of the child's birth, standing is constitutionally mandated if he both 1) acknowledges responsibility for child support or other care and maintenance, and 2) makes serious and continuous efforts to establish a relationship with the child. While [our prior] cases recognized only the importance of providing due process to fathers of illegitimate children, we conclude that the right to be heard does not cease merely because the mother is married.

While federal jurisprudence may be useful in understanding our state constitutional guarantees, *see Davenport,* 834 S.W.2d at 20, the help on the question presented here is limited by the sharp divisions present in the consideration of a claim similar to Larry's in *Michael H. v. Gerald D.,* 491 U.S. 110 (1989). *Michael H.,* the putative father, challenged the conclusive presumption created by a California statute that a man cohabiting with his wife was the biological father of a child born during the marriage. *Id.* at 119-20. Notwithstanding both his biological fatherhood and participation in rearing his daughter, *Michael H.* was found by a four-member plurality to possess no interest deserving constitutional protection, despite recognition by the other five members of the Court[289] that this holding was in apparent conflict with recent application of the federal Due Process clause to biological fathers. *Id.* at 133 (Stevens, J., concurring); *id.* at 142 (Brennan, J., dissenting); *id.* at 158-59 (White, J., dissenting).

Michael H. was, consequently, considered an aberration–"the plurality's departure" from previous federal decisional law–by the Louisiana Supreme Court in *In re Adoption of B.G.S.,* 556 So.2d at 549-50 n.2, and is perhaps best described in Justice Brennan's dissent:

> The atmosphere surrounding today's decision is one of make-believe. Beginning with the suggestion that the situation confronting us here does not repeat itself every day in every corner of the country, moving on to the claim that it is tradition alone that supplies the details of the liberty that the Constitution protects, and passing finally to the notion that the Court always has recognized a cramped vision of "the family," today's decision lets stand California's pronouncement that Michael–whom blood tests show to a 98 percent probability to be Victoria's father–is not Victoria's father. When and if the Court awakes to reality, it will find a world very different from the one it expects.

Michael H., 491 U.S. at 128 (Brennan, J., dissenting); *see also In re Adoption of Kelsey S.,* 823 P.2d 1216, 1228 (Cal.1992)(stating "we must not read too much into *Michael H.,*" and relying on that case for the proposition that five justices recognized unwed father's liberty interest). It is wholly under our Texas due course of law guarantee, which has independent vitality, separate and distinct from the due process clause of the Fourteenth Amendment to the U.S. Constitution, that we reach today's decision.

VI.

Randy and Judy insist that Larry's right to be heard may be statutorily denied. They argue that, by prohibiting an alleged biological father from asserting his paternity, the Family Code protects the marital unit from intrusion by outsiders and protects the child from delegitimation. The State has a legitimate interest in minimizing familial disruptions that are harmful to the child. But as the court of appeals observed, this marital unit was clearly

---

[289]The disputed California statute was upheld because Justice Stevens concurred with the plurality, despite his disagreement with Justice Scalia's "reject[ion] [of] the possibility that a natural father might ever have a constitutionally protected interest in his relationship with a child whose mother was married to and cohabiting with, another man at the time of the child's conception and birth." 491 U.S. at 133 (Stevens, J., concurring). Justice Stevens "assume[d] for the purpose of deciding [the] case" that Michael's relationship with his daughter deserved due process protection, noting that recent cases, such as *Stanley v. Illinois,* 405 U.S. 645 (1972), and *Caban v. Mohammed,* 441 U.S. 380 (1979), "demonstrate that enduring 'family' relationships may develop in unconventional settings." He nevertheless found sufficient safeguard for Michael's interest in California's statutory authorization for trial court discretion in allowing anyone with an interest in a child to gain visitation rights. *Id.* at 133. The Texas Family Code affords no comparable right. Section 11.03(c) permits a person "deemed by the court to have had substantial past contact with the child sufficient to warrant standing," a right of intervention in a suit filed by someone authorized to sue under subsections 11.03(a) or (b); by its terms this would exclude the putative father. Even though the tenuous coalition that produced a judgment in *Michael H.* might well have decided the instant case differently than Justices Cornyn and Enoch now suggest, speculating how another court would resolve this matter is hardly determinative of our decision.

disrupted before Larry ever filed this suit:

> [t]hat the biological mother, for whatever reason, has chosen to engage in sexual relations outside of marriage is proof itself that the "integrity and solemnity of the family unit" has been damaged at least to some degree. [Resolution of these difficulties by the husband and wife] does not, we feel, give license to the state to perpetuate the myth of "presumption of paternity" so as to deprive the biological father of at least a chance of being able to exercise those rights, duties, privileges, and responsibilities that all civilized societies have recognized to be fundamentally ingrained in the concept of parenthood.

Perhaps this asserted interest had merit in an earlier era when the true biological father could not be established with near certainty and when illegitimacy carried a significant legal and social stigma. Since this is no longer the case, the focus should more properly be directed toward what is best for the child–it may be in best interest of the child to allow development of a relationship with the natural father and it may not.[290] The effect of the alternative offered by the dissenting justices is to leave this determination of the child's best interest and the definition of family, itself, exclusively to the biological mother. In the name of protecting the family, Justice Enoch would grant rights to putative fathers who had been permitted by the mother to develop a relationship with the child but not to those not afforded that opportunity.

We do not say that our Constitution guarantees every natural father ties with his illegitimate offspring. We do say that one who is arbitrarily prevented from attempting to establish any relationship with his natural child, after making early and unqualified acceptance of parental duties as Larry has done, is denied due course of law under section 19 of our Texas Bill of Rights. Those provisions of the Family Code that bar Larry's pursuit of his parental rights violate our constitutional guarantee that every Texan shall be accorded due course of law. We, therefore, hold unconstitutional Section 11.03(a)(7) and 12.06(a) to the extent that they wholly deny a putative father's standing to sue with regard to a child who has a presumed father, and prevent the bringing of any suit affecting the parent-child relationship in which a presumption of paternity may be rebutted.

HECHT, Justice, concurring.

[I]t seems to me that two constitutionally protected interests are involved in this case–parenthood and preservation of the family–and they are in conflict. The State has chosen to resolve this conflict by denying the biological father of a child who has a presumed father any standing to assert his interest. In all such circumstances, the family interest is made paramount by statute. I agree with the Court that the State has no reason or purpose sufficient to deny every biological father the right to assert his interest in a child

---

[290] Status as a "parent" under the Family Code does not guarantee a relationship with the child. The trial court may refuse to award visitation if "it finds that parental possession or access is not in the best interest of the child and that parental possession or access would endanger the physical or emotional welfare of the child." Tex.Fam.Code § 14.03(d).

simply because there is a presumed father. When a biological father acknowledges his responsibility to help support the child and has made every reasonable effort to establish a relationship with the child, he is entitled to assert his interest in the child, notwithstanding the opposition of the mother and her husband.

He is not, however, necessarily entitled to prevail in his assertion. I agree with the Court that in determining what rights a biological father may have in his child, the best interest of the child must be considered. I do not agree with the implication in the Court's opinion–it is really only an implication and nothing more–that the best interest of the child is the only, or always the paramount, consideration. The interests of the mother and her husband in preserving their family unit exclusive of the biological father are equal in dignity to the biological father's interest and entitled to equal consideration. Such interests are especially important when the best interest of the child is unclear. For example, when it appears that a child would do as well or better with his biological father as with his mother and her husband, should the biological father be allowed visitation if his continued presence in the child's life would almost certainly imperil the stability of the mother's marriage? I suspect this situation is commonplace, and I cannot see how consideration of the best interest of the child alone supplies the solution.

The Court does not exclude family interests from consideration in determining what rights should be awarded a biological father. I presume therefore that such interests can and should be fully considered. With this understanding, I concur in the judgment of the Court.

ENOCH, Justice, dissenting.

Under the guise of denial of procedural due course of law, the Court is in fact creating a substantive due course of law interest in favor of an putative biological father to challenge paternity and obtain parental rights in derogation of the right of the marital family to protect its children from claims of illegitimacy by outsiders. With this action, I cannot agree.

In reaching its decision, the Court rejects a United States Supreme Court holding directly on point. In *Michael H. v. Gerald D.,* 491 U.S. 110 (1989), the Supreme Court held that a putative biological father was not deprived of any due process rights by a state statute that prevented him from petitioning to establish his paternity of a child born into a marriage. The Court dismisses *Michael H.* as an "aberration." To the contrary, *Michael H.* simply reflects a determination that not all parental-related rights are to be given the same stature and constitutional import, a distinction which this Court fails to recognize.

Although this Court is not bound by the decisions of the United States Supreme Court in construing the due course of law provision of the Texas Constitution, I find the decisions of the United States Supreme Court, and in particular, *Michael H.,* instructive and persuasive. Even assuming that our due course of law provision is broader and protects interests not protected by the Due Process Clause of the United States Constitution, I find nothing in the jurisprudence of this State to suggest that Texas has traditionally protected and recognized the interests of an adulterous putative father to establish and obtain parental rights over the objection of the mother and presumed father and to the derogation of the marital family's right to protect its children from claims of illegitimacy by outsiders.

Accordingly, I would conclude that Larry G., the putative biological father, does not have a constitutional interest protected under Article I, section 19 of the Texas Constitution to challenge and petition for paternity of a child born into a marriage between a woman and another man, and consequently, he has not been deprived of due course of law by sections 11.03(a)(7) and 12.06(a) of the Texas Family Code.

CORNYN, Justice, dissenting on motion for rehearing.

Respectfully, I dissent. Aware of the monumental social crisis posed by broken families in our state and nation, the legislature could have rationally chosen to protect the marital family over any right that the Texas Constitution might confer on a biological father. Elevating its will over the law, the court has substituted its own social policy preferences for those of the people's legitimate representatives.

In identifying new rights granted by the due course clause, the court relies on the "adaptability" of the Texas Constitution to social changes it deems important, rather than our traditional interpretive methods. This form of adaptation permits constitutional amendment via the courtroom, rather than the usual method of constitutional adaptation in Texas–the ballot box. Unlike the United States Constitution, which has been amended only eighteen times since the Bill of Rights was ratified in 1791, the Texas Constitution was amended 338 times between 1876 and 1993. Texans have shown no reluctance to adapt their constitution when changed circumstances so require. If the people actively maintain their constitution as a living document, then this court has even more reason than the United States Supreme Court to remain circumspect about vague notions of constitutional "adaptation" through judicial opinions.

The court here offers no explanation for why it chooses to disregard the Supreme Court's warning in *Michael H. v. Gerald D.,* 491 U.S. 110 (1989) (plurality opinion), and to follow, at least for the moment, a doctrine that has been subject to sharp criticism for more than a century and the use of which has been dramatically curtailed since the late 1930's. Substantive due process is by no means entrenched in our jurisprudence.

Because the federal due process clause and our due course clause are virtually identical, Texas courts have held for over a century that the due course clause "in so far as it is identical" to the Fourteenth Amendment, is co-extensive with the Fourteenth Amendment. *Mellinger v. City of Houston,* 68 Tex. 37, 3 S.W. 249 (1887). If the Supreme Court has ruled on an issue under the federal constitution, this court has said that it will follow that ruling unless some difference between the two clauses requires a different result. *Id.* at 253.

In reaching today's result, five members of the court explain that the due course clause has "independent vitality" and is "arguably broader" than the corresponding language in the United States Constitution. To the extent the court recognizes a due course right that was expressly rejected on due process grounds in *Michael H.,* the court necessarily holds that the due course clause is broader. This approach to the due course clause directly conflicts with the canons of constitutional interpretation that this court has followed since shortly after adoption of the 1876 Constitution. *See Mellinger,* 3 S.W. 249, 253 (Tex.1887).

Neither history nor language leads to the court's conclusion. In fact, there is as much reason to believe that the due course clause is generally narrower than the due process clause as there is reason to believe it to be broader.

Even if the Texas framers did not preclude substantive review of statutes under the due course clause, there are good reasons why the meaning of these clauses should be treated as being the same. First, the United States Supreme Court encounters due process issues far more frequently than does this court, and thus is in a better position to develop a coherent and consistent framework. Second, because federal precedent in this area is more extensive than our state jurisprudence, the *Mellinger* approach promotes certainty in the law and discourages unnecessary or duplicative litigation. Third, the dangers of substantive due process going awry are great, and a restrained method minimizes the likelihood that arbitrary decisions will call this court's legitimacy into question. Finally, a restrained method enables our due course jurisprudence to evolve–to the extent it departs from the federal cases–with maximum deliberation and care. Simply put, unless differences between the clauses give us a good reason to depart from either the direct holdings of the Supreme Court or its methodology, then we should not do so.

All members of the Supreme Court in *Michael H.* agreed that a putative father who has not established a relationship with his child has no due process right to establish any relationship. *Michael H.,* 491 U.S. at 121-30 (Scalia, J., joined by Rehnquist, C.J., O'Connor & Kennedy, JJ.), 132-33 (Stevens, J., concurring), 142-43 (Brennan, J., joined by Marshall & Blackmun, JJ.), 159-61 (White, J., joined by Brennan, J.). Justice Stevens concurred with the four-judge plurality opinion by Justice Scalia on the ground that Michael H. had no constitutional right to a declaration of paternity, *id.* at 132-33, but noted that the California statutory scheme still provided Michael H. an opportunity to sue as "any other person" to maintain his established relationship with Victoria. *Id.* at 133-36. Justice Stevens did not decide whether an established relationship results in a protected right, but "assume[d] for the purpose of deciding this case" that such a right existed between Michael H. and Victoria. Presumably, even Justice Brennan would hold that Larry K. does not have a right to sue for paternity. Thus, there are no "sharp divisions," among the justices concerning the issue presented in this case.

If this court could identify some difference between the due course and due process clauses, some other clause in the Texas Constitution, some aspect of history or a tradition unique to Texas to demonstrate that the Texas Constitution confers an authority to intervene in this case when the United States Constitution does not, then the court's conclusion might be supportable. But the court does not identify even a relevant difference, let alone a compelling one. I do not suggest that this court should never look to the Texas Constitution to determine whether the rights it provides are different from the rights guaranteed under an analogous provision of the United States Constitution. My concern is that the court's dramatic departure from our usual interpretive framework undermines this court's legitimacy.

Notes on Due Process Rights of Natural Fathers

Federal v. State Conceptions of Due Process: What were the differences between the Texas Family Code provisions regarding parental rights struck down in *In re J.W.T* and the California statute upheld by a very divided Supreme Court in *Michael H.*? In what other ways can the cases be distinguished factually? Texas law did not allow for visitation rights in Larry G.'s situation, while the dispositive factor in Justice Stevens's concurrence was that California left open such a possibility for Michael H. On the other hand, Larry G. did not have the same established relationship with his child that Michael H. did. Is it possible to predict the impact that these distinctions could have had if the United States Supreme Court had decided *In re J.W.T.*? Or is it simply impossible to tell, especially considering that the Supreme Court's composition had changed substantially between *Michael H.* and *J.W.T.*?

Is *In re J.W.T.*'s holding based on the substantive or procedural aspects of the Texas Due Course of Law Clause? Do the majority and dissenting opinions have different views on this issue? Is this a potential further distinction from *Michael H.*?

A number of other states have also considered whether statutory schemes depriving a putative father of standing to rebut the marital presumption or establish paternity violates the state constitution. While, due to variations in the statutory schemes, it is difficult to directly compare the holdings, the states have reached divergent results on the constitutional issues.[291] Other states have avoided the constitutional issue by interpreting the common law or state statutory scheme to authorize standing for the putative father. Was this avenue available to the Texas Supreme Court?

Interpretation and the Living Constitution: How persuasive are Justice Cornyn's objections to the majority's holding, particularly his charge that the court's interpretive framework undermined its legitimacy? The majority acknowledges that a strictly historical analysis would not have provided the putative father a constitutional right, but indicated that societal and scientific changes (such as the removal of legal disabilities based on illegitimacy and the accuracy of paternity testing) had rendered the historical discrimination against putative fathers obsolete. Should the court be free to make changes in constitutional doctrine based on such advancements? Or should the issue have been left to the legislature, which was (very slowly) in the process of modernizing the Family Code provisions? Is the answer dependent on whether one views due process, and constitutional meaning more generally, as historically frozen or as capable of evolution?

University of Texas Medical School v. Than, 901 S.W.2d 926 (Tex. 1995)

ENOCH, Justice, delivered the opinion of the Court, in which all Justices join.

This case concerns the procedural due process, if any, that must be afforded to a graduate student who is dismissed from a state university. The trial court found that the

---

[291] *Compare* R. McG. v. J.W., 615 P.2d 666, 672 (Colo. 1980) (state constitution required standing for putative father); Callender v. Skiles, 591 N.W.2d 182, 192 (Iowa 1999) (same) *with* Dawn D. v. Superior Court, 952 P.2d 1139, 1145-46 (Cal. 1998) (upholding state statutory scheme); Evans v. Steelman, 970 S.W.2d 431, 434-35 (Tenn. 1998) (same); A v. X, Y, & Z, 641 P.2d 1222, 1224-27 (Wyo. 1982) (same).

student's due course of law rights had been violated and granted the student a permanent injunction. The court of appeals affirmed. For the reasons expressed below, we affirm the permanent injunction as modified.

Allan Than, a medical student at the University of Texas Medical School at Houston, was dismissed for academic dishonesty. As a third year student, Than took the National Board of Medical Examiners (NBME) exam in surgery on February 22, 1991. During the exam, two proctors observed Than repeatedly looking at the answer sheet of another student. The proctors were instructed by Dr. Margaret McNeese, an associate dean of UT, to either pull Than's test or to move one of the students. Before the proctors could do either, however, the student from whom Than was allegedly cheating finished the exam and left the room. Perceiving that the threat of cheating had dissipated, and rather than disrupt the remaining students who were still taking the test, the proctors opted not to pull Than's exam and allowed him to complete the exam.

Shortly after the exam, UT requested the NBME to prepare a statistical analysis of Than and the other student's exam. The NBME compared joint wrong answers, that is, the common questions that both students answered incorrectly. Of these wrong answers, the students gave the same wrong answer on 88% of the questions.

Upon receiving the NBME's statistical analysis, UT instituted disciplinary proceedings against Than for academic dishonesty. UT gave Than oral and written notice of the charges against him, including notice of some of the evidence to be used against him at the hearing. At the hearing, Than opted to represent himself. UT was represented by Dr. McNeese. Both made opening and closing statements. UT called the two proctors as witnesses and Than extensively cross-examined them. Than called two students who had taken the same exam to testify on his behalf. After the conclusion of the hearing, the hearing officer viewed the testing room with Dr. McNeese. Although Than asked, he was not permitted to accompany them to the testing room. On the hearing officer's recommendation, Than was expelled for academic dishonesty.

Than retained legal counsel and appealed his dismissal to Dr. David Low, the president of the medical school. Dr. Low upheld Than's dismissal. Than filed this action alleging that UT had violated his right to procedural due process under the due course of law guarantee of the Texas Constitution. Tex. Const. art. I, § 19.

In January 1993, the trial court granted Than a permanent injunction ordering UT to: (1) change Than's failing grade on the surgery exam to a "B"; (2) remove from Than's school records all references to his expulsion and all documents concerning the charges against him, the investigation, recommendation, hearing and appeal; (3) treat Than as a student who graduated in good standing; and (4) issue Than a diploma and all certificates necessary for his participation in any post-graduate residency program. We agree that Than was not afforded adequate procedural due process before his expulsion and is entitled to a new hearing on the charge of academic dishonesty. We affirm the permanent injunction, but as modified.

I.

The due course of law guarantee of the Texas Constitution provides:

> No citizen of this State shall be deprived of life, liberty, property, privileges or immunities, or in any manner disfranchised, except by the due course of the law of the land.

Tex. Const. art. I, § 19. The Texas due course clause is nearly identical to the federal due process clause, which provides:

> No State shall make or enforce any law which shall abridge the privileges or immunities of citizens of the United States; nor shall any State deprive any person of life, liberty, or property, without due process of law; ...

U.S. Const. amend. XIV, § 1. While the Texas Constitution is textually different in that it refers to "due course" rather than "due process," we regard these terms as without meaningful distinction. *Mellinger v. City of Houston,* 68 Tex. 37, 3 S.W. 249, 252-53 (1887). As a result, in matters of procedural due process, we have traditionally followed contemporary federal due process interpretations of procedural due process issues. *Mellinger,* 3 S.W. at 252-53; *see also Spring Branch Indep. Sch. Dist. v. Stamos,* 695 S.W.2d 556, 560-61 (Tex.1985); *Tarrant County v. Ashmore,* 635 S.W.2d 417, 422-23 (Tex. 1982). Although not bound by federal due process jurisprudence in this case, we consider federal interpretations of procedural due process to be persuasive authority in applying our due course of law guarantee.

Our review of Than's due course claim requires a two-part analysis: (1) we must determine whether Than has a liberty or property interest that is entitled to procedural due process protection; and (2) if so, we must determine what process is due. *Logan v. Zimmerman Brush Co.,* 455 U.S. 422, 428 (1982); *Board of Regents of State Colleges v. Roth,* 408 U.S. 564, 569-70 (1972).

II.

The requirements of procedural due process apply only to the deprivation of interests protected under Article I, Section 19. Both UT and Than assume that Than has a protected liberty or property interest in continued graduate education at a state-supported university. However, UT invites this Court to conclude otherwise.

In defining the scope of protected liberty interests under the Fourteenth Amendment, the United States Supreme Court has stated that a liberty interest:

> [D]enotes not merely freedom from bodily restraint but also the right of the individual to contract, to engage in any of the common occupations of life, to acquire useful knowledge, to marry, establish a home and bring up children, to worship God according to the dictates of one's own conscience, and generally to enjoy those privileges long recognized . . . as essential to the orderly pursuit of happiness by free men.

Roth, 408 U.S. at 572 (quoting *Meyer v. Nebraska,* 262 U.S. 390, 399 (1923)). Moreover, where a person's good name, reputation, honor, or integrity is at stake because of what the government is doing to him, the minimal requirements of due process must be satisfied. *Goss v. Lopez,* 419 U.S. 565, 574 (1975); *Roth,* 408 U.S. at 573. Thus, where high school students were suspended from school for 10 days based on charges of misconduct, the school's unilateral suspension was found to deprive the students of a liberty interest in their standing with fellow students and their teachers and for later opportunities for higher education and employment. *Id.* at 575.

A medical student charged with academic dishonesty faces not only serious damage to his reputation but also the loss of his chosen profession as a physician. The stigma is likely to follow the student and preclude him from completing his education at other institutions. We hold that Than has a constitutionally protected liberty interest in his graduate education that must be afforded procedural due process.

III.

Having concluded that the due course guarantee applies, we must next determine what process is due. Due process at a minimum requires notice and an opportunity to be heard at a meaningful time and in a meaningful manner. *Mathews v. Eldridge,* 424 U.S. 319, 333 (1976); *Calvert,* 394 S.W.2d at 657. What process is due is measured by a flexible standard that depends on the practical requirements of the circumstances. *Mathews,* 424 U.S. at 334. This flexible standard includes three factors: (1) the private interest that will be affected by the official action; (2) the risk of an erroneous deprivation of such interest through the procedures used, and the probable value, if any, of additional or substitute procedural safeguards; and (3) the government's interest, including the function involved and the fiscal and administrative burdens that the additional or substitute procedural requirement would entail. *Mathews,* 424 U.S. at 335.

In student disciplinary actions involving temporary suspensions, the United States Supreme Court has held that due process requires that the student be given oral or written notice of the charges against him and, if he denies them, an explanation of the evidence the authorities have and an opportunity to present his side of the story. *Goss,* 419 U.S. at 581. *Goss* stopped short of requiring a formal hearing. Rather, *Goss* required nothing more than an "informal give-and-take" between the student and the administrative body dismissing him that would give the student the opportunity to characterize his conduct and put it in what he deems the proper context. *Id.* at 583-84.

At a minimum, when university officials seek to sanction a student for misconduct, our due course of law guarantee requires oral or written notice of the charges against the student and, if the student denies them, an explanation of the evidence the authorities have and an opportunity to present his or her side of the story. As a flexible standard, however, the process due may vary depending on the competing interests of the student and the university. When, as here, a student may be expelled and deprived not only of his or her education but of professional opportunities as well, the student's interest is entitled to more deference than would be afforded for a temporary suspension. Although university officials presumably act in good faith bringing charges of academic dishonesty against a student, there is a significant risk of error because the controlling facts are in dispute and university officials often must rely on circumstantial evidence and reports of others. *See Goss,* 419

U.S. at 580. Due process requires in this case something more than the "informal give-and-take" required for short temporary suspensions.

While we conclude that due process requires some level of process beyond the informal hearing of *Goss,* we cannot specify what process must be afforded for all disciplinary dismissals from state-supported universities. "The very nature of due process negates any concept of inflexible procedures universally applicable to every imaginable situation." *Cafeteria & Restaurant Workers Union v. McElroy,* 367 U.S. 886, 895 (1961); *Bexar County Sheriff's Civil Service Comm'n v. Davis,* 802 S.W.2d 659, 661-62 (Tex.1990). We caution, additionally, that a university "'is an academic institution, not a courtroom or administrative hearing room,' and thus should not be weighted down with formalized procedural requirements imposed by actors estranged from the academic environment." *Davis v. Mann,* 882 F.2d 967, 974 (5th Cir.1989). Judicial interposition in the disciplinary decisions of state supported schools raises problems requiring care and restraint. In addition, we are careful to admonish that the due course of law guarantee, like the due process clause, does not ensure that the academic disciplinary process is accurate and without error; it merely guards against the risk of unfair dismissal or suspension if that may be accomplished without prohibitive cost or interference with the educational process.

Mindful of these concerns, we note that UT, pursuant to its own rules and regulations, afforded Than a high level of due process. Than was given oral and written notice of the charges against him; was given written notice of evidence to be used against him in the hearing, including a witness list and summaries of their testimony; was afforded the right to counsel or other representation; and was afforded a formal hearing with the opportunity to present evidence and cross-examine witnesses. Despite this level of process, we conclude that Than's due course of law rights were violated by his exclusion from a portion of the evidentiary proceedings.

The undisputed evidence shows that at the conclusion of testimony and remarks in Than's hearing, the hearing officer personally examined the site where the test was conducted, accompanied only by Dr. McNeese. Than asked to accompany them to the testing room, but the hearing officer refused. [The] hearing officer testified by deposition that on her visit to the test site she sat in four different chairs, representing the place occupied by Than, Mr. Chiang, the student from whom Than allegedly cheated, and the two proctors. In her report concluding that Than should be expelled, she lists as one of her findings that "I sat in the chair occupied by Mr. Than during the examination and could clearly see the paper from the examination chair occupied by Mr. Chiang." In determining Than's guilt, the hearing officer relied, at least in part, on the evidence she obtained while sitting in those chairs.

If Than had been allowed to accompany the others, he would have had the opportunity to respond to this evidence and to offer his own explanation about the seating arrangements. But, because the visit was conducted ex parte and at the end of the presentation of the evidence, Than was given neither a contemporaneous nor an after-the-fact opportunity to respond.

We balance UT's failure to give Than an opportunity to rebut this evidence with the burden on UT of providing this procedural safeguard. In this case, we fail to see any burden that would have resulted from Than's presence during the visit to the examination room. We therefore conclude that Than was not accorded due course of law. *See Swank v. Smart,* 898 F.2d 1247, 1252-54 (7th Cir.1990) (holding that ex parte presentation of evidence during an employee's discharge hearing denied the employee due process).

IV.

In general, however, the remedy for a denial of due process is due process. *See Perry v. Sindermann,* 408 U.S. 593, 603 (1972) (upon proof of protected interest, professor whose contract was not renewed is not entitled to reinstatement but to hearing comporting with due process); *McIntire v. State,* 698 S.W.2d 652, 661-62 (Tex.Crim.App.1985) (remedy for failure to grant hearing on motion for new trial is a hearing, not a new trial). Than is entitled to a fair hearing with notice of the charges and evidence to be used against him and with an opportunity to defend against the charges. The injunction exceeds the proper remedy.

Moreover, the injunctive relief represents unwarranted judicial interference with the educational process. The courts should tread lightly in fashioning remedies for due process violations that affect the academic decisions of state-supported universities. What grade should be awarded and whether UT issues Than a diploma should be determined by university officials after notice and hearing.

We modify the permanent injunction and order that pending a new hearing on the charge of academic dishonesty, UT:

1. remove from Than's transcript the "F" he received for his grade in surgery; and
2. remove from Than's records the penalty of expulsion.

We affirm that portion of the permanent injunction ordering that the bond posted by Than in connection with the temporary injunction be refunded to Than. In all other respects, we vacate the permanent injunction.

Notes on State Due Course and Due Process Clauses

The Scope of the Texas Due Course of Law Clause: After reading *In re J.W.T.* and *Than*, does the interpretation of the Texas Due Course of Law Clause differ from the federal interpretation of the Due Process Clause? If so, in what ways? Are any such differences supported by the text, history, structure, or purpose of the Texas guarantee?

How far does the liberty interest recognized in *Than* extend? The Texas Supreme Court in *National Collegiate Athletic Ass'n v. Yeo* considered whether a world-class amateur swimmer had a liberty interest in her reputation and future earning potential requiring procedural due process protection before she could be declared ineligible for a NCAA swimming meet as a result of the University of Texas's mistakes in attempting to comply with NCAA rules. The court held that she did not have such a liberty interest, distinguishing

Than as a case involving graduate education rather than intercollegiate athletics.[292] The court, following its prior precedent and the "'overwhelming majority'" of decisions from federal and state courts interpreting due process and related guarantees, reasoned that students did not possess a "'constitutionally protected interest in their participation in extracurricular activities.'"[293] In the absence of such a protected interest, article I, section 19 was not implicated, just as federal due process doctrine requires a protected liberty or property interest before any process is due.

Most other state courts similarly view their state due course or due process clauses as roughly equivalent to the guarantees of the Federal Constitution.[294] Nevertheless, state court interpretations have sometimes been more flexible than the federal courts in certain situations, using the same basic methodology but seizing upon slight distinctions to reach contrary results.[295] Is that a reasonable description of the Texas Supreme Court's holding in *In re J.W.T.*?

Protection of Economic Liberties: State courts have sometimes articulated greater due process protection under state constitutions in the context of reviewing economic regulations. While the United States Supreme Court regularly protected economic liberties from 1897 to 1937 during the so-called *Lochner* era,[296] the Court has since disavowed review of economic regulations under the Due Process Clause, merely requiring the law to bear a rational relationship to a legitimate state interest.[297] But some state courts have continued to protect economic liberty through substantive due process review.

Indeed, the highest court in almost every state employed economic substantive due process to invalidate legislation from 1940-1969, after the end of the *Lochner* era.[298] Since 1969, the number of states continuing to do so has been steadily declining(at least outside the context of tort reform, a topic addressed in Chapter 5), but there are still intermittent state court decisions that rigorously enforce economic substantive due process. For example, the Florida Supreme Court in 2000 invalidated, on substantive due process grounds, a state statute prohibiting title insurance agents from negotiating partial rebates of their fees with their customers under the rationale that the statute unconstitutionally restricted a citizen's right to freely bargain for services without a reasonable relationship to

---

[292] 171 S.W.3d 863, 869-70 (Tex. 2005).

[293] *Id.* at 864 (quoting Spring Branch I.S.D. v. Stamos, 695 S.W.2d 556, 561 (Tex. 1985)).

[294] *See, e.g.*, Gray v. Hall, 265 P. 246, 252 (Cal. 1928) ("Due course of law under the state Constitution and due process of law under the Federal Constitution mean the same thing."); Ind. High Sch. Athletic Ass'n v. Carlberg, 694 N.E.2d 222, 241 (Ind. 1997) (concluding that the "same analysis" applies to both the Federal Due Process Clause and the state due course of law clause); State *ex rel.* Heller v. Miller, 399 N.E.2d 66, 67 (Ohio 1980) (reasoning that the state due course of law provision was the equivalent of the Federal Due Process Clause).

[295] *See, e.g.*, Sharrock v. Dell Buick-Cadillac, Inc., 379 N.E.2d 1169, 1173-78 (N.Y. 1978); Stanton v. Tax Comm'n, 151 N.E. 760, 764 (Ohio 1926).

[296] Lochner v. New York, 198 U.S. 45 (1905).

[297] *See, e.g.*, Williamson v. Lee Optical Co., 348 U.S. 483, 491 (1955).

[298] *See* Anthony B. Sanders, *The "New Judicial Federalism" Before Its Time*, 55 AM. UNIV. L. REV. 457, 461-63 (2005).

a public benefit.[299] The Georgia Supreme Court explained in 1987 that, under its state constitution, the right to contract and for the parties to agree on a price, even a price below cost, are protected property rights that the General Assembly cannot abridge unless the business is affected with a public interest, "no matter what other states or the Supreme Court of the United States 'may or may not have decided.'"[300]

The Texas position is somewhat unclear, as Texas courts have not always been consistent in articulating the appropriate standard of review of economic regulations under the due course of law clause.[301] Some decisions have indicated that the due course of law provides an identical guarantee to the Federal Due Process Clause.[302] But in other decisions, the Texas Supreme Court has relied on the interrelationship between the due course of law clause and the takings clause to create at least an arguably more rigorous standard for reviewing economic regulations.[303] For instance, *Eggemeyer v. Eggemeyer* relied on the substantive component of the due course of law clause as an alternative argument for invalidating a divorce decree's transfer of a husband's separate property to his wife because such a taking could not be "justified by any benefit to the public welfare."[304] Is it preferable to place the burden on the legislature to justify the public welfare benefits of the economic regulations it enacts? Or should the courts defer to the legislative judgment?

F. EQUAL PROTECTION AND EQUAL RIGHTS

The American promise from the Declaration of Independence is that "all men are created equal," even though this promise remained unfulfilled for much of American history. After the Civil War, the Fourteenth Amendment's Equal Protection Clause was added to the United States Constitution to help secure this promise as part of the nation's fundamental law. This clause prevents any state from denying "to any person within its jurisdiction the equal protection of the laws."

---

[299]Chicago Title Ins. Co. v. Butler, 770 So. 2d 1210, 1220 (Fla. 2000).

[300]Strickland v. Ports Petroleum Co., 353 S.E.2d 17, 18 (Ga. 1987) (quoting Cox v. General Elec. Co., 85 S.E.2d 514, 519 (Ga. 1955)).

[301]*Cf.* Texas Workers' Compensation Comm'n v. Garcia, 893 S.W.2d 504, 525 (Tex. 1995) (recognizing inconsistency in prior cases); Trinity River Auth. v. URS Consultants, Inc., 889 S.W.2d 259, 263-64 (Tex. 1994) (same).

[302]*See, e.g.*, Mellinger v. City of Houston, 3 S.W. 249, 252-53 (Tex. 1887); Lindsay v. Papageorgiou, 751 S.W.2d 544, 550 (Tex. App.–Houston [1st Dist.] 1988, writ denied).

[303]*See, e.g.*, Tex. Power & Light Co. v. City of Garland, 431 S.W.2d 511, 516-20 (Tex. 1968) (relying on the interrelationship between article I, section 17 and 19 of the Texas Constitution to invalidate a city ordinance ousting an electric company from exercising its franchise rights in competition with a municipally owned electric plant); State v. Richards, 301 S.W.2d 597, 602-03 (Tex. 1957) (analyzing interrelationship between the two constitutional provisions in upholding forfeiture statute). Some older Texas decisions have also applied the state's guarantee of equal rights to provide slightly more protection than the federal equal protection guarantee in the economic sphere. *See, e.g.*, San Antonio Retail Grocers, Inc. v. Lafferty, 297 S.W.2d 813, 816 (Tex. 1957) (holding that statute prohibiting sales below cost by grocery stores was invalid because there was no reasonable basis to limit the prohibition to grocery stores). However, more recent Texas cases have moved away from this position, as discussed in the next section.

[304]554 S.W.2d 137, 140-41 (Tex.1977).

Most state constitutions likewise contain some type of provision offering protection for equality interests, but these provisions diverge markedly. Around one-fourth of the states have clauses mirroring the Federal Equal Protection Clause, preventing the denial to any person of the "equal protection of the laws."[305] Other states phrase at least part of the protection in terms of recognizing or declaring the "equal rights" or "equal benefits" of all citizens,[306] while other state clauses specify certain categories of prohibited discrimination, such as race, religion, color, national origin, gender, or, in three states, disability.[307] Still other states, rather than focusing on discrimination against a minority, prohibit the award of special rights or privileges to a select few.[308] Finally, many state constitutions have combined two or more of the preceding types of clauses in their equality guarantees.[309]

The Texas Constitution mixes several of these different types of equality clauses in two provisions. The first provision, article I, section 3, has been included in some form in every Texas Constitution. It both protects "equal rights" for everyone and prevents special privileges to a select few:

> All free men, when they form a social compact, have equal rights, and no man, or set of men, is entitled to exclusive separate public emoluments, or privileges, but in consideration of public services.[310]

The second provision, article I, section 3a, was added by a 1972 amendment to the Texas Constitution. Frequently referred to as the "Texas Equal Rights Amendment," it specifies certain grounds of prohibited discrimination:

> Equality under the law shall not be denied or abridged because of sex, race, color, creed, or national origin. This amendment is self-operative.[311]

A noteworthy aspect of article I, section 3a is that it explicitly prevents equality from being denied because of "sex." This amendment was added to the state constitution

---

[305]*See, e.g.*, CAL. CONST. art. I, § 7(a); CONN. CONST. amend. XXI; HAW. CONST. art. I, § 5; ILL. CONST. art. I, § 2; LA. CONST. art. I, § 3; MICH. CONST. art. I, § 2; MONT. CONST. art. II, § 4; N.Y. CONST. art. I, §11; N.C. CONST. art. I, § 19.

[306]*See, e.g.*, CONN. CONST. art. I, § 1; FLA. CONST. art. I, § 2; KAN. CONST. BILL OF RIGHTS § 1; MO. CONST. art. I, § 2; OHIO CONST. art. I, § 2.

[307]*See, e.g.*, CONN. CONST. amend. XXI; FLA. CONST. art. I, § 2; HAW. CONST. art. I, § 5; LA. CONST. art. I, § 3; MICH. CONST. art. I, § 2; MONT. CONST. art. II, § 4; N.Y. CONST. art. I, § 11; N.C. CONST. art. I, § 19. Connecticut, Florida, and Louisiana are the three states that prevent discrimination based on "physical or mental disability," "physical disability" and "physical condition," respectively, with Louisiana also outlawing arbitrary and unreasonable discrimination due to "birth," "age," "sex," or "culture." CONN. CONST. amend. XXI; FLA. CONST. art. I, § 2; LA. CONST. art. I, § 3.

[308]*See, e.g.*, CAL. CONST. art. I, § 7(b); CONN. CONST. art. I, § 1; OR. CONST. art. I, § 20; WASH. CONST. art. I, § 12.

[309]*See, e.g.*, CAL. CONST. art. I, § 7; CONN. CONST. art. I, § 1 & amend. XXI; FLA. CONST. art. I, § 2; HAW. CONST. art. I, § 5; LA. CONST. art. I, § 3; MONT. CONST. art. II, § 4; MICH. CONST. art. I, § 2; N.Y. CONST. art. I, § 11; N.C. CONST. art. I, § 19.

[310]TEX. CONST. art. I, § 3.

[311]TEX. CONST. art. I, § 3a.

at the same time Texas ratified the Federal Equal Rights Amendment, which would have prevented the denial of equality under the law by the United States or any state on account of sex. However, the Federal Equal Rights Amendment was not ratified by the required three-fourths of all the states (falling only a handful of states short), and accordingly is not part of the United States Constitution. Yet even though gender equality failed at the federal level, approximately fifteen other states adopted their own "little equal rights amendments" prohibiting gender discrimination.[312]

Do such distinctions between the federal and state constitutional texts impact the interpretation of state equality guarantees? Despite the textual differences, Texas generally follows the same basic principles familiar from federal equal protection doctrine, especially when interpreting the original Texas Equal Rights provision in article I, section 3 (also referred to as the Texas Equal Protection Clause). Recent Texas cases have confirmed that this provision provides similar protections as afforded by the Federal Equal Protection Clause,[313] even though some older cases arguably interpreted it to provide greater protection in the realm of economic regulations.[314] Moreover, the vast majority of the states likewise interpret their equality guarantees in a manner similar to the United States Supreme Court's interpretation of the Federal Equal Protection Clause.[315]

---

[312]*See, e.g.,* ALASKA CONST. art. I, § 3; COLO. CONST. art. II, § 29; CONN. CONST. amend. XXI; FLA. CONST. art. I, § 2; HAW. CONST. art. I, §§ 3, 5; ILL. CONST. art. I, § 18; IOWA CONST. art. I, § 1; MD. CONST. DECL. OF RTS. art. 46; MASS. CONST. part I, art. 1; MONT. CONST. art. II, § 4; N.H. CONST. part I, art. 2; N.M. CONST. art. II, § 18; PA. CONST. art. I, § 28; VA. CONST. art. I, § 11; WASH. CONST. art. XXXI, § 1. The California and Louisiana Constitutions also contain some protections against gender discrimination, but these protections are more limited. *See* CAL. CONST. art. I, §§ 8, 31; LA. CONST. art. I, § 3. Finally, Utah and Wyoming have long-standing provisions in their statehood constitutions, which were adopted in the 1890's, guaranteeing women the right to vote, hold office, and enjoy all civil and political rights. UTAH CONST. art. IV, § 1; WYO. CONST. art. I, § 3 & art. VI, § 1.

[313]*See, e.g.,* Bell v. Low Income Women of Tex., 95 S.W.3d 253, 266 (Tex. 2002) (noting recent state court decisions "have clarified that the federal analytical approach applies to equal protection challenges under the Texas Constitution"); Barshop v. Medina Cnty. Underground Water Conserv. Dist., 925 S.W.2d 618, 631 (Tex. 1996) (employing rational basis test to adjudge constitutionality of economic regulation); Richards v. League of United Latin Am. Citizens, 868 S.W.2d 306, 310 (Tex. 1993) ("As under the Fourteenth Amendment, equal protection challenges under the Texas Constitution are reviewed under a multi-tiered system."); Rose v. Doctors Hosp., 801 S.W.2d 841, 846 (Tex. 1990) (stating "Texas cases echo federal standards when determining whether a statute violates equal protection").

[314]*See, e.g.,* HL Farm Corp. v. Self, 877 S.W.2d 288, 292 (Tex. 1994) (holding prohibition against open-space land designation for property owned by corporations with a majority interest owned by nonresident aliens was not rationally related to the purpose of the statute, as ascertained by the court, of promoting the preservation of open-space land devoted to farm or ranch purposes); Whitworth v. Bynum, 699 S.W.2d 194, 196-97 (Tex. 1985) (holding state guest statute unconstitutional under rational basis test of the state equal rights provision due to the overinclusiveness of the statute's irrebuttable presumption that all suits by closely related passengers against the driver of an automobile were collusive, while acknowledging the existence of contrary federal precedent); San Antonio Retail Grocers, Inc. v. Lafferty, 297 S.W.2d 813, 815-17 (Tex. 1957) (holding statute prohibiting sales below cost applicable only to grocery stores violated Texas equal rights provision as department stores and drug stores also sold similar items without such a restriction); Humble Oil & Ref. Co. v. City of Georgetown, 428 S.W.2d 405, 410-14 (Tex. Civ. App.–Austin 1968, no writ) (holding city ordinance restricting the capacity of trucks delivering gasoline to filling stations violated Texas equal rights provision because evidence established larger trucks were safer).

[315]*See* 1 JENNIFER FRIESEN, STATE CONSTITUTIONAL LAW: LITIGATING INDIVIDUAL RIGHTS, CLAIMS AND DEFENSES § 3.01[3] (4th ed. 2006) (noting only a few states reject federal equal protection methodology and terminology in interpreting their own equality guarantees).

Nevertheless, there is one major difference between the scope of equality rights under the federal and state constitutions: the states, especially those states explicitly protecting against gender discrimination, have often required more exacting scrutiny in cases of sex discrimination. Texas is in the mainstream of this trend, as it held in the following case that the Texas Equal Rights Amendment provides a textual basis for applying strict scrutiny (rather than the intermediate scrutiny employed under federal law) in cases of gender discrimination.

In re Baby McLean, 725 S.W.2d 696 (Tex. 1987)

KILGARLIN, Justice.

The Texas Equal Rights Amendment, Tex. Const. art. I, § 3a, was adopted in 1972. This case calls upon us to make an initial interpretation of the extent of its guarantees. In 1983, Laura McLean, unwed, gave birth to a child. The undisputed father of the child, Billy Dean Wise, was then, and still remains, married to another woman. McLean decided to allow the infant to be adopted and the prospective parents brought suit to terminate the parent-child relationship as to both McLean and Wise. Wise filed a cross-action for legitimation, seeking managing conservatorship. The would-be adoptive parents then took a non-suit and McLean filed a general denial, opposing Wise's legitimation request and asking that no conservator be appointed. The Child Welfare Unit of Wichita County Family Court Services intervened, seeking managing conservatorship of the child, supported by McLean's affidavit urging that the child be placed with the Child Welfare Unit and stating that Wise was an unfit person to care for the child.

After trial to the court, the Child Welfare Unit was appointed managing conservator and Wise's suit for legitimation was denied. Wise appealed and a divided court of appeals affirmed the trial court judgment. Wise filed this application for writ of error, alleging violations of both the United States and Texas Constitutions, because he was forced to prove that legitimation would be in the child's best interest. Based on the Texas Equal Rights Amendment, we reverse.

Article I, section 3a, of the Texas Constitution provides that "[e]quality under the law shall not be denied or abridged because of sex, race, color, creed, or national origin." The first step in a case invoking this provision is to determine whether equality under the law has been denied. Any discrimination which occurred in the instant case is clearly "under the law" because it is required by state statute. Our next inquiry is whether equality was denied *because of* a person's membership in a protected class of sex, race, color, creed, or national origin.

Thus, the task in this case is to examine the Family Code to see if it treats Wise differently because he is male. When a child is born to a woman not married to the child's father, she automatically exercises all of the rights, duties, and privileges of the parent-child relationship. Tex.Fam.Code Ann. § 12.04 (Vernon 1986). Circumstances are different for a man who is not married to the child's mother: the father has all of those parental rights, duties, and responsibilities *only if the mother consents.* Tex.Fam.Code Ann. § 13.21(b) (Vernon 1986). Should the mother deny her consent, she pits the acknowledged father against the state: he must convince the trier of fact that legitimation best serves the child's interest if his paternity is to be legally recognized. Tex.Fam.Code Ann. § 13.21(c) (Vernon 1986). But, a man seeking to terminate a mother's parental rights finds the burden placed on him to prove that the child's best interest compels severing the child's relationship with the mother. Without maternal consent or meeting a higher burden of proof, the father has no rights in regard to his own child. Mothers are never subjected to such a proceeding; a woman, until her rights are terminated, exercises her parental prerogatives regardless of the father's veto. This is a gender-based distinction because only men are required to satisfy the "best interest" test before being recognized as a parent.

Having determined that the challenged statute discriminates on the basis of gender, we next focus on whether such discrimination is prohibited by the Equal Rights Amendment. At the outset, we note that federal precedent is not controlling when considering a case under the Texas Equal Rights Amendment. Moreover, no federal constitutional counterpart exists, efforts to secure ratification of a national E.R.A. having met with a lack of success. Therefore, we decide this case on independent state constitutional grounds.

We decline to give the Texas Equal Rights Amendment an interpretation identical to that given state and federal due process and equal protection guarantees. Both the United States Constitution and the Texas Constitution had due process and equal protection guarantees before the Texas Equal Rights Amendment was adopted in 1972. U.S. Const.Amend. V; XIV, § 1; Tex. Const. art. I, §§ 3, 13, 19. If the due process and equal protection provisions and the Equal Rights Amendment are given identical interpretations, then the 1972 amendment, adopted by a four to one margin by Texas voters, was an exercise in futility. Instead of rendering the added guarantees meaningless, we conclude that the Equal Rights Amendment is more extensive and provides more specific protection than both the United States and Texas due process and equal protection guarantees.

Our Bill of Rights is not made up of a series of one-dimensional rules, to be applied blindly, but instead declares a guiding norm and principle to be applied and interpreted by the courts. We thus choose not to adopt a *per se* standard which would automatically invalidate gender-based distinctions, but rather seek a standard to be used to reach the evils which it was designed to combat. Our reading of the Equal Rights Amendment elevates sex to a suspect classification. Sex is clearly listed in the amendment along with other classifications afforded maximum constitutional protection.

The appropriate standard is thus one which recognizes that the Equal Rights Amendment does not yield except to compelling state interests. Further, it is not enough to say that the state has an important interest furthered by the discriminatory law. Even the loftiest goal does not justify sex-based discrimination in light of the clear constitutional prohibition. Under our model of strict judicial scrutiny, such discrimination is allowed only when the proponent of the discrimination can prove that there is no other manner to protect the state's compelling interest. *Mercer v. Board of Trust, North Forest Indep. Sch. Dis.*, 538 S.W.2d 201 (Tex.Civ.App-Houston [14th Dist.] 1976, writ ref'd n.r.e.).

In this case, the state no doubt has a significant interest in protecting the welfare of a child born to a mother not married to the child's father. Nevertheless, the state's interest can be protected without discriminating solely on the basis of sex. The state goal of protecting children's welfare is better served by keying that interest to the father's relationship to the child. A father who steps forward, willing and able to shoulder the responsibilities of raising a child should not be required to meet a higher burden of proof solely because he is male.

Because we hold that sections 13.21(b) and (c) of the Texas Family Code violates the Texas Constitution, we need not reach the federal law issues in this case. We reverse the judgment of the court of appeals and remand this cause to the trial court so that it can declare Wise's parental rights, if any, and resolve the conservatorship issue without regard to sex. Texas Family Code section 14.01 (Vernon 1986) provides an adequate basis for this determination.

GONZALEZ, Justice, concurring and dissenting, joined by Justice Wallace.

I concur with the part of the opinion that adopts strict scrutiny as the standard of review for gender-based discrimination under the Texas Equal Rights Amendment. Tex. Const. art. I, § 3a. I disagree, however, that the cause should be remanded to the trial court for further proceedings. I would hold that the trial court abused its discretion and render judgment that Wise is the legitimate father of the child. I would also terminate the mother's parental rights and name Wise managing conservator.

Within two days of the baby's birth, Wise made arrangements to pay the hospital bill and began his efforts to get custody of his child. Because the child's mother desired that the child be adopted rather than be raised by his father, this unfortunate chain of events began and the child was placed in a foster home, where he is today. It has been almost four years since the child was born and Wise has been denied every effort to establish an ongoing relationship with his son. His offer to support the child was denied and his efforts to visit his little boy have been thwarted by the State. It is time to end this nightmare.

ROBERTSON, Justice, dissenting on Motion for Rehearing, joined by Chief Justice Hill, Justice Campbell, and Justice Spears.

The classification about which Petitioner complains has less to do with gender than it does the recognition of a simple fact of life: only a woman can conceive, carry and give birth to a child. It is for this reason that the mother is the easily identifiable parent who must automatically assume responsibility for the child. From the moment of conception, it is the woman, and the woman alone, who bears the physical, emotional and financial burden of her pregnancy. The biological father, on the other hand, is totally free from any responsibility with respect to the child unless and until he chooses to step forward or some action is taken against him. Meanwhile, the mother is constantly faced with decisions about how to best care for the child.

Section 13.21 does in fact provide for consideration of the father's relationship to the child and it is the evidence of that relationship that led to the trial court's determination that it was not in the child's best interest to be legitimated as to Wise. Wise did not "step forward" until after the child was born and he was informed of the adoption proceedings, although he was told by McLean that she was pregnant several months prior to birth of the child. Further, there is no credible evidence that Wise offered to support the child or that he made arrangements to pay McLean's medical bills. In fact, the hospital bill remains unpaid. More importantly, however, the record reflects that Wise is a diagnosed chronic paranoid schizophrenic for which he has been rated 100% disabled by the Veterans Administration and for which he now receives $1,400 per month in disability benefits. He is unable to hold down a steady job due to his violent temperament. At the time of the trial of this cause, three felony indictments were pending against Wise, one of which was dismissed the day of trial when Wise made restitution. These are all factors which should be taken into consideration when awarding custody, visitation or support of the child.

Notes on Equal Rights Amendments

Gender Classifications: The first step in traditional equal protection analysis is determining the nature of the classification established by the statute or policy at issue. The dissent in *In re Baby McLean* urged that the statute was not a case of gender discrimination because it merely recognized biological differences between men and women. Should such biological differences be important in this context? Was there a different argument the dissent could have made? Did the statutory scheme always treat men differently than women, or was there a more precise classification that could explain the disparate treatment?

Other jurisdictions with state constitutional texts protecting gender equality have also held that distinctions between the rights of fathers and mothers with respect to illegitimate children constitute gender discrimination. As one example, the Washington Supreme Court held in *Guard v. State* that a statute requiring a father of a child born out of wedlock to have regularly contributed to the financial support of the child before joining a wrongful death action for the death of a child, while not placing a support requirement on the mother, discriminated against the father on account of his sex in violation of the Washington Constitution.[316] In contrast, the Supreme Court of the United States reasoned that a similar Georgia statute denying an illegitimate father the right to bring a wrongful death action did "not invidiously discriminate against the [father] simply because he is of the male sex" under the Federal Equal Protection Clause.[317]

Determining when a gender-based classification exists has caused interpretive difficulties in a number of contexts, both in Texas and in other jurisdictions. As discussed earlier in this chapter, a plurality of the Hawaii Supreme Court reasoned in *Baehr v. Lewin* that reserving marriage to opposite-sex couples constituted gender discrimination by constraining a person's individual choice of a marital partner by his or her own gender.[318] But a number of courts have disagreed that legal disabilities against same-sex couples

---

[316]940 P.2d 642, 645 (Wash. 1997); *accord* R. McG. v. J.W., 615 P.2d 666, 670-71 (Colo. 1980) (holding a statutory scheme which granted mothers of illegitimate children five years to seek a declaration of paternity against a natural father when they were married to another man but did not provide the natural father a right to seek paternity "was a gender classification that violates the equal rights amendment to the Colorado constitution").

[317]Parham v. Hughes, 441 U.S. 347, 355 (1979) (Stewart, J., plurality op.).

[318]852 P.2d 44, 56-66 (Levinson, J., plurality op.), *reconsideration and clarification granted in part*, 875 P.2d 74 (Haw. 1993).

constitute gender discrimination,[319] including the en banc decision of the Texas Fourteenth Court of Appeals in *Lawrence v. State*.[320] In holding that the Texas Penal Code's ban on certain sexual acts between members of the same sex did not violate the Texas Equal Rights Amendment, the majority of the en banc court determined that the statute did not discriminate on the basis of gender. The court reasoned that the statute applied equally to men and women and that the statute was not "intended to promote any hostility between the sexes, preserve any unequal treatment as between men and women, or perpetuate any societal or cultural bias with respect to gender."[321] In contrast, the dissenters urged that the statute did constitute gender discrimination because "the same behavior is criminal for some but not for others, based solely on the sex of the individuals who engage in the behavior. In other words, the sex of the individual, not the conduct, is the sole determinant of the criminality of the conduct."[322]

The Level of Scrutiny: Did either the concurring or the dissenting opinion in *In re Baby McLean* disagree with the plurality that gender-based classifications should be subject to strict scrutiny under the Texas Equal Rights Amendment? The application of strict scrutiny to sex-based discrimination under the Texas Equal Rights Amendment has not been controversial. Most other states with similar equal rights amendments protecting gender have also employed strict scrutiny.[323] Yet two states–Pennsylvania and Washington–have determined that a more exacting scrutiny is required that bars any classifications based on sex unless necessary to account for physical differences between men and women.[324]

Other Applications of the Texas Equal Rights Amendment: The Texas Equal Rights Amendment has been raised most frequently in family law cases. *In re Guthrie*, from the Dallas Court of Appeals, reasoned that the Texas Equal Rights Amendment precluded any type of presumptive preference for the father's surname in a petition for a minor's name change, although the court went on to hold that the trial court had not abused its discretion in determining that it was in the toddler's best interest to have his father's surname rather

---

[319]*See, e.g.*, Conaway v. Deane, 932 A.2d 571, 585-99 (Md. 2007); Baker v. State, 744 A.2d 864, 880-81 n.13 (Vt. 1999); Andersen v. King Cnty., 138 P.3d 963, 987-89 (Wash. 2006) (Madsen, J., plurality op.).

[320]41 S.W.3d 349, 357-58 (Tex. App.–Houston [14th Dist.] 2001), *rev'd on other grounds*, 539 U.S. 558 (2003).

[321]*Id.*

[322]*Id.* at 370 (Anderson, J., dissenting).

[323]*See, e.g.*, Child Support Enforcement Agency v. Doe, 125 P.3d 461, 471 (Haw. 2005); Estate of Hicks, 675 N.E.2d 89, 92-93 (Ill. 1996); *In re* Roberto d.B., 923 A.2d 115, 123 n.13 (Md. 2007); DuPont v. Comm'r of Corr., 861 N.E.2d 744, 752 (Mass. 2007); LeClair v. LeClair, 624 A.2d 1350, 1355 (N.H. 1993); *cf.* Daly v. DelPonte, 624 A.2d 876, 883 (Conn. 1993) (applying strict scrutiny to prohibition on disability discrimination contained in same clause as the ban on gender discrimination).

[324]*See, e.g.*, Henderson v. Henderson, 327 A.2d 60, 62 (Pa. 1974); S.W. Wash. Chapter, Nat'l Elec. Contractors Ass'n v. Pierce Cnty., 667 P.2d 1092, 1102 (Wash. 1983); Darrin v. Gould, 540 P.2d 882, 889 (Wash. 1975). The Washington Supreme Court reasoned that, because its prior cases held that gender discrimination triggered strict scrutiny *before* the state adopted its own equal rights amendment, the amendment necessarily entailed a heightened proscription on gender classification. *Darrin*, 540 P.2d at 889.

than his mother's ex-spouse's surname.[325] In another family law case, *Henderson v. Wietzikoski*, the Waco Court of Appeals held that the Family Code's provisions precluding a biological father from having standing to establish parental rights if his child was born into another's marriage violated both the Due Course of Law Clause and Equal Rights Amendment of the Texas Constitution.[326] The court reasoned that allowing the mother to sue to establish the father's paternity while not allowing the natural father to sue was gender-based discrimination necessitating heightened scrutiny.[327] In a case presented in the last section, *In re J.W.T.*, the Texas Supreme Court held that this same marital presumption violated due course of law, but it did not discuss the Texas Equal Rights Amendment. Is the *Henderson* court correct that the marital presumption was based on gender even though the presumed father could also deny paternity? Consider whether the following case from the Texas Supreme Court impacts *Henderson*'s holding on the existence of gender-based classifications.

Bell v. Low Income Women of Texas, 95 S.W.3d 253 (Tex. 2002)

Justice O'NEILL delivered the opinion of the Court, in which Chief Justice PHILLIPS, Justice HECHT, Justice ENOCH, Justice OWEN, Justice JEFFERSON, Justice SCHNEIDER and Justice SMITH joined.

In this case, plaintiffs challenge certain restrictions the State's Medicaid program places on abortion funding. The program provides medically necessary services for which federal matching funds are available. Before 1976, those services included abortions that were determined to be medically necessary. But after the United States Congress passed the Hyde Amendment in 1976, federal funds could no longer be used for medically necessary abortions unless the pregnancy resulted from rape or incest or placed the woman in danger of death. When federal matching funds became unavailable, the State stopped funding medically necessary abortions that did not comply with the Hyde Amendment. Plaintiffs claim that this funding restriction violates the Texas Constitution's Equal Rights Amendment and Equal Protection Clause, and their constitutional right to privacy, because the State applies a higher standard of medical necessity for treatments that involve abortion than it applies to all other medical services.

We hold that the funding restrictions do not discriminate on the basis of sex and are rationally related to a legitimate governmental purpose; thus, they do not violate the Equal Rights Amendment. We further hold that the restrictions violate neither the constitutional right to privacy nor the Equal Protection Clause.

---

[325]45 S.W.3d 719, 724-27 (Tex. App.–Dallas 2001, pet. denied); *accord In re* Custody of J.C.O., 993 P.2d 667, 669-70 (Mont. 1999) (noting similar equality concerns regarding presumption in favor of father's name).

[326]841 S.W.2d 101 (Tex. App.–Waco 1992, writ denied).

[327]*Id.* at 104-05.

I. Background

A. Statutory framework

Since 1965, the federal government's Medicaid program has offered matching funds to states that provide health services to the indigent. If a state implements a program that meets certain minimum standards, the federal government will contribute a percentage of the cost of providing indigent health services in the state. 42 U.S.C. §§ 1396-1396b. A participating state may choose, at its own expense, to provide indigent health services in addition to those which the federal government reimburses, although Texas has chosen not to do so. Tex. Hum. Res.Code § 32.024(e). All states participate in the Medicaid program.

Every year since 1976, Congress has adopted the Hyde Amendment, a rider to the federal Medicaid statute that limits the availability of federal matching funds for abortions. Texas has participated in Medicaid since 1967 through the Texas Medical Assistance Program (TMAP). The act implementing TMAP expressly provides that TMAP "may not authorize the provision of any service to any person under the program unless federal matching funds are available to pay the cost of the service." Tex. Hum. Res.Code § 32.024(e). As a result, the Hyde Amendment applies to prohibit TMAP funding for abortions unless the pregnancy results from rape or incest, or places the woman in danger of death.

B. The Present Litigation

Three physicians and three clinics that provide abortions filed this lawsuit on behalf of themselves and their Medicaid-eligible patients against the Texas Board of Health, the Texas Department of Health, and Charles E. Bell, the Texas Commissioner of Health (the State). Plaintiffs claim that certain medical conditions may be caused or aggravated by pregnancy, such as premature ruptured membrane, preeclampsia, eclampsia, hypertension, diabetes, congenital heart disease, renal failure, sickle cell anemia, asthma, epilepsy, and cancer. Some of these conditions cannot be treated while a woman is pregnant. And some of these conditions can, if the pregnancy is not terminated, cause a woman to suffer strokes, severe bleeding disorders, eye disease, heart failure, renal function deterioration, seizures, and accelerated growth of breast cancer tumors. Plaintiffs claim that the State's abortion funding restrictions cause indigent women to delay or forego medically necessary abortions, causing them to either risk or experience harm to their health.

Plaintiffs filed this suit seeking a judgment declaring that TMAP's abortion funding restrictions violate indigent women's right to privacy, and their rights under the Equal Rights Amendment and Equal Protection Clause[328] of the Texas Constitution.

II. Equal Rights Amendment

A. Discriminatory Intent

Texas passed the Equal Rights Amendment to the Texas Constitution in 1972. The Equal Rights Amendment was "designed expressly to provide protection which supplements

---

[328] Although our Constitution does not use the words "equal protection," we have typically referred to the guarantee of equal rights afforded by article I, section 3 by that term. *See, e.g., Barshop v. Medina County Underground Water Conservation Dist.,* 925 S.W.2d 618, 631 (Tex.1996); *Peeler v. Hughes & Luce,* 909 S.W.2d 494, 499 (Tex.1995).

the federal guarantees of equal treatment." TEXAS LEGISLATIVE COUNCIL, 14 PROPOSED CONSTITUTIONAL AMENDMENTS ANALYZED FOR ELECTION–NOVEMBER 7, 1972 at 24 (1972). Plaintiffs contend that the abortion funding restrictions discriminate on the basis of sex because the State funds virtually all medically necessary services for men, while refusing to fund abortions that are medically necessary. They further maintain that the restrictions serve no compelling State interest and thus are constitutionally infirm.

In *In re McLean,* a plurality of this Court described a three-step process for evaluating alleged Equal Rights Amendment violations. 725 S.W.2d 696, 697 (Tex.1987) (plurality opinion). That process is consistent with the Equal Rights Amendment's language and purposes, and the parties agree that we should apply it here. In doing so, we first decide whether equality under the law has been denied. If it has, the Equal Rights Amendment's language compels us to determine "whether equality was denied *because* of a person's membership in a protected class of sex, race, color, creed, or national origin." *Id.* If we conclude that equality was denied because of a person's membership in a protected class, the challenged action cannot stand unless it is narrowly tailored to serve a compelling governmental interest. *See id.* at 698.

In the present case, it is undisputed that the State provides virtually all medically necessary services to indigent men, yet it denies funding for abortions that are determined to be medically necessary. Because the State treats indigent women seeking abortions differently from all others, the plaintiffs have established the first prong of the *McLean* analysis, that is, that equality under the law has been denied. The question we must decide is whether equality has been denied "because of" sex. The State contends that this disparity is not sex based because the funding restriction, section 32.024(e) of the Human Resources Code, is facially neutral and merely prohibits funding any services that are not federally reimbursable. Plaintiffs, on the other hand, look solely to the Hyde Amendment's terms and argue that, because only women can become pregnant, funding is necessarily denied "because of" sex. We believe the question is not as straightforward as either party suggests.

In the present case, it is true that the funding restrictions affect only women, but that is because only women can become pregnant. If the State were to deny funding of all medically necessary pregnancy-related services, the classification might be comparable to the overt gender-based distinction in *McLean.* But while the TMAP, through the Hyde Amendment, denies funding for medically necessary abortions unless certain conditions are met, it does fund all other medically necessary pregnancy-related services. Thus, to say that the State's funding restriction discriminates on the basis of pregnancy, which in turn is gender based, misses the mark. The classification here is not so much directed at women as a class as it is abortion as a medical treatment, which, because it involves a potential life, has no parallel as a treatment method. We simply cannot say that the classification is, by its terms, "because of sex" as it was in *McLean.* But that does not end our inquiry. If the TMAP funding scheme is merely a pretext designed to prefer males over females in the provision of health care, then discrimination "because of sex" is established and the funding restrictions must withstand strict scrutiny to pass constitutional muster. *See Pers. Adm'r of Mass. v. Feeney,* 442 U.S. 256, 273 (1979) (noting that discrimination that is "overtly or covertly designed to prefer males over females would require an exceedingly persuasive justification").

In determining whether the TMAP classification is impermissibly sex based, plaintiffs would have us examine only the Hyde Amendment, while the State urges us to consider only section 32.024(e). But we believe the proper focus is the TMAP funding scheme as a whole. That scheme is based upon the interplay between section 32.024(e), a facially neutral statute, and a federal funding restriction that places indigent women seeking medically necessary abortions in a distinct class. As far as we can tell, no other state appeals court that has considered the issue had before it a statute similarly authorizing the provision of services only to the extent federal matching funds are available.[329]

In *McLean,* the plurality concluded that the statute denied equal treatment "because of sex" because the statute, by its terms, treated men differently from women based solely on gender, but did not discuss how courts should decide the issue when the classification is not so overtly gender based and arises at least in part from a facially neutral law. While the plurality "decline[d] to give the Equal Rights Amendment an interpretation identical to that given state and federal due process and equal protection guarantees," *McLean,* 725 S.W.2d at 697, we find helpful guidance on this particular issue in federal authorities.

Under federal law, unless an action challenged on equal protection grounds explicitly creates a suspect classification, a litigant must establish that the action stems from a discriminatory purpose in order to subject the action to strict scrutiny. *See Hunt v. Cromartie,* 526 U.S. 541, 546 (1999). When a federal equal protection challenge rests upon disparate impact, rather than explicit classification, the federal courts apply the analytical framework the United States Supreme Court first described in *Village of Arlington Heights v. Metropolitan Housing Development Corporation,* 429 U.S. 252 (1977).

According to *Arlington Heights,* determining whether the requisite discriminatory purpose exists "demands a sensitive inquiry into such circumstantial and direct evidence of intent as may be available." 429 U.S. at 266. Disproportionate impact is one piece of evidence. *Id.* Other factors the Court identified include the historical background providing the context for the challenged action, the specific sequence of events leading up to it,

---

[329]Three other state appeals courts have considered challenges under their own Equal Rights Amendments to abortion funding restrictions. Two have held that the restrictions violated their state Equal Rights Amendments. *See Doe v. Maher,* 40 Conn.Supp. 394, 515 A.2d 134 (1986)(holding restrictions unconstitutional under statutory scheme that did not require that services be eligible for federal matching funds); *New Mexico Right to Choose/NARAL v. Johnson,* 126 N.M. 788, 975 P.2d 841 (1998)(holding restrictions unconstitutional where statutory scheme did not require that services be eligible for federal matching funds). One court has upheld them. *See Fischer v. Dep't of Pub. Welfare,* 509 Pa. 293, 502 A.2d 114 (1985). None of these cases involved a provision similar to section 32.024(e). Likewise, none of the other published appellate cases addressing other constitutional challenges to abortion funding restrictions discuss a statute like section 32.024(e) that expressly limits services to those for which federal matching funds are available. *Dep't of Health & Soc. Servs. v. Planned Parenthood of Alaska, Inc.,* 28 P.3d 904 (Alaska 2001)(holding that denial of funds for medically necessary abortions violates Alaska equal protection guarantee); *Renee B. v. Florida Agency for Health Care Admin.,* 790 So.2d 1036 (Fla.2001)(holding that funding restrictions did not violate Florida right to privacy); *Moe v. Sec'y of Admin. & Finance,* 382 Mass. 629, 417 N.E.2d 387 (1981)(holding that funding restrictions violate fundamental right to privacy under Massachusetts constitution); *Doe v. Dep't of Soc. Servs.,* 439 Mich. 650, 487 N.W.2d 166 (1992)(holding that funding restrictions do not violate Michigan equal protection clause); *Right to Choose v. Byrne,* 91 N.J. 287, 450 A.2d 925 (1982)(holding that funding restrictions violate New Jersey equal protection provision); *Rosie J. v. N.C. Dep't of Human Res.,* 347 N.C. 247, 491 S.E.2d 535 (1997)(holding restrictions do not affect suspect class or impinge upon fundamental right).

departures from the normal procedural and substantive course, and legislative or administrative history. *Id.* at 267-68. Our consideration of these factors in the present case leads us to conclude that the TMAP funding restrictions are not based on sex.

First, the history of TMAP reveals that the Texas Legislature intended to create a program that conformed to the federal program's contours. Section 5 of the Act is now codified as section 32.024(e) of the Human Resources Code, which expressly prohibits the Department from authorizing any services "unless federal matching funds are available." This provision was plainly not directed at abortion funding, as abortion was illegal in Texas at the time it was enacted. The record contains no evidence that the State has ever deviated from adhering to the matching-funds requirement in administering its Medicaid program. Furthermore, it is undisputed that Texas has consistently funded abortions through TMAP to the extent that federal matching funds have been available. From the time that the Supreme Court struck down Texas's abortion law in *Roe v. Wade,* 410 U.S. 113 (1973), until Congress passed the Hyde Amendment, TMAP funded all medically necessary abortions. The historical background of the State's creation and administration of TMAP supports the conclusion that the funding restrictions do not discriminate "because of" sex.

Finally, we consider the Hyde Amendment's terms and effect. The State contends that we need look no further than the United States Supreme Court's decision in *Harris v. McRae,* 448 U.S. 297 (1980). There, the plaintiffs contended that the Hyde Amendment impinged upon their fundamental right to privacy under the United States Constitution by hindering indigent women's ability to obtain abortions. They also claimed that the Hyde Amendment violated the equal protection component of the Fifth Amendment's Due Process Clause by restricting abortion funding while paying the costs associated with childbirth. The Court rejected both arguments. In assessing the plaintiffs' privacy challenge, the Court differentiated between laws that place "obstacles in the path of a woman's exercise of her freedom," and the government's obligation to remove obstacles such as poverty that it did not create. The Court also determined that the Hyde Amendment classification is based on financial need, and "[a]n indigent woman desiring an abortion does not come within the limited category of disadvantaged classes so recognized by our cases." *Id.* at 323. Applying rational-basis review, the Court determined that the Hyde Amendment restrictions were rationally related to the government's interest in protecting potential life and encouraging childbirth.

While we find *Harris v. McRae* instructive, it does not control our decision for at least three reasons. First, the Texas Equal Rights Amendment, under which plaintiffs bring their challenge, has no federal constitutional counterpart. Our Equal Rights Amendment was passed many years after the equal protection and due process clauses of both the United States and Texas Constitutions, and it expressly prohibits gender discrimination. Rules of constitutional interpretation dictate that all clauses must be given effect. *McLean,* 725 S.W.2d at 697-98. Unless the Equal Rights Amendment grants additional protection against gender-based classifications than had been found in the federal and state constitutions at the time it was passed, the amendment was futile. *Id.* at 697. As we have noted, the amendment's legislative history indicates that it was intended to enlarge upon the federal equal protection guarantees. It does so by elevating sex to a suspect class and subjecting sex-based classifications to heightened strict-scrutiny review. *See McLean,* 725 S.W.2d at 698.

Second, while the Supreme Court in *Harris v. McRae* determined that the Hyde Amendment classified based on financial need, it did not specifically consider whether the Hyde Amendment discriminated on the basis of sex. Instead, the equal-protection challenge the Court considered was like the one it addressed in *Maher v. Roe,* where the Court considered "whether the Constitution requires a participating State to pay for nontherapeutic abortions when it pays for childbirth." *Maher,* 432 U.S. at 466. While both decisions concluded that the Hyde Amendment did not violate federal equal protection guarantees, neither expressly considered a gender discrimination claim.

Finally, the Court in *Harris v. McRae* considered only the Hyde Amendment, while the TMAP funding scheme we consider involves the interplay between the amendment and section 32.024(e). For these reasons, we must conduct our own analysis to determine whether the TMAP funding scheme, as a whole, discriminates because of sex. In doing so, we note that the Texas Equal Rights Amendment affords greater protection through strict-scrutiny review once gender-based discrimination is found, but it does not affect the initial determination of whether the classification is impermissibly sex based.

The State contends that, even if we ignore section 32.024(e)'s facial neutrality and look only at the Hyde Amendment's abortion funding restrictions, those restrictions implement a legitimate governmental purpose to favor childbirth over abortion. We agree. While the federal constitution prevents the State from placing undue burdens upon a woman's freedom to terminate a pregnancy, the State retains the authority to "make a value judgment favoring childbirth over abortion, and to implement that judgment by the allocation of public funds." *Maher,* 432 U.S. at 474. In the absence of any other evidence of discriminatory intent, we believe that the Hyde Amendment was intended to implement such a value judgment.

B. Rational-Basis Review

Because the TMAP funding scheme does not discriminate "because of" sex, we judge the classification by the more deferential rational-basis standard of review. *Sullivan v. Univ. Interscholastic League,* 616 S.W.2d 170, 172 (Tex.1981). Under this standard, a party asserting that a classification is unconstitutional must demonstrate that the action is not rationally related to a legitimate governmental purpose.

Plaintiffs argue that the funding restrictions cannot survive even this deferential level of review because they are not rationally related to TMAP's express purpose to provide medical assistance to needy individuals and allow the State to obtain all benefits provided by the federal act. We agree that the restrictions do not necessarily advance either of those goals. Denying medical assistance does not further the provision of medical services, and the State's ability to collect matching funds for services other than abortions would not be affected if the State elected to fund medically necessary abortions with unmatched State funds. But, as we have noted, TMAP was expressly designed from its inception to fund only those services for which federal reimbursement is available, and an additional legitimate purpose underlies the Hyde Amendment–encouraging childbirth and protecting potential life. The restriction clearly serves those purposes, and it is not for us to second-guess the Legislature's policy choices. Because the TMAP funding scheme is rationally related to legitimate governmental purposes, it does not violate the Equal Rights Amendment.

III. Right to Privacy

We have recognized that the Texas Constitution protects personal privacy from unreasonable governmental intrusions and unwarranted interference with personal autonomy. *City of Sherman v. Henry,* 928 S.W.2d 464, 468 (Tex.1996); *Tex. State Employees Union v. Tex. Dep't of Mental Health and Mental Retardation,* 746 S.W.2d 203, 205 (Tex.1987). Plaintiffs claim that the TMAP abortion funding restrictions violate their right to privacy under the Texas Constitution by interfering with the personal autonomy of indigent women. By paying medical expenses for childbirth but not for medically necessary abortions, they argue, the State effectively coerces a woman's decision whether to terminate or continue a pregnancy.

The United States Supreme Court has analyzed similar challenges under the federal Constitution on two occasions. See *Harris,* 448 U.S. at 312-18; *Maher,* 432 U.S. at 472-80. In those cases, the Court recognized a fundamental difference between governmental action prohibiting abortion, and the government's decision to encourage childbirth as a policy matter.

While we have never decided whether the Texas Constitution creates privacy rights coextensive with those recognized under the United States Constitution, we find this distinction persuasive. We disagree with those courts that have concluded that recognizing a woman's fundamental right to choose to terminate a pregnancy imposes a concomitant duty upon the State to fund that choice. As in *Maher v. Roe* and *Harris v. McRae,* the funding restrictions here leave "an indigent woman with at least the same range of choice in deciding whether to obtain a medically necessary abortion as she would have had if [the State] had chosen to subsidize no health care costs at all." *Harris,* 448 U.S at 317. We hold that the TMAP funding restrictions do not violate indigent women's privacy rights under the Texas Constitution.

IV. Equal Protection Clause

Finally, plaintiffs claim that the TMAP abortion funding restrictions cannot survive rational-basis review under Texas Equal Protection Clause. Tex. Const. art. I, § 3. They rely on two cases which they claim suggest that we have "applied a rational basis test more exacting than mere reasonableness," in which the statutory classification must be rationally related not only to a legitimate state interest as required under federal law, but to the very object or subject of the legislation. *See Whitworth v. Bynum,* 699 S.W.2d 194, 197 (Tex.1985); *State v. Richards,* 157 Tex. 166, 301 S.W.2d 597, 600-01 (1957). Plaintiffs contend that the abortion funding restrictions create a distinction between health-preserving and life-preserving abortions that is wholly unrelated to TMAP's purpose, which is to protect both life and health.

We do not read *Whitworth* and *Richards* to establish the more exacting standard the plaintiffs suggest. To the extent they might suggest such a standard, we have recently clarified that the federal analytical approach applies to equal protection challenges under the Texas Constitution. Moreover, we believe that plaintiffs oversimplify TMAP's underlying purposes. As we have discussed, the Legislature's intent from the program's inception has been to provide indigent health care only *to the extent that federal matching funds are available.* Even under the more rigorous standard plaintiffs advocate, the TMAP funding restrictions are rationally related to this underlying legislative purpose and do not violate the Texas Equal Protection Clause.

V

We hold that the TMAP abortion funding restrictions do not violate the Texas Constitution's Equal Rights Amendment, Equal Protection Clause or right to privacy. Accordingly, we reverse the court of appeals' judgment and render judgment for the defendants.

Notes on Comparing State and Federal Equality Guarantees

Classifications "Because of" Sex: Do *Bell* and *In re Baby McLean* use the same or different standards for determining whether a classification is "because of" sex? How does the rationale employed in *Bell* compare to federal equal protection analysis? Is *Bell* consistent with decisions in other jurisdictions that have considered the standards for establishing a classification under their state equal rights amendments?

As *Bell* notes, some states have concluded that state regulations singling out gender-linked conditions for less favorable treatment create a gender classification. For instance, the New Mexico Supreme Court in *New Mexico Right to Choose/NARAL v. Johnson* held that denying poor women funding for medically necessary abortions was gender discrimination as pregnancy was a condition unique to women.[330] New Mexico thus rejected the United States Supreme Court's holding in *Geduldig v. Aiello* that the exclusion of pregnancy from a disability scheme was a distinction between "pregnant women and non-pregnant persons" rather than gender discrimination.[331] But even under the holding in *New Mexico Right to Choose*, the Texas statute at issue in *Bell* was unique in that it did not single out a gender-linked condition for less favorable treatment–instead, the statute predated the abortion funding controversy and had been neutrally applied to prohibit all state funding regarding any medical procedure when federal funding was not available.

Consequences of the Level of Scrutiny: What is the primary difference between the Texas Equal Rights Amendment and the Federal Equal Protection Clause with respect to gender discrimination? Does this difference have much significance? Is it likely that many cases involving discrimination "because of" sex would be decided differently under intermediate scrutiny rather than strict scrutiny?

If strict scrutiny applies under the Texas Equal Rights Amendment to gender-based discrimination against women, would strict scrutiny also apply to affirmative action programs benefitting women? If so, would that help or hinder governmental attempts to remedy past discrimination against women? As an example, would the navy regulation that the United States Supreme Court upheld in *Schlesinger v. Ballard* that required the discharge of male officers who had not been promoted for nine years but allowed women to remain for thirteen years without a promotion have survived strict scrutiny when the regulation was designed to remedy the fewer opportunities that women had previously had

---

[330] 975 P.2d 841, 855-56 (N.M. 1998).

[331] 417 U.S. 484, 496-97 & n.20 (1974).

for promotion?[332] What about the provision of the Social Security Act upheld by the Supreme Court in *Califano v. Webster* that provided a more advantageous calculation of benefits for women as a result of the statistical salary disparity between men and women?[333] In cases such as these, the level of scrutiny applied is often dispositive, as aptly illustrated by federal cases upholding, under federal equal protection principles, affirmative action programs for women under intermediate scrutiny, while invalidating similar race-based affirmative action programs under strict scrutiny.[334]

One state has avoided this scrutiny dilemma by refusing to apply its equal rights amendment to affirmative action programs based on gender. The Washington Supreme Court reasoned that the "absolute mandate of equality" in the state's equal rights amendment does not "bar affirmative governmental efforts to create equality in fact;" thus, if the intent behind the gender favoritism is to remedy past discrimination, the state's equality guarantee is not implicated.[335] Under this reasoning, the court upheld state regulations of a political party that required both that the chairman and vice chairman of the state committee be members of the opposite sex and that the two members elected to the state committee by each county central committee be members of the opposite sex.[336] The court determined that these requirements, while classifying by gender, did not *discriminate* by sex because the statutes mandated that both genders would have "an equality of numbers and an equality of rights to be in office and to control the affairs of the state committee."[337] The dissent, however, complained that such a quota based on sex alone prevented the state's equal rights amendment "from achieving its purpose of making sex a neutral factor, one to be disregarded in favor of ability and performance."[338] In another case, the Washington high court upheld an affirmative action program that gave a preference to businesses owned by women in public works contracting, reasoning that the benign motivations supporting the preference were to ameliorate the effects of past discrimination and to combat the stereotype that women were unable to perform strenuous and mechanically complex labor.[339] Other states, however, have applied the same level of scrutiny to affirmative action programs based on gender as to gender discrimination claims,[340] which comports with federal doctrine.[341]

The Impact of State Equal Rights Amendments: Does the mere fact that a state has adopted an equal rights amendment explicitly protecting against gender discrimination

[332]419 U.S. 498 (1975).

[333]430 U.S. 313 (1977).

[334]*See, e.g.*, Coral Constr. Co. v. King Cnty., 941 F.2d 910 (9th Cir. 1991); Associated Gen. Contractors of Cal. v. San Francisco, 813 F.2d 922, 928-42 (9th Cir. 1986).

[335]S.W. Wash. Chapter, Nat'l Elec. Contractors Ass'n v. Pierce Cnty., 667 P.2d 1092, 1102 (Wash. 1983).

[336]Marchioro v. Chaney, 582 P.2d 487 (Wash. 1978), *aff'd*, 442 U.S. 191 (1979).

[337]*Id.* at 492.

[338]*Id.* at 497 (Horowitz, J., dissenting).

[339]*Nat'l Elec.*, 667 P.2d at 1103.

[340]*See, e.g.*, Hi-Voltage Wire Works, Inc. v. City of San Jose, 12 P.3d 1068, 1084-85 (Cal. 2000).

[341]*Associated Gen. Contractors*, 813 F.2d at 939-42; *cf.* Grutter v. Bollinger, 539 U.S. 306, 326-27 (2003) (holding racial affirmative action programs subject to strict scrutiny)

necessarily mean that the state right offers broader protection? Consider article I, section 11 of the Virginia Constitution, which provides that

> the right to be free from any government discrimination upon the basis of religious conviction, race, color, sex, or national origin shall not be abridged, except that the mere separation of the sexes shall not be considered discrimination.

But although Virginia apparently does not regard "separation of the sexes" as unlawful discrimination under its equal rights amendment, the United States Supreme Court has, at least in some circumstances, a different view under the Federal Constitution. In *United States v. Virginia*, the Supreme Court held Virginia's policy of excluding women from the Virginia Military Institute violated the Federal Equal Protection Clause.[342] Thus, if anything, the Virginia state provision appears narrower in certain situations than the federal standard.

Only the holdings of a relatively few decisions under state equal rights amendments actually diverge from the expected results under federal doctrine and provide greater protection against gender discrimination.[343] But the relative paucity of such decisions does not impact other benefits of enshrining constitutional protection against sex discrimination in the state charter. State equal rights amendments have led to commissions and statutory reform efforts designed to eradicate sexual bias in some state governments.[344] Moreover, a commitment to gender equality principles in the state's fundamental law is at least of strong symbolic value.[345]

Sometimes these state equal rights amendments have also extended protections to groups not recognized as suspect or even quasi-suspect classes under federal equal protection analysis. For instance, the Connecticut Supreme Court held that the explicit prohibition of discrimination based on physical disability in its state constitution required the application of strict scrutiny–rather than the rational basis test applied in federal law–to restrictions placed on a driver with a seizure disorder to keep his driver's license.[346] Such an extension of protected classes under state constitutions might also influence federal doctrine in our system of dual federalism, just as the Supreme Court was influenced by similar constitutional and statutory developments in holding that gender classifications deserved heightened intermediate scrutiny under the Fourteenth Amendment.[347]

---

[342] 518 U.S. 515 (1996).

[343] *See, e.g.*, R. McG. v. J.W., 615 P.2d 666, 670-71 (Colo. 1980); N.M. Right to Choose/NARAL v. Johnson, 975 P.2d 841, 851-57 (N.M. 1998); Guard v. State, 940 P.2d 642, 645 (Wash. 1997).

[344] *See, e.g.*, Linda J. Wharton, *State Equal Rights Amendments Revisited: Evaluating Their Effectiveness in Advancing Protection Against Sex Discrimination*, 36 RUTGERS L.J. 1201, 1283-84 (2005).

[345] *See id.*

[346] Daly v. DelPonte, 624 A.2d 876, 882-85 (Conn. 1993).

[347] *See* Mary Anne Case, *"The Very Stereotype the Law Condemns": Constitutional Sex Discrimination Law as a Quest for Perfect Proxies*, 85 CORNELL L. REV. 1447, 1461-66 (2000).

G. OTHER DUALLY PROTECTED RIGHTS

State constitutions typically contain numerous other rights provisions that are similar to guarantees protected against state governmental transgression by the United States Constitution. In Texas, these include constitutional protections against cruel or unusual punishment, double jeopardy, bills of attainder, ex post fact laws, and laws impairing the obligation of contracts.[348] For the most part, these guarantees have been presumed to be, or have been interpreted as, coextensive with the analogous guarantees protected by the United States Constitution.[349] Yet with respect to other dually protected rights under the Texas Constitution, arguments can be made that their text, history, or purpose necessitates additional protections in certain situations, despite the fact that Texas courts have not yet recognized such broader rights.

1. Takings Clause

The Fifth Amendment to the United States Constitution guarantees that private property will not "be taken for public use without just compensation." In comparison, the takings provision of the Texas Constitution is detailed and verbose. It provides for compensation for property that is "taken, damaged or destroyed," requires compensation to be made or secured in advance if the property is not taken for the use of the state, and specifies the governmental objectives satisfying the "public use" requirement.

Article I, section 17 of the Texas Constitution begins with the command that "[n]o person's property shall be taken, damaged or destroyed for or applied to public use without adequate compensation being made," while the Fifth Amendment merely provides for compensation when private property is "taken." The purpose of adding the "damaged or destroyed" language was to obviate the need for an actual physical invasion before a compensable taking occurred.[350] But the Texas Supreme Court has never decided whether this additional language supports a different standard for regulatory takings under the Texas Constitution, merely recognizing that "it could be argued that the differences in the wording of the two provisions are significant."[351] The court's decisions thus have presumed that the

---

[348]*See* TEX. CONST. art. I, §§ 13, 14, 16.

[349]*See, e.g., Ex parte* Lewis, 219 S.W.3d 335, 337 (Tex. Crim. App. 2007) (holding "proper rule under the Texas Constitution is the rule articulated by the United States Supreme Court" for the attachment of double jeopardy to mistrials); Grimes v. State, 807 S.W.2d 582, 584 (Tex. Crim. App. 1991) ("When interpreting our state constitution's *Ex Post Facto* Provision, Texas case have followed the Supreme Court lead."). *But see* Travelers' Ins. Co. v. Marshall, 76 S.W.2d 1007, 1010-11 (Tex. 1934) (refusing to follow United States Supreme Court's interpretation of the Contract Clause under the Texas Constitution).

[350]*See, e.g.,* DuPuy v. City of Waco, 396 S.W.2d 103, 108 (Tex. 1965) ("It was the injustice of requiring an actual [physical] taking which explains the inclusion for the first time in the Constitution of 1876 of the requirement that compensation be paid for the damaging of property for public use."); Trinity & S. Ry. Co. v. Meadows, 11 S.W. 145, 146 (Tex. 1889) ("The insertion of the words 'damaged or destroyed' . . . was doubtless intended to . . . afford protection to the owner of property by allowing him compensation when, by the construction of a public work, his property was directly damaged or destroyed, although no part of it was actually appropriated."). *Accord* Steele v. City of Houston, 603 S.W.2d 786, 789-90 (Tex. 1980) (discussing historical distinction between the taking, the damaging, and the destruction of property).

[351]Sheffield Dev. Co. v. City of Glenn Heights, 140 S.W.3d 660, 669 (Tex. 2004).

"comparable" state and federal takings provisions are to be interpreted coextensively in the absence of briefing on the issue from the parties.[352]

Other states, though, have concluded that similar state takings provisions offer greater protection in some circumstances than provided by the United States Constitution. For example, the Alaska Supreme Court held that a temporary loss of profits due to business interruption from a taking was compensable under the state constitution, primarily relying on the fact that the Alaska Constitution requires "just compensation" for both "damaged" and "taken" property rather than just "taken" property as under the Federal Constitution.[353] The Mississippi Supreme Court similarly held that its state constitutional text requiring compensation for "damaged" property meant that an actual physical invasion of the property was not required and that compensation was needed if an adjacent property was damaged through a public use.[354] But other states disagree that such variations in the state constitutional text are meaningful.[355] Should the decision of the Texas framers in 1876 to include protection for property that is "damaged or destroyed" provide additional safeguards against regulatory takings today?

Many states have also departed from federal guidance when interpreting state constitutional "public use" limitations on the government's eminent domain authority. In *Kelo v. City of New London*, the Supreme Court held that the condemnation of property in order to transfer it to other private parties to generate greater tax revenues and other economic benefits for local communities is a "public use" satisfying the Fifth Amendment's Taking Clause.[356] But the subsequent public backlash against this decision motivated more than forty states to enact legislation limiting or restricting the power of eminent domain.

Several state courts also rejected *Kelo*'s reasoning when interpreting the takings clauses in their own state constitutions. The Oklahoma Supreme Court, in the first such decision after *Kelo*, held in *Board of County Commissioners v. Lowery* that a county's condemnation of property for "economic development" did not satisfy the state constitution's "more stringent limitation on governmental eminent domain power."[357] The court distinguished its prior cases authorizing takings for blight removal as involving different circumstances, reasoning that permitting a mere assertion of the need for "economic development" as a public use "would blur the line between 'public' and 'private' so as to render our constitutional limitations on the power of eminent domain a nullity."[358] Similarly, in *City of Norwood v. Horney*, the Ohio Supreme Court held that a city could not use eminent domain to take private homes for the development of a business and

---

[352] *Id.*; *accord* Hallco Tex., Inc. v. McMullen Cnty., 221 S.W.3d 50, 56 (Tex. 2006); Town of Flower Mound v. Stafford Estates Ltd. P'ship, 135 S.W.3d 620, 631 (Tex. 2004); Mayhew v. Town of Sunnyvale, 964 S.W.2d 922, 932 (Tex. 1998).

[353] State v. Hammer, 550 P.2d 820, 823-25 (Alaska 1976).

[354] Gilich v. Miss. State Highway Comm'n, 574 So. 2d 8, 12 (Miss. 1990).

[355] *See, e.g.*, Temple Baptist Church, Inc. v. City of Albuquerque, 646 P.2d 565, 575 (N.M. 1982) (noting that federal and state takings provisions embodied the "same principle" despite textual differences).

[356] 545 U.S. 469, 480-85 (2005).

[357] 136 P.3d 639, 651 (Okla. 2006).

[358] *Id.* at 652.

condominium complex because a public economic or financial benefit alone was not sufficient to satisfy the public-use requirement of its constitution.[359] Other states have likewise either held or implied that *Kelo* is not controlling in the interpretation of the public use requirement in their takings clauses.[360] In addition to these judicial decisions, some states have amended their constitutions to eliminate or restrict condemnations of property for economic development purposes.[361]

While the Texas Supreme Court had not addressed the public use requirement under the state constitution for some time, its earlier decisions might be described as somewhat deferential to the legislative determination of public use,[362] as long as the public obtained some definite right or use in the business or undertaking to which the property was devoted.[363] But in response to *Kelo*, the legislature amended the Texas Government Code to prohibit most takings primarily for a private benefit or for economic developmental purposes and to specify that the condemning authority's determination of public use does not create a presumption in favor of its authorization.[364] Subsequently, article I, section 17 of the Texas Constitution was amended in 2009 to specify "public use" did not include taking property "for transfer to a private entity for the primary purpose of economic

---

[359]853 N.E.2d 1115, 1142 (Ohio 2006).

[360]*See, e.g.*, Sw. Ill. Dev. Auth. v. Nat'l City Envtl., L.L.C., 768 N.E.2d 1 (Ill. 2002) (holding before *Kelo* that economic development alone would not achieve a legitimate public use under its state constitution); Wayne Cnty. v. Hathcock, 684 N.W.2d 765 (Mich. 2004) (same); Gallenthin Realty Dev., Inc. v. Borough of Paulsboro, 924 A.2d 447, 460 (N.J. 2007) (holding that state constitutional provision specifying that redevelopment of "blighted areas" was a public use for which private property could be taken applied only to deteriorating property with a "decadent effect" on surrounding property); Ga. Dep't of Transp. v. Jasper Cnty., 586 S.E.2d 853, 855-57 (S.C. 2003) (holding before *Kelo* that economic benefit from proposed marine terminal was not a public use that could justify the use of eminent domain); Benson v. State, 710 N.W.2d 131, 146 (S.D. 2006) (noting in dicta that South Dakota employs a stricter public use requirement under its constitution mandating "use by the public").

[361]*See, e.g.*, CAL. CONST. art. I, § 19 (preventing, under most circumstances, the use of eminent domain to acquire an owner-occupied residence for conveyance to a private person or business); COLO. CONST. art. II, § 15 (specifying that issue of public use is a judicial question without any deference to the legislative assertion); LA. CONST. art. I, § 4 (defining permissible "public purposes"); FLA. CONST. art. X, § 6 (preventing private property taken by eminent domain from being conveyed to a private entity except on three-fifths vote of both legislative houses); MICH. CONST. art. X, § 2 (defining "public use" as not including economic development or enhancement of tax revenues); MISS. INITIATIVE 31 (initiative amendment approved in 2011 but not yet codified prohibiting most transfers of property acquired under eminent domain to non-governmental entities for ten years after the acquisition of the property); NEV. CONST. art. I, § 22 (defining public use as not including the transfer of private property from one owner to another); N.H. CONST. part I, art. 12-a (preventing takings for private development or other private use of the property); N.D. CONST. art. I, § 16 (prohibiting takings for economic development or for private use, unless necessary for conducting a common carrier or utility business); S.C. CONST. art. I, § 13 (prohibiting takings for economic development); VA. CONST. art. I, § 11 (defining public use as not including economic development).

[362]*See, e.g.*, Davis v. City of Lubbock, 326 S.W.2d 699, 704-09 (Tex. 1959) (upholding urban renewal law providing for redevelopment by private enterprises of slum and blighted areas in cities partially on the basis that great deference was owed to the legislative judgment); Hous. Auth. of Dallas v. Higginbotham, 143 S.W.2d 79, 83-85 (Tex. 1940) (upholding condemnation of slums for development of low rent public housing).

[363]*See, e.g.*, Maher v. Lasater, 354 S.W.2d 923, 924-26 (Tex. 1962) (invalidating taking of private road as a public highway when its only use was to provide access to land owned by another private individual); Coastal States Gas Producing Co. v. Pate, 309 S.W.2d 828, 833 (Tex. 1958) (upholding condemnation for development of oil and gas by private leaseholder when one-fourth of production was reserved to the state).

[364]TEX. GOV'T CODE § 2206.001.

development or enhancement of tax revenues," even though "the elimination of urban blight on a particular parcel of property" remains an authorized ground for a governmental taking.[365]

The Texas courts have not had an opportunity to interpret article I, section 17 as amended. But there is little question that the text, purpose, and history of this amendment indicate that the "public use" requirement in the Texas Constitution differs from the Supreme Court's interpretation of the comparable federal provision in *Kelo*.

2. Religious Liberty and Establishment

The Bill of Rights of the Federal Constitution contains one clause on religious rights: "Congress shall make no law respecting an establishment of religion, or prohibiting the free exercise thereof."[366] But in most states, constitutional provisions regarding religious liberty and establishment are more numerous, verbose, and elaborate. For example, the Texas Bill of Rights contains four sections touching on religion, with section 4 banning religious tests for public office, section 5 prohibiting the disqualification of witnesses on the basis of their religious beliefs, and sections 6 and 7 providing detailed guarantees protecting freedom of worship, preventing governmental preferences for any religious denomination, and prohibiting the appropriation of state money for religious purposes.[367] The Texas freedom of worship guarantee in article I, section 6 provides:

> All men have a natural and indefeasible right to worship Almighty God according to the dictates of their own consciences. No man shall be compelled to attend, erect or support any place of worship, or to maintain any ministry against his consent. No human authority ought, in any case whatever, to control or interfere with the rights of conscience in matters of religion, and no preference shall ever be given by law to any religious society or mode of worship. But it shall be the duty of the Legislature to pass such laws as may be necessary to protect equally every religious denomination in the peaceable enjoyment of its own mode of public worship.

Section 7 then adds the following prohibition on appropriations to benefit religion:

> No money shall be appropriated, or drawn from the Treasury for the benefit of any sect, or religious society, theological or religious seminary; nor shall property belonging to the State be appropriated for any such purposes.

The combination of these texts might be argued to furnish state constitutional protections that differ from those afforded by the United States Constitution, at least under

---

[365]TEX. CONST. art. I, § 17.

[366]U.S. CONST. amend. I.

[367]TEX. CONST. art. I, §§ 4-7.

certain circumstances.[368] But Texas decisions have yet to interpret these guarantees differently.

In addressing religious freedom claims under article I, section 6, Texas courts have typically paralleled the decisions under prevailing First Amendment doctrine.[369] Nevertheless, because "Texans repeatedly expressed their indignation over Mexico's deprivation of the right . . . to religious freedom" before the war for Texas independence,[370] it may be possible to construct an argument from section 6's history and purpose that the section provides additional rights of religious liberty. The Roman Catholic religion was established as the sole religion in Mexican Texas, with the exercise of any other religion prohibited.[371] The Texas Declaration of Independence thus complained that Mexico denied Texans "the right of worshiping the Almighty according to the dictates of our own conscience by the support of a national religion, calculated to promote the temporal interest of its human functionaries rather than the glory of the true and living God."[372] This concern with religious conscience was incorporated into the Declaration of Rights of the Republic of Texas Constitution and carried forward to the present section 6, which recognizes citizens' "natural and indefeasible right to worship Almighty God according to the dictates of their own consciences" and admonishes that human authority should not "control or interfere with the rights of conscience in matters of religion."

Some other states with clauses similarly protecting citizens' freedom of conscience from governmental interference have interpreted religious liberties more broadly under their state constitutions. For instance, several state courts have rejected the Supreme Court's holding in *Employment Division v. Smith* that a religiously neutral law of general applicability criminalizing the use or possession of peyote was not subject to strict scrutiny,

---

[368]Any such differing protections would not mean, however, that the Texas Constitution protects religious liberty more broadly under all circumstances. For instance, article I, section 4, while prohibiting religious tests as a qualification for office and disqualification for office based on religious sentiments, allows disqualification of government officeholders that do not "acknowledge the existence of a Supreme Being," a provision that violates current First Amendment doctrine. *See* Torcaso v. Watkins, 367 U.S. 488, 495-96 (1961) (invalidating similar provision in Maryland Constitution).

[369]*See, e.g.,* HEB Ministries, Inc. v. Tex. Higher Educ. Coordinating Bd., 235 S.W.3d 627, 649-50 (Tex. 2007) (explaining that the court has treated the state guarantee as coextensive with the protections under the United States Constitution absent argument to the contrary); Tilton v. Marshall, 925 S.W.2d 672, 677 n.6 (Tex. 1996) (assuming free exercise provisions of federal and state constitutions were coextensive when the parties did not argue to the contrary); City of New Braunfels v. Waldschmidt, 207 S.W. 303, 305 (Tex. 1918) (relying on federal authority to reject challenge under article I, section 6 to local ordinance requiring smallpox vaccinations). The Texarkana Court of Appeals in *Howell v. State*, 723 S.W.2d 755, 758 (Tex. App.–Texarkana 1986, no writ), opined that the state constitution "grants greater religious freedom than is provided for in the United States Constitution," but the court then employed a test virtually identical to the prevailing federal test at that time.

[370]*Ex parte* Tucci, 859 S.W.2d 1, 31 (Tex. 1993) (Phillips, C.J., concurring).

[371]CONST. OF COAHUILA Y TEJ. of 1827, art. 9 ("The Roman Catholic Apostolic Religion shall be the religion of the state. The state protects it by wise and just laws, and prohibits the exercise of any other."); *id.* art. 10 ("The state shall regulate and pay all expense that should be necessary for the preservation of religious worship, agreeably to the concordates the nation should ratify with the Apostolic See, and to the laws that shall be prescribed on the exercise of the *patronato* throughout the republic.").

[372]THE TEX. DECLARATION OF INDEPENDENCE para. 12 (1836).

even though a religious practice of the Native American Church was thereby affected.[373] These courts have reasoned that their state religious clauses, which bar infringing on or interfering with matters of conscience, provide a textually broader right that, unlike the Supreme Court's interpretation of the First Amendment, recognizes religious liberty claims when a law applying to everyone interferes with a religious practice.[374] But other states with analogous freedom of conscience clauses have instead adopted *Smith*'s approach under their state constitutions.[375]

The final resolution of this issue in Texas has become less important since the legislature enacted a state religious freedom restoration act (or state RFRA) in 1999 that specifies that state and local governments generally may not, unless necessary to further a compelling governmental interest, substantially burden a person's free exercise of religion.[376] Although the United States Supreme Court in *City of Boerne v. Flores* declared the Federal Religious Freedom Restoration Act unconstitutional to the extent that it was applied against state and local governmental actions, *Flores* did not prevent the states from enacting similar statutes under their police power to protect religious liberties.[377] Approximately a dozen other states have adopted state RFRAs that statutorily require the use of a strict scrutiny standard for all substantial infringements on religious liberties.[378] Since the adoption of the Texas RFRA, Texas cases have emphasized these statutory religious liberties more than the free exercise constitutional guarantees in article I.[379]

The other primary state constitutional religious protection, "Texas' equivalent of the Establishment Clause," is derived from the prohibition against governmental compulsion

---

[373]494 U.S. 872, 879 (1990). The Supreme Court held that the Free Exercise Clause was not violated by an Oregon drug law prohibiting ingestion of peyote when applied to religious ceremonies of the Native American Church. *See id.*

[374]*See, e.g.*, McCready v. Hoffius, 586 N.W.2d 723, 729 (Mich. 1998) (employing compelling state interest test under state constitution), *vacated in part on other grounds*, 593 N.W.2d 545 (Mich. 1999); State v. Hershberger, 462 N.W.2d 393, 397-99 (Minn. 1990) (relying on broader language of state constitution to require a compelling governmental interest to justify infringements on matters of religious conscience); Humphrey v. Lane, 728 N.E.2d 1039, 1044-45 (Ohio 2000) (concluding that state constitutional phrase barring "interference with the rights of conscience" was broader than the United States Constitution as it targeted laws tangentially affecting religion); Munns v. Martin, 930 P.2d 318, 321 (Wash. 1997) (holding that a facially neutral administrative process required under a demolition ordinance could not constitutionally be applied to a Catholic church desiring to destroy a building); First Covenant Church of Seattle v. City of Seattle, 840 P.2d 174, 186 (Wash. 1992) (reasoning state history and constitutional text, being "significantly different and stronger than the federal constitution," supported a broader reading than *Smith*'s interpretation of the First Amendment); State v. Miller, 549 N.W.2d 235, 238-42 (Wis. 1996) (relying on freedom of conscience provision to support application of strict scrutiny to free exercise claim); *cf.* Attorney General v. Desilets, 636 N.E.2d 233, 235-37 (Mass. 1994) (rejecting *Smith* despite textual similarity of federal and state free exercise provisions).

[375]*See, e.g.*, State v. DeLaBruere, 577 A.2d 254, 268-72 (Vt. 1990).

[376]TEX. CIV. PRAC. & REM. CODE § 110.003 (providing that "a government agency may not substantially burden a person's free exercise of religion" unless it demonstrates that such a burden is "the least restrictive means of furthering" a "compelling governmental interest").

[377]521 U.S. 507, 512 (1997).

[378]*See* Douglas Laycock, *Theology Scholarships, the Pledge of Allegiance, and Religious Liberty: Avoiding the Extremes But Missing the Liberty*, 118 HARV. L. REV. 155, 211-12 (2004) (listing state statutes).

[379]*See, e.g.*, Barr v. City of Sinton, 295 S.W.3d 287, 308 (Tex. 2009) (holding city zoning ordinance prohibiting a halfway house ministry violated the Texas Religious Freedom Restoration Act).

and preferences in article I, section 6 and the bar against governmental financial aid to benefit sectarian institutions in article I, section 7.[380] The Texas Supreme Court has presumed, in the absence of contrary argument, that these state protections against governmental establishment of religion are coextensive with federal protections.[381] The Texas Attorney General likewise opined in 2004 that the Texas Constitution imposes the same restraints as the Establishment Clause of the United States Constitution.[382]

Nevertheless, this presumption could be challenged in light of the separate constitutional prohibition in section 7 against the use of public funds for sectarian benefits, a prohibition that is commonly encountered in the constitutions of many other states and that is typically interpreted to provide additional restrictions on governmental aid to religion. Section 7 first appeared in the 1876 Texas Constitution and was designed to stop the prior practice in Texas of extending occasional state financial support for religious education. Article VII, section 5 reinforces this ban specifically with respect to education, preventing the legislature from appropriating or using the permanent school fund and the available school fund for the support of any sectarian school.[383] Although there have not been any Texas cases invalidating legislation under these provisions,[384] the Texas Attorney General opined in 1973 that article I, section 7 is "more restrictive than the federal charter . . . and will not tolerate, in our opinion, any aid to *sects* or sectarian schools."[385] The Texas Attorney General has accordingly advised that pupils of parochial may not be transported to their schools on a publicly owned bus,[386] that the state may not pay tuition for physically disabled individuals at denominational schools,[387] that sectarian religious instruction in the public schools is prohibited,[388] and that tax funds could not be expended for the construction and maintenance of a chapel at a county hospital.[389]

---

[380]Williams v. Lara, 52 S.W.3d 171, 186 (Tex. 2000).

[381]*See, e.g.*, HEB Ministries, Inc. v. Tex. Higher Educ. Coordinating Bd., 235 S.W.3d 627, 642 (Tex. 2007); *see also Williams*, 52 S.W.3d at 192 (concluding no discussion of the state constitutional claims was necessary when the United States Constitution had been violated).

[382]Tex. Att'y Gen. Op. GA-0252 (2004).

[383]TEX. CONST. art. VII, § 5.

[384]An early Texas case construing these provisions, *Church v. Bullock*, 109 S.W. 115 (Tex. 1908), upheld the reading, without comment, of Bible passages and the recitation of the Lord's Prayer at the beginning of each school day. The court reasoned that these exercises were not sectarian because such exercises were not supporting any particular denomination of religious people, but instead the "moral truths of the Bible." *Id.* at 117-18.

[385]Tex. Att'y Gen. Op. H-66 (1973) (emphasis in original). The state attorney general advised in this opinion that Tuition Equalization Grants could not be used for sectarian programs but could be used at denominational schools for secular courses of study. *See id.*

[386]*See, e.g.*, Tex. Att'y Gen. Op. No. 0-7128 (1946). *But see* Tex. Att'y Gen. Letter Advisory No. 105 (1975) (stating this decision is "questionable" under later attorney general opinions and subsequent United States Supreme Court decisions).

[387]Tex. Att'y Gen. Op. 0-2412 (1940).

[388]Tex. Att'y Gen. Op. 0-5037 (1943).

[389]Tex. Att'y Gen. Op. No. WW-1409 (1962). On the other hand, the Texas Attorney General has opined that supplying secular textbooks to private schools is permissible due to the minimal benefits accruing to sectarian activities, Tex. Att'y Gen. Letter Advisory No. 105 (1975), that parochial school students could receive band lessons at a public school, Tex. Att'y Gen. Op. M-1074 (1972), that a nondenominational chapel could be constructed in a public building with private funds, Tex. Att'y Gen. Op. H-1087 (1977), and a non-

Many sister states with similar bans on appropriating public funds to benefit religious groups have determined that governmental aid that does not violate the First Amendment is unconstitutional under their state constitutional text. For instance, several state courts have held (like the Texas Attorney General originally advised) that providing bus transportation to students of parochial schools violates the state constitution,[390] even though such transportation assistance has been held by the Supreme Court to be permissible under the First Amendment.[391]

Other state courts have invalidated school voucher or scholarship programs that can be used at religious institutions even though such programs satisfy the Establishment Clause.[392] *Locke v. Davey* provides an illustration.[393] Under the United States Constitution, the First Amendment is not violated by a state scholarship fund that allows otherwise qualified individuals to study at religious institutions.[394] Yet the Washington Constitution provides that tax dollars cannot be spent on "any religious worship, exercise or instruction, or the support of any religious establishment."[395] As a result, a Washington state scholarship program denied funds to students seeking a devotional theology degree. A Washington student awarded a scholarship filed suit under the First Amendment when he discovered that he could not use his scholarship to pursue his desired degree in pastoral ministries. But the U.S. Supreme Court held that Washington did not violate the Federal Free Exercise Clause by denying funding for the study of devotional theology. While Washington could fund theology degrees without violating the Establishment Clause, the state could also interpret its state constitutional provision more stringently and bar such funding without violating the Free Exercise Clause.[396] The Court reasoned that the state had a substantial interest in not funding the pursuit of devotional degrees in accord with its state constitution, and that the failure to do so did not demonstrate an animus toward religion that violated the student's religious liberty. The *Locke* case, like *PruneYard Shopping Center v. Robins* studied earlier, illustrates once again the interplay between providing more expansive state constitutional guarantees and the federal baseline of constitutional rights in our federal system.

---

sectarian Bible course could be taught at a junior college. Tex. Att'y Gen. Op. 0-5643 (1943).

[390] *See, e.g.*, Matthews v. Quinton, 362 P.2d 932, 941-43 (Alaska 1961); Bd. of Educ. for Indep. Sch. Dist. No. 52 v. Antone, 384 P.2d 911, 913 (Okla. 1963); Spears v. Honda, 449 P.2d 130, 135-38 (Haw. 1968); Visser v. Noosack Valley Sch. Dist. No. 506, 207 P.2d 198, 202-04 (Wash. 1949). Other states, however, have held that only aid that principally or primarily benefits religion violates such a provision, as it would be error to conclude that "some shadow of incidental benefit to a church-related institution is a violation." Jackson v. Benson, 578 N.W.2d 602, 621 (Wis. 1998). This view has led several other state courts to uphold the constitutionality of such transportation assistance under their state constitutions. *See, e.g.*, Bd. of Educ., Sch. Dist. No. 142 v. Bakalis, 299 N.E.2d 737, 745-46 (Ill. 1973); Att'y Gen. v. Sch. Comm. of Essex, 439 N.E.2d 770, 772-76 (Mass. 1982); Am. United Inc. v. Indep. Sch. Dist. No. 622, 179 N.W.2d 146, 152-54 (Minn. 1970); Rhoades v. Sch. Dist. of Abington Township, 226 A.2d 53, 63 (Pa. 1967).

[391] Everson v. Bd. of Educ., 330 U.S. 1 (1947).

[392] *See, e.g.*, Cain v. Horne, 202 P.3d 1178, 1182-85 (Ariz. 2009) (holding school voucher program violated aid clause of state constitution); Chittenden Town Sch. Dist. v. Dep't of Educ., 738 A.2d 539, 547-63 (Vt. 1999) (relying on compelled support clause of state constitution).

[393] 540 U.S. 712 (2004).

[394] Witters v. Wash. Dep't of Servs. for Blind, 474 U.S. 481, 486-89 (1986).

[395] WASH. CONST. art. I, § 11.

[396] Locke v. Davey, 540 U.S. 712, 720 (2004).

3. The Right to Bear Arms

A long-standing debate over the meaning of the Second Amendment to the United States Constitution focused on the scope of the right protected against federal interference. Did the amendment protect an individual right to bear arms, or only safeguard some type of collective right of state citizens to maintain militias or other organized military forces? The confusion was due in part to the curious wording of the Second Amendment, which provides: "A well-regulated Militia, being necessary to the security of a free State, the right of the people to keep and bear arms, shall not be infringed."[397] The federal courts struggled for decades over whether this provision protected an individual's right to keep and bear arms in the absence of a connection to the militia. The Supreme Court finally resolved this question in 2008 by holding in *District of Columbia v. Heller* that an individual right was protected to keep arms for self-defensive purposes in the home.[398]

Under the Texas Constitution, this is not–and has never been–an issue. The state constitution in article I, section 23 protects a citizen's "right to keep and bear arms in the lawful defense of himself or the State,"[399] a provision owing its origins to the revolutionary grievances of Texans highlighted in the Texas Declaration of Independence.[400] Based on this language, there has never been any doubt that Texas recognizes an individual right to bear arms for one's own self-defense. And Texas is not alone in this regard. Of the forty-four states with state constitutional protections for bearing arms, almost all of them have consistently interpreted their constitutional provisions to protect an individual right to bear arms rather than to preserve only some type of collective right.[401] Indeed, the United States Supreme Court relied on the state constitutional experience with the right to bear arms in *Heller*, and then did so again in holding in *McDonald v. City of Chicago* that the Fourteenth Amendment incorporated the Second Amendment's protections against state actors.[402]

This long-existing state constitutional protection of the individual's right to keep and bear arms, however, has not precluded the valid regulation of firearms in Texas or any other state. Article I, section 23 recognizes that the legislature has the "power, by law, to regulate the wearing of arms, with a view to prevent crime."[403] Under this provision, Texas

---

[397]U.S. CONST. amend. II.

[398]554 U.S. 570 (2008).

[399]TEX. CONST. art. I, § 23.

[400]THE TEX. DECLARATION OF INDEPENDENCE para. 13 (1836) ("It has demanded us to deliver up our arms, which are essential for our defence, the rightful property of freemen, and formidable only to tyrannical Governments.").

[401]*See* David P. Kopel, *What State Constitutions Teach About the Second Amendment*, 29 N. KY. L. REV. 823, 825-48 (2002) (listing state constitutional provisions and cases).

[402]130 S. Ct. 3020 (2010).

[403]TEX. CONST. art. I, § 23. This recognition was not included in early Texas constitutions. The Republic of Texas Constitution provided: "Every citizen shall have the right to bear arms in defense of himself and the Republic." In 1845, the Statehood Constitution added the right to "keep" arms, inserted "lawful" before the word defense, and substituted "State" for Republic. While some delegates to the statehood convention proposed allowing the legislature to regulate the carrying of concealed weapons, these proposals were not adopted. WILLIAM F. WEEKS, DEBATES OF THE TEXAS CONVENTION 311-12 (1846). Early Texas cases viewed the right to bear arms under these provisions as a "high power" that could not be infringed or impaired "because

courts have not yet invalidated a state statute regulating firearms, instead upholding statutes criminalizing firearm possession by felons,[404] barring machine gun possession,[405] and prohibiting the carrying of pistols or handguns outside the home except when traveling.[406] Likewise, every other state court interpreting its state guarantee has upheld reasonable regulations of firearms–only those rare regulations that are either arbitrary or amount to a complete ban have been invalidated in the hundreds of cases challenging gun regulations under state constitutions.[407]

Under the continuing federal-state dialogue in American federalism, this greater experience of the state courts in addressing the right to bear arms might guide the United States Supreme Court in future decisions addressing the scope of the Second Amendment. The Supreme Court's decisions in *Heller* and *McDonald* left many fundamental questions unanswered, including whether the right of self-defense extends beyond the home, which weapons qualify as protected "arms," whether certain individuals are categorically excluded from the right, which regulations are sufficiently burdensome to implicate the right, and the appropriate level of scrutiny.[408] Yet state courts have addressed such issues hundreds of times under their state constitutions, which may provide some assistance to the Supreme Court as it defines the parameters of the Second Amendment.[409]

CHAPTER 4 EXERCISES AND PROBLEMS

1. Despite earlier statements to the contrary, the United States Supreme Court held in *Lingle v. Chevron U.S.A. Inc.*, 544 U.S. 528 (2005), that a federal takings claim could not be maintained on the basis that a governmental regulation did not "substantially advance legitimate state interests." Construct an argument, based on text, structure, history, and precedent, that the failure of a state regulation to "substantially advance legitimate state interests" gives rise to a compensable taking under the Texas Constitution.

---

it is above the law, and independent of the law-making power." Cockrum v. State, 24 Tex. 394, 401-04 (1859); *accord* Choate v. Redding, 18 Tex. 579, 581 (1857) (noting in dicta that "the right to keep and bear arms cannot be infringed by legislation"). After the Civil War, however, the Reconstruction convention delegates, concerned about violence, crime, and perhaps the continued potential for rebellion, qualified the right to keep and bear arms, providing it was subject to "such regulations as the Legislature may prescribe." TEX. CONST. of 1869, art. I, § 13. The 1876 Texas Constitution then specified that the legislature's authority extended only to regulating "the wearing of arms" in order "to prevent crime."

[404] *See, e.g.*, Milligan v. State, 554 S.W.2d 192, 193-94 (Tex. Crim. App. 1977); McGuire v. State, 537 S.W.2d 26, 28-29 (Tex. Crim. App. 1976); Webb v. State, 439 S.W.2d 342, 343-44 (Tex. Crim. App. 1969).

[405] *See, e.g.*, Morrison v. State, 339 S.W.2d 529, 531-32 (Tex. Crim. App. 1960).

[406] *See, e.g.*, Masters v. State, 685 S.W.2d 654, 655 (Tex. Crim. App. 1985); Roy v. State, 552 S.W.2d 827, 830 (Tex. Crim. App. 1977); Collins v. State, 501 S.W.2d 876, 877-78 (Tex. Crim. App. 1973); State v. Duke, 42 Tex. 455, 458-59 (1875).

[407] *See* Adam Winkler, *The Reasonable Right to Bear Arms*, 17 STAN. L. & POL'Y REV. 597, 598-99 (2006).

[408] *See* Charles W. "Rocky" Rhodes, McDonald v. City of Chicago*: The Second Amendment Applies to State and Local Governments*, 2010 EMERGING ISSUES 5195 (LexisNexis July 2010) (discussing issues left unresolved by *Heller* and *McDonald* and the potential resolution of these issues).

[409] *Cf. Heller*, 554 U.S. at 626-27 (noting history of state prohibitions on carrying concealed weapons in public, possessing dangerous weapons, carrying firearms in sensitive places, and keeping and bearing weapons by felons and the mentally ill).

2. The United States Supreme Court has upheld a voucher program against a challenge under the First Amendment's Establishment Clause in *Zelman v. Simmons-Harris*, 536 U.S. 639 (2002). Construct an argument, based on text, structure, history, and precedent, that such a program would violate the provisions of the Texas Constitution limiting state financial aid to sectarian institutions.

CHAPTER 5

UNIQUE STATE CONSTITUTIONAL PROTECTIONS FOR INDIVIDUAL RIGHTS

In addition to guaranteeing rights that are also protected by the federal charter, state constitutions typically contain provisions that either are not mentioned in the United States Constitution or are not protected from state interference. As a result, the only source of constitutional protection for these rights is the state constitution.

Sometimes this occurs because, although there is a comparable guarantee in the United States Constitution against the actions of the federal government, the federal right has not been incorporated through the Due Process Clause to apply against the conduct of state and local governments. While most of the first eight Amendments of the United States Constitution are applicable to the states,[1] the United States Supreme Court has explicitly held that two are not: (1) the Fifth Amendment's requirement of a grand jury indictment;[2] and (2) the Seventh Amendment's guarantee of a jury trial in civil cases.[3] Thus, any constitutional protection for these rights against the actions of state and local governments must come from that state's constitution. The state courts may, of course, borrow from the Supreme Court's construction of the federal right when interpreting any similarly worded state constitutional provision, but several states have developed their own jurisprudence in these areas.

But for those state constitutional provisions that provide additional right protections not contained at all within the United States Constitution, employing a similar interpretation as the federal version is not feasible because no analogous federal right exists. The state courts therefore must adopt their own interpretation of the provision, with the only other persuasive source the jurisprudence of other states with a similar provision.

This chapter begins by considering the scope of state constitutional protections in those situations in which a comparable federal constitutional right has not been incorporated to apply against the states. It then addresses two of the oft-litigated unique individual rights under the Texas Constitution and the constitutions of some other states: (1) the "open courts" or "right to a remedy" provision; and (2) the prohibition against retroactive laws. It concludes with a summary of other unique state constitutional rights in Texas and its sister states.

---

[1] *See, e.g.*, Duncan v. Louisiana, 391 U.S. 145, 148-49 (1968) (listing the provisions of the Federal Bill of Rights that have been incorporated to apply against the states). The Court has assumed that the Eighth Amendment's prohibition against excessive bail applies against the states, *see* Schilb v. Kuebel, 404 U.S. 357, 365 (1971), but has not addressed the incorporation of the Third Amendment's guarantee against the quartering of soldiers or the Eighth Amendment's prohibition against excessive fines.

[2] Hurtado v. California, 110 U.S. 516, 538 (1884).

[3] Minneapolis & St. Louis R.R. Co. v. Bombolis, 241 U.S. 211, 217-18 (1916).

A. NON-INCORPORATED RIGHTS

Despite the fact that the United States Supreme Court has held that the protections of the grand jury and the right to a jury trial in civil cases are not so "fundamental to the American scheme of justice" as to require their incorporation against state action,[4] these rights are commonly protected in state constitutions. The Texas Constitution safeguards both these rights, sometimes affording protections exceeding those provided by the United States Constitution.

1. Grand Jury

Under the Fifth Amendment to the United States Constitution, "[n]o person shall be held for a capital, or otherwise infamous crime, unless on presentment or indictment of a Grand Jury," except in cases involving the military.[5] The grand jury was envisioned as a stalwart protection against a potentially oppressive government, precluding the initiation of felony proceedings unless a group of citizens found enough cause to proceed. But the grand jury is no longer viewed by many as a necessary bulwark for individual liberty, primarily due to concerns that it often delays the proceedings and that it does not meaningfully check prosecutorial power. As a result, the United States Supreme Court refused to incorporate the grand jury requirement against the states, and most states no longer require its use.

Article I, section 10 of the Texas Constitution, however, mandates the use of grand jury indictments in most felony cases.[6] Texas decisions have held that presentment of grand jury indictment is mandatory, unless the indictment has been waived in a noncapital felony in accordance with the statutorily required procedures.[7] The grand jury requirement is traceable to Texans' grievances against the Mexican legal system, and accordingly has been followed in Texas since the outbreak of the Texas Revolution.[8]

2. Right to Jury Trial in Civil Cases

Another concern of the early Texans with the Spanish and Mexican legal systems was their failure to provide for the right to a trial by jury. The Texas settlers attempted to incorporate this institution within the Mexican legal system, securing a promise that the congress of the Mexican federated state of Coahuila and Texas would have one of the "main objects of [its] attention . . . [establishing] the trial by jury in criminal cases, [extending] the same gradually, and even [adopting] it in civil cases in proportion as the advantages of this

---

[4]*See* Duncan v. Louisiana, 391 U.S. 145, 148-49 (1968).

[5]U.S. CONST. amend. V.

[6]TEX. CONST. art. I, § 10 (providing, in part, that "no person shall be held to answer for a criminal offense, unless on an indictment of a grand jury, except in cases in which the punishment is by fine or imprisonment, otherwise than in the penitentiary, in cases of impeachment, and in cases arising in the army or navy, or in the militia, when in actual service in time of war or public danger.").

[7]*See, e.g.*, King v. State, 473 S.W.2d 43, 49-52 (Tex. Crim. App. 1971).

[8]*See id.* at 47.

valuable institution become practically known."[9] But the Texans were not pleased with the resulting progress, and sought in their 1833 proposed state constitution to firmly establish a legal foundation for the "right to trial by jury" and to make it "inviolable."[10] Texans repeated their concern in the Texas Declaration of Independence, complaining that Mexico had "failed and refused to secure, on a firm basis, the right of trial by jury, that palladium of civil liberty, and only safe guarantee for the life, liberty, and property of the citizen."[11] The 1836 Republic of Texas Constitution accordingly established that the "the right of trial by jury shall remain inviolate,"[12] a guarantee now contained in article I, section 15.[13]

Additional protections for the jury trial right were added in the judiciary article of the 1845 Statehood Constitution. Article IV, section 16 of the Statehood Constitution provided: "In the trial of all causes in equity in the district court, the plaintiff or defendant shall, upon application made in open court, have the right of trial by jury, to be governed by the rules and regulations prescribed in trials at law."[14] The purpose of this provision was to ensure the benefit of trial by jury for equitable proceedings, such as suits for injunctive relief, even though the common law did not recognize a jury trial right in such proceedings. Another section of the judiciary article in the Statehood Constitution guaranteed the right of a jury trial in all causes arising out of a contract when the amount in controversy exceeded ten dollars.[15] The 1866 Constitution then merged these two sections of the judiciary article to preserve the right of trial by jury "in all cases of law or equity" with an amount in controversy of twenty dollars or more.[16] The 1876 Constitution replaced the separate references to "law or equity" to provide for the right of trial by jury "in all causes" in which a jury was properly requested and the jury fee paid.[17]

Texas thus currently has two constitutional provisions protecting the right to a jury trial in civil cases. Article I, section 15 in the Texas Bill of Rights is somewhat similar in wording to the Seventh Amendment, providing that "the right of trial by jury shall remain inviolate,"[18] although an additional clause provides the legislature the power to enact

---

[9] CONST. OF COAHUILA Y TEJ. of 1827, art. 192.

[10] PROPOSED CONST. FOR TEX. art. 4 (1833).

[11] THE TEX. DECLARATION OF INDEPENDENCE para. 6 (1836). The United States Declaration of Independence likewise complains of the denial of the right to jury. THE DECLARATION OF INDEPENDENCE para. 20 (U.S. 1776).

[12] CONST. OF REP. OF TEX of 1836., DECL. OF RTS. § 9.

[13] TEX. CONST. art. I, § 15.

[14] TEX. CONST. of 1845, art. IV, § 16.

[15] *Id.* § 18.

[16] TEX. CONST. of 1866, art. IV, § 20. The 1869 Constitution dropped the amount in controversy to ten dollars or more and provided exceptions to the right based on waiver or failure to appear. TEX. CONST. of 1869, art. V, § 16.

[17] TEX. CONST. art. V, § 10.

[18] TEX. CONST. art. I, § 15. The Seventh Amendment provides: "In Suits at common law . . . the right of trial by jury shall be preserved . . . ." U.S. CONST. amend. VII.

legislation to regulate and to maintain the "purity and efficiency" of the jury trial right.[19] The Texas Supreme Court has interpreted this section to preserve the right to a jury trial in those actions, or analogous actions, which were tried by jury when the Texas Constitution was adopted in 1876.[20] This provision thus protects the right to a trial by jury when the claimant asserts rights and remedies that would have been tried by a jury at common law.[21] This means the right to a jury trial in state court under the Texas Bill of Rights is analyzed similarly to the federal right under the Seventh Amendment,[22] with the only difference being that the right under the state constitution is preserved as it existed in 1876, while the federal right is preserved as it existed in 1791.[23]

The second constitutional jury guarantee, found in the judiciary article, provides additional protections in certain situations. Article V, section 10 extends the right to a jury trial to "the trial of all causes in the District Courts," upon proper application by one of the parties.[24] The supreme court has held that this protects the right to have a jury resolve fact questions in all "causes" brought in the district courts, both in law and in equity.[25] However, a few special types of proceedings are not "causes" under article V, such as civil contempt, election contests, and appeals from certain administrative proceedings.[26]

Almost all states likewise have some protection for jury trials under their state constitutions, but the extent of protection varies. The typical clause protects the rights to a civil jury that existed at the time the state constitution was adopted, similar to article I, section 15 of the Texas Constitution, but of course the relevant adoption dates vary from state to state. Very few states protect a general right to a jury trial in equitable actions similar to article V, section 10 of the Texas Constitution.[27] What might account for the decision to originally incorporate this extremely unique provision in the 1845 Texas Statehood Constitution, a constitution which has been described as motivated by a "concern

---

[19]TEX. CONST. art. I, § 15. This provision also authorizes the legislature to authorize the temporary commitment of the mentally ill for observation or treatment without a jury trial, and another constitutional provision details the procedures for permanent commitments of the mentally disabled. *See id.* §§ 15-15-a.

[20]*See, e.g.*, Barshop v. Medina Cnty. Underground Water Conservation Dist., 925 S.W.2d 618, 636 (Tex. 1996); Tex. Workers' Comp. Comm'n v. Garcia, 893 S.W.2d 504, 526 (Tex. 1995); Tex. Ass'n of Bus. v. Tex. Air Control Bd., 852 S.W.2d 440, 450-51 (Tex. 1993).

[21]State v. Credit Bureau of Laredo, Inc., 530 S.W.2d 288, 291 (Tex. 1975).

[22]*Cf. id.* at 291-92 (citing federal precedent as support for court's holding).

[23]*Cf. Barshop*, 925 S.W.2d at 636 (concluding that there was no scheme for a jury trial for regulation of natural resources in 1876); *Tex. Ass'n of Bus.*, 852 S.W.2d at 450-51 (holding agencies' assessments of environmental penalties were not analogous to actions tried to a jury in 1876); White v. White, 196 S.W. 508, 512-15 (Tex. 1917) (determining that right to jury trial for civil commitments of the insane could not be statutorily deprived because a jury trial right existed for such proceedings in 1876).

[24]TEX. CONST. art. V, § 10.

[25]*Credit Bureau*, 530 S.W.2d at 292-93.

[26]*See, e.g., Barshop*, 925 S.W.2d at 636 (appeal from administrative proceeding); *Garcia*, 893 S.W.2d at 527 (appeal from an administrative decision); *Credit Bureau*, 530 S.W.2d at 292-93 (listing examples).

[27]Fleming James, Jr., *Right to a Jury Trial in Civil Actions*, 72 YALE L.J. 655, 657 & n.13 (1963) (noting that Texas and North Carolina provide for a constitutional right to a jury trial in equitable actions and Georgia and Tennessee have established this jury trial right by statute).

for annexation [that] counseled conservatism"?[28]

How important is the right to a civil jury trial in the twenty-first century? Is it a vestige of an earlier era, no longer worth the inefficiency and expense? Can a layperson jury appropriately comprehend, deliberate, and render judgment on complex commercial disputes, products liability cases, or medical malpractice claims? Similar concerns have led most common law nations, including Britain and Canada, to curtail or eliminate the civil jury trial right in modern times. On the other hand, though, the right to a jury trial has always been a fundamental aspect of the American civil justice scheme, a component of a just "day in court" for redress of an injury. The debate regarding the utility of juries in civil cases is not new; in fact, the Texas Constitutional Statehood Convention of 1845 struggled with these same issues in considering whether to extend the jury trial right to equitable actions. Some convention delegates argued that, because juries were not equipped to handle the complex issues often arising in equitable actions, these cases should be entrusted to a chancellor.[29] The successful counter to this argument was that justice necessitated a jury, as chancellors often acknowledged by empaneling juries when not required to do so. One delegate declared: "You will often hear litigants cursing judges for improper decisions; but very seldom if they have had a jury."[30]

Some states have extended their jury trial right to bar legislative interference with the jury's damages awards for common law claims, thereby rendering legislatively imposed compensatory damages caps unconstitutional. For example, the Georgia Supreme Court held that a legislative cap on noneconomic damages in medical malpractice claims violated the state right to a civil jury trial.[31] The court reasoned that medical malpractice was a longstanding common law claim, with roots traceable to early English common law, such that the restriction on the jury's ability to determine the amount of damages suffered by the plaintiff nullified "the jury's findings of fact regarding damages and thereby undermines the jury's basic function."[32] State high courts in Alabama, Missouri, Oregon, and Washington have likewise held that damages caps on common law claims violate a state constitutional right to a jury trial in civil cases.[33] Yet a number of other states have disagreed, reasoning that the jury trial right, while encompassing the right of a jury to assess damages, does not include the right to have the jury dictate the legal consequences of its assessment.[34] Texas courts have not addressed this issue, instead considering the constitutionality of damages

---

[28]John Cornyn, *The Roots of the Texas Constitution: Settlement to Statehood*, 26 TEX. TECH. L. REV. 1089, 1092 (1995).

[29]WILLIAM F. WEEKS, DEBATES OF THE TEXAS CONVENTION 268-69 (1846).

[30]*Id.* at 269 (remarks of James Love).

[31]Atlanta Oculoplastic Surgery, P.C. v. Nestlehutt, 691 S.E.2d 218 (Ga. 2010).

[32]*Id.* at 221-24.

[33]*See, e.g.*, Moore v. Mobile Infirmary Ass'n, 592 So.2d 156, 159-64 (Ala. 1991); Watts v. Lester E. Cox Med. Ctrs., 376 S.W.3d 633, 637-41 (Mo. 2012); Lakin v. Senco Prods., Inc., 987 P.2d 463, 473-75 (Or. 1999); Sofie v. Fibreboard.Corp., 771 P.2d 711, 724 (Wash. 1989).

[34]*See, e.g.*, Evans v. State, 56 P.3d 1046, 1050-51 (Alaska 2002) (equally divided court); Kirkland v. Blaine Cnty. Med. Ctr., 4 P.3d 1115, 1118-20 (Idaho 2000); Johnson v. St. Vincent Hosp., Inc., 404 N.E.2d 585, 602 (Ind. 1980); Murphy v. Edmonds, 601 A.2d 102, 116-18 (Md. 1992); Arbino v. Johnson & Johnson, 880 N.E.2d 420, 431-32 (Ohio 2007); Judd v. Drezga, 103 P.3d 135, 144 (Utah 2004); Etheridge v. Med. Ctr. Hosp., 376 S.E.2d 525, 529 (Va. 1989); MacDonald v. City Hosp., Inc., 715 S.E.2d 405, 415 (W. Va. 2011).

caps on common law claims under a unique state constitutional guarantee, the open courts or right to a remedy provision.

B. OPEN COURTS OR REMEDY PROVISION

The most frequently litigated of the unique state constitutional provisions not found within the United States Constitution is the "open courts" guarantee, which has also been called the "right of access to the courts," the "right to courts," or the "right to a remedy." Regardless of its name, it is a longstanding Anglo-American right, derived from Sir Edward Coke's interpretation of the Magna Carta. And it is still flourishing today, as it expressly or implicitly appears in forty state constitutions.[35]

While the wording of this provision typically differs at least somewhat from state to state, it usually takes one of two basic forms. State constitutions in a minority of jurisdictions contain language devised in the seventeenth century by Lord Coke, providing something similar to the following: "That every person for every injury done him in his goods, land, or person, ought to have remedy by the due course of the law of the land and ought to have justice and right for the injury done to him freely without sale, fully without denial, and speedily without delay, according to the law of the land."[36] Most states, though, use a more compact form of these principles, which resembles the following: "That all courts shall be open, and every person, for an injury done him in his person, property, or reputation, shall have remedy by the due course of the law."[37]

Texas has adopted the more compact form, with its open courts clause in article I, section 13 providing:

> All courts shall be open, and every person for an injury done him, in his lands, goods, person or reputation, shall have remedy by due course of law.[38]

While every Texas Constitution has contained this clause, the judicial interpretation of this provision's scope has gradually expanded over the last century and a half. Early Texas cases construed article I, section 13 as mandating the existence of an actual court that could redress the grievances of the plaintiff. For instance, in *Runge & Co. v. Wyatt*, the Texas Supreme Court held that a venue statute requiring plaintiffs to sue in the county of defendants' domicile violated the open courts provision when no court or district clerk yet existed in the defendant's home county.[39] The court reasoned that plaintiffs "could have no remedy by due course of law, if there was no tribunal in which they could make their

---

[35]Thomas R. Phillips, *The Constitutional Right to a Remedy*, 78 N.Y.U. L. REV. 1309, 1310 & n.6 (2003).

[36]*Id.* at 1311.

[37]*Id.*

[38]TEX. CONST. art. I, § 13. Section 13 also contains, before the open courts guarantee, the Texas guarantees regarding excessive bail and cruel and unusual punishment: "Excessive bail shall not be required, nor excessive fines imposed, nor cruel or unusual punishment inflicted."

[39]25 Tex. Supp. 291, 294 (1860).

complaint."[40] Modern Texas cases refer to these decisions as illustrative of the first guarantee emanating from the open courts provision, that the courts must actually be open and operating.[41]

The second guarantee emanating from the Texas open courts provision, that citizens must have access to the courts unimpeded by unreasonable financial barriers, had its beginning in the case of *Dillingham v. Putnam*.[42] In *Dillingham*, the court held that the open courts provision precluded hinging a receiver's right to appeal on the payment of a supersedeas bond that was double the amount of the appealed judgment, interest, and costs. Although recognizing that the legislature had the power to regulate appeals and to provide for supersedeas in order to suspend execution of the judgment, the court reasoned that "a party's right to appeal to this court cannot be made to depend on his ability to give a bond" without denying a remedy by due course of law.[43] A few years later, the court similarly held in *Eustis v. City of Henrietta* that a statute requiring defendants to pay their property taxes before being allowed to make a defense to a tax sale violated the open courts provision because it effectively denied "the citizen the right to be heard in court" by making the tax payment a "condition precedent" to asserting a valid defense.[44] These cases stand for the proposition that the legislature cannot impose litigation taxes and prepayment requirements that unreasonably limit court access.

The final guarantee of the open courts provision, that meaningful legal remedies must be afforded to Texas citizens, did not develop until the twentieth century. This is the aspect of the open courts provision that has been used to strike down some aspects of legislative "tort reform" in the last thirty years, including statutes of limitations and damages caps in medical malpractice cases. As interpreted by Texas courts, this prevents legislative interference with well-established common law causes of action unless the governmental interest outweighs the infringement on the litigant's right to redress.

Other states have similarly gradually expanded the scope of their open courts provision from merely requiring the assurance of fair and timely judicial access to guaranteeing the preservation of certain substantive rights and remedies. But the scope of this protection varies from state to state. In some states, the open court guarantee preserves the existence of well-established causes of action unless an adequate substitute remedy is provided. In other states, legislative interference with substantive rights must satisfy some form of heightened scrutiny in order to satisfy the open courts provision. Finally, there are some states where the judiciaries have not interpreted the open courts guarantee to provide any meaningful substantive limitations on legislative authority.[45] The following article

---

[40]*Id.*; *accord* O'Shea v. Twohig, 9 Tex. 336, 341-42 (1852) (holding plaintiff could sue several defendants in a single county even though some of the defendants resided in another recently formed county when the new county did not have a district court).

[41]Tex. Ass'n of Bus. v. Tex. Air Control Bd., 852 S.W.2d 440, 448 (Tex. 1993).

[42]14 S.W. 303 (Tex. 1890).

[43]*Id.* at 304-05.

[44]39 S.W. 567, 569 (Tex. 1897).

[45]*See* 1 JENNIFER FRIESEN, STATE CONSTITUTIONAL LAW: LITIGATING INDIVIDUAL RIGHTS, CLAIMS AND DEFENSES § 6.02[3] (4th ed. 2006).

excerpt generally describes the gradual evolution in the interpretation of the open courts provision in the states and the resulting confusion in the reported decisions.

Thomas R. Phillips, *The Constitutional Right to a Remedy*, 78 N.Y.U. L. Rev. 1309 (2003)*

* * * *

I Origins of the Right to a Remedy

To understand the right to a remedy, most states look first to the guarantee's origin and development in England. Judges long have been impressed by its pedigree, dating from the Great Charter on the field at Runnymede in 1215 and confirmed as Chapter 29 of the "final version" of Magna Carta in 1225. But the modern significance of the right to a remedy began in 1641, when Sir Edward Coke's *Second Part of the Institutes of the Laws of England* was published posthumously. Coke described Chapter 29 of Magna Carta as a "roote" from which "many fruitfull branches of the law of England have sprung." One such branch was the protection of individuals' rights from official acts of oppression, the precursor to modern due process. Another was "the rights of subjects in their private relations with one another," where Coke gave this gloss on Magna Carta:

> [E]very subject of this realm, for injury done to him in goods, lands, or person, by any other subject, be he ecclesiastical, or temporall, . . . or any other without exception, may take his remedy by the course of the law, and have justice, and right for the injury done to him, freely without sale, fully without any deniall, and speedily without delay.
>
> . . .[J]ustice must have three qualities; it must be . . . free; for nothing is more odious than Justice let to sale; full, for justice ought not to limp, or be granted piece-meal; and speedily, for delay is a kind of denial; and then it is both justice and right.

Much of this language survives intact as the remedies guarantees of some state constitutions.

During the next century, Sir William Blackstone described the right to a remedy as one of the critical means through which a civilized society served its principal aim–the preservation of an individual's absolute rights to life, liberty, and property. In his *Commentaries on the Laws of England*, first published in Oxford between 1765 and 1769, Blackstone divided the rights of persons into two categories. The three absolute rights of personal security, personal liberty, and private property existed in a state of nature. Other rights were merely relative, arising only because men live in society and have relationships with other people. Absolute rights could not be protected simply by declaratory law; individuals required means of vindicating them.

The right to a remedy was one of the five subordinate rights through which people vindicated their absolute rights, and it encompassed both the substance of the law and the procedures through which courts applied that law. Once a person was injured, the right to an "adequate remedy" immediately attached, though judicial process might be necessary to ascertain the exact parameters of that right. The right to a remedy dictated that common-law courts exercise general jurisdiction, being open for all cases involving injury to individual rights, "[f]or it is a settled and invariable principle in the laws of England, that every right when withheld must have a remedy, and every injury its proper redress." Thus when Blackstone quoted Coke's dictum that justice be granted fully and without delay, he was concerned not merely with the physical availability of judicial process but with the substantive opportunity to assert claims to protect absolute rights.

Neither Coke nor Blackstone would have empowered judicial officers to protect rights against [all] government intrusion. At that time, [for all practical purposes,] no one accorded power to the courts to strike down legislative actions. As Blackstone stated, "[Parliament] being the highest and greatest court, over which none other can have jurisdiction in the kingdom, if by any means a misgovernment should any way fall upon it the subjects of this kingdom are left without all manner of remedy." Blackstone clearly saw the remedies guarantee only as a check on royal and other "private" abuses of power, not parliamentary excess.

Unlike Coke and Blackstone, the rebellious American colonists saw both the Crown and Parliament as oppressors. Parliamentary initiatives during the 1760s and 1770s convinced the colonists that the informal constitution securing English rights against royal infringement was inadequate to protect against all forms of government oppression. When independence was declared, some of the new American states began adopting formal written constitutions to structure their new governments and to help secure their most fundamental rights. As Gordon Wood notes, they recognized that laws protecting their basic freedoms must be of "a nature more sacred than those which established a turnpike road."[46]

By the end of 1776, two states–Delaware and Pennsylvania–had adopted constitutions guaranteeing the right to a remedy. Four more states adopted the right before the United States Constitution was ratified, as did all three new states that joined the Union before 1800.

In the absence of any surviving debate or discussion from the adoption of these provisions, our best opportunity to discover how the early framers intended to adapt the wisdom of Coke and Blackstone to the American experience comes from early judicial interpretations of the right. If the framers really intended to place a constitutional shield around the common law, that notion should appear in opinions applying the guarantee.

II. Early Interpretations

The first case to strike down a government action solely on the basis of the remedies clause came from Tennessee, in 1835. The action condemned was not a law, but a justice-of-the-peace court rule requiring all motions for new trial to be made on the first Saturday after trial. Because "[i]t is the business of the courts to be open, where right and justice shall be administered[,]" the rule had to yield to the constitution. Later, several state

[46]Gordon S. Wood, *Foreword: State Constitution-Making in the American Revolution*, 24 RUTGERS L.J. 911, 920 (1993).

courts voided laws that taxed access to the courts in one way or another beyond what was needed to support the judicial machinery.

The first case I have found that [invalidated] a non-revenue statute primarily on the basis of the remedies clause did not come until 1862, when the Supreme Court of Minnesota struck down a law denying access to the courts of the state to anyone "aiding the Rebellion." After expounding their support for the Union cause, the justices observed that "in the end all must regard as matter of pride and gratulation, that in this state no one, not even the worst of felons, can be denied the right to simple justice."

Not until 1901 did a court rely squarely on the right to a remedy to strike down a statute providing tort remedies. In *Mattson v. Astoria*,[47] a municipal ordinance completely eliminated all remedies for persons injured by a defective public street. The Oregon Supreme Court held that

> [t]he constitutional provision guarantying [sic] to every person a remedy by due course of law for injury done him in person or property . . . was intended to preserve the common-law right of action for injury to person or property, and while the legislature may change the remedy or form of procedure, attach conditions precedent to its exercise, and perhaps abolish old and substitute new remedies, it cannot deny a remedy entirely.

Thus, the full import of the remedies clause was not realized until the same decade when the United States Supreme Court used substantive due process to "enact Mr. Herbert Spencer's Social Statics" in *Lochner*.[48] Yet state courts were unwilling to apply the remedies clause aggressively to strike down emerging workers' compensation systems. All states eventually adopted these plans, and they were generally upheld by the courts, although in some instances constitutional amendments were necessary to satisfy or overcome judicial objections.

While inconsistent with some modern views of the right to a remedy, these early cases were surprisingly consistent with Blackstone's view. In most early American cases, the courts were willing to supply a remedy for every right, whether created by common law or statute. But they were not bound to preserve any particular remedy or procedure for vindicating the right. As long as the new law preserved the injured person's ability to vindicate his or her rights in court or provided an adequate substitute remedy, the right to a remedy was not violated. The courts also allowed legislatures to limit remedies derived from relative law, such as respondeat superior, in part because the injured person retained the right to obtain a judicial remedy against the individual who caused the injury, that is, the individual who violated the injured person's absolute right to personal security.

III. Modern Interpretations

Widely divergent outcomes resulted from challenges to the various statutes of repose passed in the 1960s and 1970s to help architects, engineers, builders, and others in

---

[47]65 P. 1066 (Or. 1901).

[48]Lochner v. New York, 198 U.S. 45, 75 (1905) (Holmes, J., dissenting).

the construction field. Because these statutes cut off certain claims before they even arose, they were in tension with the established remedies doctrine in many states. Most of these statutes were upheld against remedies attacks, though a significant minority were struck down.

Numerous remedies challenges were brought against laws passed in the 1970s and 1980s regulating medical malpractice suits. Again, while many of these laws were struck down in whole or in part on equal protection, jury trial, privileges and immunities, due process, and separation of powers grounds, as well as on the right to a remedy, state courts also have upheld a number of statutes against all such attacks.

Now, remedies challenges are being leveled against recent "tort reform" laws. Taking advantage of new state constitutional law treatises, law review articles, and increased interstate dialogue between state appellate justices, contemporary remedies opinions are often longer and more thoughtful, but as yet they are no more consistent than before. Indeed, current variations among and even within states are truly confounding. Justice Hans Linde noted that his own Supreme Court of Oregon "has written many individually tenable but inconsistent opinions" about the remedies guarantee,[49] while former [Chief] Justice [Michael] Zimmerman of the Utah Supreme Court called upon the bench and bar to develop new approaches to find "understandable standards . . . that are practically capable of predictable application."[50]

The Texas cases interpreting the open courts provision since 1980 have considered three recurring issues. First, under the "second guarantee" of the open courts provision, when has the legislature unreasonably impeded access to the courts? Second, under the "third guarantee" of the open courts clause, under what circumstances does a statute of limitations or a statute of repose unconstitutionally abrogate a well-established common law cause of action? Finally, also under the "third guarantee," under what circumstances can the legislature impose legislative "caps" or other restrictions on damages awards? These issues are addressed in turn in each of the following sections.

1. Unreasonable Financial Barriers

Federal due process and equal protection principles rarely invalidate filing fees and other costs that burden an indigent's access to the civil justice system. Only if the fee abridges the individual's right to protect a fundamental constitutional interest, such as marriage or the parent-child relationship, will the United States Supreme Court strike down the financial barrier.[51] Filing fees are constitutional in all other cases, even in those

---

[49]Hale v. Port of Portland, 783 P.2d 506, 518 (Or. 1989) (Linde, J., concurring).

[50]Lyon v. Burton, 5 P.3d 616, 641 (Utah 2000) (Zimmerman, J., concurring).

[51]*See, e.g.*, M.L.B. v. S.L.J., 519 U.S. 102, 119-24 (1996) (holding that denying appeal from a parental rights termination due to inability to pay fees violated due process and equal protection); Little v. Streater, 452 U.S. 1, 13-17 (1981) (compelling the state to pay for blood tests necessary for an indigent to contest paternity); Boddie v. Connecticut, 401 U.S. 371, 374 (1971) (requiring state to waive filing fees for divorcing indigents).

situations in which the litigation concerns the party's indigence, such as bankruptcy proceedings or welfare determinations.[52]

State open courts provisions, in contrast, provide a constitutional ground for ensuring that the courts are "open to all with legitimate disputes, not just those who can afford the fees to get in."[53] Moreover, as evidenced in the following case, this guarantee has not merely been applied to require exceptions for the indigent, but also to prohibit any unreasonable litigation taxes or prepayment requirements for judicial review.

***LeCroy v. Hanlon*, 713 S.W.2d 335 (Tex. 1986)**

SPEARS, Justice.

We are called upon to decide whether sections 31 and 32 of the Omnibus Fee Bill (House Bill 1593, 69th Leg., 1985), which direct $40 of a litigant's district court filing fee to go to state general revenues, violate the Texas Constitution. We [hold] sections 31 and 32 violate the Texas Constitution's caption requirement, Article III, § 35, and open courts provision, Article I, § 13.

I. *Facts.*

The facts are undisputed. Ben Hanlon's truck was damaged in an automobile accident on March 2, 1985. Texas Wrecker Service towed the truck to its yard. Hanlon had automobile insurance, including towing coverage, on his truck from Northern County Mutual Insurance Company. Northern County Mutual refused to pay Hanlon's claim, and Texas Wrecker Service refused to release Hanlon's truck without payment.

On September 5, 1985, Hanlon attempted to file suit under the Texas Insurance Code and Texas Deceptive Trade Practices Act against Northern County Mutual and Texas Wrecker Service with the Lubbock County District Clerk. He presented the district clerk with two checks totaling $98, the filing fee existing before September 1, 1985. The district clerk refused the petition, because Hanlon did not tender $173, the filing fee effective September 1, 1985 under House Bill 1593 §§ 31, 32. Section 31 increased the district court filing fee from $25 to $75; Section 32 allocated $10 of the increase to the district clerk and the remaining $40 to the state's general revenue fund. Mr. Hanlon did not file an affidavit of inability to pay costs under Tex.R.Civ.P. 145.

Hanlon filed a petition for writ of mandamus and amended it to request a declaratory judgment and injunctive relief against the Lubbock County District Clerk. Hanlon maintained that the fees he tendered were proper and that the new fee requirements were unconstitutional. After a hearing, the district court agreed. The court issued a mandamus directing the district clerk to file Hanlon's petition and enjoining the collection of the new fee. The Attorney General on behalf of the State appeals the declaratory judgment and the injunctive relief.

---

[52]*See, e.g.*, Ortwein v. Schwab, 410 U.S. 656, 659-60 (1973) (upholding fee for appellate review of welfare determination); United States v. Kras, 409 U.S. 434, 445-46 (1973) (upholding filing fees for bankruptcy).

[53]Griffin Indus., Inc. v. Thirteenth Court of Appeals, 934 S.W.2d 349, 353 (Tex. 1996).

* * * *

III. *The Open Courts Provision.*

The Attorney General also contends that the $40 tax allocated to state general revenues does not violate the open courts provision of Article I, § 13. We disagree.

Like the citizens of other states, Texans have adopted state constitutions to restrict governmental power and guarantee individual rights. The powers restricted and the individual rights guaranteed in the present constitution reflect Texas' values, customs, and traditions. Our constitution has independent vitality, and this court has the power and duty to protect the additional state guaranteed rights of all Texans. Article V, § 1; *Nelson v. Krusen,* 678 S.W.2d [918,] 923 [(Tex. 1984)]. By enforcing our constitution, we provide Texans with their full individual rights and strengthen federalism.

The open courts provision, Article I, sec. 13 reads:

> Excessive bail shall not be required, nor excessive fines imposed, nor cruel and unusual punishment inflicted. All courts shall be open, and every person for an injury done him, in his lands, goods, person or reputation, shall have remedy by due course of law.

The provision's wording and history demonstrate the importance of the right of access to the courts. The provision's wording indicates the high value the drafters and ratifiers placed on the right of access to the courts. First, the language is mandatory: "*shall* be open" and "*shall* have remedy by due course of law." Further, it is all-inclusive: "*all* courts" are to be open; "for *every* person"; for *all* interests, "lands" (real property), "goods" (personal property), "person" (body and mind), and "reputation" (good name); *at all times,* since there is no emergency exception. This all-inclusive language contrasts with the qualifying language used in other sections. *See, e.g.,* Article I, § 9; Article I, § 11; Article I, § 11a.

The open courts provision's history also reflects its significance. It originates from Chapter 40 of Magna Carta, the great charter of English liberties obtained from King John in 1215: "To none will we sell, to none deny or delay, right or justice." Tex.Const. art. I, sec. 13, interp. commentary (Vernon 1984); 14 Encyclopedia Britannica 576 (1967). Colonists brought to America and then to Texas their belief in the historic rights guaranteed by Magna Carta. 1 G. Braden, *The Constitution of the State of Texas: An Annotated and Comparative Analysis* 3 (1977); F. Stewart and J. Clark, *The Constitution and Government of Texas* 5 (1936). The right of access to the courts has been at the foundation of the American democratic experiment.

Every Texas Constitution has contained an open courts provision with the identical wording. 1 G. Braden, *supra,* at 45; W. Harris, *Constitution of the State of Texas Annotated,* 114 (1913). Other Bill of Rights sections, in contrast, have been amended over the years. 1 G. Braden, *supra,* at 2. Apparently, the open courts provision was uncontroversial [to the framers at the 1875 Constitutional Convention as there was no debate regarding it].

This court first enforced the open courts provision in 1852 in *O'Shea v. Twohig,* 9 Tex. 336, 341-42 (1852). The court followed with three other cases before the 1875

Constitutional Convention. *Teas v. Robinson,* 11 Tex. 774 (1854); *Clark v. Goss,* 12 Tex. 395 (1854); *Runge & Co. v. Wyatt,* 25 Tex.Supp. 291 (1860).[54] The people ratified the court's approach by passing an identical provision in the 1876 Constitution. This court then reaffirmed its commitment to the open courts provision in several cases shortly after the 1876 Constitution's adoption. *Lumpkin v. Muncey,* 66 Tex. 311, 17 S.W. 732 (1886); *Dillingham v. Putnam,* 109 Tex. 1, 14 S.W. 303 (1890); *Union Cent. Life Ins. Co. v. Chowning,* 86 Tex. 654, 26 S.W. 982 (1894); *Eustis v. City of Henrietta,* 90 Tex. 468, 39 S.W. 567 (1897).

Besides the open courts provision, every Texas constitution has also included a separate due process provision, presently Article I, § 19; 1 G. Braden, *supra,* at 67. Logically, our constitutions have included both provisions because they serve different purposes. The open courts provision must have been intended to provide rights in addition to those in the due process provision or the former would be surplusage. Furthermore, the due process provision's general guarantees contrast with the open courts provision's specific guarantee of a right of access to the courts. 1 G. Braden, *supra,* at 50.

The open courts provision specifically guarantees all litigants the right to redress their grievances–to use a popular and correct phrase, the right to their day in court. *Nelson v. Krusen,* 678 S.W.2d at 923; *Sax v. Votteler,* 648 S.W.2d [661,] 665 [(Tex. 1983)]. This right is a substantial state constitutional right. *Nelson v. Krusen,* 678 S.W.2d at 921. Because a substantial right is involved, the legislature cannot arbitrarily or unreasonably interfere with a litigant's right of access to the courts. *Neagle v. Nelson,* 685 S.W.2d 11, 12 (Tex.1985); *Nelson v. Krusen,* 678 S.W.2d at 922; *Sax v. Votteler,* 648 S.W.2d at 664, 665. Thus, the general open courts provision test balances the legislature's actual purpose in enacting a law against that law's interference with the individual's right of access to the courts. *Sax v. Votteler,* 648 S.W.2d at 665, 666. The government has the burden to show that the legislative purpose outweighs the interference with the individual's right of access. *Id.* at 666.

The question here is whether a filing fee that goes to state general revenues is an arbitrary and unreasonable interference with the right of access to the court. Section 32's purpose in allocating $40 of the $75 filing fee to the state general revenue fund is "to generate revenue and to help finance state services." House Comm. on Appropriations, Bill Analysis, Tex.H.B. 1593, 69th Leg. (1985). The Comptroller estimates that the $40 fee will

---

[54]In *O'Shea v. Twohig,* a unanimous court indicated that its statutory interpretation, allowing a plaintiff to sue several defendants although the court designated for jurisdiction was not organized, was dictated by constitutional necessity. 9 Tex. at 341. Two years later in *Teas v. Robinson,* a unanimous court held that a defective statute could not deprive an individual of his "[right] to his appeal. This is guaranteed by the constitution and cannot be withheld." 11 Tex. at 777. In *Clark v. Goss,* a unanimous court reaffirmed *O'Shea v. Twohig.* 12 Tex. 395, 397-98 (1854).

In 1860 in *Runge & Co. v. Wyatt,* a unanimous court stated specifically that these prior cases were based upon the open courts provision. 25 Tex.Supp. 291 (1860). A statute required the plaintiff to sue in the county of the defendant's domicile; however, since there was no district clerk in the defendant's county, the plaintiff sued in the pre-partition county of domicile. Quoting the open courts provision, this court reversed a trial court judgment sustaining a plea to the jurisdiction. 25 Tex.Supp. at 294.

raise $11,062,000 this fiscal year, approximately 1/10 of 1% of state revenues.

The major defect with the filing fee is that it is a general revenue tax on the right to litigate: the money goes to other statewide programs besides the judiciary. Nearly all states with similar open courts provisions have held that filing fees that go to fund general welfare programs, and not court-related services, are unconstitutional. *Crocker v. Finley,* 99 Ill.2d 444, 459 N.E.2d 1346 (1984); *Farabee v. Board of Trustees, Lee County Law Library,* 254 So.2d 1 (Fla.1971). See also *Hayes v. C.C. & H. Min. & Mill Co.,* 126 S.W. 1051 (Mo.1910). *Cf. State v. Gorman*, 41 N.W. 948, 949 (Minn.1889).

The state argues that a tax on individual litigants is reasonable as long as the amount raised for general revenues is less than the amount spent from general revenues on the judiciary. This argument, however, uses the wrong perspective: a societal perspective. When individual rights guaranteed by the state constitution are involved, an individual rights perspective is used. From that perspective, litigants must pay a tax for general welfare programs as a condition to being allowed their right of access to the courts. This the open courts provision prohibits.

We hold that filing fees that go to state general revenues–in other words taxes on the right to litigate that pay for other programs besides the judiciary–are unreasonable impositions on the state constitutional right of access to the courts. Regardless of its size, such a filing fee is unconstitutional for filing fees cannot go for non-court-related purposes.

Filing fees and court costs are usually constitutional. Charging litigants that are able to pay a reasonable fee for judicial support services does not violate the open courts provision. Such fees interfere somewhat with access to the courts, but they are permitted because they go for court-related purposes.

GONZALEZ, Justice, dissenting.

I dissent. Section 31 of the Omnibus Fee Bill increased the district court filing fee from $25 to $75. Section 32 of that same bill allows the district clerk to retain $35 and requires the clerk to send the remainder to the comptroller for deposit in the general revenue fund. Sections 31 and 32 do not violate the Texas Constitution's open courts provision, Article I, § 13, nor do they violate the constitution's caption requirement, Article III, § 35.

Open Courts Provision

The open courts provision is essentially a due process guarantee. *Sax v. Votteler,* 648 S.W.2d 661, 664 (Tex.1983). The requirements of procedural due process apply only to the threatened deprivation of liberty and property interests deserving the protection of the federal and state constitutions. *Board of Regents v. Roth,* 408 U.S. 564, 569 (1972); *Tarrant County v. Ashmore,* 635 S.W.2d 417, 422 (Tex.1982). Therefore, any assessment of proper procedural safeguards necessarily begins with a consideration of whether the particular interest at stake is a protectable interest.

A constitutionally protected right must be a vested right or something more than a mere expectancy based upon an anticipated continuance of an existing law. *City of Dallas v. Trammel,* 129 Tex. 150, 101 S.W.2d 1009 (1937). Here, Hanlon clearly did not have a vested interest or right in a $25 district court filing fee. Hanlon argues, however, that he has a vested right to sue in the Texas courts. The critical issue is whether this right has been unreasonably restricted by the act. I submit that Hanlon's right to sue has not been unreasonably abridged. Hanlon could file suit this very day; all he has to do is pay the $75 filing fee or file as a pauper under Tex.R.Civ.P. 145. Thus, the Texas courts are "open" to litigants such as Hanlon. *No explanation is given by the court for how the act actually prevents litigants from exercising their right to bring suit.*

The increase in the filing fee cannot be characterized as an "impossible condition" as in the prior cases applying the open courts provision. A person's inability to pay the filing fee will not prevent them from filing a cause of action. Texas Rule of Civil Procedure 145 provides that persons who are unable to pay court costs can be excused from payment. Filing fees are a part of court costs. *See Rodeheaver v. Alridge,* 601 S.W.2d 51 (Tex.Civ.App.–Houston [1st Dist.] 1980, writ ref'd n.r.e.). Thus, Rule 145 assures that persons unable to pay the filing fee will have open access to the courts.

The court draws a significant distinction on the fact that the fee goes into state general revenues and not into a special fund for the courts. The court holds that "filing fees that go to state general revenues–in other words, taxes on the right to litigate that pay for other programs besides the judiciary–are unreasonable impositions on the state constitutional right of access to the courts." The court thus implies that if the $50 increase went into a special fund for the benefit of the courts, the act would be constitutional. As the state observes, however, a special fund is no more than an accounting device. Since dollars are fungible and more money will be spent on the court system than will be taken in under Section 32, it is absurd to conclude money collected from fees "will pay for other programs besides the judiciary." The state's annual share of the filing fee is expected to be approximately $11,000,000 while the State's annual cost will be over $52,000,000. *See* Art. of May 27, 1985, ch. 980, art. IV, 1985 Tex.Sess.Law Serv. 7284 (Vernon). As long as the State pays more in financing the judiciary than the courts receive in user fees, the court's logic is flawed. This court need not presume that any portion of the fee increase goes to support general welfare programs unrelated to the court system. If any presumption is to be made, it should be in favor of the validity of the statute.

Notes on Financial Impediments to Court Access

LeCroy, *Filing Fees, and Litigation Taxes*: If the open courts provision protects litigants' right to their day in court for redress of grievances, how was that right infringed when Hanlon could have either paid the filing fee or obtained a waiver of the fee through an affidavit of indigence? Should it matter whether the fee is an actual financial impediment to the litigant's access to the courts? Justice Gonzalez's dissent urged that it should, contending Hanlon had not shown that the increased filing fee actually interfered with his right of access to the courts. A similar argument was made by Justice Doggett in dissent in another case, where he urged that a penalty prepayment requirement applicable to corporations should not be invalidated until it actually restricted their access to the courts.[55]

[55]Tex. Ass'n of Bus. v. Tex. Air Control Bd., 852 S.W.2d 440, 457 (Tex. 1993) (Doggett, J., dissenting).

How would the *LeCroy* majority respond to these arguments?

Once the *LeCroy* court determined that the right of access had been infringed, what test does it employ to adjudge the constitutionality of the infringement? Under this test, why does the court conclude that the individual interest outweighs the legislative purpose? Is this determination a case of form over substance? Could the legislature have enacted the exact same filing fee increase as long as it ensured the money was placed in a special fund for the benefit of the judiciary because the state's expenses for the judiciary greatly exceeded the aggregate revenue from the fees?[56] Did the court's invalidation of the fee increase employ an "individual rights perspective," a "societal perspective," or perhaps instead an "accounting perspective"?

Prepayment Requirements for Judicial Review: *LeCroy*'s principles have been frequently employed to strike down prepayment requirements for judicial review of administrative determinations. As one example, *Texas Ass'n of Business v. Texas Air Control Board* held that an environmental statute, which required prepayment through a supersedeas bond or a cash deposit as a prerequisite to obtaining judicial review of an administrative penalty imposed by the Texas Air Control Board, violated the open courts provision.[57] Although only statutory rather than common law rights were at issue, the court reasoned that the open courts guarantee of access to the courts unimpeded by unreasonable financial barriers did not depend on whether a common law or statutory right was being asserted. Instead, the controlling issue was whether the legislature had imposed an unreasonable financial barrier in light of the state interest involved.[58] While the legislature had an important state interest in requiring the expeditious payment of administrative penalties for environmental violations, this interest, according to the court, could be adequately satisfied by providing the agency with an immediate collection right unless a supersedeas bond was posted providing security for the penalties. Thus, it was not necessary to infringe "on a party's right to its day in court" because a narrower provision without a prepayment condition for judicial review would serve the legislative interest.[59]

Other Texas cases have reached similar holdings. *Central Appraisal District v. Lall* held that requiring a taxpayer to pay an amount equal to the previous year's real property tax assessment as a condition for judicial review of a tax protest was unconstitutional, but that a solvent taxpayer could be required to pay those current year taxes that were not being challenged.[60] The court reasoned that forcing a taxpayer to pay disputed taxes as a prerequisite for judicial review violated the open courts guarantee when other alternatives

---

[56]*Cf.* Fox v. Hunt, 619 So. 2d 1364, 1366-67 (Ala. 1993) (declining to follow *LeCroy* and holding that jury trial fee paid into state general fund was not a litigation tax under "economic reality" when the legislature spent over $59 million more on the courts than collected by the fee); Crist v. Ervin, 56 So. 3d 745, 747-51 (Fla. 2010) (declining to follow *LeCroy* and holding that directing portion of filing fees into general revenue fund for further appropriation was not a litigation tax but rather "an accounting mechanism reasonably related to the governmental purpose of funding the administration of justice" when the fees deposited were less than the appropriations for the judiciary).

[57]852 S.W.2d 440, 449-50 (Tex. 1993).

[58]*Id.* at 448-49.

[59]*Id.* at 450.

[60]924 S.W.2d 686 (Tex. 1996).

were available to the legislature to ensure the prompt payment of taxes.[61] *R Communications v. Sharp* concluded under analogous reasoning that conditioning judicial review of the comptroller's sales tax assessment on either the payment of the taxes or the posting of a bond equal to twice the alleged obligation was unconstitutional under the open courts provision.[62] Similarly, *State v. Flag-Redfern Oil Co.* held that requiring that state mineral lessees pay in full any disputed royalties before seeking judicial review of a General Land Office royalty determination violated the open courts provision when the state's only interest was immediate access to the disputed royalty payments.[63]

However, it is only in those cases in which prepayment is required *as a prerequisite to judicial review* that the open courts provision is implicated. Thus, the Texas Supreme Court upheld a statute authorizing the state to collect an administrative penalty immediately when such a payment was not a prerequisite to judicial review in *Barshop v. Medina County Underground Water Conservation District*.[64] As long as the collection efforts for the penalty are not a condition for a litigant's right to access the courts, there is no interference with the open courts guarantee.

While some states with open courts provisions have reached similar holdings that prepayment requirements as a condition for judicial review are invalid,[65] other states have disagreed, concluding that requiring such prepayments does not deny an individual the right of access to the courts protected by the open courts provision.[66]

Other Potential Unreasonable Financial Barriers: What else might constitute an unreasonable financial barrier to citizens' access to the courts? Could a statutory requirement that the parties must mediate or arbitrate their dispute before filing a lawsuit violate the open courts provision?[67] Could the cost of an expert affidavit required as a precondition to filing a lawsuit constitute an unreasonable financial barrier violating the open courts provision?[68] Could an indigent, pro se litigant have a right under the open

---

[61]*Id.* at 690-92.

[62]875 S.W.2d 314, 314 (Tex. 1994).

[63]852 S.W.2d 480, 484-85 (Tex. 1993).

[64]925 S.W.2d 618, 637 (Tex. 1996).

[65]*See, e.g.,* Bennett v. Davis, 37 A. 864, 865-66 (Me. 1897) (invalidating state statute under open courts provision that required property owner to deposit with the court all taxes, costs, and interest as a prerequisite to challenging the validity of a tax assessment and the sale of his land for taxes).

[66]*See, e.g.,* Heikes v. Clay Cnty., 526 N.W.2d 253, 254 (S.D. 1995) (upholding statute requiring payment of all delinquent taxes as a precondition to maintaining a quiet title action to recover property sold for nonpayment of taxes).

[67]*Cf.* State *ex rel.* Cardinal Glennon Mem'l Hosp. for Children v. Gaertner, 583 S.W.2d 107, 109-10 (Mo. 1979) (holding that statute compelling non-binding arbitration before medical malpractice suits could be filed violated state constitution's open courts provision).

[68]*Compare* Wall v. Marouk, 302 P.3d 775, 784-85 (Okla. 2013) (holding that affidavit of merit requirement for complaints alleging professional negligence was an unconstitutional burden on access to the courts) & Putnam v. Wenatchee Valley Med. Ctr., P.S., 216 P.3d 374, 376-77 (Wash. 2009) (holding certificate of merit requirement for medical malpractice complaints violated right to access discovery process of the courts) *with* Walker v. Cromartie, 696 S.E.2d 654, 656-57 (Ga. 2010) (holding costs of expert affidavit required to be filed with complaint were created by private rather than state actors and thus did not violate state due process

courts provision to an appointed attorney?[69]

2. Statutes of Limitations and Repose

The United States Supreme Court has never employed the Federal Constitution to restrict legislative interference with common law rights or remedies. Nevertheless, the open courts provisions in many state constitutions have been interpreted to limit legislative modification of causes of action, including arbitrary or unreasonable statutes of limitations and repose.

Sax v. Votteler, 648 S.W.2d 661 (Tex. 1983)

KILGARLIN, Justice.

The parents of Lori Beth Sax brought a medical malpractice suit against Dr. T.P. Votteler, alleging that he mistakenly removed one of Lori Beth's fallopian tubes, instead of her appendix, during an operation that occurred on May 10, 1976. Dr. Votteler continued to treat Lori Beth until August 5, 1976, at which time she was eleven years of age. The Saxes' suit against Dr. Votteler was filed on February 20, 1979. Dr. Votteler filed a motion for summary judgment, claiming Lori Beth's cause of action was barred by the two-year statute of limitations contained in Texas Insurance Code, article 5.82, section 4 (hereinafter referred to as article 5.82, section 4). The trial court granted the motion and the court of appeals affirmed. We reverse in part and affirm in part the judgments of the courts below and remand this cause for trial on the merits.

Historically, in Texas, minors have had varying periods of time after reaching their majority to bring an action in tort. As early as pre-statehood, Texas tolled limitations for minors until two years after their attaining majority. Act of February 5, 1841, § 11, 1841 Laws of the Republic of Texas, at 166. Thereafter, for a brief time, the Texas Constitution tolled limitations for minors for seven years after removal of disabilities. Tex. Const. art. XII § 14 (1869). Prior to the enactment of article 5.82, section 4, Texas law allowed for a tolling of limitations in all tort actions by minors until two years after attaining majority or removal of disabilities. Tex.Rev.Civ.Stat.Ann. art. 5535 [derived from Tex.Rev.Civ.Stat. art. 5708 (1911)].

In 1975, however, by enacting the Professional Liability Insurance for Physicians, Podiatrists, and Hospitals Act (Ch. 330, 1975 Tex.Gen.Laws 864), the Texas Legislature amended Chapter 5 of the Insurance Code by adding article 5.82, which changed the law with respect to limitations for minors in medical malpractice actions. Section 4 of article 5.82 provided that "no claim against a person or hospital . . . licensed to practice medicine . . . may be commenced unless the action is filed within two years of the breach or the tort

---

guarantee). Courts typically have not found an open courts violation on access to the courts when the expert affidavit can be submitted *after* filing suit, as is the case in Texas. *See, e.g.*, Mahoney v. Doerhoff Surgical Servs., Inc., 807 S.W.2d 503, 509-10 (Mo. 1991); DeLuna v. St. Elizabeth's Hosp., 588 N.E.2d 1139, 1145-46 (Ill. 1992).

[69] *Cf.* TEX. GOV'T CODE § 24.016 ("A district judge may appoint counsel to attend to the cause of a party who makes an affidavit that he is too poor to employ counsel to attend to the cause.").

complained of or from the date the medical treatment that is the subject of the claim or the hospitalization for which the claim is made is completed, except that minors under the age of six years shall have until their eighth birthday in which to file, or have filed on their behalf, such claim."

As the date of Lori Beth's last treatment from Dr. Votteler occurred in 1976, the statute of limitations in article 5.82 is applicable to the filing of her suit. It is the constitutionality of that provision which is under attack here. The Saxes urge that by removing the tolling provision after age six Lori Beth is being denied her rights to due process and equal protection of the law as guaranteed her by the fourteenth amendment of the United States Constitution. Further, the Saxes urge that article 5.82, section 4, violates the equal protection guarantee, article I, section 3, and the due process guarantees, article I, section 13, and article I, section 19, of the Texas Constitution.

While it is true that state constitutional protections cannot subtract from those rights guaranteed by the United States Constitution, there certainly is no prohibition against a state providing additional rights for its citizens. *See, e.g., PruneYard Shopping Center v. Robins,* 447 U.S. 74 (1980). Because we are of the opinion that the Texas Constitution, article I, section 13, does accord Texas citizens additional rights, we choose not to decide this case on the basis of the United States Constitution or the equal protection provision of the Texas Constitution.

The Texas Constitution contains two separate due process provisions. Article I, section 19, is the traditional due process guarantee, which states: "No citizen of this state shall be deprived of life, liberty, property, privileges or immunities, or in any manner disfranchised, except by the due course of the law of the land." Article I, section 13, provides: "Excessive bail shall not be required, nor excessive fines imposed, nor cruel or unusual punishment inflicted. All courts shall be open, and every person for an injury done him, in his lands, goods, person or reputation, shall have remedy by due course of law." While it is true that this provision is sometimes referred to as the "Open Courts Provision," it is, quite plainly, a due process guarantee. *See Hanks v. City of Port Arthur,* 121 Tex. 202, 48 S.W.2d 944, 945 (1932). Both provisions of the Texas Constitution have their origin in Magna Carta. *See* Tex. Const. art. I, §§ 13, 19, comment.

As early as 1932, this Court recognized that article I, section 13, of the Texas Constitution ensures that Texas citizens bringing common law causes of action will not unreasonably be denied access to the courts. *Hanks v. City of Port Arthur, supra.* In *Hanks,* this Court was confronted with an ordinance that exempted Port Arthur from liability for injuries caused by defective streets unless the city had received notice of the defect twenty-four hours prior to the accident. The ordinance was challenged as being violative of article I, section 13. In holding that the ordinance was unconstitutional, this Court reasoned:

> As written . . . [the ordinance] applies to all persons who may be upon the streets; to children . . . [who] have the right to use the sidewalks. . . . Are we to say that a small child running an errand, or a small boy selling newspapers to help make the family living, who is injured by reason of a defective sidewalk, due to the negligence of the city, or by reason of

> otherwise actionable negligence of the city, cannot recover because the infant, or some one for him, has not notified one of the city commissioners twenty-four hours before the accident of the existence of the defect? Would that be reasonable? *Is the requirement of a thing impossible from an infant, or one incapacitated for any other reason, due process?* We think not; and yet it is a condition precedent to a recovery. . . .

48 S.W.2d at 948 (emphasis added). In conclusion, the Court set out the test for analyzing future violations of the open courts-due process provision: A statute or ordinance that unreasonably abridges a justiciable right to obtain redress for injuries caused by the wrongful acts of another amounts to a denial of due process under article I, section 13, and is, therefore, void.

The rule in *Hanks* has been considered dispositive in at least two other cases decided by this Court. In *Lebohm v. City of Galveston,* 154 Tex. 192, 275 S.W.2d 951 (1955), an ordinance similar to the one in *Hanks* exempted Galveston from liability for injuries caused by defective streets. In striking down the ordinance on the basis of article I, section 13, this Court stated:

> [L]egislative action withdrawing common-law remedies for well established common-law causes of action for injuries to one's "lands, goods, person or reputation" is sustained only when it is reasonable in substituting other remedies, or when it is a reasonable exercise of the police power in the interest of the general welfare. Legislative action of this type is not sustained when it is arbitrary or unreasonable.

Waites v. Sondock, 561 S.W.2d 772 (Tex.1977) is the most recent pronouncement of this Court involving article I, section 13. In *Waites,* a mother seeking child support from her ex-husband had filed a motion for him to show cause why he should not be held in contempt for failure to pay child support as ordered by the court. The mother alleged that because the former husband had made no payments of child support for approximately two years, she was suffering irreparable harm. The hearing on her motion was set for a date shortly after the Texas Legislature had gone into session. Mr. Waites' attorney, who was a member of the legislature, filed a motion for continuance pursuant to article 2168a, Texas Revised Civil Statutes, which provided continuances for legislator-lawyers until thirty days after the close of the session. The trial court granted the continuance and the mother filed a motion for leave to file a petition for mandamus to require the trial judge to hear her motion for contempt. After citing article I, section 13 and *Lebohm v. City of Galveston, supra,* with approval, this Court held the statute was unconstitutional as applied to Mrs. Waites: "The legislative basis for withdrawing the mother's remedy–the presumption that the policy behind article 2168a outweighs a litigant's right of redress–is arbitrary and unreasonable when, in situations such as this, a party allegedly faces irreparable injury from inaction." *Id.* at 775.

We reaffirm today the interpretation of article I, section 13, set out in *Hanks, Lebohm,* and *Waites.* In doing so, we note that the basis for the Court's conclusion in these cases was that the litigant's right of redress outweighed the legislative basis for the respective ordinances and statute. We hold, therefore, that the right to bring a well-established common law cause of action cannot be effectively abrogated by the legislature absent a showing that the legislative basis for the statute outweighs the denial of the constitutionally-guaranteed right of redress. In applying this test, we consider both the general purpose of the statute and the extent to which the litigant's right to redress is affected.

Article 5.82 was enacted to establish standards for setting liability insurance rates for physicians and other health care providers. *See* Tex.Ins.Code.Ann. art. 5.82, caption. Specifically, the legislation's proponents argued that the number and amount of health care claims had increased to the point that it was indirectly affecting the availability and quality of health care. This effect was due to the higher costs of medical malpractice insurance and its unavailability. The general purpose of the statute, therefore, was to provide an insurance rate structure that would enable health care providers to secure liability insurance and thereby provide compensation for their patients who might have legitimate malpractice claims. The specific purpose of the provision in question was to limit the length of time that the insureds would be exposed to potential liability.

In analyzing the litigant's right to redress, we first note that the litigant has two criteria to satisfy. First, it must be shown that the litigant has a cognizable common law cause of action that is being restricted. Second, the litigant must show that the restriction is unreasonable or arbitrary when balanced against the purpose and basis of the statute.

Texas courts have long recognized that a minor has a well-defined common law cause of action to sue for injuries negligently inflicted by others. *See Texas & P. Ry. Co. v. Morin,* 66 Tex. 225, 18 S.W. 503 (1886); *Houston & Great Northern R.R. Co. v. Miller,* 51 Tex. 270 (1879). A child's cause of action, however, is distinctly separate from the parent's right to recover damages for injuries to children. A child may recover damages for pain and suffering as well as other damages he may accrue after he reaches the age of majority. *Texas & P. Ry. Co. v. Malone,* 15 Tex.Civ.App. 56, 38 S.W. 538, 539 (Tex.Civ.App.1896, writ ref'd). For example, a child is entitled to recover loss of earning capacity, commencing upon the date of attaining majority or removal of disabilities. However, since the services and earnings of an unemancipated minor belong to his parents, an infant may not recover for diminution of his earning capacity during the period intervening between the injury and his attainment of majority. *Texas and P. Ry. Co. v. Morin, supra.* Historically, in Texas, the right to recover for medical costs incurred in behalf of the minor is a cause of action belonging to the parents, unless such costs are a liability as to the minor's estate. *Bering Mfg. Co. v. Peterson,* 28 Tex.Civ.App. 194, 67 S.W. 133, 135 (Tex.Civ.App.1902, writ dism'd).

The second criterion we examine is the effect of the restriction on the child's right to bring his cause of action. A child has no right to bring a cause of action on his own unless disability has been removed. *Gulf, C. & S.F. Ry. Co. v. Styron,* 66 Tex. 421, 1 S.W. 161 (1886); *Moke v. Fellman,* 17 Tex. 367 (1856). If a minor does bring a cause of action in his own behalf, the action is subject to being abated upon a timely plea of the defendant. *Moke v. Fellman,* 17 Tex. 367 (1856). If the parents, guardians, or next friends of the child negligently fail to take action in the child's behalf within the time provided by article 5.82, the child is precluded from asserting his cause of action under that statute. Furthermore, the child is precluded from suing his parents on account of their negligence, due to the doctrine of parent-child immunity. *See Felderhoff v. Felderhoff,* 473 S.W.2d 928 (Tex.1971). The child, therefore, is effectively barred from any remedy if his parents fail to timely file suit. Respondents argue that parents will adequately protect the rights of their children. This Court, however, cannot assume that parents will act in such a manner. It is neither reasonable nor realistic to rely upon parents, who may themselves be minors, or who may be ignorant, lethargic, or lack concern, to bring a malpractice lawsuit action within the time provided by article 5.82.

We agree with Dr. Votteler that both the purpose and basis for article 5.82 are legitimate. Additionally, we recognize that the length of time that insureds are exposed to potential liability has a bearing on the rates that insurers must charge. We cannot agree, however, that the means used by the legislature to achieve this purpose, article 5.82, section 4, are reasonable when they are weighed against the effective abrogation of a child's right to redress. Under the facts in this case, Lori Beth Sax is forever precluded from having her day in court to complain of an act of medical malpractice. Furthermore, the legislature has failed to provide her any adequate substitute to obtain redress for her injuries. *See, e.g., Middleton v. Texas Power & Light Co.,* 108 Tex. 96, 185 S.W. 556 (1916).

We conclude that as to that part of the cause of action for medical malpractice unique to the minor, article 5.82, section 4, is unreasonable. This statute effectively abolishes a minor's right to bring a well-established common law cause of action without providing a reasonable alternative. Therefore, we declare the limitations provision of article 5.82, section 4, to be in violation of article I, section 13 of the Texas Constitution.

Notes on Statutes of Limitations Abrogating Meaningful Legal Remedies

Well-Established Common Law Causes of Action: The meaningful legal remedies guarantee of the Texas open courts provision protects well-established common law causes of action from a legislative restriction that is unreasonable or arbitrary. The first step of the analysis, then, is ascertaining whether the legislature is restricting a "well-established common law cause of action." How is this to be determined?

One issue is defining the cause of action being restricted. At what level of abstraction or specificity should the litigant's claim be analyzed to determine whether the legislature is infringing on a well-established common law cause of action? Does this require a consideration of all the surrounding circumstances of the claim, just the elements of the plaintiff's prima facie case, or merely the source of the remedy? For an illustration, consider the cause of action that was being infringed in *Sax*. Was it the very general right of a minor to sue for his or her injuries? Was it the more specific right of a child to bring a medical malpractice cause of action? Or was it the very specific right of an individual to bring a medical malpractice suit after reaching the age of majority for injuries suffered while a minor? If it was the last, very specifically defined right, what was the source of such a right in Texas: the common law or statute?

Another issue is determining whether a cause of action is "well established" in the common law. Does this depend on whether the cause of action had been recognized by the common law at the time of the Texas Constitution of 1876? Or is one hundred years of recognition enough? How about fifty years? Twenty-five? Could eight years of common law recognition be sufficient to make the claim "well established"?

Balancing the Legislative Purpose and Right to Redress: Assuming the legislature has restricted a well-established common law cause of action, the next step of the analysis according to *Sax* is whether such a restriction is unreasonable or arbitrary when balanced against the statute's purpose. What was the legislative purpose behind the statute in *Sax*? How did the court balance the legislative purpose of the statute against the minor's right to redress? Is this entirely a matter of a judicial value judgment, or did the court provide any meaningful standards to govern future determinations of whether the legislative restriction is reasonable? How does the *Sax* statement compare with the earlier standard adopted in *Lebohm v. City of Galveston*, which provided that "legislative action withdrawing common-law remedies for well established common-law causes of action . . . is sustained only when it is reasonable in substituting other remedies, or when it is a reasonable exercise of the police power in the interest of the general welfare"?

Subsequent Texas Developments on Tolling of Limitations for Minors: Despite *Sax*'s holding, the Texas Legislature has attempted on two other occasions to reinstate a statute of limitations for minors asserting medical malpractice actions. *Weiner v. Wasson* applied the *Sax* holding to invalidate the legislature's first attempt, a statute of limitations for minors in medical malpractice actions that tolled limitations until the minor's twelfth birthday (rather than the minor's sixth birthday as in the legislation invalidated in *Sax*).[70] The *Weiner* majority held that, as long as a minor was legally disabled from bringing suit on his own behalf, the legislature could not hinge the minor's right to redress on the possibility that an adult might bring suit for the minor.[71] The dissent disagreed, contending that the open courts provision was not violated because a reasonable substitute for the minor's own claim existed when the minor was twelve or older and had a legally competent parent or guardian without a conflict of interest to bring suit on his or her behalf.[72]

The Texas Legislature tried again in 2003, enacting House Bill 4 that, among other changes, amended section 74.251 of the Texas Civil Practice and Remedies Code to once again provide that limitations in medical malpractice claims would only be tolled until the minor's twelfth birthday. The legislature supported this amendment with specific findings that the number of health care liability claims had increased "inordinately" since 1995, causing a medical malpractice insurance crisis that was having a material adverse effect on the delivery of medical and health care in Texas.[73] The San Antonio Court of Appeals nevertheless invalidated the legislation under the open courts provision, concluding that similar legislative findings had not saved the statute at issue in *Sax*.[74] Should these new findings have made a difference?

---

[70]900 S.W.2d 316, 319 (Tex. 1995).

[71]*Id.*

[72]*Id.* at 327 (Owen, J., dissenting).

[73]2003 Tex. Sess. Law Serv. Ch. 204, § 10.11.

[74]Adams v. Gottwald, 179 S.W.3d 101, 103 (Tex. App.–San Antonio 2005, pet. denied).

Tolling of Limitations for Minors in Other States: Some jurisdictions have agreed with *Sax* and *Weiner* that statutes of limitations that operate to bar the claims of minors before they reach majority violate the state's open courts or right to a remedy guarantee.[75] Other jurisdictions have reached a contrary result.[76] This split of authority partially arises from the differences in the states' approach to interpreting the open courts provision, but it is also a result of the indeterminate task that the court must undertake in determining whether the limitation on a minor's right to redress is reasonable in light of the countervailing interests in finality and repose. Are parents' rights to bring causes of action on behalf of their children an adequate substitute remedy? How strong is society's interest in preventing the maintenance of suits for events that may have occurred two decades ago?

Restricting Limitations Periods on Common Law Remedies: The Texas Supreme Court has relied on *Sax* in several subsequent decisions considering whether applying a statute of limitations that expires before the discovery of the injury violates the open courts provision. In *Nelson v. Krusen*, the court, after concluding that the "common thread of this court's decisions construing the open courts provision is that the legislature has no power to make a remedy by due course of law contingent on an impossible condition," held that an absolute two-year statute of limitations in medical malpractice actions that barred a cause of action before the plaintiffs knew, or reasonably should have known, of the injury could not be constitutionally applied to bar the plaintiffs' claims.[77]

In that case, the Nelsons' child did not begin to demonstrate the symptoms of a neuromuscular defect until more than three years after the last treatment by the defendant doctor. But under the absolute two-year statute of limitations adopted by the legislature in 1975 for medical malpractice claims, the Nelsons' claims were nevertheless time barred. This legislation was passed a mere eight years after the Texas Supreme Court, for the first time, adopted the "discovery rule" for medical malpractice claims that precluded the statute of limitations from beginning to run on such claims until the plaintiff either knew or should have known of the injury.[78] Reasoning that applying the legislature's new absolute two-year limitations period would "require the Nelsons to do the impossible–to sue before they had any reason to know they should sue," the court held that the statute of limitations as applied to the Nelsons violated the open courts provision.

Nelson identified the "established common law cause of action" at issue in that case and in *Sax* as medical malpractice.[79] But the court did not separately address whether such a medical malpractice claim relying on the discovery rule was "well established" when

---

[75]*See, e.g.,* Barrio v. San Manuel Div. Hosp., 692 P.2d 280, 286 (Ariz. 1984) (citing *Sax*); Piselli v. 75th Street Med., 808 A.2d 508, 524-26 (Md. 2002) (citing *Sax*); Strahler v. St. Luke's Hosp., 706 S.W.2d 7, 10-11 (Mo. 1986) (citing *Sax*); Mominee v. Scherbarth, 503 N.E.2d 717, 722 (Ohio 1986) (citing *Sax*).

[76]*See, e.g.,* Barlow v. Humana, Inc., 495 So. 2d 1048, 1052 (Ala. 1986); Smith v. Cobb Cnty.–Kennestone Hosp., 423 S.E.2d 235, 239-40 (Ga. 1992); Me. Med. Ctr. v. Cote, 577 A.2d 1173, 1175-76 (Me. 1990); Dowd v. Rayner, 655 A.2d 679, 683 (R.I. 1995); Aicher v. Wis. Patients Comp. Fund, 613 N.W.2d 849, 862-65 (Wis. 2000).

[77]678 S.W.2d 918, 921-22 (Tex. 1984).

[78]Gaddis v. Smith, 417 S.W.2d 577, 580 (1967).

[79]*Nelson*, 678 S.W.2d at 922-23.

Texas courts first recognized a remedy in such a situation a mere eight years before the legislature amended the limitations statute. Since the Texas Supreme Court's adoption of the discovery rule in medical malpractice cases eight years earlier was based on statutory construction, should the legislature have had the opportunity to abolish the discovery rule in medical malpractice cases without running afoul of the open courts provision?

Restricting Limitations Periods in "Sponge" Cases: Relying on *Sax* and *Nelson*, the Texas Supreme Court in 1985 held in *Neagle v. Nelson* that the application of an absolute two-year statute of limitations violated the open courts provision when the plaintiff did not have a reasonable opportunity, within the limitations period, to discover that a surgical sponge had been left in his abdomen during an appendectomy.[80] The court opined that "[t]he open courts provision of our Constitution protects a citizen, such as Neagle, from legislative acts that abridge his right to sue before he has a reasonable opportunity to discover the wrong and bring suit."[81]

Twenty-five years later, the Texas Supreme Court affirmed *Neagle*, but indicated that "[s]ponge cases constitute a unique class of malpractice claims, thus meriting unique Open Courts treatment."[82] *Walters v. Cleveland Regional Medical Center* involved a sponge left in a patient during a tubal ligation that was not discovered until more than nine years after the surgery.[83] The Texas Supreme Court, relying on *Neagle*, held that the patient raised a fact issue as to whether she discovered the sponge and brought her suit within a reasonable time, such that the two-year limitations period could not bar her claim without running afoul of the open courts provision. The court noted that sponge cases are "unique" in part because they are both hard to discover and always indicate negligence.[84] The court also emphasized the legislature's enactment of a ten-year statute of repose for medical malpractice claims in 2003 that would have no meaning if a two-year limitations period always applied. Was the court's reliance on these "unique" aspects of sponge cases consistent with *Nelson*?

Due Diligence and Restricted Limitations Periods: Open courts issues regarding medical malpractice limitations periods continue to arise in cases such as *Walters* because neither *Nelson* nor *Neagle* facially invalidated the two-year absolute limitations period for medical malpractice claims. Instead, these cases invalidated the limitations period only as applied to plaintiffs who did not have a reasonable opportunity to discover their injury and bring suit before limitations expired. As a result, if the plaintiff could have discovered the injury through due diligence and filed suit before an absolute statute of limitations expires, the open courts provision is not violated.

In *Morrison v. Chan*, for instance, the supreme court held that the application of the absolute two-year limitations period for medical malpractice claims did not violate the open courts provision when the plaintiff had discovered her injury more than a year before the

[80]685 S.W.2d 11, 12 (Tex. 1985).

[81]*Id.*

[82]Walters v. Cleveland Reg'l Med. Ctr., 307 S.W.3d 292, 294 (Tex. 2010).

[83]*See id.*

[84]*Id.* at 297.

statutory deadline.[85] Similarly, the state supreme court has upheld in two other cases the absolute two-year statute of limitations in medical malpractice cases when the plaintiff unreasonably delayed filing suit after discovering the injury.[86] The legislature thus can curtail the limitations period for common law claims without a facial violation of the open courts provision; the open courts provision will only assist those plaintiffs who meet their burden of establishing they exercised due diligence and did not have a reasonable time to discover their injury and file suit.

Stockton v. Offenbach extended this due diligence prerequisite to the post-filing service of an expert medical report.[87] Texas Civil Practice and Remedies Code § 74.351 requires that an expert report be served on each defendant in a health care liability suit within 120 days of the suit's filing. The plaintiff patient claimed that she was unable to serve this expert report on the defendant within the 120 days because, despite her efforts to locate him, his whereabouts were unknown following the loss of his medical license for prescription drug abuse.[88] After concluding that § 74.351 required the service of an expert report in every health care case, the court addressed the patient's argument that such a result was unconstitutional under the open courts provision as applied to her. While acknowledging that the statute could "[]not apply to create an impossible condition to the pursuit of a health care liability claim," the court held that the patient and her counsel had not employed the required due diligence in attempting to serve the report.[89]

Restricted Limitations Periods on Statutory Remedies: The holdings of *Sax* and *Nelson* also do not control when the litigant seeks a remedy conferred solely by statute. For example, in *Moreno v. Sterling Drug, Inc.*, the Texas Supreme Court held that the open courts provision was not violated by applying an absolute two-year statute of limitations in wrongful death actions, even though the plaintiff allegedly could not have discovered the cause of death before limitations expired.[90] The court reasoned that wrongful death was a statutory remedy that had not been recognized by the common law, such that the Texas open courts' protection of common law remedies did not apply.[91] Because the legislature had created the right to recover for wrongful death, it could subsequently limit or abolish recovery as well.[92] Since *Moreno*, the court has frequently held that the open courts provision cannot be used to invalidate the limitations period for statutory wrongful death and survival actions.[93]

---

[85]699 S.W.2d 205, 206-07 (Tex. 1985).

[86]*See, e.g.*, Yancy v. United Surgical Partners Intern., Inc., 236 S.W.3d 778, 784-86 (Tex. 2007); Shah v. Moss, 67 S.W.836, 847 (Tex. 2001).

[87]336 S.W.3d 610 (Tex. 2011).

[88]*Id.* at 612.

[89]*Id.* at 618.

[90]787 S.W.2d 348, 355 (Tex. 1990).

[91]*Id.* at 356-57.

[92]*Id.* at 355-57.

[93]*See, e.g.*, Diaz v. Westphal, 941 S.W.2d 96, 101 (Tex. 1997) (holding open courts doctrine did not apply to limitations period in wrongful death and survival claims asserted on behalf of a minor child because the sole requested remedy was conferred by statute rather than the common law); Baptist Mem'l Hosp. Sys. v. Arredondo, 922 S.W.2d 120, 121-22 (Tex. 1996) (holding open courts provision did not apply to wrongful death

Restricted Limitations Periods in Other States: Other jurisdictions are split on whether absolute statutes of limitations that may bar a claim before the discovery of the injury violate the open courts or right to a remedy provision.[94] This split is primarily due to the differences among the states in the very meaning of the open courts provision. Some states review the reasonableness of all legislative enactments that limit the right to both statutory and common law remedies to determine whether a reasonable alternative has been substituted or the limitation is necessary to respond to an important need.[95] In contrast, other states provide very few substantive limitations on legislation under the open courts provision, instead predominantly viewing the guarantee as directed at the judiciary.[96] Finally, still other states employ a historically-based approach similar to that used in Texas, restricting the legislature's ability to modify pre-existing common law causes of action. And even the cases within a jurisdiction are not always easy to reconcile. How does the following case upholding a statute of repose compare to *Sax* and *Nelson*?

Trinity River Authority v. URS Consultants, Inc.–Tex., 889 S.W.2d 259 (Tex. 1994)

PHILLIPS, Chief Justice, delivered the opinion of the Court, joined by GONZALEZ, HIGHTOWER, HECHT, CORNYN, GAMMAGE, ENOCH and SPECTOR, Justices.

Texas Civil Practice and Remedies Code section 16.008 bars suits against architects or engineers for defective design of an improvement to real property unless brought within ten years after the improvement is completed, regardless of when the defect is discovered. The issue presented is whether this statute of repose violates either the Texas or United States Constitution. We hold that, as applied in this case, it does not, and therefore we affirm the judgment of the court of appeals.

---

action based on medical malpractice); Bala v. Maxwell, 909 S.W.2d 889, 893 (Tex. 1995) (holding an allegedly unreasonable application of a strict two-year limitations period did not violate open courts because plaintiffs had no common law right to bring either a wrongful death or survival action).

[94]*Compare, e.g.*, Kenyon v. Hammer, 688 P.2d 961, 972-79 (Ariz. 1984) (invalidating absolute three-year statute of limitations for medical malpractice claims under equal protection in conjunction with open courts); Martin v. Richey, 711 N.E.2d 1273, 1284-85 (Ind. 1999) (holding application of absolute two-year medical malpractice statute of limitations was unconstitutional as applied to plaintiff because it would have required her to file a claim before she was aware of the injury); Hardy v. VerMeulen, 512 N.E.2d 626, 628-30 (Ohio 1987) (holding statute barring medical malpractice claims brought more than four years after act of malpractice violated open courts as applied to plaintiffs who did not know or could not have reasonably known of their injuries within that period) *with* Crier v. Whitecloud, 496 So.2d 305, 310 (La. 1986) (upholding absolute three-year statute of limitations in medical malpractice action against open courts challenge); Hill v. Fitzgerald, 501 A.2d 27, 33-35 (Md. 1985) (upholding absolute five-year medical malpractice limitations period against open courts challenge); Harrison v. Schraeder, 569 S.W.2d 822, 827-28 (Tenn. 1978) (upholding similar three-year limitations period against open courts challenge).

[95]*See, e.g.*, Kluger v. White, 281 So. 2d 1, 4 (Fla. 1973) (holding that the legislature must provide a reasonable alternative remedy or an overpowering public necessity before abolishing a right to redress provided by the statutory or common law before the adoption of the 1968 Florida Constitution).

[96]*See, e.g.*, Meech v. Hillhaven W., Inc., 776 P.2d 488, 492-93 (Mont. 1989) (concluding Montana remedy clause was not "a directive to the legislature" but instead was addressed exclusively to the courts); Rivas v. Parkland Manor, 12 P.3d 452, 457-58 (Okla. 2000) (holding the Oklahoma open courts provision "is a mandate to the judiciary and is not intended to be a limitation on the authority of the legislature.").

I

In May 1972, respondent URS Consultants, Inc. ("URS") contracted with petitioner Trinity River Authority ("Trinity") to design improvements to a sewage treatment plant operated by Trinity. An equalizer basin wall designed by URS was completed and put into service at the plant in 1976. On March 11, 1990, the basin wall collapsed, spilling a large amount of raw sewage and causing extensive property damage to the plant and surrounding area. Contending that the basin wall was negligently designed, Trinity brought suit for damages against URS on March 6, 1992.

URS subsequently moved for summary judgment on the basis of Texas Civil Practice and Remedies Code section 16.008, which bars such suits against architects or engineers brought more than ten years after the improvement is completed. The trial court rendered summary judgment for URS, and the court of appeals affirmed.

II

Texas Civil Practice and Remedies Code section 16.008, which bars claims against an architect or engineer after ten years even if the alleged design defect was undiscoverable before that time, is commonly referred to as a "statute of repose." *See Johnson v. City of Fort Worth,* 774 S.W.2d 653, 654 n.1 (Tex.1989). Unlike traditional limitations provisions, which begin running upon accrual of a cause of action, a statute of repose runs from a specified date without regard to accrual of any cause of action. One court has characterized statutes of repose as "a substantive definition of, rather than a procedural limitation on, rights." *Lamb v. Wedgewood South Corp.,* 308 N.C. 419, 302 S.E.2d 868, 872 (1983). Statutes similar to section 16.008 have been enacted in a majority of states in response to a perceived need to protect designers and builders from the threat of claims arising many years after completion of a project.[97]

Trinity does not contest that URS is a design professional covered by section 16.008. The sole issue, therefore, is whether the statute is constitutional. Trinity raises challenges under the Texas constitutional guarantees of open courts, equal protection, and due course of law, as well as the federal equal protection and due process clauses. Trinity also claims that section 16.008 is a "special law" in violation of the Texas Constitution.

III

In *Lebohm v. City of Galveston,* 275 S.W.2d 951, 955 (Tex.1955), we articulated the relevant test [for the third prong of the open courts guarantee] as follows:

> [L]egislative action withdrawing common-law remedies for well established common-law causes of action for injuries to one's "lands, goods, person or reputation" is sustained only when it is reasonable in substituting other remedies, or when it is a reasonable exercise of the police power in the interest of the general welfare.

---

[97]Forty-six states have enacted statutes of repose protecting architects and engineers, with the repose period ranging from four to twenty years. *See generally Blaske v. Smith & Entzeroth, Inc.,* 821 S.W.2d 822, 827-28 (Mo.1991). Thirty-two of these jurisdictions have upheld their statutes against constitutional attack, while eleven have struck them down on constitutional grounds. *Id.*

The Court noted in *Sax* that a litigant challenging a statute on open courts grounds must satisfy two criteria: "First, it must be shown that the litigant has a cognizable common law cause of action that is being restricted. Second, the litigant must show that the restriction is unreasonable or arbitrary when balanced against the purpose and basis of the statute." 648 S.W.2d at 666.

The first step in our open courts analysis, therefore, is determining whether section 16.008 abrogates a well-established common law cause of action. We conclude that, under the circumstances of this case, it does not. Although it is clear that an owner of a structure had a right at common law to recover property damage resulting from negligent design or construction, *see, e.g., Newell v. Mosley,* 469 S.W.2d 481, 483 (Tex.Civ.App.–Tyler 1971, writ ref'd n.r.e.); *Pierson v. Tyndall,* 28 S.W. 232 (Tex.Civ.App.1894, no writ), that right is abrogated by section 16.008 only to the extent it historically could have been asserted ten years after completion of the improvement. The traditional rule in Texas, however, has been that such a cause of action accrues, and the two year negligence limitations period begins to run, as soon as the owner suffers some injury, regardless of when the injury becomes discoverable. *See Houston Water-Works Co. v. Kennedy,* 70 Tex. 233, 8 S.W. 36 (1888). In *Kennedy,* the defendant cut an arch in plaintiff's building while installing a water pipe in 1884. The arch, being concealed, was not discoverable until it eventually caused the building to settle and crack. Plaintiff brought his negligence action in 1887, three years after the alleged negligence but within two years after the injury became manifest. The Court concluded that the action was barred by limitations because the negligently cut arch constituted a legal injury, [which started the running of limitations immediately].

The holding in *Kennedy* is consistent with the general rule that a cause of action accrues as soon as the defendant's wrongful act effects *some* injury. *See Murray v. San Jacinto Agency, Inc.,* 800 S.W.2d 826, 828 (Tex.1990). The discovery rule, under which the cause of action is deemed not to accrue until the injury becomes discoverable, is merely an exception to this general rule. *See Moreno v. Sterling Drug, Inc.,* 787 S.W.2d 348, 351 (Tex.1990). Although we have adopted the discovery rule for certain causes of action, *see, e.g., Gaddis v. Smith,* 417 S.W.2d 577, 581 (Tex.1967) (medical malpractice based on leaving a foreign object in the patient's body); *Willis v. Maverick,* 760 S.W.2d 642, 646 (Tex.1988) (legal malpractice), we have not previously done so for actions based on negligent design or construction of an improvement to real property.

Taking Trinity's allegations as true, it suffered a legal injury in 1976 when it received a defective structure built to URS's negligent design specifications. Under the traditional rule as set forth in *Kennedy,* this type of action is assertable only during the two year period following completion of the improvement. As to such a case, section 16.008, which bars actions brought ten years after completion of the improvement, does not abrogate the right to bring a well-established common law action.

We emphasize that we are expressing no opinion on whether, if squarely presented with the issue, we would adopt the discovery rule in a case such as this. Rather, we hold that, because the discovery rule had not been adopted for negligent design cases at the time section 16.008 was enacted, that statute did not abrogate the right to bring a common law cause of action under these circumstances. As applied in this case, therefore, section 16.008

does not violate the Texas open courts guarantee.[98]

Notes on Statutes of Repose and Common Law Causes of Action

Revisiting Well-Established Common Law Causes of Action: What common law right did the court hold was being abrogated by the statute of repose in *Trinity River Authority*: the right to recover property damage, the right to recover property damage resulting from negligent design or construction, or the right to recover property damage resulting from negligent design or construction asserted more than ten years after completion of the improvement? Is this holding consistent with *Sax* and *Nelson*? Can the cases be reconciled on the basis that the legislation in *Trinity River* did not abrogate the ability to recover on a common law cause of action, whereas the legislation in *Sax* and *Nelson* did?

In *Computer Associates International, Inc. v. Altai, Inc.*, the Texas Supreme Court held that a two-year limitations period without a discovery rule for misappropriation of trade secrets did not violate the open courts provision when the plaintiff did not know about the misappropriation until after the limitations period expired.[99] The court, relying on *Trinity River*, explained that, in Texas, a cause of action traditionally "accrues and the two-year limitations period begins to run as soon as the owner suffers some injury, regardless of when the injury becomes discoverable. Failure to permit a discovery rule exception to the traditional rule does not abrogate a common law right."[100] After *Trinity River* and *Altai*, should the first step in the open courts analysis depend on whether the plaintiff *alleges* a common law *cause of action* historically well established under the common law, or instead on whether the plaintiff's *right of recovery* for a common law cause of action previously existed under all the relevant circumstances?

Does the well-established common law cause of action requirement help explain why *Trinity River* left open the possibility in the footnote at the end of the case excerpt that the identity of the plaintiff might make a difference in considering the constitutionality of a statute of repose? Under the common law, as the court discussed, the purchaser of a defective structure suffers a legal injury immediately upon receiving the defective structure. In contrast, would a third party injured after the repose period ends have a well-established common law cause of action?

The Constitutionality of Statutes of Repose in Other States: *Trinity River* noted that the vast majority of states have upheld their state statutes of repose against constitutional attacks. Nevertheless, at least eleven states have invalidated them on constitutional grounds. Some of these states have done so on the basis of their open courts provisions, while others have relied on equal protection grounds, the prohibition against

---

[98]We express no opinion as to whether section 16.008 would violate the open courts guarantee as applied to abrogate the claim of a third party who sustains damages from a defective structure after the ten year repose period.

[99]918 S.W.2d 453 (Tex. 1996).

[100]*Id.* at 458 (citation omitted).

special laws, or other unique state constitutional provisions.[101] Is the lack of uniformity in these decisions troubling?

Statutes of Repose versus Statutes of Limitations: What's the difference between a statute of repose and a statute of limitations? A statute of repose begins to run on a readily ascertainable date, such as the date work was completed, a product was delivered, or a service was rendered, and is not subject to the judicially crafted rules of tolling and deferral often applicable to statutes of limitations. The basic idea is that a statute of repose creates a final deadline for filing suit without any judicial exceptions, operating to create a substantive right to be free from liability after the specified time has expired. In contrast, a limitations period typically provides a shorter time frame to file suit after the accrual of a cause of action, although the date of accrual may be subject to the discovery rule and other judicially created tolling or deferral rules.

Do these differences between a statute of repose and a statute of limitations provide the legislature greater leeway in establishing a statute of repose even for a well-established common law cause of action? The Texas Supreme Court considered this issue in the following case, issued the same day as *Walters v. Cleveland Regional Medical Center* (which was discussed in the notes following *Sax*).

Methodist Healthcare System of San Antonio, Ltd. v. Rankin, 307 S.W.3d 283 (Tex. 2010)

Justice WILLETT delivered the opinion of the Court.

This case pits the ten-year statute of repose for healthcare-liability claims against the Texas Constitution's Open Courts provision. We examine for the first time whether the latter saves a malpractice claim if the former has expired. The answer is no.

The Open Courts provision does not confer an open-ended and perpetual right to sue; it "merely gives litigants a reasonable time to discover their injuries and file suit." The Legislature may set an absolute cut-off point for healthcare suits, as it has for other suits, so long as the repose period is a reasonable exercise of the Legislature's police power to act in the interest of the general welfare. The ten-year statute of repose at issues adopts a constitutionally permissible policymaking judgment of the Legislature.

I. Background

After experiencing abdominal pain, Emmalene Rankin consulted a physician in July 2006 and learned that a surgical sponge had been left inside her during a November 1995 hysterectomy. Rankin sued the hospital where the operation was performed and two physicians.

Rankin filed her suit, however, in October 2006, almost eleven years after the alleged negligence. The defendants moved for summary judgment, arguing that Rankin's claim was barred by section 74.251(b) of the Civil Practice and Remedies Code, the ten-year

---

[101] *See* 1 JENNIFER FRIESEN, STATE CONSTITUTIONAL LAW: LITIGATING INDIVIDUAL RIGHTS, CLAIMS AND DEFENSES § 6.05[2][b] (4th ed. 2006) (discussing cases).

statute of repose for healthcare-liability claims. Rankin submitted evidence that she did not know of the sponge and could not have discovered it in the exercise of reasonable care prior to expiration of the ten-year repose period.

Section 74.251(b) provides:

> A claimant must bring a health care liability claim not later than 10 years after the date of the act or omission that gives rise to the claim. This subsection is intended as a statute of repose so that all claims must be brought within 10 years or they are time barred.

The trial court granted summary judgment, but the court of appeals reversed, holding the statute unconstitutional under the Open Courts provision. This appeal followed.

II. Analysis

In *Lebohm v. City of Galveston*, the Court undertook its first in-depth analysis of the Open Courts provision. Justice Calvert, writing for a unanimous Court, formulated the test that we follow today:

> [L]egislative action withdrawing common-law remedies for well established common-law causes of action for injuries to one's "lands, goods, person or reputation" is sustained only when it is reasonable in substituting other remedies, or when it is a reasonable exercise of the police power in the interest of the general welfare. Legislative action of this type is not sustained when it is arbitrary or unreasonable.

We have quoted this language with approval in later decisions.

Rankin argues that the statute [of repose] is unreasonable, and thus unconstitutional, because it cut off her right to sue before she had an opportunity to discover her injury. But Open Courts analysis is not quite this myopic; focusing solely on Rankin's lost right to sue ignores the broader societal concerns that spurred the Legislature to act.

Section 74.251(b) was enacted in 2003 as part of House Bill 4, a top-to-bottom overhaul of Texas malpractice law to "make affordable medical and health care more accessible and available to the citizens of Texas," and to "do so in a manner that will not unduly restrict a claimant's rights any more than necessary to deal with the crisis." The omnibus bill makes explicit findings describing the Legislature's concern that a spike in healthcare-liability claims had fueled an insurance crisis that was harming healthcare delivery in Texas. The Legislature made these findings after conducting hearings and amassing evidence of the problems facing healthcare providers as a result of enduring liability claims for indeterminate periods of time. We have recognized "that the length of time that insureds are exposed to potential liability has a bearing on the rates that insurers must charge."

In enacting the repose piece of House Bill 4, lawmakers made a fundamental policy choice: the collective benefits of a definitive cut-off are more important than a particular plaintiff's right to sue more than a decade after the alleged malpractice. A few plaintiffs such as Rankin will encounter the Legislature's statutory roadblock, unable to bring claims through no fault of their own, but some defendants would likewise suffer unfortunate consequences were potential liability left indeterminate. The constitutional inquiry is whether the Legislature acted unreasonably or arbitrarily. We cannot brand as arbitrary lawmakers' policy rationales for granting healthcare providers a substantive right to be free from liability after ten years, even if a plaintiff could have discovered her injury no sooner.

Surveying legislation around the nation, repose statutes for medical-negligence cases are commonplace. [And most] other jurisdictions have rejected constitutional challenges to repose statutes in medical-malpractice cases premised on open courts provisions or similar provisions guaranteeing the right to a remedy.

Section 74.251(b) is a reasonable exercise of the Legislature's police power to provide a certain cutoff to claims after an ample period of ten years, five times longer than the general limitations period for bringing a negligence action, and five times longer than the general limitations period for bringing a healthcare-liability claim. We presume that the Legislature's judgment was not an arbitrary or unreasonable exercise of the police power, and Rankin has offered no compelling argument or proof to the contrary. Repose statutes are not exempt from Open Courts challenges, but the reviewing court cannot ignore the Legislature's broader reasons for limiting a litigant's rights and its considered judgment in exercising its police power in the interest of the general welfare.

III. Conclusion

We have never declared a statute of repose unconstitutional and decline to do so today. Section 74.251(b)'s grant of absolute protection against indefinite potential liability does not violate the Texas Constitution. The Open Courts provision confers a constitutional right of access but not an everlasting one. Texas' ten-year repose period will weigh heavily on a small number of plaintiffs like Rankin, who belatedly discover a *res-ipsa*-like injury. A statute of repose, by design, will always bar some otherwise-valid claims, but that result is the whole point of a statute of repose.

Notes on Legislative Interests and Repose

Revisiting the Open Courts Standard: Both the decisions in *Rankin* and in *Trinity River* employed the original version of the *Lebohm* test for an open courts violation rather than the *Sax* restatement of the test. What are the major differences between the *Lebohm* formulation and the *Sax* formulation? How important are these differences? Could the differences be outcome determinative in a particular case? Keep these questions in mind while reading the majority and dissenting opinions in *Lucas v. United States*, excerpted in the next subsection below.

Reasonable Abrogation of Common Law Claims: *Rankin* is one of only two cases from the Texas Supreme Court holding that a particular litigant's right to redress for a well-established common law cause of action can be completely barred without violating the open courts provision. The other case was *Owens Corning v. Carter*, which upheld a limitations borrowing statute that closed Texas courts to nonresident plaintiffs in personal injury or death actions when their claims were time barred in the state in which the wrongful act took place.[102] The *Owens Corning* court reasoned that the legislative purpose in preventing plaintiffs from obtaining greater rights in Texas than they would have had in the state of the injury outweighed the limited interest of the plaintiffs in pursuing their claims in Texas.[103]

Rankin determined that the legislature did not act unreasonably or arbitrarily in enacting a ten-year statute of repose for medical malpractice actions, as the legislature could reasonably conclude, in light of its findings on a medical insurance crisis, that the general welfare of society was best served through such an absolute deadline even if a small number of meritorious claims pursued diligently would thereby be barred. The legislative judgment that "the collective benefits of a definitive cut-off are more important than a particular plaintiff's right to sue more than a decade after the alleged malpractice" could not be, according to *Rankin*, "brand[ed] as arbitrary."[104]

How much leeway does the legislature have after *Rankin* to impose a statute of repose in medical malpractice and other cases? *Rankin* emphasized that the ten-year repose period in Texas for medical malpractice was as long as the repose period of any of the twenty other jurisdictions that imposed a repose period applicable to "sponge" or foreign-object cases. Many of these other states had upheld these statutes against open courts and other state constitutional challenges. Does this mean a six-year statute of repose, as employed by several of these other states, would also be constitutional under the Texas open courts provision? What about the three-year statute of repose a few states have adopted? Could even a two-year statute of repose be constitutional? If so, would that allow the legislature to merely re-label the absolute two-year statute of limitations for medical malpractice claims as a statute of repose and circumvent the earlier decisions in cases such as *Neagle* and *Nelson* that the legislature cannot require the plaintiffs "to do the impossible–to sue before they had any reason to know they should sue"? Or could such a two-year repose period be "brand[ed] as arbitrary"?

Medical Repose versus Tolling for Minors: What impact does upholding the ten-year statute of repose have on the Texas Supreme Court's holdings in *Sax* and again in *Weiner* that limitations must be tolled for minors until they reach the age of majority? If a toddler is injured by a physician's malpractice on his second birthday, must suit be brought on his behalf before he turns twelve in order to satisfy the statute of repose? If so, has *Sax* been effectively overruled?

The El Paso Court of Appeals confronted this situation in *Rivera v. Compton*.[105] A newborn suffered severe brain damage due to lack of oxygen during her birth which caused her permanent neurological injury. Her mother waited, however, until she was fourteen to sue the treating physician and hospital for medical malpractice. The health care defendants pled that her claims were barred by the ten-year statute of repose, contending that *Rankin* meant the ten-year repose period did not violate the open courts provision. But the El Paso

---

[102]997 S.W.2d 560, 574 (Tex. 1999).

[103]*Id.*

[104]*Rankin*, 307 S.W.3d at 288.

[105]392 S.W.3d 326 (Tex. App.–El Paso 2012, pet. granted).

Court of Appeals, after reasoning that *Sax* and *Weiner* governed rather than *Rankin,* held that applying the ten-year statute of repose to a minor under the age of eight violated the open courts provision.[106] The Texas Supreme Court then granted the defendants' petition to review the appellate court's holding, with oral argument scheduled for February 2014.

3. Damages Caps and Tort Reform

Damages caps and other aspects of tort reform routinely survive constitutional scrutiny under the United States Constitution.[107] But in several states, including Texas, the courts have invalidated certain tort reform measures under the state constitution.

Lucas v. United States, 757 S.W.2d 687 (Tex. 1988)

KILGARLIN, Justice.

This is the first case to come to us on questions certified by a federal appellate court. *See Lucas v. United States,* 807 F.2d 414 (5th Cir.1986), *questions certified,* 811 F.2d 270 (5th Cir.1987). For the reasons stated in this opinion, we answer that the damages limitations contained in sections 11.02 and 11.03 of article 4590i violate article I, § 13 of the Texas Constitution.

To put the facts of this case in perspective, we quote at length from the original opinion of the Fifth Circuit:

> When fourteen-month-old Christopher Lucas developed a swollen neck and a fever after a family outing, his parents took him to the William Beaumont Army Medical Center near El Paso, Texas, for diagnosis and treatment. An army doctor determined that the child had a cyst in his thyroglossal duct and ordered an injection of 600,000 units of Bicillin LA, a penicillin product manufactured and packaged in its own syringe by Wyeth Laboratories.
>
> A hospital nurse gave Christopher the shot in his right buttock with a 1 1/4" needle that was fully inserted. Blood appeared at the injection site, and within a few moments, Christopher's legs became mottled. The doctors were summoned. They concluded that the baby was having an allergic reaction to the antibiotic and gave injections to combat it.
>
> Several hours later, Christopher's parents noticed that his legs were not moving as they usually did when he cried. Tests conducted during the next several days indicated paralysis. An operation to remove a tumor

---

[106] *Id.* at 332-33.

[107] *See, e.g.,* Smith v. Botsford Gen. Hosp., 419 F.3d 513, 519-20 (6th Cir. 2005) (upholding Michigan's $359,000 cap on noneconomic damages in medical malpractice cases against Seventh Amendment and Equal Protection Clause challenges); Boyd v. Bulala, 877 F.2d 1191, 1196-97 (4th Cir. 1989) (upholding Virginia's $750,000 cap on medical malpractice damages against Seventh Amendment, Due Process Clause, and Equal Protection Clause challenges).

> suspected to be pressing on the nerves controlling the child's legs determined that the paralysis was the result of blood starvation of the nerves caused by a blockage created when the Bicillin LA was injected directly into an artery. Tragically, the paralysis is permanent.
>
> Christopher and his parents sued the United States under the Federal Tort Claims Act. The district court held that the injection was negligently administered and awarded the parents $498,628.72 as the present value of the past and future medical expenses they face in caring for Christopher until his majority. The court also awarded to Christopher $350,000.00 as the present value of the future medical expenses he will have after his eighteenth birthday, and $600,000.00 as the present value of the impairment of his future earning capacity. Finally, the court awarded Christopher $1,500,000.00 for pain and suffering.

Lucas v. United States, 807 F.2d 414, 416 (5th Cir.1986), *questions certified,* 811 F.2d 270 (5th Cir.1987).

On appeal, the Fifth Circuit held that the liability limit of article 4590i, section 11.02, does apply to federally operated hospitals and that its application was consistent with the due process and equal protection clauses of the United States Constitution. Our question, then, is whether the limits of liability for health care providers set out in that statute and/or section 11.03 are consistent with the Texas Constitution. Those sections provide in pertinent part:

> Limit on Civil Liability
>
> Sec. 11.02. (a) In an action on a health care liability claim where final judgment is rendered against a physician or health care provider, the limit of civil liability for damages of the physician or health care provider shall be limited to an amount not to exceed $500,000.
>
> (b) Subsection (a) of this section does not apply to the amount of damages awarded on a health care liability claim for the expenses of necessary medical, hospital, and custodial care received before judgment or required in the future for treatment of the injury.
>
> Alternative Partial Limit on Civil Liability
>
> Sec. 11.03. In the event that Section 11.02(a) of this subchapter is stricken from this subchapter or is otherwise invalidated by a method other than through legislative means, the following shall become effective:
>
> In an action on a health care liability claim where final judgment is rendered against a physician or health care provider, the limit of civil liability of the physician or health care provider for all past and future noneconomic losses recoverable by or on behalf of any injured person and/or the estate of such person, including without limitation as applicable past and future physical pain and suffering, mental anguish and suffering, consortium, disfigurement, and any other nonpecuniary damage, shall be limited to an amount not to exceed $150,000.

Tex.Rev.Civ.Stat.Ann. art. 4590i, §§ 11.02, 11.03. The limits in both sections are not absolute but instead increase or decrease depending on the consumer price index published by the federal government. *Id.* at §§ 11.01, 11.04.

At least thirteen states other than Texas have enacted damage limitation provisions into their medical malpractice statutes. Each statute has different characteristics, and the state courts have divided on the constitutionality of the various caps. *See, e.g., Smith v. Department of Insurance,* 507 So.2d 1080, 1087-89 (Fla.1987)($450,000 limit on noneconomic damages violated "open courts" provision of Florida Constitution); *Wright v. Central Du Page Hospital Ass'n,* 63 Ill.2d 313, 347 N.E.2d 736, 743 (1976)($500,000 cap constituted "special law" in violation of Illinois Constitution); *Carson v. Maurer,* 120 N.H. 925, 424 A.2d 825, 836-38 (1980)($250,000 limit on noneconomic damages violated equal protection guaranteed by New Hampshire Constitution); *Arneson v. Olson,* 270 N.W.2d 125, 135-36 (N.D.1978)($300,000 ceiling violated equal protection clause of North Dakota Constitution); *Duren v. Suburban Community Hospital,* 24 Ohio Misc.2d 25, 482 N.E.2d 1358, 1361-63 (1985)($200,000 limit on general damages violated Ohio and federal constitutions); *Fein v. Permanente Medical Group,* 38 Cal.3d 137, 695 P.2d 665, 679-84 (1985) ($250,000 ceiling on noneconomic damages held constitutional); *Johnson v. St. Vincent Hospital, Inc.,* 273 Ind. 374, 404 N.E.2d 585, 598-601 (1980)($500,000 cap upheld); *Prendergast v. Nelson,* 199 Neb. 97, 256 N.W.2d 657, 668-69 (1977)($500,000 cap upheld in plurality opinion joined by only three judges, with three others dissenting as to constitutionality, and one judge declining to reach constitutional issues because opinion was merely advisory).

We begin our state constitutional analysis by noting the findings and purposes enumerated by the Texas Legislature in Tex.Rev.Civ.Stat.Ann. art. 4590i, § 1.02 (Vernon Supp.1987). Based on these findings and purposes, the legislature enacted the damages limitations quoted in section 11.02 and, alternatively, section 11.03. Significantly, section 11.03 on its face shows that the legislature itself entertained doubts about the constitutionality of the limit of liability set out in section 11.02(a).

We have considered the arguments for and against the constitutionality of the caps. With all respect due a legislative enactment, we nevertheless conclude that the liability limits in article 4590i, sections 11.02 and 11.03, are unconstitutional as applied to catastrophically damaged malpractice victims seeking a "remedy by due course of law." Construing article I, section 13, of the Texas Constitution, this court has said:

> In analyzing the litigant's right to redress, we first note that the litigant has two criteria to satisfy. First, it must be shown that the litigant has a cognizable common law cause of action that is being restricted. Second, the litigant must show that the restriction is unreasonable or arbitrary when balanced against the purpose and basis of the statute.

Sax v. Votteler, 648 S.W.2d 661, 666 (Tex.1983).

Texas courts have long recognized that victims of medical negligence have a well-defined common law cause of action to sue for injuries negligently inflicted upon them. This much is undisputed. Under *Sax,* then, the remaining inquiry is whether the restriction on Lucas' right of recovery "is unreasonable *or* arbitrary when balanced against the purpose and basis of the statute" (emphasis added). We hold that the restriction is unreasonable *and* arbitrary and that article 4590i, sections 11.02 and 11.03, unconstitutionally limit Lucas' right of access to the courts for a "remedy by due course of law." Tex. Const. art. I, § 13. We note that there is no provision in the federal constitution corresponding to our constitution's "open courts" guarantee. Indeed, that guarantee is embodied in Magna Carta and has been a part of our constitutional law since our republic.

Our first concern with the statute is that the legislature has failed to provide Lucas any adequate substitute to obtain redress for his injuries. *See Sax*, 648 S.W.2d at 667. As did the Supreme Court of Illinois, we reject any argument that the statute may be supported by alleged benefits to society generally. *Wright,* 63 Ill.2d at 328, 347 N.E.2d at 742.

It should be remembered that the Medical Liability Act of 1977 (now article 4590i) was based on recommendations of the Texas Medical Professional Liability Study Commission, sometimes referred to as the Keeton Report. Dean Keeton, in a separate statement, recommended a victim's compensation fund as a statutory substitute for limitations upon recovery. *See* Keeton Report at 51-52. The legislature chose not to follow this recommendation.

We also question whether the restrictions in sections 11.02 and 11.03 are reasonable when balanced against the purposes and bases of the statute. The legislature, in enacting article 4590i, apparently did not intend to strike at frivolous malpractice suits for it found in section 1.02(a)(2) that "the filing of *legitimate* health care liability claims in Texas is a contributing factor affecting medical professional liability rates" (emphasis added). The legislature did find that a "medical malpractice insurance crisis" had been created and that "satisfactory insurance coverage . . . [was] often not available at any price," but it then stated that "adoption of certain modifications in the medical, insurance, and legal systems . . . *may or may not have an effect* on the rates charged by insurers for medical professional liability coverage." Tex.Rev.Civ.Stat.Ann. art. 4590i, § 1.02(a)(5), (10), (12) (emphasis added).

In the context of persons catastrophically injured by medical negligence, we believe it is unreasonable *and* arbitrary to limit their recovery in a speculative experiment to determine whether liability insurance rates will decrease. Texas Constitution article I, section 13, guarantees meaningful access to the courts whether or not liability rates are high. As to the legislature's stated purpose to "assure that awards are rationally related to actual damages," section 1.02(b)(2), we simply note that this is a power properly attached to the judicial and not the legislative branch of government. Tex. Const. art. II, § 1. In any event, we hold it is unreasonable and arbitrary for the legislature to conclude that arbitrary damages caps, applicable to all claimants no matter how seriously injured, will help assure a rational relationship between actual damages and amounts awarded.

We are supported in our decision to strike down the damages caps in article 4590i by the reasoning of the Florida Supreme Court invalidating that state's $450,000 ceiling on noneconomic damages. *Smith v. Department of Insurance,* 507 So.2d 1080 (Fla.1987). Like the appellees in *Smith,* the medical defendant in our case argues that the legislature has not totally abolished a cause of action but merely placed a cap on damages that may be recovered and, therefore, has not denied the right of access to the courts. The Supreme

Court of Florida rejected these arguments.

> Access to the court is granted for the purpose of redressing injuries. A plaintiff who receives a jury verdict for, e.g., $1,000,000, has not received a constitutional redress of injuries if the legislature statutorily, and arbitrarily, caps the recovery. Nor, we add, because the jury verdict is being arbitrarily capped, is the plaintiff receiving the constitutional benefit of a jury trial as we have understood that right. Further, if the legislature may constitutionally cap recovery at $450,000, there is no discernible reason why it could not cap the recovery at some other figure, perhaps $50,000, or $1,000, or even $1.

Smith, 507 So.2d at 1088-89.

The reasoning from the *Smith* opinion is entirely consistent with our "open courts" analysis in *LeCroy v. Hanlon,* 713 S.W.2d 335 (Tex.1986). *LeCroy* involved legislative interference with access to the courts by way of increased filing fees, much of which went to the state's general revenue fund. Clearly this was not a total abolition of the right of access. Nevertheless, the court held the fee increases invalid under Tex. Const. art. I, § 13.

We understand the legislature's concern in attempting to solve the health care problems it perceived during the middle of the 1970's. Nevertheless, we agree with the statement by the Supreme Court of New Hampshire: "It is simply unfair and unreasonable to impose the burden of supporting the medical care industry solely upon those persons who are most severely injured and therefore most in need of compensation." *Carson v. Maurer,* 120 N.H. 925, 424 A.2d 825, 837 (1980).

For the reasons stated in this opinion, our answer to the certified question is that the limitation on medical malpractice damages in Tex.Rev.Civ.Stat.Ann. art. 4590i, §§ 11.02 and 11.03, is inconsistent with and violative of article I, section 13, of the Texas Constitution.

GONZALEZ, Justice, dissenting.

I dissent. The issue is not the wisdom or fairness of the cap, but whether the cap bears a reasonable relation to a proper legislative purpose. I would hold that the limitation on recovery of nonmedical damages does not violate either the Equal Protection or the Due Process guarantees which are set forth in the Texas Constitution.

* * * *

Open Courts

Article I, Section 13 provides two separate and distinct guarantees: (1) all courts shall be open, and (2) every person shall have remedy for injury by due course of law. The former category guarantees a right of "access," while the latter category guarantees a right of "redress." No opinion of this court has discussed the independent guarantee of redress; rather, the focus of our analysis has been upon those legislative enactments which impose impossible or unreasonable conditions on a litigant's right of access to the courts. It is of course obvious that an entire abrogation of access results in an entire denial of redress.

Thus, to that extent, the right of access and redress are inextricably intertwined. However, this case presents a slightly different question because section 11.02 of Article 4590i leaves the right of access wholly intact; only the right of redress is partially restricted.

Thus, this case presents two important questions of first impression. Does a legislative enactment which partially restricts the right of redress trigger the protections of Article I, Section 13? If so, what is the appropriate standard of review to be applied?

I have found no case which interprets the open courts provision as independently protecting a litigant's right of redress. I am mindful, however, of the text of our Constitutional provision: "every person . . . shall have remedy by due course of law." I agree with the majority that the protections of Article I, Section 13 do extend to legislative enactments which allow free access but restrict redress. I further agree that the appropriate standard of review is whether the legislative purpose for the statute outweighs the partial diminution of a litigant's constitutionally-guaranteed right of redress. I vigorously disagree, however, with the majority's implication that the appropriate standard of review includes the existence of a reasonable substitute (individual quid pro quo) as a *constitutional* prerequisite to statutory validity.

This court has never expressly required an individual quid pro quo in the past; to do so now would unquestionably restrain the legislature's ability and duty to effect social change through legislative enactment. Article I, Section 13 does not guarantee the continued existence of a common law cause of action, but only proscribes the creation of an impossible or unreasonable impediment to access or redress to vindicate a recognized and justiciable substantive right. The open courts provision was never intended to create any new rights, nor was it intended to elevate the common law to constitutional stature.

Two of the stated purposes of article 4590i are to:

> (4) make available to physicians, hospitals, and other health care providers protection against potential liability through the insurance mechanism at reasonable affordable rates;
> (5) make affordable medical and health care more accessible and available to the citizens of Texas; . . . .

Although an individual quid pro quo is not constitutionally required, I nonetheless submit these two purposes reveal that the medical cap in section 11.02 of article 4590i provides both a societal and individual quid pro quo. The benefit to society is that by reducing the awards given to those injured in excess of the caps, insurance payouts are more readily calculable. This in turn allows a predictable rate structure to be erected, thus allowing policies to be written on health care providers who otherwise could not afford the exorbitant rates associated with policies of undeterminable risk. The resultant societal quid pro quo is the decrease in cost of medical malpractice insurance in the state of Texas and the increased availability of health care. I further suggest there is an individual quid pro quo because the caps enable health care providers to procure insurance in the first place. Without adequate coverage, it was reasonable for the Legislature to conclude that the plaintiff in a medical malpractice case would suffer damages with no recovery at all against an insolvent, judgment-proof defendant. I submit that a recovery of all medical costs and expenses, with a cap on $500,000 plus a Consumer Price Index adjustment on other damages, is better than a potential recovery of zero. Thus, while a reasonable substitute should not be required for legislative *modifications* of causes of action, I suggest there is in fact a sufficient quid pro quo in this case. I agree with the position taken by the California Supreme Court:

> Even if due process principles required some "quid pro quo" to support the statute, it would be difficult to say that the preservation of a viable medical malpractice insurance industry in this state was not an adequate benefit for the detriment the legislation imposes on malpractice plaintiffs.

Fein v. Permanente Medical Group, 38 Cal.3d 137, 160 n.18, 695 P.2d 665, 681-82 n.18 (1985).

In determining whether a litigant's right of redress is unreasonably or arbitrarily restricted, four distinct characteristics of article 4590i must be emphasized. First, the medical malpractice claimant is allowed to recover all past and future medical expenses without limitation. Secondly, the plaintiff may recover up to $500,000 of nonmedical damages. Thirdly, the legislature provided for an upward adjustment of the damages limit based upon the Consumer Price Index. And fourth, the statute imposes a limitation on the liability of health care providers rather than an absolute ceiling on the amount a plaintiff can recover. Thus, where multiple defendants are involved, the medical malpractice plaintiff can recover against each. The statutory limits are applied on a per defendant basis rather than on a per occurrence basis. It is clear, therefore, that the Legislature was concerned with limiting the liability of each defendant, not with unreasonably and arbitrarily limiting the amount a plaintiff can recover. These aspects of the statute serve to distinguish it from all other state versions which have undergone constitutional attack.

The majority cites with approval the language used by the Supreme Court of Florida: "[I]f the legislature may constitutionally cap recovery at $450,000 there is no discernable reason why they could not cap the recovery at some other figure, perhaps $50,000 or $1,000 or $1." This argument ignores the fact that any modification the legislature makes is subject to being stricken as unconstitutional. A reduction of nonmedical damages to a lesser cap at some point would be manifestly so insufficient as to become a denial of justice.

Plaintiffs have no vested property rights in a particular measure of damages. This is without doubt since a "vested right" must be something more than a mere expectation based on anticipated continuance of existing law. It must become a title, legal or equitable, to present or future enjoyment of property. *National Carloading Corp. v. Phoenix-El Paso Express,* 142 Tex. 141, 176 S.W.2d 564 (1944). The legislature has broad powers to modify the scope and nature of such damages. I am not prepared to hold that an award of close to $1 million ($500,000 plus consumer index adjustment provided for in § 11.04 of the Act) for nonmedical damages coupled with no limitation on past and future medical expenses is so arbitrary and unreasonable that it does not pass constitutional muster. Therefore, this cap is no more a violation of the open courts provision of the Texas Constitution than the fee increase was in *LeCroy,* 713 S.W.2d at 343 (Gonzalez, J., dissenting).

I acknowledge that there are serious questions surrounding the causes of the medical malpractice insurance crisis. I also acknowledge that the validity of some of the findings made by the Study Commission and adopted by the legislature are questionable. However, the findings are "legislative facts" which should be accorded great deference by this court, particularly because reasonable minds can differ as to the causes of the crisis. For us to "unfind" that there is a crisis on the state of this record is to act like a "super legislature" in violation of the separation of powers doctrine. We must respect the process. Whatever flaws exist in the legislative findings, the proper forum to correct them is the Texas Legislature and not this court. For the above reasons, I dissent.

PHILLIPS, Chief Justice, dissenting.

I respectfully dissent. I would hold that the $500,000 cap on non-medical damages does not violate any provision of the Texas Constitution.

* * * *

Open Courts

The plaintiffs and all aligned amici allege that the cap violates the second due process provision in the Texas Constitution, the so-called open courts provision. Although there is no similar provision in the federal constitution, a majority of state constitutions contain substantially identical guarantees.

While it is universally agreed that the open courts provision guarantees a right of access to the courts, there is great divergence among the various states regarding the extent, if any, to which it accords constitutional protection to existing substantive remedies. *See* McGovern, *The Variety, Policy and Constitutionality of Product Liability Statutes of Repose,* 30 Am.U.L.Rev. 579, 615-18 (1981).

In many states, for example, the provision is nothing more than a procedural guarantee of judicial availability. *See, e.g., O'Quinn v. Walt Disney Productions, Inc.,* 177 Col. 190, 195, 493 P.2d 344, 346 (1972); *Twin Falls Clinic & Hosp. Bldg. Corp. v. Hamill,* 103 Idaho 19, 24, 644 P.2d 341, 346 (1982); *Johnson v. St. Vincent Hosp., Inc.,* 273 Ind. 374, 404 N.E.2d at 594 (Ind.1980); *Prendergast v. Nelson,* 199 Neb. 97, 103-06, 256 N.W.2d 657, 663-65 (1977); *Freezer Storage, Inc. v. Armstrong Cork Co.,* 476 Pa. 270, 279-81, 382 A.2d 715, 720-21 (1978).

A greater number of states, however, appear to place some substantive restrictions on the legislature's authority to abolish or restrict well-established remedies and defenses, particularly common law causes of action. This restriction appears to be absolute only in those few states which also constitutionally forbid any legislative restriction on damages. *See, e.g.,* ARIZ. CONST. art. 18, § 6; KY. CONST. § 54; WYO. CONST. art. 10, § 4. Other states require, in one form or another, a judicial balancing of the individual right to assert a recognized remedy with the public necessity for abrogating or restricting that right.

The elements which are considered in that balance, and the weight accorded to them, vary widely from state to state. Sometimes the elements are simply unclear. *See, e.g., Daugaard v. Baltic Co-Op. Bldg. Supply Ass'n,* 349 N.W.2d 419 (S.D.1984). In most states, however, the courts have articulated the factors to be considered.

[I]n a few states, the balance may be satisfied in favor of the restriction only if the legislature has created an alternative remedy, or quid pro quo, in place of the abolished right. *See, e.g., Ecker v. Town of West Hartford,* 12 Conn.App. 219, 530 A.2d 1056, 1063 (1987); *Gallegher v. Davis,* 37 Del. 380, 392, 183 A. 620, 624 (Del.Super.1936).

In other states, however, an alternative remedy is only one method of satisfying the balance in favor of the restriction. The standards for determining when another method is sufficient vary from state to state. In Alabama, for instance, a common law remedy may be constitutionally abolished "if the individual possessor receives something in return for it (the individual quid pro quo . . .), or if society at large receives a benefit (thereby justifying the exercise of the police power)." *Lankford v. Sullivan, Long & Hagerty,* 416 So.2d 996, 1000 (Ala.1982)(plurality opinion). Judicial review is more rigorous in Utah, where a remedy or cause of action may not be abrogated without providing an alternative unless "there is a clear social or economic evil to be eliminated and the elimination of an existing legal remedy is not an arbitrary or unreasonable means for achieving the objective." *Berry v. Beech Aircraft Corp.,* 717 P.2d 670, 680 (Utah 1985). Florida is more rigorous still. There the statute must provide "a reasonable alternative to protect the rights of the people of the State to redress for injuries, unless the Legislature can show an overpowering public necessity for the abolishment of such right, and no alternative method of meeting such public necessity can be shown." *Kluger v. White,* 281 So.2d 1, 4 (Fla.1973). Although the standards differ, each of these states recognize that on some occasions the legislative branch may alter or even abolish existing common law remedies.

Like Alabama, Utah and Florida, Texas restricts arbitrary legislative abolition of well-recognized common law causes of action under the open courts provision, while declining to require a quid pro quo whenever common law remedies are changed. I adhere to this interpretation of the open courts provision. I am concerned, however, that the test now in use by our court obscures rather than illuminates the correct Texas standard.

In *Lebohm v. City of Galveston,* 154 Tex. 192, 199, 275 S.W.2d 951, 955 (1955), this court articulated the test under our open courts provision as follows:

> [L]egislative action withdrawing common-law remedies for well established common-law causes of action for injuries to one's "lands, goods, person or reputation" is sustained only when it is reasonable in substituting other remedies, or when it is a reasonable exercise of the police power in the interest of the general welfare. Legislative action of this type is not sustained when it is arbitrary or unreasonable.

We quoted and reaffirmed this test in *Waites v. Sondock,* 561 S.W.2d 772, 774 (Tex.1977), and *Sax v. Votteler,* 648 S.W.2d 661, 665 (Tex.1983). In my opinion, it remains the best statement of the true purpose of the open courts guarantee.

After quoting and expressly reaffirming the *Lebohm* standard, however, the court in *Sax* immediately set forth this new test:

> We hold ... that the right to bring a well-established common law cause of action cannot be effectively abrogated by the legislature absent a showing

> that the legislative basis for the statute outweighs the denial of the constitutionally-guaranteed right of redress. In applying this test, we consider both the general purpose of the statute and the extent to which the litigant's right to redress is affected.

648 S.W.2d at 665-66.

While *Sax* does not necessarily compel an incorrect analysis, in practice it has resulted in an almost exclusive focus on "the extent to which the litigant's right to redress is affected," with an almost total disregard of "the general purpose of the statute." Except in *Nelson v. Krusen,* 678 S.W.2d 918 (Tex.1984), where the court examined the legislative purpose and effect of the statute in question at some length, the court has emphasized the nature and extent of the restriction to the virtual exclusion of other factors. In *Sax* itself, in *LeCroy v. Hanlon, supra,* and in this case, the court's "first concern" has been the absence of adequate substitute remedies. This approach also dominates the other opinions in this case.

With all due respect, these approaches all suffer from a common vice: they require this court to strike a delicate balance between important competing interests without any standards for evaluating the relative importance of those interests. This unfettered discretion leaves us with little other than our personal predilections on which to rely in reaching our decision. One justice therefore finds the cap to be "reasonable", the other justices condemn the caps as "unfair and unreasonable", or "unreasonable and arbitrary."

I would, however, return to the language of *Lebohm* to strike the proper balance. That standard correctly separates the issue of a reasonable alternative remedy from the issue of a reasonable exercise of police power. If the Legislature has provided or left in place a reasonable alternative remedy, judicial scrutiny is at an end, and properly so. The Legislature should have absolute discretion to substitute one adequate remedy for another, without its choice being subjected to judicial re-evaluation. If the Legislature has not provided or left in place a reasonable alternative remedy, however, the Constitution requires a second, separate inquiry. The courts must independently determine if the legislative action constitutes a reasonable exercise of the police power.

This determination must be searching. It is not satisfied by a mere finding that the statute is rationally related to a legitimate state interest, for such limited review would give the open courts provision no separate import, at least as to redress, from due course of law. *See LeCroy v. Hanlon,* 713 S.W.2d at 340-41. Rather, I believe it is satisfied only if the statute bears a reasonable relationship to its stated goal of ameliorating a rationally perceived social evil. A "reasonable exercise of the police power in the interest of the general welfare" thus requires that the statute address an important, not merely a legitimate, state interest, that such interest be perceived and articulated by the state, and that the remedies provided bear a real relationship to the social evil being addressed. These requirements, which are similar to those employed in intermediate equal protection scrutiny, *see* L. Tribe, *American Constitutional Law* 1601-10, and are reminiscent of heightened substantive due process standards, *see State v. Richards,* 157 Tex. at 171, 301 S.W.2d at 602, assure that the right to judicial redress is protected against arbitrary or unreasonable intrusion.

In applying the *Lebohm* standard to the provision under review, the first alternative is quickly resolved. It is apparent that our citizens have long enjoyed the right to sue for unlimited damages for medical negligence, *Graham v. Gautier,* 21 Tex. 111 (1858), and that the cap has not substituted or left in place a reasonable alternative remedy for the rights withdrawn. While some restrictions on remedies may be so insignificant or marginal that the open courts guarantee is not offended, that is not the case with the malpractice cap. Even though our limits are larger than those provided under similar legislation in many other states, they still are substantially beneath what a reasonable finder of facts might award in particular instances. In the case of a permanently and catastrophically injured infant plaintiff like Christopher Lucas, for instance, even the maximum statutory limits would likely constitute inadequate compensation under currently prevailing community mores.

It is therefore necessary to proceed to the second alternative of *Lebohm.* Under the appropriate standards for striking the balance under that alternative, I conclude that the cap does not violate the open courts provision.

The cap addressed an important public issue. The Medical Liability and Insurance Improvement Act was our state's response to a national problem of maintaining the delivery of affordable and comprehensive health care to all citizens in light of rapidly increasing insurance costs for health care providers. Forty-eight other states passed some type of legislation during the 1970's in response to this crisis, and twelve of those states also enacted damages limitations. Witherspoon, *Constitutionality of the Texas Statute,* 10 Tex.Tech L.Rev. at 420. The need for available and affordable health care is of critical importance to all people, and the Legislature was addressing an important state interest in enacting this statute.

Finally, the cap does bear a real relationship to a rationally perceived malpractice crisis. The Legislature found that "the filing of legitimate health care liability claims in Texas is a contributing factor affecting medical professional liability rates." TEX.REV.CIV.STAT. art. 4590i, § 1.02(a)(2). The need to focus on legitimate claims in order to address the problem was explained by the Commission as follows:

> Large verdicts and large settlements constitute a relatively small percentage of the total claims settled or reduced to judgment, probably no more than five percent, but indemnity and allocated losses paid on this small percentage of claims account in excess of 40% of the total damages and allocated expenses paid for all claims. It is therefore apparent that substantial reductions in settlements and judgments in those cases involving severe injuries will have a significant impact on insurance costs and the pure premium rate.

This and all other findings of the Commission were expressly adopted by the Legislature.

The primary purpose of the cap was not to protect health care providers, but to protect the public. The Legislature found that "the cost to physicians and hospitals for adequate medical malpractice insurance has dramatically risen in price, with cost impact on patients and the public," and that "satisfactory insurance coverage for adequate amounts of insurance . . . is often not available at any price." The crisis having thus "caused a serious public problem," the Legislature was reasonable in concluding that the cap would make insurance protection available "at reasonably affordable rates," thereby making "affordable medical and health care more accessible and available to the citizens of Texas." The Legislature was reasonable in concluding that cheaper and more widely available insurance coverage would result in greater health care services being provided to more citizens in more areas at more economical charges, all to the public benefit.

The court harshly criticizes the Legislature for its candid conclusion that the cap "may or may not have an effect on the rates charged by insurers for medical professional liability insurance." The court finds it "unreasonable *and* arbitrary to limit [injured plaintiffs'] recovery in a speculative experiment to determine whether liability insurance rates will decrease." I disagree. In addressing complicated social and economic problems, the Legislature must be free to attempt a remedy, even when the results are uncertain. In the real world, social policy must frequently be made on the basis of incomplete and even conflicting information, and the law of unintended consequences may override even the noblest of intentions. The Legislature should be commended, not condemned, for this realization. To turn constitutionality on the presence of a declaration of certitude might serve only to reward arrogance, ignorance or hypocrisy.

Far from engaging in undisciplined speculation, the Legislature attempted in this instance to meet a complex social problem by limiting damages "in a manner that will not unduly restrict a claimant's rights any more than necessary to deal with the crisis." TEX.REV.CIV.STAT. art. 4590i, § 1.02(a)(3). The exclusion of all medical damages from the limits, the inflation adjustment provisions, the limitation on a per defendant rather a per occurrence basis, and the exclusion of *Stowers* claims from the limits all indicate a legislative solicitude for injured claimants. Thus, I find the legislative solution to be reasonably related, or an "acceptable" fit, to a rationally perceived social evil. While the impact on those catastrophically injured persons who are denied full recovery should not be minimized, I believe that the cap is "a reasonable exercise of the police power in the interest of the general welfare."

Notes on Meaningful Legal Remedies and Damages Caps

Balancing the Competing Interests and Substitute Remedies: Because the common law placed no restrictions on Lucas's right to recover, the Texas Supreme Court immediately turned to the second part of the open courts analysis, whether the restriction on Lucas's right to redress was unreasonable or arbitrary in comparison with the legislative purpose supporting the cap. What factors led the majority to conclude the restriction was unreasonable and arbitrary?

The majority first considered whether the legislature provided Lucas an adequate substitute remedy. Most jurisdictions, including Texas, have allowed the legislature to establish administrative compensation systems and other substitute remedies that replace common law claims, as long as the injured party is not entirely deprived of a remedy and the compensation scheme provides other potential benefits to the injured party.[108] For example, the Texas Supreme Court in *Texas Workers' Compensation Commission v. Garcia* upheld a new state workers' compensation scheme against multiple constitutional challenges, including a challenge under the open courts provision. The court reasoned that although the workers' benefits were "more limited than the actual damages recoverable at common law," the fact that the recovery was "more certain" was a quid pro quo that rendered the scheme an adequate substitute for purposes of the open courts guarantee.[109] But in *Lucas*, the legislature had chosen not to follow Dean Page Keeton's recommendation that a victim's compensation fund be established for those impacted by the caps, and thus, according to the majority, no substitute remedy had been provided. Yet Justice Gonzalez's dissent maintained that a quid pro quo did exist in that, in the absence of the caps, there might not be any recovery at all for plaintiffs in Lucas's position. Is the majority or dissent more convincing on this point?

The *Lucas* majority next faulted the legislature for limiting recoveries based on mere speculation that medical liability insurance rates would thereafter decrease. The court then expressed concern that such caps were inherently arbitrary and that the court would have no principled basis to distinguish a \$50,000 cap from a \$500,000 cap. And finally, the majority highlighted that the caps would only apply to those whom juries found to be the most seriously injured–and thus presumably in the most need of compensation.

After examining these concerns, what standard did *Lucas* apply in balancing the legislative purpose against the restriction on the right to redress? Is Chief Justice Phillips correct that such a balancing approach provides "unfettered discretion" to the court in weighing the competing interests, thus leaving little structured analysis other than the "personal predilections" of the judges? Would employing something similar to intermediate scrutiny help in eliminating this "unfettered discretion"? Is that the approach the Texas Supreme Court adopted in its more recent open courts decisions, such as *Rankin*?

Restrictions on Statutory Remedies: *Lucas*, like *Sax*, only applies to common law claims. *Rose v. Doctors Hospital* accordingly held that applying the Medical Liability and Insurance Improvement Act's caps to wrongful death actions did not violate the open courts provision.[110] Because wrongful death claims were not recognized under the common law, but instead are a statutory right created by the legislature, the Texas Supreme Court reasoned that the legislature could statutorily modify the claim as it saw fit without violating the open courts provision.[111] Similarly, in *Thomas v. Oldham*, the court held that limitations on claims against municipalities under the Texas Tort Claims Act did not implicate the open courts provision because at common law municipalities performing governmental functions

---

[108]*See, e.g.*, Kruszewski v. Liberty Mut. Ins. Co., 653 So. 2d 935, 937-38 (Ala. 1995) (upholding workers' compensation scheme); Eller v. Shova, 630 So. 2d 537, 542 (Fla. 1993) (same); *In re* Abbott, 653 A.2d 1113, 1116 (N.H. 1995) (same).

[109]893 S.W.2d 504, 521 (Tex. 1995).

[110]801 S.W.2d 841, 842 (Tex. 1990).

[111]*Id.* at 845; *accord* Horizon/CMS Healthcare Corp. v. Auld, 34 S.W.3d 887, 903-04 (Tex. 2000); Bala v. Maxwell, 909 S.W.2d 889, 893 (Tex. 1995).

were completely immune from liability.[112]

The Constitutionality of Damages Caps in Other States: As discussed in *Lucas*, sister state courts have divided on the constitutionality of medical malpractice damages caps. Some decisions have upheld such caps against state constitutional open courts, separation of powers, due process, equal protection, and right to jury trial challenges.[113] Other courts, however, have held, as the Texas Supreme Court did in *Lucas*, that such legislatively imposed damages caps violate one or more of these constitutional doctrines.[114] Are these divergent results to be expected, or are they further evidence of the indeterminate nature of judicial review of legislation under the open courts provision?

The Continuing Debate Regarding the Effectiveness of Damages Caps: Much of the debate in cases challenging damages caps centers on whether the caps are effective in reducing insurance rates and averting a medical crisis. In *Lucas*, the majority highlighted the Texas Legislature's uncertainty regarding the impact of caps on medical malpractice rates as a reason to invalidate the caps under the state constitution, while Chief Justice Phillips urged that the legislature should be commended for its candor in making this acknowledgment. In the interim since *Lucas* was decided in 1988, the question regarding whether damages caps reduce insurance rates still has not been definitively resolved, although caps appear to be a factor exerting downward pressure on rates.

---

[112]895 S.W.2d 352, 357-58 (Tex. 1995).

[113]*See, e.g.*, Evans v. State, 56 P.3d 1046, 1050-57 (Alaska 2002) (equally divided court); Fein v. Permanente Med. Group, 695 P.2d 665, 681-84 (Cal. 1985); Garhart v. Columbia/Helathone, L.L.C., 95 P.3d 571, 580-81 (Colo. 2004); Kirkland v. Blaine Cnty. Med. Ctr., 4 P.3d 1115, 1116 (Idaho 2000); Johnson v. St. Vincent Hosp., Inc., 404 N.E.2d 585, 602 (Ind. 1980); Miller v. Johnson, 289 P.3d 1098, 1105-08 (Kan. 2012); Butler v. Flint Goodrich Hosp. of Dillard Univ., 607 So. 2d 517, 519-21 (La. 1992); Murphy v. Edmonds, 601 A.2d 102, 114-16 (Md. 1992); Adams v. Children's Mercy Hosp., 832 S.W.2d 898, 905-06 (Mo. 1992); Gourley v. Neb. Methodist Health Sys., Inc., 663 N.W.2d 43, 78 (Neb. 2003); Arbino v. Johnson & Johnson, 880 N.E.2d 420, 439 (Ohio 2007); Judd v. Drezga, 103 P.3d 135, 141 (Utah 2004); Etheridge v. Med. Ctr. Hosps., 376 S.E.2d 525, 529-34 (Va. 1989); Robinson v. Charleston Area Med. Ctr., 414 S.E.2d 877, 883 (W. Va. 1991).

[114]*See, e.g.*, Moore v. Mobile Infirmary Ass'n, 592 So. 2d 156, 171 (Ala. 1991) ($400,000 cap on noneconomic damages in medical malpractice cases violated state jury trial and equal protection guarantees); Atlanta Oculoplastic Surgery, P.C. v. Nestlehutt, 691 S.E.2d 218, 224 (Ga. 2010) ($350,000 cap on noneconomic damages in medical malpractice cases violated state right to jury trial provision); Lebron v. Gottlieb Mem'l Hosp., 930 N.E.2d 895, 908 (Ill. 2010) ($1,000,000 noneconomic damages cap against hospital and $500,000 noneconomic damages cap against physicians violated separation of powers clause of state constitution); Best v. Taylor Mach. Works, 689 N.E.2d 1057, 1064 (Ill. 1997) ($500,000 noneconomic damages cap in negligence and products liability suits violated separation of powers and prohibition on special legislation under state constitution); Watts v. Lester E. Cox Med. Ctrs., 376 S.W.3d 633, 636 (Mo. 2012) ($350,000 noneconomic damages cap infringed on jury's constitutional domain to determine injured party's damages); Brannigan v. Usitalso, 587 A.2d 1232, 1233 (N.H. 1991) ($875,000 cap on noneconomic loss in personal injury action violated state equal protection clause); Arneson v. Olson, 270 N.W.2d 125, 136 (N.D. 1978) ($300,000 medical malpractice cap invalid under federal and state equal protection provisions); Morris v. Savoy, 576 N.E.2d 765, 770-71 (Ohio 1991) ($200,000 cap in medical malpractice cases violated state due process guarantee); Lakin v. Senco Prods., Inc., 987 P.2d 463, 473-75 (Or. 1999) ($500,000 noneconomic damages cap violated state right to jury trial); Sofie v. Fibreboard Corp., 771 P.2d 711, 724 (Wash. 1989) (noneconomic damages cap violated state right to jury trial); Ferdon v. Wis. Patients Comp. Fund, 701 N.W.2d 440, 466-89 (Wis. 2005) ($350,000 cap on noneconomic damages violated state equal protection provision).

A 2003 study from the General Accounting Office determined that, while states with damages caps *tend* to have lower insurance premiums, caps standing alone do not necessarily translate into lower medical malpractice insurance premiums as there are too many intervening factors to establish a direct link.[115] With respect to noneconomic damages caps, an empirical study in 2005 by Professor Catherine Sharkey concluded that such caps do not have a "statistically significant effect on the size of overall compensatory damages verdicts or final judgments."[116] Instead, according to Professor Sharkey, in states with such caps, attorneys often highlight economic damages that are not capped in their cases. Yet the study admittedly did not measure the effect of caps on settlements or on the screening of cases by plaintiffs' attorneys,[117] factors tending to reduce aggregate statewide medical malpractice payments.

In any event, litigation costs and medical malpractice insurance premiums are only a small percentage of the nation's health care costs. The Congressional Budget Office in 2009 determined that medical malpractice insurance premiums, settlements, and judgment awards combined comprised a mere two percent of the nation's health care costs.[118] Yet it has been claimed that the risk of malpractice suits encourages health care providers to practice "defensive medicine," ordering tests with only a minuscule likelihood of being relevant in order to reduce the likelihood of being second guessed in a subsequent malpractice action. Under these circumstances, should the courts allow the legislature to experiment, or should they protect the litigant's right to full redress?

Subsequent Developments Regarding Damages Caps in Texas: In the 2003 legislative session, the Texas Legislature enacted House Bill 4, which, among its many other tort reform measures, limited the awards of noneconomic damages in medical malpractice claims by imposing a $250,000 cap on noneconomic damages against all doctors and health care professionals and by imposing a $250,000 per-facility cap and a $500,000 aggregate cap against health-care facilities.[119] These caps, along with the other reform measures such as medical expert report requirements, stricter liability standards for emergency room physicians, and new standards for recovering health care costs, have been credited by supporters with reducing statewide medical malpractice payments by more than seventy percent and reducing medical malpractice rates by twenty to forty percent.

In order to ensure the constitutionality of the noneconomic damages limitation in light of *Lucas*, the legislature proposed a constitutional amendment that was ratified by Texas voters. This amendment authorized the legislature, notwithstanding any other

---

[115]U.S. GEN. ACCOUNTING OFFICE, MEDICAL MALPRACTICE: IMPLICATION OF RISING PREMIUMS ON ACCESS TO HEALTH CARE, PUB. NO. GAO-03-836 (2003).

[116]Catherine M. Sharkey, *Unintended Consequences of Medical Malpractice Caps*, 80 N.Y.U. L. REV. 391, 396 (2005).

[117]*Id.* at 445-46.

[118]Letter from Douglas W. Elmendorf, Director, Congressional Budget Office, to Senator Orrin G. Hatch (Oct. 9, 2009) (on file at www.cbo.gov). The CBO estimated that the combination of a noneconomic damages cap of $250,000, a punitive damages cap, abolition of the collateral source rule, shorter statute of limitations, and elimination of joint and several liability could reduce malpractice premiums by approximately 10%. *Id.*

[119]*See* TEX. CIV. PRAC. & REM. CODE ANN. § 74.301.

provision of the state constitution, to set by statute "the limit of liability for all damages and losses, however characterized, other than economic damages," including damages for "past, present, and future physical pain and suffering, mental anguish and suffering, loss of consortium, loss of companionship and society, disfigurement, or physical impairment."[120] This amendment is not merely applicable to the medical malpractice caps established in House Bill 4, but also authorizes Texas lawmakers to place limits on noneconomic damages in any civil suit, provided that three-fifths of the members of the legislature agree.[121] However, the amendment only applies to caps on *noneconomic* damages–it does not authorize caps on economic damages similar to that considered in *Lucas*.

Texas appears to be the only state that has a constitutional provision granting the legislature a general power to establish damages caps. The converse is much more common; several states have specific constitutional provisions prohibiting such caps.[122]

Punitive Damages Caps: Do caps on punitive damages violate the open courts provision? The Texas appellate courts that have considered the issue have concluded they do not.[123] What distinction between the purposes of punitive damages and noneconomic damages might justify the disparate treatment?

The Burden of Proof and Other Concerns: The Texas Supreme Court's decisions have been inconsistent with respect to the burden of proof in an open courts challenge, placing the burden on the government in *LeCroy v. Hanlon* and placing the burden on the litigant in *Sax v. Votteler* and *Trinity River Authority*. Which approach is preferable?

Are inconsistencies in Texas cases regarding issues such as the burden of proof, the right at issue, and the appropriate weighing of the competing interests a concern? What about the conflicts in the decisions among the various states? Are there other concerns that might counsel caution before the judiciary employs the open courts provision to invalidate legislation impacting common law remedies, such as the change in the relative importance of common law claims in comparison to statutory claims over the last century?

---

[120]TEX. CONST. art. III, § 66.

[121]*Id.*

[122]ARIZ. CONST. art. II, § 31 ("No law shall be enacted in this state limiting the amount of damages to be recovered for causing the death or injury of any person"); *Id.* art. XVIII, § 6 ("The right of action to recover damages shall never be abrogated, and the amount recovered shall not be subject to any statutory limitation"); ARK. CONST. art. V, § 32 (authorizing the general assembly to enact a worker's compensation scheme but providing "that otherwise no law shall be enacted limiting the amount to be recovered for injuries resulting in death or for injuries to persons or property"); KY. CONST. § 54 ("The General Assembly shall have no power to limit the amount to be recovered for injuries resulting in death, or for injuries to person or property."); PA. CONST. art. III, § 18 (authorizing worker's compensation scheme but providing "in no other cases shall the General Assembly limit the amount to be recovered for injuries resulting in death, or for injuries to persons or property"); WYO. CONST. art. X, § 4 ("No law shall be enacted limiting the amount of damages to be recovered for causing the injury or death of any person"). Two additional states have constitutional provisions preventing limitations on recoverable damages in wrongful death cases. OHIO CONST. art I, § 19a; OKLA. CONST. art. XXIII, §7.

[123]Waste Disposal Ctr., Inc. v. Larson, 74 S.W.3d 578 (Tex. App.–Corpus Christi 2002, no pet.); Seminole Pipeline Co. v. Broad Leaf Partners, 979 S.W.2d 730, 751 (Tex. App.–Houston [14th Dist.] 1998, no pet.).

C. PROHIBITION ON RETROACTIVE LAWS

Article I, section 16 of the Texas Constitution provides: "No bill of attainder, ex post facto law, retroactive law, or any law impairing the obligation of contracts, shall be made." Three of section 16's guarantees are also contained in Article I, Section 10 of the United States Constitution, which has always barred any state from enacting bills of attainder, ex post facto laws, and laws impairing the obligation of contracts.[124] Nevertheless, one of the guarantees of section 16, the prohibition on retroactive laws, is unique to Texas and a few other states, including New Hampshire, Tennessee, Missouri, Georgia, Ohio, Colorado, and Idaho.[125]

What did the Texas framers intend to cover under the retroactive law provision? The framers presumably believed they were protecting something in addition to the protections afforded by the provisions on bills of attainder, ex post fact laws, and laws impairing the obligation of contracts. A bill of attainder is a "trial by legislature," that is, a legislative conviction of a person or group of persons without judicial trial.[126] An ex post facto law is a retroactive criminal or penal law that criminalizes conduct that was legal when performed or increases the punishment for the act from the existing punishment at the time the act was committed.[127] A law impairing the obligation of contracts is a statute specifically directed against the terms of pre-existing contracts without a sufficient police power purpose.[128] What is left to be protected by the retroactivity provision?

Mellinger v. City of Houston, 3 S.W. 249 (Tex. 1887)

STAYTON, J.

[The City of Houston brought an action in 1884 against Mellinger to recover property taxes for the years of 1875-1880 on a piece of property Mellinger purchased in 1881 that was encumbered with a tax lien. Mellinger's defense was that the statute of limitations barred the suit. In 1879, though, the legislature enacted a statute that provided "no delinquent tax-payer shall have the right to plead in any court, or in any manner rely

---

[124]Article I, Section 10 of the United States Constitution provides: "No State shall . . . pass any Bill of Attainder, ex post facto Law, or Law impairing the obligation of Contracts." A separate provision, Article I, Section 9, applies to the federal government and prohibits federal bills of attainder and ex post facto laws. Unlike the rights contained in the Federal Bill of Rights, Article I, Section 10 has always explicitly applied to the states and thus did not have to be incorporated through the Fourteenth Amendment. Thus, these guarantees have been protected since Texas's statehood by both the federal and state constitutions.

[125]See, e.g., COLO. CONST. art. II, §11; GA. CONST. art. I, § 1, para. 10; IDAHO CONST. art. XI, § 12; MO. CONST. art. I, § 13; N.H. CONST. pt. 1, art. 23; OHIO CONST. art. II, § 28; TENN. CONST. art. I, § 20. Although all these provisions prohibit retroactive or retrospective legislation, they differ in whether other types of legislation are also prohibited in the same clause and, if so, which types of legislation.

[126]United States v. Brown, 381 U.S. 437, 442 (1965) (holding federal criminal statute precluding a member of the Communist Party from serving as an officer or employee of a labor union was an unconstitutional bill of attainder).

[127]*See* Calder v. Bull, 3 U.S. (3 Dall.) 386, 390 (1798); Barshop v. Medina Cnty. Underground Water Conserv. Dist., 925 S.W.2d 618, 633 (Tex. 1996) (recognizing "the prohibition against ex post facto laws applies only to retroactive criminal or penal laws").

[128]*See Barshop*, 925 S.W.2d at 634-35.

upon, any statute of limitation by way of defense against the payment of any taxes due from him or her, either to the state, or any county, city, or town." The apparent purpose of the statute was to prevent anyone, including those purchasing property encumbered by a tax lien, from using the statute of limitations as a defense in a suit to recover taxes.

At the time of the 1879 statute, the statute of limitations had expired for the taxes due in 1875 and 1876, but not from the other years. The court's opinion below first concludes that the 1879 statute, by its terms, did not expressly apply retroactively to allow the city to recover the taxes from 1875 and 1876. The court then reasoned, as support for its conclusion, that a contrary interpretation would violate the constitutional prohibition on retroactive laws. While recognizing that the United States Supreme Court had held in *Campbell v. Holt*, 115 U.S. 620 (1885), that the Due Process Clause of the Fourteenth Amendment did not preclude a state from reviving expired statute of limitations, the court rested its holding on the express retroactivity prohibition in the Texas Constitution.]

In the absence of constitutional restrictions upon the subject, it is almost universally accepted as a sound rule of construction that a statute shall have only a prospective operation, unless its terms show clearly a legislative intention that it shall have a retroactive effect. There is nothing in the statute before us to evidence the intention of the legislature to give a strictly retroactive effect to the statute under consideration, and it must be held to be a valid law, governing in all actions brought to recover taxes after its passage, against which some valid defense did not exist at the time it took effect. It is true that the statute does not in terms restrict its operation to such actions as might be founded on causes of action not barred by laws in force at the time of its passage, and that its broad and general language might make it applicable to all actions thereafter brought, even upon causes of action then barred; but, if the statute was in terms such as to require such a construction, we are of the opinion that the constitution of this state forbids such legislation.

The people of this state have provided, in all the state constitutions adopted by them, that 'no bill of attainder, *ex post facto* law, retroactive law, or any law impairing the obligation of contracts shall be made,' (Const. art. 1, § 16;) thus giving protection to rights, by prohibiting the enactment of retroactive laws, which the constitution of the United States does not give in terms.

In the construction of a constitution it is to be presumed that the language in which it is written was carefully selected, and made to express the will of the people, and that in adopting it they intended to give effect to every one of its provisions; and it cannot be presumed that separate and distinct provisions were intended to have the same and no other effect than one of them has, unless the language used, when considered in connection with the whole instrument, shows that this must have been the intention. It cannot be presumed that in adopting a constitution which contained a declaration 'that no retroactive law shall be made,' that it was intended to protect thereby only such rights as were protected by other declarations of the constitution which forbade the making of *ex post facto* laws, laws impairing the obligation of contract, or laws which would deprive a citizen of life, liberty, property, privileges, or immunities otherwise than by due course of the law of the land. [The] clause in the constitution which forbids the making of retroactive laws was intended to give protection to every citizen against the arbitrary exercise of some power not forbidden by the other clauses of the constitution referred to, which might be lawfully exercised but for this prohibition. The making of it evidences an intention to place a further restriction on the power of the legislature; and it must be held to protect every right, although not strictly a right to property, which may accrue under existing laws prior to the passage of any, which, if permitted a retroactive effect, would take away the right. A right has been well defined to be a well-founded claim, and a well-founded claim means nothing more nor less than a claim recognized or secured by law.

Rights which pertain to persons, other than such as are termed natural rights, are essentially the creatures of municipal law, written or unwritten; and it must necessarily be held that a right, in a legal sense, exists, when, in consequence of the existence of given facts, the law declares that one person is entitled to enforce against another a given claim, or to resist the enforcement of a claim urged by another. Facts may exist out of which, in the course of time or under given circumstances, a right would become fixed or vested by operation of existing law, but until the state of facts which the law declares shall give a right comes into existence there cannot be in law a right; and for this reason it has been constantly held that, until the right becomes fixed or vested, it is lawful for the law-making power to declare that the given state of facts shall not fix it, and such laws have been constantly held not to be retroactive in the sense in which that term is used. This has been illustrated by so many decisions, made upon so great a variety of facts, that it has become the settled law of the land. When, however, such a state of facts exists as the law declares shall entitle a plaintiff to relief in a court of justice on a claim which he makes against another, or as it declares shall operate in favor of a defendant as a defense against a claim made against him, then it must be said that a right exists, has become fixed or vested, and is beyond the reach of retroactive legislation, if there be a constitutional prohibition of such laws. This, so far as we have been enabled to ascertain, has been the ruling in every state in this Union which has a constitutional provision in terms forbidding retroactive laws, in which any ruling upon the question has been made.

[The court then addressed decisions from New Hampshire, Tennessee, and Missouri similarly holding or indicating that, once an action is barred by the statute of limitations, a statute reviving the limitations period violated the state constitution's explicit ban on retroactive legislation].

The section of the constitution under consideration was considered in the case of *De Cordova* v. *City of Galveston*, 4 Tex. 480; and, while the facts in that case did not call for the decision of the question before us, it did call for a determination of the character of laws which the constitution forbids. It was said that 'laws are deemed retrospective, and within constitutional prohibition, which by retrospective operation destroy or impair vested rights, or rights to do certain actions, or possess certain things, according to the law of the land, but laws which affect the remedy merely are not within the scope of the inhibition unless the remedy be taken away altogether, or incumbered with conditions that would render it useless or impracticable to pursue it, or if the provisions regulating the remedy be so unreasonable as to amount to a denial of right,–as, for instance, if a statute of limitations applied to existing causes barred all remedy, or did not afford a reasonable period for their prosecution; or if an attempt were made by law, either by implication or expressly, to revive causes of action already barred, such legislation would be retrospective, within the intent of the prohibition, and would therefore be wholly inoperative.' We have no doubt that the law is thus correctly stated.

Notes on Retroactivity Clauses and the Revival of Expired Limitations

Mellinger*'s Holding*: *Mellinger* held that the statute barring the use of a limitations defense by taxpayers against governmental entities seeking delinquent taxes did not apply retroactively to cases in which limitations had already run. In support of this holding, the court reasoned that a contrary construction would run afoul of the state constitutional retroactive law prohibition. Even though the United States Supreme Court held in *Campbell v. Holt* that reviving an expired limitations period did not violate the Fourteenth Amendment's Due Process Clause,[129] *Mellinger* determined that the defendant's right not to be sued on a claim vested once the statutory limitations period for that claim expired. As a result, the legislature could not revive a claim after the limitations period expired, because to do so was retrospective interference with a vested right prohibited by the retroactivity provision.

This basic principle from *Mellinger*–that a statute reviving a claim previously barred by limitations is an unconstitutional retroactive law–has been applied in a number of other Texas cases. The state supreme court held in 1999 that a statute adopting the discovery rule and extending the limitations period for misappropriation of trade secrets from two years to three years violated article I, section 16 when applied to resurrect a claim that previously had been barred by the two-year limitations period.[130] Other Texas decisions have also reached comparable holdings, concluding that the defendant has a vested right protected by the retroactive law provision once the statute of limitations has expired.[131] Moreover, as mentioned in *Mellinger*, other jurisdictions prohibiting retroactive laws have likewise invalidated statutes reviving expired limitations periods,[132] and even a number of states without retroactivity prohibitions have reached similar results despite the United States Supreme Court's continued adherence to the doctrine announced in *Campbell.*[133]

But under these cases, the right does not become vested until the prior statute of limitations has expired–the retroactive laws provision does not bar a state legislature from extending a limitations period for a claim that has not yet been barred by the passage of time.[134] In a similar manner, the legislature may enact statutes granting additional time to file an instrument, record a document, or perfect title without running afoul of the

---

[129] 115 U.S. 620, 628-29 (1885); *accord* Chase Sec. Corp. v. Donaldson, 325 U.S. 304, 312-15 (1945) (reaffirming *Campbell*).

[130] Baker Hughes, Inc. v. Keco R. & D., Inc., 12 S.W.3d 1, 4-5 (Tex. 1999).

[131] *See, e.g.,* Wilson v. Work, 62 S.W.2d 490, 490 (Tex. 1933) (applying longer statute of limitations to previously barred claims violated prohibition on retroactive laws); Cathey v. Weaver, 242 S.W. 447, 453 (Tex. 1922) (same).

[132] *See, e.g.,* Doe v. Roman Catholic Diocese of Jefferson City, 862 S.W.2d 338, 341 (Mo. 1993) (citing cases from other jurisdictions to support its holding that Missouri statute applying a new longer statute of limitations for cases of childhood sexual abuse to actions that were already barred by the prior applicable limitations period violated state prohibition on retrospective laws because the defendant had acquired a vested right to be free from suit once the original limitations period expired).

[133] *See, e.g.,* Johnson v. Lilly, 823 S.W.2d 883, 885 (Ark. 1992); Bd. of Educ. v. Blodgett, 40 N.E. 1025 (Ill. 1895); Wilkes Cnty. v. Forester, 167 S.E. 691, 695 (N.C. 1933).

[134] *See, e.g.,* McCutcheon & Church v. Smith, 242 S.W. 454, 456 (Tex. 1922) (holding that limitations could be extended for subsisting notes that had not previously been barred by limitations).

retroactivity prohibition.[135]

The Scope of the Retroactivity Prohibition: A difficulty confronting the interpretation of retroactivity prohibitions is the potential breadth of the ban. One of the earliest Texas cases considering the clause acknowledged that to invalidate all laws that act on past events would constitute "a latitude of signification which would embarrass legislation on existing or past rights and matters to such an extent as to create inextricable difficulties, and in fact to demonstrate that it was incapable of practical application."[136] Thus, as discussed in the latter parts of *Mellinger*, the courts early in the nineteenth century recognized a distinction between vested rights, which could not be retroactively infringed, and laws merely affecting or regulating the remedy, which could be. Were the court's definitions of rights and remedies in *Mellinger* helpful, or were they circular? Is it possible to distinguish rights from remedies?

In re A.D., 73 S.W.3d 244 (Tex. 2002)

Justice O'NEILL delivered the opinion of the Court.

Until 1997, the Family Code provided that trial courts retain jurisdiction for four years from the time a current child-support obligation ended to enter an order directing the obligor's employer to withhold part of the obligor's wages for delinquent support. *See* Act of July 16, 1989, 71st Leg., 1st C.S., ch. 25, § 29, 1989 Tex. Gen. Laws 74, 87. In 1997, amendments to the Family Code removed this four-year limitation on the court's jurisdiction to order withholding, and also authorized the Attorney General to issue writs of withholding administratively, at any time until all current support and child-support arrearages have been paid. Tex. Fam.Code §§ 158.102, .502.

In this case, the obligor's regular support obligation ended in 1990, and the enforcement period expired in 1994 while the four-year limit was still in effect. In 1998, the Attorney General, acting under the amended statute, issued an administrative writ directing the obligor's employer to withhold a part of the obligor's earnings to satisfy support arrearages. We must decide whether this writ violates the Texas Constitution's prohibition against retroactive laws. TEX. CONST. art. I, § 16. We hold that it does not and reverse the court of appeals' judgment.

I Background

Kenneth and Shirley Davis divorced in 1974. The divorce decree gave Shirley custody of their two children and ordered Kenneth to pay $160 per month in child support until the youngest child turned eighteen. The court did not then order Kenneth's employer to withhold these payments from his wages. In 1974 the Texas Constitution did not allow garnishment to enforce child-support obligations. *See* TEX. CONST. art. XVI, § 28 (amended 1983).

---

[135] *See, e.g.*, Corpus Christi People's Baptist Church, Inc. v. Nueces Cnty. Appraisal Dist., 904 S.W.2d 621, 626 (Tex. 1995) (holding statute that extended the time for determining whether a taxing exemption was warranted was not an unconstitutional retroactive law); *cf.* Beck v. Beck, 814 S.W.2d 745, 748-49 (Tex. 1991) (upholding retroactive amendment to state constitution validating previously voidable contract).

[136] De Cordova v. City of Galveston, 4 Tex. 470 (1849).

Within eight years, Kenneth had missed support payments totaling, with interest, nearly $11,000. The trial court held him in contempt in September 1982. To avoid spending six months in the Jefferson County jail, Kenneth agreed to a payment plan, but he soon resumed violating the court's orders. After September 1983, Kenneth neither made support payments nor fulfilled the payment plan that had ostensibly been a condition of his probated contempt punishment. When his youngest child turned eighteen in November 1990, Kenneth owed more than $23,000 in past-due support.

Texas voters amended the Texas Constitution in 1983 to allow wage withholding for child-support enforcement. TEX. CONST. art. XVI, § 28. By 1990, the Legislature had amended the Family Code to provide that a court retains jurisdiction to allow judicial wage-withholding orders "if the motion for income withholding is filed before the fourth anniversary of the date . . . the child becomes an adult . . . ." *See* 1989 Tex. Gen. Laws 74, 87. Like an order holding the obligor in contempt, a wage-withholding order is available to remedy past violations of a support order whether or not the court has reduced the delinquent amount to a single, cumulative judgment.

In December 1994, the Attorney General filed a motion to reduce Kenneth's unpaid support to a cumulative judgment. But the Attorney General dismissed the motion after Kenneth pointed out that the four-year limit on the court's jurisdiction for reducing his past-due support to a cumulative judgment had expired in November 1994, four years after his youngest child turned eighteen.

In 1997, the Legislature adopted a statute providing for enforcement of child-support orders by administrative writs of withholding. Tex. Fam.Code § 158.502(a). This statute has no express time limitation on the court's jurisdiction, and provides that the Attorney General may issue an administrative writ "at any time until all current support, including medical support, and child support arrearages have been paid." *Id.* At the same time it adopted the administrative withholding statute, the Legislature removed the four-year time limit for entry of a judicial writ of withholding. *See id.*

By June 1998, interest had increased Kenneth's delinquent support obligation to $41,000. That month, the Attorney General issued an administrative writ directing Kenneth's employer to withhold part of Kenneth's wages to remedy his violation of the court's child-support orders. Kenneth moved to withdraw the writ, arguing that the four-year limit that in 1994 barred a cumulative judgment or a judicial writ of withholding for past-due support barred any later action to collect the delinquent payments. The trial court granted Kenneth's motion and ordered the Attorney General to withdraw the writ. The court of appeals affirmed, holding that Kenneth had a vested right to rely on the time limitations in effect when his support obligation ended and that the Attorney General's administrative writ violated the constitutional ban on retroactive laws. 8 S.W.3d 466, 467. We granted the Attorney General's petition for review to consider the administrative withholding statute's constitutionality when applied to Kenneth's child-support obligations that became unenforceable under prior law.

II Discussion

The court of appeals reached its conclusion that the administrative writ in this case violated the Texas Constitution's ban on retroactive laws by characterizing the former four-year limit on wage-withholding as a statute of limitations, rather than a jurisdictional or remedial provision. Under this reasoning, a statute reviving the obligor's duty after it had expired would be unconstitutional. *See Baker Hughes, Inc. v. Keco R. & D., Inc.,* 12 S.W.3d 1, 4 (Tex.1999). But the court of appeals' characterization is fundamentally flawed. The former four-year limitation was on the court's jurisdiction to order withholding of child-support arrearages, not on the obligation itself.

The Texas Constitution's ban on retroactive laws forbids statutes that "create new obligations, impose new duties, or adopt new disabilities in respect to transactions or considerations past." *Ex parte Abell,* 613 S.W.2d 255, 260 (Tex.1981) (orig.proceeding). An administrative writ of withholding for delinquent child support does not seek to impose a legal liability on the obligor to support his children. Instead, it is one of several methods the Family Code provides as a remedy to secure performance of a previously adjudicated liability. In this case, the administrative writ is a remedy for Kenneth's repeated and continuing violation of the 1974 divorce decree that ordered him to pay specific amounts for his children's support. If a plaintiff sues after the statute of limitations on his or her cause of action has expired, the defendant has no obligation to defend the action on its merits; instead, the defendant has a vested right to judgment in his or her favor. *See Baker Hughes,* 12 S.W.3d at 4. For this reason, we have held in several contexts that a statute extending a cause of action's limitations period cannot apply to revive a suit that would have been time-barred before the new statute of limitations took effect. *See, e.g., id.* at 5; *Mellinger v. City of Houston,* 68 Tex. 37, 3 S.W. 249, 253-55 (1887). Such a statutory change would violate the constitutional prohibition on retroactive laws because it would impair vested, substantive rights and would impose a new obligation on the defendant that related to the defendant's past conduct. *See Mellinger,* 3 S.W. at 253.

The administrative writ at issue in this case, however, imposes no new substantive obligations on Kenneth. The 1974 divorce judgment established Kenneth's obligation to pay, and Shirley's right to receive, $160 per month in child support. The only issue that remained unresolved after 1974 was securing Kenneth's compliance with the court's order. The Attorney General attempted in 1994 to enforce Kenneth's child-support obligations after the period in section 14.41 had expired and before the 1997 amendment, but voluntarily dismissed its action. Had it not done so, the most Kenneth would have been entitled to under the statute was a dismissal for want of jurisdiction; he would not have been entitled, by the statute, to a take-nothing judgment. The 1997 amendment removed the time restriction on the court's enforcement jurisdiction. It did not resurrect dead claims or abolish defenses to such claims. And allowing the Attorney General to issue the writ administratively merely added a different procedural vehicle to secure fulfillment of the existing obligation.

When the Davises divorced in 1974, the only means available to enforce the support order were contempt and a cumulative judgment. Later, the Legislature and Texas voters added wage withholding to the court's enforcement mechanisms, and the court could have used this method to collect Kenneth's overdue support whether or not it existed as a remedy when Kenneth failed to meet his child-support obligations. Now, the Legislature has created another enforcement method, administrative wage withholding, and has made it available regardless of how long an obligor has avoided his court-ordered support duty. The Legislature has thus elected not to reward Davis's sixteen-year refusal to follow the terms of his divorce decree by forever excusing his duty to support his family. The Legislature was free to adopt new remedies for collecting delinquent child support, such as the administrative writ at issue here, and to apply those remedies in cases in which the court's enforcement power had lapsed. The administrative withholding statute, being remedial in nature, does not violate the Texas Constitution's ban on retroactive laws.

Notes on Vested Rights

Rights Versus Remedies and Procedures: When does legislation merely affect a remedy rather than a right? What's the difference between the four-year limit on the trial court's continuing jurisdiction discussed in *In re A.D.* and the statute of limitations in *Mellinger*?

Numerous other Texas cases have considered whether a statute affected a vested right or merely affected a remedy or a procedural matter. In *Ex parte Abell*, the state supreme court addressed whether two former patients suing their psychologist for engaging in sexual relations with them in his office during their psychotherapy treatment had a vested right to obtain an answer to an interrogatory served during discovery.[137] This interrogatory sought the names of any other patients with whom the psychologist had "any sexual contact of any type." The psychologist refused to answer despite being ordered to do so by the trial court, and he was held in contempt. During his habeas appeals, the Texas Legislature enacted a statute providing for the confidentiality of mental health information, which created a new statutory privilege justifying the psychologist's refusal to answer. The plaintiffs sought to avoid the application of this new privilege to their cases by arguing that, because the trial court had ordered the psychologist to answer before the statute was enacted, they had a vested right to the answer that could not be taken away without violating the retroactivity prohibition. But the supreme court held that the change in the governing evidentiary privileges was a matter of procedure rather than a vested right, such that the plaintiffs' right to an answer was "at best a mere expectation based upon the anticipated continuance of existing law."[138] Before reaching this holding, the court provided an overview of prior Texas case law regarding the distinction between vested rights and remedial matters:

> In the protection of vested rights, the courts have held that when the statute of limitations has run on a cause of action, a right to assert that as a defense vests in the defendant and cannot be taken away by legislative enactment. Likewise, the right of a married woman under disabilities of coverture to disavow a voidable contract was held to be vested at the time of the contract and could not be taken away from her by subsequent legislation.
>
> Conversely, retroactive laws have been upheld when no vested substantive right has been impaired but only the procedure or remedy has been changed. In such cases, the change will not affect or invalidate steps

---

[137] 613 S.W.2d 255 (Tex. 1981).

[138] *Id.* at 262-63.

> previously taken in pending litigation, but all subsequent proceedings will be governed by the new statute or rule as of its effective date, provided a reasonable time is afforded in which to act upon the new law. The following changes have been held to be remedial: change of jurisdiction of the court in which the litigation was pending, authorization of additional remedy for collecting past-due child support, repeal prior to filing suit of statute granting statutory cause of action, change of statutory standard of review, change in municipal annexation law, change in statute concerning admissible evidence, amendment requiring suspension of law license during appeal of conviction, change in city ordinance reducing salary of city employee, change in worker's compensation statute for determining average weekly wage, [and] change in statute defining insurable interest. Since in none of these cases was there a savings clause to exempt pending suits, the litigation was governed by the new statute or rule as of its effective date.[139]

While *Abell* thus provided a convenient summary of earlier Texas holdings, a more fundamental question was not definitively resolved: the proper analysis for distinguishing substantive vested rights from procedural or remedial matters. Some commentators have complained that the distinction between rights and remedies in the case law is frequently a conclusion rather than a means of analysis.[140] The few Texas courts that have attempted more specificity have opined that remedial matters pertain to the "practice and procedure by which substantive law is made effective," procedural matters concern all the steps in the litigation process, and substantive matters fix and declare primary rights and the type of remedy for the invasion of these rights.[141] How helpful are these definitions? Is there a better way to distinguish these concepts?

Other jurisdictions with retroactivity prohibitions in their state constitutions also struggle with the distinction between remedies or procedures and rights.[142] And even jurisdictions without a retroactivity prohibition have grappled with this problem in resolving due process and statutory construction issues arising from the retroactive application of a statute.[143] But a consistent approach has not developed.

Vested Rights Versus Expectations: Under a vested rights analysis, even assuming the matter is substantive, an additional hurdle is determining whether the right has become so fixed or certain as to vest. A mere expectation that a law will continue to govern does not satisfy the vested right requirement. As an example, in *Reames v. Police Officers'*

---

[139] *Id.* at 260-61 (citations omitted).

[140] *See, e.g.*, Bryant Smith, *Retroactive Laws and Vested Rights*, 5 TEX. L. REV. 231, 246 (1927).

[141] *See, e.g.*, Villasan v. O'Rourke, 166 S.W.3d 752, 765 (Tex. App.–Beaumont 2005, pet. denied); Blonstein v. Blonstein, 831 S.W.2d 468, 472 (Tex. App.–Houston [14th Dist.] 1992, writ denied).

[142] *See, e.g.*, Colo. Dep't of Social Servs. v. Smith, Harst & Assocs., Inc., 803 P.2d 964, 966-67 (Colo. 1991); Mo. Nat'l Educ. Ass'n v. Mo. State Bd. of Educ., 34 S.W.3d 266, 284-86 (Mo. App. 2000); Doe v. Sundquist, 2 S.W.3d 919, 923-25 (Tenn. 1999).

[143] *See, e.g.*, Edwards v. Lateef, 558 A.2d 1144, 1146-48 (D.C. 1989); *In re* Parsons' Estate, 272 N.W.2d 16, 17-19 (Iowa 1978); State Dep't of Envtl. Prot. v. Ventron Corp., 468 A.2d 150, 163-64 (N.J. 1983).

Pension Board of Houston, the Fourteenth Court of Appeals considered whether a city ordinance restructuring the divisions within the Houston Police Department could bar a retired police officer from continuing to obtain his retirement pension that he had been receiving before the restructuring while he was employed by another department.[144] The court of appeals determined that, although the ordinance was substantive as it barred the officer from obtaining the pension, it did not impair a vested right because the Texas Supreme Court had held in an earlier case that a pensioner's right to receive monthly payments from a government pension fund was subordinate to the legislature's right to abolish the fund.[145] The Texas Supreme Court had explained that a pensioner merely had an expectancy predicated on his anticipation that existing law would continue rather than a vested right to receive the funds.[146] Thus, a right cannot vest unless there is a legal entitlement to the present or future enforcement of the right. And even rights that have vested are subject to legislative modification in some situations.

Texas Water Rights Commission v. Wright, 464 S.W.2d 642 (Tex. 1971)

POPE, Justice.

This case presents the question of the constitutionality of Article 7519a, which authorizes the cancellation of water permits upon proof of ten continuous years of non-use. The Texas Water Rights Commission, after a hearing, cancelled two water permits owned by L. A. Wright, Myrlee Wright McNary, and George T. McNary, hereafter called permittees. On appeal, the District Court of Travis County rendered judgment that the order cancelling the permits was supported by substantial evidence. The court of civil appeals reversed that judgment, holding that Article 7519a is a retroactive law which violates Article I, Section 16 of the Texas Constitution. We reverse.

The parties are in agreement concerning the facts essential to our opinion. Permit No. 260 was granted in 1918, Permit No. 1083 was granted in 1928, and the permittees have succeeded to the rights under the permits. These permits authorized the permittees to divert water for irrigation purposes from the Rio Grande River at a particular point on the left bank of the river. The permits were used and exercised in conformity with statutory requirements until 1954, when a flood washed out the pumps located at the authorized point of diversion. These pumps were not replaced and no water has been diverted through the authorized diversion point from 1954 to the present time.

In 1957, the Texas Legislature enacted Article 7519a. The effective date of the statute was August 21, 1957. On February 27, 1967, the Texas Water Rights Commission, acting pursuant to the statute, gave the permittees notice of a hearing to cancel their permits. After a hearing on May 2, 1967, the Commission ordered the cancellation of the two permits in question.

The 1918 and 1928 water permits were issued under the permit system established by the Water Act of 1913, as amended by the Water Act of 1917. Section 46 of the 1917

---

[144] 928 S.W.2d 628 (Tex. App.–Houston [14th Dist.] 1996, no writ).

[145] *Id.* at 631-32 (citing City of Dallas v. Trammell, 101 S.W.2d 1009, 1012-13 (Tex. 1937)).

[146] *Trammell*, 101 S.W.2d at 1012-13.

Act, codified as Article 7544, provided that water permits were subject to forfeiture when water use was "willfully abandoned during any three successive years." It was held in City of Anson v. Arnett, 250 S.W.2d 450 (Tex.Civ.App.1952, writ ref. n.r.e.), that to establish willful abandonment of a water permit required proof, not only of non-use, but also of the subjective intent of the permittee to abandon the permit. Basically, the permittees contend that this status of the law fixed their rights under the permits. They contend that Article 7519a would operate retroactively upon their vested rights by changing the law and fixing a new basis for the forfeiture of their permit rights.

Permittees' argument that their grants of water permits were grants of vested rights is supported by a number of Texas precedents. Justice McClendon in Clark v. Briscoe Irr. Co., 200 S.W.2d 674 (Tex.Civ.App.1947, no writ) thoroughly examined the law of appropriation rights and directly held that a water right, when acquired and perfected, constituted a vested right to the use of the water appropriated. In our opinion, a matured appropriation right to water is a vested right. However, the right which one obtains by a water permit for appropriated waters is a right which is limited to beneficial and non-wasteful uses. Permittees at no time were vested with the right of non-use of the water for an indefinite period of time.

We thus confront the contention of the permittees and the basic holding of the court of civil appeals that Article 7519a is a retroactive law and invalid. The Texas Constitution, unlike the Federal Constitution, has a specific prohibition against retroactive laws. The provision in the State Constitution broadly protects rights, although they may not be rights in property. A right has been defined to be "a well-founded claim, and a well-founded claim means nothing more nor less than a claim recognized or secured by law." Mellinger v. City of Houston, 68 Tex. 37, 3 S.W. 249 (1887). Permittees urge that Article 7519a is invalid because it nullifies their vested rights.

We recognize that both in its language and in the manner in which it was applied in this case, Article 7519a has a retroactive effect. It is retroactive in two respects. First, it has a definite impact on rights created before the effective date of the statute. Second, it is retroactive in the sense that it authorizes the Water Rights Commission to take into consideration conduct, or more specifically non-conduct, taking place prior to the statute's effective date. The notice and hearing given by the Commission both occurred less than ten years after the effective date of the statute. As a consequence, some six months of the ten-year span of non-use resulting in forfeiture of the permits occurred prior to the statute's effective date.

Mere retroactivity is not sufficient to invalidate a statute. The fact that a statute authorizes the consideration of events that occurred prior to the effective date of the statute does not compel disapproval of the enactment, provided the affected parties were afforded a reasonable time to protect their interests. Cf. Bunn v. City of Laredo, 208 S.W. 675 (Tex.Civ.App.1919), affirmed, 245 S.W. 426 (Tex.Com.App.1922, jdgmt. adopted). Most statutes operate to change existing conditions, and it is not every retroactive law that is unconstitutional.

Instances of what is permissible retroactive legislation and what is not have been catalogued in a variety of ways. Retroactive laws have been upheld if the change is called a remedy, and denied if it is a right. As Justice Bradley said in Campbell v. Holt, 115 U.S. 620 (1885), "Remedies are the life of rights." While our precedents recognize and apply the distinction, they also recognize that the two terms are often inseparable. Other cases permit retroactive operation of statutes upon non-vested or inchoate rights, but not upon rights which are vested, or as defined in Mellinger, supra, a well-founded claim.

These efforts to catalogue cases have provided some aid as well as confusion in the decisions. See Smith, Retroactive Laws and Vested Rights, 5 Tex.L.Rev. 231, 244 (1927). A number of scholars have endeavored to discover the underlying rationale for the cases which either uphold or strike down a statute which is attacked as unconstitutionally retroactive. One has said that "the most important single inquiry to be made, from the standpoint of the individual and aside from the public interest, is whether the retroactive law gives effect to or defeats the bona fide intentions or reasonable expectations of the persons affected, * * *." Smith, Retroactive Laws and Vested Rights, 6 Tex.L.Rev. 409, 427 (1928). Another has said that the common characteristic in the cases holding a statute invalid is the element of surprise, by which a person has changed his position or omitted to change it in reliance upon the law in force. Stimson, Retroactive Application of Law–A Problem in Constitutional Law, 38 Mich.L.Rev. 30 (1939). Still another has said, "Where a statute has become a likely basis for substantial reliance by people who may have changed their positions to reap its benefits, the policy against retroactive change is strong." Greenblatt, Judicial Limitations on Retroactive Civil Legislation, 51 Nw.L.Rev. 540, 566 (1956).

When we measure the impact of Article 7519a on the permittees' rights to water usage by the cases and standards stated above, we conclude that the retroactive effects of the statute do not require its invalidation. We conclude that the permittees could reasonably expect that their rights would be subjected to a remedy enforcing the conditions inherently attached to those rights and enabling the state to assert and protect its own rights and interests in the water. They knew their permits were only usufructuary and that the State was charged by the Constitution to conserve its water. Moreover, the permittees were afforded a reasonable time after the enactment of Article 7519a in which to put their system into operation and to preserve their rights. The Commission did not institute proceedings until nine and one-half years after the effective date of Article 7519a and their permits were valid until the State instituted its proceedings and obtained an order of cancellation. The court of civil appeals found as a fact that there was a total non-use of the water continuously during the full ten-year period prior to the institution of the cancellation proceedings. The fact that six months of the ten-year period is drawn from the time antecedent to the statute's effective date does not defeat the fair notice to which the permittees were entitled.

Notes on the Opportunity to Preserve Rights

Wright*'s Holding*: In what two respects was article 7519a retroactive? Why didn't this retroactivity invalidate the statute? What characteristics does *Wright* indicate are important for ascertaining whether a law is retroactive? Is examining settled expectations and reliance interests a better methodology than a categorical evaluation of "vesting"?

An Adequate Time to Preserve Rights: The plaintiffs in *Wright* had nine and a half years to protect their rights by beginning to withdraw water again. The court therefore had little trouble in concluding this was a reasonable time to protect their interests, preventing the retroactive effects of the statute from being unconstitutional. But how long is a reasonable period of time? Does it depend on the circumstances?

In *City of Tyler v. Likes*, the Texas Supreme Court held that a 1987 amendment to the Texas Tort Claims Act which barred claims against municipalities for the operation and maintenance of storm sewers was not unconstitutionally retroactive as applied to Likes' common law claims that accrued in April 1986.[147] The court, following *Wright*, reasoned that Likes had a reasonable time to preserve her rights after the accrual of her cause of action in April 1986 before the amendment went into effect on September 1, 1987. Additionally, Likes had more than two months to file suit after the governor signed and the legislature passed the amendment in mid-June before it went into effect in September. While recognizing that the new statute affected her remedy, the court noted that the legislature can affect a remedy without violating the retroactivity ban if it provides a reasonable time or fair opportunity to preserve the claimant's rights.[148]

The Fifth Circuit then followed *Likes* in *Burlington Northern & Santa Fe Railway Co. v. Poole Chemical Co.*[149] The federal court reasoned that a statute of repose that applied to claims that arose from events occurring before the statute became effective was not unconstitutionally retroactive under the Texas Constitution when the company had nine months after the rupture of the storage tank, and almost two months after the effective date of the statute, to file its claim before being barred by the new fifteen-year period of repose.

Yet providing an adequate time to preserve rights is not the only means to circumvent the retroactivity provision. In the following case, the court employed another approach as the law under consideration did not provide any time whatsoever to preserve the claimant's rights.

Barshop v. Medina County Underground Water Conservation District, 925 S.W.2d 618 (Tex. 1996)

Justice ABBOTT delivered the opinion for a unanimous Court.

This case concerns water rights in Texas. The clash between the property rights of landowners in the water beneath their land and the right of the State to regulate water for the benefit of all is more than a century old. This case presents another chapter in this ongoing battle.

Historically, landowners have had property rights in the water beneath their land. Over time, however, the State has increasingly attempted to regulate water usage and its withdrawal from the ground. Indeed, the State has the responsibility under the Texas Constitution to preserve and conserve water resources for the benefit of all Texans [under] Article 16, section 59 of the Texas Constitution. Pursuant to this constitutional authority,

---

[147] 962 S.W.2d 489, 502 (Tex. 1997).

[148] *Id.*

[149] 419 F.3d 355, 359-60 (5th Cir. 2005).

the Legislature enacted the Edwards Aquifer Act and created the Edwards Aquifer Authority. Plaintiffs claim that the Act violates their right to withdraw water from their property.

The Act establishes a conservation and reclamation district named the Edwards Aquifer Authority to regulate groundwater withdrawals by well from the aquifer. The Act imposes an aquifer-wide cap on water withdrawals by non-exempt wells of 450,000 acre-feet of water per year through the year 2007 and 400,000 acre-feet per year thereafter. The Authority will allocate these caps among wells by a permit system. The permit system established by the Act gives preference to "existing users." The Act defines "existing users" as those persons who withdrew and beneficially used underground water from the aquifer on or before June 1, 1993. The Authority will grant regular permits only to existing users who properly file a declaration of historical use and who can establish, by convincing evidence, beneficial use of the water withdrawn between June 1, 1972 and May 31, 1993. The Act requires existing users to file this declaration of historical use on or before March 1, 1994. Until regular permits are granted, existing users can withdraw and beneficially use water, provided it is not wasted.

The Act entitles an existing user to a permit for an amount of water equal to the user's maximum beneficial use of water during any one calendar year of the historical period, unless the sum-total amount of such use throughout the aquifer exceeds 450,000 acre-feet. If this occurs, the Authority is required to adjust proportionately the amount of water authorized for withdrawal under the permits to meet the cap.

The Act was originally passed on May 30, 1993, and was to take effect September 1, 1993. However, it did not become effective then because the United States Department of Justice refused to give administrative preclearance to the Act under section 5 of the Voting Rights Act due to the appointment method of selecting the board of directors for the Authority. In response, the Legislature amended the Act in May 1995, changing the board's selection method from appointive to elective. In August 1995, the Department of Justice precleared the amended Act.

The amended Act was to be effective August 28, 1995. However, six days before the effective date, Plaintiffs brought this lawsuit to restrain the administration and enforcement of the Act. The district court held the Act unconstitutional and enjoined the State from enforcing the Act.

* * * *

VIII

Plaintiffs urge that the Act is a retroactive law in violation of the Texas Constitution. Under our state charter, retroactive laws affecting vested rights that are legally recognized or secured are invalid. *See Texas Water Rights Comm'n v. Wright,* 464 S.W.2d 642, 648-49 (Tex.1971). Plaintiffs maintain that the Act is retroactive because the amount of water a landowner is allowed to withdraw is determined from action or inaction taken before the passage, signing, or effective date of the Act.

Plaintiffs are correct that the Act may have retroactive effects. This Court recognized in *Wright* that a statute which allows an agency to take into consideration conduct occurring before the effective date of the statute possesses a retroactive effect. 464 S.W.2d at 648. The Edwards Aquifer Act, similar to the statute in *Wright* that was held to be retroactive, takes into account the landowner's use of water in the years preceding the effective date of the legislation in determining future entitlement to water. However, "[m]ere retroactivity is not sufficient to invalidate a statute." *Id.* A valid exercise of the police power by the Legislature to safeguard the public safety and welfare can prevail over a finding that a law is unconstitutionally retroactive. *See Texas State Teachers Ass'n v. State,* 711 S.W.2d 421, 424 (Tex.App.--Austin 1986, writ ref'd n.r.e.)(the rule against retroactive laws is not absolute and should yield to a state's right to safeguard the public safety and welfare); *Ismail v. Ismail,* 702 S.W.2d 216, 222 (Tex.App.--Houston [1st Dist.] 1985, writ ref'd n.r.e.)("overriding public interest" justified the retroactive application of a special class of marital property); *Kilpatrick v. State Bd. of Registration for Professional Eng'rs,* 610 S.W.2d 867, 871 (Tex.Civ.App.--Fort Worth 1980, writ ref'd n.r.e.)(concern for public safety and welfare can override retroactive law prohibition). We agree with the reasoning of these decisions.

The Act provides that the Authority is "required for the effective control of the [aquifer] to protect terrestrial and aquatic life, domestic and municipal water supplies, the operation of existing industries, and the economic development of the state." Act of May 30, 1993, *supra,* § 1.01. The Legislature also found that the aquifer was "vital to the general economy and welfare of this state." Based on these legislative findings, we conclude that the Act is necessary to safeguard the public welfare of the citizens of this state. Accordingly, the retroactive effect of the statute does not render it unconstitutional.

Plaintiffs argue, however, that our holding in *Wright* that the statute at issue was constitutional was premised on the fact that the statute provided the affected parties a reasonable time to protect their interests. *Wright,* 464 S.W.2d at 648. Plaintiffs point out that the Edwards Aquifer Act, in contrast, does not allow them a reasonable time to protect their interests since the historical use period ended the day after the Legislature passed the Act. While *Wright* was indeed based on the provisions in the statute providing time for the landowners to protect their interests, it does not address the issue of whether the prohibition against retroactive laws precludes the Legislature from enacting statutes that are necessary to safeguard the public safety and welfare. We conclude that article I, section 16 does not absolutely bar the Legislature from enacting such statutes. *Wright* therefore does not lead to the conclusion that the Act is an unconstitutional retroactive law.

Notes on Countervailing Governmental Interests

The Scope of the Retroactivity Prohibition: *Barshop* provided another method for upholding a statute's constitutionality against a retroactivity challenge in those cases in which retroactive application was necessary to safeguard the public welfare. As a result, a statute could be upheld against a retroactivity challenge under any one of the following circumstances: (1) the challenged legislation impacted a matter of remedy or procedure rather than a substantive right, (2) the claimant did not have sufficiently settled expectations in the alleged right, (3) the legislation provided an adequate time to protect any reasonable expectations of the claimant, or (4) the legislation was necessary to safeguard the public safety and welfare.

With all these avenues to circumvent the retroactivity provision, Texas courts rarely invalidated statutes as unconstitutionally retroactive. In fact, the courts before 2010 only employed the provision against the following categories of statutes: (1) statutes reviving a previously expired limitations period, as discussed in *Mellinger* and its progeny; (2) statutes interfering with a prior final judgment, typically one adjudicating property rights;[150] and (3) statutes applying a new ground for terminating the constitutionally protected parent-child relationship applying to past legal conduct that did not threaten the child's welfare.[151]

Balancing the Competing Interests: What guidance did the court in *Barshop* provide on ascertaining whether a statute overcomes the prohibition on retroactive laws because it is necessary to safeguard the public safety and welfare? Is a rational basis test or a more searching inquiry appropriate?

Texas cases after *Barshop* continued to hold that a police power need to protect the public safety and welfare could override the retroactivity clause.[152] The vast majority of other states with similar prohibitions likewise weigh governmental interests in evaluating the constitutionality of retroactive statutes.[153] Such cases typically balance the competing governmental and individual interests without specifying a particular level of scrutiny, just as in the open courts cases. But the Texas Supreme Court took a different approach–and may have reinvigorated the retroactivity prohibition in the process–in the following case.

Robinson v. Crown Cork & Seal Co., 335 S.W.2d 156 (Tex. 2010)

Justice HECHT delivered the opinion of the Court, in which Chief Justice JEFFERSON, Justice MEDINA, Justice GREEN, Justice WILLETT, and Justice LEHRMANN joined.

The issue we address in this case is whether a statute that limits certain corporations' successor liability for personal injury claims of asbestos exposure violates the prohibition against retroactive laws contained in article I, section 16 of the Texas

---

[150] *See, e.g.*, Jenckes v. Mercantile Nat'l Bank, 407 S.W.2d 260, 264-65 (Tex. Civ. App.–Dallas 1966, writ ref'd n.r.e.) (invalidating retroactive application of statute that interfered with vested rights in a certificate created by an earlier final judgment); *cf.* R.R. Comm'n v. Pend Oreille Oil & Gas Co., 817 S.W.2d 36, 47 (Tex. 1991) (recognizing that a Railroad Commission forced pooling order that becomes effective before the order is signed can be a retroactive interference with vested property rights obtained under then-existing commission orders).

[151] *See, e.g., In re* Shaw, 966 S.W.2d 174, 180 (Tex. App.–El Paso 1998, no pet.) (holding that retroactive application of constructive abandonment termination ground was an unconstitutional interference with vested rights in parent-child relationship); *In re* R.A.T., 938 S.W.2d 783, 784 (Tex. App.–Eastland 1997, writ denied) (same). However, retroactive applications of termination grounds were authorized when necessary to safeguard the public welfare and advance the public interest. *See, e.g., In re* A.V., 113 S.W.3d 355, 361 (Tex. 2003) (holding termination for incarceration for more than two years could be retroactively applied due to the "State's duty to protect the safety and welfare of its children").

[152] *See, e.g., In re* A.V., 113 S.W.3d at 36; *In re* E.M.N., 221 S.W.3d 815, 822 (Tex. App.–Fort Worth 2007, no pet.).

[153] *See, e.g.*, Van Sickle v. Boyes, 797 P.2d 1267, 1270-71 (Colo. 1990); Hayes v. Howell, 308 S.E.2d 170, 175-76 (Ga. 1983); Hayes v. LeBlanc, 316 A.2d 187, 189 (N.H. 1974); Doe v. Sundquist, 2 S.W.3d 919, 924 (Tenn. 1999).

Constitution as applied to a pending action. We hold that it does.

I

In 2002, petitioner Barbara Robinson ("Robinson") and her husband, John, Texas residents, filed suit alleging that John, age 63, had contracted mesothelioma from workplace exposure to asbestos products. As often happens, John had used several such products over the course of his life, and the Robinsons sued twenty-one defendants, including respondent Crown Cork & Seal Co., alleging that they were all jointly and severally liable. With respect to Crown, the Robinsons claimed that during John's service in the United States Navy from 1956 to 1976, he worked with asbestos insulation manufactured by the Mundet Cork Corporation, and that when Crown and Mundet merged, Crown succeeded to Mundet's liabilities.

Crown has never itself engaged in the manufacture or sale of asbestos products. It manufactures metal bottle-caps and other packaging for consumer goods. In November 1963, Crown's predecessor, a New York corporation with the same name, which was then the nation's largest manufacturer of crowns, acquired a majority of the stock in Mundet, another New York corporation, which besides insulation, also manufactured crowns. Within ninety days, in February 1964, Mundet sold all its assets related to its insulation business. Two years later, in February 1966, the companies merged. In 1989, Crown's predecessor was reincorporated as Crown, a Pennsylvania corporation.

Crown acknowledges that under New York and Pennsylvania law, it succeeded to Mundet's liabilities, which, as pertaining to Mundet's asbestos business, have been hefty. Over the years, Crown has been named in thousands of lawsuits claiming damages from exposure to asbestos manufactured by Mundet. While Crown acquired Mundet for only about $7 million, by May 2003 Crown had paid over $413 million in settlements, and Crown's parent company estimated in its 2003 Annual Report that payments could reach $239 million more. Mundet's aggregate insurance coverage totaled $3.683 million.

At first, Crown did not contest its successor liability to the Robinsons for any compensatory damages; consequently, the trial court granted the Robinsons' motion for partial summary judgment on that issue. But about the same time, the Texas Legislature enacted Chapter 149 of the Texas Civil Practice and Remedies Code, which limits certain corporations' successor liability for asbestos claims. Chapter 149 applies (with exceptions not relevant here) to "a domestic corporation or a foreign corporation that has . . . done business in this state and that is a successor which became a successor prior to May 13, 1968" – a date by which, the Legislature appears to have thought, the dangers of asbestos should have been commonly known. For a covered corporation (again with some exceptions not relevant here), "the cumulative successor asbestos-related liabilities . . . are limited to the fair market value of the total gross assets of the transferor determined as of the time of the merger or consolidation." By restricting application of the cap to a corporation that had never engaged in selling asbestos products itself and had succeeded to another's liability for asbestos claims at a time when the extent of that liability was not fully appreciated, the supporters of Chapter 149 intended to protect what they called the "innocent successor."

Chapter 149 contains a choice-of-law provision, making it applicable, "to the fullest extent permissible under the United States Constitution, . . . to the issue of successor asbestos-related liabilities" in Texas courts. Furthermore, the Legislature made Chapter 149 applicable to all actions:

> (1) commenced on or after the effective date of this Act; or
> (2) pending on that effective date and in which the trial, or any new trial or retrial following motion, appeal, or otherwise, begins on or after that effective date.

Because the Act of which Chapter 149 was part, House Bill 4, passed by more than a two-thirds vote in both the House and Senate, it took effect immediately on approval by the Governor.

Crown promptly moved for summary judgment under the new law, requesting that the prior order establishing its successor liability to the Robinsons be vacated and that their claims for asbestos exposure be dismissed. The trial court granted Crown's motion. Days later, John Robinson died. Barbara Robinson amended her petition to assert statutory wrongful death and survival actions against Crown and the other defendants still remaining in the case. (Several defendants had settled for amounts totaling $859,067 and been dismissed.) Without addressing these statutory actions, Crown moved to sever the summary judgment to make it final and appealable, and the trial court granted the motion.

On appeal, Robinson contends that Chapter 149 is a retroactive law prohibited by article I, section 16 of the Texas Constitution. [The Houston Fourteenth Court of Appeals disagreed in a divided opinion. The Austin Court of Appeals came to a contrary result in a similar case against Crown. The Texas Supreme Court granted review.]

II

As a threshold matter, it is important to note the precise issue before us. The Robinsons' pleading on which Crown moved for summary judgment asserted common-law causes of action for negligence and strict liability, and claimed compensatory and punitive damages. Had John lived, the summary judgment would have disposed of all the Robinsons' claims against Crown. But John died a few days after summary judgment was granted, and Robinson amended her petition to add statutory wrongful death and survival actions. The record does not reflect that Crown moved for summary judgment on Robinson's statutory claims, or that the trial court ever disposed of them specifically. The trial court and parties appear to have assumed, correctly, that the summary judgment was nevertheless final because Robinson's statutory claims are wholly derivative of John's common-law claims, and the adjudication of the latter effectively disposed of the former.

But even though the summary judgment was final, an analysis of the retroactive effect of Chapter 149 on common-law claims and statutory claims presents different considerations. As we discuss more fully below, Crown argues that in determining whether the constitutional prohibition against retroactive laws applies in this case, it is significant that successor liability is a creature of statute. The same argument could be made to Robinson's wrongful death and survival claims, though not to the common-law claims the Robinsons previously asserted. Also, Robinson argues that it is important for our constitutional analysis that the common-law claims barred by Chapter 149 had both accrued and were the subject of a pending lawsuit before the statute was enacted. But neither is true of her statutory claims.

The parties have not briefed–or even mentioned–any of these issues but have confined their arguments regarding whether Chapter 149 is an unconstitutionality retroactive law as applied to the common-law claims the Robinsons asserted before John's death, which were adjudicated by summary judgment. These arguments are the only ones we address. We intimate no view on whether Chapter 149 limits Robinson's statutory wrongful death and survival claims except insofar as they are derivative of the claims specifically adjudicated by the trial court.

III

Before we can decide whether Chapter 149 is unconstitutionally retroactive, we must first resolve the parties' dispute over the proper standards to be applied in making that determination. Robinson argues that the test is simply whether vested rights have been impaired, period; if so, the law is prohibited, regardless of the Legislature's reasons for enacting it. Crown counters that the [correct focus is] instead on the reasonableness of the Legislature's exercise of its police power; the prohibition against retroactive laws does not invalidate a proper exercise of that power despite its impairment of private rights. As each position finds support in our case law, we begin by returning to first principles.

A.

There exists in this country, as the United States Supreme Court observed in *Landgraf v. USI Film Products,* a "presumption against retroactive legislation [that] is deeply rooted in our jurisprudence and embodies a legal doctrine centuries older than our Republic.... [T]he 'principle that the legal effect of conduct should ordinarily be assessed under the law that existed when the conduct took place has timeless and universal human appeal.'" In a concurring opinion in an earlier case, Justice Scalia noted that this principle

> was recognized by the Greeks, by the Romans, by English common law, and by the Code Napoleon. It has long been a solid foundation of American law. . . . Justice Story said that "retrospective laws are . . . generally unjust; and . . . neither accord with sound legislation nor with the fundamental principles of the social compact."

The United States Constitution does not expressly prohibit retroactive laws, but "the antiretroactivity principle finds expression" in its prohibitions of bills of attainder, ex post facto laws, and state laws impairing the obligation of contracts. Texas Constitutions have contained these provisions as well as a general prohibition against retroactive or retrospective laws. This prohibition against retroactive laws, like other constitutional bars, must be governed by its purpose, for "retroactive" simply means "[e]xtending in scope or effect to matters which have occurred in the past; retrospective," and "retrospective," even more simply, means "[d]irected to, contemplative of, past time."

The presumption against retroactivity has two fundamental objectives identified by the Supreme Court in *Landgraf.* First, it protects the people's reasonable, settled expectations. In other words, the rules should not change after the game has been played. Second, the presumption against retroactivity protects against abuses of legislative power. Constitutional provisions limiting retroactive legislation must therefore be applied to achieve their intended objectives–protecting settled expectations and preventing abuse of legislative power.

B.

[The Court began with a review of its earlier cases on retroactivity and their reliance on a "vested rights" test. The Court highlighted the inconsistencies in ascertaining what was and was not a vested right before concluding:]

What constitutes an impairment of vested rights is too much in the eye of the beholder to serve as a test for unconstitutional retroactivity. This can hardly be more vividly demonstrated than in today's opinions by JUSTICE WAINWRIGHT and JUSTICE MEDINA. The arguments and authorities ably marshaled in each show a deep division over whether a retroactive restriction on a cause of action impairs vested rights. Of course it does, if a claim, no matter how flimsy, is a vested right; or not, if a claim, even a strong one, must be reduced to judgment before it becomes a vested right. The dispute over whether to call something a vested right appears driven not so much by what the words mean as by the consequence of applying the label–that its impairment is prohibited. The "impairs vested rights" test thus comes down to this: a law is unconstitutionally retroactive if it takes away what should not be taken away.

C.

In two cases this Court has held that retroactive laws were not constitutionally prohibited, despite their impairment of vested rights, because they were each a valid exercise of the Legislature's police power. [These cases] do not except a retroactive law from the constitutional prohibition merely because there was a rational basis for its enactment, or even because, on balance, it is likely to do more good than harm. The Legislature found the water-permitting scheme established in the Edwards Aquifer Act to be necessary to discharge its constitutional duty to conserve groundwater, and the necessity of providing for the welfare of children of incarcerated convicts is too obvious to require justification. But necessity alone cannot justify a retroactive law. The retroactive laws in *Barshop* and *A.V.* were not unconstitutional because they did not defeat the objectives of the constitutional prohibition. There can be no settled expectation that a limited resource like groundwater, affected by public and private interests, will not require allocation, or that a person unable to care for his children has greater rights if his inability is due to prolonged incarceration than for other reasons. And in both cases, the Legislature acted for the general public good.

D.

We think our cases establish that the constitutional prohibition against retroactive laws does not insulate every vested right from impairment, nor does it give way to every reasonable exercise of the Legislature's police power; it protects settled expectations that rules are to govern the play and not simply the score, and prevents the abuses of legislative power that arise when individuals or groups are singled out for special reward or punishment. No bright-line test for unconstitutional retroactivity is possible. Rather, in determining whether a statute violates the prohibition against retroactive laws in article I, section 16 of the Texas Constitution, courts must consider three factors in light of the prohibition's dual objectives: the nature and strength of the public interest served by the statute as evidenced by the Legislature's factual findings; the nature of the prior right impaired by the statute; and the extent of the impairment. The perceived public advantage of a retroactive law is not simply to be balanced against its relatively small impact on private interests, or the prohibition would be deprived of most of its force. There must be a compelling public interest to overcome the heavy presumption against retroactive laws. To be sure, courts must be mindful that statutes are not to be set aside lightly. This Court has invalidated statutes as prohibitively retroactive in only three cases, all involving extensions of statutes of limitations. But courts must also be careful to enforce the constitutional prohibition to safeguard its objectives.

Under this test, changes in the law that merely affect remedies or procedure, or that otherwise have little impact on prior rights, are usually not unconstitutionally retroactive. But these consequences of the proper application of the prohibition cannot substitute for the test itself. The results in all of our cases applying the constitutional provision would be the same under this test. The cases that considered only whether the challenged statute impaired vested rights implicitly concluded that any impairment did not upend settled expectations and was overcome by the public interest served by the enactment of the statute. And the cases that focused on the propriety of the Legislature's exercise of its police power implicitly concluded that the exercise was not merely reasonable but was compelling, notwithstanding the statute's effect on prior rights.

IV

Using the standards we have set out, we must now determine whether chapter 149 is unconstitutionally retroactive as applied to Robinson.

A.

We first consider the nature of the rights claimed by the Robinsons and Chapter 149's impact on them. Chapter 149 does not directly restrict the Robinsons' common law action for personal injuries due to exposure to asbestos in the workplace. Rather, it supplants the usual choice-of-law rules for determining what state's successor liability law should apply in asbestos cases in Texas by mandating Texas courts to apply Texas law, then for the first time prescribes limits on that liability, even if, as here, successor liability arose under the law of another state. Crown argues that by allowing for an expansion of liability beyond the tortfeasor to include a successor by merger, successor liability is largely remedial in nature, and in any event, is a creature of statute in which there can be neither right nor expectation. Crown cites *Dickson v. Navarro County Levee Improvement District,* where we gave immediate effect to a statute that repealed a special, statutory cause of action. Crown analogizes this case to *Owens Corning,* which upheld the change in Texas law to allow a plaintiff no more time to sue here than he would have had in his state of residence.

But the successor liability in this case is not a creature of Texas law; the parties agree that without Chapter 149, New York or Pennsylvania law would apply, and that under the law of those states, Crown's successor liability is unquestionable. So this is not a case like *Dickson,* in which the Legislature abolished a cause of action it had itself created; Chapter 149 limits liability created under other states' laws. Nor is this a case like *Owens Corning,* in which the Legislature changed the statute of limitations so that a nonresident plaintiff would gain no advantage by suing in Texas rather than in his home state; Chapter 149 disadvantages Texas residents, as well as nonresidents, who sue Crown in Texas rather than New York or Pennsylvania. Nevertheless, Crown has a point that choice-of-law rules are purely procedural and subject to change, often by courts, but certainly by the Legislature if it chooses to do so.

However, Chapter 149 extinguishes the Robinsons' claim and all other such claims against Crown in Texas, and while it does so indirectly, extinction was the Legislature's specific intent. An interest in maintaining an established common-law cause of action is greater than an interest in choice-of-law rules. We have held that an unliquidated personal-injury claim was not a property interest under the common law, but it is now assignable as other property interests. The rights protected by the constitutional prohibition against retroactive laws are no more limited to those recognized at the time the prohibition was adopted than are the rights protected by due course of law. An unliquidated claim may have little or no value, as for example when the cause of action has not been recognized or the elements of recovery cannot be proved. But here, claims like the Robinsons' have become a mature tort, and recovery is more predictable, especially when the injury is mesothelioma, a uniquely asbestos-related disease. Discovery taken in the case shows that the Robinsons' claims had a substantial basis in fact. Their right to assert them was real and important, and it was firmly vested in the Robinsons.

Crown argues that when Mundet was still selling the asbestos insulation to which John Robinson was exposed in ship boiler rooms, the Robinsons could not reasonably have expected Mundet to be able to pay all the claims that would eventually arise, or that the company would merge with a deeper pocket like Crown. But those are not the expectations the prohibition against retroactive laws protects. The Robinsons could well have expected, then as now, that a rule of law that permitted their recovery, and many others' before them, would not be changed after they had filed suit to abrogate their claim.

Crown argues that the Robinsons have alleged that all the defendants they have sued are jointly and severally liable and that they are likely to recover all their damages from those who have already settled and the others than remain. We refuse to speculate about what might happen. If Crown would otherwise be responsible for the Robinsons' injury, then by insulating Crown, Chapter 149 either reduces the recovery to which the Robinsons are entitled or requires the other defendants to pay Crown's share. Either way, the statute disturbs settled expectations. We therefore conclude that Chapter 149 significantly impacts a substantial interest the Robinsons have in a well-recognized common-law cause of action.

B.

We next consider whether Chapter 149 serves the public interest. Crown argues that the statute helps alleviate the asbestos litigation crisis that has already bankrupted many companies, resulting in lost jobs and a burden on the State's economy. The Legislature has recognized the severity of that crisis in another context, but it did not do so in enacting House Bill 4 and Chapter 149. On the contrary, the legislative record is fairly clear that chapter 149 was enacted to help only Crown and no one else. Crown itself has been unable to identify to us any other company affected by Chapter 149. There is evidence that Crown has about 1,000 employees in Texas and about the same number of former employees on retirement, and that it operates three facilities here. Crown asserts that it continues to be sued on asbestos claims in Texas, but the record is silent concerning the number of those claims or the amount of Crown's probable exposure.

The Legislature made no findings to justify Chapter 149. Even the statement by its principal House sponsor fails to show how the legislation serves a substantial public interest. No doubt Texas will benefit from reducing the liability of an employer and investor in the

State, but the extent of that benefit is unclear on this record. And in any event, there is nothing to indicate that it rises to the level of the public interest involved in *Barshop* and *A.V.*

Crown argues that the public interest has been recognized by other states' legislatures in enacting similar legislation. We are aware of ten other state legislatures that have enacted laws similar to chapter 149. In one state, Pennsylvania, the legislation was fully retroactive, just as chapter 149 is, but the Supreme Court of Pennsylvania has held the statute to violate the Open Courts provision of the Pennsylvania Constitution. Statutes adopted in three states–Florida, Indiana, and Wisconsin–apply to pending actions if trial has not commenced. Statutes adopted in three other states–North Dakota, Ohio, and Oklahoma–have the same application *unless it is found to be unconstitutional.* South Carolina's statute applies only to actions filed after the statute's effective date, and Georgia's applies only to actions that accrue after the statute's effective date. The effect of Mississippi's statute on accrued or pending claims is unclear from the text. Other states' perception of the public interest served by retroactive legislation is at best ambiguous.

It is tempting to think that the real burden of Chapter 149 on the Robinsons and other plaintiffs in their shoes will be light compared to the benefit to Crown, its current and former employees, and the State. The Robinsons' case, and most others like it, involves many defendants and large settlements funded from many pockets. The impact of Chapter 149 on individual cases may be slight, relative to the cumulative impact on Crown without Chapter 149. But we think that an important reason for the constitutional prohibition against retroactive laws is to preempt this weighing of interests absent compelling reasons. Indeed, it is precisely because retroactive rectification of perceived injustice seems so reasonable and even necessary, especially when there are few to complain, that the constitution prohibits it.

Accepting the legislative record as indicating the reasons for its actions, we conclude that the public interest served by Chapter 149 is slight.

* * *

For these reasons, we hold that Chapter 149, as applied to the Robinsons' common-law claims, violated article I, section 16 of the Texas Constitution.

Justice MEDINA, concurring.

I join the Court's opinion because I agree that a retroactive law is presumptively "unconstitutional without a compelling justification that does not greatly upset settled expectations" and that no such justification exists here. I agree that Chapter 149 here violates article I, section 16 of the Texas Constitution because it operates to retroactively abolish the Robinsons' vested property rights, or in the words of the Court–"significantly impacts a substantial interest the Robinsons have in a well-recognized common-law cause of action." I write separately because I do not share the Court's disdain for traditional vested rights analysis nor the dissent's view of that analysis. . . .

Justice WAINWRIGHT, joined by Justice JOHNSON, dissenting.

The Legislature enacted Chapter 149 of the Civil Practice and Remedies Code to protect businesses, which acquired other entities, from financial disaster based solely upon the acquired entities' past, discontinued manufacture of asbestos products. The statute limits the liability of the acquiring business, which had not engaged in the asbestos business, to the fair market value of the acquired entity at the time of the acquisition. Through Chapter 149, the Legislature balances limitations on asbestos-related recoveries against protecting the assets and employees of businesses who did not cause the illness, while leaving intact the entirety of potential liability and damages proven against companies that were involved in the asbestos business and are, perhaps, more culpable. The Court's holding that the legislation is unconstitutional prevents the Legislature from addressing an injustice arising from a crisis that caused dozens of bankruptcies and the loss of thousands of jobs in this state and throughout the country due to asbestos-related litigation.

I would hold that an accrued, but unliquidated cause of action is not a vested right because: (1) the framers of the Texas Constitution would not have considered an unliquidated cause of action to be a vested property right entitled to protection under the Retroactivity Clause; (2) a lawsuit is not a right to recover anything but a contingent and unliquidated pursuit of a claimed injury that may or may not be successful; and (3) until and unless a final judgment is rendered in favor of the claimant, there is no right to recover damages on the claim against another. [A] cause of action becomes a "vested right" for the constitutional retroactivity analysis when it has reached a final determination–that is, where it has been reduced to an enforceable judgment in the plaintiff's favor. This rule is most consistent with the understanding of vested property rights at the time of the ratification of the 1876 Constitution. It is consistent with our subsequent interpretation of the words of the Retroactivity Clause. It is consistent with our case law and the great weight of court of appeals opinions. And it is more predictable and avoids confusion and ambiguity when the Legislature attempts to constitutionally craft a law affecting past conduct.

The Robinsons did not have a vested right in their accrued causes of action when Mr. Robinson was diagnosed with mesothelioma. At most, they had contingent belief that they might be able to recover against Crown Cork or the other defendants. At the time Mr. Robinson's cause of action accrued, the Robinsons had not taken any action in reliance on the law at the time, and they had no entitlement to the law as it existed. Even after they filed their action and received a partial summary judgment that Crown Cork was liable as a successor corporation, they had an unliquidated interest in a personal injury tort claim that was not recognized as a property right–vested or otherwise–at common law. The expectation further deteriorated when Mr. Robinson passed away, and Mrs. Robinson asserted new statutory survival and wrongful death claims.

[Even assuming the Robinsons had a vested right,] there are five reasons that Chapter 149 was a legitimate exercise of the police power. The first three demonstrate that the Robinsons' expectations in the continued state of the law, as-applied, are low. The second two demonstrate that the Legislature's exercise of the police power was rational, justifiable, and reasonably limited. First, at common law, Mr. Robinson's claims were not "property," were not assignable, and were extinguished when he passed away. Second, Chapter 149 does not interfere with a claim sounding in contract or a claim for an injury to real or personal property, which was protected much more stringently at common law. Third, Chapter 149, as applied, does not deprive the Robinsons of their cause of action against Crown Cork, and it does not deprive the Robinsons of real and substantial remedies for their alleged wrongs. The Robinsons sued twenty other defendants in this case and recovered approximately $850,000 from a number of the defendants for their injuries. Fourth, the Legislature rationally drew Chapter 149 to address a problem it perceived as very important–the effects on the Texas economy and employment because of the bankruptcy of companies that never manufactured, sold, or distributed asbestos-containing products. Finally, the class of persons protected by the legislation has a rational relation to the legislative purpose of the legislation. Chapter 149 does not violate article I, section 16 of the Texas Constitution.

Notes on the *Robinson* Retroactivity Standard

Robinson*'s Retroactivity Test*: In place of the rather formalistic vested rights analysis, *Robinson* adopted a multi-factor standard that considers the following three factors in light of the retroactivity provision's objectives to protect reasonable, settled expectations and to prevent legislative abuses of power: (1) the nature and strength of the public interest served by the statute as evidenced by the legislature's factual findings; (2) the nature of the prior right impaired by the statute, and (3) the extent of the impairment. The court continued that there must be a "compelling public interest to overcome the heavy presumption against retroactive laws." While the court indicated that "[t]he results in all of our cases applying the constitutional provision would be the same under this test," the court did not provide much guidance regarding how the test would be applied under different circumstances. Indeed, even with respect to the Robinsons' claims, the court only invalidated chapter 149 as applied to the common law claims that were filed and pending before chapter 149 became effective, while expressing no opinion on whether chapter 149 could be applied to the later-asserted statutory wrongful death claims that accrued after the statute became effective.

What are the advantages of the court's new approach in comparison to the court's prior retroactivity jurisprudence? What are the disadvantages? How much guidance did *Robinson* provide to the legislature and to litigants regarding the scope of the retroactivity provision?

Statutory v. Common Law Claims: *Robinson* left open the possibility that the retroactivity provision might apply differently to statutory causes of action. Why might this be the case?

One argument is that the reasonable, settled expectations in a statutory cause of action are less than those for a common law cause of action. Texas courts have long held that the repeal of a statute creating a judicially enforceable right is to be given immediate effect, even to pending cases in the trial and appellate courts, in the absence of a savings clause to the contrary. In *Dickson v. Navarro County Levee Improvement District*, for example, the legislature's repeal–while the case was on appeal–of the statute creating the cause of action resulted in an immediate dismissal.[154] The case involved a statutory cause of action enacted during the 1920s authorizing bondholders of levee improvement districts to sue landowners for delinquent taxes when the district failed to file suit within a specified time period. A bondholder instituted suit under the statute in April 1937 against Dickson and obtained a default judgment. While the case was pending on appeal, the repeal of the statute authorizing such suits became effective. The Texas Supreme Court dismissed the case, holding that "if a statute giving a special remedy is repealed, without a savings clause in favor of pending suits, all suits must stop where the repeal finds them; and, if final relief has not been granted before the repeal goes into effect, it cannot be granted thereafter."[155] This rule from *Dickson* has been reaffirmed several times.[156] Because a statutory cause of action can thus be entirely eliminated at any time before final relief is granted, the reasonable expectations and reliance interests of the claimant are weaker for statutory causes of action than for common law causes of action.

Another argument is that the legislature does not abuse its power by retroactively modifying a cause of action it created. While retroactive interference with a pending common law claim raises the possibility of an abuse of power, the legislature arguably should have more leeway to adjust its own statutory causes of action, just as the courts can retroactively modify the common law.

Robinson did not address these issues, instead only noting that a statutory cause of action "presents different considerations." But a case currently pending before the Texas Supreme Court might provide additional guidance. A plurality of the en banc First Court of Appeals concluded in *Union Carbide Corp. v. Synatzske* that a new statutory requirement, imposed after the death of the decedent, for a pulmonary function test to maintain a statutory wrongful death claim for asbestos-related injuries violated the retroactivity prohibition.[157] The plurality opined that the statutory nature of the asserted cause of action did not impact the retroactivity analysis unless the legislature entirely repealed the cause of action or deprived the judiciary of subject matter jurisdiction. On the other hand, the dissent objected that the statutory nature of the claims "significantly" impacted the analysis. The Texas Supreme Court granted Union Carbide's petition for review and heard oral argument shortly before this book's publication. Under what circumstances (if any) should the court hold that statutory causes of action are subject to retroactivity challenges after *Robinson*?

---

[154] 139 S.W.2d 247 (Tex. 1940).

[155] *Id.* at 259.

[156] *See, e.g.*, Quick v. City of Austin, 7 S.W.3d 109, 125 (1998); Knight v. Int'l Harvester Credit Corp., 627 S.W.2d 382, 384 (Tex. 1982).

[157] 386 S.W.3d 278(Tex. App.–Houston [1st Dist.] 2012, pet. granted).

D. OTHER UNIQUE TEXAS CONSTITUTIONAL RIGHTS PROVISIONS

The Texas Bill of Rights contains a number of other unique provisions not protected by the United States Constitution, including the right to bail, the prohibition against imprisonment for debt, the bans against outlawry and exile, the prevention of monopolies, perpetuities, primogeniture, and entailment, and the rights of crime victims. These rights, though, are not as significant as the guarantees discussed earlier in this chapter, as they either are rarely discussed in judicial decisions or are covered by due process or other federal constitutional principles.

Right to Bail: One unique Texas guarantee of some note, which is also protected by approximately forty other state constitutions, is the right to bail.[158] Section 11 of the Texas Bill of Rights provides that prisoners have a constitutional right to bail, although this right can be denied in certain circumstances, such as in capital offenses with "evident" proof, in cases involving repeat offenders committing felonies, violent offenses, or sexual offenses, and for felons or family violence offenders violating conditions of release implicating the public safety.[159] While the Eighth Amendment to the United States Constitution prohibits excessive bail, it does not specifically require the availability of bail. The Supreme Court has left open the question whether the Eighth Amendment circumscribes congressional power to define the classes of criminal arrestees entitled to bail in the same manner as article I, section 11 limits the Texas Legislature.[160]

Imprisonment for Debt: Another unique state constitutional guarantee in Texas and approximately forty other states protects against imprisonment for debt.[161] Although debtors' prisons were commonplace in the early American Republic, many states began to abolish imprisonment for debt in the second quarter of the nineteenth century. The 1836 Republic of Texas Constitution guaranteed that no Texan could "be imprisoned for debt in consequence of inability to pay."[162] The Texas Statehood Constitution of 1845 deleted the qualification of an "inability to pay" and simply provided that "[n]o person shall ever be imprisoned for debt."[163] This language has been included unchanged in every subsequent Texas constitution, presently appearing in article I, section 18.[164] Despite the apparently unqualified language of this prohibition, not every monetary obligation is considered a "debt," including criminal fines, certain turnover orders, temporary spousal support

[158]*See* Donald B. Verrilli, Jr., Note, *The Eighth Amendment and the Right to Bail: Historical Perspectives*, 82 COLUM. L. REV. 328, 353 n.172 (1982) (listing state constitutional provisions on the right to bail).

[159]TEX. CONST. art. I, §§ 11, 11a, 11b.

[160]*See* United States v. Salerno, 481 U.S. 739, 754 (1987).

[161]*See* Becky A. Vogt, Note, State v. Allison*: Imprisonment for Debt in South Dakota*, 46 S.D. L. REV. 334, 335 n.9 (2001) (listing state constitutional provisions). The remaining states have abolished imprisonment for debt by statute. *See id.*

[162]CONST. OF REP. OF TEX. of 1836, DECL. OF RTS. § 12.

[163]TEX. CONST. of 1845, art. I, § 15.

[164]TEX. CONST. art. I, § 18.

payments, and child support obligations. But if the obligation is a "debt," a person may not be confined for failing to pay it, even if payment is required by court order.[165]

The extent of protection against imprisonment for debt under the United States Constitution is less certain. Although the United States Supreme Court has frequently described "the traditional aversion to imprisonment for debt,"[166] it has never specifically held that all prison terms for debts would violate any federal constitutional guarantee. The Court has, however, employed the Thirteenth and Fourteenth Amendments to invalidate statutes requiring either forced labor because of a debt or an increased prison term because of an indigent's failure to pay a criminal fine.[167] Some lower federal courts have interpreted these cases to support a general federal constitutional prohibition against imprisonment for debt.[168] Yet this federal constitutional issue may never be definitively resolved due to the existing state statutory and constitutional protections against imprisonment for debt, and similar protections afforded by various federal statutes.

Outlawry and Transportation: Article I, section 20 of the Texas Constitution precludes a citizen from being exiled through transportation out of Texas for an offense committed within the state or from being "outlawed," which was a process at English common law to deprive persons of all their legal civil rights and protections.[169] Although some other states protect against being outlawed or exiled except pursuant to the law of the land,[170] Texas appears to be the only state with constitutional bans on both practices.[171] But

---

[165]*See, e.g., In re* Henry, 154 S.W.3d 594, 596-98 (Tex. 2005) (holding husband's obligation to pay past-due property taxes under divorce decree dividing community property was an order to pay a debt owed to a third-party such that confinement for contempt for failure to pay violated the prohibition on imprisonment for debt). In determining whether a divorce obligation is a "debt," courts examine whether the divorce decree specifies specific funds to pay the obligation or particular community property from which the obligation is to be paid. If so, the surrendering spouse is not paying a debt, but rather turning over property rightfully owed to another under the decree, such that contempt imprisonment for failure to do so does not violate the state constitution. *Id.* at 597.

[166]*See, e.g.*, United States v. Bishop, 412 U.S. 346, 352 (1973); Spies v. United States, 317 U.S. 492, 498 (1943); *accord* Edwards v. Kearzey, 96 U.S. 595, 602 (1877) (describing imprisonment for debt as "a relic of ancient barbarism").

[167]*See, e.g.*, Bearden v. Georgia, 461 U.S. 660, 667 (1983) (holding that criminal fines cannot be converted into jail terms solely because the defendant's indigence precludes immediate payment); Pollock v. Williams, 322 U.S. 4, 17-18 (1944) (holding that forced labor because of debt is typically prohibited by Thirteenth Amendment).

[168]*See, e.g.*, Goldyn v. Hayes, 444 F.3d 1062, 1069 (9th Cir. 2006); Alkire v. Irving, 330 F.3d 802, 816 (6th Cir. 2003).

[169]TEX. CONST. art. I, § 20; *accord* Peeler v. Hughes & Luce, 909 S.W.2d 494, 499 (Tex. 1995). Section 20 provides: "No citizen shall be outlawed. No person shall be transported out of the State for an offense committed within the same. This section does not prohibit an agreement with another state providing for the confinement of inmates of this State in the penal or correctional facilities of that state."

[170]*See, e.g.*, MD. CONST., DECL. OF RTS., art. 24; N.C. CONST. art. I, § 19; TENN. CONST. art. I, § 8. The Texas guarantees against outlawry and transportation were likewise part of the state's due course of law provision before the 1876 Texas Constitution. *See, e.g.*, TEX. CONST. of 1845, art. I, § 16; TEX. CONST. of 1869, art. I, § 16.

[171]At least two other states absolutely prohibit the exile of a citizen. *See, e.g.*, ALA. CONST. art. I, § 30 ("no citizen shall be exiled"); AR. CONST. art. II, § 21 (barring outlawry except by the law of the land and banning exile under any circumstances).

these protections seem unnecessary today as neither outlawry nor transportation has ever been practiced in the United States. Any attempt to reinvigorate such punishments presumably would run afoul of the protections against cruel or unusual punishments and deprivations of liberty without due process of law. Not surprisingly, then, there has never been a judicial decision finding a violation of this state constitutional command.

Perpetuities, Monopolies, Primogeniture, and Entailments: State laws and constitutional prohibitions against entailments, primogeniture, monopolies, and perpetuities stemmed from early American republican egalitarianism and were designed to prevent an aristocratic perpetuation of privilege in America similar to that existing in Europe.[172] The Texas Constitution's disapproval of these practices has remained unchanged since 1836, presently appearing in article I, section 26: "Perpetuities and monopolies are contrary to the genius of a free government, and shall never be allowed, nor shall the law of primogeniture or entailments ever be in force in this State."[173] The state constitutional ban against monopolies prevents the government from granting exclusive rights or privileges to buy, sell, or make something.[174] This prohibition has invalidated several contracts between governments and public utilities,[175] although such contracts will be upheld if the contract can be interpreted to provide a nonexclusive grant, to allow competition, or to further a proprietary function of government.[176] The ban against perpetuities essentially constitutionalizes the common law rule against perpetuities.[177] Primogeniture laws, which limit inheritance to the oldest son, and the law of entailments, which establishes a mandatory order of succession to inherited property, have never been in force in Texas (as the constitution mandates), so no judicial decision has interpreted these prohibitions.

Only one other state, Oklahoma, has a similar constitutional provision encompassing bans on monopolies, perpetuities, primogeniture, and entailments.[178] Nonetheless, several other states have outlawed one or more of these practices,[179] or have interpreted a state constitutional provision preventing irrevocable grants of privileges to encompass similar ideas.[180] The United States Constitution does not afford any constitutional protection in

[172]*See* GORDON S. WOOD, THE CREATION OF THE AMERICAN REPUBLIC 1776-1787, 72 (1969).

[173]TEX. CONST. art. I, § 26.

[174]*See* City of Brenham v. Brenham Water Co., 4 S.W. 143, 153-56 (Tex. 1887).

[175]*See, e.g.*, Ennis Waterworks v. City of Ennis, 144 S.W. 930, 934-35 (Tex. 1912); *City of Brenham*, 4 S.W. at 153-56.

[176]*See, e.g.*, City of Memphis v. Browder, 12 S.W.2d 160, 161-62 (Tex. Com. App. 1929, holding approved); Sw. Broadcasting Co. v. Oil Center Broadcasting Co., 210 S.W.2d 230, 233-34 (Tex. Civ. App.–El Paso 1947, writ ref'd n.r.e.).

[177]*See* Mattern v. Herzog, 367 S.W.2d 312, 314 (Tex. 1963).

[178]OK. CONST. art. II, § 32.

[179]*See e.g.*, AR. CONST. art. II, § 19 (perpetuities and monopolies); ARIZ. CONST. art. II, § 29 (perpetuities and entailments); MD. CONST., DECL. OF RTS., art. 41 (monopolies); N.C. CONST. art. I, § 34 (perpetuities and monopolies); TENN. CONST. art. I, § 22 (perpetuities and monopolies); WYO. CONST. art. I, § 30 (perpetuities and monopolies).

[180]*See, e.g.*, Rogers v. City of Mobile, 169 So. 2d 282, 300 (Ala. 1964) (interpreting ALA. CONST. art. I, § 22 to prevent monopolies).

these areas,[181] although federal statutory regulation of anti-competitive business arrangements is pervasive.

The Rights of Crime Victims: A modern state constitutional trend is including a listing of the rights of crime victims within state bills of rights. Since 1980, more than three-fifths of the states have adopted a crime victims' bill of rights.[182] The Texas guarantee, ratified in 1989 as article I, section 30 of the constitution, is illustrative, establishing such rights for crime victims as the right to be treated with fairness and respect, to be reasonably protected from the accused, to notification of court proceedings on request, to confer with prosecutorial office representatives, to obtain restitution on request, and to obtain information regarding the status of the proceedings.[183] Section 31 then establishes a fund and auxiliary fund dedicated to compensate victims of crime, subject to legislative appropriation.[184]

The difficulty, however, is that these rights are often difficult to enforce. Most of the state constitutional provisions establishing rights for crime victims, including article I, section 30, limit the availability of damages for violations.[185] In the absence of damages, frequently no other practical remedy exists. For example, if a victim is not properly notified of a criminal proceeding, the lack of notice cannot be remedied as the proceeding cannot be repeated. An aggrieved victim's only avenues of relief are to contact the state prosecuting attorney to enforce his or her rights or perhaps to file a mandamus proceeding on his or her own behalf.

The movement to amend the United States Constitution to similarly provide a constitutional status for victims' rights has to date been unsuccessful, although federal criminal statutes provide similar legislative protection to victims.[186] Despite the state constitutional amendments and statutes protecting victims' rights, many advocacy groups believe that a federal constitutional amendment with a strong enforcement mechanism is necessary to ensure that such rights are protected.

CHAPTER 5 EXERCISES AND PROBLEMS

1. The Texas Legislature enacted a Government Code section authorizing a county to adopt a "family protection fee" in an amount not to exceed $15 that the district or county clerk would collect in suits filed for the dissolution of marriage. The fee is to be deposited into a family protection account in the county treasury and used to fund services such as family violence prevention, intervention, mental health, counseling, and marriage preservation services. What are the constitutional arguments for and against the

---

[181]*See* The Slaughter-House Cases, 83 U.S. (16 Wall.) 36 (1873).

[182]*See, e.g.*, Paul G. Cassell, *Treating Crime Victims Fairly: Integrating Victims into the Federal Rules of Criminal Procedure*, 2007 UTAH L. REV. 861, 866 & n.13 (listing state constitutional provisions).

[183]TEX. CONST. art. I, § 30.

[184]TEX. CONST. art. I, § 31.

[185]*See, e.g.*, TEX. CONST. art. I, § 30 (e).

[186]*See, e.g.*, 18 U.S.C. § 3771.

constitutionality of this fee under the open courts provision? *Compare* Tex. Att'y Gen. Op. No. GA-0231 (2004).

2. The Texas Legislature adopted a ten-year statute of repose for medical malpractice actions in 2003, which requires all actions filed after 2003 to be brought within ten years of the act or omission giving rise to the claim, notwithstanding any law to the contrary. Dr. Maim committed malpractice on an infant Z in 1998. Z's parents never filed a malpractice suit. After Z turned 18 in 2016, he brought a claim against Dr. Maim for medical malpractice. Dr. Maim defended based on the ten-year statute of repose. What constitutional arguments are potentially available to Z to circumvent the statute of repose? How would Dr. Maim likely respond to Z's arguments?

3. *Robinson v. Crown Cork & Seal Co.* addressed an as-applied constitutional retroactivity challenge to Robinson's common law claims. What would have been the arguments for and against an open courts challenge to chapter 149 as applied to Robinson's common law claims? Could an open courts challenge have been made to the application of chapter 149 to the subsequently asserted statutory wrongful death and survival claims in *Robinson*?

4. The legislature adopted a requirement in asbestos cases that a plaintiff not diagnosed with an asbestos-related cancer must serve an expert medical report opining that the plaintiff suffers from an asbestos-related impairment based on the medical expert's interpretation of a pulmonary function (breathing) test. If such an expert report is not filed within 30 days after the defendant files its answer, the case must be dismissed without prejudice to the plaintiff's right to refile upon later developing a medically certified asbestos-related impairment. The legislative purpose behind this requirement was to alleviate the asbestos litigation crisis in Texas courts by dismissing lawsuits in which the plaintiff had not been functionally impaired by exposure to asbestos while protecting the right to sue once an asbestos-related impairment developed. The requirement is to be applied to all cases filed on or after the effective date of the legislation as well as to all claims pending on the effective date and in which a trial or retrial of the cause started more than 90 days after the legislation's effective date. Consider the following questions:

(a) What are the arguments for and against a facial challenge to the constitutionality of this requirement under the open courts and retroactivity provisions of the Texas Constitution?

(b) What are the arguments for and against a constitutional challenge to the requirement as applied to a wrongful death action filed and pending before the statute became effective?

(c) What are the arguments for and against the requirement as applied to a wrongful death action in which the decedent died a year before the statute became effective but that was not filed until after the statute became effective?

Chapter 6

SEPARATION OF POWERS

The concept of separation of powers is a fundamental American constitutional principle designed as a bulwark against tyranny. As James Madison remarked, the "accumulation of all powers, legislative, executive and judiciary, in the same hands . . . may justly be pronounced the very definition of tyranny."[1]

Yet federal separation of power principles are not binding on the states' allocation of governmental authority under their own state constitutions.[2] States are free to experiment with different power distributions among the branches or departments of government, unless the result violates a specific federal constitutional constraint on the states, such as the Guarantee Clause or the ban on legislative trials under the bill of attainder prohibition.[3]

Separation of powers principles in the states, unlike the federal model, are frequently grounded in constitutional text. While the United States Supreme Court has developed its separation of power doctrine from the United States Constitution's structure, the concept of separation of powers is explicitly stated in the text of forty state constitutions. Thirty-five of these state separation of powers provisions appear relatively strict, dividing authority between the various branches and prohibiting each branch from exercising powers properly belonging to another branch; the other five provisions are more general, merely dividing the powers of government into separate and distinct branches.[4] Yet all forty of these provisions are more specific than the structural inferences that support federal separation of powers doctrine.

Although James Madison proposed a separation-of-powers amendment similar to those found in state constitutions to Congress for inclusion in the Bill of Rights, his proposal was rejected by the United States Senate.[5] Because no record was made of the Senate debate, it is not known whether the Senate rejected the proposal under the belief that it was unnecessary and redundant due to the structural inclusion of separation of powers principles in the United States Constitution, or whether the Senate rejected the proposal for substantive reasons, concerned that such an amendment would result in a stricter separation of powers

---

[1] THE FEDERALIST NO. 47 (James Madison) (Clinton Rossiter ed., 1961).

[2] *See, e.g.*, Highland Farms Dairy, Inc. v. Agnew, 300 U.S. 608, 612 (1937) ("How power shall be distributed by a state among its governmental organs is commonly, if not always, a question for the state itself."); Chicago, Rock Island & Pac. Ry. Co. v. Cole, 251 U.S. 54, 56 (1919) (noting nothing in the Federal Constitution prevents a state from conferring "legislative and judicial powers upon a commission not known to the common law").

[3] U.S. CONST. art. I, § 10; art. IV, § 4. See Chapter 2, section A for a discussion of the Guarantee Clause, and Chapter 5, section C for a brief discussion of bills of attainder.

[4] *See* Jim Rossi, *Institutional Design and the Lingering Legacy of Antifederalist Separation of Powers Ideals in the States*, 52 VAND. L. REV. 1167, 1191 & nn. 105-07 (1999) (categorizing and listing state constitutional separation of powers provisions).

[5] *See* 2 BERNARD SCHWARTZ, THE BILL OF RIGHTS: A DOCUMENTARY HISTORY 1151 (1971).

doctrine.[6] A statement of the Senate's rationale might have been of some benefit to state courts, which have had to continuously grapple with the intended import of their separation of powers clauses.

This chapter begins with an introduction to separation of powers principles under the Texas Constitution, analyzing three situations in which the explicit separation of powers provision in article II, section 1 appears to have resulted in a stricter doctrine than the federal model. The chapter then briefly considers comparative doctrine from other states.

A. SEPARATION OF POWERS IN TEXAS

The separation of powers idea in Texas is traceable to both United States and Mexican influences. In addition to the American constitutional norm of divided powers, both the Mexican National Constitution of 1824 and the Coahuila y Tejas Constitution of 1827 incorporated specific separation of powers clauses.[7] These clauses have thereafter continued to appear in every constitution for Texas, with article II, section 1 of the Texas Constitution currently providing:

> The powers of the Government of the State of Texas shall be divided into three distinct departments, each of which shall be confided to a separate body of magistracy, to wit: Those which are Legislative to one; those which are Executive to another, and those which are Judicial to another; and no person, or collection of persons, being of one of these departments, shall exercise any power properly attached to either of the others, except in the instances expressly permitted.

Of course, article II must be read in conjunction with the structure of the state constitution as a whole–specifically, the legislative article (article III of the Texas Constitution), the executive article (article IV), and the judicial article (article V)–to ascertain which powers are appropriately assigned to each of the "departments," or branches, of government.

Article III, which establishes the Legislative Department and vests legislative power in a bicameral legislature, primarily addresses the qualifications of and method of election for members of the Texas Senate and Texas House of Representatives, the process for enacting laws, and certain restrictions on the types of laws that can be enacted. The essential realm of the legislature under the Texas Constitution is to enact, alter, or repeal laws establishing public policy for the state of Texas. Article I, section 28 of the Texas Constitution buttresses this conclusion, as it specifies that only the legislature has the power to suspend valid laws.

Article IV of the Texas Constitution establishes the Executive Department, which consists of a governor, lieutenant governor, secretary of state, comptroller, land

---

[6]Both of these contradictory arguments had been raised in the House of Representatives. *See* 1 ANNALS OF CONG. 760 (1789) (statements of Roger Sherman and Samuel Livermore).

[7]FED. CONST. OF THE UNITED MEXICAN STATES of 1824, art. II, § 1, ¶ 3; CONST. OF COAHUILA Y TEJ. of 1827, art. 29.

commissioner, and attorney general. Article IV details the method of selection and the powers and duties of each of these officials, allocating to each various duties such as faithfully executing the laws, conducting relations with other states, accounting for public funds, and representing the state in legal proceedings.

Article V of the Texas Constitution then creates the Judicial Department, specifying its membership, the jurisdictional reach of the courts, certain procedural requirements, and the qualifications and method of selection of judges, clerks, county attorneys, district attorneys, and sheriffs. The judicial power in Texas encompasses the authority to consider evidence, resolve legal and factual disputes, render and effectuate judgments in cases between adversarial parties, and ascertain and protect judicial jurisdiction.

Separation of powers does not mandate an inflexible compartmentalization regarding the division of authority among these departments. Article II acknowledges that some constitutional provisions "expressly permit[]" a department to exercise a power not typically within its sphere. As an example, article V, section 8 grants district courts "general supervisory control" over county commissioners courts, despite the predominantly legislative nature of county commissioners courts. Even without explicit constitutional authorization, some intermixing is permissible to promote efficiency or to check another department's power.

Yet several related limitations cannot be transgressed without violating article II. First, a department may not aggrandize its powers by assuming powers that are more properly entrusted to the other departments of the government. In other words, the challenged arrangement may not greatly expand the powers of a department at the expense of the other departments. *Walker v. Baker* provides a good illustration of this principle through its holding that the Texas Senate could not convene on its own motion to consider recess appointments by the governor.[8] The court reasoned that authorizing the senate to do so would increase its own power at the expense of the governor's constitutional authority to make recess appointments.[9]

Second, separation of powers principles are designed to protect the integrity and independence of each department by preventing other departments from encroaching on its powers by unduly interfering with the powers of another branch. Thus, for example, the legislature may not unduly interfere with an express power of the governor, such as constraining the governor's pardon power, without violating article II.[10]

---

[8]196 S.W.2d 324 (Tex. 1946). The claim was brought on behalf of the printers of the Senate Journal who sought payment for printing services during the time period in which the senate considered the appointments. After payment was refused on the basis that the session was illegal, the assignee of the printers' claim sought mandamus relief. *Id.* at 326.

[9]*Id.* at 327-29. The court noted that the senate had never attempted to convene itself previously to consider recess appointments. Nor did the Texas Constitution specifically grant the senate authority to do so, but instead indicated that recess appointments should be addressed at the next regular session of the legislature. *See id.*

[10]*Cf. Ex parte* Redwine, 236 S.W. 96, 98 (Tex. Crim. App. 1921) (recognizing that a parole law which abridged or infringed the executive's power under the state constitution would violate separation of powers principles), *aff'd per curiam*, 261 U.S. 608 (1923).

Finally, separation of powers principles limit the ability of a department to delegate its power to agencies or other governmental departments. As a result, the legislature must ensure, for instance, that it does not grant unbridled discretionary authority to an executive official to establish the public policy of the state.[11]

Although all these limitations also exist under federal constitutional principles, Texas courts appear to apply them more strictly in three areas. First, Texas courts, especially in criminal cases, have jealously guarded core judicial functions from undue legislative interference. Second, Texas decisions have steadfastly refused to allow legislative policy functions to be reviewed de novo by any other department of the government. Finally, Texas cases have been more likely to invalidate delegations of legislative authority, especially to private entities.

1. The Protection of Core Judicial Functions from Undue Interference

Article II invalidates legislation that unduly interferes with the judiciary's exercise of its core constitutional functions. The Texas Court of Criminal Appeals applied this principle in *Williams v. State* to hold that a statute which operated to undermine prior final judgments in bond forfeiture cases was unconstitutional because the rendition of final judgments was a judicial, rather than legislative, function.[12] Once a court has rendered a final judgment, the legislature cannot modify it without encroaching on the judicial power.[13] Although federal courts would also invalidate legislative interference with a prior final judgment, the Texas courts have extended this principle to encompass other core judicial functions.

As one example, the Texas Court of Criminal Appeals held in separate cases that legislation prohibiting a trial court's rendition of a final judgment against a bond until a specified time had passed from the date of the bond's forfeiture interfered with the core judicial function of rendering final judgments in pending cases.[14] The court highlighted that such legislative control over the timing of judgments would grant the legislature "the power to render the Judiciary impotent with respect to the entry of final judgments."[15] Another related example is the criminal court's holding that the legislature unconstitutionally encroached on prosecutorial discretion and trial preparation by mandating that the state had to be ready for trial in all cases without exception within 120 days after commencement of

---

[11]*See, e.g.*, Bullock v. Calvert, 480 S.W.2d 367, 372 (Tex.1972) (holding statute designating the Texas Secretary of State as the state's chief election official did not authorize the secretary to conduct or pay for party primaries in part because such an interpretation "would be an unconstitutional delegation of legislative power in violation of the separation of powers").

[12]707 S.W.2d 40, 46 (Tex. Crim. App. 1986).

[13]*Id.*; *see also* Langever v. Miller, 76 S.W.2d 1025, 1035-37 (Tex. 1934) (holding state law could not modify prior final judgment without violating separation of powers principles).

[14]*See, e.g.*, State v. Matyastik, 811 S.W.2d 102, 104 (Tex. Crim. App. 1991) (invalidating nine month limitation in misdemeanor cases); Armadillo Bail Bonds v. State, 802 S.W.2d 237, 239-41 (Tex. Crim. App. 1990) (invalidating eighteen month limitation in felony cases).

[15]*Armadillo Bail Bonds*, 837 S.W.2d at 241.

a felony criminal action or the indictment would be dismissed with prejudice.[16] Although a similar federal "Speedy Trial Act" has been upheld by the federal courts against constitutional challenge, the Court of Criminal Appeals invalidated the state "Speedy Trial Act" on the basis that it interfered with the prosecutorial discretion of district and county attorneys, offices established as part of the judicial department in article V, section 21 of the Texas Constitution.[17] These decisions from the criminal high court all prohibited the legislature from unduly interfering with core judicial functions that occurred before a final judgment had been rendered in the case.

Yet not all legislative interference is prohibited–only undue interference.[18] The Texas Constitution's grant of procedural rule-making authority to the judiciary requires that such procedural rules must comport "with the laws of the State," subordinating the judiciary's authority over rules of court practice and procedure to that of the legislature.[19] Thus, the legislature is allowed to prescribe rules of practice and procedure, as long as these rules do not go too far and "infringe upon the substantive power of the Judicial Department under the guise of establishing 'rules of court.'"[20] Moreover, the state constitution authorizes the legislature to confer and define the jurisdiction of the courts, assuming the judiciary retains the power to interpret the law and to determine whether a case falls within its constitutional and statutory jurisdiction.[21]

Texas cases acknowledge the need for inter-department cooperation when reviewing the constitutionality of legislative intrusions on judicial functions. The Texas Supreme Court in *Government Services Insurance Underwriters v. Jones* upheld the constitutionality of a statute imposing a mandatory continuance in all pending lawsuits upon application of a member of the legislature despite its interference with a typical judicial function.[22] The court reasoned that the continuance, even though it could be subject to abuse, would tend to prevent conflicts between the legislative and judicial branches, as requiring the attendance of a legislator during the legislature's session would interfere with the legislative function.[23] This issue of inter-department cooperation surfaced again in *In re Allcat Claims Service, L.P.*[24] The legislature had granted the state supreme court "exclusive and original jurisdiction" to consider challenges to the constitutionality of its extension of the state's franchise tax to limited partnerships, but specified that the court "shall rule" on such a challenge "on or before the 120th day after the date the challenge is filed." Although no party raised the issue, Justice Willet's concurring and dissenting opinion in *Allcat* contended

---

[16]Meshell v. State, 739 S.W.2d 246, 254-55 (Tex. Crim. App. 1987); *cf.* Ex parte Young, 213 S.W.3d 327, 331-32 (Tex. Crim. App. 2006) (holding dismissal with prejudice for not meeting mandatory deadline violated separation of powers in part due to its serious disruption of a prosecutor's ability to perform duties).

[17]*Meshell*, 739 S.W.2d. at 257.

[18]Gov't Servs. Ins. Underwriters v. Jones, 368 S.W.2d 560, 564-65 (Tex. 1963).

[19]TEX. CONST. art. V, § 31.

[20]*Meshell,* 739 S.W.2d at 255.

[21]*See, e.g., In re* Dean, 393 S.W.3d 741, 748 (Tex. 2012).

[22]368 S.W.2d 560, 565 (Tex. 1963).

[23]*Id.* at 565-66.

[24]356 S.W.3d 455 (Tex 2011).

that this time limit "raise[d] separation of powers concerns" by interfering with core judicial functions regarding the court's control of its docket.[25] While first stressing that the constitutionality of the time limit was not properly before the court (such that resolving it would be an advisory opinion violating separation of powers principles), the majority's response was:

> We see no valid reason that this Court cannot cooperate with priorities expressed by other branches of government as long as we fulfill our constitutional duties and neither impair our judicial prerogatives and functions, nor impair the rights of the parties. We do not see how expediting disposition of this matter violates our constitutional duties or impairs our judicial prerogatives or functions, and the parties have neither alleged nor shown that they have been harmed or prevented from properly presenting their positions by the manner of the proceedings.[26]

Yet how far does this need for cooperation extend? Could the legislature require the courts to decide all cases within 120 days, or would this be an undue interference with a core judicial function?

2. De Novo Reviews of Legislative Determinations

The Texas Supreme Court has consistently held that a "legislative function cannot, under the separation of powers doctrine, be reviewed de novo by any other branch of government."[27] This principle has prevented the legislature from authorizing the judiciary to conduct a de novo review of a public policy determination by an administrative agency, despite several attempts by the legislature to do so.

Gerst v. Nixon, for example, held that a statute providing for de novo review of the Savings and Loan Commissioner's determination whether there was a public need for a new savings and loan violated the separation of powers provision because the determination of whether a "public need" existed was a policy matter appropriate for the legislature, not the judiciary.[28] The judiciary thus was limited to addressing whether there was "substantial evidence" to support the Commissioner's decision; in other words, the court could only determine whether the Commissioner's conclusions were arbitrary rather than redetermining in the first instance whether a public need actually existed. Similarly, in *Chemical Bank & Trust Co. v. Falkner*, the court held that the "determination of 'public necessity' by the State Banking Board involves a determination of public policy which is a matter of legislative discretion which can not constitutionally be given to the judiciary."[29] Likewise, in *Davis v. City of Lubbock,* the court held that a decision that a neighborhood was "detrimental to the public health, safety, morals or welfare of the city" was "a decision of a question of pure

[25] *Id.* at 485-93 (Willet, J., concurring & dissenting).

[26] *Id.* at 474.

[27] Quick v. City of Austin, 7 S.W.3d 109, 114-15 (Tex. 1998).

[28] 411 S.W.2d 350, 353-54 (Tex. 1966).

[29] 369 S.W.2d 427, 432 (Tex. 1963).

public policy" that involved "legislative discretion" such that "de novo judicial review of such a decision would clearly involve the exercise by the courts of nonjudicial powers."[30] In response to these decisions, the legislature proposed a constitutional amendment to require the Texas courts to undertake de novo review of administrative determinations whenever authorized to do so by statute, but this proposed amendment was defeated by the voters in 1962.

Nevertheless, not all de novo reviews of an agency determination violate the Texas Constitution. *Key Western Life Insurance Co. v. State Board of Insurance* upheld a statute requiring the judiciary to undertake a de novo review when the Board of Insurance Commissioners disapproved an insurance policy form.[31] The court reasoned that "there is a distinction between the types of decisions rendered by different administrative agencies," as some "perform judicial or quasi-judicial functions" while "others exercise powers which are essentially legislative."[32] Although acknowledging that de novo review of an agency's public policy determinations violate article II, the court concluded that judicial or quasi-judicial determinations by an agency could be reviewed de novo by Texas courts. As the agency's determination in *Key Western* did not involve public policy but instead depended solely on whether the form violated the Insurance Code or was deceptive or misleading, the court held that de novo review was permissible. Similarly, in *Scott v. Texas State Board of Medical Examiners*, the Texas Supreme Court upheld a statute providing for de novo review from a decision to revoke a medical license because the determination of whether the doctor committed the charged acts was judicial in nature as it only affected the parties to the case and was similar to decisions typically made by judges and juries.[33] As a result, only those agency determinations involving legislative policy matters cannot be reviewed de novo by the judiciary–de novo review of an agency's quasi-judicial determinations is permitted.

3. The Nondelegation Doctrine

Because lawmaking power under the United States Constitution is vested in Congress, Congress cannot wholly abdicate its essential legislative functions by delegating legislative authority without an "intelligible principle" that constrains the delegatee.[34] Similarly, under the Texas Constitution, the legislature cannot delegate lawmaking authority without establishing standards for guidance that are capable of reasonable application.[35] But while the United States Supreme Court has not invalidated a federal statute since the late 1930's under the federal nondelegation doctrine, the Texas Supreme Court has struck down two delegations of legislative authority since 1997 under state constitutional principles.

---

[30]326 S.W.2d 699, 714 (Tex. 1959).

[31]350 S.W.2d 839, 848-50 (Tex. 1961).

[32]*Id.* at 847-48.

[33]384 S.W.2d 686, 690-91 (Tex. 1964).

[34]*See, e.g.*, Mistretta v. United States, 488 U.S. 361, 371-72 (1989).

[35]*See, e.g.*, R.R. Comm'n v. Lone Star Gas Co., 844 S.W.2d 679, 689 (Tex. 1992); Martinez v. State, 323 S.W.3d 493, 501 (Tex. Crim. App. 2010); State v. Rhine, 297 S.W.3d 301, 306 (Tex. Crim. App. 2009); *Ex parte* Granviel, 561 S.W.2d 503, 514-15 (Tex. Crim. App. 1978).

Texas Boll Weevil Eradication Foundation v. Lewellen, 952 S.W.2d 454 (Tex. 1997)

PHILLIPS, Chief Justice, delivered the opinion of the Court [with Justices GONZALEZ, HECHT, OWEN, and BAKER joining in all the portions of the opinion excerpted below and Justices CORNYN, ENOCH, SPECTOR, and ABBOTT joining in Part I of the excerpt].

Subchapter 74D of the Texas Agriculture Code (the Act) provides for the creation and operation of an "Official Cotton Growers' Boll Weevil Eradication Foundation." Subject to referendum approval from the affected cotton growers, this Foundation is authorized to operate boll weevil eradication programs and assess the growers for the cost. Appellees in these consolidated direct appeals, who are cotton growers subject to the Foundation's jurisdiction, filed declaratory judgment actions challenging the Foundation's assessments on a variety of constitutional and statutory grounds. The trial court in each case invalidated the assessments and enjoined their collection.

We conclude that the Legislature made an unconstitutionally broad delegation of authority to the Foundation, a private entity, thereby violating Article II, Section 1 of the Texas Constitution. For this reason, without reaching all the other constitutional and statutory arguments raised by appellees, we affirm the judgments of the trial courts.

I

A

There is no dispute among the parties to these appeals or the numerous amici curiae that the Anthonomus grandis Boheman, an insect commonly known as the boll weevil, presents a major economic threat to the Texas cotton industry. *See* Tex. Agric. Code § 74.001. This pest, which entered Texas from Mexico in 1892, causes an estimated $20 million in crop loss in Texas every year. To aid in the ongoing battle against the boll weevil, the Legislature in 1993 authorized the creation of the Official Cotton Growers' Boll Weevil Eradication Foundation. Instead of directly creating the Foundation, however, the Legislature merely authorized the Commissioner of Agriculture to certify some nonprofit organization representing cotton growers to create the Foundation and propose geographic eradication zones. *See* Tex. Agric. Code § 74.103(a). The Act authorizes the creating organization or the Foundation to conduct referenda in each proposed eradication zone ("zone referenda") to determine whether those cotton growers desire to establish an official boll weevil eradication zone. *See id.* § 74.105. Contemporaneous with the zone referendum, the growers are also to elect a member to represent them on the Foundation's board. *See id.* § 74.106. If the growers vote not to establish a zone, their board selection is without effect. *Id.* § 74.105(d).

Under the Act, once the initial zone has been created and the first board member elected, the growers of that zone must approve the assessment to fund the eradication at a subsequent referendum. Thereafter, the board is authorized to determine the assessment needed for each additional participating zone, which must be approved by the growers at a referendum. *See id.* § 74.113. The Foundation may collect the assessment only if the assessment referendum passes. Approval of a zone and of the assessment each requires a vote of either two-thirds of the cotton growers in the zone or of those who farm more than one-half of the cotton acreage in the zone. *See id.* §§ 74.113(d), 74.114(g).

The Foundation exercises broad governmental powers. Besides being authorized to conduct elections in proposed eradication zones, Tex. Agric. Code § 74.108(a)(1), (2), the board may add an area to a zone under certain circumstances if approved by a referendum of cotton growers in the area. *Id.* § 74.108(b). The board determines what eradication programs to conduct. *Id.* § 74.108(a)(4). The Foundation may impose penalties for late payment of assessments. *Id.* § 74.115(a). A cotton grower who fails to pay an assessment within ten days of its due date must destroy his cotton crop. *Id.* § 74.115(b). If the grower fails to do so, his crop is automatically declared a public nuisance. *Id.* On the Foundation's recommendation, and after notice, the Department of Agriculture must destroy it, even if not infested with boll weevils, at the owner's cost. *Id.* In addition, a cotton grower who violates the statute (including, presumably, by failing to pay an assessment or failing to destroy his own crop if payment is more than ten days late) is guilty of a Class C misdemeanor. *Id.* § 74.126(b). Cotton which a delinquent grower has already produced and harvested is subject to a lien. *Id.* § 74.115(c). Representatives of the Foundation may enter private property which is subject to eradication without the owner's permission for any purpose under the Act, including "the treatment, monitoring, and destruction of growing cotton or other host plants." *Id.* § 74.117. Finally, the Commissioner and the Foundation may adopt rules necessary to carry out the purposes of the Act. *Id.* § 74.120(c).

While growers in a zone must approve their assessments, they do not approve the type of eradication program or the amount of debt incurred by the Foundation to finance it. These matters are left to the Foundation's discretion. If the eradication program is discontinued for any reason, the Foundation may continue collecting assessments "as necessary to pay the financial obligations of the foundation." *Id.* § 74.127(c).

Under the Act, some power is retained by the Commissioner of Agriculture. For example, the Foundation can change the number of board positions or the eradication zone representation on the board only with the Commissioner's approval. *Id.* § 74.107(b). The Commissioner must also make rules to protect life and property from pesticides and other aspects of eradication programs. *Id.* § 74.120. The Commissioner may prohibit planting cotton in zones when it would jeopardize the success of an eradication program. *Id.* § 74.118. The Commissioner may exempt a cotton grower from payment of the Foundation's assessment penalties if payment would leave the grower with less than $15,000 taxable income. *Id.* § 74.116. The Foundation may expend revenue only on "programs approved by the commissioner as consistent with this subchapter and applicable provisions of the constitution." Tex. Agric. Code § 74.109(h). Finally, the Commissioner must determine when elimination of boll weevils is no longer necessary to prevent economic loss to cotton growers. *Id.* §§ 74.102(6), 74.112.

After a referendum has passed, the cotton growers in the zone must be allowed to conduct referenda "periodically" under the terms prescribed in the initial referendum to determine whether to continue their assessments, *id.* § 74.105(f), although the Act says nothing about how often these referenda must occur. In addition, the Foundation must conduct a referendum on whether to discontinue the program on the petition of at least forty percent of the cotton growers in the zone. *Id.* § 74.112(f)-(i). As noted, however, the

Foundation may continue to collect assessments previously approved to pay its financial obligations. *Id.* § 74.127(c).

* * * *

C

In May 1993, Texas Cotton Producers, Inc., a nonprofit organization representing cotton growers, petitioned the Commissioner for authority to create the Foundation. In its petition, Texas Cotton Producers proposed nine eradication zones around the state and provided that the Foundation board would consist of a corresponding nine members. Texas Cotton Producers further provided that "[o]n creation of the proposed official cotton growers' boll weevil eradication foundation by TCP the initial board will be appointed by the board of TCP pending conduct of the board election."

While the nine-member board is consistent with the requirements of section 74.103(b)(2), which permits a six, nine, twelve, or fifteen person board, the statute never authorizes the creating organization to appoint the initial Foundation board. Despite this flaw, the Commissioner certified Texas Cotton Producers to create the Foundation. In September 1993, Texas Cotton Producers incorporated the Foundation as a Texas nonprofit corporation, appointing nine members to the board who purportedly represented each of the nine proposed eradication districts. The Foundation has since conducted six zone referenda, and in each instance the growers elected as their board representative the person previously appointed by Texas Cotton Producers to represent that proposed zone. In the meantime, the remaining appointed members apparently voted on all Foundation matters, including the setting of assessments and expenditure of funds.

In April 1995, the Foundation conducted a referendum in the proposed High Plains Eradication Zone, which comprises all or parts of thirty West Texas counties. The cotton growers approved creation of the zone. The following September, ten cotton growers from the High Plains Zone sued the Foundation in district court in Hale County, challenging the validity of the referendum and assessments. After discovery, the trial court granted summary judgment for the plaintiffs, without stating specific grounds. The Foundation appealed directly to this Court, and we accepted jurisdiction. *See* Tex. Gov't Code § 22.001(c); Tex.R.App. P. 140.

D

In April 1994, the Foundation conducted a referendum in the proposed Lower Rio Grande Valley Eradication Zone, which comprises nine South Texas counties. The cotton growers approved creation of the zone, and the following October they approved an assessment of $18 per acre on irrigated land and $12 per acre on unirrigated land. One year later, however, the growers petitioned for another referendum to cancel the program. *See* Tex. Agric. Code § 74.112(f). This referendum passed in January 1996, thus terminating the eradication program in the Lower Rio Grande Valley Zone. The Foundation, however, continued billing growers for the assessments, solely to retire the $9 million debt already incurred for eradication.

In July 1996, thirty-one Lower Rio Grande Valley cotton growers sued the Foundation to enjoin collection of the assessments. After an evidentiary hearing, the trial court rendered a temporary injunction enjoining collection of the assessments, which the

Foundation also appealed directly to this Court. We accepted jurisdiction and consolidated the two appeals.

* * * *

V

Finally, we turn to the growers' argument that the Legislature violated Article II, Section 1 of the Texas Constitution, requiring the separation of powers between the legislative, executive, and judicial branches, by improperly delegating governmental authority to the Foundation. In particular, the growers contend that the Foundation is a private entity whose directors are neither constrained before they act by meaningful standards nor made accountable after they act by administrative, judicial, or popular review. In response, the Foundation contends that both the Legislature's guidelines and the Commissioner of Agriculture's supervisory authority are constitutionally adequate.

A

"The delegation of legislative power is an old concern. . . ." Peter H. Aranson et al., *A Theory of Legislative Delegation,* 68 Cornell L. Rev. 1, 4 (1982). The prohibition on unwarranted delegation of lawmaking power is "rooted in the principle of separation of powers that underlies our tripartite system of Government." *Mistretta v. United States,* 488 U.S. 361, 371 (1989). The United States Constitution expressly vests legislative power in the Congress, *see* U.S. Const. art. I, § 1, and the Texas Constitution similarly vests legislative power in our Legislature. *See* Tex. Const. art. II, § 1; art. III, § 1. Thus, "Congress is not permitted to abdicate or to transfer to others the essential legislative functions with which it is vested." *A.L.A. Schechter Poultry Corp. v. United States,* 295 U.S. 495, 529 (1935). Likewise, in our State "[t]he power to pass laws rests with the Legislature, and that power cannot be delegated to some commission or other tribunal." *Brown v. Humble Oil & Refining Co.,* 126 Tex. 296, 83 S.W.2d 935, 941 (1935).

Yet, like many truisms, these blanket pronouncements should not be read too literally. Even in a simple society, a legislative body would be hard put to contend with every detail involved in carrying out its laws; in a complex society it is absolutely impossible to do so. Hence, legislative delegation of power to enforce and apply law is both necessary and proper. Such power must almost always be exercised with a certain amount of discretion, and at times the line between making laws and enforcing them may blur.

Even in its heyday, the nondelegation doctrine was sparingly applied, having been used by the United States Supreme Court to strike down a federal statute only three times. *See Panama Refining Co. v. Ryan,* 293 U.S. 388 (1935); *A.L.A. Schechter Poultry Corp. v. United States,* 295 U.S. 495 (1935); *Carter v. Carter Coal Co.,* 298 U.S. 238 (1936). Since the Court retreated from its opposition to New Deal initiatives, it has consistently upheld congressional delegations.

Texas courts have also generally upheld legislative delegations to state or municipal agencies. We most recently did so in *Edgewood Independent School District v. Meno,* 917 S.W.2d 717, 740-741 (Tex.1995), where we said:

> The Texas Legislature may delegate its powers to agencies established to carry out legislative purposes, as long as it establishes "reasonable

> standards to guide the entity to which the powers are delegated." *Railroad Comm'n v. Lone Star Gas Co.,* 844 S.W.2d 679, 689 (Tex.1992). "Requiring the legislature to include every detail and anticipate unforeseen circumstances would . . . defeat the purpose of delegating legislative authority." *Id.*
>
> * * * * * *
>
> The separation of powers clause [Tex. Const. art. II, § 1] requires that the standards of delegation be "reasonably clear and hence acceptable as a standard of measurement." *Jordan v. State Bd. of Ins.,* 160 Tex. 506, 334 S.W.2d [278,] 280 [(1960)].

But there are some indications that extreme judicial deference to legislative delegation may be declining. A number of Supreme Court justices have emphasized the need for adequate legislative standards. Moreover, "[m]any distinguished scholars and judges [have become] so concerned about the enormous discretionary power of agencies that they [have] urged reinvigoration of the doctrine." KENNETH CULP DAVIS & RICHARD J. PIERCE, JR., 1 ADMINISTRATIVE LAW TREATISE § 2.6, at 74 (3d ed. 1994).

State courts may have less need to reinvigorate the doctrine, since they have historically been more comfortable with striking down state laws on this basis than their federal counterparts. *See* DAVIS § 3.14, at 204 (2d ed. 1978). Texas courts are no exception. In particular, this Court has been especially willing to strike down delegations of legislative authority to the judicial department. *See, e.g., Chemical Bank & Trust Co. v. Falkner,* 369 S.W.2d 427 (Tex.1963); *Davis v. City of Lubbock,* 160 Tex. 38, 326 S.W.2d 699 (1959); *Daniel v. Tyrrell & Garth Inv. Co.,* 127 Tex. 213, 93 S.W.2d 372 (1936). In *Bullock v. Calvert,* 480 S.W.2d 367 (Tex.1972), the Court refused to read a statute as allowing the Secretary of State to decide whether state funds should be used for a political party's primary elections, because such unbridled discretion would violate the delegation doctrine. As Justice Reavley explained for a unanimous Court:

> [T]he effect of this degree of implied authority would be to give the Secretary of State the decision on whether or not state funds should be used for party primary elections and, if so, for what particular expenses and to what extent. This would be an unconstitutional delegation of legislative power in violation of the separation of powers section (Art. 2, § 1) of the Constitution.

480 S.W.2d at 372. In *Ex parte Leslie,* 87 Tex.Crim. 476, 223 S.W. 227 (1920), the Court of Criminal Appeals invalidated a statute empowering the Live Stock Commission to create a penal offense for failing to dip cattle for fever ticks, holding that the law failed to reasonably guide the Commissioner in defining the elements of the offense.

B

As difficult as the issue of proper legislative delegation may be, the considerations are even more complex when the delegation is made not to another department or agency of government, but to a private individual or group. While at first blush such delegations might seem manifestly unconstitutional, further reflection demonstrates that they also are frequently necessary and desirable. Presumably no one would argue that the state should not accord the full benefits and responsibilities of a marital union to a couple who was married by a minister, priest, or rabbi rather than a judge. *See* Tex. Fam.Code § 1.83(a). Also, the delegation of authority to private associations to promulgate certain industrial and professional standards has been of immense benefit to the public. For example, a number of states have adopted existing or future versions of the National Electrical Code, promulgated by an industry association, "turning a technical and complex task often quite beyond the competence of many city councils or even state legislatures over to a specialized private group." David M. Lawrence, *Private Exercise of Governmental Power,* 61 Ind. L.J. 647, 689 (1986).

Still, private delegations clearly raise even more troubling constitutional issues than their public counterparts. On a practical basis, the private delegate may have a personal or pecuniary interest which is inconsistent with or repugnant to the public interest to be served. More fundamentally, the basic concept of democratic rule under a republican form of government is compromised when public powers are abandoned to those who are neither elected by the people, appointed by a public official or entity, nor employed by the government. Thus, we believe it axiomatic that courts should subject private delegations to a more searching scrutiny than their public counterparts.

While the United States Supreme Court has upheld many statutes involving some degree of private delegation, state courts have frequently invalidated such provisions. Unfortunately, scholars have concluded that these cases do not yet, when taken together, evince a coherent constitutional standard. When Professor Davis issued the second edition of his treatise, for example, he abandoned his earlier effort to analyze the state law on private delegations "because identifiable principles do not emerge." DAVIS § 3.12, at 196 (2d ed. 1978). We thus begin our analysis with full recognition that, if the delegation at issue is to a private entity, we must craft our own criteria to judge its constitutionality.

* * * *

D

The only test that has been articulated by a Texas court in assessing the validity of a private delegation is this: "The delegation of authority to private entities may be lawful if the legislative purpose is discernible and there is protection against the arbitrary exercise of power." *Office of Public Ins. Counsel v. Texas Auto. Ins. Plan,* 860 S.W.2d 231, 237 (Tex. App.–Austin 1993, writ denied). This language, which is paraphrased from Professor Davis' explanation of one part of a proposed five-part test for a new public delegation standard, DAVIS § 3.15, at 208 (2d ed. 1978), is not incorrect, but seems too conclusory to give much assistance in striking the proper balance between important but competing interests and principles. Therefore, we prefer to condense the various inquiries posed by scholars and courts to these eight factors:

> 1. Are the private delegate's actions subject to meaningful review by a state agency or other branch of state government?
> 2. Are the persons affected by the private delegate's actions adequately represented in the decisionmaking process?
> 3. Is the private delegate's power limited to making rules, or does the delegate also apply the law to particular individuals?

4. Does the private delegate have a pecuniary or other personal interest that may conflict with his or her public function?
5. Is the private delegate empowered to define criminal acts or impose criminal sanctions?
6. Is the delegation narrow in duration, extent, and subject matter?
7. Does the private delegate possess special qualifications or training for the task delegated to it?
8. Has the Legislature provided sufficient standards to guide the private delegate in its work?

We emphasize at the outset that these standards apply only to private delegations, not to the usual delegation by the Legislature to an agency or another department of government. In reviewing a public delegation, we adhere to those factors set forth by this Court in *Housing Authority of City of Dallas v. Higginbotham,* 135 Tex. 158, 143 S.W.2d 79, 87 (1940), and its progeny. Furthermore, nothing in our analysis should be read as suggesting what provisions of the Act would or would not pass muster were this a public delegation. Likewise, we express no opinion as to whether any of the other statutory enactments cited by the dissenting justices would or would not pass constitutional muster. Thus, in no way does our opinion, as the dissenting justices fear, "ultimately threaten the heretofore established role of quasi-governmental entities under Texas law."

Before applying these factors, we also note that the growers have not expressly categorized their nondelegation argument as either a facial challenge or an "as applied" challenge. We conclude that it is a facial challenge. The growers argue that, based on the overall statutory structure, the Foundation's assessment, collection, and expenditure of funds for eradication violates the separation of powers mandate of our Constitution. Thus, under the growers' argument, the Foundation lacks authority to perform its core function–collecting assessments and conducting mandatory eradication programs–as to any cotton producer, regardless of that producer's particular circumstances. We will thus facially review the legislative delegation before us in light of the above eight factors.

First, while the Foundation is subject to some oversight by the Commissioner of Agriculture, the review is uneven and incomplete. The Legislature did direct the Commissioner to promulgate rules regarding certain areas of the Foundation's operations. The Commissioner could not, however, adopt any procedure for reviewing such critical decisions as the amount of assessments adopted by the growers, the total amount of funds expended on eradication, the amount of debt incurred by the Foundation, or the repayment terms for such debts. These determinations are left exclusively to the growers and the board, excluding the Commissioner or any state agency from meaningful review.

Judging the statute as it is written, rather than as it operated in practice, the second factor militates in favor of the private delegation. The growers in each zone are allowed to vote on whether to participate in the eradication program, and thereby subject themselves to the Foundation's jurisdiction, and are allowed to approve or reject any proposed assessment. Although the Foundation in actuality operated for nineteen months with a board controlled by Texas Cotton Producers' appointees, this process was inconsistent with the statutory contemplation that the Foundation should at all times by governed by the elected board.

The third factor weighs against the delegation. Far from merely devising eradication guidelines, the Foundation actually applied the programs it devised to all growers in zones where the program was approved. In accordance with its statutory authority, the Foundation collected assessments from individual growers and entered those growers' property to carry out its eradication programs.

The fourth factor also weighs against the delegation. The Foundation board members are cotton growers who have a direct pecuniary interest in the eradication programs implemented by the Foundation.

Under the circumstances of this case, the fifth factor does not weigh in our consideration of whether the statute as a whole is an unconstitutional delegation of authority to the Foundation. The Foundation is vested with authority to impose monetary penalties for late payment of the assessments and to direct the Department to destroy a delinquent growers' crops, and it is further empowered to adopt rules, a violation of which is a criminal offense. While this authority to impose penal sanctions strongly suggests an improper private delegation, principles of severability would allow us to strike down this power and still uphold the Act. Thus, even though the penalty provisions seem to represent an unconstitutional delegation of authority to the Foundation, this should not weigh in judging the validity of the Foundation's core function under the Act, *i.e.*, the levying and collecting of assessments and the expenditure of those assessments on eradication programs.

The sixth factor is inconclusive under the circumstances of this case. While the statute pertains to a specific, narrow purpose–eradication of the boll weevil and other cotton pests–it does not limit the program's cost and duration, other than to provide that the program is subject to the Sunset Act and that it should be discontinued once the boll weevil is eradicated.

The seventh factor, on its face, weighs against the delegation. While the Act is designed to allow those with firsthand experience in the cotton industry to lead the eradication effort, there is no assurance that those elected will actually have special qualifications or training regarding eradication of boll weevils, and there is absolutely no evidence that board actions were "taken for purposes which are independent of the statute," Professor Davis' salient test. DAVIS § 3.12, at 196 (2d ed.1978). The facts are thus quite distinct from a private delegation, say, for the promulgation of a municipal electrical code by an industry association consisting of electrical contractors, inspectors, and manufacturers. There is, of course, some tension between this factor and the second factor. It would ordinarily be difficult for a private delegation both to guarantee adequate representation of those affected by the delegation and to vest decisionmaking authority in a group of experts. There is no evidence in the record of a disinterested and yet eminent pre-existing entity to which the devising and implementing of a boll weevil eradication program could have been delegated. Thus, while the Act fails to meet the seventh factor, this failure is excused by the satisfaction of the second factor.

Finally, the eighth factor weighs against the delegation. The Legislature has provided very few statutory standards to guide the Foundation. While the Act provides the procedures for zone referenda and specifies the powers and duties of the board, it provides no guidance as to how assessments are to be set or the amount of debt that the Foundation may incur. Thus, in practice, the Foundation had free rein to incur over $9 million in debt in the Lower Rio Grande Valley Zone to be repaid by the growers there through several years of assessments, even though those growers voted within 21 months to discontinue their eradication program.

We recognize that the judicial branch should defer to the judgment of the people's elected representatives whenever possible, and we by no means suggest that a private delegation must satisfy all eight of these factors. We recognize also that courts should, when possible, read delegations narrowly to uphold their validity. Thus, in *Edgewood,* we accepted the State's restricted reading of a statute giving the Commissioner of Education rulemaking authority, to hold that, as limited, no authority was conveyed in violation of the nondelegation doctrine. *See* 917 S.W.2d at 740-41. Here, however, the invalidity of the delegation does not hinge on any one provision of the Act that might be narrowly interpreted; rather, the Act as a whole represents an overly broad delegation of legislative authority to a private entity, violating a majority of the eight factors we have set forth. Therefore, the Act cannot stand.

* * * * * *

The nondelegation doctrine should be used sparingly, when there is, in Justice Cardozo's memorable phrase, "delegation running riot." *A.L.A. Schechter Poultry Corp. v. United States,* 295 U.S. 495, 553 (1935) (Cardozo, J., concurring). Because we believe this is an extraordinary case, we affirm the judgments of the trial courts.

HECHT, Justice, concurring in part and dissenting in part, and concurring in the judgment.

The Texas Boll Weevil Eradication Foundation wields more legislative power with less restraint than any other privately chartered nonprofit corporation in Texas, or, as far as I can tell, in the history of Texas. Twelve other states have private foundations to help eradicate boll weevils; none has–or appears to need–the power the Legislature has ceded the Texas Boll Weevil Eradication Foundation. The Foundation is by no means a typical administrative agency; it is not even an atypical administrative agency; it is a complete anomaly in the structure of government.

Thus, I agree with the Court that the Official Cotton Growers' Boll Weevil Eradication Foundation Act delegates legislative power to the Foundation in violation of Article II, Section 1 of the Texas Constitution, but I think this conclusion is much clearer than the Court does. The Court's decision certainly does not "threaten the heretofore established role of quasi-governmental entities under Texas law," as the sky-is-falling rhetoric of Justice Cornyn's opinion forebodes. Holding the extraordinary delegation of power to the Foundation unconstitutional is no more a threat to other administrative agencies than it is to the ozone layer.

The vice in the delegation to the Foundation does not lie simply in the fact that the Foundation is a private entity or that, as I conclude, it is privately managed. Nor is the vice simply that the only standards prescribed by the Legislature to guide the Foundation are extremely broad, or that the Foundation is largely free of public supervision. The Court's decision rests on a consideration of all these factors. Plainly put, the Texas Boll Weevil

Eradication Foundation is little more than a posse: volunteers and private entities neither elected nor appointed, privately organized and supported by the majority of some small group, backed by law but without guidelines or supervision, wielding great power over people's lives and property but answering virtually to no one. The Foundation is only a private, nonprofit corporation, run mostly by individuals who have never been elected or appointed by an elected official, but the Legislature has empowered it to conduct elections of cotton growers in various areas throughout the State, to determine whether and how to conduct a boll weevil eradication program, to assess cotton farmers millions of dollars to pay for the program, to deposit those assessments in its own account not subject to state purchasing and auditing requirements, to enter private property and destroy healthy crops for failure to pay assessments, to borrow unlimited amounts and commit cotton farmers to repay its debts without their approval, and to spend the money without any state supervision. The Legislature has broad discretion to delegate authority to administrators, but for reasons the Court explains, this goes too far.

CORNYN, Justice, joined by ENOCH, SPECTOR and ABBOTT, Justices, concurring in part and dissenting in part.

I.

In striking down this statute, the Court commits four major errors that ultimately threaten the heretofore established role of quasi-governmental entities under Texas law. Repeatedly, we have recognized that legislative delegations of authority are an essential part of modern governance in an increasingly complex society. *See, e.g., National Ass'n of Indep. Insurers v. Texas Dep't of Ins.,* 925 S.W.2d 667 (Tex.1996); *Texas Ass'n of Business v. Texas Air Control Bd.,* 852 S.W.2d 440, 451 (Tex.1993). The Court's decision in this case, ironically enough, tends to prove rather than refute the arguments of those administrative law scholars who contend that state delegation cases lack a defining principle. *See, e.g.,* Greco, *Standards or Safeguards: A Survey of the Delegation Doctrine in the States,* 8 Admin. L.J. 67 (1994).

That is not to say that the concerns embodied in the nondelegation doctrine are trivial; just the opposite is true. There can be no doubt that when lawmaking power is delegated to an administrative agency to carry out the Legislature's policy goals, that agency is necessarily given the power to give substance to that legislative policy. But as the United States Supreme Court has said, given proper safeguards, this delegation is both proper and necessary:

> So long as Congress "shall lay down by legislative act an intelligible principle to which the person or body authorized to [exercise the delegated authority] is directed to conform, such legislative action is not a forbidden delegation of legislative power."

Mistretta v. United States, 488 U.S. 361, 372 (1989).

Given that the same concerns and conditions exist in our state system, it is not surprising that we have likewise acknowledged the propriety of legislative delegation to carry out legislative purposes, as long as there are established reasonable standards to guide the agency to whom those powers are delegated. *See e.g., Edgewood Indep. Sch. Dist. v.*

Meno, 917 S.W.2d 717, 740 (Tex.1995). We do not require these standards to be comprehensive. To the contrary, we have said that "[r]equiring the legislature to include every detail and anticipate unforeseen circumstances . . . would defeat the purpose of delegating legislative authority." *Railroad Comm'n v. Lone Star Gas Co.,* 844 S.W.2d 679, 689 (Tex.1992).

It is the unknown ramifications of the Court's new test that ought to be of the most concern to the Court. The Court's new test will no doubt apply to delegations ranging from "school choice" to private prisons. In fact, "private" delegations are used extensively in Texas government, have been routinely upheld by this and other Texas courts, and given proper standards and oversight by the delegating authority, these delegations raise no constitutional concerns. For instance, the Court does not consider whether or how this new test might affect the continuing viability of the Relinquishment Act, which dedicates revenue from state-owned oil and gas reserves to the Permanent School Fund, the constitutionality of which this Court upheld against a delegation challenge in *Greene v. Robison,* 117 Tex. 516, 8 S.W.2d 655, 656 (1928) (allowing private persons to sell or lease oil and gas owned by the state "upon such terms and conditions as such [private person] may deem best" subject only to minimum prices set in the statute). Similarly, in *Texas Workers' Compensation Comm'n v. Garcia,* 893 S.W.2d 504 (Tex.1995), this Court upheld the constitutionality of the Workers' Compensation Act against an open courts, equal protection, and a substantive due course of law challenge arising out of the use of the American Medical Association's Guides to the Evaluation of Permanent Impairment for determining injured workers' impairment ratings. Clearly, the Act delegates to the American Medical Association (AMA), a private national association of physicians, the task of promulgating standards for translating a worker's job-related injury into an impairment rating to determine compensation benefits. Although no separate delegation argument was advanced in that case, the constitutional complaints that were urged involve many of the same considerations that arise in a delegation challenge. Yet the Court had no trouble upholding the use of the AMA Guides.

Nor does the Court consider the impact of its decision on the Legislature's common practice of delegating eminent domain powers to private entities. *See, e.g.,* Tex. Nat. Res.Code § 111.019 *et seq.* (granting common carriers power of eminent domain); Tex.Rev.Civ. Stat. art. 1417 (granting telegraph corporations the power to condemn property); Tex.Rev.Civ. Stat. art. 1435a (granting certain private oil and gas companies the power of eminent domain); Tex.Rev.Civ. Stat. art. 1439 (granting power of condemnation to sewer companies); Tex.Rev.Civ. Stat. art. 6535 (granting certain railroad corporations right of eminent domain).

Even this Court delegates to a private entity the task of approving the law school course-of-study requirements for would-be Texas lawyers. Rather than engage in the laborious, expensive, and specialized task of assessing the nation's law schools ourselves, we delegate this function to the American Bar Association, a voluntary national association of lawyers. Not surprisingly, the Legislature has also embraced this model for a host of other certifications and licenses. Significantly, "private" delegations offer vast and varied expertise to Texas government at no additional cost to taxpayers and without bloating an already sizable bureaucracy.

Finally, only by leapfrogging a nearly unbroken string of decisions from this Court and the United States Supreme Court upholding legislative delegation of authority to various agencies, many with far less legislative guidance than was provided here, is the Court able to apply its new, stricter "private delegation" test in place of long-established Texas law. In my view, this Court's decisions provide more than sufficient guidance–and certainly more authority–for evaluating the propriety of the delegation in this case. Our decisions also compel a determination that Subchapter 74D is not facially unconstitutional.

* * * *

III.

As I have previously noted, we have repeatedly held that the Legislature may delegate authority to agencies to carry out legislative purposes so long as it establishes "'reasonable standards to guide the entity to which the powers are delegated.'" *Edgewood,* 917 S.W.2d at 740 (quoting *Railroad Comm'n v. Lone Star Gas Co.,* 844 S.W.2d 679, 689 (Tex.1992)). "'Such standards may be broad . . . [when] conditions must be considered which cannot be conveniently investigated by the legislature,'" *Lone Star Gas Co.,* 844 S.W.2d at 689, and at the same time, they should be "reasonably clear and hence acceptable as a standard of measurement." *Jordan v. State Bd. of Ins.,* 160 Tex. 506, 334 S.W.2d 278, 280 (1960). The Court has recognized six categories of allowable delegations:

> (1) delegations when the Legislature cannot practically and efficiently exercise powers (such as determining rail rates, questions of public convenience and necessity, and granting permission to drill oil wells);
> (2) delegations to administrative bodies of the authority to make rules to implement statutes;
> (3) delegations to find facts and ascertain conditions upon which an existing law may operate (for example, the authority given the Railroad Commission, the Public Utility Commission, the Texas Natural Resource Conservation Commission);
> (4) delegations of legislative authority that set up broad standards, leaving to the delegate to make rules and determine facts to which the legislative policy is to apply, when the conditions to be considered cannot be easily investigated by the Legislature;
> (5) delegations of the power to fix rates within prescribed limits to cover specified items of cost; and
> (6) delegations of the power to determine the question of necessity of taking land for public use.

Housing Auth. v. Higginbotham, 135 Tex. 158, 143 S.W.2d 79, 87 (1940).

[T]he delegation to the Foundation fits the description of at least four types of allowable delegation outlined in *Higginbotham.* First, the Legislature cannot practically and efficiently exercise many of the powers delegated to the Foundation, such as determining the level of assessments needed to achieve the statute's goals. Second, the statute delegates to the Foundation and Commissioner the authority to make rules to implement the statute. Third, the Foundation and Commissioner are given the power to find facts and ascertain conditions upon which Subchapter 74D may operate, such as determining when a field is infested and what crops present a threat to the program. Fourth, the statute sets up broad standards, leaving to the delegate to make rules and determine facts to which the legislative policy is to apply, when the conditions to be considered, such as level of infestation and which types of integrated management practices to use, cannot be easily investigated by the Legislature. *See Higginbotham,* 143 S.W.2d at 87.

Accordingly, I would hold that Subchapter 74D represents a constitutionally valid delegation of power and that petitioners' facial challenge fails.

Notes on Delegations to Private Entities

Private v. Public Delegations: Why was the *Boll Weevil* court concerned that the delegation had been made to a private entity? How did the test the court adopted for private delegations differ from the test the court previously promulgated for public delegations? Would the *Boll Weevil* delegation have been constitutional if the delegation had been made to a governmental entity?

Delegations of legislative authority to governmental entities have routinely been upheld in Texas over the last several decades.[36] Indeed, the Texas Supreme Court has only struck down one delegation to a governmental entity since 1975, in *Texas Antiquities Committee v. Dallas County Community College District*.[37] The legislature had created the Texas Antiquities Committee that could prevent the alteration and demolition of "buildings . . . and locations of historical . . . interest." A plurality concluded that this delegation provided no meaningful criteria or standards as "[a]ll unrestorable structures ordinarily hold some nostalgic tug upon someone and may all qualify as 'buildings . . . of historical . . . interest.'"[38] But Chief Justice Greenhill, while concurring in the judgment, declined to reach the nondelegation doctrine question, and four justices dissented.

The Private Delegation Doctrine in Other Contexts: The private delegation principles from *Boll Weevil* have been applied in two subsequent Texas Supreme Court decisions. In *Proctor v. Andrews*, the court upheld a delegation of authority to the American Arbitration Association and the Federal Mediation and Conciliation Service to determine whether arbitrators were qualified and neutral.[39] In evaluating the eight *Boll Weevil* factors, the court reasoned that, although the selection of qualified arbitrators was not subject to any other meaningful government review, the parties did have the right to strike arbitrators they believed were not qualified. Additionally, the delegation was both narrow and limited, and was made to respected entities that did not have any private interest at stake in the controversy between the parties.[40]

---

[36]*See, e.g.*, Edgewood Indep. Sch. Dist. v. Meno, 917 S.W.2d 717, 740 (Tex. 1995) (upholding delegation of authority to state education commissioner to adopt necessary rules to implement chapter of Education Code); R.R. Comm'n v. Lone Star Gas. Co., 844 S.W.2d 679, 685 (Tex. 1992) (upholding delegation to Railroad Commission of authority to adopt rules and orders as necessary for the conservation of oil and gas); Jordan v. Bd. of Ins., 334 S.W.2d 278, 281-82 (Tex. 1960) (upholding delegated authority of state board of insurance to determine whether officers and directors of insurance carriers were "not worthy of the public confidence").

[37]554 S.W.2d 924 (Tex. 1977).

[38]*Tex. Antiquities*, 554 S.W.2d at 927.

[39]972 S.W.2d 729 (Tex. 1998).

[40]*Id.* at 735-38.

In contrast, in *FM Properties Operating Co. v. City of Austin*, the court held that section 26.179 of the Water Code was an unconstitutional delegation as it authorized some private landowners to create, in the extraterritorial jurisdiction of certain cities, "water quality protection zones" that in specified situations were exempt from municipal regulation.[41] Employing the eight *Boll Weevil* factors, the court reasoned that the delegation impermissibly authorized interested landowners to exempt themselves from all meaningful review of their substitute plans, which replaced the water quality protection plans enacted through the representative process at the municipal level.[42]

Instead of relying on article II, section 1 as the source of limitations for private delegations, both *Proctor* and *FM Properties* relied on article III, section 1, which vests the power to make laws in the legislature.[43] Although *Boll Weevil* involved article II as well because there was some dispute as to whether the Foundation was a state administrative agency (another department of government) or a private entity, the *Proctor* court explained that, in those instances in which there is no dispute that the delegate is a private party, the only constitutional source for the doctrine is article III, section 1.[44] Nevertheless, whether analyzed under article II or article III of the Texas Constitution, the same eight-factor test applies to ascertain whether the legislature has impermissibly delegated authority to a private entity.

Federal v. State Delegations: As Chief Justice Phillips notes in his opinion, many state courts demand more specificity for legislative delegations than required for congressional delegations by the federal courts. While some state courts have followed the federal nondelegation doctrine, more states have adopted a more stringent approach. What might account for this difference of treatment?

Are there prudential institutional reasons to scrutinize more carefully legislative delegations made by the state legislature in comparison to those made by Congress? The Texas Legislature is in session far less often than Congress, only meeting in regular session for no more than 140 days every two years.[45] This may make it efficient to delegate authority. On the other hand, though, as many state legislators are only part-time, is it reasonable to expect them to exercise the same degree of oversight over agencies as full-time congressional offices? Is this a reason to exercise more care due to the concern that the state legislatures may be too prone to delegate authority rather than properly make key policy decisions?

Is the presence of an express separation of powers provision another reason supporting a state's employment of stricter standards in adjudging whether a law violates separation of powers principles? In *City of Dallas v. Stewart*, the Texas Supreme Court held

---

[41]22 S.W.3d 868 (Tex. 2000).

[42]*Id.* at 880-88.

[43]*FM Properties*, 22 S.W.3d at 873; *Proctor*, 972 S.W.2d at 733. Article III, section 1 of the Texas Constitution provides: "The Legislative power of this State shall be vested in a Senate and a House of Representatives, which together shall be styled 'The Legislature of the State of Texas.'"

[44]*Proctor*, 972 S.W.2d at 733.

[45]TEX. CONST. art. III, § 5.

that the Texas Constitution required the judiciary to make an independent, de novo determination in a takings claim whether the landowner's property was a public nuisance as a result of blight, instead of employing a substantial evidence review of an administrative body's determination of the issue.[46] The court relied in part on the state's "Separation of Powers Clause, which has no explicit federal analogue," as supporting the need for an independent judicial review of the constitutional issues raised in a takings claim. The court explained:

> The scope of separation of powers is a function of governmental structure, and because of the difference between Texas and federal government, its requirements at the state level are different. . . . In particular, the fragmentation of Texas's executive branch "attenuates" the accountability of our administrative agencies. Accountability is especially weak with regard to municipal level agencies . . . which are created by cities that "typically lack the separation of powers of the state and federal governments."[47]

Does a similar rationale support the concern for private delegations expressed in *Boll Weevil*? Is that what other states with explicit separation of powers provisions have done?

B. SEPARATION OF POWERS IN OTHER STATES

While forty states have express separation of powers clauses in their constitutions, judicial interpretations of their scope have varied. A few states have employed the federal approach that authorizes practically all delegations, some states have used what can be described as a middle ground, and other states (like Texas) have adopted a strict interpretation of separation of powers. Although some states have relied on their explicit state constitutional provisions in adopting a stricter approach for separation of powers issues,[48] other states have expressed the view that the terminology makes no difference.[49] What should the proper impact of an explicit separation of powers provision? The following high-profile case from Florida provides one answer.

Bush v. Schiavo, 885 So.2d 321 (Fla. 2004)

PARIENTE, C.J.

The narrow issue in this case requires this Court to decide the constitutionality of a law passed by the Legislature that directly affected Theresa Schiavo, who has been in a persistent vegetative state since 1990. This Court, after careful consideration of the arguments of the parties and amici, the constitutional issues raised, the precise wording of

---

[46] 361 S.W.3d 562, 564 (Tex. 2012).

[47] *Id.* at 573 (citations omitted).

[48] *See, e.g.*, Hobbs v. Jones, 2012 Ark. 293 (2012) (holding statute granting corrections officials unbridled discretion to determine state's lethal injection protocol violated explicit state separation of powers provision); Legislative Research Comm'n v. Brown, 664 S.W.2d 907, 914-20 (Ky. 1984) (invalidating legislative delegation of authority due in part to "strict construction" required by separation of powers provision).

[49] *See* Brown v. Heymann, 297 A.2d 572, 577 (N.J. 1972).

the challenged law, and the underlying procedural history of this case, concludes that the law violates the fundamental constitutional tenet of separation of powers and is therefore unconstitutional both on its face and as applied to Theresa Schiavo.

FACTS AND PROCEDURAL HISTORY

The resolution of the discrete separation of powers issue presented in this case does not turn on the facts of the underlying guardianship proceedings that resulted in the removal of Theresa's nutrition and hydration tube. [But] the procedural history is important because it provides the backdrop to the Legislature's enactment of the challenged law. As set forth in the Second District's first opinion in this case,

> Theresa Marie Schindler was born on December 3, 1963, and lived with or near her parents in Pennsylvania until she married Michael Schiavo on November 10, 1984. Michael and Theresa moved to Florida in 1986. They were happily married and both were employed. They had no children.
>
> On February 25, 1990, their lives changed. Theresa, age 27, suffered a cardiac arrest as a result of a potassium imbalance. Michael called 911, and Theresa was rushed to the hospital. She never regained consciousness.
>
> Since 1990, Theresa has lived in nursing homes with constant care. She is fed and hydrated by tubes. The staff changes her diapers regularly. She has had numerous health problems, but none have been life threatening.

In re Guardianship of Schiavo, 780 So.2d 176, 177 (Fla. 2d DCA 2001) (*Schiavo I*).

For the first three years after this tragedy, Michael and Theresa's parents, Robert and Mary Schindler, enjoyed an amicable relationship. However, that relationship ended in 1993 and the parties literally stopped speaking to each other. In May of 1998, eight years after Theresa lost consciousness, Michael petitioned the guardianship court to authorize the termination of life-prolonging procedures. *See id.* By filing this petition, which the Schindlers opposed, Michael placed the difficult decision in the hands of the court.

After a trial, at which both Michael and the Schindlers presented evidence, the guardianship court issued an extensive written order authorizing the discontinuance of artificial life support. The trial court found by clear and convincing evidence that Theresa Schiavo was in a persistent vegetative state and that Theresa would elect to cease life-prolonging procedures if she were competent to make her own decision. This order was affirmed on direct appeal, *see Schiavo I,* 780 So.2d at 177, and we denied review. *See In re Guardianship of Schiavo,* 789 So.2d 348 (Fla.2001).

The severity of Theresa's medical condition was explained as follows:

> The evidence is overwhelming that Theresa is in a permanent or persistent vegetative state. It is important to understand that a persistent vegetative

> state is not simply a coma. She is not asleep. She has cycles of apparent wakefulness and apparent sleep without any cognition or awareness. As she breathes, she often makes moaning sounds. Theresa has severe contractures of her hands, elbows, knees, and feet.
>
> Over the span of this last decade, Theresa's brain has deteriorated because of the lack of oxygen it suffered at the time of the heart attack. By mid 1996, the CAT scans of her brain showed a severely abnormal structure. At this point, much of her cerebral cortex is simply gone and has been replaced by cerebral spinal fluid. Medicine cannot cure this condition. Unless an act of God, a true miracle, were to recreate her brain, Theresa will always remain in an unconscious, reflexive state, totally dependent upon others to feed her and care for her most private needs. She could remain in this state for many years.

Although the guardianship court's final order authorizing the termination of life-prolonging procedures was affirmed on direct appeal, the litigation continued because the Schindlers began an attack on the final order. [The Schindlers filed a motion for relief from judgment in the original guardianship court, a separate complaint in a different court, and appealed adverse determinations by these courts through the Florida appellate system. After these appeals were exhausted], Theresa's nutrition and hydration tube was removed on October 15, 2003.

On October 21, 2003, the Legislature enacted chapter 2003-418, the Governor signed the Act into law, and the Governor issued executive order No. 03-201 to stay the continued withholding of nutrition and hydration from Theresa. The nutrition and hydration tube was reinserted pursuant to the Governor's executive order.

On the same day, Michael Schiavo brought the action for declaratory judgment in the circuit court. Relying on undisputed facts and legal argument, the circuit court entered a final summary judgment on May 6, 2004, in favor of Michael Schiavo, finding the Act unconstitutional both on its face and as applied to Theresa.

ANALYSIS

We begin our discussion by emphasizing that our task in this case is to review the constitutionality of chapter 2003-418, not to reexamine the guardianship court's orders directing the removal of Theresa's nutrition and hydration tube, or to review the Second District's numerous decisions in the guardianship case. Although we recognize that the parties continue to dispute the findings made in the prior proceedings, these proceedings are relevant to our decision only to the extent that they occurred and resulted in a final judgment directing the withdrawal of life-prolonging procedures.

The language of chapter 2003-418 is clear. It states in full:

> Section 1. (1) The Governor shall have the authority to issue a one-time stay to prevent the withholding of nutrition and hydration from a patient if, as of October 15, 2003:
> (a) That patient has no written advance directive;

> (b) The court has found that patient to be in a persistent vegetative state;
> (c) That patient has had nutrition and hydration withheld; and
> (d) A member of that patient's family has challenged the withholding of nutrition and hydration.
> (2) The Governor's authority to issue the stay expires 15 days after the effective date of this act, and the expiration of the authority does not impact the validity or the effect of any stay issued pursuant to this act. The Governor may lift the stay authorized under this act at any time. A person may not be held civilly liable and is not subject to regulatory or disciplinary sanctions for taking any action to comply with a stay issued by the Governor pursuant to this act.
> (3) Upon issuance of a stay, the chief judge of the circuit court shall appoint a guardian ad litem for the patient to make recommendations to the Governor and the court.
> Section 2. This act shall take effect upon becoming a law.

Ch.2003-418, Laws of Fla. Thus, chapter 2003-418 allowed the Governor to issue a stay to prevent the withholding of nutrition and hydration from a patient under the circumstances provided for in subsections (1)(a)-(d). Under the fifteen-day sunset provision, the Governor's authority to issue the stay expired on November 5, 2003. *See id.* The Governor's authority to lift the stay continues indefinitely.

SEPARATION OF POWERS

The cornerstone of American democracy known as separation of powers recognizes three separate branches of government--the executive, the legislative, and the judicial–each with its own powers and responsibilities. In Florida, the constitutional doctrine has been expressly codified in article II, section 3 of the Florida Constitution, which not only divides state government into three branches but also expressly prohibits one branch from exercising the powers of the other two branches:

> Branches of Government.– The powers of the state government shall be divided into legislative, executive and judicial branches. No person belonging to one branch shall exercise any powers appertaining to either of the other branches unless expressly provided herein.

"This Court . . . has traditionally applied a strict separation of powers doctrine," *State v. Cotton,* 769 So.2d 345, 353 (Fla.2000), and has explained that this doctrine "encompasses two fundamental prohibitions. The first is that no branch may encroach upon the powers of another. The second is that no branch may delegate to another branch its constitutionally assigned power." *Chiles v. Children A, B, C, D, E, & F,* 589 So.2d 260, 264 (Fla.1991) (citation omitted).

Encroachment on the Judicial Branch

Under the express separation of powers provision in our state constitution, "the judiciary is a coequal branch of the Florida government vested with the sole authority to exercise the judicial power," and "the legislature cannot, short of constitutional amendment, reallocate the balance of power expressly delineated in the constitution among the three coequal branches." *Children A, B, C, D, E, & F,* 589 So.2d at 268-69.

As the United States Supreme Court has explained, the power of the judiciary is "not merely to rule on cases, but to *decide* them, subject to review only by superior courts" and "[h]aving achieved finality . . . a judicial decision becomes the last word of the judicial department with regard to a particular case or controversy." *Plaut,* 514 U.S. at 218-19, 227. Moreover, "purely judicial acts . . . are not subject to review as to their accuracy by the Governor." *In re Advisory Opinion to the Governor,* 213 So.2d 716, 720 (Fla.1968).

In this case, the undisputed facts show that the guardianship court authorized Michael to proceed with the discontinuance of Theresa's life support after the issue was fully litigated in a proceeding in which the Schindlers were afforded the opportunity to present evidence on all issues. This order as well as the order denying the Schindlers' motion for relief from judgment were affirmed on direct appeal. *See Schiavo I,* 780 So.2d at 177; *Schiavo IV,* 851 So.2d at 183. The Schindlers sought review in this Court, which was denied. Thereafter, the tube was removed. Subsequently, pursuant to the Governor's executive order, the nutrition and hydration tube was reinserted. Thus, the Act, as applied in this case, resulted in an executive order that effectively reversed a properly rendered final judgment and thereby constituted an unconstitutional encroachment on the power that has been reserved for the independent judiciary.

Delegation of Legislative Authority

In addition to concluding that the Act is unconstitutional as applied in this case because it encroaches on the power of the judicial branch, we further conclude that the Act is unconstitutional on its face because it delegates legislative power to the Governor. The Legislature is permitted to transfer subordinate functions "to permit administration of legislative policy by an agency with the expertise and flexibility to deal with complex and fluid conditions." *Microtel, Inc. v. Fla. Public Serv. Comm'n,* 464 So.2d 1189, 1191 (Fla.1985). However, under article II, section 3 of the constitution the Legislature "may not delegate the power to enact a law or the right to exercise unrestricted discretion in applying the law." *Sims v. State,* 754 So.2d 657, 668 (Fla.2000). This prohibition, known as the nondelegation doctrine, requires that "fundamental and primary policy decisions . . . be made by members of the legislature who are elected to perform those tasks, and [that the] administration of legislative programs must be pursuant to some minimal standards and guidelines ascertainable by reference to the enactment establishing the program." *Askew v. Cross Key Waterways,* 372 So.2d 913, 925 (Fla.1978).

We have recognized that the "specificity of the guidelines [set forth in the legislation] will depend on the complexity of the subject and the 'degree of difficulty involved in articulating finite standards.'" *Brown v. Apalachee Regional Planning Council,* 560 So.2d 782, 784 (Fla.1990) (quoting *Askew,* 372 So.2d at 918). However, we have also made clear that "[e]ven where a general approach would be more practical than a detailed scheme of legislation, enactments may not be drafted in terms so general and unrestrictive that administrators are left without standards for the guidance of their official acts." *State Dep't of Citrus v. Griffin,* 239 So.2d 577, 581 (Fla.1970).

In *Askew,* the Court invalidated a statute that directed the executive branch to designate certain areas of the state as areas of critical state concern but did not contain sufficient standards to allow "a reviewing court to ascertain whether the priorities recognized by the Administration Commission comport with the intent of the legislature."

372 So.2d at 919. In this case, the circuit court found that chapter 2003-418 contains no guidelines or standards that "would serve to limit the Governor from exercising completely unrestricted discretion in applying the law to" those who fall within its terms. The circuit court explained:

> The terms of the Act affirmatively confirm the discretionary power conferred upon the Governor. He is given the "authority to issue a one-time stay to prevent the withholding of nutrition and hydration from a patient" under certain circumstances but, he is not required to do so. Likewise, the act provides that the Governor "*may* lift the stay authorized under this act at any time. The Governor *may* revoke the stay upon a finding that a change in the condition of the patient warrants revocation." (Emphasis added). In both instances there is nothing to provide the Governor with any direction or guidelines for the exercise of this delegated authority. The Act does not suggest what constitutes "a change in condition of the patient" that could "warrant revocation." Even when such an undefined "change" occurs, the Governor is not compelled to act. The Act confers upon the Governor the unfettered discretion to determine what the terms of the Act mean and when, or if, he may act under it.

We agree with this analysis. In enacting chapter 2003-418, the Legislature failed to provide any standards by which the Governor should determine whether, in any given case, a stay should be issued and how long a stay should remain in effect. Further, the Legislature has failed to provide any criteria for lifting the stay. This absolute, unfettered discretion to decide whether to issue and then when to lift a stay makes the Governor's decision virtually unreviewable.

We also reject the Governor's argument that this legislation provides an additional layer of due process protection to those who are unable to communicate their wishes regarding end-of-life decisions. Parts I, II, III, and IV of chapter 765, enacted by the Legislature in 1992 and amended several times, provide detailed protections for those who are adjudicated incompetent, including that the proxy's decision be based on what the patient would have chosen under the circumstances or is in the patient's best interest, and be supported by competent, substantial evidence. Chapter 765 also provides for judicial review if "[t]he patient's family, the health care facility, or the attending physician, or any other interested person who may reasonably be expected to be directly affected by the surrogate or proxy's decision . . . believes [that] [t]he surrogate or proxy's decision is not in accord with the patient's known desires or the provisions of this chapter."

In contrast to the protections set forth in chapter 765, chapter 2003-418's standardless, open-ended delegation of authority by the Legislature to the Governor provides no guarantee that the incompetent patient's right to withdraw life-prolonging procedures will in fact be honored. *See In re Guardianship of Browning,* 568 So.2d 4, 12 (Fla.1990) (reaffirming that an incompetent person has the same right to refuse medical treatment as a competent person). As noted above, the Act does not even require that the Governor consider the patient's wishes in deciding whether to issue a stay, and instead allows a unilateral decision by the Governor to stay the withholding of life-prolonging procedures without affording any procedural process to the patient.

In sum, although chapter 2003-418 applies to a limited class of people, it provides no criteria to guide the Governor's decision about whether to act. In addition, once the Governor has issued a stay as provided for in the Act, there are no criteria for the Governor to evaluate in deciding whether to lift the stay. Thus, chapter 2003-418 allows the Governor to act "through whim, show [ ] favoritism, or exercis[e] unbridled discretion," and is therefore an unconstitutional delegation of legislative authority.

CONCLUSION

The continuing vitality of our system of separation of powers precludes the other two branches from nullifying the judicial branch's final orders. If the Legislature with the assent of the Governor can do what was attempted here, the judicial branch would be subordinated to the final directive of the other branches. Also subordinated would be the rights of individuals, including the well established privacy right to self determination. No court judgment could ever be considered truly final and no constitutional right truly secure, because the precedent of this case would hold to the contrary. Vested rights could be stripped away based on popular clamor. The essential core of what the Founding Fathers sought to change from their experience with English rule would be lost, especially their belief that our courts exist precisely to preserve the rights of individuals, even when doing so is contrary to popular will.

The trial court's decision regarding Theresa Schiavo was made in accordance with the procedures and protections set forth by the judicial branch and in accordance with the statutes passed by the Legislature in effect at that time. That decision is final and the Legislature's attempt to alter that final adjudication is unconstitutional as applied to Theresa Schiavo. Further, even if there had been no final judgment in this case, the Legislature provided the Governor constitutionally inadequate standards for the application of the legislative authority delegated in chapter 2003-418. Because chapter 2003-418 runs afoul of article II, section 3 of the Florida Constitution in both respects, we affirm the circuit court's final summary judgment.

Notes on Delegations and Encroachments in Other Jurisdictions

A Delegation with Inadequate Standards?: Did Florida's "Terri's Law" really provide inadequate standards for Governor Jeb Bush? In view of the procedural history of the law, was the legislative intent clear? Or was the court correct in limiting its analysis to the plain text of the statute? In a subsequent decision, *Florida Department of State v. Martin*, the Florida Supreme Court relied on *Schiavo* to hold that a statute granting the Department of State absolute discretion to allow a candidate for elected office to withdraw within forty-two days of an election unconstitutionally delegated "unbridled" legislative authority to the department as no standards or criteria were provided to guide the determination.[50] The court was concerned that the statute neither provided factors to be considered nor the legislative purpose served in determining whether a candidate should be allowed to withdraw, allowing the potential for arbitrary decisionmaking.[51]

---

[50]916 So.2d 763, 769-73 (Fla. 2005).

[51]*Id.* at 771-73.

Would the Texas Supreme Court have reached the same holding as the Florida Supreme Court on a delegation made to the executive? Was the Florida Supreme Court's alternative holding regarding the encroachment on the judicial branch the stronger basis for invalidating the law?

Legislative Encroachment on the Judiciary: *Schiavo*'s alternative holding that the legislature cannot interfere with the judiciary's final judgments is a typical component of American separation of powers principles. As discussed in the previous section, the Texas high courts have likewise held that a statute which operates to undermine prior final judgments is unconstitutional.[52] This is also consistent with federal precedent, at least with respect to federal court judgments.[53] But the Texas courts have repeatedly noted the limitations of this rule. The legislature has the authority to prescribe rules of procedure and evidence and to modify the governing law even in pending cases,[54] as long as in doing so it does not unduly interfere with core judicial functions or prior judgments that have been finally resolved by the judicial department. Is this an appropriate balance between the legislative and judicial departments?

Should legislative encroachments on the judiciary be forbidden? A couple of states originally subordinated the judiciary to the other branches of government. For instance, article IX of the New Jersey Constitution of 1776 provided that the governor and the upper house of the legislature also constituted "the Court of Appeals, in the last resort, in all causes of law." Thus, judicial decisions were subject to political review in New Jersey at the founding. Almost all the other states, however, had independent judiciaries, which New Jersey finally adopted in 1844.

Even if legislative encroachments on the judiciary should be forbidden, is the judiciary the appropriate branch to determine when the legislature has gone too far? Does the judiciary have an inherent conflict of interest? Or does the judiciary have to undertake this role because no other branch can be trusted to do so? Such normative questions lurked beneath the New York high court's decision in *Maron v. Silver*.[55] After twelve years

---

[52]*See, e.g.*, Williams v. State, 707 S.W.2d 40, 46 (Tex. Crim. App. 1986); Langever v. Miller, 76 S.W.2d 1025, 1035-37 (Tex. 1934).

[53]*See, e.g.*, Plaut v. Spendthrift Farm, Inc., 515 U.S. 211, 218-24 (1995). While Congress cannot undermine prior final judgments of the federal courts, it has some power to undermine prior final judgments of the state courts, although how far that power extends is subject to some debate. In enacting the federal Terri's Law for the Relief of the Parents of Theresa Marie Schiavo, Pub. L. No. 109-3, Congress instructed the federal courts to engage in a de novo review, without deference to the prior state court final judgments, of whether the removal of Schiavo's nutrition and hydration violated any federal right. The federal courts determined it was unnecessary to decide the various constitutional challenges raised against the law because an adequate showing for injunctive relief had not been made, *see* Schiavo *ex rel.* Schindler v. Schiavo, 403 F.3d 1223, 1227 (11th Cir. 2005), even though one judge believed the law violated separation of powers principles. Schiavo *ex rel.* Schindler v. Schiavo, 404 F.3d 1270, 1272-75 (11th Cir. 2005) (Birch, J., specially concurring to denial of en ban rehearing).

[54]*See, e.g.*, *In re* Ford Motor Co., 165 S.W.3d 315, 321 (Tex. 2005) (giving effect to statute providing for mandatory legislative continuances despite tension with article II, section 1); Gross v. State, 308 S.W.2d 54, 55 (Tex. Crim. App. 1957) (legislature has power to change or alter rules of evidence); Martinez v. State, 114 S.W.2d 874, 876 (Tex. Crim. App. 1938) (courts must follow procedural statutes enacted by legislature).

[55]925 N.E.2d 899 (N.Y. 2010).

without a judicial pay raise, New York was nearly last in the level of compensation for its judges, adjusted for the cost of living. After several attempts to secure a judicial pay raise were unsuccessful due to political wrangling over unrelated issues, several lawsuits were filed by judges attempting to secure a retroactive pay raise. While not ordering specific relief but instead presuming that the legislature would rectify the constitutional violation, New York's high court held that the independence of the judiciary was being improperly jeopardized in violation of separation of powers principles by the legislature's failure to independently examine judicial compensation on the merits.[56] Was this an appropriate resolution of this issue, or should the New York courts have refused to entertain the matter due to judges' self-interest?

CHAPTER 6 EXERCISES AND PROBLEMS

1. The Texas Legislature adopted a requirement that a claimant in a health care liability claim must serve an expert medical report meeting certain criteria within 120 days of the filing of the petition or the case is to be dismissed with prejudice and reasonable attorney's fees and court costs are to be awarded to the defendants. What are the arguments for and against the constitutionality of this requirement under separation of powers principles?

2. A city creates a "citizen review committee" to review disciplinary actions against civil servants. The committee is composed of three city residents, one appointed by each side in a particular disciplinary case and the third who is to be appointed by the other two appointees. The only qualification for members of the committee is that they are registered city voters. The determinations of the committee are final and not subject to appeal, and the committee is empowered to make its own rules. What are the arguments for and against the constitutionality of the committee under separation of powers principles?

[56] *Id.* at 914-15. After additional maneuvering, the legislature finally created a judicial pay commission that convenes every four years to make recommendations for judicial compensation, which recommended a 27% pay raise for judges that the legislature adopted and went into effect on April 1, 2012.

Chapter 7

LEGISLATIVE POWERS, DUTIES, AND LIMITATIONS

The federal government is a government of limited and enumerated powers, which means that legislation adopted by the United States Congress without constitutional authorization is void. In contrast, state legislatures are typically viewed as holding an inherent power to govern, subject only to *limitations imposed* by the federal and state constitutions. As the Texas Supreme Court recognized: "The power and authority of a state legislature is plenary and its extent is limited only by the express or implied restrictions thereon contained in or necessarily arising from the Constitution itself."[1] Courts from other states have likewise concluded that their legislatures may act unless prohibited from doing so.[2]

In viewing state legislative power, then, the operative question is not whether the action is authorized by the state constitution, but rather whether the action is *prohibited by* the state constitution or the United States Constitution. The United States Constitution, of course, places several restrictions on state legislative powers, including that the legislation cannot infringe upon equal protection and due process rights,[3] unduly burden interstate commerce,[4] discriminate against citizens of other states with respect to certain privileges and immunities,[5] violate any federal statute or administrative regulation,[6] create a state monetary system, impair the obligation of contracts, increase the punishment for crimes previously committed, or impose convictions without a judicial trial.[7] In addition to these federal constitutional limitations, state constitutions often impose a number of unique restrictions

---

[1]Gov't Servs. Ins. Underwriters v. Jones, 368 S.W.2d 560, 563 (Tex. 1963). *Accord* Shepherd v. San Jacinto Junior College Dist., 363 S.W.2d 742, 743 (Tex. 1962) ("'All power which is not limited by the Constitution inheres in the people, and an act of a state legislature is legal when the Constitution contains no prohibition against it.'"); Bexar Cnty. Hosp. Dist. v. Crosby, 327 S.W.2d 445, 447 (Tex. 1959) ("There can be no dispute but that in this State the provisions of the Constitution serve only as a limitation on the power of the Legislature, and not as a grant of power."); Brown v. City of Galveston, 75 S.W. 488, 492 (Tex. 1903) ("[E]xcept [when] restrained by the Constitution of the United States, the legislative department may exercise all legislative power which is not forbidden expressly or by implication by the provisions of the Constitution of the state of Texas."); State v. Brownson, 61 S.W. 114, 114 (Tex. 1901) ("The legislative department of the state government may make any law not prohibited by the constitution of the state or that of the United States.").

[2]*See, e.g.,* The Italia Am. Shipping Corp. v. Nelson, 154 N.E. 148, 203 (Ill. 1926) ("The State constitution is not a grant of, but is a limitation upon, legislative power"); Sherwood Sch. Dist. 88J v. Wash. Cnty. Educ. Serv. Dist., 6 P.3d 518 (Or. App. 2000) (noting "the state constitution does not grant the legislature authority but, rather, only limits it").

[3]U.S. CONST. amend. XIV. The Supreme Court has held that "due process" incorporates many of the guarantees contained in the first eight amendments of the Bill of Rights, as well as providing the basis for both substantive due process and procedural due process.

[4]U.S. CONST. art. I, § 8, cl. 3.

[5]U.S. CONST. art. IV, § 2 ("The Citizens of each State shall be entitled to all Privileges and Immunities of Citizens in the several States.").

[6]U.S. CONST. art. VI.

[7]U.S. CONST. art. I, § 10, cl. 1.

on state legislative power, and sometimes even place affirmative duties on the legislative branch.

This chapter focuses on the limitations and duties placed on the Texas Legislature under the Texas Constitution. The chapter addresses legislative qualifications and disqualifications, procedural requirements for legislation, the prohibition on special or local laws, restrictions on taxation and state public debt, and the legislative duties of providing for an efficient public school system and reapportioning congressional and state legislative seats. The chapter also incorporates a comparative analysis, as many of these limitations and duties are frequently encountered in other state constitutions.

A. THE LEGISLATURE AND LEGISLATORS

The Texas Constitution, like every other state constitution other than the Nebraska Constitution, establishes a bicameral legislature.[8] Article III, section 1 provides:

> The Legislative power of this State shall be vested in a Senate and House of Representatives, which together shall be styled "The Legislature of the State of Texas."

The Texas Legislature has 181 members in both houses, with 31 senators and 150 representatives.[9] Senators typically serve four-year terms, although half the senators chosen in the first election after any apportionment (in which the entire senate is elected) serve only a two-year term.[10] Members of the Texas House are elected to two-year terms, corresponding to the biennial regular legislative sessions established by the Texas Constitution.[11]

The Texas Constitution directs the schedule and limits the length of these every-other-year regular legislative sessions. During the first thirty days, legislators introduce bills

---

[8]NEB. CONST. art. III, § 1.

[9]TEX. CONST. art. III, § 2. Under the prior version of article III, section 2, the Texas House originally consisted of ninety-three members. But the provision authorized the number of representatives to be increased in a ratio of one representative for every fifteen thousand inhabitants up to a maximum of 150 representatives. The Texas House reached the maximum of 150 in 1923. JANICE C. MAY, THE TEXAS STATE CONSTITUTION, A REFERENCE GUIDE 77 (1995). In 1999, article III, section 2 was amended to state more simply: "The Senate shall consist of thirty-one members. The House of Representatives shall consist of 150 members."

[10]TEX. CONST. art. III, § 3. Although the Texas Constitution creates staggered four-year terms for senators, the requirement that all senate seats are up for election after each apportionment prevents senators from always enjoying their four-year terms. Assuming apportionment is carried out once each decade, one-half the senate seats have a two-year term followed by two four-year terms while the other half of the seats have two four-year terms followed by a two-year term. However, in recent decades, reapportionment has occurred more than once every ten years, resulting in even more two-year terms for senators. *See infra* section F.

[11]TEX. CONST. art. III, §§ 4-5. Biennial regular legislative sessions used to be more common in other states, with only six states holding annual legislative sessions at the turn of the twentieth century. G. ALAN TARR, UNDERSTANDING STATE CONSTITUTIONS 121 (1998). Most current state constitutions, though, provide for annual regular legislative sessions. *Cf.* THE COUNCIL OF STATE GOVERNMENTS, THE BOOK OF THE STATES 114-17 (2012). Texas is one of only a few states currently providing for regular sessions every other year–others include Montana, Nevada, North Dakota, and Oregon. *See id.*

and resolutions, the legislature acts upon emergency appropriations, and the senate considers confirmation of the governor's recess appointments.[12] The next thirty days are devoted to committee hearings on bills and resolutions, with the remainder of the session reserved for acting upon bills and resolutions.[13] But the governor may submit emergency matters at any time and either house may suspend this schedule by a four-fifths vote.[14] Regular legislative sessions are limited by the constitution to no more than 140 days,[15] although the governor can also convene the legislature in special sessions of not longer than thirty days to consider specifically designated subjects.[16]

While such constitutional limitations on the length and frequency of legislative sessions used to be common in other states, only a few state constitutions today still retain them. Session length and frequency limitations became popular after the Civil War as a reform measure to constrain legislative power and to encourage efficiency. This system sought to encourage a part-time, citizen legislature, with legislators focusing on pressing issues rather than having the opportunity for mischief. Yet during the twentieth century, most states moved away from constitutional constraints on legislative sessions, while Texas has not. Are there unique attitudes toward governmental power in Texas that might explain why the nation's second most populous state retains a nineteenth century view regarding the legislature?

Even though the constitution vests the state's legislative power in the Texas Legislature,[17] the legislature is not the sole constitutional repository of lawmaking authority. Home rule cities may enact laws,[18] the governor has the power to veto laws,[19] and constitutional amendments (along with rare types of legislation) require the concurrence of the citizenry of the state.[20] Yet the Texas Legislature does not share general legislative power with the citizenry, as do the legislatures in the approximately twenty states that authorize lawmaking through the citizen initiative process. A proposed Texas constitutional amendment to adopt the initiative and referendum in 1914 did not pass, leaving the legislature preeminent as the lawmaker for the state.

This plenary legislative authority does not, however, extend to non-legislative constitutional functions that are shared with another department of government. As an example, the legislature may not convene itself in special session to address recess appointments made by the governor–the power to make recess appointments is vested in the

---

[12]TEX. CONST. art. III, § 5.

[13]*Id.*

[14]*Id.*

[15]TEX. CONST. art. III, § 24 (b).

[16]TEX. CONST. art. III, § 40.

[17]*See* TEX. CONST. art. III, § 1 ("The Legislative power of this State shall be vested in . . . 'The Legislature of the State of Texas.'").

[18]TEX. CONST. art. XI, § 5.

[19]TEX. CONST. art. IV, §§ 14-15.

[20]TEX. CONST. art. XVII, § 1. An example of legislation that requires a statewide citizen referendum before it can become effective is a state income tax. *See* TEX. CONST. art. VIII, § 24.

governor and the legislature's only constitutional role is that the senate considers confirmation of recess appointees at the beginning of the next regular legislative session.[21] Similarly, because punishing for contempt is not an inherent aspect of legislative power but rather is part of the judicial power, legislative punishments for contempt must strictly adhere to constitutional requirements.[22] On the other hand, though, despite the lack of an explicit constitutional authorization, the legislature may convene itself to consider the impeachment of the governor, because the house and senate have the sole authority under the Texas Constitution to impeach and remove the governor from office, without sharing that power with any other governmental department.[23]

In addition to establishing the basic Texas legislative framework, article III also establishes the qualifications for legislators. Section 6 provides that a senator must be at least twenty-six years old when elected, a Texas resident for the preceding five years with at least the last year spent in his or her senatorial district, and a qualified voter and United States citizen.[24] The qualifications for representatives are outlined in section 7, which are similar to those for a senator other than the representative must only be twenty-one years old at the time of election and reside in Texas for the last two preceding years.[25] Each house is to judge the qualifications and election of its own members, but the legislature may delegate by law the power to judge contested elections, which it has shared with the judiciary, subject to various restrictions.[26]

These basic qualifications are supplemented by a number of constitutional ineligibility provisions. For example, an individual who has been convicted of giving or offering a bribe is constitutionally disabled from serving in the legislature or any other state office.[27] More commonly encountered, though, are the various prohibitions on holding more than one governmental office that apply both to legislators and to candidates for legislative office.

---

[21]Walker v. Baker, 196 S.W.2d 324, 327-29 (Tex. 1946).

[22]*See Ex parte* Youngblood, 251 S.W. 509, 511-12 (Tex. Crim. App. 1923). The Texas Constitution provides: "Each House may punish, by imprisonment, during its sessions, any person not a member, for disrespectful or disorderly conduct in its presence, or for obstructing any of its proceedings; provided, such imprisonment shall not, at any one time, exceed forty-eight hours." TEX. CONST. art. III, § 15. *Youngblood* held that this provision neither authorized the exercise of the contempt power by a legislative committee nor allowed the legislature to impose a punishment of more than forty-eight hours. 251 S.W. at 512. The legislature subsequently circumvented these limitations by enacting a substantive criminal offense of refusing to answer questions before a legislative committee and then leaving prosecution and enforcement to the criminal justice system. *See* Ferrantello v. State, 256 S.W.2d 587, 590-91 (Tex. Crim. App. 1953), *overruled in part on other grounds*, *Ex parte* Shorthouse, 640 S.W.2d 924 (Tex. Crim. App. 1982).

[23]Ferguson v. Maddox, 263 S.W. 888, 890-91 (Tex. 1924).

[24]TEX. CONST. art. III, § 6. The constitutional qualifications for both senators and representatives must be met as of the date of the general election (rather than the date of the primary election or the date of taking office). *See* Luna v. Blanton, 478 S.W.2d 76, 77-78 (Tex. 1974).

[25]TEX. CONST. art. III, § 7.

[26]TEX. CONST. art. III, § 8.

[27]TEX. CONST. art. XVI, §§ 16, 41. The legislature is also constitutionally authorized to enact laws to exclude anyone from state office convicted of bribery, perjury, forgery, or other high crimes. *Id.* § 2. Moreover, any person convicted of giving or offering a bribe to secure election or appointment is disqualified from holding any state office. *Id.* §5.

Article III, section 18 prohibits a legislator, during his or her elected term, from serving in any other state office that either (1) was created or had its "emoluments" increased during the legislative term or (2) is subject to legislative appointment or confirmation.[28] A similar prohibition has existed in every Texas constitution, and also exists in the United States Constitution and almost every other state constitution. The purpose of this prohibition is to further separation of powers by preventing the people's representatives from bartering with the executive branch for appointments, as had occurred in many colonial legislatures.[29] Texas decisions have addressed the nature of "emoluments" that cannot be increased, and have abided by the general American rule that emoluments necessitate an actual pecuniary gain rather than some contingent insurance or retirement benefit. As a result, the legislature's enactment of an across-the-board three percent pay increase per year for all state employees, even though it was less than the rate of inflation, was held to be a prohibited increase in "emoluments" disqualifying a sitting state senator from running for attorney general.[30] Conversely, a law potentially increasing retirement benefits for state officials was held not to increase "emoluments," thereby allowing a sitting senator to be a candidate for attorney general despite section 18.[31]

In addition to section 18's limits on legislators' ability to seek state offices, the Texas Constitution also contains several provisions preventing state officers from seeking legislative office. Article III, section 19 prevents a "judge of any court, Secretary of State, Attorney General, clerk of any court of record, or any person holding a lucrative office under the United States, or this State, or any foreign government" from being eligible to the state legislature "during the term for which he is elected or appointed."[32] Section 20 prohibits anyone who has been a "collector of taxes" or otherwise "entrusted with public money" from serving as a state legislator or other state officer unless he or she obtains "a discharge" for such moneys.[33] Article XVI, section 12 contains a more generic prohibition on dual office-seeking, preventing any legislator or officer in the government of the United States, another state, or a foreign government from serving in the Texas Legislature or in a state "office of profit or trust."[34] Article XVI, section 40 then generally prohibits any person from holding or exercising more than one "civil office of emolument," although there are numerous exceptions, including allowing state officials to be members of the National Guard or military reserves.[35]

What is the purpose of all these disqualifications? Is it merely to further separation of powers principles and to prevent legislators from benefitting personally by their position in the legislature during their term of service? Or are there less noble purposes at work?

---

[28]TEX. CONST. art. III, § 18. This section also prohibits legislators from having either a direct or indirect interest in any state or county contract authorized by any law passed during their elected terms. *See id.*

[29]*Cf.* THE FEDERALIST NO. 76 (Alexander Hamilton) (Clinton Rossiter ed., 1961).

[30]Strake v. First Court of Appeals, 704 S.W.2d 746, 748 (Tex. 1986).

[31]Brown v. Meyer, 787 S.W.2d 42, 45 (Tex. 1990).

[32]TEX. CONST. art. III, § 19.

[33]TEX. CONST. art. III, § 20.

[34]TEX. CONST. art. XVI, § 12.

[35]TEX. CONST. art. XVI, § 40.

Dawkins v. Meyer, 825 S.W.2d 444 (Tex. 1992)

CORNYN, Justice.

In this original proceeding we decide whether Pattilou Dawkins, a member of the Board of the Texas Department of Mental Health and Mental Retardation (hereinafter, MHMR) whose term of office will end after the next regular session of the legislature begins, is eligible to be a candidate for the state House of Representatives.

I.

Pattilou Dawkins was appointed to a term on the board of MHMR which ends on January 31, 1993, shortly after the next general session of the legislature is to begin. Board members, under a series of appropriation acts, have been entitled to receive reimbursement for expenses for transportation, for meals and lodging up to $75 per day, as well as compensation of $30 per day for each day of service. On January 3, 1992, Dawkins applied to be a candidate in the Republican primary for State Representative, District 87.

Fred Meyer, Chairman of the Republican Party of Texas, [declared] Dawkins ineligible for the legislative term she sought under the provisions of article III, section 19 of the Texas Constitution[36] on the grounds that she held, for an overlapping term, a "lucrative office" of the state. Meyer explained that the public record established that Dawkins was appointed to a term on the MHMR board which was to end on January 31, 1993, after the legislative term was to begin. He further explained that, as a member of the MHMR board, Dawkins was entitled to receive per diem compensation above and beyond reimbursement for actual and necessary expenses.

Dawkins filed this original proceeding, countering that her office cannot be considered lucrative because her expenses incurred in performing her duties on the MHMR board exceed the total of funds she is paid. In her uncontroverted affidavit Dawkins avers that in her four and half years on the board she has incurred unreimbursed expenses of at least $2,000. Second, Dawkins contends that this court should conclude that her board membership is not the type of office which makes her ineligible to run for the legislature. We cannot agree with either of Dawkins' assertions.

II.

Dawkins' first argument directly challenges this court's holding in *Willis v. Potts* that any compensation, no matter how meager, renders an office "lucrative." *See* 377 S.W.2d 622, 623 (Tex.1964). Doyle Willis was a Fort Worth city councilman who was

---

[36]Article III, section 19 provides:

> "No judge of any court, Secretary of State, Attorney General, clerk of any court of record, or any person holding a lucrative office under the United States, or this State, or any foreign government shall during the term to which he is elected or appointed, be eligible to the Legislature."

This provision has been characterized by the United States Supreme Court as imposing a "waiting period" for state officials before they become eligible for the legislature. *Clements v. Fashing*, 457 U.S. 957, 967 (1982). That is, they must wait until their term of office expires before they are eligible for service in the legislature.

entitled to receive $10 per diem for attending meetings, up to $520 per year, in addition to all necessary expenses. The Court rejected Willis's argument that $10 per day was not "adequate" compensation and that, therefore, his office was not "lucrative" within the meaning of the constitution. This court held, relying on a case decided by the Wyoming Supreme Court, that the amount of the salary or compensation attached to an office is not material. *Id.* (citing *Baker v. Board of Comm'rs*, 9 Wyo. 51, 59 P. 797 (1900)). Dawkins offers no compelling reason for overruling *Willis*.

Had Dawkins received only reimbursement for her expenses and no compensation for her activities with the MHMR, her position would not be considered lucrative. Reimbursement for expenses alone does not render an office "lucrative". *Whitehead v. Julian*, 476 S.W.2d 844, 845 (Tex.1972). In *Whitehead*, the Court held that a mayor who received a $50 per month expense allowance, and whose expenses were greater than or equal to the expense allowance did not hold a "lucrative office." The court continued to define a lucrative office as one in which the holder received a salary, fees, or "other compensation." In this case, Dawkins receives more than reimbursement for expenses—she is compensated $30 per day independent of any expenses she incurred.

Dawkins' argument that her position cannot be considered lucrative because her expenses exceed her compensation is superficially attractive but, on closer scrutiny, is fraught with insurmountable problems. First, were we to adopt such a test, MHMR board members who do not incur additional expenses for meals or lodging because they live in or near Austin, or because they stay with relatives, would not be eligible to run for the legislature; and those, like Dawkins, who spend in excess of their allotment for expenses and per diem would be eligible. Such disparate treatment of eligibility based on geography and differences in individual spending habits is insupportable.

Second, such a test could render article III, section 19 an irrational standard against which to judge eligibility for legislative office. If the test for whether an office is "lucrative" is that an office holder's compensation exceeds his or her expenses, an office holder's eligibility would be determined based purely on the level of his or her expenses. The resulting lack of a certain, meaningful standard is obvious.

These factors militate heavily against adopting a test for "lucrative" which measures an office holder's compensation against his or her expenses. Instead, we stand by the rule we announced in *Willis v. Potts* that an office is lucrative if the office holder receives any compensation, no matter how small.

III.

* * * *

B.

Dawkins contends that the framer's intent in adopting article III, section 19 will not be defeated by allowing a person holding a part-time, unprofitable position on an appointed board to run for the legislature.

Article III, section 19's historical antecedents date to a 1701 act of Parliament which rendered a "Person who [had] an Office or Place of Profit under the King or receive[d] a Pention from the Crown" ineligible to serve in the House of Commons. 12 & 13 Gul., ch.

II, § 3. A 1707 statute stated that if a member of the House of Commons accepted an "Office of Profit" from the Crown, that member's election to the House would be void "as if such Person so accepting was naturally dead." 6 Anne, ch. 41, § 25. The policy underlying such prohibitions, including article III, section 19, is the doctrine of separation of powers which was considered a means of mitigating undue influence by the executive upon the legislative branch.

The framers' intent behind article III, section 19—to bolster the separation of powers doctrine—as well as this court's decisions interpreting that section, control our decision in this case. Whether we agree or disagree with the wisdom of the constitutional method chosen to accomplish the framers' intent is beside the point.

C.

Dawkins [ignores] the fact that we have held other offices, dissimilar to those specifically mentioned in article III, section 19, to be covered by the terms of the provision. Thus, having held that article III, section 19 applies to a city councilman, a county commissioner, a district attorney, a county superintendent of schools, and a mayor, [we] cannot compel a different result for an MHMR board member.

D.

Dawkins herself concedes that the purpose of section 19 is to mitigate the executive's influence on the legislature. The doctrine would therefore require disqualification of all officeholders who were members of the executive branch in a way akin to the offices enumerated in section 19, for example, a "clerk of any court of record." It logically follows, then, that a member of the MHMR board, which is an agency within the executive department holding significant policy-making powers, is even closer to the intended purpose of the prohibition than a clerk of court would be. The purposes of separation of powers are better served by preventing a policy-making member of the executive department from running for the legislature than a clerk of the court.

IV.

The language of the constitution and our previous interpretations of article III, section 19 constrain us to hold that Dawkins is not currently eligible to be a candidate for the House of Representatives. We acknowledge the harshness of the result of the decision we make today. However, the power to change such a result by amending our constitution lies not in our hands, but in the hands of the sovereign people of the State of Texas.

GONZALEZ, Justice, dissenting, joined by Hightower, J.

The fundamental issues in this case depend on how we interpret the scope of the prohibition under article III, section 19. The broadest interpretation of this provision would disqualify someone from running for the legislature if he or she holds a "lucrative" office which, according to the Court, is one for which the legislature denominates payment as "compensation" rather than "reimbursement." This simplistic analysis of the constitutional provision is the basis for today's inequitable holding. Thus, the legislature's choice of words, not the amount of money involved, determines whether a job is "lucrative." If the legislature designated $30,000 remuneration for an office as reimbursement, then that job would not be "lucrative," and the officeholder could run for the legislature. But if the legislature designated $1 as payment for a particular position, and called it compensation, then that office is "lucrative" and prohibits candidacy. I object to hinging the right of public spirited officeholders like Ms. Dawkins to run for the legislature on the legislatively-selected label placed on an office's remuneration.

If possible, we should adopt an interpretation of section 19 that preserves the principle, recently reiterated by this court, "that constitutional provisions which restrict the right to hold public office should be strictly construed against ineligibility." *Brown v. Meyer*, 787 S.W.2d 42, 45 (Tex.1990); *see also Sears v. Bayoud*, 786 S.W.2d 248, 251 (Tex.1990). We can construe section 19 to preserve *Brown v. Meyer*'s directive by applying section 19 only to those offices which are the holder's principal, if not exclusive, occupation. Compensation is relevant in that these offices provide a livelihood so that the officeholder can dedicate his or her efforts exclusively to the work required. The MHMR board of which Ms. Dawkins is a member meets about four times a year, and the $30 per diem she receives does little to change the essentially charitable nature of her service. Under this preferable interpretation of section 19, Ms. Dawkins would not be prohibited from running. We should permit neither sketchy history nor poor precedent to steamroll Ms. Dawkins' rights; but the Court does just that.

The Court states that the amendment's history supports the Court's result, asserting that section 19 is descended from a 1707 English statute that prohibited employees of the Crown from serving in the House of Commons. That statute, however, essentially proscribed dual officeholding; it said nothing of the rights of a Crown employee to run for the House of Commons. The policy advanced by this historical reference seeks, as the Court notes, to preserve the separation of powers by preventing dual officeholding. This policy argument neither fits this case nor supports the Court's decision to deny Ms. Dawkins' candidacy. For *Ms. Dawkins is not seeking to hold two offices at the same time*. Reading the Texas Constitution as a whole, which we must do, reveals that article III, section 19 is not principally a prohibition against dual officeholding, because that problem is addressed by other articles of our constitution. TEX. CONST. ART. XVI, §§ 12, 33, 40. These other constitutional provisions would compel Ms. Dawkins, upon election to the legislature, to resign her position with MHMR. These provisions also indicate that section 19 must stand for something other than separation of powers.

The United States Supreme Court analyzed article III, section 19 in *Clements v. Fashing*, 457 U.S. 957 (1982). *Clements* involved several justices of the peace running for the legislature. They challenged section 19 on First Amendment and equal protection grounds, and a plurality of the court held that section 19 did not violate the United States Constitution. 457 U.S. at 971. The court concluded that a rational predicate for the "temporary" denial of candidacy existed due to: 1) Texas' interest in maintaining the integrity of the judiciary; 2) the likelihood that the demands of a political campaign would tempt a judge to devote less than was required by his or her current office; and 3) the need to discourage a judge from leaving office before the end of the term. 457 U.S. at 968. These three purposes are ill-served (or irrationally served) by the group of officeholders covered by section 19. Only those officeholders whose terms happen to overlap with the legislative term are prohibited from running for the legislature. Those whose terms do not overlap with that of the legislature are left free to campaign for the legislature while remaining in office.

Additionally, if these are legitimate state interests, then why do they only apply to officeholders who run for the legislature and not to those running for other offices? And why do these interests only limit the rights of an officeholder whose term overlaps the legislative term? And what of a federal judge who is appointed to a lifetime position; is he or she forever precluded from running for the state legislature, despite resignation from the judicial post? What if an officeholder like Ms. Dawkins waives compensation?

The dissent in *Clements* [by] Justice Brennan commented that section 19, as interpreted in our prior opinions, served no purpose but to function as a legislative incumbent's protection "act." *Clements*, 457 U.S. at 979. He concluded that "[t]he only conceivable state interest in barring these candidacies would be the impermissible one of protecting Texas legislative seats against outside competition." *Id.* I agree; and because such a policy cannot have been the intent of the framers and ratifiers of our constitution, we must reexamine whether this provision as interpreted by existing precedent frustrates rather than effectuates the framers' conceivable intent.

[The dissent of Justice Gammage, joined by Justice Mauzy, has been omitted].

Wentworth v. Meyer, 839 S.W.2d 766 (Tex. 1992)

COOK, Justice.

In this original proceeding, we must determine whether the Texas Constitution prevents Relator Jeff Wentworth from serving as a state senator in the Texas legislature. The legislative term would overlap, by twenty-one days, Wentworth's previous term of appointment to the Board of Regents of the Texas State University System. The question is whether article III, section 19 of the Texas Constitution renders Wentworth ineligible because of this overlap. Wentworth denies his candidacy violates the constitution because he resigned his position on the Board long ago, and seeks mandamus relief to ensure his place on the ballot as the Republican nominee. Because we determine that Wentworth's resignation prior to running for office places him outside the prohibitions of the constitution, we conditionally grant the writ.[37]

I.

On March 24, 1987, the Governor appointed Wentworth to the Board of Regents for a six year term that would expire on February 1, 1993. On May 10, 1988, Wentworth resigned as regent, before assuming office as a state representative on May 11, 1988, after a special election. Wentworth was re-elected to the House of Representatives in November 1988 and November 1990, and his current term as a representative would not expire until the legislature convenes on January 12, 1993, when his prospective term as state senator, should he prevail, would begin.

Wentworth won the Republican nomination for State Senator from District 26 in a runoff election on April 14, 1992. On April 24, Fred Meyer, State Chairman of the Republican Party of Texas, certified to the Secretary of State that Wentworth was the Republican Party's nominee for the office. Three weeks later, Meyer notified the Secretary

[37] We reserve the issue when an officeholder must resign to avoid article III, section 19.

of State by letter that he had determined and declared Wentworth ineligible as the Republican nominee. Meyer further informed the Secretary that the district executive committee, or the State Republican Executive Committee, would be selecting a replacement nominee for the general election. Meyer based his decision on article III, section 19 of the constitution:

> No judge of any court, Secretary of State, Attorney General, clerk of any court of record, or any person holding a lucrative office under the United States, or this State, or any foreign government shall during the term for which he is elected or appointed, be eligible to the Legislature.

II.

We consider the question whether Wentworth's resignation from the Board, four years before his victory in the recent runoff election, saves his candidacy from the prohibition of section 19. Resolution of the issue requires interpretation of the words "during the term for which he is elected or appointed." The words support two interpretations. If the "term" which cannot overlap is the entire six-year Board term, then Wentworth cannot become a state senator. If Wentworth's "term" ended when he resigned, then he is free to run for legislative office.

In interpreting any constitutional provision, we begin with the text of the constitution. When there is doubt as to the meaning of the literal text, we must then consider the intent of the people who adopted the constitution, although the history of that intent is often difficult to discern. *See Edgewood v. Kirby*, 777 S.W.2d 391, 394 (Tex.1989) (citation omitted). We remain aware that the constitution was ratified to function as an organic document to govern society and institutions as they evolve through time. *Id.* These general principles are buttressed by another, more specific, rule of interpretation in disputes involving elections: Any constitutional or statutory provision which restricts the right to hold office must be strictly construed against ineligibility. *Brown v. Meyer*, 787 S.W.2d 42 (Tex.1990). This rule is particularly important where, as here, the language is susceptible of varied interpretations.

In *Dawkins v. Meyer*, 825 S.W.2d 444 (1992), we discussed the purpose of section 19. The provision bolsters the separation of powers within our state government. Specifically, the section protects the legislature from undue influence by certain officeholders. *Id.* at 448; *see also* TEX. CONST. art. III, § 8, interp. commentary.

It is consistent with this purpose to interpret section 19 as prohibiting those officeholders from sitting in the legislature during the time they hold their offices. On the other hand, the purpose of section 19 is not advanced by denying legislative office to someone who abandons his office four years before seeking a legislative seat. That this is so is illustrated by the case before us today. Wentworth can exert no influence over the legislature by virtue of his former position as a regent, for he resigned that position four years ago. It was filled and is now occupied by someone else. Moreover, Wentworth has already served two terms in the legislature as a member of the House of Representatives. The purpose of section 19 cannot be fostered by an interpretation that denies this former regent the opportunity to run for the state senate.

III.

We are aware that the views we express today conflict with previous opinions of this court. In *Lee v. Daniels*, 377 S.W.2d 618 (Tex.1964), a case remarkably like the one we consider today, we construed section 19 in favor of ineligibility. In *Lee*, a county commissioner resigned office to run for the House of Representatives. His term as commissioner overlapped the house term by nearly two months. A petition for writ of mandamus was filed to remove his name from the ballot. We conditionally granted the writ. *Id.* at 620. It made no difference that the office seeker in *Lee* resigned prior to seeking office. We stated that it is the term which controls, and it makes no difference when the office-holder resigns, even if he resigns only a day after he begins holding office.

This interpretation of section 19 is at odds with the rule that requires us to strictly construe election law restrictions against ineligibility. The interpretation narrows, rather than expands, the potential for eligibility. Because we are bound to decide in favor of eligibility whenever possible, we must reevaluate our opinion in *Lee*.

We initially review our contention that, by adopting the disputed language of section 19, the framers intended to insure that "term of office" meant an entire term, not just the officeholder's tenure in the term. Without this meaning, we said, the language is mere surplusage. *Lee*, 618 S.W.2d at 620. The interpretation is plausible, but it is only one possible suggestion for adoption of the phrase. Addition of the critical language could carry other meanings. The phrase could mean that officeholders are disqualified only during their tenure in office, and not perpetually. Given the two interpretations, and absent an adequate history of the constitutional convention to guide us, we must advance the purpose of section 19 and adhere to the rule requiring us to decide in favor of eligibility. We can no longer view the language at issue as preventing eligibility where an officeholder has resigned before running for the legislature.

We do not, however, overrule or disturb in any way our holding and opinion in *Dawkins v. Meyer*, 825 S.W.2d at 448. The facts and issue in that case were entirely different than those presented here. *Dawkins* was argued and decided on the issue whether the office which prevented Dawkins' candidacy was lucrative within the meaning of section 19. Unlike Wentworth, when Dawkins moved for leave to file the petition for writ of mandamus, she had not resigned the office and had expressed no intent to resign.

IV.

Wentworth resigned his position as a member of the Board of Regents of the Texas State University System years before he ran for the Senate. During part of the intervening years, he served as a state representative. His position as regent was filled by someone else. To allow Wentworth to take his seat as a senator does not violate either the express language or the purpose of article III, section 19 of the Texas Constitution.

MAUZY, Justice, concurring.

I dissented from the majority's decision in *Dawkins*, and adhere to my view that article III, section 19 should not be lightly applied to prevent voters from electing the candidate of their choice. For that reason, and for additional reasons specific to this case, I join the majority's decision to grant the writ of mandamus.

This is not the first time since Wentworth's appointment to the Board of Regents that the Chairman of the Republican Party has been asked to certify him as eligible for the legislature. Nor is it the second, third, fourth, fifth, or even the sixth. After certifying Wentworth as eligible for the Texas Legislature half a dozen times, the Chairman now argues that Wentworth has been ineligible ever since his 1987 appointment to the Board of Regents. This change apparently arises from nothing more than mere whim: the main cases on which the Chairman relies are almost thirty years old, and there has been no change in Wentworth's status to make him any less eligible now than he was in 1988.

I would hold that, under these circumstances, Respondent Chairman Meyer is estopped from declaring Wentworth ineligible. When a candidate has been certified as eligible on six prior occasions, and there has been no subsequent change affecting his eligibility, a sudden decertification by the party's chairman is both arbitrary and unfair. This sort of game-playing by party officials harkens a return to the days of political bosses and smoke-filled rooms, when the ordinary voter was effectively shut out of the decision-making process.

HECHT, Justice, concurring.

I join in JUSTICE COOK's opinion for the Court and in JUSTICE CORNYN's concurring opinion. To summarize the Court's decision, five Members of the Court—JUSTICE COOK, JUSTICE GONZALEZ, JUSTICE HIGHTOWER, JUSTICE CORNYN and myself—hold that article III, section 19 of the Texas Constitution does not prohibit an officeholder who resigns his position from serving in the Legislature during a time when he would otherwise have remained in his former office. These five Justices also hold that *Lee v. Daniels*, 377 S.W.2d 618 (Tex.1964), and *Kirk v. Gordon*, 376 S.W.2d 560 (Tex.1964), are overruled to the extent that they conflict with today's decision. No one who joined in the Court's opinion in *Dawkins v. Meyer*, 825 S.W.2d 444 (Tex.1992), has expressed disagreement with that decision today. I write separately only to respond to the dissenting opinions of CHIEF JUSTICE PHILLIPS and JUSTICE DOGGETT.

Article III, section 19 makes certain specific officials—judges, the Secretary of State, the Attorney General, and court clerks—and any other person "holding" lucrative office in any government (except one of our sister states) ineligible to serve in the Legislature. If this were all section 19 said, its construction would be a simple matter. A person who resigns his office is no longer "holding" office and therefore is not made ineligible by this provision. However, section 19 adds that a person's ineligibility lasts "during the term for which he is elected or appointed". This additional phrase creates an ambiguity in the text. On the one hand, section 19 applies only to persons "holding" office, not persons who have ever held office. On the other hand, if section 19 does not apply to persons who have resigned office, it is not clear what the additional phrase adds to the meaning of the provision.

[I]f the word "term" in article III, section 19 is given what I concede is its more common meaning, the provision has no sound rationale. A person who served the first day of a full term of office and then resigned would be ineligible for the Legislature for varying periods of time, depending on the office held: two years for most city council members, four years for district judges, six years for most university regents, eight years for a federal magistrate, fourteen years for a bankruptcy judge, and life for a federal district or appellate judge. It is not at all clear why the period that an officeholder is ineligible to the Legislature should depend upon the fixed term of the office held, nor why, to take the extreme case, a federal district judge who retires from office should be ineligible to serve in the Texas Legislature for the remainder of his or her life (even if the judge did not regard the disability as too serious). The reason CHIEF JUSTICE PHILLIPS and JUSTICE DOGGETT offer—and the only reason that appears ever to have been put forward for this application of article III, section 19—is that the purpose of the constitutional provision is to discourage trafficking in offices and the neglect of those offices occasioned by campaigning for the Legislature. Now if the dissenters are right about this, the provision does little to further its purpose, for it does not disqualify all officeholders from all other offices for the duration of their "terms", but only certain officeholders from legislative office. It is an odd rule that allows a person who resigns from the Santa Fe city council and moves to El Paso to serve in the Texas Legislature before the fixed term of his council seat expired, but prohibits a member of the El Paso city council or a member of the government of Ciudad Juárez from doing the same thing. And it is an odd rule to prevent trafficking in offices and distracting campaigns that allows an officeholder to resign and run for any other office in Texas *except* the Legislature.

The dissenters attempt to show that the framers actually intended this construction of article III, section 19, odd consequences and all. Yet the historical evidence available to us indicates only that the provision did not contain the phrase, "during the term for which he is elected or appointed", prior to 1875, when it was added by amendment on the floor of the constitutional convention. Despite the absence of any record of debate concerning the purpose of the amendment, the dissenters conclude that it must have been intended to operate as they now construe it. But this is not the only conclusion to be drawn from the evidence. Indeed, I doubt whether it occurred to the framers that article III, section 19 would operate to disqualify someone in relator's position from running for the Legislature. If we were to resort to speculation—which is all we *could* do in the absence of any evidence of what the framers actually intended—we might as well suppose that the phrase was added to clarify that a person holding office was ineligible for the Legislature only so long as the "term" of office, and not thereafter. But we are not allowed to speculate, and the history of section 19 does not illumine the matter.

[The concurrences of Justices Gonzalez, Cornyn, and Gammage have been omitted].

PHILLIPS, Chief Justice, dissenting.

* * * *

Wentworth was appointed to a six-year term on the Board of Regents of the Texas State University System. Wentworth's resignation did not bring an end to this term. When a public officer resigns, dies or is otherwise unable to serve, a successor is elected or appointed to fill the *unexpired portion* of the term. For example, our Constitution elsewhere provides:

> In case of a vacancy in the office of the Chief Justice or any Justice of the Supreme Court, the Governor shall fill the vacancy until the next general election for state officers, and at such general election the vacancy for the

> *unexpired term* shall be filled by election by the qualified voters of the state. . . .

Tex. Const. art. V, § 2 (emphasis added). A "term," therefore, refers to the length of time the officeholder is elected or appointed to serve, not to the actual length of service.

[T]here is some ambiguity on the face of Section 19 because it applies in the first instance to persons "holding" lucrative office. If the officer has resigned, he or she is no longer "holding" office and arguably does not fall under the restriction. Justice Hecht goes on to suggest that, under this interpretation, the phrase "during the term for which he is elected or appointed" is not surplusage because it can interpreted as a *limitation* on the restriction; i.e., clarification that the restriction does not apply to officers who are holding over in office beyond their terms, awaiting qualification of their successors.

If we were construing Section 19 in a vacuum, I might be inclined to resolve this ambiguity in favor of eligibility. However, this Court has twice interpreted this provision as precluding a lucrative officeholder from serving in the legislature for the entire term of the office, even if he or she resigns before its expiration. *Lee v. Daniels*, 377 S.W.2d 618 (Tex.1964); *Kirk v. Gordon*, 376 S.W.2d 560 (Tex.1964). The history of Section 19, as well as Section 18 preceding it, persuade me that these decisions were correct and should not be overruled.

As originally drafted by the Legislative Committee of the 1875 Constitutional Convention, Section 19 provided as follows:

> No judge of any court, Secretary of State, Attorney General, clerk of any court of record, or any person holding a lucrative office under the United States or this State, or any foreign government, shall be eligible to the Legislature.

Journal of the Constitutional Convention of the State of Texas, 1875 156 (1875) [hereinafter *Journal*]. This draft in relevant respects matched the restriction contained in earlier Constitutions. Thus, the Committee draft, like the earlier Constitutions, disqualified the designated officeholders from legislative candidacy only while holding office, not for their entire term. On the floor of the Convention, however, delegate J.B. Murphy of Nueces County moved to amend the section by inserting after the word "shall" the phrase "during the term for which he is elected or appointed." *Journal* at 210. This change was adopted.

The wording of Murphy's amendment was almost identical to language in the Legislative Committee's draft of the preceding provision of the Constitution, Section 18, which provided:

> No senator or representative shall, *during the term for which he may be elected*, be eligible to any civil office of profit under this State, which shall have been created, or the emoluments of which may have been increased during such term; no member of either house shall, *during the term for which he is elected*, be eligible to any office or place, the appointment to

which may be made, in whole or in part, by either branch of the Legislature.

. . .

Journal at 156 (emphasis added). This language was adopted without change and remains in effect today. Tex. Const. art. III, § 18. Thus, the temporal restriction of Section 18 ("during the term for which he may be elected") was added to Section 19 in almost identical form.

Clearly, in Section 18 the meaning of the phrase "during the term for which he may be elected" is unambiguous. The purpose of that section is to prevent a legislator from voting to create an office or make an office more lucrative, then resigning his or her legislative seat to accept that office. *See* 1 George D. Braden, et al., *The Constitution of the State of Texas: An Annotated and Comparative Analysis* 132-34 (1977). To accomplish that purpose, the "during the term" language must encompass the legislator's entire term, not just the portion served. *See generally* Tex. Const. art. III, § 18, interp. commentary ("The language is designed to prevent legislators from resigning to take state offices which have been created, or the emoluments of which may have been increased during their term of office.").

By using virtually identical words in Sections 18 and 19, I believe that the framers intended the same result. *Cf. Boriack v. Boriack*, 541 S.W.2d 237, 240 (Tex. Civ. App.—Corpus Christi 1976, writ dism'd) (phrase used in different parts of a statute should be interpreted the same throughout).

Texas is apparently the only state that bars officeholders from the legislature "during the term" of the office. Other states extend the restriction only to persons currently "holding" office, as did Texas prior to 1876. However, many other states impose restrictions similar to Article III, Section 18, limiting a legislator's ability to hold other office during the term for which the legislator was elected. Many of these provisions contain language virtually identical to the language at issue in the present case. Most courts have construed this language as referring to the legislator's entire term, regardless whether he or she resigns.

Wentworth's Board of Regents term overlaps his potential Senate term by only 19 days. Wentworth argues that this overlap is de minimis and should be ignored.

Tex. Const. art. III, § 18 was amended in 1968 to allow for a de minimis term overlap when legislators move to some other civil office. Wentworth argues that by amending Section 18, the State has recognized that a de minimis overlapping of terms is not against the public interest. However, the people adopted a de minimis exception only for Section 18, not Section 19. Even if we accept Wentworth's argument that the policy rationale underlying the change in Section 18 would apply with equal force to Section 19, we cannot judicially amend the plain language of the Constitution based on policy reasons.

DOGGETT, Justice, dissenting.

The issue of whether resignation of a prior office removes the candidacy restrictions for the Legislature set forth in article III, section 19 of the Texas Constitution has already been clearly decided. After serving more than three of the four years of his term as county commissioner, Sam Jorrie resigned in order to run for state representative. Making precisely the same argument presented today, he contended that the constitutional bar extending for "the term for which he is elected or appointed" applied only to his tenure of office, the actual period of service, and not the entire term. This court flatly rejected that argument. *Lee v. Daniels*, 377 S.W.2d 618, 619 (Tex.1964).

Ordinarily, constitutional provisions are not read or construed in isolation. *Vinson v. Burgess,* 773 S.W.2d 263, 265 (Tex.1989). Of at least twenty-seven provisions in which our state charter uses the word "term," none suggests that the term ends on resignation. Indeed, some provide for filling "unexpired terms." *See, e.g.*, TEX. CONST. art. XVI, § 27. If "term" means "tenure," how can there ever be an unexpired term? Today's redefining of the word "term" injects chaos into consistent constitutional construction.

While debate has occurred over the public policy underlying article III, section 19, there has until today been a rather clear understanding of its meaning. A study commission recommended its removal to our most recent constitutional convention:

> [New section 3(d)] has made a substantial change in Article III, Section 19 of the Constitution of 1876. The 1876 document does not allow an officeholder to resign and to run for the Legislature during the term for which that officeholder was elected or appointed. This prevents many elected officials of state and local government from running for the Legislature.

Texas Constitutional Revision Comm'n, A New Constitution for Texas: Text, Explanation, Commentary 79 (Nov.1973). This proposal was rejected, however, in a committee report that retained the language "during the term for which he is elected or appointed," with the explanation that:

> [New subsection (f)] prohibits certain appointed or elected officers from running for the legislature during the term for which they were appointed or elected. This provision is the same as Article III, Section 19, of the Constitution of 1876. . . . This subsection would prohibit those persons from running for the legislature during the term for which they were appointed or elected *whether or not* they resigned before running.

1 Texas Constitutional Convention, Official Journals, January 8, 1974-July 30, 1974, at 656, 659 (emphasis in original). Floor debate further indicated that resignation would not remove the candidacy bar. Texas Constitutional Convention, Official Proceedings, January 8, 1974-July 30, 1974, at 1115, 1334. The "during the term" limitation was retained in the final version.

Nor does the plurality consider the history of Article VII, section 16 under which the position for Wentworth's previous appointment was created. Adopted in 1928, that provision responded to an educational survey under the direction of one of the nation's leading educators, determining that:

> The personnel of the governing boards of higher institutions is a matter of the most serious consequence to the institutions themselves and in general to the development of higher education. . . . [T]hese [appointees] are shaping the State's policy relative to its most fundamental interest, not only for the present, but for years in the future. . . . [C]ertainly [appointees should] refuse to use such honors as a step to political preferment.

6 George A. Works, Texas Educational Survey Comm'n, Texas Educational Survey Report 346 (1925). This report further concluded:

> The people of the State must realize that the institution cannot render to the State the largest possible measure of service if membership on the board is regarded as a political office. . . . [T]his service [must engage] the attention and devotion of men of consequence and attainment who will not under any circumstances undertake any other public career.

8 *id.* at 238-39; *see also* TEX. CONST. art. VII, § 16 (interp. commentary). Barring candidacy for the full term of the appointment is consistent with the objective of this companion provision.

Ignoring the invaluable history of article III, section 19, and its unambiguous text, the plurality frames the sole issue as whether the asserted interpretation promotes its underlying purpose to "bolster[ ] the separation of powers within our state government." Certainly "the evils intended to be remedied" are of importance in our constitutional inquiry. *Davenport*, 834 S.W.2d at 79. They do not, however, provide a clear explanation, since the predecessor to article III, section 19 in the Constitution of 1869 also arguably sought to bolster the separation of powers. The general purpose cannot explain why the "during the term" clause was added in 1875. The objective remained the same, but the means of effectuating it was altered.

This court should interpret the Texas Constitution with respect for its text and history to give full effect to the will of the people. Because today's decision markedly veers from that path, I dissent.

Notes on Prohibitions on Dual Office Holding

***Comparing* Dawkins *and* Wentworth**: Dawkins was ineligible to be a candidate for the state House of Representative under article III, section 19 because she was serving in a "lucrative office" as a member of the Board of the Texas Department of Mental Health and Mental Retardation. Although her term on the board of MHMR was to end just weeks after the next general session of the legislature was to begin, the court held that the overlap prevented her from running for the legislature because her $30 per day compensation rendered her office "lucrative," despite her claim that her actual expenses exceeded the combination of her compensation and reimbursement per diem. The majority asserted that such a result was necessary to further fundamental separation of powers concerns, although the dissent viewed the prohibition as incumbent protectionism rather than a necessary incident of divided government.

But article III, section 19 did not render Wentworth ineligible from serving as a state senator when his legislative term would overlap, by twenty-one days, Wentworth's previous term of appointment to the Board of Regents of the Texas State University System. The court held the difference was that Wentworth had resigned as a regent before he assumed office as a state representative after a special election A concurrence argued that the Republican Party chairman was estopped from declaring Wentworth ineligible after he had been certified as a candidate at least a half dozen times previously after he resigned as a regent.

Wouldn't Dawkins have presumably resigned from her $30 a day position if she was aware that such an action would have allowed her to run for the legislature? Presumably she didn't do so because prior precedent held that the resignation was irrelevant as the phrase "during the term for which he is elected or appointed" included the entire term, not just the portion served. Is the different treatment of Dawkins and Wentworth in these two opinions–which were issued just months apart–justified?

Textualism v. Prudential Considerations: What modes of constitutional interpretation supported the various interpretations of the phrase "during the term for which he is elected or appointed" in *Wentworth*? Did the dissenters have the better argument based on text, structure, history, and precedent? Even Justice Hecht conceded the dissenters' interpretation of "term" was the "more common reading" textually. Structurally, the court never responded to the dissenters' arguments that the word "term" is consistently used throughout the state constitution to encompass the legislator's entire term, not just the portion served. Nor did the court have much of a response based on history, and prior precedent supported the position of the dissenters. Was it appropriate, then, to rely on an admittedly less common meaning of the word "term" to achieve a contrary result based on prudential considerations? Should the court have waited for the people of the state to amend the constitution if they did not like the result of *Lee v. Daniels*? Or is there perhaps a concern that the legislature would not have submitted an amendment to the people by the necessary two-thirds vote of both houses when sitting legislators benefit from less competition for their seats, as Justice Gonzalez contended in his *Dawkins* dissent?

The Timing of the Resignation: *Wentworth* reserved the issue of when an officeholder must resign to avoid article III, section 19. How should that issue be resolved? Is it merely required that the officeholder resign before the primary or general election, or should the officeholder be required to resign before announcing his or her candidacy for legislative office? Or is the officeholder required to resign at some earlier juncture? Which juncture best serves the separation of powers purposes discussed in *Wentworth* and *Dawkins*?

The Republican Party's position appears to be that the resignation must at least occur before the application deadline to become a candidate, although the courts still have not resolved the issue. *In re Carlisle* addressed whether a school district trustee held a lucrative office under section 19 precluding her from running for the legislature.[38] The chair of the Republican Party of Texas ruled that she was ineligible because her position as a

---

[38] 209 S.W.3d 93 (Tex. 2006).

trustee allowed her to receive expense reimbursements for meals without receipts, and further argued that she could not then resign from her position because the application deadline to be a legislative candidate had passed. The Texas Supreme Court, though, did not reach the resignation argument, instead holding that the trustee did not hold a "lucrative office" when the school district's policy allowed only reimbursement for expenses rather than compensation for services.[39]

B. LEGISLATIVE PROCEEDINGS AND JUDICIAL REVIEW

The Texas Constitution, like almost all other state constitutions, sets forth more detailed and restrictive procedural requirements for enacting legislation than the United States Constitution does. These procedural requirements first appeared in state constitutions during the 1830's as a means to constrain the legislature and prevent legislative abuses.[40]

Early American history was replete with examples of such abuses, including the notorious Yazoo Act hastily enacted by the Georgia Legislature in early 1795. While the Yazoo Act stated its purpose was to protect and support Georgia's frontier settlements, the Act in fact sold some 35 million acres of land at less than 1.5 cents per acre to four companies, which, in return for their speculative coup, arranged for money and land to be distributed to legislators, state officials, newspaper editors, and other influential Georgians. Other states also experienced legislative corruption and favoritism to the privileged few during the late eighteenth and early nineteenth centuries. Such excesses spurred states to adopt constitutional provisions designed to enhance legislative transparency and accountability while combating special privileges and the threat of corruption.[41]

These restrictions took both substantive and procedural forms. Substantive restrictions, including prohibiting special or local laws and establishing constraints on taxation, debt, and spending, were intended to rein in legislative favoritism, and are discussed in the following two sections of this book. The procedural restrictions sought to increase legislative transparency and accountability by combating disfavored legislative practices, such as combining dissimilar provisions that could not pass individually into a single act to force simultaneous passage (known as logrolling) and hastily enacting important measures without due consideration.[42] The constitutional measures to remedy these abuses included requiring a bill to have an adequate title that disclosed its subject matter to the legislature and the citizenry, specifying that a bill could only address a single subject in order to prevent logrolling and reduce voter confusion, necessitating that a bill be considered in committee before being acted on by the entire legislature in order to ensure adequate legislative contemplation, mandating that the vote on a bill must be reflected in a legislative journal to prevent fraud, and prohibiting a bill from being amended to such an extent to change its original purpose to limit confusion and ensure full legislative

---

[39] *Id.* at 95-96.

[40] G. ALAN TARR, UNDERSTANDING STATE CONSTITUTIONS 118-19 (1998).

[41] *See id.*

[42] *See* Robert F. Williams, *State Constitutional Limits on Legislative Procedure: Legislative Compliance and Judicial Enforcement*, 17 PUBLIUS: THE JOURNAL OF FEDERALISM 91, 91-95 (1987).

deliberation.[43] Once adopted by a state, these remedies spread to other states through the interstate borrowing of state constitutional provisions.

Article III of the Texas Constitution contains many of these procedural requirements under the heading "Proceedings," including:

> All laws must have an enacting clause stating: "Be it enacted by the Legislature of the State of Texas."[44]
>
> A bill cannot be amended to such an extent as to change its original purpose.[45]
>
> A bill must be read with the opportunity for debate for three days in each house before it can become a law (unless a four-fifths majority suspends the requirement).[46]
>
> A bill containing the same substance as a bill considered and defeated earlier in the session cannot be enacted into law during the same session.[47]
>
> Bills cannot contain more than one subject (except that general appropriation bills can embrace all subjects and accounts dealing with appropriating money), and the subject of each bill must be expressed in its title in a manner that gives the legislature and the public reasonable notice of the subject (although compliance with the title requirement is explicitly made solely the province of the legislature).[48]
>
> A bill amending or reviving a prior law must publish the prior law at length rather than just referencing the prior law's title.[49]
>
> A bill cannot be considered unless it is referred to and reported on by a committee at least three days before the final adjournment of the legislature.[50]

---

[43] *See id.*

[44] TEX. CONST. art. III, § 29 ("The enacting clause of all laws shall be: 'Be it enacted by the Legislature of the State of Texas.'").

[45] TEX. CONST. art. III, § 30 ("No law shall be passed, except by bill, and no bill shall be so amended in its passage through either House, as to change its original purpose.").

[46] TEX. CONST. art. III, § 32.

[47] TEX. CONST. art. III, § 34. The same requirement also applies to legislative resolutions, which do not have the force of law. *See id.*

[48] TEX. CONST. art. III, § 35.

[49] TEX. CONST. art. III, § 36.

[50] TEX. CONST. art. III, § 37.

> Laws passed by the legislature, except the general appropriation act, cannot become effective until ninety days after the adjournment of the session, unless two-thirds of the members of each House vote otherwise.[51]
>
> The legislature may not, when convened in special session, consider a subject not designated in the proclamation of the governor or otherwise presented to them by the governor.[52]

The Texas Legislature usually diligently self-polices its compliance with these constitutional requirements and the other procedural requirements each house has adopted by rule. Yet on occasion, bills are signed into law by the presiding officer of each house and the governor when one of these requirements was not satisfied.[53] May the constitutionality of the law be challenged in a judicial proceeding on the basis of the failure to abide by one of these requirements? If so, what evidence should be considered? Or should separation of powers principles counsel against judicial review of legislative proceedings? The Texas Supreme Court was faced with these questions shortly after the ratification of the 1876 Constitution.

Williams v. Taylor, 19 S.W. 156 (Tex. 1892)

GAINES, J.

[Williams sought a writ of mandamus to compel Taylor, a district court clerk in Tarrant County, to issue citation in a trespass to try title action for a term of the court to begin on the second Monday in May, 1892. Taylor refused to do so on the basis that the statute that purported to require the May term of court was invalid because the legislative journals did not show, among other things, that the underlying bill was properly presented to and reported on by a committee at least three days before the final adjournment of the legislature. The Texas Supreme Court held that the journals could not be employed to invalidate the act when the act on its face appeared proper.]

The power of the courts, under the form of government common to the states of this Union, to declare void an act of the legislature on the ground that such legislation is prohibited by the constitution of the state was questioned at an early day in the history of our jurisprudence, but that the power exists is now settled beyond controversy. In passing a law the legislature acts under the authority conferred by a written constitution, and whether or not it has exceeded its authority in the passage of any particular act is a judicial question. The constitution is the superior law, and when attempted legislation conflicts with its restrictions and purports to make a law which is thereby prohibited it is clearly the duty of the courts to declare such legislation void, and to give it no effect. In every such case the vice of the enactment appears upon its face, and no one who takes the proper steps to inform himself as to the law need be misled by it. But, in addition to certain laws which the

---

[51] TEX. CONST. art. III, § 39.

[52] TEX. CONST. art. III, § 40.

[53] *See* TEX. CONST. art. III, § 28 (providing the presiding officer of each house shall "sign all bills and joint resolutions passed by the Legislature"); TEX. CONST. art. IV, § 14 (allowing the governor to sign or veto laws).

constitutions of most of our states in terms more or less explicit prohibit their respective legislatures from making, it has become customary to prescribe in the fundamental law certain rules of procedure by which the two bodies which compose the legislature are to be guided in framing and passing statutes. Such is the constitution of our own state, and it is for the supposed violation of these rules of procedure that the act in question in this case is claimed to be void. It would seem upon first blush that there should be a broad distinction between the authority to declare an act of the legislature void for want of power to pass the law in any manner, and the jurisdiction to annul a statute upon the ground that some provision of the constitution as to the mode of its passage has not been observed. The same distinction exists with reference to the judgments of the courts themselves. If, when the validity of a judgment is called in question, it appear that the court was without jurisdiction,–that is to say, that it had no power to hear and determine the case and to render any judgment in the premises,–the judgment will be held void in any suit in which its validity may be involved. But if the court have jurisdiction, no other court would have power in any collateral proceeding to revise its judgment, however irregular its proceedings may have been. Much stronger reasons exist why we should hesitate to annul the action of the legislature upon grounds of irregularity in its procedure than exist when we are asked to declare void the judgment of a court. Our constitution devolves the executive, legislative, and judicial functions of the government each upon a separate magistracy, and declares that no person or a collection of persons attached to either of the departments shall exercise the functions belonging to either of the others. Const. 1876, art. 2, § 1. The courts certainly have no power to revise or amend the statutes passed by the legislature, and we think they should ponder well before undertaking to revise the proceedings of either house of the legislature, and to declare its action void merely on account of its failure to observe some rule of procedure prescribed in the constitution. That it was competent to confer such a power upon the courts by the organic law we see no good reason to doubt. But when we consider the consequences of the exercise of such power, we think the authority should very plainly appear in the constitution before the courts should undertake of exercise it. In those tribunals in which it has been held that the journals of the two branches of the legislature could be looked to in order to determine whether or not the requirements of the constitution had been observed in passing a statute, with a view to test its validity, the decision has been placed upon the ground that the constitution required each house to keep a journal of its proceedings, and that the object of that requirement is to provide evidence by which the courts may determine whether the provisions of the constitution have been complied with or not. The constitution of our state does not declare such to be the object of requiring the journals to be kept, and we know of none that does. On the contrary, we think the more obvious purpose of the provision was to preserve a record of the action of the individual members of the house, to the end that these constituents should fix upon them a proper responsibility for their conduct. In the absence of some declaration or language in the constitution showing that it was intended that the journals of the two houses should have a conclusive effect in determining whether the acts of the legislature have properly ripened into laws, we should hesitate long before conceding to them such an effect by remote implications. . . .

The policy of modern legislation is to stamp upon each statute evidence of unquestioned authority. That evidence at common law was the enrolled bill, and behind it the courts were not permitted to go. Rex v. Arundel, Hob. 110. Our constitution provides that after the passage of a bill it shall be signed by the presiding officer of each house, in presence of the house; and we are of the opinion that when a bill has been so signed, and has been submitted to and approved by the governor, it was intended that it should afford conclusive evidence that the act had been passed in the manner required by the constitution. Such being the rule of the common law, we think, in the absence of something in the constitution expressly showing a contrary intention, it is fair to presume that it was intended that the same rule should prevail in this state. There is no provision of the constitution indicating in any direct manner such contrary intention; and the fact that it is provided that journals shall be kept, and that certain things shall be entered thereon, we think insufficient to show any such purpose.

There exists, as we have seen, another very satisfactory reason for these provisions; and in view of the consequences which are likely to flow from the rule we are of the opinion they afford no sufficient ground for holding that they were intended to furnish a record by which the validity of the statutes should be tested. As was held in Blessing v. Galveston, 42 Tex. 641, whether a statute be valid or not is a question of law, to be determined by the court from such sources of information as it may see proper to resort to, and is not to be decided as a matter of fact upon such evidence as may be adduced. If invalid, it cannot be made good by estoppel, acquiescence, or any lapse of time. If its validity is to be tested by the journals, we see no reason why the courts should not look to them; and there could never be an assurance of the validity of any statute until the journals had been examined, and it had been found that the procedure prescribed in the constitution had been followed. It seems to us that such a rule would lead to inextricable confusion. It is probable that there are few titles of land in this state which do not depend upon some statutory enactment. Let us suppose that some statute for the granting of land certificates, or for the acknowledgment and recording of deeds, or for fixing liens, or for the sale of lands under execution, or even fixing the terms of holding the courts, should, when tested by the journals of the two houses of the legislature, be found not to have been passed in strict compliance with the procedure provided for in the constitution in force at the time of its passage. If the journals are to control, as soon as the court's attention should be called to the fact it would be constrained to hold that the statute was void, and that all titles dependent upon it should fall to the ground. From our knowledge of the manner in which the journals of the legislature are ordinarily made up, the supposition is by no means a violent one, and hence we conclude that a rule fraught with such consequences was never entered. In order to maintain that the journals should prevail over an enrolled bill duly signed and approved, it should be held that they are a more certain and reliable record of what occurred during the progress of the bill than the signatures of the presiding officers, which the constitution provides as the evidence of its passage. Such can hardly be said to be the fact. It should be assumed that the highest officer in the body, who is sworn to support the constitution, and upon whom is devolved the important function of finally attesting the bill in presence of the house over which he presides, will bring to the discharge of that duty that judgment and circumspection which the occasion demands. The journals are the work of the clerks, perhaps hastily performed, and, as the official copies in this state, in some instances at least, will show, their reading is frequently dispensed with by vote. When such is the case, the journals are merely the work of the recording clerk, and even when read there is no assurance that the reading has led to the correction of every error.

Upon the question under discussion there is a very decided conflict of authority in the courts of the different states of our Union. We shall not consider them here in detail.

They are ably reviewed in the case of State v. Swift, 10 Nev. 176. The opinion in that case was delivered in 1875, and we concur in the conclusion there announced, that at that date the decided weight of authority was in favor of the rule that generally the enrolled bill as signed and approved should be taken as conclusive evidence of the law. The tendency of the latter decisions is to uphold the contrary rule. See Suth. St. Const. 44, and cases cited. Our conclusion upon the point that we cannot look to the journals in order to invalidate the statute is decisive of both questions presented by this appeal. The last section of the act under consideration would indicate that it was intended to pass the bill under a suspension of the rules as 'an imperative public necessity.' Without looking to the journals, we cannot say that the act was not regularly passed without suspending the rules, and therefore we need not decide whether the language used in the third section were sufficient to have authorized such suspension or not. In Ewing v. Duncan, (Tex. Sup.) 16 S. W. Rep. 1000, the question was not whether the bill had passed, but whether it had been carried by a sufficient majority to put it into immediate effect. The signatures of the presiding officer and the approval of the governor attested the passage of the act, but did not determine that it had taken effect from the date of its passage. There being no method of attesting the fact that a bill which purports to take effect from its passage has received the required two-thirds majority, we deemed the journals the best evidence upon the question, and looked to them for that purpose only. For the reasons given, the judgment is reversed, and here rendered for appellant, awarding the peremptory writ of *mandamus* as prayed for.

Notes on the Enrolled Bill Doctrine

Competing Visions of Legislative Deference: The *Williams* court refused to examine whether the procedural requirement of a bill being reported to a committee three days before adjournment was satisfied, instead concluding that such an evaluation would violate separation of powers principles and could have far-reaching and deleterious consequences. The court adopted what is known as the enrolled bill doctrine, under which courts will not look beyond duly enrolled legislation, once it is signed by the presiding officer of each house and either signed by the governor or allowed to become law without his or her signature, for evidence of procedural irregularities in its passage.

The majority of states, as well as the United States Supreme Court, follow at least some version of the enrolled bill doctrine.[54] The U.S. Supreme Court adopted the enrolled bill rule in *Marshall Field & Co. v. Clark*, decided just days before *Williams*.[55] The plaintiffs in *Marshall Field* contended that congressional journals demonstrated that neither house of Congress actually passed the exact bill that was subsequently enrolled. But the Supreme Court held that, once a bill was attested to by the signatures of the presiding officers of both houses and approved by the President, it had to be accepted by the federal judiciary as properly authenticated.[56] The Court reasoned that such a result followed from the "respect due to coequal and independent departments" and the "absolutely intolerable"

[54] 1 GEORGE D. BRADEN ET AL., THE CONSTITUTION OF THE STATE OF TEXAS: AN ANNOTATED AND COMPARATIVE ANALYSIS 121 (1977).

[55] 143 U.S. 649 (1892). *Marshall Field* issued on February 29, 1892, less than two weeks before *Williams* was decided.

[56] *Marshall Field*, 143 U.S. at 672.

mischiefs that would result if every legislative act could be "impeached by the journals, loose papers of the legislature, and parole evidence."[57] Since *Marshall Field*, federal courts consistently have refused to examine whether a duly enrolled bill actually passed Congress.[58]

But not all states subscribe to this rule. Some states, such as Florida, follow the "journal entry rule," authorizing a court to consider any evidence in the legislative journal that may contradict the otherwise prima facie valid enrolled bill.[59] The rationale behind the journal entry rule is that the journals, being mandated by the state constitution, are at least equal in dignity to an enrolled bill.

Exceptions to the Enrolled Bill Doctrine: Even in those states adhering to the enrolled bill rule, some exceptions exist. A number of states, including Texas, have recognized an exception when the evidence conclusively establishes a clerical error in the enrolled bill. In *Association of Texas Professional Educators v. Kirby*, the Texas Supreme Court addressed a constitutional challenge to an enrolled bill signed by the governor that contained a clerical change from the version actually passed by the legislature.[60] The challenge was based on more than just the legislative journals, though–the presiding officers of both houses testified that the enrolled bill was not the bill actually passed, and the attorney general, acting in his official capacity, stipulated in court that the enrolled bill had been changed from the version that passed the legislature. The Texas Supreme Court first noted that a number of states recognized some exceptions to the enrolled bill rule under similar circumstances, including Pennsylvania, Illinois, Kansas, and Missouri. The court then held that an exception was required under the presented circumstances "to avoid elevating clerical error over constitutional law."[61] The court therefore recognized a narrow exception to the doctrine when conclusive evidence from official journals, the presiding officers, and the attorney general establishes that "the enrolled bill signed by the governor was not the bill passed by the legislature."[62] Does such an exception contravene the purposes of the enrolled bill rule?

The Breadth of the Enrolled Bill Doctrine and the Prior Conflict Between the Texas High Courts: Another issue is the scope of the enrolled bill rule. This issue is not always easy, illustrated by the conflict that existed for some time in Texas between the state's two high courts on whether the doctrine prevented constitutional challenges to duly enrolled legislation based on article III, section 40. This section requires the legislature,

---

[57]*Id.* at 672-75 (quotations omitted).

[58]*See, e.g.*, OneSimpleLoan v. U.S. Sec'y of Educ., 496 F.3d 197, 200-03 (2d Cir. 2007) (employing enrolled bill rule to dismiss plaintiff's claims that the Deficit Reduction Act of 2005 was not passed by both chambers of Congress); Pub. Citizen v. U.S.D.C. for D.C., 486 F.3d 1342, 1349 (D.C. Cir. 2007) (same); Gibson v. Anderson, 131 F. 39, 42-43 (9th Cir. 1904) (holding enrolled bill rule barred argument that an authenticated bill was approved on a different date than stated).

[59]Robert F. Williams, *State Constitutional Limits on Legislative Procedure: Legislative Compliance and Judicial Enforcement*, 17 PUBLIUS: THE JOURNAL OF FEDERALISM 91, 106-12 (1987).

[60]788 S.W.2d 827 (Tex. 1990).

[61]*Id.* at 829-30.

[62]*Id.* at 830.

when convened in a special session called by the governor, to consider only those subjects designated or presented by the governor. The Court of Criminal Appeals in several early twentieth century cases examined legislative compliance with article III, section 40, without viewing the inquiry as barred by the enrolled bill rule.[63] But the Texas Supreme Court later held in *City of Houston v. Allred* that a duly enrolled bill precluded judicial examination of whether the subject matter of the legislation had been presented to the legislature by the governor.[64] Finally, in 1971, in *Maldonado v. State*, the Texas Court of Criminal Appeals adopted the position of the Texas Supreme Court.[65] In that case, Maldonado argued that his murder conviction was void because the legislation creating the criminal district court was enacted in a special session without an authorization from the governor. But the criminal high court rejected his contention, reasoning:

> There is no reason why the Court of Criminal Appeals and the Supreme Court of Texas, the two courts of last resort of our State, should have a different rule construing the constitutionality of statutes passed at special sessions of the Legislature.
>
> To carry out our early rule to its logical conclusion, . . . the act creating [these] courts could be void and cases tried in these courts could be subject to attack. If the rule adopted by the Supreme Court were followed, the judges and other personnel of the courts created in the [Act] would be entitled to hold office, continue to act and to be paid.
>
> The Supreme Court cases are more recent than ours and no doubt have been relied upon by the Legislature and by the Governor.
>
> We will not look behind the engrossed bill to see if the Governor issued a proclamation including the subject matter of the enacted legislation. All cases holding to the contrary are overruled.[66]

What other potential difficulties could have arisen during the time the state's two high courts had different understandings of the scope of the enrolled bill doctrine?

The Enrolled Bill Doctrine and Procedural Omissions Apparent on the Face of the Bill: The differing views of the two high courts were possible in part because the enrolled bill rule does not apply to every procedural requirement in the Texas Constitution. Rather, the doctrine prevents duly enrolled legislation from being contradicted or impeached by the legislative journals or similar evidence–the judiciary may still ensure that no procedural irregularities are apparent on the face of the enrolled bill.

---

[63] *See, e.g.*, *Ex parte* Fulton, 215 S.W. 331, 334 (Tex. Crim. App. 1919); Howard v. State, 178 S.W. 506, 509 (Tex. Crim. App. 1915); Long v. State, 127 S.W. 208, 210 (Tex. Crim. App. 1910); Brown v. State, 22 S.W. 596, 601 (Tex. Crim. App. 1893).

[64] 71 S.W.2d 251, 257 (Tex. 1934); *see also* Jackson v. Walker, 49 S.W.2d 693, 694-95 (Tex. 1932).

[65] 473 S.W.2d 26 (Tex. Crim. App. 1971).

[66] *Id.* at 28.

For example, Texas courts review whether legislation comports with the single subject rule of article III, section 35 of the Texas Constitution, despite the enrolled bill doctrine.[67] Texas courts also require that the exact language specified in article III, section 29 ("Be it enacted by the Legislature of the State of Texas") must appear on the face of the legislation for the law to be valid.[68] These decisions are based on the rationale that the judiciary only needs to examine the face of the enrolled legislation–not the underlying journals–to ascertain compliance with these constitutional provisions.

The face of duly enrolled legislation contains the bill number, a title, the enacting clause, operative sections indicating additions, revisions, or deletions to existing statutory provisions by underlining new provisions and striking out provisions to be deleted, the bill's effective date, and the signature of presiding legislative officers, clerks, and the governor. The following bill enacted by the Texas Legislature and approved by the governor in 2011 illustrates each of these components:

H.B. No. 692

AN ACT

relating to high school graduation requirements for a student who is unable to participate in physical activity due to disability or illness

BE IT ENACTED BY THE LEGISLATURE OF THE STATE OF TEXAS:

SECTION 1: Section 28.025, Education Code, is amended by amending Subsection (b-1) and adding Subsection (b-11) to read as follows:

(b-1) The State Board of Education by rule shall require that:

(1) except as provided by Subsection (b-2), the curriculum requirements for the recommended and advanced high school program under Subsection (a) include a requirement that students successfully complete:

(A) four credits in each subject of the foundational curriculum under Section 28.002(a)(1), including at least one-half credit in government and at least one-half credit in economics to meet the social studies requirement;

(B) for the recommended high school program, two credits in the same language in a language other than English under Section 28.002(a)(2)(A) and, for the advanced high school program, three credits in the same language in a language other than English under Section 28.002(a)(2)(A); and

[67] *See, e.g.*, Moore v. Sheppard, 192 S.W.2d 559 (Tex. 1946).

[68] Am. Indem. Co. v. City of Austin, 246 S.W. 1019 (Tex. 1922).

(C) for the recommended high school program, six elective credits and, for the advanced high school program, five elective credits;

(2) one or more credits offered in the required curriculum for the recommended and advanced high school program under Subsection (a) include a research writing component; and

(3) the curriculum requirements for the minimum, recommended, and advanced high school programs under Subsection (a) include a requirement that students successfully complete:

(A) one credit in fine arts; and

(B) <u>except as provided by Subsection (b-11)</u>, one credit in physical education under Section 28.002(a)(2)(C).

<u>(b-11) In adopting rules under Subsection (b-1), the State Board of Education shall allow a student who is unable to participate in physical activity due to disability or illness to substitute one credit in English language, arts, mathematics, science, or social studies or one academic elective credit for the physical education credit required under Subsection (b-1)(3)(B). A credit allowed to be substituted under this subsection may not also be used by the student to satisfy a graduation requirement other than completion of the physical education credit.</u>

SECTION 2: This Act takes effect immediately if it receives a vote of two-thirds of the members elected to each house, as provided by Section 39, Article III, Texas Constitution. If this Act does not receive the vote necessary for immediate effect, this Act takes effect September 1, 2011.

/s/________________
President of the Senate

/s/________________
Speaker of the House

I certify that H.B. No. 692 was passed by the House on April 21, 2011, by the following vote: Yeas 148, Nays O, 1 present, not voting.

/s/________________
Chief Clerk of the House

I certify that H.B. No. 692 was passed by the Senate on May 24, 2011, by the following vote: Yeas 31, Nays O.

/s/________________
Secretary of the Senate

Approved:

____
Date

/s/________________
Governor

While the enrolled bill doctrine prohibits the Texas judiciary from reviewing the legislative journals to contradict such an enrolled bill, it does not bar the courts from considering any procedural irregularities apparent in the text of the enrolled bill itself.

The Rise and Fall of Judicial Review of the Adequate Title Requirement: One procedural requirement that does not require an examination of the legislative journal is whether the bill contains an adequate title as required by article III, section 35. The adequate title requirement used to be the subject of frequent litigation. As one commentator noted, "The title requirement of [section 35] has generated more pages of appellate court opinion than all the other legislative process requirements in [article III] combined."[69] One example is that the title requirement was an alternative basis for striking down the filing fee at issue in *LeCroy v. Hanlon*, a case that was discussed in Chapter 5.[70] But soon after *LeCroy*, in November 1986, Texas voters ratified an amendment to section 35 adding the following subsections:

> (b) The rules of procedure of each house shall require that the subject of each bill be expressed in its title in a manner that gives the legislature and the public reasonable notice of that subject. The legislature is solely responsible for determining compliance with the rule.
>
> (c) A law, including a law enacted before the effective date of this subsection, may not be held void on the basis of an insufficient title.[71]

Under this November 1986 amendment, the courts no longer have the power to declare legislation invalid solely as a result of a defect in its title.[72] Yet Texas courts can still ensure compliance with the other requirement in section 35, the single subject limitation.

Moore v. Sheppard, 192 S.W.2d 559 (Tex. 1946)

SHARP, Justice.

[Moore and three other Texas appellate court clerks sought a writ of mandamus to compel the Texas Comptroller, George Sheppard, to pay their salaries. Sheppard argued that the clerks were not entitled to payment because they were indebted to the state. All three clerks had received money for furnishing uncertified and unofficial copies of court opinions, and they had not deposited this money in the state treasury. But the clerks maintained that they were not indebted to the state because the law allowed them to keep any extra compensation for the services they provided outside the scope of their official duties. Their entitlement to their salary, then, depended on whether the clerks had an official duty to deposit with the state treasury the money they had collected for uncertified, unofficial copies.]

---

[69] 1 GEORGE D. BRADEN ET AL., THE CONSTITUTION OF THE STATE OF TEXAS: AN ANNOTATED AND COMPARATIVE ANALYSIS 170 (1977).

[70] 713 S.W.2d 335, 337-38 (Tex. 1986).

[71] TEX. CONST. art. III, § 35.

[72] *See, e.g.*, Baggett v. State, 722 S.W.2d 700, 702 (Tex. Crim. App. 1987).

[Since 1933, the legislature had appended to appropriation bills for the judiciary a section directing that fees paid to clerks for unofficial copies of opinions had to be paid into the state treasury. But the clerks maintained in their petition that this rider violated the single-subject requirement.]

Petitioners do not question the power of the Legislature to enact general legislation prescribing a duty to furnish unofficial copies of court opinions and records, and prescribing the circumstances under which they shall be furnished, and fixing the amount to be charged therefor. It is their contention, however, that such legislation would be 'general legislation,' and could not therefore constitutionally be appended to another enactment on a different subject,–that is, the subject of appropriations. The inhibition of the Texas Constitution cited is: 'No bill, (except general appropriation bills, which may embrace the various subjects and accounts, for and on account of which moneys are appropriated) shall contain more than one subject.' Art. III, Sec. 35.

That the fixing of official fees is a matter of general legislation, and is a 'subject' of general legislation within the meaning of Article III, Section 35, above, cannot be questioned. There are many such enactments in our statutes. These statutes have been strictly construed against allowing a fee by implication, as regards both the fixing of the fee and the officer entitled thereto. McLennan County v. Boggess, 104 Tex. 311, 137 S.W. 346. We therefore hold that the fixing of fees for furnishing unofficial copies of opinions of the Courts of Civil Appeals, and the disposition of such fees, are matters of general legislation, and are 'subjects' within the meaning of Article III, Section 35, of the Texas Constitution.

Similarly, the appropriating of funds to be paid from the State Treasury is a 'subject' within the meaning of Article III, Section 35, of our Constitution. Therefore, since Article III, Section 35, provides that, 'No bill * * * shall contain more than one subject * * *,' that portion of the Appropriation Bill setting out for the first time matters not germane thereto, and dealing with general legislation on the different and wholly unrelated 'subject' of fees charged by petitioners for unofficial copies, and prescribing the disposition of such fees, is in conflict with the mandate of Article III, Section 35, and is unconstitutional. State v. Steele, 57 Tex. 200; Linden v. Finley, 49 S.W. 578.

There being no statutory duty requiring petitioners to furnish uncertified, unofficial copies of opinions of the Courts of Civil Appeals, no statute fixing any fee for such services, and no valid statute requiring that money received therefore be deposited in the State Treasury, there is no debt owing by petitioners to the State.

Dellinger v. State, 28 S.W.2d 537 (Tex. Crim. App. 1930)

CHRISTIAN, J.

Appellant was convicted of the offense of assaulting Adolpho Esqubiel, in concert with two others, while he (appellant) and his companions were masked. The punishment was assessed at confinement in the penitentiary for twenty-five years.

Adolpho Esqubiel was in his home at night when appellant and two companions, with masks covering their faces, forcibly entered the room in which he, his wife, and small children were asleep. Appellant shot at Esqubiel with a pistol, and he and his companions beat him, dragged him from his family, and carried him into the state of New Mexico, where they imprisoned him. Responding to a summons by the grand jury, Esqubiel had, prior to the assault, testified that appellant had sold him intoxicating liquor. At the time of the assault an indictment was pending against appellant charging him with the offense of selling intoxicating liquor to Esqubiel. The purpose of the imprisonment of the injured party was to remove him from the jurisdiction of the court in order that he might not appear against appellant as a witness. All of the foregoing facts were uncontroverted.

Section 5 of chapter 63 of the Acts of the Thirty-ninth Legislature, Regular Session (Vernon's Ann. P. C. art. 454e), reads as follows: "If any two or more persons acting in concert, or aiding and abetting each other, when either or all of whom are masked, or in disguise, shall assault or shall falsely imprison any other person, each of such persons so offending shall be guilty of a felony and upon conviction shall be punished by confinement in the penitentiary for any term of years not less than five. The terms 'masked' or 'in disguise' used in this article means that such person by artificial means has so changed or obscured his usual appearance as to render his identification impossible, or more difficult than it would have been if such mask or disguise has not been used."

It was under the foregoing provision that the indictment was drawn. It is appellant's contention that the statute above set out is inoperative as being in contravention of section 35 of article 3 of the Constitution of Texas, his position being that the act contains more than one subject. He asserts that the controlling or dominant subject-matter of the act is the regulation and prohibiting of secret masked societies and organizations, as indicated by the title, and that section 5, under which the prosecution herein proceeded, has no legitimate relation to or connection with said subject. The caption of the act (Acts 1925, c. 63) reads as follows: "An Act prohibiting the doing of acts hereinafter recited, to-wit: (a) Going into or near any public place masked or disguised and defining a public place. (b) Going masked or disguised into or near any private house, or who demand or seek entrance therein, or disturb the inhabitants thereof. (c) Going masked into a church or other place where people are assembled for religious purposes or services. (d) The acting in concert of two or more persons when masked or disguised, or the aiding or abetting by said persons of each other, and the assaulting, when so disguised, by such persons of any other person, or the false imprisonment by such person of any other person. (e) The parading of any secret society or organization or a part of the members thereof when masked or disguised upon or along any public road, or any street, or alley of any city or town of this State, and declaring equally guilty other members of such society who aid, abet or encourage such parading, and declaring them to be offenses; and defining and fixing penalties for violation of the provisions of this Act, and declaring an emergency."

A liberal construction will be applied in determining whether or not a statute violates section 35 of article 3 of our Constitution, and, where the provisions are germane in any degree, the law will be upheld. Mercer v. State, 111 Tex. Cr. R. 657, 13 S.W.(2d) 689; Davis v. State, 88 Tex. Cr. R. 183, 225 S. W. 532. The word "subject" is used in the same sense as the word "object" in former Constitutions. Fielder v. State, 40 Tex. Cr. R. 184, 49 S. W. 376. The word "object" under former Constitutions was construed by the courts to mean "end" or "purpose." Mercer v. State, supra, and authorities cited.

The object and purpose of the act is to prohibit the commission of the acts described therein while the offender is masked. Such object is fairly indicated by the title. The opinion is expressed that an application of the principles controlling renders untenable appellant's contention.

Notes on the Single Subject Requirement

The Doctrine and Its Purposes: The purpose of the unity of subject or single subject requirement is to prevent legislative logrolling, or the inclusion in a bill of several unconnected subjects in order to create a composite bill with more widespread legislative support.[73] Although logrolling is a common legislative practice, critics contend that it hampers political transparency and legislative accountability to voters. As a result, more than forty states have single subject requirements in their state constitutions.[74]

Yet does the interpretation afforded to the single subject requirement by Texas courts meaningfully prevent the opportunity for legislative logrolling? *Dellinger* acknowledged that a "liberal construction" is employed favoring legislative compliance with the single subject requirement, and that the entire law will be upheld if the provisions "are germane in any degree." The Texas Supreme Court has likewise opined that the various provisions in a single bill are to be construed "liberally to uphold validity, rather than construing them strictly to invalidate."[75] This means that "a bill satisfies the unity of subject requirement, even if it contains numerous provisions, however diverse, as long as these provisions relate directly or indirectly to the same general subject and have a mutual connection."[76]

This is not a difficult standard for the legislature to satisfy in most cases. In *LeCroy v. Hanlon*, for instance, the Texas Supreme Court declined to hold that the Omnibus Fee Bill, a law containing eighty-nine substantive sections covering widely disparate areas of law, violated the unity of subject requirement.[77] The court reasoned that, because the general subject of the bill was "the imposition of new fees," provisions increasing filing fees and allocating a portion to general revenue related to the bill's general subject.[78] In the vast majority of cases, as long as the legislature defines the subject matter of the bill broadly, the Texas judiciary will not invalidate any portion of the legislation.

The only exception recognized to date by Texas courts is general legislation altering existing substantive law in appropriation bills, as in *Moore v. Sheppard.* An appropriations

---

[73] *See, e.g.*, LeCroy v. Hanlon, 713 S.W.2d 335, 337 (Tex. 1986); Robinson v. Hill, 507 S.W.2d 521, 524 (Tex. 1974).

[74] *See* Kurt G. Kastorf, *Logrolling Gets Logrolled: Same-Sex Marriage, Direct Democracy, and the Single Subject Rule*, 54 EMORY L.J. 1633, 1641 (2005).

[75] *LeCroy*, 713 S.W.2d at 337. *Accord* Jessen Assocs., Inc. v. Bullock, 531 S.W. 2d 593, 600-01 (Tex. 1975); *Robinson*, 507 S.W.2d at 524.

[76] *LeCroy*, 713 S.W.2d at 337.

[77] 713 S.W.2d 335 (Tex. 1986). The court did, however, invalidate the law under the open courts provision and the adequate title requirement. *See id.*

[78] *Id.* at 337.

bill designates that funds are to be paid from the state treasury for specified purposes. While an appropriations bill may direct payment of funds for an infinite number of purposes without violating the single subject requirement, those provisions without any relationship to expending or dedicating appropriated funds are subject to invalidation under the single subject requirement. In *Moore*, for instance, the rider to the appropriations bill on the fees that the clerks could collect was a general legislative matter that did not relate to the spending of money from the state treasury. As a result, the rider was invalid under the unity of subject requirement as it was outside the subject matter of the remainder of the act.

The Texas Supreme Court followed *Moore* in *Strake v. First Court of Appeals*.[79] In *Strake*, the legislature had adopted an across-the-board three percent pay increase for all state employees, including elected state officials, in its general appropriation act. Recognizing that this pay increase likely would disqualify sitting legislators from running for executive offices under article III, section 18 of the Texas Constitution (discussed earlier in this chapter), the legislature included a provision in the general appropriations act that nullified the pay increase if a sitting legislator was elected to a state civil office. But the Texas Supreme Court concluded that the attempted nullification of the pay increase was invalid because it was a general law attempting to circumvent article III, section 18, not a provision relating to the appropriation of funds that could be included in an appropriations act.[80] Other than prohibiting such general legislative provisions contained in appropriations acts, however, the single subject requirement has had minimal impact in Texas.

The Single Subject Requirement in Other States: Most state courts likewise interpret their single subject limitations liberally to uphold legislation, merely requiring that the various provisions in a bill be reasonably related to the same subject matter, logically connected, or germane to each other.[81] But there are some other state courts that, despite articulating a similar standard, apply it with less deference to the legislative judgment.

The Oklahoma Supreme Court, for instance, acknowledges that the single subject requirement is satisfied "if the provisions are germane, relative, and cognate to a readily apparent common theme and purpose," yet it does not liberally construe statutory provisions. Instead, the court ensures that the resulting combination is not misleading and is unlikely to force legislators to "an unpalatable all-or-nothing choice" in casting their votes.[82] This approach, which is predicated on the underlying purposes of the single subject requirement, has led to the invalidation of a number of bills by the Oklahoma Supreme Court, including a bill authorizing revenue bonds by the Oklahoma Capitol Improvement Authority for three

---

[79] 704 S.W.2d 746 (Tex. 1986).

[80] *Id.* at 748-49.

[81] *See, e.g.*, Legislature v. Eu, 816 P.2d 1309, 1320 (Cal. 1991) (holding single subject requirement not violated if "all of its parts are 'reasonably germane' to each other"); Dakota Sys., Inc. v. Viken, 694 N.W.2d 23, 29 (S.D. 2005) (various provisions must merely "fairly relate" to each other and have a common basis).

[82] Fent v. State *ex rel.* Okla. Capitol Improvement Auth., 214 P.3d 799, 805 (Okla. 2009) (internal quotations omitted).

different capital projects and a bill involving several different aspects of freedom of conscience.[83]

The Ohio Supreme Court employed similar reasoning to invalidate an omnibus tort reform package that contained noneconomic damages caps, punitive damages caps, limitations on agency liability in actions against a hospital, qualified immunity for athletic coaches, evidentiary rules regarding seat belt usage, and several other disparate matters in part under the state constitutional one subject rule.[84] Although the court acknowledged that the single subject rule merely mandated "a common purpose or relationship . . . between the topics," the court refused to embrace the legislature's proposed relationship that the provisions all pertained to "tort and other civil actions," reasoning that accepting such a proposition would abdicate its judicial duty to enforce the state constitutional requirement.[85]

Is the deference the Texas and most other state courts have afforded to the legislature when interpreting the single subject requirement appropriate? Would it be better to adopt the more searching inquiry employed in Ohio and Oklahoma? What impact might that have had on the tort reform package in House Bill 4 enacted in 2003 by the Texas Legislature,[86] which also embraced numerous disparate provisions, including (among many other topics) setting damages caps in certain cases, expanding the Texas Supreme Court's jurisdiction over certain interlocutory appeals, establishing a judicial panel on multidistrict litigation, creating incentives for parties to make and accept reasonable settlement offers, amending the proportionate responsibility scheme, establishing various defenses in products liability cases, and modifying rules regarding post-judgment interest, pre-judgment interest, and appeal bonds?

C. THE PROHIBITION ON LOCAL AND SPECIAL LAWS

The procedural state constitutional limitations on legislatures discussed in the last section were later buttressed by substantive limitations on legislation, such as the prohibition on local and special laws. This limitation became common during the latter half of the nineteenth century and was designed to combat perceived legislative acquiescence to demands by railroads, corporations, and wealthy individuals for private grants and special privileges.

Nineteenth century state legislatures enacted numerous laws benefitting particular individuals, businesses, or localities in the state.[87] Antebellum state constitutions

---

[83]*See, e.g.*, Nova Health Sys. v. Edmonson, 233 P.3d 380, 381-82 (Okla. 2010) (discussing prior Oklahoma decisions).

[84]State *ex rel.* Ohio Acad. of Trial Lawyers v. Sheward, 715 N.E.2d 1062, 1099-1102 (Ohio 1999).

[85]*See id.*

[86]Act of June 2, 2003, 78th Leg., R.S., ch. 204, 2003 Tex. Gen. Laws 847.

[87]*See* Sheyl G. Snyder & Robert M. Ireland, *The Separation of Government Powers under the Constitution of Kentucky: A Legal and Historical Analysis of* L.R.C. v. Brown, 73 KY. L.J. 165, 168 (1984) (detailing that the quantity of local and private legislation had grown unmanageable after the Civil War throughout the United Stats as evidenced by the 94% of the Kentucky Legislature's 1883-84 legislative output that concerned local or private matters).

occasionally sought to restrain legislatures from enacting some of these private laws; the Texas Constitution of 1845, for example, barred the legislature from granting divorces and creating private corporations by special law.[88] These early provisions, though, did not constrain the onslaught of special legislation enacted in the wake of American industrialization in the postbellum period. Corporations sought franchises and monopolies for transportation and utility services that state legislatures often granted, in exchanges that many citizens viewed as corrupt.[89] Even in the absence of the specter of corruption, there was a widespread concern that enacted laws advanced personal and private interests rather than the public interest.[90] Legislators were thought to widely engage in vote trading to support each other's personal and constituent interests.[91] State constitutional prohibitions on special and local laws, designed to protect the majority of citizens from legislative favoritism to the privileged few, were viewed as a solution to these problems.

Although the terms "special law" and "local law" are frequently used interchangeably, their meaning is not identical. A "special law" is a law that does not apply uniformly to all similarly situated subjects, providing special privileges to certain persons, corporations, or other businesses. A "local law" is one that applies to particular geographical segment of the state, providing special privileges to one local area or political subdivision over other portions of the state.

A prohibition on local and special laws is contained in the constitutions of approximately three-fourths of the states, although various forms of the prohibition exist. First, some states, like Illinois, Indiana, Michigan, and Montana, prohibit all special or local laws when a general law can be made, or perhaps already is, applicable. Other states, such as Florida, Louisiana, North Carolina, and Washington, only prohibit special or local laws in certain specified situations, thereby allowing the legislature to enact special or local laws in all other instances outside the constitutionally precluded areas. Some state constitutions, while allowing special and local laws in at least certain circumstances, include additional legislative procedures that must be followed before the legislature can enact such a law.

The Texas Constitution combines all these limitations. First, Texas Constitution article III, section 56(a) provides that the legislature shall not enact thirty specified categories of local or special laws, unless otherwise authorized by the Constitution. In addition to these thirty categories, there is also a "catch-all" provision in section 56(b), barring the legislature from enacting local or special laws "in all other cases where a general law can be made applicable."[92] Finally, in those limited situations when a local or special law is authorized by the state constitution, section 57 requires that a notice of an intention

[88] *See* 1 GEORGE D. BRADEN ET AL., THE CONSTITUTION OF THE STATE OF TEXAS: AN ANNOTATED AND COMPARATIVE ANALYSIS 272 (1977) (discussing provisions).

[89] G. ALAN TARR, UNDERSTANDING STATE CONSTITUTIONS 120 (1998).

[90] *See* Miller v. El Paso, 150 S.W.2d 1000, 1001 (Tex. 1941).

[91] *See id.*

[92] TEX. CONST. art. III, § 56(b).

to enact such a law with a description of its substance must be published, at least thirty days before the legislative introduction of the bill, in the affected locality.[93]

Such limitations, however, do not result in uniform application of all Texas laws. The constitutional prohibition on local and special laws requires only that the distinctions established by the law are legitimate and reasonable. In other words, some real difference must justify the law's application to certain persons, places, or things, but not to others. The legislature does not violate the local or special law prohibition by enacting non-uniform laws when there is a reasonable basis for the classification and the law operates equally on all within the class.

Moreover, the Texas Constitution specifically authorizes the legislature to enact special and local laws in defined circumstances. For instance, article III, section 56(b) allows local fencing laws and wildlife conservation laws, article VIII, section 9(e) permits the legislature to enact local or special laws for the maintenance of public roads and highways without prior notice, and several sections in article V of the Texas Constitution allow the legislature to establish courts on a local basis. Thus, a law will only violate the constitutional ban on local or special laws if its application is based on unreasonable distinctions and the state constitution does not otherwise authorize such disparate treatment. The following case illustrates these concepts.

Maple Run at Austin Mun. Utility Dist. v. Monaghan, 931 S.W.2d 941 (Tex. 1996)

PHILLIPS, Chief Justice.

Section 43.082 of the Texas Local Government Code, enacted in 1995 and expiring on the last day of 1996, purportedly authorizes certain municipal utility districts lying within a municipality's extraterritorial jurisdiction to dissolve, requiring the affected municipality to take ownership of the district's assets and assume its debts. Because of extremely specific requirements about the amount and character of outstanding debt and other factors, Maple Run at Austin Municipal Utility District is the only district in the state qualifying for the special treatment under section 43.082. The parties stipulate to this fact, and they further stipulate that the Legislature intended for the statute to apply only to this district. In this direct appeal, we must decide whether section 43.082 violates the Texas Constitution. The trial court invalidated the statute and enjoined its enforcement. Because we hold that section 43.082 is an invalid local law under Article III, Section 56, we affirm the judgment of the trial court.

---

[93]TEX. CONST. art. III, § 57. This section provides:

> No local or special law shall be passed, unless notice of the intention to apply therefor shall have been published in the locality where the matter or thing to be affected may be situated, which notice shall state the substance of the contemplated law, and shall be published at least thirty days prior to the introduction into the Legislature of such bill and in the manner to be provided by law. The evidence of such notice having been published, shall be exhibited in the Legislature, before such act shall be passed.

Other provisions of the Texas Constitution provide exceptions to section 57, including that notice is not required before the creation of a school district under article VII, section 3. In addition, the Texas Constitution contains independent notice requirements for local laws creating conservation districts in article XVI, section 59.

I

Maple Run at Austin Municipal Utility District (hereinafter "Maple Run" or "the District") was formed in 1983 in an area south of the City of Austin to provide utility service to the area's residents. The District, created under Chapter 54 of the Texas Water Code, is authorized to, among other things, construct and operate plants and facilities for supplying water and wastewater services. The District is a political subdivision of the state, with the power to incur bonded indebtedness and levy ad valorem taxes.

Because Maple Run lies within the City of Austin's extraterritorial jurisdiction, the Maple Run landowners were required under section 54.016 of the Texas Water Code to obtain consent from the City to create the district. In connection with the City's grant of consent, the District and the City entered into a written agreement concerning the creation and operation of the District (the "Consent Agreement"). This agreement recognizes that the District lies within the City's extraterritorial jurisdiction, and that its area "is scheduled for annexation by the City in accordance with the Annexation Plan of the City."

The District subsequently issued $20,900,000 in "contract revenue bonds," repayable out of revenues from the District's utility operations. The District also issued $3,750,000 in "combination tax and revenue bonds," repayable out of a combination of ad valorem taxes and revenues. All facilities for which the District issued its bonds have been constructed. Based on its projected use of the District facilities, the City agreed to bear 84.83 percent of the debt service for the contract revenue bonds. The City assumed no liability, prior to annexation, for the remaining part of the contract revenue bonds, or any part of the combination tax and revenue bonds.

Real estate development did not occur in Maple Run as expected. The District initially anticipated that as many as 2,000 single family and multi-family units would be developed, as well as a substantial number of commercial projects. Since 1983, however, only about 450 homes have been built, and there has been no multi-family or commercial development. Accordingly, revenues from water and wastewater services have been much lower than expected, forcing the District to assess relatively high taxes and monthly surcharges to homeowners. Despite these high rates, the District contends that it is still experiencing serious financial trouble.

In 1995, the Legislature passed Senate Bill 1261, which was codified as section 43.082 of the Texas Local Government Code. This act authorizes the municipal utility district that meets its specific requirements to dissolve upon resolution of the district's board, without consent from the adjacent municipality, and upon dissolution requires the municipality to assume the assets and liabilities of the district.

When a district dissolves under section 43.082, the municipality is required to provide full municipal services to the area, and the municipality may annex the district by simple resolution, without following the normal notice and hearing procedures. The municipality may assess a $25 monthly surcharge on utility customers in the former district and, importantly, may also assess a platting fee surcharge on developers desiring to subdivide land in the former district. The surcharge may be in an amount sufficient to offset the financial burden imposed on the municipality from assuming the district's indebtedness.

The application of section 43.082 is restricted as follows:

> (a) This section applies to any district created in or after 1983 within the extraterritorial jurisdiction of a municipality with written consent by ordinance or resolution as required by Section 42.042 if the district has:
> (1) issued not less than $17 million nor more than $21 million in bonds, excluding refunding bonds, repayable in a manner authorized under Section 54.503(2), Water Code;
> (2) issued at least $3.5 million of bonds repayable in a manner authorized under Section 54.503(3), Water Code, before June 1, 1993; and
> (3) constructed all of the facilities for which the bonds were issued prior to December 31, 1991.

Tex. Local Gov't Code § 43.082(a). The parties stipulate that Maple Run is the only district in the State meeting these criteria, that only Maple Run requested its enactment, and that the Legislature intended for section 43.082 to apply only to Maple Run. In other words, while Maple Run is not mentioned by name in the statute, the Legislature selected the criteria for the purpose of restricting the statute solely to that district. Moreover, because section 43.082 expires on December 31, 1996, there is no chance that it will ever apply to any other districts. The legislative history accompanying Senate Bill 1261 confirms that the statute was enacted to relieve the financial problems of Maple Run. *See Bill Analysis of S.B. 1261* (May 11, 1995).

In January 1996, the Maple Run board of directors adopted a resolution dissolving the District in accordance with section 43.082, effective May 10, 1996. Prior to dissolution, Maple Run landowners James G. Monaghan, Maple Run Joint Venture and S.R. Ridge Limited Partnership (collectively "Monaghan") sued the District and the City of Austin seeking to enjoin enforcement of section 43.082, contending that it violated the Texas Constitution. Monaghan argued that section 43.082 was a special or local law prohibited by Article III, Section 56, a grant of public money and credit prohibited by Article III, Sections 50, 51, and 52, and an extinguishment of public debt prohibited by Article III, Section 55. The City filed a cross-claim against the District raising a similar constitutional challenge, thus aligning itself with Monaghan on this issue. After stipulating to the essential underlying facts, the parties filed cross motions for summary judgment directed solely to the constitutional issues.

On May 6, 1996, the trial court signed a final judgment declaring the statute unconstitutional and permanently enjoining its operation. The District perfected a direct appeal to this Court, challenging this ruling. *See* Tex. Gov't Code § 22.001(c); Tex.R.App. P. 140.

II

A

Article III, Section 56 of the Texas Constitution provides in relevant part:

> LOCAL AND SPECIAL LAWS. The Legislature shall not, except as otherwise provided in this Constitution, pass any local or special law . . .

> [r]egulating the affairs of counties, cities, towns, wards or school districts.
> . . .
> And in all other cases where a general law can be made applicable, no local or special law shall be enacted. . . .

While the terms "local law" and "special law" have at times been used interchangeably, a local law is one limited to a specific geographic region of the State, while a special law is limited to a particular class of persons distinguished by some characteristic other than geography.

The purpose of Section 56 is to "prevent the granting of special privileges and to secure uniformity of law throughout the State as far as possible." *Miller v. El Paso County,* 136 Tex. 370, 150 S.W.2d 1000, 1001 (1941). In particular, it prevents lawmakers from engaging in the "reprehensible" practice of trading votes for the advancement of personal rather than public interests. *Id.*

A law is not a prohibited local law merely because it applies only in a limited geographical area. We recognize the Legislature's broad authority to make classifications for legislative purposes. *See Miller,* 150 S.W.2d at 1001. However, where a law is limited to a particular class or affects only the inhabitants of a particular locality, "the classification must be broad enough to include a substantial class and must be based on characteristics legitimately distinguishing such class from others with respect to the public purpose sought to be accomplished by the proposed legislation." *Miller,* 150 S.W.2d at 1001-02. "The primary and ultimate test of whether a law is general or special is whether there is a reasonable basis for the classification made by the law, and whether the law operates equally on all within the class." *Rodriguez v. Gonzales,* 148 Tex. 537, 227 S.W.2d 791, 793 (1950).

For example, in *County of Cameron v. Wilson,* 160 Tex. 25, 326 S.W.2d 162 (1959), we upheld a law providing for the development of public parks that applied only in counties "border[ing] on the Gulf of Mexico within whose boundaries is located any island, part of an island, or islands, suitable for park purposes." 326 S.W.2d at 165. We held that "[t]he coastal geography of Texas affords a reasonable distinction between the island park on the one hand and the mainland park on the other," noting that the "demand for the conveniences usually provided by county parks may be greater along the coast than in many inland areas." *Id.* at 166.

Similarly, in *Robinson v. Hill,* 507 S.W.2d 521 (Tex.1974), the Court upheld a law imposing special bail bond regulations in counties with a population of 150,000 or more. We held that there was a reasonable basis for this classification, concluding that

> [t]he Legislature in this instance may well have concluded that bail bondsmen in the more populous counties should be regulated and required to secure their obligations because of the high incidence of crime and the difficulties involved in enforcing bond forfeitures . . . , but that the same safeguards and procedures were not necessary and would be unduly burdensome in more sparsely populated areas.

On the other hand, we have struck down several laws under Section 56 where no reasonable basis supported the classification. For example, in *Miller,* we invalidated a law authorizing an economic development tax that applied only in counties

> having a population of not less than 125,000 nor more than 175,000 inhabitants, and containing a city having a population of not less than 90,000 inhabitants, as shown by the last preceding Federal census.

150 S.W.2d at 1002. We held that these population brackets, which included only El Paso County, bore no substantial relation to the objects sought to be accomplished by the act.

Similarly, in *City of Fort Worth v. Bobbitt,* 121 Tex. 14, 36 S.W.2d 470, 471-72 (1931), the Court struck down a public works law that applied only in cities with a population between 106,000 and 110,000. The Court held that the bracket advanced no legitimate purpose, but rather was simply a means of singling out one city for special treatment.

Likewise, in *Bexar County v. Tynan,* 128 Tex. 223, 97 S.W.2d 467 (1936), the Court invalidated an act reducing the compensation of certain officers in counties with a population between 290,000 and 310,000, which included only Bexar County. The Court concluded that

> the attempted classification is unreasonable and arbitrary to such degree as to indicate beyond doubt that the purpose of the Legislature was to single out one county and to attempt to legislate upon the question of the compensation of its officers, and not upon the subject generally. . . .

Id. at 470. *See also Smith v. Decker,* 158 Tex. 416, 312 S.W.2d 632, 636 (1958) (striking down act imposing special bail bond rules in counties with population between 73,000 and 100,000); *Rodriguez v. Gonzales,* 148 Tex. 537, 227 S.W.2d 791, 793-94 (1950) (invalidating act providing for special procedures for collecting ad valorem taxes applicable only in certain counties along the Mexican border).

Here, there is no dispute that the Legislature singled out Maple Run for special treatment. No one contends that the brackets selected by the Legislature have anything to do with the purpose of the statute; rather, these brackets serve solely to restrict section 43.082 to the District without actually identifying it by name. Further, the District offers no legitimate reason, and none appears in the record, why the statute is limited to Maple Run. The parties have stipulated that there are other districts in the state 1) with serious financial troubles, 2) with tax rates higher than Maple Run, 3) with annual debt service higher than Maple Run, and 4) with overall indebtedness higher than Maple Run.

Because the Legislature singled out the District for special treatment without any reasonable basis for doing so, section 43.082 has all the appearances of a local law within the meaning of Article III, Section 56.

B

The District argues, however, that section 43.082 is not a local law because it affects a matter of statewide interest. This argument, as framed by the District, consists of three components: 1) section 43.082 serves a conservation purpose; 2) Article XVI, Section 59 of the Texas Constitution mandates that conservation of our natural resources is of statewide importance; and 3) laws affecting matters of statewide importance are by definition not local or special laws. We conclude that this approach is flawed.

We assume for purposes of this discussion that section 43.082 does in fact serve a conservation purpose. The District relies on Article XVI, Section 59 of the Texas Constitution for the general proposition that conservation of our natural resources is a matter of statewide importance. Section 59 provides in relevant part:

> The conservation and development of all the natural resources of this State, including the control, storing, preservation and distribution of its storm and flood waters, the waters of its rivers and streams, for irrigation, power and all other useful purposes, . . . are each and all hereby declared public rights and duties; and the Legislature shall pass all such laws as may be appropriate thereto.

Tex. Const. art. XVI, § 59(a). While we agree that all Texans have an interest in protecting this State's natural resources, we disagree that one may simplistically conclude that any law having a conservation purpose is ipso facto not a local or special law. The District relies on a series of cases in which this Court has espoused the principle that a law is not local, even if its operation is restricted to a specific area, if it affects a matter of statewide interest. *See Lower Colorado River Authority v. McCraw,* 125 Tex. 268, 83 S.W.2d 629, 636 (1935); *Stephensen v. Wood,* 119 Tex. 564, 34 S.W.2d 246, 248 (1931). The statutes involved in these cases, however, affected a substantial class of persons over a broad region of the state, as opposed to section 43.082, which applies to one municipal utility district. Moreover, our later cases have clarified that the ultimate question under Article III, Section 56 is whether there is a *reasonable basis* for the Legislature's classification. *See, e.g., Robinson v. Hill,* 507 S.W.2d 521, 525 (Tex.1974); *Rodriguez v. Gonzales,* 148 Tex. 537, 227 S.W.2d 791, 793 (1950); *Miller v. El Paso County,* 136 Tex. 370, 150 S.W.2d 1000, 1001 (1941). The significance of the subject matter and the number of persons affected by the legislation are merely factors, albeit important ones, in determining reasonableness. For example, in *City of Irving v. Dallas/Fort Worth Int'l Airport Bd.,* 894 S.W.2d 456, 467 (Tex.App.--Fort Worth 1995, no writ), the court upheld legislation giving certain municipal airport authorities the exclusive power to make land-use decisions for property within the geographic boundaries of the airport. Because the statute applied only to airports operated jointly by two cities with population exceeding 400,000, only D/FW Airport qualified. The court upheld this classification as reasonable, however, noting the tremendous statewide importance of the facility and the special zoning conflicts that can arise for a jointly operated airport. It does not follow, however, that any legislation having some incidental effect on the environment must be upheld, regardless of whether there was any legitimate basis for the classification drawn by the Legislature. This would seriously undermine the purpose of Article III, Section 56.

Because section 43.082 singles out one specific municipal utility district for special treatment without any reasonable basis for doing so, we hold that it is a local law within the meaning of Section 56.

III

The District next argues that, even if section 43.082 is a local law, it is not a *prohibited* local law. The first sentence of Section 56 bars the Legislature from passing local or special laws "except as otherwise provided in this Constitution." The District contends that section 43.082 is specifically authorized under Article XVI, Section 59, and thus falls under this exception.

As noted earlier, Section 59(a) provides that the conservation and development of the State's natural resources are "public rights and duties," and directs the Legislature to pass "all such laws as may be appropriate thereto." Tex. Const. art. XVI, § 59(a). To accomplish these purposes, Section 59(b) specifically authorizes the Legislature to create conservation and reclamation districts. Section 59(c) authorizes conservation and reclamation districts to incur bonded indebtedness to achieve their purposes, and to levy taxes for the purpose of repaying the debt. Maple Run is a district created under and subject to the authority of Section 59.

It is well settled that Section 59(b) authorizes the Legislature to pass local legislation creating specific conservation and reclamation districts without violating Article III, Section 56. *See Lower Neches Valley Authority v. Mann,* 140 Tex. 294, 167 S.W.2d 1011, 1014 (1943); *Harris County Flood Control Dist. v. Mann,* 135 Tex. 239, 140 S.W.2d 1098, 1101 (1940). Indeed, the Legislature has created hundreds of these districts by special law. *See* WATER AUXILIARY LAWS, Table III, 1996 pamphlet.

Moreover, the Legislature has *dissolved* numerous conservation and reclamation districts by special act. While these special dissolution acts are not before us and we express no opinion on their validity, they are notably different from section 43.082. In every other instance that we have examined, the Legislature either 1) determined that the district had no outstanding indebtedness, 2) required the District to develop a plan to liquidate its indebtedness prior to dissolution, or 3) conditioned dissolution on a municipality's *consent* to take over the indebtedness and service requirements of the district.

Section 43.082, on the other hand, requires the City to assume the assets and indebtedness of the District without the City's consent, requires the City to provide full municipal services to the District immediately, and requires landowners desiring to subdivide property in the District to pay a substantial platting fee to offset the City's financial burden. While we presume that legislative enactments are constitutional and, if possible, interpret them in a manner to avoid constitutional infirmities, *see Barshop v. Medina County Underground Water Conservation Dist.,* 925 S.W.2d 618, 629 (Tex.1996), Section 59 cannot be read so broadly as to specifically authorize this local legislation. Section 59 allows the Legislature to create conservation and reclamation districts when essential to accomplish the purposes of the amendment; it does not authorize the Legislature to intimately regulate the financial affairs of a specific community–without that community's consent–in the name of conservation. Indeed, forcing indebtedness upon a political subdivision goes against the tenor of Section 59. While Section 59 grants the

Legislature a broad mandate to protect our natural resources, it recognizes local control of financial obligations. Under these circumstances, Section 59 cannot reasonably be read as authorizing local legislation that arbitrarily singles out a community for financial regulation.

For the foregoing reasons, we hold that section 43.082 is not authorized under Article XVI, Section 59 of the Texas Constitution, and therefore is a prohibited local law.

Notes on Local and Special Laws

Prohibited Local and Special Laws in Texas: How reasonable does the legislative classification have to be to avoid characterization as a prohibited local or special law? Is there a difference between local laws and special laws in this regard?

Maple Run invalidated a local law intended and designed to authorize one particular municipal utility district to dissolve and be annexed by the City of Austin. The court reasoned that there was no basis for singling out this particular district for favorable treatment when other such districts in the state faced even more severe financial difficulties. The court relied on many of its prior decisions that had invalidated laws as local laws that applied to a single area of the state or political subdivision when there was no indication that the classification had any legitimate purpose.

On the other hand, it has been more than sixty years since Texas courts have invalidated a law as a special law, even when the law applies only to a single entity.[94] Although the governing standard is identical, identifying a reasonable basis for a classification is typically easier when the classification does not favor selected political subdivisions of the state.

Ford Motor Co. v. Sheldon provides an illustration.[95] Section 6.06(g) of the Texas Motor Vehicle Commission Code authorized the Texas Supreme Court to review on interlocutory appeal a court of appeals' decision about the grant or denial of class certification involving a motor vehicle licensee, while in all other interlocutory appeals from a class certification decision (at that time)[96] review was final in the court of appeals (unless there was a dissent or a conflict with the opinion of another court of appeals). The plaintiffs, who had prevailed in the court of appeals, contended that Section 6.06(g) was an unconstitutional special law as it unreasonably distinguished "class actions involving cars and trucks from class actions involving the goods and services provided by every other business in the world."[97] But the supreme court disagreed:

---

[94]*See, e.g.*, August A. Busch & Co. v. Tex. Alcoholic Beverage Comm'n, 649 S.W.2d 652, 654 (Tex. App.–Texarkana 1982, writ ref'd n.r.e.) (upholding against a special law challenge a prohibition against vertical integration in the alcoholic beverage industry even though only a single entity was impacted).

[95]22 S.W.3d 444 (Tex. 2000).

[96]Subsequently, the Texas Legislature granted the Texas Supreme Court appellate jurisdiction over all interlocutory appeals of class certification decisions. *See* TEX. GOV'T CODE § 22.225(d).

[97]22 S.W.3d at 450.

> We conclude that there is a reasonable basis for distinguishing class actions involving motor vehicle licensees from other class actions and that Section 6.06(g) operates equally on all within the class. First, "[a] statute is not local or special . . . if it operates on a subject in which people at large are interested." *Langdeau v. Bouknight,* 162 Tex. 42, 344 S.W.2d 435, 441 (1961). Automobiles and related issues such as automobile safety are important subjects to the public. Automobiles are the primary means of transportation for most people; many, if not most, travel many thousands of miles each year and hence spend hundreds of hours each year in an automobile. In fact, acquiring an automobile is one of the largest and most important purchases that many consumers will make. As a result, automobiles have often been the subject matter of Texas class action suits. Thus, it is reasonable for the Legislature to ensure heightened judicial scrutiny of these class actions that affect so many individuals. This justification is sufficient to sustain Section 6.06(g) against constitutional challenge.
>
> Second, Section 6.06(g) applies uniformly to all members of the affected class, as any party to a class action suit involving a licensee may assert a claim thereunder. Under the circumstances, Section 6.06(g) is not a special law that violates Article III, Section 56 of the Texas Constitution.[98]

How much deference should be given to the legislative judgment on the reasonableness of the classification? Is the deference afforded by Texas courts, especially with respect to special laws, appropriate?

Judicial Review in Other Jurisdictions: Texas is not alone in its deference to the legislative judgment on the reasonableness of the classification, especially with respect to special laws. Indeed, a number of early state court decisions held that the determination of whether a general law could be made applicable was the province solely of the legislative branch, stripping away judicial review of the question.[99] While subsequent state constitutional amendments and state court decisions have resulted in most state courts today reviewing whether legislation is a prohibited special or local law,[100] the judiciary is typically deferential to the legislative judgment, especially when addressing a claim that legislation

[98]*Id.* at 451.

[99]*See, e.g.,* Anderson v. Bd. of Comm'rs, 95 P. 583, 585 (Kan. 1908) (noting state courts at the time had "almost uniformly held it to be the province solely of the Legislature to determine when a general law can be made applicable"); Thomas F. Green, Jr., *A Malapropian Provision of State Constitutions*, 24 WASH. U. L.Q. 359, 369 (1939) (concluding a majority of jurisdictions at that time would not review whether a general law could be made applicable).

[100]*See* NORMAN J. SINGER, 2 SUTHERLAND STATUTES AND STATUTORY CONSTRUCTION § 40:3 (6th ed. 2001). Some states, such as Illinois and Missouri, overturned the earlier cases through state constitutional amendments providing that whether a general law is or can be made applicable is a "judicial question" or a "matter for judicial determination." *See* ILL. CONST. art. IV, § 13; MO. CONST. art III, § 40.

is a special law.[101] Although local laws favoring a particular political subdivision of the state for no apparent legitimate reason, like the statute at issue in *Maple Run*, are frequently invalidated,[102] the legislative judgment will not be disturbed if a legitimate basis for the classification is apparent.[103]

At least a couple of state courts, however, engage in more rigorous review, providing less deference to the legislature, even when considering alleged special laws. The Illinois Supreme Court and the Oklahoma Supreme Court, for example, have invalidated certain aspects of tort reform legislation under their state special law prohibition, reasoning that the legislation impermissibly favored health care providers or product manufacturers.[104]

If local laws and special laws are the product of a "reprehensible" practice, as Texas cases suggest, why isn't judicial review more robust in Texas and most other jurisdictions? Is the problem that laws are frequently responsive to a constituent concern, such that distinguishing between general and special laws is not a simple proposition? Is that why local and special laws are not prohibited by the United States Constitution? James Madison, in Federalist No. 57, wrote that Congress "can make no law which will not have its full operation on themselves and their friends, as well as on the great mass of society." Nevertheless, he admitted that this restraint was not explicit in the Constitution but based on the "genius of the whole system; the nature of just and constitutional laws; and above all, the vigilant and manly spirit which actuates the people of America."[105] Yet despite these implicit restraints, Congress frequently enacts "private" laws. For example, Congress enacted the federal "Terri's law" in 2005, which applied exclusively to allow Terri

---

[101]*See, e.g.*, Med. Soc'y of S.C. v. Med. Univ. of S.C., 513 S.E.2d 352, 357 (S.C. 1999) (holding a law is not unconstitutional as a special law unless its constitutional repugnance "is clear beyond a reasonable doubt" and "there has been a clear and palpable abuse of legislative discretion"); Mandell v. Haddon, 121 S.E.2d 516, 524-25 (Va. 1961) (highlighting that the "necessity for and the reasonableness of the classification are primarily questions for the legislature" in upholding Sunday closing law against special law challenge).

[102]*See, e.g.*, Op. of the Justices, 672 So.2d 1294, 1296-98 (Ala. 1996) (holding proposed bill authorizing the sheriff of a single county to collect a processing fee from each inmate would violate local law prohibition); City of South Bend v. Kimsey, 781 N.E.2d 683, 697 (Ind. 2003) (holding law, applying only to a single county in the state, which permitted a majority of landowners to block annexation by a municipality was unconstitutional); O'Reilly v. City of Hazelwood, 850 S.W.2d 96, 99 (Mo. 1993) (concluding that laws singling out one or a few political subdivisions based on permanent, closed characteristics are presumed invalid); Keiderling v. Sanchez, 572 P.2d 545, 546-47 (N.M. 1977) (holding law that provided additional disqualifications of judges by parties in one particular judicial district in the state was an unconstitutional "special law"); Pa. Tpk. Comm'n v. Commonwealth, 899 A.2d 1085, 1087 (Pa. 2006) (holding legislation applying to a single public employer in the state was unconstitutional special legislation).

[103]*See, e.g.*, *O'Reilly*, 850 S.W.2d at 99 (noting that open-ended classifications of political subdivisions based on population or assessed valuation are upheld if rationally related to a legitimate legislative purpose).

[104]*See, e.g.*, Best v. Taylor Mach. Works, 689 N.E.2d 1057, 1069-78 (Ill. 1997) (holding $500,000 noneconomic damages cap on personal injury and property damage claims violated separation of powers and prohibition on special legislation); Wright v. Cent. Du Page Hosp. Ass'n, 347 N.E.2d 736, 741-43 (Ill. 1976) (holding $500,000 damages cap for medical malpractice claims was an unconstitutional special law); Wall v. Marouk, 302 P.3d 775, 781-84 (Okla. 2013) (holding expert affidavit requirement for "professional negligence" claims was an impermissible special law); Zeier v. Zimmer, Inc., 152 P.3d 861, 865-68 (Okla. 2006) (holding that expert affidavit requirement for medical malpractice claims violated the prohibition on special laws as tort victims of medical malpractice faced additional procedural requirements that did not apply to other tort victims).

[105]THE FEDERALIST NO. 57 (James Madison) (Clinton Rossiter ed., 1961).

Schiavo's parents the right to challenge de novo in federal court the removal of her nutrition tube after the Florida Supreme Court struck down the state "Terri's law" on separation of powers grounds. Do such "private laws" comport with Madison's ideals?

D. RESTRAINTS ON DEBT, SPENDING, AND TAXATION

In addition to the prohibition on local or special laws, other substantive state constitutional restraints on legislative power include limitations on debt, spending, and taxation. In the nation's formative years, state constitutions typically did not impose many restrictions in these areas. But a number of states experienced financial crises and scandals both before and after the Civil War, including defaulting on state-issued bonds, incurring heavy debt loads that were difficult to service, providing aid to corporate and railroad interests that did not, in the opinion of many, benefit the citizens of the state, and enacting taxing schemes that placed inordinate burdens on some while imposing lesser burdens on others. These experiences led almost all of the states to either amend their constitutions or adopt new constitutions during the latter half of the nineteenth century to constrain the traditional legislative prerogative on setting tax rates, undertaking public debt, aiding private enterprises, and controlling tax revenues. In many states, these limitations were quite draconian, which severely restricted the ability of legislatures to combat the challenges facing state governments in the twentieth century. As a result, the state constitutions had to be amended to ease some of these restrictions so that the government could undertake projects thought to be necessary functions of modern state governments. This amendment process has resulted in a detailed maze of constitutional prohibitions and exceptions to these prohibitions in a number of state constitutions.

The Texas Constitution provides a good example. The 1876 Texas Constitution was extremely restrictive, placing financial controls on the state government in all the key areas of financial functioning, including debt restrictions, spending controls, and taxing limitations.[106] But over the years, these restrictions have had to be eased, primarily by constitutional amendment, so that the state government could ensure that it had the financial ability to build highways, assist veterans, create programs for water conservation and development, develop state parks, guarantee student loans, and perform other similar governmental functions.

The general debt limitation in Texas Constitution article III, section 49 prohibits the state from incurring any debt except as specifically authorized by the constitution. This bars the state from issuing general obligation bonds supported by the full faith and credit of the state of Texas in the absence of a constitutional exception (although revenue bonds that are repaid by the operation of a constructed facility, such as toll roads, are not prohibited under the section 49 bar).[107] In addition, the legislature is required to balance the biennial budget, preventing appropriations during the two-year budget period from exceeding the available treasury funds and anticipated state revenues, except "in the case of emergency and imperative public necessity and with a four-fifths vote of the total membership in each

[106]*See* John Walker Mauer, *State Constitutions in a Time of Crisis: The Case of the Texas Constitution of 1876*, 68 TEX. L. REV. 1615 (1990) (excerpted in Chapter 1).

[107]*See, e.g.*, Tex. Pub. Bldg. Auth. v. Mattox, 686 S.W.2d 924, 927-28 (Tex. 1985) (citing cases).

House."[108] But a number of constitutional exceptions exist to the section 49 prohibition on debt. For instance, section 49 itself allows debt needed to repel invasion, suppress insurrection, defend the state in war, or supply "casual deficiencies of revenue" of less than $200,000.[109] Section 49 also establishes a procedure through which the legislature, by a resolution approved by two-thirds of the members of each house, may submit to the state's voters a proposition to authorize the creation of any disclosed amount of state debt for any purpose specified in the resolution.[110] The state constitution also contains specific amendments allowing the legislature to issue bonds to assist veterans,[111] for water development and storage facilities,[112] for the development of Texas state parks,[113] to make loans for the purchase of farm and ranch lands,[114] to establish a state economic stabilization fund to prevent temporary state cash deficiencies,[115] for correctional institutions and mental health institutions,[116] for state highways,[117] and for student loans,[118] among other exceptions.[119] Many of these provisions are quite intricate and extremely specific, outlining the agency in charge of the program, the amount of bonds that can be issued, and the purposes for which the moneys may be spent.

The taxation and revenue provisions in the Texas Constitution are similarly complex. The nineteenth century concern with special privilege led Texas, along with most other states, to mandate uniformity and equality in taxation.[120] This mandate, which has been included in every Texas state constitution, is presently contained in the first section of article VIII and provides: "Taxation shall be equal and uniform."[121] But although this provision appears simple, its application is more complex. *Taxes* are *not* required to be

---

[108]TEX. CONST. art. III, § 49a. The comptroller is charged with the duty to prepare and submit to the governor and legislature a sworn statement regarding the financial condition of the state and anticipated revenues before the beginning of each regular legislative session. *Id.* Moreover, before any appropriations bill is sent to the governor from the legislature, the comptroller must certify that the amounts appropriated fall within the estimate of available funds. *Id.* If the comptroller finds that the appropriation exceeds estimated revenue, the legislature must fix the deficiency in the bill by either providing additional revenue or reducing the appropriation. *Id.*

[109]TEX. CONST. art. III, § 49(a)(1)-(2).

[110]TEX. CONST. art. III, § 49(b)-(f).

[111]TEX. CONST. art. III, § 49-b.

[112]*See, e.g.*, TEX. CONST. art. III, §§ 49-c, 49-d, 49-d-1 through 49-d-11.

[113]TEX. CONST. art. III, § 49-e.

[114]TEX. CONST. art. III, § 49-f.

[115]TEX. CONST. art. III, § 49-g.

[116]TEX. CONST. art. III, § 49-h.

[117]*See, e.g.*, TEX. CONST. art. III, §§ 49-k through 49-n.

[118]*See, e.g.*, TEX. CONST. art. III, §§ 50a & 50b-4 through 50b-7. Article III, section 50 generally prohibits the legislature from pledging the credit of the state to assist any person, association, corporation, or municipality. Once again, however, there are quite a few exceptions to this bar in the Texas Constitution, including the authorization for student loans to be guaranteed by the state.

[119]*See, e.g.*, TEX. CONST. art. III, § 49-i (Texas Agricultural Fund), § 49-o (Texas Rail Relocation and Improvement Fund).

[120]*See* 2 WADE NEWHOUSE, CONSTITUTIONAL UNIFORMITY AND EQUALITY IN STATE TAXATION 1704-16 (2d ed. 1984); G. ALAN TARR, UNDERSTANDING STATE CONSTITUTIONS 170 (1998).

[121]TEX. CONST. art. VIII, § 1.

equal and uniform; rather, only the *process of taxation* must be equal and uniform.[122] Thus, while a property tax must be levied in uniform proportion to the reasonable market value of the property, appropriate property tax exemptions are not prohibited by the equal and uniform guarantee.[123] Moreover, the legislature does not violate the guarantee by making classifications reasonably related to the object of an occupation, use, or sales tax, as long as equality and uniformity exist within the classes.[124] On the other hand, this mandate is violated if the legislature imposes double taxation on some taxpayers but not others.[125] But subject to such limits, and other constitutional constraints, the legislature is allowed to exercise reasonable discretion in structuring the tax laws.

These other constitutional restraints, though, are fairly numerous. The state is prohibited, for instance, from levying an ad valorem tax upon property,[126] and this restraint, as will be discussed in the next section, has played a key role in the school finance litigation. The so-called Bullock Amendment ratified in 1993 bars a tax on the net incomes of natural persons unless the tax is approved by a majority of voters in a statewide referendum,[127] which presumably will ensure that Texas will remain one of only a handful of states without a state income tax.[128] The legislature may, though, impose occupation taxes on businesses and individuals (with the exception of persons engaged in mechanical and agricultural pursuits).[129] Texas courts have interpreted the term "occupation tax" broadly, including any fee levied on a business, profession, trade, or calling with a primary purpose of raising revenue rather than regulating.[130] The Texas Legislature also retains the plenary power to impose other taxes not prohibited by the constitution, such as sales, use, and other business and franchise taxes, assuming all constitutional requisites are satisfied.[131] The legislature is restricted in the appropriations that can be made from state tax revenues, as the growth

---

[122]*See In re* Nestle USA, Inc., 387 S.W.3d 610, 618-24 (Tex. 2012).

[123]*See id.*

[124]*See, e.g.*, *id.* (upholding exemptions and special deductions allowed by the state franchise tax); State v. Sw. Gas & Elec. Co., 193 S.W.2d 675, 677 (Tex. 1946) (upholding differential tax treatment of public utilities); Tex. Co. v. Stephens, 103 S.W. 481, 485 (Tex. 1907) (upholding higher tax on oil wholesalers than other wholesalers).

[125]*See* Tracfone Wireless, Inc. v. Comm'n on State Emergency Commc'ns, 397 S.W.3d 173, 180 (Tex. 2013).

[126]TEX. CONST. art. VIII, § 1-e.

[127]TEX. CONST. art. VIII, § 24. The Texas Supreme Court held that this prohibition did not prohibit a franchise tax on limited partnerships because Texas follows the entity theory under which the tax is on the partnership entity, not its individual members. *In re* Allcat Claim Serv., LP, 356 S.W.3d 455, 468-70 (Tex. 2011).

[128]Only seven states do not have any type of income tax: Alaska, Florida, Nevada, South Dakota, Washington, Wyoming, and Texas. If an income tax on natural persons was approved by the legislature and Texas voters, the revenues from the tax must be used to reduce ad valorem taxation by school districts and to support education. TEX. CONST. art. VIII, § 24.

[129]TEX. CONST. art. VIII, § 1(c).

[130]*See, e.g.*, Lowenberg v. City of Dallas, 261 S.W.3d 54, 57-58 (Tex. 2008); Hurt v. Cooper, 110 S.W.2d 896, 899 (Tex. 1937).

[131]TEX. CONST. art. VIII, § 17 ("The specification of the objects and subjects of taxation shall not deprive the Legislature of the power to require other subjects or objects to be taxed in such manner as may be consistent with the principles of taxation fixed in this Constitution.").

of appropriations from state tax revenues not dedicated by the constitution cannot exceed the estimated growth of the state's economy,[132] and no appropriation of money can be made for a period of more than two years.[133] In addition, throughout article VIII, there are detailed requirements on homestead and other tax exemptions and on the maximum ad valorem tax and occupation tax rates that may be imposed by local governments.[134]

Due to the detail in these provisions, as well as their frequent amendment, an in-depth study of all the various financial limitations imposed on the legislature by the Texas Constitution would be impracticable. But that does not diminish their importance, as the *Edgewood* and *West Orange-Cove* school financing cases discussed in the next section demonstrate. Even if a legislative program itself does not violate the state constitution, the method for funding the program might.

E. EFFICIENT SYSTEM OF PUBLIC FREE SCHOOLS

Public education has been an important function of state and local governments since at least the mid-nineteenth century. Before that time, formal education consisted of private schools and private tutors, which typically only were available to the upper class. Public schools expanded educational opportunities to a broader range of the state's citizens.

Each state constitution accordingly directs the legislature to establish a system of public schools. Many state constitutions further require that the public school system be "uniform,"[135] "efficient,"[136] "adequate,"[137] "thorough,"[138] or a combination of these or similar descriptive terms.[139] A purpose behind such clauses was to ensure that all qualified children benefitted equally from the public educational system.[140]

---

[132] TEX. CONST. art. VIII, § 22.

[133] TEX. CONST. art. VIII, § 6.

[134] *See generally* TEX. CONST. art. VIII, §§ 1-24.

[135] *See, e.g.*, ARIZ. CONST. art. XI, § 1 ("general and uniform" system); IND. CONST. art. VIII, § 1 (same); MINN. CONST. art. XIII, § 1 (same); NEV. CONST. art. XI, § 1 ("uniform system"); TENN. CONST. art. XI, § 12 (same); WASH. CONST. art. IX, § 2 ("general and uniform system"); WYO. CONST. art. VII, § 1 ("complete and uniform system").

[136] *See, e.g.*, DEL. CONST. art X, § 1 ("general and efficient system"); KY. CONST. § 183 ("efficient system").

[137] *See, e.g.*, GA. CONST. art VIII, § 1 ("adequate public education").

[138] While "thorough" is contained in the educational provision of several state constitutions, it is always in combination with another term. The following note contains examples.

[139] *See, e.g.*, ARK. CONST. art. XIV, § 1 ("general, suitable, and efficient system . . . suitable" for educational opportunities); COLO. CONST. art. IX, § 2 ("thorough and uniform system"); FLA. CONST. art. IX, § 1 ("uniform, efficient, safe, secure, and high quality system"); IDAHO CONST. art. IX, § 1 ("general, uniform, and thorough system"); ILL CONST. art. X, § 1 ("efficient system of high quality"); MD. CONST. art. VIII, § 1 ("thorough and efficient system"); N.J. CONST. art. VIII, § 4 (same); N.M. CONST. art. XII, § 1 ("uniform system . . . sufficient for" education); N.C. CONST. art. IX, § 2 ("general and uniform system . . . [with] equal opportunities"); OHIO CONST. art. VI, § 2 ("thorough and efficient system"); PA. CONST. art. III, § 14 (same); VA. CONST. art. VIII, § 1 ("educational program of high quality"); W. VA. CONST. art. XII, § 1 ("thorough and efficient system").

[140] *See* G. ALAN TARR, UNDERSTANDING STATE CONSTITUTIONS 199 (1998).

In Texas, article VII, section 1 of the state constitution, after recognizing that "[a] general diffusion of knowledge" is essential to the rights and liberties of the people, directs the legislature "to establish and make suitable provision for the support and maintenance of an efficient system of public free schools." This constitutional mandate has provided the basis for some of the most important constitutional decisions rendered by the Texas Supreme Court, the *Edgewood* school finance decisions and their progeny.

The Texas public school finance laws were initially challenged in federal court over a decade before the *Edgewood* case began. In *San Antonio Independent School District v. Rodriguez*, the United States Supreme Court upheld the state finance system, which relied heavily on local taxes on property within a school district, against an equal protection challenge brought by residents of poorer school districts.[141] While expressing some dismay at the Texas school finance system, the Supreme Court, in a five to four decision, declined to find a violation of equal protection, concluding that no fundamental federal constitutional right to an education existed and that classifications based on wealth were only subject to rational basis review.[142] The Court opined that, while the Texas financing system was in need of reform, federalism principles counseled that such efforts should be left to the state since the desire for local control over school education was sufficient to satisfy the federal rational basis standard.[143]

After *Rodriguez* prevented any federal constitutional remedy against the public school financing systems in Texas and other states with extreme in-state disparities regarding available educational funds, poorer districts and their students turned to state constitutional provisions for relief. In response to these challenges, approximately one-third of the state judiciaries held that the school financing scheme established in their state violated either the state constitutional educational directive or the state constitutional equality guarantee. The Texas Supreme Court addressed such a challenge in the case below.

Edgewood Independent School District v. Kirby, 777 S.W.2d 391 (Tex. 1989)

MAUZY, Justice.

At issue is the constitutionality of the Texas system for financing the education of public school children. Edgewood Independent School District, sixty-seven other school districts, and numerous individual school children and parents filed suit seeking a declaration that the Texas school financing system violates the Texas Constitution.

The basic facts of this cause are not in dispute. The only question is whether those facts describe a public school financing system that meets the requirements of the Constitution. As summarized and excerpted, the facts are as follows.

There are approximately three million public school children in Texas. The legislature finances the education of these children through a combination of revenues supplied by the state itself and revenues supplied by local school districts which are

---

[141] 411 U.S. 1, 55 (1973).

[142] *Id.*

[143] *Id.* at 55-59.

governmental subdivisions of the state. Of total education costs, the state provides about forty-two percent, school districts provide about fifty percent, and the remainder comes from various other sources including federal funds. School districts derive revenues from local ad valorem property taxes, and the state raises funds from a variety of sources including the sales tax and various severance and excise taxes.

There are glaring disparities in the abilities of the various school districts to raise revenues from property taxes because taxable property wealth varies greatly from district to district. The wealthiest district has over $14,000,000 of property wealth per student, while the poorest has approximately $20,000; this disparity reflects a 700 to 1 ratio. The 300,000 students in the lowest-wealth schools have less than 3% of the state's property wealth to support their education while the 300,000 students in the highest-wealth schools have over 25% of the state's property wealth; thus the 300,000 students in the wealthiest districts have more than eight times the property value to support their education as the 300,000 students in the poorest districts. The average property wealth in the 100 wealthiest districts is more than twenty times greater than the average property wealth in the 100 poorest districts. Edgewood I.S.D. has $38,854 in property wealth per student; Alamo Heights I.S.D., in the same county, has $570,109 in property wealth per student.

The state has tried for many years to lessen the disparities through various efforts to supplement the poorer districts. Through the Foundation School Program, the state currently attempts to ensure that each district has sufficient funds to provide its students with at least a basic education. *See* Tex.Educ.Code § 16.002. Under this program, state aid is distributed to the various districts according to a complex formula such that property-poor districts receive more state aid than do property-rich districts. However, the Foundation School Program does not cover even the cost of meeting the state-mandated minimum requirements. Most importantly, there are no Foundation School Program allotments for school facilities or for debt service. The basic allotment and the transportation allotment understate actual costs, and the career ladder salary supplement for teachers is underfunded. For these reasons and more, almost all school districts spend additional local funds. Low-wealth districts use a significantly greater proportion of their local funds to pay the debt service on construction bonds while high-wealth districts are able to use their funds to pay for a wide array of enrichment programs.

Because of the disparities in district property wealth, spending per student varies widely, ranging from $2,112 to $19,333. Under the existing system, an average of $2,000 more per year is spent on each of the 150,000 students in the wealthiest districts than is spent on the 150,000 students in the poorest districts.

The lower expenditures in the property-poor districts are not the result of lack of tax effort. Generally, the property-rich districts can tax low and spend high while the property-poor districts must tax high merely to spend low. In 1985-86, local tax rates ranged from $.09 to $1.55 per $100 valuation. The 100 poorest districts had an average tax rate of 74.5 cents and spent an average of $2,978 per student. The 100 wealthiest districts had an average tax rate of 47 cents and spent an average of $7,233 per student. In Dallas County, Highland Park I.S.D. taxed at 35.16 cents and spent $4,836 per student while Wilmer-Hutchins I.S.D. taxed at $1.05 and spent $3,513 per student.

The amount of money spent on a student's education has a real and meaningful impact on the educational opportunity offered that student. High-wealth districts are able to provide for their students broader educational experiences including more extensive curricula, more up-to-date technological equipment, better libraries and library personnel, teacher aides, counseling services, lower student-teacher ratios, better facilities, parental involvement programs, and drop-out prevention programs. They are also better able to attract and retain experienced teachers and administrators.

The differences in the quality of educational programs offered are dramatic. For example, San Elizario I.S.D. offers no foreign language, no pre-kindergarten program, no chemistry, no physics, no calculus, and no college preparatory or honors program. It also offers virtually no extra-curricular activities such as band, debate, or football. At the time of trial, one-third of Texas school districts did not even meet the state-mandated standards for maximum class size. The great majority of these are low-wealth districts. In many instances, wealthy and poor districts are found contiguous to one another within the same county.

Based on these facts, the trial court concluded that the school financing system violates the Texas Constitution's equal rights guarantee of article I, section 3, the due course of law guarantee of article I, section 19, and the "efficiency" mandate of article VII, section 1. The court of appeals reversed. We reverse the judgment of the court of appeals and, with modification, affirm the judgment of the trial court.

Article VII, section 1 of the Texas Constitution provides:

> A general diffusion of knowledge being essential to the preservation of the liberties and rights of the people, it shall be the duty of the Legislature of the State to establish and make suitable provision for the support and maintenance of an efficient system of public free schools.

The court of appeals declined to address petitioners' challenge under this provision and concluded instead that its interpretation was a "political question." Said the court:

> That provision does, of course, require that the school system be "efficient," but the provision provides no guidance as to how this or any other court may arrive at a determination of what is efficient or inefficient. Given the enormous complexity of a school system educating three million children, this Court concludes that which is, or is not, "efficient" is essentially a political question not suitable for judicial review.

761 S.W.2d at 867. We disagree. This is not an area in which the Constitution vests exclusive discretion in the legislature; rather the language of article VII, section 1 imposes on the legislature an affirmative duty to establish and provide for the public free schools. This duty is not committed unconditionally to the legislature's discretion, but instead is accompanied by standards. By express constitutional mandate, the legislature must make "suitable" provision for an "efficient" system for the "essential" purpose of a "general diffusion of knowledge." While these are admittedly not precise terms, they do provide a standard by which this court must, when called upon to do so, measure the constitutionality

of the legislature's actions. *See Williams v. Taylor,* 83 Tex. 667, 19 S.W. 156 (1892). We do not undertake this responsibility lightly and we begin with a presumption of constitutionality. Nevertheless, what this court said in only its second term, when first summoned to strike down an act of the Republic of Texas Congress, is still true:

> [W]e have not been unmindful of the magnitude of the principles involved, and the respect due to the popular branch of the government. . . . Fortunately, however, for the people, the function of the judiciary in deciding constitutional questions is not one which it is at liberty to decline. . . . [We] cannot, as the legislature may, avoid a measure because it approaches the confines of the constitution; [we] cannot pass it by because it is doubtful; with whatever doubt, with whatever difficulties a case may be attended, [we] must decide it, when it arises in judgment.

Morton v. Gordon, Dallam 396, 397-398 (Tex.1841). If the system is not "efficient" or not "suitable," the legislature has not discharged its constitutional duty and it is *our* duty to say so.

The Texas Constitution derives its force from the people of Texas. This is the fundamental law under which the people of this state have consented to be governed. In construing the language of article VII, section 1, we consider "the intent of the people who adopted it." *Director of Dep't of Agriculture and Env't v. Printing Indus. Ass'n,* 600 S.W.2d 264, 267 (Tex.1980); *see also Smissen v. State,* 71 Tex. 222, 9 S.W. 112, 116 (1888). In determining that intent, "the history of the times out of which it grew and to which it may be rationally supposed to have direct relationship, the evils intended to be remedied and the good to be accomplished, are proper subjects of inquiry." *Markowsky v. Newman,* 134 Tex. 440, 136 S.W.2d 808, 813 (1940). However, because of the difficulties inherent in determining the intent of voters over a century ago, we rely heavily on the literal text. We seek its meaning with the understanding that the Constitution was ratified to function as an organic document to govern society and institutions as they evolve through time. *See generally Printing Indus.,* 600 S.W.2d at 268-269.

The State argues that, as used in article VII, section 1, the word "efficient" was intended to suggest a simple and inexpensive system. Under the Reconstruction Constitution of 1869, the people had been subjected to a militaristic school system with the state exercising absolute authority over the training of children. *See* Tex. Const. art. VII, § 1, interp. commentary. Thus, the State contends that delegates to the 1875 Constitutional Convention deliberately inserted into this provision the word "efficient" in order to prevent the establishment of another Reconstruction-style, highly centralized school system.

While there is some evidence that many delegates wanted an economical school system, there is no persuasive evidence that the delegates used the term "efficient" to achieve that end. *See Journal of the Constitutional Convention of the State of Texas* 136 (Oct. 8, 1875); S. McKay, *Debates in the Texas Constitutional Convention of 1875* 107, 217, 350-351 (1930). It must be recognized that the Constitution requires an "efficient," not an "economical," "inexpensive," or "cheap" system. The language of the Constitution must be presumed to have been carefully selected. *Leander Indep. School Dist. v. Cedar Park*

Water Supply Corp., 479 S.W.2d 908 (Tex.1972). The framers used the term "economical" elsewhere and could have done so here had they so intended.

There is no reason to think that "efficient" meant anything different in 1875 from what it now means. "Efficient" conveys the meaning of effective or productive of results and connotes the use of resources so as to produce results with little waste; this meaning does not appear to have changed over time. *E.g.*, IV *Oxford English Dictionary* 52 (1971); *Webster's Third New International Dictionary* 725 (1976). One dictionary used by the framers defined efficient as follows:

> Causing effects; producing results; actively operative; not inactive, slack or incapable; characterized by energetic and useful activity. . . .

N. Webster, An American Dictionary of the English Language 430 (1864). In 1890, this court described "efficient" machinery as being "such as is capable of well producing the effect intended to be secured by the use of it for the purpose for which it was made." *Maxwell v. Bastrop Mfg. Co.,* 77 Tex. 233, 14 S.W. 35, 36 (1890).

Considering "the general spirit of the times and the prevailing sentiments of the people," it is apparent from the historical record that those who drafted and ratified article VII, section 1 never contemplated the possibility that such gross inequalities could exist within an "efficient" system. At the Constitutional Convention of 1875, delegates spoke at length on the importance of education for *all* the people of this state, rich and poor alike. The chair of the education committee, speaking on behalf of the majority of the committee, declared:

> [Education] must be classed among the abstract rights, based on apparent natural justice, which we individually concede to the State, for the general welfare, when we enter into a great compact as a commonwealth. I boldly assert that it is for the general welfare of all, rich and poor, male and female, that the means of a common school education should, if possible, be placed within the reach of every child in the State.

S. McKay, *Debates in the Texas Constitutional Convention of 1875* 198 (1930). Other delegates recognized the importance of a diffusion of knowledge among the masses not only for the preservation of democracy, but for the prevention of crime and for the growth of the economy. *See, e.g., id.* at 199- 200, 216-217, 335.

In addition to specific comments in the constitutional debates, the structure of school finance at the time indicates that such gross disparities were not contemplated. Apart from cities, there was no district structure for schools nor any authority to tax locally for school purposes under the Constitution of 1876. B. Walker and W. Kirby, *The Basics of Texas Public School Finance* 5, 86 (1986). The 1876 Constitution provided a structure whereby the burdens of school taxation fell equally and uniformly across the state, and each student in the state was entitled to exactly the same distribution of funds. *See* Tex. Const. art. VII, § 5 (1876). The state's school fund was initially apportioned strictly on a per capita basis. B. Walker and W. Kirby at 21. Also, a poll tax of one dollar per voter was levied across the state for school purposes. *Id.* These per capita methods of taxation and of revenue distribution seem simplistic compared to today's system; however they do indicate that the people were contemplating that the tax burden would be shared uniformly and that the state's resources would be distributed on an even, equitable basis.

If our state's population had grown at the same rate in each district and if the taxable wealth in each district had also grown at the same rate, efficiency could probably have been maintained within the structure of the present system. That did not happen. Wealth, in its many forms, has not appeared with geographic symmetry. The economic development of the state has not been uniform. Although local conditions vary, the constitutionally imposed state responsibility for an efficient education system is the same for all citizens regardless of where they live.

We conclude that, in mandating "efficiency," the constitutional framers and ratifiers did not intend a system with such vast disparities as now exist. Instead, they stated clearly that the purpose of an efficient system was to provide for a "*general* diffusion of knowledge." (Emphasis added.) The present system, by contrast, provides not for a diffusion that is general, but for one that is limited and unbalanced. The resultant inequalities are thus directly contrary to the constitutional vision of efficiency.

In the context of article VII, section 1, the legislature has expressed its understanding of the term "efficient" for a long time even though it has never given the term full effect. Sixty years ago, the legislature enacted the Rural Aid Appropriations Act with the express purpose of "equalizing the educational opportunities afforded by the State. . . ." 1929 Tex. Gen. Laws, ch. 14 at 252 (3rd called session). Again, in creating the Gilmer-Aikin Committee to study school finance, the legislature indicated an awareness of this obligation when it spoke of "the foresight and evident intention of the founders of our State and the framers of our State Constitution to provide equal educational advantages for all." Tex.H.Con.Res. 48, 50th Leg. (1948). Moreover, section 16.001 of the legislatively enacted Education Code expresses the state's policy that "a thorough and efficient system be provided . . . so that each student . . . shall have access to programs and services . . . that are substantially equal to those available to any similar student, notwithstanding varying economic factors." Not only the legislature, but also this court has previously recognized the implicit link that the Texas Constitution establishes between efficiency and equality. In *Mumme v. Marrs,* 40 S.W.2d at 37, we stated that rural aid appropriations "have a real relationship to the subject of equalizing educational opportunities in the state, and tend to make our system more efficient. . . ."

By statutory directives, the legislature has attempted through the years to reduce disparities and improve the system. There have been good faith efforts on the part of many public officials, and some progress has been made. However, as the undisputed facts of this case make painfully clear, the reality is that the constitutional mandate has not been met.

The legislature's recent efforts have focused primarily on increasing the state's contributions. More money allocated under the present system would reduce some of the existing disparities between districts but would at best only postpone the reform that is necessary to make the system efficient. A band-aid will not suffice; the system itself must be changed.

We hold that the state's school financing system is neither financially efficient nor efficient in the sense of providing for a "general diffusion of knowledge" statewide, and therefore that it violates article VII, section 1 of the Texas Constitution. Efficiency does not require a per capita distribution, but it also does not allow concentrations of resources in property-rich school districts that are taxing low when property-poor districts that are taxing high cannot generate sufficient revenues to meet even minimum standards. There must be a direct and close correlation between a district's tax effort and the educational resources available to it; in other words, districts must have substantially equal access to similar revenues per pupil at similar levels of tax effort. Children who live in poor districts and children who live in rich districts must be afforded a substantially equal opportunity to have access to educational funds. Certainly, this much is required if the state is to educate its populace efficiently and provide for a general diffusion of knowledge statewide.

Under article VII, section 1, the obligation is the legislature's to provide for an efficient system. In setting appropriations, the legislature must establish priorities according to constitutional mandate; equalizing educational opportunity cannot be relegated to an "if funds are left over" basis. We recognize that there are and always will be strong public interests competing for available state funds. However, the legislature's responsibility to support public education is different because it is constitutionally imposed. Whether the legislature acts directly or enlists local government to help meet its obligation, the end product must still be what the constitution commands–i.e. an efficient system of public free schools throughout the state. This does not mean that the state may not recognize differences in area costs or in costs associated with providing an equalized educational opportunity to atypical students or disadvantaged students. Nor does it mean that local communities would be precluded from supplementing an efficient system established by the legislature; however any local enrichment must derive solely from local tax effort.

Although we have ruled the school financing system to be unconstitutional, we do not now instruct the legislature as to the specifics of the legislation it should enact; nor do we order it to raise taxes. The legislature has primary responsibility to decide how best to achieve an efficient system. We decide only the nature of the constitutional mandate and whether that mandate has been met. Because we hold that the mandate of efficiency has not been met, we reverse the judgment of the court of appeals.

Because of the enormity of the task now facing the legislature and because we want to avoid any sudden disruption in the educational processes, we modify the trial court's judgment so as to stay the effect of its injunction until May 1, 1990. However, let there be no misunderstanding. A remedy is long overdue. The legislature must take immediate action.

Notes on the Constitutional Duty to Finance and Maintain Public Schools

Edgewood ***and an "Efficient System of Public Free Schools"***: *Edgewood* held that legislative compliance with article VII, section 1 was justiciable and that the legislature had failed to comply with its constitutional duty "to establish and make suitable provision for the support and maintenance of an efficient system of public free schools." The court determined that the state's school financing system, with "glaring" disparities among school districts due to the heavy reliance on local property taxes, was not financially efficient. Nor was it efficient in the sense of providing for a "general diffusion of knowledge" statewide. The court reasoned that such a system was not "productive of results" or "effective" when "gross inequalities" existed between the districts that were not contemplated by the framers and ratifiers of the state constitution. Although acknowledging that "efficiency" does not require a per capita distribution, the court proclaimed that "districts must have substantially equal access to similar revenues per pupil at similar levels of tax effort." The court did not attempt to compel the legislature to enact specific legislation, but instead left it to the legislature to create a system satisfying the constitutional standard.

Higher Education and the Texas Constitution: Does article VII, section 1 provide a constitutional right for higher education? In *Richards v. League of United Latin American Citizens*, the Texas Supreme Court held that it does not.[144] The court relied primarily on the structure of article VII as a whole, noting that sections 1 through 8 were contained within a subdivision entitled "Public Free Schools," whereas a separate subdivision in article VII was entitled "University." The court also relied on prudential concerns, reasoning that the state would be hard pressed to operate all its universities as free schools as required by article VII, section 1.[145] While some other state constitutions include a legislative duty to provide higher education as part of the "free public school system," they typically authorize tuition to be charged at such institutions.[146]

School Finance Litigation in Other Jurisdictions: The Texas Supreme Court is not alone in considering the constitutionality of its state system of public school finance. More than forty other state high courts have addressed state constitutional challenges to public school financing under a state educational mandate or equality guarantee.

A number of these challenges have been based on equality concerns as in *Edgewood.* At least fifteen other states have, like Texas, invalidated at least one system of public financing of state education due in part to disparities in school district resources.[147]

---

[144] 868 S.W.2d 306, 316-17 (Tex. 1993).

[145] *Id.* at 317.

[146] *See, e.g.*, N.D. CONST. § 148 ("The legislative assembly shall provide for a uniform system of free public schools throughout the state, beginning with the primary and extending through all grades up to and including schools of higher education, except that the legislative assembly may authorize tuition, fees and service charges to assist in the financing of public schools of higher education.").

[147] *See, e.g.*, Roosevelt Elementary Sch. Dist. No. 66 v. Bishop, 877 P.2d 806 (Ariz. 1994) (concluding financing scheme violated state constitutional requirement of "a general and uniform public school system"); Lake View Sch. Dist. No. 25 v. Huckabee, 91 S.W.3d 472 (2002) (holding revised system still unconstitutional under text requiring state to maintain a "general, suitable and efficient system of free public schools"), *mandate recalled on other grounds*, 142 S.W.3d 643 (Ark. 2004); DuPree v. Alma Sch. Dist. No. 30, 651 S.W.2d 90 (Ark. 1983) (relying on both state constitutional equal protection and education clauses); Serrano v. Priest (Serrano II), 557 P.2d 929 (Cal. 1976) (finding education is a fundamental interest under state equal protection clause); Serrano v. Priest, 487 P.2d 1241 (Cal. 1971) (same); Horton v. Meskill, 376 A.2d 359 (Conn.1977) (relying on state "free public elementary and secondary schools" and equal protection clauses to invalidate financing scheme); Rose v. Council for Better Educ., Inc., 790 S.W.2d 186 (Ky.1989) (holding state constitutional education mandate for efficient system of common schools violated); McDuffy v. Sec'y of Educ., 615 N.E.2d 516 (Mass. 1993) (finding state constitutional legislative duty to "cherish the interests of literature and the sciences" through public schools and grammar schools not met); Helena Elementary Sch. Dist. No. 1 v. State, 769 P.2d 684 (Mont.1989) (invalidating financing scheme under state guarantee of "equality of educational

Yet a slightly greater number of state high courts have upheld state school financing schemes against such constitutional challenges, typically concluding that the state constitution did not require the legislature to equalize financial resources among districts or that the existing variations among districts were not substantial enough for a constitutional violation.[148]

In addition to equality-based challenges such as *Edgewood*, state courts have also considered another group of challenges to school financing systems based on the adequacy of funding. While equality and adequacy issues are frequently intertwined and often arise in the same case, equality-based challenges focus on funding disparities among districts, whereas adequacy-based challenges focus on the sufficiency of the aggregate level of educational funding to meet constitutional requirements.

Adequacy claims have prevailed slightly less often than equality-based challenges. Several state high courts have refused to address adequacy challenges on the merits at all, holding that judicial review of the legislative allocation of resources and the aggregate funding of education is inappropriate under either separation of powers principles or the political question doctrine.[149] Those state high courts reaching the merits are frequently

---

opportunity"); Claremont Sch. Dist. v. Governor, 703 A.2d 1353 (N.H. 1997) (holding financing scheme violated state constitutional provision requiring proportional and reasonable tax assessments); Abbott v. Burke (Abbott V), 693 A.2d 417 (N.J. 1997) (holding system still violated provision mandating "thorough and efficient system of free public schools"); Robinson v. Cahill, 303 A.2d 273 (N.J. 1973) (same); DeRolph v. State, 677 N.E.2d 733 (Ohio 1997) (holding educational funding violated "thorough and efficient" system of common schools requirement of state constitution); Tenn. Small Sch. Sys. v. McWherter, 851 S.W.2d 139 (Tenn. 1993) (finding violation of state educational guarantee and equal protection clause); Brigham v. State, 692 A.2d 384 (Vt. 1997) (applying state education and common benefits clauses to strike down funding scheme); Seattle Sch. Dist. No. 1 v. State, 585 P.2d 71 (Wash. 1978) (finding violation of state constitutional duty to make ample provision for the education of all children within the state); Pauley v. Kelly, 255 S.E.2d 859 (W. Va. 1979) (holding inequalities violated state requirement of a "thorough and efficient" education); Washakie Cnty. Sch. Dist. No. 1 v. Herschler, 606 P.2d 310 (Wyo. 1980) (holding financing scheme violated state equal protection clause).

[148] *See, e.g.*, Matanuska-Susitna Borough Sch. Dist. v. State, 931 P.2d 391 (Alaska 1997); Lujan v. State Bd. of Educ., 649 P.2d 1005 (Colo.1982); Coalition for Adequacy & Fairness in Sch. Funding, Inc. v. Chiles, 680 So.2d 400 (Fla. 1996); McDaniel v. Thomas, 285 S.E.2d 156 (Ga. 1981); Thompson v. Engelking, 537 P.2d 635 (Idaho 1975); Comm. for Educ. Rights v. Edgar, 672 N.E.2d 1178 (Ill. 1996); Unified Sch. Dist. No. 229 v. State, 885 P.2d 1170 (Kan. 1994); Sch. Admin. Dist. No. 1 v. Comm'r, 659 A.2d 854 (Me. 1995); Hornbeck v. Somerset Cnty. Bd. of Educ., 458 A.2d 758 (Md. 1983); Skeen v. State, 505 N.W.2d 299 (Minn. 1993); Comm. for Educ. Equality v. State, 294 S.W.3d 477 (Mo. 2009); Bd. of Educ. v. Nyquist, 439 N.E.2d 359 (N.Y. 1982); Britt v. State Bd. of Educ., 357 S.E.2d 432 (N.C. 1987); Fair Sch. Fin. Council of Ok., Inc. v. State, 746 P.2d 1135 (Okla.1987); Olsen v. State, 554 P.2d 139 (Or. 1976); Danson v. Casey, 399 A.2d 360 (Pa. 1979); City of Pawtucket v. Sundlun, 622 A.2d 40 (R.I. 1995); Richland Cnty. v. Campbell, 364 S.E.2d 470 (S.C. 1988); Scott v. Commonwealth, 443 S.E.2d 138 (Va. 1994); Kukor v. Grover, 436 N.W.2d 568 (Wis. 1989).

[149] *See, e.g., Ex parte* James, 836 So.2d 813 (Ala. 2002); Bonner v. Daniels, 907 N.E.2d 516 (Ind. 2009); Neb. Coalition for Educ. Equity & Adequacy v. Heineman, 731 N.W.2d 164 (Neb. 2007); Okla. Educ. Ass'n v. State, 158 P.3d 1058 (Okla. 2007); Marrero v. Commonwealth, 739 A.2d 110 (Pa. 1999). Several state high court decisions have refused to address adequacy challenges on the merits while reaching the merits on equality-based claims in the same case. *See, e.g.*, Coalition for Adequacy & Fairness in Sch. Funding, Inc. v. Chiles, 680 So.2d 400 (Fla. 1996); Comm. for Educ. Rights v. Edgar, 672 N.E.2d 1178 (Ill. 1996); City of Pawtucket v. Sundlun, 662 A.2d 40 (R.I. 1995); *accord* King v. State, 818 N.W.2d 1 (Iowa 2012) (holding no cause of action existed on adequacy while considering equality claim).

quite deferential to the legislative judgment.[150] Nevertheless, several state courts have invalidated financing schemes at least in part on adequacy grounds,[151] with a few state high courts issuing or affirming remedial orders against the legislature requiring a third-party commissioned study or even mandating the appropriation of additional state educational funds.[152]

In addition to these systematic funding challenges, state courts have also addressed a number of other issues related to state constitutional education mandates. For example, some state courts have addressed whether special needs children have a state constitutional right to receive an educational program catered to their particular situation and whether a constitutional duty exists to provide bilingual education. Although these related questions have not been addressed by Texas courts under the state constitution (primarily because of the state's choice to provide such services and obtain related federal educational funding), other states have concluded that their state constitutional educational guarantee encompasses at least some of these rights.[153] Another issue that has arisen is whether the legislative duty to maintain public schools creates a constitutional right to attend state public schools free of any additional charges or fees, such as for books, school supplies, or transportation. Decisions from other jurisdictions are inconsistent. While some state supreme courts have held that their state constitutional "free public schools" guarantees prevent such charges,[154] other state high courts with similar constitutional provisions have reached a contrary

---

[150] *See, e.g.*, Lobato v. State, 218 P.3d 358 (Colo. 2009); Conn. Coalition for Justice in Educ. Funding, Inc. v. Rell, 990 A.2d 206 (Conn. 2010); Pendleton Sch. Dist. 16R v. State, 200 P.3d 133 (Or. 2009); Abbeville Cnty. Sch. Dist. v. State, 515 S.E.2d 535 (S.C. 1999); Davis v. State, 804 N.W.2d 618 (S.D. 2011); Brigham v. State, 889 A.2d 715 (Vt. 2005).

[151] *See, e.g.*, Rose v. Counsel for Better Educ., Inc., 790 S.W.2d 186 (Ky. 1989); Idaho Sch. for Equal Educ. Opportunity v. State, 129 P.3d 1199 (Idaho 2005); McDuffy v. Sec'y of Educ., 615 N.E.2d 516 (Mass. 1993); Columbia Falls Elementary Sch. Dist. v. State, 109 P.3d 257 (Mont. 2005); Londonberry Sch. Dist. SAU No. 12 v. State, 907 A.2d 988 (N.H. 2006); Hoke Cnty. Bd. of Educ. v. State, 599 S.E.2d 365 (N.C. 2004); Derolph v. State, 677 N.E.2d 733 (Ohio 1997); Seattle Sch. Dist. No. 1 v. State, 585 P.2d 71 (Wash. 1978).

[152] *See, e.g.*, Montoy v. State, 112 P.3d 923 (Kan. 2005); Lake View Sch. Dist. No. 25 v. Huckabee, 220 S.W.3d 645 (Ark. 2005); Abbott v. Burke, 693 A.2d 417 (N.J. 1997); Campaign for Fiscal Equity, Inc. v. State, 801 N.E.2d 326 (N.Y. 2003); State v. Campbell Cnty. Sch. Dist., 32 P.3d 325 (Wyo. 2001).

[153] *See, e.g.*, State v. Stecher, 390 A.2d 408, 410-11 (Conn. Super. 1977) (concluding special education provided to children at state institutions must be free under state constitution); Levine v. State Dep't of Institutions & Agencies, 418 A.2d 229, 237-38 (N.J. 1980) (concluding that, while the plaintiffs were so severely mentally impaired as to be unable to benefit from education, mentally disabled individuals with the capacity for improvement through education had a constitutionally protected right to receive free educational instruction); *In re* G.H., 218 N.W.2d 441, 446 (N.D. 1974) (holding state had constitutional duty to educate child with severe physical handicaps).

[154] *See, e.g.*, Paulson v. Minidoka Cnty. Sch. Dist. No. 331, 463 P.2d 935, 938-39 (Idaho 1970) (holding textbooks must be provided free of charge under state constitutional mandate for "public, free common schools"); Bond v. Pub. Schs. of Ann Arbor Sch. Dist., 178 N.W.2d 484, 487-88 (Mich. 1970) (determining textbooks must be provided for free under state constitutional directive to provide a system of "free public elementary and secondary schools"); Cardiff v. Bismarck Pub. Sch. Dist., 263 N.W.2d 105, 113-14 (N.D. 1978) (concluding state constitutional provision requiring "free public schools" precluded rental fees for textbooks); Randolph Cnty. Bd. of Educ. v. Adams, 467 S.E.2d 150, 158-60 (W. Va. 1995) (holding textbooks and other items necessary to accomplish the goals of a school system must be provided free of charge under state constitutional provision mandating a "thorough and efficient system of free schools").

holding.[155] In Texas, this issue is governed by article VII, section 3(b) of the state constitution, which mandates that the State Board of Education has a duty to set aside enough funds to provide "free text books for the use of children attending the public schools of this State." Finally, one state (Florida) has held that the state constitution's requirement of creating a system of uniform free schools bars a voucher program allowing students to use state money at private schools,[156] although other states disagree.[157] This issue has not arisen frequently, however, because most states (including Texas) do not have voucher programs.

The Texas School Finance Saga Continues: In several states, the school financing decisions have become quite a saga, with repeated decisions by the state supreme court invalidating legislative responses.[158] Mark G. Yudof, Chancellor of the University of California System and formerly Dean of the University of Texas Law School, colorfully compared such school finance litigation to Russian novels: "long, tedious, and everybody dies in the end."[159] For Texas, the first *Edgewood* opinion was merely the first chapter in a long and tedious ongoing affair.

After *Edgewood*, the Texas Legislature passed Senate Bill 1 in an attempt to alleviate the constitutional infirmities in the public school finance system. But, in *Edgewood Independent School District v. Kirby* (*Edgewood II*), the court held unanimously that Senate Bill 1, while making some improvements "by providing a wide array of biennial studies to detect deviations from fiscal neutrality and inform senior policy makers when increased state funding is required," left "essentially intact the same funding system with the same deficiencies" identified in *Edgewood I*.[160] The court reasoned that Senate Bill 1 failed to adequately restructure the system, as most property owners still had to carry a heavy tax burden to provide a less expensive education for students in their district while other property owners in the wealthiest districts in the state had a much lighter tax burden that provided more educational funds on a per student basis in their district.

In an opinion denying the motion for rehearing in *Edgewood II*, a majority of the court clarified that unequal local supplementation would be constitutionally permissible once the legislature had established and maintained an efficient statewide public school

---

[155] *See, e.g.*, Arcadia Unified Sch. Dist. v. State Dep't of Educ., 825 P.2d 438, 442-46 (Cal. 1992) (holding bus transportation fee not unconstitutional under state free school guarantee); Sneed v. Greensboro City Bd. of Educ., 264 S.E.2d 106, 108-09 (N.C. 1980) (holding incidental course and instructional fees not precluded under state constitutional guarantee for "free public schools"); Harner v. Bd. of Educ. of Sch. Dist. No. 109, 265 N.E.2d 616, 619-20 (Ill. 1970) (upholding rental fees for textbooks against challenge under free common school education clause).

[156] Bush v. Holmes, 919 So.2d 392, 398 (Fla. 2006).

[157] *See, e.g.*, Jackson v. Benson, 578 N.W.2d 602, 627-28 (Wis. 1998).

[158] *See, e.g.*, Abbott v. Burke (Abbott VI), 748 A.2d 82 (N.J. 2000) (discussing thirty-year "major judicial involvement" in state educational reform); Lake View Sch. Dist. No. 25 v. Huckabee, 91 S.W.3d 472 (Ark. 2002) (highlighting twenty years of continuing judicial oversight).

[159] Mark G. Yudof, *School Finance Reform in Texas: The* Edgewood *Saga*, 28 HARV. J. ON LEGIS. 499, 499 (1991).

[160] 804 S.W.2d 491, 495 (Tex. 1991).

finance system.[161] The court also reemphasized that the Texas Constitution limits the ability of the state to enact a statewide ad valorem tax as a means to resolve the school financing dilemma. But despite this warning, the next legislative solution was held to be a prohibited state ad valorem tax in *Edgewood III*.

Carrollton-Farmers Branch Independent School District v. Edgewood Independent School District, 826 S.W.2d 489 (Tex. 1992) (*Edgewood III*)

GONZALEZ, Justice.

We are again called upon to determine whether the state public school finance system violates the Texas Constitution. Article VII, section 1 of the Texas Constitution gives the Legislature the duty "to establish and make suitable provision for the support and maintenance of an efficient system of public free schools." We have twice recently held that the state public school system, because of the way in which it is financed, is not "efficient" as required by this provision of the Constitution. To try to cure the system's constitutional infirmity, the Seventy-Second Legislature enacted Senate Bill 351, as amended by House Bill 2885 ("Senate Bill 351"), making various changes in the school finance scheme. At issue before us now is whether the method prescribed by this statute violates other provisions of the Texas Constitution.

Appellants, composed of numerous school districts and individual citizens, challenge the constitutionality of the school finance system devised by Senate Bill 351 on three grounds: (1) that it levies a state ad valorem tax in violation of article VIII, section 1-e; (2) that it levies an ad valorem tax without approval of the voters in violation of article VII, section 3; and (3) that it creates county education districts ("CEDs") in violation of article VII, section 3 and article III, sections 56 and 64(a). Appellees include the State of Texas, certain CEDs created by Senate Bill 351, and other interested school districts and individual citizens. In this proceeding, all appellees are aligned with the State in defending Senate Bill 351 against the challenges by appellants.

After careful consideration of the constitutional principles in issue, we sustain two of the appellants' challenges to Senate Bill 351. First, we hold that Senate Bill 351 levies a state ad valorem tax in violation of article VIII, section 1- e; and second, we hold that the Bill levies an ad valorem tax without an election in violation of article VII, section 3 of the Texas Constitution.

* * * *

To ameliorate disparities among school districts due to local property wealth, Senate Bill 351 creates 188 county education districts. Most of these CEDs consist of school districts in a single county, although some of them include school districts in more than one county. Tex.Educ.Code § 20.941. CEDs have only tax functions; they perform no educational duties. They employ no teachers, provide no classrooms, and educate no children. CEDs do not even determine their own tax rate. That rate is effectively prescribed by statute. *Id.* at § 16.252(a). The CEDs' sole function is to levy, collect, and distribute property taxes as directed by the Legislature. *Id.* at § 20.942.

---

[161] *Edgewood II*, 804 S.W.2d at 499-500.

* * * *

[S]ince *Edgewood I,* some aspects of the public school system have been changed, but others have not. The reliance on local ad valorem taxes for more than half of the revenue for education has not changed. However, the manner in which local funds are contributed to the system has changed dramatically. The State has moved from encouraging school districts to contribute local tax revenue, to conditioning state funds on such contribution, to mandating a specified contribution. This has reduced the geographical disparities in the availability of revenue for education. It has accomplished this, however, by requiring the taxpayers in one school district, without a vote of approval, to fund the schools in other districts over which they have no control. These changes present the constitutional issues now raised before us.

II

Article VIII, section 1-e of the Texas Constitution states: "No State ad valorem taxes shall be levied upon any property within this State." Appellants contend that the taxes which the CEDs are required by Senate Bill 351 to levy are state ad valorem taxes prohibited by this provision. We agree.

Senate Bill 351 mandates the tax CEDs levy. No CED may decline to levy the tax. The tax rate for all CEDs is predetermined by Senate Bill 351. No CED can tax at a higher rate or a lower rate under any circumstances. Indeed, the very purpose of the CEDs is to levy a uniform tax statewide. The distribution of the proceeds is set by Senate Bill 351. No CED has any discretion to distribute tax proceeds in any manner except as required by statute. Every function of the CEDs is purely ministerial. *See* Letter from John Hannah, Jr., Texas Secretary of State, to Assistant Attorney General, United States Department of Justice, Voting Section (May 3, 1991). If the State mandates that a tax be levied, sets the rate, and prescribes the distribution of the proceeds, the tax is a state tax, regardless of the instrumentality which the State may choose to use.

Appellees advance several reasons why the tax should not be characterized as a State ad valorem tax. First, the State points out that while the Legislature has mandated the yield, it is the CED that sets the rate to achieve that yield. A witness in the district court testified that Senate Bill 351 does not mandate a tax rate because a CED is allowed to take into account projected tax delinquencies in arriving at the rate necessary to obtain the CED's share. One district court concluded that because collection rates will vary, the State does not set the rate, and therefore it is not a state tax. As one commentator observes:

> The court's logic is precarious because: (1) the state sets the amount of the local share at a fixed dollar figure, and (2) the CED taxable base is also fixed by the certified tax roll it receives from one or more appraisal districts. The rate, then, is self-calculating (levy divided by tax base). In effect, the state sets a *de facto* rate when it mandates a specific tax levy. The fact that each CED's *collection* rate will vary is a thin distinction to draw between a state-established tax rate and a locally-established tax rate.

[Billy D.] Walker, *supra,* at 19 (footnotes omitted) [unpublished monograph]. The collection rate is based on objective facts, another fixed number in the formula mandated by the State.

Despite this contention that it does not set the CED tax rate, the State concedes, as it surely must, that if the proceeds of the tax levied by the CEDs under Senate Bill 351 were deposited into the state treasury, the tax would be a state tax prohibited by article VIII, section 1-e. But the State argues that because the proceeds are not deposited into the state treasury, the tax is not a state ad valorem tax. The distinction the State attempts to draw is not viable. If the State could avoid the prohibition of article VIII, section 1-e simply by requiring that tax proceeds be deposited in some lesser instrumentality's account, that provision would be essentially meaningless. The State could create County Highway Districts, or County Prison Districts, or all-purpose County Funding Districts to levy taxes at set rates for prescribed purposes, and by such means accomplish what it could not do itself. CEDs are mere puppets; the State is pulling all the strings. Though the hands collecting the tax be Esau's, the voice of authority is unmistakably Jacob's. The depository for CED taxes does not govern whether they are state or local.

By the same analysis, the dedication of the proceeds of each CED's tax to activities conducted wholly within its boundaries does not make the tax a local one outside the prohibition of article VIII, section 1-e. Again, were it otherwise, the State could simply divide itself into districts and prescribe the funding for activities conducted within each district. Although the activities funded by CED taxes are conducted within the district, their funding is part of the state public education scheme mandated by Senate Bill 351.

The State argues that the CED taxes required by Senate Bill 351 simply reflect the historical uses of both local and state funds for public education, authorized by article VII, section 3 of the Constitution. However, neither the plain language of article VIII, section 1-e nor its history reveals any exception that permits state ad valorem taxes for education. Prior to January 1, 1951, the State could levy ad valorem taxes for general purposes. Effective that date, article VIII, section 1-a proscribed state ad valorem taxes for general revenue purposes, still allowing such taxes for specific purposes, including education. Article VIII, section 1-a did not eliminate the state ad valorem tax for public schools authorized by article VII, section 3. However, when article VIII, section 1-e was adopted in 1968, this special state ad valorem school tax was repealed. In 1982, article VIII, section 1-e was amended to remove any remaining authority to impose state ad valorem taxes, resulting in the blanket prohibition now in effect. The history of article VIII, section 1-e thus establishes that its framers and ratifiers specifically intended to eliminate the state ad valorem tax as a source of funds for public education.

The State argues that CED taxes uniform statewide are necessary to meet the requirement of article VII, section 1 that the public school system be efficient. Assuming that this argument is correct, it does not follow, nor does the State argue, that this system is the only one which would comply with article VII, section 1. While the Legislature has some latitude in the manner it chooses to discharge its duty to establish and maintain an efficient public school system, it cannot go so far as to violate another constitutional provision in attempting to comply with article VII, section 1.

An ad valorem tax is a state tax when it is imposed directly by the State or when the State so completely controls the levy, assessment and disbursement of revenue, either directly or indirectly, that the authority employed is without meaningful discretion. How far the State can go toward encouraging a local taxing authority to levy an ad valorem tax before the tax becomes a state tax is difficult to delineate. Clearly, if the State merely authorized a tax but left the decision whether to levy it entirely up to local authorities, to be approved by the voters if necessary, then the tax would not be a state tax. The local authority could freely choose whether to levy the tax or not. To the other extreme, if the State mandates the levy of a tax at a set rate and prescribes the distribution of the proceeds, the tax is a state tax, irrespective of whether the State acts in its own behalf or through an intermediary. Between these two extremes lies a spectrum of other possibilities. If the State required local authorities to levy an ad valorem tax but allowed them discretion on setting the rate and disbursing the proceeds, the State's conduct might not violate article VIII, section 1-e. It is difficult, perhaps impossible, to define for every conceivable hypothetical precisely where along this continuum such taxes become state taxes. Therefore, if the Legislature, in an effort to remedy Senate Bill 351 with as few changes as possible, chose to inject some additional element of leeway in the assessment of the CED tax, it is impossible to say in advance whether that element would remove the tax from the prohibition of article VIII, section 1-e. Each case must necessarily turn on its own particulars. Although parsing the differences may be likened to dancing on the head of a pin, it is the Legislature which has created the pin, summoned the dancers, and called the tune. The Legislature can avoid these constitutional conundra by choosing another path altogether.

Two things are clear, however, among many which are not. One is that local revenue may play a role in achieving an efficient system of free public schools. The other is that article VIII, section 1-e prohibits the State from doing indirectly through CEDs what it cannot do directly, that is, levy an ad valorem tax. We have not attempted to dictate to the Legislature what part local revenue should play in funding public education, viewing that decision as properly the Legislature's prerogative in the first instance. Although the Constitution requires the Legislature to "establish and make suitable provision for" free public schools, it contains no specific requirement that public education be funded completely with state revenue. The Constitution prohibits, however, heavy reliance on grossly disparate local revenue to provide the funding essential for public schools. *Edgewood II,* 804 S.W.2d at 496-97, 500. Were local revenue but an insubstantial part of the total funding, the disparities in school district property wealth might be inconsequential to the system as a whole. But when local revenue pays a very significant part of the cost of a fundamental education–now more than half–those disparities dominate the entire system.

In sum, we conclude that the tax mandated by Senate Bill 351 is a state ad valorem tax prohibited by article VIII, section 1-e of the Constitution.

Notes on Educational Funding Restrictions

The Remainder of the* Edgewood III *Opinion: After holding that Senate Bill 351 ran afoul of the constitutional prohibition on a state ad valorem tax, the court also held that the legislation violated state constitutional constraints on education funding contained in article VII of the constitution. In addition to imposing a duty on the legislature to support and maintain an efficient system of public schools, article VII establishes educational funding mechanisms and limitations. One of these limitations, in section 3, requires in part that local voters must approve ad valorem taxes imposed by local school districts.

Edgewood III held CEDs were accordingly prohibited from levying ad valorem taxes without the approval of the voters in the CED.[162] Although noting that article VII, section 3-b obviated the necessity of a tax authorization election whenever a school district's boundaries were changed or consolidated with another district, the court reasoned that the section 3-b exception did not apply to CEDs as they were not preexisting school districts but instead newly created taxing districts.[163] As a result, the CEDs had to comply with the article VII, section 3's prerequisite that the qualified voters of a school district approve the levying of any additional ad valorem taxes, which had not been done.

The court did, however, conclude Senate Bill 351 was not invalidated by the prohibition against local or special laws. The court explained that the mere "fact that sections of the statute assign particular school districts to CEDs does not make the law a special one inasmuch as it affects school districts throughout the state."[164]

The court also highlighted that its holding, and the holdings in the earlier *Edgewood* opinions, were all limited to the financing of public schools. But the court cautioned that "money is not the only issue, nor is more money the only solution."[165] Although it was constrained to the parties' arguments, the legislature could make more fundamental reforms, such as eliminating gross wastes in the bureaucratic administration of the system or otherwise overhauling the system itself, to ensure that the system met the efficiency mandate.

Justice Doggett, joined by Justice Mauzy, dissented from the majority's conclusion that Senate Bill 351 created a state ad valorem tax. Justice Doggett contended:

> The tax authorized by Senate Bill 351 is not assessed by the state, nor is it placed into the state treasury or appropriated by the Legislature. The levy is made by the CEDs, goes into the treasuries of the CEDs and is used to finance schools within the CEDs. The tax rate is not predetermined by Senate Bill 351. The legislation does impose upon each CED the responsibility for raising a share of the cost of education in that district. That share is not a specified dollar amount, but rather is initially calculated as a percentage of its tax base equal to \$0.72 per \$100.00 of value, with adjustments in subsequent years. Tex.Educ.Code § 16.252. The tax rate is not \$0.72. The amount of the levy will vary among CEDs depending upon collection rates and other factors unique to the district. Tr. 740. The State thus does not impose the tax nor set the rate, but imposes a burden that can only be met by the local government's levy.
>
> Absent from the majority's analysis is any consideration of whether the CEDs' levy serves a local purpose, a key factor in classifying the tax as state or local. Although claimed by some parties in this case to be purely

[162]*Edgewood III*, 826 S.W.2d at 506.

[163]*Id.* at 508-09.

[164]*Id.* at 510.

[165]*Id.* at 524.

> a state function, education has undeniably significant local benefits and has traditionally been viewed as a joint responsibility shared by state and local governments. The Texas Constitution clearly permits the state to share the burden of financing education with localities and the power to determine most of the terms of that partnership.[166]

Is the majority's or the dissent's position more convincing on the characterization of the tax imposed by the CEDs?

***The Legislative Response and* Edgewood IV**: After the Texas Supreme Court's decision in *Edgewood III*, the Texas Legislature first attempted to amend the Constitution to authorize the system established by Senate Bill 351, but the amendment was soundly defeated by Texas voters.

The Legislature then enacted Senate Bill 7, which established a two-tiered Foundation School Program. Tier 1 guaranteed a sufficient minimum level of financing for all school districts to provide a basic program of education to meet accreditation and other legal standards. If the school district could not, at a \$0.86 tax rate, generate revenue equal to a "basic allotment" per weighted student that ranged over the years between \$2300 and \$2550, the district received state funds for the difference. Then, Tier 2 provided for partially state-supported local supplementation. For each penny a district raised the tax rate between the minimum and a \$1.50 cap, the state guaranteed a certain yield per weighted student, which ranged from about \$20 to \$27. Senate Bill 7 also equalized school district's wealth per student (taxable property value divided by the weighted average daily attendance) by requiring school districts with wealth per student greater than a certain amount to transfer the excess, or the tax revenue generated from it, to provide funding for school districts with less wealth. This equalization process led to Senate Bill 7's common description as a "Robin Hood" financing scheme.

Senate Bill 7 was upheld initially in *Edgewood Independent School District v. Meno* (*Edgewood IV*) against a variety of constitutional attacks brought by both property-poor school districts alleging that the system was still not efficient and by property-rich districts complaining of the new taxation scheme.[167] In response to the property-poor district's complaints, the court noted that the constitutional efficiency mandate had to be measured in both qualitative and financial terms.[168] The qualitative aspect, the court opined, was satisfied by Senate Bill 7's accountability system of student assessment and district standards to measure whether the districts were progressing toward meeting the goals of public education.[169] The court next reasoned that the system was financially efficient because, although it did not mandate complete equality in funding between school districts, the combined tier system achieved an effective ratio in access to funds of 1.36 to 1, which

---

[166] *Id.* at 552-53 (Doggett, J., dissenting).

[167] 917 S.W.2d 717 (Tex.1995).

[168] *Id.* at 730.

[169] *Id.*

provided the necessary "substantially equal access to the funds necessary for a general diffusion of knowledge."[170] The court continued:

> As long as efficiency is maintained, it is not unconstitutional for districts to supplement their programs with local funds, *even if* such funds are unmatched by state dollars and *even if* such funds are not subject to statewide recapture. We caution, however, that the amount of "supplementation" in the system cannot become so great that it, in effect, destroys the efficiency of the entire system. The danger is that what the Legislature today considers to be "supplementation" may tomorrow become necessary to satisfy the constitutional mandate for a general diffusion of knowledge.[171]

The court thereafter rejected the various challenges of the property-rich districts, including their complaint that Senate Bill 7 created an impermissible state ad valorem tax. The court reasoned that the school districts retained discretion in setting the amount of the tax, especially as a general diffusion of knowledge could be attained at tax rates of between $1.20 and $1.31. But the court cautioned that this discretion would probably not last indefinitely:

> if the cost of providing for a general diffusion of knowledge continues to rise, as it surely will, the minimum rate at which a district must tax will also rise. Eventually, some districts may be forced to tax at the maximum allowable rate just to provide a general diffusion of knowledge. If a cap on tax rates were to become in effect a floor as well as a ceiling, the conclusion that the Legislature had set a statewide ad valorem tax would appear to be unavoidable because the districts would then have lost all meaningful discretion in setting the tax rate.[172]

Although it upheld the system, the court offered a less than ringing endorsement of the new legislative scheme: "Surely Texas can and must do better."[173] The court observed that its holding "should not be interpreted as a signal that the school finance crisis in Texas has ended."[174]

***The* West Orange-Cove *Challenge*:** The subsequent challenge foreseen in *Edgewood IV* began six years later when four school districts filed suit in April 2001 and asserted that the public school finance system had again become an impermissible state ad valorem tax because school districts were forced to tax at the $1.50 maximum rate. The trial court dismissed their claim on the pleadings, and the court of appeals affirmed. But the supreme court in *West Orange-Cove Consolidated Independent School District v. Alanis*

---

[170] *Id.* at 730-31.

[171] *Id.* at 732.

[172] *Id.* at 738.

[173] *Id.* at 726.

[174] *Id.* at 725.

(*West Orange-Cove I*) concluded that the trial court erred in dismissing the claims on the pleadings because the plaintiffs had at least alleged a viable claim that the system once again constituted an impermissible ad valorem tax.[175] The court then remanded the case back to the trial court for further proceedings.

On remand, additional groups of school districts intervened, contending that school funding was still inefficient under article VII, section 1 because the property-poor districts did not have substantially equal access to education revenue. All the school districts, both property-rich and property-poor, contended that the system was underfunded and could therefore not satisfy the "general diffusion of knowledge" standard required by the state constitution. The trial court found in favor of the school districts, and the Texas Supreme Court accepted the state's subsequent direct appeal in *Neeley v. West Orange-Cove Consolidated Independent School District* (*West Orange-Cove II*).[176]

In its lengthy opinion in *West Orange-Cove II*, the supreme court invalidated the school finance system again under the prohibition against state ad valorem taxes, although the court held that the system was at least marginally acceptable under the standards of article VII, section 1.[177] The court first reviewed its prior *Edgewood* decisions interpreting article VII, section 1, noting that these decisions mandated that the public school system must be: (1) "efficient" both qualitatively and financially, (2) "adequate" to achieve a general diffusion of knowledge, and (3) "suitable" to accomplish its educational mission.[178] After rejecting the state's justiciability challenges to the school districts' claims, the court then analyzed whether the current Texas public education system violated article VII, section 1.

The court first recognized that its prior cases had not explicitly established a standard of review for determining whether the public finance system satisfied the efficient, adequate, and suitable mandates of article VII.[179] Yet *Edgewood IV*, the court reasoned, had implicitly employed an analysis of whether the legislation was "arbitrary" or "unreasonable," which comported with pre-*Edgewood* precedent discussing article VII. The court distinguished this "arbitrary" standard, which ascertains whether the legislative act is adopted without reference to guiding rules and principles, from the rational basis test, which is the "minimal requirement a classification must meet to be consistent with the constitutional guarantee of equal protection when no suspect class or fundamental right is involved."[180] Although recognizing that the testimony and fact findings in the district court indicated troubles with the dropout rate and gaps in educational quality that predicted a "drift toward constitutional inadequacy," the court determined that it could not presently conclude "that the Legislature has acted arbitrarily in structuring and funding the public

---

[175]107 S.W.3d 558, 578-83 (Tex. 2003).

[176]176 S.W.3d 746 (Tex. 2005).

[177]*Id.* at 800.

[178]*Id.* at 752-53.

[179]*Id.* at 783.

[180]*Id.* at 784.

education system" when standardized test scores indicated that public education in Texas had improved in comparison to other states.[181]

But while rejecting the article VII, section 1 challenge, the court accepted the article VIII, section 1-e complaint that the funding scheme under Senate Bill 7 had become an unconstitutional state ad valorem tax. Relying on the standards from *Edgewood III*, and the cautionary note in *Edgewood IV* quoted above, the court reasoned that the previously discretionary tax rate had effectively become a state ad valorem tax because numerous districts "lacked meaningful discretion" to set their tax rates under the $1.50 maximum in order to satisfy state accreditation standards. Thus, the system was "virtually indistinguishable from one in which the State simply set an ad valorem tax rate of $1.50 and redistributed the revenue to the districts."[182]

The court's judgment gave the legislature until June 1, 2006 to cure the constitutional deficiencies in the finance system. While not providing a specific suggested solution, the court cautioned that "structural changes, and not merely increased funding, are needed in the public education system to meet the constitutional challenges that have been raised."[183]

The legislative response was to provide additional state funding to the districts through a variety of taxes such that the districts would again have "meaningful discretion" to set their tax rates under the $1.50 maximum. But this text's author was skeptical at the time:

> Despite repeated warnings from the courts that "a band-aid will not suffice" and that "Texas can and must do better," the legislature keeps trying to patch the system rather than overhauling it. The only stated justification for our present system, including more than 1,000 school districts ranging in size from only 16 to over 210,000 students, is to maintain local control over the schools. Admittedly, local involvement, especially by parents, in the education of the community is an important goal, and may be the key factor in success. But the crazy patch-work of school districts in Texas varying widely in size, student populations, and taxable wealth does not serve this worthy objective.
>
> Many districts obviously have too few students, with 11 Texas school districts having less than 60 pupils and over 200 districts having less than 350 students. These very small independent school districts require redundant staffing, facilities, and administration, making them more expensive on a per-student basis. In contrast, other districts are extremely large, with two having more than 160,000 students. While such large districts may have better economies of scale, the goal of local input in the education of the community has likely been lost.

---

[181] *Id.* at 789-90.

[182] *Id.* at 796-97.

[183] *Id.* at 800.

> Somewhere in between there is an optimum range for the student population in a district, which will insure both efficiency in administration and responsiveness to the needs of the community. The community should have a meaningful voice in the decisionmaking process. On the other hand, unnecessary duplication of administrative expenses should be avoided. An administrative bureaucracy does not teach our children–we should spend our resources on the teachers that do.
>
> Every decade the state must change the boundaries of state and federal political districts to correct for population shifts. In contrast, though, the population and economic shifts that have occurred in our school districts haven't been corrected in generations. The inefficiencies and inequities of the present system need to be eliminated. Instead, the legislature's most recent effort merely swaps some state dollars for local dollars without making any long-term changes. When costs increase, and enough more local dollars are required, the system will become unconstitutional again. The Texas Supreme Court warned that money may delay constitutional challenges to our educational scheme, but these problems "will repeat until the system is overhauled." It's unfortunate that this advice has been ignored again.[184]

Five years later, during the 2011 legislative session, over $4 billion of state financial support was cut from public education, reducing funding by nearly $500 per student. Several groups of school districts, students, parents, and taxpayers responded to these cuts with yet another set of legal challenges to the Texas education system. Property-poor districts claimed the system was constitutionally inadequate and inefficient, and wealthy districts contended that schools were inadequately financed and the new system constituted an illegal statewide property tax. These consolidated lawsuits were tried before Travis County District Court Judge John Dietz. At the conclusion of the trial in February 2013, Judge Dietz orally ruled that the school finance system was unconstitutionally inefficient and inadequate. Yet during the 2013 legislative session, the legislature restored much of the previously cut funding for public education, as well as adopting new testing and graduation requirements. As a result, Judge Dietz announced that a new six-week trial would begin before him on January 6, 2014 to consider the impact of the 2013 legislation on the constitutionality of the Texas education system.

The Legislative and Judicial Struggle over School Finance: Texas is not the only state that has had continuing difficulties with its state constitutional education guarantee. One intriguing case came from Nevada, *Guinn v. Legislature.*[185] The Nevada Constitution has, since its 1864 inception, mandated: "The legislature shall provide for a uniform system of common schools, by which a school shall be established and maintained in each school district at least six months in every year . . . ."[186] In 2003, as the legislature was attempting

---

[184]Charles W. "Rocky" Rhodes, *Another Short-Term Fix for the Ailing Texas School System*, THE BEAUMONT ENTERPRISE, Apr. 2006.

[185]71 P.3d 1269 (Nev. 2003).

[186]NEV. CONST. art. XI, § 2.

to create the state budget within the confines of other provisions of the state constitution requiring both a balanced budget[187] and a two-thirds vote of both legislative houses to enact a tax increase,[188] a difficulty arose. The legislature's budget had appropriated almost all expected income, even though no appropriations had been budgeted for education as required by the state constitution. After two special sessions, a legislative majority had come to an agreement on the education budget and the necessary tax increases to balance the budget, but was one vote short of the necessary supermajority for a tax increase. The governor filed a mandamus proceeding in the state supreme court seeking to require the legislature to enact the tax increase. The supreme court granted the petition and ordered the legislature to proceed under a simple majority rule, concluding that the education mandate conflicted with the supermajority tax increase requirement, and that the fundamental right to a state-sponsored education trumped the procedural two-thirds majority provision.[189] When the matter returned to the legislature, one of the holdout legislatures voted for the tax increase, allowing it to be passed by the required two-thirds majority.

What lessons, if any, should be taken from the experiences in Texas and Nevada, the thirty-plus year educational reform saga in New Jersey, and the twenty-plus year see-saw between the legislature and the judiciary in Arkansas? In many jurisdictions, state constitutional challenges to public school systems initially involved equality of funding, a matter that seemed relatively easy to rectify. Subsequently, however, these challenges have expanded to include both the sufficiency of the funding and the adequacy of education, issues closer to the legislature's prerogative. Yet is the role of the state courts in ensuring the legislature provides an adequate education to poor and disadvantaged students much different from the oversight role that the federal courts played in ending intentional public school racial segregation through busing programs and other judicial decrees?

F. APPORTIONMENT OF LEGISLATIVE DISTRICTS

A traditional state legislative power is the power to reapportion itself. Many state constitutions explicitly impose a duty on the legislature, or sometimes a commission, to apportion the state into legislative districts following the decennial federal census. The state redistricting process possesses added significance because the United States Constitution does not require that Congress determines the boundaries of any federal congressional districts, instead allowing that determination to be made by the states, subject to federal constitutional and statutory constraints.[190]

Of course, these federal constitutional and statutory constraints can be vitally important. As discussed in Chapter 2, constitutional amendments and federal statutes

---

[187]NEV. CONST. art. IX, § 3.

[188]NEV. CONST. art. IV, § 18, c. 2. At least fifteen other states also have similar supermajority requirements for tax increases. *See* Max Minzner, *Entrenching Interests: State Supermajority Requirements to Raise Taxes*, 14 AKRON TAX. J. 43, 55 (1999).

[189]71 P.3d at 1275-76.

[190]U.S. CONST. art. I, § 4 ("The Times, Places and Manner of holding Elections for Senators and Representatives, shall be prescribed in each State by the Legislature thereof; but the Congress may at any time by Law make or alter such Regulations . . . .").

provide for uniform federal election dates and require that the right to vote cannot be denied to any citizen, who is at least eighteen years of age, based on gender, race, ethnicity, disability, or failure to pay a poll tax. Other federal requirements have had a more direct impact on the redistricting process itself. For example, some states employed at-large elections for members of the House of Representatives until federal apportionment statutes beginning in 1842 required states to draw congressional election districts, eventually ending statewide at-large voting for Congress.[191]

Two other critical federal limitations on the redistricting process are the Equal Protection Clause and the Voting Rights Act. During the first half of the twentieth century, many states refused to reapportion themselves as urban migration caused cities to become underrepresented in relation to rural areas. But the United States Supreme Court held, in a series of cases, that the Equal Protection Clause mandated that all legislative districts be approximately the same in population size under the one-person, one-vote principle.[192] These decisions fundamentally changed the selection of state legislators and federal representatives in forty-six states,[193] including Texas.[194] In addition, federal equal protection principles also limit racial considerations in drawing legislative districts.[195] Finally, the Voting Rights Act prevents minority voting strength from being unlawfully diluted and authorizes various remedial measures to ensure a state's compliance.[196]

Yet the states still retain wide discretion within these federal constraints, being authorized to subdivide into legislative districts in the manner provided by their own constitutions and laws. Under the Texas Constitution, state senatorial districts must be divisions of contiguous territory.[197] In addition, state representative districts must be based,

---

[191]Act of June 25, 1842, ch. 47, § 2, 5 Stat. 491 (current version at 2 U.S.C. § 2c). Even though this statute was first enacted in 1842, the House repeatedly refused to enforce it and subsequent versions against states employing at-large elections, at least partially because of fears that the statute was unconstitutional. *See* Paul E. McGreal, *Unconstitutional Politics*, 76 NOTRE DAME L. REV. 519, 618-31 (2001).

[192]*See, e.g.*, Reynolds v. Sims, 377 U.S. 533, 568 (1964) ("We hold that, as a basic constitutional standard, the Equal Protection Clause requires that the seats in both houses of a bicameral state legislature must be apportioned on a population basis."); Gray v. Sanders, 372 U.S. 368, 379-81 (1963) (holding that "all who participate in the election are to have an equal vote" because the American "conception of political equality . . . can mean only one thing–one person, one vote").

[193]G. ALAN TARR, UNDERSTANDING STATE CONSTITUTIONS 146 (1998).

[194]*See, e.g.*, Kilgarlin v. Hill, 386 U.S. 120, 121-25 (1967) (holding aspects of 1965 Texas reapportionment scheme violated one-person, one-vote principles).

[195]*See, e.g.*, Bush v. Vera, 517 U.S. 952 (1996) (holding three Texas congressional districts were racially gerrymandered in violation of the Fourteenth Amendment); Shaw v. Reno, 509 U.S. 630, 642 (1993) (holding race-conscious redistricting can violate equal protection rights); White v. Regester, 412 U.S. 755, 765-69 (1973) (holding multi-member districts in Dallas and Bexar counties invidiously discriminated against minority groups in violation of the Equal Protection Clause).

[196]42 U.S.C. § 1973 et. seq.

[197]TEX. CONST. art. III, § 25. Before 2001, section 25 also provided that "no single county shall be entitled to more than one Senator," a provision that led to massive underrepresentation in urban counties such as Harris and Dallas until it was invalidated by the federal courts in the 1960's under the one-person, one-vote principle. *Kilgarlin*, 386 U.S. at 121-25.

"as nearly as can be," on population, employing county lines whenever possible.[198] The Texas Constitution places the initial duty for apportionment on the legislature, specifying that, at the first regular legislative session following the United States decennial census, it is to apportion the state into senatorial and representative districts that comply with the constitution.[199]

The Texas Constitution also provides a back-up plan in case the Texas Legislature fails to accomplish its state legislative apportionment responsibilities, the Legislative Redistricting Board of Texas.[200] This board, whose members are the lieutenant governor, the speaker of the house, the attorney general, the comptroller, and the land commissioner, must assemble within ninety days after the adjournment of the legislative session that failed to make the apportionment and then create an apportionment plan within sixty days which, when approved by at least three members of the board, shall have the force and effect of law.[201]

The Texas Constitution does not, however, contain a provision addressing congressional redistricting. Nevertheless, because the Texas Legislature may legislate in any area unless prohibited by the federal or state constitution, this constitutional silence does not prohibit the legislature from undertaking congressional redistricting. As the Texas Supreme Court noted, the Texas Legislature "is the department constitutionally responsible for apportioning the State into federal congressional legislative districts."[202]

Any apportionment plan that is adopted, of course, is then subject to court challenges under the federal and state constitutions and laws. Numerous cases have considered Texas state constitutional challenges to apportionment schemes. In *Smith v. Craddick*, the Texas Supreme Court held that the 1971 apportionment scheme for the state house violated the Texas Constitution's requirement that county lines be used.[203] While acknowledging that the one-person, one-vote principle might require the cutting of county lines in some instances, the court held that there was no evidence offered in that particular case that "the wholesale cutting of county lines" in the apportionment plan was necessary to comply with the principle.[204] Ten years later, the Texas Supreme Court again invalidated a legislative apportionment plan under this provision of the state constitution.

---

[198]TEX. CONST. art. III, § 26. A since-repealed provision of the Texas Constitution previously limited the number of state representatives from large metropolitan counties to one per 100,000 people before it too was invalidated by the federal courts in the 1960's. *Kilgarlin*, 386 U.S. at 121-25.

[199]TEX. CONST. art. III, § 28.

[200]*Id.*

[201]*Id.*

[202]Perry v. Del Rio, 67 S.W.3d 85, 91 (Tex. 2001). Justice Baker's opinion in *Perry* did, however, err by citing Texas Constitution article III, section 28 as support for this proposition. This provision of the Texas Constitution only addresses state redistricting, not federal congressional redistricting. *See* TEX. CONST. art. III, § 28 ("The Legislature shall, at its first regular session after the publication of each United States decennial census, apportion the state into *senatorial and representative districts*, agreeable to the provisions of Section 25 [specifying requirements for state senatorial districts] and 26 [specifying requirements for state representative districts] of this Article.") (emphasis and bracketed materials added).

[203]471 S.W.2d 375, 378-79 (Tex. 1971).

[204]*Id.*

Clements v. Valles, 620 S.W.2d 112 (Tex. 1981)

RAY, Justice.

By House Bill 960 the Legislature has redrawn the representative districts of the State from which members of the House of Representatives of the Texas Legislature are elected. The only question presented to us in this direct appeal is whether this redistricting statute violates Article II, § 26 of the Texas Constitution.

Article III, § 26 of the Texas Constitution provides the following:

> The members of the House of Representatives shall be apportioned among the several counties, according to the number of population in each, as nearly as may be, on a ratio obtained by dividing the population of the State, as ascertained by the most recent United States census, by the number of members of which the House is composed; provided, that whenever a single county has sufficient population to be entitled to a Representative, such county shall be formed into a separate Representative District, and when two or more counties are required to make up the ratio of representation, such counties shall be contiguous to each other; and when any one county has more than sufficient population to be entitled to one or more Representatives, such Representative or Representatives shall be apportioned to such county, and for any surplus of population it may be joined in a Representative District with any other contiguous county or counties.

In Smith v. Craddick, 471 S.W.2d 375 (Tex. 1971), we declared a statute redrawing the representative districts of the state invalid for its "wholesale cutting" of county lines in violation of Section 26. The boundaries of thirty-three counties were cut under the terms of the statute, eighteen of which had less than sufficient population to form a separate representative district. We noted that although the burden is one on attacking an act to establish its invalidity, once it is established that the statute violated Article III, § 26 of the constitution by cutting county lines, the proponents were then required to justify the redistricting plan by presenting evidence that the cutting of county lines was necessary to satisfy the requirements of equal representation. We found that the provisions of the statute violated the constitution because appellants (state and local officials) failed to present evidence that the cutting of county lines was justified to comply with the equal population requirement of the Fourteenth Amendment of the United States Constitution.

In reviewing a statute for compliance with the equal representation requirement, the paramount consideration is the variation, per representative, between the populations of the various districts. As described in Smith v. Craddick, supra, at 377, this variation is computed by beginning with an ideal district population. In Texas, with a 1980 population of 14,288,383 and 150 representatives, that ideal is 94,856. The total variation in the present case is 9.4 percent. This is derived by figuring the percent by which the district of the smallest population is overrepresented and the percent by which the district of the largest population is underrepresented, and then adding the two figures together to obtain the total deviation of variation percentage between the largest and smallest districts.

Equality of population within representative districts is required in so far as practicable. A reapportionment plan, in order to be constitutional, must not contain impermissible deviations from population equality. In White v. Regester, 412 U.S. 755 (1971), the United States Supreme Court reviewed the apportionment plan prepared by the Legislative Redistricting Board after the decision in Smith v. Craddick, supra. Under the plan only twenty-three districts were overrepresented or underrepresented by more than three percent, and only three of those districts were overrepresented or underrepresented by more than five percent. The plan resulted in a total variation between representative districts of 9.9 percent and an average deviation from the ideal of 1.82 percent. The Court held that plaintiffs failed to prove a prima facie case of invidious discrimination under the Equal Protection Clause from these deviations and approved as constitutionally acceptable the plan's efforts to conform to Section 26.

House Bill 960 cuts the boundaries of thirty-four counties as compared to the thirty-three counties cut in Smith v. Craddick, supra. Twenty-four of those counties have surplus populations, and ten have populations less than sufficient to form a separate representative district. In addition, three counties, Nueces, Denton, and Brazoria, which are entitled to one or more representatives, are cut so that their surplus populations are joined to two, rather than one, adjoining district. Nueces County, with a population of 268,215 entitling it to 2.82 representative districts, is given only one district wholly within its boundaries. The overall deviation of the plan is 9.4 percent, and the average deviation among the districts is 2.11 percent. No district has a deviation over five percent, and only ten districts have a deviation above four percent.

We hold that House Bill 960 fails to follow the requirements of Section 26. In Smith v. Craddick, supra, we held that the state constitution requires that a county constitute a separate district if the population of the county is slightly under or over the ideal population but within constitutional limits of variation. The plan in House Bill 960 divides eight surplus population counties (Potter, Webb, Gregg, El Paso, Tarrant, Bexar, Dallas, and Harris), and appellants argue that retaining surplus populations within those urban counties would result in a systematic underrepresentation of minorities in violation of the equal representation requirement. However, appellants failed to prove that the retention of surplus populations within the boundaries of the eight counties would result in impermissible deviations. In fact, appellees presented evidence of a number of alternate redistricting plans which maintain more of the surplus populations within county lines than House Bill 960 and result in deviations less than the 9.9 percent approved in White v. Regester, supra.

The statute also divides at least three counties with less than sufficient populations for separate districts. While appellants argue that it was necessary to divide the counties in order to comply with equal representation requirements, appellees presented evidence of numerous alternative plans, some of which were statewide, which kept the counties intact and resulted in population variances well under 9.9 percent.

Finally, the failure of the plan in House Bill 960 to allot two representative districts to Nueces County is not justified by the necessity of complying with the Voting Rights Act, 42 U.S.C. § 1973 et seq., as appellants contend. Appellees introduced evidence of two alternate plans which created two districts wholly within Nueces County and maintained the voting strength of the Hispanic population, as required by the Voting Rights Act.

Although a legislative enactment is entitled to a presumption of validity, it is our opinion that House Bill 960 violates the Texas Constitution and must be declared invalid in its entirety.

Notes on State Apportionment

Texas Constitutional Limits on Apportionment: The Texas Constitution provides minimal limitations on state legislative apportionment, merely requiring population-based state representative districts that respect (to the extent possible) county lines, and contiguous state senatorial districts. Yet these limits are judicially enforceable, as *Clements* illustrates. *Clements* reasoned that the cutting of thirty-four county boundaries was unnecessary when other alternative plans had been proposed that better respected county boundaries without violating the one-person, one-vote principle. During the course of its opinion, the *Clements* court twice remarked that a legislative enactment is entitled to a presumption of validity. But did the court presume the validity of House Bill 960? While the court never explicitly articulated a standard of review, the court's analysis primarily relied on the fact that the plan's opponents had formulated alternative plans with less cutting of county lines while still limiting population deviations to below ten percent. Does this mean that any violation of article III, section 26 requires a least restrictive means analysis? Would this provide much discretion to either the legislature or the redistricting board in drawing house districts to serve other purposes, such as incumbency protection, preserving communities of interest in the same district, and other political considerations?

Permissible Population Deviations: A state apportionment scheme must also satisfy federal constitutional and statutory limitations, such as the one-person, one-vote principle emanating from the Equal Protection Clause. As *Clements* indicates, the United States Supreme Court has upheld population deviations in state apportionment schemes of up to ten percent without requiring a state justification,[205] and even larger deviations have been affirmed when adequately justified by the state.[206] Yet the Court has invalidated extremely small deviations for federal congressional districts, concluding that "precise mathematical equality" is typically required.[207] Is this broader latitude given to state legislative

---

[205] *See, e.g.*, Brown v. Thomson, 462 U.S. 835, 842 (1983) (noting that apportionment plans with a maximum population deviation under 10% are minor deviations which are insufficient to establish a prima facie case of invidious discrimination); White v. Regester, 412 U.S. 755, 764 (1973) (upholding Texas apportionment scheme with 9.9% deviation). *But see* Cox v. Larios, 542 U.S. 947 (2004) (affirming summarily district court's holding that Georgia apportionment scheme with less than 10% deviation nevertheless was invalid under one-person, one-vote principles based on deliberate and systematic policy of overpopulating Republican and suburban districts while underpopulating Democratic and inner-city districts).

[206] *See, e.g.*, Mahan v. Howell, 410 U.S. 315, 324-25 (1973) (upholding a Virginia state redistricting plan with a maximum deviation of 16.4% because of the state's interest in preserving its political subdivision boundary lines).

[207] Kirkpatrick v. Preisler, 394 U.S. 526, 530-31 (1969); *see also* Karcher v. Daggett, 462 U.S. 725, 727 (1983) (affirming invalidation of congressional apportionment with a deviation of less than one percent when the state had not established that the deviations were the result of a good-faith effort to achieve population equality). *But see* Tennant v. Jefferson Cnty. Comm'n, 133 S. Ct. 3 (2012) (upholding population deviation of less than one percent when justified by the state's interests in avoiding placing two incumbents in the same district, refraining from splitting county lines, and not moving a substantial percentage of the state's population into a new district).

redistricting appropriate under federalism principles, or should the Equal Protection Clause be interpreted similarly in either a state or federal election district?

Minority Representation: Another federal statutory requirement under the Voting Rights Act is that minority voting strength cannot be diluted under an apportionment scheme. Did *Clements* adequately address the claim that county lines in urban surplus population counties had to be cut to prevent an underrepresentation of minority voters? Isn't this underrepresentation argument distinct from the argument that one-person, one-vote would otherwise be violated?

The minority representation issue took center stage in the state redistricting process after the 1990 census. The legislature's redistricting plan was challenged on the basis that the federal census on which it was based had undercounted minorities in Texas. The state attorney general, governor, and some state senators worked with the plaintiffs to adopt an alternate redistricting plan that would increase the number of minority-dominated districts in the state. The parties then submitted this agreement to settle the pending litigation, and the district court adopted this new redistricting plan. Other affected individuals then sought mandamus from the Texas Supreme Court.

Terrazas v. Ramirez, 829 S.W.2d 712 (Tex. 1991)

HECHT, Justice.

Following publication of the 1990 United States decennial census, the Seventy-Second Legislature enacted Senate Bill 31 and House Bill 150, reapportioning state senatorial and representative districts, respectively, as required by article III, section 28 of the Texas Constitution. In litigation challenging the accuracy of the 1990 census and the validity of any redistricting based upon it, Hon. Mario E. Ramirez, Judge of the 332nd District Court in Hidalgo County, Texas, has ordered that all elections for the Texas Senate and House of Representatives be based, not upon the reapportionment statutes enacted by the Legislature, but upon districts reconfigured by the court.

Two judgments rendered by the district court affect state senatorial districts, one dated October 11, 1991, in *Mena v. Richards*, and the other dated October 7, 1991, in *Quiroz v. Richards*. Both judgments were based upon a settlement agreement between the plaintiffs in the two cases and three of the defendants, the Governor and the director and executive director of the Texas Legislative Council. These defendants are represented by the Texas Attorney General, who executed the settlement agreement on their behalf.

In the original mandamus proceeding now before this Court, five individuals who were not parties in either suit request us to direct the district court to vacate these two judgments. They argue, in essence, that the district court, in redistricting the State by merely approving an agreement of the Governor, the Attorney General, and a few other individuals, encroaches upon a power which the Constitution commits to the Legislature. They also ask that the Attorney General be directed to rescind his agreement to the judgments, and that the Secretary of State be directed to withdraw the districting plan created by the judgments from preclearance consideration by the United States Department of Justice under section 5 of the Voting Rights Act of 1965, 42 U.S.C. § 1973c.

We hold that a district court cannot order a reapportionment plan for the State based upon nothing more than the agreement of the Governor, the Attorney General, and a few citizens. Accordingly, we conditionally grant the requested relief directed to Judge Ramirez. We deny relief against the Attorney General and Secretary of State.

* * * *

II

A

The responsibility for apportioning the State into legislative districts belongs primarily to the Legislature. TEX. CONST. art. III, § 28. The judiciary, however, is both empowered and, when properly called upon, obliged to declare whether an apportionment statute enacted by the Legislature is valid. *Reynolds v. Sims*, 377 U.S. 533 (1964); *Baker v. Carr*, 369 U.S. 186 (1962); *Clements v. Valles*, 620 S.W.2d 112 (Tex.1981). A judicial determination that an apportionment statute violates a constitutional provision is no more an encroachment on the prerogative of the Legislature than the same determination with respect to some other statute. The Legislature, as well as the judiciary, must comply with the United States Constitution and the Texas Constitution. Yet a court's duty to consider a party's constitutional challenge to a statute, never to be taken lightly, and the deference owed a coordinate branch of government, are rarely more sensitive or serious matters than when the statute attacked involves the highly politically charged subject of apportionment.

Although state courts in Texas have invalidated apportionment statutes, none has ever imposed a substitute plan upon the State. Nevertheless, we do not doubt the power of our courts to do so. United States District Courts have this power, *Reynolds*, 377 U.S. at 586-87, and have exercised it in Texas. State courts in other jurisdictions have also ordered apportionment plans after invalidating legislative plans. Reason and experience argue that courts empowered to invalidate an apportionment statute which transgresses constitutional mandates cannot be left without the means to order appropriate relief. While this power has generally been exercised by a state's highest court, we see no constitutional reason why it does not also reside in a trial court of general jurisdiction.

Although Texas courts may order apportionment, that power ought to be used only after investigation and careful consideration of the many, diverse interests affected, after due deference to the Legislature to rectify its own statutes, and after due regard for the effect of the court's order on the election process. We comment on each of these considerations in turn.

1

Apportionment affects every person in the State, yet only a very few parties can be involved in any lawsuit challenging redistricting. The trial court must attempt to consider the interests, not only of the parties in the case, but of others who are not present. For this reason, the agreement of the parties in a reapportionment lawsuit cannot alone be conclusive of either the validity of the statute or, if it is found to be invalid, the relief to be granted.

* * * *

2

Furthermore, the court must give due deference to the Legislature before ordering a substitute apportionment plan. Apportionment involves uniquely political judgments, and for sound practical as well as theoretical reasons is constitutionally committed to the legislative branch. As the United States Supreme Court stated in *Connor v. Fitch*, 431 U.S. 407, 414-15 (1977): "a state legislature is the institution that is by far the best situated to identify and then reconcile traditional state policies within the constitutionally mandated framework of substantial population equality." Thus, "judicial relief becomes appropriate only when a legislature fails to reapportion according to . . . constitutional requisites in a timely fashion after having had an adequate opportunity to do so." *Reynolds*, 377 U.S. at 586. After a legislative plan has been invalidated, respect for the separation of powers explicitly recognized in article II, section 1 of our Constitution requires that the Legislature be given a reasonable opportunity to enact a substitute statute. Only in the most exigent circumstances should a court intrude into this arena without affording the Legislature a full opportunity to remedy any defects.

Moreover, the court must attempt to give effect to as many of the Legislature's redistricting decisions as are not invalid. There are a vast number of possible plans for apportioning state legislative districts that fully comply with all applicable laws. When a court sets aside the plan chosen by the Legislature, the beginning point for fashioning a substitute plan must be those aspects of the legislated scheme which are valid. *White v. Weiser*, 412 U.S. 783 (1973).

3

Finally, the court must consider the impact of its decision upon the electoral process. In lieu of postponing the elections, the court may determine that it is more advisable to allow elections to proceed under the lines drawn by the Legislature. Many courts have permitted impending elections to proceed under lines already declared unconstitutional in order to permit the legislative process to perform in an orderly fashion. *See, e.g.*, *Upham*, 456 U.S. at 44. Such deference, in the absence of unconscionable delay, is entirely appropriate.

* * * *

B

To reiterate, only after giving full and careful consideration to the interests affected by its ruling and the effect upon the election process, and after affording the Legislature sufficient opportunity to correct the constitutional infirmities in apportionment legislation, may the district court order its own apportionment plan. The judgments challenged in this proceeding do not meet these standards.

In *Mena*, the only parties were a few citizens as plaintiffs, the Governor and two other state defendants represented by the Attorney General, and the county defendants. Only the plaintiffs and the state defendants joined in the settlement agreement upon which agreed judgments were rendered in both *Mena* and *Quiroz*.

The parties in this proceeding have focused much of their argument on the power of the Attorney General to execute the settlement agreement. The concurring opinions of JUSTICE GONZALEZ and JUSTICE CORNYN would hold that the Attorney General exceeded his authority. We do not agree with their views. The Attorney General, as the chief legal officer of the State, has broad discretionary power in conducting his legal duty and responsibility to represent the State. *See* TEX. CONST. art. IV, § 22; TEX.GOV'T CODE

§ 402.021; *see also Maud v. Terrell*, 109 Tex. 97, 200 S.W. 375 (1918); *Lewright v. Bell*, 94 Tex. 556, 63 S.W. 623 (1901). This discretion includes the authority to propose a settlement agreement in an action attacking the constitutionality of a reapportionment statute. The Attorney General has participated in such settlements on previous occasions. *Terrazas*, 581 F.Supp. at 1321; *Graves*, 408 F.Supp. at 1052. Although the Attorney General appears to have acted throughout this litigation only on behalf of the state defendants and not for himself, he had the authority, certainly for his clients and even on his own, to suggest possible remedies after the district court rendered an interlocutory summary judgment holding Senate Bill 31 unconstitutional. He also had the power to negotiate a settlement with the plaintiffs and to execute an agreement with them. To hold that he did not would be to give him less authority than any party or any other attorney participating in the case.

The real issue, however, is not whether the Attorney General had the power to do what he did in this case, but what the effect of his action was. As he conceded at oral argument, he certainly had no power to effectuate a valid reapportionment of senatorial districts himself; that could be done only by judgment of the district court. The settlement agreement may have been a valid agreement between plaintiffs and the state defendants. It alone could not, however, support rendition of a judgment without evidence and without other interested parties being encouraged to intervene in the litigation.

In *Quiroz*, where the agreed judgment regarding senatorial districts was first rendered, the court heard no evidence concerning the settlement agreement. The suit and answer were filed, and judgment was rendered, all in one day, in the span of a few minutes. There was literally no opportunity at all for comment. This irregular procedure was designed to avoid our stay of proceedings in *Mena*, and we do not approve it. A few days later, the same judgment was rendered in *Mena* on the same basis, again with no opportunity to be heard. Two State Senators directly affected by the judgment attempted to intervene in both cases and set aside the judgments, but their interventions were struck by the district court. The manner in which the judgments were rendered in these cases excluded any comment by anyone not a party to the settlement agreement.

The district court ordered a reapportionment plan without a determination that Senate Bill 31 was invalid. Although the court granted summary judgment in *Mena* invalidating the statute, the state defendants appealed that ruling. In the settlement agreement the state defendants reserved their contention that the statute is valid, just as plaintiffs reserved their claims. The court expressly based its judgment upon the settlement agreement and not upon any prior evidence or findings. Indeed, to have adjudicated the invalidity of the statute in the agreed judgment would have been contrary to the settlement agreement. Without a determination that Senate Bill 31 is invalid, the district court was prohibited from suspending its effect by article I, section 28 of the Texas Constitution which states: "No power of suspending laws in this State shall be exercised except by the Legislature." We are aware of no instance in any other jurisdiction when a court reapportioned state legislative districts without first deciding that the statutory plan was invalid.

Under these circumstances, the settlement agreement does not provide sufficient basis for the rendition of the judgment.

GONZALEZ, Justice, concurring.

The Texas Constitution explicitly provides for the separation of powers among three branches of government: the legislature, the executive, and the judiciary. TEX. CONST. art II, § 1. And the Constitution prohibits any branch exercising "any power properly attached to either of the others, except in instances expressly permitted." *Id.* Here, the legislature and the LRB have the express power to reapportion the senate voting districts, and the Attorney General has no statutory or constitutional power to alter this process. Thus, he exceeded his authority, and his unauthorized action did not bind the state. * * * *

CORNYN, Justice, concurring.

Because the constitution expressly grants the redistricting power for senatorial and representative districts to the legislature and the LRB and describes the means for exercising the power, such are the exclusive means by which the power can be exercised. Accordingly, the executive branch, including the Attorney General, has no reapportionment power.

This conclusion is also compelled by the doctrine of separation of powers, implicit in the federal constitution, *A.L.A. Schechter Poultry Corp. v. United States*, 295 U.S. 495, 529 (1935), but explicit in the Texas Constitution. TEX. CONST. art. II, § 1. Thus, under our constitution, it is only by *express* constitutional provision that the executive department could legitimately exercise the redistricting power. As has been noted, under article III, § 28, that power is expressly granted to the legislature and the LRB, not to the executive department.

Finally, this holding is compelled by the absence of specific constitutional authorization for the Attorney General's agreement to the substitute senate districts ordered by the trial court's judgment. It is true that the Constitution and laws of this state generally grant the Attorney General broad authority in exercising his role as the state's lawyer. *Maud v. Terrell*, 109 Tex. 97, 200 S.W. 375, 376 (1918) (upholding the exclusive constitutional grant to the Attorney General to represent the Comptroller, as a state official); *Bullock v. Texas Skating Assoc.*, 583 S.W.2d 888, 894 (Tex.Civ.App.—Austin 1979, writ ref'd n.r.e.) (holding that it is within the authority of the Attorney General to decide whether to appeal an adverse judgment). But, it is fundamental to our jurisprudence that the Attorney General may only act within his constitutional or statutory authority. *Day Land & Cattle Co. v. State*, 68 Tex. 526, 4 S.W. 865, 867 (1887). Any of his actions beyond the scope of his delegated power are not binding on the state.

The general discretionary power of the Attorney General to settle lawsuits on behalf of the state is not the issue here. As a general rule, he has such authority. *Executive Condominiums, Inc. v. State*, 764 S.W.2d 899, 902 (Tex.App.—Corpus Christi 1989, writ denied). However, the Attorney General as a member of the executive department, simply cannot settle a case in a manner that usurps the express constitutional authority of another department of government. * * * *

MAUZY, Justice, dissenting, joined by Doggett, J.

* * * *

Since today's writings will affect not only these parties but also the course of future redistricting litigation, I note those important issues on which at least seven justices agree:

> 1. The attorney general is constitutionally empowered to execute a settlement agreement in litigation challenging a legislative redistricting plan.
> 2. A trial court is constitutionally empowered to invalidate an unconstitutional legislative redistricting plan.
> 3. A trial court is constitutionally empowered to adopt a constitutional legislative redistricting plan as a remedy for an unconstitutional legislative redistricting plan.
> 4. Before rendering judgment to adopt a substitute legislative redistricting plan, a trial court, to the extent possible without disrupting the election process, should show due deference to the legislative and executive branches affording them a reasonable opportunity to remedy constitutional deficiencies.
> 5. Before rendering judgment to adopt a substitute legislative redistricting plan, recognizing the particular public interest involved in ensuring the integrity of the election process, a trial court should afford a full opportunity for all interested persons to be heard. This should include public notice of its intention to adopt a substitute plan, a reasonable opportunity for interested persons to intervene and be heard concerning same, even if the substitute represents a settlement, and a requirement that evidence be heard to support adoption of the substitute plan.

Our conflict centers on whether the trial court abused its discretion in failing to apply these principles first announced today to these Relators, who never petitioned the trial court for this relief but consciously chose to sit, watch and complain later to this court when dissatisfied with the result he reached. * * * *

HIGHTOWER, J., dissenting, joined by Gammage, J.

The court should have denied mandamus relief because relators purposefully chose to not seek their legal remedy of intervention and appeal. Since mandamus relief does not lie, this court should not have reached the merits of the trial court judgments. On reaching the merits, the court should have concluded the judgments are not void. The trial court, if it conducts further proceedings and approves an agreed interim redistricting plan, should protect the public interest by considering the factors identified in the plurality opinion. If the court fails to do so, its judgment is voidable. The plurality opinion, however, may serve to confuse the trial court because it does not clearly state the weight to be given competing interests. The court errs in issuing the writ of mandamus in this proceeding, and compounds its error through opinions the trial court may well have difficulty following.

Notes on the Redistricting Roles of Texas Governmental Departments

Apportionment Responsibilities of the State Legislature, Executive, and Judiciary: The *Terrazas* plurality detailed the role of each governmental department in legislative apportionment in Texas. First, the primary constitutional responsibility belongs to the legislature, or, if the legislature does not act timely, the legislative redistricting board. In any state court challenges to the adopted apportionment plan, the attorney general represents the state in litigation and has broad authority to negotiate and propose settlements, like any other attorney. But a substitute redistricting plan may only be imposed by court order, and the court must act with due deference to the legislative will and a careful consideration of the many, diverse interests affected by redistricting. Because these standards had not been satisfied, *Terrazas* invalidated the state trial court's rendition of a judgment creating a new state redistricting scheme based on a settlement agreement between a handful of Texas citizens and a few state defendants that terminated ongoing litigation.

The Settlement Authority of the Texas Attorney General: Another case addressing the authority of the Texas Attorney General, this time his authority to settle federal voting rights litigation against the state, was the Fifth Circuit's decision in *League of United Latin American Citizens, Council No. 4434 v. Clements*.[208] Ten individual voters and the League of United Latin American Voters sued alleging that Texas's system of electing state trial judges countywide violated the Voting Rights Act. Toward the end of a lengthy litigation process, Attorney General Dan Morales entered into a consent agreement with the plaintiffs which he requested the court to enforce despite the objections of many of the named state defendants. The Fifth Circuit held that, while *Terrazas* established that the attorney general's power to settle a case was "certainly no less than that of other lawyers," it also was not any greater, precluding him from forging "a settlement agreement over the express objection of his client."[209] As a result, the court refused to enforce the consent decree when certain of the "State's policymakers" were opposed.[210]

Mid-Decade Redistricting: *Terrazas* addressed another important state constitutional issue of first impression: whether the legislature has the authority to enact state legislative apportionment plans later than the constitutionally-specified first regular session after the United States census. The court reasoned that nothing prohibited the legislature from acting after the first regular session once the constitutional authority of the legislative redistricting board expired. Was the court's holding limited to those situations in which the initial plan is being challenged in court, or can the legislature redistrict as often as it desires?

In the millennial decade, the state judicial challenges shifted from state legislative apportionment to congressional redistricting. The 2000 census entitled Texas to two additional members of Congress, mandating that the state's congressional districts had to be redrawn. However, the 2001 Texas Legislature did not redraw the districts before its adjournment. Because the powers of the legislative redistricting board only apply to state

---

[208] 999 F.2d 831 (5th Cir. 1993) (en banc).

[209] *Id.* at 842.

[210] *Id.* at 840.

senatorial and representative districts, the matter had to be settled by the courts. In such a situation, the federal courts must defer to the state courts, but can set a deadline for final action by the state court system.[211]

Several state court actions were filed in Travis County and Harris County, by persons identified with the Democratic Party and Republican Party, respectively. Four of these cases were set for trial on the same day, two in Travis County and two in Harris County. The parties sought review by the Texas Supreme Court to determine which case had dominant jurisdiction, and the court determined that the Travis County case filed immediately after the legislature adjourned had dominant jurisdiction because it was the first case that was ripe when filed.[212] Afterwards, the Travis County district court rendered judgment outlining a new redistricting plan. But another appeal was taken to the Texas Supreme Court.

Perry v. Del Rio, 67 S.W.3d 85 (Tex. 2001)

Justice BAKER delivered the opinion of the Court, in which Justice ENOCH, Justice O'NEILL, Justice JEFFERSON, and Justice RODRIGUEZ joined.

This matter is yet another chapter in the 2000 congressional redistricting controversy. Governor Rick Perry and former Secretary of State Henry Cuellar (the State defendants), Susan Weddington, several congressional members, the Associated Republicans of Texas, and Charles Babb directly appeal the final judgment from a bench trial held in Travis County, Texas. We determine two issues:

- Does the Attorney General, under the separation-of-powers doctrine, have the authority to require the trial court to adopt his redistricting plan and render judgment that his plan is the baseline state court plan for the federal court redistricting proceedings?

- Did the trial court violate the parties' due course of law rights when it rendered a judgment based on a party's new plans not in evidence at trial without giving the parties an opportunity for a meaningful hearing?

We conclude that the Attorney General's assertion that he speaks for the Legislature and thus the trial court must adopt his plan violates the separation-of-powers doctrine. Moreover, under the facts here, we conclude that the manner in which the trial court rendered its judgment violated the parties' due course of law rights. Accordingly, we vacate the trial court's October 10, 2001 judgment and remand the case to the trial court for proceedings consistent with this opinion.

I. BACKGROUND

On September 10, 2001, this Court determined that the Travis County trial court had dominant jurisdiction to hear the plaintiffs' claims that, under the 2000 census, the existing

---

[211] *See, e.g.,* Growe v. Emison, 507 U.S. 25, 35-37 (1993).

[212] Perry v. Del Rio, 66 S.W.3d 239, 256 (Tex. 2001).

Texas congressional districts are unconstitutional and that the trial court must adopt a new redistricting plan. *Perry et al. v. Del Rio et al.*, 66 S.W.3d 239. Following our decision, the Travis County trial court set the case for trial beginning September 17, 2001. The trial court received evidence and heard testimony and arguments from all the parties about the various proposed congressional redistricting plans they urged the trial court to adopt. On September 28, 2001, the parties rested, closed, and presented arguments to the trial court.

On October 1, 2001, the trial court notified the parties that it was, on its own motion, appointing the Texas Legislative Council to act as the trial court's expert in deciding the issues in this case. The trial court issued an order to this effect and required the Texas Legislative Council's staff to maintain as confidential the trial court's dealings and communications with the staff. The State defendants objected to this order. They argued that not only was the trial court's order impermissible under the Texas Rules of Civil Procedure, but it also created a conflict of interest because the Texas Legislative Council's staff are the Lieutenant Governor's and Speaker of the House's employees.

Two days later, on October 3, 2001, the trial court entered an order announcing its intent to adopt Plan 1065C for Texas' congressional districts. The trial court attached Plan 1065C to the order and identified an Internet site where the parties could view the plan. Further, the trial court invited all parties to file comments, proposed changes, or requested modifications to this plan by October 9, 2001. The trial court also stated that it was preparing findings of fact and conclusions of law.

On October 9, 2001, the Democratic Congressional Interveners and the Del Rio and Cotera Plaintiffs filed objections to Plan 1065C. On that same day, Speaker Laney submitted proposed modifications to Plan 1065C and requested that the trial court incorporate his proposed new plans, different from those he offered during the trial, into Plan 1065C.

Sometime after 10:00 a.m. on October 10, 2001, the trial court notified the parties by facsimile that it was "seriously considering" adopting several changes Speaker Laney proposed. The trial court briefly explained the changes it was considering making to Plan 1065C and asked the parties to submit comments on these proposed changes by noon that day. Unlike its previous order identifying Plan 1065C as the proposed plan, the trial court did not attach a map showing what the new proposed plan looked like. Also, it did not refer the parties to an Internet site where they could view the plan.

Later that day, the trial court rendered its final judgment. And, rather than adopting Plan 1065C, the trial court adopted a new plan designated Plan 1089C. The trial court's judgment states that Plan 1089C incorporates certain proposals the parties submitted. Moreover, the trial court's judgment permanently enjoins further use of the existing thirty Texas congressional districts in any primary or general election.

* * * *

A. Separation of Powers

The Legislature is the department constitutionally responsible for apportioning the State into federal congressional legislative districts. U.S. Const. amend. XIV, § 2; Tex. Const. art. III, § 28; *Wise v. Lipscomb*, 437 U.S. 535, 539 (1978). When the Legislature does not act, citizens may sue and, then, it is the judiciary's role to determine the appropriate redistricting plan. *See Terrazas*, 829 S.W.2d at 717-20.

Because of our Constitution's explicit prohibition against one government branch exercising a power attached to another, unless specific circumstances exist, "it is only by *express* constitutional provision that the executive department could legitimately exercise the redistricting power." *Terrazas*, 829 S.W.2d at 733 (Cornyn J., concurring) (emphasis in original). This is because "[t]he powers conferred by the Constitution upon the state officials are generally held to be exclusive, and except in the manner authorized by the Constitution, these powers cannot be enlarged or restricted." *Garcia v. Laughlin*, 285 S.W.2d 191, 194 (Tex. 1955).

The Attorney General is a member of the Executive Department whose primary duties are to render legal advice in opinions to various political agencies and to represent the State in civil litigation. *See* TEX. CONST. art. IV, §§ 1, 22; TEX. GOV'T CODE § 402.021. We have recognized that the Attorney General, as the State's chief legal officer, has broad discretionary power in carrying out his responsibility to represent the State. *Terrazas*, 829 S.W.2d at 722. But we have held that this power does not permit the Attorney General "to effectuate a valid reapportionment of senatorial districts himself," because only the trial court's judgment can accomplish this when the Legislature fails to act. *Terrazas*, 829 S.W.2d at 722. This is because the Attorney General can only act within the limits of the Texas Constitution and statutes, and courts cannot enlarge the Attorney General's powers. *Terrazas*, 829 S.W.2d at 735 (Cornyn, J., concurring).

* * * *

We disagree with the State defendants' argument that the trial court violated our separation-of-powers doctrine when it did not defer to, or adopt, the redistricting plan the Attorney General proposed during the trial. To the contrary, it is the Attorney General's position—that in congressional redistricting controversies he steps into the Legislature's shoes if the Legislature does not act—that violates the separation-of-powers doctrine.

To accept the State defendants' position that the Attorney General becomes the Legislature's voice when the Legislature fails to act would condone a constitutional violation. *See* TEX. CONST. art. II, § 1 (no branch of government "shall exercise any power properly attached to either of the others, except in the instances herein [the Constitution] expressly permitted."). As a member of the executive branch, the Attorney General may not perform legislative functions unless expressly authorized to do so. *See* TEX. CONST. art. II, § 1; *Garcia*, 285 S.W.2d at 194-95; *Terrazas*, 829 S.W.2d at 733 (Cornyn, J., concurring). Neither our Constitution nor Chapter 402 of the Government Code expressly authorizes the Attorney General's position here. *See* TEX. CONST. art. IV, §§ 1, 22; TEX. GOV'T CODE § 402.021. And the State defendants provide us with no other authority giving the Attorney General the Legislature's power to resolve the congressional redistricting controversy. As we stated in *Terrazas*, under these circumstances, only courts have the authority to effectuate a valid congressional reapportionment plan unless or until the Legislature acts.

Accordingly, we agree with Speaker Laney's and the Plaintiffs' contentions that the Attorney General does not have the authority to act in the Legislature's stead and dictate the remedy in a congressional redistricting case.

B. Due Course of Law

We agree with Weddington, ART, and Babb that the manner in which the trial court arrived at its October 10 final judgment violated our Constitution's due course of law provision. For all we know, the redistricting plan could very well dictate our State's congressional elections for the next decade. Court-ordered redistricting cases require close scrutiny of several important factors and interests, including: compactness, regularity, contiguity, preservation of communities of interest, equal protection, and the integrity of natural and traditional county and city boundaries. *See generally Bush v. Vera*, 517 U.S. 952 (1996). Therefore, it is imperative in these cases that a court's procedures protect all interests involved.

Indeed, we have recognized that court-ordered redistricting could affect not only the parties to the litigation but also others in our State who should have the opportunity to intervene and be heard. *Terrazas*, 829 S.W.2d at 726. Also, we have recognized that courts in these cases must take careful consideration of the many, diverse interests affected. *Terrazas*, 829 S.W.2d at 718.

Undoubtedly, redistricting will impact nearly all Texas voters, because it will determine who they choose to represent their interests in Congress. Furthermore, there is a significant risk that all Texas citizens' interests may not be protected in redistricting litigation. This is why a court cannot order a reapportionment plan for the State based upon nothing more than an agreement between the Governor, the Attorney General, and a few citizens. *See Terrazas*, 829 S.W.2d at 714. And this is why we have held that, in redistricting cases, Texas courts may order apportionment only after investigation and careful consideration of all diverse interests affected. *Terrazas*, 829 S.W.2d at 718.

The unique circumstances and constitutionally protected interests involved in court-ordered redistricting cases require that, before entering its final judgment on a redistricting plan, a trial court must afford all the parties a meaningful hearing. This does not unduly burden our courts; it is simply what our Constitution and the state-wide interests a court-ordered redistricting case affects require.

Here, the manner in which the trial court entered its final judgment did not comport with *Terrazas* and violated the parties' due course of law rights. On October 3, 2001, the trial court advised the parties that it intended to adopt Plan 1065C and gave the parties a meaningful period of time to comment on this plan. To this point, the trial court provided an adequate procedure by which it could give full and careful consideration to the interests its ruling may affect.

In its October 10 mid-morning facsimile to the parties, the trial court set a noon deadline for any party to comment on Plan 1089C, a plan significantly different than the plan the trial court originally proposed to adopt. The trial court's facsimile made clear that it would not entertain any comments received after noon because the Tyler federal court's filing deadline was 5:00 p.m. Thus, the parties not only had little time to object to the new changes, they were deprived of a meaningful opportunity to present a motion for new trial. Once the trial court determined that it intended to substantially change its proposed redistricting plan, the constitutionally-protected interests involved, *Terrazas*, and our

Constitution's due course of law provision required the trial court to provide the parties a meaningful opportunity to be heard.

We do not mean to suggest that a trial court cannot make de minimis changes to its proposed redistricting plan without reopening the evidence. The proceedings must end at some point. But, here, the trial court's changes to Plan 1065C were extensive and significant—not de minimis. As the Tyler court noted in its October 11, 2001 order, the trial court made "major changes" to its initially proposed plan. Because the trial court did not provide the necessary due course of law when it made these wholesale changes, its October 10, 2001, judgment violated the parties' due course of law rights and therefore is invalid.

Justice OWEN, concurring.

I join in the Court's decision to remand this case and its analysis of the due process issue and the scope of the Attorney General's authority. But this Court should give guidance and instructions to the trial court on the substantive law that should govern the selection of a plan on remand if the case is to proceed. The modifications to Plan 1065C that led to Plan 1089C were based in part, if not in whole, on political considerations, including incumbent protection. I would remand this case with directions to the trial court that it cannot consider political factors.

Justice RODRIGUEZ, joined by Justice ENOCH and Justice JEFFERSON, concurring.

I join fully in the Court's opinion, but I write separately because I share the concerns raised by JUSTICE HECHT in Part II(B) of his opinion regarding the propriety of the trial court's consideration of incumbency protection issues in formulating its plan. The changes asked for by Speaker Laney and ultimately adopted by the trial court in plan 1089C, while not couched in terms of incumbent protection, are not so distinct from incumbent protection as to escape suspicion. And I would caution on remand that the trial court may not consider incumbent protection in drawing Congressional district lines.

That the trial court used incumbent protection as a factor in drawing the district lines for plan 1089C is an issue raised by the Attorney General in his Appellant's Brief and by others. I believe it is appropriate for this Court to provide guidance to the trial court on this issue on remand. *See, e.g., Dallas Mkt. Ctr. Dev. Co. v. Liedeker*, 958 S.W.2d 382, 385 (Tex.1997) (considering an issue raised by a party to provide guidance to the district court on remand); *Edinburg Hosp. Auth. v. Trevino*, 941 S.W.2d 76, 81 (Tex.1997) (considering an issue "not essential to [the Court's] disposition of th[e] case . . . to provide the trial court with guidance in the retrial of [the] case").

Justice HECHT, dissenting.

In my view: the Court's remand to the district court is essentially pointless because the state judiciary is not prepared to adopt a congressional redistricting plan in time to avoid disrupting the 2002 elections, and under the United States Supreme Court's decision in *Growe v. Emison*, the litigation should now shift once and for all to the federal court; and judgment should instead be rendered adopting Plan 1065C, in accordance with the district court's stated intention, because the only objections to that plan, and all of the changes the court made to it, were based on an improper consideration—the protection of incumbents. Therefore I respectfully dissent.

[The dissenting opinion of Chief Justice Phillips, joined by Justice Hankinson, has been omitted].

Notes on State and Federal Judicial Review of Apportionment

State Judicial Review of Congressional Redistricting: Because the legislature had not acted on federal congressional redistricting during its 2001 session, the courts had to undertake the task. In this situation, state courts have the first opportunity to draw the districts, with parallel litigation typically pending in federal court. In *Perry*, the Travis County state district court, after announcing an intent to adopt one redistricting plan a week earlier, rendered judgment on a new plan with only hours of notice given to the parties. The aggrieved parties filed a direct appeal with the Texas Supreme Court, arguing (1) that the state trial court should have used the plan proposed by the state attorney general, and (2) that the notice provided violated the state due course of law guarantee.

In rejecting the claim that the state court should have deferred to the plan submitted by the attorney general, *Perry* quoted extensively from then-Justice Cornyn's concurrence in *Terrazas* regarding the powers of the Texas Attorney General. At first blush, this is somewhat surprising as Justice Cornyn's *Terrazas* opinion, while concurring in the court's judgment, disagreed with the majority of the court on the scope of the attorney general's power. Between *Terrazas* and *Perry*, though, Justice Cornyn had become Texas Attorney General Cornyn. Was it appropriate for the court to employ against General Cornyn a position he expressed in an opinion that did not command a court majority when he was Justice Cornyn?

The Texas Supreme Court proceeded to invalidate the trial court's congressional redistricting plan under the alternative argument, that the court had not provided interested parties a sufficient opportunity to present objections before it adopted a scheme favored by the Speaker of the House. When the legislature has been unable to adopt an apportionment plan, the court reasoned, the judiciary must closely scrutinize factors such as compactness, regularity, contiguity, local boundaries, and compliance with federal law before adopting a scheme. The judiciary should not, however, consider purely political considerations, such as incumbency protection. According to some of the separate writings in *Perry*, Speaker Laney's and others' objections to the trial court's initial plan were predicated on prohibited judicial redistricting considerations regarding incumbency protection. The majority did not reach this issue, instead merely remanding the case back to the trial court for further proceedings over Justice Hecht's complaint that the remand was pointless.

Federal Judicial Review and Further Legislative Action: Justice Hecht correctly prophesied that the state courts would not be able to adopt a redistricting plan in time. As a result, the litigation then shifted to the three-judge federal district court in Tyler, which created a redistricting plan for Texas, employing neutral, non-political factors to make the necessary changes to the existing apportionment plan from the prior decade (which had been drawn by and favored Democrats). This federal court apportionment plan governed the 2002 congressional elections, and resulted in the election of seventeen Democrats and fifteen Republicans to the House, despite the fact that a solid majority (nearly sixty percent) of Texans voted Republican in statewide races that year.

In 2003, the Texas Legislature revisited the redistricting issue that it was unable to accomplish during the 2001 session. After a great deal of political maneuvering, including both the Texas Senate and House Democrats fleeing the state at separate times to deny the quorum required for legislative action,[213] and the lieutenant governor suspending the operation of a senate rule requiring a two-thirds supermajority, the legislature passed a new congressional redistricting plan in a third special legislative session. Senior officials at the Justice Department then precleared the plan despite an initial determination by Justice Department staff lawyers that the new plan violated the Voting Rights Act.[214]

This new congressional redistricting plan was then challenged in federal court under a variety of grounds, including that the state could not redistrict mid-decade, the plan unconstitutionally discriminated on the basis of race, the plan was an unconstitutional partisan gerrymander, and minority voting strength was unlawfully diluted in certain districts in violation of the Voting Rights Act. A three-judge district court upheld the plan, but its decision was vacated and remanded in light of the Supreme Court's decision in *Vieth v Jubelirer* that it was possible at some point that a political gerrymander would violate the Equal Protection Clause.[215] On remand, the three-judge district court again affirmed the plan, concluding that the claims of excessive partisanship in the redistricting process "suffer from a lack of any measure of substantive fairness."[216]

The three-judge court's judgment was then appealed to the United States Supreme Court, which upheld most of the plan in *League of United Latin American Citizens v. Perry*.[217] The Supreme Court invalidated one of the congressional districts in the plan, holding that it impermissibly diluted minority voting rights under the Voting Rights Act, but otherwise affirmed.[218] The Supreme Court's invalidation of this district eventually required modifications to be made to five congressional districts to remedy the statutory violation.[219]

The final congressional lines for the millennial decade, then, were not completed until the 2006 election, six years after the census. A similar delay appears to be underway again for redistricting after the 2010 census. Once the Texas Legislature adopted redistricting plans during its 2011 legislative session for Congress and the state house and

---

[213]TEX. CONST. art. III, § 10 ("Two-thirds of each House shall constitute a quorum to do business, but a smaller number may adjourn from day to day, and compel the attendance of absent members, in such manner and under such penalties as each House may provide.").

[214]Dan Eggen, *Justice Staff Saw Texas Districting as Illegal*, WASH. POST, Dec. 2, 2005, at A1.

[215]Session v. Perry, 298 F. Supp. 2d 451 (E.D. Tex. 2004), *vacated sub nom.* Henderson v. Perry, 543 U.S. 941 (2004) (vacating judgment for further consideration in light of *Vieth v. Jubelirer*, 541 U.S. 267 (2004)).

[216]Henderson v. Perry, 399 F. Supp. 2d 756, 758 (E.D. Tex. 2005).

[217]548 U.S. 399 (2006).

[218]*Id.* at 442-47.

[219]League of United Latin Am. Citizens v. Perry, 457 F. Supp. 2d 716, 721 (E.D. Tex. 2006).

senate, these plans were challenged in federal court under the Voting Rights Act. These challenges led the federal court to order interim plans that were employed for the 2012 election cycle. The legislature then proceeded during its 2013 session to adopt by statute these court-ordered interim plans for Congress and the senate, while enacting an amended version of the court-ordered plan for the house. Although these 2013 legislative plans will be used for elections in 2014, ongoing challenges to the congressional and state house plans are pending in federal court and are unlikely to be resolved before 2015. To avoid such litigation, would it be better to have a nonpartisan commission draw district lines after a census? Or is it practically impossible to remove politics from the apportionment process?

CHAPTER 7 EXERCISES AND PROBLEMS

1. Article XVI, section 59 of the Texas Constitution authorizes the legislature to create conservation and reclamation districts throughout the state, but requires that before such a bill can be introduced, notice must be given in the newspapers having a general circulation in the affected areas and a copy of the proposed bill must be delivered to the commissioners court of each county and the governing board of each city or town within the district's boundaries. This provides the affected citizens, counties, and cities an opportunity to voice objections and lobby against the creation of the district. If the legislature specifies in a properly enrolled bill, signed by the presiding legislative officers and the governor, that the required newspaper notice and the copies of the bill have been furnished to necessary persons and entities as required by law, can the statute be challenged on the basis that the required notice was not in fact given? What are the arguments for and against employing the enrolled bill doctrine under these circumstances? *Compare Save Our Springs Alliance, Inc. v. Lazy Nine Mun. Util. Dist.*, 198 S.W.3d 300 (Tex. App.–Texarkana 2006, pet. denied).

2. In 2003, the Texas Legislature enacted House Bill 7, which was entitled "An act relating to the reorganization of, efficiency in, and other reform measures applying to governmental entities and certain regulatory practices; providing a penalty." The act's thirty-three substantive articles, which impact approximately forty chapters of at least twelve separate legislative codes, include provisions on such diverse topics as alcoholic beverage permits for sexually oriented businesses in dry counties, the treatment of unclaimed wages under the unclaimed property statute, the content of solid waste management plans, the membership of the State Boards of Pardons and Paroles, extensions of eligibility for state employee benefits, authorization for the Legislative Budget Board to have telephonic meetings, the role of state officials in overseeing regional planning commissions, training requirements for the Insurance Commissioner, and authorization for the City of Austin to sell small tracts of land, to name a few. What are the arguments that House Bill 7 violates the single subject requirement? What are the arguments that it does not? *Compare Tex. Alcoholic Beverage Comm'n v. Silver City Club*, 315 S.W.3d 643 (Tex. App.–Dallas 2010, pet. denied).

3. What are the arguments for and against a special law challenge under the Texas Constitution to the law challenged in *Robinson v. Crown Cork*, discussed in Chapter 5?

Chapter 8

EXECUTIVE POWER

Under Article II of the United States Constitution, the federal executive power is vested in the President of the United States of America.[1] The only other federal executive officer named in the U.S. Constitution is the Vice President, whose constitutional duties are presiding over the Senate, succeeding to the presidency upon the death, removal, or resignation of the President, and acting as President if the President is unable to discharge the office's powers and duties.[2] The vesting of the federal executive power in a single office has led to the common understanding that the President has at least some measure of executive authority outside the powers specifically enumerated in the Constitution or delegated to the executive by Congress.[3]

But the structure of the executive branch and the allocation of executive authority is much different in state constitutions. While the executive structure of each of the fifty states is somewhat unique, state constitutions typically create several executive offices in addition to the governor and lieutenant governor.[4] In all but a handful of states, four or more of these executive officials are independently elected.[5] While many states still nevertheless vest the "supreme executive power" in the governor, this allocation of authority must be interpreted in light of the specific constitutional powers and duties assigned to the other various executive officers created by the state constitution.[6] Moreover, a couple of states that independently elect a plural executive do not "vest" supreme executive authority in a single office, but instead specifically allocate and divide executive powers among the various executive offices.[7]

Texas is one of these latter states. Article IV, section 1 of the Texas Constitution provides that the state's executive department shall consist of the governor, lieutenant governor, secretary of state, comptroller of public accounts, land commissioner, and attorney

---

[1]U.S. CONST. art. II, § 1.

[2]U.S. CONST. art. I, § 3; art. II, § 1; amends. XII & XXV.

[3]*See, e.g.*, Free Enter. Fund v. Pub. Co. Accounting Oversight Bd., 130 S. Ct. 3138, 3151-52 (2010) (citing the vesting clause in support of the proposition that the President is empowered to keep executive officers accountable, including by removing them from office); Nixon v. Fitzgerald, 457 U.S. 731, 749-54 (1982) (citing the vesting clause as supporting the President's absolute immunity from civil lawsuits for official acts).

[4]*See* THE COUNCIL OF STATE GOVERNMENTS, THE BOOK OF THE STATES 231-36 (2012).

[5]*See id.* The states that elect less than four executive officials are often operating under more recent state constitutions. *See, e.g.*, ALASKA CONST. art. III, §§ 3, 8 (effective 1959); HAW. CONST. art. V, § 6 (effective 1959); N.J. CONST. art. V, § 4 (ratified 1947).

[6]*See, e.g.*, ALA. CONST. art. V, §§ 112-14; ARK. CONST. art. VI, §§ 1-2; CAL. CONST. art. V, §§ 1, 11; COLO. CONST. art. IV, §§ 1-2; CONN. CONST. art. IV, §§ 1, 5; FLA. CONST. art. IV, §§ 1-5; ILL. CONST. art. V, §§ 8, 15-18; OHIO CONST. art. III, §§ 1, 5; OKLA. CONST. art. VI, §§ 1-2; PA. CONST. art. IV, §§ 1-2; WASH. CONST. art. III, §§ 1-2.

[7]*See, e.g.*, VT. CONST. ch. II.

general.[8] While section 1 describes the governor as "the Chief Executive Officer of the State,"[9] the Texas Constitution no longer contains a clause vesting the "supreme executive power" of the state in the governor as did the Texas Constitutions of 1845, 1861, and 1866.[10] Instead, article IV divides and allocates executive authority among all these members of the executive department. Section 2 specifies that separate elections are to be held for each of these offices, with the exception of the secretary of state,[11] who is appointed by the governor with the advice and consent of the state senate.[12] This "long ballot" for the executive department weakens the governor's power as the other members of the department are not subject to his or her direct control.

As a result of this plural executive, Texas courts have held that the governor does not possess inherent executive power. For example, in *Day Land & Cattle Co. v. State*, the court rejected the argument that the general powers of the governor of the state as chief executive officer granted him the power to require the attorney general to institute a legal proceeding when in his judgment the welfare of the state required it.[13] The court reasoned that "in a government in which the duties of all officers, as well as their powers, are defined by written law, no power ought to be exercised for which warrant is not there found."[14] Thus, the exercise of executive authority in Texas is limited to those powers granted either through the state constitution or state legislation enacted by the people's representatives to each member of the executive branch.

The powers of the Texas Governor, then, must be addressed in conjunction with the following constitutional and statutory duties assigned to the other executive offices in Texas:

Lieutenant Governor: The Texas Lieutenant Governor is both an executive officer and a legislative officer.[15] The lieutenant governor is elected at the same time for the same four-year term as the governor, and must meet all constitutional qualifications to be governor.[16] Under the Texas Constitution, the lieutenant governor is the acting governor during any temporary period when the governor is unable to serve, is absent from the state, or is impeached and then acquitted.[17] The lieutenant governor is also the successor to the

---

[8]TEX. CONST. art. IV, § 1.

[9]*Id.*

[10]1 GEORGE D. BRADEN ET AL., THE CONSTITUTION OF THE STATE OF TEXAS: AN ANNOTATED AND COMPARATIVE ANALYSIS 301 (1977).

[11]TEX. CONST. art. IV, § 2.

[12]TEX. CONST. art. IV, § 21.

[13]4 S.W. 865, 867 (Tex. 1887).

[14]*Id.*

[15]*In re* Tex. Senate, 36 S.W.3d 119, 120 (Tex. 2000) (noting the dual constitutional roles of the lieutenant governor).

[16]TEX. CONST. art. IV, § 16(a). The lieutenant governor and governor must be at least thirty years of age, be a United States citizen, and have resided in Texas for the five years preceding the election. TEX. CONST. art. IV, § 4. Both the lieutenant governor and the governor are elected for four-year terms in between elections for the President of the United States. *See id.*

[17]TEX. CONST. art. IV, § 16(c).

governorship if it becomes vacant for any reason.[18] In addition, the lieutenant governor is a member of the legislative redistricting board and certain executive branch agencies.[19]

Yet the real powers of the lieutenant governor stem from his or her constitutional position as the presiding officer and president of the Texas Senate,[20] a position which is granted immense power under Texas law and typical senate rules. The Texas Constitution empowers the lieutenant governor both to vote on all questions when the senate is in the committee of the whole and to cast the deciding vote when the senate is equally divided.[21] Thus, a lieutenant governor can use his or her vote to create a tie in the committee of the whole, and then use the power to cast deciding votes to kill a motion that would have passed in his or her absence by one vote.[22] In addition, state law provides that the lieutenant governor is a member of several key legislative boards, including co-chairing the legislative budget board that initially proposes the biennial state budget and the legislative council that provides bill drafting, computing, and research services to the Texas Legislature.[23] Finally, the rules the senate adopts to govern its proceedings at the beginning of each legislative session have granted the lieutenant governor numerous other important legislative powers, including the power to appoint the membership of senate committees, refer bills to senate committees, guide the debate and agenda of the senate, and decide all parliamentary questions and the order in which bills are considered.[24] Primarily as a result of these legislative powers, the lieutenant governorship is sometimes described as the most powerful political office in the state.[25]

Attorney General: The attorney general's constitutional obligations include representing the state in legal proceedings, supervising charter rights of private corporations and instituting appropriate legal actions, and providing legal advice to the governor and

---

[18]TEX. CONST. art. IV, § 16(d).

[19]*See, e.g.*, TEX. CONST. art. III, § 28 (legislative redistricting board); TEX. GOV'T CODE § 404.122 (cash management committee); TEX. GOV'T CODE § 1231.021 (bond review board).

[20]TEX. CONST. art. IV, § 16(b); *accord In re* Tex. Senate, 36 S.W.3d at 120 (holding that the lieutenant governor is a senate officer).

[21]TEX. CONST. art. IV, § 16(b). In contrast, the Vice President of the United States may only vote in case the United States Senate is equally divided. U.S. CONST. art. I, § 3 ("The Vice President of the United States shall be President of the Senate, but shall have no Vote, unless they be equally divided.").

[22]*See, e.g.*, 32 S.J. Reg. 938-39 (1911) (documenting Lieutenant Governor A.B. Davidson's "nay" vote on a motion that caused a 15-15 tie in the senate, which he then broke by casting the deciding vote to kill the motion).

[23]*See* TEX. GOV'T CODE § 322.001 (establishing lieutenant governor as joint chair of Legislative Budget Board with the power to appoint three senators to the board); TEX. GOV'T CODE § 323.001 (providing lieutenant governor is co-chair of the Texas Legislative Council with the power to appoint six senators to the council). The lieutenant governor is also the co-chair of the legislative audit committee. *See* TEX. GOV'T CODE § 321.002.

[24]*See, e.g.*, Rules of Senate of the 82nd Texas Legislature, Rules 1.01, 5.15, 7.06, 11.01-.04, 12.01 & 20.01. Article III, section 11 of the Texas Constitution grants the state senate the power to write its own rules, which it does at the beginning of each new legislative session. As a result, these rule-based powers of the lieutenant governor are subject to modification by the Texas Senate through its internal procedures for adopting and amending its rules.

[25]*See, e.g.*, JANICE C. MAY, THE TEXAS STATE CONSTITUTION, A REFERENCE GUIDE 194 (1995); Kathleen Sylvester, *Lieutenant Governors: Giving up Real Power for Real Opportunity*, 2 GOVERNING 46 (Feb. 1989).

other executive officers.[26] The attorney general, like the other elected state executive officers, serves a four-year term,[27] and is obligated to perform other duties assigned by law.

The primary constitutional powers of the attorney general have been considered in prior chapters in this book. As discussed in Chapter 7, the attorney general has essentially the same power to represent his or her client (which is the state) as other lawyers do. The attorney general's power does not usually exceed that of other attorneys, as the judiciary is not bound by his or her agreements to settle litigation nor can the attorney general settle cases against the will of named state parties.[28] Yet the attorney general's power to represent the state does contain one unique facet: the attorney general's office, unlike a private law firm, can represent state agencies on opposing sides in the same lawsuit.[29]

As discussed in Chapter 3, the attorney general, rather than the judiciary, is given the constitutional power to provide advisory opinions to Texas officials on legal issues.[30] The Government Code specifies the state and local officials who are authorized to request formal attorney general opinions on legal questions regarding the meaning of existing laws.[31] When the attorney general is requested to write such an opinion, a group of assistant attorneys general known as the opinions committee researches the questions, solicits briefs from persons and groups likely to be affected, and then drafts an opinion which is reviewed by the attorney general and the first assistant attorney general before being issued under the attorney general's signature.

Comptroller: The comptroller is to "perform such duties as are or may be required by law,"[32] which predominantly revolve around the constitutional duties to submit a verified statement to the legislature and governor of the financial condition of the state and to review all appropriation bills to ensure that the amount appropriated is within the state's estimated revenues.[33] Before each regular legislative session, the comptroller reports on the state's current financial situation and forthcoming expected state revenues. The legislature is prohibited from sending any appropriations bill to the governor until the comptroller certifies that the appropriated amounts fall within the comptroller's estimate of available funds. If the comptroller finds that the appropriation exceeds estimated revenue, the Texas

---

[26]TEX. CONST. art. IV, § 22.

[27]TEX. CONST. art. IV, § 23.

[28]*See, e.g.*, League of United Latin Am. Citizens, Council No. 4434 v. Clements, 999 F.2d 831, 840-42 (5th Cir. 1993) (en banc); Perry v. Del Rio, 67 S.W.3d 85 (Tex. 2001); Terrazas v. Ramirez, 829 S.W.2d 712 (Tex. 1991).

[29]*See* Pub. Util. Comm'n v. Cofer, 754 S.W.2d 121, 124-25 (Tex. 1988). Most other states likewise allow the attorney general's office to appear on opposite sides in cases involving state parties. *See* William P. Marshall, *Break up the Presidency? Governors, State Attorneys General, and the Lessons from the Divided Executive*, 115 YALE L.J. 2446, 2463 (2006).

[30]*See* Morrow v. Corbin, 62 S.W.2d 641 (Tex. 1933).

[31]*See, e.g.*, TEX. GOV'T CODE § 402.043.

[32]TEX. CONST. art. IV, § 23.

[33]TEX. CONST. art. III, § 49a.

Constitution requires that the Texas House and Senate must fix the deficiency in the bill by either providing additional revenue or reducing the appropriation.[34]

Land Commissioner: The land commissioner heads the state's constitutionally created General Land Office, which registers "all land titles which have emanated or may hereafter emanate from the State."[35] The land commissioner is also to perform any other duties required by law. The land commissioner is also a member, along with the comptroller, attorney general, and lieutenant governor, on the legislative redistricting board discussed in Chapter 7.[36]

Secretary of State: The secretary of state is the one constitutional executive official appointed by the governor, with the advice and consent of the senate.[37] The secretary of state authenticates the publication of the laws, records all official acts and proceedings of the governor, keeps and uses the state seal under the direction of the governor, attests all state commissions signed by the governor, and performs certain duties directed by the legislature and the governor, especially with regard to the office's statutory position as the chief election officer of the state.[38]

Governor: While the governor is the "Chief Executive Office of the State," the governor's constitutional power over the other elected executive officials and the performance of their duties is limited to requiring reports from them regarding their budgets and the management of their offices.[39] The Texas Constitution does, however, grant several important explicit powers to the governor. The governor, who must be at least a thirty-year old United States citizen residing in Texas for the last five years, is elected to a four-year term in between national presidential elections.[40] Once elected, the governor becomes the commander-in-chief of the state's military forces and is charged with the duties to ensure that the laws are faithfully executed and to provide a biennial state of the state message to the legislature.[41] The governor also may convene thirty-day special legislative sessions, which are limited to legislating upon those subjects designated by the governor.[42] The governor is also immune from mandamus issued by any court, unlike the other constitutional

---

[34]*Id.*

[35]TEX. CONST. art. XIV, § 1.

[36]TEX. CONST. art. III, § 28. The other member is the Speaker of the House. *See id.*

[37]TEX. CONST. art. IV, § 21.

[38]TEX. CONST. art. IV, §§ 2, 19-21. The statutory duties of the secretary of state as the state's chief election officer are discussed in chapter 31 of the Texas Election Code. *See* TEX. ELEC. CODE § 31.001 *et seq.*

[39]TEX. CONST. art. IV, § 24.

[40]TEX. CONST. art. IV, § 4.

[41]TEX. CONST. art. IV, §§ 7, 10.

[42]TEX. CONST. art. III, § 40; art. IV, § 8. Although the legislature may be limited to *legislating* on the subjects designated by the governor, the legislature may consider non-legislative matters, including conducting impeachment trials, *see* Ferguson v. Maddox, 263 S.W. 888, 891 (Tex. 1924), establishing a study committee, *see* Tex. Att'y Gen. Op. No. M-309 (1968), petitioning Congress to propose an amendment to the United States Constitution, *see* Tex. Att'y Gen. Op. No. M-1167 (1972), proposing state constitutional amendments, *see* TEX. CONST. art. XVII, § 1, and approving gubernatorial appointments.

executive officials.[43] In addition, the governor has been granted constitutional authority to veto legislation, to grant clemency, and to appoint certain state officers and judges, as discussed in greater detail in the following sections.

A. VETO POWER

The governor has the power to "disapprove" a bill passed by the Texas Legislature and prevent it from becoming law unless the veto is overridden by a two-thirds majority of both houses.[44] Under the Texas Constitution, the governor's disapproval of a bill requires an affirmative statement of his objections; if the governor does not sign a bill within the designated time period (either ten days not including Sundays if the legislature has not adjourned or twenty days after the legislature's adjournment), the bill becomes law without the governor's signature.[45] This practice differs from the federal practice, which allows the United States President to "pocket veto" a bill after the adjournment of Congress by not signing it within the prescribed ten-day period.[46]

A governor's disapproval of a bill is rarely overridden by the Texas Legislature. Due to the relatively short biennial legislative sessions, most bills (and almost all controversial ones) are passed during the last ten days of the session. The governor has twenty days after the session has adjourned to disapprove these bills, and the legislature does not have any opportunity to override the veto.[47] And even if the bill is passed earlier in the session, a two-thirds vote in both houses is required to override the governor's disapproval. As a result, in the last seventy years, only once has a governor's disapproval of a bill been overridden by the legislature.[48]

In addition to disapproving an entire bill, the Texas governor may, if a bill contains "several items of appropriation," "object to one or more of such items, and approve the other portion of the bill."[49] But this limited line-item veto raises two important issues. First, how broadly or narrowly should "item" be interpreted? Second, which bills are appropriations bills?

---

[43]*See* TEX. CONST. art. V, § 3 (a) ("The Legislature may confer original jurisdiction on the Supreme Court to issue writs of quo warranto and mandamus in such cases as may be specified, except as against the Governor of the State.").

[44]TEX. CONST. art. IV, § 14.

[45]*Id.*

[46]U.S. CONST. art. I, § 7.

[47]TEX. CONST. art. IV, § 14.

[48]*See* 66 S.J. Reg. 1431 (May 17, 1979) (documenting senate and house override of governor's veto of House Bill 2153 regarding hunting and fishing regulations approved by the Commissioners Court of Comal County).

[49]TEX. CONST. art. IV, § 14.

Jessen Associates, Inc. v. Bullock, 531 S.W.2d 593 (Tex. 1976)

GREENHILL, Justice.

This suit is an original petition for writ of mandamus to compel the Respondent Bob Bullock, Comptroller of Public Accounts, to issue a warrant on the State Treasury for $2,590.25 for architectural services performed by Relator, Jessen Associates, Inc., for The University of Texas at Austin.

It is our conclusion that the warrant should be issued. In reaching this conclusion, we hold that a rider to the latest General Appropriations Act was not subject to the veto of the Governor. The Governor has the power to veto an entire appropriations bill; but his power to veto part of an appropriations bill is limited to vetoing "items of appropriation." This rider, authorizing the construction of certain enumerated projects without the consent of the College Coordinating Board, was not intended by the Legislature to appropriate funds, and therefore was not an "item of appropriation" which was subject to veto apart from the remainder of the bill.

The constitutional provisions dealing with the Governor's power to veto legislation are found in Article IV, Section 14 of the Texas Constitution:

> "Sec. 14. Every bill which shall have passed both houses of the Legislature shall be presented to the Governor for his approval. If he approve he shall sign it; but if he disapprove it, he shall return it, with his objections . . . . *If any bill presented to the Governor contains several items of appropriation he may object to one or more of such items, and approve the other portion of the bill.* In such case he shall append to the bill, at the time of signing it, a statement of the items to which he objects, and no item so objected to shall take effect."

This language is the sole source of the Governor's authority to veto legislation. His veto power is a legislative function and not an executive function, and it exists only to the extent granted by the Constitution. To the extent that the Governor's actions exceed this authority, they have no effect. *Fulmore v. Lane*, 104 Tex. 499, 140 S.W. 405 (1911). Therefore the first question for our consideration is whether the Governor's attempted veto was permitted under the constitutional language set out above.

The case of *Fulmore v. Lane*, supra, is a leading Texas authority on the veto power of the Governor. That case, like this one, involved an attempt to veto a portion of a General Appropriations Act. In the opinion by Justice Dibrell, there appears the following discussion:

> The executive veto power is to be found alone in section 14, art. 4, of the Constitution of this state. By that section he is authorized to disapprove any bill in whole, or, if a bill contains several items of appropriation, he is authorized to object to one or more of such items. Nowhere in the Constitution is the authority given the Governor to approve in part and disapprove in part a bill. The only additional authority to disapproving a

> bill in whole is that given to object to an item or items, where a bill contains several items of appropriation. It follows conclusively that where the veto power is attempted to be exercised to object to *a paragraph or portion of a bill other than an item or items, or to language qualifying an appropriation or directing the method of its uses*, he exceeds the constitutional authority vested in him, and his objection to such paragraph, or portion of a bill, or language qualifying an appropriation, or directing the method of its use, becomes noneffective. 140 S.W. at 412.

Consequently, if the provision which the Governor attempted to veto in the present case is not *an item of appropriation*, but is merely language qualifying an appropriation, or directing its uses, then the veto is of no effect. See also Texas Attorney General Opinion No. V–1196 (1951).

There is no Texas authority other than the *Fulmore* case which deals with the question of what is meant by "item of appropriation." However, that term has been discussed by courts in other jurisdictions with similar constitutional provisions. In *Bengzon v. Secretary of Justice*, 299 U.S. 410 (1936), the Supreme Court of the United States held that such term "obviously means an item which in itself is a specific appropriation of money . . ." The Supreme Court of Florida, in *Green v. Rawls*, 122 So.2d 10 (Fla.1960), made its determination based on the presence of two factors. Where a certain provision designates a specified purpose and the amount to be used therefor, it is an item of appropriation even though it may be included in a larger, more general item.

It can be said then that the term "item of appropriation" contemplates the setting aside or dedicating of funds for a specified purpose. This is to be distinguished from language which qualifies or directs the use of appropriated funds or which is merely incidental to an appropriation. Language of the latter sort is clearly not subject to veto. *Fulmore v. Lane*, supra; *Bengzon v. Secretary of Justice*, supra; *Fairfield v. Foster*, 25 Ariz. 146, 214 P. 319 (1923); *Turner v. Iowa State Highway Comm'n*, 186 N.W.2d 141 (Iowa 1971).

[I]f the rider contains any language of appropriation, it must be found in subdivision (1), which authorizes the Regents "to expend such amounts of its Permanent University Fund bond proceeds and/or other bond proceeds and such amounts of its other available moneys as may be necessary." Although this is not the traditional language of appropriation, it might be construed as setting aside funds under certain circumstances.

A fundamental rule in the construction of statutes is to ascertain and give effect to the intent of the Legislature. *Calvert v. Texas Pipe Line Co.*, 517 S.W.2d 777 (Tex.1974); *Flowers v. Dempsey-Tegeler & Co.*, 472 S.W.2d 112 (Tex.1971). This rule applies also in determining what constitutes an item of appropriation. See *Fulmore v. Lane*, supra. If the language is intended to set aside funds for a specified purpose, it is an "item of appropriation" and is therefore subject to veto by the Governor. Otherwise, the Governor must veto the entire bill or let the objectionable part stand.

When the rider is read in connection with the requirements of Section 61.058, Texas Education Code, its purpose becomes clear. What the Legislature intended was to give its approval to the enumerated projects, and thereby eliminate the need for approval by the Coordinating Board. There was no intent for the language of the rider to set aside funds for these projects, because such funds were appropriated elsewhere. The rider was intended merely to direct the use of those funds by giving express legislative approval to the projects specified.

Consequently, the rider cannot be construed as an "item of appropriation" as that term is used in the Constitution. The Governor, therefore, exceeded the power granted to him in the Constitution in attempting to veto the rider; and his actions therefore have no effect.

Notes on Item Vetoes

The Genesis of the Item Veto: All state constitutions, as well as the United States Constitution, allow the executive to veto legislation. Vetoes traditionally were "all or nothing" propositions, requiring either the approval of all parts of the bill or the rejection of the entire bill by the executive.[50]

Authorization for an item veto first appeared in the Constitution of the Confederate States, which allowed the President of the Confederacy to disapprove of individual items in appropriation bills.[51] Texas and Georgia were the first states to adopt this provision in their post-Civil War constitutions.[52] The concept then spread to other states during the retrenchment era and progressive movement, even though an item veto is still not authorized by the United States Constitution.[53]

Today, all but six states allow the governor to partially veto at least some types of legislation.[54] While most states, including Texas, limit the governor's partial veto authority to "items of appropriation" in an appropriations bill, ten states have broader provisions authorizing the governor to exercise an item veto on all bills.[55]

Defining "Items of Appropriation": The limitation of the partial veto to "items of appropriation" in Texas and other states has caused interpretive difficulties. *Jessen* defined "item of appropriation" as "the setting aside or dedicating of funds for a specified purpose," distinguishing an "item of appropriation" from matters that are incidental to the appropriation, such as language qualifying or directing the use of appropriated funds. Even though such incidental language may appropriately be included in an appropriations bill, the incidental language is not itself something that can be vetoed. In accord with this

---

[50]*See, e.g.*, Clinton v. City of New York, 524 U.S. 417, 438-41 (1998).

[51]*See* Roger H. Wells, *The Item Veto and State Budget Reform*, 18 AM. POL. SCI. REV. 782, 782-83 (1924). However, Jefferson Davis, the President of the Confederacy, never exercised this power. *See id.*

[52]GA. CONST. of 1865, art. III, § 2, cl. 6; TEX. CONST. of 1866, art. V, § 17.

[53]*Clinton*, 524 U.S. at 438-41.

[54]THE COUNCIL OF STATE GOVERNMENTS, THE BOOK OF THE STATES 219-20 (2012). The exceptions are Indiana, Nevada, New Hampshire, North Carolina, Rhode Island, and Vermont. *See id.*

[55]*See id.* The tens states with broader provisions are Alabama, Delaware, Hawaii, Illinois, Maryland, Massachusetts, Mississippi, New York, Washington, and Wyoming. *See id.*

understanding, *Jessen* held that the governor could not veto the rider in question because the rider merely approved the enumerated projects rather than setting aside the funds for them. But in a nice illustration of the subtlety of this distinction, the rider was considered to be sufficiently related to the appropriation to be upheld against a single subject challenge.

Other practical and conceptual difficulties also exist with the item veto. As Professor Richard Briffault explained:

> The use of the item veto assumes that a bill is composed of separable parts, some of which a governor may subtract after the legislature has passed the bill without doing violence to the idea that the bill is still the legislature's product. There is, however, no obvious definition of an "item;" that is, there is often no easy way to determine whether a particular provision of a bill is itself a free-standing item and not an inseparable part of a larger item. Moreover, legislation is not just a matter of cobbling together discrete provisions into a bill. It is a process of negotiation and compromise in which the votes essential to the passage of a bill are attained by tying different elements together or by modifying minority proposals with new provisions, conditions, or restrictions until there is a majority ready to support the result. By putting asunder what the legislature has put together, the item veto results in laws that the legislature has never passed. As a result, the item veto poses a profound challenge to the view of legislation as the domain of the legislature.[56]

Not surprisingly in light of these difficulties, states are divided on the appropriate scope of the governor's item veto power. Some states define "item" to encompass only an appropriation for a set purpose (like a governmental department), so that the governor has to disapprove all appropriations for that purpose to properly exercise the item veto power.[57] Other states define "item" to include specified sums within a purpose (like salary for employees of a department), so that the governor has more power to disapprove individual expenditures.[58] Frequently, though, the definition of "item" appears to depend in large measure on the specificity of the legislative appropriation–if the legislature has made detailed specifications of appropriations without contingencies, then the governor may employ the item veto against the specific provisions.[59] What additional problems does this solution cause?

---

[56]Richard Briffault, *The Item Veto in State Courts*, 66 TEMPLE L. REV. 1171, 1174 (1993).

[57]*See, e.g.*, Commonwealth v. Dodson, 11 S.E.2d 120, 127-31 (Va. 1940) (holding governor could not veto separately legislative provisions enabling attorney general to hire special counsel and creating new governmental positions).

[58]*See, e.g.*, Green v. Rawls, 122 So. 2d 10, 17 (Fla. 1960) (authorizing governor to veto appropriation for two specific salaries within appropriation for wages and salaries).

[59]Briffault, *Item Veto*, 66 TEMPLE L. REV. at 1182.

B. CLEMENCY POWER

Historically in Texas, the governor had almost complete power to pardon criminal convictions, reprieve (or postpone) the execution of sentences, and commute punishments from a more to less severe form. In 1936, however, a constitutional amendment placed limitations on the governor's clemency power, allowing the governor to typically act only on the written recommendation and advice of a newly created department, the Board of Pardons and Parole.[60] This amendment was primarily motivated as a reform in response to the perceived excessive issuance of pardons, particularly during the gubernatorial administrations of James ("Pa") and Miriam ("Ma") Ferguson from 1915-1917, 1925-1927, and 1933-1935. Nevertheless, the general scope of the clemency power still belongs to the executive, as illustrated by the following case.

State ex rel. Smith v. Blackwell, 500 S.W.2d 97 (Tex. Crim. App. 1973)

ONION, Presiding Judge.

This writ of prohibition proceeding presents the question of the Legislature's authority to enact legislation empowering district judges to resentence under a new law those individuals who were previously convicted of offenses involving marihuana under a prior law.

The petitioner under the provisions of Section 4.06 of the Texas Controlled Substances Act, Frank Allan Demolli, was convicted of the offense of possession of marihuana in 1971 in the 167th District Court of Travis County. His punishment was assessed by the jury at twenty-five (25) years' confinement in the Texas Department of Corrections. See former Article 725b, Vernon's Ann.P.C. 1925. The evidence reflects he possessed a little over twenty-one (21) pounds of marihuana.

Subsequent thereto, the Texas Controlled Substances Act was enacted, and Demolli now seeks benefit of the provisions of Section 4.06 thereof by petitioning the convicting court for resentencing. The respondent, judge of the convicting court, set the petition for hearing, and the [district attorney] brought these proceedings contending the said Section 4.06 is unconstitutional.

Article IV, Section 11, Vernon's Ann.St. Constitution, grants to the Governor the power, after conviction, and upon the recommendation of the Board of Pardons and Paroles to grant reprieves and commutations of punishments and pardons. He is also given the power to remit fines and forfeitures.[61]

---

[60] TEX. CONST. art. IV, § 11. The governor may grant one thirty-day reprieve in capital cases and may revoke conditional pardons without the recommendation of the Board of Pardons and Paroles. *Id.* In addition, in cases of treason, the governor may grant clemency with the advice and consent of the Legislature rather than on recommendation of the Board of Pardons and Paroles.

[61] Article IV, Section 11, of our State Constitution reads in part as follows:

> "In all criminal cases, except treason and impeachment, the Governor shall have power, after conviction, on the written signed recommendation and advice of the Board of Pardons and Paroles, or a majority thereof, to grant reprieves and commutations of punishment and

In drafting a constitution, the people of a state are at liberty to lodge this power in any branch of government that they may so desire. *See Ex parte Miers*, 124 Tex.Cr.R. 592, 64 S.W.2d 778, 780 (1933). History teaches us that for many years Texans placed almost complete pardoning power in the office of the Governor. Texas Constitutions from that of 1845 through the Constitutions of 1861 and 1866 and the original section of the present 1876 Constitution were very similar in their phraseology touching on the pardoning power.

The present constitutional provision, Article IV, Section 11, Vernon's Ann.T.S., Constitution, was amended on November 3, 1936. It placed a limitation upon the Governor's power and provided that he must act upon the written recommendation of the Board of Pardons and Paroles in granting reprieves and commutations of punishments and pardons after conviction in all criminal cases except treason and impeachment. He also was given the authority to remit fines and forfeitures upon recommendation of the Board.

While a limitation was placed upon the executive's power, the general scope of the power of clemency still rests with the Governor.

Over the years the courts have had occasion to strike down any encroachment by other branches of government upon the power granted to the executive by the people. In 1930 the Supreme Court of Texas in *Ferguson v. Wilcox*, 119 Tex. 280, 28 S.W.2d 526, declared unconstitutional an act passed by the legislature providing a pardon for a former impeached governor. Earlier, the Court of Criminal Appeals held that whenever the power to discharge convicts before they had served their terms was conferred upon other officials the statutes were invalid. *Ex parte Gore*, 109 Tex.Cr.R. 244, 4 S.W.2d 38 (1928).

It is also to be observed Article II, Section 1, of our State Constitution divides the powers of government into three distinct departments, Executive, Legislative and Judicial, and further provides ". . .; *and no person, or collection of persons, being of one of these departments, shall exercise any power properly attached to either of the others, except in the instances herein expressly permitted.*" (emphasis supplied).

This clearly worded Article has been interpreted to mean that a power which has been granted to one department of government may be exercised only by that branch to the exclusion of the others. *Snodgrass v. State*, 67 Tex.Cr.R. 615, 150 S.W. 162 (1912). And any attempt by one department of government to interfere with the powers of another is null and void. *Ex parte Rice*, 72 Tex.Cr.R. 587, 162 S.W. 891 (1914). This has long been a maxim of constitutional law.

---

pardons; and under such rules as the Legislature may prescribe, and upon the written recommendation and advice of a majority of the Board of Pardons and Paroles, he shall have the power to remit fines and forfeitures. The Governor shall have the power to grant one reprieve in any capital case for a period not to exceed thirty (30) days; and he shall have power to revoke paroles and conditional pardons. With the advice and consent of the Legislature, he may grant reprieves, commutations of punishment and pardons in cases of treason."

See also Article 48.01, Vernon's Ann.C.C.P. Cf. former Article 955, Vernon's Ann.C.C.P. (1925).

If there has been any remission of the Governor's power of clemency after conviction in criminal cases, it is to be found in Article IV, Section 11A, Vernon's Ann.St. Constitution, which provides:

> "The Courts of the State of Texas having original jurisdiction of criminal actions shall have the power, after conviction, to suspend the imposition or execution of sentence and to place the defendant upon probation and to reimpose such sentence, under such conditions as the Legislature may prescribe."[62]

This section of the Constitution is a limited grant of clemency to the courts by the people and does not encompass the general authority to grant commutation and pardons. The section itself has been held not to be self-enacting. *State v. Klein*, 154 Tex.Cr.R. 31, 224 S.W.2d 250 (1949).

With this constitutional background we now turn to the new enactment which has been called into controversy by this proceeding.

Section 4.06, Texas Controlled Substances Act

Said Section 4.06, supra, provides as follows:

> "Sec. 4.06 (a) Any person who has been convicted of an offense involving a substance defined as marihuana by this Act prior to the effective date of this Act may petition the court in which he was convicted for resentencing in accordance with the provisions of Section 4.05 of this Act whether he is presently serving a sentence, is on probation or parole, or has been discharged from the sentence.
>
> "(b) On receipt of petition, the court shall notify the appropriate prosecuting official and shall set the matter for a hearing within 90 days.
>
> "(c) At the hearing the court shall review the record or the prior conviction. The court *shall* resentence the petitioner in accordance with the appropriate

[62]The background of the adoption of this constitutional provision is interesting. The first suspended sentence law (Acts 1911, 32nd Leg., Ch. 44), which authorized courts to suspend the execution of the sentence and also to set aside and annul the former judgment, was held invalid on several grounds, one of which was that it infringed upon the pardoning power of the Governor. *See Snodgrass v. State*, 67 Tex.Cr.R. 615, 150 S.W. 162 (1912).

The subsequent action of the Legislature in enacting a suspended sentence law (Acts 1913, 33rd Leg., Ch. 7) was upheld in *Baker v. State*, 70 Tex.Cr.R. 618, 158 S.W. 998 (1913). It was held that the legislation did not conflict with the Governor's pardoning power in that it did not relieve from punishment after conviction but provided that in certain types of cases no punishment should be assessed unless the individual should once again violate the law. It was held that defining crimes and fixing penalties was a legislative function and the Legislature was authorized to provide that in certain cases no punishment should be fixed.

To remove any question, Section 11A of Article IV was adopted by the voters in 1935 and grants to the court clear constitutional authority to grant probation after the suspension of the imposition or execution of the sentence.

provision of Section 4.05 and shall grant him credit for all time served on the original sentence prior to the resentencing hearing.

"(d) If the time served on the original sentence exceeds the revised sentence imposed by the court under the appropriate provision of Section 4.05, the court shall order the petitioner discharged.

"(e) In no event may resentencing under this section lengthen the petitioner's sentence or require him to pay an additional fine." (emphasis supplied)

The Effect of Section 4.06

If the said Section 4.06 is valid, it appears from the use of the word "shall" that the convicting court is given no discretion but is required to set the resentencing petition for a hearing and upon such hearing "shall" resentence in accordance with the provisions of Section 4.05 of the Act.

Section 4.06 further prevents the convicting court from lengthening petitioner's original sentence or from requiring an additional fine, thus placing a qualification upon resentencing under the provisions of Section 4.05 of the Act.

Thus it appears that in Demolli's case the trial judge must reduce his twenty-five year sentence. The new maximum sentence that could be imposed in view of the amount of marihuana possessed would be ten years (for a felony of the third degree). Therefore, if the respondent acted upon Demolli's petition, there would be at least a fifteen year reduction in sentence.

Putting aside the facts of the instant case, it is observed that if the amount of marihuana involved in the prior marihuana-related conviction is four ounces or less, the convicting court upon resentencing petitioner would be required to change the former conviction from that of a felony to a misdemeanor conviction, either a Class A or Class B misdemeanor, thus in effect restoring certain disabilities lost as a result of the earlier felony conviction.

It seems too clear to question that if said Section 4.06 is applied in Demolli's case or those similarly situated it would result in a less severe punishment being imposed. This would result in a "commutation" as that term "means the change of the punishment assessed to a less severe one." *Ex parte Lefors*, 165 Tex.Cr.R. 51, 303 S.W.2d 394 (1957).

From the very wording of the statute it is clear that it extends commutation to those previously convicted of certain offenses as a mere gift or a matter of clemency upon a filing of a resentencing petition. This is clearly violative of the constitutional provision placing the power of clemency in the hands of the Governor, acting upon the recommendation of the Board of Pardons and Paroles. *Ex parte Anderson*, 149 Tex.Cr.R. 139, 192 S.W.2d 280 (1946).

It would also appear that where the resentencing results in a misdemeanor conviction the same would be a partial pardon. A pardon is partial when it remits only a portion of the punishment or absolves from only a part of the legal consequences of the crime. *Carr v. State*, 19 Tex.App. 635 (1885); *Warren v. State*, 127 Tex.Cr.R. 71, 74 S.W.2d 1006 (1934).

Any statute which in any wise abridges or infringes upon the power granted to the Governor by Article IV, Section 11, would be unconstitutional. *Ex parte Redwine*, 91 Tex.Cr.R. 83, 236 S.W. 96 (1922). When the power of clemency has been conferred by the Constitution, it cannot be exercised by the Legislature. *Ex parte Miers*, 124 Tex.Cr.R. 592, 64 S.W.2d 778 (1933).

Conclusion

We therefore hold that the Legislature exceeded its power in enacting Section 4.06 of the Texas Controlled Substances Act since it is violative of Article IV, Section 11, of our Constitution. To hold that said Section 4.06 should be given effect would, in our opinion, be equivalent to announcing that the Legislature, in enacting such Section, clothed district judges with the power to grant commutation, etc., after conviction, thus usurping the Governor's powers granted to him by the Constitution.

Of course, the Legislature is invested with the law-making power of the people and may define crimes and prescribe penalties. *See* Article III, Section 1, Vernon's Ann.St. Constitution. And under such authority it may prevent punishment *before conviction*. *Baker v. State*, 70 Tex.Cr.R. 618, 158 S.W. 998 (1913); *Ex parte Muncy*, 72 Tex.Cr.R. 541, 163 S.W. 29 (1914). Section 4.06 authorizing resentencing clearly applies, however, to those who are presently serving a sentence, are on probation or parole, or who have been discharged from the sentence. The Section obviously applies to those who have been convicted, and comes within the meaning of the term "after conviction" used in Article IV, Section 11, of our Constitution.

The Texas Controlled Substances Act clearly represents a re-thinking, a change in attitude toward marihuana-related offenses and the penalties to be imposed. It was in fact remedial legislation as it related to possession of marihuana. And the Legislature was not unaware of the large number of inmates in the Department of Corrections as well as those who have already been released who suffered some of the harsher penalties authorized by the former law which will no longer be imposed for the same type of offense. Undoubtedly the Legislature was also aware of difficulties and obstacles inherent in the current commutation policy of the Board of Pardons and Paroles. There can be no question but that the Legislature acted with worthy motives in mind, but today's holding cannot come as a surprise to the Legislature, for prior to the final passage of the Act Attorney General John Hill in Letter Advisory Opinion No. 38 (dated May 16, 1973) concluded that the resentencing provision was unconstitutional on the same basis that we today hold the same to be unconstitutional.

Notes on the Allocation of Clemency Powers

Post-Conviction Legislative Changes as Clemency: *Blackwell* held that legislation requiring new sentencing under more lenient standards for those previously convicted of a crime constituted an unconstitutional intrusion on the clemency powers of the executive department. The court later extended this reasoning in *Ex parte Giles*, holding that the legislature also violated separation of powers by providing for re-sentencing in cases pending on appeal on the statute's effective date.[63] Although acknowledging the legislature's right to reduce sentences before a trial court conviction, the court reasoned that only the executive may make such a change after conviction.[64]

Is the court correct that a post-conviction legislative reduction in the punishment for a crime constitutes an unconstitutional intrusion on the clemency power of the executive? Other state courts are split on the issue. Some state courts have reached a similar result as *Blackwell*.[65] But other states have disagreed. The Ohio Supreme Court, for example, upheld the legislature's power to retroactively apply a post-conviction change reducing criminal penalties.[66] The court reasoned that because the state constitution only limits legislative power rather than grants such power, the grant of clemency power to the governor did not preclude the legislature from enacting statutes that effectively constituted a commutation or pardon.[67]

The Possibility of Relief from the Board of Pardons and Paroles: *Blackwell* invalidated the legislation allowing Demolli to have his sentence reduced from twenty-five years to the ten years he would serve under the new punishment scheme. What options were then left to Demolli? Did he have to serve his entire twenty-five year sentence? Could he request a commutation from the Board of Pardons and Paroles? Was he likely to obtain relief if he did? The court noted the "difficulties and obstacles inherent in the current commutation policy of the Board of Pardons and Paroles." The following case highlights these problems.

Ex parte Tucker, 973 S.W.2d 950 (Tex. Crim. App. 1998)

PER CURIAM.

On April 19, 1984, applicant was convicted of the offense of capital murder. After the jury returned affirmative answers to the special issues, punishment was assessed at death. This Court affirmed applicant's conviction on direct appeal. *Tucker v. State*, 771 S.W.2d 523 (Tex. Cr. App.1988). The trial court has scheduled applicant's execution to take place on February 3, 1998.

In the instant cause, applicant presents nine allegations. We have reviewed the application and find it fails to satisfy the requirements of Art. 11.071, Sec. 5, V.A.C.C.P., and accordingly dismiss the application as an abuse of the writ. We also deny applicant's request for a stay of execution.

---

[63] 502 S.W.2d 774, 786-87 (Tex. Crim. App. 1973).

[64] *Id.*

[65] *See, e.g.,* People v. Herrera, 516 P.2d 626, 628 (Colo. 1973); People v. Freleigh, 54 N.W.2d 599, 600-01 (Mich. 1952).

[66] State v. Morris, 378 N.E.2d 708 (Ohio 1978).

[67] *Id.* at 713-14. *See also In re* Briggs, 47 S.E. 403, 405 (N.C. 1904) (holding state legislature had power to grant pardons to testifying witnesses).

McCORMICK, Presiding Judge, concurring, joined by MANSFIELD, KELLER, PRICE and HOLLAND, JJ.

I agree that our duty is to dismiss applicant's successive habeas corpus application as mandated by our Legislature in Article 11.071, Section 5, V.A.C.C.P. Our state law is clear and well-settled. "Clemency powers embodied in the parole system are beyond the reach of interference by the judicial branch," and any judicial action that interferes with the exercise of that power by the executive branch "is as much of an unconstitutional interference as is an attempted usurpation of that power." *Sanders v. State*, 580 S.W.2d 349, 352 (Tex.Cr.App. 1979). Clemency decisions are not the business of the courts; they belong solely to the executive branch.

The dissenting opinion's reliance on *Ex parte Patterson* about some "entitlement doctrine of an inmate's liberty interest" under Texas' due course of law constitutional provision is misplaced and does not apply to this case. *Patterson* deals with an inmate's "liberty interest" in such things as good time credits that affect his eligibility for parole. *See Patterson*, 740 S.W.2d at 769.

This case deals with whether a lawfully convicted and sentenced death row inmate has any kind of a "liberty interest" in executive clemency. Under our state law, this inmate has no such "liberty interest" as the decision whether to grant clemency is and has been solely within the unfettered discretion of the executive branch. There is no tradition or practice in this state's history that recognizes any kind of fundamental right to executive clemency. Since there is no underlying "liberty interest" or fundamental right to executive clemency, there are no minimum due course of law procedures due relating to the executive branch's decision to grant clemency. *Cf. Meachum v. Fano*, 427 U.S. 215, 225-26 (1976); *Wolff v. McDonnell*, 418 U.S. 539, 556-58 (1974). Therefore, applicant and the dissenting opinion must demonstrate that our state law and the manner in which executive clemency decisions are made in Texas violate federal due process principles.

The foregoing discussion as well as the United States Supreme Court's decision in *Connecticut Board of Pardons v. Dumschat*, 452 U.S. 458 (1981), answer the federal due process arguments adversely to the positions taken by applicant and the dissenting opinion. An inmate has "'no constitutional or inherent'" right to commutation of her sentence. *Dumschat*, 452 U.S. at 464. And, a state law which, like Texas', confers "unfettered discretion" in granting executive clemency does not create such a right. Therefore, no minimum federal due process procedures apply to the manner in which executive clemency decisions are made in Texas. *See Dumschat*, 452 U.S. at 463-65.

OVERSTREET, Judge, concurring.

Applicant's complaints about the inadequacies of our Texas executive clemency procedures are not unheard of. Not only are they not unheard of, but her complaints are pretty much accurate. I would say that clemency law in Texas is a legal fiction at best. In recent years, we have likewise heard similar complaints, with much clamor, in cases involving Gary Graham and Leonel Torres Herrera. *See State ex rel. Holmes v. Third Court of Appeals*, 885 S.W.2d 389 (Tex.Cr.App.1994) and *Ex parte Herrera*, 860 S.W.2d 106 (Tex.Cr.App.1993). However, those clemency procedures remain the same.

It is, and has been, apparent to all that the clemency process has some real problems—no standards or definitive factors or criteria to consider, and nothing to ensure uniformity and consistency in consideration. Yet these procedures remain the same.

It is within the Legislature's prerogative to enact laws to correct some of these problems. Yet it has chosen not to do so. Thus the people of Texas, acting through the elected Legislature, must be satisfied with the current clemency process, or lack thereof. It is not the prerogative of this Court to by judicial fiat alter what in Texas is called the clemency process.

The executive clemency process is a vehicle for mercy. Applicant's application presents a great deal of information suggesting and arguing that she is entitled to such mercy. However, applicant does not have a constitutional right to mercy. "[A]n inmate has 'no constitutional or inherent right' to commutation of his [or her] sentence." *Connecticut Board of Pardons v. Dumschat*, 452 U.S. 458, 464 (1981).

Accordingly, I concur with the Court's order dismissing applicant's current application. If the people of Texas want the clemency process changed, they must let the Legislature know that they demand such change.

BAIRD, Judge, dissenting.

This habeas application presents a question of first impression, namely: whether a death row inmate has a due process right to meaningful consideration of a commutation request in the clemency process. For the following reasons, I believe the question should be answered in the affirmative.

I.

In its finality, death is different from any other punishment. Because of the gravity of capital punishment, Texas has both constitutional and statutory provisions for clemency. TEX. CONST., art. IV, § 11; TEX.CODE CRIM. PROC. Ann. art. 48.01; TEX. ADMIN. CODE, Title 37, Chapter 143 et. seq. (Executive Clemency; Reprieve of Execution). Under the present clemency scheme, the Board of Pardons and Paroles (hereafter, the Board) has the authority to either conduct a hearing or summarily recommend or deny commutation. 37 TAC § 143.43. Upon the Board's recommendation, the Governor may commute a death sentence to life imprisonment. TEX. CONST. art. IV, § 11; 37 TAC § 143.41(b).

Even though procedures are in place to request commutation, applicant asserts the clemency process, as applied, does not provide meaningful consideration of such a request. In support of her argument, applicant has supplemented her application with the 1997 records of the Board. Of the 37 inmates executed in 1997, 16 sought commutation and requested a clemency hearing. Yet no hearings were held and no board member voted for commutation in any case.[68] And despite the Constitutional mandate that the Board "keep

---

[68] According to applicant, since *Furman v. Georgia*, 408 U.S. 238 (1972), the Board has held only one live clemency hearing. Additionally, applicant has provided an affidavit from Debbie Crosby, sister of David Stoker, who was executed in June 1997 after his commutation request was denied. Crosby called members of

records of its actions and the reason for its actions," Tex. Const. art. IV, § 11(a), applicant contends the Board keeps no such records.[69] Consequently, applicant fears there will be no meaningful consideration of her commutation request because the "board has no guidelines stipulating the factors that must be used in reviewing clemency requests" and "each member decides individually on what basis to recommend or deny action."

II.

Since our Constitution and statutes provide for clemency, there must be, at the very least, a modicum of due process. The United States Constitution guarantees that no State shall "deprive any person of life, liberty, or property, without due process of law." U.S. CONST. amend XIV. This constitutional guarantee applies to the inmate population. Therefore, inmates "may not be deprived of life, liberty, or property without due process of law" subject though they may be "to restrictions imposed by the nature of the regime to which they have been lawfully committed." *Wolff v. McDonnell*, 418 U.S. 539, 557 (1974). In *Ex parte Patterson*, 740 S.W.2d 766 (Tex.Cr.App.1987), this Court adopted the entitlement doctrine of an inmate's liberty interest which Justice Stevens expressed in his dissent in *Meachum v. Fano*, 427 U.S. 215, 230 (1976):

> . . . neither the Bill of Rights nor the laws of sovereign States create the liberty which the Due Process Clause protects. The relevant constitutional provisions are limitations on the power of the sovereign to infringe on the liberty of the citizen. The relevant state laws either create property rights, or they curtail the freedom of the citizen who must live in an ordered society. Of course, law is essential to the exercise and enjoyment of individual liberty in a complex society. But it is not the source of liberty, and surely not the exclusive source.

---

the Board and states the following:

> . . . After I learned of the denial of my brother's commutation request, I attempted to call the board members to learn of their reasons for denying commutation. I was only able to reach two of the eighteen board members: Charles Shipman of Abilene and Thomas Moss of Amarillo. As I recall, I had a lengthy conversation with Shipman (about eight minutes), who told me that he did not read my brother's commutation request, and gave me the sense that he generally did not read the commutation requests. He said he did not put a lot of stock into reading about the capital cases. He said he did not see any reason to give these cases further review, because they had gone through the court appellate process.

[69]The Texas Constitution mandates the Board of Pardons and Paroles "keep records of its actions and the reason for its actions." TEX. CONST. art. IV, § 11(a).

Regarding the workload of the Board, applicant submits the following:

> According to statistics published by the Texas Sunset Commission in its 1996 report, each of the eighteen board members votes in an average of 14,900 non-death penalty cases, as follows: Consideration of parole (8,400), Revocation of parole (4,300), Conditions of mandatory supervision (2,200). Averaging 40 hours a week for 50 weeks, this meant that each board member voted on 7.45 cases per hour, or one every eight minutes. Bill Habern, in his article in the 1997 Advanced Criminal Law Course, estimated an average of one vote every 5.13 minutes. *Id.* at Chapter Z-5. Of course, the board members have far more duties than just voting.

> I had thought it self-evident that all men were endowed by their Creator with liberty as one of the cardinal unalienable rights. It is that basic freedom which the Due Process Clause protects, rather than the particular rights or privileges conferred by specific laws or regulations.

Patterson, 740 S.W.2d at 771. In light of that liberty interest, the role of the State to extend and enforce the guarantees of due process is inherent and "[o]nce the State established the baseline of how it customarily treats the prison population, whether by statute, administrative rule, or simply unwritten policy or practice, any substantial deviation from that line in a particular case will impact a liberty interest." *Patterson*, 740 S.W.2d at 772 (internal quotations and citations omitted).

In *Connecticut Board of Pardons v. Dumschat*, 452 U.S. 458, 465 (1981), the Supreme Court held that the liberty interest in clemency review as a ground for a constitutional claim "must be found in statutes or other rules defining the obligations of the authority charged with exercising clemency." In our clemency scheme:

> The Executive Department is constitutionally required to adopt and follow rules that comport with due process and due course of law. Now that the Supreme Court of the United States has spoken in *Herrera v. Collins*, 506 U.S. 390 (1993), concerning the role of the executive clemency in providing a forum for testing claims of "actual innocence," *this Court has the power, duty and responsibility to assure that due process and due course requirements are met.* (Emphasis added.)

Ex parte Graham, 853 S.W.2d 565, 570 (Tex.Cr.App.1993) (Clinton, J. concurring).

Because clemency provides the "fail safe" in our criminal justice system, *Herrera v. Collins*, 506 U.S. at 414-15, our clemency process must provide meaningful consideration of a commutation request. Therefore, even though the power of commutation is vested in the Executive Branch, this Court has an appropriate and important role to ensure the clemency process comports with due process and due course of law. U.S. CONST. amend. XIV; and, TEX. CONST. art I, § 19.

III.

Since the reinstatement of capital punishment in 1972, Texas has executed 144 inmates but not a single death sentence has been commuted solely by request of the condemned. Presently 444 inmates await their execution. If those inmates are constitutionally guaranteed the right to seek commutation, due process commands they know what criteria is examined in the clemency process, otherwise there can be no meaningful consideration of their commutation requests.

The instant application raises questions sufficient to warrant further review. Therefore, I would stay applicant's imminent execution and remand this matter to the habeas court to conduct a hearing to determine whether the procedures and policies in the clemency process, if any, comport with the requirements of due process and due course of law.

Notes on the Texas Clemency Process

Judicial Review of Clemency: *Ex parte Tucker* held that clemency decisions in Texas, being the sole prerogative of the executive department, are not subject to interference by the judiciary. As a result, despite Tucker's apparently accurate complaints regarding the inadequacy of clemency procedures in Texas, the court dismissed her subsequent application for habeas corpus relief.

The court did not recount the facts of the underlying case, but they were well known. Karla Faye Tucker and Daniel Garrett gruesomely murdered two people, Tucker striking them repeatedly with a pickax and later claiming to have experienced a sexual thrill in doing so. While awaiting her execution on death row, Tucker became a born-again Christian and a prison minister. Her attorneys filed *Ex parte Tucker* with the Texas Court of Criminal Appeals two weeks before her scheduled execution date. After the Texas Court of Criminal Appeals decided *Ex parte Tucker*, the eighteen members of the Texas Board of Pardons and Paroles unanimously (with two abstentions) rejected her plea to commute her sentence to life in prison, apparently without conducting a live clemency hearing. Despite international publicity, including a story on "60 Minutes" and an appeal by the Pope, Governor George Bush declined to grant her a one-time, thirty-day stay as authorized by the state constitution. On February 3, 1998, she became the first woman to be executed in Texas since 1863.

The Need for Reform? Do the statistics recounted in Judge Baird's dissent raise concerns regarding the efficacy of the present clemency system in Texas? Has the system morphed from one of unbridled discretion in the hands of the governor to an overworked bureaucracy? Is the political process likely to change the system? If not, does this justify judicial intervention, or was Judge Overstreet correct in laying the responsibility at the feet of the people of Texas?

C. APPOINTMENT POWER

Although the governor does not have the power to appoint constitutional executive officers other than the secretary of state, the governor's appointment power is still important. The Texas executive branch consists of an ever-increasing list of independent agencies, boards, commissions, and departments.[70] Texas Constitution article IV, section 12 provides that the governor may fill all vacancies in "State or district offices, except members of the Legislature."[71] During a four-year term, a governor typically makes approximately 3,000 appointments to agencies, task forces, and vacated state elective offices.

Such appointments are to be made with the advice and consent of two-thirds of the state senate when in session, but the governor may also make recess appointments and then

[70] *See* 1 GEORGE D. BRADEN ET AL., THE CONSTITUTION OF THE STATE OF TEXAS: AN ANNOTATED AND COMPARATIVE ANALYSIS 303 (1977).

[71] TEX. CONST. art. IV, § 12 (a). When a legislative seat is vacant, the governor is to issue a writ of election to fill the vacancy within twenty days after the vacancy occurs. TEX. CONST. art. III, § 13.

submit the appointee or another nominee to the senate within ten days after the next legislative session begins.[72] Once confirmed, appointees to elected offices serve until the next general election, while appointees to other offices serve the remainder of the term. The governor may remove appointed officers only with the advice and consent of two-thirds of the senate.[73]

In addition to the general power of appointment contained in article IV, section 12, the governor has other grants of constitutional authority to appoint specific officers. For example, the constitution specifies the governor's appointment authority with respect to the Texas Ethics Commission, the Veterans Land Board, and the Water Development Board.[74] And the constitution also has provisions in article V relating to the governor's appointment power with respect to state judges.[75] The following case considers the intersection of the various constitutional provisions relating to judicial appointments.

State ex rel. Angelini v. Hardberger, 932 S.W.2d 489 (Tex. 1996)

ENOCH, Justice, delivered the opinion of the Court in which PHILLIPS, Chief Justice, and HECHT, CORNYN, OWEN and ABBOTT, Justices, join.

This is an original proceeding for writ of quo warranto. The State of Texas, on relation of the Governor's appointee, Karen Angelini, seeks a declaration that the Honorable Phil Hardberger has vacated his office as Justice of the Court of Appeals for the Fourth District of Texas. Because we conclude on constitutional grounds that Justice Hardberger has not yet vacated his office, and that there will be no vacancy in his office until the effective date of his resignation, we deny the writ.

By letter dated June 20, 1996, Justice Hardberger advised the Governor of his intention to resign his office effective January 1, 1997. The term of Justice Hardberger's office does not expire until December 31, 2000, but Justice Hardberger is a candidate for election to the office of Chief Justice of the Fourth Court of Appeals. Because he is unopposed, Justice Hardberger will be elected in the November general election and will be entitled to take office on January 1, 1997, for a full term of six years. Believing Justice Hardberger's resignation to be effective by statute eight days after the Governor received the resignation, or June 28, 1996, the Governor appointed Karen Angelini to fill the unexpired term of Justice Hardberger's office, until the next general election. *See* TEX.ELEC.CODE § 201.023. Justice Hardberger has refused to vacate his office. By writ of quo warranto, the State seeks to have the office declared vacant.

I

A writ of quo warranto is an extraordinary remedy available to determine disputed questions about the proper person entitled to hold a public office and exercise its functions.

---

[72] TEX. CONST. art. IV, § 12 (b)-(c).

[73] TEX. CONST. art. XV, § 9.

[74] *See* TEX. CONST. art. III, §§ 24a, 49-b, & 49-c.

[75] TEX. CONST. art. V, §§ 2, 4, & 12.

State ex rel. R.C. Jennett v. Owens, 63 Tex. 261, 270 (1885). The Legislature has conferred original jurisdiction on this Court to issue writs of quo warranto. TEX.GOV'T CODE § 22.002(a); TEX. CONST. art. V, § 3.

II

The Texas Constitution gives to the Governor the power to fill by appointment vacancies in higher judicial offices. Article V, Section 28 of the Constitution provides:

> Vacancies in the office of judges of the Supreme Court, the Court of Criminal Appeals, the Court of Civil Appeals and the District Courts shall be filled by the Governor until the next succeeding General Election; . . .

TEX. CONST. art. V, § 28. *See also* TEX. CONST. art. V, § 2 (providing that a vacancy in the office of Chief Justice or Justice of the Supreme Court is to be filled by appointment by the Governor "until the next general election for state officers"); *id.* § 4 (providing that a vacancy in the office of Judge of the Court of Criminal Appeals is to be filled by appointment by the Governor "until the next succeeding general election"). Article IV, Section 12 also gives the Governor the power to fill by appointment vacancies in state or district offices:

> Sec. 12. (a) All vacancies in State or district offices, except members of the Legislature, shall be filled unless otherwise provided by law by appointment of the Governor.
> (b) An appointment of the Governor made during a session of the Senate shall be with the advice and consent of two-thirds of the Senate present.
> . . . .
> (g) Appointments to vacancies in offices elective by the people shall only continue until the next general election.
> (h) The Legislature by general law may limit the term to be served by a person appointed by the Governor to fill a vacancy in a state or district office to a period that ends before the vacant term otherwise expires or, for an elective office, before the next election at which the vacancy is to be filled, if the appointment is made on or after November 1 preceding the general election for the succeeding term of the office of Governor and the Governor is not elected at that election to the succeeding term.
> (i) For purposes of this section, the expiration of a term of office or the creation of a new office constitutes a vacancy.

TEX. CONST. art. IV, § 12. As is plain from the text of Article V, Section 28, and Article IV, Section 12(g), the Constitution grants the Governor the power to make interim appointments to the next succeeding general election.

Justice Hardberger has indicated in his resignation letter to the Governor that he intends to remain in office and to fully discharge his duties until January 1, 1997. Barring some change in circumstances, Justice Hardberger's office will become vacant upon the effective date of his resignation, January 1, 1997.

A

The State claims that Justice Hardberger, whatever his expressed intent, cannot deliver his letter of resignation in June 1996, to be effective January 1, 1997, because the Texas Election Code creates a vacancy in his office no later than eight days after his letter of resignation is received by the Governor. The State points to section 201.023 of the Texas Election Code, which provides:

> If an officer submits a resignation, *whether to be effective immediately or at a future date*, a vacancy occurs on the date the resignation is accepted by the appropriate authority or on the eighth day after the date of its receipt by the authority, whichever is earlier.

TEX.ELEC.CODE § 201.023 (emphasis added). In short, the State would have us read section 201.023 as ousting Justice Hardberger from his office months before he intends to vacate the office. Neither the statute nor the Texas Constitution permits such a construction.

Section 201.023 does not create an actual vacancy in office. That section and others in Subchapter 201(b) deeming vacancies for purposes of Title 12 of the Election Code are limited in application to that title. Section 201.021 specifically states:

> *For purposes of this title*, a vacancy in office occurs at the time prescribed by this subchapter.

On its face, section 201.023 expressly defines the time at which a vacancy occurs after resignation only for purposes of initiating the electoral process to fill that vacancy.

The dissent contends that section 201.023 could reasonably be read to oust Justice Hardberger from office because of his announced prospective resignation. However, under that reading, section 201.023 would unconstitutionally restrict the tenure of a duly elected officeholder. Having won election to the court in 1994, Justice Hardberger is entitled to serve for six years unless he dies, is constitutionally removed from office, or leaves of his own accord. While an appellate justice in this State may be constitutionally removed for several reasons, such as willful or persistent violation of rules promulgated by the Supreme Court, *see* TEX. CONST. art. V, § 1-a(6), incompetence in performing the duties of the office, *id.*, willful violation of the Code of Judicial Conduct, *id.*, or accepting another office of civil emolument, *see* TEX. CONST. art. XVI, § 40; *Pruitt v. Glen Rose Indep. Sch. Dist.*, 126 Tex. 45, 84 S.W.2d 1004, 1006 (1935), submitting a future resignation is not one of them. If his service is ended by voluntary resignation, he controls the right to decide when he leaves. *See State ex rel. Dosland v. Holm*, 202 Minn. 500, 279 N.W. 218, 220 (1938). The Constitution permits his service to be extended, *see* TEX. CONST. art. XVI, § 17, but not truncated. *Cf. Opinion of the Justices of the Supreme Judicial Court*, 343 A.2d 196, 203 (Me.1975) ("When the Constitution fixes the tenure of a civil office, it is beyond the power of the Legislature to affect the tenure."); *Fitzgerald v. Kuppinger*, 163 Neb. 286, 79 N.W.2d 547, 552 (1956) (constitutional provision stating circumstances under which vacancy exists are exclusive and legislature has no power to add other or different grounds); *State ex rel. Thompson v. Seigler*, 230 S.C. 115, 94 S.E.2d 231, 233 (1956) (legislature cannot provide conditions for removal of constitutional officer unless authority for such action is found in the constitution).

B

On the other hand, reading section 201.023, as urged by Justice Hardberger, as "creating" a vacancy only for purposes of triggering an election runs afoul of another provision of the Texas Constitution. Section 201.023 would deem a vacancy for purposes of triggering an election before there is an actual vacancy in office. In these circumstances, section 201.023 would violate Article V, Section 28 of the Texas Constitution, which mandates that "[v]acancies . . . shall be filled by the Governor until the next succeeding General Election." TEX. CONST. art. V, § 28.

When Justice Hardberger actually leaves office, he will vacate his office in the constitutional sense. *See Leander Indep. Sch. Dist. v. Cedar Park Water Supply Corp.*, 479 S.W.2d 908, 912 (Tex.1972) (words used in constitution are to be interpreted as the people generally understood them). *Cf. Youngblood v. Marr*, 253 Ind. 412, 254 N.E.2d 868, 871-72 (1970) (legislature cannot declare a vacancy under the constitution when in fact no vacancy exists); *State ex rel. Foughty v. Friederich*, 108 N.W.2d 681, 690-91 (N.D.1961) (legislature may not create a vacancy in the constitutional sense when one does not naturally exist); *Friedman v. Lewis*, 143 Pa.Cmwlth. 367, 598 A.2d 1361, 1363 (1991) (words in constitution must be given their common or popular meaning, and the plain meaning of "vacancy" is "[a] place or position which is empty, unfilled, or unoccupied"); *State ex rel. Witcher v. Bilbrey*, 878 S.W.2d 567, 573-74 (Tenn.Ct.App.1994) ("[T]he Constitution of Tennessee uses the term 'vacancy' in its ordinary sense. . . . Thus, a vacant office is one that is unoccupied or without an incumbent."). When the office is vacant, the Governor has the exclusive constitutional authority under the Judicial Article to appoint a successor to serve until the next general election. By deeming a vacancy to occur when Justice Hardberger merely submits his resignation, thereby mandating an election to fill the vacancy that has not yet occurred, section 201.023 infringes upon that power.

Because "[t]he Texas Constitution suffers from a surplus of provisions for filling judicial vacancies," 1 GEORGE D. BRADEN, THE CONSTITUTION OF THE STATE OF TEXAS: AN ANNOTATED AND COMPARATIVE ANALYSIS 478 (1977), it is possible that the Governor's appointment authority could be modified by some other constitutional grant to the Legislature. The only other provision of the Constitution that speaks to the appointment of court of appeals justices is located in the Executive Article, which provides in part:

> (a) All vacancies in State or district offices, except members of the Legislature, shall be filled *unless otherwise provided by law* by appointment of the Governor.
> (b) An appointment of the Governor made during a session of the Senate shall be with the advice and consent of two-thirds of the Senate present.

TEX. CONST. art. IV, § 12(a, b) (emphasis added). By including the language "unless otherwise provided by law," section 12(a) subjects the Governor's appointment power to at least some degree of legislative modification. One could argue, perhaps, that the Legislature may restrict the Governor's appointment power by enacting election laws deeming a vacancy to occur prior to the true vacancy.

The potential conflict between Article IV, Section 12 and Article V, Section 28 has been examined before. In *White v. Sturns*, 651 S.W.2d 372 (Tex.App.-- Austin 1983, writ ref'd n.r.e.), the plaintiff had been appointed district judge by an outgoing governor, but prior to Senate confirmation the new Governor had obtained a return of the nomination and had made a new appointment. Plaintiff sought to have himself declared judge on the basis that Article V, Section 28 did not require Senate confirmation of judicial appointees. The court of appeals rejected this argument on several grounds. It looked to the consistent practice of all governors in submitting judicial appointments for confirmation, as well as to the Legislature's failure to clarify the issue by constitutional amendment despite two other changes to Section 28 since 1876. *Id.* at 376. Its primary holding, however, was that no conflict existed between the two constitutional provisions because the confirmation requirement in Section 12 was an additional, not a contradictory, requirement:

> We hold that Sturns' theory is totally without merit because it is an argument solely from silence, that is, because art. V, § 28 does *not* state that the advice and consent of the Senate are required, it is in conflict with art. IV, § 12 which *does* specifically require such action by the Senate. We think, however, that this circumstance merely lends conclusive force to the proposition that no conflict is possible, and certainly not found in the express terms of the two constitutional provisions, leaving full scope for the operation of the fundamental rule of construction that no conflict was intended and that the two provisions were meant to operate in conjunction.

Sturns, 651 S.W.2d at 376 (emphasis in original). Two attorney general opinions accord with this holding. *See* OP.TEX.ATT'Y GEN. NOS. JM-1161(1990), O-1092 (1939).

Texas law does not support the conclusion that the "unless otherwise provided by law" language of Article IV, Section 12 permits the Legislature to foreclose the Governor's appointment power under the circumstances of this case. In *Denison v. State*, 61 S.W.2d 1017 (Tex.Civ.App.--Austin), writ ref'd, 122 Tex. 459, 61 S.W.2d 1022 (1933), the court examined whether the Legislature could alter the requirement in Article IV, Section 12 that the Governor's appointees be confirmed by two-thirds of the Senate. The court of appeals answered no, concluding that the "otherwise provided by law" language only allowed the Legislature to change the *appointing authority* for an office, not the other requirements of Section 12, and to that extent only for offices not provided for in the Constitution. *Id.* at 1020. Thus, while the Legislature could have provided that members of the Highway Commission be appointed by someone other than the Governor, it could not do so for appellate judges. This Court refused to grant writ, expressly adopting the first part of the court of appeals' holding in its per curiam opinion. *Denison v. State*, 122 Tex. 459, 61 S.W.2d 1022 (1933).

Denison prohibits the Legislature from circumventing the Governor's appointment power by redefining the meaning of the constitutional term "vacancy." In the teeth of a specific constitutional provision mandating that the Governor shall fill vacancies in this office by appointment, the Legislature cannot cede to a resigning justice the discretion to time that resignation in a manner that instead fills that vacancy by election. When read to deem a vacancy for purposes of election, section 201.023 unconstitutionally abridges the Governor's constitutional power of appointment when an officeholder tenders a resignation before a general election to be effective after the election.

SPECTOR, Justice, joined by GONZALEZ, Justice, concurring.

I concur in the majority's judgment, but I cannot join its holding that section 201.023 unconstitutionally infringes the Governor's appointment power. That conclusion is inconsistent with sound principles of construction and a recent decision of this Court. Without a constitutional amendment, the appointment power of the Governor does not trump the people's right to elect their judges.

As long as the method established by our Constitution for selecting judges remains unchanged, section 201.023 should be upheld as a legitimate effort by the Legislature to ensure that the people may exercise their most fundamental constitutional right at the earliest opportunity. It seems clear that our Constitution establishes the gubernatorial appointment as a stopgap measure; appointees serve only "*until* the next succeeding General Election." TEX. CONST. art. V, § 28 (emphasis added); *see also* TEX. CONST. art. V, §§ 2, 4. The majority's approach thwarts the preference in our current Constitution for the election of judicial officers.

The relief the State requested was a holding that Justice Hardberger's delivery of his prospective resignation triggered the Governor's power to appoint a successor to serve only *until* the November general election. Consequently, the contention that section 201.023 is unconstitutional under the circumstances of this case, although mentioned in passing, was neither briefed nor argued. Both major political parties have nominated candidates to be placed on the November 1996 ballot. The majority's decision makes that election a nullity and allows the Governor's appointee to serve until the November 1998 election.

I would hold that Justice Hardberger's prospective resignation triggered an election under section 201.023 of the Election Code. Because, however, I agree with the majority's holding that it did not create a present vacancy for appointment purposes, I concur in the judgment of the Court and would deny the writ of quo warranto.

BAKER, Justice, dissenting.

Governor Bush appointed Angelini to fill the vacancy in Place 4 on the Fourth Court of Appeals. The Election Code provides that a vacancy in office may occur as the result of any one of eight events: (1) death, § 201.022; (2) resignation, § 201.023; (3) removal, § 201.024; (4) acceptance of another office that may not be held simultaneously, § 201.025; (5) declaration of ineligibility, § 201.026; (6) creation of a new office, § 201.027; (7) if the election was won by a deceased or ineligible candidate, § 201.028; and (8) if an officer-elect declines to qualify for office, § 201.029.

Only one of these provisions, section 201.023 of the Election Code, concerns a vacancy created by a prospective resignation. It provides:

> If an officer submits a resignation whether to be effective immediately or at a future date, a vacancy occurs on the date the resignation is accepted by the appropriate authority or on the eighth day after the date of its receipt by the authority, whichever is earlier.

The Legislature amended section 201.023 following our decision in *Texas Democratic Executive Comm. v. Rains*, 756 S.W.2d 306 (Tex.1988). In *Rains*, a Justice of the Fourth Court of Appeals, Justice Rudy Esquivel, submitted a prospective resignation, to be effective January 1, 1989. Governor William P. Clements, Jr. received the resignation on June 21, 1988. However, Governor Clements declined to accept it, choosing instead to wait until November 1988, which would have allowed him to appoint Justice Esquivel's successor rather than have his successor chosen at the November general election.

The Secretary of State also refused to certify Ron Carr as the Democratic candidate for Justice Esquivel's unexpired term in the November general election. The Secretary of State claimed that he could not certify Carr's candidacy in the absence of a "vacancy" in office. He asserted that no vacancy existed until the Governor accepted Esquivel's resignation. Relators sought to compel the Governor to accept Esquivel's resignation immediately, contending that given an otherwise proper resignation, the Governor had no discretion but to accept it. We agreed. *Rains*, 756 S.W.2d at 307.

The pivotal holding in *Rains* was that the Governor could not unilaterally delay acceptance of an officeholder's resignation to manipulate the method–whether by election or appointment–by which an officeholder's successor is chosen. In 1989, the Legislature effectively codified *Rains* when it amended section 201.023 of the Election Code to provide that a resignation must be accepted no later than the eighth day after it is received.

While the Legislature clearly intended by section 201.023 to limit the Governor's ability to delay acceptance of a tendered resignation for essentially political purposes, the question before us is the other side of that coin: whether an officeholder may resign prospectively to deny the Governor an appointment and force an election to choose a successor.

It is true that many Texas judges–fifty-three percent of those currently in office–are chosen by popular, partisan elections. Forty-seven percent of the judges currently in office were appointed by a governor. OFFICE OF COURT ADMINISTRATION (information on file with Office of General Counsel). Our Constitution has expressly provided since 1876 that the Governor's appointees fill vacancies in judicial offices until the next general election. Rather than indicating a preference for one method of judicial selection over the other, our Constitution treats these as alternative methods, each available under different circumstances.

It is also telling that the Constitution carves out a legislative exception to the Governor's general authority under Article IV, Section 12 to appoint state and district officers. The Governor has no authority to appoint legislators; they must be chosen by special election. TEX. CONST. art. IV, § 12. If the framers of our Constitution had determined to prefer judicial elections to interim appointments by the Governor, they could have readily provided for special elections for judicial vacancies. Instead, they chose a method combining both elections and gubernatorial appointments by the Governor, again, depending on the timing of a vacancy.

If any vacancy created by section 201.023 is solely for the purposes of an election, as Justice Hardberger contends, I believe the statute cannot be constitutionally implemented because such a statute would abridge the Governor's constitutional appointment power. The Legislature has broad lawmaking power, but that power is circumscribed by express or implied restrictions contained in or necessarily arising from the Constitution itself. *See Government Serv. Ins. Underwriters v. Jones*, 368 S.W.2d 560, 563 (Tex.1963). Under Article II, Section 1, our Constitution's express separation of powers provision, the Legislature cannot abridge or otherwise impair the constitutional prerogatives of the Executive Department. *See, e.g., Rose v. State*, 752 S.W.2d 529, 535 (Tex.Crim.App.1989); *State ex rel. Smith v. Blackwell*, 500 S.W.2d 97, 104 (Tex.Crim.App.1973); *Walker v. Baker*, 145 Tex. 121, 196 S.W.2d 324, 327 (1946). Because there is no constitutional basis for favoring elections over appointments, the Legislature cannot do so by statute, which is exactly what Justice Hardberger's interpretation of section 201.023 would allow.

If a plausible alternative construction of a statute exists that will allow a court to avoid constitutional problems, we will adopt that construction. *Public Citizen v. United States Dep't of Justice*, 491 U.S. 440, 442 (1989); *Key W. Life Ins. Co.*, 350 S.W.2d at 848-49. We should thus assume that the Legislature intended to treat the resigning officeholder and the Governor with parity. Otherwise, we would be forced to the conclusion that the Legislature intended to unconstitutionally elevate the power of the officeholder to determine whether a successor will be chosen by an election and thus deny the Governor a power the Constitution itself confers. *See, e.g., Green v. Bock Laundry Mach. Co.*, 490 U.S. 504, 527-30 (1989) (Scalia, J., concurring). Framing the issue this way, as I believe we must, I would hold that Justice Hardberger vacated his office effective June 28, 1996.

Further, to accept Justice Hardberger's construction of section 201.023 leads to at least one other difficulty, one that can be avoided by construing the statute as I suggest. *See State v. Standard Oil Co.*, 130 Tex. 313, 107 S.W.2d 550 (1937) (stating that a court must construe a statute in a way that makes all relevant laws harmonious). Justice Hardberger, if his prospective resignation had been otherwise effective, intended to resign on January 1, 1997. Texas Government Code section 601.004, prevents that prospective date from being effective. That section provides:

> Persons elected to unexpired terms in the various state . . . offices . . . shall be entitled to qualify and assume the duties of their respective offices . . . immediately following the official canvass of the results of the election at which they were elected, and they shall take office as soon thereafter as possible.

In other words, the candidate elected at the November 5, 1996 general election may, if he or she so chooses, assume office before Justice Hardberger intends to depart on January 1, 1997. See *Texas Democratic Executive Comm. v. Rains*, 756 S.W.2d 306, 309 (Tex.1988) (Phillips, C.J., dissenting). Under these circumstances, Justice Hardberger's contention that he has the unilateral right to determine the timing of his resignation is plainly untenable.

Notes on Appointments to the Judiciary and Executive Agencies

Hardberger's *Aftermath*: The *Hardberger* majority did not accept the primary argument of either party. The state asserted that Justice Hardberger's prospective resignation letter, which was dated June 20, 1996 and intended to be effective January 1, 1997, created a vacancy no later than June 28 that Governor Bush could fill by appointment. Justice Hardberger, in contrast, urged that, while his resignation letter triggered a November election to replace him under Election Code § 201.203, he had not yet vacated his office. The supreme court agreed with Justice Hardberger that his office was not vacant, but held that section 201.023 could not create a vacancy solely for purposes of triggering an election without running afoul of the governor's constitutional authority to fill judicial vacancies by appointment until the next election. While acknowledging that article IV, § 12 allowed the legislature to provide by law for other means to fill vacancies in state or district offices, the court concluded that the legislature's authority in this regard only extended to non-constitutional, legislatively created offices.

As a practical matter, this prevented the holding of an election in November 1996 to replace Justice Hardberger. Instead, only after Justice Hardberger resigned to become Chief Justice of the San Antonio Court of Appeals on January 1, 1997 did a vacancy exist, which Governor Bush filled through the appointment of Karen Angelini to serve as a justice until the next general election held in November 1998.

Yet like so many state constitutional law issues, that was not the end of the story. The League of United Latin American Citizens challenged the supreme court's holding in *Hardberger* in federal court, claiming that the decision constituted a new state election law that had to be precleared by the Department of Justice under the Voting Rights Act. Although the three-judge federal district court hearing the challenge declined to call a special election or remove Justice Angelini, the federal court ordered the State of Texas to seek preclearance and not to follow the *Hardberger* decision until preclearance was obtained.[76] Texas subsequently did obtain preclearance to continue to implement the decision.

Why did this appointment become such a high stakes affair? Mostly it was politics, both writ large and small. In a narrow sense, the justices on the San Antonio Court of Appeals at the time were closely split between Republicans and Democrats, with the Angelini appointment giving Republicans a four-to-three majority on the court. But from a larger perspective, Hardberger's contention that he could manipulate his resignation before the end of his term to prevent the governor from having an appointment had serious separation of powers implications. As Justice Baker's dissent notes, although judges in Texas must run for election, almost half of the judges serving at that time had been appointed rather than elected. These appointees then have the advantage of incumbency when seeking to be elected for a subsequent term. Indeed, Justice Angelini has been elected four times since her appointment, with her current term ending on December 31, 2018. Does the prevalence of initially-appointed judges in the state have any impact on the

---

[76] League of United Latin Am. Citizens v. Texas, 995 F. Supp. 719, 724-25 (W.D. Tex. 1998).

argument for a merit system of selection rather than maintaining Texas's partisan judicial elections?

Selection Methods for Executive Agencies: As discussed in *Hardberger*, the governor has the ability to appoint all state and district officers, although the legislature can provide by law for other means of selection of non-constitutional executive offices. As one example, the Texas Agricultural Commissioner, a statutory office created by the legislature, is elected statewide rather than appointed by the governor.

Moreover, specific constitutional provisions control the method of selection for some offices. Texas Constitution article XVI, section 30 provides that the commissioners of the Railroad Commission of Texas, a powerful state agency regulating oil and gas production, are to be elected statewide.[77] The constitution also grants the legislature the authority to determine the method of selection of the board members of the state board of education.[78]

The governor appoints the members of most other executive agencies. But despite this initial appointment, the governor has limited authority after the appointment to hold appointees accountable for failing to abide by his or her policy preferences. Unlike the United State President, whose executive authority extends to removing appointed officers (although sometimes limited to removal for good cause),[79] the governor can only remove an appointed officer with the approval of two-thirds of the senate.[80] Moreover, the fragmentation of the executive branch further attenuates the accountability of agencies.[81] As a result, the governor does not have the same structural mechanisms under the Texas Constitution to ensure that his appointees follow his or her positions. Yet because Texas does not have term limits for the governor, a long-serving governor can hold appointees accountable through other informal mechanisms.

---

[77]TEX. CONST. art. XVI, § 30. The Railroad Commission was originally created during the administration of Governor James Hogg in 1891 to regulate railroads as common carriers. Over the years, the commission's authority has expanded to include regulation of oil and gas, although the commission no longer regulates railroads.

[78]TEX. CONST. art. VII, § 8. By law, board members are elected from districts within the state.

[79]Free Enter. Fund v. Pub. Co. Accounting Oversight Bd., 130 S. Ct. 3138, 3151-52 (2010).

[80]TEX. CONST. art. XV, § 9.

[81]*See* City of Dallas v. Stewart, 361 S.W.2d 562, 573 (Tex. 2012).

CHAPTER 8 EXERCISES AND PROBLEMS

1. Assume you are a legislator drafting the appropriations bill at a time when the legislature and the governor are at odds regarding whether the attorney general should be pursuing litigation against corporations allegedly engaging in deceptive trade practices. The legislature wants to appropriate funds to allow the attorney general to hire additional staff to pursue such litigation, but the governor believes the funds would be better spent on other state needs. The appropriations bill is typically long (over 1000 pages) and detailed, providing goals, strategies, and specific allocations of funds for each purpose, such as:

Items of Appropriation:	Year ending 8/31/12	ending 8/31/13
A. Goal– Provide legal services		
A.1.1. Strategy–Legal services	95,000,000	82,000,000
B. Goal–Enforce child support law		
B.1.1. Strategy–Child support enforcement	270,000,000	260,000,000
B.1.2. Strategy–State disbursement unit	13,000,000	12,000,000
C. Goal–Refer Medicaid Crimes		
C.1.1. Strategy–Medicaid investigation	14,000,000	14,000,000

What would be the best way to appropriate funds for the additional staff to pursue deceptive trade practices? How would the governor likely respond?

2. Assume you are part of a task force assigned to provide recommendations on amending the state constitution to establish a new process for clemency. What are your recommendations for establishing a new clemency procedure that ensures a meaningful review but limits the possibility for abuse of the pardon power?

www.ingramcontent.com/pod-product-compliance
Lightning Source LLC
LaVergne TN
LVHW062242200926
848484LV00006B/1596
* 9 7 8 1 6 0 0 4 2 2 1 5 7 *